MW00999242

SCIENTIFIC FOUNDATIONS
OF
NEUROLOGY

Scientific Foundations
of
Neurology

Edited by

MACDONALD CRITCHLEY

C.B.E., M.D., F.R.C.P., Hon. F.A.C.P.

Honorary Consulting Physician, The National Hospital, Queen Square;
Honorary Consulting Neurologist, King's College Hospital, London;
President, The World Federation of Neurology

JAMES L. O'LEARY

Ph.D., M.D.

Professor of Neurology and of Experimental Neurological Surgery;
Washington University School of Medicine;
Associate Neurologist, Barnes Hospital, St. Louis;
Consultant Neurologist, Jewish and St. Lukes Hospitals

and

BRYAN JENNETT

M.D., F.R.C.S.

Professor of Neurosurgery,
Institute of Neurological Sciences, Glasgow,
and the University of Glasgow

 F. A. DAVIS COMPANY, PHILADELPHIA

First published 1972

ISBN 0 8036 2190 6

Text set in 10/11 pt. Monotype Times New Roman, printed by letterpress,
and bound in Great Britain at The Pitman Press, Bath

PREFACE

Over the past two decades, clinical neurology has extended so much that it now subsumes a considerable package of investigative and therapeutic techniques. Its scientific basis is no longer restricted to a simple description of the underlying physiological anatomy of the nervous system. When diagnosis was largely confined to a shrewd assessment at the bedside of subtle signs and symptoms, it was enough to incorporate within a contemporary text-book a brief account of the structure and function of the central and peripheral nervous systems. Present day workers within the fields of neurology and neurosurgery now ask for something more. The Editors of this volume assume a certain familiarity among their readers with the current fundamental concepts of nervous function and dysfunction. Their object is to high-light some of the more recent work upon various topics, including trends in clinical, physiological and psychological thinking. No such book can possibly be comprehensive and this one is limited to those topics which the Editors believe merit review, either because of recent advances, or because of current re-thinking. A number of gaps will be obvious—perhaps also a certain overlap—for which no apology is offered.

Thus brain metabolism and cerebral blood flow are dealt with in depth, because they are clearly relevant not only to cerebrovascular disease, but also to a number of other more distantly related conditions. On the other hand, it was decided not to discuss neuroradiology, because justice could not be done to such an important subject, and in any event several comprehensive works are already available.

The rationale of several investigative measures and therapeutic methods is reviewed: the emphasis has been upon principles, so that interpretation and application can take account of the limitations imposed by various alternative techniques. A few clinical essays are included which are related to other articles dealing with theoretical aspects of the same topics, or which are concerned with subjects still controversial.

It is hoped that this book will interest those neurological clinicians or research-workers who are anxious for information as to the scientific principles of their own studies or those of colleagues in cognate fields. Advice as to further reading follows most of the articles. These reference lists, too, are obviously incomplete, but they are designed to lead the way into the literature of their various subjects. The literary purist will observe certain inconsistencies both of spelling and of style. This is because the Editors in their permissiveness have deliberately not prevented American and English authors from adopting their own individual orthographies.

The Editors would like to express their recognition of the efficiency and diligence of their secretaries. Mr. Richard Emery has been particularly patient and helpful in organising the work of the individual authors and of the Editors.

Macdonald Critchley
Bryan Jennett
James O'Leary

September 1972

CONTENTS

SECTION I

PHYSIOLOGY IN GENERAL

SECTION II

THE PERIPHERAL NERVOUS SYSTEM

SECTION III

MOTOR SYSTEM

SECTION IV

EPILEPSY

CONTENTS

CONTENTS

SECTION VII

CEREBRAL CIRCULATION

SECTION VIII

CEREBROSPINAL FLUID AND INTRACRANIAL PRESSURE

SECTION IX

DIAGNOSTIC AND THERAPEUTIC TECHNIQUES

CONTENTS

SECTION X

SOME INTERESTING CONDITIONS

LIST OF CONTRIBUTORS

HUME ADAMS, M.B., Ch.B., Ph.D., M.R.C.Path.
Professor of Neuropathology University of Glasgow and Institute of Neurological Sciences, Glasgow.

ARNOLD APPLEBY, M.B., B.S., F.F.R., D.M.R.D.
Consultant Radiologist, Royal Victoria Infirmary, Newcastle upon Tyne; Clinical Teacher, University of Newcastle, Newcastle upon Tyne; Consultant Neuroradiologist, Newcastle General Hospital, Newcastle upon Tyne.

REGINALD G. BICKFORD, M.B., B.Chir., F.R.C.P.
Professor of Neurosciences, Department of Neurosciences, University of California, San Diego, School of Medicine; Consultant in Neurology, Veterans Administration Hospital San Diego; Head, EEG Laboratory, Division of Neurology, Department of Neurosciences, University of California, San Diego, School of Medicine, UCSD University Hospital of San Diego County.

M. R. BOND, M.D., Ph.D., F.R.C.S.E., D.P.M.
Lecturer in Neurology Institute of Neurological Sciences, Glasgow, and University of Glasgow.

E. M. BRETT, D.M., M.R.C.P.
Consultant Neurologist, The Hospital for Sick Children, Great Ormond Street, The National Hospitals for Nervous Diseases and Queen Mary's Hospital for Children, Carshalton.

JAMES B. BRIERLEY, M.D., F.R.C.Path., F.R.C.Psych.
Senior Lecturer in Neuropathology, Institute of Psychiatry, Scientific Officer (Clinical) M.R.C. Neuropsychiatry Unit, M.R.C. Laboratories, Carshalton, Surrey.

MACDONALD CRITCHLEY, C.B.E., M.D., F.R.C.P., Hon, F.A.C.S.
Honorary Consulting Physician, The National Hospital, Queen Square; Honorary Consulting Neurologist, King's College Hospital, London; President, The World Federation of Neurology.

J. N. CUMINGS, M.D., F.R.C.P., F.R.C.Path.
Professor of Chemical Pathology (Emeritus); Recently Professor of Chemical Pathology, Institute of Neurology, The National Hospital, Queen Square, London.

JAMES ALEXANDER DOIG, M.B., F.R.C.S. (Ed.).
Consultant Surgeon to the Department of Otolaryngology, Glasgow Royal Infirmary and Department of Neuro-Otology, Institute of Neurological Sciences, and Honorary Clinical Lecturer, Glasgow University.

J. W. DUNDEE, M.D., Ph.D., F.F.A.R.C.S.
Professor of Anaesthetics, Queen's University of Belfast.

R. J. FALLON, B.Sc., M.D., M.R.C.Path.
Consultant in Laboratory Medicine, Ruchill Hospital, Glasgow; Honorary Lecturer in Bacteriology and Immunology, University of Glasgow.

A. J. GAY, M.D.
Associate Professor Clinical Ophthalmology and Clinical Neurology; Washington University School of Medicine, St. Louis, Missouri 63110, U.S.A.

D. I. GRAHAM, M.B., Ch.B., M.R.C.Path.
Lecturer in Neuropathology, University Department of Neuropathology, Institute of Neurological Sciences, Glasgow.

ROBERT G. GROSSMAN, M.D.
Associate Professor of Neurological Surgery, The Albert Einstein College of Medicine, Yeshiva University, The Bronx, New York, U.S.A.

A. N. GUTHKELCH, M.A., M.Ch., F.R.C.S.
Consultant Neurosurgeon, Hull Royal Infirmary, Hull.

A. MURRAY HARPER, M.D.
Reader in Surgical Physiology, University of Glasgow; Honorary Consultant Clinical Physiologist, Royal and Western Infirmaries, and Institute of Neurological Sciences, Glasgow.

DAVID HELLERSTEIN, Ph.D.

M. E. HUMPHREY, M.A., B.Sc.(Oxon.), F.B.Ps.S.
Senior Lecturer in Psychology, St. George's Hospital Medical School, Tooting, London.

BRYAN JENNETT, M.D., F.R.C.S.(Eng.).
Professor of Neurosurgery, the University of Glasgow, Institute of Neurological Sciences, Glasgow.

RALPH H. JOHNSON, M.A., M.D., D.M., D.Phil.
Senior Lecturer in Neurology, University of Glasgow; Consultant Neurologist, Institute of Neurological Sciences, Glasgow.

J. W. LANCE, M.D., F.R.C.P., F.R.A.C.P.
Chairman, Division of Neurology, The Prince Henry and Prince of Wales Hospitals, Sydney; Associate Professor of Medicine, University of New South Wales, Sydney, Australia.

L. P. LASSMAN, M.B., B.S.(Lond.), F.R.C.S.
Neurological Surgeon, Newcastle General Hospital and the Royal Victoria Infirmary, Newcastle upon Tyne; Clinical Lecturer in Neurological Surgery, University of Newcastle upon Tyne.

I. McA LEDINGHAM, M.B., Ch.B.
Senior Lecturer in the Department of Surgery and Intensive Therapy Unit, Western Infirmary, Glasgow.

N. G. LUNDBERG, M.D., D.M.
Professor of Neurosurgery, University Hospital, Lund, Sweden. Director of the Neurological Department B, University Hospital, Lund, Sweden.

W. McCARTNEY, B.Sc., Ph.D., F.R.I.C.
Late Scientific Assistant, Chilean Iodine Educational Bureau and Commonwealth Bureau of Animal Nutrition.

D. G. McDOWALL, M.D. (Edin.), F.F.A., R.C.S.
Professor of Anaesthesia, The University of Leeds; Hon. Consultant Anaesthetist, The United Leeds Hospitals; Hon. Consultant Anaesthetist, Leeds (St. James's) University Hospital.

V. H. MACMILLAN, M.D., F.R.C.P.(C.).
Assistant Professor Medicine (Neurology) University of Toronto, R. S. McLaughlin fellow 1970–1972; Staff

Neurologist Toronto General Hospital, Toronto, Canada.

C. Mawdsley, M.D., F.R.C.P., (Lond)., F.R.C.P. (Edin).
Senior Lecturer in Medical Neurology, Edinburgh University. Head, University Department of Medical Neurology. Consultant Neurologist, Royal Infirmary and Northern General Hospital, Glasgow.

Ronald Melzack, Ph.D.
Professor, Department of Psychology, McGill University, Montreal, Quebec, Canada.

Douglas Miller, M.D. (Glas.), F.R.C.S. (Ed. and Glas.)
Senior Lecturer, University Department of Neurosurgery, Consultant Neurosurgeon, Institute of Neurological Sciences, Glasgow.

Willi, K. Müller, M.D.
Lecturer in Neurology, University of Wurzburg, Germany; Head Dept. Neurovirology, Laboratory of Medical Microbiology, University of Leiden, Netherlands.

Freda, G. Newcombe, M.A., D.Phil. (Oxon.).
Fellow of Linacre College; Senior Research Officer, Department of Neurology, Oxford.

N. M. Newman, A.B., M.D.
Fellow in Neuro-Ophthalmology, Departments of Ophthalmology and Neurosurgery, University of California Medical Center, San Francisco.

Robert G. Ojemann, M.D.
Associate Neurosurgeon, Massachusetts General Hospital; Assistant Clinical Professor of Surgery, Harvard Medical School.

R. C. Oldfield, M.A. (Cantab.).
Director, Medical Research Council, Speech and Communication Unit and Honorary Professor, University of Edinburgh.

James L. O'Leary, Ph.D., M.D.
Professor of Neurology and of Experimental Neurological Surgery, Washington University School of Medicine; Associate Neurologist, Barnes Hospital, St. Louis; Consultant Neurologist, Jewish and St. Lukes Hospitals.

I. Oswald, M.A., M.D., D.Sc., D.P.M.
Reader in Psychiatry, University of Edinburgh; Consultant Psychiatrist, Royal Infirmary of Edinburgh, and Royal Edinburgh Hospital.

Fred Plum, M.D.
Anne Parrish Titzell Professor of Neurology Cornell University Medical College Neurologist-in-Chief, New York Hospital, New York.

Theodore Rasmussen, M.D., M.S., F.R.C.S. Director, Montreal Neurological Institute and Hospital; Professor of Neurology and Neurosurgery, McGill University, Canada.

R. W. Ross Russell, M.D. (Cantab.), D.M. (Oxon.), F.R.C.P.
Physician, The National Hospital, Queen Square, London; Physician to the Neurological Department, St. Thomas' Hospital, and to Moorfields Eye Hospital, City Road, London.

J. O. Rowan, F. Inst. R.
Principal Physicist, The Institute of Neurological Sciences Glasgow, and The Department of Clinical Physics and

Bioengineering, Western Regional Hospital Board, Glasgow.

Bo K. Siesjö, M.D., Ph.D.
Career Investigator, Swedish Medical Research Council, Director, Brain Research Laboratory, University Hospital, Lund, Sweden.

J. A. Simpson, M.D. (Glas.), F.R.C.P. (Lond. Edin. and Glas.), F.R.S. (Edin.).
Professor of Neurology, University of Glasgow; Physician-in-Charge, Department of Neurology, Institure of Neurological Sciences, Glasgow; Hon. Consultant Neurologist to the Army in Scotland.

G. D. Smellie, M.B., Ch.B., F.R.C.S. (Glas., Ed., Eng.), D.Obst., R.C.O.G.
Consultant Surgeon, Victoria Infirmary, Glasgow.

R. S. Snider, Ph.D.
Professor, Center for Brain Research, University of Rochester U.S.A.

W. Eugene Stern, M.D., F.A.C.S.
Professor and Chief, Department of Surgery/Division of Neurosurgery, University of California, School of Medicine, Los Angeles, California; Consultant, Wadsworth Veterans Administration Hospital, Los Angeles, California.

David Sumner, T.D., B.Sc., M.R.C.P.
Consultant Neurologist, Leeds (St. James's) University Hospital; Honorary Senior Lecturer in Neurology, University of Leeds.

John W. Turner, M.B., B.S., F.R.C.S., (Ed.).
Consultant Neurosurgeon, Institute of Neurological Sciences and Consultant Neurosurgeon, Victoria Infirmary, Glasgow; Honorary Lecturer, University of Glasgow.

R. Tym, M.B., F.R.C.S.
Associate Professor of Neurology, University of Toronto; Neurosurgeon, The Wellesly Hospital, Toronto.

Ronald T. Verrillo, Ph.D.
Associate Professor, Laboratory of Sensory Communication, Syracuse University, Syracuse, New York.

Sir Francis M. R. Walshe, M.D., D.Sc., F.R.C.P., F.R.S.
Honorary Consulting Physician to University College Hospital, London and to the National Hospital for Nervous Diseases, Queen Square, London.

Arthur A. Ward, Jr., M.D.
Professor and Chairman, Department of Neurological Surgery, University of Washington School of Medicine, Seattle, Wash., U.S.A.

E. S. Watkins, M.D., B.Sc.Hons., F.R.C.S.
Professor of Neurosurgery, The London Hospital Medical College. Honorary Consultant Neurosurgeon, The London Hospital, Whitechapel, London.

A. G. M. Weddell, M.D., M.A., D.Sc.
Reader in Human Anatomy, University of Oxford; Fellow, Medical Tutor and Vice Provost, Oriel College, Oxford.

Professor R. Wüllenweber, Dr. Med., Dr. Phil.
Oberarst, Neurochirurgische, Universitäts-Klinik, Bonn-Venusberg.

MELVIN D. YAHR, M.D., F.A.C.P.
Merritt Professor Neurology, Columbia University College of Physicians and Surgeons, Attending Neurologist, Neurological Institute and Director, Clinical Center for Parkinsonism and Allied Diseases, Columbia University.

SECTION I

PHYSIOLOGY IN GENERAL

1. THE NERVE CELL AND ITS PROPERTIES

JAMES L. O'LEARY

INTRODUCTION

The functioning of the CNS rests largely upon the exercise of its information gathering capacities. This is subject to the activities of a wide variety and distribution of outlying receptors, each sensitively attuned to a particular change in external or internal environment. Different receptors are responsive to special modalities of information, and each is a transducer set at the end of a sensory nerve terminus. The unique qualities of a receptor restrict its nerve fibre to the transmission of one kind of information, but the enormous potential the entire system has for information gathering is suggested by a totality of 1,200,000 nerve fibres in the sensory roots of the human spinal nerves alone. The various spinal and brain stem relay stations reached by such information re-route it to those parts of the CNS where the appropriate response can be synthesized. In the case of simple reflexes such as the stretch reflex, the site of synthesis is close to hand. More lengthy and complex paths are required to carry the code to the successively forward levels of the neuraxis where higher syntheses occur. In any case, the executive organs are the muscles and glands. They are reached by whatever intermediary routes are required, but always necessitate a final common path leading from neuraxis through motor nerves to the body part innervated.

Within the nervous system structure and function are so intimately related that they represent the two sides of a coin. Nevertheless they can be segregated for purposes of description and comment and we have done so in the following account.

STRUCTURAL CONSIDERATIONS

1. The Neuronal Population

A fabulously large population of ten billion neurons comprises the bulk of the human brain. Nerve cells differ from all others in possessing a complex of branched extensions called dendrites which increase the surface of the cell and thus enlarge its field of receptivity to many times that provided by the soma alone. Each cell also possesses a single axon, the all-or-none conductor of signals generated by the cell.

Neurons show much the same internal make-up as do other somatic cells, including their companion elements of nervous tissue, the glia. Yet the constituent organelles of neuroplasm show characteristics unique to nerve cells.

Cell and axon size varies both in different species and in different neuron types of the same species. Some types, such as the motoneurons of spinal cord and Betz cells of motor cortex, are quite large for all species, approaching the lower visibility limit of the human eye. Others, such as the granule cell of cerebellar cortex, are a little smaller than a red blood corpuscle. No clearly stated reasons have been given for the size differences between cell types. However, large cells tend to be less numerously represented, to be surrounded by much more neuropil, and to possess more discrete sources of synaptic activation. Their axons conduct more rapidly and have a lower threshold of excitability. They also support more extensive end-arborizations, often referred to as the telodendrial periphery. To the contrary, small cell populations are numerously represented, their field of receptivity is limited, and the effect of a single one is scarcely distinguishable in the record of mass activation.

Based on the distance traversed by an axon between its issue from the axon hillock and its final arborization, neurons can be divided into two broad categories. In one the axon divides repeatedly shortly after its issue to arborize about the nerve cells of its vicinity. This is the short axon cell which is generally believed to provide local synchronizing, and perhaps specifically inhibitory, action.

The other category includes all cells having axons which pursue a lengthy course before re-entering grey matter to terminate. Each CNS tract is composed of myriad axons which function to link associated neural activities into longitudinal systems of common functional import. The primary sensory and motor neurons providing the peripheral inflow and outflows which relate the organism to its environment also belong to the long axon category. In summary, short axon cells have to do with very local aspects of integration, whereas cells of long axon operate over extended distances providing effective fore-aft integration. However, there is no sharp cleavage between categories; long axon cells sometimes provide significant collateralization in their own vicinities as well as remote connections at higher or lower CNS levels.

Many secrets of nervous organization lie concealed in the processes of growth, differentiation and migration by which the embryonic nerve cell reaches the ultimate site of its functioning, lays down its dendritic arbor, and directs the axon toward its ultimate destination. All connections necessary for normal coordination arise in accordance with a biochemically directed plan that ultimately connects precisely the various nerve endings to their corresponding points throughout brain and spinal cord and establishes the corollary external relations.

Hamburger has said that there are more types of nerve cell than there are for all the other body tissues taken together, and the adaptive features of neurons with respect to size, number, branching of processes, and of synaptic connections are countless. Even so, many more nerve cells are laid down in embryonic life than remain to function, and the time of death of the supernumeraries during embryonic development, as well as the exact character of the connectivities of each neuron destined to remain permanently, is programmed into the genome of the individual. Such exactly ordered specification, leading to differentiation of a variety of cell types, is, then, the keystone of patterning for the nervous system. For the mature cell it is inherent in the differences in size, shape and character of dendritic arborizations, and in the connectivities existing between the numerous cell groupings which make up the grey matter.

Neurons occur in a rich variety of architectonic formats, each recognizable from others by unique congruities which exist between the neuronal bodies and their dendritic overlaps. A few of these are: six layered cerebral cortex, the neuron somata being packed into five overlying horizontal layers, their major dendrites rising through the layers to partake of a terminal imbrication occupying the relatively acellular plexiform layer just beneath the cortical surface; cerebellar cortex which is bilaminate and shows strong directional tendencies in both its axonal and dendritic plexuses; reticular neurons having dendritic arbors that overlap continuously from lower spinal cord through upper brain stem; closed-in configuration of the circumscribed motor nuclei of the cranial nerves; hilar arrangements in which axons of egress of neurons collect within a central hilus whereas the opposite cell surfaces are embedded in a close knit investiture of arriving axons.

2. Nerve Cell Internal Organization

The cytoplasmic matrix of the neuron soma and dendrites is called neuroplasm; that of the axon is sufficiently distinguishable from it structurally and functionally to warrant a separate designation, axoplasm. The neuroplasm contains the usual organelles found in other somatic cells, including aggregates of Nissl substance (granular ergastoplasm), a Golgi apparatus (agranular ergastoplasm), mitochondria, neurofibrils, microtubules, and synaptic vesicles. All have counterparts in other somatic cells, and it is only by their appearances in neuroplasm as such that we recognize them as unique constituents of nerve cells. Figure 1 schematizes the ultrastructural appearance of the perikaryon and its organelles.

Nissl Substance-Granular Ergastoplasm

In light microscopy sections Nissl substance occurs as variously shaped aggregates of small round granules which stain brightly with aniline dyes. In different kinds of nerve cells such aggregates show differences in size, abundance and distribution. By electron microscopy the tiny granules which compose them can be shown to relate to an underlying system of membrane-bound profiles which vary in shape from circular to oblong and in diameter from 30–50 mμ, occasional spaces reaching 100–250 mμ across. The system of spaces is interconnected to produce a tridimensional net which extends longitudinally into the dendrites.

The granules (ribosomes) are distributed between and also overlie these spaces, the particles often being arranged in rows upon the underlying membranes. Each granule has a high content of RNA and where several cluster together they are sometimes called polysomes. The ribosomes function in protein synthesis, and similar combinations of ribosomes with ergastoplasmic spaces occur in other somatic cells, such as those of the pancreatic acinus, for example.

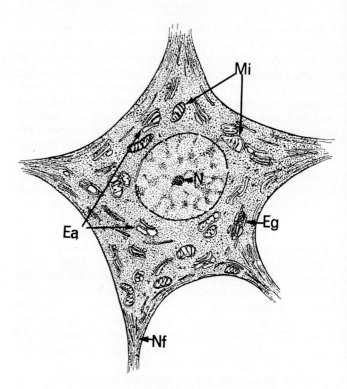

FIG. 1. Diagrammatic representation of the perikaryon of a nerve cell from an ultrastructural preparation. Shows nucleus with bilaminar nuclear membrane and nucleolus (N), granular (Eg) and agranular ergastoplasm (Ea), neurofibrils (Nf), mitochondria (Mi).

Agranular Ergastoplasm

In ultrastructural preparations another system of spaces is also seen within the neuroplasm. These spaces are agreed to be identical with the Golgi apparatus of light microscopy where they appear as a closed system of canals outlined by osmic acid fixatives. By electron microscopy they are not surrounded by ribosomes, although they have been said to be contained in a cloud of tiny vesicles. They appear as elongated flattened cisternae and other vacuoles.

It has been proposed for other somatic cell types that they interconnect with the spaces of the granular ergastoplasm, the proteins synthesized by the ribosomes being transported into the cisternae where they become concentrated. An enzyme called thiamine pyrophosphate is also known to exist in these vacuoles. The system surrounds the nucleus and lies midway between it and the surface membrane of the soma.

The Nucleus

This is surrounded by a double membrane, the inner component smooth and 130 Å across, the outer one 75 Å thick, and presenting a wavy appearance. The nuclear membrane shows pore-like spaces which do not necessarily participate in nucleocytoplasmic interchange. Structural continuities with membranes of the ergastoplasm have been seen. The nuclear sap is similar to that of all other cell types, whereas the nucleolus is made up of small granules of somewhat greater density and may be composed of RNA particles.

Mitochondria

These are present in all parts of the cytoplasm, their lengths being measurable in microns. Each shows a smooth outer limiting membrane and an inner one which forms inward projections called cristae running longitudinally as well as cross-wise. In the mitochondria of other cells so-called elementary particles have been identified which are evidently composed of mitochondrial ATPase. However these may be bound particles and not a part of the membrane structure.

Other Organelles

These are seen with relative rarity and random distribution and include multivesicular bodies, lysosomes and pigment granules.

3. Neuroplasmic Specialization in Dendrites and Axons

Dendrites

By light microscopy dendrites, like neuroplasm of the soma, contain Nissl granules; like axons they show neurofibrils. In the larger dendrites the Nissl granules appear along anastomosing slender tubules with shallow cisternae, and accumulate particularly at points of branching. Palay considers long straight canaliculi 200 Å in diameter to be a characteristic of dendrites. In transverse sections these appear as small thick circles having clear centres.

Mitochondria occur throughout the lengths of the dendrites and do not diminish proportionately in number as branching diminishes dendrite diameter. Large dendrites can have frequent, peripherally placed mitochondria.

Axons

For the moment we disregard the structure of the investing sheath of the myelinated nerve fibre (p. 5). Large axons are characteristically filled with fine neurofilaments 100 Å in diameter which appear solid and which differ from the somewhat thicker canaliculi of the dendrite. The aggregate of neurofibrils of an axon sometimes end in a ring-like formation in the presynaptic terminus. Mitochondria of axons are often elongate and quite slender.

Similarities Exist Between Small Axons and Dendrites

Even by electron microscopy it may be difficult to make this differentiation by comparison of the smaller cross-sections of the two types of terminal cell process, particularly where they interlace bewilderingly in the so-called formless neuropil which intervenes between nerve cell bodies and constitutes the main synaptic substrate. Neurofibrils splay out terminally in the smaller axon branches and but few canalicular structures can be identified there together with widely spaced mitochondria. It is not until the actual axon terminus is reached, ordinarily containing a collection of synaptic vesicles, that one can clearly identify a terminal axonal segment and suspect that a synapse is nearby.

4. Axonal End Specialization and the Synaptic Membrane

Forms of Axonal Terminals

Some manner of terminal axonal swelling, containing an aggregate of synaptic vesicles and several mitochondria, identifies the sites of synapses (Figs. 2B and C). The

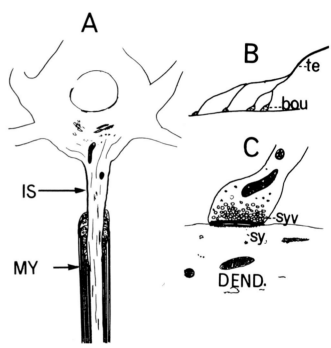

FIG. 2. A, shows the initial amyelinate segment of a CNS axon characterized by a sub-membrane addition of dense material. This portion of the axon has a highly developed detonator function and issues the code transmitted to the axon terminals. IS, initial segment. MY, myelin sheath. B, several telodendria, amyelinate axon twigs (te), that provide collateral and terminal boutons (bou), synapsing in this instance with a small dendrite. C, a single bouton showing apposition between pre- and postsynaptic membranes (sy), a cluster of synaptic vesicles (syv) and two mitochondria. DEND, dendrite.

commonest of these are the minute end-bulbs (boutons) which closely cover the somadendrite membranes of many kinds of nerve cells. The innumerable small dendritic spines of cortical pyramids, each showing an interior system of membrane-bound spaces separated by zones of intervening dense cytoplasm, also establish their contacts with axonal boutons. Corresponding dendritic spines of cerebellar neurons form similar axon contacts but lack the spine apparatus. Thus the axonal bouton is the generalized type of somadendritic apposition.

Besides boutons there are more specialized bearers of the sites of synaptic apposition. These include the mossy and climbing axodendritic and basket axo-axonic synapses of cerebellar cortex. Other large axons produce terminal outfoldings which grasp much of the soma of the synapsing cell. The axon clubs which appose the lateral dendrite of the Mauthner cell of the teleost fish medulla is another prime example of a very specialized synapse.

Let us revert momentarily to the preterminals which are transitional between the myelinated CNS axon and its terminal axoplasm. The branching undergone is known chiefly from the study of Golgi material which indicates that when the stem axon is reduced to a critical diameter it loses its myelin sheath, becoming amyelinate. Some such naked axons terminate bluntly in contact with the soma surface or that of a major dendrite. Others continue to arborize within the neuropil following dendrites and sometimes establishing bouton contacts with both dendrites and soma.

The Synapse

Two kinds of synaptic appositions, differing in details of their lengths and their positions relative to dendrites (type I) or somata (often type II), have been reported by Gray. In type I synapses upon dendrites increase in thickness, and density of the membrane is present over 90–100 per cent of the contact region between pre- and postsynaptic processes (Fig. 2C). The synaptic vesicles ordinarily lie near the presynaptic membrane, and the cell processes are about 200 Å apart. For type II synapses the thickening regions of the membranes occur only over a short part of the length of apposition between pre- and postsynaptic membranes. The axo-dendritic synapse on the lateral dendrite of the giant Mauthner neuron provides a special case. The synaptic region presents a succession of segments each $1/2 \mu$ long, with gaps between. The usual cleft between pre- and postsynaptic membranes is occluded by an added membrane which gives a trilaminated appearance to the disc-shaped synapses.

The Motor End Plate

Axons that arise from motoneurons form the final common path to striated muscle. After branching and loss of the myelin sheath the terminal collaterals come to lie partially embedded in an eccentric disc of sarcoplasm called the sole plate. In electron microscopy preparations this is made up of an intricately folded plasma membrane (corresponding to the postsynaptic membrane of the central synapse) which is separated by a space of 250–300 Å from the corresponding presynaptic plasma membrane of the axon terminal. Elsewhere than at the interface with sarcoplasm the axon terminal is covered by a thin layer of cytoplasm which evidently belongs to the terminal neurilemmal cell of the investing sheath of the axon. Synaptic vesicles are recognized in the axon terminals as in the synaptic end boutons of many CNS synapses.

Synaptic Vesicles and Other Neural Transmitters

A synaptic vesicle is round, 200–650 Å in diameter, and bounded by a smooth line of 50–70 Å thickness. Synaptologists agree generally that each of the usual round vesicles contains a packet of acetylcholine, the chemical excitatory transmitter which is presumed to be operative at most CNS synapses and at the motor endplates of skeletal muscle. In the latter site quanta of transmitter release have been shown to exist electrophysiologically as a form of graded response, and to be equated with the packet release of ACh for diffusion to muscle receptor sites.

There is no general agreement concerning a mammalian chemical inhibitory transmitter, although GABA (gamma aminobutyric acid) has acceptance as an invertebrate one. The question of the synaptic storage sites of the inhibitory versus the excitatory synapse remains undecided although there is considerable support for vesicles of ovoid shape as the containers of the inhibitory transmitter (Uchizono). Some terminal boutons, then, appear to show only round vesicles, others only ovoid ones, and perhaps still others a mixture of the two. The findings indicate a dispersion of the excitatory type over the dendrites, of the inhibitory type over somata, and particularly in the neighbourhood of the axon hillock.

Other vesicles have been described in CNS synaptic structures of dense appearance and perhaps reminiscent of the epinephrine and norepinephrine granules of adrenal medulla, and these, too, may play a role in central synaptic transmission.

There is also the fact of neurosecretion to be noted. Hormones which are extractable from the pars nervosa of the hypophysis are not made there; rather they are produced in bodies of nerve cells in the paraventricular and supraoptic nuclei of the hypothalamus and pass to the nerve endings in the pars nervosa. Neurosecretory granules observed in these hypothalamic nuclei are elaborated in the cytoplasm of cells which have all the characteristics of nerve cells. The product passes along the axons to the posterior lobe where it is discharged into the capillaries of the portal circulation.

The existence of free ribosomes, particles known to be concerned in the synthesis of proteins in the soma, and their scantiness, if not complete absence, at the axonal periphery suggests that protein replacement might be furnished by the soma for transport along the axon to the periphery. The axon flow theory was first evolved by Weiss and Hiscoe, and more recent workers have used radioautographic methods centering upon labelled amino acids to prove that proteins indeed migrate centrifugally at a rate of 1·5 mm. a day. Recent studies have supported a faster axon transport mechanism as well. Bishop examined the same problem from the viewpoint of the axonologist. Since a large nerve cell ordinarily supports a profusely arborized telodendrial periphery with numerous (or large) specialized terminals, the soma under these circumstances must produce replenishment material. A large axon is usually issued by a large cell, and by the laws governing transport the volume increases as the diameter squared, the larger the fibre the greater its transport capacity at a given pressure gradient. Resistance to flow caused by friction decreases with increase in size by a still larger factor, also facilitating axon flow.

5. The Sheath Structure of Myelinated and Non-myelinated Fibres

The investments of peripheral and central myelinated axons are essentially alike, their development in both instances resulting from a spiral wrapping of the axon by the enveloping sheath cell. In the case of peripheral axons the investing sheath is the cell of Schwann which individually builds an entire internodal stretch; for the central axon it is the oligodendroglia cell which apparently can provide wrapping for more than one myelinated central axon and also share with others in the coverage of single internodal segments.

The way in which the sheath of the peripheral myelinated fibre is constructed is described here, for it was the first to be understood and provides the simpler case. Analogy of the investing membrane to the mesentery which suspends the gut from the abdominal wall is appropriate. Conceive of the tubular gut as rotating through a number of complete turns whilst the mesentery is stretching to accommodate the spiral wrapping which results. The inner mesaxon illustrated in Fig. 3, then, is comparable with the attachment of the mesentery to the gut, the outer mesaxon to the

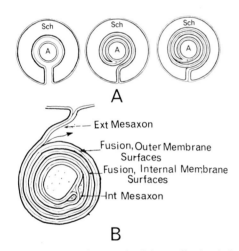

Fig. 3. A, stages in histogenesis of the myelin sheath showing several steps in wrapping of the axon by the Schwann (Sch) cytoplasm. B, alternation between dense and thin (intraperiod) lines during the wrapping of the sheath. These are produced respectively by the fusion during wrapping of the inner (dense) and outer (attenuated) Schwann cell membranes. Inner and outer mesaxon positions are labelled.

body wall fixation. The much attenuated cell process which is twisted about the axon by the rotation of the latter consists of inner and outer membranes separated by a thin intervening layer of the cytoplasm. The axon at first lies within a groove of the wrapping membrane. As the cell membrane lining one side of the groove is brought into proximity with that lining the other side, the inner surfaces fuse together, resulting ultimately in a series of rings made up of double lines. As the Schwann cell continues to encircle the nerve fibre the outer layers continue to come into contact and fuse, the second dark line so formed becoming the fine *intraperiod line* (Fig. 3). Next the cytoplasm of the Schwann cell is squeezed out leaving the

lipid behind (i.e. becomes compacted). Thus the myelin which forms the space between the two major dense lines is derived chiefly from the lipid that existed in the middle layers of the two cell membranes. Also the lamellae of the mature myelin sheath consist of a series of densely staining fusions of inner lines representing protein, an intervening light line made up of lipid. It is the light line that is bisected by the intraperiod line. The whole width of a segment of the laminated membrane is 75 Å. The clothing of peripheral non-myelinated fibres is not constructed along the lines of syncitium. Rather, multiple axons, each perhaps with its own mesaxon, if deeply embedded, lie within the confines of one Schwann cell.

The Node of Ranvier, Schmidt–Lantermann Incisure, and Origin of the Axon

Nodes of Ranvier represent myelin-free intervals along the lengths of myelinated axons of both CNS and peripheral nerve (Fig. 4). As the myelin sheath reaches the

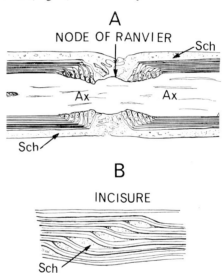

Fig. 4. A, Node of Ranvier from an ultrastructural preparation, diagram. Schwann cell cytoplasm (Sch); Ax, axon. The termini of two Schwann cells interdigitate at the node. There the axon is naked and shows the surface density which also features the amyelinate initial segment of the axon. B, funnel-shaped interruptions occur in the internodal segments called Incisures of Schmidt–Lantermann. Each is produced by a transitory separation of the fused dense lines of the laminated sheath. Each separation encloses a bit of Schwann cell cytoplasm.

nodal region it becomes progressively thinner and the spirally arranged lamellae terminate successively from within outwards along the axon. As they do so, the major dense lines of the sheath open up to enclose the terminal cytoplasm of the Schwann cell. Then each cross-section of a terminating line produces a pocket-like appearance. Axon branching frequently occurs at nodes of Ranvier and this further alters the relation of the parent axon to its daughter branches. Between successive nodes of Ranvier funnel-shaped incisures interrupt the myelin in light microscopy preparations. Ultrastructural preparations reveal that these represent discontinuities in the myelin sheath in which the unit membranes separate along the major dense lines by 500–1,000 Å. Considering the spiral arrangement, a long strand of cytoplasm was apparently not squeezed out at the time of fusion. Some believe that each of these incisures represents a long spiral pathway of Schwann cytoplasm extending from the outside to the inside of the myelin sheath, perhaps serving a transport function. Schmidt–Lantermann incisures as seen in ultrastructural preparations are illustrated in Fig. 4B.

At the node the axon, bare of myelin, shows an accumulation of dense material underlying the axolemma. Similar material has also been described for the initial segment of the axon before it acquires a myelin sheath (Fig. 2A).

FUNCTIONAL CONSIDERATIONS

This section commences with a very simplied version of how resting potential across the nerve cell membrane is maintained and how, through its breakdown, it produces the all-or-none nerve impulse for speedy non-decremental propagation over long stretches of axon. Thereafter, neuromuscular transmission is considered as an example of graded postsynaptic events. This in turn forms the basis for examining excitatory and inhibitory processes in neural membrane and their applicability to the problem of spinal transmission.

1. General Review of Membrane Processes

By biophysical definition a neuron is a semiporous bag of excitable membrane which contains a considerable preponderance of K^+ in its interior and is immersed in an outer environment in which Na^+ is in excess. We still do not know how the excitable membrane acts differentially with respect to ions, but each of these cations and the Cl anion act to produce electrochemical potentials as a result of differences in their concentration (i.e. "concentration potential") on the two sides of the membrane.

The succeeding simplified account of membrane potential is believed generally in accord with evidence collected upon squid giant axons (Hodgkin and Huxley) and other axons where the membrane is the site of a self-regenerative process that serves to propagate the nerve impulse. Some inaccuracies may have been introduced in the effort to simplify the story.

The ionic imbalance between in- and outsides of the resting nerve fibre is sufficient to maintain a voltage difference across the membrane such that the interior is ordinarily about 0·07 V. (70 mV.) negative to the exterior. Receiving and transmitting functions of neurons reside in the excitable membrane, whereas the interior is concerned with metabolism, participating in recovery from activity and the maintenance of the biochemical integrity of the neuron.

In the interval between nerve impulses there is a continuing exchange of Na^+ and K^+ brought about by a pumping action of these ions against their normal diffusion gradients across the membrane, Na^+ out, K^+ in. Considering the initiation of an impulse in the frame of reference of the resting membrane, either an electric shock or activity in a neighbouring region produces an initial depolarization which starts a rapid influx of Na ion carrying a surge of current. The interior of the axon falls to zero potential and even reverses in sign so that it temporarily becomes somewhat positive to the outside. This depolarization produces the rise phase of the axon potential spike. That rise is halted by an "inactivation process" which terminates the permeability of the membrane to Na^+. Even before that moment, however, K^+ has commenced to pass out of the membrane along its concentration gradient. After the sodium flux stops, K^+ flow is restored to its original state by a process called repolarization.

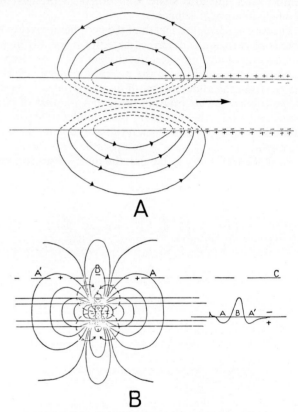

Fig. 5. A, lines of current flow which accompany the propagation of an impulse, in peripheral nerve. B, corresponding lines of current flow in CNS axon, a volume conductor situation.

It is important that axonal conduction is all-or-none and nondecremental, impulses in myelinated axons skipping from one node of Ranvier to the next and thus speeding up conduction over long distances. Figure 5 diagrams the lines of current flow which accompany the passage of the impulse along a myelinated axon in peripheral nerve (Fig. 5A) and in the volume conductor situation of central white matter (Fig. 5B). Corresponding postsynaptic processes of soma and dendrite which also result from ion flow are graded and decremental in type. The next section upon neuromuscular transmission serves as an introduction to the characteristics of graded processes such as are also found in generator potentials of peripheral sensory receptors. In considering the transfer of excitation from nerve to muscle what has been said of nerve membrane also applies to muscle membrane in so far as the known facts of excitation are concerned.

2. Transfer of Excitation from Nerve to Muscle

Axons that arise from motoneurons form the final common path to striated muscle. Each ramifies into slender terminals which form partially submerged plaques upon the muscle fibres (p. 4).

The transition at the neuromuscular junction from the rapidly propagating axon impulse to the *graded* end-plate potential (EPP) of the postsynaptic membrane teaches us much about membrane properties which is applicable to the operation of CNS synapses. The end-plate, in fact, comes close to completely satisfying the several criteria necessary to establish mediation by a chemical excitatory transmitter. These are: existence of the substance in sufficient quantities in the presynaptic terminals which must also contain a synthesizing enzyme; stimulation of presynaptic nerve fibres must release the substance in adequate quantities from the terminals; when directly applied (iontophoresis) the action of the substance upon the postsynaptic cell must be identical with that of synaptic action.

At the neuromuscular junction impulses normally travel but one way—from axon to muscle. Intricate experiments have been devised to answer the question of how the presynaptic membrane, separated by a significant cleft from the postsynaptic one, effects the depolarization of the latter. The events proved to occur take place in this order: upon invasion of the terminal filaments of the axon by the nerve impulse, the depolarization of the nerve endings causes acetylcholine (ACh) molecules stored in the axoplasm (in synaptic vesicles) to be released into the synaptic cleft. ACh thus liberated diffuses across the synaptic cleft to reach the postsynaptic membrane. Eccles has shown that the width of the cleft is balanced critically between the needs for rapid diffusion between membranes and for sufficient width to lower the resistance to passage of ionic current. There the ACh becomes attached to certain specific sites of the postsynaptic membrane called ACh receptors. A receptor protein has been studied which binds ACh strongly. This could be the factor which accounts for the permeability and the potential changes that occur during neuromuscular transmission. The other receptor substance is ACh-binding cholinesterase. The structural change in postsynaptic membrane effected by combination of ACh with the receptor protein increases the ionic permeability of the membrane. Most ions of the type mentioned hitherto can cross the activated end-plate membrane carrying an ionic current. With a muscle resting potential of –90 mV. and a normal ionic environment the synaptic flow into the muscle fibre is thought to be through highly localized spots, the inward current of the end-plate potential being carried largely by sodium ions. The neighbouring polarized membrane of the muscle fibre then short-circuits through this point. When the resulting depolarization reaches threshold for the muscle, a propagated action current is generated there in turn.

The mechanism by which the conducted muscle current activates the contractile apparatus is unknown. The active state of the postsynaptic membrane, as indicated by the end-plate potential (EPP), persists as long as the ACh concentration in the synaptic cleft is maintained. How-ever, provisions exist for rapid decay resulting from diffusion of ACh molecules out of the space and its fast removal due to the hydrolytic activity of the enzyme cholinesterase.

An interesting development in the area of neuromuscular transmission was the discovery of miniature end-plate potentials (called MEPP's to distinguish them from the usual EPP's recorded during transmission from nerve to muscle). Fatt and Katz recorded spontaneous low-voltage fast activity from microelectrodes thrust into the junctional regions. This activity resolves into numerous tiny discharges having peak amplitude of 1 mV. Pharmacological tests have proved that those, too, result from action of ACh upon the receptor surface of the end-plate. Under favourable circumstances transitions are demonstrable. For example, decreasing calcium or increasing magnesium in the extracellular fluid causes the size of successively evoked EPP's to show stepwise fluctuations. This led to the interpretation that each represents the impact of quanta of ACh on the postsynaptic membrane and that the quanta result from the way in which ACh is stored in the presynaptic endings—as the content of separate synaptic vesicles which cluster together in the synaptic terminals. Spontaneous MEPP's and the quantal nature of transmission has also been proved for the neuromuscular junction of the crayfish, thus demonstrating that this method operates over a wide phylogenetic span (Dudel and Kuffler). There is also evidence for quantal transmission in motoneurons.

When a muscle fibre is deprived of its motor innervation the ACh-sensitive region at the end-plate increases in size until ultimately it covers the whole surface of the fibre (Axelsson and Thesleff). Botulinus toxin also increases the size of the chemosensitive area (Thesleff).

3. Synaptology

General Attributes applicable to all Neurons

The resting potential of the membrane which covers soma and dendrites does not have an absolute value but fluctuates about a median which approximates that of squid axon. Within that range increase in permeability to Na^+ lowers (and decrease raises) resting potential value. Upon the low side (increased ionic permeability) depolarization occurs immediately when a critical level is exceeded. Opposite shift (i.e. toward hyperpolarization) gives no such membrane breakdown. Rather, that change simulates the process called hyperpolarization which is associated with synaptic inhibition.

Even excluding its elongated axon a neuron may be a remarkably extended cell, major dendrites sometimes passing as much as 0·6–2·0 mm. away from the soma. Only the excitable membrane covering the axon produces potentials of all-or-none self-regenerating type suitable for conveying impulses without decrement to the axon terminals. By contrast potentials of soma and dendrites are graded in amplitude and die away with increasing distance from the stimulus point. However, the surface of soma and dendrites is studded with a swarm of synapses, each capable of producing a local graded response at a tiny spot of subsynaptic membrane. Such excitatory post-synaptic potentials are ordinarily equated with "pre-potentials" of axonal conduction. Those are graded local disturbances set off by subthreshold shocks below that required for firing of a nerve impulse. In propitious records of neuron somata prepotentials may be detected as notches upon the rise phase of all-or-none spikes recorded from the soma at the time of discharge of the cell. The term prepotential seems sometimes to be used synonomously with "generator potential", a term ordinarily applied to the initiation of impulses at the receptors in skin and muscles.

The two kinds of synapses

Two kinds of synapses have been proved electro-physiologically for motoneurons (Eccles) and several other species of nerve cells—excitatory and inhibitory ones. No sure morphological differences have been detected between them, although Uchizono equated round synaptic vesicles with excitatory and ovoid ones with inhibitory transmitter (p. 4). Chemical mediation across synaptic clefts of excitatory synapses in vertebrates by acetylcholine has been proved for motor end-plates and Renshaw cells of the spinal cord, although it is presumed to take place elsewhere as well. An indisputably accepted inhibitory transmitter has not been isolated for vertebrate inhibitory synapses.

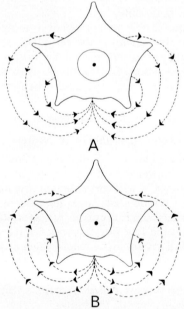

A

B

FIG. 6. Theoretical interpretation of the lines of current flow as they might exist about the soma of a nerve cell during excitation (A) and inhibition (B) occurring at a synapse. All such closed lines of flow are conceived of as entering and then leaving the cell or axon in question, or vice versa. In the excitatory situation current enters at the synapse (arrows inward) over lines of flow which converge exteriorly indicating the drawing of current from the remainder of the soma membrane. This produces the EPSP or excitatory postsynaptic potential. In the inhibitory situation (B) current flows outwards at the synapse and returns over exterior lines to close-by and distant points upon the soma surface. This hyperpolarizes the site of the synapse and produces the IPSP or inhibitory potential.

Activity at an excitatory synapse (EPSP, excitatory postsynaptic potential) involves a spot depolarization necessitating transport of Na^+, K^+, and Cl ions. Inward flow of current conveyed by Na^+ across the synaptic cleft results in the postsynaptic potential (Fig. 6A). Return current flow is through the remainder of the soma-dendrite membrane, shifting resting potential value there in the direction of depolarization. Depending upon the distance the active synapse is from axon hillock, a postsynaptic excitatory process at a single point could decrement too rapidly to make an effective contribution to the issuance of all-or-none impulses. Thus we are likely to invoke a process called electrotonus to explain how a distant synaptic site could influence the detonator region at the axon hillock.

Consider that when current passes inward through the cell membrane at one point, it must leave at other loci, completing the circuit through the internal core of the element (soma or dendrite) involved. In the case of the dendrite the element is linear, and the core has a significantly high resistance. Thus, a decreasing amount of current flows per unit area of membrane at increasing distance along the dendrite from the point of origin. Excitable membrane also has capacity which is charged with increasing slowness at successively longer distances from the source of excitation. For that reason voltage peaks recorded at increasing distances along the dendrite are attained at successively later times, and although current starts to flow simultaneously to all loci, the voltage peaks move later in time with greater distances from the entry of the current, giving the appearance of conduction by electrotonus. Such flow can occur despite the fact that there is no associated membrane breakdown, and (in theory at least) the cumulative effects of many point impacts on dendrites can be summed to regulate the output of all-or-none impulses from the axon hillock.

The postsynaptic inhibitory potential (IPSP) is also graded, but the membrane becomes permeable only to K^+ and, possibly, Cl ions. In this instance current flow is inward over most of the neuron membrane and outward at the point of the synapse (Fig. 6B). As a result the potential of the interior of the soma shifts negatively, and the membrane becomes hyperpolarized. However, that is not the universal case for inhibition. It has been shown for the crustacean stretch receptor neuron that inhibition can occur even though the membrane potential remains fixed. However, in the situation membrane conductance presumably increases.

Extraneous agents can mimic postsynaptic excitatory and inhibitory synaptic actions. In general, anaesthetics reduce or prevent the excitatory increase in membrane permeability. On the other hand, facilitatory agents increase permeability and permit depolarization to occur more readily, the effect being to heighten excitability. Negative currents applied from an external source (as a battery) excite axonal membranes exactly as does the current generated locally by physiological means. Positive currents should prevent excitation quite as does inhibitory activity by diverting a local excitatory current through the permeable inhibitory area of the membrane itself.

As a nerve cell dies, or as its oxygen supply is diminished, its metabolism decreases, permeability to all ions increases, the concentration potential falls, and the element becomes inexcitable. When narcotized, to the contrary, the permeability of the membrane is decreased. Stronger stimuli are then required to excite it, leading to the membrane becoming inexcitable for the opposite reason.

FURTHER READING

Bishop, G. H. (1965), "My Life Among the Axons," *Ann. Rev. Physiol.*, **27**, 1.

Bodian, D. (1937), The Structure of the Vertebrate Synapse: "A Study of Axon Endings on Mauthner's Cell and Neighboring Centers of the Gold-fish," *J. comp. neurol.*, **68**, 117.

Bullock, T. H. (1959), "Neuron Doctrine and Electrophysiology," *Science*, **129**, 997.

de Reuck, A. V. S. and Knight, J. (1966), "Concluding Discussion," in *Touch, Heat and Pain*, A Ciba Foundation Symposium. Boston: Little, Brown and Company.

del Castillo, J. and Katz, B. (1954), "Quantal Components of the End Plate Potential," *J. Physiol.* (*Lond.*), **124**, 560.

Gabe, M. (1966), *Neurosecretion*. Oxford: Pergamon Press.

Gray, E. G. (1956), "Axosomatic and Axodendritic Synapses of the Cerebral Cortex. An Electron Microscopic Study," *J. Anat.* (*Lond.*), **193**, 420.

Ham, A. W. (1969), *Histology*. Phila.: J. B. Lippincott Company.

Hamburger, V. (1957), "The Life History of a Nerve Cell," *Amer. Sci.*, **45**, 326.

Hartman, J. F. (1968), "Newer Knowledge of the Neurons in the Central Nervous System," in *The Central Nervous System* (O. T. Bailey and E. Smith, Eds.). Baltimore: Williams and Wilkins.

Iggo, A. (1959), "A Single Unit Analysis of Cutaneous Receptors with C Afferent Fibers," from *Pain and Itch*, Ciba Foundation, Study Group No. 1 (G. A. Wolstenholme and M. O'Connor, Eds.), p. 41. Boston: Little, Brown and Company.

Katz, B. and Miledi, R. (1963), "A Study of Spontaneous Miniature Potentials in Spinal Motoneurons," *J. Physiol.* (*Lond.*), **170**, 389.

Katz, B. (1966), *Nerve, Muscle and Synapse*. New York: McGraw-Hill.

Lowry, O. H. (1966), "Energy Metabolism of the Nerve Cell," in *Nerve as a Tissue*, (K. Radahl and B. Issekutz, Eds.). N.Y.C.: Harper and Row.

O'Leary, J. L. (1962), "A Liter and a Half of Brains. Contemporary Survey in Electrophysiology," *Arch. Neurol.*, **7**, 487; **8**, 35; **8**, 178.

Palay, S. L. (1958), "The Morphology of Synapses in the Central Nervous System," *Exp. Cell. Res. Suppl.*, p. 275.

Palay, S. L. (1964), "The Structural Basis of Neural Action," in *Brain Function* (M. A. B. Brazier, Ed.). Los Angeles: U. of Calif. Press.

Peters, A. (1968), "The Morphology of Axons of the Central Nervous System," in *The Structure and Function of Nervous Tissue* (G. H. Bourne, Ed.). New York: Academic Press.

Robertson, J. D. (1966), "Design Principles of the Unit Membrane," in *Principles of Biomedical Organization*, A Ciba Foundation Symposium (G. E. W. Wolstenholme and M. O'Conner, Eds.), p. 357. Boston: Little, Brown and Company.

Sperry, R. W. (1959), "The Growth of Nerve Circuits," *Sci. Amer.*, **201**, 68.

Zachs, S. I. (1964), *The Motor End Plate*. Phila.: W. B. Saunders and Company.

2. THE GLIA

ROBERT G. GROSSMAN

In 1846 Virchow designated the substance which intervenes between neurons as neuroglia or nerve glue. Later Deiters saw individual corpuscles or cells in the interstitial substance of brain tissue, and in 1893 Andriezen first described the fibrous and protoplasmic astrocytes. Cajal used metallic impregnation to study the astrocytes in more detail. He also characterized smaller glial cells and called them "the third element". This third element was subsequently divided by del Rio-Hortega into oligodendrocytes and microglial cells.

Astrocytes and oligodendrocytes are termed macroglia in contrast to microglial cells. The Schwann cells of peripheral nerves and the satellite cells of sensory ganglia can be designated the glial cells of the peripheral nervous system. They resemble the oligodendrocytes of the CNS in many ways. The cells of the ependyma and the epithelial elements of the choroid plexus might also be included in a survey of non-neural cells of nervous tissue, as they have properties in common with those of the macroglia.

A marked increase in knowledge of the physiology of glia has occurred over the past fifteen years as a result of the study of these cells in invertebrate and vertebrate *in vitro* and *in vivo* preparations, and by the techniques of light and electron microscopy, radioautography, histochemistry, microchemistry and microelectrode recording. Many of the current concepts which concern glia may require modification or clarification in the near future. A recurrent problem regarding the experimental attack on the problem has been the histological identification of the type of cell under study. As yet insufficient information has been obtained about glia to generalize concerning their properties, since most findings have resulted from experimental work conducted in a few areas of the nervous system (nerves, ganglia, cerebral cortex) in a small number of species (leech, necturus, rat, cat). This chapter will deal with the morphology, development, physiological properties, functions in normal brain, and reactions to injury, of the glia. In certain instances, the probable type of glial cell that is responsible for a known glial activity is indicated by means of parentheses and a question mark.

MORPHOLOGY OF GLIA AND RELATIONSHIPS TO NEURONS AND BLOOD VESSELS

The glia of the mammalian brain are generally smaller than neurons. Figure 1 illustrates the relative sizes of the glia and neurons in the cortex. In contrast to neurons, glia do not have axons, nor do axon terminals synapse upon them. The staining reactions of glia differ from those of neurons. Besides the nuclei which stain in both cell types, aniline dyes such as thionine stain the Nissl substance of nerve cell cytoplasm strongly; on the contrary the cytoplasm of the astrocyte stains weakly, perhaps due to the lesser amount of endoplasmic reticulum it contains, and it is principally the nuclei of glia that stain by thionine. Metallic impregnation techniques are used to reveal the more obscure details of glial morphology by light microscopy. Electron microscopy has shown that the nuclei of glia have nucleoli.

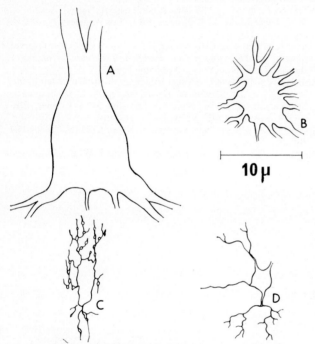

FIG. 1. Relative sizes of glia compared to an average pyramidal neuron of the motor cortex of the cat. A, pyramidal neuron. B, astrocyte. C, oligodendrocyte. D, multipolar form of a microglial cell. (After Ramon–Moliner, E. (1961) *J. Comp. Neurol.*, **117,** 43.)

Astrocytes

Astrocytes in the mammalian brain have elliptical or triangular bodies from which a number of tapering and branching processes arise, giving these cells star-like appearances. The diameters of astrocytic somata in the cortical grey matter of the cat average 8–10 μ, and astrocytic processes can extend for five or six times the diameter of the soma, or perhaps more. In electron micrographs the astrocytes have more electron-lucent cytoplasm than oligodendrocytes and neurons (Fig. 2). Astrocytic perikarya and processes contain mitochondria and glycogen granules (the latter 200–400 Å in diameter), both of which may constitute gliosomes as seen by light microscopy. Their cytoplasm also contains fibrils 80–90 Å in diameter, each having an electron-lucent core. These occur principally in bundles as also seen by light microscopy. Occasionally 250 Å microtubules can be observed as well.

On the basis of silver impregnation studies, astrocytes have been subclassified into protoplasmic and fibrous varieties. Fibrous astrocytes are found largely in white matter and show larger, straighter processes with more prominent cytoplasmic fibrils. The protoplasmic astrocytes are found in grey matter and present a bushy appearance due to the radiation of blunt cytoplasmic processes. These occur in a variety of morphological forms some of which are shown in Fig. 3 taken from a silver impregnation of cortex. This illustration also shows the layer of astrocytic cells and processes which lie just below the pia mater and form the external membrane (*glia limitans*) of the brain.

There are no striking qualitative differences in fine structure between normal astrocytes that derive from different areas of the CNS, although protoplasmic astrocytes have more convoluted membranes and fewer fibrils than do the fibrous ones. It is not known if astrocytes of different morphology have different functional properties, or whether these differences are only structural adaptations to the neurovascular matrix in which they develop.

Relationships of Astrocytes to Other Cells

The largest volume of the grey matter is made up of neuropil and consists of a tangle of neuronal and glial processes. Many of the glial processes have irregular shapes that appear to conform to surrounding neural structures. The distance between neural and glial membranes is not known with certainty for the living brain. In perfusion-fixed tissue the plasma membranes of neuronal and glial perikarya and processes are separated by extracellular clefts 150–200 Å in width. With freeze substitution fixation the extracellular space has been shown to be larger than the 150–200 Å width found using aldehyde or osmium perfusion fixation. When neuronal and astrocytic somata adjoin each other some interdigitation of their membranes can be seen, but areas of specialized contact between their surface membranes have yet to be adequately described.

When in contact with each other astrocytic membranes can show small areas of specialized contact. One type is the gap junction, in which small areas of membrane are apposed with a separation of about 20 Å between them. A second type of specialized contact is the *puncta adhaerentia*, a small spot of parallel apposition of membranes that are separated by a wider than normal extracellular cleft.

Many astrocytes have one or more processes which terminate as end-feet on capillaries. Although the end-feet have the appearance of specialized structures by light microscopy, electron microscopy has not revealed any specializations within the glial membranes which contact capillaries. The glial membrane and basement membrane of the capillary endothelial cell are generally closely apposed, but in some sites in the CNS they are separated by a cleft which contains collagen.

It is not known if central blood vessels are always completely ensheathed by the astrocytic processes which

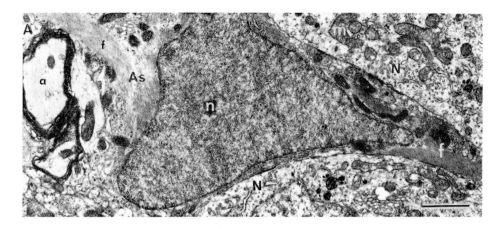

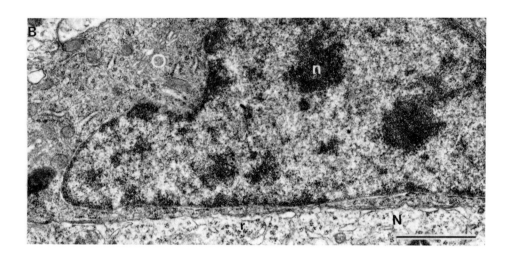

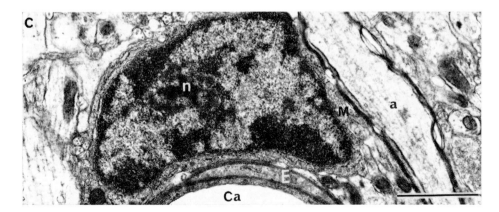

FIG. 2. Morphology of macroglia (A, B), and of pericytes (C). Motor cortex of the cat. A, Reactive astrocyte As. one month after a cortical injury produced by local freezing. The astrocytic cytoplasm surround the irregular nucleus n, contains bundles of fibrils f, which extend into a glial process lying between two neurons, N. B, Perineuronal satellite oligodendrocyte O, with a small amount of dense cytoplasm, adjacent to the soma of a neuron. C. Perivascular cell (pericyte?) M, adjacent to a capillary Ca, Endothelial cell E. Additional abbreviations: a, axon; m, mitochondrion; r, ribosomes of endoplasmic reticulum. Bar represents 1μ. Electron micrographs of Dr. Vick F. Williams.

make up the perivascular *glia limitans*. Some studies have shown an incomplete sheath with about 85 per cent of capillary surface in contact with astrocytic membranes and the remainder with oligodendrocytes, neural proceses, and pericytes. There are clefts between the adjacent cell membranes of the perivascular *glia limitans*, and small protein molecules like peroxidase can pass through them.

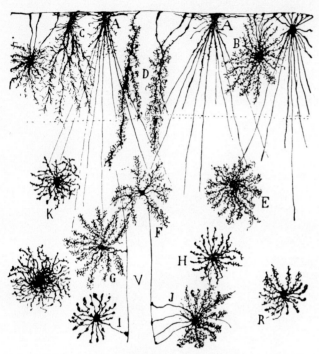

FIG. 3. Morphology of astrocytes of the gray matter of the human cortex (age 2 months). A–D, astrocytes of the molecular layer which form the external *glia limitans*. E–H, protoplasmic astrocytes. I, J, protoplasmic astrocytes with end-feet on a small blood vessel, V. (From Ramón y Cajal, S. (1911), Histologie du Systeme Nerveux. Vol. II, Paris: Maloine.)

Oligodendrocytes

Oligodendrocytes are smaller than astrocytes with shorter processes. Their cytoplasm is also more electron dense and contains a more compact endoplasmic reticulum (Fig. 2B). They also show 250 Å tubules, like those of neurons. Oligodendrocytes have generally been typified as interfascicular, lying in rows between axons in white matter, and perineuronal or satellite, in positions adjoining the neuronal perikarya. As noted above they also lie adjacent to capillaries. Interfascicular oligodendrocytes have a morphological relationship to axons, the myelin wrappings of which are formed of spirally wound condensed oligodendroglial membrane. An oligodendrocyte can have processes which wrap more than one axon. Oligodendrocyte membranes and adjacent myelin sheaths may come into very close apposition with each other.

Microglia

The microglia are fewer in number than the macroglial cells and are more difficult to identify as a distinct cell type.

With light microscopy when studied with metallic impregnation they generally have one to five spindly processes which have small spiny projections along their length. Their morphology depends to some degree on the matrix they lie in. In the white matter their processes can be spread in layers between nerve fibres (lamellar forms). They are more common in the grey matter, where they often are found in the position of perineuronal satellite cells. Electron microscopic identification of microglia is still controversial.

Pericytes are small, dark cells found in expansions of the basement membranes of capillaries (Fig. 2C). Pericytes may act as macrophages after brain injury.

Pericytes, macrophages from the bloodstream, and a recently described "third glial cell type" which somewhat resembles the satellite oligodendrocyte, but which may be a multipotential glial precursor cell, probably all have been described as microglial cells on light microscopy.

Distribution of Glial Cells in the Brain

The number of glial elements increases in complex brains by comparison with those which are more primitive. It has been estimated that there are about one-half as many glia as neurons in the rat cortex, but there are about twice as many in the human frontal cortex. More satellite neuroglia (oligodendrocytes?) are found around large neurons with large axons than around smaller neurons.

In certain areas of the brain there are greater numbers of one type of glial cell than of others. There are slightly more oligodendrocytes than astrocytes in the cortex (cat). The distribution of astrocytes is fairly constant throughout the different cortical layers, but the oligodendrocytes increase in number towards the white matter. The microglia are more numerous subpially than deeper in the cortex, and comprise about 10 per cent of the cortical glia. In the molecular layer of the cerebellum, particularly in lower animals, astrocytes are the preponderant glial cell. In the optic nerve oligodendrocytes are found only in the myelinated part of the nerve behind the lamina cribrosa. This portion of the nerve also contains astrocytes. Small astrocytic-like cells only are found in the nerve near the retina. A cluster of astroglial cells above the *area postrema* projects into the fourth ventricle. Other examples of areal congregations could also be given.

DEVELOPMENT OF GLIA

Glial development has been extensively studied in the rodent brain which undergoes a significant amount of postnatal development. Radioautographic studies of glial and neural uptake of ^{3}H-thymidine, which is incorporated into nucleic acids in dividing cells, and electron microscopy, have shown that there is a definite sequence of progression of neuronal and glial development. Neuroblasts first migrate outward from the subependymal cell layer or matrix layer, adjacent to the wall of the lateral ventricle, and begin to differentiate into neurons. After this process has started the spongioblasts migrate from the subependymal layer and develop into astroblasts and oligoblasts. Glial-vascular relationships are then established. Myelination begins to occur after neural development has progressed to a significant degree, and oligodendrocytes differentiate in large number at this time.

The origins of the microglia are still unclear. Some investigators consider them to be of reticulo-endothelial cell origin. During early development of the brain microglial cells appear to migrate into the brain from the pia-arachnoid. Other cells may enter from the blood vessels. Other investigators have labelled the cells of the subependymal layer with ^{3}H-thymidine and have found labelled microglial cells which appear to have migrated from the subependymal layer into the white matter.

Labelling of cells by ^{3}H-thymidine has also shown that the microglia and perhaps the astrocytes have a continual low rate of mitotic activity or turnover in adult life. There is no strong evidence that oligodendrocytes can proliferate in adult life.

PHYSIOLOGICAL PROPERTIES OF GLIA

Physiological properties of glia grown from explants of brain of newborn mammals have been studied in tissue culture (where they are dissociated from their normal vascular and neuronal relationships), in the abdominal ganglia of the leech, and optic nerves of amphibia and mammals where a glial cell envelops a number of axons. They have also been examined in the CNS of mammals, where the glial somata can be anatomically juxtaposed to neuronal perikarya as well as to axons, and where glial-vascular relationships are more extensive. The glia in all of these preparations are electrically and synaptically inexcitable.

Intracellular recording in vertebrate glia has shown that some glial cells exhibit slow depolarizing and hyperpolarizing potentials in response to neural activity. It is not yet known if these recordings were made in astrocytes or oligodendrocytes or both types of glia. It is probable that most were taken from astrocytes. It would be of

interest to know the electrophysiological activities of the oligodendrocyte membrane, inasmuch as myelin, which is the spirally wound condensed membrane of the oligodendrocyte, has a high resistance to current flow.

Membrane Properties of Mammalian Glia (Astrocytes?)

These properties, which are used to identify glia penetrated with intracellular recording electrodes, are illustrated in Fig. 4, for a glial cell in the cerebral cortex. The glial membrane behaves passively during the transmembrane passage of depolarizing and hyperpolarizing currents, as shown in Fig. 4B. Similar depolarization of neurons evokes graded responses or action potentials (regenerative responses), as shown in Fig. 4C. Very strong depolarization of glia produces a depolarizing response which is thought to be due to breakdown of the dielectric properties of their membranes. In contrast to neurons, which exhibit postsynaptic potentials (PSPs) due to neurotransmitter mediated changes of ionic conductance, glia do not exhibit PSPs when afferent projections terminating on neurons in their vicinity are fired. The absence of postsynaptic and spike potentials in glia has led to their being called "silent" or "idle" cells. Glia nevertheless do exhibit another type of potential change in response to neuronal activity, which will be described below. In tissue culture glial cells (oligodendrocytes?, astrocytes?) and ependymal cells have membrane potentials of up to 70 −mV., and in the brain glial cells (astrocytes?) have membrane potentials of up to −95 mV. (Fig. 4A). Whether some glia in the brain may normally have low membrane potentials is not known, but it can be said that some glial cells have a membrane potential about 20 mV. larger than that of the neurons adjacent to them.

In addition to these differences in glial and neural membrane excitability and potential, mammalian glial cells with high membrane potentials have membranes that appear to have much lower specific resistance than neurons.

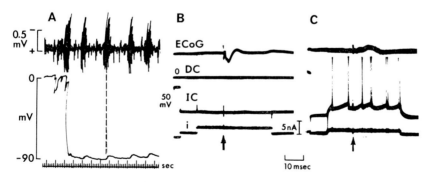

FIG. 4. Electrophysiological identification of glia and neurons. Motor cortex, cat. A, upper line, recording of electrocorticogram (ECoG); lower line, penetration of a glial cell with a micropipette, recording of a large membrane potential and slow depolarizing potentials. B, inexcitability of the glial membrane to the intracellular passage of depolarizing current, and to firing of synaptic terminals in the area of the cell. On the lowest line the passage of current is shown, and on the line above it the intracellular recording from the cell. The upper line is the cortical surface ECoG recording. At the arrow thalamo-cortical afferent fibres were stimulated. C, excitability of the neuronal membrane with similar stimulation which evokes action potentials. (Figs. 4, 7 and 9 from Grossman, R. G., Whiteside, L. and Hampton, T. (1969), *Brain Res.*, **14**, 401,)

The specific resistance of their membranes expressed as ohm cm.^{2} of the membrane, has been measured to be as low as 10 to 100 ohm cm.^{2} in tissue culture and about 500 ohm cm.^{2} *in vivo*. These measurements are subject to considerable error and require assuming the surface area of the cell, but it appears that the glial membrane is highly permeable to some ion species, and it will be seen below that K$^+$ is one of the ions to which the glial membrane is highly permeable.

An alternative explanation of the apparently low resistance of glial membranes in the brain is that the glia may be electrically coupled together and form a syncytium, in the manner of cardiac muscle fibres. Electrical coupling of glia in the optic nerve of amphibia has been demonstrated, and as will be discussed below, is the reason why glial potentials can be recorded from the surface of the optic nerves with gross electrodes. As discussed in relationship to glial anatomy it has recently been found that gap junctions of apposing membranes which are seen in electrically coupled cells, such as heart muscle, are found between astrocytes. Whether the extent of gap junctions between astrocytes is sufficient to couple them is unknown. A direct electrical test of coupling requires passage of current into one glial cell with simultaneous recording in another, which has not yet been accomplished in glia in the brain. Therefore there is no direct evidence at present that the glia of the brain form a functional syncytium.

Ionic Permeability and Ionic Content of Glia and the Glial Membrane Potential

The very large membrane potentials of some glia, which are larger than those of mammalian neurons, and as large as those of muscle fibres, suggest that these glia should be cells with high internal concentrations of K$^+$ and a membrane which is selectively highly permeable to K$^+$ as are muscle and nerve. This idea has been tested directly by measuring the membrane potentials of glia while varying the concentration of K$^+$ in the extracellular fluid around the glia. In glia in leech ganglia and in the amphibian optic nerve the glial membrane potential decreased with increasing concentration of extracellular K$^+$ with a slope of 58 mV. for a tenfold change in K$^+$ ECF. This relationship, which is shown in Fig. 5, is in exact agreement with the electrochemical equilibrium predicted by the Nernst equation that relates the potential across a semipermeable membrane to the concentrations of the ion, to which the membrane is permeable, on the inside and the outside of the cell membrane. In fact, the slope of the change in membrane potential with changes in extracellular K$^+$ is closer to that predicted by the Nernst equation over a wider range of K$^+$ for glia than for neurons. Varying Na$^+$ and Cl$^-$ has no effect on the membrane potential, suggesting a selective permeability to K$^+$. Both calculation of the internal concentration of K$^+$ and direct measurement give an internal concentration of K$^+$ of about 100 mequiv./l.

Similar experiments on the K$^+$ dependence of the membrane potential of mammalian optic nerve and cortical glia have found a change of potential of about 40 mV. for a tenfold change of K$^+$ ECF. Whether this means that the membrane potential of mammalian glia is in part determined by permeability to other ions, or that the results are due to technical difficulties, is not known.

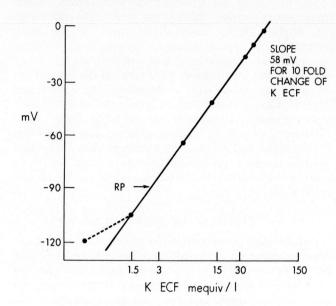

FIG. 5. Relationship of the membrane potential of a glial cell in the amphibian optic nerve to changes in the concentration of K$^+$ in the extracellular fluid (ECF). RP indicates the initial level of membrane potential. The dotted line indicates the deviation from the predicted slope at very low K$^+$ concentrations. (After Kuffler, S. W., Nicholls, J. G. and Orkand, R. K. (1966) *J. Neurophysiol.*, **29**, 768.)

The ionic content of mammalian glia is not definitely known. The brain contains a large amount of Na$^+$ in comparison with muscle, another tissue containing excitable cells. The major ions in these tissues, in mequiv./l. are:

	Na$^+$	K$^+$	Cl$^-$
Brain	50	100	30
Muscle	20	100	15

It has been suggested that the glia (astrocytes) contain high concentrations of Na$^+$. However, the Na$^+$ content of the brain can be theoretically accounted for by the distribution of Na$^-$ in both neurons and glia, that contain high concentrations of K$^+$ and smaller concentrations of Na$^+$, without assuming that there must be certain cells with high levels of Na$^+$. Probable ranges of ionic concentration in compartments of the brain are shown in Fig. 6.

Slow Depolarizing Potentials of Glia

Glial depolarization following neuronal activity was first described in the optic nerve glia of amphibia. In the optic nerve and in the mammalian cortex following the firing of neurons, glia (astrocytes?) adjacent to the active neurons exhibit a graded slow depolarizing potential. If

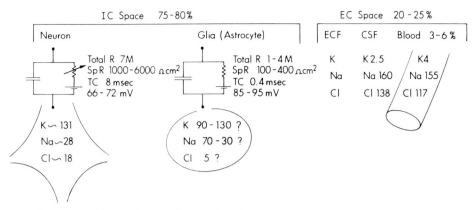

FIG. 6. Probable distribution of major ions in compartments of the brain, and average membrane properties and ionic content of cortical pyramidal neurons and astrocytes, based on data from cat cortex. Abbreviations: SpR, specific resistance of 1 cm² of membrane; TC, time constant of membrane.

the firing is repetitive the depolarizations summate as shown in Fig. 7. In Fig. 7A the motor cortex was activated by repetitive afferent volleys evoked by stimulation of thalamo-cortical fibres. In the upper trace (IC) the intracellular depolarizing responses of a glial cell are shown in response to volleys delivered at 8 sec. In the lower trace (EC), with the electrode just outside of the cell, small field potentials of the neuronal activity evoked

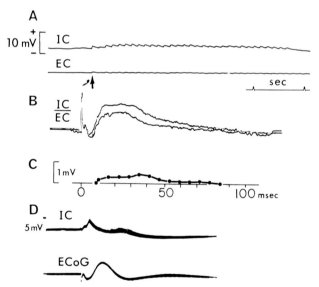

FIG. 7. Relationships of glial potentials evoked by neuronal activity in the brain to the time course of neuronal potentials. A, intracellular recording (IC) from a cortical glial cell and extracellular recording adjacent to the cell during 8 sec stimulation of thalamo-cortical afferents. B, intracellular and extracellular potentials compared. C, time course of glial depolarization after a single thalamic volley. D, intracellular potentials of a pyramidal neuron of the same area of the cortex, and ECoG response after a single thalamic volley.

by the stimuli are recorded. The time course of glial depolarization in this situation can be seen without contamination by the neural potentials by subtracting the

extracellular record from the intracellular record (Fig. 7B). The glial depolarization is shown in Fig. 7C. It follows the neuronal field potentials and intracellularly recorded postsynaptic potentials of adjacent neurons (Fig. 7D) with a latency of about 10 msec.

During extremely strong electrocortical activity as in a seizure or during spreading depression of cortical activity during which extra cellular K⁺ rises to high levels the glia may depolarize by 30 to 40 mV. The level of a glial cell's membrane potential appears to fluctuate with the level of activity of adjacent neurons, and in about one-fifth of the cortical glia studied with micropipette recordings, slow depolarizations of up to 5 mV. occur during the synchronous activity of cortical neurons which generate the alpha-rhythm-like spindle burst waves of the electrocorticogram, as shown in Fig. 4A. Following cessation of neuronal activity that evokes glial depolarization, cortical glia repolarize over several seconds.

Mechanism of Glial Depolarization. Slow depolarization of glia appears to be mediated by the release of substances from neurons. It has been calculated that the amounts of K⁺ released during neural activity could produce the observed glial depolarization if the glial cell behaved as a K⁺ electrode. In the case of a cell with a membrane potential of −95 mV. bathed in ECF with a K⁺ concentration of 3·0 mequiv./l., the increase in the extracellular K⁺ concentration required to produce a depolarization of 10 mV. would be 1·4 mequiv./l. There is no strong evidence that transmitter substances liberated by neurons can produce changes in conductance of the glial membrane, i.e. by the mechanism generating PSPs in neurons. Mechanisms thought to be involved in glial potential changes are shown in Fig. 8. The rate of glial depolarization and repolarization is a function of the rate of neuronal release of K⁺ and the removal of K⁺ from the surface of the glial cell. K⁺ may be removed by diffusion and by neuronal re-uptake, and possibly by glial uptake. This possibility will be discussed further below.

It has recently been found that after the depolarization of cortical glia evoked by a period of intense neuronal activity, as during a seizure, the glial membrane often will hyperpolarize for about a minute. It is not known if this represents a passive response of the glial membrane to changes in extracellular ions, or is a sign of mediated uptake or active transport of ions into the glia.

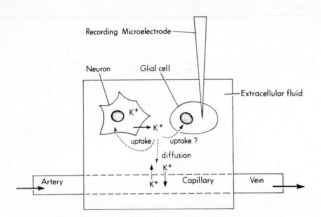

FIG. 8. Model of the mechanism of depolarization of a glial cell by K^+ liberated from neurons. See text for description.

The Contribution of Glial Potentials to Potentials Recorded from the Nervous System

Slow potentials recorded extracellularly during neuronal activity. If there is differential depolarization of two points on the surface of a cell an extracellular current will flow between them, as illustrated in Fig. 10. Whether this potential drop across the resistance of the extracellular fluid can be detected by extracellular electrodes depends on the size of the potential dipole and the size and relationship of the recording electrodes. In the amphibian optic nerve the glia are connected by low resistance bridges so that current can flow through them as if they were a syncytium, and therefore glial depolarization in one portion of the nerve can be recorded from the surface of the nerve with gross electrodes which are much larger than the individual glial cells.

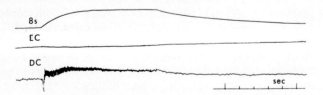

FIG. 9. Relationship between glial depolarization evoked by 8/sec thalamic stimulation, shown in the upper line and slow potential shift (DC potential) recorded from the cortical surface shown on the lower line. The middle line EC is an extracellular recording made just outside of the glial cell.

It can be seen from inspection of Fig. 7A that glial potentials evoked by fast neural activity tend to summate into slow potentials, and therefore they tend to follow the envelope of bursts of fast EEG activity, as in Fig. 4A.

Therefore it is unlikely that glial potentials contribute to fast EEG activity. However, glial potentials might contribute to the slow potential shifts which can be recorded from the cortex and other brain areas. An example of the temporal correspondence of glial depolarization and a slow potential shift which were both evoked in the cortex by repetitive thalamic volleys is shown in Fig. 9. The proof of whether glial potentials contribute significantly to slow potential shifts in the brain and spinal cord would appear to depend on demonstrating that they can form long dipoles, which could be formed by long glial fibres in the brain (cf. Fig. 3) or by electrical coupling.

Blood–Brain Potentials. If an electrode is placed in the CSF and another in the blood a potential will be recorded with the CSF 2 to 7 mV. positive to the blood. This potential might be generated across ependymal or perivascular glial cells. The interior of the ependymal cells covering the choroid plexus is about 64 mV. negative to the ventricular fluid, and 50 mV. negative to the interstitial tissue of the plexus. Therefore there is a potential across the ependyma with the CSF positive to the interior of the plexus. The CSF-blood potential might be set by the concentration of ions in cerebral compartments, or it might partially regulate the distribution of ions in these compartments (cf. Fig. 6). There are species differences in this potential and in its sensitivity to changes in the blood and CSF. In the dog where the CSF is positive the potential is inversely related to the pH of the blood, being $+15$ mV. at an arterial pH of 7·1 and -3 mV. at a pH of 7·6. The H^+ sensitivity of the potential has a slope of 42 mV. per pH unit change in the blood, whereas a slope of about 60 mV. would be predicted for a perfect pH electrode. In the cat and monkey the CSF-blood or transvascular potential is shifted negatively by intravenous injection of beta-adrenergic catecholamines.

Aspects of Metabolism of Glia Related to Ionic Movements

Study of the biochemical activities of individual types of glia has been hampered by the difficulty of separating glia from neurons, and until recently data have been obtained on glial enriched fractions of brain homogenates, or on single cells or lumps of glia dissected from the brain. Methods of separation which involve partial digestion of brain tissue with enzymes and mechanical and centrifugal dissociation of neurons and glia have recently been developed.

Histochemical stains for enzymes give some information about possible metabolic pathways in individual glia. Astrocytes have much lower concentrations of some enzymes used in oxidative metabolism than do neurons or oligodendrocytes. Glial perikaryal membranes contain Na^+–K^+ activated ATPase. Astrocytes in tissue culture swell when exposed to low concentrations of ouabain, a drug which reduces Na^+ and K^+ transport dependent upon ATPase. Increasing extracellular K^+ stimulates glial respiration. Increasing extracellular K^+ also mediates uptake of Cl^- into glia (astrocytes?) and produces glial swelling. K^+ enter as well. It is not clear if this process involves active transport, and which ion (K^+, Cl^-) is the primary and which the counter-ion. K^+ mediated swelling of glia is dependent upon the presence of Cl⁻ and Na⁺ in the ECF and can be prevented by substituting other anions for Cl⁻.

FUNCTIONS OF GLIA IN NORMAL BRAIN

With the exception of the participation of oligodendrocyte membranes in the formation of the myelin wrappings of axons the functions of the glia in the normal brain are unknown. Many roles have been proposed on the basis of their anatomical relationships to neurons and blood vessels and on the basis of their physiological and metabolic activities. These functions can be classified as structural and as metabolic with respect to the activity of neurons. Most of the theories of normal glial function have been advanced for the astrocytes, although some of these roles could also be discussed with respect to oligodendrocytes.

Astrocytes

Structural Functions. Historically one of the first functions proposed for the glia was that it was a structural matrix binding the nervous system together. The cytoplasmic filaments of astrocytes have been considered as possibly providing rigidity for the astrocyte and thereby for the brain tissue. In contrast, however, the plasma membrane of astrocytes in tissue culture is more delicate than that of the neuron.

Cajal suggested another structural role for glia, that of insulating the neurons from each other. It has been suggested that astrocytic processes form compartments around neurons which separate axonal terminals belonging to functionally different systems from each other. This type of partitioning is shown schematically for a single afferent fibre terminal for each of two systems in Fig. 12. The glial processes might act as barriers to the diffusion of different neurotransmitters.

Metabolic Functions. It has often been suggested that astrocytes function in the metabolism of neurons. This role has been thought of in two ways, one of supplying metabolites to the neuron, possibly transporting substances from pericapillary end-feet to neurons, and secondly, of removing metabolic byproducts of neural activity. It has been shown that the extracellular clefts in the leech nervous system are adequate channels for diffusion of metabolites and ions to the neurons, and that neurons isolated from glia continue to function for long periods of time. These findings, however, do not rule out the possibility that glia may interact metabolically with neurons. Metabolic interaction might occur in periods of increased neural activity. This might be more important in the mammalian brain where the metabolic activity of neurons is much greater than in invertebrates or cold-blooded vertebrates.

K⁺ Regulation. The glial-neural interaction for which there is most evidence is that of the possible glial uptake from the extracellular fluid of K⁺ released from active neurons. A way in which this could occur as a result of the depolarization of part of a glial process adjacent to a site of K⁺ release is shown in Fig. 10. As a result of the difference in transmembrane potential between the depolarized and normally charged portion of the membrane current flows in the extracellular space, carried largely by Na⁺ which is the predominant extracellular cation, and to a lesser extent by K⁺. Since the glial membrane is thought to be selectively permeable to K⁺, the inward current into the cell and the outward current will be carried by K⁺. The effect of the current flow is to passively transport K⁺ from a site of high concentration in the extracellular fluid to a site of lower concentration, thereby buffering the extracellular space against increases in K⁺ which might depolarize neurons or axon terminals.

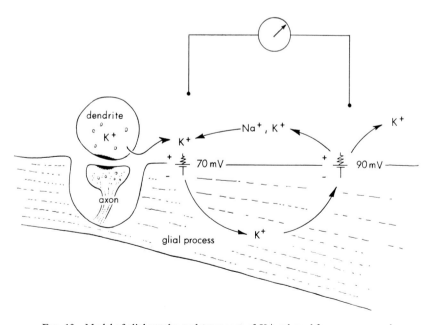

FIG. 10. Model of glial uptake and transport of K⁺ released from neurons and their processes.

This mechanism of buffering the extracellular clefts against local increases in K^+ would break down in the face of a general increase in neural activity with a widespread release of K^+, as during a seizure, a situation in which a mechanism for regulating extracellular K^+ would be most important. There is some electrophysiological and metabolic evidence that active transport or uptake of K^+ or Cl^- by mammalian glia might occur, as discussed above in the sections on glial physiology and metabolism.

CO$_2$ and H$^+$ Regulation. Neuronal metabolism results in the production of large amounts of CO_2. The high concentration of carbonic anhydrase in some glia seen on histochemical study (astrocyctes?) suggests that these cells might be involved in CO_2 removal. A mechanism by which H^+ excretion into the blood is linked with Na^+ transport into the extracellular fluid has been proposed which also might explain the higher concentration of Na^+ in the CSF than in the blood.

Glia and the Blood–Brain Barrier. It is currently thought that the tight junctions between endothelial cells of capillaries are the structural basis of the blood–brain barrier. Tracer molecules such as peroxidase which can be visualized on electron microscopy are prevented from entering the brain past the endothelial cells by these junctions. It is not known if the endothelial cell is the barrier to highly charged lipophobic molecules such as trypan blue. The inability of these dye molecules to penetrate the brain from the blood gave rise to the barrier concept. However, since the perivascular *glia limitans* may not completely ensheath capillaries and since there are clefts between the cells of the sheath, it does not seem to be a candidate for the barrier. Nevertheless if glia have ion-transporting activity it might contribute to barrier functions and to the brain–blood potentials.

Transmitter Metabolism. It has been suggested that glia may inactivate or metabolize neurotransmitters. There is no evidence that glia is involved in the metabolism of acetylcholine and catecholamines. The presence of glutamic decarboxylase in glia suggests that it could function in the metabolism of the amino acids which are also putative neurotransmitters, although this is a tenuous hypothesis at present.

Supply of Metabolic Substrates to Neurons. Most of the evidence for this possible function comes from the experiments of Hydén and coworkers who isolated single neurons and satellite glia (oligodendrocytes?, astrocytes?) of the lateral vestibular nuclei by microdissection and studied their metabolism after animals were subjected to procedures which presumably increased, and in other cases decreased, neuronal activity. Reciprocal relationships of the level of cytochrome oxidase, succinoxidase and RNA in neurons and glia after presumed high and low levels of neuronal activity were considered evidence of a metabolic inter-relationship of neurons and glia, with the suggestion that glia supplies energy-rich compounds to neurons.

Oligodendrocytes

The role of these cells in the formation and maintenance of the myelin sheath of axons appears to be established. However, the functions of oligodendrocytes seen as satellite cells around central neuronal perikarya and adjacent to blood vessels are not clear. In a so-called satellite position oligodendrocyte membranes in the cortex show no specializations with respect to neuronal perikarya, and their perineuronal position may be functionally unrelated to the neuronal soma. Their actual function may relate to axons out of the plane of the section. Oligodendrocytes in tissue culture exhibit a remarkable pulsatile activity with a periodicity of 5–6 min., contracting over about 1 min. and expanding over about 3 min. The function of this activity, if it occurs *in vivo*, can only be speculated upon, but might be related to the wrapping of processes around axons.

At present no function can be assigned to microglia in normal brain, unless it is in relationship to a role as macrophages.

Possible Role of Glia in "Plastic Changes" in Neural Function

The idea has been put forward that reactions of glia to neural activity might in turn modify subsequent neural activity and thereby produce modifications of neural behaviour. Both structural changes in the relationship of glial processes to nerve terminals and synapses, and changes in metabolic efficiency with respect to neurons have been suggested. The motility of glia in tissue culture, and its electrophysiological activity *in vivo* indicate that there may be heuristic value in thinking of the glia as an active participant in neural activity. However its role in modifying normal neuronal activity has not yet been subjected to rigorous testing.

REACTIONS OF GLIA IN INJURY
AND DISEASES

Injury produces regressive and developmental changes which occur at different rates in neurons, glia and blood vessels. Although the mechanisms of these changes are not well understood, a common factor in many types of injury appears to be the interference with the supply of oxygen and metabolites. After 1–2 min. of anoxia synaptic transmission fails in the cortex, and the EEG is therefore absent. After 3 min. of anoxia, the membrane potentials of cortical neurons start to decrease, a process which is reversible for a few additional minutes. The sensitivity of the membrane potentials and other properties of glia to anoxia are unknown. Metabolic studies suggest that oligodendrocytes are more sensitive to anoxia than astrocytes. Similar findings are suggested by studies of chronic cyanide poisoning of the cytochrome system of cells, which produces damage to oligodendrocytes and neurons and subsequent demyelination, with lesser effects on astrocytes.

Repair of an injury occurs by means of at least three processes. The first is the reversal of regressive changes, or development of hypertrophic changes of injured cells. The second process is migration of new cells into the damaged area. The third process is the proliferation of the fixed cells at the site of injury, and of cells which have entered the site of injury. The cellular responses of hypertrophy, migration and proliferation which will be referred to as glial reaction are largely confined to the astrocytes and microglia, and to the endothelial cells if blood vessels have been injured. Evidence for the formation of collateral sprouts of central axon terminals, in response to the degeneration of adjacent synaptic terminals, has recently been found but proliferation of neurons or oligodendrocytes is not known to occur after an injury in adult life.

The stimulus which triggers the glial reaction after injury is unknown. The reaction develops more quickly and is more intense around traumatic injuries in which capillary permeability is increased than around degenerating axons in an area of intact capillaries. The reaction is also more intense around a cortical puncture wound made with a solid needle which crushes tissue than around a surgical excision made with a hollow trocar that cleanly removes a core of tissue. These findings and a correlation between the duration and spread of oedema fluid and the rate of development and distribution of astrocytic reaction have led to the suggestion that some substance in the oedema fluid, which is not normally present in the ECF, stimulates glial reaction. Serum proteins and increases in K$^+$ concentration may be the factors. Since glial reaction also occurs around degenerating neurons it is possible that some substance released from degenerating neurons, or a change in the surface contacts of the cells can be a stimulus for reaction.

Reactions of Astrocytes

Astrocytes in an area which has sustained an injury produced by mechanical trauma or vascular occlusion respond acutely by swelling. Serum proteins and blood cells enter the extracellular clefts to a variable degree depending upon the severity of the injury. Oedema and red cells are largely cleared from the tissue in one to two weeks although the blood–brain barrier may be abnormally permeable to dyes for a month or longer. Axonal degeneration and chromatolysis can appear in a few days and be present for several weeks. Injury generally results in atrophy of the tissue due to the loss of neural processes, whose bulk is not compensated for by glial hypertrophy. These relationships are shown schematically in Fig. 11.

If the injury is severe enough to kill the astrocytes, degenerating processes surrounded by microglia can be seen within a week. Reactive glial changes occur in 48–72 hr., and consist of hypertrophy of cells, and of mitoses. Mitoses are maximal at 72–96 hr. and are largely gone by 1 week. Although binucleated astrocytes, and astrocytes in groups of four are frequently seen in injured brain, suggesting mitotic division of these cells, mitotic figures were not found in astrocytes until very recently, and these negative findings gave rise to the

concept that astrocytes divide amitotically. The recent observation of mitoses appears to be due to better methods of tissue fixation. What happens during mitosis to the astrocytic processes which are intricately extended between neural processes and around capillaries, and how are the relationships of the astrocytes to other cells shared by the daughter cells? Perhaps some degree of dissociation of contacts with other cells is required for astrocytic division. However they develop, new astrocytic-vascular relationships appear to be formed in injured brain due to astrocytic proliferation and to the ingrowth of new capillaries.

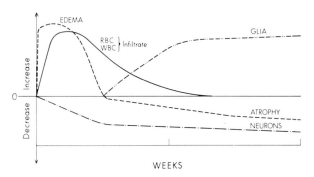

FIG. 11. Time course of development of changes in the number and size of glia and neurons following a local brain injury.

In 2–4 weeks after injury the astrocytic population studied by silver staining or electron microscopy consists of many hypertrophied cells with somas about 15 μ in diameter, or about twice the normal size. The proportion of these cells that develop as a result of cell division, compared to those that hypertrophy wthout dividing, and the relationships between hypertrophy and cell division are not known. The hypertrophied cells of experimental lesions are probably equivalent to the gemistocytic (fattened or plump) astrocytes of Nissl of human neuropathology.

In addition to hypertrophied astrocytes smaller cells are also present which resemble developing astrocytes. The hypertrophied astrocytes contain large numbers of fibrils (Fig. 2A), mitochondria, and glycogen granules. Lipid containing vacuoles are often present. The lipid appears to be derived from degenerating myelin. The astrocyte can also engulf degenerating axon terminals. There is some evidence, that astrocytes have a role as phagocytes after injury. The glial fibres seen on phosphotungstic acid—haematoxylin stained sections of the brain, which appear to be extracellular on light microscopy, may by electron microscopy be seen to be bundles of fibrils contained within astrocytic processes. These fibrils give old areas of injury their sclerotic, gliotic or scarred appearance. The fibrils may be arranged in whorls, or without any preponderant pattern, or may be arranged parallel to surviving axons, producing an isomorphic pattern of gliosis.

Glial reaction and cerebral oedema appear to be less

marked following injury in the neo-natal period than in the adult brain.

The most general astrocytic reaction to injury is hypertrophy with increased numbers of fibrils and glycogen granules. The functional significance of this response is unknown. Astrocytic processes appear to replace degenerating terminals at synaptic contact sites, as shown schematically in Fig. 12. They may have a role in preventing or determining new contacts which might be made. Increased numbers of fibrils may provide structural support for the injured tissue. Reactive astrocytes show a striking increase in enzymes used in oxidative metabolism. The rate of accumulation of glycogen in these cells after injury, and its significance are unknown.

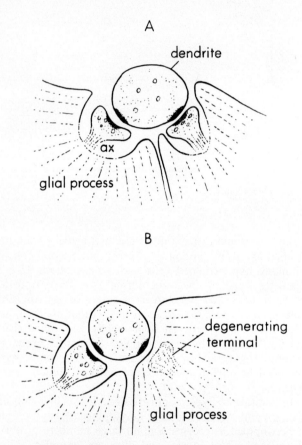

FIG. 12. Diagram of the replacement of a degenerating axonal terminal synapsing on a dendrite by a reactive glial process. On the left, two axonal terminals, represented as belonging to different afferent projections, each surrounded by a glial process. On the right, one of the terminals is degenerating and has been surrounded by a glial process which is also covering the site of the synaptic junction.

It has been suggested that one cause of the epileptic activity of cortical scars is the failure of astrocytes in the scar to buffer the extracellular clefts against increases in neuronally liberated K$^+$. Intracellular recording in areas of astrocytic scarring has shown that some glial cells in the scar have electrical activities similar to normal glia. However, many low-membrane potential cells (injured glia?) are present, and the behaviour of these cells may be quite important in the physiology of injured brain if the glia does function to regulate K$^+$ and other ions in the ECF.

Reactions of Oligodendrocytes

Acute swelling and vacuolization of the cytoplasm and pyknotic changes of the nucleus have been described in oligodendrocytes in a wide variety of diseases. The conditions under which this change occurs are not clearly defined. The change can be associated with the appearance of a mucinous glycolipid material in the cytoplasm.

Damage to oligodendrocytes is thought to produce demyelination. Demyelination can be produced by experimental allergic encephalomyelitis, CSF barbotage, and cyanide poisoning which damages both oligodendrocytes and axons so that the relationship of the demyelination to axonal and to glial damage is not completely clear in all of these cases.

Reactions of Microglia

Studies of the reactions of these cells in brain injury have been hampered by inability to distinguish clearly between reactive microglia and mononuclear leukocytes which enter the injured area from the blood. There are two populations of microglial-like cells at the site of an injury, those which have pre-existed in the tissue, and which undergo mitosis 48–72 hrs. after the injury in a zone several hundred microns wide around a puncture wound, and those which enter from the blood and which appear to have their peak period of proliferation from the third to seventh day after the injury.

The microglial cells pre-existing in tissue which has been damaged hypertrophy and appear to retract some of their processes. After section of the VII and XII nerves microglia increase in numbers around the neuronal somata which are undergoing chromatolysis, and these microglia exhibit peak numbers of mitoses in 72–96 hrs.

Phagocytosis of cellular debris in injured brain is largely carried out by mononuclear phagocytic cells. These cells have also been called lipid phagocytes, compound granular cells, and gitter cells. A series of stages in the transformation of microglia to these cells can be constructed but the proportions of the cells developing from microglia and developing from monuclear leukocytes remains unknown.

The rod cells (*Stäbchenzellen*) are bipolar forms of microglia with elongated nuclei which develop in certain diseases, notably in general paresis where they are vertically oriented in the cortex.

FURTHER READING

Bourke, R. S., Nelson, K. M., Naumann, R. A. and Young, O. M. (1970), "Studies of the Production and Subsequent Reduction of Swelling in Primate Cerebral Cortex Under Isosomotic Conditions *in vivo*," *Exp. Brain Res.*, **10**, 427.
Brightman, M. W. and Reese, T. S. (1969), "Junctions Between Intimately Apposed Cell Membranes in the Vertebrate Brain", *J. Cell Biol.*, **40**, 648.

Bunge, R. P. (1968), "Glial Cells and the Central Myelin Sheath," *Physiol. Rev.*, **48**, 197.

Castelluci, V. F. and Goldring, S. (1970), "Contribution to Steady Potential Shifts of Slow Depolarization in Cells Presumed to be Glia," *Electroenceph. clin. Neurophysiol.*, **28**, 109.

Cavanagh, J. B. (1970), "The Proliferation of Astrocytes Around A Needle Wound in the Rat Brain," *J. Anat. (Lond.)*, **106**, 471.

Friede, R. L., Hu, K. H. and Johnstone, M. (1969), "Glial Foot-plates in the Bowfin. I. Fine Structure Chemistry," *J. Neuropath. exp. Neurol.*, **28**, 513.

Kuffler, S. W. (1967), "Neuroglial Cells: Physiological Properties and

a Potassium Mediated Effect of Neuronal Activity on the Glial Membrane Potential," *Proc. roy. Soc. B*, **168**, 1.

Mori, S. and LeBlond, C. P. (1969), "Electron Microscopic Features and Proliferation of Astrocytes in the Corpus Callosum of the Rat," *J. comp. Neurol.*, **137**, 197.

Nakai, J. (Ed) (1963), *Morphology of Neuroglia*. Springfield: C. C. Thomas.

Pollen, D. A. and Trachtenberg, M. C. (1970), "Neuroglia: Gliosis and Focal Epilepsy," *Science*, **167**, 1252.

Vaughn, J. E., Hinds, P.L. and Skoff, R. P. (1970), "Electron Microscopic Studies of Wallerian Degeneration in Rat Optic Nerves, I. The Multipotential Glia," *J. Comp. Neurol.*, **140**, 125.

3. CEREBRAL ENERGY METABOLISM

VERNON MACMILLAN and BO K. SIESJÖ

This chapter on cerebral energy metabolism has two main objectives. The first will be to present an account of the main features of the production and utilization of energy by the intact brain. The second will be to describe the sequence of biochemical events found in a number of clinically applicable experimental situations in which disturbances of energy metabolism occur, or at least have been implicated in the genesis of the pathological state. By necessity this account will be brief and only a selected number of key references will be given; for more detailed accounts reference is made to recent reviews and articles.[2,3,9,24]

ENERGY PRODUCTION AND UTILIZATION IN THE BRAIN

General Aspects

Energy can be defined in simplest terms as the capacity to do work. The principles of energy flow as applied to neural tissues are shown in Fig. 1. The structural energy of the fuel molecule (glucose) is converted by cellular metabolic processes to usable chemical energy in the form of adenosine triphosphate (ATP). Since the brain does not perform any external mechanical or osmotic work, the energy derived from respiration is utilized for the internal transport of ions and for biosynthetic work, which includes the synthesis of transmitter substances and proteins, and

the constant rebuilding of cellular structural units. The relative proportion of energy required for transport or biosynthetic work is poorly known; however, as neural tissue is continually involved in utilizing and re-establishing electrochemical membrane gradients, that is performing osmotic work via energy-requiring membrane transport systems, estimates of up to 40 per cent of its energy production being used for ion transport do not seem unreasonable. A minimal amount of energy is also required to maintain cellular structural integrity, and more knowledge is required concerning this amount as it may provide clues to the magnitude of the energetic defect that the brain can tolerate before loss of cellular structure makes the damage irreversible.

Overall Glucose Metabolism

Glucose is normally the only substrate which can maintain an adequate energy production in the brain under *in vivo* conditions. In spite of the fact that the brain comprises only 2·5–3·0 per cent of the total body weight, it receives 15 per cent of the cardiac output, utilizes up to 25 per cent of the total body glucose consumption, and accounts for 20 per cent of the O_2 utilized by the body as a whole. A number of factors, including high and continuous energy needs, low energy reserves, a low O_2 storage capacity and a relatively sparse capillarity, all contribute to make normal brain function critically dependent on a continuous

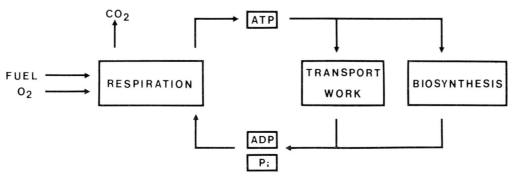

FIG. 1. Principles of energy flow in neural tissues.

and adequate supply of substrates (glucose and oxygen) via the cerebral circulation. The major changes between the blood entering and the blood leaving the brain (Table 1)

TABLE 1

CHANGES IN CEREBRAL BLOOD CONTENTS ON PASSAGE THROUGH THE BRAIN

Substance	Venous-arterial difference per 100 ml. blood
Oxygen:	
Content (ml./100 ml.)	−6·7
Saturation %	−31·7
Carbon dioxide:	
Content (ml./100 ml.)	+6·6
Tension (mm.Hg.)	+10·0
Glucose:	
(mg./100 ml.)	−9·8
Lactic acid:	
(mg./100 ml.)	+1·6

Values are from Gibbs *et al.* (1942) for 50 healthy men 18–29 years of age. Blood from internal jugular vein and femoral artery.

are seen in an oxygen content difference of about 6·7 ml. O_2/100 ml. blood and an equivalent change in the CO_2 content. The glucose content difference between arterial and venous blood is slightly larger than that which corresponds to the oxygen consumed; however, the difference can be accounted for when the changes in the lactate and pyruvate contents of the venous blood are considered.

The production of energy as ATP from glucose in normal cerebral tissues proceeds via the pathways of glycolysis and the mitochondrial tricarboxylic acid cycle and electron transport system. The complete oxidation of 1 mole of glucose ("respiration") will yield 38 moles of ATP, whereas the anaerobic conversion of 1 mole of glucose to lactate ("glycolysis") will only yield 2 moles of ATP, viz:

Aerobic state:

$$\text{Glucose} + 6\,O_2 + 38\,\text{ADP} + 38\,\text{Pi} \rightarrow 6\,CO_2 + 44\,H_2O + 38\,\text{ATP} \quad (1)$$

Anaerobic state:

$$\text{Glucose} + 2\,\text{ADP} + 2\,\text{Pi} \rightarrow 2\,\text{lactate} + 2\,\text{ATP} \quad (2)$$

Although a maximal increase in the glycolytic rate of 5–7 times normal is possible under conditions of hypoxia,[13] the energy which is produced by this accelerated degradation of glucose to lactate falls short of the resting energy requirements of the tissue. Also to be noted is that this increase in glycolysis can be maintained only as long as the endogenous stores of glucose and glycogen are adequate. When these stores have been exhausted the rate of glucose transport from blood to tissue may impose a restriction to glycolysis, and thereby to energy production, due to substrate depletion. It is therefore evident that not only is the brain dependent on glucose, but also upon its complete oxidation, to maintain normal energy relationships. The glycolytic process, however, warrants a more detailed discussion at this point for a number of reasons. These are:

(1) Glycolysis is the compulsory first step in the oxidation of glucose, and the glycolytic sequence is the site of important metabolic control mechanisms.

(2) Glycolysis is rapidly activated in many situations and its product, lactic acid, may give valuable diagnostic information concerning the presence of these situations.

(3) The lactacidosis occurring under hypoxic conditions plays an important homeostatic role in that it induces vasodilatation in the tissue, and thereby enhances oxygen delivery to the cells in the brain.

Glycolysis

The glycolytic sequence is schematically shown in Fig. 2. After phosphorylation of glucose to glucose 6-phosphate, and of fructose 6-phosphate to fructose 1·6-diphosphate, the original glucose molecule is split into two freely inter-convertible 3 carbon fragments—glyceraldehyde phosphate (GAP) and dihydroxyacetone phosphate (DAP). Two molecules of ATP are consumed in the phosphorylation of glucose and of fructose 6-phosphate; however, 4 ATP molecules are formed later in the sequence and thus the net yield is 2 ATP per molecule of glucose converted to lactate (or pyruvate). This ATP formation is associated with oxidative reactions, i.e. with removal of electrons (or hydrogen atoms) from the compound which is being oxidized. The first of these reactions is the oxidation of 3-phosphoglyceraldehyde (GAP) to 1,3-diphosphoglycerate —the oxidant being the pyridine nucleotide coenzyme NAD^+ which is reduced to NADH (eq. 3):

$$\text{GAP} + NAD^+ + \text{Pi} \rightarrow \text{1,3-DPG} + \text{NADH} + H^+ \quad (3)$$

The second ATP-forming reaction is the intramolecular oxidation which occurs when phosphoenolpyruvate is converted to pyruvate. Each oxidative step is associated with a large release of free energy from the substrate molecule, which is trapped and stored in the high energy structure of ATP.

When glycolysis proceeds to lactic acid formation the NADH produced at the first oxidative step is reoxidized according to equation (4):

$$\text{pyruvate} + \text{NADH} + H^+ \rightarrow \text{lactate} + NAD^+ \quad (4)$$

There is thus no net oxidation or reduction and glycolysis can proceed until glucose or glycogen are exhausted. If glycolysis proceeds only to pyruvate, as occurs when the pyruvate molecules are further oxidized in the mitochondria, there will be one NADH formed for each pyruvate. If the glycolytic reactions are not to come to a halt due to a deficiency of NAD^+ needed in reaction (3), the cell must have a means of reoxidizing cytoplasmic NADH to NAD^+. This can be done in the mitochondria, but since NADH cannot freely cross the mitochondrial membrane, the cell must use a "shuttle" system which carries the electrons into the mitochondria for further processing. In brain tissue the malate-oxaloacetate shuttle is the most probable means of achieving this.

It should be noted that in the brain the reversal of the glycolytic sequence (gluconeogenesis) is prevented by the virtual absence of the hydrolytic enzymes needed to circumvent the phosphofructokinase and hexokinase steps (Fig. 2).

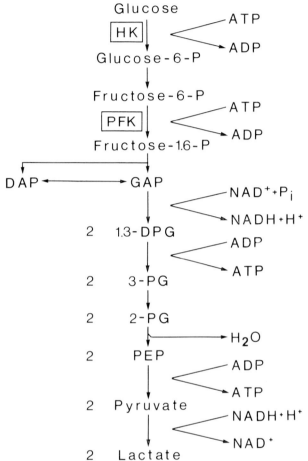

FIG. 2. Glycolytic sequence (GAP—glyceraldehyde phosphate; DAP—dihydroxyacetone phosphate; 1,3-DPG—1,3-diphosphoglyceric acid; 3-PG—3-phosphoglyceric acid; 2-PG—2-phosphoglyceric acid; PEP—phosphoenolpyruvate).

Cytoplasmic Redox State

A brief discussion of the significance of the cytoplasmatic redox state as determined from the lactate/pyruvate ratio is appropriate at this point. An increased lactate/pyruvate ratio has frequently been proposed as being a sensitive indicator of tissue hypoxia. This is due to the fact that the lactate dehydrogenase (LDH) reaction exists close to equilibrium in the cell according to equation (6).

$$\frac{NADH}{NAD^+} = \frac{Lactate}{Pyruvate} \cdot \frac{K}{H^+} \qquad (6)$$

The equation predicts that an increase in the cytoplasmatic $NADH/NAD^+$ ratio will be accompanied by increases in the lactate/pyruvate ratio. As the $NADH/NAD^+$ ratio would be expected to increase in hypoxia, it has been proposed that measurements of intracellular or extracellular lactate and pyruvate can be used to determine the presence of hypoxia. However, it should be noted that the

LDH equilibrium is pH sensitive and that increases in the lactate/pyruvate ratio can occur in acidotic states in the absence of hypoxia and in the presence of an unchanged $NADH/NAD^+$ ratio. It follows that valid use of the lactate/pyruvate ratio to derive the cytoplasmatic $NADH/NAD^+$ ratio requires accurate determination of the intracellular pH (see later sections for examples).

The Tricarboxyclic Acid Cycle and Electron Transport

The pyruvate formed from glucose during glycolysis is further oxidized in the mitochondria through the reactions of the tricarboxylic acid cycle (Krebs cycle). In the TCA cycle (Fig. 3) the pyruvate molecule is oxidized in a cyclic series of reactions which constantly replenishes its starting material—oxaloacetate. In these oxidative reactions, the electrons removed from the substrate molecules are accepted either by mitochondrial NAD^+, or by the oxidized form of a flavoprotein (FAD). The TCA cycle also provides entrance and exit points to other important metabolites—especially the glutamate group of amino acids. These points also provide for replenishment of the citric acid intermediates via transaminase and carbon dioxide fixation reactions.[24]

The further handling of the NADH (and $FADH_2$) produced by the TCA cycle occurs in the mitochondrial electron transport system—a system of redox couples which allows the energy release to be graded and controlled as the electrons proceed to the final electron acceptor—molecular O_2 (Fig. 3). Each electron passing along the system from NADH releases enough energy to result in the formation of 3 molecules of ATP from 3 molecules of ADP and Pi. In all 34 molecules of ATP are formed in the electron transport system, plus 2 from glycolysis and 2 more from GTP formation in the TCA cycle, thus equating a net total of 38 molecules of ATP per molecule of glucose oxidized.

CONTROL MECHANISMS

The overall rate of glucose utilization by the brain is considerably lower than the potential rates observed for the individual enzymatic steps involved. By way of example, brain phosphofructokinase has a maximal catalytic capacity of about 30 m. mol. substrate/kg. wet weight/min., yet the normal rate of aerobic glycolysis is only 0·3 m. moles glucose/kg. wet weight/min. It follows that the rates of the individual steps must be subjected to *in vivo* limitations and in some cases to specific control, and that the normal aerobic glycolytic rate represents a state of inhibition. A number of possible control mechanisms exist but two main concepts with examples will serve to introduce the problem.[21] The first is the control of enzyme activity via metabolic effectors—familiar in the concept of *feedback inhibition* of the first unique enzyme of a metabolic sequence by the end product of that sequence. The strict application of this principle to the general *in vivo* control of the pathways involved is difficult, as the sequences are shared at many points by the antagonistic processes of energy production and energy utilization (biosynthesis).

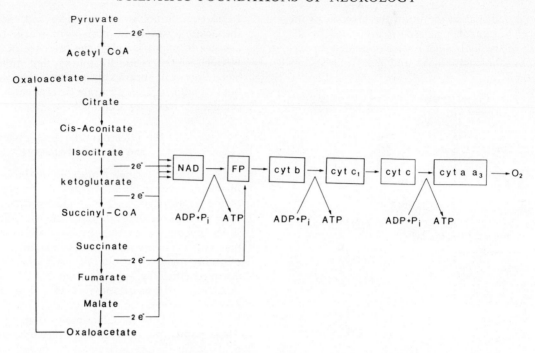

Fig. 3. The tricarboxylic acid cycle and electron transport system.

A broader concept of control is envisioned by Atkinson[1] who proposes that the control of the metabolic flux in these common pathways is via the energy state of the adenine nucleotide system—i.e. the balance between energy utilization and production. He compares the adenine nucleotide system of the tissue to an electrochemical storage cell, considering the extent to which the ATP–ADP–AMP system is filled with high energy phosphate bonds. The charge of the adenine nucleotide pool can be expressed as equation (7).

$$\text{Energy charge potential} = \frac{[\text{ATP}] + 0\cdot5\,[\text{ADP}]}{[\text{ATP}] + [\text{ADP}] + [\text{AMP}]} \quad (7)$$

Changes in the ECP are strongly resisted by the cell, since many ATP-consuming and ATP-producing reactions respond to changes in the energy charge. For example, if the need for energy increases there will be an imbalance between rates of utilization and regeneration of ATP, and the energy charge will decline. Even a slight fall in the energy charge will result in stimulation of the energy-producing sequences and inhibition of the energy-using (biosynthetic) pathways, thus acting to normalize the ratio. This concept allows metabolic control to be explained in terms of the ever changing needs of the cell—the coupling of energy production to function.

A number of control points of major importance have been localized. The most important of these are (1) the phosphofructokinase reaction which has been proposed as being the main control point of glycolysis. Phosphofructokinase is a complex allosteric enzyme, which is inhibited by ATP, citrate and H^+, and activated by ADP, AMP, cyclic AMP, Pi, and NH_4^+, as well as by the substrate (fructose 6-phosphate) and the product (fructose 1,6-diphosphate) of the reaction. (2) The main control of the

rate of electron transport and thereby oxidative phosphorylation (in the normoxic state) appears to be the ADP availability. This sensitivity of both the glycolytic and oxidative phosphorylation rates to the tissue contents of the adenine nucleotides allows for a close adjustment of the two processes in providing for the energy needs of the cells.

ENERGY FLOW AND ENERGY STATE IN THE BRAIN

Under normal conditions the rate of energy production in the brain is finely adjusted to the energy use rate, and this delicate balance between the rates of production and utilization of ATP constitutes a strongly poised energy state. A distinction must be made between energy state and energy flow. The *energy state* may be defined in terms of the energy charge potential (see above), and this should be clearly separated from *energy flow* which is the turnover rate of ATP. As oxygen consumption and production of ATP from ADP and Pi are normally tightly coupled, the oxygen consumption in the steady state therefore constitutes a measure of ATP utilization. This coupling between functional activity and rate of oxidative metabolism is such that as long as the brain receives adequate amounts of oxygen and substrate, oxygen will be used up in proportion to the work done. At any given moment, therefore, a measured metabolic rate for O_2 can only be judged nutritionally adequate if related to the energy requirements of the tissue. This can rarely be done, thus making evaluations of a deranged energy state impossible from measurements of energy flow.

What cellular parameters can be used to assess the energy state of the tissue most accurately? As proposed, the energy charge of the adenine nucleotide system may be the relevant parameter to evaluate. Conventionally, however, the energy state of the tissue has been considered in terms of the ATP concentration, or in terms of certain "emergency" reactions which all have the effect of minimizing or retarding a fall in ATP, or an increase in ADP. It has been recognized that a measurable fall in ATP, which occurs in the tissue at a concentration of 3 m.mol./kg. of wet tissue, is a relatively late phenomenon, and that it may be preceded by changes which are the result of such emergency reactions. These reactions are (1) an accelerated anaerobic glycolysis which leads to increased lactate contents (and L/P ratios) and (2) shifts in the creatine phosphokinase equilibrium (equation 8) and in the myokinase (adenylate kinase) equilibrium (equation 9).

$$PCr + ADP + H^+ \rightleftharpoons Cr + ATP \qquad (8)$$

$$2\,ADP \rightleftharpoons ATP + AMP \qquad (9)$$

these reactions allow for a rapid interconversion of energy between phosphocreatine and ATP, and among the adenine nucleotides.

As a consequence of the accelerated glycolysis, and of the shifts in the creatine phosphokinase and the myokinase equilibria, there will be increases in the tissue concentrations of lactate and AMP, as well as an increase in the lactate/pyruvate ratio, and the phosphocreatine concentration will fall. All these changes have previously been considered to be sensitive indicators of tissue hypoxia. However, the creatine phosphokinase equilibrium, like the lactate dehydrogenase equilibrium, is pH-dependent. Reductions in the phosphocreatine content can therefore be produced by acidosis alone, without primary disturbances of the ATP/ADP ratio, exactly as an acid shift in pH may cause an increased lactate/pyruvate ratio in the absence of a primary increase in the NADH/NAD$^+$ ratio. For these reasons, the tissue content of AMP, which is normally around 0·03 m.mol./kg. (i.e. about 1 per cent of the ATP concentration), may be the most sensitive and unequivocal indicator of an imbalance of the tissue energy state. It is evident that the energy charge potential will also serve as a sensitive indicator of an imbalance in the energy state. Its determination, utilizing fluorometric methods for measurement of the adenine nucleotides, reveals a variation of less than 1 per cent under normal circumstances, thus reinforcing its usefulness as a valuable parameter.

ACID-BASE METABOLISM OF BRAIN

Indirect estimations of brain intracellular pH give values close to 7·0. Since the extracellular pH is around 7·3–7·4, it can be deduced that H$^+$ and HCO$_3^-$ are not passively distributed in the electrical field across the neuronal and glial cell membranes. Such a disequilibrium is usually taken to imply an active transport of H$^+$ from the cells to the extracellular fluid (ECF), and it is conceivable that part of the energy consumed by the tissue is used up in transporting H$^+$ or HCO$_3^-$. It should be noted that the CSF [H$^+$] is out of equilibrium with plasma [H$^+$], but since this disequilibrium may be caused by an outflux of acid from cells to ECF an active H$^+$ transport between plasma and CSF seems less clear.

Extracellular acid-base changes play an important homeostatic role in that the ECF pH seems to determine both pulmonary ventilation and cerebral blood flow.[6] Adjustments in lung ventilation and in CBF undoubtedly guard energy homeostasis in the brain in e.g. hypoxemia but, as will be discussed, extracellular acidosis also seems to abolish autoregulation and thereby to compromise capillary flow whenever the cerebral perfusion pressure is decreased.

The intracellular pH in the brain may be changed if either the tissue CO$_2$ tension or the buffer base concentration varies. Under normal conditions, the cell pH is well regulated during hyper- and hypocapnia. Part of this regulation occurs by means of compensatory changes in the intracellular buffer base concentration. Thus, in hypercapnic acidosis inhibition of one or several rate-limiting metabolic steps (phosphofructokinase, isocitrate dehydrogenase?) leads to a partial depletion of substrates distal to those steps, chiefly lactate and glutamate. Since this depletion probably occurs by means of oxidation to carbon dioxide and water, a corresponding amount of H$^+$ disappears from the system. In *hypocapnia*, an activation of the same rate-limiting steps leads to increased tissue levels of metabolic acids, chiefly lactic acid, and the mechanism is so efficient that the intracellular pH stays within 0·05 pH units of the normal value even under conditions of extreme hypocapnia. It should be mentioned that deep barbiturate anaesthesia, which is associated with an increase in the intracellular buffer base concentration (see above), gives a larger alkaline shift in pH$_i'$ than even vigorous hyperventilation. Thus, the regulation of pH$_i'$ in hypercapnia and hypocapnia is intimately connected with the control of energy metabolism.

When brain hypoxia leads to an increased glycolytic rate, and especially in conditions of ischemia, there are few mechanisms to guard the constancy of the intracellular pH, and excessive pH shifts may occur. Under such conditions the acidosis is mainly caused by lactic acid. However, if total ischemia occurs, the CO$_2$ liberated from bicarbonate cannot escape, and the CO$_2$ tension may rise to 200–300 mmHg, thereby significantly contributing to the acidosis. Figure 4 shows the pH$_i'$ changes which are obtained when rats are exposed to 0–40 per cent CO$_2$ for 45 min., and when the tissue lactate content is increased during normocapnic hypoxemia. The figure demonstrates that an increase in the tissue lactate content to 10 m.Eq./kg. of wet tissue, such as occurs with a lowering of the PaO$_2$ to about 25 mmHg., gives a decrease in pH$_i'$ comparable to that observed when about 20 per cent CO$_2$ is administered. With this degree of acidosis (pH 6·80) the phosphocreatine content falls from 5·0 to 3·8 and the lactate/pyruvate ratio increases from 15 to 40, simply due to pH-dependent shifts in the CPK and the LDH equilibria (see above).

Acidosis has been incriminated as one of the main causes of irreversible cell damage in various hypoxic conditions, but there are few results which directly support this assumption. The brain can tolerate complete ischemia for 6–8 min. and since this may lower pH$_i'$ to 6·0, an excessive but shortlasting acidosis is evidently not harmful by itself. Furthermore, 40 per cent CO$_2$ can be administered for much longer periods without causing loss of consciousness, fall in ECP, or permanent damage. From this we can conclude that a fall in pH_i' to 6·65, or of the ECF pH to much lower values, does not seem to affect the energy state of the tissue. It may therefore be that the harmful effects of tissue acidosis is exerted on the capillary circulation, and that the combination of acidosis and ischemia is what causes cellular damage.

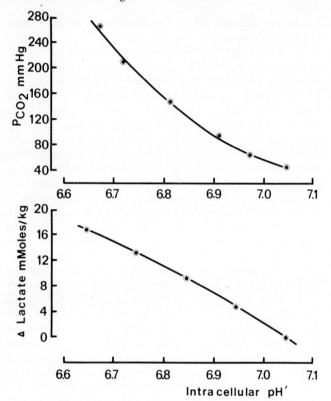

Fig. 4. The intracellular pH of brain tissue at various PCO_2 levels (upper) and at various tissue lactate concentrations (lower).

Cerebral Energy Metabolism in Hypoxic and Ischemic States

Disturbances of brain function secondary to hypoxic and ischemic states are a common clinical occurrence. *Hypoxia* is definable as a restriction of tissue oxygen supply sufficient to interfere with normal physiological and biochemical function, while *anoxia* is taken to mean a total lack of oxygen in the tissue. *Hypoxemia* means a reduced arterial oxygen tension, while *ischemia* signifies underperfusion of the tissue with blood. Although ischemia is a form of hypoxia (stagnant hypoxia) a fundamental difference exists from the usual forms of hypoxia, in that during ischemia the tissue experiences both oxygen and substrate lack, plus has the added insult of defective metabolic end-product removal (such as CO_2). Detailed classifications of hypoxic and ischemic states are available in the standard textbooks of medicine and neurology and will not be discussed here. The experimental studies quoted here will be mainly concerned with acute anoxia (asphyxia), subacute hypoxia (arterial hypoxemia), acute total ischemia, and incomplete ischemia (arterial hypotension).

A consideration of the arterial and cerebral venous blood oxygen contents (Table 1) shows that the brain extracts about 6·7 vol. per cent from the arterial blood, leaving an oxygen content of about 12·5 vol. per cent and an oxygen saturation of 65–70 per cent in the outflowing venous blood. This suggests that there is an ample reserve of oxygen which the tissue can draw on in states of increased activity or decreased supply. The delivery of oxygen to the tissues, however, occurs by means of physical diffusion and thus depends on the partial pressure differences between capillary blood and the site of oxygen consumption—the mitochondria. By reasoning, it can be deduced that the lowest tissue oxygen tensions will be found in those areas farthest from the capillary and that the PO_2 at any given tissue point will depend on capillary PO_2 distance of the point from the capillary, diffusion rate of oxygen in the tissue, and the oxygen consumption rate.

Application of these variables to the mathematical solution of tissue capillary models has led to attempts to calculate "critical" tissue oxygen tensions, and to correlate these to cerebral venous oxygen tensions. In these studies it has generally been assumed that the venous PO_2 represents end-capillary PO_2 values, and that the venous PO_2 measured in any hypoxic situation, whether caused by hypoxemia or ischemia, reflects a corresponding lowering of the tissue PO_2. The following relationships have been predicted:

(1) When the venous PO_2 is lowered from a normal value of about 35 mmHg. to 25–28 mmHg., the PO_2 in tissue areas distant from the capillary will fall below the minimal requirements for full mitochondrial function, and regional hypoxia will exist. This will result in physiological compensatory mechanisms such as vasodilatation with a resulting increase in cerebral blood flow ("reaction threshold").

(2) At cerebral venous PO_2 of 17–19 mmHg. the PO_2 in larger areas is inadequate for continued mitochondrial function, and regional anoxia ensues with loss of consciousness, electroencephalographic abnormalities, and decreased oxygen consumption ("critical threshold").

(3) At cerebral venous PO_2 of 12 mmHg., or less, the tissue is grossly anoxic and death is imminent, usually secondary to hypoxic cardiovascular collapse ("lethal threshold").

Although some clinical observations have tended to agree with the above proposals (Table 2), objections have

TABLE 2 CEREBRAL VENOUS PO_2 AND FUNCTION

Functional state	Cerebral venous PO_2 mmHg.
1. Normal—alert	35–40
2. Impaired learning Minor EEG change	30–32
3. Psychological testing abnormalities	23–29
4. Loss of consciousness EEG slowing	17–19
5. Imminent death	12–14

pH_i': the equivalent of pH_i, calculated for the intracellular space as a homogeneous system at the measured mean PCO_2 and bicarbonate concentration of the tissue.

been raised concerning the general validity of the proposals (see Siesjö and Plum[24] for recent review). Some of the objections concern the assumptions made in the calculations. Thus, whereas it was originally assumed that the cerebral metabolic rate for oxygen ($CMRO_2$) is around 3·5 ml. O_2/100 g./min., and that the local PO_2 required for unimpaired mitochondrial function is about 10 mmHg., recent studies indicate that $CMRO_2$ for cerebral cortex may be as high as 10 ml. O_2/100 g./min., and that mitochondria may respire maximally down to PO_2 of 1–2 mmHg. The errors in the assumptions will change the values for the calculated tissue PO_2 but an even more serious objection concerns the capillary models used. Thus, the conventional capillary models entailing symmetrical capillaries with parallel flow may be inadequate in describing the real capillary pattern, which probably is more complex with asymmetrical parallel-antiparallel flows coexisting. As we will see, recent experimental results prove that the venous PO_2 may be grossly dissociated from the energy state in the tissue, and they emphasize that there are fundamental differences between hypoxemic and ischemic states. Consequently, we must judge the oxygenation of the brain from the cerebral venous PO_2 with great caution.

Acute Anoxia

When the brains' oxygen supply is suddenly and totally restricted, as in asphyxia, rapid and dramatic metabolic changes occur. The brain's oxygen stores have been estimated to be about 7–10 ml., adequate for only 8–12 seconds of physiological function before consciousness is lost. Once the oxygen stores are depleted, a rapid reduction of the mitochondrial redox systems occurs with resultant cessation of ATP formation by the mitochondria. The emergency responses detailed in previous sections occur, with stimulation of glycolysis and shifting of the phosphocreatine reaction in favour of ATP formation. Within 3 minutes of the onset of the asphyxia, a nearly complete depletion of phosphocreatine and a moderate to marked fall in ATP content occurs. The lactate rises to near 25 mm./kg. intracellular H_2O, pH' falls to near 6·5 and the NADH/NAD^+ ratio increases to 3–4 times its normal value. If oxygen is reintroduced at this phase rapid normalization of the biochemical abnormalities occurs.[10]

The brain can tolerate only about 4–5 minutes of this type of insult before evidence of irreversibility occurs. The precise mechanisms contributing to irreversibility are unclear (see section on ischemia for further discussion). However, it seems established that the brain cells may withstand complete anoxia for slightly longer periods, and that the survival of the organism as a whole is limited by the greater vulnerability of the heart to anoxia.

Subacute Hypoxia

Experimental observations on the brains' metabolic responses to graded hypoxia—induced by arterial hypoxemia—reveal that once the PaO_2 is reduced to below 50 mmHg. a progressive tissue lactacidosis and increased lactate/pyruvate ratio develops. This corresponds to the PaO_2 range at which compensatory increases in the cerebral blood occur. Further reductions of the PaO_2 to below 35 mmHg. results in a progressive decrease in the phosphocreatine content (Fig. 5). These findings of an increasing lactate/pyruvate ratio and declining phosphocreatine content have previously been used as indicators of tissue hypoxia; however, as has earlier been pointed out, these parameters are pH sensitive and their critical evaluation requires knowledge of the intracellular pH'.

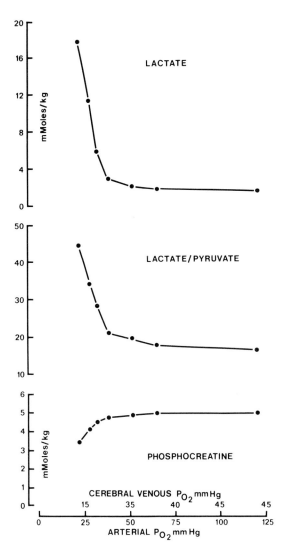

FIG. 5. Brain tissue contents of lactate and phosphocreatine, and the lactate/pyruvate ratios related to arterial and cerebral venous oxygen tension in animals subjected to a 30 min. decrease in the arterial O_2 tension.

A better indicator of the presence of tissue hypoxia would be an assessment of the ability of the mitochondria to maintain the energy state of the tissue at a normal level. In the series of animals shown in Fig. 5 the tissue contents of adenine nucleotides were measured and related to the arterial and sagittal sinus PO_2. Figure 6a reveals that no changes in the tissue contents of ATP, ADP, or AMP occurred and that the ECP remained unchanged to PaO_2

of below 20 mmHg. and cerebral venous PO_2 down to 10 mmHg. Moreover, calculations of the cytoplasmic $NADH/NAD^+$ ratios utilizing the lactate/pyruvate ratios and derived intracellular pH′ revealed no changes suggestive of an altered cytoplasmic redox state (Fig. 6b). These relations held as long as the blood pressure was maintained

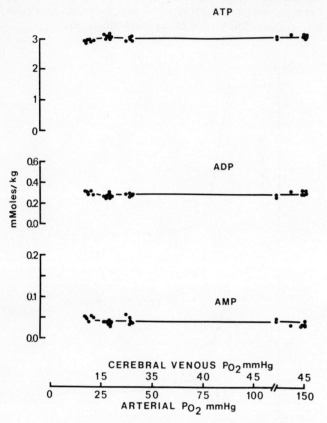

FIG. 6(a). Brain tissue contents of ATP, ADP and AMP related to arterial and cerebral venous oxygen tensions in animals exposed to a 30 min. decrease in the arterial O_2 tension.

at normal levels, as in some animals dramatic changes were observed in the presence of relatively small and often transient falls in the mean blood pressure.

Thus at these severe degrees of hypoxemia the only detectable alteration of cellular metabolism is an accelerated glycolytic rate as evidenced by the lactic acidosis. As the tissue contents of the adenine nucleotides and the ECP remained unchanged no final conclusions can be made concerning the trigger mechanism for the increased glycolytic rate. This is all the more so when it is considered that the citrate content and the H^+ concentration are elevated, both of which are known to be inhibitory to the activity of the main glycolytic regulatory enzyme—phosphofructokinase (see section on control mechanisms). These findings may mean that the control systems respond to very small metabolite changes, possibly regionally in the cell and undetectable by present analytical methods; however, the findings may also signify that other, as yet undefined, control mechanisms exist which are activated in hypoxemia. Whatever the mechanism, the resulting lactic acidosis does seem to play a homeostatic role, as the acidosis acts to increase the cerebral blood flow and to shift the creatine phosphokinase equilibrium in favour of ATP formation.

The results support the findings that only very low O_2 tensions are required to saturate the mitochondria *in vivo*. They also suggest that a re-evaluation of current theories of oxygen supply and diffusion in the brain is needed; since the venous PO_2 can be lowered to below 10 mmHg. without detectable changes in the energy state of the tissue, it seems difficult to maintain a concept of a "lethal threshold" occurring at venous PO_2 of about 12 mmHg. It should be stressed, however, that although the tissue energy state and oxygenation are far better upheld in hypoxemia than previously assumed, there are results which indicate that function suffers earlier. Since there is little correlation between energy state and consciousness in severe hypoxemia, we may have to consider other metabolic changes as the cause of loss of function; or we may have to assume

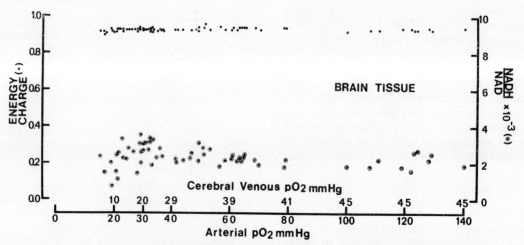

FIG. 6(b). Energy change potential of brain adenine nucleotides (([ATP] + 0·5 [ADP])/([ATP] + [ADP] + [AMP])), and cytoplasmatic $NADH/NAD^+$ ratio related to arterial and cerebral venous oxygen tensions in animals subjected to a 30 min. decrease in the arterial O_2 tension.

that metabolic changes in only a few neurones, or in localized cellular area (i.e. synaptic areas), may disrupt the complex circuits supporting conscious behaviour.

Ischemia

As both the supply of substrates and oxygen, and the removal of metabolic waste products, are dependent on an intact cerebral circulation, disturbances of cerebral blood flow are potentially important causes of disturbances in cerebral energy metabolism. The physiology and control of the cerebral circulation are outside the scope of this chapter (see Section VII), but some salient features must be considered. The cerebral blood flow (CBF) is determined by the arterio-venous pressure head and the vascular resistance (F = P/R). The resistance is governed by a complex set of mechanisms, which act to increase the CBF under conditions of hypoxemia, and which maintain the CBF constant over a relatively wide range of pressure alterations (autoregulation). In hypoxemia, but not in ischemia, the decrease in cerebrovascular resistance seems to be coupled to the lactacidosis; since the mean arterial blood pressure may be reduced to 40–50 mmHg. without causing any lactacidosis in the tissue, the autoregulation may be caused by myogenic mechanisms. Normally autoregulation is adequately upheld at blood pressures of 60–70 mmHg., but can be lost in circumstances of tissue acidosis, hypercapnia and trauma, thus converting the system into a passive system sensitive to relatively minor blood pressure variations.

The metabolic effects of acute total cerebral ischemia have been recently reviewed[16] and only the main features will be summarized. In the presence of total ischemia the brain is converted to a closed system, with energy production limited to the metabolism of endogenous substrates. As the tissue oxygen stores are adequate for only a few seconds of aerobic metabolism, the sole source of energy is the anaerobic conversion of glucose to lactate. Theoretical calculations and experimental observations show that the brain energy stores become virtually completely depleted after 2–3 minutes of total ischemia.[13]

The problem of subtotal cerebral ischemia is of greater clinical interest and importance because of the many potentially reversible situations in which it may occur (i.e. hypotension, shock, local vascular occlusive disease, and increased intracranial pressure). Difficulties in the experimental study of the problem are encountered due to autoregulatory mechanisms which act to maintain flow adequate for metabolic needs, until a "critical point" is reached at which the tissue quickly takes on the metabolic characteristics of total ischemia. The perfusion pressure at which this happens is in the range of 35–40 mmHg.

Utilizing an animal model with bilateral carotid artery ligation and graded hypotension Eklöf and Siesjö[5] have been able to obtain more gradual flow reductions and to relate them to the energy state of the tissue. Bilateral carotid artery ligation at normal blood pressures resulted in a 50 per cent decrease in CBF, but in no changes in the tissue energy state, whilst bilateral carotid artery ligation at a blood pressure of 100 mmHg. or of 70 mmHg., resulted in a further decrease in CBF and a marked decline

in the energy state. However, with this degree of ischemia the correlation between flow and energy state is uncertain since the decrease in flow does not seem uniform. An important observation was that the changes in metabolism occurred at a cerebral venous PO_2 of 25–30 mmHg. If it is recalled that in normotensive hypoxemia a cerebral venous PO_2 of less than 10 mmHg. was associated with a normal energy state, one must conclude that the ischemic model caused gross inhomogeneities of flow, in such a way that well-perfused areas contributed to the high venous PO_2, while other areas with virtual cessation of flow were responsible for the deranged energy state.

These observations have led to the hypothesis that tissue acidosis and abolished autoregulation predispose the tissue to regional nonperfusion, and that combinations of hypotension and acidosis may lead to cessation of flow in some capillary areas with resultant total anoxia.

The discrepancy between the cerebral venous PO_2 and the energy state of the tissue in the above experiments casts additional doubts on the value of the cerebral venous PO_2 as an indicator of "critical" end-capillary O_2 tensions. An additional example is found in the combination of hypotension and moderate hypercapnia (60–65 mmHg.) where dramatic changes in the energy state can be seen at cerebral venous oxygen tensions as high as 50–55 mmHg.

RECOVERY AFTER CEREBRAL ANOXIA

It was long believed that the brain cells could survive complete anoxia for only 3–4 min. but later results have shown that if special measures are taken to support the heart, or if a selective brain anoxia (ischemia) is induced, there may be complete electroencephalographic and biochemical restitution after 7–8 min. of cerebral circulatory arrest. Since isolated retina preparations may recover functionally even after a 20 min. anoxic period, it has been suggested that the shorter survival of brain cells *in vivo* is due to secondary vascular changes which prevent adequate reperfusion of the tissue in the postanoxic period. These vascular changes, which are assumed to consist of swelling of the capillary endothelium and vascular compression by swollen glial processes, form the basis of the non-reflow phenomenon. The importance of these vascular phenomenon is at present unclear and it is not known if recent reports of functional recovery after circulatory arrest for 20–30 min. may have been influenced by anaesthesia, or by an accidental fall in brain temperature; nor is it known how complete was the neurological recovery. However, even if the inherent revival time of the brain cells is shorter than has been assumed in some of these recent reports, the results give a novel aspect to the pathophysiology of cerebral anoxia by emphasizing such important factors as cerebrovascular resistance and perfusion pressure; undoubtedly, experimental results in this field may be of great clinical importance.

CEREBRAL ENERGY METABOLISM IN ANAESTHESIA

There is a large literature concerning the effects of various anaesthetics upon the energy metabolism of the brain. Previous *in vitro* studies have suggested that the barbiturates, especially oxybarbiturates, inhibit electron transport and energy transfer reactions in the mitochondria. These findings originally led to the suggestion that anaesthetics reduce the metabolic rate by restricting energy producing reactions, and consequently that the anaesthetic state is an energy depleted state. *In vivo* studies have shown that anaesthetics, in particular barbiturates, protect the brain against hypoxia, which is the converse of the *in vitro* situation, in that anaesthetics act primarily to depress energy utilization and therefore result in a "high energy state".

The problem of anaesthetic effect on brain energy metabolism has recently been carefully re-evaluated.[7,18]

In summary the results revealed no significant effect on the tissue contents of ATP, ADP and AMP produced by the various agents studied (nitrous oxide, halothane, diethyl ether, cyclopropane, phenobarbital, pentothal and amobarbital). The barbiturate group led to significant increases in the tissue phosphocreatine content; however, as the barbiturates are associated with an intracellular alkalosis, the increases could be explained on the basis of a H^+ ion effect, shifting the creatine phosphokinase equilibrium to the left (equation 8). The barbiturate animals also showed decreased tissue contents of lactate and pyruvate, and more recent studies have revealed a moderate reduction of other metabolites (malate, citrate, α-ketoglutarate). Further studies have revealed a significant protective influence of the barbiturates on brain metabolism in conditions of restricted oxygen and substrate supply, induced by graded arterial hypotension. This effect seemed most likely to be due to the reduced rate of energy utilization in the presence of barbiturates.

CEREBRAL ENERGY METABOLISM IN COMA STATES SECONDARY TO SYSTEMIC METABOLIC DISEASE

A number of metabolic disorders with broad systemic manifestations and profound imbalances in body chemistry ultimately result in coma. The problem of the neurochemistry and neurophysiology of metabolic coma states has recently been reviewed.[25] There appears to be no common biochemical basis for the various disorders of consciousness, and since they may be the result of dysfunction at any one of a number of levels in the structural and functional organization of the nervous system, each must be studied individually. Deficiency in the supply of substrates, and impairment of the processes for the production, conservation and utilization of energy are possible mechanisms by which systemic disease may interfere with cerebral energy metabolism. A large number of other mechanisms, with and without biochemical correlates exist and the reader is referred to recent reviews for details.[20,25]

Regardless of cause or mechanism, a reduced cerebral metabolic rate for oxygen ($CMRO_2$) is a characteristic feature of the coma state. Table 3 summarizes the $CMRO_2$ in a variety of clinical conditions associated with disturbances of consciousness. Except for hypoglycemia,

the depressed $CMRO_2$ is not associated with an inadequate supply of oxygen or oxidizable substrate, and thus one must attribute the depressed $CMRO_2$ in most cases to a reduced demand or a toxic effect interfering with energy production.

TABLE 3

CEREBRAL METABOLIC RATE AND BLOOD FLOW IN VARIOUS DISORDERS OF CONSCIOUSNESS

Condition	Mental state	Cerebral blood flow ml./100 g./min.	$CMRO_2$ ml./100 g./min.
1. Normal	alert	54	3·3
2. Normal sleep	asleep	65	3·4
3. Hepatic insufficiency	coma	33	1·7
4. Insulin Hypoglycemia arterial glucose			
74 mg.%	alert	68	2·6
19 mg.%	confused	61	1·9
8 mg.%	coma	63	2·1
5. Diabetic acidosis	confused	45	2·7
6. Coma	coma	65	1·7

Adapted from Sokoloff (1971).

Substrate Deficiency

The metabolic alterations associated with disturbances of oxygen supply have been presented in an earlier section.

During *hypoglycemia*, the onset of functional and metabolic change is quite slow. With the continued function of the TCA cycle, and at the low level of oxygen consumption prevailing in hypoglycemic coma, it has been estimated that the endogenous substrates (glucose, glycogen and amino acids) are sufficient to maintain energy production for up to 90 minutes. Beyond this point the coma frequently becomes permanent and irreversible, presumably secondary to irreversible structural and enzymatic changes occurring when substrate is exhausted. Changes in phosphocreatine and ATP content occur late in the hypoglycemic process, often when deep shock is present, and thus it is difficult to be certain that circulatory factors are not involved in the production of this deterioration in the energy state.

Systematic Metabolic Disease

Diabetes mellitus progressing to the stage of acidosis and ketosis almost inevitably leads to mental confusion and ultimately to coma, with a depressed $CMRO_2$. The basis for the depression of consciousness and $CMRO_2$ in diabetic coma are unclear, as substrate, cerebral blood flow and oxygen supply are all intact. There is no convincing evidence that the brain is dependent on insulin for the normal uptake and utilization of glucose. The role of the systemic metabolic acidosis and ketosis is unclear. It has been suggested that elevated blood levels of acetoacetate may cause coma via succinyl-CoA depletion and via depletion of free CoA in the acetoacetyl CoA thiolase reaction. These depletions could theoretically interfere with Krebs cycle function and thus energy production. Experimental evidence confirming this mechanism is lacking.

Non-ketoacidotic hyperosmolar diabetic coma appears to be primarily due to severe brain dehydration, and no studies of brain energy metabolism in this condition are available.

The disturbances of consciousness seen in *hepatic insufficiency syndromes* has been attributed to an effect of ammonia on the oxidative metabolism of the brain. It has been proposed that with increased brain tissue ammonia contents, the rate of α-ketoglutarate diversion to glutamate via reductive amination increases (equation 10)

$$\alpha\text{-ketoglutarate} + NH_3 + H^+$$
$$+ NADH \rightarrow glutamate + NAD^+ \quad (10)$$

and that the increased ammonia will also favour the conversion of glutamate to glutamine via the glutamine synthase reaction (equation 11)

$$Glutamate + NH_3$$
$$+ ATP \rightarrow glutamine + ADP + Pi \quad (11)$$

Since this reaction requires ATP, an extra demand is placed on the available ATP. From considerations of the energy generations in the TCA cycle, it has been estimated that up to 75 per cent of the potential energy yield is lost for each mole of glucose diverted to glutamine via this mechanism. Another possible coma mechanism is the conversion of glutamate to γ-aminobutyric acid (GABA) via the glutamic decarboxylase reaction. Accumulation of GABA, an inhibitory neurotransmitter, could then conceivably cause reduced excitability of the brain to a point persistent with loss of consciousness.

Experimental observations on acute ammonia intoxication in animals have revealed:

(1) A moderate decrease in the phosphocreatine content, but no significant changes in the ATP, ADP and AMP contents of the cerebral hemispheres.

(2) Moderate decreases in phosphocreatine and possibly mild changes in ATP content in the cerebellum and brain stem.

(3) Increased lactate contents and L/P ratios, most pronounced in the cerebellum and brain stem.

(4) An elevated $NADH/NAD^+$ ratio approaching 3–4 times the normal value. There was no evidence of α-ketoglutarate depletion, and in fact α-ketoglutarate was noted to increase with increasing ammonia loads. From these findings, it would appear that the theories implicating α-ketoglutarate and ATP depletion as major factors in the genesis of ammonia coma require re-evaluation. The finding of an elevated $NADH/NAD^+$ ratio has been attributed to a possible interference with the malate-oxaloacetate shuttle.[8]

CEREBRAL ENERGY METABOLISM IN EPILEPSY

Until recently, it was widely believed that brain metabolism increased so greatly during seizures that it outstripped its oxygen supply, resulting in relative cerebral hypoxia. An inference of the early studies was that seizure activity stopped because cerebral oxidative energy reserves became so depleted that they could no longer sustain the necessary neuronal membrane potentials required for activity. Most of these studies on brain metabolism during seizures, however, were not controlled for ventilation and muscle metabolic demand. In fact, the combination of increased neural and muscular activity, and respiratory-cardiovascular insufficiency during seizures creates conditions resembling hypoxia-ischemia. If care is taken to maintain oxygenation and cerebral blood flow, there is neither a fall in the tissue contents of ATP or glucose, nor any rise in the lactate contents, despite a 3–4 times increase in the energy flow rate. These findings strongly suggest that previously observed energy metabolism disturbances have been secondary to systemic hypoxemia and hypotension; they emphasize the importance of ventilatory and circulatory control in the clinical management of these patients.[4,19]

REFERENCES

[1] Atkinson, D. E. (1968), "The Energy Charge of the Adenylate Pool as a Regulatory Parameter. Interaction with Feedback Modifiers," *Biochemistry*, 7, 4030–4034.

[2] Bachelard, H. S. and McIlwain, H. (1969), *Comprehensive Biochemistry*, Vol. 17, pp. 191–218 (M. Florkin and E. H. Stotz, Eds.), Amsterdam: Elsevier Publ.

[3] Balacz, R. (1970), "Carbohydrate Metabolism," in *Handbook of Neurochemistry*, Vol. 3, pp. 1–36 (A. Lajtha, Ed.). New York: Plenum Press.

[4] Collins, R. C., Posner, J. B. and Plum, F. (1969), "Cerebral Metabolic Response to Electroconvulsions in Paralyzed Ventilated Mouse," *Trans. Amer. neurol. Ass.*, 94, 242–244.

[5] Eklöf, B. and Siesjö, B. K. (1971), "Cerebral Blood Flow and Cerebral Energy State," *Acta physiol. scand.*, 82, 409–411.

[6] Fencl, V., Vale, J. R. and Broch, J. A. (1969), "Respiration and Cerebral Blood Flow in Metabolic Acidosis and Alkalosis in Humans," *J. appl. Physiol.*, 27, 67–76.

[7] Goldberg, N. D., Passoneau, J. V. and Lowry, O. H. (1966), "Effects of Changes in Brain Metabolism on the Levels of Citric Acid Cycle Intermediates," *J. biol. Chem.*, 241, 3997–4003.

[8] Hindfelt, B. and Siesjö, B. K. (1971), "Cerebral Effects of Acute Ammonia Intoxication. II. The Effect upon Energy Metabolism," *Scand. J. clin. Lab. Invest.*, 28, 365–374.

[9] Jöbsis, F. F. (1965), *Handbook of Physiology—Respiration*, Vol. 1, pp. 63–124 (W. O. Fenn and H. H. Rahn, Eds.). Washington: American Physiological Society.

[10] Kaasik, A. E., Nilsson, L. and Siesjö, B. K. (1970), "The Effect of Asphyxia upon the Lactate, Pyruvate and Bicarbonate Concentration of Brain Tissue and Cisternal CSF, and upon the Tissue Concentrations of Phosphocreatine and Adenine Nucleotides in Anesthetized Rats," *Acta physiol. scand.*, 78, 433–447.

[11] Kety, S. S. (1957), "Determinants of Tissue Oxygen Tension," *Fed. Proc.*, 16, 666–670.

[12] King, L. J., Lowry, O. H., Passonneau, J. V. and Venzon, V. (1967), "Effects of Convulsants on Energy Reserves in the Cerebral Cortex," *J. Neurochem.*, 14, 599–611.

[13] Lowry, O. H., Passonneau, J. V., Hasselberger, F. X. and Schulz, D. W. (1964), "Effects of Ischemia on Known Substrates and Cofactors of the Glycolytic Pathway in Brain," *J. biol. Chem.*, 239, 18–30.

[14] Lübbers, D. W. (1968), "The Oxygen Pressure Field of the Brain and its Significance for the Normal and Critical Oxygen Supply of the Brain," in *Oxygen Transport in Blood and Tissues*, pp. 124–139 (D. W. Lübbers, V. C. Luft, G. Thews and E. Witzleb, Eds.). Stuttgart: Georg Thieme Verlag.

[15] MacMillan, V. and Siesjö, B. K. (1971), "Critical Oxygen Tensions in the Brain," *Acta physiol. scand.*, **82,** 412–414.

[16] Maker, H. S. and Lehrer, G. M. (1970), *Handbook of Neurochemistry*, Vol. 4, pp. 267–310 (A. Lajtha, Ed.). New York: Plenum Press.

[17] McIlwain, H. and Bachelard, H. (1971), *Biochemistry and the Central Nervous System*. London: J. & A. Churchill, Ltd.

[18] Nilsson, L. and Siesjö, B. K. (1970), "The Effect of Anesthetics upon Labile Phosphates and upon Extra- and Intracellular Lactate, Pyruvate and Bicarbonate Concentrations in the Rat Brain," *Acta physiol. scand.*, **80,** 235–248.

[19] Plum, F. (1971), "The Effect of Epileptic Seizures and Comatose States on the Oxidative Metabolism of the Brain," in *Ion Homeostasis of the Brain*, pp. 439–456 (B. K. Siesjö and S. C. Sørensen, Eds.). Copenhagen: Munksgaard.

[20] Plum, F. and Posner, J. (1966), *Stupor and Coma*. Davies Publ.

[21] Scrutton, M. C. and Utter, M. F. (1968), "The Regulation of Glycolysis and Gluconeo-genesis in Animal Tissues," *Ann. Rev. Biochem.*, **47,** 249–302.

[22] Siesjö, B. K., Nilsson, L., Rokeach, M. and Zwetnow, N. N. (1971), *Brain Hypoxia*, pp. 79–93 (J. R. Brierley and B. S. Meldrum, Eds.). London: William Heinemann Medical Books Ltd.

[23] Siesjö, B. K. and Nilsson, L. (1971), "The Influence of Arterial Hypoxemia upon Labile Phosphates and upon Extracellular and Intracellular Lactate and Pyruvate Concentration in the Rat Brain," *Scand. J. clin. Lab. Invest.*, **27,** 83–96.

[24] Siesjö, B. K. and Plum, F. (1972), "Pathophysiology of Anoxic Brain Damage," in *Biology of Cerebral Dysfunction*. Plenum Press.

[25] Sokoloff, L. (1971), *Neurochemistry of Hepatic Coma*, pp. 15–33 (E. Polli, Ed.). Basel: S. Karger.

1. SPINAL MOTOR AND SENSORY MECHANISMS

JAMES L. O'LEARY

INTRODUCTION

From the remote beginnings of the evolution of the CNS two types of neural organization have played prime participatory roles. One, the partial pattern type, had local operational significance and so became particularly effective in establishing the quasi-autonomy of spinal segments; the other includes the total patterns that make possible the integration of local activities over wide ranges of the nervous system.

The CNS of the lowest vertebrates is essentially a spinal segmental apparatus reinforced cephalically by an integrative centre situated in the lower medulla where swimming movements are initiated, and another in the upper brain stem which provides coordination of head and feeding movements, the two interconnected in their activities. These centres were forerunners of sites of brain stem integration which evolved for generalized control over respiration, circulation, posture, righting and other activities of total organismic significance.

Spinal segmentation is already distinguishable at an early stage of vertebrate embryogenesis. Each of a succession of segments, 31 in man, is provided with a pair of spinal nerves for each side. Each pair is made up of a dorsal, ganglion bearing, sensory root, and a ventral one containing the segmental motoneuron outflow. These pairs join to produce each of the spinal nerves.

All such spinal nerves contain a minimum complement of two functional components, general somatic afferent and efferent. In addition the thoracolumbar and the several sacral roots contain general visceral afferent and efferent components, providing respectively the outflows and inflows of the thoracolumbar and sacral autonomic systems. A nerve component can be defined as the aggregate of those axons possessing distinctive physiological and morphological attributes which enable them to react in a common mode.

It is also important that as compared with the 31 spinal nerves, the 12 cranial ones possess those 4 and additional components not duplicated elsewhere in the body. A second segmental apparatus, the gill arches, and their important derivatives in the higher vertebrates, require special visceral motor and sensory connections within the brain stem. The optic and auditory nerves contain a special somatic afferent component leading to sense organs (distance receptors) uniquely different from those of the body wall and viscera as supplied by spinal nerves.

STRUCTURAL CONSIDERATION OF SPINAL GREY AND WHITE MATTER

Embryogenesis

A section across the embryonic neural tube taken just after its closure and submersion beneath the body wall ectoderm (Fig. 1) reveals a quadrilateral cellular plate separated into bilaterally equal halves by a slit-shaped central cavity. Upon either side, midway of the slit, there is a longitudinal groove called the *sulcus limitans.* Its site demarcates dorsal sensory from ventral motor quadrants of the primitive tube. Next to each dorsal quadrant lies a longitudinal column of undifferentiated cells, the neural crest, which separated from the alar plate at the time of closure. From the crest, through segmental aggregation, cellular elements differentiate which ultimately become spinal ganglion cells; others get to be sheath cells which come to encase the out-growing embryonic axons of both sensory and motor roots. The cellular elements from which the autonomic nervous system derives also have a crest origin.

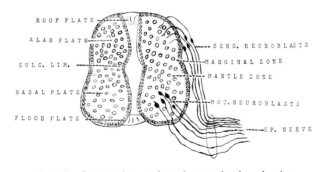

FIG. 1. Cross-section, embryonic neural tube, showing essential landmarks. Indicates relation of sensory and motor neuroblasts to the origin of dorsal and ventral roots and the formation of a spinal nerve.

Originally the developing spinal ganglion cell is bipolar. Its centrally directed process contributes to the dorsal root and ultimately establishes a synaptic relationship with differentiating neuroblasts of the alar plate to establish the reflex and relay connections of the future dorsal horn; the distally directed process grows from the opposite pole of the soma to establish sensory receptors in skin, muscles, tendons, joints or viscera. During cellular differentiation a dendritic arbor fails to develop and the centrally and distally directed processes come together to join the soma by a single stem.

Neuroblasts which differentiate from the basal plates largely evolve into motoneurons. Through a genetically determined plan based upon principles of organization not yet fully understood but involving over-production and death of supernumeraries, survivors aggregate into groups and even subgroups of longitudinal arrangement (cell columns) which extend through many segments. The constituents of particular cell columns of intersegmental extent bear a provable relation to corresponding parts of the myotome (muscle) mass, and intrasegmentally to the innervation of particular muscles. Sprouting axons that derive from these future motoneurons at each segmental level break through the cord surface and join the similarly directed peripheral processes of spinal ganglion cells to produce the corresponding segmental spinal nerve. In turn, through the primary and secondary divisions of the spinal nerves and the plexuses which develop out of combinations between them, the axons make their way to their sites of motor or sensory termination. Figure 2

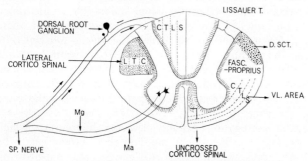

FIG. 2. Cross-section of the cervical spinal cord illustrating the positions of the fasciculus proprius and the principal long tracts described in the text.

shows the apperance of a transverse section of an adult spinal cord, including the shape of the grey interior, the disposition of long tracts in the surrounding white matter, and the roots of entry and exit.

Architectonics, Spinal Grey

A simple cell classification applicable to any transverse section through the spinal grey divides all such elements into three principal classes, sensory relay neurons of the dorsal horn, interneurons everywhere in evidence, and motoneurons of the ventral horn. The ventral horn also contains a population of small nerve cells called gamma motoneurons which tonically innervate the muscle spindles (p. 41). Such a structural classification fills the simpler needs of reflex physiology and accounts for the central latency differential between the monosynaptic and poly-synaptic reflexes. The former includes only the stretch reflex mechanism; the latter make up the circuitry of the flexor withdrawal and crossed extensor reflexes, among others, and also the more complex phenomena of reciprocal innervation.

A much needed revision of the architectonics of the spinal grey was provided by Rexed for the cat. He took into account the abundant small-celled component of the dorsal grey and the marked tendency there towards a laminar arrangement, and substituted for the older

columnar designations a generalized lamination plan covering the entirety of the spinal grey (Fig. 3). It is also referred to in current experimental work, so the locations of the ten laminae are summarized here. Rexed divided

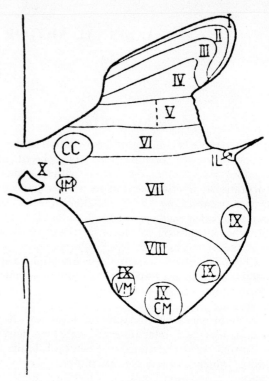

FIG. 3. Cell lamination pattern of the spinal grey. Taken from Rexed, B., 1954, Fig. 21, *J. comp. Neurol.*, **100**, 297. Wistar Institute Press.

the whole of the dorsal grey into six laminae from head to base of the horn. For these and the other laminae the fields designated are based upon size distribution, disposition, and other features of the contained cells. Laminae I, II and III, labelled progressively inwards across the outer cap, follow the contour of the head of the dorsal horn. Lamina IV cuts across the crown of the head, lamina V straight across the body, and VI occupies the base. Lamina VII takes in much of the intermediate grey with extensions into the ventral grey. Lamina VIII occupies the medial part of the ventral grey and consists of small and large densely coloured cells. Lamina IX contains the medial and lateral motoneuron columns of the older nomenclature, cells which supply striated muscle. Lamina X includes the cellular surround of the central canal.

In two monographs listed under "Further Reading", the Scheibels, using principally Golgi and Golgi Cox material from the cat spinal cord, have provided a wealth of detailed information concerning the axonal and dendritic neuropil components of the spinal grey. Their observations can be related without difficulty to the Rexed lamination plan outlined above. These workers cover the distributions of interneurons and short axon neurons, the recurrent collaterals of the axons of the large multipolar neurons, and the terminal distributions of sensory dorsal root axons within the cell laminae of the dorsal horn.

The Scheibels defined Golgi type II cells as possessing locally arborizing axons of non-projective nature. The Renshaw elements, whose function has been worked out in detail by Eccles, were presumed by him to be short axon cells of the medial border of the ventral horn favourably situated to receive the axon collateral termini of the segmental motoneurons and to provide through their own axons an inhibitory control over the firing of the motoneurons as a feed-back phenomenon. Willis marked the sites of 19 Renshaw cells studied by extracellular recording. Most of them were located in the ventral part of lamina VII near the egress of motoneuron axons to the ventral root. The Scheibels, covering an extensive Golgi material, found no short axon cells in that locale, but did identify interneurons with branching axons which decussated (in part at least) and entered the fasciculus proprius system of the opposite side of the cord to distribute plurisegmentally. They found the motoneuron somata to lie outside the range of the axonal arbors of such interneurons. Thus in Golgi material they could not identify any neuron which might produce the Renshaw effect.

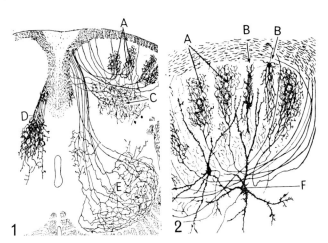

FIG. 4. Arborization of dorsal root axons, and post-synaptic elements relabelled from Ramon y Cajal. 1, A, termini of collaterals in the substantia gelatinosa, laminae III, II and I, Rexed. C, afferent plexus, lamina IV, Rexed. D, afferents to Column of Clarke. E, collaterals to motoneurones. 2, A, as in 1. B, neurones of substantia gelatinosa, laminae II and III, Rexed. F nerve cells, lamina IV, Rexed.

The Scheibels also examined the internuncial pools of the dorsal horn in the three major planes of histological section. This was necessary in order to define the characteristics of the branched terminals that arise out of the arborizations of dorsal root axons (Fig. 4, 1 and 2 from Ramon y Cajal). For the dorsal horn two such terminal arbors can be differentiated having somaesthetic and proprioceptive functions respectively. The somaesthetic projection relates to lamina III Rexed with extensions into lamina II. It is seen as a series of densely arborizing neuropil sheets which are oriented longitudinally. Small cells of the substantia gelatinosa are embedded within, their dendritic domains arranged in the sagittal plane. The proprioceptive (muscle spindle, tendon organ) projection

terminates largely as transversely oriented neuropil sheets in which most of the spinal interneurons are embedded. The dendrites of these generate a broadly interlocking coverage as seen in the transverse plane. From the sagittal perspective they appear as stacked modules set on end. Clarke's and lesser cell columns at the base of the dorsal horn are an exception, for in them the neuropil spreads rostrocaudally. Some of these features are revealed in Fig. 4, 1D.

A unique marginal cell of Waldeyer belonging to lamina I should also be mentioned. Collectively these present flat, transversely compressed dendritic fields which hug the undersurface of dorsomedial and dorsolateral white matter, their dendritic arbors not being reached by presynaptic afferents deriving from III and II below. The Waldeyer cell appears to have three sources of synaptic activation, two deriving from coarse terminals of axons arising from gelatinosal cells.

Using the methods of conventional neurohistology Romanes has also contributed significantly to our understanding of the motor cell groupings of the ventral horn. There are two aspects to the problem. One concerns the location within the cell columns of the elements which supply individual muscle or groups of muscles. For the cat, at least, such localization is fairly well established (Fig. 5) for some muscles. The second aspect relates to whether or not different degrees of differentiation exist between species showing various limb specializations. Is the plan for the cat universal regardless of the form and function of the limb supplied?

In the whale the muscles of the hand are lacking and those of the forearm grossly reduced, yet the relevant cell groupings are closely akin to those of other mammals. Romanes finds a comparison of extremity innervation in mole and bat to have a corresponding interest. For both species the cell groups show an unusual difference in complexity between cervical and lumbar enlargements, those of the cervical region being similar in disposition to other mammals, whereas the lumbar cell groups, although alike in appearance for the two species are low in number by comparison with other animals. Yet both species have highly differentiated forelimbs, each organized on an entirely different plan, and hind limbs that are also unlike. Romanes concludes that so far as the evidence goes the motor cell groups represent in part the morphological divisions of the muscles, but in most mammals they also have a topographical significance related to the joints moved, with occasional subdivisions representing single muscles. Typical motoneurons in Golgi sections are represented schematically in Fig. 6.

The synaptic contacts of monkey motoneurons have been thoroughly investigated by Bodian who described them spatially in terms of four zones of functional differentiation, soma, proximal dendrites, distal dendrites, and axon. The usual case for large motoneurons is the coverage of more than one-half of the soma surface by synaptic boutons, the spaces between containing glial processes. Large synaptic bulbs occur upon the motoneuron somata and usually near the bases of the dendrites. Bodian viewed them as distinctly different from the generality of smaller

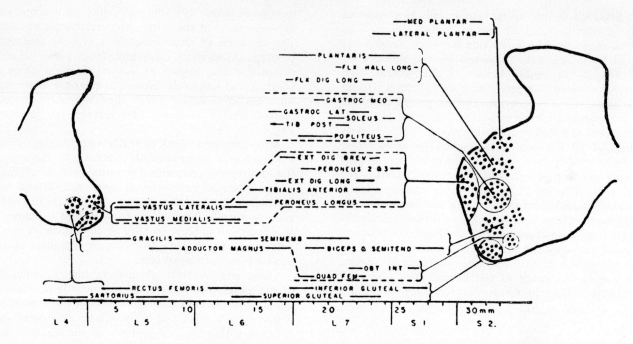

FIG. 5. Lumbosacral cord, cat, illustrating cell columns from which different muscles are innervated. From Romanes, G. J., 1951, *J. comp. Neurol.*, **94**, 339. Wistar Institute Press.

boutons seen on dendrites and somata. Their size range is 3–6 μ and they are regularly associated with subsynaptic Nissl substance and an underlying cisterna which is separated from the postsynaptic membrane by a space of 75 Å. The large bulbs tend to be packed with synaptic vesicles of spherical type, and to contain several mitochondria placed at the junction of end-bulb and terminal axonal segment. Other large synaptic bulbs seen on motoneuron dendrites arise from big myelinated axons and lack the subsynaptic cisternae situated beneath the postsynaptic membrane. Experimental evidence indicates that such bulbs are the termini of dorsal root axon collaterals. Beyond the proximal dendritic trunks the density of synaptic boutons increases until at the cross-sections of the finest dendrites of the arbor they become tightly packed.

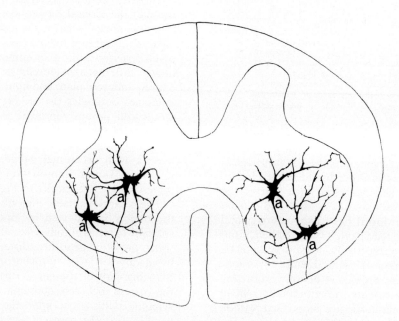

FIG. 6. Schema showing several motoneurones of the ventral grey, Golgi preparation.

Two basic types of small synaptic bulbs were observed. One, the more numerous, contained agranular vesicles with circular profiles of 250–400 Å, hereafter referred to S vesicles. The other type contains flattened elongated agranular vesicles which may be 100–200 Å wide and 500–600 Å long, called F vesicles. These types were found not only on dendrites and somata of motoneurons but on smaller interneurons and Clarke's column neurons as well. The F type bulb is of widespread distribution but is consistently in the minority by comparison with those of S type. Evidence from other sources indicates that the S type bulbs are excitatory, F type inhibitory in nature.

Fibre Tracts

The white matter includes three major columns, dorsal, lateral and ventral of which only the dorsal one is sharply circumscribed by the septum and the medial edge of the dorsal horn (Fig. 2). The division between lateral and ventral columns is an arbitrary one. The notion should be dispelled that each of the ascending and descending spinal long tracts (fasciculi) occupies a sharply delimited sector of the white matter. Rather the concept of a discretely localized spinal tract is an abstraction which arises from its definition as an axon bundle having the same origin and termination and a readily definable function. At best there is considerable overlap between neighbouring tracts and probably much individual variability as to exact extent and position. Also the fibres of ascending and descending tracts may have overlapping distributions, covering the same territory. A brief description of some of the principal cord tracts of clinical significance follows:

Fasciculus Proprius System

These comprise the association bundles and are largely composed of interneuron axons which may issue a diffuse collateralization at several successive ascending or descending segmental levels including the one of origin. Proprius components are both decussated and non-decussated. Long and short, ascending and descending, axons are knit together in a close investiture of the grey matter contour (Fig. 2) as it follows the dorsal and ventral horns and the intermediate grey. Besides the short association systems which link together neighbouring cord segments in to and fro connections, there are corresponding long systems which extend between cervical and lumbar enlargements. These even include proprius elements which pass the length of the cord to and from the brain stem reticular substance. We view the distribution of proprius connections as determined by functional requirements, those innervation levels heavily interrelated physiologically having a rich array of communication links.

Dorsal Column System

The dorsal column is largely composed of the ascending branches of dorsal root axons which are added in rising sequence from a lateral approach, segment by segment, the latest arrival always pushing medially those which had entered just below. The descending branches pass downwards four to six segments and establish reflex connections.

In this fashion the dorsal column is built up by successive accessions from a series of root entry zones. The innermost tract of the column, the fasciculus gracilis, receives all of its accessions between the lowest sacral segments and T–6 and continues upwards to terminate in the nucleus gracilis at the caudal end of the medulla. Beginning at T–6 and receiving accessions to C–1, the laterally placed tract of the column terminates within the nucleus cuneatus which corresponds functionally with the nucleus gracilis. Phylogenetically there is a marked increase in dorsal white column area between cat and monkey and monkey and man, with the inference that a corresponding increase occurs in complexity of function. Functionally the fibres of the dorsal columns are mechanoreceptors serving three aspects of mechanoreceptive sensibility, identified as touch-pressure, position sense and flutter-vibration (Mountcastle). Wall disagreed with this view as to function of the dorsal columns (see "Further Reading").

Two other tactile paths also exist. One, called Morin's tract, ascends through the ipsilateral lateral column to the nucleus cervicalis lateralis at spinal levels C–1 and C–2. That nucleus relays fast cutaneous impulses to the opposite thalamus and cortex. The other such path relays almost immediately within the dorsal grey horn and decussates, the tract axons passing through the opposite ventrolateral area (herein called Gowers' tract) whence they reach higher levels in brain stem and thalamus. Thus for each spinal site of entry touch is represented by ascending paths on both sides of the cord. In the upper brain stem, of course, the majority of tactile impulses have already crossed the midline of the neuraxis and end with those of the Morin's tract relay system in the ventral nucleus of the thalamus. In contrast with the tactile path that of pain and temperature is not projected upwards on the side of entry, its activity being transferred to the secondary path which decussates entirely at the level of cord entry.

The tract of Lissauer (dorsolateral fasciculus) is situated at the apex of the dorsal horn overlying laminae I, II and III of Rexed which cap the dorsal horn. The medial portion of this tract is the sensory analogue of the dorsal column, constituting the entry zone for all small myelinated and non-myelinated dorsal root axons. Such have a short ascending course and function in large part in the conveyance of pain and temperature through the cord gateway to a terminus within the underlying laminae.

The lateral extent of the tract of Lissauer completes the bridge to the lateral fibre column. It contains axons of a size with the foregoing but belonging to an intersegmental association system also believed to establish its principal contacts within laminae I, II and III of Rexed and to participate in the organization of pain and pain equivalent information for transmission to higher CNS levels.

Ventrolateral Cord Tracts

Ascending Systems

For simplification only two such bundles are described. Both arise as relays (secondary systems) from the dorsal horn cellular laminae. The one described first is a composite of ascending bundles belonging to the ventrolateral area, for the whole of which we prefer the older terminology of Gowers' tract because the several components differ in their functional connotations. Gowers' tract has several termini including reticular substance of the brain stem, cerebellum, tactum and thalamus, and is especially well-known clinically because the lateral spinothalamic tract is the secondary pain path, decussating between its origin in the dorsal horn (laminae II and III) and its entry into the ventrolateral area of the opposite side. Because Gowers' tract contains this pain component it has been sectioned many times in man for relief of intractable pain upon the opposite side of the body, the sections being made either in high thoracic or the high cervical cord. The tract is more widespread in the ventrolateral column than is usually supposed, and to be successful in alleviating pain a surgical section usually must extend from the ventral fissure to the denticulate ligament.

Secondary degeneration which ensues from severance of the tract fibres can be followed to the several high termini of Gowers' tract. It is important that we do not know for any of these termini whether the axons ending in them had pursued an independent course throughout. Presumably the ventral spinocerebellar bundle is a separate component and arises from laminae VI or VII of the dorsal and intermediate grey. On the contrary, the spinoreticular, spinotectal and spinothalamic tracts could be the product of a common sensory path from which issue groups of collaterals to each of the several regions of termination.

It is important that in the case of the dorsal column the accession of new bundles occurs at the root entry zone, whereas for the ventrolateral column the accessions take place from the inside of the cord (Fig. 2) since they arise after synapse and are distributed from the base of the dorsal horn. At least the lamination of pain fibres can be verified by section of the ventrolateral area at upper thoracic or upper cervical levels. The lamination revealed at the site of cervical section, for example, shows sacral dermatomes represented exteriorly, cervical dermatomes interiorly, with thoracic and lumbar ones between.

The other important ascending tract of the lateral column is the dorsal spinocerebellar which lies superficially at the dorsal extremity of the lateral column, external to the position of the corticospinal tract. It originates from the ipsilateral Clarke's cell column situated at the base of the dorsal horn which extends downwards to L–1. Cord segments below that level probably connect with Clarke's column through ascending branches of the dorsal root axons. The tracts contain some of the largest and fastest fibres in the spinal cord which conduct impulses of muscle receptor origin and provide a direct route via the restiform body to the anterior lobe of the cerebellum.

Descending Systems

The corticospinal system (Fig. 2) is composed of axons which originate from pyramidal cells of the precentral motor cortex, inclusive of the primary motor and supplementary motor areas. In man each tract contains over a million axons of which two-thirds are myelinated. It is the largest and most important descending system of the

human cord, and with the corticobulbar tract which leads to the motor nuclei of the brain stem it is the chief direct outlet of cerebral cortex to lower levels.

The fibres pass through the medullary pyramid before entering the cord and the large majority cross in the pyramidal decussation, moving dorsally and laterally to occupy a cord position in the dorsal part of the lateral column interior to the dorsospinocerebellar tract. The uncrossed remainder decussate gradually from a position in the ventral white column blending in their distribution with the crossed component. The uncrossed bundles (Fig. 2) may be entirely absent.

Of the myelinated fibres the large majority are under 4 μ in size. A few are large myelinated with a maximum size of 15–20 μ. Within the cord the tract axons terminate in the internuncial pools of the intermediate grey (lamina VII), or, to a significantly lesser extent, make direct contact with the soma-dendrites of the motoneurons to provide a monosynaptic path leading from motor cortex to the muscle innervated. The monosynaptic route is said to be confined to the distal limb innervation, proximal musculature being innervated over a polysynaptic path.

Other motor paths exist, passing between the several levels of the brain stem and the internuncial pools (Rexed VII) of the segmental cord levels. Some are crossed, others uncrossed. In most cases the exact positions and sizes of these tracts is conjectural and in human cord it is difficult to assign a specific function to any of them. They are: tectospinal, rubrospinal, vestibulospinal, olivospinal and reticulospinal.

PHYSIOLOGICAL CONSIDERATIONS

The term reflex may cover any form of automatic behaviour, simple or complex. Our primary interest lies with the spinal reflexes and their role in the activities of the segmental neuromuscular mechanism. Since Sherrington these have been studied intensively in experimental animals—chiefly the cat—and the accumulated knowledge has become applicable to the interpretation of the pathological expressions of postural tone and motor deficit which result in paralysis, spasticity and rigidity as it occurs in human neurological lesions.

The spinal reflex substrate has been alluded to earlier. Two neural elements, entering afferent and leaving efferent, make up an irreducible arc for the consummation of the monosynaptic spinal reflex; and this simple a path is only operative for one reflex, the proprioceptive stretch (myotatic) response. The shortening which follows a muscle stretch takes place across a single cord hemi-segment, and afferent and efferent termini lie within the same muscle. By contrast, the flexor withdrawal reflex, which is ordinarily activated by a cutaneous nociceptive stimulus as a defensive safeguard is propagated inwards over delta myelinated (perhaps also non-myelinated) fibres, and is polysynaptic and plurisegmental. The triple flexion at hip, knee and ankle requires the integrated action of many flexor muscles together with the inhibition of their antagonists; yet the whole of the response can be activated by stimulation of any cutaneous or mixed nerve of the leg, or even a cutaneous spot within one dermatome. The same stimulus activates the crossed extensor reflex which is also polysynaptic and utilizes the opposite cord hemi-segments to produce a generalized accession of extensor tone in the musculature of that extremity.

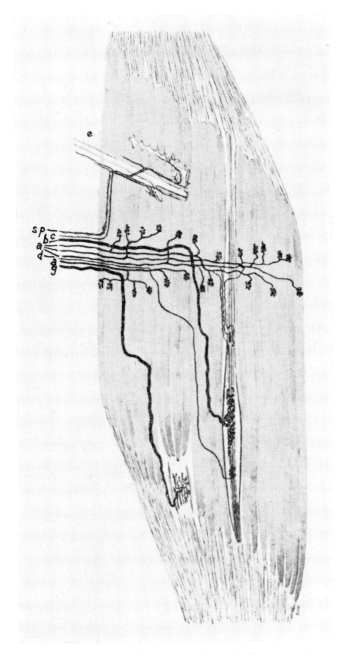

FIG. 7. Scheme of innervation of muscle fibres and of sensory receptors in muscle (Denny-Brown). Four motor axons innervate 23 extrafusal motor fibres. c, large axon of I a group provides the afferent terminals of a muscle spindle. g, large axon of 1 b group innervates a Golgi tendon organ. From Creed et al., The Clarendon Press, 1932.

The stretch response mechanism is basic to the causation of spasticity (Landau), one of the prime results of neurological deficit in upper motoneuron lesions. The initial stretch produced by a tendon tap in a normal muscle results in a two-phased efferent response which is due to the successive activation of the two major stretch receptors of the muscle—the spindle and the Golgi tendon organs. Spindle sensitivity to stretch is provided by a tonic state of contraction which is maintained in the intrafusal muscle fibres of the spindle. Those are innervated by a special cell population of the ventral horn called the gamma or fusimotor* motoneurons. The word *gamma* as used here derives from their small-sized myelinated axons in the ventral roots which belong to the gamma elevation of the conducted action potential of nerve. By contrast, the extrafusal muscle fibres which make up the main body of the muscle are innervated by the alpha group (Fig. 7). The spindle receptors are placed in parallel with extrafusal fibres, whereas the Golgi organs distribute to the musculotendinous junctions with which they are placed in series. In the latter case sensitivity is not regulated by a spinal outflow such as the gamma motoneuron population issues to the intrafusal muscle fibres.

The sequence of action in an augmenting muscle stretch is signalled by an increasingly asynchronous discharge from an increasing number of spindle stretch receptors whose activity results in muscle contraction. At a lesser rate the Golgi tendon organs also show an increase in asynchronous activation. As the extrafusal fibres of the muscle mass shorten, the input from the parallel spindle afferents diminishes, the tension upon them decreasing. Meanwhile the input from the series-linked tendon organs also reflects a continuous increase in both passive stretch and muscle contraction tension. Ultimately increase in inhibitory influence together with relative diminution of spindle tone produces a net motoneuron inhibition, resulting in relaxation of the muscle to its steady state. With a hyperactive cord mechanism such as is believed to explain clinical spasticity, the initial response to stretch results in an abrupt muscle contraction followed by a similarly rapid unloading relaxation; the latter is the clasp knife release, a cardinal sign of spasticity in human upper motoneuron lesions.

Clonus, like spasticity, is a manifestation of the hyperactive reflex mechanism we associate with upper motoneuron lesions. It illustrates well the rhythmicity inherent in even the normal spinal cord. The stimulus here is a square wave of tension the rise phase of which is equivalent to the patellar tap. The initial event is again a synchronous volley from the excitatory spindle receptor and a consequent sudden strong contraction of the stretched muscle. This is followed by a silent period of muscle relaxation due primarily to the sudden unloading of the parallel spindle receptors by contraction of the main muscle. In a sense the silencing of muscle by sudden unloading of the parallel spindle receptors is just the opposite of the preceding muscle contraction which is due to sudden increase in receptor activity as in the tendon jerk. As the contraction is relaxed and the muscle restretched the persistently applied pressure sets up another synchronized spindle receptor burst, recycling the continuing clonus.

* fusi-, der. Latin, *fusus*, spindle.

The Afferent Systems

Receptor Function

Receptors respond to mechanical, thermal or electro-magnetic (as light) activation. Different receptors are specific for different kinds of energy. An unusual example is the infrared organ situated in the facial pit of the viper. This has been shown to be a sensitive detector of the snake's prey. Besides specificities as to type of energy, the sensitivity to particular frequency bands within a sense modality and the time course over which a stimulus is effective is important. The former may be inherent in the mechanical properties of the system or unique to the receptor units. Receptors divide into rapidly and slowly adapting types. For rapidly adaptive units (called phasic) discharge frequency falls to zero during a continuing stimulus. For slowly adapting units, called tonic, the frequency of discharge declines slowly to a steady state characteristic of the applied force. The fast touch receptors and the slowly adapting muscle spindles are the prototypes of the two categories.

The transformation of mechanical energy to trains of nerve impulses for inward transit is mediated through a graded receptor potential. In the Paccinian corpuscle, a receptor sensitized to rapid mechanical events, the last node of Ranvier upon the nerve fibre is situated proximally within the corpuscle. Distally thereto the fibre becomes a naked terminal axoplasmic filament 2 μ in diameter which lies at the hub of the corpuscle. It is in this segment that the receptor potential arises through radial displacement of surrounding lamellae. Current flow generated by the disturbance is at first transmitted electrotonically along the axon. It can still be recorded from the fibre just proximal to the position of the receptor.

Fibre Types in Nerve and Sensory Modalities

Since original studies by Erlanger, Gasser, Bishop and Heinbecker, a spectrum of fibre sizes has been recognized having correlates in threshold, conduction rate, refractory period, and other properties. The conducted action potential, compounded from excitation and recording of whole nerve during step-wise increases in stimulus strength, shows 3 major elevations, the first (A) and the last (C) containing the sensory components (Fig. 8). The A, or initial, elevation of the potential recorded after conduction is composed of 4 submaxima which increase in threshold and diminish in conduction rate from alpha (100–85 m./sec.) through beta (50–70 m.) and gamma (30) to delta (15–30). Quite slow, high threshold small fibres of the B group are exclusively autonomic motor in function, and discussion of them is omitted here. Afferents of the C wave have a high threshold for direct stimulation and conduct very slowly (1–2 m./sec.). A roman numeral alternative classification of dorsal root axons is in vogue in spinal reflexology. This includes groups I–A (muscle spindle) and I–B (Golgi tendon organ) afferents as subdivisions of the A alpha elevation. Group II axons include the beta–gamma axons of the A spike and Group III the delta axons. Group IV contains exclusively non-myelinated fibres.

Using a combination of clinical and experimental methods it was concluded some time ago that touch is conveyed over large myelinated axons of the A group and pricking pain by smaller more thinly myelinated axons of the delta elevation and over C fibres as well. In man, after subarachnoid novocain block, pain and temperature sensations disappear before those of touch and pressure. With pressure block the reverse order of sensory loss is observed. These observations have been related to corresponding ones which concern the order of loss of potential maxima in experimental nerves *in vivo* and *in vitro*.

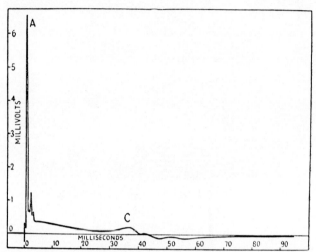

FIG. 8. Three principal elevations of the compound conducted action potential of peripheral nerve, from Gasser, H. S., 1938, *J. applied Physics*, **9**, 88.

Meanwhile another line of evidence was developing. Adrian recorded nerve potentials *in situ* from the ulnar nerve of the cat while stimulatng skin over the receptor area. A light touch was shown to produce both large spikes attributable to large rapidly conducting myelinated axons and small ones perhaps attributable to axons conducting in the delta range. Zotterman noted that small thinly myelinated axons convey thermal sensations, and also showed for the cat saphenous nerve dissected into fine strands the existence of potentials but one-twentieth the amplitude of the next largest ones. These were best seen following a firm stroke or burning stimuli. Later it became possible to further improve the technique for isolating sensory axons *in vivo* and to prove that either stroking the skin or heating gave rise to spikes in non-myelinated (C) axons.

More recently Iggo has further perfected the technique of recording both myelinated and C axons *in vivo* in animals using multi-fibre strands. By different kinds of skin stimulation he defined categories of response to mechanical, thermal and chemical stimuli. It is important that in cat and rabbit delta axons can be shown to supply cutaneous receptors very sensitive to light stroking of skin or fur. Thus it must be concluded that not all delta axons convey noxious impulses. Bessou and Perl performed similar isolation experiments upon the non-myelinated axons of the cat and differentiated low threshold receptors which could be excited by weak mechanical stimuli or marked cooling of the skin. High threshold C axon receptors were responsive to intense mechanical stimuli or noxious heat. Thus among non-myelinated (like delta) axons there was not a pure occupation of the parallel elements by conduction of noxious activity. We return to this matter in the next section which concerns the transfer of activity at the dorsal root entry zone.

Dorsal Root Entry Zone

All past evidence has indicated that impulses are re-grouped at entry to the spinal cord so that, irrespective of source, those which are transmitted within the same sensory modality project together to a higher level. In animal experiments conducted in 1915 Ranson severed separately the small (laterally placed) and large (medially placed) fibre components of the L–7 (lumbosacral) dorsal root. Thereafter faradic stimulation strong enough to engender a rise of blood pressure such as goes with the avoidance of a noxious stimulus was abolished by section of the lateral division. Others confirmed this experiment by recording from the contralateral tegmental fasciculus in the midbrain and from the ventralis lateralis nucleus of the thalamus. The path through midbrain tegmentum was interrupted by lateral division section, again indicating that the small myelinated and non-myelinated axons of Lissauer's tract constitute the principal input of pain impulses to the higher levels of the nervous system.

In cats Wall examined the spinal terminus of primary neurons distributed to cutaneous receptors. Using microelectrodes he found that pressure sensitive A fibres form a continuous group in which threshold varies with fibre diameter. Some smaller fibres were found to respond to both pressure and temperature. Cells responding to light touch were arranged in a definite lamina situated dorsally in the posterior horn, the peripheral leg being represented medially, the proximal leg laterally. All cells responded to heavy pressure and to temperature. Christensen and Perl similarly used microelectrodes to investigate the activation of specific kinds of cutaneous sensory units which lie at the dorsal horn margin of the spinal grey. At such loci postsynaptic units activated only by slowly conducting myelinated delta axons and/or non-myelinated (C) axons were regularly encountered, results which are in accord with the old theory of regrouping of impulses by sensory modality upon entry to the cord.

Ascending Pathways

Neurologists have always had an absorbing interest in the ascending path through the ventrolateral column of the cord. Two types of evidence have accumulated, clinicoanatomical and electrophysiological. The former conceives of a lamellated dermatomal disposition of fibres in the ventrolateral column, and has been dealt with previously. In résumé it seems established that between high thoracic and high cervical cord a gradual dorsolateral and external shift takes place resulting in movement of the fibres representing the sacral dermatomes to the outside, and leaving those to the cervical dermatomes on the inside,

with lumbar and thoracic components between. Besides the direct route to the thalamus the lateral column (at least in the monkey) contains a deep system of fibres which distributes massively to various cell groups of medullary and pontine reticular substance, whereas the more super-ficially situated spinal system connects with the lateral reaches of the midbrain grey matter and with the nucleus ventralis posterolateralis of the thalamus.

The pursuit of greater clinical knowledge of the ventro-lateral column tract components has led to physiological studies on animals in which peripheral nerves have been stimulated and conducted ventrolateral cord potentials recorded contralaterally, related to the A delta and C (non-myelinated) afferents of peripheral nerve. The dorsal columns, to the contrary, are made up of axons belonging to the beta elevation of the A nerve potential.

Influence of Higher Centres upon the Spinal Sensory Relays

Hagbarth and Kerr found that stimulation of various higher centres influences the size of an afferent volley evoked by a dorsal root stimulus and recorded from dorsal and ventrolateral white columns, midbrain, cerebellum, and sensory cortex. The relayed response was invariably depressed. These effects were found to be abolished by anaesthesia. With Fex, Hagbarth explored the dorsal grey and spinal paths of decerebrated, unanaesthetized cats for unit responses to naturally occurring peripheral stimuli. Thereafter they attempted to modify unit activity by electrical stimulation of various stations in the brain, care being taken to avoid the complications introduced by antidromic stimulation. The results indicate that post-synaptic spinal elements are exposed to excitatory as well as inhibitory influences from above. It is also argued that spontaneous activity of the spinal sensory neurons is somehow conditioned by tonic cerebral influences, the two streams mingling at the spinal level. Others have shown inhibitory influences of higher level centres upon dorsal column, trigeminal, cochlear and visual systems. Such work has instigated the histological search for corticofugal fibres reaching the sensory cranial nerve nuclei. Using the Glees method, such have been found extending downwards principally from frontoparietal cortex. Among lower nuclei investigated have been those of sensory trigeminal and solitary tracts of the brain stem.

SUMMARY

Many advances have been made in spinal anatomy and physiology since the era of Cajal and Sherrington. The former established the structural plan of the spinal apparatus, the latter the principles of its reflex physiology.

Cytoarchitectonic mapping of the grey matter by Rexed was a necessary prelude to the interpretation of synaptic potentials activated over reflex and sensory relay channels. The Scheibels have studied short axon cells and other cord interneurons in a voluminous material, thus signifi-cantly contributing to our knowledge of the synaptic substrate and removing an important obstacle to a complete understanding of the afferent relay to second order nerons in the dorsal root entry zone.

The Eccles group has examined in great detail the electrophysiological processes involved in the Sherringtonian reflexes including excitatory and inhibitory postsynaptic potentials, the chemical transmitters, and Renshaw inhibition. Wall, Perl and others have studied unit postsynaptic potentials evoked in the dorsal root entry zone by cutaneous receptor activation. Those studies give promise of making a major contribution to vexing problems of sensory physiology. Finally, Hagbarth and Kerr discovered descending paths leading to the first sensory cell station which modulate incoming activity before its projection to higher centres.

FURTHER READING

Bessou, P. and Perl, E. R. (1969), "Response of Cutaneous Sensory Units with Unmyelinated Fibers to Noxious Stimuli," *J. Neurophysiol.*, 32, 1025.

Bodian, D. (1964), "An Electron Microscopic Study of the Monkey Spinal Cord," *Bull. Johns Hopk. Hosp.*, 144, 13.

Bodian, D. (1966), "Synaptic Types on Spinal Motoneurons; An Electron Microscopic Study," *Bull. Johns Hopk. Hosp.*, 119, 16.

Christensen, B. N. and Perl, E. R. (1970), "Spinal Neurons Specifically Excited by Noxious or Thermal Stimuli: Marginal Zone of the Dorsal Horn," *J. Neurophysiol.*, 33, 293.

Creed, R. S., Denny-Brown, D., Eccles, J. C., Liddell, E. G. T. and Sherrington, C. S. (1932), *Reflex Activity of the Spinal Cord.* Oxford: The Clarendon Press.

Eccles, J. C. (1961), "The Mechanism of Synaptic Transmission," *Ergebn. Physiol.*, 51, 299.

Hunt, C. C. (1951), "The Reflex Activity of Mammalian Small-Nerve Fibers," *J. Physiol.*, 115, 456.

Hunt, C. C. and Perl, E. R. (1960), "Spinal Reflex Mechanism Concerned with Skeletal Muscle," *Physiol. Rev.*, 40, 538.

Iggo, A. (1966), "Cutaneous Receptors with a High Sensitivity to Mechanical Displacement," in *Touch, Heat and Pain* (A. V. S de Reuck, and J. Knight, Eds.), Ciba Foundation Symposium. Boston: Little Brown and Company.

Landau, W. M. (1969), "Spasticity and Rigidity" in *Recent Advances in Neurology*, by F. Plum. Phila.: F. A. Davis and Co.

Manfredi, M. and Castellucci, V. (1969), "Fiber Responses in the Ventrolateral Columns of Cat Spinal Cord," *Science*, 165, 1020.

Mountcastle, V. B. (1968), *Medical Physiology*, Vol. II, pp. 1378–80. St. Louis: C. V. Mosby Company.

Ranson, S. W. and Clark, S. L. (1947). *The Anatomy of the Nervous System.* Phila.: W. B. Saunder Company.

Rexed, B. (1954), "A Cytoarchitectonic Atlas of the Spinal Cord in the Cat," *J. comp. Neurol.*, 100, 297–380.

Romanes, G J (1953), "The Motor Groupings of the Spinal Cord," in *The Spinal Cord* (G. E. W. Wolstenholme, Ed). Boston: Little Brown and Company.

Scheibel, M. D. and Scheibel, A. B. (1968), "Terminal Axonal Patterns in Cat Spinal Cord. II. The Dorsal Horn," *Brain Research*, 9, 32.

Scheibel, M. E. and Scheibel, A. B. (1969), "A Structural Analysis of Spinal Interneurons and Renshaw cells," in *The Interneuron*. Berkeley: U. of Calif. Press.

Wall, P. D. (1960), "Cord Cells Responding to Touch, Damage, and Temperature of Skin," *J. Neurophysiol.*, 22, 305.

Wall, P. D. (1970), "The Sensory and Motor Role of Impulses Travelling in the Dorsal Columns Toward Cerebral Cortex," *Brain*, 93, 505.

Willis, W. D. Jr. (1969), "The Localization of Functional Groups of Interneurons," in *The Interneuron*, UCLA Forum in Medical Sciences.

2. MUSCLE

J. A. SIMPSON

Development of Muscle

The skeletal muscle mass develops from the mesodermal layer of the embryo which splits into segmentally arranged *myotomes* around the developing skeletal elements. The pre-muscle masses derived from the myotomes split longitudinally or tangentially and the portions so derived may remain separate or fuse with portions of adjoining myotomes, carrying with them the original segmental innervation. Thus a developed muscle may have its nerve supply from a number of segments of the neuraxis.

The primitive mononuclear *myoblasts* fuse into multinucleated *myotubes*. They are striated from an early age. Fusion depends on cell surface factors and is paced by the mitotic cycle. Myotubes soon begin to synthesize myosin, actin and tropomyosin. The multinucleated cells show an increasing capacity for contractile activity accompanied by a progressive rise in the contribution of myofibrillar fractions to the total cell protein. Even at an early embryonic age some enzymic specialization can be seen, foreshadowing the different types of muscle fibre found in fully developed muscle. Near the time of birth the concentration of enzymes rises sharply but in some instances, such as lactic dehydrogenase, there are isoenzymes in which the relative proportion differs in the foetus from the infant or adult.

In some muscular dystrophies and congenital myopathies some of the muscle fibres show resemblances to primitive myotubes and the foetal types of isoenzymes predominate. A hypothesis that these genetic disorders are due to maturation failure remains unproved. The abnormal finding may be associated with regeneration of damaged muscle fibres. There is also evidence that biochemical maturation of sarcoplasmic enzymes is sensitive to the activity pattern of the muscle. The type of muscle fibre may be modified by the motor nerve supply it receives. The levels of enzymes associated with formed structures such as mitochondria and myofibrils appear to be less susceptible to the activity pattern of muscle. Developing muscle is a self-limiting system. As the tissue matures, cell proliferation subsides and the number of muscle fibres becomes constant.

Regeneration

Injured skeletal muscle is capable of regeneration. There are two main mechanisms. *Terminal budding* is the predominant method when damage has been relatively extensive. Multinuclear buds grow out from the ends of the sound portions of surviving fibres. *Cellular fusion* is the second type. It is seen when injury is mild and has affected few fibres so that many sarcolemmal nuclei and endomysial sheaths remain intact. Isolated surviving nuclei enlarge to form spindle-shaped cells. These fuse into cellular bands which make contact with the healthy portions of the fibres, restoring their continuity. The origin of these cells is not certain. Some are believed to be developed from sarcolemmal nuclei, others may be *satellite cells* which some research workers believe are transported by the blood stream. A former belief that absent or defective regeneration was a characteristic of dystrophic muscle has been disproved.

Structure of Skeletal Muscle

All skeletal muscles shorten when activated. If physical constraints forbid significant shortening the force produced is termed "*isometric tension*". In most instances the muscle is attached to the skeleton at both ends, frequently through a tendon, so that muscle shortening produces movement with little increase in tension. This is termed "*isotonic contraction*". Skeletal muscles can only pull— they cannot push, except by using the principle of the lever (see for instance the actions of opening the mouth and protruding the tongue). In order to produce the complex movements of the body the muscles have to act together but in changing patterns. A single muscle may act as a prime mover, antagonist or synergist according to the demands of the central nervous system (Chapter II : 1).

The tension developed by a muscle depends on the number of activated fibres rather than on their length. It is, therefore, rare for muscle fibres to run the whole length of the muscle. They are usually fixed to tendinous insertions over a large area within the muscle. A common arrangement is the bipennate muscle where contraction is normally required to produce force (e.g. m. gastrocnemius) and linear where the main function is to shorten in order to move a lever (e.g. m. biceps brachii).

The muscle, enclosed in *perimysium*, is composed of muscle fibres surrounded by a variety of interstitial tissues. Each fibre is surrounded by a reticulin sheath (*endomysium*). Within the interstitial tissue is an abundant arteriovenous circulation, a lymphatic system, and the distribution of the nerve supply. The motor and sensory innervation of muscle are discussed in Chapter II : 1. There are also pain receptors and nerve fibres within the muscle. The function of certain fine non-myelinated nerve fibres is unknown. They may be autonomic. Certainly the blood supply of muscle is more complex than generally realized. There is, for instance, a greater capillary network around those muscle fibres with aerobic metabolism. Dilatation of the intramuscular capillaries is stimulated by metabolites released from contracting muscle, probably adenosine triphosphate (ATP), but autonomic control is important. It has long been believed that intramuscular vasoconstriction occurs after taking food, to release blood to the alimentary system. There is considerable evidence that the microcirculation of the muscle is of dual type, one part of the capillary bed supplying the muscle fibres, the other being a bypass "shunt" to which blood is diverted by a precapillary sphincter under autonomic control. Some authors have suggested that a disorder of this system would lead to chronic anoxia of muscle fibres and hence to muscular dystrophy but the experimental findings may be explained in other ways.

The *muscle fibre* is a cylindrical structure which may be many centimetres long (Fig. 1). Its multiple nuclei normally, in the mature fibre, lie under a thin membranous covering, the *sarcolemma*. This sheath is distinct from the endomysium. It has a basement membrane and a *plasma membrane* of the muscle cell which is important in regulating the ionic composition of the cell's protoplasm, the sarcoplasm. Between the two layers of membrane are satellite cells believed to be dormant myoblasts. The *sarcoplasm* of the muscle fibre fills the spaces between myofibrils which are the contractile part of the fibre. There are also numerous *sarcosomes*, mitochondria, ribosomes, lipochrome pigment, lipoid granules, glycogen and a Golgi apparatus concerned with the cell's metabolism. In diseased muscle *lysosomes* (containing proteolytic enzymes) may be detected but it is still uncertain whether they are present in normal fibres.

After staining, or when suitably illuminated, the skeletal muscle fibre is seen to have regular striations which extend

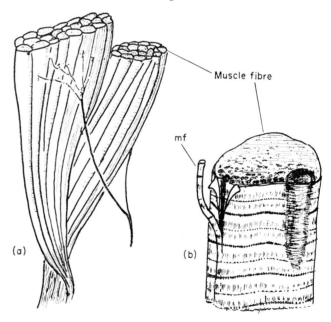

Fig. 1. (a) Human skeletal muscle to show motor nerve entry zone on deep surface. (b) Longitudinal segment of a muscle fibre. The striped appearance results from the precise alignment of its striated myofibrils (mf). The cell nucleus lies under the sarcolemmal sheath which consists of two layers, the basement membrane and the plasma membrane.

right across inside the fibre, dividing it up into sarcomeres about 2 μ long. This segmentation is due to the structure of the *myofibrils* running from one end of the fibre to the other (diameter about 1 μ). There is no explanation why the associated structure of each myofibril should be so aligned as to impose the same pattern on the whole muscle fibre. The myofibrils are composed of alternating bands, birefringent; anisotropic (A-band) and isotropic (I-band) under polarized light. Under ordinary light the appearance is reversed, so that the A-band appears dark and the I-band appears light. The structural and functional division of fibril into segments is by thin partitions called Z-lines or Z-discs. A Z-disc runs across the middle of the I-band and, since the fibrils are aligned as described above, the Z-discs are continuous from fibril to fibril right across the fibre, thus dividing it into sarcomeres. Each end of a sarcomere is, therefore, half of an I-band and in the middle of the sarcomere is the A-band of high refractive index. In the A-band is a less refractile central H-zone (Fig. 2).

The bands seen by the histologist form different proportions of the sarcomere when the muscle fibre is contracted,

also caused by the higher concentration of protein in the former.

The *protein filaments* are of two types, thick and thin, which interdigitate (Fig. 3). Thin filaments are attached to each side of Z-discs. They run towards the equator of the sarcomere but do not meet, the H-zone being that part of the A-band from which thin filaments are absent. They are connected end to end across the H-zone by fibrous connections (s-filaments). Interleaved between thin filaments are thick filaments. They are confined to the A-band. They are the only filaments crossing the H-zone and in that area have a smooth surface. The ends interdigitating in the denser parts of the A-band away from the equator have projections sticking out to either side, forming a flexible ratchet linkage with the thin filaments believed to be important in the contractile mechanism (p. 47).

In relaxed muscle an *M-line* can be distinguished at the equator of the sarcomere, within the H-band. Short M-line bridges link the thick filaments laterally and no doubt anchor the thick filaments to the equator of the sarcomere.

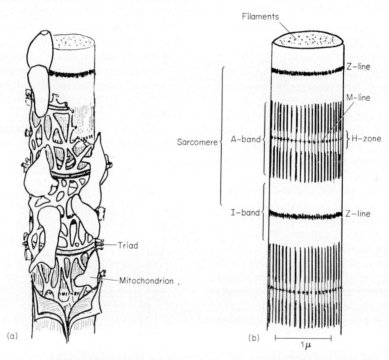

FIG. 2. (a) Diagram of a myofibril from human skeletal muscle. It is surrounded by the membrane-limited tubular network of the *sarcoplastic reticulum* and the *T-system*. An intermediate transverse tubule of the T-system bounded on each side by a transverse cisterna of the sarcoplasmic reticulum forms a complex called the *triad*. In the human muscle fibre this is near the junction of the A and I bands of the myofibril. (b) Diagram of a myofibril without the T-system. The banded appearance is the result of the disposition of the thick and thin myofilaments.

at its resting length, or passively stretched. This is because the bands result from the organization of longitudinal fine protein filaments. Anisotropy is a sign that the structure is highly ordered right down to molecular dimensions and the higher refractive index of the *A-discs* than the *I-discs* is

Structure of Myofilaments

A fine axial periodicity (400 Å) seen on electron microscopy and X-ray diffraction indicates a precise localization of interstitial substances. The thin filament is composed of two strings of globular protein units wound round each other. The globular protein unit is probably formed from a capsized protein chain which has a cylindrical structure. The cylinder in turn is formed from a chain of protein units with a coiled α-helix central spine and radially orientated amino acid groups. The principal protein of the thin filaments is *actin*, a protein which undergoes mechanical change if its bound ATP is hydrolysed to ADP (at the same time liberating energy and inorganic phosphate).

Thick filaments, the structural basis of the A-discs, are composed mainly of *myosin*. The myosin molecule has a globular head (yielding heavy meromyosin (HMM) on tryptic digestion) and a tail (yielding light meromyosin (LMM) on digestion), the whole resembling a spermatozoon in an electronmicrograph. The "tails" have a structural function, being assembled into a rod which is also probably composed of a two-stranded rope of two α-helices coiled round each other. The "head" has special properties. The HMM has a globular structure with two reactive sites. At one of these binding to actin can occur and at the other the hydrolysis of ATP is catalysed. This part of the myosin molecule appears to be very suitable for producing a mechanical effect by linkage with the thin filament actin as well as for producing breakdown of the immediate source of energy (ATP). Myosin molecules aggregate into rods with their heads arranged in an orderly way which suggests that they are important in the cross-bridges of the thick filaments. Further discussion of the chemical structure of muscle is best postponed until the mechanism of contraction has been described. The type of protein described has configurational properties which change when ATP is split and it is natural that an explanation of muscular shortening should be sought in these terms. Nonetheless, the known physical characteristics of muscle during shortening and lengthening can be accounted for by postulating that the process of contraction involves only a translational shifting of these macromolecular species with respect to one another.

Mechanism of Contraction

There are various theories based on sliding of myofilaments when the muscle cell is stimulated. The more important were described independently around 1950 by A. F. Huxley and H. E. Huxley. According to A. F. Huxley the transversely oriented bridges linking the thick and thin filaments are the basis of relative translation of the two types of fibres. In this model, the bridges are an integral structural component of the thick (myosin) filaments as described above, and shortening is accomplished when the ATP-ase active sites at the extremities of the bridges shift their points of attachment from periodically located sites on the thin (actin) filaments to adjacent sites, thus causing one filament to slide or creep over the other (Fig. 3). (To account for the extent of sliding it is necessary to postulate that the re-attachment of active sites is repeated five or six times.)

If the cross-bridges become firmly attached to the actin filaments the resulting shortening is irreversible (e.g. *rigor mortis* and other forms of *contracture*). In physiological contraction the sliding of the interdigitated fibres is reversible. Unfortunately the fixation of tissue required for electronmicroscopy produces changes of rigor type. Nevertheless, X-ray diffraction data on living muscle support the

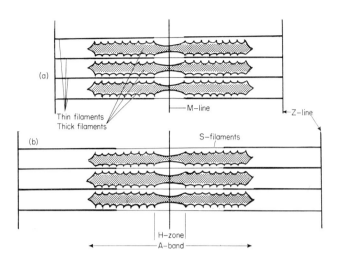

FIG. 3. Diagram of protein filaments within a myofibril: (a) contracted; (b) relaxed.

sliding filament model. For instance, it accounts well for the relative dimensions of A- and I-discs and of the H-zone in muscle at different lengths. It would, however, be expected that the muscle would become unable to shorten or develop tension if the fibril were stretched until thick and thin myofilaments no longer overlapped. Buchthal found that structural continuity is preserved and small but significant shortening is still possible in these conditions. It is also difficult to account for the directionality of the shift of bridge-links unless there is an asymmetrical chemical mechanism or sequential shortening of the axially repeating units within the thick myofilaments, causing a caterpillar-like movement. Nevertheless, there is general agreement that a sliding filament mechanism accounts for the shortening of muscle fibres when stimulated.

Neuromuscular Transmission

Functional contact between a branch of a motor nerve fibre (Chapter II : 1) and a muscle fibre is achieved through the *motor endplate* where there is intimate contact between the respective surface membranes, the two membranes remaining intact. The endoneurium becomes continuous with the endomysium and the neurilemma with the sarcolemma but the myelin sheath of the nerve fibre is lost at the point where the nerve axon divides into terminal branches with expansions within the soleplate area which consists of a depression on the surface of the muscle fibre (Fig. 4). The terminal expansions lie in a *synaptic gutter* in the soleplate area separated by a space of about 400 Å (in the human). There are different types of structure, some described according to their appearance in stained preparations as "en plaque" or "en grappe". Most skeletal muscle fibres in man have a single endplate but multiple innervation may be found in some fibres. These morphological differences vary from one muscle to another and are probably correlated with differences in the type of muscle fibre (see below) and the response to pharmacological agents. The author has suggested that pathological changes of endplate morphology would account for the pathophysiology of some neuromuscular disorders, notably myasthenia gravis.

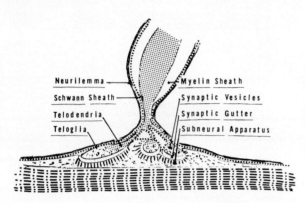

FIG. 4. Diagram of typical human neuromuscular junction.

Although electrical transmission occurs at some synapses in lower animals, it is certain that transmission at the neuromuscular junction in the human is entirely chemical. The transmitter is *acetylcholine* (ACh). It is stored in vesicles in the motor nerve terminal. Small amounts leak out and can be detected by their action on the muscle. When a nerve action potential invades the nerve ending there is a massive discharge of ACh which is related to the frequency of the nerve impulses. The ACh is liberated into the cleft between the membranes of nerve and muscle in the endplate. The adjacent muscle membrane is thought to have chemoreceptor sites to which ACh molecules become attached. The number of these receptor sites is increased by the fact that the synaptic gutter (*primary synaptic cleft*) has secondary synaptic clefts, derived from infolded muscle surface membrane, projecting downwards and laterally from it. The ACh liberated into the clefts diffuses rapidly from the edges of the clefts into extramuscular space. The activity of the ACh molecules which become attached to postjunctional receptors is also terminated by *cholinesterase* (ChE) present in rodlets ("organites") of a *subneural apparatus* in the sarcoplasm underlying the soleplate area and radiating normal to the receptor membrane.

The efficiency of the neuromuscular transmission depends on the integrity of production, storage and release of ACh from the nerve terminal, the dimensions of the primary and secondary synaptic clefts and the function of ChE which rapidly hydrolyses ACh. At normal junctions in the human there is a surplus of ACh over the amount required to depolarize the postsynaptic membrane adequately unless rapid trains of nerve action potentials occur for a comparatively long period of time. There is, then, a high "safety-factor".

The liberation of ACh from the nerve terminal is facilitated by repeated stimulation by a train of action potentials and also by the presence of Ca^{++} in the tissue fluid bathing the terminal but is reduced by excess of Mg^{++} ions. It is suggested that depolarization of the nerve terminals caused by the nerve action potential is produced by influx of *calcium ions*, following which the synaptic vesicles are broken down, releasing ACh, a mechanism which is blocked competitively by extracellular magnesium ions.

Defects of Neuromuscular Transmission

Neuromuscular Block

Abnormality of any of the factors listed above will lower the safety factor of transmission and may lead to transmission failure. Thus a deficit of calcium or surplus of magnesium ions at the endplate will block liberation of ACh from vesicles. (The number of ACh quanta released is reduced; the size of each quantum is normal.) A similar defect has been described in the carcinomatous syndrome associated with bronchogenic carcinoma (Eaton-Lambert syndrome). The output of ACh per stimulus increases progressively with successive stimuli faster than 10/sec. and is also increased by raising external calcium ion concentration or with the addition of guanidine. Hemicholinium-3 and similar substances arrest the synthesis of acetylcholine. Any ACh which is already formed and stored in vesicles is liberated normally in response to depolarization of the nerve terminal, but once the store is exhausted, further transmission becomes impossible. Hemicholinium-3 may also have a postjunctional action. The toxin of *Clostridium botulinum* causes failure of release of ACh, accounting for the paralysis of botulism.

Acetylcholine may be formed and released in normal amounts but fail to evoke a full response, especially if stimulation is repeated in any situation which lowers the safety factor for transmission. The classical example is myasthenia gravis where the morphological changes at the endplate (widening of the primary cleft and relative absence of secondary clefts) are sufficient to explain the failure to sustain an indirectly evoked tetanus. The changes are apparently due to immunological damage. This can also account for the reduction in size of endplate potentials though the original describers have interpreted this as an indication that the ACh quantum released from terminal vesicles is reduced in size.

Competitive Block

Neuromuscular transmission may be blocked by substances that compete with acetylcholine for the receptors on the endplate and thus prevent its depolarization. This is considered to be the mode of action of *d*-tubocurarine, gallamine *tri*-ethiodide and other substances. Many of these are quaternary ammonium compounds like ACh. They resemble ACh sufficiently to occupy the same receptors but do not cause depolarization of the endplates. They can be displaced from the receptors by increasing the local concentration of ACh as by the use of anticholinesterase substances such as neostigmine.

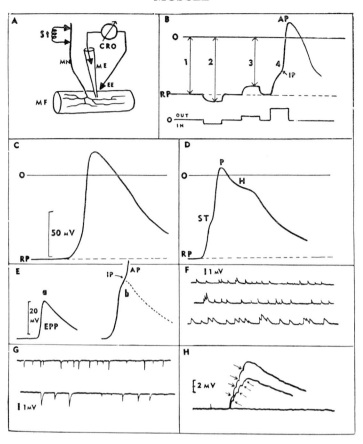

FIG. 5. Diagrams showing some of the electrical events associated with the process of neuromuscular transmission. *A.* Experimental arrangement to record the potential changes occurring across the end-plate membrane during transmission. The tip of a microelectrode is shown inserted into the junctional region of a muscle fibre (MF). The potential changes between the intracellular microelectrode (ME) and an external electrode (EE) are displayed by a cathode ray oscilloscope (CRO). Stimulating electrodes (ST) are placed in the motor nerve (MN). *B.* This diagram shows the way in which the potential changes across the muscle membrane appear in the CRO screen. When the microelectrode tip is outside the muscle fibre, both electrodes are at the same potential and the position of the electron beam in the screen is taken as zero (0). The recording system is arranged conventionally so that negativity of the microelectrode tip results in a downward deflection of the baseline. The impalement of the muscle fibre with the microelectrode tip is accompanied by a sudden downward deflection of the trace to RP. The difference between O and RP is the resting potential (1). A second microelectrode can be inserted into the end-plate region of the muscle fibre and used to inject electric current across the membrane. An inward current (i.e. carried by positive ions entering the muscle fibre) causes an increase in the resting potential or hyperpolarization (2). If the current flows out of the fibre, there will be a reduction of the resting potential or depolarization (3). If the depolarization reaches a value of between 30 and 40 mV., the muscle fibre is electrically stimulated, and an action potential (4) is generated. Note the inflection point (IP) marking the transition between the passive depolarization and the beginning of the action potential. The lower trace in B indicates the direction and relative duration and intensity of the current applied across the membrane. *C.* Action potential of the muscle fibre elicited by direct stimulation. *D.* Action potential of the muscle fibre elicited by synaptic action and recorded at the end-plate region (*St*, step; *P*, peak; *H*, hump). See text. *E*: (a) represents an end-plate potential such as recorded in preparation blocked by curarine. Note fast-rising phase and slower decay; (b) a just threshold end-plate potential that succeeds in firing an action potential. Note inflexion point (IP) showing the transition between synaptic depolarization and action potential. The dotted line shows the hypothetical decay curve of this end-plate potential. *F.* Tracings of recordings of miniature end-plate potentials (m.e.p.ps). The lower record was obtained on a faster baseline. Note the general resemblance between end-plate potentials and m.e.p.ps. *G.* Tracings of recordings of external m.e.p.ps (see text). *H.* Shows two superimposed end-plate potentials recorded from a magnesium-blocked frog's muscle at 5°C (see text). Note steps in the rising phase, indicated by the arrows, suggesting a desynchronization in the liberation of ACh quanta. (After J. del Castillo, 1960. *Res. Publ. Assoc. Res. Nerv. Ment. Dis.*, **38**, 90–143.)

Depolarization Block

If the receptor site remains occupied by ACh the initial twitch response is followed by neuromuscular block, but transmission failure is not progressive as this type does not depend on lowering of the safety factor. As endplate depolarization is prolonged it has been termed "depolarization block". In fact the endplate membrane does repolarize, though later than usual, but block persists. It appears that continuous occupation of the receptors renders the postjunctional membrane "insensitive" though the mechanism is not understood. Prolonged occupation by ACh occurs with administration of anticholinesterase substances such as edrophonium, neostigmine, pyridostigmine and organic phosphorus compounds, some of which are used as insecticides or toxic war gases. Depolarization block is also produced by decamethonium iodide and succinylcholine, used in anaesthetic practice, and by choline. These substances depolarize the endplate but are then resistant to hydrolysis by cholinesterase. Block of this type is, of course, increased by neostigmine and its analogues.

Endplate Physiology

Endplate Delay

The liberation of ACh by nerve impulses, its transfer to the receptor sites and the provocation there of an endplate potential requires an appreciable time of the order of 0·5–2 msec. The major part of the delay is in the mechanism by which the action potential raises the probability of quantal release. The delay may be appreciably increased at some junctions in myasthenia gravis, increasing the "*jitter*" or time variation between action potentials of muscle fibres innervated by a single neurone.

Endplate Potential

When ACh fixes to receptors on the endplate it evokes a change in the membrane potential (*see* below). Although the endplate is a very sensitive electric indicator for small doses of ACh, it is not sensitive enough to show up the action of single molecules. A microelectrode in or near the postsynaptic membrane records *miniature endplate potentials* (m.e.p.p.) even when no stimulus has been applied and the muscle fibre is completely at rest. These "spontaneous m.e.p.ps" occur at random intervals, summate without a refractory period, and show discontinuous gradation of size indicating that they are multiples of minimum sized potentials. It is accepted that the smallest m.e.p.p. results from stimulation of the receptor surface by a single *quantum of ACh*, probably the contents of one presynaptic vesicle and that the larger m.e.p.ps are due to spontaneous discharge of several quanta. The frequency of the spontaneous discharge (but not the quantal size) can be "driven" over a wide range by altering the membrane potential in the terminal part of the motor axon.

Depolarization of the nerve terminal by a nerve action potential or by potassium liberates many quanta of ACh almost synchronously causing a large *endplate potential* (e.p.p.) at the subsynaptic membrane, which immediately triggers an *action potential* in the muscle fibre if it reaches a threshold level of depolarization (Fig. 5). This is an indication that electrical current has flowed across the subsynaptic membrane. It is now necessary to examine the chemical correlates of this electrical change.

Membrane Permeability

Acetylcholine diffusing across the narrow synaptic cleft reacts with receptors in the outer surface of the muscle membrane, causing this area to become permeable to ions. A flow of ionic current takes place across this localized area of membrane, mainly sodium ions passing out of the muscle cell and potassium and calcium ions passing in. (The ionic species are probably limited by the diameter of pores opened up in the subsynaptic membrane and not indiscriminately as originally believed.) The ions move down their electrochemical gradients and not in response to an ionic pump. The endplate potential also differs from

the action potential of nerve or muscle in not having a regenerative link, the local conductance change being independent of the level of membrane potential.

The receptor sites at which ACh produces this change in ionic conductance are probably not restricted to the actual subsynaptic membrane, but extend in progressively diminishing concentration for up to 300 μ away from the endplate. When muscle is denervated receptor sites may be found in most parts of the muscle membrane so that even small amounts of ACh in the blood (and possibly from Schwann cells) may depolarize the muscle fibre. This is probably the mechanism giving rise to spontaneous *fibrillation* (*see* Chapter IX : 2). It is not known how contact with the motor nerve limits the excitable area to the endplate zone. "*Neurotrophic factors*" have been proposed but, like the ether of the nineteenth century physics, better understanding may remove the need to postulate these undetectable substances. (In truth the evidence for specific receptor sites is little better.) At the endplate (which can be investigated in curarized muscle) there is a rapid depolarization of the membrane, reaching a maximum in about 1 msec, from which decline is at first very rapid and then slower, depending on the concentration of cholinesterase and the possibility for ACh to diffuse away from the synaptic cleft and the recharging of membrane capacitance by potassium and chloride ions. The endplate response is a graded one and therefore it can be modified. It is not "all or none". Local circuit action causes a redistribution of the electrical charge over the membrane away from the endplate. It spreads decrementally along the muscle membrane.

Action Potential of Muscle

The muscle cell has a resting potential of approximately 90 mV, the interior being negative with respect to the exterior, caused by the ionic distribution across the cell membrane which acts as a diffusion barrier. In the resting state there is a low concentration of sodium and chloride and high concentration of potassium and organic ions within the cell, the reverse obtaining in the extracellular fluid (Fig. 6a).

The maintenance of concentration differences depends mainly upon the net movement of ions against their electrochemical potential gradients due to the semipermeable nature of the membrane and active transport of Na^+ out of and K^+ into the muscle cell. The transporting system for these "*ionic pumps*" is metabolically energized but the type of energy coupling remains uncertain. It is the potassium conductance of the membrane which ultimately determines the level of the resting potential. As the membrane is lipoprotein it also exhibits capacitance. The membrane, therefore, has electrical resistance and capacitance in parallel. This gives it an electrical time constant which affects the velocity with which depolarization can be obtained.

If the local current at the endplate zone causes a critical level of depolarization of the adjacent membrane there is a sudden rise in the membrane's permeability to inflowing sodium ions from the Na^+ rich interstitial fluid. This response is an "all or none" event. The sodium inflow becomes greater than the potassium outflow due to activation of a *"sodium carrier mechanism"* described below. Increased sodium conductance (as this is called in electrical parlance) leads to further depolarization. This important step is regenerative (unlike the ionic flow at the endplate) as the entry of positive sodium ions (down their concentration and potential gradients into the negatively charged interior of the cell, assisted by the sodium carrier) brings

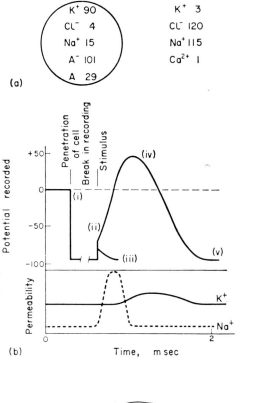

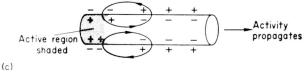

Fig. 6. (a) The distribution of ions inside and outside a muscle fibre. Approximate concentrations in gram-ions per litre. A and A are non-diffusible organic substances, ionized and non-ionized respectively. (b) The changes in potential recorded by a microelectrode inside a muscle fibre (upper curves). The lower curves show the underlying changes in membrane permeability. (c) The currents generated by an active region flow in such a way as to stimulate neighbouring resting regions. (After D. R. Wilkie, 1968. *Muscle*, Arnold, London.)

positive charges inside the membrane. This depolarizes it further leading to more increase in sodium conductance and more sodium entry. The influx of sodium ions is great enough to reverse the membrane potential. It becomes positive internally with reference to the outside of the cell. Potassium permeability also increases but more slowly and insufficient to balance the inflow of sodium ions. However, potassium permeability is still increasing after sodium permeability has reached its maximum and is beginning to

fall (Fig. 6b) so there is a rapid net outward flux of potassium ions, the electrochemical gradient being added to by a *"potassium carrier"*. Because of this potassium flow the peak of depolarization is past and repolarization is well on its way before the increased sodium conductance has ceased. The original resting potential is rapidly restored (often within a millisecond) but the cell now contains a surplus of sodium and deficit of potassium ions until these are restored by the sodium-potassium metabolic "pump" referred to above. Note that metabolic energy is required to restore the resting situation rather than to produce the action potential which depends on electrostatic energy. A similar principle is used in providing the energy for muscular contraction.

To summarize these events—the acetylcholine released from motor nerve terminals becomes attached to discrete receptor sites at the motor endplate where the membrane permeability is altered. The rapid flow of ions into and out of the muscle cell at different rates according to the ionic species causes a net ionic current to flow. As the membrane has high electrical resistance the current passing through it generates a potential difference across the membrane (by Ohm's law). As the initial flow of positive ions is from outside the cell to the inside this leads to depolarization of the outside of the membrane. Slower restorative processes then restore the original polarization, outside positive to inside. The sequence of events is called the *action potential*. The cell membrane now has an area of negative potential at the active region, the remaining membrane still being positively charged externally. There is therefore a current flow from the positively charged areas into the negatively charged "sink" of the active area, the circuit being completed through the "inactive" membrane (see Fig. 6c). Thus adjacent areas of membrane in turn become depolarized while the original area of stimulation is being repolarized by the metabolic pump. The result of this is that the action potential propagates in each direction from the endplate zone towards the poles of the muscle fibre. When recorded by an intracellular electrode, as in Fig. 6b, the action potential is a positive variation but consideration of the diagram will show that the same potential change is "seen" by an external electrode (referred against a remote inactive area) as a negative "spike". A stigmatic electrode applied to the outside of the muscle cell in a conducting medium will record the voltage change associated with the outflow of current immediately ahead of the active region, then the current inflow as the active region passes under the electrode, and finally the outflowing current as that area again becomes a "source" of current.

It follows, therefore, that an extracellular electrode in a volume conductor "sees" the electrical changes associated with a propagating wave of depolarization as a positive-negative-positive variation with the negative phase indicating when the area of depolarization is close to the electrodes. If, furthermore, the reference electrode (since only potential *differences* can be recorded) is affected by changes in the potential field it will undergo the same sequence but with amplitude and timing dependent on the distance of the reference electrode from the generator and the homogeneity of the conducting medium. However, if suitable precautions are taken to make the reference electrode comparatively indifferent the changes at the stigmatic or "active" electrode associated with the propagation of the muscle action potential are triphasic. Where a number of muscle fibres are active the electrode records a compound potential. By suitable analysis it can be recognized whether a recorded potential was generated by one fibre or by a group such as a motor unit. This is the basis of electromyography (Chapter IX : 2).

Refractory Period

It has been shown above that the depolarizing effect of ACh at the endplate may be summed. This is true even if quanta of ACh do not reach the receptor surface synchronously. The excitable membrane of the muscle cell differs in this respect because of the sodium-carrier mechanism, which gives it an explosive "all or none" type of response. The intense depolarization during the propagated impulse largely inactivates the sodium-carrier and this causes a refractory state. A second stimulus during this time, (which approximates to the negative spike in volume conduction) is unable to depolarize the cell to the critical level. An additional factor is that the potassium-carrier mechanism continues after the action potential and this raises the level of depolarization which is required in order that the inward sodium current should exceed the outward current due to flux of potassium and chloride ions. There is, therefore, a *"relative refractory period"* following the *"absolute refractory period"*. The refractory period is the shortest time interval between conditioning and testing stimuli at which a testing stimulus of given strength evokes a propagated action potential. The response to the testing stimulus at this shortest interval occurs with a slightly greater latency than that to the conditioning stimulus so that the shortest interval between action potentials at a given strength of the testing stimulus, the *irresponsive period*, is in fact slightly longer than the refractory period as just defined. Furthermore, the absolute refractory and irresponsive periods increase with increasing repetition rate of paired stimuli. This indicates that the recovery time after paired responses considerably exceeds the recovery time after a single action potential. Both these recovery periods are prolonged by anoxia.

In the human, different fibre types have different relative and absolute refractory periods. With a repetition rate of paired stimuli of 1 per sec. the absolute refractory periods fall into two groups, one of 2·2–3·1 msec. and the other of 3·4–4·6 msec. (at 34–36·5°C) but both groups appear to have the same absolute irresponsive periods. In patients and carriers of Duchenne type muscular dystrophy the absolute refractory period of muscle is shorter than normal. This may be associated with the decrease in intracellular potassium which has been found in dystrophic muscle and would correlate with the lowered resting potential of the dystrophic muscle fibres which has been demonstrated by intracellular recording.

Accommodation

The inactivation of the sodium-carrier caused by depolarization of the cell membrane can be shown in other ways. A continued depolarization at a level too low to cause appreciable activation of the sodium-carrier (i.e. subthreshold) nevertheless brings about a relatively slow decline of the effectiveness of a testing stimulus, indicating that it partially inactivates the sodium-carrier. The response to a slowly rising stimulus has a higher threshold than the response to an abrupt depolarization (Chapter IX : 2). This property—termed *accommodation*—is less prominent in muscle than in nerve fibres. Nevertheless, a continuous current applied to normal muscle does not evoke a prolonged train of action potentials but only a cathodal "make" or anodal "break" response (at threshold). Repetitive firing to continuous current occurs if the concentration of calcium or magnesium ions is reduced in the extracellular fluid (note that nerve membrane is more sensitive to these changes and that the phenomena of tetany are neural rather than muscular).

When the property of accommodation is reduced, the membrane response to even a brief stimulus tends to be oscillatory and, if accommodation is abolished, the cell may "fire" spontaneously as its resting potential is unstable. Certain substances such as veratrine alkaloids accentuate the oscillatory response whereas calcium, cocaine and other local anaesthetics and cardiac glycosides tend to prevent it without hyperpolarizing the cell. This has led to the concept of *membrane stabilizers*. An extended discussion is beyond the scope of this review. In some diseases of muscle there is a marked tendency for the muscle membrane to fire repetitively when depolarized by neural activity or by injury (if not spontaneously). If the train of action potentials evokes a series of twitches the phenomenon of *myotonia* results. Membrane stabilizers such as quinine, procaine amide, or phenytoin reduce the oscillatory response of the muscle cell membrane and so abolish myotonia (but they do not, of course, influence any associated weakness of muscular contraction).

Sarcoplasmic Reticulum

The exact mechanism of excitation—contraction coupling is obscure. One problem has been to account for the virtually simultaneous activation of myofibrils throughout the muscle fibre. It is probable that the link involves a specialized internal conduction system within the muscle fibre. This is the *sarcoplasmic reticulum*, a system of tubules ramifying between the myofibrils (Fig. 2a). From openings on the surface of the fibre, *transverse tubules*, sometimes called the T-system, run inwards conducting some sort of electrical signal into the interior. Each sarcomere has *terminal cisternae* linked by *longitudinal tubules* in a reticular fashion. Two cisternae (outer vesicles) in close contact with the interpolated transverse tubule form structures called *triads*. They are located near the junction of the A- and I-bands in human skeletal muscle (i.e. two per sarcomere), unlike the frog and other lower vertebrates where the triad is at the Z-line. The cisternae are believed to pump calcium ions from the sarcoplasm, thus lowering the concentration below that at which ATP splitting can occur. When an action potential propagates along the surface of the fibre, the electrical change produced in the

T-system causes the calcium ions to be released from the outer vesicles into the sarcoplasm where the level of calcium becomes sufficient to allow ATP splitting and contraction is initiated. Unless another action potential comes along the calcium ions are rapidly pumped back into the vesicles and the muscle relaxes. Caffeine is thought to act directly on the vesicles, initiating a contracture of muscle fibre without altering the membrane potential. The possibility for uncoupling by disease of the action potential-contraction mechanism, will be apparent but no such disorder has been identified. In familial periodic paralysis the sarcoplasmic reticulum is dilated.

Muscular Contraction

As described above muscular contraction is believed to occur from the sliding of thin actin filaments between thick myosin filaments due to movement of cross bridges. Myosin acts as an ATP-ase, splitting ATP in the presence of a suitable concentration of calcium and magnesium. When ATP is present the actin and myosin do not stick together. The muscle action potential transfers calcium from the sarcoplasmic reticulum into the sarcoplasm, the ATP is split by ATP-ase, the actin and myosin then bind strongly together and the fibres shorten. A sliding filament theory is highly probable, but different explanations of the function of the cross-bridges have been proposed. Whatever the physical mechanism, it is agreed that the proteins make up the machinery of the muscle cell and that the breakdown of ATP provides the energy. But there are other proteins than actin and myosin in the muscle cell, and the amount of ATP in the fibre would suffice for about ten contractions only unless it is regenerated.

Tropomyosin

Originally thought to be a building block of myosin, it is now believed that tropomyosin B may give mechanical strength to the Z-disc but there is some evidence that in a complex with *troponin* it also affects the reactions of the contractile proteins to calcium. SH groups in troponin are considered to be necessary for the calcium action. Relaxation of myofibrils is accompanied by transfer of calcium ions back into the sarcoplasmic reticulum. Possible *relaxing factors* are still under investigation.

It may be worth noting the importance of the Z-line. It is the "anchor" area for the thin filaments without which no tension could be produced by sliding or contracting filaments. In a number of myopathies one of the earliest disorders seen by electronmicroscopy is a disruption of the Z-line.

Storage and Release of Energy

It has been pointed out above that muscle contains insufficient ATP to provide energy for more than a short series of twitches if the reaction was irreversible. The muscle fibre contains a large store of carbohydrate in the form of granules of *glycogen* but the rate of liberation of

energy from oxidation of glycogen is too slow to drive the muscle engine. The compromise used is to supply energy from a high energy source, *adenosine triphosphate* (ATP), and to "recharge" it from a series of progressively slower chemical processes. Thus a metabolic debt is accumulated during muscular contraction, which is repaid when contraction has ceased.

The energy comes from two sources, (1) hydrolysis of *phosphocreatine*, which is replenished by metabolizing glycogen to lactic acid. (2) Oxidation of *carbohydrate and fat*, a slow but almost limitless source of energy requiring oxygen. The following is a simplified scheme of the chemical changes providing the energy for muscular contraction.

(1) The action potential causes transfer of calcium ions from sarcoplasmic vesicles to actomyosin, influenced by tropomyosin, and makes it function as ATP-ase which hydrolyses ATP to ADP with liberation of phosphorus and energy.

$$ATP \rightarrow ADP + P_1$$

(2) Hydrolysis of phosphocreatine to creatine regenerates the ATP for further use.

$$ADP + PC \underset{cpt}{\leftrightharpoons} ATP + C$$

This is a reversible transphosphorylation catalysed by the enzyme *creatine phosphotransferase* (creatine kinase).

(3) The stores of phosphocreatine are restored after contraction stops by reversing the first two reactions. The energy for the rephosphorylations is obtained from the step by step hydrolysis of *glycogen*, a substance stored as granules in muscle fibres, by enzymes contained in soluble form in sarcoplasm.

In the first stage of *glycolysis* the glycogen, by reacting with phosphate, is broken into 6-carbon units (hexoses) and then to 3-carbon units ending as *pyruvic acid* ($CH_3.CO.COOH$). Some of the breakdown stages fail if appropriate enzymes are missing as in the glycogen storage diseases.

In the second stage pyruvic acid enters the tricarboxylic (Krebs) cycle which progressively breaks it—and other substrates including fatty acids—into *carbon dioxide*, a waste product, and hydrogen which is carried away by special carriers for further metabolic use in the third stage.

The second and third stage enzymes are in mitochondria. The third stage oxidizes the hydrogen to form *water* by the action of a series of iron-containing enzymes, the *cytochrome chain*. In the second and third stage considerable free energy is available for oxidative phosphorylation to convert ADP back to ATP.

If there is insufficient available oxygen the level of hydrogen carried by, for example, nicotinamide-adenine nucleotide (NAD), rises until the NADH reacts with pyruvic acid to form *lactic acid*. This provides a source of energy which, though dependent on the early stage of glycolysis, does not require oxygen. It is a valuable energy reserve during exercise. Later the lactic acid is oxidized via the Krebs cycle in the muscle and in other organs such as heart muscle to which it is carried by the blood stream or resynthesized to glycogen in the liver. A phosphorylase required for this anaerobic process is missing in McArdle's syndrome. No lactic acid is produced by muscle exercising under ischaemic conditions in that disorder. Muscular exercise is followed by pain in the muscles due to accumulation of unidentified metabolites. Similar pain is noted in muscles deprived of a normal blood supply through atheroma, causing intermittent claudication.

The importance of glycolysis for rephosphorylation of ATP and so ultimately for providing the energy for muscular contraction is undoubted but it is certain that fat provides a more important metabolic fuel for muscle than has been conceded in the past. There is evidence that more efficient use of fatty acids by muscle is one of the metabolic adaptations induced, presumably hormonally, by physical training. As the surface membrane and mitochondrial membranes are also of a lipid nature and abnormal accumulation of fat in muscle ("pseudohypertrophy") is a feature of some types of hereditary muscular dystrophy there are many who feel that the full importance of fat metabolism of muscle has yet to be revealed.

Fibre Types

Histochemical studies indicate that muscle fibres differ in their metabolism and that this may correlate with differences in function. There are three main types and other fibres which are difficult to classify within these groups.

Type I fibres have high mitochondrial enzymic activity, low phosphorylase activity and abundant fat droplets. These fibres usually have a smaller diameter and correspond to the red fibres of an older nomenclature.

Type II fibres have lower mitochondrial enzymic activity, higher phosphorylase and fewer fat droplets. These fibres, which tend to have a larger diameter, correspond to the white fibres of the older nomenclature.

Intermediate fibres include fibres showing intermediate features with variable mitochondrial content.

Myoglobin is a soluble protein found in the sarcoplasmic matrix of muscle fibres. It gives the muscle its red colour. It is more abundant in Type I than in Type II fibres. It is a pigment resembling haemoglobin and presumably has an oxygen storage function.

Physiologists have grouped muscle into *red* ("tonic or slow") and *white* ("phasic or fast") types but this functional classification has a poor correlation with the histological type. The latter may be determined by the motor neurone innervating it, as all muscle fibres belonging to one motor unit are of the same type. There is some evidence that the endplate structure differs in each type of muscle fibre.

Fibres of extraocular muscles have also been classified according to the structure of their myofibrils and sarcoplasm. *Fibrillenstruktur* fibres have clearly defined, round sectioned, myofibrils separated by abundant sarcoplasm. *Feldenstruktur* fibres have myofibrils of varying siqe, irregularly separated. Fibrillenstruktur fibres have "*en plaque*" motor endings but feldenstruktur fibres have "*en grappe*" endings.

It is tempting to link motor neurone type, endplate structure and muscle fibre type but present evidence does not allow this to be done with reasonable certainty as most of the work on "slow" and "fast" contraction has been done on whole muscle consisting of mixtures of fibre types in different proportions.

Heat Production in Muscle

It is convenient at this point to remind the reader that very little energy is required to produce an action potential—the acetylcholine liberated from nerve endings pulls the trigger of a loaded gun and energy is expended in resetting the trigger. The action potential is coupled to a system of proteins which contract with energy provided very rapidly but sparingly at the very site of contraction. This is possible because that energy source is constantly restored by a series of chemical reactions occurring while contraction is still taking place (hydrolysis of phosphocreatine) or after it is over (glycolysis and fatty acid oxidation). The muscle takes up most of its oxygen from the blood after it has contracted. The "oxygen debt" is not paid until the fatty acids have been oxidized. The importance of these backing-up reactions is shown by measuring the heat production of muscle.

A short time after the action potential, heat is produced explosively in the muscle fibre. This *activation heat* begins before the tension rises and increases rapidly. It results from the breakdown of ATP associated with the in and out movement of calcium. There is then *contraction heat* up to the peak of contraction, followed by *relaxation heat* associated with phosphocreatine hydrolysis. The glycolytic and fatty acid reactions following the contraction are associated with *recovery heat*, which continues for 20–30 min. after contraction.

Although muscle transforms chemical energy directly into mechanical work, with heat as a waste product rather than an intermediary form of energy, the efficiency of the conversion is low—about 20–25 per cent. Nevertheless the heat is valuable for the other metabolism of the body and indeed muscle *shivering* is one of the major methods the body has for heat production.

Development of Tension

It is generally accepted that the muscle fibre develops force by a contraction in length of sarcomeres produced by a sliding of the actin filaments between the myosin filaments to which they are linked by "bridges". The maximum tension it can develop is related to the extent of the overlap between thick and thin filaments, a relationship dependent on muscle length. It follows that the tension varies with the length of the muscle. The *tension-length curve* differs in muscle fibres of different types. This depends partly on the length of thick and thin filaments and their overlap, and partly on the elasticity and viscosity of the muscle connective tissue and associated tendon. The elasticity of the connective tissue is in parallel with the contractile component; the elasticity of the tendon is in series with it. A stretched muscle produces less tension when stimulated as the filament overlap is reduced beyond a certain optimal length.

Isometric Contraction (with no shortening permitted)

This produces most tension at a degree of shortening less than maximal.

Isotonic Contraction

This is the change in length when the muscle is allowed to shorten while lifting a load. The greater the load, the smaller the total shortening and the smaller the maximum speed of shortening. These relationships are defined by a *force–velocity curve*. (Fig. 7). The factors governing this relationship are not fully understood. The curve shows that the mechanical work done by the isotonically contracting muscle is greatest when the force of the muscle and its speed of shortening are about one-third of their maximum. These facts, that the muscle contracting isometrically has an optimum length, and the muscle contracting isotonically has an optimum load and speed of shortening, each less than maximal, must be understood by physiotherapists, gymnasts and others using muscular power.

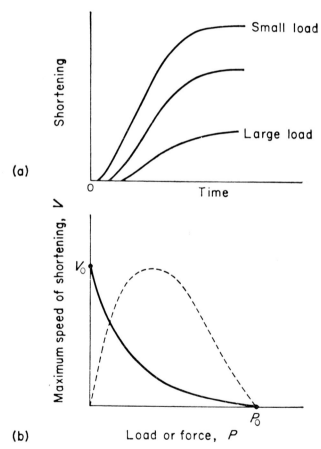

FIG. 7. (a) Records of shortening against time from a muscle lifting various loads. Tetanic stimulation started at time zero. (b) Force-velocity curve. The interrupted line shows how mechanical power produced (= force × velocity) varies with the force on the muscle. (After Starling and Lovatt Evans, 1962. *Principles of Human Physiology* (13th Edition), Eds. Davson and Eggleton; Churchill, London.)

It has been shown that the contracting muscle develops chemical energy very rapidly and that this is almost immediately translated into mechanical energy. Nevertheless tension and/or shortening are not developed immediately when a muscle is stimulated. This is due to the elastic element in series with the contractile one. Thus a muscle *twitch* rises to a peak and then relaxes in a time which may be up to $\frac{1}{2}$ sec. The variation in this is recognized by the classification of fibres into fast twitch and slow twitch as described above. By special techniques the internal series elastic effect can be eliminated and it is then seen seen that the contractile activity shows an *"active state"* which rises very rapidly to reach maximum a few milliseconds following the stimulus. Thereafter there is a plateau of active state followed by a slow decline. In the muscle fibre with

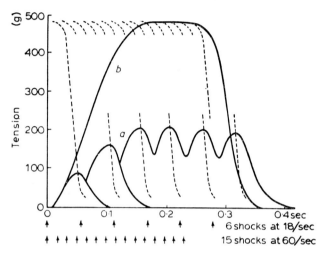

FIG. 8. Relationship between active-state curve and isometric tension during repetitive activation (frog gastrocnemius muscle stimulated by way of the sciatic nerve, 20°C): (a) time—courses of tension—development in response to 1, 2 and 6 shocks at 18/sec; (b) response to 15 shocks at 60/sec. The traces have been brought into coincidence at the moment of the first shock in each series. Portions of the active-state curves associated with each of the shocks are shown by dotted lines. (After T. D. M. Roberts, 1967. *Neurophysiology of Postural Mechanisms*, Butterworths, London.)

intact series elastic elements the active state after a single stimulus will actually have started to fall before the tension of the fibre (measured between its origin and insertion) has reached the plateau value of the active state. Thus the elastic tissue prevents a single twitch response from being maximal. However, if the muscle is again stimulated before the active state declines the plateau value may be maintained and the subsequent twitch tensions will more nearly approximate to it (Fig. 8). A train of rapid stimuli will therefore cause more tension to be developed than a single twitch, i.e. the *twitch/tetanus ratio* is less than unity (about 1:4 at 37°C). Note that each stimulus causes the same "all or none" action potential so that the electrical response to a train of stimuli at 2/sec. or more may be constant (but see Chapter I:1) while the contractile response shows a *staircase phenomenon*, a rise in tension following a transient drop. If the stimuli are repeated regularly at a high enough frequency, the result is a smooth *tetanus* with tension maintained at a high level as long as the train of stimuli continues or until fatigue occurs.

Fatigue of muscle is a term used without precision. It has been used to include progressive failure of skilled movements which probably has a central component, the failure of neuromuscular transmission associated with lowering of the safety factor for transmission by blocking agents or in myasthenia gravis (v.s.), as well as the normal fatigue of continuously activated muscle which is increased by ischaemia of the muscle. In the latter, the muscle action potenial continues to be evoked (by voluntary effort or by nerve stimulation) so that the failure is either in the contractile mechanism or its coupling to the action potential mechanism. The muscle fibre has little reserve against fatigue. It is, however, protected by the neural mechanism which governs its rate of stimulation and recruitment. This constitutes a servo-control which automatically regulates the activity of the muscle as a whole to compensate for diminished tension production by any of its component fibres.

Gradation of Muscular Tension

It has been shown that the activation of the action potential mechanism of the muscle fibre is an "all or none" phenomenon. It is not certain whether this is also true of excitation-contraction coupling but it may well be so. The contractile mechanism shows "fatigue". Muscular contraction/tension can be graded because it is produced by the regulated activity of a large number of component fibres with differing twitch characteristics. The mechanisms controlling firing rate and recruitment are discussed on page 343. The extent of shortening or the tension produced by the integrated activity of many motor units is regulated by facilitatory and inhibitory feedback from proprioceptors in muscle, tendon and joints acting via segmental reflexes (p. 341). In this chapter only the musculo-tendinous components will be described.

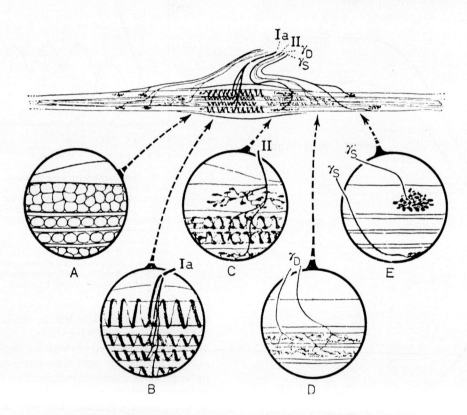

FIG. 9. Diagram of a typical mammalian muscle-spindle. Less than half of the whole length is shown and the transverse dimensions have been exaggerated to show some of the details. The ends of the nuclear chain fibres would be just out of this picture (typical length—4 mm.). The nuclear bag fibres extend a further 2 mm. or so at each end (say 8 mm. overall). Inset A: Arrangement of nuclei in the central region of the intrafusal muscle-fibres as seen after all the nervous elements have been allowed to degenerate. From the above downwards: capsule, lymph-space, nuclear bag fibre, 2 nuclear chain fibres, part of a nuclear bag fibre (in a typical spindle, there will be 2 nuclear bag fibres and 4 nuclear chain fibres). Inset B: primary sensory receptor connected to group Ia afferent (there is always one and only one of these to each spindle). Inset C: secondary sensory receptor connected to a group II afferent (there may be up to five secondary endings, some on each side of the primary ending). Inset D: trail ending of a dynamic gamma fusimotor fibre. Inset E: Plate ending of a static gamma fusimotor fibre. In some stituations plate endings are more commonly associated with nuclear bag fibres and trail endings with nuclear chain fibres. In other places, both types of ending occur on both types of intrafusal muscle-fibre. (After T. D. M. Roberts, 1967. *Neurophysiology of Postural Mechanisms*, Butterworths, London.)

Muscle Spindles

Some of the striated muscle fibres of skeletal muscle have a specialized function. Though arranged in parallel with the "power" fibres discussed hitherto, their contraction produces little tension at the muscle insertion. However, the tension produced by their shortening is sufficient to modify the activity of specialized sensory receptors near their equator. Bundles of intrafusal fibres have their receptor areas invested in a capsule—the muscle *spindle*. The muscle fibres of the spindle are described as *intrafusal fibres* to differentiate them from the power fibres which are then described as *extrafusal*.

Intrafusal muscle fibres are analogous to the slow muscle fibres of amphibia (not to be confused with the slow-twitch fibres described above). They are innervated by small motor nerve fibres (mainly gamma fibres) ending in discrete endplates or "trail" type endings on the intrafusal fibres. These muscle fibres have more than one motor nerve ending on each side of the sensory area. There are more than one type of gamma motor nerve fibre. It is premature to attempt a correlation between gamma fibre type, motor ending, spindle fibre type and function. Two major types of spindles can be described. *Nuclear bag muscle fibres* contain numerous large nuclei packed together in the equatorial region of the spindle. These fibres contract more slowly than even a slow-twitch extrafusal fibre. Still slower are the *nuclear chain intrafusal fibres*. These are usually shorter than the nuclear bag fibres and each contains a single row of central nuclei in the equatorial region. The ends of the nuclear chain fibres are attached to the nuclear bag fibres and both ends of the spindle are attached to extrafusal muscle bundles.

nuclear chain muscle fibres in the myotube regions and their structure is either annulo-spiral or "flower spray" in type (Fig. 9).

Primary sensory endings, formerly named type A endings, have low thresholds to extension and are excited by stretching the muscle, especially the dynamic component of stretch, but also fire more slowly with maintained stretch. They have a tendency to adapt to continuing stretch. The large dynamic response of the primary ending is probably caused by its lying on relatively nonviscous regions of the intrafusal fibres. *Secondary sensory endings* have less dynamic response (firing frequency related to velocity) but signal mainly the instantaneous length (Fig. 10). This differentiation is convenient for a simplified presentation but classification, though convenient from a histological point of view has not yet been rigidly established from a functional point of view.

Fusimotor Nerve Fibres

This name is now given to the small efferent fibres supplying the motor endings on the muscle spindles. They are mainly but not exclusively, gamma (γ) fibres (slowly conducting) (p. 41). The intrafusal fibres also receive some β fibres and collaterals from large (α) nerve fibres to extrafusal muscle fibres. It is an attractive idea to link different types of fusimotor nerve supply with different types of spindle function but this is not possible at present. Undoubtedly the intrafusal muscle fibres vary in the type of motor response. Contraction of intrafusal fibres applies tension to the regions carrying sensory endings. If not actually initiating sensory nerve potentials, the effect would be to partially depolarize the receptor and hence to

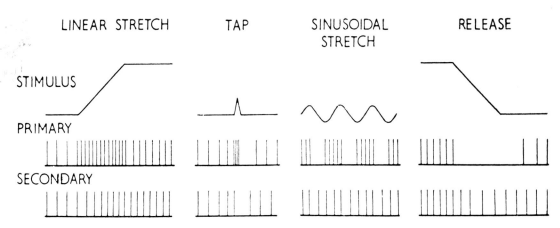

FIG. 10. Diagrammatic comparison of the responses of "typical" primary and secondary endings to various stimuli. The responses are drawn as if the muscle were under moderate initial stretch and as if there were no fusimotor activity. (After P. B. C. Matthews, 1964. *Physiological Reviews*, **44**, 219–288.)

Each spindle has one primary sensory nerve ending supplied by one group Ia afferent nerve fibre, and from 0–5 secondary nerve endings, each supplied by one group II afferent nerve fibre. The *primary sensory terminations* lie on the equator of both nuclear bag and nuclear chain muscle fibres and have an annulo-spiral structure. The *secondary sensory terminations* lie predominantly on the

"bias" it so that a minimal stretch applied to the whole muscle will suffice to bring the depolarization to the critical level. In this way the central nervous system acting through the fusimotor nerves may lower the threshold for stretch reflexes or for any other motor response involving the stretch reflex arc. (It has been suggested that this may be involved in voluntary motor activity.) The mechanism of excitation of the secondary sensory endings is less clear. Indeed the striated region of intrafusal fibres supplied with a secondary ending might shorten rather than undergo stretch when the fusimotor nerves are activated. It has been postulated that activity in γ_1 fibres (causing contraction of nuclear bag intrafusal fibres) will excite mainly the primary endings and that activity in the γ_2 fibres (causing contraction of nuclear chain intrafusal fibres) will excite both the primary and the secondary endings. This is a rapidly advancing field of physiological study and the final story has yet to be written. Quite obviously the muscle spindles and their innervation are extremely important for the functional control of muscle. It is, therefore, surprising that little is known about the pathophysiology of the system in disease.

Function of Muscle Spindles

It was formerly believed that spindles were sensory organs for conscious proprioception ("position sense", "muscle-joint sense"). There is little evidence to support this. The sensory signals arising from the different spindle receptors are now believed to play a part in the subconscious nervous control of muscular contraction, both during movement and during steady contraction, mainly through the stretch reflexes but also by spinocerebellar influences. A simple stretch reflex, even if modified by applying fusimotor innervation to maintain the afferent flow from spindles during muscular shortening, would tend to maintain the muscle at one length only. Fusimotor discharge provides one way by which the muscle can be set reflexly to a variety of lengths independent of the load on the muscle. Indeed the fusimotor nerves could initiate movement by "driving" the spindles and hence the extrafusal fibres via the stretch reflex loop. The evidence for the latter function is not satisfactory. There is little doubt that the spindles and their fusimotor control provide a mechanism by which the central nervous system controls the rate of shortening of muscle and the stiffness or damping of reflex responses but it seems unlikely that voluntary contraction is initiated through the "γ route".

Golgi Organs

These are sensory endings (formerly named B-type) found characteristically in tendons of muscles but also within the muscle belly, often at the end of a spindle. They are similar to spray endings but give rise to group Ib fast conducting afferent fibres. These endings are in series with the extrafusal fibres so it is believed that the deformation of the receptor is normally the result of the application of tension to the tendon. (There is at present no direct information about the quantitative relationship between stimulus and response for the tendon organs.) It seems likely that the tension stimulus can be consciously appreciated but, like the spindle response, the signals from the tendon organs are largely used for reflex control of muscular contraction. The appropriate reflexes are largely inhibitory (p. 41).

Pain Nerve Endings

The muscle, like other tissues, contains pain nerve endings which are mainly bare endings for which the appropriate stimulus is chemogenic, by polypeptides released from damaged tissue. Normal muscle metabolites accumulated during anoxic exercise also produce pain. Local muscle contraction may be caused by means of axon reflexes. More generally, impulses arising in pain receptors evoke spinal reflexes leading to contraction of flexor muscles and inhibition of extensor muscles, the basis of the withdrawal reflexes.

This chapter has summarized some of the properties of muscle fibres and their nervous connections. It has been shown that there are different varieties of muscle fibre and of apparently similar nerve fibres. It is tempting to construct simple links such as "tonic" and "phasic" systems. This must be resisted. Although some specialization of function seems to be certain, the central nervous system undoubtedly imposes controls offering a much higher degree of plasticity than this simple scheme would allow.

FURTHER READING

Bourne, C. H. (Ed.) (1960), *Structure and Function of Muscle*, Vols. 1 and 2. London and New York: Academic Press.

Coërs, C. and Woolf, A. L. (1959), *The Innervation of Muscle. A Biopsy Study*. Oxford: Blackwells.

Gergely, J. (1969), "Biochemical Aspects of Muscular Stimulation," in Walton (1969), 89–141 (loc. cit.).

Granit, R. (Ed.) (1966), Nobel Symposium I. *Muscular Afferents and Motor Control*. Stockholm: Almqvist & Wiksell; New York, London and Sydney: John Wiley & Sons.

Granit, R. (1970), *The Basis of Motor Control*. London and New York: Academic Press.

Gray, J. (1953), *How Animals Move*. London, Cambridge University Press.

Guth, L. (1968), " 'Trophic' Influences of Nerve on Muscle," *Ann. Rev. Physiol.*, **48**, 645–687.

Hill, A. V. (1960), "The Heat Production in Muscle," in *Molecular Biology* (D. Nachmansohn, Ed.). London and New York: Academic Press.

Hubbard, J. I., Llinas, R. and Quastel, D. M. S. (1969), *Electrophysiological Analysis of Synaptic Transmission*. London: Edward Arnold (Publishers) Ltd.

Huxley, A. F. (1957), "Muscle Structure and Theories of Contraction." *Progr. Biophys.*, **7**, 255–318.

Katz, B. (1966), *Nerve, Muscle and Synapse*. New York: McGraw-Hill.

Matthews, P. B. C. (1972), *Mammalian Muscle Receptors and their Central Action*. London: Arnold.

Simpson, J. A. (1969), "The Defect in Myasthenia Gravis," in *The Biological Basis of Medicine*, Vol. 3, pp. 345–387 (E. E. Bittar and N. Bittar, Eds.). London and New York: Academic Press.

Walton, J. N. (Ed.) (1969), *Disorders of Voluntary Muscle*, 2nd edition. London: J. & A. Churchill.

Wilkie, D. R. (1956), "The Mechanical Properties of Muscle." *Brit. Med. Bull.*, **12**, (3), 177–182.

Zacks, S. I. (1964), *The Motor Endplate*. Philadelphia: Saunders.

SECTION III

MOTOR SYSTEM

1. CEREBRAL CORTEX

JAMES L. O'LEARY

INTRODUCTION

The cerebral cortex, external grey mantle which covers the cerebral hemispheres, is divided generally into *neo-* or *isocortex* and *archi-* or *allocortex*. Isocortex makes up a large part of the exposed surface, and includes both cortical areas which present a six layer architectonic plan in the adult stage, and those in which the six layer plan is only evident during ontogenetic maturation. This takes in much of the frontal, temporal, parietal, occipital and insular cortex, but might include other parts such as the gyrus cinguli, the anterior 5 cm. of the temporal lobe, and the interhemispheric cortex of the inferior frontal area. We prefer to designate these latter as transitional in character.

Allocortex, roughly identical with archicortex, contains both hippocampus and related structures and the palaeo-cortex of the pyriform lobe. Allocortex by definition did not pass through a six layer stage during its ontogenetic development. The following account of cortical structure is restricted to isocortex or modifications thereof, and for want of space passes over allo- and transitional cortex.

STRUCTURAL CONSIDERATIONS

Cytoarchitectonics

Some knowledge of the surface topography of the human brain is presumed (Fig. 1). *In toto* cortex is said to have an area of 250,000 mm.², a thickness of 1·5–3·5 mm. and a weight one-third to one-half that of whole brain. The human brain is gyrencephalic and only the cortex which covers the convolutions is exposed to view; the remainder is buried in the sidewalls of sulci having variable depth and tortuosity, and may include one-third of the total cortex of this complexly convoluted organ. The cytoarchitecture of deep as well as of surface parts must be considered in deriving any comprehensive structural plan, even though the function of the former is off effective limits for the exploring electrodes of the neurosurgeon.

Parcellation into cytoarchitectonic fields should have as one of its purposes the detection of areas of histological uniformity which have a discoverable functional signific-ance. However, relatively few functions of cortex have been shown to be *area specific*, and within cortex reside generalizing functions which belong to the cortex as a whole. Evolution-wise all human cortex derives ultimately from but a speck of primordial reptilian pallium called *generalized cortex*, and features of both structure and function which denote equipotentiality as opposed to

specificity have had overriding significance during most of the duration of cortical evolution. As to the cogency of establishing the functional specificity of fields of uniform structure, the exact localization of a retinal half-field within the histologically defined area striata, and of the somatotopic localization to the corresponding structural features of the somatosensory cortex, are unusual rather than usual relationships of cortical architectonics. In the instances of many designated fields we can provide no more than wordy abstractions as functional correlates.

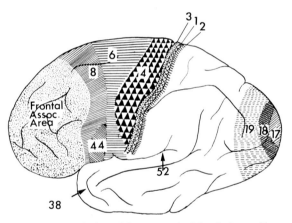

FIG. 1. Lateral view of human cerebral hemisphere with important Brodmann areas indicated. (Modified from von Bonin, Chapter II, *Precentral Motor Cortex*; Ed., P. C. Bucy; Urbana, University of Illinois Press.)
Area 4—Motor cortex
Area 6—Premotor cortex
Area 8—Frontal eye field
Area 44—Motor speech area
Area 52—Auditory cortex
Areas, 17, 18, 19—Visual cortex
Area 38—Tip of temporal lobe

Using the criteria to be set forth in the subsequent paragraphs, up to 150 fields of presumedly uniform structure have been delimited for human cortex. However, critical studies have demonstrated significant structural variability between identical areas studied in different brains of the same species. Neither need architectonic detail be exactly the same for homologous areas of the cortex of the several species used as exemplary of the stages of mammalian cerebral evolution.

The base method of architectonic parcellation involves coloration of cell bodies in 20–40 μ relatively thick perpendicular sections stained by analine dyes. Glial cells as well as nerve cells stain, and the former may comprise as much as one-half of all cells identified in a low power reconnoitre of a section. Thus variations in the distribution of the non-neural elements of cortex could considerably complicate the application of criteria given for areal parcellation. Regardless of this certain cortical areas such as the visual, auditory, somatosensory and somatomotor present specific features not elsewhere evident.

Besides analine dye coloration, two precarious histological methods are usefully applied to the structural analysis of cortical fields. The Golgi method was successfully used by Ramon y Cajal to analyse the principal motor and sensory fields of human and lower cortices. By silver chromate deposition upon the membranes of soma-dendrite and axon it is possible to render all parts of a single neuron selectively opaque against a relatively colourless background of similar unstained elements. Since very few neurons stain *in extenso* in the thick sections used, it is possible to visualize the entire spread of a neuron and its dendrites. Under some circumstances the axonal plexuses may stain as well, permitting differentiation between cells of short and of long axon and defining the cortical levels of the principal axonal plexuses and the sources which contribute to their make-up. A modified Golgi method (the Cox) using mercury instead of silver salts stains many more of the soma-dendrites but few or none of the axons. Cut perpendicular to the cortical surface, such preparations facilitate understanding of how neurons which are principally oriented vertically can produce horizontally disposed cell layers in much thinner

sections coloured by analine dyes. Finally the Golgi methods stain selectively the spines upon the cortical dendrites. These are often the termini of synapses of exogenous axons, and their absence in experimental preparations over limited sectors of the dendritic shafts suggest the ending there of one or another of the exogenous cortical afferent systems.

The Weigert method stains only myelin sheaths and is principally useful for defining the myelinated components of the axonal plexuses as well as the main avenues of entry and exodus.

Marchi and Nauta Gygax are experimental anatomical methods which can be used to trace secondary degeneration extending from lesions at the sources of primary and secondary afferent systems to their cortical terminals. The Nauta–Gygax has largely replaced the Marchi for it stains as well the degenerating preterminals as they pass outwards and upwards across the cortical neuropil. The primary afferent systems have sources within one or another of the principal relay nuclei of the thalamus (somatosensory, visual or auditory). Each terminates at the intermediate level of its respective cortical area. Callosal afferents perhaps terminate throughout the cortical thickness but with particular emphasis upon the superficial level. Association axons deriving from cortical areas of the same hemisphere tend to end superficially as well.

Electron microscopy has yet to be exploited fully for its

FIG. 2. Lower mammal, the VI layer plan showing dendritic plexuses. Right, a and b, thalamic axon afferents; other non-specific afferent c, d, e and f. (From Lorente de Nó, Chapter XV, *Physiology of the Nervous System*, 3rd Ed.; J. F. Fulton, author. Oxford University Press.)

contribution to the analysis of cerebral cortical fields. Szentágothai has differentiated pyramidal from stellate cells and examined their synapses. Both he and Collonier have shown the flattened synaptic vesicles of supposed inhibitory type (Uchizono) to be concentrated upon the somata and the origins of the dendrites, the spherical vesicles of excitatory type to make contacts with more distally situated elements of the cortical neuropil. Szentágothai has also called attention to horsetail-shaped terminal axon ramifications related to the cortical dendrites. Gray, of course, has recognized the spine apparatus upon the dendritic shafts as exemplary of the type of synapses which occur there.

The essential features of the generalized six layer plan are presented below, reading downwards from cortical surface to white matter (Fig. 2).

I Plexiform layer. Relatively acellular and made up principally of the overlapping terminal dendritic arbors that derive from pyramidal neurons belonging to all subjacent layers. Includes axonal arborizations deriving from short axon cells and those belonging to the recurrent collaterals of pyramidal axons.

II Layer of small and medium-sized pyramids. Pear-shaped bodies, obliquely directed basal dendrites. Lengths of ascending dendrites vary with depths of somata.

& Within the limits of an apparently random distribution larger somata tend to be disposed in lower

III range of the layer, smaller bodies in the upper range. Axonal plexuses composed of short axon ramifications intermingle with terminal twigs of the afferent plexus.

IV Layer of star cells and granular pyramids. Former may exist with or without a dendritic shaft reaching layer I. Latter have small-sized somata with slender lengthy dendrites also reaching layer I. The major afferent plexus of extraneous origin blankets this layer.

V Layer of large pyramids. Have extended lateral and basal dendrites and a thick shaft ascending to layer I. Pyramids with smaller bodies and thinner dendrites also occur.

VI Basal dendrites are projected downward and arise from short shafts. Taken with the typical apical dendrite the cell body often assumes a fusiform shape. Apical dendrites reach and arborize within the plexiform layer.

It is to be noted that some variant of the pyramidal cell is seen in all of the five cellular layers (Fig. 3). In large part the axons of these enter the white matter for distribution as projection, commissural or association connectors; however, there are specific instances where such axons lose their descending shafts and produce only arciform ascending tributaries which end in the plexiform layer. Each conventional pyramidal axon, whatever its layer of origin, produces a system of recurrent collaterals which pass obliquely upwards to reach the plexiform layer. Within that superficial plexus there is both an axonal

and a dendritic component traceable to each pyramidal soma of the cortex. Thus the superficial cortical stratum provides a powerful integrative mechanism for the entire pyramid population distributed through the cellular layers.

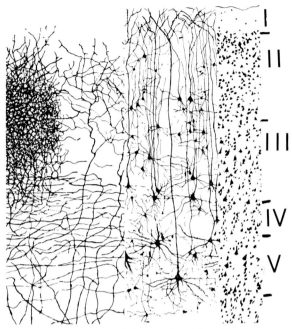

Fig. 3. A composite of the axonal and dendritic plexuses of motor cortex. From: Ramon y Cajal (left), a Golgi Cox drawing (center), and a Nissl drawing (right). Note that the principal range of the afferent plexus (left) covers lamina III with upward extent into II.

Short axon cells (Fig. 4) ordinarily having much simpler dendritic systems also inhabit all cellular layers and contribute extensively to their intrinsic axonal plexuses. A variety of these cell types has been identified. However, sub-typing is unsure and some may even exist which have not been recognized due to failures in Golgi impregnation. Based on features of their axonal arbors, these cells divide into diffusely and restrictively arborizing types. Among the latter are those which provide basket contacts with the somata of immediately neighbouring pyramids. In some instances short axons of the diffuse type break up into vertically arborizing tendrils which form chains of synapses extending along the dendrite shafts of neighbouring pyramids. In general the uppermost short axon somata issue descending axonal arbors, the more deeply situated ascending, and those of mid-cortex transversely directed ones. Some of the latter provide terminals about the somata of the large deep pyramids. Short axon elements can only be surely identified and studied in Golgi preparations, and represent a hiatus in all usual architectonic studies. In current electrophysiological theory they are primarily inhibitory in function; a contrary view suggests a locally operated synchronizing function which coordinates the discharge of pyramidal units.

The architectonic classification that has become best entrenched in experimental and clinical research is that of

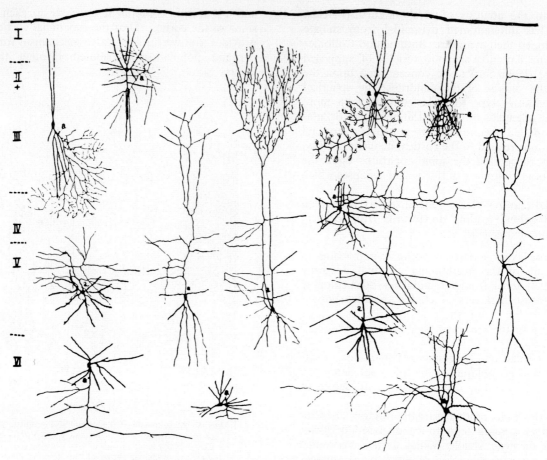

FIG. 4. Selected short axon cells, visual cortex, rabbit, illustrating types which occur at different cortical depths.

Brodmann. Both it, and its competitor, the Economo classification, recognize three broad divisions of isocortex: that in which the granular layer (IV) shows an ordinary degree of development separating the inner and outer groups of classical pyramids; that in which the granular layer is much over-developed at the expense of inner and outer pyramids (granulous cortex); and that in which it has been replaced entirely by a merger of the inner and outer pyramidal layers (agranular cortex). In general, the sensory arrival platforms (visual, auditory, somatosensory) show granulous cortex, the cortical association areas (prefrontal, parietal and temporo-occipital) granular cortex, and the motor, premotor and supplementary motor areas agranular cortex. Figure 1 is a map indicating for human cortex the locales of a number of Brodmann areas of functional significance. These include: frontal lobe, areas 4, 6, 8, 44, and the frontal association areas; parietal lobe, areas 3, 1 and 2; occipital lobe, areas 17, 18, 19, visual cortex; temporal lobe, area 52, auditory cortex; tip of the temporal lobe, area 38.

In conclusion there is the need for searching out more objective criteria for delimiting architectonic fields than presently exist. This could lead to significant reduction in the number of existing fields and thus prove a salutary advance. In the few instances in which distinctive structure and function have already been shown to co-exist (visual, sensorimotor cortex) we still lack any concept of why one structural pattern has preference over another as the requisite substrate for a function in a locus of cortex.

Chemical Architectonics

Over the past quarter century significant advances have been made in microchemical techniques which permit the quantitative analyses of tissue samples weighing a microgram or less. Proceeding from frozen cylinders of biopsy or autopsy material which can be cut horizontally from surface to white matter in serial 40 μ sections, it is possible to use alternate sections for cytoarchitectonic identification and neurobiochemical analyses. In this way intralaminar distributions of a variety of biochemical components and enzyme activities can be made and compared layer for layer throughout a sample of cortex. The assay method obviously have their greatest value in neuropathological studies. Thus comparisons of normal adult and senile cortex with that from subjects of presenile and senile dementia can be made by laminar analyses, and thereafter the results from one cytoarchitectonic area compared with those from another.

The following table was made up for the International Academy of Pathology Monographs No. 9 by Alfred Pope (*see* reading list). It illustrates the versatility of the biochemical determinations which can be undertaken.

STRUCTURAL COMPOUNDS AND ENZYMES ANALYSED MICRO-CHEMICALLY IN ARCHITECTONIC LAYERS AND SUBJACENT WHITE MATTER OF HUMAN ISOCORTEX

Biochemical Structural Components	Enzyme Activities
Total solids	Cytochrone oxidase
Total proteins	Adenosine triphosphatases
Proteolipid proteins	Mg++—activated
Residue proteins	Ca++—activated
	Na+—, K+, Mg++—
	activated
Ribonucleic acids	
Deoxyribonucleic acids	Dipeptidase (v. L-alanylglycine)
Total lipids	Lipase (v. tri-N-butyrin)
Total phospholipids	
Gangliosides	
Cerebrosides	Acetylcholinesterase
Cholesterol	

EVOKED POTENTIALS AND UNIT ACTIVITY

Evoked Potentials

There are two broad classes of electrical activity of cerebral cortex, the spontaneous and the evoked. The former present wave patterns characterized by unique frequency, amplitude, wave shape and locus of origin within the hemisphere. The 8–12 per sec. alpha rhythm of man is a classic example. The interpretation of the spontaneous cerebral rhythms belongs to the speciality of Electroencephalography and is considered elsewhere in the text.

With two exceptions the initial components of evoked potentials (the components most rigorously studied) are di- or multiphasic and reflect a neural disturbance which rises from a site of origin corresponding to the afferent plexus of the lower superficial pyramid and granular layers (lower III and IV, Fig. 3). In an evoked potential such as the visual response of the cat, evoked by a brief electrical shock to the contralateral optic nerve, the initial phase is surface-positive in electrical polarity and is featured by three successive faster spikes which appear upon its rise phase (Fig. 5, 1). This is followed by a surface-negative phase of longer duration. The neural disturbance which initiates such a pattern rises through the cortex involving in upward succession the upper superficial pyramids as well. The ensuing negative component is believed to relate to the progressive involvement of cortical dendrites in the disturbance (*see* direct cortical response, ensuing paragraph).

In contrast to the visual evoked response which is exogenous in its activation, the *direct cortical response* is an electrical process locally activated in the superficial cortex and presumed to have a dendritic origin. The potential is a monophasic surface-negative deflection, the amplitude of which increases with rise in stimulus intensity (Fig. 5, 4). Like the surface-negative phase of the visual evoked response it is presumed to arise from elements of the dendritic plexus which undergo a wealth of branching in

the surface cortical layers. From there it spreads downwards along the dendritic shafts.

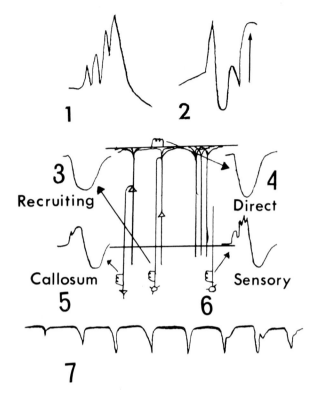

FIG. 5. Different kinds of evoked potentials drawn with reference to the depths of the cortex from which they arise (central schema). 1, Visual evoked response. 2, Augmenting wave, visual cortex, arrow; it undergoes augmentation on slowly repetitive stimulation. 3 and 7, Recruiting response. 3, Single recruiting wave of negative sign. 7, Recruiting series to show increase in amplitude during slowly repetitive stimulation. 4, Direct cortical response arising from a surface stimulus; presumably of dendritic origin. 5 and 6, Callosal and sensory evoked responses as recorded from mid-cortex. (This figure modified from W. M. Landau, Fig. 13, "Evoked potentials", p. 478, *The Neurosciences, A Study Program.* New York, Rockefeller University Press, 1967.)

All cortical potentials evoked by either natural stimulation of sense organs or brief electric shocks to their nerves of supply remain confined to their corresponding sensory receiving areas. (*See* Fig. 5, 6, a somewhat more generalized version of the sensory response than illustrated in Fig. 5, 1). We speak of visual, auditory and somatosensory evoked responses having as their common denominator the fast positive-negative sequence described previously for the evoked response. For all, the neural disturbance which gives rise to the potential develops in mid-cortex at a depth corresponding to the terminal axonal plexus which derives from thalamic projection axons. By mapping visual, auditory and somatosensory cortices, one obtains a distribution of points which can be related respectively to opposite retinal field, base to apex of the cochlear coil, and for somatosensory cortex to the parts of the body as projected to the cortical surface.

Three special types of potential require brief mention. The augmenting potential is similar in form to the evoked type, but the initial diphasic deflection is trailed by a late positive wave which increases significantly in amplitude during repetitive stimulation at slow rates (Fig. 5, 2, arrow). Another special type is the recruiting response (Fig. 5, 3 and 7). It results from repetitive stimulation within the midline thalamus and is quite generalized in its distribution over the cortex. Like the direct cortical response of local origin (Fig. 5, 4) is is a monophasic negative deflection, exogenously activated, which grows in amplitude with successive, slowly repeating stimuli. Finally, the callosal evoked potential is activated by stimulation within the corresponding cortical field of the opposite hemisphere. It develops from a wider fraction of the cortex than the evoked response but resembles evoked response in shape and diphasic sequence, and probable dendritic origin.

Comparable evoked responses can also be recorded through the skull and scalp and in restricted usage have produced useful clinical data. The localization of the scalp-recorded potential is far less accurate than that recorded directly from the brain, due to volume conductor considerations. Those most often recorded are visual, auditory and somatosensory. The results are best obtained by a computer processing technique which rejects random waves of the electroencephalogram while adding those evoked by repetitive stimulation at one per second.

Unit Activity

Earlier references have been made to units in other connections. Figure 6 illustrates a sequence of spontaneously discharging units recorded extracellularly from human somatosensory cortex.

A clear question remains however; it concerns how far such impulses pass outward along the dendritic shaft. His findings indicated that rapid discharge rates can occur under conditions of intracellular recording, but he questioned the extent to which the probing of the interior of a cell by microelectrodes can stir up abnormal discharges. After comparing central neurons to sense organs, he noted that both are systems responding to graded stimuli with appropriate rhythmic firing of all-or-none impulses. He saw the neuron as possessing both pacemaker and generator functions, the former a property of dendrites, the latter evidently of the initial segment of the axon. Intracellular records from the Betz cell show waves of depolarization interpreted as surges of generator activity, each of which brings the axon hillock region to threshold, forcing it to fire impulses repeatedly. These were interpreted as resulting from massive synaptic actions which converge on soma and dendrites from neurons upstream.

Mountcastle studied the responses of single units of the postcentral gyrus of the barbiturized monkey to a variety of peripheral stimuli. The studies were referred to a cytoarchitectonic analysis of the somatosensory cortex showing three different fields in the locale of the recording electrodes. Area 3 (Brodmann) was typical of granulous cortex, whereas 1 and 2 were transitional to usual parietal cortex (Fig. 1). Correlations with the properties of neurons showed that over 90 per cent of those of Area 2 related to deep tissue receptors, whereas the majority of those in Area 3 could be activated only by cutaneous stimuli. His evidence from depth recording supported the hypothesis that the firing pattern of activated cortical cells responding to a peripheral stimulus is that of vertically

FIG. 6.   Units recorded extracellularly, human somatosensory cortex, discharging spontaneously. Note variable spacing between units.

Extracellular traces have been obtained from numerous cortical areas, including sensorimotor of cat and monkey, suprasylvian of cat, visual and auditory for experimental animals. In different studies anaesthetized (pentobarbitol sodium), immobilized, *cerveau isolé* and unanaesthetized cats have been used. Responses to visual, auditory and tactile stimuli have been recorded from the respective receiving areas, and also responses of motor cortex pyramidal cells subsequent to antidromic stimulation.

Phillips (studies by extracellular and intracellular recording) examined the unit behaviour of cortical pyramidal cells in a manner similar to that of earlier contributions upon membrane physiology at the spinal level. By extracellular recording he observed the passage of the antidromically derived impulses into the soma (from a stimulus applied to bulbar pyramid), noting the hesitation upon the rise phase of the unit which signifies the traverse of the initial segment of the axon upon invasion of soma.

oriented modules extending across all the cellular layers of the cortex.

In another study he worked out with collaborators the details of the activation pattern resulting from cutaneous sensibility. Cortical cells were able to respond at frequencies well in excess of those normally set up in first order afferent fibres by natural stimuli. The peripheral receptive field of a cortical neuron is surrounded by a belt of skin within which stimulation will inhibit the cell under study. The activation of units of postcentral gyrus also gives evidence of a class of cells that subserve the senses of position and movement (joint, not muscle), depicting by their pattern of activity the steady angles of the joints and the transient changes which take place.

In corresponding studies upon motor-sensory (MS I) cortex, V. B. Brooks tested units for their responses to natural stimuli applied to body surface. Sixty per cent had wide skin inputs driven by hair-bending, and the large fast conducting PT cells (those cortical neurons having axons that pass spinalwards through the pyramidal tract) were outstanding targets for such cutaneous input. Such cell units, superficial small as well as deep large, form radial columns of shifted overlapping topography like those of sensory cortex previously described by Mountcastle. Cells possessing localized and wide cutaneous receptive fields exist together within a column, the cells of localized field relating to the same skin area: Output-wise the PT cells of the cortical neuron population also show, radially aligned columns of origin, each pool, however, containing lesser pools reaching to different spinal termini. Since it has been shown that both visual and somatosensory cortex have a similarly modular arrangement, it would appear that this feature is common to the functional arrangement of the whole cerebral cortex.

In other hands unit studies conducted at retinal, geniculate and cortical levels of the visual system have provided valuable results. In mapping the receptive fields of the retinal ganglion cells by unit potential responses Kuffler noted that diffuse lighting of the retina does not affect a ganglion cell nearly so much as does a tiny spot of light. He described two types of receptive field, one having an "on" centre and an "off" periphery, and the other the reverse attribute. Hubel and Wiesel observed that each cell element in the lateral geniculate relay to cerebral cortex is also driven from a corresponding tiny retinal region, and the receptive pattern is similarly constructed from "on" and "off" centres. However, the peripheries of geniculate loci are much better able to cancel the effects of the centre, leading to the interpretation that the neurons one step higher in the visual hierarchy respond more sensitively to spatial differences in retinal illumination.

It was in the visual cortex that Hubel and Wiesel discovered new properties and relations indicative of change in structural relations. There, two kinds of cells, characterized as simple and complex, could be differentiated. As with Mountcastle, electrodes placed to record unit discharges from simple cells demonstrated columns oriented perpendicularly to the cortical surface. In this case all elements responded similarly to line stimuli, such as dark bars on a white background. Here the orientation of the figure displayed to the retina was found to be most important in determining whether a cell did or did not respond, a bar shown vertically producing responses in different elements than a bar shown horizontally. The complex cells were like the simple ones in responding to bars, slits or edges in the event that the shape was suitably oriented. However, in eliciting a response from a particular neuron, the exact position of the stimulus applied to the retina was much less consequential than for simple cells. With movement but without changes in orientation such cells responded with sustained firing.

The phenomena of more diffuse activation and complex elements could find an explanation if large numbers of simple cells situated at different loci in the visual field converged their activities upon a single complex locus. That theory would, of course, presuppose a vast network of connections. Whatever the complexity of organization required to support such spatial and directional effects,

all the facts discovered so far can be explained in terms of relatively simple phenomena of nerve cell excitation including impulse transmission, convergence, excitation and inhibition. The striate cortex is by no means the apex of the visual hierarchy; there is the possibility of further elaboration effected at still higher cortical levels.

ELECTRICAL EXCITATION OF CEREBRAL CORTEX

The electrical excitability of cerebral cortex (in particular of motor cortex) was discovered by Fritsch and Hitzig in 1890. Since then the motor points for excitable cortex have been mapped for many species using different sources of electrical current and bipolar or monopolar electrodes. Motor points have no fixed relationship to cortical landmarks. The movements discerned over the opposite half of the body can be flexion, extension or rotation of an extremity, twitching of face, or torsion of

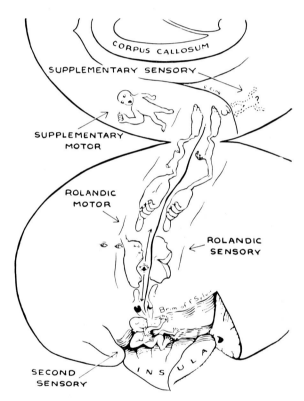

FIG. 7. Somatic figurines drawn upon the paracentral area of the left hemisphere. (From W. Penfield and H. Jasper, *Epilepsy and the Functional Anatomy of the Human Brain*, Fig. III–36, p. 105. Boston, Little Brown and Company.)

body and tail. In primates and man discrete movements of the digits can be localized, and in man speech arrest can result from stimulation of the posterior part of the left third frontal convolution. Just above threshold (but depending upon type and depth of anaesthesia) the most discretely localized movements are obtained; maximal stimuli produce spread, one loses the detailed character of the motor map, and seizure activation may result. At the end of a systematic exploration of the cortex neighbouring upon the central sulcus in primates or man it may be possible to define a distribution of points which bear a clear relationship to the parts of the body where movements are elicited, the foot and leg being represented more medially in the motor cortex backing upon the central sulcus, head laterally, face and arm in an intermediate position (Fig. 7, Penfield, human cortex).

The most important variables in the elicitation of the motor map of man and animals are the anaesthetic used, the frequency, waveform and current density of the stimulus employed, and the mode of application of the electrodes, monopolar or bipolar. In animal experimentation ether is generally a more satisfactory anaesthetic than the barbiturates unless the level of the latter is kept quite light. In man local anaesthesia, if feasible, produces the most reliable results.

It is important that different motor maps can be elicited using several forms of electrical stimulation. Fritsch and Hitzig used galvanic stimulation but Ferrier who followed them changed to faradic current because he believed it evoked a wider range of movements. Liddell and Phillips have been particularly aware of the importance of depth of anaesthesia and form of stimulation. They used a square wave stimulator which affords a wide choice of strength, frequency and duration of pulses, and found that by using single pulses of 5 msec. duration upon quiet (unfacilitated) cortex the movements elicited were confined to distal segments of the contralateral limbs and face. Commonly elicited from wide areas of motor cortex were those of thumb-index, face and hallux, effects comparable to the signal symptoms of the Jacksonian epileptic march. Under special circumstances of anaesthesia and stimulation others have been able to reduce the stimulus effect produced from a particular cortical point to the contraction of a single muscle.

In considering such marked discrepancies it is important to recognize that sufficiently strong cortical activation may stimulate the pyramidal axons of subcortical white matter directly related to a monosynaptic path which leads through the motoneurons to the muscles activated. A weaker stimulus confined to cortex alone releases a complex of excitatory and inhibitory effects out of which activation of a movement develops. Those are just beginning to be understood through the use of unit recording.

Over the past quarter century maps based on surface stimulation have been supplemented by others produced through an adaptation of the techniques used to record evoked potentials. Electrical or mechanical stimuli can be applied to the skin covering the body parts of the experimental animal, or electrical shocks given the nerves of supply. For each site stimulated a distribution of points on the corresponding cortical fields of sensory projection are sampled. Using widely separated points on the body surface it is possible to plot the potential maxima on cortex of each of the body regions studied, producing a sensory homunculus which complements the motor homunculus mapped by cortical stimulation.

Through comparative electrophysiological studies upon the sensorimotor, auditory and visual receptive areas of cerebral cortex in mammals, Woolsey of Wisconsin and

his colleagues have made valuable contributions (Fig. 8, for example). The admirable detail with which they have worked out the plan of cortical localization and their recourse to many species to review the phylogenetic origin of the human map makes it impossible to do justice to these developments in a limited space.

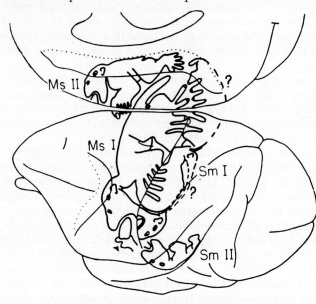

MONKEY

FIG. 8. Motor and sensory figurines, Macaque monkey, primary and supplementary motor and senory fields. The two sensory and two motor zones face each other in mirror image relationship across the line of the central sulcus. (From C. N. Wolsey, Fig. 3–1, Chapter 3, *Cerebral Localization and Organization*, G. Schaltenbrand and C. N. Woolsey, eds., The University of Wisconsin Press, Madison, 1964.)

The stage for this work was set early by lack of general agreement among histologists upon the purely anatomical criteria for parcellation of fields. Out of the application of the cathoderay oscillograph to cortical electrophysiology came evoked potential studies and the comprehension of the importance of the contribution such mapping could make to the problems of cortical localization.

At first the principal projection areas for cutaneous, visual and auditory sensibility were delimited. These were generally consistent with the cortical areas designated for these modalities by clinicoanatomical techniques. However, the mapping technique allowed the extent of cortex concerned with each sensory mechanism to be mapped and in addition permitted field homologies between widely disparate species to be established. As the mapping technique developed, it became evident that the cutaneous sensory field overlapped areas of motor projection previously delimited by electrical stimulation techniques. Thus it became necessary to reevaluate cortical motor areas previously defined. As a result it was established generally that sensory cortical areas are not exclusively afferent nor are motor areas entirely motor. Postcentral gyrus, for example, has a well-organized motor outflow which functions months after complete removal of hitherto recognized motor areas of frontal lobe; conversely, afferent projections to the frontal motor area exist which are independent of the parietal afferent projections. Delimitation of the entire visual and auditory cortical projections (in addition to the above) permitted construction of a composite cortical map for each species by subtracting the size of the association areas in proportion to their growth during mammalian phylogenesis. Indeed one of the unique contributions of these studies has been the shrinkage of the territory which can be allotted to association fields as compared with those represented in the plan of cortical localization constructed on a purely clinicoanatomical basis.

The relation of the two sensory (S I and S II) and the two motor (M I and M II) areas, as they face each other in mirror image relationship across the line of the central sulcus, (Fig. 8) is selected here as an example of the refinements which evoked potential and motor response mapping has made possible. The general aspects of the caricature figurines, called motor and sensory homunculi by Penfield and Rasmussen, started a trend toward the body image depiction of the distribution of motor and sensory points. This type of representation (with body parts enlarged proportionate to the extent of their representation in cortex) has been adopted for apes and other species as well. As lesser motor and sensory areas were discovered, having relatively constant relations to the primary ones, these were shown as smaller body images positioned on the maps with respect to the larger ones. Thus, M II, the supplemental motor area of Woolsey, was discovered in the midline cortex of the paracentral area as a lesser system of points related to rump and tail of the larger M I figurine. The smaller sensory figurine of the primate was discovered to bear a constant relationship to the face area of the larger S I figurine. Reviewing the primate distribution from the perspective of that of lower forms, it is important that for all four figurines the points for the apices of the limbs are nearest the hypothetical line projected for the central sulcus, the points for the back furthest away. Considerable detail proving the dynamics of the phylogenetic development of the plan of representation is omitted here.

When the distribution of points upon postcentral gyrus (S I) for both motor response and evoked potential are compared for topographical relationship between parts of the body, remarkable similarities in somatotopical organization are noted. Thus, a base relationship appears to exist between input and output for the S I (Sm I, newer nomenclature) field. The S II (Sm II) field situated upon parietal operculum of the monkey also shows somatotopic coincidence of motor and sensory patterns.

A variety of studies indicate an afferent projection to the precentral gyrus (M I, or more recently Ms I because it has a lesser number of sensory points). Malis, Pribram and Krueger reported, for example, that precentral sensory responses could be evoked by electrical stimulation of cutaneous nerves alone, even after ablation of parietal lobe or cerebellum. Supporting evidence for this comes from the squirrel monkey and from a number of studies upon unit recording. Penfield et al., have obtained evidence of a sensory function of the supplemental motor area (M. II or Ms II).

In summary, four principal areas concerned with somatic sensibility and motor response are organized about the central sulcus. All show evidence of somatotopic localization. None is exclusively sensory or motor. In the areas where both patterns have been studied in detail the point distributions show consistency in somatotopic localization.

Clear separation of easily excitable Ms cortex from weakly excitable Sm cortex is present in rodents, carnivores, primates, anthropoids and man. Yet in primitive animals such as marsupials and monotremes motor and sensory cortices are one (so-called sensory-motor amalgam) and then Ms-I and Sm-I are oriented identically.

ABLATION STUDIES IN PRIMATES

Since the pioneer studies of John Fulton a quarter of a century ago the criteria for parcellation of the motor areas of the frontal lobe have changed markedly. Fulton depended upon the cytoarchitectonic map of Brodmann (Fig. 9), using the line at which Betz cells disappear on the

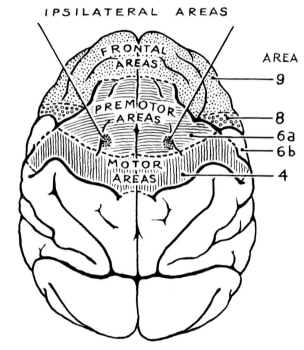

FIG. 9. Macaque brain, dorsal surface, showing distribution of motor and premotor areas in terms of Brodmann fields. (From J. F. Fulton, *Proc. Cal. Acad. Med.*, 1933–1934, Fig. 1, p. 6.)

maps as the boundary between motor and premotor cortices. This line was established by the criteria of stimulus mapping, and involved a significant elevation in the threshold of movements in the opposite extremity and the shift from a discrete to a generalized movement pattern.

As described by Fulton and his associates, ablations sharply restricted to the motor area, area 4, (precentral motor cortex) caused immediate flaccid paralysis of the opposite arm and leg with profound depression of deep and superficial reflexes. Voluntary power commensurate with the weakness persisted for a few days, then to return, first in the proximal muscles and somewhat later in the digits.

Isolated ablation of the premotor area, (area 6) which extends rostrally from area 4 to the margin with area 8 and the frontal association area (Fig. 1), produced a spastic hemiplegia with exaggerated tendon jerks and signs reminiscent of the human pathological reflexes. Here, too, much of the deficit disappeared in the course of a few weeks. Combined ablations of motor and premotor areas upon one side gave a permanent spasticity and exaggerated tendon jerks but paralysis never became complete. With bilateral loss of both motor and premotor cortex the animals became permanently paralysed. It will be noted that isolated lesions of motor cortex alone gave rise to a flaccid type paralysis, of the premotor area to a spastic type paralysis, both recoverable, and only bilateral removal of both resulted in permanent paralysis. Hines complicated the simplicity of this interpretation by showing that the whole syndrome allocated by Fulton to the premotor cortex could be produced by a strip lesion placed at the boundary between areas 4 and 6.

Recent studies by Travis of the Woolsey associates do not altogether correspond but the criteria for the areas of ablations differed from those of Fulton in significant respects. Woolsey defined the precentral motor cortex as the entire area of electrically excitable cortex as plotted in a formalized manner from specific criteria. Points for the distal extremities lie at the central sulcus and for the back extend forwards into area 6. Mesially (Fig. 8) this cortex meets the supplementary motor area and this boundary is the important one for deciding the limits between motor and supplemental motor removals. The remaining portion of area 6 was unaffected by Travis' ablations which were carried out by cortical aspiration. Travis' results in macaques upon motor area removal were immediate severe impairment in voluntary movement, hypotonia and diminished reflexes. Partial recovery of motor performance took place, and movements reappeared as soon at distal as at proximal joints. Within 12 weeks the animals were again able to pick up objects by apposition of thumb and index finger.

Treating supplementary motor area lesions as those of a distinct somatotopically organized field (Fig. 8), unilateral lesions produced weak, transient grasp reflexes in the opposite limbs and within 1 week moderate bilateral hypotonia of the shoulders. With simultaneous bilaterally symmetrical lesions there was practically no paresis but posture and tonus were disturbed and there was increased resistance to passive movements of the limbs. Ablation of parts of area 6 not included in the precentral and supplementary motor area lesions resulted in no motor impairment, no grasp reflex and no hypertonia.

Adult animals could walk and right themselves after bilateral removal of areas 4 and 6 including the supplementary motor areas, or after total removal of both frontal lobes except for one precentral face area and the adjoining frontal operculum. Animals with complete removals of both frontal fields retained some ability to use the hands and to perform other acts involving prehension. In successive operations two of the animals were carried to total removal of neocortex of both hemispheres. One of these was able to right and walk without assistance and the other showed remarkable retention of both righting and walking ability.

From comparison of these two studies conducted a quarter century apart it will be evident that the motor area 4 lesions showed roughly comparable but not identical results, that Fulton's premotor deficit does not require removal of the entire area 6 but is more closely akin to the supplementary motor area lesion, and that bilateral extensive removals as in the case of Travis' decorticate monkeys still leave the animal capable of executing righting and walking.

SUMMARY

An immense amount of new data has accumulated concerning cerebral cortical functioning. However, these relate chiefly to evoked and unit potential recording. Significant differences still exist concerning cytoarchitectonic parcellation and the interpretation of the results of motor cortex ablation. For the latter the studies by Woolsey and associaites promise clarification.

FURTHER READING

Bailey, P. and von Bonin, G. (1951), *The Isocortex of Man*. Urbana of Ill. Press.

Brodmann, K. (1909), *Vergleichende Lokalisationslehre der Grosshirnrinde*. Leipsig, Barth.

Bucy, P. C. (1933), *Electrical Excitability and Cytoarchitecture of the Premotor Cortex in Monkeys*, **30**, 1205.

Brooks, V. B. (1969), "Information Processing in the Motorsensory Cortex," in *Information Processing in the Nervous System* (K. N. Leibovic, Ed.). New York: Springer-Verlag.

Economo, C. V., *The Cytoarchitectonics of the Human Cerebral Cortex*. London: Oxford Univ. Press.

Fulton, J. F. (1933), "Paralyses of Cortical Origin," *Proc. Calif. Acad. Med.*

Fulton, J. F. and Viets, Henry R. (1953), "Upper Motor Neuron Lesions. An Analysis of the Syndromes of the Motor and Premotor Areas," *J.A.M.A.*, **104**, 357.

Hines, M. (1937), "The Motor Cortex," *Bull. Johns Hopk. Hosp.*, **60**, 313.

Hubel, D. H. and Wiesel, T. N. (1959), "Receptive Fields of Single Neurons in Cat's Striate Cortex," *J. Physiol. (Lond.)*, **148**, 574.

Lashley, K. S. and Clark, G. (1946), "The Cytoarchitecture of the Cerebral Cortex of Atetes: A Critical Examination of Architectonic Studies," *J. comp. Neurol.*, **85**, 233.

Liddell, E. G. T. and Phillips, C. G. (1950), "Thresholds of Cortical Representation," *Brain*, **73**, 125.

Mountcastle, V. B. and Powell, T. P. S. (1959), "Neural Mechanisms Subserving Cutaneous Sensibility with Special Reference to the Role of Afferent Inhibition in Sensory Perception and Discrimination," *Bull. Johns Hopk. Hosp.*, **105**, 201.

Phillips, C. G. (1965), "Changing Concepts of the Precentral Motor Area," in *Brain and Conscious Experience* (J. C. Eccles, Ed.), Springer, New York, **389**, 1965.

Pope, A. (1968), "Structural and Enzymatic Microchemistry of Human Cerebral Cortex," in *The Central Nervous System*, Int. Acad. Path. Monographs. Baltimore: Williams and Williams, p. 42.

Travis, A. M. (1955), "Neurological Deficiencies Following Supplementary Motor Area Lesions in Macaca Mulatta," *Brain*, **78**, 174.

Travis, A. M. and Woolsey, C. M. (1956), "Motor Performance of Monkeys after Bilateral Partial and Total Cerebral Decortications," *Amer. J. phy. Med.*, **35**, 273.

Travis, A. M. (1955), "Neurological Deficiencies after Ablations of the Precentral Motor Area in Macaca Mulatta," *Brain*, **78**, 155.

Walshe, F. M. R. (1948), "The Giant Cells of Betz, the Motor Cortex and the Pyramidal Tract," in *Critical Studies in Neurology*. Edinburgh: E. and S. Livingston, Inc.

Walshe, F. M. R. (1951), "On the Interpretation of Experimental Studies of Cortical Motor Fuction," *Brain*, **74**, 249.

Woolsey, C. N., "Organization of Somatic Sensory and Motor Areas of the Cerebral Cortex," in *Biological and Biochemical Bases of Behavior* (H. F. Harlow and C. M. Woolsey, Eds.). Madison: The University of Wisconsin Press.

2. THE CEREBELLUM

RAY S. SNIDER

INTRODUCTION

The cerebellum arises from bilateral expansions of the embryological alar (dorsal) quadrants of the hind-brain. These fuse over the IVth ventricle and from the resultant anlagen arises the entire circuitry of both cerebellar cortex and nuclei. Afferent pathways reach the cortex over three cerebellar peduncles to convey information from exteroceptors, enteroceptors and proprioceptors as well as from special cephalic receptors providing vestibular, auditory and visual information, and from higher levels of the neuraxis which relay other specialized information through the pontine and inferior olivary nuclei. Most of the efferent fibres pass to the vestibular nuclei, reticular formation, and thalamus.

In contrast to the highly variable structure of cerebral cortex that of cerebellum is noted for its over-all computer-like structural uniformity. Basically, it presents a single layer of Purkinje cells, the prime integrative elements, each provided with a directionally oriented dendritic arbor and an axon which goes to cerebellar or to extrinsic nuclei. Purkinje cells are activated over monosynaptic (climbing fibre) and disynaptic (mossy fibre) paths of external origin which terminate upon the dendritic expansions. Since lesions of the cerebellum produce disturbances of muscular coordination, it has long been postulated that the cerebellum is the "head ganglion of the proprioceptive system" (Sherrington). However, as noted below there are several sensory modalities represented in the cerebellum and the modern trend is to ascribe a much broader function to this organ.

Structural Features

There are three cerebellar lobes each containing a median vermian and a right and left hemispheric portion. In submammalian animals the cerebellum is composed almost entirely of the vermis. In man, the vermis is small compared to the hemispheres. The *anterior* lobe extends from the most anterior tip to the primary fissure (Fig. 1). The bulk of the human cerebellum is made up of the *posterior* lobe which extends caudally from the primary fissure to the postero-lateral fissure. The latter is located

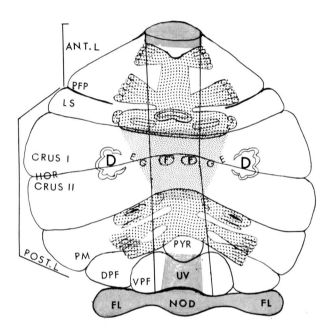

Fig. 1. Composite drawing of cerebellum flattened to show the anterior, posterior, and flocculo-nodular lobes and subdivisions.
The five sensory areas are:
(1) *dark shading*—anterior and posterior vestibular areas;
(2) *light stippling*—head, trunk, arm and leg regions related to anterior and posterior co-extensive proprioceptor and tactile areas;
(3) dark stippling—co-extensive auditory and visual areas.
These data are extrapolated from near threshold-evoked potential studies on the monkey.
(See text for afferent and efferent connections. Not shown are the extensive cortico-ponto-cerebellar and cortico-olivo-cerebellar projections to the cerebellar hemispheres and vermis.)

ANT.L—Anterior lobe	PM—Paramedian
PFP—Primary fissure	POST.L—Posterior lobe
LS—Simplex lobule	DPF, VPF—Dorsal and
Crus I	Ventral Para-
Crus II	flocculus
HOR—Horizontal fissure	PYR—Pyramis
D—Dentate	UV—Uvula
E—Emboliform	FL, NOD—Flocculus and
G—Globose	Nodulus
F—Fastigii	

in front of the *flocculo-nodular* lobe which extends to the caudal margin of the cerebellum (Fig. 1). All *vestibular* pathways connect with the flocculo-nodular lobe, the caudal vermian portion of the posterior lobe, and the cephalic tip of the anterior lobe. The *spinal* connections pass to medial and intermediate areas of anterior lobe and the caudal areas of the posterior lobe (both stippled areas in Fig. 1).

Virtually all cerebellar areas receive connections from the pontine and olivary nuclei. These afferent fibres are especially numerous in the hemispheres and the mid-

questioned. Cerebellar connections to the vestibular nuclei and reticular formation pass through the inferior peduncle.

There are direct vestibular root fibres to the flocculo-nodular lobe and indirect vestibular fibres which are relayed through the vestibular nuclei to the anterior part of anterior lobe and posterior part of posterior lobe. The return pathway synapses in the nucleus fastigii (medialis) and terminates in the vestibular nuclei. Special connections from Purkinje cell axons in the flocculo-nodular lobe go directly to the vestibular nuclei. Functional

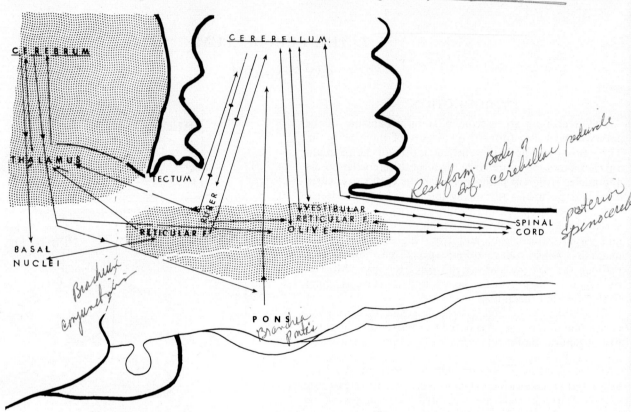

Fig. 2. Outline showing afferent and efferent connections drawn on midsagittal section of brain (showing cerebellum, cerebrum, basal nuclei, thalamus, tectum, reticular formation, nucleus ruber, pontine nuclei, vestibular nuclei, olivary nuclei, and spinal cord). The four major reverberating circuits indicated by arrows are:

(1) Spino-cerebello-spinal   (2) Cerebro-cerebello-cerebral
(3) Vestibulo-cerebello-vestibular   (4) Reticulo-cerebello-reticular

vermian areas. The horizontal cerebellar fissure divides the posterior lobe into approximately equal anterior and posterior areas.

As shown in Fig. 2 the cerebellum has to and fro connections with (1) spinal cord, (2) cerebrum, (3) vestibular nuclei and (4) ascending and descending components of reticular formation. The ascending spinal pathways include not only the dorsal and ventral spinocerebellar, but also the spino-olivo-cerebellar, spino-vestibulo-cerebellar and the spino-cuneo-cerebellar tracts. Some evidence exists for spinal connections through the pontine and the tectal nuclei. Cerebellar influences on the spinal cord are exerted by way of the vestibulo-spinal, rubro-reticulo-spinal and olivo-spinal pathways. The existence of a direct cerebello-spinal tract to cervical levels is

but not structural considerations make the flocculo-nodular lobe the equivalent of a vestibular nucleus. All vestibular pathways traverse the inferior peduncle.

Cerebro-cerebellar influences exist because of intermediate relays in pontine, olivary and reticular nuclei. Direct cerebello-cerebral connections do not exist, but there are relays in thalamic nuclei, i.e. ventralis lateralis, ventralis posterior, ventralis anterior, centrum medianum, reticularis and medial geniculate. Most of the ascending connections pass through the superior cerebellar peduncle and arise from cell bodies in nucleus dentatus (lateralis). Some ascending fibres arise from nucleus fastigii (medialis) and synapse in midbrain and thalamus.

There are numerous efferent connections arising from the cerebellar nuclei which go to the ascending reticular formation where they synapse with cells which in turn relay the impulses to the thalamus thence to both sensory and motor areas of the cerebrum. In addition, there are direct fibres connecting the cerebellar nuclei with the thalamus and thence with the cortex. The return loop fibres from the cerebrum to the cerebellum synapse in the pontine, olivary and reticular nuclei (Fig. 2). Undoubtedly, many ascending reticular influences reach the basal nuclei of the cerebral hemispheres. The functional significance of most of the ascending connections is not known.

Nuclei in the midbrain and medullary reticular formation give rise to direct reticulo-cerebellar fibres which pass through the superior and inferior cerebellar peduncles. Regardless of the origin of afferent fibres, the bulk of them are distributed to Purkinje cells by way of mossy and climbing fibres. Except for the flocculo-nodular lobe, the Purkinje cell is an internuncial cell to 1 of 4 nuclei which give rise to the efferent tracts. Purkinje cells in the vermis send axons to the medial (fastigii) nuclei while laterally located Purkinje cell axons synapse in the lateral (dentate) nuclei.

Functional Considerations

Numerous physiological studies have established the electrical characteristics of various cell types in the cerebellar cortex. Curiously, four of the five cell types are inhibitory in function (see Fig. 3). This figure also summarizes the principal intracortical circuits. Afferent (CF) impulses (from olivary nuclei, for example) excite the primary and secondary dendrites of the Purkinje cells which in turn send inhibitory impulses to the nuclear cells. All nuclear cells are excitatory to extracerebellar centres where they synapse. A second pathway through the cerebellar cortex results from conveyance of excitatory impulses from the mossy fibres via granule cell dendrites to ascending axons and parallel fibres to synapse on tertiary Purkinje cell dendrites. The Purkinje cell axon exerts an inhibitory effect on the cerebellar nuclei. Climbing fibres can activate Golgi II, basket and stellate cells which have an inhibitory function. Mossy fibres synapse on Golgi II dendrites, but do not contact basket and stellate cells. Inhibitory influences are exerted on (a) granule cell dendrites by Golgi II cells, (b) Purkinje cell somata by basket cells, (c) Purkinje dendrites by stellate cells and (d) cerebellar nuclear cells by Purkinje cell axons.

Without doubt, a major function of the cerebellum is control of muscular movements which result from extracerebellar activity. Fast conducting pathways from spinal, vestibular and reticular nuclei indicate significant coordinating influences on opposing muscle groups during voluntary and reflexly induced movements, as well as maintenance of posture. Exteroceptor, and especially proprioceptor end organs send signals to the spinal areas (Fig. 1) where "corrections" appear to be made between actual movements (example, muscle spindle discharges to cerebellum) versus intended movements (example, discharges from higher motor centres). It is not known how this is done. However, it is known that the anterior lobe can regulate activity in gamma and alpha spinal motor

neurons which in turn influence muscle spindle activity returning back to the anterior lobe, thus closing the spinal loop with the cerebellum.

As shown in Fig. 1, there are five so-called sensory areas which have been determined by electrophysiological studies. The vestibular areas have already been described, are the oldest, and are represented in the most anterior and posterior folia. Adjacent to these folia are the proprioceptor and tactile areas as represented by the afferents from the spinal cord. Note that there are 2 areas; the anterior one is represented ipsilaterally in the medial and intermediate regions of the anterior lobe. A trigeminal projection from face region goes to the lobulus simplex which is situated caudal to the primary fissure. Much of the sensory representation from the lips and mouth are

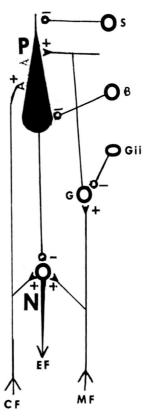

FIG. 3. Outline summary of intracerebellar circuitry. Plus signs indicate sites of excitatory synapses and minus signs indicate sites of inhibitory synapses.

B—Basket cell
CF—Climbing fibres
EF—Efferent fibres arising in cerebellar nuclei
G—Granule cell
G II—Golgi cell
MF—Mossy fibres
N—Cerebellar nuclei
P—Purkinje cell
S—Stellate cell.

Note that afferent climbing fibres send collaterals to cerebellar nuclei but the main synaptic area is on proximal and secondary dendrites of Purkinje cells. Afferent mossy fibres send collaterals to cerebellar nuclei but the main synaptic area is the granule cell dendrite. Afferent connections to Golgi II, basket and stellate cells are not shown.

deep on the banks of this fissure. Much of the experimental data show that the proprioceptor and tactile areas are co-extensive.

The posterior tactile and proprioceptor area is mainly located in the paramedian lobule (called gracilis and biventer in man) with the small face region in front of large hand and foot regions. There is some doubt about the existence of the posterior face area; however, there is no question concerning the existence of the bilateral representation of hand and foot regions and the coexistence of proprioceptor and tactile areas.

The coextensive auditory and visual areas are located between the two tactile areas and occupy vermian and intermediate zones. At the anterior and posterior margins they overlap the face regions of the anterior and posterior tactile areas (Fig. 1). The pathways from the auditory and visual endorgans synapse in the tectum on their way to the cerebellum. Most afferent impulses reach the various sensory areas of the cerebellum as fast as or faster than they reach the sensory areas of the cerebrum. After synapsing in the cerebellar cortex efferent impulses pass via relays in the reticular formation and thalamus to the cerebral sensory areas. Thus, ascending cerebellar influences can be exerted on sensory areas as well as motor and premotor areas which receive their afferents from thalamic nucleus ventralis lateralis, a cerebellar relay nucleus. Reverberating circuits through the cerebropontine and cerebroolivary pathways close the cerebro-cerebellar loops. The function of these cerebello-cerebro-cerebellar circuits are not known.

Clinical Considerations

The most meaningful information about functional significance has come from the study of deficits occurring after cerebellar lesions. In man a common symptom is a disturbance in gait but lateralized ataxia of the upper extremity is usually more prominent than that of the lower extremity. Nystagmus is not a persistent symptom unless the base of the cerebellum is involved. Acute lesions of the cerebellar cortex may produce transitory ataxia but there are consistent findings which show that man can recover completely from large cortical lesions. Since the hemispheres make up the bulk of the cerebellum, traumatic lesions and tumors in the posterior fossa often damage them. The first symptoms appear ipsilaterally and consist of ataxia and hypotonia often accompanied by hyporeflexia. Muscular weakness is often seen, but tremor may be transitory unless the cerebellar nuclei are involved. Involvement of the dentate nucleus not only exaggerates the above symptoms but also make them more enduring.

Lesions limited to the anterior lobe are rare, and the symptoms differ from some of those described above. Common signs are a wide base with a stiff-legged gait due to increased positive supporting reactions; hypertonia may even be present. Tremor is seldom seen unless there is nuclear damage. Nystagmus may be present if the lesion extends anteriorly. The term "cerebellar seizures" appears to be a misnomer because of the frequency of brain stem damage accompanying large anterior lobe lesions adjacent to the tentorium. An increasing amount of electrophysiological data indicates that seizure discharges are difficult to elicit and maintain in the cerebellar cortex probably due to the extensive inhibitory circuitry which exists within it. However, any sizeable anterior lobe damage must impair proprioceptive and tactile input from the spinal cord as well as interfere with efferent connections to the spinal cord via the vestibular nuclei and reticular formation. The interruption of these pathways in the brain stem is the most likely basis for the abnormal muscular activity described above.

Some clinicians recognize a syndrome associated with damage to the vermian part of the posterior lobe. The dominating signs are disturbance of equilibrium and so called "ataxia of the trunk". The latter is of interest since the individual appears to have limited control of trunk musculature. As shown in Fig. 1, medial parts of the posterior proprioceptor-tactile area represent trunk rather than limb and digit musculature. However, such observations are difficult to analyse since damage to the nearby vestibular area would interfere with the ability to orient the body in space. Nystagmus and abnormal head posturing are less commonly observed unless the lesion is asymmetrical.

Symptoms related to lesions of the auditory-visual area (Fig. 1) have never been studied in man. Electrical stimulation of this area in monkeys elicits complex eye movements which may be related to head turning.

Deficits resulting from lesions of the flocculo-nodular lobe have been studied extensively in monkeys and they resemble deficits reported in patients suffering from medulloblastoma of that lobe. Such individuals have disturbance in gait due to difficulty in balance. There may be abnormal head posture and nystagmus if the lesion is asymmetrical. Tremor, ataxia of individual limbs, and hypotonia are not associated with restricted flocculo-nodular lesions. Neither is there a loss of sensory perception of any kind. The latter statement may also be applied to a description of any cerebellar lesion. Obviously, more sensitive clinical tests need to be developed, especially those related to sensory deficits.

FURTHER READING

"The Cerebellum" (1970), *International Journal of Neurology*, Vols. 2, 3 and 4, pp. 91–318.

Dow, R. S. and Moruzzi, G. (1958), *The Physiology and Pathology of the Cerebellum*, 675 pages. The University of Minnesota Press, Minneapolis.

Eccles, J. C., Ito, M. and Szentágothai, J. (1967), *The Cerebellum as a Neuronal Machine*, 335 pages. Berlin–Heidelberg–New York, Springer-Verlag.

Fields, W. S. and Willis, W. D. Jr. (1970), *The Cerebellum in Health and Disease*, 557 pages. W. H. Green, St. Louis.

Fox, C. A. and Snider, R. S. (1967, "The Cerebellum," *Progress in Brain Research*, Vol. 25, 355 pages. Elsevier Publishing Company, Amsterdam.

Larsell, O. (1970), *The Comparative Anatomy and Histology of the Cerebellum from Monotremes through Apes* (J. Jansen, Ed.). The University of Minnesota Press, Minneapolis.

Llinas, R. (1969), *Neurobiology of Cerebellar Evolution and Development*, 931 pages. American Medical Association Press, Chicago.

3. THE BASAL GANGLIA

E. S. WATKINS

Strictly defined the term basal ganglia encompasses the cellular masses of the caudate nucleus, putamen, globus pallidus, substantia nigra, subthalamic nucleus and the red nucleus and does not include the thalamus. But the functional inter-relationships are such that exclusion of the thalamus from consideration on anatomical grounds is entirely artificial and it is significant that much of the modern surgical therapy of so-called basal ganglia disease in humans is directed to the thalamus.

The anatomical connections both between these structures themselves, and between the cerebral cortex, cerebellum and spinal cord, are intricate and bewildering. Much remains unknown or disputed and, in terms of physiological function, unravelled; from the point of view of pathological study the changes in these structures in basal ganglia disease may appear insignificant and undramatic despite their devastating clinical effects.

THE THALAMUS

Anatomy

Broadly speaking the thalamus can be considered anatomically and functionally in four systems related to anatomical subdivisions:

(1) *Medial thalamic mass and system*—nucleus medialis (dorsalis medialis) and the anterior nucleus.

(2) *Lateral thalamic mass and system*—nucleus intermedius, nucleus ventro-caudalis internus and externus.

(3) *The intralaminar system*—centro-medianum, nucleus parafascicularis and intralaminar cells.

(4) *The pulvinar and geniculate bodies.*

The Medial Thalamic Mass

The nucleus medialis (dorso-medialis) and smaller paraventricular nuclei are related to the emotional and limbic system by afferents from the hypothalamus and by efferent projections to the orbital and frontal cortex. Functionally the anterior nucleus may also be considered part of the medial system by virtue of its projection to the cingulate cortex and its connection via the mamillo-thalamic tract to the mamillary body, fornix, hippocampus and rhinencephalon. Stereotaxic destruction of the medial nucleus or of its projection to the frontal cortex, and also cingulectomy have been employed for the treatment of mental disorders. Accidental inclusion of the medial nucleus in stereotaxic lesions for the treatment of patients with dystonia or intractable pain may result, particularly if the lesions are bilateral, in unwanted mental confusion with social and intellectual defects.

The Pulvinar and Geniculate Bodies

The medial and lateral geniculate bodies are concerned with specific sensory systems of hearing and vision while the function of the pulvinar remain unknown. Recently, however, attention has been drawn to the claim of beneficial effects of stereotaxic lesions in the pulvinar in the treatment of spasticity in humans. Whether there is any specificity of interruption here rather than the effects of lesions generally in the thalamus is unknown, but most previous experience indicates that lateral thalamotomy has little to offer in spastic motor disorders.

The Lateral Thalamic Mass

This large and complex mass is intimately concerned with exteroception and proprioception and with the regulation of muscle tone and the maintenance of normal movement patterns and posture. Unfortunately much confusion results from the wealth of terminology used to distinguish its subdivisions. Anatomically it is divided into:

(1) The posterior somato-sensory nuclei—ventro-caudalis internus and externus.

(2) An intermediate cellular mass—nucleus intermedius.

(3) An anterior cellular mass—nucleus oralis.

The Posterior Group of Somato-sensory Nuclei—Ventro-caudalis Internus (Ventro-posterio-medialis) and Ventro-caudalis Externus (Ventro-posterior Lateralis)

On histological grounds the cellular patterns of these nuclei are dissimilar and individually characteristic making for ease of delineation; even macroscopically the inferior part of ventro-caudalis internus is readily visible as a semilunar structure infero-lateral to centro-medianum.

This nuclear group receives the afferent fibres of the lateral spino-thalamic system in a somatopically organized manner in the thalamic homunculus, the face and tongue areas lying most medial and inferior with the leg most lateral and superior. The projections from these nuclei to the parietal cortex and the primary sensory area are similarly topographically organized, with the face and arm lying inferiorly.

During stereotaxic physiological micro-electrode exploration in the human the pattern of spontaneous electrical activity, and the response pattern of potentials evoked by peripheral cutaneous or joint stimulation, can be utilized to determine the position of these nuclei with precision. Elegant recording techniques have shown a sensory fractionation within the nuclei, in that evoked responses from joint and muscle stimulation are found mainly anteriorly while responses from cutaneous stimuli are found posteriorly. There are suggestions that in man the topographic organization is less precise than in primates and that the thalamic homunculus is more complex.

The Nucleus Intermedius

This nucleus lies in the middle part of the lateral mass; its cellular pattern of large darkly staining cells distinguishes it from the posterior group and from the nucleus oralis. It receives afferents from the globus pallidus (ansa and fasciculus lenticularis) and cerebellum (dentato-rubro-thalamic fibres); and it projects to and receives afferents from the motor cortex. The nucleus thus receives proprioceptive information and electro-physiologically its spontaneous activity shows characteristically slow waves (20–25 c./s.) and large, spiking action potentials. In parkinsonian

patients tremor rhythms contemporaneous with (but independent of) peripheral tremor may be detected and this region of the thalamus has been called "the Tremorogenic zone". This part of the thalamus now seems to be the best site for stereotaxic lesions intended to control tremor, increased tone and abnormal movements due to basal ganglia disease regardless of the site of the primary pathology or the exact nature of the dyskinesia.

The Nucleus Oralis

This nucleus lies anterior to the intermediate nucleus and its cellular characteristics are such as to distinguish an internal portion containing large, palely staining cells and a lateral portion of small, irregular darkly staining cells. It receives afferents from the globus pallidus similarly to the intermediate nucleus (ansa and fasciculus lenticularis). In the early days of thalamic surgery this part of the thalamus

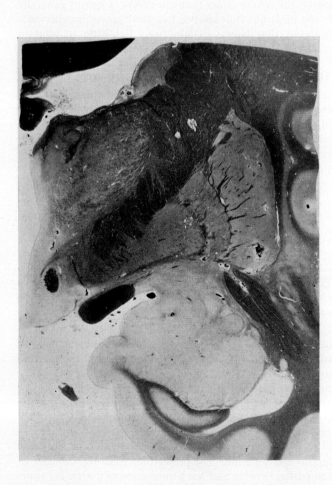
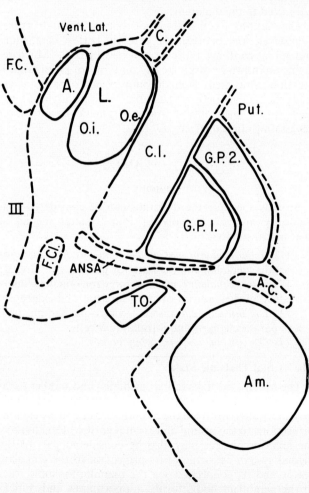

FIG. 1A and B. Coronal section of thalamus and basal ganglia just behind the Foramen of Monro. (Reproduced by kind permission of Williams and Wilkins.)

III	= Third ventricle		G.P.1	= Globus pallidus, medial crus
A	= Anterior Nucleus		G.P.2	= Globus pallidus, lateral crus
A.C.	= Anterior Commissure		L.	= Lateral Thalamic Mass
Am.	= Amygdalum		O.e.	= Oral nucleus, external part
Ansa	= Ansa lenticularis		O.i.	= Oral nucleus, internal part
C.	= Caudate Nucleus		Put.	= Putamen
C.I.	= Internal capsule		T.O.	= Optic tract
F.C.	= Fornix Body		Vent. Lat.	= Lateral Ventricle
F.Cl.	= Fornic Column			

was often chosen as the "surgical target", but subsequently more posteriorly placed lesions were found to be of more lasting benefit particularly for the control of tremor.

The Centro-medianum and the Intralaminar System

The centro-medianum is a large nucleus with a rich network of fibres and widely scattered medium size cells. It lies centrally in the thalamus and the fibres of the internal lamina of the thalamus enclose the cellular body. In relation to the internal lamina aggregation of cells occur and comprise the smaller intralaminar nuclei. The nucleus parafascicularis lies medial to the centro-medianum and the cells are smaller and darkly staining. The centro-medianum and parafascicularis receive ascending afferents from the lateral spino-thalamic system to some extent, but mainly from the brain stem reticular formation as well as from frontal cortex, cerebellum, globus pallidus, putamen and caudate nucleus. The projections from this system are to the putamen, caudate nucleus and to some extent, directly or through collateral fibres, to frontal cortex. Despite the great size of the centro-medianum and associated nuclei its functions are not precisely known. Generally it is regarded as part of the non-specific central activating system in view of the cortical arousal that results from experimental stimulation within it. Surgically this region is of importance as a target for stereotaxic interruptions in the treatment of intractable pain. Guarded hints as to the system's role in motor mechanisms result from functional interpretations of its connections to the globus pallidus, etc., and its inclusion as a surgical target for the treatment of spasmodic torticollis and dystonia.

Function

Despite the vast experience of stereotaxic surgery in humans, including much electrophysiological exploration involving stimulation and recording studies, the exact functions and finite workings of the thalamus remain obscure. It is fashionable to link the thalamic subdivisions functionally with the other basal ganglia by a series of line drawings indicating wiring arrangements broadly divided into motor and sensory categories although the relationship of this sort of interpretation of central nervous activity to reality is as obscure as the functions it purports to simplify.

It is recorded that very large areas of the thalamus can be damaged and destroyed in humans by stereotaxic lesions with apparently little motor or sensory effect (other than beneficial!). Certainly this is true of unilateral interruptions, while bilateral interruptions can be tolerated remarkably well in selected patients of suitable age. From the neuropathological point of view disease rarely affects the thalamus in isolation from other structures; but it is not unusual to find lesions in the thalamus with cavitation and atrophy occurring naturally, presumably vascular in origin, with no evidence prior to death of disturbed neurological function. That the syndrome of "thalamic pain" does not regularly follow posterior stereotaxic thalamic lesions suggests that the significant pathological lesion in this state does not lie in the thalamus. The more regular production of such serious hemi-dysaesthesia by stereotaxic mesencephalotomy favours a disturbance of brain stem mechanism as the cause.

THE SUBTHALAMIC NUCLEUS

Anatomy

This nucleus lies ventral to the lateral mass of the thalamus, its lateral margin abuts the medial fibres of the internal capsule and the nucleus is in close relation to the zona incerta and fields of Forel. It is known to receive afferents from and send efferent connections to the globus pallidus, and possibly has connections with the lateral thalamus, red nucleus and substantia nigra.

Function

For many years on clinical and neuropathological grounds damage to the nucleus in man has been thought to be associated with the production of wild, choreiform or ballismic movements in the contralateral limbs. Experiments in monkeys indicate that lesions causing damage to more than 20 per cent of the nucleus produce hemichorea or hemiballismus;[19,32] the persistence of such movements depends on the integrity of the globus pallidus or lenticular fascicularis and can be partially or totally abolished by extension of the lesion to involve these structures.[3]

Martin[16] has drawn attention to the extreme sensitivity of patients with mild hemiballismus to changes of posture and argues that the involuntary movements are exaggerated responses of the postural reflexes to instability. He concludes that the subthalamic nucleus normally controls and suppresses the postural reflexes excited by instability.

In the human the subthalamic nucleus is dangerously and strategically situated in relation to the ventro-lateral mass of the thalamus so that the nucleus may be damaged accidentally during stereotaxic thalamotomy. Some authorities[12] describe a post-operative incidence of hemiballismus occurring in 1–3 per cent of all thalamotomy cases. It has similarly been confirmed in humans that the spontaneously occurring disorder of hemiballismus can be abolished by thalamotomy[17] as can the iatrogenic form by extending the surgical lesion either to the globus pallidus or making a larger thalamic lesion. However, while the relationship of lesions in the subthalamic nucleus to hemiballismus seem clearcut, all cases of hemiballismus do not show damage to the subthalamic nucleus.[4,12]

THE RED NUCLEUS

Anatomy

This large nucleus lies between the ventral border of the thalamus, above the substantia nigra and medial to the subthalamic nucleus. It is easily distinguished in fibre and cellular stains, and is divided into magnocellular and parvocellular parts in lower mammals. In man the red nucleus is homologous to the parvocellular part of the mammalian red nucleus. It receives important cerebellar connections through the brachium conjunctivum from the contralateral dentate nucleus and is connected to the ipsilateral thalamus and olivary nucleus (dentato-rubro-thalamic system). The magnocellular part gives the descending tract—the contralateral rubrospinal tract; this, together with the connection to the precentral cortex and to the cerebellum implies a role in motor control, the system being facilitatory to flexor muscles and inhibitory to extensor muscles. However, the regression of the magnocellular part in man is marked and coincides with a marked reduction in the size and length of the rubrospinal tract to an almost rudimentary state.

Function

The function of the parvocellular part of the red nucleus is unknown but clinico-pathological observations have assigned two syndromes to lesions affecting the nucleus in man. One in which oculomotor nerve paralysis is associated with tremor of the contralateral limbs which are weak and hypertonic (Benedikt's syndrome). The second syndrome in man consists of contralateral ataxia, dysmetria and hypotonus and is said to result from lesions confined to the red nucleus (Claude's syndrome). However, experimental studies in animals have not reproduced the tremor state when the lesions were confined to the red nucleus, but alternatively tremor has resulted from ventral lesions in the brachium conjunctivum. As is common in basal ganglia disturbances, the situation is not clear-cut and both syndromes may result from apparently identical lesions in different patients. From the anatomical connections and the sparse physiological knowledge of the parvocellular part Massion[18] has suggested that the dentato-rubro-olivo-cerebellar system plays a part in the feedback control of the motor system.

THE GLOBUS PALLIDUS

Anatomy

The globus pallidus is a conical structure lying alongside the thalamus and separated from it by the internal capsule. The base of the cone lies externally so that in coronal and horizontal sections of the brain the globus pallidus appears triangular with the tip of the cone pointing medially towards the thalamus and other basal ganglia. The putamen lies lateral to the external edge of the globus pallidus and separated from it by the external medullary lamina. The internal medullary lamina separates the globus pallidus into a medial and lateral mass or "crus". A large mass of efferent fibres (fasciculus and ansa lenticularis) connect across and around the internal capsule with the ventral and lateral thalamus; other efferent connections to the centro-medianum and subthalamic nuclei are known to exist and possibly also to the substantia nigra. Afferent connections to the globus pallidus arise from the subthalamic nucleus, substantia nigra, putamen and caudate nuclei, the cerebral cortex and the intralaminar nuclei.

Function

The globus pallidus has the distinction of being the first popular stereotaxic target for destruction in man to treat the rigidity and tremor of Parkinson's disease. Its development as a target resulted from early open operations on the ansa lenticularis, section of which was found to improve the rigidity and tremor of parkinsonism. Subsequently with the development of stereotaxic techniques "ansotomy" and then "pallidotomy" were performed. In humans bilateral surgical lesions may be tolerated without obvious neurological deficit added to the parkinsonian patient but

Martin[16] suggests that severe pathological changes in the globus pallidus in parkinsonian patients are associated with loss of postural reflexes. However, pathological changes in the globus pallidus are not uncommon in senile brains whether or not the patient had parkinsonism. From the experimental point of view Denny Brown[6] has shown in the monkey, bilateral lesions do produce disturbances of posture and loss of postural righting reflexes together with increased tone in the limbs producing a plastic rigidity. Denny Brown drew attention to the sensitivity of the globus pallidus in man to anoxia and relates a clinical state of rigid akinetic mutism seen in patients with carbon monoxide poisoning with lesions in the globus pallidus.

It is clear however, that surgical interruption of the globus pallidus or its outflow in man and experimental animals can abolish the mild movements of hemiballismus, and the rigidity and to some extent the tremor of parkinsonism in man.

SUBSTANTIA NIGRA

Anatomy

This structure is normally pigmented and is composed of large cells containing melanin granules. It lies closely below and lateral to the red nucleus and in relationship to the cortico-spinal fibres of the cerebral peduncle. Its superior and lateral borders form the boundary of the fields of Forel in coronal section and its superior anterior surface is in close proximity to the subthalamic nucleus. Undisputed connections to the globus pallidus, putamen, caudate nucleus, ventro-lateral thalamus and motor cortex are efferent; an afferent fibre system from globus pallidus to substantia nigra is held to run with the pallido-fugal outflow.

Function

Clinico-pathological studies have demonstrated that degeneration of the substantia nigra with loss of pigmented cells is a characteristic finding in many parkinsonian patients and it is clear that reduction or loss of nigral activity results in muscular rigidity. The closest association of these events is found in cases of post-encephalitic parkinsonism but the relationship is not a constant finding and the substantia nigra may appear unaffected in cases of parkinsonism due to arteriosclerosis.

Similarly confusing results have been obtained in experimental lesions in the substantia nigra in animals. Lesions confined to the structure itself in the monkey have not produced any changes in muscle tone nor tremor, but ventral paramedian lesions in the mid-brain tegmentum have been successful in mimicking the tremor and hypokinesia of Parkinsonism although not the disturbed tone.[31]

From the physiological point of view the simple relationships so envisaged cannot be easily reconciled. Evidence exists that the substantia nigra has a profound inhibitory influence on the activity of the ventral lateral thalamus in a direct manner and also on cells in the caudate nucleus. It has also been established biochemically that lesions in the substantia nigra in monkeys produce a reduction in dopamine content of putamen and caudate nucleus. The projection system from substantia nigra to caudate nucleus and putamen is known to be dopaminergic and following its interruption there is secondary degeneration of neurones in these structures.[26,27] Dopamine depletion in these ganglia in parkinsonian patients has been found[9] and the administration of L-Dopa to parkinsonian patients profoundly improves the muscular rigidity and akinesia but not the tremor.

The situation is thus so complex that a comprehensibly simple interpretation is not yet possible.

THE PUTAMEN

Anatomy

This structure lies lateral to the external aspect of the globus pallidus and contributes to the generally wedge shaped form of the two structures by providing the base of the cone.

Although topographically it is closely related to the globus pallidus, functionally its relationship to the caudate nucleus is overriding. The cell types in both caudate and

putamen are similar, both ganglia containing large and small nerve cells in similar proportions so that the histological similarity is close.

It projects to the globus pallidus and substantia nigra, and receives afferents from the centro-medianum, cerebral cortex and the caudate nucleus.

Function

Clinical-pathological associations in man concerning putamenal degeneration and disordered function have long been recognized and are well established, but conflict exists in relation to the results of making experimental lesions in this structure in primates; the effect on motor function is minimal with only mild disturbances of tone and no consistent abnormalities of posture. The following motor disturbances have been associated with putamenal degeneration in man:

(1) The disorder of tone and movement of Wilson's hepato-lenticular degeneration—although there is in

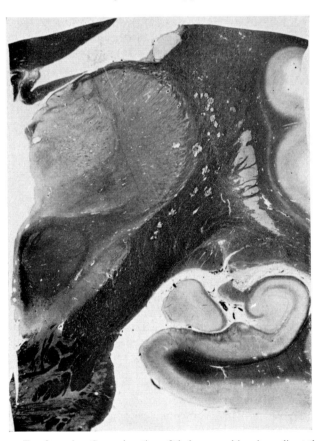
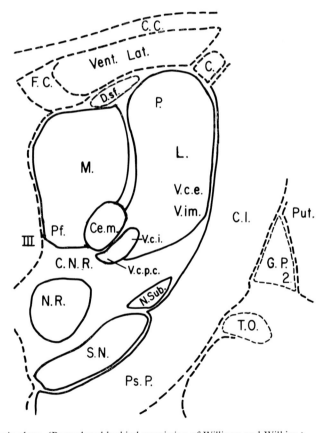

Fig. 2A and B. Coronal section of thalamus and basal ganglia at the mid-thalamic plane. (Reproduced by kind permission of Williams and Wilkins.)

III	= Third ventricle		N.Sub.	= Subthalamic Nucleus
C.	= Caudate Nucleus		P.	= Pulvinar
C.C.	= Corpus Callosum		Pf.	= Nucleus Parafascicularis
Ce.m.	= Centro-medianum		Ps.P.	= Cerebral penduncle
C.I.	= Internal capsule		Put.	= Putamen
C.N.R.	= Capsule of Red Nucleus		S.N.	= Substantia Nigra
D.sf.	= Dorso-superficial Nucleus		T.O.	= Optic tract
F.C.	= Fornix Body		V.c.e.	= Ventro-caudalis externus
G.P.2	= Globus pallidus; lateral crus		V.c.i.	= Ventro-caudalis internus
L.	= Lateral Thalamic Mass		V.c.p.c.	= Ventro-caudalis parvo-cellularis
M.	= Medial Thalamic Mass—Nucleus Medialis		V.im.	= Ventro-intermedius
N.R.	= Red Nucleus		Vent. Lat.	= Lateral Ventricle

addition widespread damage and gliosis in cortex, thalamus and cerebellum.

(2) The chorea of Huntington's syndrome—here again the caudate nucleus and frontal cortex are universally atrophic as well.

(3) Double athetosis—with marble-scarring of the putamen bilaterally.

(4) Dystonia musculorum deformans—although this most severe dyskinesia may occur without any obvious neuropathological change in the putamen or elsewhere.

(5) Striatal hemiplegia—in association with caudate atrophy.[22]

(6) Hemiballismus.[28]

The above disorders are widely different in aetiology and clinical effects but in general it seems clear that widespread degeneration of the putamen results in the human in increased muscle tone with rigidity and dystonic movements of an athetoid type. According to Denny Brown[6] the progression of damage in the putamen is accompanied by an initial disturbance of athetosis followed later by a rigid posture with flexion of the upper limbs and extension of the lower limbs. Oppenheimer[22] points out that in his case of striatal hemiplegia rigidity and spasms in the contralateral limbs were present from the time of onset and that in the early years the patient could move her fingers and her foot between the muscular spasms.

The mechanism by which the putamen exerts its influence on muscle tone remains unknown, but Martin[16] infers that putamenal control is exerted normally over postural fixation and that the control is probably exerted through and upon the activity of the globus pallidus.

THE CAUDATE NUCLEUS

Anatomy

This structure forms the lateral margin of the floor and the inferior margin of the lateral wall of the lateral ventricle in close relationship to the superior surface of the lateral thalamus. The anterior part of the structure is larger than its caudal portion and loosely the terms head, body and tail of the caudate nucleus are applied; the head and tail straddling the whole length of the thalamus.

Histologically its appearance is similar to that of the putamen and the connections are similar receiving fibres from the centro-medianum and intralaminar nuclei, from the substantia nigra and from cerebral cortex. It projects to putamen and to cerebral cortex.

Function

Pathologically degeneration of the head of the caudate nucleus is a constant finding in cases of Huntington's chorea and, in consequence, the occurrence of choreiform movements and caudate atrophy have become associated. As has been stated earlier, however, such patients show cortical and putamenal degeneration in addition. Moreover, the movement disorder of Huntington's chorea may encompass, as well as the characteristic chorea, myoclonus, rigidity and dystonic posturing so that the correlations are not clear.

Denny Brown[6] has shown that in monkey bilateral destruction of the caudate nucleus produced an intractable state of restless motor behaviour but that apart from these abnormal movements there were no other major disturbances of tone, reflexes or reactions. Other caudate ablation experiments in lower animals have resulted in a stereotyped forward locomotor response even to point of running and a disregard of visual stimuli, e.g. obstacles which would normally alter the motor behaviour are ignored.

Unilateral destruction of the caudate nucleus has been found to produce repetitive circling movements, and stimulation experiments to cause head and trunk turning to the contralateral side. These phenomena have been interpreted as evidence that the caudate nucleus has a suppressing influence over locomotion, and that it is concerned with the control of automatic motor patterns and visually determined responses.

Biochemical investigations mentioned earlier have shown that the neurones in the caudate and putamen undergo degeneration after nigral lesions and that a depletion of dopamine content of these structures occurs. Recent physiological studies indicate that the substantia nigra exerts an inhibitory influence on the large cells of the caudate nucleus but that the controlling pathways may not all be dopaminergic in nature.

It is of significance that one of the striking side-effects of L-Dopa treatment in parkinsonian patients is the production of choreiform and athetoid involuntary movements; indeed the whole spectrum of involuntary movements may be observed in a series of patients, each individual exhibiting a particular response to the drug therapy.

THE FIELDS OF FOREL

Anatomy

The dorsal and ventral tegmental areas of white matter (H_1 and H_2) lie in the subthalamic region in relation to the zona incerta, the subthalamic nucleus, the red nucleus and substantia nigra. These areas contain major fibre projection systems between the basal ganglia including anteriorly the fasciculus lenticularis, the ansa lenticularis and the thalamic fascicularis. In the posterior part connections from the red nucleus, subthalamic nucleus, substantia nigra and brain stem reticular formation are highly concentrated.

Function

The functions of this compact zone are those related to all the systems which contribute major connections through these areas.

Surgically the zone is of importance in that the area in relation to the ventrolateral thalamus has been used as a stereotaxic target for the treatment of parkinsonism and also myoclonus. Jinnai[13,14] and Bertrand[2] regard the anterior Forel area as a useful target for the treatment of cases of intractable, generalized, non-focal epilepsy which is unsuitable for other surgical treatment and is therapeutically unmanageable. The potential dangers of imprecise stereotaxic interruption in so highly eloquent an area do not need to be further elaborated.

SURGERY OF THE BASAL GANGLIA

The early open transventricular operations of Russell Meyers[20,21] in which the head of the caudate nucleus and the medial globus pallidus were excised, interrupting the ansa lenticularis, gave place to closed stereotaxic ansotomy (Spiegel and Wycis[29]), then pallidotomy, and ultimately thalamotomy. The most popular surgical target at present is the intermedius part of the lateral thalamic mass ("the tremorogenic zone"). Various techniques are used for precise identification prior to lesion making and these are described in Chapter 7, section VIII.

Indications

The following disorders may be treated by thalamotomy with success of varying grades:

Dyskinesias

(1) Parkinsonism—particularly unilateral tremor and rigidity.

(2) Familial intention tremor—surgery is strikingly successful.

(3) Intention tremor of disseminated sclerosis—the possibility of bilateral treatment is limited.

(4) Ballismic disorders following stroke, severe choreioid tremor following head injury.

(5) Dystonia musculorum deformans—particularly when abnormal limb movements are prominent.

(6) Spasmodic torticollis—placing bilateral lesions perhaps in centro-medianum.

(7) Choreo-athetotic disorders—in patients with mentality and voluntary power well preserved. The results in this group of patients are not as good as in the other groups.

(8) Spastic states—cerebral palsy—placing lesions perhaps in pulvinar; recently attempts have been made to derive benefit by making cerebellar dentate lesions.

Intractable Pain

Placing lesions in posterior medial thalamus in relation to centro-medianum; bilateral interruptions are usually necessary for patients with a benign basis for the pain state.

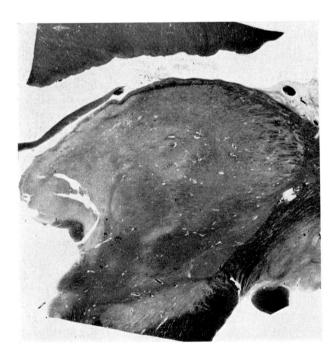

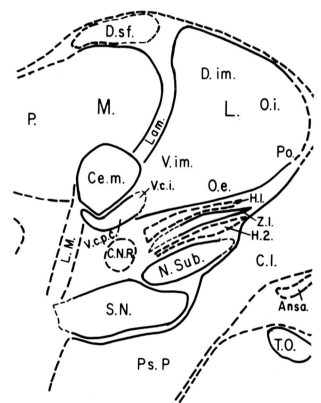

FIG. 3A and B. Sagittal section of thalamus and basal ganglia at 10 mm. from the midline. (Reproduced by kind permission of Williams and Wilkins.)

Ansa	= Ansa lenticularis		N.Sub.	= Subthalamic Nucleus
Ce.m.	= Centro-medianum		O.e.	= Oral nucleus, external part
C.I.	= Internal capsule		O.i.	= Oral nucleus, internal part
C.N.R.	= Capsule of Red Nucleus		P.	= Pulvinar
D.im.	= Dorso-intermedius Nucleus		Po.	= Polaris nucleus
D.sf.	= Dorso-superficial Nucleus		Ps.P.	= Cerebral Peduncle
Hl.	= Dorsal Tegmental Area		S.N.	= Substantia Nigra
H2.	= Ventral Tegmental Area		T.O.	= Optic tract
L.	= Lateral Thalamic Mass		V.c.i.	= Ventro-caudalis internus
Lam.	= Internal Medullary Lamina		V.c.p.c.	= Ventro-caudalis parvo-cellularis
L.M.	= Medial Lemniscus		V.im.	= Ventro-intermedius
M.	= Medial Thalamic Mass—Nucleus Medialis		Z.I.	= Zona Incerta

Epilepsy

In patients with non-focal epilepsy who are unmanageable despite heavy medication and who are not suitable for orthodox cortical resection or temporal lobectomy.

Complications

The mortality of stereotaxic operations on the basal ganglia is now extremely low (1–2 per cent) and the morbidity such as hemiplegia (2–3 per cent overall) much reduced owing to improvements in anatomical knowledge, electrophysiological aids, and control of lesion production by thermal measurements in cryogenic and radiofrequency interruptions.

Bilateral operations offer more risk particularly to seriously disturbed or old patients and caution is advisable to avoid blunting effects on mentality and drive in such cases. Deeply placed posterior lesions carry a slight risk of akinetic mutism or severe confusional states due possibly to incrimination of the central grey matter or the Forel inputs. Bilateral operations in parkinsonian patients offer some risk to speech volume, swallowing and balance and should be avoided in patients who are found to have these difficulties on pre-operative assessment. However, young patients will tolerate large and even repeated thalamic lesions bilaterally as Cooper[4] has shown, and for the treatment of severe dystonia he has stressed the need for early and radical treatment to gain control over this condition.

PATHOPHYSIOLOGY OF MOVEMENT DISORDERS

This subject remains in a confused and highly controversial state. It is best discussed under the headings of the principal disturbances of tone and movement as so many named disorders are composite disturbances of power, posture, tone and involuntary movement. For example, in cases of dystonia musculorum deformans tremor, athetoid movements of the limbs, spasmodic torticollis, facial grimacing, and torsion spasms of the trunk with increased tone and dystonic posturing of the limbs are present.

Disturbances of Tone—Rigidity and Spasticity

In man increased tone may be due to increased activity of the alpha motoneurons of the spinal cord supplying the extrafusal muscle fibres.[23] A striking example of intense rigidity of all four limbs in a patient with a cervical intramedullary tumour was described by Rushworth et al.[24] The interpretation of this phenomenon was based on the concept that functional isolation of anterior horn motoneuron cells resulted in spontaneous discharge, the posture of the patient and his limbs depending on the size of the muscle groups involved, and in whether or not there was any response of the spontaneously firing cells to reflex or voluntary mechanisms. Tarlov[30] ascribed rigidity in a similar case to loss of spinal interneurones with resulting spontaneous discharge of the alpha motoneurons.

In the rigid state of Parkinsonism facilitation of alpha motoneurons, as a result of suprasegmental influences produced by the disorder, might be expected and some believe this to be the basis.[7] However, Rushworth[23] has shown that procaine injections near the motor points of muscles effectively reduces Parkinsonian and dystonic rigidity by blocking gamma motor fibres whereas voluntary power actually increases, suggesting that hyperactivity of the gamma system is the prime mechanism. Directly contrary views have been expressed by Hassler[11] concerning the gamma system, while other authorities believe that parkinsonian rigidity is due to hyperactivity of both alpha and gamma systems. The suprasegmental influences responsible for these changes have not yet been precisely defined, although there is evidence suggesting that activation of the gamma system may be reduced by thalamic or pallidal interruptions. Rushworth[23] has shown that spasticity due to a variety of causes responds similarly to procaine experiments and that excessive gamma activity seems to be responsible for this disturbed state of muscle tone.

Oppenheimer[22] notes that in his patients with striatal damage, a rigid state was produced without any evidence of damage to the pyramidal tract. He draws attention to the evidence of Bucy that a pure pyramidal lesion does not produce a spastic hemiplegia. The inference is clear that a spastic hemiplegia in the usual sense attributed to an upper motoneuron lesion is a composite condition resulting from an insult to a variety of structures—cortical and subcortical.

Tremor

Postural or parkinsonian tremor (5/sec.) probably originates in the thalamus in the tremorogenic zone. Though so frequently associated with rigidity, the latter may be relieved by pallidal or anterior thalamic lesions without affecting the former at all—or only transiently. The only lesions to effectively and permanently abolish tremor are either in the corticospinal system, when the effect is proportional to the degree of paralysis, or in "the tremorogenic zone" of the thalamus when no added deficit is induced.

Cooper[4] believes that cerebellar (intention) tremor is basically similar to parkinsonian tremor, the clinical difference resulting from the differing aetiology and differing physiological background of muscle tone. He concludes that postural tremor identical to parkinsonian can be produced in patients with cerebellar pathology by manoeuvres which heighten gamma input to the muscles. Certainly cerebellar tremor in disseminated sclerosis and other intention tremors can be abolished by thalamotomy. He argues that an effective lesion interrupts pallido-fugal and dentato-fugal connections in the tremorogenic zone of the thalamus.

It has been suggested that the cells of this zone of thalamus, when functionally partly isolated by disease processes from the influences of the nigro-striatal or dentato-cerebellar (or brachium conjunctivum) systems, respond by spontaneous discharge at 5/sec. tremor rates—the tremor then being easily abolished by accurately placed lesions in this zone. However, Earl Walker et al.[8] have pointed out that under normal conditions none of the central neural systems has a spontaneous rhythm at such a rate.

Abnormal Movements and Posture

The movements of chorea, athetosis and dystonia although clinically separable have been regarded by Denny

Brown[6] as fluctuations of posture which are interrelated. The involuntary movements of Huntington's chorea are rapid, momentary posturings with repetition of the same or varied postures, while in dystonia the postural abnormality becomes a relatively fixed attitude. In athetosis two conflicting or "basic" postures with fluctuation between constitute the abnormal movement—from flexion-supination to hyperextension-pronation of the fingers, wrist and forearm. A relationship between chorea and ballismus is disputed by Denny Brown owing to the rotary character of the movements in ballismus but most observers would disagree and regard the extent and violence of the movements as the criteria. Purdon Martin [16] has considered the relationships in great detail in relation to postural reflexes, and regards the mechanism of control of equilibrium as dependent on the normal function of the basal ganglia in controlling the postural reflex mechanisms.

NEUROCHEMISTRY OF THE BASAL GANGLIA

No attempt is to be made here to review in detail this massive topic which is now a subject in its own right. Earlier in the text references have been made to the findings of low dopamine content in the basal ganglia of Parkinsonian brains and the normally high concentration found in the striatum in normal brains.[9] Depletion of dopamine content is found concurrently with secondary degeneration of neurones of the caudate nucleus and putamen following interruptions of the nigro-striatal pathway in monkeys.[27] These changes in the striatum in man, it is argued, produce the increased tone and akinesia of the striatal syndrome. The administration of L-Dopa to rigid, akinetic patients dramatically reverses these effects but tends not to improve Parkinsonian tremor and may produce involuntary choreoathetotic movements. The effects of L-Dopa administration in the other dyskinetic syndromes is not predictable. In animals L-Dopa administration raises dopamine concentration lowered by neuroleptic drugs, e.g. reserpine, and reduces rigidity and akinesia induced by these agents along with changing alpha and gamma activity to the peripheral musculature—reducing the former and increasing the latter.

The importance of these biochemical findings cannot be over-emphasized and the role of chemical transmitters in central neural mechanisms is considered of such significance that Yahr stated in 1966 "classical anatomical concepts may have to be revised and the nervous system viewed in terms of its chemo-architecture".

FURTHER READING

[1] Andrew, J. and Watkins, E. S. (1969), *Stereotaxic Atlas of the Human Thalamus.* Baltimore: Williams and Wilkins.
[2] Bertrand, C. (1971), Personal communication.
[3] Carpenter, M. B., Whittier, J. and Mettler, F. A. (1950), *J. Comp. Neurol.,* **92,** 293.
[4] Cooper, I. S. (1969), *Involuntary Movement Disorders.* New York: Harper & Row.
[5] Costa, E., Cote, L. J. and Yahr, M. D. (1966), *Biochemistry and Pharmacology of the Basal Ganglia.* New York: Raven Press.
[6] Denny Brown, D. (1962), *The Basal Ganglia.* Oxford University Press.
[7] Denny Brown, D. (1969), *Third Symposium on Parkinson's Disease.* Edinburgh: Livingstone.
[8] Earl Walker, A. (1969), *Third Symposium on Parkinson's Disease.* Edinburgh: Livingstone.
[9] Ehringer, H. and Hornykiewicz, O. (1960), *Klin. Wschr.,* **38,** 1236.
[10] Gillingham, F. J. and Donaldson, I. M. L. (1969), *Third Symposium on Parkinson's Disease.* Edinburgh: Livingstone.
[11] Hassler, R. (1966), *The Thalamus* (D. P. Purpura and M. D. Yahr, Eds.). New York: University of Columbia Press.
[12] Hughes, Brodie (1965), *J. Neurol. Neurosurg. Psychiat.,* **28,** 291.
[13] Jinnai, D. (1963), *1st International Symposium Stereoencephalotomy (Philadelphia),* p. 222. New York: Karger.
[14] Jinnai, D. (1965), *2nd International Symposium Stereoencephalotomy (Vienna),* p. 129. New York: Karger.
[15] Martin, J. P. (1959), *Lancet,* **i,** 999.
[16] Martin, J. P. (1967), *The Basal Ganglia and Posture.* Philadelphia: J. B. Lippincot Co.
[17] Martin, J. P. and McCaul, I. (1959), *Brain,* **82,** 104.
[18] Massion, J. (1967), *Phys. Rev.,* **47,** 383.
[19] Mettler, F. A. (1945), *J. Neuropath. exp. Neurol.,* **4,** 99.
[20] Meyers, Russell (1942), *Res. Publ. Ass. neuro. ment. Dis.,* **21,** 602.
[21] Meyers, Russell (1951), *Acta Psychiat. Neurol. Supp.,* **67,** 1.
[22] Oppenheimer, D. R. (1967), *J. Neurol. Neurosurg. Psychiat.,* **30,** 134.
[23] Rushworth, G. (1960), *J. Neurol. Neurosurg. Psychiat.,* **23,** 99.
[24] Rushworth, G. (1961), *J. Neurol. Neurosurg. Psychiat.,* **24,** 132.
[25] Sourkes, T. L. and Poirier, L. J. (1963), *Second Symposium on Parkinson's Disease (Washington).*
[26] Sourkes, T. L. and Poirier, L. J. (1966), *J. Neurosurg.,* **24,** 194.
[27] Sourkes, T. L., Poirier, L. J. and Singh, P. (1969), *Third Symposium on Parkinson's Disease.* Edinburgh: Livingstone.
[28] Smith, Marion C. (1972), Personal communication.
[29] Spiegel, E. A. and Wycis, H. T. (1954), *Arch. Neurol. and Psychiat.,* **71,** 598.
[30] Tarlov, I. M. (1967), *Arch. Neurol.,* **16,** 536.
[31] Ward, A. A., McCulloch, W. S. and Magoun, H. W. (1948), *J. Neurophysiol,* **11,** 317.
[32] Whittier, J. and Mettler, F. A. (1949), *J. comp. Neurol.,* **90,** 281.

4. INVOLUNTARY MOVEMENTS

MELVIN D. YAHR

Involuntary movements, frequently encountered as a symptom of central nervous system dysfunction, consist of hyperkinetic or dyskinetic activity of a single segment or of multiple segments of the body which present in a variety of forms. Most are uncontrollable, inconstant, inappropriate movements which usually appear during wakefulness and regress during sleep. They vary in velocity, intensity, extent and duration ranging from rapid, slight flicks of a finger lasting for a fraction of a second, to slow gross bizarre writhing movements of the arm, shoulder and neck

4

lasting for several minutes. Some occur only when the affected musculature is at rest, others during contraction of the musculature in the performance of voluntary movements, and some are initiated by contactual, auditory, or proprioceptive stimuli. Many involuntary movements become super-imposed upon or replace normal voluntary motor activity with the result that functional activities become markedly impaired. The major types of involuntary movements have been termed athetosis, chorea, dystonia, ballism, myoclonus and tremor. Unfortunately, these terms have been used with dual meanings, on the one hand to describe a type of movement and on the other to denote particular disease entities. Since one or more of these abnormal movements may occur in a number of different disease entities, resulting from quite different etiological and pathological mechanisms, it is preferable to use these terms in a descriptive sense.

A wide variety of disease processes are manifested by the appearance of involuntary movements. Some are primary diseases of the brain while others represent secondary involvement of the nervous system as a result of a widespread systemic disturbances of essential metabolic processes or as a reaction to toxic factors. The etiology and pathogenesis of many of these disorders have not been defined and in some even the anatomical site of central nervous system involvement has not been precisely localized. However, it is generally agreed that most of the involuntary movements result from disease or at least dysfunction in the basal ganglia and their connections.

The term "basal ganglia" has defied precise definition. Originally applied to the nuclear masses situated at the base of the forebrain, caudate nucleus, putamen and pallidum, the term has been expanded to include a number of closely related nuclei in the diencephalon, such as the corpus Luysi, and in the mid brain, the substantia nigra and the red nuclei. These interconnected nuclear masses, commonly termed the "extrapyramidal system" probably function chiefly in relation to the control of movement and posture. Dysfunction within this system results in abnormal involuntary movements, often associated with alterations of muscle tone, i.e. the resistance to passive manipulations of the limbs. Apart from a small body of information, much of it controversial, the physiological mechanisms underlying these symptoms have not been clearly defined.

PHYSIOLOGICAL ANATOMY

Traditionally, clinical neurologists have separated motor disorders into those produced by lesions of the pyramidal system and those produced by the extrapyramidal system. As a practical means of localizing lesions in the nervous system, this approach has proved useful. However, in physiological terms and in the light of our current concepts of the integrative nature of the nervous system, it is an anachronism to separate the motor functions of the nervous system into these two categories. Recent physiological studies in animals have demonstrated that neurons of the pyramidal tract discharge in relation to active movements of the limbs. However, neurons located within elements of the "extrapyramidal system" and the cerebellum also discharge in relation to the same active movements.

Additionally, in most human diseases the classical symptoms attributable to interruption of the pyramidal tract, spasticity with hyperreflexia, probably require damage to extrapyramidal projections to the spinal cord as well. It is also quite apparent that symptoms of extrapyramidal dysfunction may not be evident when the pyramidal tract is damaged. Consequently, it has become increasingly evident that the pyramidal and extrapyramidal systems are intimately related and operate in close unison.

Our concepts of the anatomical localization and physiological mechanisms underlying many movement disorders have developed slowly and incompletely because most movement disorders do not result from discrete focal lesions of the nervous system, and it has proved difficult to replicate movement disorders of humans using animal models. Much of our knowledge concerning the structures involved has been derived from clinical-pathological correlations in human diseases. The accompanying diagram Fig. 1, indicates the structures and connections most

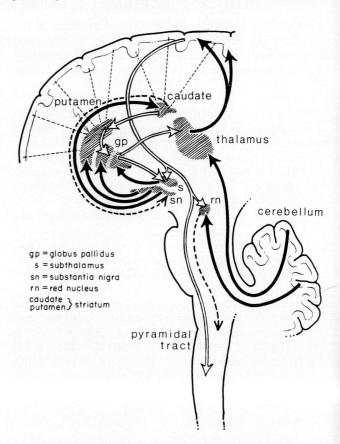

FIG. 1. Basal ganglia and its major connections. Schematic representations of the basal ganglia and its major connections. For illustrative purposes the cerebrum is shown in caronal section, the brain stem and cerebellum in sagittal view.

frequently implicated. It should be recognized that involuntary movements may arise from interruption of these pathways, but that inactivation of other parts of the nervous system may also produce these movement disorders.

CHEMICAL ANATOMY

In certain disease states such as parkinsonism and dystonia musculorum deformans, the degree of neuropathological involvement is disproportionately small in relation to the severity of the clinical disorder. In parkinsonism the neuropathological abnormalities are slight and in dystonia musculorum deformans morphological abnormalities have as not yet been demonstrated with certainty. However, a growing body of knowledge indicates that the abnormalities in such cases may be chemical rather than morphologic. A striking example of the importance of this concept can be found in parkinsonism. Recent studies have demonstrated that the striatum, particularly the caudate nucleus, contains abundant amounts of dopamine and acetylcholine, which are thought to be neurotransmitters having opposing actions. The former usually appears to be involved in neural inhibition while the latter, in many instances produces excitation. According to our current concepts, in the healthy nervous system their opposite actions are delicately balanced, resulting in smooth coordinated activity within the striatum. In parkinsonism striatal dopamine has been found to be markedly diminished although no morphological abnormality has been demonstrated consistently in the cellular elements of the striatum. Indeed, the major site of pathological alteration is in the substantia nigra. Experimentally produced lesions in the substantia nigra of animals result in a depletion of dopamine in the striatum similar to the depletion found in parkinsonian patients. This and other evidence currently available indicates that neurons of the substantia nigra produce dopamine but store and release it through nerve endings in the striatum. Owing to a deficiency of dopamine in the striatum of parkinsonian patients from neuropathological involvement of neurons in the substantia nigra, an imbalance of pharmaco-physiological mechanisms occurs in the striatum resulting in unrestrained cholinergic activity. Presumably the resulting abnormal striatal activity underlies the symptoms of parkinsonism. It is conceivable that analogous biochemical abnormalities may be found in other involuntary movement disorders and that their discovery will lead to a better understanding of and more rational therapy for these bizarre and distressing conditions.

CLINICAL SYNDROMES

Until the biochemical and pathological features are more fully worked out, a reasonable and practical approach to diagnosis can be achieved by defining carefully the characteristics of each of these movement disorders and relating these characteristics to the specific parts of the nervous system which are at present known to be involved. Accordingly, the following discussion will define the characteristics of the most common involuntary movement disorders, relate these disorders to the disease processes in which they most commonly occur, and comment upon the underlying pathological anatomy.

Tremor

One of the commonest of the abnormal involuntary movements, tremor consists of the rhythmic, repetitive movement of a segment of the body owing to alternating contractions of opposing muscle groups. Usually the tremor follows a stereotyped movement pattern, such as alternating flexion and extension of the digits, pronation and supination of the wrist, or flexion and extension of the foot. The pattern, frequency, and the factors provoking tremor are helpful in its classification into various types and, in many instances, in localizing the site of nervous system involvement. Tremor may be divided into three categories: (1) tremor-at-rest; (2) static (postural) tremor; and (3) kinetic (action or intention) tremor.

Tremor-at-rest

By definition, this type of tremor is evident when the involved segment of the body is placed at complete rest and is fully supported. It is most frequently associated with parkinsonism, in which it occurs as the initial manifestation or during the course of the disorder in a large proportion of patients. Characteristically, it is of moderate amplitude and with a frequency of 5–6 c./s., though these features are extremely variable. Although many parts of the body may be involved, it begins most often in the upper limbs, primarily in the distal segments. Alternate flexion and extension of the index fingers combined with abduction and adduction of the thumb give rise to the classical "pill rolling" movement which has become the hallmark of parkinsonism. Other conditions frequently associated with tremor-at-rest are anxiety reactions resulting from psychiatric disorders, the tremor affecting the face, tongue and hands resulting from general paresis, and some forms of familial tremor. The anatomical and physiological substrate of tremor-at-rest have not been defined with certainty. In Parkinson's disease the substantia nigra invariably undergoes degeneration, but not all such patients develop tremor and it remains a controversial issue whether the pathological changes are entirely limited to this structure. A few reports have implicated the pallidum neuropathologically. Certain thalamic nuclei, particularly the nucleus lateralis posterior have been implicated physiologically, since spike discharges synchronous with the rhythmicity of limb tremors have been recorded from this region. Ablation in this area abolish both the tremor and the spike discharges, a finding that has been taken as evidence that alteration of intrinsic neuronal rhythms of thalamic neurons underlies parkinsonian tremor. However, it is equally plausible that such electric abnormalities in thalamus may be secondary discharges, resulting from interruption of activity reaching it from other elements of the nervous system, particularly the basal ganglia. Experimentally, tremor-at-rest simulating that of parkinsonian tremor has been produced in monkey by lesions placed in the ventro-medial tegmental area of the mesencephalon at the level of the substantia nigra and red nuclei. Histological analysis of the lesions in these preparations suggests that in order to produce tremor it is necessary to destroy neurons in the pars compacta of the substantia nigra and interrupt pathways to the striatum, pallidum and thalamus as well as rubrospinal and tegmento-spinal tracts.

Static (Postural) Tremor

A form of tremor which is activated by the simultaneous co-contraction of antagonistic muscles when attempting to sustain a posture, such as extending the arm, supporting the leg, or maintaining the head upright. Static tremor is associated with a variety of neurological disorders, and its characteristics are helpful in defining the anatomical site of involvement and thereby, the type of disease process. In general, proximal static tremors, i.e., those generated at the shoulder, pelvic girdle, or neck, are produced by lesions of the cerebellum or its brainstem connections. In contrast, distal static tremors, i.e., those occurring at the wrist or finger joints, result from diseases of the basal ganglia or midbrain. In addition, distal static tremors of small amplitude and rapid frequency, often at 10/sec., commonly occur in toxic disorders such as alcoholism, and with endocrinological dysfunction such as hyperthyroidism. An inherited form of tremor with varying rates of genetic penetration, termed familial or benign essential tremor, though having characteristics in common with parkinsonian tremor is a prime example of postural tremor. It commonly affects the head and neck and the distal segments of the upper limbs. Although its rate and amplitude are similar to those of parkinsonism, essential tremor is more apt to occur when the limbs are held in an extended position than when they are supported and at complete rest. Additionally, this tremor occurs in the absence of the muscular rigidity, postural abnormalities and akinesia which so frequently accompany parkinsonism. Commonly essential tremor affects the neck, producing a characteristic nodding or to and fro motion of the head. Both static tremor and tremor-at-rest occurs in some parkinsonian patients. In such instances, the rest tremor disappears temporarily when the patient raises the arm outward, only to reappear when the limbs are held in a static posture. In sharp contrast, patients with diseases of cerebellum show no tremor-at-rest, but develop a rhythmical proximal tremor when the limbs are held in an extended outward position. Postural tremor in such instances is of a slower frequency, oscillating and pendulous in nature. It results from the marked loss of muscle tone with inability to fix a segment into position or prevent its displacement which is characteristic of involvement of the cerebellum.

Kinetic Tremor

Also termed "action tremor" and "intention tremor" as it is provoked by and occurs during active voluntary movement. It may be limited to proximal or distal protions of the limbs. A distinction which is helpful in identifying the site of nervous system involvement. Characteristically, intention tremor is most prominent as the termination of a goal-directed motor activity is being completed at which time rhythmic gross oscillations of moderate frequency and amplitude develop. As in static tremor, those generated at proximal joints such as shoulder and pelvis indicate disease involving the cerebellum and/or its pathways. It occurs in a number of disease entities, particularly demyelinating diseases, and the spinocerebellar degenerations, as well as toxic, degenerative, vascular and neoplastic involvement of the cerebellum. Commonly it is associated with static tremor and with other signs of cerebellar disease, including hypotonia, ataxia of gait and disturbances of the rate and rhythm of voluntary movements such as dysdiadockokinesis and dysrhythmokokinesis. Kinetic tremor generated chiefly at distal segments of the limbs usually occurs in diseases of the basal ganglia, such as parkinsonism and hepato-lenticular degeneration.

It should be emphasized that these generalities have many exceptions, in that a given patient with one or another of these disease processes may show a combination of proximal and distal tremors and that many diseases have various admixtures of these various tremor types.

Athetosis (Mobile Spasms)

The term athetosis was originally introduced to describe bizarre, writhing movements of the fingers and toes which appeared to be in continuous motion and incapable of maintaining a fixed posture. However, it has subsequently become clear that segments of the body other than the digits may be involved and that such movements occur only when active movements are initiated. Consequently the term athetosis has come to indicate an instability of posture characterized by irregular, writhing, sinuous movements which may be slow, especially when associated with spasticity, or more rapid in rate when such increase in tone is absent. Although athetotic movements appear to be continuous, they actually are not, since they result from an intermittent build-up of muscle tension in antagonistic muscle groups. The movements are superimposed on an abnormal posture, produced when both extensor and flexor muscles are activated so that alternating powerfully sustained contractions occur in one or the other. For reasons not fully understood the hand is invariably involved with the typical posture being that of hyperextension of the fingers with flexion of the wrist and pronation of the hand. Jaw, lips, tongue and foot are other sites in which athetotic movements occur. Athetoid movements have many similarities to choreiform movements though they are in the main slower and more sustained. They are closely allied to dystonic movements though in the latter more proximal muscles are involved and the discontinuous nature of the movement is more readily apparent.

The anatomic substrate and pathophysiology of this movement disorder is at present ill-defined. Experimental studies designed to reproduce athetosis have been singularly unrewarding. The basis of our present concepts rest on a limited number of correlated clinical and pathological reports. In most instances disruption of the putamen or pallidum has been found in individuals who have suffered from athetotic movements. The cause of such lesions is speculative but appear to be a result of pre- or perinatal factors either developmental or traumatic in nature. Some appear to have been acquired during adult life due to metabolic disturbances or vascular lesions which involve these areas. Athetosis occurring during childhood most often involves both sides of the body (double athetosis) and is associated with characteristic morphological changes in the putamen. This structure grossly gives the appearance of a marbleized scar produced by an excessive amount of myelinated nerve fibers irregularly arranged against a background of cell loss and gliosis. In adult life, athetosis involves one or the other side of the body (hemiathetosis) and occurs during or following secondary involvement of the cortico-spinal pathway at the level of the internal capsule. Such involvement is primarily caused by vascular lesions which extend to structures such as the pallidum and putamen. The frequent occurrence of cortico-spinal damage in instances of athetosis has led some investigation to consider this disorder as resulting from a combination of pathophysiological factors.

Chorea

Characteristically choreic movements are brief, forceful, jerky and occur in abrupt explosive non-stereotyped fashion. Though seemingly purposeful and coordinated their random irregular, irrelevant nature is readily apparent on closer inspection. Their presence at rest prevents the involved segment from being kept immobile for more than a fraction of a second before uncontrollable movement recurs. Similarly volitional movements are interrupted or distorted so that they cannot be performed or appear awkward in nature. Choreic movements may be confined to limited segments of the body but more often are generalized. In its mildest form chorea appears as restless fidgeting movements or as exaggerated gestures of normal associated movements. In more severe instances frequent rapid jerking movements of the distal members of the limbs, the trunk, neck, face and tongue are evident. Grimacing of the face, darting movements of the tongue, dancing movements of the feet with gesturing of the upper limbs are all frequently encountered. These many features give the overall appearance of an excess of motor activity and an exaggerated character to all movements. Choreic movements have been ascribed to lesions occurring in many different parts of the brain and as a result of variable pathogenetic processes. It is the exception rather than the rule to find single discrete lesions in the brains of those who have manifested this type of dyskinesia. In fact the multiplicity of areas involved have suggested that a combination of lesions may be operative. One of the most frequently involved structures, however, is the striatum particularly the caudate nucleus. Cellular loss particularly of small nerve cells is found in most instances. Their loss is particularly striking in Huntington's chorea, a genetically determined progressive disorder in which various admixtures of chorea and dementia occur. In Syndenham's chorea, a self-limited form of chorea thought to be infectious in origin, the pathology is more obscure but areas of necrosis in relation to vasculitis are frequently found in the striatum. It must, however, be appreciated that in both these conditions other regions of the brain particularly the cerebral cortex and thalamic areas are also involved and may well play a role in the production of the choreic movements. Attempts to reproduce chorea in experimental animals by destruction of the caudate nucleus has led to controversial reports. Some investigators have claimed that choreic movements can be produced by regional destruction of the caudate particularly in its anteroventral portion. Implied is that this area is a major "inhibitory center" which affects the pallidum. Others have indicated, however, that such lesions

merely interrupt circuits originating in cerebral cortex and destined for striatum and other basal ganglia structures.

Recently interest has centered on the pharmacological projections of the striatum in view of the induction of choreiform movements by a number of drugs capable of altering its monoamine content. As previously indicated a balance between the neurotransmitters dopamine and acetylcholine is important for normal physiological activity of the striatum. In contrast to parkinsonism where the balance favors acetylcholine, it is postulated that in chorea it is shifted to dopamine. Support for this concept derives from the observation that in patients with parkinsonism treated with levodopa, the immediate precursor of dopamine, choreiform movements may develop. The administration, however, of levodopa to normal individuals has not resulted in such movements, which suggests that some substrate of damaged neurons within the basal ganglia complex is a necessity for their induction. It is conceivable that in chorea as well as in parkinsonism that alteration in the dopaminergic receptor sites have undergone changes which increase their sensitivity to dopamine. In both conditions an induced state of denervation hypersensitivity of striatal neurons may exist. In chorea it results from striatal cells in various stages of degeneration while in parkinsonism loss of presynaptic nerve terminals induces alterations in post synaptic receptor sites. The resultant pharmocological reactivity is similar in each instance.

Dystonic or Torsion Movement

Slow turning or twisting movements of the head, neck, trunk or proximal segments of the limbs are included in this category of involuntary movements. Produced by powerful contractions of the musculature, the build up of muscle tone occurs gradually, reaching a crescendo in which it is sustained for a variable period of time. The involved segment becomes fixed in an abnormal posture which gradually relaxes until a new cycle of mobile activity recurs. The movements are readily induced by attempts at voluntary movement or by contactual stimulae. Posture abnormalities such as a retraction of the head (retrocollis) or its deviation to the side (torticollis) as well as rotation of the pelvis (tortipelvis) are frequently seen. The abnormal movements and postures which develop can neither be voluntarily inhibited, nor modified nor terminated and they seriously impair functional activities. The pathophysiological mechanism and underlying pathology of dystonic movements are at present unknown. The movements most characteristically occur in dystonia musculorum deformans, a genetically determined disorder. To date no consistent abnormalities have been found at autopsy in this disorder. The induction of dystonic symptoms by various chemotherapeutic agents such as phenothiazenes and levodopa have raised the possibility that disturbances in catechol amine metabolism in the nervous system may be the underlying cause.

Ballism

One of the more violent forms of dyskinesia is ballism which consists of uncontrollable flinging movements of the limbs. The movements are produced by forceful muscular contractions of the large proximal muscles of the limbs. A complex random pattern of flexion, extension and rotation of shoulder or hip joint results, which contorts and tosses the limb in various directions. The patterns of movements change continuously and their speed of execution and purposeless nature have many characteristics in common with chorea. However, the severity and sustained nature of these movements far outweighs any which are encountered in the latter disorder. Most frequently ballism is localized to a single limb or side of the body and its bilateral occurrence is only rarely encountered. The upper limbs are more often and severely involved than the lower. Ballism is one of the few involuntary movements for which a somatotopic localization has been established. In the monkey destruction of the subthalmic nucleus (corpus Luysii) results in ballistic movements involving the contralateral limbs. In man a variety of lesions involving this nucleus or its surrounding neural pathways produce these movements. Vascular lesions, both thrombotic and hemorrhagic, tumor infiltrations, infectious processes and the effects of trauma have all been found at autopsy.

The neural mechanism by which ballism occurs has often been pointed to as a prime example of a release phenomena in the nervous system. In this instance the destruction of the subthalamic nucleus or its adjacent connecting fiber pathways removes an important subcortical influence on the corticospinal pathway. Presumably the loss of this input into the major motor pathway removes one of the essential modulating or controlling ingredients for orderly motor behavior.

Myoclonic Movements

The sudden brief contraction of a functionally synergistic group of muscles of sufficient degree to cause movement of a segment of the body are included in this category. The contractions may be isolated, diffuse and infrequent or rhythmic and confined to a segment of the body. The latter is definable as a particular neurological entity involving primarily the palate (palatal myoclonus). In this disorder rhythmic contractions of the soft palate and pharyngeal muscles occur in rapid uncontrollable fashion as a result of lesions involving inferior olivary nucleus and olivicerebellar tracts. Isolated myoclonic phenomena however occur in a wide variety of neurological disorders. They are not infrequent in the epilepsies, and disorders with widespread degenerative lesions in the nervous system such as subacute sclerosing panencephalitis and cortico-striatal-spinal degeneration. In these disorders they may be triggered by various stimulae such as auditory or contactual.

CONCLUSION

It should be readily evident from the foregoing there is at the present time inadequate information regarding the neural mechanisms underlying the various involuntary movements. Not only is our knowledge regarding the anatomical sites essential for their production imperfect, but even less is known about their pathological physiology. Though as yet no single theoretical concept has been forthcoming which satisfactorily explains all of these movements, it is apparent that they result from interruption or loss of critical neuronal circuits within the basal ganglia complex. Increasing evidence is accumulating that this region of the brain has a distinctive biochemical topography and pharmacological reactivity. Further elucidation of these aspects will hopefully bring us to a better understanding and treatment of these bizarre motor phenomena.

FURTHER READING

Vinken, P. J. and Bruyn, G. W. (1968), "Diseases of the Basal Ganglia," *Handbook of Clinical Neurology*, Vol. 6. Amsterdam: North-Holland Publishing Company.
Denny Brown, D. (1962), *The Basal Ganglia and their Relation to Disorders of Movement*. Oxford Neurological Monographs.
Yahr, M. D. and Purpura, D. P. (Eds.) (1967), *Neurophysiological Basis of Normal and Abnormal Motor Activities*. New York: Raven Press.

SECTION IV

EPILEPSY

1. BASIC MECHANISMS OF THE EPILEPSIES

ARTHUR A. WARD, JR.

INTRODUCTION

The word epilepsy is derived from the Greek word "epilepsia" or seizure. As the term has evolved, epileptic seizures are characterized as being spontaneous, episodic, recurrent, and paroxysmal: that is—"a fit of disease". Such a definition of the general clinical phenomenon thus excludes those convulsive seizures induced by intense electrical stimulation of the brain or by convulsant drugs, as well as those which occur during toxic states such as uremia. Some of these phenomena may provide useful models for studying certain components of seizure mechanisms, but since they do not occur in self-perpetuating, recurrent episodes, they are not, strictly speaking, considered to be clinical epilepsy.

As Hughlings Jackson first proposed a century ago, an epileptic seizure is a state produced by an abnormal excessive neuronal discharge within the central nervous system. The advent of electroencephalography, beginning with the pioneer work of Hans Berger some 40 years ago, marked the beginning of the modern era of research in the epilepsies and amply confirmed the definition of epilepsy as a sudden paroxysmal, excessive neuronal discharge. Since that time, the explosion of knowledge in the neurosciences has made possible a better understanding of the basic mechanisms of the epilepsies and, in turn, the challenge and opportunity provided by the clinical problem has added much to our knowledge in the brain sciences. Much of this progress is summarized in a recent monograph.[1]

The elemental problem in epilepsy deals with the "highly explosive" discharges, as Jackson called them, which characterize the epileptogenic focus. How does the behavior of this cluster of neurons at the epileptogenic focus differ from normal neuronal activity? Furthermore, if seizures arise in a geographically restricted mass of neurons, what are the mechanisms of propagation of the seizure discharge to the rest of the brain? Answers to these questions would clearly provide an understanding of the major mechanisms underlying epilepsy of focal onset in the cortex. Such insight is necessary before more complex manifestations of human epilepsy can be understood, since we do not know, at the present time, that all human epilepsy arises in a restricted epileptogenic focus located somewhere in the brain.

The necessary answers require that we define the mechanisms operating at the focus when clinical seizures are not evident (interictal activity); as well as those mechanisms responsible for the propagating seizure (ictal activity). There is evidence to indicate that interictal and ictal phenomena are not simply different degrees of the same phenomenon but probably involve different underlying mechanisms. Thus, to use a crude analogy, the focus is the campfire continuously burning in the forest; at relatively infrequent intervals, the fire spreads to set the forest afire and a clinically evident seizure occurs.

Thus, the essential feature is the epileptogenic focus since, in its absence, a propagating seizure does not arise. The primary concern is then to try and determine the biological characteristics of the focus and identify the mechanisms generating the interictal hyperactivity in this neuronal aggregate. The mechanisms involved in the spread or propagation of the seizure discharge will then be discussed; finally, these concepts will be related to some of the clinical phenomena of epilepsy.

INTERICTAL ACTIVITY—THE FOCUS

It is generally agreed that the hallmark of the epileptic process is the epileptic "spike" as recorded from either the exposed brain or scalp with the electroencephalograph. Such EEG potentials appear to be almost entirely the consequence of postsynaptic activity set up in the graded response membrane of vertically oriented neurons. There is negligible contribution to such potentials from action potentials of either the neuron soma or axons, and glial cells probably do not make a significant contribution to such potentials under normal conditions. Such EEG spike activity is utilized to localize the cortical focus and this operational definition of the epileptogenic focus has obviously been clinically useful. However, it should also be recognized that any aggregate of neurons will respond to a relatively synchronous synaptic input with an EEG "spike" and this can introduce certain ambiguities. It is well known that the experimental application of strychnine to a small area of cortex will evoke spontaneous spikes which have certain superficial similarities to the epileptic spike. In this instance, the point of origin of the strychnine spike is known with certainty. Yet, from the examination of the EEG recorded from distant points of the cortex of the same or opposite hemisphere of the animal, it may be impossible to distinguish the spikes recorded at the strychnine focus from those recorded from distant cortex to which the spikes are monosynaptically propagated over well known projections. Thus additional resolution is desirable.

Epileptic Neuron

Such additional resolution might well be provided by examining the behavior of individual neurons in the epileptogenic focus. This can be undertaken in monkeys exhibiting spontaneous clinical seizures of focal onset some months or years after the intracortical injection of alumina. Utilizing fine microelectrodes, whose tips are 5 microns or less in diameter, it is possible to record the activity of single cortical neurons in undrugged, awake, epileptic monkeys.

high frequency firing in bursts have been recorded which are indistinguishable from those recorded in the awake monkey. When the cortical focus is well localized, the bursts are stereotyped and have the unusual properties of timing characterized by a long first-interval between the first action potential and the subsequent action potentials in the burst.

Since neurons in the brain do not normally fire in high frequency bursts, it might be anticipated that this kind of signal might have unusual effects on the next neuron in the

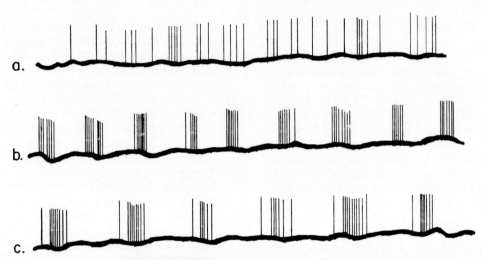

FIG. 1. Diagrammatic representation of firing patterns of cortical neurons.
a. Normal firing patterns.
b. Varieties of burst firing patterns characteristic of neurons in epileptogenic focus.
c. Stereotyped firing patterns observed only in the focus characterized by a long first-interval between the first and subsequent spikes in each burst.

In contrast to the random but well-ordered, low-frequency firing patterns of normal cells (Fig. 1a), a variety of patterns of neuronal hyperactivity may be observed at the epileptic focus (Fig. 1b and c). In unanesthetized cortex, the most frequently encountered interictal pattern of unit discharge is regular, recurrent, bursts of action potentials. The frequency of firing within each burst is high and may range from 200 to 900/sec. The burst starts at high frequency and there is no decrement in frequency during the burst. There are few if any spikes between bursts; the bursts usually repeat 5–15 times/sec. The bursts tend to be stereotyped and, particularly in the center of the focus, they may have special properties of timing characterized by a long first-interval between the first spike of the burst and the rest of the burst. In addition, the subsequent spikes in the burst (when recorded with an extracellular microelectrode at some distance) may exhibit a fairly characteristic "notching" of the waveform of the action potential. This and other data might be interpreted as evidence for an abnormal site of spike generation in the epileptic or "pacemaker" neuron.

These findings in experimental animals have also been confirmed in man where patterns of firing of single neurons in the epileptogenic focus have been examined during the course of operations for epilepsy. Patterns of

chain receiving this input. In normal spinal motoneurons, asynchronous firing of 2 per cent of the synapses ending on that motoneuron can either elicit slow, rhythmic firing from a previously silent cell or increase a pre-existing firing rate. Furthermore, it is estimated that 8 per cent of a motoneuron's inputs, firing at a nominal 20/sec. each, will drive the cell to fairly high firing rates. Epileptic neurons, on the other hand, instead of firing at 20/sec. often fire at rates of 200–900/sec. during their bursts. Assuming rates of only 200/sec. within an epileptic burst, these need to project to only 80 input boutons on another cell to cause high-frequency firing in that post-synaptic cell. Thus less than 0·2 per cent of the 60,000 synapses of a cortical neuron need to be bursting to convert this cell into another bursting cell. It is thus clear that the epileptic burst is a very efficient "packaging" compared to the firing patterns of normal cortical neurons.

A group of such primary epileptic bursting neurons in the center of an epileptic focus might be expected to have an appreciable density of synaptic connections to normal neurons in the surrounding cortex allowing recruitment of normal neurons to widen the extent of the "focus". Background synaptic activity should bias such recruitment. On this basis, the size of the epileptic focus should expand and shrink depending on background synaptic activity and upon synchronizing factors. Thus, even at the cellular level, it may be difficult to distinguish between the "primary" or pacemaker epileptic neurons and the "follower" normal neurons which receive this optimal bursting input.

Morphologically, the chronic epileptogenic focus in both monkey and man is characterized by a depopulation of neurons in which the remaining small neurons are embedded in a striking astrocytic gliosis. These epileptic neurons are characterized, in the Golgi stain, by a striking loss of dendritic spines and other changes in their dendritic morphology. Moving radially away from the primary electrographic focus, all of the dendritic changes appear less marked and gradually blend into relatively normal cortex. This appears to correlate well with the electrophysiological data which also shows a transition from maximal unit hyperactivity to apparently normal activity a few millimeters away from a well localized focus.

The morphological evidence suggesting that the input to the epileptic neuron is altered is consistent with physiological observations indicating that it is difficult to evoke the activity of epileptic neurons by synaptic input. Thus one might propose that epileptic neurons are partially denervated. It is unlikely that all synaptic input is lost since epileptic seizures can be modified by events that are presumably synaptically mediated. The thesis that a reduction in synaptic input can result in autonomous hyperactivity is supported by other lines of data. De-afferentation of neurons in the spinal trigeminal complex of animals by trigeminal rhizotomy is followed, after some weeks, by dramatic neuronal hyperactivity. It has been proposed that this might account for the high incidence of parethesiae following trigeminal rhizotomy in man. In the spinal cord, the deafferentation induced by multiple level rhizotomy may also induce spontaneous hyperactivity of the denervated second order spinal neurons. This may be the basis for some of the sensory and motor phenomena seen in causalgia and spinal cord lesions.

Thus, in epilepsy, a modification of input to an ensemble of neurons appears to occur as the result of a certain degree of cortical scarring which follows injury whether this injury is the result of trauma, vascular occlusion, brain tumor or birth injury. Why such a modification of input or other features of the local pathology should result in the hyperactivity which characterizes the epileptogenic focus is poorly understood. There is some evidence that this pacemaker activity may be the consequence of generator potentials at the denervated subsynaptic sites in dendrites and, possibly, by mechanical deformation of the dendritic tree. In normal neurons, it is thought that synaptic activity locally depolarizes post-synaptic membrane; this relatively slow synaptic potential reduces soma membrane potential to a level where the low threshold membrane of the axon hillock is activated and an action potential is triggered. In the epileptic neuron, it may be that the denervated subsynaptic sites become "leaky" and produce generator potentials much as in denervated muscle. Mechanical deformation can also induce local depolarization in some circumstances. These depolarizing potentials might trigger repetitive firing

arising in the initial segment or proximal axon. Another possibility is that action potentials may be generated at abnormal sites elsewhere in the membrane of epileptic neurons and that such sites may be located in the dendrites. The remaining synaptic inputs to such neurons (such as those from the non-specific thalamic system) may bias or serve to actually trigger the burst discharges. Clearly the factors involved in the generation of such burst activity are not simple ones and multiple mechanisms are probably involved.

The dendritic abnormalities appear to include membrane alterations such that K^+ ion leakage occurs. If the interstitial potassium concentration exceeds a certain threshold, it may trigger a regenerative all-or-none process. This factor might be potentiated by abnormalities of the extracellular space secondary to the scarring at the focus or to changes in the metabolic activity in the astrocytes which are thought to play a role in maintaining extracellular K^+ ionic concentrations.

In addition there are changes in excitability of the axonal terminals of cells engaged in repetitive activity. It is known that, subsequent to conditioning by a high frequency volley, axons respond to a single spike with brief trains of repetitive action potentials. It is thought that the tetanic conditioning volley induces hyperpolarization of the terminal branches of the axon possibly as a consequence of activation of an electrogenic sodium pump. This post-tetanic hyperpolarization not only accounts for post-tetanic repetitive firing in axons but also is invoked as the mechanism for the post-tetanic potentiation (PTP) of muscle response and the PTP of the monosynaptic reflex in the spinal cord. Furthermore, post-tetanic hyperpolarization is augmented by increases in extracellular potassium and such increases in K^+ efflux have been demonstrated in the epileptic focus. It is of interest that one of the best documented physiological actions of the well known anticonvulsant drug diphenylhydantoin is to suppress both post-tetanic repetive firing and PTP in the cord.

It has been recently shown that a conditioning orthodromic volley may enhance the excitability of axonal terminations to the point that a discharge in the postsynaptic neuron will evoke an antidromically conducted discharge in the pre-synaptic fiber. This neuron-presynaptic coupling might be grossly augmented in the epileptic focus. This or the mechanisms mentioned above might provide models for the firing patterns observed in epileptic foci including the unusual properties of timing of spikes within the burst such as the long first-interval phenomenon.

Although no detailed insight is yet available regarding these factors, it is apparent that these epileptic neurons in the focus are engaged in continuous abnormal activity characterized by intermittent bursts and these bursts of action potentials are conducted down their axons to the next synaptic relay. This abnormal activity (which has been continuously recorded during interictal periods for many hours) only at relatively rare intervals develops into a propagating seizure with clinical concomitants. Yet these abnormal signals may well disrupt adjacent normal function. This accounts for the paradoxical improvement of motor function that can follow excision of an epileptogenic focus in the motor cortex as Penfield first pointed out. The improvement is paradoxical because structural lesions of motor cortex commonly result in a motor deficit; but removal of a discharging focus in the same cortical area may permit normal functioning of adjacent neural nets with an improvement in function. As Lennox graphically pointed out, when normal circuits are subjected to such abnormal input, "the harmony of the orchestra becomes a single note".

The role of this relatively continuous interictal activity in disrupting normal ongoing activity may be clinically identified when a very specific function like finger dexterity is involved; it may be very difficult for more complex functions of the brain. However, there are hints from isolated clinical observations that this process is of greater clinical importance than generally realized. As an example, temporal lobe seizures in a child may be effectively controlled by anticonvulsant medication with no improvement in coexisting behavioral problems and little change in the interictal EEG abnormalities. A further increase in medication then results in marked behavioral and EEG improvement as well. Thus interictal epileptic activity may not be functionally benign. There are even some hints in experimental animals that there may be structural consequences of this continuous hyperactivity in which neurons die, presumably as a consequence of excessive metabolic demands. The experimental evidence is now becoming quite clear that some neurons in the vicinity of the focus may die when clinical seizures are occurring. Thus the goals of effective therapy may have to be more rigorously defined.

ICTAL ACTIVITY—PROPAGATION OF THE SEIZURE

At relatively infrequent intervals, the interictal activity at the focus becomes augmented and builds up into a seizure. The mechanisms involved in the precipitation of interictal activity into a propagating seizure are largely unknown. It is known that, in both the primate model as well as in man, seizures may be precipitated by stress. In addition, metabolic factors presumably play a role since seizures may be precipitated in epileptic patients by mild water intoxication (the pitressin test) and by unknown changes associated with menstrual periods in the female. Seizures may occur following alcohol ingestion and may preferentially occur at certain hours of the day or night. Those seizures which appear to be precipitated by certain phases of sleep may be a consequence of the increase in cortical excitability associated with sleep.

Thus, at relatively infrequent intervals, the interictal activity at the focus becomes augmented and builds up into a seizure. In both the primate model as well as man, recording of single neuron activity reveals that the onset of a spontaneous seizure is indicated by an increase in the frequency of interictal burst activity which progresses until the cell is firing tonically at high rates up to 1,000/sec.

Once a seizure is initiated at an epileptogenic focus, it appears to spread in two ways. The first of these is a rather rapid and almost explosive spread of the seizure discharge to more distant parts of the brain occurring over known cortical projections. The second is a slow, local spread.

Local Spread

The slow, creeping invasion of adjacent cortex is well documented clinically in Jacksonian epilepsy. As Hughlings Jackson pointed out so well a century ago, this spread of the seizure over a relatively few centimeters of cortex requires a period of several minutes and the rate of spread is of the order of magnitude of 5 mm./min. There are many similarities between this observation and a phenomenon known as spreading depression. The latter propagates at 2–3 mm./min. across the cortex and is associated with marked depolarization of neuronal membranes and release of K^+ into the extracellular space. It has thus been proposed that the gross hyperactivity of epileptic neurons results in the release of abnormal amounts of potassium which now either directly depolarizes the next neuron into transient hyperactivity or which facilitates synaptic mechanisms which are known to operate in the more usual propagation of intracortical discharges.

At some stage, one would assume that local synaptic circuits within the cortical feltwork would be involved in spread. Since little is known regarding the details of the local circuitry in the cerebral cortex, one can only speculate regarding the interactions between excitatory and inhibitory synaptic actions involved. Certainly the high frequency signals generated by the epileptic neurons must be extraordinarily effective in "capturing" the activity of normal neurons and driving them into abnormal patterns of activity.

Generalized Propagation

The neurons engaged in the high frequency firing at the focus during the onset of a seizure propagate these signals widely through the brain over their axonal projections. There appear to be preferential pathways for spread to subcortical structures including basal ganglia, thalamus and midbrain reticular formation. Neurons located in such distant loci respond to this high frequency synaptic input with excessive membrane depolarization and a tonic discharge of action potentials. These signals, in turn, will be propagated over axonal projections to activate still other neuronal circuits. Thus the seizure process rapidly becomes generalized. The form and clinical expression of such generalization will be determined by the neuronal circuits involved.

Intracellular recording in normal cortical neurons synaptically driven into seizure activity demonstrates that the synaptically induced tonic-clonic sequence is followed by an enduring hyperpolarization which characterizes the postical electrical silence. The mechanisms involved in this active inhibition of neuronal discharge are poorly understood though it has been suggested that this may be the result of activation of inhibitory circuits in mesial thalamus or midbrain reticular formation. This may account for the observation that the seizure may terminate abruptly in the entire brain at the same moment.

Chemical Changes

Very shortly after the onset of a propagating seizure, a marked increase in blood flow occurs which appears to be localized to the portion of cortex involved in the seizure and extends to other areas only when the convulsion becomes generalized. There is no evidence that cerebral ischemia initiates the convulsion and the increased flow is a consequence of vasodilatation, probably secondary to increased metabolic demand and an increase in tissue CO_2. During the seizure there is a rapid depletion of substrate and high energy reserves in the brain. Energy utilization during convulsions exceeds energy replacement and energy reserves in cerebral tissue are markedly reduced despite increased glucose uptake and metabolism to lactic acid and beyond. As might be anticipated, following the seizure there is a reactive hyperemia. However, the once popular concept that metabolic deprivation is the mechanism of postconvulsive depression is not supported by current data.

The search for a "biochemical lesion" as the primary mechanism underlying the properties at the epileptogenic focus or in initiating seizures has not yet been successful. It is doubtful that changes in energy metabolism are fundamental to the mechanism of seizure induction. However, since there are many clues from the physiological and morphological data indicating that membrane abnormalities may be related to the epileptic properties of neurons at the focus, alterations of membrane properties of either a conformational or neurochemical type might be anticipated. The differential distribution of monovalent cations across neuronal membrane is maintained by an active transport system which is apparently based on the Mg-dependent, Na-K-ATPase system. Cellular respiratory metabolism is heavily involved in supporting this system since 30–50 per cent of cellular energy generation is controlled by the rate of cation transport. Since information is now being generated indicating defects in processes involved in membrane stability of neurons in the epileptic focus, additional insight may be forthcoming in the future.

Genetic Mechanisms

Studies in comparative genetics have identified a rather large number of hereditary diseases of mammals of which counterparts are also found in man and epilepsy is one of these. The best studied has been the case of audiogenic seizures in mice. In man, it appears that the major gene in the form of epilepsy associated with the centrencephalic EEG trait is an irregular, autosomal, dominant gene. Thus approximately 37 per cent of the siblings of probands with spike-wave epilepsy have the spike-wave EEG trait, compared with 5 per cent of comparable controls. A lower incidence of EEG abnormalities has been shown in the siblings of probands with febrile convulsions. If the spike-wave EEG trait is due to an autosomal dominant gene, it would be carried by approximately 4 per cent of a randomly mating population. Whether or not the trait can be demonstrated depends in great part on the age of the individual (5–15 years) and thus the EEG trait may not be demonstrable in more

than 1 per cent of the general population. Of greater interest to this discussion is the preliminary information obtained from studying families of patients who have been operated upon for focal epilepsy. Although the numbers are small, Metrakos reports that the prevalence of EEG abnormalities among the siblings, parents and offspring of epileptic probands is significantly higher than in a control group.

The mechanisms by which genic DNA can influence the epileptic process are unknown. It has been suggested that the end product of the gene is formation of an abnormal protein and that the seizure is a far removed neurophysiological consequence. Genetically determined alterations in the conformational properties of neuronal membrane might, in rather subtle ways, modify excitability in neuronal nets so that propagation of the seizure discharge occurs more easily. Even events at the focus may be dependent upon genetically determined variations in the extent of astrocytic scar formation as Pollen has suggested.

CLINICAL EXPRESSIONS OF SEIZURES

Aura

A local seizure at the focus which does not develop to the point where propagation occurs may, by activation of local neurons, produce a sensation or feeling which the patient can describe. This has been called an aura. The aura is not strictly a warning, but rather is the first event in a seizure. Its characteristics are determined by the function of the cells at the focus and thus it provides very specific information regarding the localization or origin of the epileptic discharge.

Partial Seizures

As the seizure begins to propagate, the activation of specific neuronal circuits will evoke specific clinical functional manifestations. Thus seizures with local motor phenomena arise in the sensorimotor cortex. Similarly, sensory phenomena are localized primarily to the paracentral cortex, visual sensations to occipital cortex, and the like. Seizure discharges arising in the insular cortex may evoke epigastric sensations and the subsequent propagation to the limbic circuits of the temporal lobe can evoke hallucinations which may resemble dreams and often progress into automatisms in which the patient engages in automatic motor activity of a variety of kinds. Such a seizure pattern has been called psychomotor epilepsy in the past. The patterns and detailed evidence for localization they provide have been well described by Penfield.[3]

It should be obvious that when the seizure discharge engages a neuronal circuit, it evokes a parody of normal, orchestrated function of that neuronal circuit. The phenomena are much the same as those induced by local electrical stimulation of the same circuit. Thus epileptic activation of the visual cortex evokes flashes of light and even in parastriate cortex only complex shapes. Such activation never reproduces the visual pattern evoked by normal visual input. Similarly, such activation of speech cortex does not evoke speech but rather blocking of speech or at most a noise. In fact, one can almost say that such activation (either by the epileptic discharge or by the stimulating current) blocks the normal integrative function of these particular circuits and this blocking will be most marked when the function involved is the most complex.

Many areas of cortex have projections to medial thalamus and upper brain stem reticular formation. It is well known that these circuits are intimately involved in the maintenance of consciousness. Thus the propagation of the seizure discharge not infrequently results in loss of consciousness and this propagation may be so rapid that the patient loses awareness early in the seizure and is unable to recall any events of the ictus. This is particularly true of much of frontal lobe cortex.

Generalized Seizures

Seizures arising in a focus may, when appropriate axonal projections are involved, propagate widely through much of the brain and will be clinically manifested by a major convulsive seizure. Such a terminal generalized convulsion, or *grand mal* seizure, has no localizing pattern or significance except to indicate the general susceptibility of the brain as a whole to the spread of an epileptic process.

However, there are other types of seizures where the clinical manifestations are generalized from onset and are associated with more or less well-synchronized epileptiform discharges from both hemispheres in the EEG. Such clinical manifestations have, in the past, been called classic *petit mal* seizures, or a combination of *petit mal* and *grand mal* attacks with sudden bilateral onset. Much less is known of the mechanisms involved in such phenomena. In some of these patients, deep epileptogenic foci have been found in the cerebral cortex and particularly in the cortex of the medial frontal and orbital frontal lobes. Jasper has proposed that such cortex has

strong projections to the central core of the diencephalon and brain stem with widespread reciprocal interconnections to the cortex of both hemispheres, and this functional system has been termed the centrencephalic system by Penfield. Involvement of this system by seizure discharges might then be the mechanism by which consciousness is suddenly snuffed out for a few seconds and equally suddenly turned on again, or by which a major convulsive seizure involving both sides of the body from onset could be induced. Our knowledge regarding buried cortex or subcortical nuclei is currently fragmentary and, for this reason, we know the least about these kinds of generalized seizures.

CONCLUSION

It is clear that complex mechanisms must be operating in the genesis and spread of seizure discharges in the process we call epilepsy. The process involves an organ composed of ten billion neurons with rich interconnections in which each cell may have 60,000 synaptic inputs from other cells. The membrane properties accounting for the excitability of the individual cell and the ability of the neuron to integrate its input, which is both excitatory and inhibitory, coupled with the properties of the neural nets composed of such elements, must be better understood before complete insight into the mechanisms of the epilepsies is possible. This will require the talents of all the neurosciences applied to this problem and represents the challenge as well as the excitement of the field.

FURTHER READING

[1] Jasper, H. H., Ward, A. A., Jr. and Pope, A. (1969), *Basic Mechanisms of the Epilepsies*. Boston: Little, Brown and Co.
[2] Penfield, W. and Jasper, H. (1954), *Epilepsy and the Functional Anatomy of the Human Brain*. Boston: Little, Brown and Co.
[3] Penfield, W. and Kristiansen, K. (1951), *Epileptic Seizure Patterns*. Springfield, Ill: Charles C. Thomas.

2. EPILEPSY AND CONVULSIONS IN INFANCY AND CHILDHOOD

EDWARD M. BRETT

INTRODUCTION

There are many points of difference between epilepsy and seizures in the young and in older subjects. The most important of these is the ease with which attacks may be induced in infants and children by transitory changes such as pyrexia and chemical disturbances in contrast to the relative stability of the adult. It follows that a clear distinction must be made at the outset between the child who has had one or more seizures *only* in association with fever or with a transient biochemical or other disorder in the newborn period, and one who has had recurrent attacks in the absence of such provoking factors. The latter can properly be regarded as "epileptic", since the

concept of *recurrent* attacks is implicit in the word "epilepsy", whereas the former should not be so regarded until a clear pattern of unprovoked attacks has emerged. Although the word "epileptic" is necessarily used to describe particular *events*, strict criteria should be used in applying it to individual children, since the distinction may have prognostic, therapeutic and even genetic implications.

TYPES OF ATTACK

Neonatal Convulsions

Seizures are common in the newborn period and usually take the form of twitching, generalized or variably focal, or tonic attacks. Neonatal apnoeic episodes may also represent seizures. In this age-group convulsions are rarely, if ever, due to idiopathic epilepsy but occur in two main circumstances. The first is in relation to difficulties in delivery (foetal distress, asphyxia or intracranial bleeding), severe hyperbilirubinaemia, and infection of the nervous system, notably meningitis, and is often associated with a poor prognosis. The second group includes the transient biochemical disorders, hypoglycaemia, hypocalcaemia and hypomagnesaemia. Hypoglycaemia, common in babies born "light for dates" after toxaemic pregnancies, carries a bad prognosis for later development, whereas the outlook is better in the other two disorders. In the rare condition of pyridoxine-dependent epilepsy fits may occur in the newborn period or even *in utero*. A therapeutic test with large doses of pyridoxine parenterally will allow the diagnosis to be made. Occasionally neonatal convulsions occur as a withdrawal phenomenon in the infants of mothers taking barbiturates and certain other drugs.

The three serious and treatable causes of neonatal seizures, meningitis, hypoglycaemia and pyridoxine-dependent epilepsy, should be excluded by lumbar puncture, blood glucose estimation and a therapeutic trial of glucose and pyridoxine. Apart from the specific treatment of the underlying cause, where possible, anticonvulsants are often needed and phenobarbitone, phenytoin and rectal paraldehyde or chloral hydrate may be used.

Infantile Spasms

Known by many synonyms (including lightning, salaam or propulsive attacks), these attacks generally start between the ages of 3 and 36 months with their peak onset at 5 or 6 months. The word "salaam" well describes the typical episode with sudden flexion of neck and trunk, raising of arms, sometimes flexion of thighs and often a cry. The child, if sitting, may fall forward. Sometimes the limbs and trunk extend rather than flex. For the recognition of their nature, the pattern of the attacks (which is often more usefully *imitated* than described by a parent) and their tendency to occur in prolonged series several times daily at regular intervals of a few seconds for periods up to several minutes, numbering between three and several score, are equally important. These points distinguish them from startle reactions, attacks of colic and attempts to sit up, with all of which confusion may occur. Almost always the infant's development slows down or regresses when the spasms begin. Social responsiveness and skills are lost, so that deafness or blindness may be wrongly suspected. The usual, though not invariable, electro-encephalographic correlate of these clinical features is a severely disorganized pattern of a type known as "hypsarhythmia".

The triad of infantile spasms, retardation and hypsarhythmia is not diagnostic, but occurs, like most other forms of childhood epilepsy, in symptomatic or idiopathic (cryptogenic) forms. The idiopathic group makes up about half of the cases in most series, tending to lessen as more detailed investigation discloses underlying

syndromes, structural or biochemical. In this group the child has usually appeared normal neurologically and developmentally before the onset of the spasms. In the symptomatic group there is often evidence of previous neurological abnormality with retardation and/or cerebral palsy, attributable to known problems in pregnancy, delivery or newborn period, so that the onset of attacks is merely one milestone in a pattern of aberrant development. Tuberous sclerosis may present with infantile spasms, before adenoma sebaceum and other lesions of the skin develop, and can be recognized by the white "achromic naevi" which are its earliest stigmata. Phenylketonuria and other inborn metabolic errors account for a few cases, as do various cerebral malformations. Infantile spasms sometimes begin soon after immunization, especially with diphtheria-pertussis-tetanus (DPT) vaccine, and an "allergic" reaction to the pertussis element is suspected in these cases.

The prognosis in infantile spasms is worse than in any other form of childhood epilepsy. In untreated cases severe mental retardation is almost invariable. The attacks may cease at 2 or 3 years of age but major convulsions often supervene. Treatment with ordinary anticonvulsants is usually unhelpful, although some good results have been reported with diazepam (Valium) and nitrazepam (Mogadon). ACTH or adrenal cortical steroids offer the best hope of success, improving the EEG abnormality in most cases and often reducing the number of spasms, but seldom improving the long-term outlook for mental development. There is some evidence that the prognosis is better in idiopathic cases than in those which are symptomatic, and in cases treated early than those treated late.

Febrile Convulsions

It has long been known that convulsions associated with fever due to infection outside the nervous system are common, but the relationship of these attacks to epilepsy has been controversial. Some workers have regarded them as a form of epilepsy differing from other forms only in that the trigger mechanism is recognized, while others believe that they are quite distinct from the epilepsies. The occurrence of short, generalized seizures in children between the ages of 1 and 6 years in association with fever, often due to respiratory infection, without electro-encephalographic abnormalities, is well known, and these are usually known as febrile convulsions. There is often a family history of similar episodes in siblings or parents, so that genetic factors may be important. The outlook is usually regarded as good, and in most series only a minority of children have continued to have convulsions without provocation after the age of 6 or 7 years, and thereby graduated to epilepsy proper.

Three factors have recently led to a re-appraisal of the significance of febrile convulsions. One is the recognition that they are very common, occurring for example in 2 to 3 per cent of children under the age of 5 in the United States. Another is that they are often prolonged, lasting 30 min. or more, and are therefore the commonest "cause" of status epilepticus in young children. (Some writers have excluded prolonged seizures from the category of febrile convulsions, but this seems illogical, since short or long attacks may occur with fever at different times in the same child or the same sibship.) The third factor is the realization, from small prospective and larger retrospective studies, that serious neurological sequelae may follow febrile convulsions. Dementia, spasticity and other permanent neurological deficit have been seen in some children immediately after prolonged fits with fever. Although "encephalitis" has sometimes been blamed in such cases, the evidence for this has usually been un- convincing, and neuropathological studies have often shown neuronal damage which can be correlated with particular episodes of febrile convulsion. Retrospective clinical studies have suggested that febrile fits are an important aetiological factor in the later development of temporal lobe epilepsy, and similar findings have been observed in a study of adults treated by temporal lobectomy.

The management of febrile convulsions involves attempts to prevent them or shorten their duration by reducing fever and by giving anticonvulsants. Simple measures such as tepid sponging, the use of a fan, and aspirin are often effective when fever develops. Parents must be warned against wrapping up the febrile child in extra blankets, so increasing his fever. Anticonvulsants may be given regularly until the age of 6 or 7 when fever is unlikely to provoke fits, or intermittently at the first sign of a febrile episode. In some children the first indication of fever, however, may be a convulsion, so that there is no time for preventive measures. Recent studies have shown the preventive value of continuous phenobarbitone, but not phenytoin, in febrile convulsions. (Faerø *et al.*, 1972. Epilepsia, **13**, 279.)

The treatment of prolonged convulsions and status epilepticus with fever is of great importance. For the reasons mentioned these should be terminated as soon as possible (*see* page 100).

Grand mal attacks and other forms of major epilepsy

Grand mal attacks in infancy and childhood may fail to show the classical features seen in older patients, with a prodromal period of irritability and malaise, an aura, a tonic followed by a clonic stage and post-ictal confusion, drowsiness or headache. One or more of these stages may be lacking. A history of an aura (which may itself represent a focal seizure preceding a generalized convulsion) is seldom obtained in a young child, but as he matures he may be able to describe the symptoms. A careful parental account of the child's attacks may suggest a focal origin. In some attacks tonic features may be the main or only element present; they may be bilateral, unilateral or confined to one limb or part of a limb.

Temporal lobe or psychomotor seizures are among the commonest focal attacks and are more frequent in childhood than is sometimes realized. Any of the complex psychic, autonomic and motor phenomena of older patients may occur in children, although they usually cannot describe their symptoms. Temporal lobe attacks in children are often misinterpreted and confused with hysteria, behaviour disorder or petit mal attacks. When the motor features of the seizures are mild, they may be unobserved or forgotten by parents, who may describe only episodes of unresponsiveness. They should be asked about the occurrence of chewing, lip-smacking or swallowing movements, automatic-type movements such as fumbling with clothing or buttons, more complex bizarre, stereotyped actions or autonomic symptoms, such as pallor, flushing, borborygmi or a rapid heart-beat. In general, motor features other than rhythmic blinking suggest that an episode is not a petit mal absence. Since parents are fallible historians, an attempt should be made to provoke an attack by hyperventilation (best achieved by the child repeatedly blowing at a handkerchief or tissue held a few inches from his mouth). Other points of distinction from petit mal absences are mentioned later.

Temporal lobe epilepsy always suggests focal pathology, but in children it is usually difficult to demonstrate the lesion which is unlikely to be neoplastic, and is often due to perinatal difficulties or to previous prolonged febrile seizures. This form of epilepsy is often accompanied by severe behaviour problems, particularly by hyperkinetic behaviour and catastrophic outbursts of rage, which may be more handicapping than the seizures themselves and prevent normal education.

The electroencephalogram often shows discharges or other abnormality in one or both temporal areas, but may on the other hand be normal. The use of sphenoidal electrodes may disclose abnormalities missed on routine recording, but this technique is seldom indicated in childhood.

Jacksonian epilepsy and *epilepsia partialis continua* occur in children but, like other forms of focal epilepsy, are rarely due to neoplasms, so that their investigation need not usually be as rigorous as in adults.

Petit mal Absences, Akinetic and Myoclonic attacks

The term "petit mal triad" is sometimes used for three types of minor seizure, the absence, the akinetic, and the myoclonic attack, but this seems no longer justified, since the attacks differ markedly.

It seems wiser to limit the term "petit mal" to the episode known as the absence, an abrupt and brief cessation of activity with unresponsiveness, eyes staring or upturned, sometimes with rhythmic blinking, associated with a typical electroencephalographic pattern of bilaterally symmetrical 3 c./s. spike and wave activity. This form of epilepsy occurs in the young rather than in adults, tends to cease with increasing age and is often the only type of attack which the patient has. It is usually "primary" or idiopathic, and is generally responsive to the dione and succinimide group of drugs, and not to those which are effective in cases and grand mal.

Although often confused with temporal lobe attacks, petit mal absences can usually be distinguished by their brevity, by the lack of motor events (other than eye movements and blinking), of post-ictal confusion, and by the typical EEG pattern. Rarely, a therapeutic test with succinimide is needed.

The akinetic attack is a type of "drop attack'" in which, as a result of a sudden brief loss of power or postural tone without obvious change in the level of consciousness, the patient falls or sags at the knees, but recovers immediately. In myoclonic attacks a sudden, rapid, single jerk of one or more limbs occurs, usually without alteration in consciousness, so that the child may fall, or drop what he is holding. Myoclonic attacks often occur soon after waking in the morning.

Electroencephalography in patients with akinetic and myoclonic attacks does not show the regular 3 c./s. spike and wave pattern of petit mal absences, but atypical spike and wave complexes with varying frequency often mixed with polyspike discharges. Akinetic and myoclonic attacks usually respond less well to succinimide and the diones than do petit mal absences.

The individual attacks may be of little more than nuisance value, but their timing and frequency may make them more disabling, as with petit mal absences. Akinetic or myoclonic attacks may occasionally occur without interruption and then constitute a form of status epilepticus ("minor epileptic status") in which the patient is grossly incapacitated by the intrusion of myoclonic jerks of small or larger range and may fall repeatedly as a result of jerks affecting the legs or akinetic drop attacks, his level of alertness being transiently impaired. This condition may be confused with cerebellar ataxia, drug intoxication and degenerative brain disease. Rarely petit mal absences also occur continuously, causing the condition of petit mal status, distinguished from "minor epileptic status" by the lack of motor features, apart from blinking, and the characteristic electroencephalographic findings.

Major status epilepticus, in which grand mal convulsions continue without interruption, is a medical emergency particularly dangerous in young children. The risks of asphyxia, hyperpyrexia, hypoglycaemia, inhalation of vomit and secretions and permanent neurological damage or death make it essential to terminate the condition as soon as possible.

Precipitating factors in childhood convulsions and epilepsy

Fever has been mentioned in relation to the common condition of febrile convulsions in young children, but in some older children with epilepsy, whether idiopathic or symptomatic, fever with infection may at times act as one of a number of non-specific "triggers" in provoking an attack. Infections, especially of the upper respiratory tract, are potent factors in causing an increase in fits, or even status epilepticus. Emotional factors of all kinds, whether pleasant or unpleasant, are equally potent triggers.

Some children have attacks only in response to flickering light of a certain frequency, and these photically induced convulsions occur most often today when watching television. The effect can be reduced by sitting the patient at least six feet from the screen. Other rarer forms of reflex epilepsy involve auditory stimuli, touch, startle and sudden movement.

Management of convulsions and epilepsy in childhood

Assessment

The nature of the episodes must first be decided. Many children are referred with possible epilepsy whose attacks are found, on careful enquiry, to be of another type. Thus infantile spasms may be wrongly suspected when it transpires that it is abdominal colic which causes a baby to flex his legs and cry. Breath-holding attacks in infancy are often mistaken for convulsions: a careful history should prevent this error. Syncopal attacks also enter the differential diagnosis of seizures, as do episodes of unconsciousness in children with congenital heart disease and, *very rarely*, hysterical attacks and tetany.

A complete neurological and general examination, after the history, should include examination of the skin for stigmata of neurocutaneous syndromes such as tuberous sclerosis and neurofibromatosis, and of the fundus of the eyes for signs of raised intracranial pressure, phakoma, choroido-retinitis or abnormal retinal pigmentation which might suggest previous toxoplasmosis, cytomegalovirus, rubella or other infection.

Investigations are dictated by the clinical picture. In general in childhood epilepsy, where cerebral neoplasms are a rare cause unlike epilepsy of late onset, they do not need to be as detailed as in adults. Skull X-rays and EEG are advisable with recurrent attacks. Hypoglycaemia and hypocalcaemia should be excluded as they are uncommon (except in the newborn) but treatable causes of convulsions. The association of fits with mental retardation and a history of affected siblings makes it important to exclude inborn metabolic errors, such as phenylketonuria, by aminoacid chromatography of plasma or urine. Serological tests may be needed to exclude intrauterine infections with toxoplasma, cytomegalovirus, rubella and syphilis. Focal epilepsy, sometimes but not always associated with focal EEG changes, may suggest a localized cerebral lesion, but it is unusual in childhood in such cases for contrast radiography (pneumoencephalography, arteriography, or brain scan) to demonstrate a solid lesion. Cerebral atrophy, which may be general or focal, may be shown by special X-rays especially in mentally subnormal children, but this radiological feature is of limited diagnostic and prognostic value.

Drug Treatment

The decision whether to treat must depend on the frequency and severity of the attacks. Febrile convulsions may be treated by anticonvulsants regularly, or intermittently in febrile episodes, and there is no clear evidence that one method is more effective than the other. An isolated seizure is seldom an indication to start treatment; many children may have only one or two attacks, so that it is usually reasonable to defer a decision to treat until a more definitive pattern has emerged.

The regime of treatment should be as simple as possible, not exceeding two drugs when possible. Compound preparations of two or three drugs are best avoided since they allow no flexibility of dose. The drugs must be carefully prescribed and *regularly reviewed* according to the weight of the patient. Even spacing of drugs throughout the day is desirable in order to maintain effective blood levels, but larger doses may be given at particular times, e.g. at bedtime in the case of nocturnal or early morning convulsions.

The anticonvulsant drugs used in childhood are similar to those used for adults and classified as those effective in major epilepsy including temporal lobe attacks, and those effective in petit mal absences, there being little overlap between the two.

Children usually tolerate well anticonvulsants in correct doses. A common exception is phenobarbitone which may cause behaviour disorders and overactivity in children and aggravate these features if already present, making the drug unacceptable. Phenytoin is well tolerated by children in the correct dose of about 5 mg./kg. of body weight 24 hr. (not exceeding 8 mg./kg.). Hypertrophy of the gums. and hirsuties are the commonest side-effects. Ataxia is unusual with the appropriate dose. Primidone, though sometimes initially causing nausea, vomiting or abdominal pain, is usually well tolerated if introduced gradually and increased to a dose of 20–25 mg./kg./body weight/24 hr. A combination of phenytoin with phenobarbitone or primidone is often effective in grand mal and temporal lobe epilepsy. The combination of phenobarbitone and primidone often causes drowsiness and should be avoided. Prolonged treatment with these three drugs may lower the blood level of folic acid and produce changes in the peripheral blood, bone-marrow, general health and mental state which can be counteracted by treatment with folic acid. Although folic acid treatment of the folate-deficient *adult* has been found to provoke increased fit-frequency or status epilepticus, this has not been the general experience in paediatric practice in which the addition of folic acid may benefit both general health and mental state. Other drugs sometimes used for children include pheneturide, sulthiame, carbamazepine, acetazoleamide, diazepam and nitrazepam. These may be more helpful when added to one of the major anticonvulsants than when used alone.

Myoclonic and akinetic attacks often prove resistant to anticonvulsant treatment. Some workers have found nitrazepam effective in myoclonic epilepsy and some success has also been claimed for it in infantile spasms.

The succinimides and oxazolidinediones are the two groups of drugs effective in petit mal absences. The diones (troxidone and paramethadione) have been largely superseded by ethosuximide which is usually effective in true petit mal absences with the typical EEG pattern and well tolerated, hiccoughs being among the commoner side-effects. The belief that treatment of petit mal with ethosuximide may provoke grand mal attacks has led many workers to advise combining it with a major anticonvulsant but this risk is by no means generally recognized.

Occasionally vigorous treatment will fail to reduce a child's attacks to a level which would be acceptable for an adult patient. In such intractable cases it is important to avoid progressively increasing the dose and numbers of drugs so that the child suffers severe side-effects and becomes mentally obfuscated. A ketogenic diet has been found helpful in some children with drug-resistant epilepsy. In some children complete suppression of attacks leads to behaviour-problems of such degree that their parents may prefer them to be allowed to have occasional fits as the price for tolerable behaviour.

Status epilepticus must be treated energetically as an emergency. The first treatment is usually in the hands of the family doctor who should be prepared to give an intramuscular injection of paraldehyde in a dose of 0·2 ml./kg. of body weight, or of phenobarbitone. Paraldehyde can also be given rectally with an equal volume of olive oil. Hospital admission is often needed, but treatment should never be delayed until it can be arranged. Intravenous diazepam has been found helpful by some workers in controlling status but may cause respiratory depression, especially when used in combination with barbiturates or paraldehyde. The patient's airway must be kept clear, inhalation of vomit and secretions avoided, oxygen given and fluid and electrolyte balance maintained in prolonged status epilepticus. Hyperpyrexia should be combated by tepid sponging or fanning in cases of febrile convulsion.

The duration of anticonvulsant treatment cannot be pre-determined, but must be decided in each case individually. It is a reasonable practice to discontinue treatment after two years of freedom from attacks, although an EEG showing frequent paroxysmal discharges will make this inadvisable. Treatment should not be stopped abruptly but reduced gradually. One means of achieving this is deliberately to fail to increase the dose as the child becomes heavier. Parents and child should be warned that there is a risk of recurrence of seizures after stopping treatment so that they will not be too greatly upset if a relapse should occur.

Surgical Treatment

The place of surgery in the treatment of childhood epilepsy is limited. Cerebral hemispherectomy has helped certain carefully selected hemiplegic children with intractable epilepsy and behavioural disorders, but may have long-delayed post-operative complications. Temporal lobectomy has been of value in a few children with temporal lobe seizures and associated behaviour-problems. Surgery should not be considered until adequate medical treatment has been tried and found wanting.

Genetic implications of epilepsy

Assessment of the risk of children having epilepsy if a parent is epileptic, or of further children having epilepsy when one child is already affected, depends largely on the type and cause of the epilepsy. When one parent has idiopathic epilepsy the chances of having an epileptic child are 1 in 40. With symptomatic epilepsy the risk depends on the underlying disease. In acquired conditions such as brain-damage due to perinatal problems, head-injury and inflammatory brain-disease, they are no greater than in the general population. When epilepsy is due to tuberous sclerosis, inborn errors of metabolism or progressive degenerative brain-disease, the risk of later children having fits is related to that of the underlying disease being inherited.

General management

As with other chronic handicaps the aim should be to allow the child to lead as normal a life as possible and to develop his potential to the full. Often it is the associated problems, such as hyperkinesis, short attention-span, outbursts of rage, and other behavioural or intellectual difficulties rather than the epilepsy itself which limit the child's potential and necessitate special educational and other arrangements. Most children with epilepsy can be educated in ordinary schools, with understanding teachers, but residential or day special schools are needed by some because of associated problems. Restrictions placed on the child's activities by parents and teachers in swimming, sports, cycling and travelling should be as few as seems consistent with common sense and safety. The school-child with epilepsy feels himself to be "different" from other children as a result of his mysterious attacks, his need to take medicine and the often misguided attitudes of adults and cruel reactions of school-mates towards his disability. Severely limiting his activities has the effect of isolating him further. The doctor concerned has the responsibility in each case of educating parents, teachers and others in enlightened attitudes towards the whole subject of epilepsy, and should be ready to spend time discussing with the child himself his worries about his condition. Parents are usually anxious to know the cause of the epilepsy and the prospects of the fits stopping, and may ask these questions repeatedly. The doctor must give frank answers, avoid the temptation to be dogmatic, and be prepared to explain the reasons for the fact that, though hope of improvement can often be held out, his answers must to some extent be indefinite.

FURTHER READING

Brett, E. M. (1966), "Minor Epileptic Status," *J. Neurol. Sci.*, **3**, 52.

Bridge, E. M. (1949), *Epilepsy and Convulsive Disorders in Children.* New York: McGraw-Hill Book Co.

Crichton, J. U. (1966), "Infantile Spasms and Skin Anomalies," *Develop. Med. Child Neurol.*, **8**, 273.

Gibberd, F. B. (1966), "The Prognosis of Petit Mal," *Brain*, **89**, 531.

Harper, J. R. (1968), "True Myoclonic Epilepsy in Childhood," *Arch. Dis. Childh.*, **43**, 28.

Jeavons, P. M. and Bower, B. D. (1964), "Infantile Spasms," *Clinics in Developmental Medicine*, No. 15. London: Heinemann.

Myer, A. (1967), In Greenfield's *Neuropathology* (W. Blackwood, W. H. McMenemey, A. Meyer and R. M. Norman, Eds.). Baltimore: Williams and Wilkins Co.

Millichap, J. G. (1968), *Febrile Convulsions.* New York: MacMillan.

Ounsted, C., Lindsay, J. and Norman, R. M. (1966), "Biological Factors in Temporal Lobe Epilepsy," *Clinics in Developmental Medicine*, No. 22. London: Heinemann.

Taylor, D. C. (1969), "Differential Rates of Cerebral Maturation between sexes and between hemispheres. Evidence from Epilepsy," *Lancet*, **2**, 140.

Wilson, J. (1969), "Drug Treatment of Epilepsy in Childhood," *Brit. med. J.*, **4**, 475.

3. SURGICAL THERAPY OF FOCAL EPILEPSY

THEODORE RASMUSSEN

INTRODUCTION

Epileptic seizures, regardless of their nature or severity, represent a symptom of some cerebral or, less frequently, some systemic dysfunction. Thus epilepsy, or the tendency to recurring seizures, is not a disease, but is only a symptom indicating the presence of some underlying disease or disorder of the brain or the body. It may be a symptom of some systemic disorder, such as hypoglycemia induced by insulin or by an adenoma of the pancreas, or uremia, carotid sinus irritability, abnormal calcium metabolism, eclampsia, pheochromocytoma of the adrenals, etc. It is important, therefore, that a systemic cause for the attacks should always be ruled out before the convulsive tendency is considered to be a symptom of cerebral dysfunction, as is actually the case in the great majority of patients coming for treatment.

The term "epilepsy" is ordinary used, however, to refer to seizures arising from some disturbance of brain function. Seizures are a frequent and important symptom of a wide variety of lesions and diseases of the brain. Some of these conditions are acute and can be treated more or less effectively (meningitis, encephalitis, eclampsia, toxic states such as lead and arsenic poisoning, etc.); some are chronic, potentially life-threatening but treatable conditions (brain tumours, arteriovenous malformations, etc.); some are progressive and untreatable (certain chronic degenerative brain diseases, etc.). Many lesions of the brain that produce seizures are, however, static, such as gross or microscopic scarring of the brain, and do not require treatment for the lesion itself. It is important to emphasize, however, that benign and slowly-growing tumours, particularly certain astrocytomas both in children and in adults, may produce seizures for years, without showing evidence of progressive neurological deficit or increased intracranial pressure. Both carotid angiograms and pneumoencephalograms are often normal during the early years in these patients, so that it is often advisable to repeat X-ray contrast studies periodically in patients with focal epilepsy, in whom some definite etiology for the attacks cannot be established.

The basic neuronal mechanisms responsible for seizure phenomena are probably similar, regardless of the nature of the underlying brain lesion or disease. Although rapid strides are being made in neurophysiological, neuro-chemical, neuropharmacological and neuroanatomical studies in experimental animal models, and in patients with various types of epilepsy, an understanding of the intimate details of the seizure discharge in the brain has not yet reached the level of providing much therapeutic guidance to the physician. The principles of treatment, medical and surgical, have been developed largely on an empirical basis.

A general discussion of the initial investigation of a patient with epilepsy, after a systemic etiology has been ruled out, is outside the scope of this chapter, but it is important to emphasize that the severity of a seizure does not give any hint as to the underlying brain lesion. Thus, extremely severe and frequent seizures are often due to static brain lesions, such as scarring and gliosis, whereas mild and infrequent seizures may be caused by potentially lethal lesions, such as brain tumours.

If the seizure is focal in nature, its pattern of onset frequently indicates the *area* of the brain giving rise to the initial seizure discharge, but rarely gives any clue as to the *nature* of the underlying brain lesion. The attack pattern and the EEG may thus give good evidence as to *where* the lesion is, but contrast X-ray studies are usually required to determine the nature of the lesion.

THE NEUROSURGICAL HYPOTHESIS

The history of surgical efforts to cure the epileptic patient dates back to Hippocratic times, and perhaps earlier, in addition to spanning the modern era of neuro-surgery. The list of discarded surgical procedures carried out for epilepsy since prehistoric times is a lengthy one, and bears eloquent testimony to the fanciful ideas concerning the nature of epilepsy that existed well into this century, and, more significantly, emphasizes the desperation of the epileptic patient in his search for relief.

The technique of cortical excision, guided by detailed study of the patient's attack pattern, special localizing EEG studies, plus cortical electrographic and electrical stimulation studies during craniotomy carried out under local anaesthesia, has stood the test of time and constitutes a valuable addition to the therapeutic armamentarium for selected patients with intractable focal epilepsy. Following the pioneering work of Foerster on cortical excisions for the treatment of post-traumatic epilepsy, the principles underlying this surgical approach to the treatment of focal epilepsy have been developed over the past forty years mainly at the Montreal Neurological Institute. As a result of continuing study of follow-up records on patients undergoing this procedure, and of repeated correlations of these with the operative and pre-operative clinical and EEG data, the operative techniques were

TABLE 1.

RESULTS OF REOPERATION IN PATIENTS WITH NON-TUMORAL EPILEPTOGENIC LESIONS

127 patients reoperated upon from 1928 through 1968

No attacks following last operation	11 pts. (10%)	36 pts. (32%)	56 pts. (50%)
Became attack-free after some early attacks	25 pts. (22%)		112 pts. with follow-up data of 2-38 yrs.
Marked reduction of seizure tendency	20 pts (18%)		
Moderate to no reduction of seizure tendency	56 pts. (50%)		median 11 yrs.
Less than 2 years follow-up data	10 pts.		
Postoperative deaths	5 pts. (pt. mortality rate 4.7%)		
Total	**127 pts.**		

The initial treatment of the symptom, epilepsy, is medical in nature, once it has been established as completely as possible that the seizure tendency is not due to some brain lesion that requires surgical treatment for its own sake. If a medical regime of anticonvulsant medication, avoidance of general and specific precipitating factors, etc., keeps the seizure tendency under satisfactory control, so that the patient can lead a reasonably normal life, the question of possible surgical therapy ordinarily does not arise. When this degree of seizure control cannot be achieved after a thorough trial of various combinations of anticonvulsant medications, in maximum tolerable doses, the question of possible surgical therapy may be raised for patients with certain types of seizure problems.

progressively refined and the indications for operation widened. This surgical series now consists of approximately 1,600 patients in whom nearly 1,900 craniotomies have been carried out. During the first 30 years of this experience, the operations were carried out by Dr. Wilder Penfield and his associates, and during the past 10 years by his successors. Dr. Herbert Jasper and, more recently, Dr. Peter Gloor have provided the electroencephalographic and clinical neurophysiological expertise that has made them indispensable members of the team.

Small, discrete epileptogenic lesions of the brains of a variety of experimental animals are providing valuable data on the neuronal mechanisms involved in epilepsy, but the clinical data that have accumulated in the patients in the above series indicate that small, discrete epileptogenic foci in man are rare. The great majority of the patients in this series were found to have epileptogenic lesions of considerable extent, with the region of lowest threshold ordinarily giving the local sign to the attack pattern. This area of lowest threshold, however, rarely gives any clear idea as to the total extent of the epileptogenic cortex. For this, it is necessary to rely on the EEG.

Success in stopping the seizures seems to be reasonably well correlated with the completeness of the removal of the epileptogenic cortex. The surgical aim, therefore, is to identify and map out the total epileptogenic area of the cortex, and to remove the involved cortex as completely as possible, without running too great a risk of producing a significant neurological deficit, or of increasing one that is already present. Cortical excision limited to the areas of maximum epileptogenicity frequently produced only minimal or moderate reduction in the seizure tendency, whereas re-operation and more complete excision of the epileptogenic area often reduced the patient's seizure tendency and further converted an unsuccessful into a successful result (Table 1). Thus one-third of the 112 patients who have undergone one or more re-operations, and have accurate follow-up data of 2 years or longer, have become seizure-free following excision of additional cortical tissue, after the initial cortical excision had failed to reduce the seizure tendency satisfactorily. In an additional 18 per cent there was a marked, but not quite complete, reduction in seizure tendency, with the patients continuing to have 1–2 per cent as many attacks, or less, compared to before operation. Thus half of these 112 patients experienced a complete or nearly complete reduction in seizure tendency as a result of additional removal of epileptogenic cortex, after an inadequate reduction had been produced by the initial, more limited, excision.

SELECTION CRITERIA FOR SURGERY

(1) The first specific criterion for selection of a patient as a possible candidate for surgical therapy is failure of an adequate trial of various combinations of anticonvulsant medications in maximal tolerable doses, to keep the attacks under control to the point where the patient can live a reasonably normal life.

(2) Clinical and EEG evidence must indicate that the attacks are focal in origin, and are arising in an area of the brain that can be excised without producing a significant neurological deficit, or without increasing one that is already present.

(3) The attacks must have been present for a long enough period of time to be reasonably sure that all potentially epileptogenic areas of the brain have matured and become symptomatic. Operation is rarely recommended earlier than 3–5 years after onset of the seizures, unless the seizure tendency is unusually severe or is becoming progressively worse. In the case of children, operation is rarely carried out until repeated investigations, over a period of one or more years, have indicated that the seizure pattern is a stable one, and is not changing with maturation of the brain. Our data suggest that the likelihood of cortical excision producing a satisfactory reduction in seizure tendency is as good when operation is carried out 10, 20 or 30 years after the onset of seizures, as when the attacks have been present for only 1, 2 or 3 years. Particularly frequent and severe seizures, however, may make early operation advisable.

(4) The seizures must have been present long enough to make spontaneous regression of the seizure tendency within a reasonable period of time unlikely. A certain percentage of patients with post-traumatic seizures following brain injury in adult life, for example, show a spontaneous regression of the seizure tendency in the first 2–5 years after the onset of the attacks.

(5) Lastly, the patient himself, if over 12–13 years of age, must be well motivated toward considering a major surgical procedure. The patient's complete and enthusiastic co-operation is essential for some of the more complicated diagnostic procedures, and for the operation when it is carried out under local anaesthesia.

INVESTIGATION

(1) The prime aim in surgical therapy of the epileptic patient is elimination of the clinical seizures, so the cornerstone of the investigation is the analysis of the patient's attack pattern or patterns. This begins with repeated questioning of the patient as to what he feels and does at the onset of his attacks, detailed descriptions from relatives and friends as to what they see in an attack, particularly at the beginning of the spell. To this is added recorded descriptions of attacks witnessed in hospital by nurses trained to look for localizing features of the attack, and to describe them in objective terms. It is then usually possible to localize the cerebral area, or areas, of lowest seizure threshold with reasonable certainty and accuracy.

(2) The EEG, when carried out with special localizing techniques and with anticonvulsant medication reduced or stopped, gives the most valuable objective evidence as to both the localization and the extent of the epileptogenic area of the brain. The epileptic tendency fluctuates in some patients so that a minimum of two EEG examinations is essential, regardless of the clarity of the diagnosis and localization in the initial studies, in order to be as sure as possible that the epileptiform abnormality is stable and not one that shifts from day to day. In patients with temporal-lobe epilepsy it is particularly important to carry out several EEG studies routinely, since the decision as to which temporal lobe is responsible for the seizures often rests completely in the EEG evidence; in addition, the presence of independent bitemporal EEG abnormality requires special investigations and safeguards, if operation is to be carried out.

(3) Many patients with complicated seizure problems require special EEG procedures. These include pharyngeal and sphenoidal leads, activation procedures with sleep, metrazol (pentamethylenetetrazol), megamide (ethylmethyl glutamic acid) or pentothal, use of closely spaced leads in suspected parasagittal or central lesions and the use of chronic implanted subdural or depth electrodes for stimulation and recording. We currently employ these implanted leads much less frequently than in earlier years,

because the recently developed intracarotid amytal-metrazol (amobarbitalpentamethylenetetrazol) EEG test seems to be giving us more valuable practical therapeutic guidance in many of these patients with complex seizure problems. The technique of telemetering the EEG during normal every-day activities and during normal sleep gives promise of providing additional guidance in certain selected patients.

(4) Skull X-rays are studied with special reference to asymmetries, since focal atrophic lesions of the brain, dating from birth or early infancy, are frequently associated with smallness of the related cranial fossa, loss of normal brain markings or increased thickness of the skull over the involved area of the brain. These bony changes are sometimes more significant than the appearance of the ventricles or the subarachnoid spaces. Usually, however, a focal atrophic lesion of the brain manifests itself as well by a more or less localized enlargement of the related portion of the ventricular system and/or the overlying subarachnoid space. Intracranial calcification is seen in certain uncommon epileptogenic lesions (tuberous sclerosis, toxoplasmosis, tuberculoma, certain hamartomas or indolent neoplasms, and Sturge-Weber pial angiomatosis).

Carotid angiograms are not done as a routine, unless a cerebral neoplasm is suspected, as is *always* the case when attacks start in adult life. Angiography is, however, carried out as a general rule when the skull X-rays and air studies *fail* to show atrophy in the area implicated by the patient's attack pattern and EEG studies, since a certain percentage of such patients will be found to have either indolent neoplasms or vascular malformations. Radioactive brain scans are valuable in identifying the latter, but are usually normal in the indolent gliomas that sometimes cause seizures for years before neurological deficits or intracranial pressure symptoms appear.

(5) Special psychological testing, as developed by Dr. Brenda Milner, is of increasing value in indicating that certain brain regions are not performing as well as the level of brain function as a whole. In addition, these psychological tests sometimes give warning that the patient may have an unusual lateralization of speech functions in the brain, when this is not otherwise suspected.

(6) The carotid amytal (amobarbital) speech test devised by Wada is carried out when the lateralization of speech representation is uncertain, as is the case in all left-handed and ambidextrous individuals. This special speech test is also carried out in those right-handed patients in whom there is some hint from the history, seizure pattern or X-ray studies, that the speech representation may not have developed in the left hemisphere. Thus, the test is carried out in right-handers who have historical or X-ray evidence of injury to the left hemisphere in infancy, and in those right-handed patients with epileptogenic lesions near the speech zones of the left hemisphere, who do not show ictal or postictal dysphasia, and in those right-handers with epileptogenic lesions in the right hemisphere, who do show some hint of ictal or postictal speech disturbance. It is now clear that early injury to the left cerebral hemisphere may result in development of speech functions in the right hemisphere, without a comparable shift in handedness and without evidence of right hemiparesis.

During this intracarotid amytal (amobarbital) speech test, memory functions are also tested, and this now gives considerable safety in avoiding significant postoperative memory deficit, when operating on temporal-lobe seizure patients who have some EEG or X-ray evidence of damage to the opposite temporal lobe as well.

THE NEUROSURGICAL PROCEDURE

Certain special technical aspects of the surgical procedure have proved to be important in securing maximal reduction of the seizure tendency, and in reducing the risks of producing significant neurological deficits.

(1) The operation is done under local anaesthesia as a general rule, unless the patient is under 12 or 13 years of age or is unable to co-operate satisfactorily for other reasons. The use of local anaesthesia permits one to map out the epileptogenic area with maximum accuracy, by recording the brain waves unaltered by any anaesthetic agent.

(2) The use of local anaesthesia also permits the mapping out of the motor, sensory, and speech zones in appropriate detail, so that maximal removals of the epileptogenic area can be planned with the least possible risk of encroaching on non-dispensable cortex. Periodic testing of motor, sensory and speech functions during the removal also gives additional safety in minimizing the risk of producing a significant neurological deficit.

(3) The cortical excisions are made with a suction-tip technique, designed to produce the least possible trauma and vascular disturbance in the adjacent remaining gyri and in the underlying white matter. The removal is planned to follow sulci as much as possible, and the cortex is then gently sucked away from the pial margins of the removal bank with as little retraction and massaging of the remaining convolutional banks as possible.

(4) If the post-excision cortical EEG shows a significant amount of epileptiform abnormality, further excision is carried out, provided this can be done without incurring too great a risk of producing a significant neurological deficit. One, two or sometimes three further excisions are often done before a satisfactorily clean cortical EEG is obtained, or the attempt to do so abandoned.

(5) Analysis of our long-term follow-up data shows that only 3 per cent of the patients who have become seizure-free soon after operation, develop any recurrence of seizures in later years, and this recurrence usually consists only of rare and sporadic attacks. It thus seems clear that, with this technique of cortical resection, failures to reduce the seizure tendency satisfactorily are due to inadequate resection of the original epileptogenic cortex, and not to the development of a new epileptogenic lesion as a result of the surgical cicatrix.

NEUROPATHOLOGICAL FINDINGS

In 20 per cent of the patients in this series, operation disclosed the presence of a tumour or arteriovenous malformation. In about three-quarters of these patients the diagnosis of tumour had been made pre-operatively, but the operation was carried out as a seizure operation under local anaesthesia, because the patient's presenting problem was the seizure tendency without increased intracranial pressure or progressive neurological deficit. In the remaining one-quarter, however, the pre-operative studies did not show any evidence of a tumour, and the diagnosis was made only during the surgical procedure itself. Indolent astrocytomas constituted three-quarters of the tumours encountered in this series. Most of these fail to show a tumour stain or tumour vessels on angiographic examination, and fail to show up on radioactive brain scans, but do show some hint of a space-occupying lesion in the pneumoencephalogram.

In the patients with non-neoplastic lesions, the findings at operation usually consisted of atrophy, scarring or gliosis of the brain of varying extent and severity. The principal causes of the brain damage were (1) birth compression, trauma or anoxia, (2) post-natal brain trauma, and (3) post-inflammatory brain scarring (Table 2).

In earlier years a persistent hemiparesis, of variable severity and permanence, followed a small percentage of temporal lobectomy operations. Since the importance of avoiding any manipulation of the middle cerebral artery branches in the insula was appreciated, this complication has been avoided, and it has not occurred in over 400 consecutive temporal lobectomies carried out at the Montreal Neurological Institute since 1958.

In cortical excisions above the fissure of Sylvius the incidence of persistent hemiparesis, as an operative complication, is approximately half of 1 per cent, unless the epileptogenic area involves mainly the sensorimotor region itself. When this is the case it is sometimes necessary to take a calculated risk of producing some weakness of the arm or leg, or of increasing a pre-existing weakness, in patients with particularly severe or frequent Jacksonian seizures.

A partial or complete upper quadrantic hemianopia will be produced by temporal lobectomy with increasing

TABLE 2.

ETIOLOGY - Total Surgical Seizure Series

Patients operated upon from 1928 through 1968

Tumors	277 pts.	(19%)
AV Malformations	18 pts.	(1%)
Non-tumoral lesions		
Birth trauma, anoxia or compression	352 pts.	(25%)
Postnatal trauma	275 pts.	(19%)
Postinflammatory brain scarring	179 pts.	(12%)
Miscellaneous	74 pts.	(5%)
Unknown	281 pts.	(19%)
Total	**1456 pts.**	**(100%)**

Among the miscellaneous non-neoplastic lesions encountered at operation in this series are capillary and venous vascular malformations, hamartomas, tuberous sclerosis, Sturge–Weber pial angiomatosis and chronic encephalitis, as well as a variety of other less common causes of brain damage.

In many of the patients classified as being of unknown etiology two or more potential etiological factors were present, and it was not possible to differentiate which was actually responsible for the development of the epileptic tendency.

SURGICAL RISKS

Cortical resections, controlled by cortical electroencephalographic recording and cortical stimulation, are lengthy but relatively safe operations. In approximately 900 consecutive seizure operations carried out since 1957, there has been only 1 operative death, a 2-year-old girl with chronic encephalitis who died 5 days after operation of tracheostomy complications. The over-all operative mortality rate in patients with non-neoplastic epileptogenic lesions over the past 40 years, in approximately 1,400 operations, is 1·1 per cent.

frequency, as the line of excision moves posterior to the level of the fissure of Rolando at the Sylvian fissure. This upper quadrantic defect, however, is rarely noticed by the patient, and does not constitute a significant handicap, when it does occur. On rare occasions it is worthwhile to produce a complete homonymous hemianopia, in order to eradicate a large epileptogenic area in the posterior third of the hemisphere, which is producing particularly severe and intractable seizures. This decision most frequently arises in patients who are hemispherectomy candidates. If such a patient has a preserved visual field, and if the principal EEG abnormality is anterior to the occipital lobe, only the anterior two-thirds of the hemisphere is removed, as a rule sparing the occipital lobe and posterior portions of the parietal and temporal lobes, in order to preserve as much as possible of the contralateral homonymous visual field. This tactic has usually resulted in a satisfactory reduction of the seizure tendency, with preservation of the visual field. In a few instances, however, persistence of seizures has made it necessary to complete the hemispherectomy later on, and to sacrifice the homonymous visual field in order to stop the seizures.

Dr. Brenda Milner's psychological investigations on the

localization of higher intellectual functions have identified subtle deficits produced by cortical epileptogenic lesions and by excisions of various regions of the brain, but these are rarely of clinical significance. An exception is the production of a serious global memory deficit by removal of one temporal lobe including the hippocampal region, in a patient whose opposite hippocampus is non-functioning. This complication, which has occurred in three patients after unilateral temporal lobectomy and was reported in detail by Penfield and Milner, has subsequently been avoided by carrying out special memory tests during temporary inactivation of first one and, on another day, the other cerebral hemisphere by the intracarotid injection of sodium amytal (amobarbital) in all patients who have EEG, X-ray or psychological test evidence of damage to both temporal lobes.

RESULTS OF CORTICAL RESECTION ON THE SEIZURE TENDENCY

Continuing follow-up examinations and inquiries have been carried out from the beginning of this series, so that complete follow-up data, much of it on a yearly basis, are available in over 85 per cent of the patients. After excluding patients who, in early years, had craniotomy and exploration only without any cortical resection, the series consisted by the end of 1970 of 1,508 patients who had undergone 1,751 craniotomies with cortical resection of epileptogenic brain tissue, including some with tumours and other space-occupying lesions. It is emphasized that the seizures in all patients in this series had been refractory to medical anticonvulsant therapy, often for many years.

Analysis of the results in the 1,161 patients who had been operated upon for non-tumoral epileptogenic lesions up to the end of 1968 (to permit a minimum follow-up period of 2 years) (Table 3), shows that 40 per cent have

reduction in seizure frequency, ranging from moderate reduction to none.

In the continuing follow-up analysis of the effects of cortical excisions on the different types of seizure patterns it has been fruitful to divide the patients into anatomical groups, on the basis of the brain area primarily involved in the epileptogenic process. The great majority of patients in this series clearly fall into one of six groups: temporal, frontal, parietal, central, occipital and those with large destructive lesions involving more than one lobe of the brain.

Just over 50 per cent of the patients in the total series had cortical resections of epileptogenic areas that were largely limited to the temporal lobe of one hemisphere. Some of these patients had, in addition, smaller removals of the adjacent portions of the frontal, central or parietal regions, but the main bulk of the epileptogenic cortex was in the temporal lobe. The results of the cortical resection on the seizure tendency were comparable to those in the total series, 44 per cent became seizure free and another 21 per cent had a marked reduction in number of seizures, so that a complete or nearly complete reduction in seizure tendency followed the cortical resection in 65 per cent (Table 4).

The statistics were similar in the smaller anatomical groups: frontal, parietal, central, occipital, and those with large destructive lesions, with the seizure-free percentage ranging from 37 to 47 per cent, and the total percentage with complete or nearly complete reduction in seizure tendency ranging from 61 to 67 per cent. Thus the effectiveness of cortical resection is about the same, regardless of the principal anatomical area involved in the seizure process.

When the patients are classified according to the nature of the original brain lesion, the results are also quite similar. Thus in patients whose epileptogenic lesion

TABLE 3.

RESULTS OF CORTICAL RESECTION FOR NON-TUMOURAL EPILEPTOGENIC LESIONS

Patients operated upon from 1928 through 1968

Seizure free since discharge	229 pts. (22%)	419 pts. (40%)	641 pts. (61%)	1044 pts. with follow-up data of 2–40 yrs.
Became seizure free after some early attacks	190 pts. (18%)			
Marked reduction of seizure tendency	222 pts. (21%)			
Moderate to no reduction of seizure tendency	403 pts. (39%)			median 10 yrs.
Less than 2 years follow-up data	104 pts.			
Postoperative deaths	13 pts. (pt. mortality rate 1.1%)			
Total	**1161 pts.**			

become seizure-free and another 21 per cent had a marked reduction in frequency of seizures, to as few as 1–2 per cent as were occurring pre-operatively. Thus a complete or nearly complete reduction of seizure tendency followed the cortical resection in 61 per cent of the patients in this series. The remaining 39 per cent had a less satisfactory

seemed clearly due to birth trauma, anoxia or compression, 50 per cent became seizure free and a total of 69 per cent have shown a complete or nearly complete reduction in seizure tendency. In the post-traumatic group, 40 per cent became seizure free, and a total of 66 per cent have shown a complete or nearly complete reduction in seizure tendency. In the post-inflammatory group, 49 per cent became seizure free, and a total of 73 per cent have shown a complete or nearly complete reduction in seizure tendency. In those classified as of unknown etiology, often because there was more than one potential etiological factor, 38 per cent became seizure free, and a total of 58 per cent have shown a complete or nearly complete reduction in seizure tendency.

It seems clear from these data that the effectiveness of cortical resection in the treatment of intractable focal epilepsy is correlated with the completeness with which the epileptogenic cortex can be removed, rather than with the anatomical location of the principal epileptogenic

patients with well-categorized seizure problems treated with these methods.

CONCLUSION

The ultimate therapeutic goal in epilepsy is the correction of the basic neuronal abnormality responsible for the seizure discharge. Until such time, however, as our basic understanding of the mechanisms underlying the epileptic process permits the development of a definitive medical treatment, cortical resection, controlled with cortical EEG recording and cortical stimulation studies, carried out in institutions with the necessary facilities and interest in this aspect of epilepsy and neurosurgery, can

TABLE 4.

RESULTS OF CORTICAL RESECTION FOR TEMPORAL LOBE NON-TUMORAL EPILEPTOGENIC LESIONS

Patients operated upon from 1928 through 1968

Seizure free since discharge	146 pts. (26%)	248 pts. (44%)	367 pts. (65%)	566 pts. with follow-up data of 2-35 yrs. median 9 yrs.
Became seizure free after some early attacks	102 pts. (18%)			
Marked reduction of seizure tendency	119 pts. (21%)			
Moderate to no reduction of seizure tendency	199 pts. (35%)			
Less than 2 years follow-up data	56 pts.			
Post-operative deaths	3 pts. (pt. mortality rate 0.5%)			
Total	**625 pts.**			

area, or the nature of the underlying cause of the original brain damage.

OTHER NEUROSURGICAL PROCEDURES

Space does not permit detailed discussion of recent interesting efforts, in other centres in North America, Europe and Asia, to lessen the epileptic patient's seizure tendency by interruption of the neuronal pathways of spread of the seizure discharge, rather than by excision of the epileptogenic cortex. These efforts began with Van Wagenen's procedure of sectioning the corpus callosum in 1940, and with the pioneering stereotactic studies of Spiegel and Wycis soon after. Recent refinements in techniques of chronic recording and stimulation studies with fine wire electrodes stereotactically placed in the brain, as well as increasing experience with placement of subcortical lesions by stereotactic methods, have revived interest in the possibility of aborting the development of clinical seizures by the stereotactic placement of lesions, to interrupt the pathway of spread of the seizure discharge.

Stereotactic destruction of the amygdaloid nuclei gives hope of a surgical approach to certain patients with epileptogenic lesions of both temporal lobes, in whom standard unilateral temporal lobectomy is rarely justified. Stereotactic lesions in other subcortical regions have recently given some encouragement to the possibility of treating certain other types of seizure problems, suspected of arising in subcortical regions. Evaluation of the potential therapeutic roles of such procedures, however, must await longer and more detailed follow-up studies of

play an important role in the treatment of certain specially selected groups of patients with intractable focal seizure problems, and can bring about important expansion in the social and economic horizons for many of them.

FURTHER READING

Bailey, P. (1953), "Treatment of Psychomotor States by Anterior Temporal Lobectomy," *Res. Publ. Ass. nerv. ment. Dis.*, **31**, 341.

Baldwin, M. and Bailey, P. (Eds.) (1958), *Temporal Lobe Epilepsy*. Springfield, Illinois: Charles C. Thomas.

Branch, C., Milner, B. and Rasmussen, T. (1964), "Intracarotid Sodium Amytal for the Lateralization of Cerebral Speech Dominance," *J. Neurosurg.*, **21**, 399.

Crandall, P. H., Walter, R. D. and Rand, R. W. (1963), "Clinical Applications of Studies on Stereotactically Implanted Electrodes in Temporal Lobe Epilepsy," *J. Neurosurg.*, **20**, 827.

Falconer, M. A. (1968), "Surgical Treatment of Drug-Resistant Epilepsy due to Mesial Temporal Sclerosis," *Arch. Neurol.*, **19**, 353.

Foerster, O. and Penfield, W. (1930), "Structural Basis of Traumatic Epilepsy and Results of Radical Operation," *Brain*, **53**, 99.

Green, J. R. (1967), "Temporal Lobectomy with Special Reference to Selection of Epileptic Patients," *J. Neurosurg.*, **26**, 584.

Jasper, H. H., Ward, A. A. and Pope, A. (Ed.) (1969), *Basic Mechanisms of Epilepsy*. Boston: Little, Brown & Co.

Jennett, W. B. (1962), *Epilepsy After Blunt Head Injuries*. London: Heinemann.

Milner, B. (1964), "Some Effects of Frontal Lobectomy in Man," in *The Frontal Granular Cortex and Behaviour*, pp. 313-334 (J. M. Warren and K. Akert, Eds.). New York: McGraw-Hill.

Milner, B. (1966), "Amnesia Following Operation on the Temporal Lobes," in *Amnesia*, pp. 109-133 (O. L. Zangwill and C. W. M. Whitty, Eds.). London: Butterworth.

McRae, D. and Castorini, G. (1963), "Radiological Findings in Temporal Lobe Epilepsy of Non-Tumoral Origin," *Acta radiol.*, **1**, 541.

Niedermeyer, E., Walker, A. E. and Blumer, D. (1967), "EEG and Behavioural Findings in Temporal Lobe Epileptics before and after Temporal Lobectomy," *Electroenceph. clin. Neurophysiol.*, **23**, 493.

Penfield, W. and Jasper, H. (1954), *Epilepsy and the Functional Anatomy of the Human Brain*. Boston: Little, Brown & Co.

Penfield, W. and Milner, B. (1958), "Memory Deficit Produced by Bilateral Lesions in the Hippocampal Zone," *Arch. Neurol. Psychiat.*, **79**, 475.

Penfield, W. and Rasmussen, T. (1950) *The Cerebral Cortex of Man, A Clinical Study of Localization of Function*. New York: The Macmillan Company.

Rasmussen, T. and Blundell, J. (1961), "Epilepsy and Brain Tumor," in *Clinical Neurosurgery*, Vol. 7, Chap. X, pp. 138–156. Baltimore: The Williams and Wilkins Company.

Rasmussen, T. and Branch, C. (1962), "Temporal Lobe Epilepsy: Indications for and Results of Surgical Therapy," *Postgrad. med. J.*, **31**, 9.

Rasmussen, T. and Gossman, H. (1963), "Epilepsy due to Gross Destructive Brain Lesions," *Neurology*, **13**, 659.

Rasmussen, T. (1963), "Surgical Therapy of Frontal Lobe Epilepsy," *Epilepsia*, **4**, 481.

Rasmussen, T. (1969), "Surgical Therapy of Post-Traumatic Epilepsy," in *Late Effects of Head Injury*, pp. 277–305 (A. E. Walker, W. F. Caveness and M. Critchley, Eds.). Springfield, Illinois: Charles C. Thomas.

Schwab, R. S., Sweet, W. H., Mark, V. H., Kjellberg, R. N. and Ervin, F. R. (1965), "Treatment of Intractable Temporal Lobe Epilepsy with Stereotactic Amygdala Lesions," *Trans. Amer. neurol. Ass.*, **90**, 12.

Walker, A. E. (1969), "Pathogenesis and Pathophysiology of Post-Traumatic Epilepsy," in *Late Effects of Head Injury*, pp. 306–314 (A. E. Walker, W. F. Caveness and M. Critchley, Eds.). Springfield, Illinois: Charles C. Thomas.

Wilson, P. J. E. (1970), "Cerebral Hemispherectomy for Infantile Hemiplegia. A Report of 50 Cases," *Brain*, **93**, 147.

4. THE CLINICAL PHARMACOLOGY OF ANTICONVULSANTS

C. MAWDSLEY

Epilepsy was regarded by the ancient Greeks as a "seizing" of the sufferer by mysterious external forces. Hippocrates and Galen later suggested that epilepsy was due to a disturbance of the brain. In the seventeenth century Willis attributed epileptic fits to an explosion of animal spirits within the brain. Treatment reflected these theories of supernatural causation and included trephining, the drinking of blood and the wearing of a sheet of paper bearing the words Melchior, Jasper and Balthazar. However, the first effective therapy, as so often is the case, was discovered by chance. Sir Charles Locock in 1857, introduced potassium bromide to dampen down the sexual excess to which he ascribed epilepsy. It reduced the incidence of fits and bromide salts were the mainstay of treatment for more than half a century.

In 1870, the experiments of Fritsch and Hitzig showed that electrical stimulation of the dog's cortex produced fits and in the same year Hughlings Jackson put forward the concept that epilepsy arose from occasional, brief, discharges of neurones. These postulates marked the beginning of a scientific understanding of the disease. Further effective treatments were introduced in the early part of the twentieth century when phenobarbitone and later diphenylhydantoin were synthesized. The use of these and later drugs was empirically based and the mechanism of anticonvulsants' actions still remains incompletely understood. It is, however, now possible to consider rationally the pharmacology of anticonvulsants in the light of modern insights into the basic mechanisms of epilepsy.

MECHANISMS OF EPILEPSY

Common to all forms of epilepsy is a paroxysmal electrical discharge of high voltage relative to the normal cerebral background activity. This discharge arises from the hypersynchronous firing of an aggregation of neurones. The basic mechanism of epilepsy depends on what Schmidt has called the hyperexcitable neurone.

The neuronal cell membrane is normally polarized to maintain a potential difference of -70 mV. within the cell compared to its extracellular environment. This membrane potential is mediated by active exclusion of sodium ions from the cell by the sodium "pump". The energy demanded by this active metabolic process is derived from oxidative activity dependent on adenosine triphosphate. Movement of sodium ions into, and potassium ions out of, the cell causes a reduction in the membrane potential. After a fall of approximately 20 mV. an action potential is generated.

During a seizure discharge there is a relative increase in intracellular sodium and a fall in its extracellular concentration (Woodbury) and it may be that in cortical epileptic foci there is a permanent deficit of intracellular potassium and excess of sodium causing a tendency to instability of neuronal membranes.

Calcium and magnesium ions are incorporated into the cell membrane and play a part in maintaining its stability. A fall in the extracellular content of these ions, thus reducing their content in the membrane renders the latter permeable to sodium and potassium and thus more excitable.

The susceptibility of neuronal membranes to depolarize underlies the generation of epileptic discharges. The action potentials generated from epileptic neurones are abnormally large and of abnormally high frequency; up to 1,000 per sec. compared to the normal 150 per sec.

Epileptic neurones do not function in isolation. The epileptic focus is a population of neurones on which a number of external influences play. Chemical transmitters released from the terminals of other neurones, acting on the dendrites and cell bodies of epileptic neurones, render the membranes of the latter more excitable or more stable. Excitatory transmitters tend to depolarize membranes and inhibitory transmitters lead to hyperpolarization. The discharge of cells is, therefore, influenced by the balance between these two opposing influences.

Acetylcholine is known to be an excitatory transmitter in the central nervous system. An increase of acetylcholine has been found in epileptic foci compared with adjacent neural cortex and during electrically induced seizures there is an increase in free (active) acetylcholine preceding the onset of the epileptic discharge. Some amino acids such as L-glutamic and L-aspartic acids may also act as excitatory neuro-transmitters. The intracarotid injection of L-glutamic acid can induce convulsions.

Gamma-aminobutyric acid (GABA) is found in high concentration in cerebral grey matter and functions as a transmitter of inhibitory postsynaptic activity. The formation of GABA is governed by pyridoxine-dependent enzymes and the fits which result from pyridoxine deficiency are probably mediated by reduced intracerebral GABA. Glycine is also an inhibitory transmitter to spinal neurones and it may play a part in the cortex. All inhibitory transmitters may be considered to be anticonvulsants and the role of such substances may be of therapeutic importance in the future.

Fits can be produced experimentally by metrazol which amplifies excitatory postsynaptic potentials and by strychnine which blocks some inhibitory influences, notably those produced by glycine.

When the abnormal high frequency discharge arises it is then propagated to involve masses of other neurones which are inherently normal. Spread of the abnormal discharge may occur to adjacent neurones or via conducting pathways to distant groups of neurones or to brain stem structures and thence via the diffuse projection system to become generalized.

The bombardment by high frequency discharges not only potentiates the firing of normal cells but sometimes induces permanent changes in such cells, thus creating secondary abnormal foci which themselves may initiate epileptic discharges.

The clinical fit resulting from an epileptic discharge depends on its site of origin and the extent and direction of its propagation. In focal fits the discharge arises in a group of cortical neurones; it may remain localized there or may spread to nearby cortical structures; it may spread to the opposite hemisphere via the corpus callosum; or it may spread to brain stem structures causing loss of consciousness and evoking symmetrical discharges over both hemispheres. It has been suggested that generalized fits are due to discharges arising in mid-line diencephalic areas which are then propagated diffusely over the cortex to give rise to so-called centrencephalic epilepsy. Williams has recently cast doubt on this mechanism and has speculated that generalized fits may have a cortical origin.

During the development of the epileptic discharge and its spread there is a concurrent recruitment of inhibitory influences which may arise from adjacent neurones or may be due to the activity of distant neurones.

ANTICONVULSANTS IN GENERAL

The above review of the mechanisms of epilepsy suggests that anticonvulsant drugs might be effective either by suppressing the abnormal discharge or by preventing its propagation. Suppression of the initiating discharge could be achieved by stabilizing the epileptic neural membranes by (1) modifying intracellular metabolism, or (2) reducing excitatory influences acting on the abnormal neurones from the surrounding extracellular medium or from transmitter release at synapses. Restriction of the propagation of the discharge could be accomplished by (1) restricting the release of excitatory neuro-transmitters, (2) protecting the target neurones by rendering them less excitable, or (3) enhancing the effects of the inhibitory neuronal system.

It is possible to evaluate the actions of anticonvulsants by studying their efficacy in experimentally produced seizures. Fits may be produced in animals by electrical stimulation of differing intensities, by the topical application of penicillin and strychnine and other convulsants to the cortex, and by the injection of metrazol. Chronic epileptic animals may be produced by the implantation of alumina or metallic cobalt into their brains. Drugs may raise the threshold to such stimuli or modify the pattern of the seizures produced. In general, drugs which are active against grand mal modify maximal fits produced by electrical stimulation, whilst drugs which in man are helpful in petit mal elevate the threshold and modify the pattern of metrazol-induced attacks in animals. However, these experimental assessments are fallible and their forecasts need to be supplemented by clinical information about the various drugs.

Most effective anticonvulsants are chemically similar, sharing a cyclic structure, usually composed of five atoms, and many contain the grouping:

$$
\begin{array}{ccc}
R & & \\
\diagdown & & \\
& C & C=O \\
\diagup & | & | \\
R & | & | \\
& O=C—N &
\end{array}
$$

the introduction of phenyl rings at the points marked "R" is common to many drugs which suppress grand mal fits whilst alkyl groups in these positions confer efficacy against petit mal discharges.

Many drugs are useful anticonvulsants and are best considered in chemically determined groups.

BARBITURATES

Introduced as hypnotics some derivatives of malonyl urea (barbituric acid) were found to have anticonvulsant as well as sedative effects. Phenobarbitone and primidone are among the most widely used and most effective anticonvulsants. Methyl phenobarbitone and methbarbital are occasionally employed.

Phenobarbitone

Phenobarbitone exerts a depressive effect on metabolisms throughout the body. Heat production, oxygen consumption, respiration and cardiac output are all reduced by the drug. Its anticonvulsant activity is not merely a reflection of its hypnotic effect. Phenobarbitone may act partly by suppressing the epileptic discharge. It impairs the transport of sodium and potassium ions across neuronal membranes, thus rendering the membrane potential more stable. Its principal effect is on synaptic transmission which it depresses. This is particularly evident in multisynaptic pathways. It reduces excitatory postsynaptic potentials of motor neurones. It has been suggested that phenobarbitone may also enhance presynaptic inhibition. The anticonvulsant effect of phenobarbitone is probably due both to suppression of the initiating discharge and to prevention of its propagation.

The drug has other effects when given in higher than therapeutic doses. It causes a depression of the synthesis of adenosine triphosphate and acetylcholine, and of plasma acetylcholinesterase. When phenobarbitone is withdrawn the production of acetylcholine rises at a faster rate than that of cholinesterase, and it is interesting to speculate that a continuing relative excess of acetylcholine may be a factor in the production of fits after the drugs administration is suddenly stopped.

Phenobarbitone is rapidly absorbed from the stomach, and slowly from the lower gastro-intestinal tract. The maximal rise in blood levels occurs about 12 hours after oral ingestion. About a quarter of administered phenobarbitone is excreted unchanged in the urine. The remainder is hydroxylated in the liver and there stimulates the production of the enzymes needed for its own metabolism.

The usual adult dose is 30–60 mg. thrice daily. It is a cheap and effective treatment of grand mal and focal epilepsy. It is occasionally effective in the treatment of petit mal but more often it increases the frequency of petit mal fits.

The most common side effect of treatment is sedation whose occurrence limits its usefulness in isolation. Often the dose of phenobarbitone which would effectively suppress fits, produces unacceptable somnolence. This effect is sometimes used, to advantage, when the drug is prescribed at night to prevent nocturnal seizures. It means, however, that effective control of fits during the day requires the combination of phenobarbitone with other drugs, particularly phenytoin.

In elderly patients and in children phenobarbitone may induce restlessness and irritability. Rashes result from its administration occasionally. Cerebellar ataxia and megaloblastic anaemia are of rare occurrence.

Primidone

This drug is closely related chemically to phenobarbitone. Approximately one-fifth of ingested primidone is metabolized to phenobarbitone in the liver. Its mode of action is similar to that of phenobarbitone but its effectiveness in modifying electrically induced fits is greater than that of phenobarbitone as is its clinical efficacy in temporal lobe fits. Its principal use is in grand mal and focal seizures but it is sometimes helpful in petit mal attacks.

The usual adult dose lies between 250 mg. and 500 mg. three times daily. Its half-life in the plasma is approximately one-and-a-half hours.

Primidone frequently causes somnolence and sometimes ataxia and double vision. These effects are particularly liable to occur during the week after its exhibition and can be mitigated by introducing it in small doses and gradually increasing it. The drug gives rise to rashes fairly frequently, sometimes causing megaloblastic anaemia, and rarely leukopenia. It occasionally evokes paranoid and psychiatric reactions in mentally retarded patients and in those suffering from temporal lobe fits.

THE HYDANTOINATES

Diphenylhydantoin

Diphenylhydantoin (phenytoin, dilantin) was the first of this group to be used as an anticonvulsant, remains the most useful, and has been extensively studied.

The neuropharmacological effects of phenytoin are legion. It enters the nucleus of neurones and at the time when it is active as an anticonvulsant it is found in the mucrosomal fraction. It may be incorporated into messenger-R.N.A. Phenytoin causes a fall in the intracellular concentration of sodium and prevents the rise therein which usually results from electrically induced convulsions. It enhances the effect of the sodium pump and actively extrudes sodium from cortical neurones. The cerebral concentration of glutamic acid falls and GABA concentration rises. All these effects tend to produce cell membrane stability.

The principal anticonvulsant action of phenytoin is probably due to the prevention of spread of the abnormal discharge. It markedly reduces post-tetanic potentiation which is thought to be an important factor in the spread of the high frequency trains of impulses arising in the epileptic focus.

Phenytoin is metabolized in the liver by parahydroxylation and the metabolites are excreted in the urine. A small amount of the drug is excreted unchanged in the saliva. Metabolism of phenytoin in the liver is subject to alterations which are of clinical importance. There is a genetic variation. In a few patients there is a deficiency of the enzyme which mediates parahydroxylation; in other instances excessively fast metabolism occurs. Other drugs modify the metabolism of phenytoin. Phenobarbitone stimulates the production of the liver enzymes responsible for the metabolism of phenytoin as well as those involved in its own breakdown. Since the two drugs "compete" for the same enzymes the effects of the concurrent administration of the two drugs is variable but usually the initial effect of phenobarbitone is to produce a rise in serum levels of phenytoin; long continued ingestion of phenobarbitone causes a fall in the blood levels of phenytoin. Other drugs, notably sulthiame, para-aminosalicylic acid, isoniazid, dicoumarol and occasionally chlorpromazine impair the metabolism of diphenylhydantoin and raise its serum level.

These variations are reflected in the plasma half-life of the drug whose average is 22 ± 9 hours.

The usual adult dose of phenytoin is 100 mg. three times daily but the effective dose is not simply or easily presented since its metabolism is variable and toxic serum levels are close to therapeutic concentrations. The optimal therapeutic serum levels lie between 10 and 20 μg./ml. Levels above 25 μg./ml. are almost always associated with toxic effects. Because of these difficulties, the administration of phenytoin to epileptics, should whenever possible, be monitored by frequent estimations of blood levels.

Diphenylhydantoin is the most effective treatment for grand mal epilepsy and for focal seizures. It is ineffective in petit mal.

Toxic effects are numerous and fairly common. Minor disturbances include gum hypertrophy, rashes which are sometimes photosensitive, and hirsutism. A low serum protein bound iodine is common in those taking phenytoin but this is probably due to impaired binding of thyroxine by protein and does not presage hypothyroidism. A generalized lymphadenopathy, sometimes accompanied by splenomegaly is a rare complication of phenytoin therapy. The picture regresses within 1–2 weeks of withdrawal of the drug.

A number of neurological side effects occur. A cerebellar syndrome of acute or chronic development is common. It often develops in patients who have taken the drug without ill effect for years. Ataxia, nystagmus and dysarthria are manifest and these features usually disappear within a week after the drug's withdrawal. There is good evidence that toxic doses of phenytoin cause permanent damage to the cerebellar cortex.

Psychoses, intellectual deterioration, peripheral neuropathy and pyramidal signs are less common neural complications of phenytoin.

Low serum folate levels are sometimes associated with phenytoin administration and are less often found after the ingestion of primidone and phenobarbitone. All three drugs, particularly phenytoin, may cause macrocytosis and a megaloblastic anaemia. It may be that some of the neuropsychiatric complications of phenytoin therapy are related to folate deficiency. The mechanism by which anticonvulsants induce folate deficiency is obscure. The serum folate should be estimated in any patient who develops a neurological complication or anaemia whilst taking phenytoin. Blood counts should routinely be performed in all epileptics taking these drugs. Concurrent administration of folic acid (5 gm. three times daily) will rapidly cure the megaloblastic anaemia and will often help the psychiatric disturbances. It has been suggested that the anticonvulsant action of phenytoin might be due to its anti-folate effect and that the administration of folic acid causes a deterioration in the control of fits. Several recent studies have not confirmed these hypotheses.

A recently discovered side effect of phenytoin, which is also produced by primidone and phenobarbitone, is a disturbance of calcium metabolism. Hypocalcaemia and a raised alkaline phosphatase, together with osteomalacia have been found in a significant proportion of epileptics taking phenytoin. It may be that a drug induced increase in hepatic enzymes leads to increased breakdown or inactivation of vitamin D. Treatment with vitamin D effectively reverses these biochemical changes.

Mesantoin (Methoin, Mephenytoin)

Has anticonvulsant properties similar to phenytoin, but has an increased tendency to depress bone marrow function and to cause liver necrosis. The usual dose is 50 to 100 mg. three times daily, but it should be used in the treatment of grand mal seizures only if other drugs are ineffective.

Ethotoin

Is less effective as an anticonvulsant than phenytoin. It is sometimes useful in doses of 250 to 500 mg. three times daily.

ACETYLUREAS

These drugs are closely related to the barbiturates and hydantoinates. Phenylacetylurea is the only one of the group usually prescribed. Its mode of action and metabolism are similar to those of phenytoin. It is an effective treatment of grand mal and focal fits and has some value in petit mal. It is, however, liable to produce hepatic and renal failure and should rarely be used.

SUCCINIMIDES

This group of drugs, relatively recently introduced, has not as yet been extensively studied experimentally. It would seem likely that they are effective in blocking multisynaptic pathways.

Ethosuximide

Is effective in animals in preventing metrazol-induced fits and clinically is perhaps the drug of greatest benefit in the control of petit mal attacks.

The dose is 250 mg. three times daily. Though highly successful, at this dosage, in suppressing petit mal episodes it sometimes tends to evoke grand mal attacks and should, therefore, be given in conjunction with phenytoin or primidone if the clinical picture suggests that a patient may be predisposed to grand mal fits.

Ethosuximide is a relatively safe drug, but may cause rashes, somnolence and rarely, bone marrow depression.

Methsuximide

This drug is effective in the treatment of petit mal seizures and has no tendency to precipitate grand mal attacks. It is occasionally helpful in the suppression of temporal lobe seizures.

The dosage is 300 mg. twice or three times daily.

It occasionally gives rise to rashes and rarely to profound loss of appetite.

Phensuximide

Phensuximide too is useful in the treatment of petit mal, but is less so than ethosuximide or methsuximide, and has a greater tendency than these two drugs to produce side effects. Its dose is 500 mg. three times daily, and occasionally doses up to 1 g. three times daily are employed.

It frequently produces nausea and vomiting and in high

doses causes episodes of depersonalization. It occasionally causes renal failure and this, together with its reduced potency when compared to ethosuximide relegates phensuximide to a role as an alternative when other, safer, succinimides have proved ineffective.

THE OXAZOLIDINEDIONES

The oxazolidinediones were the first drugs which were regularly effective in the treatment of petit mal.

Trimethadione (Troxidone)

Like the other oxazolidinediones trimethadione most effectively prevents experimental metrazol-induced fits. The drug prolongs recovery time at the synapse and seems to inhibit polysynaptic transmission. Some experimental findings suggest that the drug acts presynaptically. It reduces the response to repetitive electrical stimulation. Probably its major therapeutic effect is to interrupt the spread of the epileptic discharge from the cortex to the thalamus.

The dose in children is 300 mg. three times daily, and in adults twice this dose is usually effective.

The drug is rapidly absorbed from the gut, and is metabolized in the liver by demethylation.

Trimethadione is an effective treatment of petit mal, but because of its side effects it is now usually used only when ethosuximide has failed.

There are a number of toxic effects from trimethadione. Rashes are fairly common. An unusual untoward effect is the intolerance of bright lights which it evokes.

Bone marrow depression is uncommon and the nephrotic syndrome and hepatic necrosis are rare. Occasional patients develop lupus erythematosus whilst taking the drug.

When it is necessary to use trimethadione the patient should be frequently observed during the few months after its introduction and repeated blood counts, and liver function tests and urine examination should be carried out.

Paramethadione

The effects of paramethadione are similar to those of trimethadione. The dose and side effects are similar. There is some evidence that paramethadione is less toxic than is trimethadione, but it can also lead to severe bone marrow depression.

Aloxidone

This is another variant of the oxazolidinediones. The dose and side effects being similar to those of trimethadione.

All the oxazolidinediones occasionally seem to precipitate grand mal convulsions and where the clinical or electroencephalographic picture raises the possibility of associated grand mal convulsions, phenobarbitone or primidone should be introduced as well. There is some evidence that diphenylhydantoin reduces the potency of the oxazolidinediones, and, therefore, the barbiturate preparations are preferred for combined therapy.

THE BENZODIAZEPINES

These drugs were originally introduced as tranquillizers, but there is much recent evidence of their effectiveness as anticonvulsants. They suppress both metrazol-induced and electrically-induced fits. The major effect of the benzodiazepines is the inhibition of EEG arousal from brain stem stimulation. They raise the after-discharge threshold of the thalamus. Their therapeutic effects as anticonvulsants seems to depend on the enhancement of an inhibitory mechanism. At present nitrazepam would seem to be the most effective anticonvulsant of this group of drugs. It is particularly helpful in the control of myoclonic epilepsy and has also been used in the control of infantile spasms associated with hypsarrhythmia. The dose of nitrazepam is 2·5 mg. to 5 mg. three times daily.

Diazepam also seems to be effective occasionally in the treatment of grand mal and is particularly helpful in suppressing the hyperkinesis and aggressive behaviour sometimes associated with epilepsy. The dose varies between 2 mg. three times daily and 5 mg. three times daily.

Diazepam given intravenously in an initial dose of 10 mg. and thereafter given by continuous intravenous drip is a most effective treatment in status epilepticus.

It is likely that the benzodiazepines will prove to be significantly useful adjuncts in the treatment of epilepsy.

MISCELLANEOUS ANTICONVULSANTS

In addition to the groups of anticonvulsants listed above there are a number of preparations which are either useful as alternatives to the more commonly used preparation or have specific indications in certain varieties of epilepsy.

Corticosteroid Preparations

Adrenocorticotrophic hormone is of specific value in the treatment of infantile spasms associated with the EEG picture of hypsarrhythmia. ACTH seems to work by causing the exclusion of sodium from neurones. The dose is 25 international units daily. This will usually lead to marked improvement of infantile spasms and of the EEG picture, within a month of its institution. Oral preparations such as dexamethasone are also sometimes effective.

Pyridoxine

As outlined above, pyridoxine is specifically indicated for those rare instances where convulsions develop due to a deficiency of the vitamin. In addition there is a form of epilepsy presenting within three or four days of birth which is probably of genetic origin and recessively inherited. These infantile spasms respond well to 10 mg. of pyridoxine daily. It has been suggested that fits are due to a disturbance of tryptophan metabolism but this observation has yet to be confirmed.

Carbamezapine

This drug is chemically related to imipramine and is most used in the treatment of trigeminal neuralgia. It has, however, some effectiveness in controlling grand mal attacks and focal fits. It has little value in the treatment of petit mal. The dose in adults is 100 to 200 mg. three times daily.

Rashes, drowsiness and occasional jaundice are the main side effects. Bone marrow depression is a rare complication.

Sulthiame

This drug is occasionally useful in the treatment of focal epilepsy and less often is of value in the treatment of grand mal seizures. It is often given together with phenytoin but its effect in this combination is probably mainly due to the increase which it produces in the serum level of phenytoin. The dosage is 100 to 200 mg. three times daily.

Side effects include hyperventilation and paraesthesiae affecting the hands and the snout area. Somnolence and confusion are occasional complications.

Acetazolamide

Acetazolamide is a sulphonamide derivative which has a marked inhibitory effect on carbonic anhydrase. It causes a generalized fall in cerebral, including intra-neuronal, sodium concentration. It also results in a fall in intra-cellular pH associated with an elevation of carbon dioxide.

The dose in children is 125 mg. twice or thrice daily.

Acetazolamide is occasionally effective in the treatment of petit mal and it is a useful ancillary in its therapy when the major drugs have failed. It can also be used to supplement the activity of the succinimide or oxazolidinedione therapy.

Side effects are rarely serious. Paraesthesiae, rashes and occasional cyanosis occur. Rare examples of sulphonamide side effects have been described.

Bromides

Although potassium bromide was the earliest effective anticonvulsant, it is now rarely used. Bromide replaces chloride in cerebral intra- and extra-cellular compartments and presumably suppresses neuronal excitability by decreasing the movement of sodium and potassium across the membranes. Bromide intoxication is common and leads to confusion, memory disturbance and somnolence, and in severe instances to hallucination and coma.

CLINICAL APPLICATIONS

Effective anticonvulsant treatment rests on a detailed clinical history, combined whenever possible, with observation of the patient's attacks, together with the EEG pattern presented. It is important to institute therapy in effective doses but the patient should not be over treated so that the side effects of the drugs given cause more disability than the patient's occasional fits.

An isolated fit should not lead to the immediate institution of long-term drug treatment. After a single fit it is usually wise to observe the patient for a period, and only if further convulsions occur should anticonvulsants be introduced. When it is clear that specific constellations of circumstances are needed to evoke fits, the avoidance of these precipitants may obviate the need for drugs. Thus, children who develop convulsions only when exposed to flickering light, as from a malfunctioning television set, may be adequately treated by simply avoiding this stimulus. Those patients, of fairly common occurrence, whose fits occur only during the hours of sleep, may effectively be treated by a single dose of a slow-release preparation of barbiturate when they retire to bed, rather than by the regular ingestion of drugs during the day. In each patient treatment should be flexibly tailored to meet the individual problem.

Certain patterns of fit usually respond to predictable combinations of drugs.

For grand mal and focal epilepsy phenytoin, primidone and phenobarbitone are the mainstays of treatment. The combination of phenytoin with either primidone or phenobarbitone probably represents the most effective treatments for grand mal epilepsy. Phenobarbitone and primidone should not be given together since the two drugs are so similar in action that they often cause unacceptable drowsiness. Where the primary drugs are ineffective then carbamezapine or nitrazepam may be added to one of the above combinations to enhance their effect. Ethosuximide is probably the drug of choice in the treatment of petit mal. Should this prove ineffective, methsuximide, trimethadione or paramethadione may be used. When these drugs of first choice are ineffective in isolation then acetazolamide may be added.

If the appropriate drugs are given in effective doses and their effects monitored, at least three-quarters of all epileptics can be significantly improved. It is poor practice continually to alter drugs on insufficient information. Each drug or combination of drugs should be prescribed for one or two months before their ineffectiveness is assumed. Before rejecting a drug because of its presumed lack of effect it is important to cross-examine the patient about his mode of taking the drug and his adherence to the prescribed regime. Whenever a change in treatment is envisaged it is important not to withdraw one drug suddenly and substitute the newer preparation. It is wise in all instances slowly to withdraw one drug and to introduce the new drug gradually. A sudden cessation of anticonvulsant remedies, particularly phenobarbitone and phenytoin, may lead to status epilepticus.

In the treatment of epileptics it is important to remember that the mere control of fits by anticonvulsants is but one aspect of treatment and that anticonvulsant therapy should be supplemented by encouragement to live as full a life as possible. The aid of social workers and employment agencies should be invoked so that epileptics can perform to their fullest effect within the community and by this means it is possible to minimize the secondary psychiatric manifestations of paranoia and aggression which are particularly liable to supervene in long standing epileptics.

FURTHER READING

Butler, T. C. (1953), "Quantitative Studies of the Demethylation of Trimethadione," *J. Pharmacol.*, **108**, 11–17.

Butler, T. C. (1956), "The Metabolic Hydroxylation of Phenobarbitone," ibid., **116**, 326–336.

Esplin, D. W. (1957), "Effects of Diphenylhydantoin on Synaptic Transmission in Cat Spinal Cord and Stellate Ganglion," *J. Pharmacol.*, **120**, 301–323.

Esplin, D. W. and Curto, E. M. (1957), "Effects of Trimethadione on Synaptic Transmission in the Spinal Cord; Antagonism of Trimethadione and Pentylenetetrazal," *J. Pharmacol.*, **121**, 457–467.

Gastant, H., Glaser, G. H. and Magnus, O. (Eds.) (1969), "Symposium on Laboratory Evaluation of Antiepileptic Drugs," *Epilepsia*, **10**.

Goodman, L. S., Toman, J. E. P. and Swinyard, E. A. (1946), "The Anticonvulsant Properties of Tridione," *Amer. J. Med.*, **1**, 213–228.

Jasper, H. H., Ward, A. A., Jr. and Pape, A. (Eds.) (1969), *Basic Mechanisms of the Epilepsies*. Boston: Little, Brown.

Millichap, J. G. (1965), *Anticonvulsant Drugs in Physiological Pharmacology* (W. S. Root, and F. G. Hofman, Eds.). N.Y.: Academic Press.

Noach, E. L., Woodbury, D. M. and Goodman, L. S. (1958), "Studies on the Absorption Distribution, Fate and Excretion of 4-C^{14}-labelled Diphenylhydantoin," *J. Pharmacol.*, **122**, 301–314.

Raines, A. and Standaent, F. G. (1969), "Effects of Anticonvulsant Drugs on Nerve Terminals," *Epilepsia*, **10**, 211–227.

Salmoiraghi, G. C. and Bloom, F. E. (1964), "Pharmacology of Individual Neurones," *Science*, **144**, 493–499.

Schmidt, R. P., Thomas, L. B. and Ward, A. A., Jr. (1959), "The Hyperexcitable Neurone," *J. Neurophysiol.*, **22**, 285–296.

Schmidt, R. P. and Wilder, B. J. (1968), *Epilepsy*. Philadelphia: F. A. Davis.

Swinyard, E. A. and Castellion, W. A. (1966), "Anticonvulsant Properties of Some Benzodiazepines," *J. Pharmacol.*, **151**, 369–375.

Toman, J. E. P., Swinyard, E. A. and Goodman, L. S. (1946), "Properties of Maximal Seizures and their Alteration by Anticonvulsant Drugs and Other Agents," *J. Neurophysiol.*, **9**, 231–239.

Waddell, W. J. and Butler, T. C. (1957), "The Distribution and Excretion of Phenobarbital," *J. clin. Invest.*, **36**, 1217–1226.

Ward, A. A., Jr. (1961), "Epilepsy," *International Review of Neurobiology*, **3**, 137–186.

Williams, D. (1965), "The Thalamus and Epilepsy," *Brain*, **88**, 539–556.

Woodbury, D. M. and Esplin, D. W. (1959), "Neuropharmacology and Neurochemistry of Anticonvulsant Drugs," *Proc. Ass. Res. Nerv. Dis.*, **37**, 24–56.

Woodbury, J. W. (1963), "Interrelationships between Ion Transport Mechanisms and Excitatory Events," *Federated Proceedings*, **22**, 31–35.

Woodbury, D. M. and Kemp, J. W. (1971), "Pharmacology and Mechanisms of Action of Diphenylhydantoin," *Psychiatria, Neurologia, Neurochirurgia*, **74**, 91–115.

Woodbury, D. M. (1955), "Effect of Diphenylhydantoin on Electrolytes and Radio Sodium Turnover in Brain and Other Tissues of Normal, Hyponatremic and Postictal Rats," *J. Pharmacol.*, **115**, 74–95.

SECTION V

SENSORY SYSTEM

1. COMMON SENSIBILITY

GRAHAM WEDDELL AND RONALD T. VERRILLO

I. INTRODUCTION

Common sensibility is still most often divided into modalities. These comprise touch (including pressure and proprioception), warmth, cold and pain. A lot is now known about touch, and details concerning its peripheral terminations and central connections are available in most text-books. There is little disagreement about what is known and what is, as yet, unknown.

The position in respect of pain and thermal sensibility is very different so that we shall use all the space at our disposal to the consideration of pain, for this is likely to be of most interest to practising physicians. As evidence of its importance it may be noted that in the three decades between 1940 and 1970 no less than 30 volumes have been devoted to the subject of pain.

Concepts of pain have changed considerably in the course of history. Aristotle considered pain "a passion of the soul", but most modern definitions include statements concerning its rôle in the defence of the body against harm or potential damage. On the other hand Leriche (1949) regarded pain as "a sinister gift which diminishes man, which makes him sicker still than he would have been without it". Whatever attitude is adopted towards the phenomenon of pain, it is the primary symptom which brings patients to the doctor. Thus physicians should be as fully acquainted with what is known about this sensation as possible for it is their responsibility to determine its cause, alleviate it and, where possible, correct the condition which brought it about. The concept of pain sensibility has always been difficult to verbalize. Compared with other sensory modalities it has a more private or personal quality and it is this which makes unambiguous communications with others about pain so difficult. Whilst sights and sounds appear *out there*, or externalized, to be shared with others, pain appears *in here* and has always defied simple definition. Sensations aroused by the stimulation of specialized sense organs can for the most part be defined in terms of the physical parameters (electromagnetic energy, acoustical energy, mechanical displacement or chemical activity) that have activated them and their related sensory systems. Such a convenience is not available to the investigator of pain. Indeed, it is not yet fully agreed that pain ranks as a unique sensation. The investigator can only record what his subjects report in response to noxious stimuli or what patients report as the result of pathology. Above all he must keep an open mind and not attempt to verbalize *for* his subject or patient. It is only too easy for physicians to suggest to a patient with paraesthesiae that his symptoms are those of pain, i.e. that the sensation "hurts".

Two schools of thought have persisted regarding the nature of pain. One, the *sensory* viewpoint, states that pain is a separate and distinct sense modality and must therefore have neural elements for its detection, communication and appreciation. The other position has been called the *intensive* viewpoint which regards pain not as a separate modality but rather as the consequence of excessive stimulation of any sensory system. In recent years the trend has been to incorporate elements of both these viewpoints and to add a considerable measure of such complex factors as the social, personal and immediate environmental situation in which the sensation is perceived.[35,41,64]

Regardless of the theoretical position, there is one common denominator in all definitions of pain; it is a sensation that *hurts*. In what follows we shall stand by this simple and perhaps naïve definition without attempting further analysis of the word "hurts".

II. THEORETICAL POSITIONS

The theoretical positions taken by most contemporary workers in pain research will now be summarized so that readers may become familiar with some of the concepts and terminology they will encounter in the literature on pain. It is easy to disparage the making of theories for it is often the case that the less that is known about a phenomenon the more numerous and elaborate are the theories which attempt to explain it. Theories do, however, serve the indispensable function of providing a framework or background against which facts may be evaluated and they form the context within which scientific questions may be formulated. Theories serve these ends well but only so long as they are used as a setting for experimental findings and not as a tunnel through which to view the evidence.

A. Specificity Theory

The specificity theory is the earliest of the contemporary theories and has its origins in the ideas of Charles Bell (1811) and Johannes Müller (1838) which suggested that nerves are selective in the type of information which they will transduce and carry. This concept was formalized by Müller into the *doctrine of specific energies* and, in respect of common sensibility, experimentally supported by Blix (1884), Donaldson (1885) and Goldsheider (1884) who all reported that stimulation of different spots on the skin could arouse only a single sensation. Goldsheider in particular, reported that stimulation with the fine needles aroused pain from some spots in the skin and not from others. This seemed to imply that under each spot lay a nerve terminal that was uniquely qualified to respond exclusively to the type of stimulation used in the arousal of a sensation from that spot. Indeed, the most comprehensive formulation of this position was given by Von Frey (1894) who consigned each of the cutaneous sensory modalities to specific morphological neural entities in the skin. Thus we have the direct matching of touch with hair follicle nerve-baskets and Meissner corpuscles together with oft repeated but erroneous matching of cold to Krause end-bulbs and warmth to Ruffini end-organs. By a process of elimination pain was matched with the ubiquitous "free" nerve endings.

The specificity theory thus regarded pain as a separate and unique sense modality with neural units, pathways and central receptive areas designed expressly for the mediation of the sensation of pain. The idea won wide and immediate support. One of its weaknesses, however, lies in the fact that subsequent histological investigations have failed to confirm that anatomically specific receptors always lie beneath sites from which specific sensations are evoked.

More recently Lim (1966) has proposed that pain is a specific modality mediated by specific chemoreceptive neural elements served by fibres which vary from C to A-gamma-delta in size. Stimulation of these fibres is by chemical agents released primarily by supra-normal itensities or by damage to the tissues in which they lie. The perception of pain is completed by information from mechano- and thermo-receptors which contribute to the total image of a pricking, stabbing, or burning, pain sensation. The degree to which the pain component predominates is a function of "central factors" (fascilitation and inhibition) as well as the past experience and personality of the individual.

B. Pattern Theory

The idea of a one-to-one relationship between stimulus, end-organ, neural pathway and perception is rejected by the pattern theorists. They propose instead, non-specific endings and pathways carrying spatio-temporally encoded messages that contain all of the information required to elicit a specific sensation. Whilst it is now clear from anatomical and physiological investigations carried out in the past three decades that *all* communications via the nervous system are composed of spatiotemporal impulse patterns, the pattern theorists have unfortunately devoted more publication space to attacking the concept of specificity rather than providing concrete evidence that particular spatiotemporal patterns are related either to specific sensations or to the physical parameters of the stimulus.

The pattern theory was first proposed by Nafe (1927) and was later extended and refined by Kenshalo and Nafe (1962). In a series of papers, the Oxford group under Weddell provided considerable experimental evidence in support of the theory.[60,71] The position is put forcefully by Sinclair in his statement, "thus, activity in a given fibre could at one time contribute towards the experience of a sensation of touch, and at another, towards the experience of pain, cold or warmth".[60]

Closely related to the attempts to account for pain by neural firing patterns are explanations that employ the concept of reverberating circuits. Livingston (1943) suggested that intense pathological stimulation of the body set up a reverberating pattern of impulses within the spinal cord which could later be reactivated by a non-noxious stimulus. Activation of such a circuit is interpreted as pain at higher neural centres. Hebb (1949) and Gerard (1951) have proposed similar mechanisms operating at the cortical level.

These mechanisms, though they may be important in specific instances, are not necessarily relevant to the pains associated with the wear and tear of everyday life. Nevertheless, they serve to remind physicians that the early relief of pain of a potentially disabling nature is something which must never be overlooked.

Most researches in the field of pain today do not adhere strictly to the purer forms of either the specificity or the pattern theories because it is difficult to ignore experimental evidence put forth by proponents of either system. As might be expected, there have been numerous attempts to reconcile the two viewpoints and most of these have combined features of both positions into what may be called duplex theories.

C. Duplex Theories

Henry Head's (1920) classical experiments, in which he sectioned a nerve in his own arm and then noted the sequential return of sensations, as regeneration of the nerve proceeded, form the basis of the duplex theories. He concluded that the cutaneous sensations are served by two distinct systems of nerves; one more primitive (*protopathic*) to mediate pain and extremes of temperature, and another, more slowly regenerating system (*epicritic*), for light touch, localization and temperature discrimination.

The common feature of all modern duplex theories is that they postulate two interacting systems of nerve-fibres and often invoke or imply a pattern of impulses based on this interaction. Mountcastle (1961) has suggested a highly specific, fast conducting system utilizing the dorsal column-medial lemniscal pathway to mediate pressure, touch and vibration. The perception of pain and temperature is relegated to a less specific and less organized system conducting more slowly over the spinothalamic tract.

Noordenbos (1959) stressed the summation of impulses over time and space within a network of short spino-spinal fibres which he called the Multisynaptic Afferent System (MAS). Any stimulus, if strong enough and persistent enough, can activate this system and cause pain. He stressed that pain is not the result of the stimulation of specific fibres but rather of the activation of the MAS by an interaction of slow and fast fibre-impulses from the periphery. The resultant pattern of summation and inhibition within the dorsal roots at several cord levels governs the activity of the MAS and thus the experience of pain.

Perhaps the most ambitious attempt in recent years to reconcile the positions of specificity and non-specificity is that of Melzack and Wall (1965) who have combined elements of specificity, pattern and duplex theories into the *gate control theory*. They proposed nerve-terminals at the periphery which respond optimally to mechanical or thermal energies. The type of stimulus is encoded in the neural firing pattern and proceeds by large and small fibres to the cord. The temporal pattern of impulses acts upon the synaptic pattern of fibres within the substantia gelatinosa setting up a pattern of excitatory-inhibitory activity. Large fibre-activity inhibits small fibre-activity, thus forming a gate. The balance of activity between large and small fibres determines the position of the gate. If opened, the message signals *pain* over the lateral spino-thalamic pathway. If large fibre-activity predominates, the gate closes and no pain is felt. In order to account for the effects of personal experience on the perception of pain, a central control mechanism was proposed as a monitor over the activity of the gate mechanism. While the theory is specific enough to provide a springboard for research,

neither the authors nor other workers in the field have provided much substantiation for tenets of the theory.

III. ANATOMICAL CONSIDERATIONS

It is obvious from the plethora of past and current theoretical positions which have just been condensed and summarized that the mechanism by which physical energy is transduced, transmitted and ultimately appreciated as pain, is very poorly understood. The extent of our knowledge about the antomy of the system ranges from relative certainty to pure speculation. The remainder of the chapter is devoted to a discussion of that anatomy beginning with central structures and working toward the periphery. This seemingly reversed sequence was chosen because it represents a continuum of increasing certainty in our knowledge (but *see* Fig. 1).

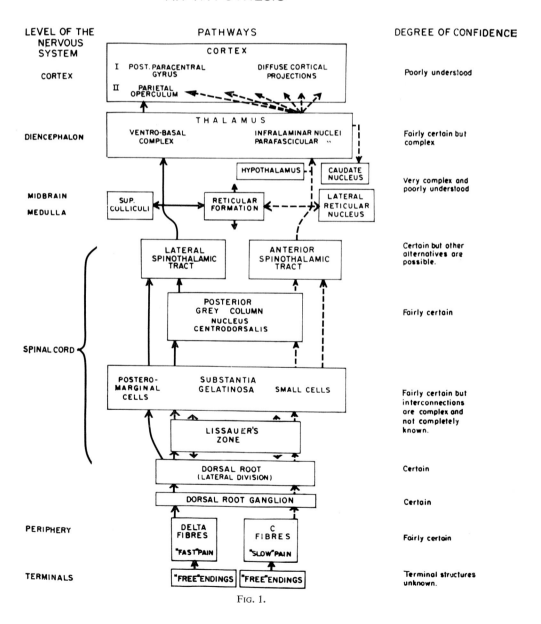

FIBRE PATHWAYS FOR PAIN SENSIBILITY
AN HYPOTHESIS

FIG. 1.

It is important that a word of caution be added regarding sensory pathways. For reasons of clarity these pathways are often depicted in a way which implies a series of wires strung out in an orderly sequence with well defined coupling areas along the path. Any such characterization must be regarded only as a rough outline of a system which involves complicated and as yet poorly understood structural inter-relationships at practically all levels. There are known to be reflex areas and short collaterals leaving fibres all along the way for unknown destinations as well as diversions to the reticular formation and interconnections with the cerebellum that are not included in this general description. It must also be remembered that a great deal of research on pain has to be performed on animals in which it is extremely easy to make the mistake of equating neurophysiological activity with human perception. Moreover, Casey (1966) has shown how great are the variations in recorded activity in anaesthetized animals compared with those which are alert. Evidence must be collated from many sectors, but it must not be forgotten that "pain" is a personal phenomenon and can be directly studied only in man.[74]

A. The Cortex

In the absence of the cerebral cortex fine sensory discrimination such as two-point discrimination, point localization and sense of position is impossible. We also know that there is no place on the cortex to which we can point and say, "that is the area for the reception of pain", as we can do with a fair degree of accuracy for hearing, vision and touch. The most likely candidate for such an area is the region of the somatosensory cortex (postcentral gyrus). Early attempts to arouse pain by the direct electrical stimulation of this region proved disappointing. Although a host of other sensations sometimes even vague tingling mixed with pain could be aroused, pure pain was rarely evoked.[53,65] Also, although destruction of small portions of the area sometimes leads to a reduction in pain sensitivity, it only rarely leads to complete analgesia.[33,40]

Later reports, however, have shown that a greater degree of success in arousing pain can be achieved if the region of stimulation is shifted to the posterior paracentral gyrus buried within the central sulcus.[18,33] This is an important observation because this area of the cortex receives projection fibres from the most caudal portion of the ventrobasal complex of the thalamus which has long been associated with the relay of pain sensations.

The somatosensory area II in the parietal operculum is also implicated in the sensation of pain by studies that report interference with pain perception after parietal lobe damage.[15,65] Direct electrical stimulation of thalamo-cortical (and corticothalamic) projections from this region have evoked sensations of pain and relief from pain without disturbing other sensory functions has been achieved by sectioning these projections.[67] Very relevant in this connection is that portions of the second somatic area in the cat can be activated only by noxious stimuli.[7]

The evaluation of pain pathways to, and projections onto the cerebral cortex are inherently difficult, for they are investigated only in patients with intractable pain whose brains are exposed and stimulated in the hope of finding a pathway which can be interrupted or an area excised which will relieve the symptoms without side effects. Moreover, it is only in patients who are experiencing severe pain in whom it is possible to evoke unequivocal reports of the pain they are experiencing on cortical stimulation.

After a decade of further research we must conclude as did Weddell and Miller (1962) that although cortical involvement is necessary in the perception and appreciation of pain, its precise rôle in this connection is impossible to define. But clearly the posterior paracentral gyrus and the somatic area II are indicated as fruitful areas for future research into cortical pain projection.

B. The Thalamus

Two groups of thalamic nuclei have been shown to be primarily involved in the mediation of pain. They are (1) the ventrobasal complex (lateral and posterior nuclei or the posterolateral ventral nuclei) and (2) the intralaminar nuclei of the dorsal thalamus.[46,61] The ventrobasal complex receives projections from the lateral spinothalamic tract (neospinothalamic system) and it displays a good somatotopic representation.[11,12,54] The posterior portions of the ventrobasal complex receives fibres from both the lateral spinothalamic tract and from the dorsal-column medial-lemniscal system in a very poor somatotopic patterning.[55a] This has been termed a thalamic "no-man's-land"[61] and its involvement with pain is open to question. The entire ventrobasal complex appears to receive projections primarily from delta peripheral fibres with a minimal representation of C-fibres.[46]

The intralaminar and parafascicular group of nuclei receive fibres from the anterior spinothalamic tract (paleo-spinothalamic system) and are very strongly activated by the stimulation of peripheral C-fibres.[46] Lesions in this region of the thalamus bring relief from pain but have no effect on the appreciation of touch or temperature.[37,38,39,59] The postoperative emotional status of patients does not appear to have been altered by the procedure, unlike that which follows leucotomy. Projections from this area go to the caudate nucleus and to all parts of the cortex in what has been termed the "diffuse thalamic projection system"[44] and is regarded by some to be the proximal portion of the reticular activating system. Once again it is necessary to sound a note of caution. The placing of lesions in the thalamus may give relief in some patients with intractable pain but this can only be interpreted within the context of the individual concerned and the precise extent and location of the lesion which was made. It is not proof that nerve-impulses perceived as pain all project via the regions in which the lesions were placed in every individual. Nevertheless, these zones are clearly deserving of continuous study and evaluation.

C. Spinal Cord

In the spinal cord there is reasonable agreement that impulses signalling pain are carried within specific regions of the cord, namely the anterolateral system. This system comprises the lateral spinothalamic tract (or neo-spino-thalamic system) and the anterior spinothalamic tract (or paleo-spinothalamic system). Full transection of these pathways always results in loss of pain and temperature sensations on the contralateral side, temporarily at least.[23,65,66,81] It has also been shown by direct electrical stimulation of the anterolateral columns in man that approximately 54 per cent of the fibres carry nociceptive information while the remainder are divided between perceptions of warmth (37 per cent) and cold (9 per cent).[82]

Both delta and C-fibres involved in nociception enter the cord over the lateral division of each dorsal root and many fibres then pass into Lissauer's tract before entering the substantia gelatinosa.[27] Delta fibres terminate primarily on cell bodies in the postero-marginal region of the dorsal horn which in turn project fibres to the ventrobasal complex of the thalamus by way of the lateral spinothalamic tract. The C-fibres are believed to terminate on the small cells of the substantia gelatinosa and project upwards primarily in the anterior spinothalamic tract to the intralaminar and parafascicular thalamic nuclei. Whilst most fibres cross to the contralateral side through the anterior white commissure a few ascend the cord on the side of entry. Some of the fibres project to the hypothalamus and both systems send fibres into the reticular formation.

D. Periphery

There is universal acceptance that the nerve-impulses giving rise to pain originate in networks of chiefly non-myelinated axons[80,83] and are transmitted over the delta and C-range of fibres.[9] This is not to imply that pain is the exclusive domain of these fibres, for it has been shown that fine peripheral fibres can be activated by touch, warmth, cold as well as nociceptive stimuli.[17,28,31] However, it is certain that activation of these small fibres is a necessary condition for the experience of pain.

There is evidence, also, that the two fibre-sizes are differentially specific in function; that the delta fibres convey "fast pain", the initial, bright, pricking pain of short latency and duration, whereas the longer lasting, less bearable and burning "slow pain" is transmitted by C-fibres.[5,62,85] Collins et al. (1960, 1966) have demonstrated by stimulating exposed peripheral cutaneous nerves in human subjects, that stimulation of large fibres produced no pain; stimulation of delta fibres resulted in a sharp, pricking bearable pain, but that unbearable pain was elicited by the stimulation of C-fibres. Iggo (1962) found that roughly half of the C-fibres investigated responded only to very intense levels of stimulation and accordingly classified them as nociceptive. Compare this to the finding of Sweet et al. (1950) cited above, that about half (54 per cent) of the fibres in the anterolateral quadrant of the cord in man when activated give rise to pain.

So far, we have been discussing the effect of impulses transmitted along peripheral nerves. When we seek to identify the sites and the mechanism by which energy is transduced into neural impulses which give rise to pain we return to the realm of speculation. The identification of sites of transduction of energies for vision in the rods and cones of the retina or for audition in the hair-cells of the cochlea would arouse little controversy today. The cutaneous sensations present more of a problem although research has recently identified transduction sites for vibration[68,69] and other types of mechanical stimulation.[43] Temperature sensations still pose a problem although it can be stated most assuredly that the Krause end-bulbs and Ruffini endings are *not* the primary sensors for cold and warmth.

The end-organ for the transduction of painful stimuli has been traditionally and consistently identified as the "free nerve-ending" for example, the non-encapsulated endings of fibres that make up the dermal nerve networks. No other end-organ has ever been seriously considered for this rôle. The problem is that no one has ever actually seen a "free nerve-ending". The literature is replete with photomicrographs of the nerve plexus and portions of axons which seem to disappear into or between dermal and epidermal cells, but the free nerve *ending* has not been unequivocally figured. Lim (1966) avoided this problem by proposing, as did Sherrington (1906), that either the ending itself or the axon leaving it may serve as the site for the initiation of propagated disturbances. The idea that the nerve-impulse is activated by chemicals released from cells into the neighbourhood of the pre-terminal axon or its ending is gaining wider acceptance. The mechanism for the release of these chemicals is either potentially damaging thermal[24] or mechanical[35] stimuli and a host of chemical agents have been suggested as neural activators.[3,24,35,56] Mountcastle (1968) has summarized the transduction process as follows: tissue-injury releases a proteolytic enzyme which causes the formation of polypeptides by its action upon the globulin in the intercellular fluids. These polypeptides are powerful stimulators of nociceptive nerve-endings.

The evidence available then suggests the following tentative anatomical pathway for impulses which will be perceived as pain. Stimuli which produce tissue-damage activate a chemical mechanism in nerve-endings or pre-terminal axon which results in the propagation of a spike potential. The nerves which carry these impulses are specific for the reception of noxious stimuli and signal one of two types of pain. Fast pain is a sensation of very short latency and short duration often described as a sharp bright prick. This type of pain is mediated by delta fibres which measure $1 \cdot 0$–$6 \cdot 0 \, \mu$ dia. in the periphery. Slow pain, which has a longer latency and duration and can grow to unbearable intensities is believed to be the consequence of activating C-fibres ($0 \cdot 4$–$1 \cdot 2 \, \mu$ dia.). The actual site of transduction from physical energy to nerve-impulse is believed to be situated at the endings or preterminal axons of "free" or unencapsulated nerve fibres. This will be discussed later in greater detail.

Both sets of fibres pass via the lateral division of the dorsal root into Lissauer's tract to synapse on the small cells of the substantia gelatinosa, on the postero-marginal cells and in the nucleus centro-dorsalis (central magnocellular nucleus) of the posterior grey horn. There are probably collateral branches as well as synaptic connections within Lissauer's tract and the substantia gelatinosa. At this level the delta and C systems are undistinguishable, but they divide now into two tracts.

The delta fibres sweep contralaterally through the anterior white commissure to ascend in the lateral spinothalamic (neo-spinothalamic) tract and to synapse within the ventro-basal complex of the thalamus. The most likely site for the termination of these fibres is in the lateral and posterior (postero-lateral ventral) thalamic nuclei. Between the first synapse in the cord and the thalamic termination, collaterals leave the ascending fibres and enter the reticular formation at a number of ill defined levels between the medulla and the mid-brain. A third major set of fibres carries these impulses from the thalamus, through the posterior limb of the internal capsule to terminate within the posterior paracentral gyrus of somatic area I.

The C-fibres at the level of the spinal cord sweep from the posterior grey horn through the anterior white commissure to the contralateral anterior spinothalamic (paleo-spinothalamic) tract. These second order neurons ascend in this tract but they also give rise to collaterals some of which enter the reticular formation between the medulla and mid-brain, others go to the hypothalamus. Most of the fibres terminate in the intralaminar and parafascicular nuclei of the thalamus. However, this system is far more diffuse than that ascending dorsal tract. From the thalamus third order fibres radiate to all parts of the cortex and downwards into the caudate nucleus.

Visceral pain is probably carried over similar fibres whose cell bodies also lie in the dorsal root ganglia, the difference being that they course peripherally along autonomic nerve-pathways. The splanchnic and cardiac nerves have an abundance of delta and C-fibres and mechanical stimulation of the peritoneum and parietal pleura is extremely painful. The adequate stimulus for visceral pain is most probably tension in the gut wall. It is likely that deep muscular pain arises in the rich innervation of delta and C-fibres found in all muscle-fibres.[29,51]

The phenomenon of referred pain is perplexing. It is pain perceived at a site which is remote from the source of the disturbance. Most commonly it is cutaneous pain with tenderness evoked by stimuli bombarding structures deep to the skin, i.e. viscera, muscle attachments or ligaments. Because both areas are related most commonly to the same or closely adjacent cord segments, knowledge of the reference sites becomes a valuable diagnostic tool for locating diseased or malfunctioning organs.[57] However, there are some notable exceptions to the mapping of referred pain by dermatomes which makes caution imperative.

A number of theories have been put forward to account for the phenomenon; for example the release of chemical mediators within the nervous system;[34,56] the division of the same nerve into deep and superficial branches[63] and the most favoured current view that cutaneous and visceral nerves converge into common synaptic pools at various levels of the spinal cord.[72] There is experimental evidence in animals of the confluence in the spinal cord of fibres serving touch from widely different areas onto one and the same cell.[22] Some mechanism of this kind must be invoked to explain pains referred from such widely different areas as the skin of the face to that of the leg. That such odd connections might occur in the course of the development of the nervous system is not impossible. Each view is logical but unfortunately the experimental evidence is often lacking, contradictory, or inconsistent with other facts. Although it is a most useful diagnostic aid, the phenomenon of referred pain has no adequate explanation at this time.

IV. Discussion

A serious gap in our knowledge clearly exists at the very beginning of the pathways outlined above, it is about the elusive nerve-*ending* where it is assumed that the impulse is initiated. It was indeed a surprising and distressing revelation to one of us (RTV), who is not an anatomist, to discover that these oft mentioned sensory terminals have never in fact been seen or photographed in their entirety. Munger (1965) has traced neurites in the snout of the opossum into the epidermis. He finds them not in the intercellular spaces but penetrating within the epidermal cells which have now, supposedly, assumed the functions of the Schwann cells. But the ending itself is never shown. Zander and Weddell (1951) have demonstrated abundant intra-epithelial fine nerve-processes in the cornea and beaded filaments are found toward the terminations of the intra-epidermal nerve fibres,[10,78] but still the ending itself has not been pictured.

It is probable that free nerve-endings do not terminate in the same way as a solid structure such as a piece of string, for nerve-fibres are not static entities, formed during development and until death maintaining a constant structure. They are living, cytoplasmic processes which undergo a continuous process of change. In the skin, conjunctiva and walls of the carotid sinus there is known to be a continuous cycle of degeneration and repair of peripheral axons and with increasing age the process of repair is often incomplete with the formation of sterile end-bulbs.[73,78] It is thus likely that the tips of cutaneous axoplasmic filaments consist of condensations of dead material which are sometimes seen as terminal beads. The beaded segments seen in the stratum corneum of the skin are most likely the products of degenerated axons which are being carried passively toward the surface to be shed with the keratin or surface squames.[9,48]

Regenerating fibres are often surmounted by small growth-cones and such fibres can be found in the epidermis shortly before an increase in its mitotic index.[52] If the skin is damaged or diseased there is a marked increase in the number of fine axons present and in the amount of degeneration and repair which goes on among them. If a parent fibre is cut or injured by disease the filaments surrounding the receptive field of the injured nerve send forth sprouts which invade the denervated or partially denervated zone.[1,70,75,76]

The period of active growth is characterized by the presence of new filaments passing along pre-existing strands of Schwann cells whilst growth-cones are found surmounting axons which appear to be leaving one strand of Schwann cells and approaching adjacent ones. Spirals comparable with those described by Perroncito (1907) are found where there is mechanical blocking preventing growth. When, in time nerves re-enter and grow down the denervated stump from above, the invading axons from neighbouring nerves start to degenerate and when the process of re-innervation is complete they are found to have retreated to the territories they originally occupied. There is an interesting and perhaps significant correlation between the period of most active growth, during which many growth-cones appear, and the experience of pain. The threshold for pain and the character of the pain change dramatically 48–64 hr. after nerve or tissue damage. During this period of active nerve invasion pain of unbearable intensity can be elicited by light mechanical brushing or light touch to the margin of the affected area. Before and after this period pain can be elicited only by stimuli which are normally painful such as a pin-prick though the sensation evoked always has an unusually unpleasant quality.

To summarize what is known about peripheral nerve-terminations of the kind which must serve pain-sensibility, a recurrent cycle of degeneration and regeneration takes place at the distal ends of all unencapsulated peripheral nerves. The morphological change occurring during this cycle have characteristics which are broadly similar to those occurring in abnormal conditions such as nerve or tissue damage, and disease. During the regenerative phase after nerve injury there are abnormalities of pain sensations that include, (a) the lowering of pain threshold i.e. such that skin pain can be evoked by light touch and (b) alterations in pain tolerance such that though the stimulus threshold is unaltered the *quality* of the sensation evoked is intolerable. This much is fairly well established and brings us to the limit of our knowledge of the structures and the events in the periphery. To make any further progress in our understanding of pain, certain questions must be answered. How close are the events which take place in the course of regeneration following abnormal conditions, to those which occur in the course of everyday life? Is there a relationship at all between the pain experienced during the course of regeneration after injury and the pain that is evoked in everyday experiences? What, in detail, are the morphological similarities, at the level of the electron microscope, that occur in the regeneration of neural turnover and that following tissue insult? In particular, what changes occur in the perineurium in the preterminal and terminal regions? Recent research has emphasized the importance of the neural coverings, especially the perineurium, in the normal (or abnormal) functioning of the axon.[79] The final, and in many ways the most important question, which must be answered: do "free nerve-endings" really exist, if so, where and how do they end and what is their ultrastructure? If "free nerve-endings" do not have neural characteristics, just how and where do peripheral, unencapsulated nerve fibres terminate from the functional point of view? If and when these questions are answered then, perhaps, we shall know a little more about how stimuli which evoke pain are transduced.

The account of what is known about pain has unfortunately raised more questions than it has answered. One thing is clear, the mechanism of its arousal and its pathways to the brain which result in its perception are complex. Thus the treatment of pain is unlikely to be straightforward nor is it probable that the same remedies will apply to all patients alike. Certain guide lines to treatment are indicated but no more. Above all the physician must always seek for the cause of the pain and it must be assumed that, with very few exceptions, pain is the result of impulses reaching the central nervous system along delta and C-fibres. Receptors for pain are ubiquitous though they have not yet been defined anatomically, but as every clinician knows pain can also be evoked by a lowering of the threshold to stimulation of the nerve-fibres serving pain (so that light touch is effective) anywhere in their passage from the periphery to the spinal cord. Indeed roots can be so affected that pain appears to be continuous. Pain should never be treated symptomatically until its site of origin and the process which is evoking it have been defined. In patients in whom the site of origin of the pain is in doubt it is usually possible to search for and find it by blocking the suspected pathway with local anaesthetics.

Once the site and probable cause of the pain has been defined it should be treated as expeditiously as possible. From what we already know it can be treated at many levels and in many different ways. Local inflammation, pressure, and degenerative changes often cause pain, and each of these is necessarily accompanied by changes in blood-supply and in consequence in some cases in local environmental changes also. There are many ways of influencing such changes, ranging from the use of anti-biotics to counter-irritants. All have at times and in some people proved efficacious. Pain resulting from skeletal degenerative changes can sometimes be treated by surgical correction of the affected parts but it is important to remember that mere anatomical deformity is not in itself necessarily the cause of pain; it is the resulting change in the neural environment which matters and to which attention must be primarily directed. In patients with chronic pain in whom a low grade inflammatory change is suspected at the site of the lesion (which has been defined by local anaesthesia) it may be possible to inject anti-inflammatory agents locally. When local treatment of this kind fails, and only provided the site and cause of the pain is in no doubt i.e. osteoarthritis, it may be possible to alleviate suffering by persuading the patient to divert his attention away from it just as a games player can ignore injuries until the match is over, i.e. to persuade patients to learn to live with their pain. Surgical intervention on the central nervous system should be used only as a last resort, for it is irreversible, and by its very nature it is impossible to avoid some side-effects—however minor—due to interference with nerve-pathways unconnected with pain.

Neurosurgeons are aware of this and have reported that a few patients complain of the side-effects as being worse than the original pain, for pain leaves no distinct memory trace.

REFERENCES

[1] Allenby, C. F., Palmer, Elizabeth and Weddell, G. (1966), "Changes in the Dermis of Human Hairy Skin Resulting from Stripping the Keratinized Layer off the Epidermis," *Z. Zellforsch.*, **69**, 566–572.

[2] Bell, C. (1811), *Idea of a New Anatomy of the Brain*. Privately Distributed Monograph; *J. Anat. Physiol.* (1869), **3**, 154–157.

[3] Benjamin, F. B. (1968), "The Release of Intracellular Potassium as a Factor in Pain Production," in *The Skin Senses* (D. R. Kenshalo, Ed.). Springfield, Ill.: C. C. Thomas.

[4] Bishop, G. H. (1946), "Neural Mechanisms of Cutaneous Sense," *Physiol. Rev.*, **26**, 77–102.

[5] Bishop, G. H. and Landau, W. M. (1958), "Evidence for a Double Peripheral Pathway for Pain," *Science*, **128**, 712–713.

[6] Blix, M. (1884), "Experimentelle Beiträge zur Lösung der Frage Über die specifische Energie der Hautnerven," *Z. Biol.*, **20**, 141–156.

[7] Carreras, M. and Andersson, S. A. (1963), "Functional Properties of the Anterior Ectosylvian Gyrus of the Cat," *J. Neurophysiol.*, **26**, 100–126.

[8] Casey, K. L. (1966), "Unit Analysis of Nociceptive Mechanisms in the Thalamus of the Awake Squirrel Monkey," *J. Neurophysiol.*, **29**, 727–750.

[9] Cauna, N. (1959), "The Mode of Termination of the Sensory Nerves and its Significance," *J. comp. Neurol.* **113**, 169–210.

[10] Cauna, N. (1966), "Fine Structure of the Receptor Organs and its Probable Functional Significance," in *Touch, Heat and Pain* (A. V. S. De Reuck and J. Knight Eds.). London: J. and A. Churchill.

[11] Chang, H. T. and Ruch, T. C. (1947), "Topographical Distribution of Spinothalamic Fibers in the Thalamus of the Spider Monkey," *J. Anat.*, **81**, 150–164.

[12] Clark, W. E. Le Gros (1936), "The Termination of the Ascending Tracts in the Thalamus of the Macaque Monkey," *J. Anat.*, **71**, 7–40.

[13] Collins, W. F., Nulsen, F. E. and Randt, C. T. (1960), "Relation of Peripheral Nerve Fiber Size and Sensation in Man," *Arch. Neurol. Psychiat.*, **3**, 381–385.

[14] Collins, W. F., Nulsen, F. E. and Shealy, C. N. (1966), "Electrophysiological Studies of Peripheral and Central Pathways Conducting Pain," in *Pain* (R. S. Knighton and P. R. Dumke, Eds.). Boston: Little, Brown and Co.

[15] Critchley, M. (1953), *The Parietal Lobes*. London: Edward Arnold.

[16] Donaldson, H. H. (1855), "On the Temperature Sense," *Mind*, **10**, 399–416.

[17] Douglas, W. W. and Ritchie, F. M. (1957), "A Technique for Recording Functional Activity in Specific Groups of Medullated and Non-medullated Fibres in Whole Nerve Trunks," *J. Physiol.* (*Lond.*), **138**, 19–30.

[18] Erickson, T. C., Bleckwenn, W. J. and Woolsey, C. N. (1952), "Observations on the Post Central Gyrus in Relation to Pain," *Trans. Amer. neurol. Ass.*, **77**, 57–59.

[19] Frey, M. Von (1894), "Beiträge Zur Physiologie des Schmerzinnes," *Ber. Verhandl. sächs. Ges. Wiss.*, **46**, 185–196.

[20] Gerard, R. W. (1951), "The Physiology of Pain: Abnormal Neuron States in Causalgia and Related Phenomena," *Anesthesiology*, **12**, 1–13.

[21] Goldscheider, A. (1884), "Die specifische Energie der Temperaturnerven," *Mh. Prakt. Derm.*, **3**, 198–208.

[22] Gordon, G. (1957), "The Physiological Basis of Referred Pain," *Proc. roy. Soc. Med.*, **40**, 586–588.

[23] Grant, F. C. and Wood, F. A. (1958), "Experiences in Cordotomy," *Clin. Neurosurg.*, **5**, 38–65.

[24] Hardy, J. D. (1953), "Thresholds of Pain and Reflex Contraction as Related to Noxious Stimulation," *J. Appl. Physiol.*, **5**, 725–729.

[25] Head, H. (1920), *Studies in Neurology*. London: Kegan Paul.

[26] Hebb, D. O. (1949), *The Organization of Behavior*. New York: Wiley.

[27] Hyndman, O. R. (1942), "Lissauer's Tract Section," *J. Internat. Coll. Surgeons*, **5**, 394–400.

[28] Iggo, A. (1960), "Cutaneous Mechanoreceptors with Afferent C Fibres," *J. Physiol.* (*Lond.*), **152**, 337–353.

[29] Iggo, A. (1962), "Non-myelinated Visceral, Muscular and Cutaneous Afferent Fibres and Pain," in *The Assessment of Pain in Man and Animals* (C. A. Keele and R. Smith, Eds.). Edinburgh: Livingstone.

[30] Kenshalo, D. R. and Nafe, J. P. (1962), "A Quantitative Theory of Feeling: 1960," *Psychol. Rev.*, **69**, 17–33.

[31] Lele, P. P. and Weddell, G. (1956), "The Relationship between Neurohistology and Corneal Sensibility," *Brain*, **79**, 119–154.

[32] Leriche, R. (1949), *La chirurgie de la Douleur*. Paris: Masson et Cie. Quoted in A. Soulairac, "On an Experimental Approach to Pain," in *Pain* (A. Soulairac, J. Cahn and Charpentier, Eds.). London: Academic Press.

[33] Lewin, W. and Phillips, C. G. (1952), "Observations on Partial Removal of the Post-central Gyrus for Pain," *J. Neurol. Neurosurg. Psychiat.*, **15**, 143–147.

[34] Lewis, T. (1942), *Pain*, New York: Macmillan.

[35] Lim, R. K. S. (1966), "A Revised Concept of the Mechanism of Analgesia and Pain," in *Pain* (R. S. Knighton and R. R. Dumke, Eds.). Boston: Little, Brown and Co.

[36] Livingston, W. K. (1943), *Pain Mechanisms*. New York: Macmillan.

[37] Mark, V. H., Ervin, F. R. and Hackett, T. P. (1960), 3, "Clinical Aspects of Stereotactic Thalamotomy in the Human," *Arch. Neurol.*, **3**, 351–367.

[38] Mark, V. H., Ervin, F. R. and Yakovlev, P. I. (1963), "Stereotactic Thalamotomy. III. The Verification of Anatomical Lesion Sites in the Human Thalamus," *Arch. Neurol.*, **8**, 528–538.

[39] Mark, V. H. and Yakovlev, P. I. (1955), "A Note on Problems and Methods in Preparation of a Human Stereotactic Atlas," *Anat. Rec.*, **121**, 745–752.

[40] Marshall, F. (1951), "Sensory Disturbances in Cortical Wounds with Special Reference to Pain," *J. Neurol. Neurosurg. Psychiat.*, **14**, 187–204.

[41] Melzack, R. and Casey, K. L. (1968), "Sensory, Motivational, and Central Control Determinants of Pain," in *The Skin Senses* (D. R. Kenshalo, Ed.). Springfield, Ill.: C. C. Thomas.

[42] Melzack, R. and Wall, P. D. (1965), "Pain Mechanisms: A New Theory," *Science*, **150**, 971–979.

[43] Merzenick, M. M. and Harrington, T. (1969), "The Sense of Flutter-vibration Evoked by Stimulation of the Hairy Skin of Primates," *Exp. Brain Res.*, **9**, 236–260.

[44] Morison, R. S. and Dempsey, E. W. (1942), "A Study of Thalamocortical Relations," *Amer. J. Physiol.*, **135**, 281–292.

[45] Mountcastle, V. B. (1961), "Some Functional Properties of the Somatic Afferent System," in *Sensory Communication* (W. A. Rosenblith, Ed.). New York: Wiley.

[46] Mountcastle, V. B. (1968), "Pain and Temperature Sensibilities," *Medical Physiology*, 12th edition, Vol. II (V. B. Mountcastle, Ed.). St. Louis: Mosby.

[47] Müller, J. (1838), *Handbuch der Physiologie des Menschen*, Vol. 2, Book V, Coblenz.

[48] Munger, B. L. (1965), "The Intraepidermal Innervation of the Snout Skin of the Opossum," *J. Cell Biol.*, **26**, 79–97.

[49] Nafe, J. P. (1927), "The Psychology of Felt Experience," *Amer. J. Psychol.*, **39**, 367–389.

[50] Noordenbos, W. (1959), *Pain*. Amsterdam: Elsevier.

[51] Paintal, A. S. (1960), "Functional Analysis of Group III Afferent Fibres of Mammalian Muscles," *J. Physiol.*, **152**, 250–270.

[52] Pawlowski, A. and Weddell, G. (1967), "The Lability of Cutaneous Neural Elements," *Brit. J. Derm.*, **79**, 14–19.

53 Penfield, W. and Boldrey, E. (1937), "Somatic Motor and Sensory Representation in the Cerebral Cortex of Man as Studied by Electrical Stimulation," *Brain*, **60**, 389–443.

54 Perl, E. R. and Whitlock, D. G. (1961), "Somatic Stimuli Exciting Spinothalamic Projections to Thalamic Neurons in Cat and Monkey," *Exp. Neurol.*, **3**, 256–296.

55 Perroncito, A. (1907), "Die Regeneration der Nerven," *Beitr. path. Anat.*, **42**, 354–446.

55a Poggio, G. F. and Mountcastle, V. B. (1960), "A Study of the Functional Contributions of the Lemniscal and Spinothalamic Systems to Somatic Sensibility. Central Nervous Mechanisms in Pain," *Bull. Johns. Hopk. Hosp.*, **106**, 266–316.

56 Rosenthal, S. R. (1968), "Histamine as the Chemical Mediator for Referred Pain," in *The Skin Senses* (D. R. Kenshalo, Ed.). Springfield, Ill.: C. C. Thomas.

57 Ruch, T. C. (1965), "Pathophysiology of Pain," in *Physiology and Biophysics* (T. C. Ruch and H. D. Patton, Eds.). Philadelphia: Saunders.

58 Sherrington, C. S. (1906), *The Integrative Action of the Nervous System*. New Haven: Yale University Press.

59 Sano, K., Yoshioka, M., Ogashiwa, M., Ishijima, B. and Ohye, C. (1966), "Thalamolaminotomy," *Confini. neurol.*, **27**, 63–66.

60 Sinclair, D. C. (1955), "Cutaneous Sensation and the Doctrine of Specific Energy," *Brain*, **78**, 584–614.

61 Sinclair, D. C. (1967), *Cutaneous sensation*. London: Oxford.

62 Sinclair, D. C. and Stokes, B. A. R. (1964), "The Production and Characteristics of 'Second Pain'," *Brain*, **87**, 609–618.

63 Sinclair, D. C., Weddell, G. and Feindel, W. H. (1948), "Referred Pain and Associated Phenomena," *Brain*, **71**, 184–211.

64 Sternbach, R. A. (1968), *Pain, A Psychophysiological Analysis*. New York: Academic Press.

65 Sweet, W. H. (1959), "Pain," in *Handbook of Physiology, Sec. 1, Neurophysiology Vol. 1*, (J. Field, Ed.). Washington D.C.: American Physiological Society.

66 Sweet, W. H., White, J. C., Selverstone, B. and Nilges, R. G. (1950), "Sensory Responses from Anterior Roots and from Surface and Interior of Spinal Cord in Man," *Trans. Amer. neurol. Ass.*, **75**, 165–169.

67 Talairach, J., Tournax, P. and Bancaud, J. (1960), "Chirurgie parietale de la douleur," *Acta neurochir.*, **8**, 153–250.

68 Verrillo, R. T. (1966), "Specificity of a Cutaneous Receptor," *Percep. Psychophys.*, **1**, 149–153.

69 Verrillo, R. T. (1968), "A Duplex Mechanism of Mechanoreception," in *The Skin Senses* (D. R. Kenshalo, Ed.). Springfield, Ill.: C. C. Thomas.

70 Weddell, G. (1942), "Axonal Regeneration in Cutaneous Nerve Plexuses," *J. Anat.*, **77**, 49–62.

71 Weddell, G. (1955), "Somesthesis and the Chemical Senses," *Ann. Rev. Psychol.*, **6**, 119–136.

72 Weddell, G. (1957), "Referred Pain in Relation to the Mechanism of Common Sensibility," *Proc. roy. Soc. Med.*, **50**, 581–586.

73 Weddell, A. G. M. (1962), "Observations on the Anatomy of Pain Sensiblity," in *The Assessment of Pain in Man and Animals* (C. A. Keele and R. Smith, Eds.). Edinburgh: E. and S. Livingstone.

74 Weddell, G. (1966), "The Relationship between Pain Sensibility and Peripheral Nerve Fibres," in *Pain*, (R. S. Knighton and P. R. Dumke, Eds.). Boston: Little, Brown & Co.

75 Weddell, G., Guttmann, L. and Gutmann, E. (1941), "The Local Extension of Nerve Fibres into Denervated Areas of Skin," *J. Neurol. Psychiat.*, **4**, 206–225.

76 Weddell, G., Jamison, D. and Palmer, Elisabeth (1959), "Recent Investigations into the Sensory and Neurohistological Changes in Leprosy," in *Leprosy in Theory and Practice* (R. G. Cochrane, Ed.). Bristol: John Wright & Sons.

77 Weddell, G. and Miller, S. (1962), "Cutaneous Sensibility," *Ann. Rev. Physiol.*, **24**, 199–222.

78 Weddell, G., Pallie, W. and Palmer, Elisabeth (1954), "The Morphology of Peripheral Nerve Terminations in the Skin," *Quart. J. Micr. Sci.*, **95**, 483–501.

79 Weddell, A. G. M., Palmer, Elisabeth and Rees, R. J. W. (1971), "The Fate of *Mycobacterium leprae* in Mice (CBA)," *J. Path.* In press.

80 Weddell, G. and Sinclair, D. C. (1953), "The Anatomy of Pain Sensibility," *Acta neuroveg. (Wein)*, **7**, 135–146.

81 White, J. C. and Sweet, W. H. (1955), *Pain Mechanisms and Neurosurgical Control*. Springfield, Ill.: C. C. Thomas.

82 White, J. C., Sweet, W. H., Hawkins, R. and Nilges, R. G. (1950), "Anterolateral Cordotomy: Results, Implications and Causes of Failure," *Brain*, **73**, 346–367.

83 Woollard, H. H., Weddell, G. and Harpman, J. A. (1940), "Observations on the Neurohistological Basis of Cutaneous Pain," **74**, 413–440.

84 Zander, E. and Weddell, G. (1951), "Observations on the Innervation of the Cornea," *J. Anat.*, **85**, 68–99.

85 Zotterman, Y. (1933), "Studies in the Peripheral Nervous Mechanism of Pain," *Acta med. scand.*, **80**, 185–242.

FURTHER READING

De Reuck, A. V. S. and Knight, J. (1966), *Touch, Heat and Pain*. London: J. and A. Churchill.

Kenshalo, D. R. (1968), *The Skin Senses*. Springfield, Ill.: C. C. Thomas.

Knighton, R. S. and Dumke, P. R. (1966), *Pain*. Boston: Little, Brown and Co.

Melzack, R. and Wall, P. D. (1965), "Pain Mechanisms: A New Theory," *Science*, **150**, 971–979.

Mountcastle, V. B. (1968), "Pain and Temperature Sensibilities," in *Medical Physiology*, 12th edition, Vol. II (V. B. Mountcastle, Ed.). St. Louis: C. V. Mosby and Co.

Ruch, T. C. (1965), "Pathophysiology of Pain," in *Physiology and Biophysics* (T. C. Ruch and H. D. Patton, Eds.). Philadelphia: Saunders.

Sinclair, D. C. (1967), *Cutaneous Sensation*. London: Oxford University Press.

Sternbach, R. A. (1968), *Pain. A Psychophysiological Analysis*. New York: Academic Press.

Sweet, W. H. (1959), "Pain," in *Handbook of Physiology. Sec. 1, Neurophysiology, Vol. 1* (J. Field, Ed.). Washington, D.C.: American Physiological Society.

Weddell, G. and Sinclair, D. C. (1953), "The Anatomy of Pain Sensibility," *Acta neuroveg. (Wein)*, **7**, 135–146.

White, J. C. and Sweet, W. H. (1955), *Pain: Its Mechanisms and Neurosurgical Control*. Springfield, Ill.: Thomas.

Wolff, H. G. (1963), *Headache and Other Head Pains*. New York: Oxford University Press.

2. EYE MOVEMENTS AND THEIR DISORDERS:
an analytical evaluation

ANDREW J. GAY AND NANCY M. NEWMAN

Eye movement disorders in man can, with few exceptions, be logically analysed and precisely described, thus aiding neurological diagnosis and providing a basis for correlating abnormal extraocular movements and intracranial lesions. The most important step in the evaluation of these movements is the realization that there are different eye movement mechanisms (five of which are discussed below) each of which may be affected separately by disease processes. This realization must be reflected throughout the examination and be incorporated into the patient's record. Thus, it is not sufficient to say that "the optokinetic response is deficient to the right" but it must be stated whether it is the fast phase, or the slow phase, or both together that are affected and also which of the other fast and slow eye movements are defective.

The analytical evaluation of eye movements requires no elaborate equipment, no time-consuming methods of examination. All that is required is that the examiner test all five eye movement mechanisms, paying attention both to qualitative and quantitative disturbances affecting each mechanism.

It is our intention to present (1) an account of how to examine eye movements, (2) a functional division of eye movement mechanisms, (3) a description of the anatomical substrates for eye movements, and (4) illustrations of how such an analytical evaluation is applied to disorders of eye movements.

In spite of the availability of a voluminous literature and many excellent experimental and clinical studies, there is still a lack of precise understanding of the anatomical and physiological substrates for eye movement. We are still further from a correlation of clinical disorders of eye movements with their anatomical bases. The following material is presented in a didactic fashion. It represents a series of working hypotheses which have served as the basis for our study of eye movements. While these hypotheses are consistent with the best clinical and experimental data available, it is fully realized that conflicting evidence and alternate concepts abound. It is hoped that the hypotheses presented here may serve as a basis for further study which will allow a fuller understanding of the anatomical and physiological substrates for eye movements.

For a complete review and a clear presentation of much of the data on which this chapter is based, the reader is referred to a definitive text such as that of Walsh and Hoyt,[1] or, for a more concise analysis, to the text of Cogan.[2] Many of the newer concepts are examined in more detail in the book edited by Bach-y-Rita and Collins.[3] The bibliographies in these texts provide a nearly complete list of source material on eye movements. Numerous

syndromes involving eye movements are not discussed as they are well described in the above references.

EXAMINATION OF EYE MOVEMENTS

The initial procedure in the examination of the oculomotor system is the evaluation of fixation (the position maintenance system); for if the patient is unable to maintain fixation, the subsequent evaluation of other eye movements necessarily will be affected. Fixation is tested by having the patient look steadily at an object, preferably both at a distant object (at least 20 feet away) and a near object. A convenient near object is the patient's thumb. If the patient fails to fixate, is it because the eye movement mechanism responsible for position maintenance (fixation) is disturbed, or is the failure due to the patient's lack of effort, or to his obtundity? Is fixation interrupted by abnormal eye movements; e.g. nystagmus; flutter (rapid horizontal conjugate oscillations in primary position usually of 2 to 4 beats, indicative of lesions of cerebellar pathways); opsoclonus (rapid conjugate eye movements in any direction, also associated with cerebellar pathway disturbances); or bobbing (rapid downward eye movements followed by a slow upward eye movement most often conjugate, seen in severe caudal pontine disorders)?

Next, the smooth pursuit mechanism and range of movement are evaluated. The patient is asked to follow a *slowly* moving target into the six diagnostic positions of gaze (Fig. 1). Each diagnostic position represents the field of isolated action of a single extraocular muscle.

Double vision (diplopia) if present will be greatest when the patient attempts to gaze into the field of action of a paretic muscle. Such loss of individual muscle function usually indicates a nuclear or an infranuclear lesion. In contrast, if both eyes show equally limited movement in one direction, a gaze paresis exists and the lesion is supranuclear, involving one or more of the conjugate gaze mechanisms. In supranuclear lesions there is no diplopia and the eyes are tracking together (conjugate).

If the patient has followed a slowly moving object, the pursuit (following) mechanism also will have been tested. Often an inability to follow is associated with occipito-mesencephalic pathway lesions. Interruption of smooth pursuit by saccades (rapid eye movements or jerks) may be indicative of an anxious patient, of drug effect (barbiturates, dilantin), of parietal, or of cerebellar pathology. In these cases, the patient is unable to follow smoothly and the pursuit movement is interrupted by jerks—even in fields of gaze where no nystagmus or other abnormal

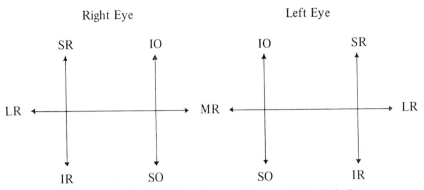

FIG. 1. Cardinal positions of gaze: each represents the field of isolated action of a single extraocular muscle as indicated.

eye movements are present. This jerky pursuit is also called "cogwheeling".

When nystagmus is present, it, too, should be evaluated carefully. The fast and slow phases must be noted as well as changes in the character of the nystagmus in different positions of gaze. This may easily be represented graphically with arrows indicating the fast component (Fig. 2).

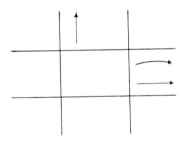

FIG. 2. Represents a patient with horizontal and rotary nystagmus on left gaze with the fast component clockwise, and vertical nystagmus on upward gaze with fast component up.

Thus, two of the eye movement mechanisms—position maintenance (fixation) and pursuit (following) have been tested. The saccadic (rapid eye movement, "voluntary" eye movement) system is tested next. This eye movement mechanism is used in looking from one place to another and is tested by having the patient look from one object to another. It is noted whether the saccades are as rapid as they should be. This is a qualitative judgment that takes some time to master but is of diagnostic significance in diseases such as progressive supranuclear palsy, where a slower eye movement may take the place of saccades.[4]

A slight undershoot in looking from one object to another is a normal finding. However, an overshoot, especially if associated with several oscillations at the end point, is called ocular dysmetria—a symptom of disturbed cerebellar function.

Convergence (the vergence system) is tested by having the patient fixate on an object of interest which is slowly brought toward the nose in the midline. (Do *not* use a light—the *patient's* finger is an appropriate and available stimulus.) The eyes should turn in smoothly and equally.

The vestibular system (one of the non-optic reflex systems) is tested by irrigating the external auditory canals with water. Warm (44°C) caloric stimulation is a greater stimulus than cold (30°C). Irrigation is usually carried out for 40 sec. with the head elevated 30° such that only the horizontal semicircular canal is stimulated. If no response is obtained, the test should be repeated with ice water and the irrigation continued for at least a 200 c.c. injection or until a response is elicited. This represents the maximal stimulus available to test the integrity of the oculomotor pathways in the obtunded or unconscious patient. The normal response is a jerk nystagmus. With cold calorics, the fast phase is away from the stimulated ear and the slow phase toward it, and the opposite is true when warm water is used. (Again, the quality of both fast and slow components is noted separately.) Simultaneous bilateral stimulation of the semicircular canals evokes vertical movements.

Additional tests are utilized to gain additional information and these may evaluate more than one eye movement mechanism at a time.

Optokinetic nystagmus (OKN) is tested horizontally and vertically with tape or drum. The normal response is a slow or following phase in the direction of the moving target. This tests the smooth pursuit mechanism. Normally, the slow phase is then interrupted by a contraversive fast phase which rapidly returns the eyes to pick up the next moving target in the series. This tests the saccadic mechanism. Both the slow and fast phases are evaluated separately.

The oculocephalic (doll's head) maneuver is carried out by (1) briskly turning the patient's head from side-to-side for horizontal movements, and (2) flexing and extending his neck for vertical movements. In examining the conscious patient, the patient is asked to fix on an object in primary position. In this case, the oculocephalic maneuver tests both fixation (the position maintenance system) and, especially, the pursuit (following) mechanism. In the comatose patient, fixation is not possible, and the oculocephalic maneuver is a test of non-optic reflexes; i.e. primarily the vestibular mechanism. In either case, a normal response (turning of the eyes in the direction opposite to that in which the head was turned) indicates that the nuclear and infranuclear pathways are intact.

TABLE 1

CONTROL MECHANISM

	Position Maintenance	Pursuit	Saccadic	Vergence	Non-Optic Reflex (Vestibular)
Function	Maintain eye position vis-à-vis target	Maintain object of regard near fovea—matches eye and target	Place object of interest on fovea rapidly	Align visual axes to maintain bifoveal fixation	Maintain eye position with respect to changes in head and body posture
Stimulus	Visual interest and attention?	Moving object near fovea	Object of interest in peripheral field	Retinal disparity	Stimulation of semicircular canals
Latency (from stimulus to onset of eye movement)		125 msec.	200 msec.	160 msec.	Very short
Velocity	Both rapid (flicks, microsaccades) and slow (drifts)	To 100°/sec., accurately to 30°/sec.	To 400°/sec.	Around 20°/sec.	To 300°/sec.*
Feedback		Continuous	Sampled data		

* Slow phase only. The fast phase, although initiated in the pontine reticular formation is discharged via the saccadic mechanism.

In such a case, any gaze paresis must result from a supranuclear lesion affecting conjugate gaze pathways prior to their termination in the pons.

Lastly, the patient is asked to close his eyes forcibly (as in testing VII nerve function). Normally, if the lids are raised by the examiner while the patient continues his effort at closure both eyes will be up and out—(divergent) (the Bell's phenomenon). In many patients with parieto-occipital lesions, the eyes deviate in parallel toward the side opposite the lesion. This abnormal deviation with eyes closed is termed "spasticity of conjugate gaze" (Cogan's sign), implying that the eyes deviate due to increased "tone". Frequently this sign is associated with "cogwheeling"—jerky pursuit movements—when following a moving target toward the side of the lesion. It is likely that this jerky following movement toward the side of the lesion is the result of the effort needed to work against the hypertonus in the opposite direction.

MECHANISMS

Eye movements are generated by five functionally different systems:

(1) the position maintenance (fixation) system;
(2) the smooth pursuit system (following);
(3) the saccadic system (generating fast eye movements, fast phase of optokinetics, fast phase of vestibular nystagmus, and (?) microsaccades);
(4) the vergence system (convergence and divergence); and
(5) the non-optic reflex system including the vestibular system (i.e. semicircular canal and otolith reflexes) and tonic neck reflexes.

Each of these systems has its uniquely adequate stimulus, latency of response, range of velocities, and sampling conditions (Table 1). The output of each of these separate systems is in one of two modes—rapid eye movement

(including saccades and "flicks" or microsaccades); or slow eye movement (including pursuit, vergence, the slow phase of optokinetic nystagmus, the slow phase of vestibular nystagmus, and drifts).

THE POSITION MAINTENANCE SYSTEM
(Fixation)

TABLE 2

THE POSITION MAINTENANCE SYSTEM (FIXATION)

I. Location
 A. Occipito-Parietal Area.
II. Characteristics
 A. Micromovements.
  1. Microsaccades or Flicks.
  2. Drifts.
III. Function
 A. Maintains Gaze on Stationary Target.
IV. Pathway
 A. Presumably Same as for Saccades and Pursuit.
V. Deficit
 A. Inability to Maintain Fixation ("Impersistence of Gaze").
VI. Tests
 A. Fixation.

We have used the position maintenance system to refer to the eye movements utilized to maintain fixation on a stationary target. This system has been less completely studied than other mechanisms and may utilize other gaze pathways as well as a system of micromovements (rapid micromovements, microsaccades or flicks, and slow micromovements or drifts). The functional and anatomical relationships between the "macro" and "micro" eye movement systems are not fully understood, but it is assumed that saccades and microsaccades share the same substrates as drifts and pursuit movements share the same substrates. It had been thought that drifts are the result of the inherent instability of the oculomotor system, while microsaccades are corrective movements which return the target to the fovea. However, recent studies under binocular conditions indicate that both drifts and flicks correct fixational errors and that drifts are also stimulated by vergence errors (St. Cyr and Fender[5]).

THE SMOOTH PURSUIT SYSTEM
(Following, Pursuit, Tracking)

TABLE 3

THE SMOOTH PURSUIT SYSTEM (FOLLOWING, PURSUIT, TRACKING)

I. Location
   A. Occipital-parietal lobe. Right occipital lobe responsible for tracking to left; maybe some bilateral responsibility.

II. Characteristics
   A. Slow movement.
   B. Short delay from stimulus to execution relative to saccadic and vestibular systems.
   C. Continuous monitoring system.
   D. EMG shows gradually increasing contraction of the agonist and gradual concomitant relaxation of the antagonist.
   E. May be interrupted by a saccadic movement when target moves faster than velocity of slow movement.

III. Function
   A. Responsible for following or tracking a target once the saccadic system places it on the fovea.

IV. Pathway
   A. Occipital lobes to brain stem reticular formation. Mostly crossing at level of III and IV nuclei. Termination in paramedian pontine reticular formation (mostly opposite to side of origin).

V. Test
   A. Ask patient to follow moving target.
   B. Slow phase of OKN.
   C. Ask patient to fix on object while head is rotated (oculocephalic maneuver, doll's head). This is a better test because it is more "automatic", seems to eliminate any "voluntary" effort, but contains some non-optic reflex influence.

VI. Result of Lesions
   A. Smooth movement interrupted by saccades ("cogwheeling").
   B. Unilateral above the decussation.
      1. Breakdown in tracking or following objects to opposite field.
   C. Unilateral below the decussation.
      1. As above, but deficit is ipsilateral.
   D. Bilateral.
      1. Usually associated with visual loss. When bilateral, cannot be tested.

Pursuit movements have a short latent period relative to saccadic movements (about 125 msec.), are slow, are linearly related to target velocity (tracking accurately to 30°/sec. maximum velocity about 90°/sec. in patients with central scotomata), and do not affect the visual threshold. They appear to be controlled by continuous feedback. The electromyogram of the extraocular muscles in pursuit movements shows a pattern of gradual recruitment in the agonist and gradual inhibition in the antagonist.

THE SACCADIC SYSTEM
(Fast Eye Movements, "Voluntary")

TABLE 4

THE SACCADIC SYSTEM (FAST, "VOLUNTARY", EYE MOVEMENT SYSTEM)

I. Location
   A. Diffuse in frontal lobes.
   B. Right frontal lobe responsible for horizontal conjugate gaze to left, and vice versa.
   C. Both frontal lobes active in vertical saccades, therefore no defect of vertical saccades seen in unilateral lesions.

II. Characteristics
   A. Rapid eye movement.
   B. Long delay from stimulus to execution.
   C. Automatic, predetermined movement.
   D. Very precise, a slight undershoot is normal, cerebellar influence.
   E. Electromyogram shows abrupt contraction of agonist, immediate silence of antagonist.

III. Function
   A. Refixation movements.
   B. Fast phases of vestibular nystagmus.
   C. Fast phases of optokinetic nystagmus.
   D. Microsaccades (probably).

IV. Pathway
   A. Fronto-mesencephalic: from frontal lobe to opposite paramedian pontine reticular formation crossing at level of oculomotor nuclei.

V. Tests
   A. Ask patient to look from one point in space to another.
   B. Optokinetic nystagmus (OKN) (fast phase).
   C. Vestibular nystagmus (fast phase).

VI. Result of lesions
   A. Unilateral, above the decussation.
      1. Eyes deviate toward side of lesion during coma. Vestibular stimulation may move eye to the side opposite the lesion during the *slow* phase movements only. Fast phase movements to the side opposite the lesion are defective or absent—including decreased fast phases of OKN and vestibular nystagmus.
      2. Gaze paretic nystagmus (see text) after coma on gaze to side opposite the lesion.
   B. Unilateral after the decussation.
      1. As above but deficit is ipsilateral.
   C. Bilateral.
      1. Total loss of ability to make refixation saccades (oculomotor apraxia, global saccadic paralysis).
      2. Loss of fast phase of optokinetic nystagmus, bilaterally.
      3. Loss of fast phase of vestibular nystagmus, bilaterally.
      4. "Spasm" of fixation (inability to refixate or reverse by means of saccade).
   D. Cerebellar Pathways.
      1. Degeneration of the precision of saccadic movement (ocular dysmetria, ocular flutter, opsoclonus).

Saccades are rapid eye movements mediated by the frontal cortex and descending fronto-mesencephalic pathways to the paramedian pontine reticular formation (Figs. 4a, b). Saccades are utilized in looking from one object to another—in bringing the object of interest onto the fovea. Hence, they also are frequently termed voluntary eye movements, fast eye movements, or rapid eye movements. (However, it should be noted that following may also be voluntary, while saccades often are part of totally reflex eye movements such as vestibular nystagmus.) All fast eye movements are saccadic in form. Thus, not only refixation movements, but also the fast phase of vestibular nystagmus and the fast phase of optokinetic nystagmus are saccades. In man, all of these eye movements appear to require the same descending fronto-mesencephalic pathways, and total interruption of these pathways produces a complete absence of saccades.

The stimulus for saccades is an object of interest distant from the fovea. Saccadic eye movements occur after a relatively long latent period (about 200 msec.), are very rapid (about 400°/sec. with the velocity being determined by the size of the movement), and are accompanied by an increase in visual threshold. Once a saccade is triggered, the predetermined movement is executed despite subsequent changes in stimulus conditions indicating dependence on a sampled data feedback system (i.e. if the stimulus is a light, that light may be moved during the 200 msec. latent period, yet the saccade will carry the eyes to the position of the original stimulus). In contrast to the activity of the extraocular muscles in pursuit movements, the EMG recordings during saccades are characterized by a rapid burst in the agonist and immediate and complete inhibition of the antagonist muscle groups. The electromyographic pattern is identical in all saccadic eye movements: (1) voluntary gaze, (2) the fast phase of vestibular nystagmus, or (3) the fast phase of optokinetic nystagmus.

In addition to the cerebral and brain stem lesions (to be discussed below) which affect saccades, it is interesting to note that most, if not all, cerebellar lesions that affect eye movements, affect this system.

THE VERGENCE SYSTEM

TABLE 5

VERGENCE SYSTEM

I. Location
  A. Occipito-parietal area.
II. Characteristics
  A. Very slow.
  B. Disjugate movements.
III. Function
  A. Aligns fovea on targets.
IV. Pathway
  A. Occipito-tegmental.
V. Deficit
  A. Deficient vergence movements.
  B. Diplopia.
VI. Test
  A. Near objects.

A stimulus which falls on non-corresponding retinal elements elicits a vergence movement. This system generates the slowest eye movements (about 20°/sec.). It also is the only oculomotor subsystem which produces predominantly disjugate eye movements (i.e. eye movements in which the visual axes converge or diverge rather than remaining parallel). The latency of the system is about 160 msec. The anatomical substrates for the vergence system are not well defined but appear to arise in the parieto-occipital cortex. The efferent discharge passes to the midbrain tegmentum and paramedian pontine reticular formation.

THE NON-OPTIC REFLEX SYSTEMS

TABLE 6

NON-OPTIC REFLEXES (INCLUDING VESTIBULAR)

I. Location
  A. Medulla and pons.
II. Characteristics
  A. Short delay.
  B. Tonic deviation, followed by fast phase.
III. Function
  A. Coordinates eye and head movements.
IV. Pathway
  A. For slow phase of vestibular nystagmus—vestibular apparatus, VIII nerve and vestibular nuclei via MLF, and pontine reticular formation to oculomotor nuclei.
  B. For fast phase of vestibular nystagmus—pontine reticular formation requiring intact fronto-mesencephalic saccadic pathway.
V. Test
  A. Calorics.
  B. Oculocephalic maneuver.
  C. Rotation.
VI. Result of lesions
  A. Defective slow phase with peripheral or central defect of brain stem vestibular connections only.
  B. Defective fast phase—mediated by fronto-mesencephalic pathways, therefore may occur with brain stem *and* cerebral lesions.

The non-optic reflex systems are concerned with the relationship between eye movements and body movements. The vestibular system (semicircular canal portion) is the most important clinically. Reflexes of the otolith organs of the vestibular system and neck receptors also belong in this category, but will not be considered here.

The vestibular impulse travels to the vestibular nucleus and from there to the oculomotor nuclei by way of the medial longitudinal fasciculus (MLF) and surrounding reticular formation. Impulses controlling the slow phase travel predominantly in the MLF while discharges related to the fast phase (as well as some slow impulses) are dependent upon the reticular formation.

The stimulus for the vestibular system is disruption of the usual balanced input from the semicircular canals. This may be by an increased input (i.e. rotation, caloric stimulus) or by a decrease in input as with a lesion of the eighth nerve. The latency of the vestibular system is very short. The slow movement of vestibular nystagmus may reach a velocity of 300°/sec. in contrast to the maximum velocity of 90°/sec. of the pursuit system. The fast component is set-off within the brain stem but very little is understood about the factors which control it. However, it is dependent on the same efferent fronto-mesencephalic paths as refixation saccades, and the fast phase of optokinetics.

ANATOMICAL SUBSTRATES

Most normal eye movements are conjugate movements in which the eyes track together—saccades, pursuit, optokinetic, and vestibular nystagmus are of this nature. The micromovements of the position maintenance system appear to be conjugate in part; i.e. microsaccades; and, in part, disjugate, as is the vergence system.

The pathways subserving conjugate gaze mechanisms—saccades, pursuit, and the non-optic reflexes—have been well studied and there is general agreement as to their location. The anatomical substrates of the vergence system are much less clearly understood and those of the position maintenance system have not been studied at all. Nevertheless, most conclusions concerning the oculomotor pathways are drawn from clinical observation. Anatomical or neurophysiological efforts have been unable to define them more accurately.

OCCIPITO-MESENCEPHALIC PATHWAYS (Fig. 3)

(Subserving Pursuit [Following] Movements)

The areas subserving pursuit movements are located in the anterior occipital lobes. Horizontal pursuit movements are mediated by the contralateral occipital areas; i.e. the right occipital lobe mediates pursuit movements to the left and vice versa. There is evidence for some ability for the occipital lobe to generate ipsilateral, as well as contralateral horizontal pursuit movements. For example, after occipital lobectomy, pursuit movements ipsilateral to the remaining occipital lobe recover if the corpus callosum is not damaged. Vertical pursuit movements are obtained by simultaneous bilateral stimulation in these same occipital areas.

The axons of the occipital lobe neurons descend in the internal sagittal stratum through the pulvinar to the pretectal area, then join the frontal lobe projections in the mesencephalic reticular formation (probably after crossing in the midbrain) to terminate in the paramedian pontine reticular formation near nucleus VI (Daroff and Hoyt[6] present evidence that this system decussates twice).

NON-OPTIC REFLEX SYSTEM

(Vestibular and Tonic Neck Reflexes)

Only the vestibular system will be considered here. The vestibular system consists of the semicircular canals, the VIII cranial nerves, and the vestibular nuclei and their projections. The pathways subserving this system ascend from the vestibular nucleus to the oculomotor nucleus in the MLF and pontine reticular formation. The superior, medial, and Dieters' nuclei are those portions of the vestibular nuclei most closely related to the oculomotor nuclei. These connections are both crossed and uncrossed and appear to be specific, such that vestibular subnuclei are connected with oculomotor subnuclei subserving extraocular movements in a specific plane; e.g. the superior

OCCIPITO-MESENCEPHALIC PATHWAYS FOR PURSUIT MECHANISM
(Smooth Pursuit, Following)

PATH FOR HORIZONTAL MOVEMENTS

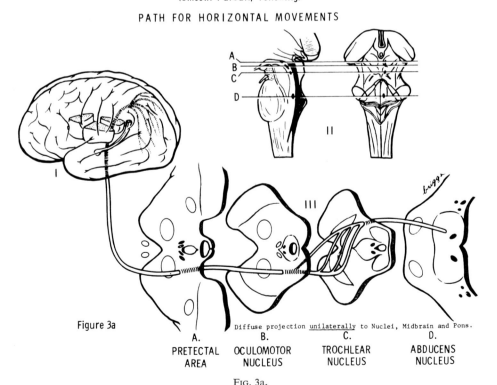

Figure 3a

Diffuse projection unilaterally to Nuclei, Midbrain and Pons.

A. PRETECTAL AREA
B. OCULOMOTOR NUCLEUS
C. TROCHLEAR NUCLEUS
D. ABDUCENS NUCLEUS

FIG. 3a.

OCCIPITOMESENCEPHALIC PATHWAYS FOR PURSUIT MECHANISM
(Smooth Pursuit, Following)

PATH FOR VERTICAL MOVEMENTS

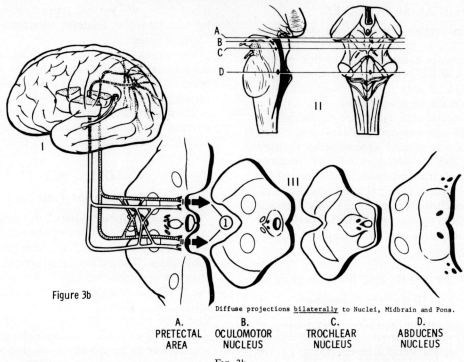

Figure 3b

Diffuse projections bilaterally to Nuclei, Midbrain and Pons.

| A. PRETECTAL AREA | B. OCULOMOTOR NUCLEUS | C. TROCHLEAR NUCLEUS | D. ABDUCENS NUCLEUS |

FIG. 3b.

vestibular nuclei and the dorsal oculomotor nuclei which send impulses to the ipsilateral inferior recti.[7] The fibers transversing the MLF are related to the slow phases of vestibular nystagmus while connections in the reticular formation are concerned primarily with fast phases. The situation for other eye movement mechanisms is probably different as saccades are defective in MLF lesions. It is generally agreed that projections from the pontine and mesencephalic reticular formation to the frontal and occipital cortex exist and are active during vestibular activity. Thus, the fast phase of vestibular nystagmus is generated in the paramedian reticular formation but is dependent upon the same fronto-mesencephalic path as saccades and the fast phase of OKN.

FRONTO-MESENCEPHALIC PATHWAYS

(Subserving Rapid Eye Movements)

The areas subserving conjugate rapid eye movements (saccades, fast phase of optokinetics, fast phase of vestibular nystagmus) (Fig. 4) are diffusely located in the frontal lobes. In general, horizontal rapid eye movements are mediated by the contralateral frontal lobe; i.e. horizontal conjugate rapid eye movements to the left are mediated by the right frontal lobe and vice versa. However, upon stimulation the frontal lobes also have the capacity to produce ipsilateral movements. On the other hand, vertical conjugate rapid eye movements are dependent on simultaneous bilateral activity within the frontal lobes in

essentially the same cerebral areas that generate horizontal eye movements. The frontal lobes are active in all rapid eye movements. Some of these impulses may originate within the brain stem (i.e. the fast phase of vestibular nystagmus), but ultimately are dependent upon this same fronto-mesencephalic path.

The axons of the frontal lobe neurons descend through the anterior internal capsule, globus pallidus and subthalamus. The fibers for horizontal movements proceed to the midbrain reticular formation while the fibers for vertical movements pass to the pretectum. This is a crossed system which decussates between nuclei III and IV, and terminates in the contralateral paramedian pontine reticular formation in the area of the nucleus of the VI nerve.

Interruption of these pathways anywhere in their course produces a supranuclear disturbance of conjugate saccadic gaze including refixation saccades, fast phase of OKN, and fast phase of vestibular nystagmus. Deficits in vertical rapid eye movements are rare in cerebral lesions and not seen then unless both fronto-mesencephalic pathways are involved. They are much more commonly seen in midbrain disorders. Thus, such deficits are not seen clinically except in massive lesions.

OCCIPITO-PRETECTAL PATHWAYS

(Pathways Subserving Vergence Movements)

The anatomical substrates for these pathways have received little study. The vergence pathways probably

FRONTOMESENCEPHALIC PATHWAYS FOR SACCADIC MECHANISM
(Saccades, Fast Eye Movements, Voluntary Eye Movements)

PATH FOR HORIZONTAL MOVEMENTS

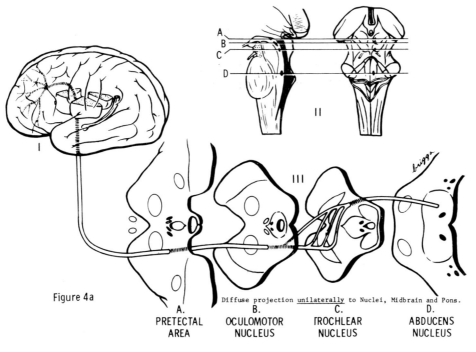

Figure 4a

Diffuse projection *unilaterally* to Nuclei, Midbrain and Pons.

A.	B.	C.	D.
PRETECTAL AREA	OCULOMOTOR NUCLEUS	TROCHLEAR NUCLEUS	ABDUCENS NUCLEUS

FIG. 4a.

FRONTO-MESENCEPHALIC PATHWAYS FOR SACCADIC MECHANISM
(Saccades, Fast Eye Movements, Voluntary Eye Movements)

PATH FOR VERTICAL MOVEMENTS

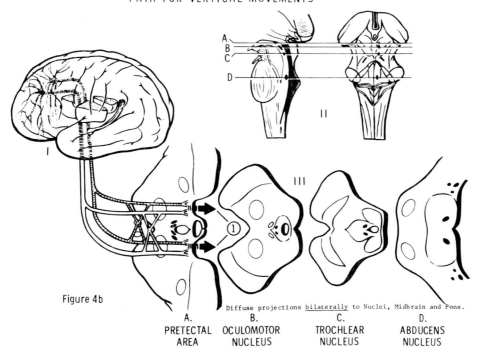

Figure 4b

Diffuse projections *bilaterally* to Nuclei, Midbrain and Pons.

A.	B.	C.	D.
PRETECTAL AREA	OCULOMOTOR NUCLEUS	TROCHLEAR NUCLEUS	ABDUCENS NUCLEUS

FIG. 4b.

originate in the anterior occipital areas slightly anterior to the pursuit pathways and are thought to descend with them to the pretectal area and subsequently to the oculomotor nucleus and other areas in the midbrain and pons.

The Third Nucleus

This nucleus is divided into subnuclei innervating single muscles. The schema of Warwick best describes the organization of the third nucleus (Fig. 5). The ventral

SUBNUCLEI OF THE OCULOMOTOR COMPLEX
(After the diagrams of Prof. R. Warwick, J. Comp. Neurol. 98:480, 1953 from his studies on the rhesus monkey)

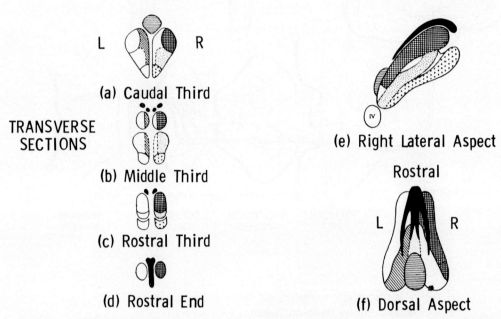

SUBNUCLEUS	REPRESENTS	DISTRIBUTION
Dorsal	(R) Inferior Rectus	Uncrossed
Intermediate	(R) Inferior Oblique	Uncrossed
Ventral	(R) Medial Rectus	Uncrossed
Medial	(R) Superior Rectus	Crossed ✓
Caudal Central	(R & L) Levator Palpebrae	Mixed ✓
Parasympathetic (Edinger-Westphal + anterior median)	(R & L) Iris Sphincter & Ciliary Muscle	Mixed ✓

CLINICAL CORRELATES

Physical Findings

1. Unilateral third nerve palsy with contralateral superior rectus palsy
2. Bilateral total third nerve palsies with spared levators   } Lesion must be NUCLEAR
3. Unilateral total third nerve palsy with normal contralateral superior rectus } Lesion cannot be NUCLEAR
4. Unilateral internal ophthalmoplegia
5. Unilateral ptosis

Figure 5

nucleus supplies the medial rectus; the dorsal nucleus: the inferior rectus; the intermediate cell column: the inferior oblique; the medial cell column supplies the superior rectus; the caudal central nucleus: the levator palpebrae; and the parasympathetic subnucleus of Edinger and Westphal supplies the ciliary body and pupil. Fibers innervating the medial rectus, inferior rectus, and inferior oblique are uncrossed. Those to the superior rectus are crossed, and those to the levator are completely mixed. The pathway of the III nerve after leaving the nucleus is well described in classical texts.

DISORDERS

Disorders of the oculomotor system may be classified as supranuclear, nuclear, and infranuclear. Thus, supranuclear dysfunction results from lesions of the fronto-mesencephalic and occipito-mesencephalic pathways (for saccades, pursuit, and vergence), lesions of the pretectum, lesions of the reticular formation, and lesions of the MLF (internuclear ophthalmoplegia).

With the exception of vergence and MLF lesions, supranuclear lesions affect conjugate mechanisms and, therefore, are not associated with diplopia or strabismus (squint) in primary position. However, lesions involving the vergence system, pretectum, and MLF, may be associated with diplopia; nevertheless, with lesions in these areas the eyes remain parallel in primary position in contrast to a nonparallel position in nuclear and infranuclear lesions. With lesions of the vergence system, pretectum, and MLF, diplopia may be present in other fields of gaze away from primary position.

Additionally, in supranuclear lesions, one or more oculomotor mechanisms may be deficient, but one modality remains intact, thus demonstrating the integrity of the nuclear and infranuclear paths (The paresis is "dissociated").

In nuclear and infranuclear lesions, the eyes are not parallel in the primary position. (There may be diplopia.) and because of the organization of the oculomotor nucleus, nuclear involvement of the central caudal nucleus causes *bilateral* ptosis and nuclear involvement of the medial cell column causes *crossed* superior rectus paresis. Internal ophthalmoplegia secondary to nuclear lesions is bilateral. Consequently, lesions that in theory must be nuclear include: (1) unilateral III with contralateral superior rectus paresis and bilateral ptosis, (2) total bilateral III (±) internal ophthalmoplegia (±) spared levator. Lesions that cannot be nuclear include: (1) unilateral complete ophthalmoplegia with normal contralateral superior rectus, and (2) unilateral internal ophthalmoplegia and (3) unilateral ptosis. Because of the location of the caudal central nucleus, levator palpebrae function may be spared with third nucleus lesions.

Peripheral lesions are well covered in classical texts and will not be considered here.

Supranuclear Lesions

Any interruption of the fronto-mesencephalic fibers for fast eye movements from the frontal cortex to the decussation causes a deficit of rapid eye movements to the opposite side; thus, a left-sided lesion will affect saccades to the right, the fast phase of optokinetic nystagmus when it is to the right, and the fast phase of vestibular nystagmus when it is to the right. On looking right, there may be gaze paretic nystagmus (a relatively slow beating nystagmus with the fast phase to the right, of varying amplitude and rhythm). The appearance of gaze paretic nystagmus is dependent on effort by the patient. Such lesions usually produce a transient tonic ipsilateral deviation (in the case above, a deviation to the left) lasting a few days unless the patient is comatose or the opposite descending pathway is deficient, in which case the deviation may persist. If the patient is comatose, the tonic deviation may last longer, while if the opposite descending path is damaged, compensation may be completely lacking. Bilateral lesions lead to a total absence of rapid eye movement, a total lack of saccades (global saccadic paralysis) including lack of the fast phase of optokinetic nystagmus, and lack of the fast phase of vestibular nystagmus). After the decussation, lesions of this pathway produce the same type of deficit, but ipsilaterally.

Fibers for vertical gaze are located in the pretectum, more rostrally and dorsally than fibers for horizontal gaze; thus, lesions in the midbrain frequently involve vertical gaze and spare horizontal gaze (Parinaud's syndrome). Less often, vertical gaze may be spared while horizontal gaze is deficient.

Destruction of the occipito-mesencephalic pathways affects the pursuit mechanisms predominately, although the vergence and fixation systems also may be influenced because of their anatomical proximity. Again, lesions anywhere from the cortex to the decussation produce peficits in contralateral following movements; lesions after the decussation produce ipsilateral deficits. As with the saccadic system, fibers for vertical pursuit movements pass to the pretectum and, therefore, may be involved in mesencephalic lesions, while the horizontal gaze mechanism is spared; less frequently, the opposite situation may be observed.

Deficits in the pursuit mechanism lead to "cogwheeling" in which the smooth pursuit movement is interrupted by saccades.

All cortico-mesencephalic fibers for horizontal eye movements become associated in the mesencephalon around the level of the decussation. Thus, lesions at this level produce deficits in both saccadic and pursuit mechanisms; vertical gaze mechanisms may or may not be spared. With lesions at this level, vestibular stimuli may produce a tonic deviation only.

Lesions in the pretectal area also may affect eye movements differentially. Most frequently vertical movements are affected before horizontal movements and the saccadic mechanism before the pursuit mechanism.

Cerebral lesions, unless very large, or multiple and diffuse, tend to affect saccadic and pursuit mechanisms separately. Conversely, simultaneous defects in both horizontal saccades and pursuit, without evidence of very widespread lesions, indicate mesencephalic damage in the lower midbrain or pons while simultaneous defects in vertical saccades and pursuit indicate damage of the pretectal area.

In the conscious patient, the oculocephalic maneuver, by utilizing the fixation reflex to move the eyes, is useful in demonstrating selective involvement of the pathways for fast eye movements. Thus, even if the patient cannot refixate voluntarily (because he cannot make saccades), the integrity of the pursuit (occipito-mesencephalic) pathway can be demonstrated by this maneuver. Perhaps, because it is reinforced by the non-optic reflexes, it provides a more consistent test than does pursuit alone, especially if the patient is less than perfectly alert and cooperative.

Pontine Conjugate Gaze Center

The fronto-mesencephalic and occipito-mesencephalic fibers for horizontal gaze decussate and are united with ascending vestibular fibers in the paramedian pontine reticular formation in the area of the "parabducens nucleus". Although not a discrete anatomical entity, this area is considered functionally as the pontine center for horizontal conjugate gaze. It projects directly to the ipsilateral VI nerve nucleus, and by way of the MLF to the contralateral III nerve nucleus. Lesions at this level produce a complete paralysis of ipsilateral horizontal conjugate gaze, involving saccades, pursuit and vestibular nystagmus. In contrast to the transient deviations with lesions of the fronto-mesencephalic fibers, deficits due to lesions of the pontine gaze center persist for a long period.

LESIONS OF THE MEDIAL LONGITUDINAL FASCICULUS
(Internuclear Ophthalmoplegia)

Lesions of the MLF between the III and VI nerve nuclei produce the clinical picture termed internuclear ophthalmoplegia (INO). The typical MLF syndrome consists of medial rectus paresis in the eye on the side of the lesion, nystagmus of the abducting eye on lateral gaze to the side opposite the lesion, and normal medial rectus activity on convergence. The "anterior internuclear ophthalmoplegia" of Cogan in which, in addition to the above, convergence is absent, probably is found only with III nuclear involvement. The MLF syndrome is a typical supranuclear lesion in that the apparently paretic muscle is able to produce normal convergence, and in the lack of diplopia in primary position (heterotropia). Since, at this level, conjugate gaze fibers to the yoke lateral rectus have already branched off, a MLF lesion produces disconjugate eye movements and diplopia. Mild degrees of internuclear ophthalmoplegia in which the abducting nystagmus is not obvious may be emphasized by asymmetric convergence or by stimuli which produce fast movements in the direction of the abducting nystagmus; (i.e. with a right MLF lesion producing abducting nystagmus in the left eye on left lateral gaze, the abducting nystagmus may be augmented by optokinetic or vestibular nystagmus with fast phases to the left.)[8]

Until recently, there has been no reasonable explanation for the abducting nystagmus. We have evidence that it is partly due to asymmetric convergence efforts, i.e. since the connection of the conjugate gaze center with the III nucleus is interrupted, the patient utilizes the only intact eye movement mechanism—convergence—to adduct with the "paretic" medial rectus. This causes the other (abducting) eye to momentarily *adduct*. Then the abducting eye makes a "corrective" saccade to the laterally displaced target. Consistent with this hypothesis are the facts that (1) asymmetric convergence stimuli produce an increased amplitude in pre-existing abducting nystagmus or may elicit abducting nystagmus unapparent under usual examining techniques, and (2) in "anterior internuclear ophthalmoplegia" where there is true medial rectus paresis, abducting nystagmus is absent or much decreased.[8]

CEREBELLAR DISORDERS

The anatomy and neurophysiology of the cerebellar control of extraocular movements are not well understood. However, the cerebellum appears to be important in the precise control of eye movements and of saccades in particular. Thus, cerebellar lesions result in a spectacular group of oculomotor disorders: dysmetria, flutter and opsoclonus. All three are conjugate disturbances. These eye movements may be considered as a continuum in which saccadic movements become less and less precise; frequently, all three are seen sequentially or simultaneously in patients with cerebellar lesions.

Dysmetria is analogous to dysmetric movements of the limbs. It is characterized by an overshoot in saccadic extraocular movements followed by compensatory swings, until a stable end point is reached. (In contrast, a slight saccadic undershoot often is seen in normal subjects.)

Flutter is seen in primary position as the result of fixation efforts and consists of a short burst of horizontal oscillations. This could be considered a manifestation of the loss of cerebellar control over the "position maintenance" system, a system that likely utilizes saccadic as well as other gaze mechanisms.

Opsoclonus is a sequence of saccadic movements, apparently unrelated to any specific stimulus. The movements may be in any direction but are predominantly horizontal. It might be postulated that this continuum of disordered extraocular movements represents disruption of finer and finer saccades; i.e. refixation saccades (dysmetria), small fixation saccades (flutter) and microsaccades (opsoclonus).

Cogwheeling (saccadic following) is seen also in cerebellar lesions and probably represents the superimposition of the disorders of saccadic movements described above on following movements. All other extraocular movement disorders described in cerebellar lesions are most likely the result of concomitant brain stem involvement.

PARIETAL LOBE LESIONS

Cortical lesions of the parietal lobe produce no characteristic defect of eye movements. In contrast, deep or massive parietal lesions produce the typical disturbance of OKN—decrease of the fast phase to the side opposite the

TABLE 7

SUMMARY

Area of Lesion	Mechanism Involved	Defect

Frontal
  Unilateral
  Bilateral
	Saccadic	Absence of contralateral rapid eye movements (saccades, fast phase of vestibular nystagmus, fast phase of OKN); tonic deviation; gaze paretic nystagmus. Bilateral defects as above and absence of vertical saccades.

Parietal	Disconnection of occipital to frontal fibers	Defective fast phase of OKN. Spasticity of conjugate gaze. Cogwheeling. Impersistence.

Occipito-Parietal
  Unilateral
 	
  Bilateral
	Pursuit
	Vergence
	Position Maintenance
	Pursuit
	Vergence
	Position Maintenance
		Inability to fixate.
		Inability to follow to contralateral side.
		
		Cortical blindness, defective vertical following, and bilateral horizontal deficits.

Capsule/Subthalamus	Saccadic and/or following	Defective saccades and/or following.
Pretectum	Vertical saccadic and pursuit	Limitation of vertical gaze, retraction nystagmus, pupillary abnormalities. "Parinaud's syndrome".
Paramedian Pontine Reticular Formation (PPRF)	Saccadic	Absence of ipsilateral saccades, fast phase of vestibular nystagmus, and fast phase of OKN.
Internuclear Ophthalmoplegia (INO)	Saccadic and pursuit	Abducting nystagmus. Supranuclear paresis of ipsilateral medial rectus sparing convergence.
Pontine Gaze Center	Saccadic, pursuit, vestibular	Loss of all ipsilateral eye movements.

Diffuse Supranuclear
  Degeneration
  (Progressive Supranuclear
  Palsy, Huntington's Chorea)
	Saccadic	Loss of saccades which are replaced by slow eye movements (? following).

Nuclear Lesions	All	Loss of all movements in field of muscles controlled by involved subnuclei.
Cerebellum	Saccadic	Dysmetria, flutter, opsoclonus.

lesion. In analogy to other parietal lobe lesions, this, too, may be thought of as a disconnection syndrome. In this case the cortico-cortical pathways from the occipital lobes to the ipsilateral frontal lobe are affected as they pass deep within the parietal lobe. Thus, the slow phase of OKN (dependent on occipito-mesencephalic pathways) is present, but the path to the frontal lobes is destroyed and, therefore, no fast phase results. However, the preservation of the fronto-mesencephalic paths may be demonstrated by normal voluntary saccades and by a normal fast phase of vestibular nystagmus.

Two other less understood phenomena—"spasticity of conjugate gaze" and "cogwheeling"—are frequent concomitants of parietal lobe lesions. Spasticity of conjugate gaze is a tonic horizontal or diagonally upward contralateral deviation of the eyes under forcibly closed lids. Its mechanism is not understood, but may be considered a loss of intracerebral inhibitory processes with consequent hypertonicity. Cogwheeling is the interruption of smooth pursuit movements by saccades when following is attempted *toward* the side of the lesion. Since this usually is associated with spasticity of conjugate gaze, and since the spasticity is in the opposite direction (i.e. opposite the parietal lesion) the cogwheeling in this situation likely represents merely a difficulty in following movements working against the spasticity (i.e. when following is performed *toward* the side of the parietal lesion).

Impersistence of conjugate gaze and impersistence of steady fixation on a stationary target are also seen in parietal lobe lesions. In these conditions, the patient is unable to maintain any one ocular position for more than a few seconds. This may be thought of as some abnormality of the "position maintenance" system; and since we believe this system utilizes both occipital and frontal gaze mechanisms, again, impersistence may represent a loss of pathways interconnecting these two areas.

SUMMARY

All information provided herein is summarized in Table 7.

ACKNOWLEDGMENT

The material in this chapter has been supported in part by USPHS Research Grant NS 08033 from National Institute of Neurological Diseases and Stroke (Dr. Gay); and by National Eye Institute Grant EY 00016 (Dr. Newman); both from National Institutes of Health, Bethesda, Maryland.

FURTHER READING

[1] Cogan, D. G. (1956), *Neurology of the Ocular Muscles*, 2nd edition. Springfield: Chas. C. Thomas.

[2] Walsh, F. B. and Hoyt, W. F. (1969), *Clinical Neuro-Ophthalmology*, 3rd edition. Baltimore: Williams & Wilkins Co.

[3] Bach-y-Rita, P. and Collins, C. (Eds.) (1971), *The Control of Eye Movements*. New York: Academic Press.

[4] Newman, N. M., Gay, A. J., Stroud, M. H. and Brooks, J. (1970), "Defective Rapid Eye Movements in Progressive Supranuclear Palsy: An Electromyographic Study," *Brain*, **93(4)**, 775–784.

[5] St. Cyr, G. S. and Fender, D. H. (1969), "The Interplay of Drifts and Flicks in Binocular Fixation," *Vision Res.*, **9**, 245–265.

[6] Daroff, R. and Hoyt, W. F. (1971), "Supranuclear Disorders of Ocular Control Systems in Man," in *The Control of Eye Movements* (P. Bach-y-Rita and C. Collins, Eds.). New York: Academic Press, pp. 175–236.

[7] McMasters, R. E., Weiss, A. H. and Carpenter, M. B. (1966), "Vestibular Projections to the Nuclei of the Extraocular Muscles," *Amer. J. Anat.*, **118**, 163–184.

[8] Stroud, M. H., Newman, N. M. and Gay, A. J., *Abducting Nystagmus*. In preparation.

3. AUDITORY AND VESTIBULAR FUNCTION AND DYSFUNCTION

J. A. DOIG

Nature has given man one tongue, but two ears, that we may hear twice as much as we speak. (Epictetus)

Some knowledge of the anatomy and physiology of the ear and its central nervous connections will be assumed, and only an outline given except where practical applications demand a fuller account. Although it may not always be clear from the text, many of the following statements on function are controversial—this is necessary for the sake of brevity. This deficiency can be corrected by reference to the bibliography.

AUDITORY FUNCTION AND DYSFUNCTION

The Middle Ear

Conduction of Sound Energy

Since 99·9 per cent of the energy of sound in air is reflected when it meets a solid or liquid the transmission from air to the fluids of the inner ear and cochlea requires the mechanism of the middle ear. Compression/rarefaction waves are converted to vibrations of the tympanic membrane and ossicles. It is assumed that in ordinary circumstances fluids are incompressible and so it is essential that both windows (fenestrae ovale and rotunda) are free to move, and allow vibration of the fluids and the basilar membrane. How successful this is may be judged by the fact that while the roar generated at an international football match has only sufficient energy to light up a small torch bulb a soft whisper can be heard at six metres.

Disorders of Sound Conduction

Disorders of sound conduction range from the trivial and slight (wax in the meatus; blood or mucus covering the round window) to the serious and profound (disruption of the ossicular chain due to cholesteatoma or

injury; infective granuloma of the scala vestibuli). Tests will reveal reduced hearing by air conduction (AC) (Fig. 2) and usually an absent stapedius reflex, but the other tests may give normal results (Table 1).

TABLE 1

Test	Site of Disorder			
	Normal	*Conduction Mechanism*	*Cochlea*	*Auditory Nerve or Nuclei*
Air conduction (pure tones)	Unchanged	Reduced	Reduced	Unchanged or reduced
Bone conduction (pure tones)	Unchanged	Unchanged (or improved)	Reduced	Unchanged or reduced
Speech discrimination	80–100%	80–100%	60–100%	0–40%
Békésy	Type I	Type I	Type I or II	Type III or IV
Tone decay	0–5 dB.	0–5 dB.	<25 dB.	>20 dB.
Recruitment (loudness balance)	Absent	Absent	Present	Absent or partial
S.I.S.I.*	0–20%	0–20%	60–100%	0–60%
Loudness discomfort	Present	Absent	Increased	Absent
Stapedius reflex†	Present	Absent	Present	Absent

N.B. "Normal" here does not include the ageing process, which may affect any part of the auditory system.

* Short Increment Sensitivity Index (S.I.S.I.).

† Involves input of stimulus in tested ear and stapedial reflex in opposite ear.

The Cochlea

Hydrodynamics

Movement inwards of the stapes footplate causes a displacement of fluid in the scala vestibuli so that the basilar membrane of the basal coil leans towards the scala tympani and the round window membrane bulges outwards. A wave can be seen to travel along the basilar membrane from the base towards the apex. High tones have their maximal effect at the base, with a fairly sharp cut-off, while lower tones affect more and more of the length of the basilar membrane with maximum effect towards the apex. Increasing intensity produces greater amplitude of basilar membrane excursion.

Loss of Elasticity of the Basilar Membrane is thought to be a factor in one form of presbyacusis which typically begins in middle age and advances slowly, with a descending audiogram and no loudness recruitment.

Transduction

How mechanical movement of the basilar membrane is converted into electrical energy is not known. It *is* known that bending of the hairs in the cupula of the semicircular canals in one direction increases the rate of firing whereas bending in the opposite direction decreases the rate. By analogy it seems probable that a similar mechanism applies in the cochlea. Bending of the hairs embedded in the tectorial membrane would occur when the basilar membrane vibrates, and this could be translated into electrical energy. It has been shown, however, that at threshold levels the tiny excursion of the basilar membrane could not possibly be responsible for all the electric potential produced. It is more likely that bending of the hairs changes the electrical resistance of the cell membrane and that this allows the current (from the 160 mV. store) to flow across the membrane.

A chemical transmitter is almost certainly involved between the hair cells and the nerve endings. This is supported by the fact that (a) discharge of nerve impulses is not in phase with vibration of the basilar membrane (b) there is a slow afterpotential following cessation of sound stimulus and (c) it is difficult to see how an efferent influence would be effective without this medium.

Hair Cell Degeneration occurs in numerous conditions including trauma (noise and mechanical), congenital abnormalities, drug ototoxicity, ageing, infection, and tumours of the auditory nerve and cerebellopontine angle. It is probable that there is a hair cell dysfunction in Menière's disease. The main clinical characteristic of hair cell disorders is sensorineural deafness with loudness recruitment (the ability of a partially deaf ear to hear intense sounds just as well as a normal ear). Discrimination of small increments of sound intensity and discomfort on exposure to loud noise are increased. Degeneration is often localized so that the hearing for only one or two octaves may be effected. In the early stages of hair cell disorders the deafness may fluctuate, but once degeneration of hair cells has taken place there is no recovery of those cells, and so deafness in the related frequency is permanent.

Electrical Activity

(1) **Resting State.** The scala media maintains a resting potential of + 80 mV. (the endolymphatic potential) supplied by the stria vascularis, while the intracellular potential of the hair cells is − 80 mV. The maintenance of the voltage is dependent on the integrity of the stria vascularis and a good oxygen supply.

Atrophy of the stria vascularis has been shown to accompany deafness with a flat audiogram but without recruitment or tone decay. This deafness is usually slowly progressive but occasionally reversible. There is some evidence that salicylate poisoning produces reversible deafness via the stria.

(2) **Fluctuations on Stimulation.** Voltage variations around the cochlea are almost identical in frequency, amplitude and wave form to an applied sound. These "*cochlear microphonics*" were at first thought to be the sum of the action potentials in the auditory nerve. It was later demonstrated that they are derived from three sources:

(a) *Cochlear microphonic potential* arising in the stimulated outer hair cells.

(b) *Summation potential.* There is a shift in the mean potential level during the application of a high intensity sound. This is usually negative but can be positive. The summation potential probably arises in the inner hair cells.

(c) *Auditory nerve action potentials.*

Each fibre responds to an adequate stimulus with an "all or none" spike followed by a refractory period which limits the rate of discharge to 1,000/sec. There are two groups of fibres, each group having a different threshold and presumably connecting with the inner and outer hair cells respectively. Each fibre has a "best" frequency to which it responds, and while it is in action it cannot respond to another stimulus (hence "masking"). The central effect of each fibre may be excitatory or inhibitory depending on its destination in the brain stem.

Whole nerve response is the sum of all the single fibre spikes. It is generally held that loudness depends on the rate of firing and the number of fibres in action.

Innervation of the Cochlea

Three types of nerve fibres supplying the cochlea are recognized, *afferent, efferent* and *adrenergic*. While there are about 34,000 hair cells and 34,000 afferent fibres, about 500 efferent fibres branch repeatedly to outnumber the afferents in number of nerve endings. Both systems lose their myelin sheaths as they approach the organ of Corti. One afferent neuron innervates several outer hair cells while several neurons supply one (histologically different) inner hair cell. This may explain why outer hair cells respond to low intensity sounds while inner cells respond only to high intensity sounds, and it is a possible explanation for the loudness recruitment phenomenon (the ability of a partially deaf ear to hear intense sounds just as well as a normal ear) which is characteristically present when the function of the outer hair cells is disturbed, for example in acoustic trauma, Menière's disease, and yet another form of presbyacusis.

It is probably also significant that the afferent fibres run in a short radial course to the inner hair cells but a long spiral course to the outer cells, while nearly the opposite holds good for efferent fibres. The complexity of the innervation is such that it should be possible eventually to explain how the various characteristics of sound—intensity, frequency, quality and direction, and the enormous variation within each category—can be handled by the cochlea.

The peripheral dendrites survive destruction of the cell body and so are presumably nourished by the cochlea.

Stimulation of *efferent* fibres causes a rise in acetylcholine in the hair cells, and a rise in the threshold for afferent impulses. This may be the mechanism involved in discarding unwanted sound. Loss of this ability occurs at an early stage of presbyacusis and is responsible for difficulty in hearing at cocktail parties. It has been shown that stimulation of one cochlea produces inhibition of the opposite cochlea, and it seems probable that this is an important factor in localization of sound.

An *adrenergic* nerve plexus has been demonstrated close to the inner hair cells and this is independent of blood vessels. The function is unknown but it has been suggested that it may have some direct influence on the cochlear neurons within the organ of Corti.

The Central Auditory System

The central axons of the bipolar cells of the spiral ganglion maintain the spatial relationship started in the cochlea, but by the time they reach the cochlear nuclei they have uncoiled and each has bifurcated, one branch ending in the ventral cochlear nucleus, the other continuing to the dorsal nucleus, those from the apex (low tones) of the cochlea tending to end first and those from the base last. The fibres end in arborizations which connect with many more second order neurons. The latter follow three main routes in their ascent, ventral in the trapezoid body, intermediate, and dorsal across the floor of the 4th ventricle, to the opposite superior olivary complex, while some break from the trapezoid body to ascend on the same side. From the superior olive on both sides the 2nd and 3rd order neurons travel via the lateral lemniscus and nucleus to the inferior colliculus and thence to the medial geniculate body and primary auditory cortex in the temporal lobe. Further relays connect with secondary and eventually with tertiary areas. During this ascent there is an exceedingly rich connection between the two sides at all levels below the medial geniculate body. There is also branching with offshoots going to the cerebellar vermis, superior colliculus, brain-stem motor nuclei and reticular formation.

The *efferent* system would appear to follow parallel routes and may be equally intricate, making contact with the afferent system at numerous points and no doubt modifying its role. It has an inhibitory effect on both cochleae and may also have a facilitatory effect. The muscles of the middle ear, eyes, neck and rest of the body come under its influence.

DISORDERS OF AUDITORY FUNCTION

(1) **Lesions of the Cochlear Nuclei and Nerve.** Destruction on one side produces total loss of hearing in the ear on the same side provided the opposite ear is masked. In a free field there may be little change in the level of hearing but location of sound and ability to hear speech in the presence of background noise may be reduced. Fifty per cent of fibres may be destroyed without any effect on the hearing for pure tones (cf. the inner ear), but there may be a marked reduction in hearing for speech on the affected side. Again, in the free field this may not be noticed. Tone decay is greatly increased. Provided the cochlea is not also implicated (as it may well be in auditory nerve tumours) there is no loudness recruitment.

(2) **Lesions of 4th Ventricle and Pons.** Because of the complex links on each side and between the two sides, a unilateral lesion in this area is unlikely to disturb the hearing level for pure tones and ordinary speech, but localization of sound and appreciation of pitch may be impaired. Special speech tests, including SSW (described below), may give a poor result in lesions at this level. Bilateral involvement may slightly increase the threshold for pure tones and ordinary speech and cause bilateral decay.

(3) **Lesions of the Inferior Colliculus and Medial Geniculate Body.** Appreciation of pitch, directional hearing and body reaction to sounds may be upset in lesions at this level.

(4) **Lesions of the Temporal Lobe.** Removal of both temporal lobes produces a rise in threshold for pure tones of about 15 dB., while loss of one lobe has a negligible effect. Symptomatically, there may be difficulty in locating sounds and, in irritative disorders, auditory hallucinations may occur. Filtered and time compressed speech may be poorly understood when presented to the opposite ear, but ordinary speech discrimination and appreciation of temporal sound patterns are reduced only in bilateral lesions.

TESTS OF HEARING

A large number of tests of the various aspects of auditory function have been developed, and a description of the more useful procedures is given below. There is no place for dogmatism in the interpretation of the results, particularly perhaps in the more complicated tests, where there are many possible sources of error, and the use of a simple tuning fork (256 or 512 c.l.s.) can prevent some serious blunders. It must be remembered too that a definitive diagnosis cannot be made on the basis of these tests alone, but they do give valuable help in topognosis. Also, although the results may indicate a peripheral cochlear disorder, this may be secondary to a central lesion, for example, when a posterior fossa tumour compresses the blood supply of the inner ear. One must bear in mind too that the conductive, cochlear and retrocochlear portions of the auditory system are serially placed and so lesions affecting two or more parts tend to be additive in their effects. Affections of the auditory system are common,

TABLE 2

Test	Site of Disorder						
	Normal	Pons Unilateral	Pons Bilateral	Mid Brain Unilateral	Mid Brain Bilateral	Temporal Lobe Unilateral	Temporal Lobe Bilateral
Air conduction (pure tones)	Unchanged	Unchanged	Unchanged or reduced	Unchanged	Unchanged or reduced	Unchanged	Unchanged or reduced
Bone conduction (pure tones)	Unchanged	Unchanged	Unchanged or reduced	Unchanged	Unchanged or reduced	Unchanged	Unchanged or reduced
Speech discrimination	80–100%	80–100%	Unchanged or reduced	Unchanged	Unchanged or reduced	Unchanged	Poor
Swinging, S.S.W., and interrupted speech	Good	Poor	Poor	Poor	Poor	Poor	Poor
Filtered and fast speech	Good	Good	Good	Probably Good	Poor	Poor	Poor
Localization	Good	Poor	Poor	Poor	Poor	Poor	Poor
Békésy	Type I	Type I	Type IV	Type I	Type IV	Type I	Type I
Tone decay	0–5 dB.	0–5 dB.	>20 dB.	0–5 dB.	20 dB.	0–5 dB.	0–5 dB.
Startle reflex	Unchanged	Unchanged	Unchanged or poor	Unchanged	Poor	Unchanged	Unchanged
Pitch discrimination	Good	Good	Poor	Good	Poor	Good	Good

especially with advancing age; and when a patient presents with a recently developed ear problem it is more likely than not to be superimposed on an old-standing lesion. It helps if one remembers this when trying to interpret apparently conflicting results in the audiological investigation.

The first four tests can be carried out with the simple pure tone audiometer found in any ear, nose and throat clinic. The remainder require special attachments and more sophisticated equipment.

Pure Tone Audiometry

This is the most generally used measure of hearing. The patient's hearing for air conduction and bone conduction is compared, in 5 dB. steps, at frequencies from 125–8,000 c.s. in octave steps, with the average hearing threshold of a number of normal young persons (0 dB.).* There are three standards, British, American and International, the last now being the generally accepted one. *Masking* of the opposite ear is necessary when the air conduction threshold is more than 50 dB. and always when testing for bone conduction thresholds (Figs. 1–3).

* dB. = decibel = $\frac{1}{10}$ Bel. A Bel is the logarithm of the ratio of 2 intensities of sound. In clinical practice the reference level is 0·0002 dyn./sq. cm. (0 dB.) at 1,000 c.s. 20 dB. then, is 100 × 0·0002 = 0·02 dyn. cm.$^{-2}$; 30 dB. = 0·2 dyn. cm.$^{-2}$; 100 dB. = 2,000,000 dyn. cm.$^{-2}$; 103 dB. = 4,000,000 dyn. cm.$^{-2}$.

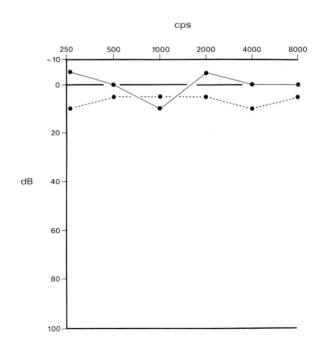

Fig. 1. Pure-tone audiogram showing *normal* hearing in one ear. The hearing-level in decibels* is recorded at each frequency from 250 to 8000 c/s. Air conduction is shown as a continuous line, bone conduction as an interrupted line.

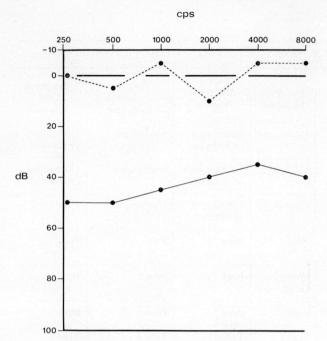

FIG. 2. Pure-tone audiogram as in Fig. 1, showing *conductive* deafness (bone conduction better than air conduction).

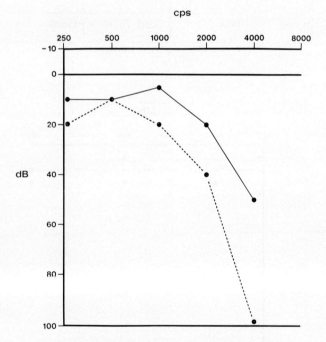

FIG. 3. Pure-tone audiogram as in Fig. 1, showing *high-tone sensorineural deafness*.

Tone Decay Test

This is a simple test which is useful for showing up *retrocochlear disorders*. Abnormal adaptation at threshold, auditory threshold fatigue, and temporary threshold drift are other terms used for the same phenomenon: an abnormal rate of increase in auditory threshold for a continuous tone. A sustained tone is presented at 5 dB.

above threshold and the intensity is increased 5 dB. when it can no longer be heard. This is repeated until the tone can be heard for 60 sec. In the normal ear and in conduction deafness the +5 dB. sound can be heard for 60 sec. In cochlear deafness +20 dB. and in retrocochlear deafness +25 dB. or more may be required. The test is repeated at various frequencies. Tone decay may be present in an auditory nerve disorder even though the pure tone audiogram is normal and in brain stem lesions tone decay may be bilateral.

Loudness Recruitment Test

The ability of a deaf ear to hear intense sounds (around 100 dB.) just as well as a normal ear is a characteristic of *cochlear* disorders. The patient is asked to compare the loudness of a Bárány noise box in each ear, or in the more sophisticated **loudness balance test,** to say when a brief pure tone, alternately presented to each ear, seems of equal loudness, starting with threshold sounds and increasing in steps to about 100 dB. A ladder graph is constructed (Fig. 4). To do the test there must be a reasonable difference between the two ears, one of which should be normal. The test does not exclude the possibility of an underlying acoustic or posterior fossa tumour, both of which may

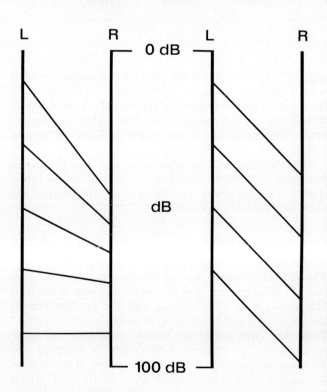

FIG. 4. Loudness balance step-ladder graphs. In the example on the right the deafness shows no recruitment, while in the left-hand graph the two ears hear equally well at 90 dB. and therefore in this instance the right ear shows recruitment.

produce inner ear changes by altering the blood supply or flow of labyrinthine fluids, by direct invasion of the cochlea, or by pressure on the efferent nerve fibres.

Loudness Discomfort Level

This requires an audiometer capable of delivering tones up to 120 dB. Unlike the loudness balance test it can be used when both ears are affected. The "discomfort" level is normally reached at 100–120 dB. and this is also true for *cochlear* deafness. A superadded conduction or nerve fibre deafness usually abolishes the discomfort.

Short Increment Sensitivity Index (SISI)

Another characteristic of cochlear deafness is its ability to detect very small increases in intensity of a sound about 20 dB. above threshold. In the normal ear a jump of 5 dB. in intensity, but *not* of 1 dB., can easily be heard. The test is carried out 20 dB. above threshold and a jump of 1 dB. of one-fifth of a second duration occurs every five seconds.

A high score (60–100 per cent) points to a *cochlear* disorder but does not exclude a retrocochlear lesion.

Speech Discrimination

A rough test of the hearing for speech can be made by asking the patient to repeat loudly spoken words while the opposite ear is masked with a moving finger or a noise box, care being taken that the patient does not see the examiner's lips. A more accurate estimation can be made using tape recorded monosyllabic words at 30 dB. above the threshold at the speech frequencies. A poor score (below 40 per cent words heard correctly) suggests a lesion of the *auditory nerve* while an intermediate score (60–75 per cent) is found in cochlear lesions. Nevertheless one in ten of patients with an auditory nerve tumour has a normal score (80–100 per cent).

Not surprisingly, in view of bilateral representation, *supranuclear lesions* seldom show any abnormality in the above tests. This is not the case however with modified speech tests. The speech frequency range can be reduced by *filters*, and speech can be *compressed in time*, and these alterations will often detect a lesion of the opposite temporal lobe. In the staggered spondaic word (SSW) test, one monosyllable of each spondee overlaps the other in time, but in opposite ears—this may be affected in lesions of the pons and fourth ventricle when the thresholds for pure tones and speech are normal.

Békésy Audiometry

A self-recording audiometer is used. The frequency slowly changes from low to high and the intensity increases until a button is pressed when it decreases until the button is released. The subject is instructed to press the button as soon as the tone is heard and release it as soon as it disappears. This can be done with an interrupted or

pulsed tone and then with a continuous tone. Two tracings are obtained on the same paper using different coloured ink for clarity.

It is possible to classify the results into five types. In *type I* the two tracings are superimposed (normal or conductive deafness). In *type II* the two tracings are superimposed up to 500–1,000 c./s. and they then diverge—but not more than 20 dB. (cochlear deafness). *Type IV* is very similar to *type II* but the separation between the two curves is greater than 20 dB. and starts below 500 c./s. (retrocochlear deafness). In *type III* the divergence is dramatic, the tracing for the continuous tone plunging towards the bottom of the graph paper (retrocochlear deafness). Where there is a difference between the two tracings the pulsed tone is above the continuous tone tracing except in *type V* which is suggestive of psychogenic deafness.

The *amplitude* of the tracing is also of interest. A small amplitude at high tones is usually found in cochlear lesions.

Acoustic Impedence

The resistance which a sound has to overcome in its passage from the outer to the inner ear can be measured on an electro-acoustic instrument. The resistance varies physiologically with the action of the stapedius and tensor tympani tendons and pathologically in altered pressure in the middle ear, or with fixed or dislocated ossicles. In the normal subject the stapedius muscle contracts on both sides when an intense sound, 85–95 dB., is presented to either ear, but this reaction is weakened or does not take place at all in deafness unless recruitment is present. An abnormal rate of decay of the stapedius muscle-contraction may be one of the earliest signs of an auditory nerve lesion. An advantage of these tests is that they are *objective* and do not require the co-operation of the patient —other than permission to do the test. The stapedius reflex can also help in locating the lesion in facial palsy.

Cortical-Evoked Response Audiometry

With computerized signal averaging it is possible to produce a clear response to sound stimuli. The thresholds appear to correspond with the subjective thresholds of hearing. There is reduced latency and increased amplitude in auditory nerve lesions. It is thought that the third component of the wave is related to the understanding of the sound. Evaluation of the procedure is difficult at this stage and further evidence of its value will be required before it is widely adopted.

Directional Hearing Tests

Localization of a sound source is reduced in the presence of considerable unilateral deafness of any type. With otherwise normal hearing it may be affected, however, in lesions of the afferent auditory pathway at the contralateral accessory olive, the floor of the fourth ventricle, the homolateral superior olive and in the cerebellopontine angle.

VESTIBULAR FUNCTION

The Sense Organs

Semicircular Canals

The hair-cells are of two types corresponding to the inner and outer cells of the cochlea. *Type I* is flask-shaped and is more numerous on the summit of the ampullary cristae of the semicircular canals, while *type II* is cylindrical and more numerous on the sides of the cristae. Each cell has many sensory hairs consisting of slender stereocilia and only one stout kinocilium which is always to one side. In the ampulla of the lateral semicircular canal the kinocilia are always on the vestibular side of the cells whereas in the vertical canals they are on the side away from the vestibule. This arrangement may be related to Ewald's experimental findings (*see below*). The hairs project into the jelly-like cupula and it seems probable that bending of the hairs with movement of the cupula is the trigger mechanism for the firing of the cells. An adequate stimulus is movement of the fluids in a semicircular canal. Each cell is supplied by two types of nerve endings—afferent and, presumably, efferent.

Utricle

The macula of the utricle lies horizontally on the floor of the vestibule with the hairs of its cells projecting upwards into a flat gelatinous mass covered with calcium carbonate crystals (the otoliths). The main stimulus is tilting of the head with subsequent bending of the hairs due to the pull of the relatively heavy otoliths. In this way the utricles give information about the position of the head in space, and may therefore be referred to as the static labyrinth.

Since the semicircular canals respond to movement, and in particular angular acceleration and deceleration, they are referred to as the kinetic labyrinth. The lateral canals work together as a pair, while each superior canal acts with the opposite posterior canal.

The following rules arose from experiments on pigeons by Flourens and Ewald but are still useful today:

(1) Stimulation of a semicircular canal tends to elicit nystagmus in its own plane (Flourens).

(2) Movement of endolymph produces a deviation of eyes in the direction of flow (Ewald).

(3) In the horizontal canal the greatest effect is produced when the flow is towards the ampulla (Ewald).

(4) In the vertical canals the greatest effect is produced when the flow is away from the ampulla (Ewald).

It has been widely debated whether the last two apply to man, but so far it has not been proved that they do not apply. If more than one canal is stimulated on one side then a rotary nystagmus is produced. In the resting state there is a continuous discharge from the hair cells of the canals and utricle. If the head is tilted the discharge from the utricles is increased. If the cupula of the lateral canal is deflected towards the vestibule the discharge is increased and if away from the vestibule the discharge is decreased. In rotation one increases while the opposite decreases.

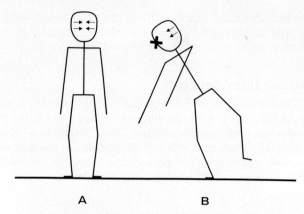

FIG. 5. A—the vestibular system on each side is intact. B—the right labyrinth (or vestibular nerve or nuclei) has been destroyed, resulting in falling, past pointing and deviation of the eyes to the right. The same can be produced by irrigating the right ear with cold water.

The effect of *destruction of one labyrinth* (Fig. 5) is deviation of the eyes, head, upper limbs and trunk towards the side of the lesion—and the same applies to a lesser degree to any paretic lesion. One might say that the normal half of the vestibular system is pushing the body towards the opposite side. Indeed it is the opposing action of the two halves of the vestibular system which helps to maintain the equilibrium. It should be noted however that while the slow drift of the eyes (and body) is towards the lesion the quick correction is towards the normal side. The subjective sensation of *vertigo* is also towards the normal side. Vertigo in this chapter is taken to mean an illusion of movement of the head or body, and is the symptom which arises from conflicting information about the body's orientation.

Sudden complete destruction in man causes violent vertigo, nausea, vomiting, and obvious dysequilibrium but this rapidly subsides so that three weeks later equilibrium may be restored except in special situations or tests. At first the subject tends to lie with the affected ear up. There is no loss of consciousness. The same effects arise from division of the 8th cranial nerve, or extirpation of the vestibular nuclei.

Blood Supply

The internal auditory artery usually arises from the anterior inferior cerebellar artery, but not infrequently directly from the basilar artery. The saccus endolymphaticus may have an independent blood supply from the posterior meningeal artery, while the bony labyrinth also is supplied by various branches of the external carotid system. However, there is no anastomosis, and so the labyrinth is highly vulnerable to interruption of its blood supply. Sympathetic nerve fibres accompany the vessels and although evidence of the functional activity of the fibres is scanty it seems highly probable that they are there to influence the blood flow. If this is correct it might explain how anxiety affects the labyrinth.

Labyrinthine Fluids

Perilymph resembles tissue fluid in its composition and it seems probable that it is formed as a transudate from the blood vessels, although enzyme analysis suggests that it may be actively secreted. The protein content is raised in Menière's disease, and markedly raised in acoustic neuroma —before there is a rise in the protein level of the CSF.

Endolymph resembles intracellular fluid. Its formation and absorption are uncertain but perhaps the most acceptable theory at present is that it is derived from perilymph and absorbed by the stria vascularis and the saccus endolymphaticus.

It has been shown that in Menière's disease there is usually distension of the cochlear duct (scala media), due to increased volume of endolymph. The explanation of this finding may be reduced formation of perilymph and reduced absorption of endolymph, secondary to vascular changes brought about by autonomic imbalance.

Innervation of the Labyrinth

As in the cochlea there are afferent, efferent and sympathetic nerve-fibres.

The *sympathetic* nerve-fibres have been shown to be in two groups (1) perivascular, and (2) independent of blood vessels, beneath the vestibular sensory epithelium. The latter arise in the central nervous system and reach the periphery via the cochlear nerve.

The *efferent* system is known to exist but anatomical details are rather sketchy. The cell-bodies are located in the lateral and descending vestibular nuclei and in the reticular formation. The axons, crossed and uncrossed, are carried in the vestibular nerve and their nerve endings are presumed to constitute one of the two types of nerve-endings which impinge on the hair-cells. There is some evidence to suggest that the system can facilitate one labyrinth while inhibiting the other. It is probable that it is partly responsible for habituation of the vestibular system in ballet dancers and skaters.

Central Connections

Although the system corresponds with the spinal reflex, in this case the afferents influence the anterior horn cells at all levels and certain cranial motor nuclei.

The central axons arising from the bipolar cells in the vestibular ganglion are covered with myelin and neurilemmal sheaths. The superior and inferior divisions fuse one with the other, and then with the cochlear nerve, within the internal auditory meatus. The vestibular nerve enters the brain-stem, medial to the cochlear nerve, at the lower border of the pons, and at the level of the lateral recess of the 4th ventricle. It passes between the inferior cerebellar peduncle and the spinal tract of the trigeminal and then divides into ascending and descending branches, which go to the four main *nuclei* and to the cerebellum. Below the level of entry the nuclei are largely concerned with the utricle while above this level the semicircular canals are represented. In a similar way, a broad distinction can be made with the connections of these regions—the lower (utricle) connects with the anterior spinal horn cells, and the upper (semicircular canals) with the eye muscle centres on both sides.

Fibres radiate directly and indirectly via the inferior cerebellar peduncle to the "vestibular" parts of the cerebellum—the flocculus, nodulus, uvula and probably the paraflocculus. Other fibres connect the vestibular nuclei with the reticular formation and are probably responsible for visceral reactions following vestibular stimulation.

The cortical projection appears to be almost exclusively the contralateral postcentral gyrus (area 2 of Brodman). There are probably however secondary connections with other areas, notably the posterior part of the temporal lobe where lesions are known to cause vertigo.

The cerebellum exerts a strong inhibiting influence over the vestibular nuclei and labyrinthine reflexes. It has been noted that a lesion of the nodulus produces a marked positional nystagmus.

VESTIBULAR DYSFUNCTION

Features of a Peripheral Disorder

Unequivocal signs are few, but would include a *"fistula" sign* where change of pressure in the external auditory canal, by pressing on the tragus with the finger, or by inflating with a Politzer bag, produces sudden vertigo and nystagmus. This occurs in erosion of the bony labyrinth. By touching with a probe a trigger area in a mastoid cavity following operation, it is sometimes possible to produce a similar effect.

Suggestive features include peripheral type deafness (conductive or inner ear) and infection or neoplasm of the middle ear. Severe rotary vertigo with nausea and vomiting is more common in peripheral than central disorders. The *spontaneous nystagmus* typical of peripheral disease is horizontal or rotary, with slow and quick components, and is maximal when the eyes are deviated in the direction of the quick component and least when deviated in the opposite direction; the movements of the eyes are conjugate; on *electro nystagmography*, the nystagmus is increased on eye closure and in the dark (Fig. 10a), and when the mind is diverted e.g. in doing calculations. The vertigo is also increased on eye closure. If *positional nystagmus* is present, it is typically produced when the affected ear is down; it comes on after a brief delay; it lasts only about forty seconds (adaptation); the nystagmus has the characteristics of the spontaneous nystagmus mentioned above; if the critical position is resumed immediately the reaction is greatly reduced or absent (fatigability); vertigo accompanies the nystagmus. If there is any departure from this description of the positional reaction a central lesion should be suspected. Unfortunately, even the entirely typical picture has been found in a few cases of acoustic neuroma and lesions of the cerebellar nodulus.

Features of Central Lesions

Nystagmus may occur without vertigo and may last for more than three weeks; it may vary in direction and occur in different positions; it may be vertical or oblique; the movement of the eyes may be dissociated; on *electro-nystagmography*, closing the eyes, or darkness, does not increase the vertigo or the amplitude of the nystagmus, and may abolish it (Fig. 10b), and saccadic movements and dysrhythmia (cerebellar lesion) may be seen. *Positional nystagmus* may be nonfatiguing and nonadapting, and may or may not be accompanied by vertigo. The calorically induced nystagmus may reveal an unusually high amplitude and dysrhythmia (cerebellar lesion).

Diminution in consciousness, drop attacks, eye bobbing, strabismus and other neurological features favour a central cause.

Tests of Vestibular Function

When vertigo or vestibular nystagmus is present it can usually be accepted that there is a vestibular disorder and special tests of vestibular function are then only of value if they help to decide the side of the lesion or its level. There are occasions when a vestibular disorder will only be revealed by special testing—not an uncommon situation in acoustic neuroma and some weeks after trauma.

Testing is usually based on the nystagmus of the eyes induced by stimulation of the lateral semi-circular canals. Although rotation is the more physiological stimulus, the technical difficulties are greater than a caloric stimulus. A simple and quick test for use in the clinic is the *Linthicum Test*. The external auditory canals must be clear and the tympanic membranes normal. The head is tilted to the side so that ice water (0·2 ml.) will flow easily to the drum. After 20 sec. the water is discharged from the ear and the head is placed 70° back, nystagmus noted, and 30° forward and nystagmus noted. The reaction is normal if nystagmus occurs in either position for both ears. If there is no reaction the amount of ice water is doubled and the test repeated.

One disadvantage of the above method is that it can give misleading information in the case of directional preponderance with regard to the side affected, and can give a normal result in other cases believed to demonstrate combined canal and utricular lesions. The *Fitzgerald-Hallpike caloric test* is more informative in this respect—but more time-consuming. Water at 30°C is run into the left ear for 40 sec. and the duration of the nystagmus from the start of the irrigation is noted. This is repeated for the right ear, and then with water at 44°C (a normal result is shown in Fig. 6). Calorigram I demonstrates a right canal paresis, while II would seem to suggest a left lesion with cold water and a right lesion with hot—this apparent anomaly is seen when there is a latent drift of the eyes to the right. In this connection it must be noted that *cold* water irrigation of the *right* ear and *hot* water irrigation of the *left* ear always tend to produce a nystagmus to the left. In the example in II a prolonged nystagmus to the left can easily be induced, while it is difficult to induce a nystagmus to the right—this has been called a directional preponderance to the left, but it can equally be regarded as a deviation or drift of the eyes to the right. This would be brought about by reduced action of the right vestibular system. Such a state can be due either to a lesion on the

right anywhere from the inferior vestibular nucleus to the vestibule, or a supratentorial lesion on the left.

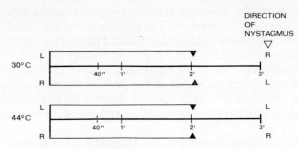

FIG. 6. *Norman calorigram* after irrigation of each ear with water at 30·C and 44°C for 40 sec. The triangles show when the induced nystagmus ceases (about 2 min.). The direction of the quick component of the nystagmus in each instance is shown.

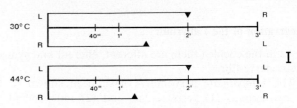

FIG. 7. *Right "canal" paresis.*

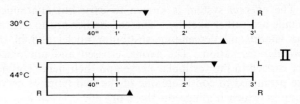

FIG. 8. *Preponderance to the left* (or drift to the right).

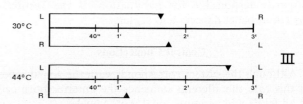

FIG. 9. *Combined lesion of the right vestibular system.*

Calorigram III occurs when there is a lesion of the right vestibular system involving both the kinetic and the static portions. It is of academic interest to note that III is very nearly the result of averaging I and II. An important practical point, however, is that III would appear normal in a caloric test which omits hot water.

Bilateral diminution in response to both cold and hot water occurs in bilateral lesions (e.g. vestibular neuronitis), vestibular habituation (e.g. ballet dancers), and anxiety states.

Electro-nystagmography is useful in that it (a) allows recording of the nystagmus, (b) shows up nystagmus which may not be apparent to the naked eye, and (c) enables recordings to be made with the subject's eyes shut or in the dark.

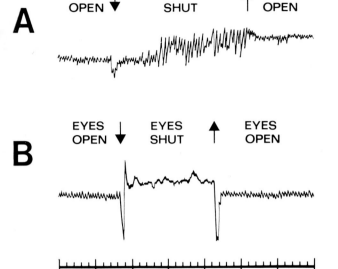

FIG. 10. Electro-nystagmograms. A—shows nystagmus to the left and effect of closing the eyes in a *peripheral* disorder.
B—shows nystagmus to the right and effect of closing the eyes in a *central* disorder.

Since the cornea is positively charged in relation to the fundus, movements of the eye in one plane can be recorded by placing electrodes on either side. Amplification may be D.C. but, more commonly A.C. Calibration is carried out by asking the subject to look 10° to the right, then 10° to the left. Knowing the speed of the paper, it is then possible to determine the speed of the slow component of nystagmus in degrees per second, and the amplitude and frequency of the nystagmus.

Recording the nystagmus in this way helps to show the level of the lesion (Fig. 10) but does not indicate the side involved. There may however be clues to this such as unilateral deafness, "canal" paresis, or other cranial nerve abnormalities.

FURTHER READING

Békésy, G. von (1960), *Experiments in Hearing*. New York and London: McGraw-Hill Book Co.

Brodal, A. (1969), *Neurological Anatomy*, 2nd edition. New York and London: Oxford University Press.

Dix, M. R. (1969), "Modern Tests of Vestibular Function, with Special Reference to their value in Clinical Practice," *Brit. med. J.*, **2**, 317–323.

Fitzgerald, G. and Hallpike, C. S. (1942), "Studies in Human Vestibular Function," *Brain*, **65**, 115.

Graham, A. B. (Ed.) (1967), *Sensorineural Hearing Processes and Disorders*. Boston: Little, Brown & Co.

Harrison, M. S. and Naftalin, L. (1968), *Menière's Disease*. Springfield: Charles C. Thomas.

McNally, W. J. and Stuart, E. A. (1967), *Physiology of the Labyrinth*. American Academy of Ophthalmology and Otolaryngology.

Maran, A. G. D. (1966), "The Evaluation of Nystagmus as a Clinical Sign," *Scot. med. J.*, **11**, 379–387.

Symposium (1967) on Vertigo, *Archives of Otolaryngology*, **85**, 497–560.

Whitfield, I. C. (1967), *The Auditory Pathway*. London: Edward Arnold (Publishers) Ltd.

Wolfson, R. J. (Ed.) (1966), *The Vestibular System and its Diseases*. London: Oxford University Press.

Wolstenholme, G. E. W. and Knight, J. (Ed.) (1970), *Sensorineural Hearing Loss*. London: Churchill.

Wright, M. I. (1971), *The Pathology of Deafness*. Manchester: The University Press.

4. OLFACTION

W. McCARTNEY

Welcher Organsinn ist der undankbarste und scheint auch der entbehrlichste zu sein? Der des Geruchs. Es belohnt nicht, ihn zu kultivieren oder wohl gar zu verfeinern, um zu geniessen; denn es gibt mehr Gegenstände des Ekels als der Annehmlichkeit, die er verschaffen kann. Der Genuss durch diesen Sinn kann immer nur flüchtig und vorübergehend sein, wenn er vergnügen sol.   *Kant*

In the year 1909, writing of the olfactory powers of the tracker dog, Zell remarked that he was studying "ein von der Wissenschaft fast gänzlich vernachlässigtes Gebiet", and while it is true that the study of human olfaction had not, at that time, been entirely neglected, comparatively little attention had been paid to it either by neurologists or by other scientific or medical workers. However, since about 1953 when the New York Academy of Sciences held its first symposium on the subject ("Basic Odor Research Correlation") interest in human and animal olfaction has grown enormously particularly in France, Germany, Switzerland and the USA where the Monell Chemical Senses Center was established in 1968 and it has recently been proposed that an international society for research on chemoreception should be formed.* As would be expected, the work that has been described

* A recently founded journal, *Olfactologia*, devoted entirely to olfaction has unfortunately ceased publication.

since 1953 has not been concerned with the human species only and, although neurologists who wish to study olfaction will naturally be interested chiefly in the human sense of smell, it may be worth while first briefly to consider olfaction in some other species, namely fish, birds and dogs remembering that considerable caution should be maintained when physiological evidence from lower animals (for example frogs and other experimental animals) is used to support odour theories based on human psychophysical responses.

Despite the fact that, in the middle of the eighteenth century, Monro held that fish have an acute sense of smell, it was for long thereafter thought that animals living in water could not have such a sense. However, there is now strong evidence that salmon and possibly other migratory fish, even after long absence at great distances from their home areas, are able to locate the streams in which they were hatched by means of their sense of smell, that some fish react vigorously to very low concentrations (e.g. one part in several million parts of water) of the "alarm" substances which are sometimes released from the intact or damaged skin of their own or other species, and that eels can smell substances such as phenylethyl alcohol which has no biological significance, detecting 1 cm.^{3} of it in a volume of water 58 times as great as that of Lake Constance which is 30 miles long, 10 miles wide and 827 ft. deep at its deepest part.

Since the days of Audubon, the results of a great number of studies of avian olfaction have been extraordinarily conflicting probably chiefly because, as Bernice Wenzel has pointed out, the question asked should not have been "can birds smell?" but, "can they perceive olfactory stimuli, regulate some of their behaviour by olfactory cues and learn so to regulate it?". Stager's experiments with turkey vultures and those of Wenzel herself with kiwis make it now seem certain that these birds do indeed have a sense of smell and that the kiwis, at least, utilize it in locating food.

But the animal that has attracted most attention from the olfactory point of view is, of course, the tracker dog. The very large numbers of laboratory and field tests that have been conducted with these animals, particularly in Germany, have given, it is true, results that were frequently contradictory but it seems beyond doubt that, if properly selected, treated and trained, they can detect by smell, for example, 1 mg. of butyric acid in 100,000,000 m.^{3} of air, can follow fresh and old human scent tracks on various kinds of surface under various weather conditions, can distinguish between such tracks when they are not less than a few minutes old and, when following a particular track, can ignore cross and diversionary tracks. It should be remembered, however, that the odour of the track usually includes, together with the scent from the feet of the quarry, a great variety of other scents and that it changes with time and place so that some investigators assert that it is not the scent of the quarry but that of the track that serves as a guide. Nevertheless, it is certain that highly trained and experienced dogs are capable of astonishing tracking feats and it seems at least possible that they may be able to detect, by means of their sense of smell, buried articles such as land mines, drugs, explosives and the "black boxes" of crashed aircraft if these boxes have previously been rendered suitably odorous.

The scientific study of the human sense of smell only began in the early years of the nineteenth century when Cloquet's treatise *Osphrésiologie* was written and it was not until the early part of the next that the still useful works of Zwaardemaker, Henning and Heyninx appeared.* Then, as now, the study was found to be very difficult because of the inaccessibility of the end organ and the lack of means to measure and classify the stimuli. And although techniques such as those of electro-physiology and gas chromatography are now available as aids to research, the progress that is being made is far from rapid.

It has occasionally been suggested that the olfactory receptors, probably the cilia of the sensory cells which may be the site of the transduction action concerned, can be excited without coming into contact with odorous material but the evidence against this is overwhelming and it can be accepted that sensation is normally produced only when an adequate amount of the material, carried by the inspired air, is adsorbed on or absorbed in the mucus that covers these cells and so produces the signal transmitted to the brain by the olfactory nerve. The amount of odorous substance required is often exceedingly small, possibly not more than a few molecules per cell stimulated. Thus, as long ago as 1886, Fischer and Penzoldt showed that they could smell as little as 1/460,000,000 mg. of ethyl mercaptan, and similar, although probably more accurate results have been obtained many times since. Thus it was recently found that 2-methoxy-3-*iso*butylpyrazine a volatile constituent of bell peppers, can be smelled at a concentration of only 2 parts per 10^{12} parts of water.

People vary very appreciably, of course, in their olfactory acuity and there are differences in acuity associated with age and sex but, apart from differences subject, apparently, to hormonal control or to partial anosmia that may be hereditarily transmitted, it seems that the variations are not at all pronounced in healthy individuals. Infants and young children probably have greater acuity than have adults and, as with other senses, acuity decreases in adults in their later years. Savages and blind persons it seems, have no greater acuity than have civilized people and people who have not lost their sight. Amongst other factors that may influence acuity considerably are: temperature, relative humidity, rate of flow of inspired air, state of health of the perceiving subject, extent to which he smokes, length of period that has elapsed since he has taken food and extent to which he has trained himself to smell. Everybody knows, too, that olfactory fatigue (or adaptation) develops rapidly in an odorous atmosphere and, indeed, advantage has been taken of this in classifying odours since like odours are readily affected by the condition, unlike odours being scarcely if at all influenced. Weak odours, of course, can be completely masked by

---

* For recent descriptions of the ultra-structure of the olfactory epithelium and its connections, *see* the report of the CIBA Foundation Symposium on "Taste and Smell in Vertebrates" (1970).

strong but it has not been convincingly shown that mutual cancellation ("compensation") ever occurs.

Because of the great difficulties encountered in measuring odorous strength—sources of error are difficult or impossible to eliminate even with the most modern instruments—many olfactometers and several olfactoria (rooms or cubicles into which the odorant under examination is released) have been devised. In all these, the pure substance or mixture of substances, generally previously dissolved in water or other odourless solvent, is diluted until it can no longer be detected or, alternatively, a concentration so low that it cannot be smelled is gradually increased until it can. Some investigators have chosen to inject odorous air into the nose but it is much more usual, and probably more satisfactory, to allow the subject to sniff at atmospheric pressure. As regards the relationship between increase in concentration of odorant and perceived increase in intensity of odour, as expressed by the "just noticeable difference", it is thought that the Weber-Fechner psycho-physical law or some modification of it may hold.

To measure odorous intensity accurately is very difficult. Perhaps it is even more difficult to classify odours, although perfumers, for their own purposes, are certainly able to make useful, albeit far from scientific classifications. Zwaardemaker's nine classes (aromatic, burnt or empyreumatic, ambrosiacal, alliaceous, fragrant, caprylic, repulsive, nauseating and ethereal) and Henning's six (fragrant, ethereal and putrid; spicy, resinous and burnt) located at the corners of his triangular "odour prism" are clearly anything but satisfactory; and most, if not all, of the investigators who have later entered this field have not been appreciably more successful. In 1952, Amoore revived the hypothesis that there are seven primary odours (camphoraceous, pungent, ethereal, floral, pepperminty, musk, putrid) from which all others could be compounded, and sought during the succeeding fifteen years to confirm his opinion. He was of the opinion that on the olfactory receptors, there are corresponding sites into which the differently shaped molecules of the odorants concerned would fit—the "site-filling" theory. Apparently he now prefers to search for subjects who exhibit specific anosmia, i.e. those who are anosmic to a particular odour while exhibiting normal ability to perceive other odours. He has also claimed to have identified another primary odour, namely, the sweaty odour of *iso*valeric acid, using in his researches models of the odorant molecules concerned and a pattern-recognition machine consisting of a television-type camera linked to a special computer.

Although Amoore's views have received a considerable degree of recognition, it is worthy of note that Schneider, a distinguished student of olfactory problems, maintains that "almost all of the so-called 'hard tests' for this theory, which at best can be termed a hypothesis, collapse at closer examination".

A different and very promising approach to the problem has been made by Hamilton Wright. Following Dyson's suggestion that "the only property of chemical compounds that can be correlated with odour is the periodic movement of the atoms or groups of which the molecules of odorous

substances are built" he has supposed that distinctive odours can be correlated with specific combinations of low-frequency molecular vibrations and he has been able, by examining many odorants having similar odours to show that these also have similar "osmic frequencies". It is, in fact, difficult to believe that, since physical and physiological properties depend on chemical constitution, there is not likewise a close correlation between constitution and odour although the many attempts to demonstrate this conclusively have had only limited success.

In a still more important direction, namely that of olfactory theory, much progress remains to be made. Just a century ago, Ogle suggested that there might be a correlation between the yellow–brown pigment in the olfactory epithelium of mammals, and olfactory acuity. His suggestion that the coloured protein-bound carotenoids concerned may be molecular receptors of odours has been renewed from time to time and Campbell has recently remarked that the carotenoids of the olfactory hair cells may serve as quasi-metallic conductors in which the standing potential is suddenly altered on contact with an odorous substance. Still more recently, Rosenberg and his co-workers have advanced a transduction theory involving formation of a pigment-odorant complex. But it is still far from certain that the pigment plays anything more than a minor part in olfactory perception.

The fact that many biological processes are greatly influenced by enzymes is the basis of the theories of Alexander and others. He believed that odorants may affect the enzyme balance of the olfactory cells by modifying existing enzymes, by forming new enzyme complexes, by inhibiting all or part of the normal cellular enzymes, or in all these ways, and Kistiakowsky has made similar suggestions. Another and more up-to-date enzyme theory is that of Martin who took as his basic postulate the idea of an enzyme with two clefts, one of which will synthesize or break down something to liberate a substance that is a common excitant of cells. This enzyme, however, would only act when an odorant molecule is introduced into the other cleft.

Quite different is the "cell penetrating and puncturing" theory of Davies. His view was that the molecules of odorants are bulky, rather rigid, and awkwardly shaped, and that they puncture the cell walls, acting like a trigger which produces effects that are then greatly amplified, while potassium passes out of the cells to be replaced by sodium. Threshold values, he claimed, depend quantitatively on the adsorption energies of the odorants passing from the air to the lipoid-aqueous surfaces of the olfactory membranes and on the sizes and shapes of the odorant molecules, while—on the basis of a study of more than fifty compounds having musk odour—he maintained that odour is a purely physical property of these molecules, determined by their rate of desorption, cross-sectional areas and the dimension ratio length-breadth. His theory, however, has been adversely criticized by Adey and by Martin.

Another group of fifty pure substances having a good variety of odours was studied by Laffort who has concluded that it is possible, from three physico-chemical properties of odorants to calculate the corresponding olfactory thresholds. These properties are: an apolar factor dependent on molecular volume at the boiling point, hydrogen-bonding index, and atomic volume polarizability. It is too early to say, however, whether this theory is generally applicable.

It is evident from this brief review in which there is no space to deal with psychological and other aspects of olfaction, that our understanding of the olfactory process, or at least of its initial stages, is now increasing, and that we may expect it to continue to expand at an accelerating pace. But presumably we may yet agree with Cloquet who wrote a century and a half ago: "Quel que soit au reste, le mode d'action de ces organes, notre intention ne sera point de vouloir remonter à l'essence de la sensation, ni de démontrer comment elle peut être éprouvée. C'est une cause placée hors de la sphère de nos recherches, et derobée, probablement pour toujours, aux moyens d'investigation que l'homme a reçu avec la vie. L'être animé présente une foule de problèmes qu'il n'est point donné aux sciences accessoires à la médecine, ni à la médecine elle-même de résoudre."

FURTHER READING

"Airkem," (1952), *Odors and the Sense of Smell*, 320 B.C.—1947. New York: Airkem.

Cadilhac, J. (1969), "Olfaction et neurologie," *J. Franc. Oto-Rhino-Laryngol. Chir. Maxillo-Faciale*, **18**, 17–23.
Cloquet, H. (1821), *Osphrésiologie, ou traité des odeurs, du sens et des organes de l'olfaction*, 2nd edition. Paris: Méquignon-Marvis.
Harper, R., Bate-Smith, E. C. and Land, D. G. (1968), *Odour Description and Odour Classification. A Multidisciplinary Examination*. London: Churchill.
Hasler, A. D. (1966), *Underwater Guideposts*. Madison, Milwaukee and London: University of Wisconsin Press.
Henning, H. (1924), *Der Geruch*. Leipzig: Barth, 2 Aufl.
Heyninx, A. (1919), *Essai d'olfactique physiologique*. Brussels: Larcier.
Kleerekoper, H. (1969), *Olfaction in Fishes*. Bloomington and London: Indiana University Press.
McCartney, W. (1968), *Olfaction and Odours*. Berlin, Heidelberg, New York: Springer-Verlag.
McCord, C. P. and Witheridge, W. N. (1949), *Odors: Physiology and Control*. New York: McGraw-Hill.
Michels, K. M., Phillips, D. S., Wright, R. Huey and Pustek, J. (1962), "Odor and Olfaction," a bibliography 1948–1960, *Percept. Motor Skills*, **15**, 475–529.
Monro, A. (1785), *The Structure and Physiology of Fishes Explained and Compared with those of Man and other Animals*. Edinburgh.
Olfaction and Taste—International Symposia. Vol. I and II, London: Pergamon Press, 1963 and 1967. Vol. III, New York: Rockefeller University Press, 1969.
Theories of Odor and Odor Measurement (1968), Istanbul: Robert College.
Wright, R. Hamilton (1964), *The Science of Smell*. London: Allen & Unwin.
Zwaardemaker, H. (1895), *Die Physiologie des Geruchs*. Leipzig: Engelmann.

5. CLINICAL ASPECTS OF ANOSMIA

DAVID SUMNER

The first problem to face the clinician when considering the sense of smell or the lack of it, is what he should use as a test-substance and whether he can make his test quantitative. Many techniques have been described to measure olfactory acuity in a quantitative fashion but in clinical practice they are either too complex for routine use—as, for example, the use of alpha blocking on the EEG in response to odours (Sarteschi and Ardito) or are too inaccurate, as were the earlier methods described by Elsberg and by Proetz. All these quantitative methods suffer from the disadvantage that they are critically dependent on a free and constant flow of air through the nose but as there are cyclical changes in the calibre of the air-passages in any individual from day to day, hour to hour and even from minute to minute, flow is equally variable.

In clinical neurology, however, quantitative assessment of the sense of smell is for the most part quite unnecessary, and reliance is placed on "clinical" testing. This is usually undertaken by presenting a series of bottles to the patient and asking him to name the contents—often with results as confusing to the examiner as to the patient. This confusion is usually due to the test-substances employed, a wide variety of which have been recommended for the purpose in standard text-books.

No one has yet devised any satisfactory classification of odours and systems such as those dividing odours into ethereal, aromatic, fragrant, ambrosial, garlic, burnt, goat-like, repulsive and nauseating, although admirably descriptive, do little to enhance our understanding of the subject. Two important considerations in the choice of test-substances, however, must be borne in mind. The first is that few common substances stimulate the olfactory system alone; many stimulate the fifth nerve to a greater or lesser degree. The second consideration is that the test-substance should not be unfamiliar to the patient. A satisfactory test-odour therefore is one that not only has an overwhelming olfactory component but one that can be readily identified by the majority of patients. In a study of this problem it has been shown that if the following four substances are used—coffee, oil of lemon, benzaldehyde (almond) and crude tar, four out of five patients can identify any two of these and nine out of ten at least one. Failure to *identify* any of the four is very suggestive of some disturbance of olfaction, for the ability to identify odours seems to be independent of intelligence—at least within very wide limits.

Temporary loss of the sense of smell is a not uncommon occurrence and in the majority of cases results from local inflamation of the olfactory mucosa during an upper respiratory tract infection. The sense of smell may also be lost in the presence of more persistent local lesions of the nose, e.g. atrophic rhinitis or nasal polypi. Although such causes of anosmia do not strictly concern the neurologist, they are of importance for they must be excluded before considering a neurogenic or central basis for any disturbance of olfaction.

The principal central causes of anosmia are listed in the table. This list is not necessarily complete; from time to time other causes of anosmia may be recorded but the conditions described are those most commonly seen, or—and this is by no means the same thing—commonly mentioned in standard texts.

CENTRAL CAUSES OF ANOSMIA

(1) Trauma
(2) Pressure on the olfactory bulbs and tracts
(3) Viral infections
(4) Familial and congenital conditions
(5) Post-ictal states
(6) Anoxia
(7) Cerebro-vascular disease
(8) Demyelinating, inflammatory and degenerative conditions of the central nervous system
(9) "Idiopathic"

Trauma

This is by far the commonest cause of central anosmia and while its detection in clinical practice is rarely of great diagnostic importance, its medico-legal significance may be enormous.

Anosmia after closed head injuries is seen in about 7 per cent of all cases of whatever severity, this incidence rising broadly with the severity of the causative head injury as measured by the length of the post-traumatic amnesia. The incidence in a recent series is shown in Fig. 1 and from this it will be seen that in about half of the cases (with the exception of the most severe injuries) the anosmia is only temporary. Recovery, when it occurs, takes place after a period of time varying from a few days to several years. The mechanism of this recovery is by no means clearly understood but as Fig. 2 demonstrates there is a sharp change in the number of cases recovering at about ten weeks. It seems likely that up to this point recovery occurs with the reduction of oedema and the removal of blood clot, but that after this period recovery must take place as the result of change in neural tissue itself. What, however, can be happening after five years to lead to functional improvement, is obscure.

It is often stated that traumatic anosmia is produced only by a serious head injury with fracture of the anterior fossa. This is not so and as we can see from Fig. 1, permanent anosmia in a small proportion of cases can be seen after the most trivial of head injuries with no loss of consciousness and no amnesia.

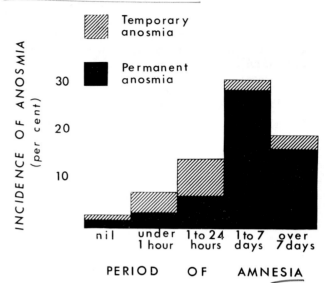

FIG. 1. The incidence of anosmia after head injuries (from *Brain* (1964), **87**, 107–120). (Reproduced by kind permission of the Editor of *Brain*.)

There is controversy concerning the site of the lesion which produces anosmia after head injuries. Classically this is supposed to result from tearing of the olfactory filaments as they pass through the cribriform plate. While this can occur, and undoubtedly does, particularly in more severe injuries, it is certainly not always the case. Experimental work has shown that the cribriform plate is relatively well protected against the shearing stresses

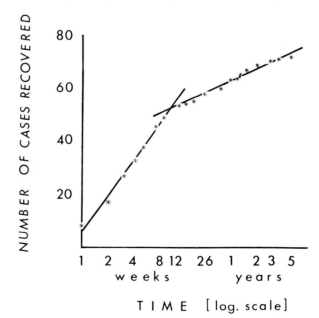

FIG. 2. Traumatic anosmia. The relationship between the time after injury and the number of cases recovered (from *Brain* (1964), **87**, 107–120). (Reproduced by kind permission of the Editor of *Brain*.)

produced after dynamic head-injuries for one thing, while for another it is very difficult to conceive of any mechanism operating at that site which will lead to recovery after a delay of five years. The most compelling reason, however, to doubt this mechanism is provided by the fact that at times, after the most trivial of head injuries, permanent anosmia is seen accompanied by total ageusia—that is loss of primary taste. Such a combination of sequelae after a trivial injury can occur only by a single lesion in some, as yet undetermined, central area.

Pressure on the Olfactory Bulbs and Tracts

Although much less commonly seen than anosmia after head injuries, the anosmia resulting from local pressure on or involvement of the olfactory bulbs and tracts is of disproportionate significance because of its diagnostic value. Any space-occupying lesion in the anterior fossa may be responsible for anosmia in this fashion but the principal cause is the olfactory groove meningioma. Although the anosmia is usually an early symptom this is not always so and it will be often missed unless specifically looked for. Unexplained bilateral anosmia (and even more so unexplained unilateral anosmia) must always suggest the possibility of the presence of frontal space occupation. It is only too easy, for example, to explain anosmia seen in an epileptic as resulting from a head injury incurred in a fit, but while this may of course be so, it is a very rash assumption to make. Anosmia may be seen as part of the Foster Kennedy syndrome, that is the association of anosmia with optic atrophy on one side, papilloedema on the other and a frontal tumour on the side of the atrophy. Tumours involving the olfactory pathway proximal to the tracts may produce olfactory hallucinations but very rarely indeed do they produce anosmia.

In addition to anosmia being seen as the result of pressure from a neoplasm, it may result from a diffuse meningeal infiltration with neoplastic cells, most commonly metastatic, but sometimes meningiomatous. Recovery from anosmia occurring as the result of either local pressure or particularly from infiltration is most uncommon.

Viral Infections

Anosmia in association with herpes zoster is well described but although the evidence is not so convincing, there seems little doubt that it can occur as the result of infection by other neurotropic viruses. From time to time there can be seen the spread of an illness from person to person where there are headache, malaise, minimal neck-stiffness and anosmia without any obvious upper respiratory tract involvement. It is wise to give a guarded prognosis in anosmia of this origin for recovery does not always take place. It is presumably this type of illness that has been referred to in the past as "influenzal" anosmia.

Familial and Congenital Conditions

Although in the past there has been some debate as to whether anosmia can be inherited, this seems now to be undoubted and many pedigrees have been published showing its inheritance either as an autosomal dominant or as a sex-linked recessive. As an autosomal dominant it is not unduly rare, but much less often seen is the combination, as an inherited condition, of anosmia, eunuchoidism and colour-blindness, an association which has been reported from many parts of the world.

A congenital (as distinct from familial) type of anosmia is recognized, and is often associated with absence of some part of the olfactory pathway. Congenital anosmia has also been reported in association with 13–15 trisomy.

Allied perhaps to familial and congenital anosmia is the condition of "smell-blindness" to one or more specific chemical substances (commonly n. butyl-mercaptan). This is familial and corresponds to the much more widely described condition of "taste-blindness".

Post-ictal States

Although not often seen, anosmia may occur for a matter of hours or days following a seizure with an olfactory aura in patients who suffer from uncinate epilepsy. In this context the anosmia corresponds to a Todd's paralysis after a motor focal fit and is perhaps the result of neuronal exhaustion. The management of such anosmia is of course the management of the underlying disease.

Anoxia

Anoxia may rarely give rise to anosmia. This has been seen after massive blood-loss where it has been reported as being permanent and in unacclimatized mountaineers climbing at high altitude. In this case it is reversible. The interest here is that in both the anoxia of blood-loss and of high altitude the anosmia is usually associated with ageusia, suggesting again that there may be some common functional point in the pathways for smell and taste which is susceptible to oxygen-lack. It has been postulated that the anosmia after head injuries may be mediated in some instances by anoxic mechanism.

Cerebro-vascular Disease

Hughlings Jackson first pointed out that anosmia may be found on the hemiplegic side of a patient who has had a stroke, but like so many of his observations, this has been largely forgotten. It is however often possible to demonstrate such unilateral anosmia, but this finding has no associated diagnostic or prognostic value.

Demyelinating, Inflammatory and Degenerative Conditions of the General Nervous System

Anosmia, usually unilateral, but at times bilateral, may be demonstrated in disseminated sclerosis. It may occur in conjunction with retrobulbar neuritis, or it may arise independently. Like other physical signs in this disease it may be transitory (and early in the disease this is usually the case) or it may be permanent. If a patient is seen, however, with the combination of optic atrophy and anosmia, it is wise always to regard this as the presentation of a frontal tumour until there is ample evidence to the contrary.

Reference is made in many standard texts to anosmia occurring in the course of tabes dorsalis and subacute combined degeneration of the cord. There seems no reason why this should not be so, particularly in the case of subacute degeneration of the cord where the anosmia may be considered analogous to the well-recognized optic atrophy. Anosmia in these two conditions must however be rare indeed.

"Idiopathic"

There is no doubt that from time to time, anosmia is seen, sometimes of sudden, sometimes of insidious onset and for which no obvious cause can be found. While it is tempting to postulate an unremembered head injury, a subclinical virus infection or an isolated episode of demyelination, the explanation is never wholly satisfactory. While some of these diagnoses may from time to time be true it is probably wiser to regard the aetiology as unknown, bearing in mind the very real possibility that such anosmia may be the first indication of a frontal lobe lesion. Such patients should therefore be carefully followed up and if necessary should be fully investigated by X-ray examination of the skull, electro-encephalography and by a gamma scan of the brain.

FURTHER READING

Elsberg, C. A. and Levy, I. (1935), "A New and Simple Method of Olfactometry," *Bull. neurol. Inst. N.Y.*, **4**, 5.

Kallman, F. J., Schoenfeld, W. A. and Barrera, S. E. (1944), "The Genetic Aspects of Primary Eunochoidism," *Amer. J. ment. Defic.*, **48**, 203.

Laskiewicz, A. (1951), "Disturbance of Smell in the Course of Herpes Zoster Encephalitis," *Acta oto-laryng.*, **39**, 291.

Miller, J. Q., Picard, E. H., Alkan, M. K., Warner, S. and Gerard, P. S. (1963), "A Specific Congenital Brain Defect in 13–15 Trisomy," *New Engl. J. Med.*, **268**, 120.

Patterson, P. M., and Lauder. B. (1948), "The Incidence and Probable Inheritance of 'Smell Blindness" to n. Butyl Mercaptan," *J. Hered.*, **39**, 295.

Proetz, A. W. (1953), *The Applied Physiology of the Nose*. St. Louis: Annals Publishing Co.

Sarteschi, P. and Ardito, R. (1960), "L'utilita dell olfattoelettroencefalografia nella obbiette-vazione delle anosmie," *Riv. Neurol. (Nap.)*, **30**, 555.

Singh, N., Grewal, M. S. and Austin, J. H. (1970), "Familial Anosmia," *Arch. Neurol. (Chicago)*, **22**, 40.

Spiegel, E. A. and Sommer, I. (1944), *Neurology of the Eye, Ear, Nose and Throat*. New York: Grune & Stratton.

Sumner, D. (1962), "On Testing the Sense of Smell," *Lancet*, **2**, 895.

Sumner, D. (1964), "Post-Traumatic Anosmia," *Brain*, **87**, 107

Zilstorff-Pederson, K. (1955), "Anosmia and Ageusia, presumably resulting from Anoxia," *Acta oto-laryng.*, **45**, 371

6. MECHANISMS OF PATHOLOGICAL PAIN

RONALD MELZACK

Pain produced by peripheral nerve injury usually decreases and vanishes by the time healing has occurred. Sometimes, however, pain persists and may even increase in severity. Causalgia (intense burning pain after a limb-nerve injury), in its most severe form, continues more than six months after injury in 85 per cent of cases, and for more than a year in 25 per cent.[12] Phantom limb pain (which is referred to particular areas of the phantom limb, in contrast to actual stump pain) subsides within a year after onset in only about 30 per cent of patients and may continue for many years.[63] The neuralgias (which may occur after peripheral nerve infections or degenerative diseases, but sometimes have unknown origin) are similarly characterized by severe pain that persists for months or years after onset.[35,54]

Several additional properties illuminate the nature of these pains: (i) they occur in about 2–5 per cent of people who sustain peripheral nerve injuries;[12,63] (ii) the initiating injuries may vary from commonplace bruises or cuts to destruction of a major nerve or loss of limb;[35,63] (iii) the onset of pain is highly variable—usually starting immediately after injury, but sometimes appearing weeks, months, even years later;[63] (iv) there are autonomic manifestations such as altered temperature and sweating, and motor disabilities such as weakness or jactitations in the affected limb;[35] (v) pain and trigger sites may spread to distant parts of the body, including perfectly healthy "mirror image" areas on the opposite side of the body;[11,35] (vi) pain may be triggered by normally non-noxious somatic stimuli, such as gentle rubbing with cotton wool, vibration, mildly warm or cool objects, and even by non-somatic stimuli such as noises and visual inputs;[35,54,72] (vii) there is an obvious psychological contribution since pain is often triggered by emotional disturbances[31] and is sometimes diminished by distraction-conditioning,[49] hypnosis[8] and psychotherapy;[31,47] (viii) the pain is tragically resistant to conventional forms of therapy such as surgical section of the sensory nerves or spinal cord pathways;[33,63] (ix) the pain may, on occasion, be permanently stopped by temporary decreases[35] or increases[14] of somatic inputs; (x) these pains, as Weir Mitchell (who coined the terms "causalgia" and "phantom limb") has noted, are the worst known to man:

"Perhaps few persons who are not physicians can realize the influence which long-continued and unendurable pain may have upon both body and mind. The older books are full of cases in which, after lancet wounds, the most terrible pain and local spasms resulted. When these had lasted for days or weeks, the whole surface became hyperesthetic, and the senses grew to be only avenues for fresh and increasing tortures, until every vibration, every change of light, and even . . . the effort to read brought on new agony. Under such torments the temper changes, the most amiable grow irritable, the soldier becomes a coward, and the strongest man is scarcely less nervous than the most hysterical girl."[72]

The mechanisms underlying these pain states remain a mystery. The purpose of this study, therefore, is to examine the theoretical concepts that have been proposed to account for them, and to discuss possible mechanisms of long-term changes in neural activity.

THEORIES OF PAIN

Specificity Theory

The traditional theory of pain on which most forms of therapy are based, proposes[32,50] that injurious stimuli activate specific pain receptors which transmit pain impulses along the small-diameter A-delta and C fibres to the spinothalamic tract (the pain pathway) and thence to a pain centre in the brain (Fig. 1). On the basis of this theory, the causes of causalgic, phantom limb and neuralgic pains are conceived to be chronic irritation of pain receptors or fibres, and therapy has focused on surgical section of the pain system.

Specificity theory, which proposes a simple one-to-one relationship among stimulus, pathway and sensation, cannot account for severe, spontaneous pain in the absence of any obvious input. Yet in many of these cases, especially causalgia, pain occurs spontaneously or may be triggered by vibration or light touch, which are inadequate stimuli for "pain receptors". Peripheral irritating factors such as neuromas (abnormal neuron growths in damaged peripheral nerves) are clearly not the main cause in most cases, because surgical section of peripheral nerves[73] or special procedures[16] to prevent neuroma formation often fail to stop pain. Similarly, surgical section of the dorsal roots (rhizotomy), which are the sole avenue of sensory input into the spinal cord, should produce total pain relief. But rhizotomy, even over an extensive area, is notoriously ineffective for causalgia or phantom limb pain.[35,63]

If the cause of the prolonged pain were a chronic irritating lesion, a minor form of therapy such as injection of the affected area, nerve, or roots with anaesthetic drugs could not by itself remove the pathological cause, since the drug effects wear off after two or three hours. Yet one or more injections may provide relief that lasts days, weeks, sometimes permanently.[28,35] Even injections of tender areas or nerves distal to the lesion[28,35] may produce prolonged or permanent relief of pain, so that irritation at the site of a lesion can be ruled out as a major cause. The

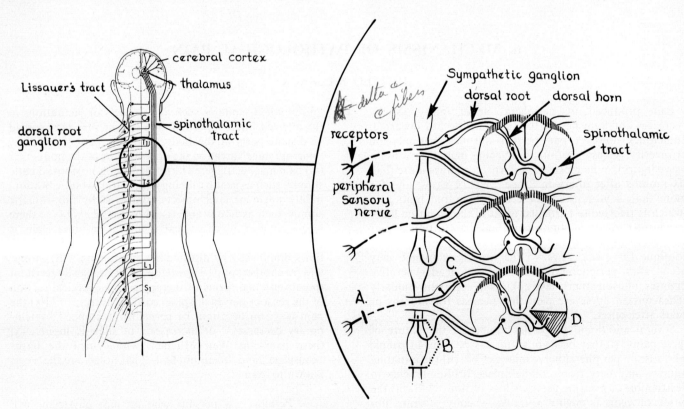

FIG. 1. Specificity theory of pain. Left: Larsell's diagram of the pain pathway: pain fibres from the skin enter the spinal cord, ascend a few segments (in Lissauer's tract) and connect with fibres that cross the cord and form the spinothalamic tract to the thalamus. Fibres from the thalamus project to the cortex. Right: Diagram of spinal-cord cross-sections and adjacent sympathetic ganglia, showing several neurosurgical procedures to stop pain. A: neurectomy; B: sympathectomy; C: rhizotomy; D: cordotomy.

data suggest, however, that chronic, low-level sensory inputs *contribute* to the pain, since modulation of the input by anaesthetic blocks clearly influences it, sometimes dramatically.

Once the pain syndrome is well established, attempts to relieve it by surgery of the so-called pain pathway in the spinal cord are usually ineffective. The data on surgical methods to relieve pain in causalgia or the phantom limb have been summarized by Sunderland:

"Operations have been performed for pain at nearly every possible site in the pathway from the peripheral receptors to the sensory cortex, and at every level the story is the same—some encouraging results, but a disheartening tendency for the pain to recur. At whatever level pain is attacked, the impression is conveyed that the whole nervous system makes a co-ordinated effort to re-establish the pathway. Livingston[35] was impressed 'with its remarkable ability to find a new route when the customary channels have been blocked'. Leriche[33] was also discouraged by the failure of surgical attacks to relieve pain: 'nerves are not made to be divided, a demonstration . . . which surgery was long in discovering, and which is not even yet universally admitted as an established fact'."[63]

Since surgical block of the sensory input often ends in failure—a patient sometimes undergoes several operations at successively higher levels—two hypotheses have been proposed in an attempt to salvage specificity theory. First, it is assumed that pain fibres travel through the sympathetic ganglia, since surgical section of the ganglia (sympathectomy) usually produces permanent relief of causalgic pain.[63,73] Sympathectomy, however, is ineffective for phantom limb pain: less than 10 per cent of cases report complete pain relief 1 to 4 years after surgery.[23] It is difficult to conceive of sympathetic "pain fibres" that specifically evoke causalgia but not phantom limb pain. Indeed, there is no convincing evidence that any afferent fibres from the limbs ascend in the sympathetic ganglia.[35,63] Second, it has been proposed, to explain causalgia, that sympathetic efferent fibres directly activate sensory afferents by way of pathological fibre-to-fibre connections called ephapses.[3] This explanation, however, fails to account for the permanent relief of pain afforded by nerve blocks of the skin itself, or of the nerve distal to the lesion. Moreover, rhizotomy should prevent ephaptic connections from transmitting signals into the spinal cord, yet the pain may persist. Even though these explanations are unsatisfactory, there is little doubt that the sympathetic nervous system *contributes*, in some way, to all of these pain states.[35,54]

The failure of traditional surgical therapy has generated a further hypothesis: that the patient is a malingerer or is simply making up or imagining the pain because of psychopathological personal needs. It is true that patients suffering these pains often have emotional disturbances such as anxiety, worries about social adjustment, unpleasant associations with amputees in the family,[31] or fear of losing one's mind (often subtly reinforced by the physician's insinuation that something is "wrong" with

the patient because none of the conventional therapies work). The hypothesis, however, cannot explain the sudden relief produced by nerve blocks.[28,35] It would be wrong to assume that the injections have psychotherapeutic (or placebo) value, because injection of an inappropriate nerve, sometimes by error, fails to relieve pain, although injection of the appropriate nerve in the same patient is effective.[28,35] Statistical analysis of the data presented by Ewalt *et al.*,[13] moreover, indicates that patients with phantom limb pain do not have a greater incidence of neuroses than those without pain in the phantom limb. Emotional problems undoubtedly *contribute* to the pain[31,35,47] but are not the major causal agency.

Pattern theory

This is a general heading for several theories which propose that pain is caused by particular patterns of nerve impulses. Goldscheider[18] was the first to suggest that stimulus intensity and central summation are the two critical determinants of the pattern underlying pain. Within this conceptual framework, Livingston[35] proposed specific neural mechanisms to account for the remarkable temporal and spatial phenomena in clinical pain syndromes. He suggested that the traumatic sensory input after injury initiates abnormal firing patterns in reverberatory circuits in spinal cord internuncial neurons. This self-sustaining cord activity sends volleys of nerve impulses to the brain

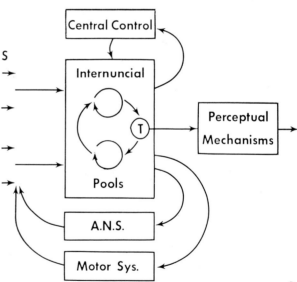

FIG. 2. Schematic diagram of W. K. Livingston's[35] theory of pathological pain states. The intense stimulation (S) resulting from nerve and tissue damage activates fibres that project to internuncial neuron pools in the spinal cord, creating abnormal reverberatory activity in closed self-exciting neuron loops. This prolonged, abnormal activity bombards the spinal-cord transmission (T) cells that project to brain mechanisms that underlie pain perception. The abnormal internuncial activity also spreads to lateral- and ventral-horn cells in the spinal cord, activating the autonomic nervous system (ANS) and motor system, producing sweating, jactitations, and other manifestations. These, in turn, produce further abnormal input, thereby creating a "vicious circle". Brain activities such as fear and anxiety evoked by pain also feed into and maintain the abnormal internuncial pool activity.

that give rise to pain. Moreover, the abnormal reverberatory activity in the cord may spread to neurons in the lateral and ventral horns which give rise to autonomic and muscular manifestations in the limb, such as sweating, immobility, or jactitations. These, in turn, produce further sensory input, creating a "vicious circle" between central and peripheral activity patterns that maintains and produces spread of the abnormal cord activity (Fig. 2). Emotional disturbance, moreover, may evoke neural activity that feeds into and maintains the abnormal neuron pool. Once the abnormal cord activity has become self-sustaining, removal of the peripheral sources of input may not stop it. Neurectomy, rhizotomy, or sympathectomy may have little effect. Rather, clinical procedures that modulate the sensory input to bring about normal sensory patterns may again reinstate normal cord activity.

Gerard[16] has proposed a theory that is similar in concept, although different in hypothetical mechanism. He suggests that a peripheral nerve lesion may bring about a temporary loss of sensory control of firing in spinal cord internuncial neurons. These may then begin to fire in synchrony, just as isolated bits of nerve tissue in an appropriate solution fire synchronously, possibly due to DC spread.[16] Such synchronously firing neuron pools "could recruit additional units, could move along in the grey matter, could be maintained by impulses different from and feebler than those needed to initiate it, could discharge excessive and abnormally patterned volleys to the higher centres".[16]

These concepts have remarkable power in their ability to explain many of the clinical phenomena of pain. None of them, however, is anchored to the more recent facts of somatosensory mechanisms. They are based, moreover, on a concept of patterning that fails to recognize the high degree of physiological specialization of receptor-fibre units. The concept of prolonged, self-sustaining central neural activity, however, can be integrated into a more recent theory of pain mechanisms that retains the facts of physiological specialization without also accepting a narrow, one-to-one psychophysical specificity.[44,45]

Gate control theory

This[45] provides an alternative to specificity and pattern theories. Conceptually, it proposes (Fig. 3a) that the input-output function of spinal cord cells is modulated by specialized inhibitory and facilitatory mechanisms. Sensory fibres, in this framework, have two functions: (i) they carry patterned information, depending on the specialized properties of each receptor-fibre unit,[44,45] about pressure, temperature and chemical changes at the skin, and (ii) they activate a specialized system (the substantia gelatinosa) which modulates or "gates" the *amount* of information projected by spinal cord transmission (T) cells to the brain. The large fibres are assumed to activate an inhibitory mechanism that diminishes or blocks transmission (closes the gate) while the small fibres activate a facilitatory mechanism (which opens the gate). Tonic activity descending from the brainstem has also been shown[20] to decrease the T-cell output, presumably by means of the inhibitory

mechanism, thus suggesting that the input-output functions of the T-cells are controlled by brain activities. In addition, it is now evident[57] that the dorsal-horn lamina-5 cells which are believed to be the T-cells,[20,57] receive input from all small fibres, whatever their somatic origin: skin, viscera, or muscle. The inhibitory and facilitatory mechanisms have yet to be ascertained, but they are assumed[45] to involve both pre- and postsynaptic changes mediated by the substantia gelatinosa. The output of the T-cells, then, is determined by the activity in large and small fibres, and by information descending from the brain. If the integrated neural activity projected to the action system exceeds a critical level (in terms of number of impulses per unit time), mechanisms that subserve pain experience and response are activated.

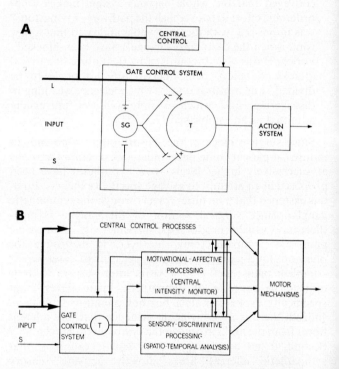

FIG. 3. A: Schematic diagram of the gate control theory of pain, from Melzack and Wall.[75] L, the large-diameter fibres; S, the small-diameter fibres. The fibres project to the substantia gelatinosa (SG) and first central transmission (T) cells. The inhibitory effect exerted by SG on the afferent fibre terminals is increased by activity in L fibres and decreased by activity in S fibres. The central control trigger is represented by a line running from the large fibre system to the central control mechanisms; these mechanisms, in turn, project back to the gate control system. The T-cells project to the entry cells of the action system: +, excitation; −, inhibition. B: Melzack and Casey's[39] conceptual model of the sensory, motivational, and central-control determinants of pain. The output of the T-cells of the gate control system projects to sensory-discriminative mechanisms (via neospinothalamic fibres) and to motivational-affective mechanisms (via the paramedial ascending system). The central control trigger (comprising the dorsal-column and dorso-lateral projection systems) is represented by a line running from the large fibre system to central control processes; these, in turn, project back to the gate control system, and to sensory-discriminative and motivational-affective mechanisms. All three processing systems interact with one another, and project to motor mechanisms.

Gating of the input in the spinal cord marks the beginning of repeated modulation and selection.[45] Melzack and Casey[39] have noted (Fig. 3b) that the output of the dorsal-horn T cells, after transmission through the anterolateral spinal cord, is projected to two major brain systems: via neospinothalamic fibres to the ventrobasal and posterolateral thalamus and the somatosensory cortex, and via medially coursing fibres to the brainstem reticular formation and the limbic system. Recent behavioural and physiological studies have led Melzack and Casey[39] to propose that (i) the selection and modulation of the sensory input through the neo-spinothalamic projection system provides, in part at least, the neurological basis of the sensory-discriminative dimension of pain, (ii) activation of reticular and limbic structures, which are assumed to comprise a "central intensity monitor", underlies the powerful motivational drive and unpleasant affect that trigger the organism into action, and (iii) neocortical or higher central nervous system processes, such as evaluation of the input in terms of past experience, exert control over activity in both the discriminative and motivational systems. All three forms of activity could then influence motor mechanisms responsible for the complex pattern of overt responses that characterize pain.[45]

Gate control theory is able to account for many of the properties of pain.[39,45] Selective degenerative changes in the large, myelinated fibres in post-herpetic[54] and trigeminal[27] neuralgia, for example, would shift the large-to-small fibre ratio in favour of the small fibres, which would open the spinal gate. All somatic inputs would then be transmitted at maximal amplification, and central summation would provide the basis for hyperalgesia and dysaesthesia. Moreover, since the gate is permanently in a relatively open position, tonic, spontaneous activity from local and more distant sources would be summated to provide prolonged, spontaneous pain. Prolonged pain, however, can occur in the absence of any pathological shift in the large-to-small fibre ratio.[21] Furthermore, it may persist after elimination of all input from an injured area by extensive dorsal root section.[63] It is proposed, therefore, that excessive or otherwise abnormal stimulation can bring about a *prolonged bias* in the activity of the gate mechanism. Clinical and experimental observations suggest four properties of the gate bias.

PROPERTIES OF THE GATE BIAS

I. Excessive or Otherwise Abnormal Sensory Input may Produce a Prolonged Bias in the Gate Mechanism

After teeth on both sides of the mouth are drilled and filled in man, without local anaesthetic, pin-pricks of the lateral nasal mucosa, as long as 70 days later, produce pain in the treated teeth on the stimulated side. The effect is permanently abolished on one side by a single novocaine block of the trigeminal nerve, but persists in the opposite, non-blocked side.[21] These referred pains necessitate the assumption of a long-term central neural change. The data suggest that the trauma produced by

treatment of the teeth evokes volleys that change firing patterns in the central nervous system. This change, once initiated, is presumably maintained by continuous, low-level input from the treated teeth. The single block of a peripheral nerve, which could not have affected the teeth, permits resumption of normal activity and the end of pain. That the *input* as such, rather than conscious awareness, is essential in initiating the abnormal central activity is evident in the observation[21] that a subject who had four teeth extracted under nitrous oxide anaesthesia felt pain referred to the jaw when the nasal mucosa was pricked 33 days after treatment.

The importance of the input is also indicated by the fact that phantom limb pain is more likely to develop in patients who have suffered pain in the limb for some time prior to amputation.[63] The pain may closely resemble, in both quality and location, the pain that was present before amputation, suggesting a causal relationship between pain before and after amputation. It is also more common in above than below-knee amputations, presumably because of the greater tissue and nerve involvement.

Prolonged changes may be determined more by the patterning than by the amount of the input. Causalgia is more common after partial than after total nerve lesions, and is characteristically associated with rapid, violent deformation of nerves by missiles such as bullets.[12,63] Pain, moreover, is not necessarily associated with irritative lesions: nerves that undergo deformation and are associated with causalgia may be histologically indistinguishable from normal nerves.[30] The importance of the input pattern is further indicated by laboratory studies of afterglows:[40] momentary stimulation of the skin with the tip of a warm probe sometimes produces a sensation of warmth followed, after a delay, by a welling-up of sensation into a sharp stinging pain that persists for many seconds, sometimes as long as minutes. These afterglow sensations may spread beyond the site of stimulation and, occasionally, the mirror-area on the other side may begin to tingle. The spread, after-sensations, delays and unpleasant sensory qualities produced by punctate stimuli resemble the properties of stimulus-evoked neuralgic pain[54] and may help illuminate their underlying mechanisms.

II. The Gate Bias may be Returned to Normal Levels by Increases or Decreases of the Sensory Input

Once causalgia and phantom limb pain are under way, almost any somatic input augments the pain. Pressure on tender neuromas or trigger points, even gentle brushing of hyperaesthetic areas, can evoke severe, prolonged pain.[35] Paradoxically, increases in the sensory input may sometimes relieve the pain.[14] Injection of 0·2–1 c.c. of 6 per cent saline into the interspinous tissue of amputees produces a sharp, localized pain that radiates into the phantom limb, lasts only about 10 min., yet may produce dramatic partial or total relief of pain for hours, weeks, sometimes indefinitely (Fig. 4). Moreover, painless phantom limbs of decades' duration may suddenly disappear, or take on a different shape.

Decreasing the sensory input, however, is the most

reliable method of relief. Injection of 2–10 c.c. of 1 per cent procaine, a local anaesthetic, into the interspinous tissue in amputees[14] produces a progressive numbness of parts of the phantom limb, and total or partial relief of pain for hours, days, sometimes permanently. A change in "emphasis" of the phantom pattern may also remain as a permanent state: in one subject who had painful phantom

anaesthetic injections of an area to which neuralgic pain is referred, from which only spontaneous impulses originate, may relieve pain at both the referred site and at the primary pain site,[26,35] and that injection of a nerve to abolish pain at the primary pain site usually also abolishes pain referred to more distant sites.[28]

There is also evidence that pain from one site on the

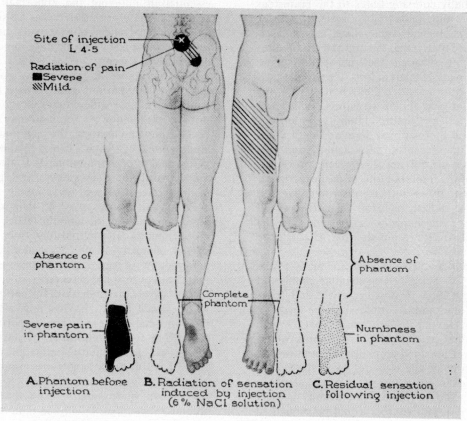

FIG. 4. Observations by Feinstein *et al.*[14] on the effect of hypertonic saline injection into L4–L5 interspinous tissues on phantom limb pain. The saline injection, in this case, produced a radiation of pain to the right hip and thigh, and sudden, detailed awareness of the complete phantom limb. After injection, numbness was felt in the previously painful area. Pain relief, after this procedure, may last for minutes, weeks, sometimes permanently.

toes, the toes were barely felt after injection and pain, instead, now arose from the heel—a condition that persisted for more than 2 months. Similarly, nerve blocks[28] distal to the site of the lesion, may stop the pain or paraesthesiae (unpleasant sensations) in a variety of neuralgic states for days, sometimes permanently, even though the anaesthesia wears off within hours.

III. The Gate Bias may be Influenced by Activity in Spatially Distant Areas of the Central Nervous System

The phenomena of referred pain, spread of pain and trigger points at a distance from the original site of body damage, which commonly occur in causalgia, phantom limb pain, and the neuralgias, suggest that activities at distant body sites converge on the gate mechanism and contribute to maintaining it in an open position for prolonged periods of time. This conception is supported by the observations that pressure on a healthy arm or on the head (Fig. 5) may trigger phantom limb pain,[11] that

body may evoke pain that is referred to a spatially distant site which was injured long before. Thus, 2 ml. of 5 per cent hypertonic saline injected under the skin of the right side of the back in patients that have anginal-effort syndrome, with pain referred only to the left side, may give rise to a diffuse, deep-seated pain that soon disappears; 2 hr. later, long after the pain has passed, exertion and anginal pain causes its reappearance.[10] Similarly, amputees who develop anginal pain as long as 25 years after amputation may suffer severe pain in the phantom limb during each bout of anginal pain, although phantom limb pain may never before have been experienced.[10]

The recent discovery of convergence of visceral and cutaneous afferents onto the same cells in lamina 5 of the dorsal horns[57] makes many of these patterns explicable. Low-level input from a skin site may summate with input from diseased viscera to produced pain that is referred to both sites. Similarly, cutaneous or muscle sites may act as trigger points,[26] so that pressure on one of these points may trigger cardiac (or other visceral) pains, presumably by summation of inputs from both sources. The fact[26] that pressure on trigger points often evokes severe pain that may persist for hours in cardiac patients, but for only minutes or not at all in normal subjects, suggests that the cardiac input has produced a prolonged bias on the gate, permitting maximum summation and pain.

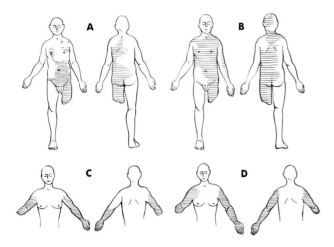

FIG. 5. Cronholm's[11] observations on stimulation sites which evoke pain sensation in the phantom limb. Top: 59-year-old man, who received compound fractures of the lower left leg at age 21; amputation 4 months later. Pressure (A) or pin-pricks (B) were applied to the skin. Stimulation of effective sites (cross-hatched areas) produced severe shooting pains and other sensations in the phantom limb. Bottom: 34-year-old woman; amputation at age 14. Pressure (C) or pin-pricks (D) were applied to the skin. Stimulation of effective sites (cross-hatched areas) produced sensations of a diffuse, unpleasant "irritation" in the phantom hand.

IV. The Gate Bias is Affected by Brain Mechanisms Underlying Psychological Processes such as Memory and Emotion

Several pain phenomena have properties similar to those of imagery, learning and memory of visual and auditory inputs.[35,52] Pain is often associated with abnormal, fixed positions of the phantom limb—such as tightly clenched fingers digging into the palm of the hand, or the arm locked in position behind the head—and relief of pain by local blocks may be accompanied by release and movement of the phantom fingers or arm.[35,54] It is apparent that the phantom limb depends, in part, on sensory input from the stump: extensive spinal cord injury stops the usual fading and shrinkage of the phantom limb.[5] However, the fact that phantom limbs are reported by children born without limbs[71] and that the phantom limb has the same shape as the sensory representation of the limb at the cerebral cortex,[22] indicates a built-in substrate on which the sensory input can act to bring about permanent or semi-permanent changes.

Complex memory mechanisms are also suggested by the fact that the quality and location of phantom limb pain may closely resemble the pain that was present before amputation.[52,63] The phantom limb may not only have a particular spatial shape and position, but may even

include minor anomalies. Thus, a patient[52] who was suffering from an ingrown toe-nail and, at that time, sustained a total cord lesion, subsequently reported a painful ingrown toe-nail in his phantom foot. These effects, moreover, may remain for years. In one case, 6 years after a young woman suffered a painful fracture of the right knee, followed by patellar removal and relief of pain, stimulation of particular parts of the body with a pin (to test the effects of a bilateral cordotomy) produced pain at the site of stimulation and, at the same time, sensations in the right knee which "reproduced all the sensations which she had at the time of the fracture of the patella".[52] In another case, saline injections of the stump of an amputee who, 5 years before amputation had a severe laceration of the leg by an ice skate, later produced vivid imagery of the pain of the skating accident: "It was not that he remembered having had this injury; he felt all the sensations again that he had felt at the time."[52]

MECHANISMS UNDERLYING PROLONGED CHANGES

Spinal Mechanisms

There is convincing behavioural evidence of prolonged changes in spinal neural activity. Temporary inflammation of a cat's paw by subcutaneous injection of turpentine produces, after the inflammatory process has healed completely and the animal walks normally, an abnormal flexion-extension pattern in the limbs when the animal is decerebrated.[15] Similarly, postural asymmetries produced by cerebellar lesions persist after transection of the spinal cord only if they are maintained for at least 45 min. before cord section.[9] Impulses descending from the cerebellum for 45 min. or longer thus appear to bring about a permanent change in neuron networks in the spinal cord.

There is now more direct physiological evidence that begins to approximate these behavioural observations (Fig. 6). Spencer and Wigdor[62] have shown that a 7-min. period of high-frequency tetanic stimulation of sensory fibres produces a post-tetanic potentiation of a monosynaptic reflex for more than 10 min. in the acute spinal cat (Fig. 6a). Twenty minutes' stimulation produces potentiation for more than 2 hr. (Fig. 6b). Potentiation lasting an hour or so occurs even with frequencies as low as 100/sec. for 20–30 min.[62] Since injury may produce intense, abnormal sensory input that lasts for several hours or days, a change in central neural activity of much longer durations can be extrapolated.

The substantia gelatinosa could fulfil the 4 properties of the gate bias. At each level, it receives fibres from specific body segments, from the brain, and from the substantia gelatinosa associated with spatially distant areas on both sides of the body.[65] The complex, diffuse cell connections in the substantia gelatinosa,[56] moreover, could permit the development of closed, self-exciting neuron loops, capable of consolidation,[19] that might underlie a permanent or semi-permanent biasing mechanism. It is possible, of course, that side-chains of internuncial neurons[61] could also contain the simple feedback circuits described by Eccles[1,2] and Kandel[24,70] as the basis of prolonged neural activity. The evidence, however, requires that such internuncial side-chains have the spatial integrating properties exhibited by the substantia gelatinosa.

In the context of gate control theory, it is proposed that intense or otherwise abnormal sensory inputs may bring about a prolonged change in the level of tonic activity in the substantia gelatinosa. The inhibitory influence on the T-cell may be decreased or the facilitatory influence increased. Either effect would provide the basis of the

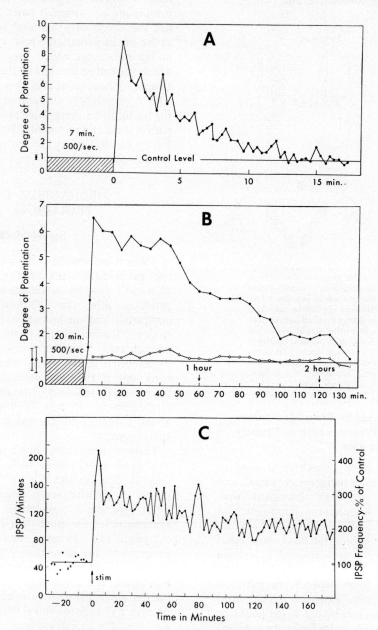

FIG. 6. A, B: Spencer and Wigdor's[62] observations on the effects of prolonged tetanizing shock of the tibial nerve on the post-tetanic potentiation of a monosynaptic reflex recorded from L7 ventral root in the acute spinal cat. Shock was applied for 7 min. (A) and 20 min. (B). Each plotted point in A represents the amplitude (as a multiple of the control level) of the monosynaptic reflex response to test stimuli at 20 sec. intervals. Each plotted point in B is an average of 10–20 responses to test stimuli delivered at 10 sec. intervals. Open circle plot in B shows the response of the contralateral control. C: Observations by Waziri et al.[70] on prolonged neural activity in the marine mollusc, Aplysia. A single stimulus train (arrow) to the brachial nerve produces a striking increase in the frequency of spontaneous inhibitory postsynaptic potentials (IPSP's) in interneuron I that persists for several hours.

long-term gate bias suggested by the clinical and experimental data. It is further possible that these changes may be produced by chemical mediators as well as the sensory input. One or more of the metabolites associated with tissue damage and stress could conceivably affect activity in the substantia gelatinosa.

Supraspinal Mechanisms

Prolonged abnormal activity could also occur at more central levels, which would maintain a continuous descending influence on the spinal gate. Thus, the central tegmental area in the reticular formation appears to exert a tonic descending inhibitory influence: stimulation of the

opening the gate, and provide the basis for hyperalgesia and hyperaesthesia.

It is significant, therefore, that prolonged changes in tonic electrical activity can be evoked in the reticular formation by brief somatic stimulation.[42] The majority of the changes produced by rubbing a paw or electrical stimulation of a cutaneous nerve for 10–20 sec. have durations of 3–12 min. but sometimes last for more than 30 min. (Fig. 7). Prolonged increases or decreases in activity, depending primarily on the recording site, have also been observed at several levels of the somatic and visual systems, and in the pyramidal tract.[4,41] Since stimulation of the brainstem reticular formation produces prolonged changes similar to those produced by somatic

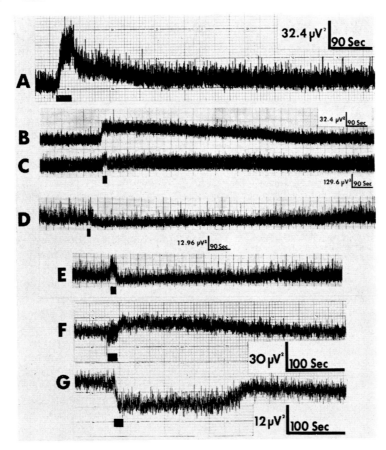

FIG. 7. Prolonged changes in central neural activity produced by brief stimulation.[41,42] Duration of stimulation is indicated by the black bar under each record. A: Prolonged changes in reticular formation activity produced by rubbing a paw in a moderately anesthetized cat. B, C: Changes in medial lemniscus (B) and dorsal column nuclei (C) activity elicited by electrical stimulation (15 μa-rms., 60 c/s.) of the midbrain tegmental reticular formation. D, E: Prolonged change in nucleus VPL produced by pinching (D) or gentle rub (E) applied to the ipsilateral hindpaw. F, G: Prolonged tonic activity increase in the pyramidal tract (F) and decrease in the visual radiations (G) produced simultaneously by electrical stimulation of the sciatic nerve.

area decreases the size of cutaneous receptive fields of cells in the spinocervical tract;[66] lesions of the area, which would remove the inhibition, produce hyperaesthesia and hyperalgesia in cats.[43] It is conceivable, then, that abnormal reticular activity could reduce the level (or change the pattern) of descending inhibition, thereby

stimulation, it appears likely that reticular mechanisms mediate the effects of somatic input on other neural structures. Since these effects are characteristically seen when the animals are in a state of moderate anaesthesia, but not when they are awake or deeply anaesthetized,[4,41,42] it is possible that anaesthetic agents block reticular or other activity that normally inhibits or occludes activity in self-sustaining, reverberatory circuits, so that a brief somatic-evoked volley produces prolonged repetitive activity.

There is now evidence for closed, self-sustaining, reverberatory circuits (Fig. 8) comprising a recurrent

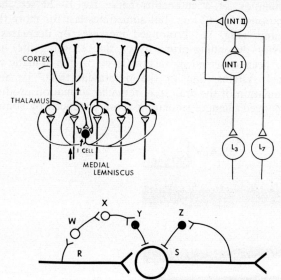

FIG. 8. Models to explain long-term changes in central neural activity. Top left: Model proposed by Andersen and Eccles[1] to account for repetitive, rhythmic bursts of activity in the ventrobasal thalamus. Input arriving along lemniscal fibres activate thalamic neurols that (i) project to cortex and (ii) send axon collaterals to an inhibitory neuron (I cell) that projects back to the thalamic-cell bodies. The thalamic cells are inhibited briefly, then (after disinhibition and rebound excitation) fire spontaneously, reactivating the recurrent inhibitory loop. This repetitive activity within the closed loop could continue for prolonged periods of time in the absence of any further input. Top right: Schematic representation proposed by Kandel et al.[24] to explain prolonged activity in inhibitory interneurons in the marine mollusc Aplysia. A closed neuron chain (interneuron II and interneuron I) is formed by mutually inhibitory connections. The inhibition of each interneuron is followed by disinhibition and rebound excitation which leads to a sustained alternation of activity in the two interneurons. Actual records[24] of activity from L3 (a follower cell on interneuron I) and L7 (a follower cell of interneuron II) provide indirect evidence of alternating IPSP bursts that persist for as long as 30 min. Bottom: Schematic model to account for prolonged activity shown in Fig. 7. Impulses in axon R normally excite neuron S and the neuronal side-chain-W-X-Y. Excitation of S produces repetitive discharges in the recurrent inhibitory loop S–Z, followed rapidly by inhibition of S by activity in the side-chain. Moderate doses of anaesthetic drugs selectively block the vulnerable multisynaptic side chain, so that excitation of S leads to prolonged activity in the S–Z loop. Additional anaesthetic doses block the S–Z loop, and the prolonged activity ceases.

axon collateral and inhibitory interneuron in the thalamic somatic relay nucleus VPL,[1,2] in the lateral geniculate nucleus of the visual system,[60] and in the hippocampus,[25] so that a volley of impulses may produce bursts of firing that continue for prolonged periods. A single volley can produce repeated after-discharges for as long as 5 sec.,[60] and interlinked groups of such circuits have been proposed by Eccles[2] to be the basis for much longer lasting activity. Networks such as these have now been described for both

excitatory[2] and inhibitory[24] neuron systems (Fig. 8), so that either excitation or inhibition could be rhythmically maintained for prolonged periods of time. It is possible, then, that neurons at reticular or other levels, which normally limit the duration of stimulus-evoked activity by inhibition or occlusion, could be selectively inactivated (Fig. 8), so that stimulation would set off excitation in reverberatory loops that is maintained for long time-periods. There is reason to believe that selective inactivation may be produced by anaesthetic agents.[42] Conceivably, it may also be produced by foci of abnormal activity, brain lesions, or metabolic agents produced by injury.[34]

Whatever the mechanism, there is now convincing evidence for experimentally induced supraspinal neural phenomena that may last indefinitely. Electrical stimulation of the amygdala or other limbic structures at low current levels (which initially have no pathological behavioural or neural effects) once a day for several consecutive days may produce after-discharges, behavioural convulsions, and a lowering of the stimulus threshold necessary to produce these effects that may persist for months.[17] These phenomena are attributed to localized changes in firing pattern, since more frequent or more intense lesion-producing stimulation fails to bring them about. More recently, Melzack and Bailey[38] have found that 1 or 2 daily periods of 1-sec. stimulation in the somatosensory thalamus or the midbrain reticular formation produces, after several weeks, epileptiform spikes that begin to appear even in the absence of stimulation.

Prolonged pathological electrical activity, then, may be produced by brief, low-intensity stimulation over long periods of time. Changes such as these, in the somatic projection systems, may underlie pathological pain states. Epileptiform discharges have been recorded[51] in the brainstem of human patients after cerebro-vascular accidents, which are highly correlated with bouts of trigeminal and other neuralgic pains. It is not surprising, then, that Tegretol (Carbamazepine), a powerful anticonvulsive agent, often relieves[73] trigeminal neuralgia (tic douloureux). It is possible that particular patterns of trigeminal input may set up abnormal, epileptiform patterns of activity in the brainstem, which become self-sustaining or are maintained by low-level input.[29] Tegretol would dampen down this activity.

IMPLICATIONS OF THE CONCEPT

The concept that the gate mechanism can be biased for long periods of time appears to be essential to explain phenomena such as causalgia, phantom limb pain and neuralgia. Since the abnormal central activity is conceived to be a change in firing pattern rather than a lesion, the main aim of therapy should be to bring about a return to normal activity patterns. The data suggest that increases or decreases of sensory or autonomic inputs may bring this about.

The paradox that increased input can diminish pain is balanced by the further paradox that decreasing the input, by anaesthetic block of the cord or sympathetic ganglia, may produce agonizing pain in a phantom limb.[48]

These data are not paradoxical if the gate activity is considered to reflect an interaction between inhibitory and excitatory influences at several neural levels. Blocks which selectively decrease the inhibitory influence would open the gate, "reinforce" the abnormal activity, and make the pain worse. In contrast, the fact that hypertonic saline injections,[14] vibration[53,73] and electrical stimulation of the skin or nerves[68,73] may relieve pain suggests that particular inputs can "break up" or abolish the abnormal activity patterns among the cells which bias the gate. The inputs which are effective would depend on the specialized properties of the active fibres, such as pre- and postsynaptic inhibitory[59] or facilitatory[46] effects, and adaptation rates,[6] which are known to vary complexly among different fibre groups.

This conceptual framework, which has its roots in Livingston's concept of abnormal activity in spinal neuron pools, thus proposes that the aim of pain therapy is (i) to abolish the abnormal gate bias, and (ii) to initiate more normal patterns of activity in the central nervous system. This concept is consistent with the evidence that neuralgic, causalgic, and phantom limb pain may be relieved by successive anaesthetic blocks of peripheral nerves, tender skin areas, trigger points, or sympathetic ganglia.[28,35] One or more blocks, temporarily diminishing or abolishing the input, would remove the gate bias, close the gate, and permit resumption of normal modulating functions by substantia gelatinosa cells. It is equally consistent with observations that pain may be relieved by vibration of the skin,[53,73] by increasingly vigorous massage and active movement of the limb,[36] or by percussion of the stump with a rubber mallet.[58]

It also encompasses the exciting discovery[68] that electrical stimulation of peripheral nerves at threshold level may abolish neuralgic pain in the arm or hand. The electrical stimulation, which selectively activates the large fibres that are assumed to close the gate, clearly brings about changes for prolonged periods of time. Stimulation for 2 min. may abolish severe neuralgic pain for more than 2 hr.[73] Successive periods of stimulation, in one case,[73] produced pain relief lasting for months. The use of analgesic drugs together with stimulation permits a further degree of control over pain.[73] The fact that even temporary pain relief allows active movement of the hand, with ensuing normal proprioceptive input, may be a decisive factor in producing enduring relief in these cases.[55] The technique is new and, as White and Sweet[73] note, holds great promise. It stands in marked contrast to surgical section of nerves, which (i) produces sudden, massive, abnormal input volleys, (ii) permanently disrupts normal input patterning, (iii) may result in abnormal inputs from irritating scars and neuromas, and (iv) destroys channels that may be potentially useful to control pain by input modulation methods.[36]

Brain activities can also have a powerful effect on transmission through the spinal gate. The brain is known to exert a tonic inhibitory influence (via pyramidal and reticular fibres) on dorsal horn neurons.[20,67] It is possible, then, that psychological factors could bring about a prolonged selective removal of inhibition at one or more

synaptic levels. Thus, attentional mechanisms appear to produce a prolonged "zone of awareness" after brief, gentle stimulation of the skin, so that all cutaneous events, including vascular pulsations, are perceived.[40] In "psychogenic pain", psychodynamic personal needs could also keep the gate open to produce maximal summation and pain.[45] Mechanisms such as these could provide the basis for the syndrome characterized as "homme douloureux"[64] in which all sensory inputs produce pain. Conversely, inhibitory mechanisms controlled by the brain could block input transmission to bring about other psychologically determined phenomena such as glove anaesthesia.[69]

In "psychogenic" pain, certain inputs but not others may be continuous sources of pain. Similarly, in normal man, inputs from body areas suspected to be diseased may be perceived as painful for long periods of time, whereas, the same inputs from other body areas may merely be felt as touch or warmth. (Pain may vanish the moment suspicion of disease is removed.) Such conditions require that the signals be identified, evaluated in terms of prior experience, localized and facilitated or inhibited before the action system responsible for pain perception and response is activated. It has been proposed,[20,39] therefore, that there exists in the nervous system a mechanism—*the central control trigger*—that activates the particular, selective brain processes that exert control over the sensory input (Fig. 3). The dorsal-column and dorsolateral systems could fulfil these functions. They carry precise information about the nature and location of the stimulus and they conduct so rapidly that they may not only set the receptivity of cortical neurons for subsequent afferent volleys but could activate selective brain processes that influence the transmission of information which is still arriving over slowly conducting fibres or pathways.

SUMMARY AND CONCLUSIONS

The mechanisms underlying pathological pain states such as causalgia, phantom limb pain and neuralgia remain a mystery. Observations that (i) inadequate stimuli may trigger pain, (ii) surgical lesions are usually unsuccessful in abolishing these pains permanently, (iii) new pains and trigger zones may spread unpredictably to unrelated parts of the body where no pathology exists, and (iv) pain may persist indefinitely, cannot be accounted for by the traditional specificity theory of pain. Rather, the key to an understanding of these pain states lies in recognizing that injurious stimulation may produce long-lasting changes in central nervous system activity. It is more than 25 years since W. K. Livingston[35] proposed a memory-like mechanism as their basis, and Nathan,[52] Sunderland,[63] and others[11,29] have recently supported this view. Yet the concept has failed to gain recognition, partly because so little has been known about long-term neural changes.

The gate control theory of pain permits the proposition that the gate can be biased for long periods of time. The properties of the bias, moreover, can be understood in terms of recent physiological data on mechanisms underlying long-term activity in the central nervous system.

The extensive speculation about these mechanisms indicates the degree of our ignorance of pain phenomena which, because they represent the worst suffering known to man, should demand our attention. The road to an understanding of these pain states was illuminated greatly by Weir Mitchell and W. K. Livingston. Livingston, shortly before he died, wrote what he imagined Weir Mitchell would say if he returned to life to address a medical audience:

"Everything we can learn about pain is important to medical science and human welfare. Go on with your studies of experimentally induced pain in normal human subjects who can give their full attention to the tests. Under these conditions the severity of the pain experienced tends to be directly proportional to the intensity of the causative stimulus. Go on with your efforts to trace the responses to noxious stimuli into the brains of normal experimental animals. These studies of pain in normal individuals are all to the good, for a knowledge of how a brain functions normally must be well founded before we can hope to understand and control its pathological states. But don't tell your students that studies based on normal subjects can tell the whole story about pain, or leave your students with the impression that whenever a patient's complaints of pain seem excessive in relation to its apparent cause he must be 'hysterical' or "malingering". Tell your students that the pains which will offer the greatest challenge to his therapeutic skills are the chronic pains that can undermine the patient's health by disrupting any of his normal body functions, which erode his morale and may eventually destroy him. Above all, teach your students all you can about causalgic states, both major and minor; convince them of the reality of these syndromes and let your students understand the challenge presented by these pathological pain states. For, in my humble opinion, our understanding of human pain problems will never be complete until we have solved the enigma of 'causalgia'."[37]

ACKNOWLEDGMENT

This study was supported by Contract DAHC-15-68-C0396 from the Advanced Research Projects Agency.

REFERENCES

[1] Andersen, P. and Eccles, J. C. (1962), *Nature*, **196**, 645.

[2] Andersen, P. J. and Eccles, J. C. and Sears, T. A. (1964), *J. Physiol.* (*Lond.*), **174**, 370; Eccles, J. C. (1965), *Epilepsia*, **6**, 89.

[3] Barnes, R., in *Peripheral Nerve Injuries* (Medical Research Council Report, Series 282, H.M. Stationery Office, 1954).

[4] Bindman, L. J. and Boisacq-Schepens, N. (1966), *J. Physiol.* (*London*), **185**, 14; Boisacq-Schepens, N. and Bindman, L. J. (1967), *J. Physiol.* (*Paris*), **59**, 355.

[5] Bors, E. (1951), *Arch. Neurol. Psychiat.* (*Chicago*), **66**, 610.

[6] Burgess, P. R., Petit, D. and Warren, R. M. (1968), *J. Neurophysiol.*, **31**, 833.

[7] Campbell, J. B. (1966), in *Pain*, (R. S. Knighton and P. R. Dumke, Eds.). Boston: Little, Brown & Co., and personal communication.

[8] Cedercreutz, C. and Uusitalo, E. (1967), in *Hypnosis and Psychosomatic Medicine* (J. Lassner, Ed.). Berlin: Springer-Verlag; Barber, T. X. (1959), *Psychol. Bull.*, **56**, 430.

[9] Chamberlain, T. J., Halick, P. and Gerard, R. W. (1963), *J. Neurophysiol.*, **26**, 662.

[10] Cohen, H. (1944), *Trans. med. Soc. Lond.*, **64**, 65; (1947), *Lancet*, **253**, 933.

[11] Cronholm, B. (1951), *Acta Psychiat. Neurol. Scand. Suppl.*, **72**, 1.

[12] Echlin, F., Owens, F. M. and Wells, W. L. (1949), *Arch. Neurol. Psychiat.* (*Chicago*), **62**, 183.

[13] Ewalt, J. R., Randall, G. C. and Morris, H. (1947), *Psychosom. Med.*, **9**, 118.

[14] Feinstein, B., Luce, J. C. and Langton, J. N. K. (1954), in *Human Limbs and their Substitutes* (P. Klopsteg and P. Wilson, Eds.). New York: McGraw-Hill.

[15] Frankstein, S. I. (1947), *Science*, **106**, 242.

[16] Gerard, R. W. (1951), *Anesthesiology*, **12**, 1.

[17] Goddard, G. V., McIntyre, D. C. and Leech, C. K. (1969), *Exp. Neurol.*, **25**, 295; Racine, R. J. (1969), *The Modification of Afterdischarge and Convulsive Behavior in the Rat by Electrical Stimulation*. Unpublished Ph.D. Thesis, McGill University, Montreal.

[18] Goldscheider, A. (1894), *Ueber den Schmerz in physiologischer und klinischer Hinsicht*. Berlin: Hirschwald.

[19] Hebb, D. O. (1949), *The Organization of Behavior*. New York: Wiley.

[20] Hillman, P. and Wall, P. D. (1970), *Exp. Brain Res.* In press.

[21] Hutchins, H. C. and Reynolds, O. E. (1947), *J. dent. Res.*, **26**, 3. Reynolds, O. E. and Hutchins, H. C. (1948), *Amer. J. Physiol.*, **152**, 658.

[22] Jalavisto, E. and Sourander, P. (1948), *Ann. acad. scient. fenn. Ser. A*, **5**, 17.

[23] Kallio, K. E. (1950), *Acta orthop. scand.*, **19**, 391.

[24] Kandel, E. R., Frazier, W. T. and Wachtel, H. (1969), *J. Neurophysiol.*, **32**, 496.

[25] Kandel, E. R., Spencer, W. A. and Brinley, F. J. (1961), *J. Neurophysiol.*, **24**, 225.

[26] Kennard, M. A. and Haugen, F. P. (1955), *Anesthesiology*, **16**, 297.

[27] Kerr, F. W. L. and Miller, R. H. (1966), *Arch. Neurol.*, **15**, 308.

[28] Kibler, R. F. and Nathan, P. W. (1960), *J. Neurol. Neurosurg. Psychiat.*, **23**, 91.

[29] King, R. B. (1958), *J. Neurosurg.*, **15**, 290; Crue, B. L., Alvarez-Carregal, E. and Todd, E. M. (1964), *Bull. Los Angeles neurol. Soc.*, **29**, 107.

[30] Kirklin, J. W., Chenoweth, A. I. and Murphy, F. (1947), *Surgery*, **21**, 321.

[31] Kolb, L. C. (1954), *The Painful Phantom: Psychology, Physiology and Treatment*. Springfield: C. C. Thomas.

[32] Larsell, O. (1951), *Anatomy of the Nervous System*. New York: Appleton-Century.

[33] Leriche, R. (1939), *The Surgery of Pain*. London: Baillière, Tindall and Cox.

[34] Lim, K. S. (1968), in *The Skin Senses* (D. Kenshalo, Ed.). Springfield: C. C. Thomas; Benjamin, F. B. ibid.; Rosenthal, S. R., ibid.

[35] Livingston, W. K. (1943), *Pain Mechanisms*. New York: Macmillan.

[36] Livingston, W. K. (1948), *Ann. N.Y. Acad. Sci.*, **50**, 247.

[37] Livingston, W. K. (1966), in *Pain*, p. 571 (R. S. Knighton and P. R. Dumke, Eds.). Boston: Little, Brown & Co.

[38] Melzack, R. and Bailey, G., unpublished observations.

[39] Melzack, R. and Casey, K. L. (1968), in *The Skin Senses* (D. Kenshalo, Ed.). Springfield: C. C. Thomas.

[40] Melzack, R. and Eisenberg, H. (1968), *Science*, **159**, 445.

[41] Melzack, R., Konrad, K. and Dubrovsky, B. (1968), *Exp. Neurol.*, **20**, 443; Melzack, R. and Casey, K. L. (1967), ibid., **17**, 276.

[42] Melzack, R., Konrad, K. W., and Dubrovsky, B. (1969), *Exp. Neurol.*, **25**, 416.

[43] Melzack, R., Stotler, W. A. and Livingston, W. K. (1958), *J. Neurophysiol.*, **21**, 353.

[44] Melzack, R. and Wall, P. D. (1962), *Brain*, **85**, 331.

[45] Melzack, R. and Wall, P. D. (1965), *Science*, **150**, 971.

46 Mendell, L. M. and Wall, P. D. (1964), *J. Physiol. (Lond.)*, **172**, 274; Mendell, L. M. and Wall, P. D. (1965), *Nature*, **206**, 97.

47 Merskey, H. and Spear, F. G. (1967), *Pain: Psychological and Psychiatric Aspects*. London: Baillière, Tindall and Cassell; Sternbach, R. A. (1968), *Pain: A Psychophysiological Analysis*. New York: Academic Press.

48 Moore, B. (1946), *Med. J. Aust.*, **2**, 645; Walker, A. E. (1942), *Arch. Neurol. Psychiat. (Chicago)*, **48**, 865.

49 Morgenstern, F. S. (1964), *J. Neurol. Neurosurg. Psychiat.*, **27**, 58.

50 Mountcastle, V. B. (1961), in *Sensory Communication* (W. A. Rosenblith, Ed.). Cambridge: Massachusetts Institute of Technology; Sweet, W. H. (1959), "A-delta Fibers are the Smallest Myelinated Fibers, C Fibers are the Unmyelinated Fibers, in Peripheral Nerve," *Handbook Physiol.*, **1**, 459.

51 Nashold, B. S. and Wilson, W. P. (1966), *Confin. neurol.*, **27**, 30.

52 Nathan, P. W. (1962), in *The Assessment of Pain in Man and Animals* (C. A. Keele and R. Smith, Eds.). Edinburgh: Livingstone.

53 Nathan, P. and Wall, P. D., personal communication.

54 Noordenbos, (1959), *Pain*. Amsterdam: Elsevier.

55 Noordenbos, W., personal communication.

56 Pearson, A. A. (1952), *Arch. Neurol. Psychiat. (Chicago)*, **68**, 515.

57 Pomeranz, B., Wall, P. D. and Weber, W. V. (1968), *J. Physiol.*, **199**, 511; Selzer, M. and Spencer, W. A. (1969), *Brain Res.*, **14**, 331. (1969), ibid., 349.

58 Russell, W. R. and Spalding, J. M. K. (1950), *Brit. med. J.*, **2**, 68.

59 Schmidt, R. F., Senges, J. and Zimmermann, M. (1967), *Exp. Brain Res.*, **3**, 234; Zimmermann, M. (1968), *Science*, **160**, 896; Franz, D. N. and Iggo, A. (1968), ibid., **162**, 1140.

60 Sefton, A. J. and Burke, W. (1965), *Nature*, **205**, 1325; Burke, W. and Sefton, A. J. (1966), *J. Physiol.*, **187**, 213; Burke, W. and Sefton, A. J. (1966), ibid., **187**, 231.

61 Spencer, W. A., Thompson, R. F. and Neilson, D. R. (1966), *J. Neurophysiol.*, **29**, 253.

62 Spencer, W. A. and Wigdor, R. (1965), *Physiologist*, **8**, 278, and unpublished observations.

63 Sunderland, S. (1968), *Nerves and Nerve Injuries*, p. 432. Edinburgh: Livingstone.

64 Szasz, T. S. (1968), in *Pain* (A. Soulairac, J. Cahn and J. Charpentier, Eds.). London: Academic Press.

65 Szentagothai, J. (1964), *J. comp. Neurol.*, **122**, 219; Heimer, L. and Wall, P. D. (1968), *Exp. Brain Res.*, **6**, 89.

66 Taub, A. (1964), *Exp. Neurol.*, **10**, 357.

67 Wall, P. D. (1967), *J. Physiol.*, **188**, 403.

68 Wall, P. D. and Sweet, W. H. (1967), *Science*, **155**, 108.

69 Walters, A. (1961), *Brain*, **84**, 1.

70 Waziri, R., Kandel, E. R. and Frazier, W. T. (1969), *J. Neurophysiol.*, **32**, 509.

71 Weinstein, S. and Sersen, E. A. (1961), *Neurology*, **11**, 905; Weinstein, S., Sersen, E. A. and Vetter, R. J. (1964), *Cortex*, **1**, 276.

72 Mitchell, S. Weir (1864), *Injuries of Nerves and their Consequences*, p. 196. Philadelphia: Lippincott.

73 White, J. C. and Sweet, W. H. (1969), *Pain and the Neurosurgeon*. Springfield: C. C. Thomas.

FURTHER READING

Kenshalo, D. (Ed.), (1968), *The Skin Senses*. Springfield: C. C. Thomas.

Knighton, R. S. and Dumke, P. R. (Eds.) (1966), *Pain*. Boston: Little, Brown & Co.

Lim, R. K. S. (Ed.) (1968), *Pharmacology of Pain*. New York: Pergamon Press.

Livingston, W. K. (1943), *Pain Mechanisms*. New York: Macmillan.

Melzack, R. and Wall, P. D. (1962), "On the Nature of Cutaneous Sensory Mechanisms," *Brain*, **85**, 331–356.

Melzack, R. and Wall, P. D. (1965), "Pain Mechanisms: A New Theory," *Science*, **150**, 971–979.

Merskey, H. and Spear, F. G. (1967), *Pain: Psychological and Psychiatric Aspects*. London: Baillière, Tindall and Cassell.

Noordenbos, W. (1959), *Pain*. Amsterdam: Elsevier.

Sinclair, D. (1967), *Cutaneous Sensation*. London: Oxford University Press.

Soulairac, A., Cahn, J. and Charpentier, J. (Eds.) (1968), *Pain*. London: Academic Press.

Sternbach, R. A. (1968), *Pain: A Psychophysiological Analysis*. New York: Academic Press.

Sunderland, S. (1968), *Nerves and Nerve Injuries*. Edinburgh: Livingstone.

White, J. C. and Sweet, W. H. (1969), *Pain and the Neurosurgeon*. Springfield: C. C. Thomas.

Yamamura, H. (Ed.) (1970), *Anaesthesia and Neurophysiology*. Boston: Little, Brown & Co.

7. PSYCHOLOGICAL ASPECTS OF PAIN

M. R. BOND

Pain in organic disease has structural, functional and perceptual components which variously unite as a subjective experience that can only occur as part of consciousness. Through the centuries attempts to provide a universally accepted definition have failed but it is reasonable to accept pain as an emotional event which is reported to us and which we understand by reference to our own experience. Most human beings in pain describe it in terms of damage to the body irrespective of the relative contributions of organic and psychological mechanisms, and an operational description by Merskey and Spear[9] takes account of this fact. In their view pain is:

"An unpleasant experience which we primarily associate with tissue damage, or describe in terms of such damage, or both."

Many still regard pain as two events, first the primary painful sensation, and second the reaction to this sensation. However, it is more reasonable to reserve the word "pain" for the whole complex of events forming the subjective experience describing the stimuli which provoke it as "noxae".

In physical illness there is often a discrepancy between the apparent severity of tissue destruction and the point at which different individuals, or the same individual in differing circumstances, experience pain. Thus G. J. Guthrie wrote in 1827: "In two persons apparently suffering from the same kind of injury and with the same detriment, one will writhe with agony whilst the other will smile with contempt." The incongruity between the presence of potentially noxious disorders and the experience of pain arouses interest in factors which influence the time at which it becomes apparent in any disease, its intensity, and the freedom with which complaints of suffering are made.

Maturation and Development of the Pain Experience

Although the ability to experience pain is usually regarded as inherent, there is evidence that learning plays an important rôle in the development of its full physiological and behavioural characteristics. Adequate environmental stimulation is important in this respect, for example, young animals reared in a world of restricted sensory stimulation have considerably increased thresholds for pain.[8] Similarly, children deprived of normal sensory experiences in their early years fail to fully develop their perceptual skills. In normal circumstances the central nervous system is immature at birth, possibly accounting for the higher thresholds of neonates and infants for noxious stimuli. As physical maturation proceeds the pattern of behaviour exhibited by a child in pain increasingly reflects both family and wider cultural influences. Thus complaints of pain in later life are more frequent in those from disturbed homes where there were punitive or quarrelsome parents, and in the younger members of large families. In rare instances there is an incomplete development of the nervous system which leaves the unfortunate individual concerned without ability to experience pain, or with a very delayed development of this faculty. This defect is clearly a serious handicap as severe injury may occur quite unknown to the person concerned. In later years of life, there appears to be gradual lessening of pain experienced in most situations and this may be one aspect of the general decline in sensitivity to sensory stimuli associated with increasing age.

The Significance of Pain

The significance of pain to the individual should be considered in all problems of pain analysis. Szarz[11] and Engel[3] agreed that it is distinguished at three levels of symbolism of increasing complexity. Firstly, pain may be a signal indicating damage or danger to bodily structure. Next, in a situation where two or more persons are

neurotic symptoms in those for whom it has acted as a defence against intolerable stress.[6] The study of pain and its relation to inflammatory changes in the appendix of patients presenting typical features of acute appendicitis, is a common situation while pain may represent a psychological disturbance masquerading as organic disease. Various studies show that approximately 40 per cent of all appendices removed are normal, but in young women between the ages of 15–35 the proportion rises to two-thirds. Investigation suggests that for many, emotional problems of adolescence or early adult life play a major rôle in the genesis of their pain. In injury the significance of pain appears to influence its severity. For example, in a study of the analgesic requirements of battle casualties and civilian patients, Beecher[1] showed that the needs of the former were significantly lower than of the latter. There was no clear relation between the extent of wounding and pain reported. It was concluded that to the soldier wounding meant release from battle and the threat of death, but for the civilian it could mean loss of earning power and social position.

Measurement of Pain

In order to quantify the effects of personal and environmental factors upon pain, methods have been devised for its evaluation both in disease and in the experimental situation. In animal experiments, most of which are used to determine the relative potency of analgesics, objective measures of pain are chiefly based upon reflex responses evoked by noxious stimulation. In man objective assessments of pain by trained observers are commonly used. However, conventional measuring processes involve categorization resulting in coarse gradings for a continuous phenomenon, and the descriptive scales in which pain is classed as nil, slight, moderate or severe are inaccurate and subject to considerable observer bias. In order to overcome the unavoidable approximations of language to describe feeling, increasing use is being made of an analogue scale: a line the boundaries of which are the extremes of the sensations being measured. This technique avoids verbal ambiguity and the use of a 100 mm. line gives fine gradings which have much greater sensitivity than descriptive scales. A pain analogue is shown in Fig. 1. Patients are required

I DO NOT
HAVE ANY PAIN ━━━━━━━━━━━━━━━━━━━━━━━ MY PAIN IS AS
BAD AS IT COULD
POSSIBLY BE

FIG. 1. The Pain Analogue

together complaints may form a means of expressing a need for help. Lastly, it may have a wider meaning and represent a complaint about being unfairly treated, or be used as a means whereby others may be manipulated. Pain may reflect guilt feelings and be regarded as a punishment for real or imagined misdemeanours. This is evidenced by the derivation of the word from the Latin "poena", or Greek "poine" meaning penalty or punishment. As a further complicating factor, organic and psychiatric illness may coexist, and although patients with chronic pain constantly seek relief successful treatment can unmask

to make a pencil mark on a line bearing the words, "I have no pain at all" at the left end; and, "My pain is as bad as it could possibly be" at the right end. The distance from th eleft end of the line to the point of intersection is measured in millimetres and designated a pain score. Using this method scores are obtained regularly throughout a period of days and then a "pain profile" is constructed. It is emphasized that each pain score represents the end point of the many factors which collectively influence both the patient's pain experience and the freedom of communication. With this method the effects of medical and surgical treatment for pain may be assessed and examples of pain profiles are shown in Figs. 2 and 3.

As indicated, it is difficult to obtain reliable quantitative measures of pain. There is one notable exception however where changes in respiratory function have been used to assess pain severity and the effectiveness of analgesics upon it following abdominal surgery. It has been shown that vital capacity is reduced to between 20–30 per cent of the pre-operative level following upper abdominal operations, and to about 50 per cent after lower abdominal surgery. Depending upon their potency, analgesics increase vital capacity to between 40–85 per cent of the pre-operative value.

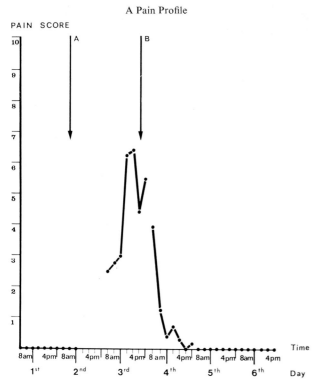

A Pain Profile

FIG. 2. Pain scores before, during and after the insertion of intrauterine radium. A: Radium inserted. B: Radium removed.

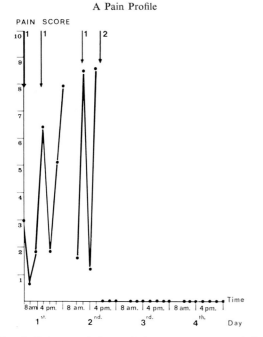

A Pain Profile

FIG. 3. Pain scores before and after percutaneous cervical cordotomy for intractable limb pain. 1: Analgesic administration. 2: Cordotomy.

Thresholds for Pain

In health or disease it is possible for an observer to induce pain using methods which permit the evaluation of pain thresholds. Although nomenclature varies it is generally agreed that there are two such thresholds; the first is when the quality of the experience evoked by a noxious stimulus changes and is regarded as painful, and the second is where it becomes unbearable. The first level may be termed the pain perception threshold (PPT), and the second the severe pain threshold (SPT). It is widely held that the PPT is primarily determined by physiological factors whereas the SPT is much more subject to psychological influences. Therefore, the SPT represents the intensity of pain at which an individual makes a verbal, or even an overt escape response, and the interval between thresholds is a measure of tolerance.

A wide range of methods has been developed for producing pain and the stimuli that have been used include heat, electric current, muscle ischaemia, the injection of various chemical agents and pressure. The use of pressure gives consistent results and specific techniques include pressure on the styloid process, the use of a rough metal grater beneath an inflated cuff, and air pressure to force a metal disc against the skin. Using a spring loaded plunger or algometer, Keele[5] found that thresholds varied between 0·5–6 kg. Subjects were arbitrarily divided into three groups, normosensitives with thresholds ranging from 2–4 kg., hyposensitives with thresholds above 4 kg. and hypersensitives with thresholds below 2 kg. In physical illness there is an increase in the number of hypersensitives at the expense of the other groups. Hyposensitive patients appear to make relatively few demands for medical help when experiencing noxious stimulation from disease processes, whereas those who are hypersensitive make complaints to their doctors more frequently than others. Keele also observed that pain thresholds for pressure correspond with those for ischaemic muscle pain, and pain induced chemically by stimulation of a blister base with solutions of potassium chloride.

Pain thresholds are normally lower in women than in men, in those from lower socio-economic groups, and those in sedentary occupations compared with individuals involved in hard or dangerous physical work. Studies in which the PPT and SPT have been measured show that both are reduced in physical illness. The latter is most affected and the resulting reduction of pain tolerance is greatest in the presence of apprehension, anxiety and fear. Tolerance is also reduced by cold, hunger and physical fatigue, but is increased by analgesic drugs most of which appear to have a primary effect upon the SPT.

Personal Factors Influencing the Pain Experience

With the development of concepts of personality amenable to quantitative assessment the link between pain, complaint behaviour and personality structure has been investigated. Using the Eysenck Personality Inventory (EPI) two fundamental dimensions of personality may be identified, namely, extroversion/introversion and neuroticism/stability. Briefly, extroversion implies the presence of an outgoing personality with relatively uninhibited social tendencies, whereas introversion indicates a withdrawn and solitary personality. Neuroticism is defined as emotional lability or over-responsiveness, and a liability to neurotic breakdown under stress. With this inventory thresholds for experimentally induced pain have been found to be lowest in introverts and those with high degrees of neuroticism, and highest in the stable or extroverted person. Thresholds for other forms of sensation show a similar relationship to personality. There is evidence suggesting that very stable extroverts may not become aware of pain in any given disease state until a late stage in their illness and this has significant implications as it may account in part for those individuals in the general population who do not seek early medical advice.

Complaint behaviour is closely related to personality. Although they have higher sensory thresholds, extroverts complain more freely than introverts about any symptoms they may experience. A study of married and unmarried mothers in childbirth showed that extroverted patients rated their pain in labour as greater than those who were introverted and this agreed with nurses ratings of the difficulties of labour in the two groups.[4] It was considered that the higher ratings of pain by extroverts reflected a tendency for them to "exaggerate" the painfulness of the situation whereas introverts minimized it. The concept of exaggeration arises from previous work by Petrie et al.[7] which showed that some people subjectively process stimuli by reducing them (reducers), some by increasing them (augmenters), whilst others do neither (moderates). Reducers are more than usually tolerant of pain and less tolerant of sensory deprivation, whereas augmenters are less tolerant of pain and more tolerant of sensory deprivation. Therefore, reducers may be equated with extroverts and augmenters with introverts. Observations upon sensory thresholds and complaint behaviour clearly indicate a difference between awareness of pain on the one hand and its acceptance or tolerance on the other.

It has long been known that anxiety bears a close relation to pain. It may be assessed physiologically using striated muscle tension and measures of autonomic activity, or psychologically with rating scales. Irrespective of the method used, results of many and varied studies show that the more anxious a person the greater his or her experience of pain, whether it is experimentally induced, or results from organic disease. Anxiety prone subjects complain significantly more often than those with little or no anxiety when subjected to experimentally induced pain.

The practical consequence of attempts to reduce anxiety and pain in organic disease have resulted in the combined treatment of both emotional and physical aspects of illness.

Saunders[10] described the treatment of intractable pain in terminal disorders emphasizing the need to relieve patients' distress by discussion of problems presented to themselves and their families by the illness, and by the judicious use of analgesic and psychotropic drugs. She also commented that enthusiasm on the part of a doctor combined with the effectiveness of suggestion does much to allay fear, anxiety and pain.

The complex difficulties presented by patients with chronic pain has led to the formation of "pain clinics" at which physicians, surgeons, psychiatrists, anaesthetists and radiotherapists have variously combined to contribute their expertise. Their observations indicate that persistent pain is associated with a long history of pain, anxiety and depression, poor general health, a disagreeable environment, resentment and lack of confidence in the doctor.

Surgical attempts to reduce anxiety or alter personality, and therefore pain, followed the introduction of prefrontal leucotomy. The operation, which has since been modified several times, is designed to divide connections from the posterior and medial nuclei of the thalamus passing forwards through the anterior limb of the internal capsule to the orbital surfaces of the frontal lobes. After operation, ability to experience pain persists but associated anxiety, fear and guilt are lessened. There appears to be a personality change for leucotomy does not alter a patient's ability to discriminate noxious stimuli, but it does alter pain.

Environment and Its Influence upon the Pain Experience

The experience of pain and readiness to complain are influenced by cultural factors. A study of attitudes towards pain and its expression amongst American Veterans and their families who were of varied ethnic origins revealed clear-cut differences. Following surgical operations patients who were of "Old American" stock showed a matter-of-fact and optimistic attitude towards pain with reluctance to make their suffering known publicly. Patients of Jewish origin showed concern about the practical implications of their pain and were suspicious of measures designed only to relieve symptoms, but open complaints about pain were numerous and indeed patients believed that their behaviour had a beneficial effect. Demands for immediate relief of pain with frequent complaints were observed for patients of Italian origin, and although their pain thresholds were lowest of all, these varied little between the three groups investigated. From this and similar studies cultural factors appear to influence attitudes, tolerance and complaint behaviour rather more than the pain perception threshold.

Within any social group the attitudes of those caring for patients in hospital vary in ways which influence both the severity of pain and complaint behaviour. In a study of patients with cancer the pattern of staff-patient relations was examined in terms of pain experienced, frequency of complaints of pain and patterns of analgesic administration.[2] Differences between the sexes were marked. Men experienced pain more often and made greater numbers of requests for drugs than women. However, men were refused analgesics more often which, when given, were of low potency. The times of drug administration were more closely allied to fixed medicine rounds on the men's than on the women's ward. It was concluded that the more authoritarian attitude towards male patients, deemed to be primarily cultural in origin, generated anxiety, fear and hostility with associated increases in pain and requests for analgesics. For both sexes there was only a very limited relation between subjective measures of pain and analgesic potency. The nature of the drug given was governed chiefly by the source of request; thus if patients requested medication they tended to receive the least potent analgesics, whereas drugs given on staff initiative were more often the most powerful forms.

Pain is not necessarily an immediate accompaniment of severe tissue damage. The intense emotion of physical combat, whether in sport or in the heat of battle, is associated with a change in awareness of noxious stimuli. In such situations the very limited and intense focusing of perception upon "fight or flight" excludes from awareness other sensory stimuli which, under normal circumstances, would in themselves be keenly appreciated. Recently, this principle, which might be termed "sensory flooding", has been used clinically. Thus in dental surgery brief but intense auditory stimulation has been effectively used to reduce pain and, if combined with the effects of suggestion, it reduces suffering still further. The converse commonly occurs where those in pain are isolated, in darkness, or other situations where there is a relative degree of sensory deprivation. Then anxiety and pain mount, thresholds fall and analgesic requirements increase.

In conclusion, the reason for a knowledge of the psychological aspects of pain and thereby its treatment was summarized long ago by Sophocles who wrote:

"To exert an influence on pain, it is more useful to know the minds of men than their physiology."

FURTHER READING

[1] Beecher, H. K. (1956), "Relationship of Significance of Wound to Pain Experienced," *J. Amer. med. Ass.*, **161**, 1609.

[2] Bond, M. R. and Pilowsky, I. (1966), "Subjective Assessment of Pain and its Relationship to the Administration of Analgesics in patients with Advanced Cancer," *J. Psychosom. Res.*, **10**, 205.

[3] Engel, G. L. (1959), " 'Psychogenic' Pain and the Pain Prone Patient," *Amer. J. Med.*, **26**, 899.

[4] Eysenck, S. G. B. (1961), "Personality and Pain Assessments in Childbirth of Married and Unmarried Mothers," *J. Ment. Sci.*, **107**, 417.

[5] Keele, K. D. (1954), "The Pressure Algometer," *Lancet*, **1**, 636.

[6] Penman, J. (1954), "Pain as an Old Friend," *Lancet*, **1**, 633.

[7] Petrie, A., Collins, W. and Solomon, P. (1960), "Tolerance for Pain and Sensory Deprivation," *Amer. J. Psychol.*, **73**, 80.

[8] Melzack, R. and Scott, T. H. (1957), "The Effect of Early Experience on the Response to Pain," *J. comp. physiol. Psychol.*, **50**, 155.

[9] Merskey, H. and Spear, F. G. (1967), *Pain, Psychological and Psychiatric Aspects.* London: Ballière, Tindall and Cassells.

[10] Saunders, C. (1963), "The Treatment of Intractable Pain in Terminal Cancer," *Proc. roy. Soc. Med.*, **56**, 195.

[11] Szarzs, T. S. (1955), "The Nature of Pain," *Arch. Neurol. and Psych.*, **77**, 74.

8. HEADACHE

JAMES W. LANCE

The head may ache because of excessive discharge of nerve-fibres arising from intracranial, cranial or extracranial structures, or from an abnormal psychological reaction to a relatively normal afferent discharge from these structures. Most of us are subject to headache from time to time as the result of fatigue, nervous tension or the abuse of the more socially acceptable drugs, yet there are some people who claim never to have experienced a headache. Perhaps such persons should volunteer for a histamine infusion or pneumoencephalogram to reassure the headache-prone majority that freedom from headache is only a matter of degree. Fortunately, headache becomes a clinical problem in only a minority of patients but there is no agreement among epidemiological studies as to the numbers who are incapacitated or inconvenienced by recurrent headache. The incidence of migraine is variously estimated at 3–9 per cent of the population,[22] probably because of the disregard in most published series of the frequency of recurrence of headache which is one of the indices essential for determining the morbidity due to the illness. Probably the most helpful survey is that of Brewis *et al.* (1966) who found that 6·3 per cent of the population suffered from migraine or other forms of chronic headache which were sufficiently frequent and severe to cause loss of time from work or school.

The study of headache divides itself fairly naturally into considerations of the serious or life-threatening causes of headache which are mostly acute and of intracranial origin, and of the chronic or recurrent forms of headache which are of predominantly extracranial origin and do not endanger life but are nevertheless extremely unpleasant.

Most forms of headache are of vascular origin. All large intracranial and extracranial vessels are sensitive to pain produced by distension and displacement and, under certain circumstances, by dilatation. Intracranial headache may also arise from irritation of the dura of the anterior and posterior fossa or by compression of those cranial nerves containing afferent fibres. Generally speaking, headache from supratentorial structures is referred to the area innervated by the first division of the trigeminal nerve, anterior to a line drawn vertically above the ear, and pain from the posterior fossa is referred to the area behind that line supplied by the second and third cervical segments.[28] Kerr (1961) has emphasized that pain can be referred from trigeminal to cervical regions and vice versa because afferent neurons from the second and third cervical roots and fibres of the descending spinal tract of the trigeminal nerve converge on second order neurons in the upper part of the cervical spinal cord, so that neurons of the secondary trigeminal tract may be activated from either source. That there is considerable interaction between trigeminal and cervical volleys was shown by Denny-Brown and Yanagisawa (1970) in the monkey. They were able to show both inhibitory and excitatory effects from the cervical segments on trigeminal function, the inhibitory effects being reversed by the use of strychnine.

Intracranial Sources of Headache

If we exclude the cranial neuralgias (trigeminal and glossopharyngeal neuralgia) and compression of cranial nerves by tumours or other disorders afflicting the base of the skull—which are relatively uncommon—intracranial headache results either from meningeal irritation or is of vascular origin. Intracranial vascular headache may simply be the result of excessive dilatation of the internal carotid artery and its branches or be the result of their displacement by space-occupying lesions, internal hydrocephalus or cerebral oedema. Intracranial vascular headache is aggravated by coughing, sneezing and jarring.

Meningeal Irritation

Meningeal irritation is most commonly the result of subarachnoid haemorrhage, meningitis, encephalitis or diagnostic pneumoencephalography. The presence of blood in the subarachnoid space induces a sterile inflammatory reaction, probably because of the release of pain-producing substances such as serotonin and bradykinin. The posterior cervical muscles contract by a polysynaptic reflex mechanism to cause neck rigidity, an important sign of meningeal irritation.

Intracranial Vasodilatation

The following factors may cause painful intracranial vasodilatation:

Reactions to toxins as in various systemic infections, foreign protein reactions, hangover headache after excessive alcohol intake, and carbon monoxide poisoning.

Metabolic disturbances such as hypoxia, hypoglycaemia and hypercapnia.

The use of vasodilator drugs like histamine, amyl nitrite or nitroglycerin.

Low cerebrospinal fluid pressure after lumbar puncture. Concussion.

Epileptic seizures, presumably as the result of hypoxia.

Hypertension, if severe, in which case the headache is usually present in the early morning and disappears after the patient gets up and about. Hypertension may also aggravate other forms of headache such as migraine. A sudden increase in blood pressure is likely to cause headache. This may occur in acute nephritis, or the paroxysms induced by a phaeochromocytoma, or the ingestion of tyramine-containing substances (cheese, red wines) in a patient taking drugs which inhibit the enzyme monoamine oxidase.

Cerebral vascular insufficiency may be associated with headache during transient ischaemic attacks, occipital if the vertebrobasilar territory is involved or unilateral over temple and vertex in the case of the internal carotid artery. The mechanism is uncertain. Dilatation of extracranial vessels which comprise the collateral circulation may play a part, as well as dilatation of intracranial vessels surrounding the ischaemic area. Internal carotid thrombosis can cause unilateral cerebral oedema which simulates a tumour on radiological investigation.

Distension of the wall of the internal carotid artery is responsible for the pain of an enlarging aneurysm in this region, and probably makes an important contribution to cluster headache and some cases of migraine as well. The association of acute pain behind one eye and a partial third nerve or other ocular palsy suggests the enlargement of a carotid aneurysm.

Displacement of Intracranial Vessels

Space-occupying lesions within the cranial cavity (haematoma, tumour or abscess) cause headache by displacement of the large cerebral arteries. In this context the association of a headache of recent onset with progressive dilatation of one pupil, whether or not it is accompanied by other components of a third cranial nerve palsy, suggests tentorial herniation compressing the third nerve on the side of the lesion and requires immediate neurosurgical intervention.

Intracranial pressure may be increased as any mass expands to a size which can no longer be compensated by compression of the soft accommodating cerebrum. Pressure may increase early in the case of tumours or inflammations which block cerebrospinal pathways, thus producing an internal hydrocephalus.

If the source of obstruction to the flow of cerebrospinal fluid is outside the ventricular system, in the basal meninges or subarachnoid space, the hydrocephalus is said to be communicating. This may evoke headache if intracranial pressure increases rapidly, but in the recently described condition of occult hydrocephalus which evolves slowly in late middle age or in the elderly, there is usually no headache.

Failure of absorption of cerebrospinal fluid because of thrombosis of the superior sagittal sinus, or the lateral sinus which drains it, is most commonly the result of head-injury or infection. Spread of otitis media through the mastoid process to the lateral sinus may cause the syndrome of "otitic hydrocephalus", in which headache and papilloedema are often accompanied by paralysis of the sixth cranial nerve on the side of the ear infection as the result of apical petrositis. It should be noted that the lateral rectus muscle may sometimes be paralysed on both sides whatever the cause of raised intracranial pressure because of compression of both sixth cranial nerves by their lateral displacement.

Rarely venous pressure may be raised sufficiently to elevate intracranial pressure.

One of the most interesting subdivisions under the classification of increased intracranial pressure is "benign intracranial hypertension" which is a syndrome of headache and papilloedema in which the cerebral ventricles are normal or small in size as the result of cerebral oedema without any evidence of venous obstruction. There are many known causes but the mechanism by which cerebral oedema is produced is not yet understood. The syndrome has been described in pregnancy, and women who are taking hormonal preparations to avoid pregnancy. It has been reported in Addisonian crises and also during treatment with adrenal corticosteroids or after the cessation of long-term treatment. It may be caused by hypocalcaemia, vitamin A intoxication or head-injury. It has appeared as an idiosyncratic reaction to certain drugs such as nalidixic acid and the tetracyclines. The condition is treated by correcting the cause whenever possible and by the reduction of intracranial pressure, using a potent diuretic such as frusemide and repeated lumbar puncture, to prevent optic atrophy. In many instances the prefix "benign" appears to be justified because this form of intracranial hypertension may persist, fluctuating in intensity, for 2 years or more without loss of visual acuity.[23]

Cranial Sources of Headache

It is unusual for disease of the skull itself to give rise to headache but the possibility of an unrecognized depressed fracture, osteomyelitis, secondary carcinoma, multiple myeloma and Paget's disease must be borne in mind. It would seem self-evident that the source of any headache may be in the cranial vault or the tissues which surround it and yet inspection, palpation and auscultation of the skull is often neglected.

Extracranial Sources of Headache

Examination of the scalp may reveal the tender thrombosed vessels of temporal (giant-cell) arteritis or signs of a local inflammatory process overlying the skull. More commonly no abnormality is found since the origin of most forms of extracranial headache lies in the vessels or muscles of the scalp, and the arterial changes may be episodic as in migraine and cluster headache. Over-contraction of the scalp muscles is a feature of chronic tension headache, and also of imbalance of the bite, which leads to a secondary jaw-clenching syndrome. Disorders of the eye, frontal sinuses and upper cervical spine may refer pain to the first division of the trigeminal nerve. Cervical spondylosis may also cause diffuse pain in the neck and head by the process of secondary muscle contraction. Disorders of the teeth refer pain only to the second and third division of the trigeminal nerve unless one includes the pain which may radiate diffusely from the temporomandibular joints in patients with an unbalanced bite (Costen's syndrome) or those who are subject to nocturnal fang-sharpening movements of the jaw which occur during sleep as an indication of repressed aggression.[10] The latter syndrome may be recognized by the association of chronic headache with pain in the temporomandibular joints and jaw muscles and a raw tender spot on the buccal mucosa opposite the posterior part of the upper gum, which results from excessive lateral movement of the mandible during sleep. This disorder responds to psychological management rather than measures directed solely to the correction of malocclusion.

Chronic Tension Headache

Tension headache is a dull headache, usually described as a feeling of pressure or band around the head which is commonly associated with over-contraction of the scalp muscles, and underlying anxiety or depression. The majority of patients with this symptom, which may recur daily in the absence of any obvious source of worry, have great difficulty in relaxing the scalp muscles. They may be chronic frowners with frontal headache, chronic jaw-clenchers with bi-temporal headache or they may hold the neck stiffly and suffer from pain in the neck and occiput. The feeling of pressure or dull pain may spread to involve several of these areas or the whole head. It is doubtful whether excessive muscle-contraction can be the sole factor responsible for this form of headache since there are many tense unrelaxed people whose brow is continually furrowed and yet who are not subject to headache. Migraine is not more common in the families of patients with tension headache than in control subjects but there is a family history of some sort of headache in 40 per cent,[11] which arouses speculation about the possibility of an hereditary factor which renders some tense patients unduly sensitive to the effects of contraction of the scalp muscles. There has long been speculation that scalp arteries are relatively constricted in tension headache, thus diminishing the blood supply to overcontracting muscles.[28] This view has not been supported by a study of blood-flow, using radioactive sodium injected into the posterior cervical musculature, which showed that the clearance was greater during tension headache than in headache-free periods.[21] It is possible that the increase in blood-flow during headache is insufficient to supply the metabolic demands of overactive muscle. Alternatively, there may be additional factors in the pathophysiology of tension headache. The Florentine school of headache-research believes that a chronic sterile inflammation is responsible for tension headache and that bradykinin and vasoactive amines may be implicated in the perpetuation of this state. These humoral substances are now thought to play an important part in the conspicuous vascular changes of migraine, and it is possible that some defect in their formation, adsorption to vessels or removal from the circulation may be in some way responsible for the more subtle vascular disturbance of tension headache. It is of interest to note that aspirin, which is effective in the milder forms of tension headache, is a bradykinin antagonist. In the more severe and chronic forms, relaxing agents such as diazepam and antidepressants such as amitriptyline have been found useful to support treatment by relaxation exercises and psychotherapy.[16] It can be seen that present knowledge of the pathophysiology of chronic tension headache is unsatisfactory and its treatment largely empirical.

Migraine

The Research Group on Migraine and Headache of the World Federation of Neurology agreed on the following definition of migraine: "Migraine is a familial disorder characterized by recurrent attacks of headache widely variable in intensity, frequency and duration. Attacks are commonly unilateral and are usually associated with anorexia, nausea and vomiting. In some cases they are preceded by, or associated with, neurological and mood disturbances."

All the above characteristics are not necessarily present in each attack or in each patient. Conditions which are generally accepted as falling within the above definition are as follows: **"Classical migraine,"** in which headache is preceded or accompanied by transient focal neurological phenomena, e.g. visual, sensory or speech disturbances.

"Non-classical migraine," which is not associated with sharply defined focal neurological disturbances. This is the more common variety encountered.

Conditions which may fall within the category of migraine were listed by the Research Group on Headache as follows: **"Cluster headache."** Unilateral intense pain involving the eye and head, usually associated with flushing, nasal congestion and lacrimation on the same side, attacks recurring one or more times daily and commonly lasting for 20–120 min. as a general rule. Such bouts continue for weeks or months and are separated by remissions of months or years (synonyms: "Harris' ciliary or migrainous neuralgia", "Horton's histaminic cephalgia").

"Facial migraine." Unilateral episodic facial pain associated with symptoms suggestive either of migraine or of cluster headache (synonym: "lower-half headache").

"Ophthalmoplegic migraine." Episodic migraine-like attacks associated with objective evidence of paresis of the extraocular muscles, usually those supplied by the third nerve, often outlasting the headache. A structural abnormality must be excluded before this diagnosis is made.

"Hemiplegic migraine." A rare condition which may exhibit a dominant inheritance, characterized by episodic migrainous attacks associated with hemiplegia outlasting the headache.

To this list we could add the variation of "vertebro-basilar migraine," described by Bickerstaff, in which brain-stem symptoms, such as vertigo and ataxia are associated with visual disturbance and an increased tendency to faint at the time of the migraine attack. The syndrome is thought to be caused by the constriction of the basilar and posterior cerebral arteries, and the fainting to result from ischaemia of the reticular formation. One is prepared to withdraw "cluster headache" from the migraine syndrome for reasons which are presented later in this chapter. For further clinical details of migraine, the reader is referred to Wolff (1963), Pearce (1969) and Lance (1969).

Migraine, like chronic tension headache, is predominantly a female disorder in adult life athough it affects the sexes fairly equally in childhood. Scandinavian studies have shown that the incidence increases from about 1 per cent at the age of 7 to about 5 per cent at the age of puberty. The incidence continues to increase in females until it may reach 19 per cent during the reproductive years of life. Migraine is an episodic disorder of the vascular system in which some intracranial arteries constrict while others dilate. Extracranial arteries and veins commonly dilate while the arterioles and capillaries of the skin constrict to cause the characteristic pallor during the attack. The classical work of the late H. G. Wolff and his colleagues demonstrated the importance of distension of the scalp arteries in causing the pain of migraine headache. Heyck (1956) showed that the arterio-venous oxygen differences of vessels supplying intracranial and extracranial structures diminished during migraine headache, indicating that blood was shunted away from the periphery, presumably by the opening up of arterio-venous communications. Supporting evidence for this concept has come from recent thermographic studies which have shown that the radiation of heat from the skin is usually less on the side of migraine headache in spite of dilatation of the scalp arteries.[17] Even in headache-free periods thermograms showed that heat loss from the forehead was asymmetrical in 8 out of 15 patients prone to vascular headache, compared with 1 of 15 normal controls. This bears out Wolff's earlier observations that the amplitude of arterial pulsation in the scalp was more variable in migrainous than normal subjects.

The application of radioactive isotope techniques to the study of cerebral blood flow has recently given further information. In the prodromal phase of migraine when neurological symptoms such as visual disturbance and paraesthesiae are commonly present, blood-flow is reduced by up to 50 per cent in the appropriate areas of the brain, even though angiograms do not always show constriction of the large intracranial arteries. In contrast to the prodromal phase, cerebral blood flow is increased during the headache.[20,24]

It is probable that the focal neurological symptoms of migraine do not depend solely upon constriction of small vessels supplying the cerebral cortex but that the "slow march of migrainous symptoms" is associated with some inhibitory process in the cerebral cortex analogous to, or identical with, the "spreading depression" described by Leão in experimental animals when the brain was dehydrated.

The cause of vascular changes of migraine is still not known. There is reason to believe that neural mechanisms are not directly involved and considerable evidence to suggest that humoral agents play a part in the altered calibre of large and small vessels, and in the production of pain from those arteries which become distended. The evidence has been summarized by Lance (1969) and Lance and Anthony (1971c).

Whatever systemic humoral changes may be demonstrated at the time of migraine headache it is still necessary to postulate an hereditary end-organ susceptibility in that the vessels are commonly affected on one side of the head only, and the side affected may alternate from one headache to another. This may be related to observations of Sicuteri (1963) that mast cells were reduced in number and in granulation in biopsy specimens taken at the time of headache. This would be consistent with the findings of Thonnard–Neumann and Taylor (1968) that the number of basophil cells increases in the blood on the side of headache and suggests that the local release of heparin and histamine may be associated with the accumulation of kinins in the vessel wall and possibly with the local action of serotonin in the production of pain from distended arteries during migraine. Such a mechanism could account for the period of freedom experienced by most migrainous patients after a headache, in that sufficient time would have to elapse for mast cells and other metabolic "batteries" to be recharged before another headache could be triggered by some systemic change.

What are the triggers for this local pain-producing system and by what mechanism do they act? Bille (1962) found that the incidence of allergy and epilepsy was no higher in migrainous children than in normal controls, but that the personality of migrainous children was more anxious and sensitive. It has been known for many years that stress or relaxation after stress may induce headache and that hypoglycaemia or the taking of certain foods may precipitate a headache in susceptible persons. Recently, Hanington and her colleagues have shown that the ingestion of tyramine is a specific trigger factor for many patients. Hormonal changes are also relevant since many women experience headache particularly at the time of their menstrual periods and 60 per cent of women lose their migraine during the last six months of pregnancy. Hormonal studies by Somerville (1971a, b) have shown that the levels of progesterone throughout the menstrual cycle were no different in normal and migrainous women, and that headache developed during the falling phase of both progesterone and oestradiol plasma levels, immediately before menstruation. Preliminary studies indicate that the maintenance of an artificially high level of progesterone at this time will not prevent the usual menstrual migraine, but that injections of oestrogen will postpone the migraine headache until the oestrogen level in the blood is allowed to fall. These observations are relevant to the clinical reports of migraine becoming worse in patients taking contraceptive hormonal pills although the mechanism is not yet clarified.

A possible end pathway for all these trigger factors is alteration of the humoral control of cranial vessels, which in turn may initiate the pain producing mechanisms considered earlier. Sicuteri first reported that the main catabolites of serotonin and noradrenaline were often present in increased amounts at the time of migraine headache. This was confirmed by Curran, Hinterberger and Lance who also found that plasma serotonin was low during migraine headache. Anthony, Hinterberger and Lance (1968) summarized this earlier work and added the observations that plasma serotonin fell suddenly to a mean of 40 per cent of its former level, that the fall was caused by some plasma agent which released serotonin from

platelets and not by any change in the character of the platelets, and that the serotonin level returned to normal as the headache subsided. Plasma serotonin did not drop in other forms of headache such as cluster headache or in the headache which follows pneumoencephalography, even when the latter was associated with vomiting. Since serotonin generally constricts large vessels and dilates small ones, it was postulated that a fall in the normal plasma serotonin would permit dilatation of the scalp arteries and constriction of arterioles, which appears to be the situation in migraine. In addition, the liberated serotonin could be adsorbed to the vessel wall and enhance the local action of bradykinin or histamine. Recent studies have shown a slight rise in histamine content of the blood after migraine headache.[1]

That the changes in plasma serotonin play a significant role in the genesis of migraine is suggested by the fact that the injection of reserpine, which releases serotonin and catecholamines from body-stores, will precipitate a headache in migrainous subjects and that reserpine-induced headaches, or spontaneous attacks of migraine, can be ameliorated by the intravenous injection of serotonin.

Carlson, Ekelund and Orö (1968) reported that the intravenous infusion of the prostaglandin PGE_1 into non-migrainous subjects produced visual disturbance and severe unilateral headache. Prostaglandins may play a part in the pathogenesis of spontaneous migraine.

If migraine is a low serotonin syndrome, how does methysergide or any other serotonin "antagonist" prevent migraine? There is good experimental evidence that methysergide simulates the action of serotonin in that it potentiates the effects of vasoconstrictor agents such as norepinephrine and would thereby promote tonic constriction of the scalp arteries in the absence of adequate amounts of the naturally occurring vasoconstrictor, serotonin. A competitive blocking action in the periphery could also diminish any local pain-producing effect of serotonin on the dilated scalp arteries. A drawback to the long-term use of methysergide is the occasional occurrence of pleural, retroperitoneal or myocardial fibrosis[12] but since the introduction of a rest period of one month in every six and the restriction of the dose of methysergide to 6 mg. daily, no further fibrotic complications have been reported. The use of prophylactic agents such as methysergide does not prevent the use of the customary ergotamine tartrate preparations at the onset of migraine attacks. Indeed it renders these preparations more effective. It is of interest that ergotamine also has the property of a "serotonin antagonist". The properties of methysergide, its side-effects, indications and contraindications have been summarized by Curran, Hinterberger and Lance (1967).

Cluster Headache

A brief description of cluster headache has already been given at the beginning of the section on migraine, but the syndrome of cluster headache can be clearly differentiated from migraine on clinical grounds[8,18] and biochemical grounds.[1]

Cluster headache affects males more often than females in the ratio of approximately 6:1. It is extremely rare for the first symptoms to start under the age of 10 years. The pain is more often strictly unilateral than that of migraine, is usually centred on the eye, although radiating upwards or downwards over the head or face, comes on rapidly and passes off after a period of 15 min. to 2 hr, rarely longer. Paroxysms of such pain may recur two or more times each 24 hr for a period of weeks or months then remit for months or years. Each episode is usually accompanied by lacrimation and blockage of the nostril on the affected side and in about one-third of the patients a partial Horner's syndrome may be observed, presumably caused by compression of the pericarotid sympathetic plexus due to distension of the wall of the internal carotid artery. Narrowing of the lumen of the intracranial portion of the intracarotid artery just proximal to the carotid siphon has been demonstrated by angiography during cluster headache.[9] A "cold spot" was observed over one eye in 2 out of 5 patients studied by thermography in the early phase of cluster headache,[17] which would be consistent with diminished flow in the internal carotid artery, which supplies this area of the forehead through the terminal branches of the ophthalmic artery. In the latter part of cluster headache, the cold spot disappeared and skin temperature over the temple and forehead usually became warmer than the unaffected side. Broch *et al.* (1970) found that blood-flow in the internal carotid artery remained constant in 3 patients during cluster headache, but this does not alter the significance of the local changes observed in some patients by angiography and thermography. These changes, and the retro-orbital pain experienced in cluster headache, suggest that oedema of the wall of the internal carotid artery may be responsible for part of the syndrome while dilatation of the extracranial arteries usually adds an additional component of pain, the mechanism of which is more closely allied to that of migraine.

Kunkle (1959) demonstrated an acetylcholine effect in the cerebrospinal fluid of 4 out of 14 patients with cluster headache which was not present in 7 patients with typical migraine. Recently Anthony and Lance (1971) found that plasma histamine was significantly increased during cluster headache, thus reviving Horton's concept that the condition is a histaminic cephalgia. It is of interest that plasma serotonin does not drop in cluster headache as it does in migraine.

It can be seen that the only feature in common between migraine and cluster headache is dilatation of the extracranial arteries and this does not seem sufficient justification for retention of the misleading term "migrainous neuralgia". In support of this contention, a family history of migraine was found by Ekbom (1970) in only 16 per cent of his patients with cluster headache compared with 65 per cent of his migrainous patients. In spite of this culling of cluster headache from the migrainous fold, the only satisfactory treatment of cluster headache known at the moment is the prophylactic use of ergotamine tartrate and methysergide during each bout to prevent dilatation of the extracranial arteries.

CONCLUSIONS

Much more could have been said about each variety of headache in this brief review. Psychological aspects of headache have been barely mentioned and the purely psychogenic headache of some psychotic states has been entirely omitted. The review has concentrated on the development of thought about the pathogenesis of headache with emphasis on recent work concerning some of the humoral mechanisms involved. References have been limited to those which provide evidence for controversial statements or which contain a full bibliography to assist in further reading. It is probable that ideas on the pathophysiology of headache will alter as much in the next ten years as they have in the past ten years.

FURTHER READING

[1] Anthony, M. and Lance, J. W. (1971), *Histamine and Serotonin in Cluster Headache. Arch. Neurol.,* **25**, 225–231.

[2] Anthony, M., Hinterberger, H. and Lance, J. W. (1968), "The Possible Relationship of Serotonin to the Migraine Syndrome," in *Res. clin. Stud. Headache,* **2**, 29–59 (A. P. Friedman, Ed.). Basel/New York: Karger.

[3] Bille, B. (1962), "Migraine in School Children," *Acta paed.,* **51,** *suppl.* 136, 1–151.

[4] Brewis, M., Poskanzer, D. C., Rolland, C. and Miller, H. (1966), "Neurological Disease in an English City," *Acta neurol.* (*Scand.*), **42,** *Suppl.* 24, 9–89.

[5] Broch, A., Hørven, I., Nornes, H., Sjaastad, O. and Tønjum, A. (1970), "Studies on Cerebral and Ocular Circulation in a Patient with Cluster Headache," *Headache,* **10,** 1–8.

[5a] Carlson, L. A., Ekelund, L.-G. and Orö, L. (1968), "Clinical and Metabolic Effects of Different Doses of Prostaglandins in Man," *Acta Med. Scand.,* **183,** 423–430.

[6] Curran, D. A., Hinterberger, H. and Lance, J. W. (1967), "Methysergide," in *Res. clin. Stud. Headache,* **1,** 74–122 (A. P. Friedman, Ed.). Basel/New York: Karger.

[7] Denny Brown, D. and Yanagisawa (1970), "The Descending Trigeminal Tract as a Mechanism for Intersegmental Sensory Facilitation," *Trans. Amer. neurol. Ass.* In press.

[8] Ekbom, K. (1970), "A Clinical Comparison of Cluster Headache and Migraine," *Acta neurol.* (*Scand.*), **46** *Suppl.* 41, 1–48.

[9] Ekbom, K. and Greitz, T. (1970), "Carotid Angiography in Cluster Headache," *Acta Radiol.* (*Diagn.*), **10,** 1–10.

[10] Every, R. G. (1960), "The Significance of Extreme Mandibular Movements," *Lancet,* **2,** 37–39.

[11] Friedman, A. P., Von Storch, T. J. C. and Merritt, H. H. (1954), "Migraine and Tension Headaches. A Clinical Study of Two Thousand Cases," *Neurology,* **4,** 773–788.

[12] Graham, J. R. (1967), "Cardiac and Pulmonary Fibrosis during Methysergide Therapy for Headache," *Amer. J. med. sci.,* **254,** 23–32.

[13] Heyck, H. (1956), *Neue Beiträge zur Klinik und Pathogenese der Migräne.* Stuttgart: Verlag.

[14] Kerr, F. W. L. (1961), "Trigeminal and Cervical Volleys," (1961), *Arch. Neurol.,* **5,** 171–178.

[15] Kunkle, E. C. (1959), "Acetylcholine in the Mechanism of Headaches of the Migraine Type," *Arch. Neurol. Psychiat.* (*Chicago*), **81,** 135–141.

[16] Lance, J. W. (1969), *The Mechanism and Management of Headache.* London: Butterworths.

[17] Lance, J. W. and Anthony, M. (1971a), "Thermographic Studies in Vascular Headache," *Med. J. Aust.* **1,** 240–243.

[18] Lance, J. W. and Anthony, M. (1971b), "Migrainous Neuralgia or Cluster Headache?" *J. Neurol. Sci.,* **13,** 401–414.

[19] Lance, J. W. and Anthony, M. (1971c), "The cephalgias," in *The Cellular and Molecular Basis of Neurologic Disease* (S. H. Appel and E. S. Goldensohn, Eds.). Philadelphia: Lea and Febiger. In press.

[20] O'Brien, M. D. (1970), "Cerebral Cortex Perfusion Rates Measured in Carotid Artery Distribution in the Migraine Syndrome," in *Kliniske aspekter i migraeneforskningen*, pp. 40–42. Copenhagen: Nordlundes Bogtrykkeri.

[21] Onel, Y., Friedman, A. P. and Grossman, J. (1961), "Muscle Blood Flow Studies in Muscle-contraction Headaches," *Neurology*, **11**, 935–939.

[22] Pearce, J. (1969), *Migraine. Clinical Features, Mechanisms and Management*. Springfield: Thomas.

[23] Rabinowicz, I. M., Ben-Sira, I. and Zauberman, H. (1968), "Preservation of Visual Function in Papilloedema," *Brit. J. Ophthal.*, **52**, 236–241.

[24] Skinhøj, E. (1970), "Determination of Regional Cerebral Blood Flow Within the Internal Carotid System During the Migraine Attack", in *Kliniske aspekter i migraeneforskningen*, pp. 43–50. Copenhagen: Nordlundes Bogtrykkeri.

[25] Sicuteri, F. (1963), "Mast Cells and their Active Substances. Their Role in the Pathogenesis of Migraine," *Headache*, **3**, 86–92.

[26] Somerville, B. (1971a), "The Role of Progestogen in Menstrual Migraine," *Neurology*, **21**, 853–859.

[26a] Somerville, B. (1971b), "The Role of Estradiol Withdrawal in the Etiology of Menstrual Migraine," *Neurology*. In press.

[27] Thonnard-Neumann, E. and Taylor, W. L. (1968), "The Basophilic Leukocyte and Migraine," *Headache*, **8**, 98–107.

[28] Wolff, H. G. (1963), *Headache and Other Head Pain*. New York: Oxford University Press.

9. DRUG TREATMENT OF PAIN

JOHN W. DUNDEE

This is essentially a survey of opiates, tranquillizers and similar drugs used in pain relief, rather than a review of local anaesthetics and neurolytics which can be used to interrupt pain-carrying fibres. The principles applying to effective analgesic therapy will be discussed more than the clinical pharmacology of individual drugs. However, to put the use of analgesics in its true perspective, one must compare their effect with that of division of nerve fibres or tracts (Table 1).

TABLE 1

SOME DIFFERENCES BETWEEN THE EFFECTS OF SECTION OF PAIN-CARRYING FIBRES AND THOSE OF ADMINISTRATION OF POTENT ANALGESICS

	Nerve block or section	Analgesics-Sedatives
Pain relief	Complete	Usually only partial Acute pain unaffected
Systemic side-effects	Few	Often marked
Local effects	May be troublesome	Nil
Ease of therapy	Requires skill; effective block may be impossible	Requires patience and attention to detail
General applicability	Limited	Widespread

Ideally one should be able to abolish all pain sensation by blocking transmission in the appropriate nerve and furthermore this may be achieved without the unpleasant side-effects which are frequently associated with analgesic therapy. However, the pathological factors which are the cause of pain, such as tumours or scar tissue, often make nerve-blocks difficult or impossible and a return of pain is not unknown after a "successful" cordotomy. Damage to sensory and autonomic pathways is also common after nerve-blocks and one can easily convert an ambulant patient into a bed-ridden incontinent cripple. Under these circumstances the concomitant pain-relief is not always appreciated. Thus, for a variety of reasons there is a place for potent analgesic drugs in the relief of intractable pain and for many people these are the only feasible form of therapy.

In contrast to interruption of nerve-fibres, tolerated doses of the available potent analgesic drugs are not usually effective against severe spasms of pain. They will control the background pain which is constant in many patients with cancer, but they are not powerful enough to relieve the sharp pain which may occur in the absence of movement and often awaken the patient from a drug-induced sleep.

It is generally agreed that there are two components of pain, (i) the original sensation and (ii) the reaction to this sensation, and the relative importance of these will vary in different situations. The patient's psychological reaction is often related to the significance of pain to him. A good example of this is the pain of battle casualties[2] to whom a wound often meant a passage home. The actual pain-stimulus here may be greater than that occurring with cancer where there is the overlying fear of the eventual outcome and its effect on friends and dependants. This is mentioned to show that the pain-experience can be mitigated by drugs, such as tranquillizers, which are not true analgesics. In fact it is often said that the main action of morphine is on the reaction to pain and this may explain why Morrison (1970) showed that it did not raise the threshold to experimentally produced somatic pain in man.

Principles of Use of Analgesics

In the management of pain, probably more than in any other branch of medicine, one has to adjust the nature of the drug, dosage, frequency of administration and several other factors to the needs of the individual patient. This requires time and patience and above all an interest in the whole patient and not only in his pain. One appreciates this on reading of the excellent results obtained at special centres such as the work of Dr. Cicely Saunders (1963, 1966, 1967). However, there are certain principles which one can follow and which help in obtaining the best treatment for any individual patient:

(1) If at all possible do not use potent opiate narcotics as the first analgesics. When faced with cancer pain one is inclined to forget that there are good non-addictive analgesics which may make the patient comfortable for some time and only too often at Pain Clinics one sees a patient with early pain of malignancy who has already become tolerant to the only drugs which can eventually offer effective pain relief. It is obvious that with pain of non-malignant origin, the value of milder analgesics should be explored to its limit.

(2) The oral route of administration should be used where possible, particularly in non-hospitalized patients. This is not only more pleasant for the patient but it gives them, at home, a much needed feeling of independence from their attendants, although on occasions patients may be inclined to make "martyrs" of themselves and may feel that too large doses of analgesics are not good for them. Even when oral analgesics do not give adequate pain-relief they can be given between intramuscular injections and the combination of a potent narcotic given by injection and a milder oral analgesic between injections has much to recommend it.

(3) Timing of dosage. It is well known that it is easier to prevent pain returning than to relieve it. Where possible one dose of analgesic should be given within the expected duration of the next dose, particularly early on in the treatment so that patients do not lose confidence in their attendants. One might expect this to lead to an early increase in tolerance to the potent analgesic but experience has not shown this to happen.

(4) Avoid supra-optimal dosage of analgesics. As has been found in postoperative pain[8] there is for each individual patient a dose of opiates above which the increasing pain-relief component is more than outweighed by the side-effects produced. The patient is interested in general comfort rather than specific pain-relief and may, in fact, feel worse because of the side-effects from supra-optimal dosage. Furthermore, the use of unnecessarily large dosage leads to early development of tolerance.

(5) Mention has already been made of avoiding tolerance to potent opiates by keeping dosage down to the minimum required to give adequate pain-relief and also paying attention to the frequency of their administration. One should always make sure that an increasing dose of opiate is actually required rather than a drug to treat some other symptom of the patient's disease-process such as anti-tussive linctus or even a simple deodorant.

Full use should always be made of non-opiate adjuvants which may help to increase the general well-being of the patient. These can be tranquillizers such as diazepam or chlorpromazine which may, in fact, potentiate the action of the analgesic. The beneficial effects of amphetamines as adjuvants to analgesic therapy should not be forgotten. Suitable doses of these increase the patient's well-being and there is some evidence to suggest that they do potentiate opiates.[5,6] Parasympathetic agents such as neostigmine are also of some value in potentiating analgesics.[1,11]

(6) The use of potent opiates should not be abandoned because of side-effects without trying to treat these specifically. While there are some drugs which suit some patients better than others, one occasionally is faced with the problem of uncontrollable vomiting, intractable constipation or intolerable dryness of the mouth from effective doses of any analgesic.

(a) Nausea and vomiting are common at the beginning of analgesic therapy and usually pass off with time if the patient is asked to lie down for a short time after taking the drug. No other treatment may be necessary but where emetic effects persist a phenothiazine may be administered, or ambulant patients may be given less toxic drugs such as cyclizine. One must not forget that the anti-emetics themselves cause side-effects and one has come across patients on opiate therapy whose main problem has been oculogyric crises due to fluphenazine or perphenazine. On the whole it is more difficult to treat nausea and the resulting anorexia than actual vomiting.

(b) Dizziness. This has been related to nausea and may be affected by posture.

(c) The soporific effects of an analgesic may be desirable at the beginning of therapy and they usually pass off with time. However, the amphetamines may be valuable when this is a problem.

(d) Constipation. This is one side-effect of opiates to which tolerance does not appear to develop. It is less troublesome with the piperidine (pethidine-like) group and can be relieved by senna compounds.

(e) Dry mouth. This is a very persistent side-effect which is made worse by the concomitant use of phenothiazines but which can be relieved to some extent by neostigmine.

(f) Addiction. Both mental and physical dependence can occur but should not contra-indicate the use of opiates in terminal malignancy. This constitutes a much smaller problem than tolerance.

One can give no guidance as regards which dose of analgesic will give the patient most complete relief but if one remembers Dr. Cicely Saunders' excellent statement "the art of giving analgesics is to keep them continually on the patient's own optimum dose" then the best interests of the patient will certainly be guarded. One should never hesitate to try a number of analgesics to find which one is best.

Available Potent Analgesics

One cannot possibly review all of these in a chapter of this size but Table 2 gives useful information. Most people are agreed that it is better to get used to a small number of compounds and know their use and limitations. For oral administration one has levorphanol and methadone. For mild pain dihydrocodeine has much to recommend it. There is very little one can say to support the widespread popularity of papaveretum which is really no better than the equivalent dose of morphine but either of these drugs or diamorphine are those most commonly used for injection.

Pethidine has its advocates and has the advantage of not causing as much constipation on long term use as the other potent opiates, but it can cause a high incidence of side-effects. Like diamorphine it has an earlier onset of action and shorter duration of action than morphine.[3,4]

night before operation, resulting from noise in the ward will also lower the pain-threshold to a marked degree. Post-operative pain may be associated with restlessness and disorientation, particularly in old people, and with general physical exhaustion due to worry and lack of sleep. The presence of intragastric tubes or intravenous infusions and the occurrence of intestinal atony, flatulence

TABLE 2

POTENT ANALGESICS (ESTABLISHED DRUGS IN CAPITALS)

Generic name and classification according to origin	Potency (relative to Morphine)	Dose range (average adult) (mg.)	Duration (approximate in hours)	Comments
NATURAL ALKALOIDS OF OPIUM				
MORPHINE	100	8–16	4–6	
CODEINE	8–15	30–60	3–4	Very weak analgesic
PAPAVERETUM	—	—	—	Regard 20 mg. as equivalent to 13 mg morphine sulphate
SEMI-SYNTHETIC OPIUM ALKALOIDS				
DIHYDROCODEINE	30	30–60	—	Good oral absorption: Mild analgesic, Constipating
DIAMORPHINE	200–300	4–8	2	Indicated in terminal malignancy
DIHYDROCODEINONE	70			
DIHYDROMORPHINONE	200–500	1–2	2–4	
Oxymorphone	500–1,000	1–3	4–6	Probably as toxic as morphine
SYNTHETIC COMPOUNDS				
Morphinans and Benzmorphinans				
LEVORPHANOL	330–500	2–4	4–6	Good oral absorption
PHENAZOCINE	500	2–4	4–6	Probably as toxic as morphine
PENTAZOCINE	50	20–40	2–4	Antagonist used as analgesic
Piperidine Derivatives				
PETHIDINE	10	75–125	2–3	Disappointing. High toxicity
Anileridine	25	30–60	2–3	Good oral absorption
Alphaprodine	25	30–50	1–2	Very short acting
PHENOPERIDINE				Too potent and toxic for routine clinical use
Diphenylheptane Derivatives				
METHADONE	100–130	5–15	6–8	Good oral absorption
Dipipanone	40	10–25	5–6	Diconal = dipipanone + cyclizine
Dextromoramide	200	5–8	2–3	Probably as toxic as morphine
DEXTROPROXYPHENE				Usually given in a mixture with mild analgesics such as Distalgesic

Mention should be made of pentazocine, an allyl-opiate which has undoubtedly less addiction potential than morphine and whose use deserves full exploration in long term treatment where there is no malignancy. One hopes that there may be similar compounds available in the next few years.

Post-operative Pain

This is quite different from chronic pain[9,15] and on account of its intensity and brevity, treatment has to be different. First of all it must be appreciated that the severity of the pain varies with the nature of the operation but within any group of patients there is a great individual variation, some patients requiring large doses of analgesics after a minor operation and others requiring nothing after a very major procedure. Unless the likelihood of severe post-operative pain is explained to the patient before operation, its occurrence may come as a surprise and the reaction to it will be exaggerated. A sleepless

and abdominal distension may cause more discomfort to the patient than the actual pain of the wound.

While complete relief of post-operative pain is best achieved by extradural injection of local anaesthetics this may lead to hypotension. The exacting nature of the technique, necessity for scrupulous asepsis and the large number of injections required make it unsuitable for routine use.

The natural or synthetic opiates are still the standby for the majority of patients and little can be said here as regards choice of drug. Despite many enthusiastic claims for new compounds, Keats (1956) found that equivalent degrees of analgesia were accompanied by the same amount of respiratory depression and the same incidence of nausea and vomiting. Drowsiness after the opiates can be combated by the concomitant use of amiphenazole or tacrine, but in the case of the latter drug, although patients are more alert, they are no better off in other ways.

Parenteral injection of local anaesthetics is often of

value as a short term procedure and the continuous intravenous injection of a dilute (0·05 per cent) solution of lignocaine can be used, but it also requires constant supervision. Single (or even repeated) intramuscular doses of 5 mg./kg. can sometimes produce dramatic results with little respiratory depression, but lignocaine causes an appreciable—and often useful—degree of drowsiness. Various local nerve-blocks have been employed without much success and hypnotism has also been used.

The most hopeful of the recent advances in this field is the use of 25 per cent concentrations of nitrous oxide in oxygen[12] which produced a greater improvement in vital capacity than 10 mg. morphine. The combined use of morphine and nitrous oxide gave better results than either agent alone. With the introduction of cylinders of pre-mixed gases, the use of 25 per cent nitrous oxide in oxygen may find a permanent place as an adjuvant to physiotherapy or even for prolonged use after abdominal or thoracic operations. The high oxygen content of this mixture would counteract any tendency to post-operative hypoxia.

REFERENCES

[1] Abaza, A. and Gregoire, M. (1952), "Potentiation of Analgesic Effect of Opiates by Combination with Prostigmine," *Presse méd.*, **60**, 331.
[2] Beecher, H. K. (1946), "Pain in Men Wounded in Battle," *Ann. Surg.*, **123**, 96–105.
[3] Dundee, J. W., Clarke, R. S. J. and Loan, W. B. (1965), "A Comparison of the Sedative and Toxic Effects of Morphine-pethidine," *Lancet*, **2**, 1262.
[4] Dundee, J. W., Clarke, R. S. J. and Loan, W. B. (1967), "Comparative Toxicity of Diamorphine, Morphine and Methadone," *Lancet*, **1**, 221–223.
[5] Goetzl, F. R., Burrill, D. Y. and Ivy, A. C. (1944), "The Analgesic Effect of Morphine Alone and in Combination with Dextro-amphetamine," *Proc. Soc. exp. Biol. (N.Y.)*, **55**, 248.
[6] Ivy, A. C., Goetzl, F. R., Harris, S. C. and Burrill, D. Y. (1944), "The Analgesic Effect of Intracarotid and Intravenous Injection of Epinephrine in Dogs and of Subcutaneous Injection in Man," *Quart. Bull. Northw. Univ. med. Sch.*, **18**, 298.
[7] Keats, A. S. (1956), "Postoperative Pain: Research and Treatment," *J. chron. Dis.*, **4**, 72.
[8] Lasagna, L. and Beecher, H. K. (1954), "The Optimal Dose of Morphine," *J. Amer. med. Ass.*, **156**, 230–234.
[9] Loan, W. B. and Morrison, J. D. (1967), "The Incidence and Severity of Postoperative Pain," *Brit. J. Anaesth.*, **39**, 695–698.
[10] Morrison, J. D. (1970), "Alterations in Response to Somatic Pain Associated with Anaesthesia. XIX: Studies with the Drugs used in Neuroleptanaesthesia," *Brit. J. Anaesth.*, **42**, 838–848.
[11] Oehlandt, G. (1955), "Clinical Observations on the Increased and more Prolonged Action of Dromoran when Combined with Mestinon," *Med. Klin.*, **50**, 2022.
[12] Parbrook, G. D., Rees, G. A. D. and Robertson, G. S. (1964), "Relief of Postoperative Pain: Comparison of a 25 per cent Nitrous Oxide and Oxygen Mixture with Morphine," *Brit. med. J.*, **2**, 480–482.
[13] Saunders, C. (1963), "The Treatment of Intractable Pain in Terminal Cancer," *Proc. roy. Soc. Med.*, **56**, 195–197.
[14] Saunders, C. (1966–67), "The Management of Terminal Illness (1), (2), (3)," *Hosp. Med.*, **1**, 225–228, 317–320, 433–436.
[15] Simpson, B. R. J. and Parkhouse, J. (1961), "The Problem of Postoperative Pain," *Brit. J. Anaesth.*, **33**, 336–344.

FURTHER READING

Beecher, H. K. (1957), "The Measurement of Pain," *Pharmacol. Rev.*, **9**, 59–268.
Beecher, H. K. (1959), *Measurement of Subjective Responses.* New York: Oxford University Press.
Bonica, J. J. (1953), *The Management of Pain.* London: Henry Kimpton.
Dundee, J. W. (1967), Chapter entitled "Pain" in *Scientific Foundations of Surgery.* (C. Wells and J. Kyle, Eds.). London: William Heinemann Medical Books Ltd.
Foldes, F. F., Swerdlow, M. and Siker, E. S. (1964), *Narcotics and Narcotic antagonists.* Springfield: Thomas.
Keele, C. A. and Smith, R. (Eds.) (1961), *The Assessment of Pain in Man and Animals.* Edinburgh: Livingstone.
Lasagna, L. (1964), "The Clinical Evaluation of Morphine and its Substitutes as Analgesics," *Pharmacol. Rev.*, **16**, 47.
Loan, W. B., Morrison, J. D. and Dundee, J. W. (1968), "Evaluation of a Method for Assessing Potent Analgesics," *Clin. Pharmacol. Ther.*, **9**, 765–776.
Morley, J. (1931), *Abdominal Pain.* Edinburgh: Livingstone.
Murphree, H. B. (1962), "Clinical Pharmacology of Potent Analgesics," *Clin. Pharmacol. Ther.*, **3**, 473–504.
Penman, J. (1954), "Pain as an Old Friend," *Lancet*, **1**, 633.
Vandam, L. D. (1962), "Clinical Pharmacology of the Narcotic Analgesics," *Clin. Pharmacol. Ther.*, **3**, 827–38.

1. THE NEUROPHYSIOLOGICAL APPROACH TO THE PROBLEM OF CONSCIOUSNESS

F. M. R. WALSHE

"The human physiologist, at least, must be interested in the nature of the brain–mind relationship. What he does not have to do is to claim the problem as wholly within his own field of science, and to put himself forward with his experimental techniques as the sole expositor, competent to discuss more general views in terms of scientific disciplines that are not his own; namely, those of physics, chemistry and mathematics. Physical scientists are, in general, not so bold."

(H. M. Pirenne, *Brit. J. Phil. Sci.*, 1950)

"Our common meeting ground is the faith to which we all subscribe, I believe, that the phenomena of behavior and mind are ultimately describable in the concepts of the mathematical and physical sciences."

(K. Lashley, *The Hixon Symposium*, 1951)

Hypotheses on the genesis, nature and flux of conscious states are numerous and diverse. They derive from philosophy, logic, psychology, neurophysiology and recently from cybernetics and communication theory. The abstract term "consciousness" commonly used in expositions of the subject embraces a many-sided problem. Hence we meet wide disparities of opinion, unreconciled and in some instances irreconcilable, not to mention the internal inconsistencies of ideas and terminology to be found in particular hypotheses. It is suggested that the time has come for a fresh and critical look at a subject that seems not to fit comfortably in the Procrustean bed of neurophysiology. The present approach is primarily concerned with the current neurophysiological hypotheses on conscious states, and meets at once the paradox that most neurophysiologists at the present time hold and pronounce that these states in their origin and nature obey the laws of physics, chemistry and mathematics, and are explicable in terms of these laws, if not yet demonstrably, ultimately to be so. Lashley's confession of faith, quoted at the head of this account, makes this clear, and at the symposium at which he made it, none of the participants dissented from it, or felt called upon to discuss so bold an affirmation.

There are, of course, two separate tenets here; that they obey these laws and are explicable in terms of them. The second one is indeed far-reaching, and is implicit in the currently dominating views of mechanistic and reductionist physiology, although physical scientists do not hold that sentience, or consciousness, is a property of chemical substances or processes.

Another remarkable feature of neurophysiological explanations of consciousness and integration is that they do not have clear and consistent references for the terms in question, and wide variations in the use of the words "consciousness" and "mind" characterize the abundant literature on these subjects. The several major symposia of recent years have tolerated this semantic chaos which, born of erroneous conceptual thinking, perpetuates its growth. The past half-century has seen an increasingly mechanistic trend in experimental neurophysiology, which

has become an abstraction from the sum of the biochemical and metabolic processes in the nervous system without which neurons would not function. For a generation it has been greatly preoccupied with electronic recording techniques and their widening application.

These have proved of great value, but have tended to channel thought too exclusively into biophysics and have not been appreciably useful in illuminating the wider problem of consciousness and the brain–mind relationship.

It is with these issues that we shall be here concerned, and as a preliminary it may be useful to point out that while we speak of consciousness and integration, what we encounter in nature are conscious states and integrative processes and not abstractions.

Unfortunately, ever since the brain has been regarded as the organ of mind, we have developed a tradition of hypostatizing our abstractions and thereupon of "localizing" them in various restricted regions of the brain, regarding them as things *in rebus naturae*, and speaking of them as "seats" of consciousness and integration. When, at the beginning of the century, Sherrington wrote his classic, *The Integrative Action of the Nervous System*, he named an essential property of the entire system, and formulated his problem in terms of events and activities rather than of abstract entities. It has proved unfortunate that his example has not been followed more closely. Defects of conceptual thinking inevitably flow from the misuse of abstractions. Had we kept in mind the idea of process more consistently, and this, after all, is a prime business of physiology, we would not have treated the problem of the genesis of conscious states from unconscious nerve impulses so casually, or be so prone to "localize" the abstraction "integration" to the degree revealed by the relevant literature: e.g. in the Laurentian Symposium on *Brain Mechanisms and Consciousness* (1954).

In this, biophysics dominated the proceedings, with few exceptions, and used a stilted terminology on conscious states: e.g. "cerebral alertness", "vigilance", "arousal", "the human state awake" etc.: all taken from the language of common usage, and not from that of science. If we consider these terms, nothing more precise can be derived from them than the notion of a low threshold of excitability in the relevant neuronal systems, or that figment, a conscious state with no specifiable content. This is a gravely inadequate equipment with which to embark upon the analysis of conscious states.

Yet in the symposium few went any deeper. Adrian is quoted as asking significantly "who reads the patterns of nerve impulses"? No answer came. Kubie reminded the participants that we must be conscious "of something", while Bremer, declaring that integration is a dynamic abstraction not localizable in space added:

> "At present we are completely unable to explain consciousness in neurophysiological terms . . . when a tune is perceived by the auditory organ it must have, as Adrian has suggested, a topographical organization in space which someone must interpret. But who is this someone? After all, this is the problem of perceptual consciousness." (p. 501, loc. cit.)

It might have been expected that two so challenging pronouncements from such an authority would have evoked an eager and informative discussion on so central a topic, one widening the selective viewpoint of neurophysiology. But the waters of debate were not stirred from their electronic preoccupations. No one was moved to enquire about the identity of the "who" or "we" that translate the busy subconscious patterns of nerve impulses into conscious states, or about how this remarkable and unspecified transformation takes place. The "someone", of whom Bremer spoke, found no further mention. Indeed, he was later to be described by Lashley (1958) as "an unnecessary postulate".

The earlier Hixon symposium on *Cerebral Mechanisms and Behavior* (1951), though its participants included a number of Professors of Psychology, was not less mechanistically oriented in the views expressed. Electronics and cybernetics predominated while the phenomenology of conscious states was barely noticed. Indeed, Lashley's first interest, psychology, so strongly urged by him in 1930, (*vide infra*) as the fundamental science in which to discuss the present subject, had lost favour with him over the lapse of years. It seems clear, therefore, that the problems surrounding the study of conscious states are wider than the scope of neurophysiological enquiry as we find it today. There is a sense in which this may also be the, perhaps unrecognized, feeling of neurophysiologists that finds expression in their growing urge to invoke the physical sciences for a solution of this problem, while at the same time rejecting any infusion of philosophic notions. Even today the latter tendency persists and where in their days Jackson and, later, Sherrington, failed to interest their fellow neurophysiologists in a philosophy of science, a like disregard is the probable response today to any renewed endeavour to draw attention to the need for it. Nevertheless, it would be pusillanimous to remain content with the present confused state of knowledge and opinion which offers no significant prospect of growing agreement, or of advance. "Philosophy", "Metaphysics", are terms that embody ideas not attractive to neurophysiologists, though one of Whitehead's definitions should calm the dread these words inspire. "By metaphysics I mean the science which seeks to discover the general ideas which are indispensably relevant to the analysis of everything that happens."

No scientific discipline can claim exemption from the cultivation of general ideas and still retain its claim to the status of a science.

THE LOCALIZATION OF FUNCTION, OR THE ANATOMIZING OF ABSTRACTIONS?

From ancient times philosophers and physicians have sought to find a local habitation for the mind, and ultimately the brain became the favoured organ and thenceforward the search for a regional seat for it began to preoccupy scientists. In the eighteenth century Prochaska chose the basal region of the brain and named it the *sensorium commune*. In the following century Johannes Müller endorsed both the region and the name, while in England W. B. Carpenter (1853) localized consciousness in what he called the "automatic apparatus", which consisted of the olfactory and gustatory nuclei, the corpora quadrigemina and the thalamus.

In the 1860s, the papers of Hughlings Jackson began to be published and for the first time—if only for the time being—the reifying and anatomizing of abstract notions was challenged. "There is no such thing as consciousness," he averred, "in health we are from moment to moment differently conscious." At greater length, he declared:

> "We spoke of the substrata of consciousness as being the highest nervous arrangements. Yet to avoid misinterpretation we pointed out explicitly that we do not really suppose there to be one fixed seat of consciousness. . . . Consciousness arises during activity of some of our highest nervous arrangements by which correspondence of the organism with its environment is being affected. Our present consciousness is our now mental state. It is such or such according to the correspondence now being effected. As this consciousness is constantly changing, the nervous arrangements are continually different." (1931).

Years later, Jackson commented that he had never seen his views on this subject referred to; an example of the perennial difficulty in science in gaining acceptance of *a new way* of looking at things even when old ways have become an obstacle to advance. In this instance even a century has not yet wholly sufficed. However, some role as a substratum in conscious states has been allowed to the cerebral cortex, though its primacy of importance is still subject to recurrent challenge.

Jackson's view on the brain–mind relationship made little impact upon his successors, and we are still postulating "seats" of consciousness and of integration: e.g. in Penfield's "centrencephalic" system:

> "The seat of consciousness is that portion of the nervous system in which circumscribed injury or

functional inactivation produces loss of consciousness. On the basis of our present information this would place the seat of consciousness somewhere in the higher brainstem."

(*Penfield, IVth Internat. Cong. Neurol.*, 1949, **3**, 425.)

Comparable attributions have been made in respect of Magoun's reticular activating system in the higher brainstem, on the dubious hypothesis that if a function is lost upon ablation of a restricted brain region, that region must be regarded as the "seat" of the lost function, whereas in fact we can say no more than that we have localized *a symptom of a lesion*. In what Bridgman has called "the operational view" of experimental procedures (1951) he points out that an experiment provides a primary datum for logical study in which the nature of the procedure as well as that of the result must be taken into account in any interpretation of the experiment. Thus, an abnormal stimulus (Sherrington's "inadequate stimulus") will evoke a physiologically abnormal response or none. Until—and even since—Sherrington and Leyton's series of cerebral cortical stimulations there have been as many theories of the cortical control of movements and theories of representation as there have been experiments and experimentalists, owing to omissions to observe this operational view. (cf. Walshe, 1951.) Some experiments recorded by Adametz and O'Leary (1959, 1960) reveal the relevance of it to the problem of consciousness. It had been found that acutely produced ablations within the reticular system of Magoun result in permanent unconsciousness in the surviving animal, but such lesions produced slowly (ingravescent lesions) resulted in a temporary unconsciousness only, showing a phenomenon familiar to clinical neurologists: that the disturbance of function produced by a destructive lesion may vary widely in depth according to the momentum of the lesion, as well as to its site. (cf. W. Riese, 1950.)

Thus, conscious states must surely escape some of the more absurd topographical dispositions imposed upon them. Indeed, it is not easy to believe that anything less than the total resourceful living organism can be the true "seat" of consciousness, however shocking the neurophysiologist may find this proposition.

Recently, Stallknecht has raised this question (1969), thus:

"Consciousness, and with consciousness the individual selfhood that characterizes its higher development, cannot be identified or located in the spatial layout of an organism as it exists at any moment of observation. In this Leibnitz was right. If the human brain and nervous system were expanded in size to equal that of a mill or factory and we were allowed to walk within it, we would observe nothing but moving parts, of one kind or another, in their intricate relationship. We would not come face to face with feelings, perceptions and ideas."

There can be no activity of the nervous system—or to use the crude current term—no "product of brain"—less amenable to topographical exercises in "localization"

than the physiological substrata of "mind" and conscious states. Lashley's unrewarded search for the "engram" has been a lesson unregarded by us.

The principle of localization of function within the nervous system has a wide range of valid applications, but the localization of *ideas*, such as the concepts of consciousness and integration, is not one of them. For example, the somatotopic plan of the disposition of the afferent sensory paths on the cortex is a useful example, but the attempt to treat the so-called motor or excitable cortex in this way was a grave disaster, for it engendered the fiction of the fixed "cortical mosaic", which, when reinforced by the largely illusory cytoarchitectonics of the Vogts and others, proved for years a grave obstacle to the recognition of the "lability" of that cortical region and the measure of equipotentiality it shows. Even at this date, that too little known work, *The Principles of Neurology*, of Walther Riese (1950) contains the most comprehensive statement of the general principles of the localization of function in the nervous system that we have. It contains much that is lacking in the literature of academic experimental neurophysiology.

CONSCIOUS STATES AND NEURONAL ACTIVITY: "THE GHOST IN THE MACHINE" AND "THE MACHINE IN THE GHOST"

"The hope of understanding all aspects of intellectual life on the principles of classical physics is no more justified than the hopes of the traveller who believes he will have obtained the answer to all problems once he has journeyed to the end of the world."

W. Heisenberg, *Philosophic Problems of Nuclear Science* (1952).

Consciousness and the brain–mind relationship are generally held by neurophysiologists to be within the purview of their discipline. This is taken for granted rather than argued from defined and generally agreed premises. Thus we read of the "electrogenesis of consciousness" as if this were a comprehensive all-embracing account of the mode of genesis of conscious states, established beyond dispute. Yet it is nothing of the sort, for as Bremer has reminded us, we have no neurological explanation of consciousness. A still larger assumption is the view that conscious states are ultimately to be revealed as explicable in the concepts of the mathematical and physical sciences, as claimed by Lashley to be the accepted view of neurophysiologists. However, these affirmations, and at the present time they are nothing more, have a verbal advantage as they appear to leap the conceptual gap between the unconscious patterns of nerve impulses within the nervous system and our conscious states, allowing us to overlook the fact that one exists.

Here we come to the "mechanistic" and to the naïve "reductionist" views of the genesis and nature of conscious states. At this point, the human physiologist begins to notice that *homo sapiens* is fading from the scene, and that Ryle's "ghost in the machine" is being replaced by "the machine in the ghost". A mechanistic physiologist accepts the role of machine-like processes in the living organism, but with this begins also to lose sight of the irreducible structures of life and conscious states, which are integral to biological machine-like processes in the living organism, but lacking in inanimate nature. In recent years physical scientists have interested themselves in the relation of animate to inanimate nature. In the volume of lectures entitled *Modes of Thought* (1938), the mathematician-philosopher, A. N. Whitehead contrasts "nature lifeless" and "nature alive" and deals exhaustively with the problems of consciousness and mind. To those who know no other presentation of this complex question than the neurophysiological, Whitehead's views are a stimulating corrective to so inadequate and so largely irrelevant a presentation of its subject. It is unfortunate that his views are so little known to biologists for they give a broad and clear picture of the irreducibility of life to the inanimate.

Another scientist, H. M. Pirenne (1950) has commented that:

"We are under no compulsion to believe that physiology gives us the whole truth about life and about ourselves. Physiology can be taken as referring only to certain aspects of reality. . . . The fundamental problem of the body–mind relationship then remains, but as a metaphysical problem, not a scientific one. . . . However, the human physiologist, at least, must be interested in the nature of the brain–mind relationship.

"What he does not have to do is to claim the problem as wholly within his own field of science, and to put himself forward with his experimental techniques, as the sole expositor, competent to discuss more general views of the subject and to explain the problem in terms of scientific disciplines that are not his own; namely, those of chemistry, physics and mathematics.

"Physical scientists are, in general, not so bold."
(*Brit. J. Phil. Sci.*, 1950, **1**, 43.)

E. P. Wigner (1969), a Nobel Laureate in Physics, has expressed the view that

"The endeavour to understand the functioning of the mind in terms of the laws of physics is doomed to have no more than temporary and partial success."

He proceeds to comment on the "greatest schism in the sciences" namely, that between the physical sciences and the sciences of the mind. Returning to biology, we find C. F. Pantin, the zoologist, describing as the "analytic fallacy" (1969) the idea that the understanding of a complex entity is to be gained only by the study of the rules governing its component parts. Indeed, taken to its logical conclusion this requirement would find the biologist lost in a world of molecular and sub-molecular physics, remote from biology.

There are many machine-like processes and machines that can be analysed without this infinite regress. "Higher order configurations", Pantin declares, "have properties to be studied in their own right. The key to the understanding of nervous action is the determination of the class to which a phenomenon belongs."

It is particularly to the writings of Polanyi, a distinguished physical chemist and philosopher of science, that we owe the clearest and most penetrating recent analyses of the relation of nature lifeless to nature alive. His concepts of focal and subsidiary awareness and of tacit knowing are notable additions to the subject here under discussion, but like his predecessor in this important field, A. N. Whitehead, he has failed to penetrate the neurophysiological fortress.

Discussing machine-like processes in the living organism and their postulated "reduction" to terms of mathematics, physics and chemistry, Polyani analyses the essential properties of a machine, man-made or biological. Both possess (i) operational principles and (ii) a physico-chemical constitution. In a man-made machine the operational principles are specified by its inventor and a suitable physico-chemical constitution provided, and, as it were, harnessed to the principles. The two constitute a dual entity of which the operational principles are the higher level.

Of necessity such a machine obeys the laws of the physics and chemistry of its constitution in the sense that is activities are dependent upon this constitution, but its operational principles are *not determined by* this constitution nor explicable in terms of it.

Consider a clock. If its mechanism is smashed, its operational principles cease to be, but its physico-chemical constitution remains intact; and a strictly physico-chemical analysis of its residue would not reveal that it had once been a clock. A biological "machine"; the nervous system, for example, also has operational principles and a physico-chemical constitution. It must obey the laws of this constitution, but its operational principles while *dependent on* this constitution are not *determined by* or explicable in terms of this constitution. A biological machine is not just "physics and chemistry" until after its operational principles have been abolished and it has been reduced to the level of inanimate matter, and belongs to another class of phenomenon.

A sound theory gives quantitative and qualitative insight into the processes and structures that function at all levels in a given system. Current mechanistic hypotheses do not give this. Thus *the Achilles heel* of a mechanistic and a reductionist neurophysiology lies in a double conceptual failure (i) to distinguish between the operational principles of a machine and its physico-chemical constitution, and (ii) to realize that while the machine must obey the laws of its physical constitution, its operational principles are not determined by, or explicable in terms of physics and chemistry.

Perhaps the most explicit example of these errors is found in R. B. Livingston's dictum:

"The whole of the nervous system is controlled by its molecular mechanism: its development, the processes of perception, judgement, emotion, learning, memory and behavior." (1970.)

It would be as easy to say that the molecular mechanisms of his bicycle control the movements of the cyclist. Yet they do not determine his choice of his destination, which is the conscious purpose of his journey. The neuro-physiological literature of conscious states blossoms with such misleading half-truths as Livingston's. Polanyi has exposed this error in another way. Reminding us of the game of chess, he points out that it is played according to rules, but that a knowledge of the rules does not make the master player, who is a master because of the *stratagems he devises within the boundaries of the rules*. He obeys the rules but they do not dictate the pattern of his game. A further feature of the neurophysiological literature on conscious states is its minimal interest in their phenomenology, most noteworthy in respect of the human subject where the problem is met in its most complex manifestations. Can it be right, following O'Leary's advice, to abandon "mentalistic thinking" because of its "obvious bankruptcy", in favour of a sophisticated technology in the field of the physical sciences?

Surely, a prior task is to seek to elucidate how the unconscious "patterns" and "bursts" of our unconscious nerve impulses become transformed into the flux and variety of our conscious states. Yet we find the relevant literature as secretive on this issue as on the phenomenology of conscious states. Even awareness of the need for an hypothesis on the subject seems lacking. As will be seen in the following chapter, where we learn that "nerve impulses" become "neural-mental events" and are then "translated" into "impressions of objects and sensations", of the *how* of these metamorphoses and of the *who* that effects them, we hear no mention.

These things are affirmed to happen, and somehow they do happen, and there we are left with the unsatisfying statement that molecular mechanisms are responsible. This is not an elucidation, but the evasion of one, and with it we are referred to the physical sciences, and the exodus from psychology and biology continues. Examples of this "progress" are given in the following chapter.

AN ANALYSIS OF SOME MECHANISTIC AND REDUCTIONIST VIEWS OF THE NATURE AND GENESIS OF CONSCIOUS STATES

The foregoing criticisms of current beliefs upon this subject require detailed references to some of their more authoritative presentations, and for quotations from them, if the viewpoint here advanced is to receive consideration.

In a review entitled *Cerebral Universe* (1965, i) O'Leary writes as follows:

"No barrier reef separates mental from neurological events, or the realms of the nerve impulse into two distinguishable worlds of brain and mind. Information collected at the body surface is encoded into spaced trains of impulses which reaching the spinal level are decoded for entry into the content of reflexes and transmission through the intervening relays to higher centres for further analysis. . . . At the forebrain this provides the material basis for the sense data upon which all our consciousness of the world around us depends. There, messages arriving over the multiple

channels must be regrouped to provide impressions of objects which include their weight, form, perspective, noise, heat, colour, or relative motion. . . .

"Together these events encompass a class of neural-mental events readily translatable either into sensation or motor patterns used to explore the reality of an object under study. This stratum of functioning lies at the threshold through which the mind examines the external world. . . . The view here adopted is that consciousness is a product of brain and amenable to treatment as a function of that entity. . . . Our cleavage arbitrarily concedes what is called mind to philosophy and keeps only consciousness and its contents as neural correlates."

This pronouncement cannot be acquitted of several obscurities, and it does not offer any clear account of the process by which the patterns of nerve impulses, of which we are not conscious become transformed into conscious states. Their "regrouping" cannot suffice to achieve this end. How a neural event becomes a "neuralmental" event and is subsequently "translated" into sensory and motor patterns remains a mystery. Further if there be no barrier between brain and mind nor two distinguishable worlds of brain and mind, how comes it that a "cleavage" is necessary into "consciousness" and "mind"; the first a neural "correlate" and the second a philosophic notion? This cleavage calls up the vision of a judgement of Solomon, dividing the declared indivisible into two entities, bifurcating mind and brain. This point of view is broadly representative of all such mechanistic hypotheses on brain and mind. It unifies and then bifurcates brain and mind. It takes no cognizance of the distinction between the operational principles of the neural machine and its physico-chemical constitution, between what is biological and what physics and chemistry, and finally does not offer any explanation of the mysterious translation of nerve impulses into conscious states. We have to be content with the bare statement that it is so.

A comparable thesis is propounded by the "biological psychologist", D. O. Hebb, thus:

"My proposition is that mind and consciousness, thoughts and perceptions, feelings and emotions, all consist of *nothing but* the transmission of messages—nerve impulses—in and through the paths of the nervous system. This is the working assumption of the biological psychologist. . . . We must at the same time keep in mind the other side of the problem, *all those aspects of mind that such theory does not comprehend*." (italics added) (1962).

Here, once more, we meet the bifurcation of the avowedly indivisible, but do not add anything whatever to our knowledge of the problem at issue.

In his work, *The Organization of Behavior* (1949), Hebb's introduction is in essence a kind of apologia for this gap in our knowledge. Thus, we read:

"Modern psychology takes for granted that behavior and neural function are perfectly correlated, that *one is completely caused by the other* [*sic*]. There is no separate soul or life force to stick a finger into the brain now and then. . . . Actually, of course, this is a working assumption only—as long as there are un-explained aspects of behavior . . . yet the working assumption is a necessary one, and there is no real evidence against it."

Again:

"All we can know of another's feelings and awareness is an inference from what he does. . . . These observ-able events are determined by electrical and chemical events in nerve cells."

Yet conscious states are not "determined" by physico-chemical events, and the confusion between the notion of "dependence on" and that of "determination by" runs iike a thread through the writings on this subject. Polanyi in his book, *Tacit Dimension* illustrates the logical in-dependence of the principles of a higher level from laws of lower levels:

"The operation of a higher level cannot be accounted for by the laws governing its particulars forming the lower level. You cannot derive a vocabulary from phonetics; you cannot derive the grammar of a language from its vocabulary; a correct use of grammar does not account for good style; and a good style does not provide the content of a piece of prose. We may conclude then quite generally . . . that it is impossible to represent the organizing principles of a higher level by the laws governing its isolated particulars."

Seymour Kety (1960) has put the matter more bluntly: "you cannot assess the content and style of a printed page in terms of the physics and chemistry of printing ink and paper".

Yet this is the order of proposition inherent in the desire to account for conscious states in terms of mathe-matics, physics and chemistry, and no one seems to note its absurdity in the form in which it is presented. A point of view in the same category is provided by J. Z. Young in his work *A Model of the Brain* (1965), where he has chosen to adopt the language of mechanics in preference to that of biology because he believes it more effective than the latter and is also "more exciting". Thus:

"When we say that living systems have 'needs' we emphasize that they are self-maintaining systems; 'homeostats' in modern terminology . . . so organized that they are able to interchange with their surroundings without merging into them.

"One of the features of a homeostat is the presence of detectors that indicate tendencies of imbalance within it and set in motion actions that tend to correct them. These are the systems of 'need' and 'motivation' which, more than any other features, seem to set living beings apart from the rest of the universe. . . . The use of the language of the physical sciences is already commonplace in biology. Indeed it is the central part in much that is considered most exciting in the subject."

Finally, he adds: "It is not absurd that those actions of the brain that take place in what we ordinarily call our 'minds' should be discussed in terms of machines,

for thus we learn a language more useful than our present one for speaking about brains and their products, such as mind."

Opinions will differ as to the credibility of this remark-able proposition. Can we envisage a science of psychology framed in the language of mechanics, or indeed of any philosophical, scientific or literary discourse on the human mind couched in such terms? This is surely an affectation, the more unreal since the author ignores the dual nature of a machine or machine-like process: its operational principles and its physico-chemical constitution.

This is not to assert that a scientific use of communica-tion theory, such as D. M. Mackay's *Mind's Eye View of the Brain* (1965) does not make a considered endeavour to fill the gap between nerve impulses and conscious states, if not wholly convincing one.

Finally, we come to Lashley's views. His many brilliant contributions to psychology and neurophysiology are remarkable for the very notable changes of view on the relative roles of psychology and physiology to the prob-lems of consciousness and the brain-mind relationship, that they display over the years. These are best illustrated by quotations from his writings, but they remain difficult to account for. A contempt for philosophers and philo-sophy appears intermittently in his writings, as though a scientist had no need of a philosophy of science. That brilliant scientists have at times been also philosophers seemed unknown to, or disregarded by, him. The fluctua-tions of his views are quoted from the posthumously published volume of his papers, entitled *The Neuro-psychology of Lashley* (1960).

(1) *From the Psychol. Review,* **37,** 1, (1930)

"Most of our psychological textbooks begin with an exposition of the structure of the brain and imply that this lays a foundation of a later understanding of behavior. It is rare that a discussion of any psycho-logical problem avoids some reference to the neural substratum. . . . In reading this literature I have been impressed chiefly by its futility. . . . Psychology today is a more fundamental science than neurophysiology. By this I mean the latter offers few principles from which we may predict or define the normal organization of behaviour, whereas the study of psychological processes furnishes a mass of factual material to which the laws of neural action in behavior must conform."

(2) *From the Hixon Symposium,* (1951)

"our common meeting ground is the faith to which we all subscribe, I believe, that the phenomena of behavior and mind are ultimately describable in the concepts of the mathematical and physical sciences".

I discern no common idea in these two pronouncements.

(3) *Cerebral Organization and Behavior,* (1958)

This was Lashley's final published paper and is a wide ranging and remarkable collection of his current views, couched in challenging and even satirical terms. Having 'disposed of' some views earlier expressed by Jackson, Sherrington, Eccles and the present writer that had a metaphysical flavour, he concluded of them that:

"These views are based on a thorough misconception of the facts of consciousness. They fail to analyse the problem and show no conception of what phenomena are to be explained by the action of the brain. The problem requires an entirely different approach; a thorough analysis of the phenomena of consciousness, oriented with reference to the phenomena of neural activity."

This last is the analysis we still await from any source.

As has been earlier mentioned, in reading the literature of neurophysiology on brain and consciousness, what strikes the clinical neurologist is the virtual disappearance of *homo sapiens* from the scene by a Freudian-like forgetfulness on the part of the authors. He has been replaced by a homeostat, or dismissed as Lashley's "unnecessary postulate".

In spite of all this, the personal pronouns "we" and "who" creep into all mechanistic stories of how the "brain" achieves this and that in the making of its "products", mind and consciousness. So we find them also in Lashley's last account:

(i) "The only conclusion that can be derived from experience is that thought exists. No psychologist has ever discovered the thinker. . . . There are neither empirical nor logical grounds for assuming that the existence of consciousness implies a distinct entity which is in the relation to it of a knower or doer."

(ii) "No activity of mind is ever conscious. . . . There are order and arrangement, but there is no experience of that order."

(iii) "Experience gives no clue to the means by which it is organized. . . . If the brain is capable of producing such organization then it may be considered the organizer."

(iv) "The brain is only here and now, but mind leaps into the past and brings it into the present. Mind crosses the ocean when *we* think of scenes in London and Paris. Mind reaches into the future when *we* foresee events."

Here, (ii) and (iii) must refer to the unconscious activity of nerve impulses within the nervous system, but (i) and (iv) can hardly do so. Who, then are Bremer's "someone", or the "we" and "who" that think of "scenes in London and Paris" and "foresee events". These cannot be the "ever unconscious mind". Surely "a thinker" is hidden somewhere in this story, and the "unnecessary postulate" has had to be resurrected to provide a live entity in it.

It is difficult to see how these irreconcilable propositions can throw any light upon the genesis of conscious states, or on the relation of "mind" to neuronal activities.

We have seen that J. Z. Young has reduced man to a homeostat, and thus Shakespeare's "paragon of animals" (cf. Hamlet) has become a paragon of machines. Yet, human nature will out! and the homeostat and the "unnecessary postulate" in these strange theses are given

the honorary titles of "who" and "we", and neuro-mythology acquires new *personae dramatis* who at once both are and are not. Such are the horns of the dilemma upon which, sooner or later, the mechanistic neurophysiologist is impaled.

Finally, we cannot fail to note the fluctuating relations that come and go between "consciousness" and "mind": sometimes synonyms, they also represent distinct entities, sometimes both are biophysical phenomena, but "mind" sometimes only a philosopher's fancy. Since the building of the tower of Babel and its linguistic results were described in the Book of Genesis, we may wonder whether a greater confusion of words and ideas has ever been created.

The more exclusively the neurophysiologist's experience is restricted to the lower forms of animal life, the simpler it is to view the living organism as just a homeostat, and to identify "mind" as a synonym for "consciousness". For the human physiologist it is by no means as simple, for his life is lived with the present and the past of human history and human life. How can he restrict himself to the animal world and neglect *homo sapiens* in the study of conscious states and mind?

Whitehead has provided good reasons why he should not:

"When we come to mankind, nature seems to have burst through another of its boundaries . . . there is the introduction of novelty of feeling by the entertainment of unexpressed possibilities. This second side is the enlargement of the conceptual experience of mankind. The characterization of this conceptual feeling is the sense of what might be and what might have been. It is the entertainment of the alternative. In its highest development, this becomes the entertainment of the Ideal.

"It emphasizes the sense of Importance. And this sense exhibits itself in various species, such as, the sense of morality, the mystic sense of religion, the sense of that delicate adjustment which is beauty . . the expression of these various feelings produces the history of mankind as distinct from the narrative of animal behaviours . . . the life of a human being receives its worth, its importance, from the way in which unrealized ideals shape its purpose and tinge its actions."

(*Modes of Thought*, Ch. II.)

This gives us a glimpse of the vast task that awaits the seeker of the mystery that still surrounds conscious states and "mind". Pascal has reminded us that "Man is not a geometrical proposition," and Whitehead that the history of man is not a mere narrative of animal behaviours.

THE PHILOSOPHERS AND CONSCIOUS STATES

Stress has been laid on the importance of a philosophy of Science, but it has to be said that the academic philosopher with no science is no better placed than the physiologist with no philosophy to cope with the problem of conscious states of mind. For example, J. C. C. Smart (1959) writing as a philosopher commits himself to the following opinions:

"It seems to me that science is increasingly giving a viewpoint whereby organisms are able to be seen as physico-chemical mechanisms: it seems that even the behavior of man himself will one day be explicable in mechanistic terms. There does seem to be, as far as science is concerned, nothing in the world but increasingly complex arrangements of physical constituents. . . . For a full description of what is going on in a man, you would have to mention not only the physical processes in his tissues, glands, nervous system, and so forth, but also his states of consciousness. . . . That these should be correlated with brain processes does not help, for to say that they are correlated is to say they are something "over and above". You cannot correlate something with itself.

"So sensations, states of consciousness, do seem to be one sort of thing left outside the physicalist picture, and for various reasons I cannot believe that this can be so. That everything should be explicable in terms of physics except the occurrence of sensations seems to me frankly inexplicable."

Like other mechanistic accounts this one is appropriately described by its author as "largely a confession of faith", for even if we except neurophysiologists, most physiologists hold that there are biological processes that cannot be adequately described as "physico-chemical mechanisms" as these are encountered in inanimate nature, but which are found only in living systems.

Smart states that philosophy does not require us to hold a dualistic concept of man, for "A man is a vast arrangement of physical particles, but there are not, over and above this, sensations of states of consciousness. There are just behavioral facts about this vast mechanism." There follows a lengthy scholastic-type disputation, reminiscent of the middle ages, on the meaning of words, which leave the problem untouched and unsolved. This is not the order of philosophic thought to which the neurophysiologist has been urged here to follow. Another unique feature of both types of discussion on the genesis and nature of conscious states is the appearance of the "confession of faith", by both philosophers and neurophysiologists. This is certainly unique in physiological disquisitions and suggests that the writers do not know where they are or where they are going in the search for an understanding of conscious states, physiologically.

The one confession we so rarely hear is that the problem may not be amenable to any scientific analysis (Eccles, 1965). It is one the mechanist cannot allow himself to make, though in their times both Jackson and later Sherrington were bold enough to make it, and even at the present time some physical scientists do not shrink from it.

O'Leary, in the review cited, regrets that Jackson did not adopt a more erudite doctrine than that of psychophysical parallelism, which we have just seen Smart reject, but two questions arise: how many know precisely what Jackson did say on this matter, and is there any current hypothesis more satisfactory than the one he proposed? It may be useful to quote his words, thus (*Selected Writings*, Vol. **2**, p. 84):

"I am not competent to discuss the metaphysical question of the nature of the relation of mind to nervous activities. . . .

There are three doctrines: (a) that mind acts through the nervous system (through highest centres first); here an immaterial agency is supposed to produce physical effects; (b) that activities of the highest centres and mental states are one and the same thing, or are different sides of one thing. (c) A doctrine I have adopted: that nervous states are utterly different from states of consciousness. The two occur in parallelism, there is no interference of one with the other, but for every nervous state there is a co-relative conscious state. Psychical states occur during—not from—highest nervous activities." Of these three propositions he regards (b) as complacently assuming that there is nothing to explain. "To merely solidify the mind into a brain is to make short work of a difficult problem."

Yet this (b) is precisely the position of today's mechanistic neurophysiology. Jackson then makes a significant qualification:

"If (c) is erroneous, I ask that the doctrine of concomitance be provisionally accepted as an artifice in order that we may study the most complex diseases of the nervous system; that is, as a methodological postulate."

Faced as we are by an admittedly unsolved problem, in respect of which both philosophers and physiologists have little to offer other than "confessions of faith", the cry for a more erudite doctrine from Jackson, our predecessor of nearly a century ago, sounds rather hollow, since no one has improved upon his hypothesis, modestly stated as it was, while the exodus from psychology and biology continues to move over the desert of the mathematical and physical sciences where nature is inanimate. There is now a growing literature of the philosophy of science, which is more than a linguistic exercise, but which has not penetrated the world of neurophysiology to any depth, yet which is essential to its advance, and I have named Whitehead and Polanyi as amongst its most stimulating exponents, though by no means its only ones. Without what they have to offer, neurophysiology—at the level here under consideration—will remain the deficiency syndrome it is, looking to the physical sciences for the ideas they do not contain, or their exponents claim to possess.

CONCLUSIONS

From its beginning the foregoing critical commentary has run counter to majority opinion in academic neurophysiology. For the present writer there was no alternative, and no justification for yet another docile resumé of views that have been reiterated, but seldom questioned from within, for a generation.

The view here advanced holds that the topic of conscious states—not only in the lower animals but also more manifestly in man—overflows the bounds of academic neurophysiology which is dominantly a neurobiophysics, and thus a brilliant yet only a half-told tale of the nervous system and of consciousness. The subject demands also a psychological approach, and, like every other special science, some reference to a philosophy of science. Of both, neurophysiology has been starved: of psychology by neglect, of philosophy by a perverse and damaging antipathy, shown by no other special science.

Collingwood, the historian of Roman Britain and a philosopher also, in his work, *The Idea of Nature* (1945) wrote:

"It cannot be well that natural science should be assigned exclusively to one class of persons called scientists and philosophy to another class called philosophers. A man who has never reflected on the principles of his work has not achieved a grown-up man's attitude towards it; a scientist who has never philosophized about his science can never be more than a second hand and imitative journeyman scientist. A man who has never enjoyed a certain type of experience cannot reflect upon it; a philosopher who has never studied and worked at natural science cannot philosophize about it without making a fool of himself. . . .

"In the nineteenth century a fashion grew up separating natural scientists and philosophers into two professional bodies, each knowing little about one another's work and having little sympathy with it. It is a bad fashion that has done harm to both sides, and on both sides there is an earnest desire to see the last of it and to bridge the gulf of misunderstanding it has created. The bridge must be begun from both ends."

In their time, Jackson, Sherrington and J. S. Haldane were well aware of this situation, but their efforts to bridge the gap and to remind us of its existence failed of effect.

We have seen that a distinguished neurophysiologist has advised that neurophysiologists should abandon mentalistic thinking and turn to the physical sciences in the search for an understanding of conscious states and of the brain–mind relationship. We have followed this course for a generation and with no result but an increasing confusion of opinions, but with no advance to the desired goal. It is submitted therefore that we take to mentalistic thinking; that is, to a philosophy of science as this is now developing, particularly amongst physical scientists, who look with no sanguine opinion upon the biologists' wanderings in the realm of the physical sciences. The structure of life and of conscious states are irreducible to the level of inanimate nature, and we cannot be hopeful that the particular problem of the brain–mind relationship will be resolved within the naïve limits of a mechanistic

psychology or physiology. The words "science" and "omniscience" are not synonyms.

FURTHER READING

Bremer, F. (1954), in *Brain Mechanisms and Consciousness*, p. 245. Oxford: Blackwell Scientific Publications.
Bridgman, P. (1951), *Brit. J. Phil. Sci.*, **1**, 257.
Carpenter, W. B. (1853), *Principles of Human Physiology*. London: Churchill.
Collingwood, R. G. (1945), *The Idea of Nature*, p. 2. Oxford: Clarendon Press.
Eccles, J. C. (1965), *The Brain and the Unity of Conscious Experience* (Eddington Lecture). Cambridge University Press.
Fessard, A. E. (1954), in *Brain Mechansims and Consciousness*, p. 201. Oxford: Blackwell Scientific Publications.
Haldane, J. S. (1919), *The New Physiology*. London: Griffin and Sons.
Hebb, D. O. (1949), *The Organization of Behavior*, Introduction, p. xiii. New York: Wiley and Sons.
Hebb, D. O. (1962), *McGill Medical Journal*, 33.
Jackson, J. H. (1931), *The Selected Writings of John Hughlings Jackson*. London: Hodder & Stoughton; and New York: Basic Books Inc. Vol. 2., p. 84.
Kubie, L. (1954), in *Brain Mechanisms and Consciousness*, p. 444. Oxford: Blackwell Scientific Publications.
Lashley, K. S. (1930), "Basic Neural Mechanisms in Behavior," *Psychol. Rev.*, **37**, 1–24. Also in *The Neuropsychology of Lashley*, p. 191. New York: McGraw-Hill Book Co., Inc.
Lashley, K. S. (1951), "Cerebral Mechanisms in Behavior," in *The Hixon Symposium*, p. 112. New York: John Wiley and Sons; and in *The Neuropsychology of Lashley*, p. 506. McGraw-Hill Book Co.
Lashley, K. S. (1958), "Cerebral Organization and Behavior," *Proc. Ass., Res. nerv. ment. Dis.*, **36**, p. 1; and in *The Neuropsychology of Lashley*, p. 529. McGraw-Hill Book Co.
Livingston, R. B. (1970), "Some General Integrative Aspects of Brain Function," in *Control Processes in Multicellular Organisms*, p. 384. Ciba Foundation Symposium, Churchill, London.
O'Leary, J. L. (1965), "Cerebral Universe," Parts 1 and 2, *J. nerv. ment. Dis.*, **141**, 135.
O'Leary, J. L. (1965), "Matter and Mind," *Brain*, 1965, 777.
O'Leary, J. L. and Adametz, J. (1960), *J. Neurosurg.*, **17**, 1045.
Pantin, C. F. A. (1969), "Organism and Environment," in *The Anatomy of Knowledge*, p. 103 (M. Greene, Ed.). London: Routledge and Kegan Paul.
Pirenne, H. M. (1950), *Brit. J. Phil. Sci.*, **1**, 43.
Polanyi, M. (1966), *The Tacit Dimension*. New York: Doubleday and Co.
Polanyi, M. (1965), "Life's Irreducible Structure," in *Knowing and Being: Essays by Michael Polanyi*. London: Routledge and Kegan Paul.
Polanyi, M. (1965), "The Structure of Consciousness," *Brain*, **88**, 799.
Riese, W. (1950), *The Principles of Neurology*.
Smart, J. C. C. (1959), "Sensations and Brain Processes," *Phil. Rev.*, **68**, 141.
Stallknecht, N. P., (1969), "Philosophy and Civilization," in *The Anatomy of Knowledge*, pp. 219–233. London: Routledge and Kegan Paul.
Whitehead, A. N. (1938), *Modes of Thought*. Cambridge University Press.
Wigener, E. P. (1969), in *The Anatomy of Knowledge*, pp. 31–46. London: Routledge and Kegan Paul.
Young, J. Z. (1964), *A Model of the Brain*, Chap. 1, pp. 6–10. Oxford: Clarendon Press.

2. SLEEP

IAN OSWALD

We spend nearly a third of our lives in sleep, a state in which our central nervous system functions very differently from the waking state in which a neurologist's patients are most often examined. Sleep is a state of inertia and unresponsiveness. The unresponsiveness is general and it affects our reflexes, so that, for example, the respiratory centre, normally highly sensitive to carbon dioxide, tolerates a considerably higher concentration of blood carbon dioxide during sleep. We tend to think of sleep as a continuous state extending over periods of hours, but it is important to remember that not only can the individual awaken from sleep for a few seconds at a time, but that the awake person can slip into a light sleep for a period of only a couple of seconds at a time, particularly if he is very sleep-deprived or bored.

In the past twenty years there have been rapid advances in knowledge about sleep and these have been made possible by the widespread use of the electroencephalogram (EEG). As someone passes from wakefulness to sleep the alpha rhythm of the EEG, at about 10 c./sec., becomes lost in drowsiness and is replaced by irregular, slightly slower waves of low voltage. As the minutes pass, stages 2, 3 and 4 appear and these are characterized by *sleep spindles* at about 14 c./sec., prominent over the front of the head, and by large slow waves in the EEG, as slow as 1 c./sec. Large slow waves in the EEG occur in a great many conditions where there is inefficiency or impairment of cortical function, for example, hypoxia, hypothyroidism, or coma from poisoning or head injury. The sleep spindles, however, are a much more specific sign of sleep.

Our lives are governed by rhythms or cycles and one of the most obvious is the sleep-wakefulness cycle of about 24 hr. We feel sleepy, not simply because we may be bored, or short of sleep, but because we are reaching that particular time of the 24 hr. in which sleep is customarily taken, and this powerful rhythm is not easily shaken off if we suddenly fly to another part of the world. Superimposed upon this 24-hr. rhythm is another rhythm, which in the adult has a period of about 90 min. There is increasing evidence that this rhythm is present throughout the 24 hr. By day it may be masked, but, in a relatively unstructured environment, may reveal itself by spontaneous fluctuations in general motor activity, or in eating and drinking behaviour. In the case of the patient with idiopathic narcolepsy the times of irresistible periods of sleepiness are governed by this 90 min. rhythm. It is, however, during prolonged nocturnal sleep that the 90 min. rhythm is most clearly apparent and in its timing is in some measure entrained by the onset of sleep. About one hour after the beginning of sleep the normal individual undergoes a considerable change in his physiology and enters what is called paradoxical or rapid eye movement (REM) sleep. In fact we now recognize two different kinds of sleep and the second we call orthodox, non-rapid eye movement (NREM), or EEG slow wave sleep. The cyclical alternation between a higher voltage slow wave EEG with sleep spindles, on the one hand, and a low voltage non-spindling EEG, on the other, can still be seen in some patients who are comatose after head injury, and in cases where only slow waves continue uninterruptedly the prognosis for recovery is poor.

Paradoxical sleep occupies only about 20–25 per cent of the night's sleep in the normal adult, but in some ways is a more spectacular kind of sleep so that it has attracted a great deal of research. It possesses what are known as *tonic* features and *phasic* features. The tonic features include EEG of fairly low voltage, devoid of spindles, and without the very large slow waves that may be seen in orthodox sleep. Other tonic features are erection of the penis, or increased vaginal blood flow in the female, and profound loss of muscle tone. Among the phasic features are sudden rises in blood pressure, and sudden changes in heart-rate and respiration, often coupled with brief bodily twitches and a burst of rapid conjugate eye-movements. The loss of skeletal muscle-tone is of particular interest. The knee-jerk reflex can be elicited by sudden stretching of the patellar tendon, or alternatively by an electrical stimulus direct to the sensory nerve. The electrically induced reflex, or Hoffman reflex, cuts out the muscle spindles. When the Hoffman reflex is repeatedly elicited during orthodox sleep, by stimulation of the posterior tibial nerve, its amplitude differs very little from that found during wakefulness. When attempts are made to elicit it during paradoxical sleep, however, it is either zero or of negligible amplitude. Japanese authors studied a patient with a lesion of the anterior cervical cord and found that during paradoxical sleep the Hoffman reflexes did not diminish to zero but remained similar to those of orthodox sleep. Elegant animal studies by Pompeiano and his colleagues in Italy have demonstrated that at the precise moment of a sudden flurry of rapid eye movements, muscle tone falls to its lowest level, electrical stimuli applied to the motor cortex are least able to elicit movement, and electrically induced reflexes are at their minimum. In other words the profound loss of muscle-tone and unresponsiveness during paradoxical sleep can be interpreted as a positive state determined by impulses that descend from the brain-stem and inhibit anterior horn cells.

Another tonic feature of paradoxical sleep is raised cerebral blood-flow. In orthodox sleep of the cat cerebral blood-flow differs little from that of wakefulness, but during paradoxical sleep it may rise to almost twice that of wakefulness in certain parts of the brain. In the case of the human it appears that cerebral blood-flow may rise somewhat above waking levels during orthodox sleep but there is a very large rise during paradoxical sleep. The rise appears to be related to a high rate of cerebral metabolism during paradoxical sleep and accompanying vasodilatation. In patients with space-occupying cerebral lesions the vasodilatation and consequent rise of intracranial pressure can impede the blood-flow and reduce available oxygen.

Mental life probably continues without interruption throughout the whole of sleep, but, because the laying down of memories or engram-formation is impaired during sleep, unless the individual is actually awakened from sleep and immediately questioned about what was passing through his mind, he remembers little or nothing of it. When people are awakened from orthodox sleep they generally describe mental life of a fairly mundane character, often related to events of the previous day, that they characterize as "thinking". When awakened from paradoxical sleep they are much more likely to characterize the mental life as "dreaming" and it tends to be more colourful and adventurous in nature.

Claims were made at one time that dreaming ceased in some patients who had had a leucotomy or in others who had suffered parieto-occipital injury. These claims must be regarded as obsolete and could be sustained only if patients failed to recall dreams when questioned under optimum conditions. In fact when patients who have had leucotomy are awakened from their periods of paradoxical sleep and questioned, they too recall having just been dreaming.

Among the most fascinating of recent discoveries is that the colourful features that distinguish "dreaming" from "thinking" during our sleep are themselves phasic events in that they appear to be injected intermittently into mental life at the very moment of the rapid eye movements. Rapid eye movements tend to occur in brief bursts which may be separated by half a minute or so and during that half minute mental life tends to be just as mundane as during orthodox sleep.

THE CONTROL OF SLEEP

Sensory stimulation is an obvious means of maintaining wakefulness and when Pavlov and his colleagues made dogs blind, deaf and anosmic and observed that their dogs appeared to sleep much longer, they concluded that it was the lack of sensory inflow that was responsible, and conversely that sensory inflow is of principal importance in maintaining wakefulness. In 1935 Bremer described his experiments with the *encéphale isolé* and the *cerveau isolé*. In the former a transection was made through the lower end of the brain-stem and in the latter through the upper midbrain. The characteristics of the EEG and the behaviour of the eyes suggested that the *encéphale isolé* passed through periods of both wakefulness and sleep, whereas the *cerveau isolé* appeared to be in a state resembling perpetual sleep. The difference that Bremer could see between these two preparations lay in the differences in sensory inflow, in particular, the fact that the trigeminal nerve was excluded from

influencing the cortex in the case of the *cerveau isolé*. In the 1950s, however, the notion that wakefulness was maintained simply by the sensory inflow along classical paths was superseded by the concept of the ascending, activating, reticular formation of the brain-stem.

It had been known since the nineteenth century that the drowsiness and impairment of consciousness in many cases of encephalitis was associated with postmortem lesions apparent, not in the cortex, but in the central grey matter of the brain stem. Neurosurgeons like Jefferson and Johnson remarked upon the fact that supratentorial lesions were not very potent in causing loss of consciousness, whereas infratentorial space-occupying lesions, which caused compression of the brain-stem, very readily gave rise to clouding or loss of consciousness. The brain-stem looked as if it might hold the key.

Moruzzi and Magoun then discovered that electrical stimulation of the mesencephalic reticular formation could cause "awakening" of the *encéphale isolé*. It was later demonstrated that, from all the main sensory tracts, collateral afferents fed into the central core of the brain-stem, so that even when the classical sensory paths themselves were interrupted above the point where the collaterals branched off, sensory stimulation of the modality concerned would still lead to awakening. The brain-stem activating reticular formation, extending from medulla to thalamus, came to be seen as a sort of master-zone for consciousness, from which non-specific impulses ascended to the cortex and descended to the spinal cord, in order, as it were, that both should be pepped-up and so improved in their degree of responsiveness, making possible both conscious perception and effective motor action. Sleep was conceived of as merely the time when these non-specific impulses had died away, although the work of Dell and others demonstrated that the cerebral cortex and the carotid sinus exerted tonic inhibitory effects which positively damped down the excitement of the reticular formation and so tended to bring about sleep.

The concept of sleep as an essentially negative state was at variance with the ideas put forward in the 1940s by W. R. Hess who had demonstrated that there were brain-stem areas which, when stimulated electrically, caused the waking cat to groom itself, to settle peacefully, and to go off into apparently natural sleep. In the 1960s several groups of workers have confirmed that there are indeed both forebrain and hindbrain areas which seem to have a specifically sleep-promoting function, and if the forebrain areas are destroyed then cats will simply not sleep at all and eventually die.

The demonstration of two very different states of sleep has also made it clear that the simple notion of sleep as a unitary state dependent upon the withdrawal of activating impulses from the reticular formation is inadequate. The main controlling mechanisms for paradoxical sleep, as Jouvet's research especially has shown, seem to be located in the pons. The action of drugs has also given much food for thought. Barbiturates had been held to induce sleep by some selective inhibitory action on the reticular formation, and amphetamines to cause wakefulness by a stimulant action thereon. In fact both these categories of drugs bring about a selective decrease in the proportion of paradoxical sleep, accompanied in the case of barbiturates by an increase of orthodox sleep, and in the case of amphetamine by an absolute reduction of orthodox sleep. The possibility that humoral agents may help to tip the balance from wakefulness to sleep is now also much more seriously considered.

SLEEP PHENOMENA

Drowsiness at night, or occurring by day in association with sleep-deprivation, is accompanied by *hypnagogic hallucinations*, by loss of direction of thought, loss of contact with the environment, and by a variety of sudden, brief, sensory phenomena, often associated with a bodily jerk. The most common of these sensory phenomena is the feeling of falling with sudden arrest of motion, but a flash of light, a bang inside the head, with or without an electric feeling passing right through the body are also common. They are all entirely normal phenomena, though there are individual variations in the degree to which they are noticed and remembered, and they are more likely to be remembered at times of raised anxiety or when there is difficulty in falling asleep. The drowsy state facilitates EEG electrical discharges of the kind associated with epileptic phenomena and seizures in some patients are especially common in drowsiness. Individual differences are considerable and whereas, in some, the paradoxical sleep-phase is a time when epileptic spike and wave phenomena will disappear from the EEG, in other patients they are enhanced.

Idiopathic narcolepsy is now much better understood in patients who have also attacks of cataplexy. These patients are unusual in that, instead of passing first into orthodox sleep, as we normally do, they first pass for a period of about 15 min. into paradoxical sleep. The vivid dream experiences and awareness of paralysis, as they come to from their sleep, can now be understood as features of paradoxical sleep. Cataplexy itself has been interpreted as a partial manifestation of the paradoxical sleep-phase into which these patients have a peculiar liability to pass, as if cataplexy occurs as a state in which the loss of muscle-tone is present without the full picture of sleep. The drug imipramine, which selectively alters sleep by reducing paradoxical sleep duration, is effective in eliminating cataplectic attacks without reducing the liability to attacks of sleepiness (it is a drug that should not be combined with amphetamines).

When people have become dependent upon large quantities of hypnotic drugs or alcohol, all of which suppress paradoxical sleep, their brain-mechanisms have changed as they have developed tolerance, and when the drugs are withdrawn, the abnormal cerebral components, of a kind which had been serving to counteract the effects of the drugs, now bring about increased anxiety, decreased sleep, increased restlessness and increased paradoxical sleep. The full-blown picture is that of delirium tremens with terror, restlessness, insomnia and vivid dream experiences that intrude into wakefulness. The patient with delirium tremens, in so far as he gets sleep

at all, may get up to 100 per cent of it as paradoxical sleep and can be seen repeatedly to pass from wakefulness into paradoxical sleep.

The new knowledge about sleep has also illuminated other disorders not so closely related to paradoxical sleep. A proportion of patients with narcolepsy or hypersomnia, who do not have cataplectic attacks, have no special liability to fall into paradoxical sleep. The obese Pickwickian, contrary to former belief, sometimes has quite normal daytime respiratory function, but he does have a neurophysiological peculiarity in that, not merely does he tend to be sleepy at times during the day, but at night his respiration is characteristically periodic. About every half minute there is a short series of explosive snorts followed by apnoea, followed by ineffectual respiratory movements, culminating in another burst of snorts.

Many of the episodic abnormalities of sleep occur in orthodox sleep, namely, sleep-walking, enuresis, snoring and night-terrors in children. Head-banging and body-rocking (*jactatio capitis nocturna*) can occur in either phase of sleep and may be extremely violent and last for a minute or more without causing awakening. Sudden awakenings in a state of terror in adults as well as in children will occur from orthodox sleep, while the more prolonged nightmares, often with awareness of inability to move (sleep paralysis), are phenomena of paradoxical sleep.

The commonest of all sleep-disorders remains insomnia, with anxiety as its chief cause. Insomnia is, nevertheless, much more common in older groups, in whom it has now been shown by Feinberg and his colleagues, that the increasing tendency towards brief awakenings, and reduction of the proportion of paradoxical sleep, are closely correlated with diminishing cognitive abilities. Indeed these objective and parallel signs of ageing in the brain can be detected from 30 years and onwards.

Much recent research has been directed to the hypnotic drugs used for the treatment of insomnia and this has taken place in an era when many doctors have become uneasy at the heavy rate of prescription of drugs of this kind. When sedative drugs are given by night or day their effects gradually diminish, though tolerance is never complete. When the time comes to stop them, the brain will no longer function normally without them. Sleep does indeed become more difficult, more broken (especially by frightening dreams) than would have been the case had the drugs never been given, and it takes about two months for the brain to recover to normal. Unless, therefore, there are good grounds for forecasting termination of some current anxiety, it may be a disservice to place a patient on sleeping pills. The chronic worrier, or individual with life-long difficulties in interpersonal adjustments, is unlikely to receive lasting benefit from the prescription of such drugs. In an era when the commonest single category of emergency admission to general hospitals is deliberate self-poisoning, especial care should be taken in the selection of a hypnotic, so that slowly-eliminated drugs, such as phenobarbitone, should not be used, and those which, even in large doses will not produce coma, should be selected, for example, nitrazepam.

SLEEP AND THE BODY *= Stimulus*

Sleep occurs in great amounts in young and growing creatures and has, too, been thought of as serving a restorative function in those who are fully grown. In recent times attention has been directed to links between sleep and synthetic processes, whether for growth or restoration. A considerable (fillip) to this work was given by the Japanese discovery that orthodox sleep with very large slow EEG waves, is a necessary condition for the major nocturnal outpouring of human growth hormone, an agent that increases biosynthesis of RNA and protein. The same stages of sleep are increased after physical exercise and by the administration of thyroid hormone in those who have been hypothyroid, so it seems likely that stages 3 and 4 sleep are particularly associated with bodily synthetic processes. There is growing evidence to link secretion of the female sex hormones and also testosterone, another anabolic hormone, with intra-sleep patterns, and there are grounds for thinking that paradoxical sleep, with its increased cerebral blood-flow and increased cerebral metabolism may be especially related to synthetic processes in the brain, including those required for the laying down of permanent memories of daytime events. New knowledge accumulates rapidly and it is perhaps of special interest that the central nervous system may be the co-ordinator of wholesale restorative processes for other organs.

FURTHER READING

Books
A short general review:
Oswald, I. (1970), *Sleep*, 2nd revised edition, p. 152. Penguin Books: Harmondsworth, Middlesex.
Specialist symposia, including papers by Jouvet, Dement and Feinberg:
Kales, E. (Ed.) (1969), *Sleep: Physiology and Pathology*, p. 360. Philadelphia: Lippincott.

Kety, S. S., Evarts, E. V. and Williams, H. L. (1967), *Sleep and Altered States of Consciousness*, p. 591. Baltimore: Williams and Wilkins. (Volume 45 of Research Publications of the Association for Research in Nervous and Mental Disease).

Papers
Bergamasco, B., Bergamini, L., Doriguzzi, T. and Fabiani, D. (1968), "EEG Sleep Patterns as a Prognostic Criterion in Post-traumatic Coma," *Electroenceph. clin. Neurophysiol.*, **34**, 374–377.
Cooper, R. and Hulme, A. (1966), "Intracranial Pressure and Related Phenomena During Sleep," *J. Neurol. Neurosurg. Psychiat.*, **29**, 564–570.
Gastaut, H. and Broughton, R. (1967), "A Clinical and Polygraphic Study of Episodic Phenomena During Sleep," *Recent Adv. Biol. Psychiat.*, **7**, 197–221.
Goas, J. Y., Seylaz, J., Mamo, H., MacLeod, P., Caron, J. P. and Houdart, R. (1969), "Variations du débit sanguin du cortex de l'homme au cours du sommeil," *Rev. Neurol., (Paris)*, **120**, 159–176.
Kuhlo, W. (1968), "Neurophysiologische und klinische Untersuchungen beim Pickwick-Syndrom," *Arch. Psychiat. Z. ges. Neurol.*, **211**, 170–192.
McGinty, D. J. and Sterman, M. B. (1968), "Sleep Suppression After Basal Forebrain Lesions in Cats," *Science*, **160**, 1253–1255.
Molinari, S. and Foulkes, D. (1969), "Tonic and Phasic Events During Sleep; Psychological Correlates and Implications," *Percept. mot. Skills*, **29**, 343–368.
Naitoh, P., Kales, A., Kollar, E. J., Smith, J. C. and Jacobson, A. (1969), "Electroencephalographic Activity After Prolonged Sleep Loss," *Electroenceph. clin. Neurophysiol.*, **27**, 2–11.
Oswald, I. (1968), "Drugs and Sleep," *Pharmacol. Rev.*, **20**, 273–303.
Oswald, I. (1969), "Human Brain Protein, Drugs and Dreams," *Nature (Lond.)*, **223**, 893–897.
Pompeiana, O. (1970), "Mechanisms of Sensorimotor Integration During Sleep," *Progr. Physiol. Psychol.*, **3**, 1–179.
Roth, B., Bruhová and Lehovský (1969), "REM Sleep and NREM Sleep in Narcolepsy and Hypersomnia," *Electroenceph. clin. Neurophysiol.*, **26**, 176–182.
Sassin, J. F., Parker, D. C., Mace, J. W., Gotlin, R. W., Johnson, L. C. and Rossman, L. G. (1969), "Human Growth Hormone Release: Relation to Slow-wave Sleep and Sleep-waking Cycles," *Science*, **165**, 513–515.
Shimizu, A., Yamada, Y., Yamamoto, J., Fujiki, A. and Kaneko, Z. (1966), "Pathways of Descending Influence on H-reflex During Sleep," *Electroenceph. clin. Neurophysiol.*, **10**, 425–431.
Zanchetti, A. (1967), "Brain Stem Mechanisms of Sleep," *Anesthesiology*, **28**, 81–99.

3. ORGANIC DISTURBANCES OF CONSCIOUSNESS

FRED PLUM

INTRODUCTION AND DEFINITIONS

Consciousness is psychological awareness of the self and the environment and the content of man's consciousness is evolution's highest prize. Man is the only animal who expresses his mental content through language rather than mere somatic motor behaviour; this unique faculty inevitably imposes a somewhat parochial and possessive view when we consider the conscious state and its alterations. Our consciousness equals our identity and as a result disturbances of consciousness rank high as medical problems. Stupor or coma mean that the brain has at least temporarily failed and both patients and doctors rightfully sense that survival of the body without an intact brain is a questionable benefit.

Medically, one identifies two components of consciousness, its content and its on-off or arousal quality. The content of consciousness has qualitative and quantitative dimensions, but this chapter concerns only the latter. The basis for purely qualitative differences in human consciousness, the factors that govern hope and despair, genius, dull mediocrity or even delusion, have until now unbendingly resisted chemical, physical or anatomical dissection, and their causes and mechanisms remain a mystery both at the cellular and the molecular level. On the other hand quantitative changes in consciousness do provide a presently understandable medical problem whose mechanisms are biologically quite well understood, and whose appearances closely parallel the development and progression of certain kinds of abnormal changes in the brain.

A later section will review the anatomy and physiology of consciousness, and will stress that full conscious behavior depends upon the physiological interaction between arousal systems located in a normal brainstem and the extensive neuronal populations of the intact cerebral hemispheres. But let us first define the states of quantitatively altered or depressed consciousness and discuss briefly how one tests for them.

Specific Focal Losses in Mental Content include dementia, aphasia, memory loss and other more or less circumscribed psychological defects. These abnormalities are usually due to restricted lesions of the cerebral hemispheres (although admittedly sometimes bilateral ones). They are often irreversible and they are not usually considered as states of altered consciousness unless their causative lesions also produce at least some degree of reduced arousal. Profound dementia in which the mental content has entirely disappeared is akin to unconsciousness.

Acute Generalized Psychological Losses (the confusional and delirious states) are usually due to diffuse anatomic or metabolic lesions of the brain. They combine a generalized reduction or alteration in the content of consciousness with at least some reduction in total arousal. Patients with such clouding of consciousness can be lethargic or hyper-irritable when awake, but they almost always sleep more than the usual fraction of the twenty-four hour day and they often tend to invert the normal pattern, sleeping during the day and awakening at night. Patients with clouded consciousness are bewildered and have difficulty in following commands. They have at least a minor disorientation for time, and sometimes for place and person as well and their short attention span and poor memory truncates their ability either to recite numbers forward or backward or to complete serial 7's within a reasonable time or accuracy. *Delirium* includes the agitation and characteristic dreamlike, rapidly-changing delusional episodes during which patients are out of contact with the environment and psychologically unreachable by the examiner. Most delirious patients are frightened, noisy and confused even between their delusions.

Defects in the Arousal Mechanism

Defects in arousal include stupor and coma and their appearance usually precludes any chance of testing whether the content of consciousness also is impaired. Stupor and coma are usually the result of acutely developing processes that attack the brain rapidly. By contrast more insidious and chronic hemisphere-damaging lesions empty the mind to produce an overwhelming or complete dementia.

Stupor is unresponsiveness from which the subject can be aroused only by vigorous and repeated stimuli. Most stuporous patients have organic cerebral dysfunction although deep physiological sleep or catatonic schizophrenia both can lead to stupor and their identification can require great skill in differential diagnosis.

Coma is unrousable unresponsiveness, "the absence of any psychologically understandable response to external stimulus or inner need".[8] When evaluating patients in coma it is important it distinguish between the psychological state and the primitive motor responses which are purely reflex, and are mediated by very different subcortical pathways. *Hypersomnia* refers to excessive drowsiness and is sometimes applied to states of sleeplike coma; since the physiological relation of sleep to coma is unclear this term is potentially confusing.

Akinetic Mutism (coma vigile) describes the silent, alert-looking and wakeful immobility that accompanies certain subacute or chronic states of altered consciousness; the cerebral hemispheres and their efferent pathways can be morphologically largely intact yet the subject displays neither psychological awareness nor movement, usually because of a failure of deep diencephalic mechanisms to activate the cerebrum. This condition vividly illustrates a dissociation between preserved arousal (wakefulness) and a loss of the psychological functions of the cerebral hemispheres. Because of the presence of sleep-wake cycles some workers consider akinetic mutism and similar states to be conditions of profound dementia rather than disorders of consciousness; such a distinction is entirely semantic, and probably unimportant as long as one demands accurate descriptions.

The Apallic State describes the constellation of diffuse bilateral cerebral cortical degeneration and its accompanying behavioral abnormalities which usually include psychological unresponsiveness and bilateral diffuse muscular rigidity or spasticity.

The De-efferented State is a condition that includes paralysis of all four extremities and the lower cranial nerves due to a lesion that interrupts the motor pathways but spares the brainstem reticular activating system and the cerebral hemispheres. Although a peripheral neuropathy can rarely produce such a condition, the commoner cause is a pontine infarct that interrupts the corticospinal and lower corticobulbar pathways but spares the more dorsally lying tegmentum. Patients with such lesions retain only their vertical eye movements to communicate with and can be erroneously considered to be in coma unless closely and thoughtfully evaluated.

THE ANATOMY OF CONSCIOUSNESS AND COMA

Experimental studies in animals, and clinical-pathological analyses of disease in man, generally paint a similar picture for the basis of consciousness. Whatever uncertainties or discordances remain reflect largely the difficulties of trying on the one hand to infer the conscious state of animals entirely from their motor behavior, and on the other of finding clinically well-studied human cases who not only have small and restricted lesions of the brain at autopsy, but also lack the obscuring effects of other cerebral abnormalities or uncontrolled cardiovascular and metabolic perturbations. In both animals and man the rate at which lesions develop determines the extent to which they alter the conscious state. As a result, small, rapidly produced and precisely localized neurolytic lesions often paralyze arousal far more than do much larger but more slowly evolving abnormalities.

The Brainstem Reticular Formation

Modern thinking about consciousness and its activation dates mainly from the physiological studies of Moruzzi and Magoun on the reticular formation of the brainstem,[6,10] but also from earlier human pathological studies by Mauthner, von Economo and others which indicated that destructive lesions of the central mid-brain and posterior diencephalon gave rise to sleep-like states.[3,7]

The reticular formation of the brainstem diffuses its way rostrally along the central brainstem core lying just ventral to the cerebral ventricular system from the medullary-cervical junction caudally to the posterior hypothalamus and diencephalon rostrally, whence it blends into the limbic system. The components essential to arousal, or the "ascending reticular activating system" (ARAS) as Magoun called it, occupy a more anatomically restricted but not well-defined zone extending along the paramedian center of the reticulum from a caudal level at about the lower third of the pons to a rostral level that includes the posterior hypothalamus, the thalamic intralaminar nuclei and the septal area. The reticular formation is closely linked with the limbic system but just how much the functions of different parts can be fractionated, and how much must be destroyed to interrupt consciousness, is not fully elucidated. In the early experiments which underlay the original concepts of the ARAS as the basis for all of cerebral arousal, most conclusions emanated from studies where relatively large and bilateral reticular lesions were created at the level of the posterior hypothalamus and the adjacent midbrain tegmentum. Subsequently, studies of naturally occurring pathological lesions in man, as well as of smaller and more chronically studied experimental lesions in animals, have demonstrated:

(a) Lesions that destroy the reticular formation below the lower third of the pons do not produce coma.

(b) Above this level a lesion must destroy both sides of the paramedian brainstem reticulum to interrupt consciousness.[2,13]

(c) The arousal effects of reticular stimulation on behavior and on the EEG are separable (a corollary to this is that bilateral lesions of the pontine tegmentum which produce coma can be associated with a normal "awake" EEG).

(d) Sleep, whatever its function, depends on active physiological processes, not a mere failure of arousal,[9] and it is a separable condition from pathological stupor and coma.

(e) Sleeping and waking behavior can occur in man before the hemispheres develop and after they have been bilaterally and perhaps totally destroyed by disease.[1]

In brief, damage to or depression of the brainstem reticular formation can cause stupor or coma by interrupting or destroying normal arousal mechanisms but the adequate lesion must:

(1) Occupy both sides of the midline.

(2) Be located somewhere between the lower third of the pons and the posterior diencephalon.

(3) Be either abruptly acquired or fairly large in its extent.

The Cerebral Hemispheres

If the findings of clinical-pathological studies in man are compared with those of behavioral analyses after forebrain ablation in animals, the cerebral hemispheres are seen to exert a far greater influence on aroused consciousness in man than in lower forms. Consequently the conclusions of this section are based mainly upon observations from human disease, as documented elsewhere.[13]

In contrast to the brainstem, where relatively small and well-localized lesions can cause coma, only very extensive depression or dysfunction of the hemispheres appears adequate to blunt or prevent the conscious state. As with the brainstem, the rate at which disease intrudes is important, so that cerebral degenerations which evolve slowly may never dampen arousal or change waking and sleeping patterns, even when they eventually destroy so much cortex that only mindless vegetation remains. But with rapidly evolving disorders, impairment of the cerebral hemispheres reduces arousal as well as the content of consciousness roughly in proportion to the size of the lesion. However, purely unilateral abnormalities never seem sufficient to cause stupor or coma. Whether the particular anatomical locus of the bilateral cerebral lesions influences the degree of alertness is uncertain. Some observers have concluded that bilateral limbic system injury particularly devastates the conscious state. But the evidence on this point is not altogether clear and the only cerebral area that unequivocally exerts a disproportionately large effect on consciousness for its anatomic size is the language area of the dominant hemisphere. This influence can be observed in patients with acute lesions causing severe global aphasia, who often appear less alert and are harder to arouse than would be expected merely from the estimated anatomic size of the cerebral abnormality. Likewise, although there has been some controversy about the explanation for it, amylobarbital injections into the carotid artery of the dominant hemisphere that block language function appear temporarily to blunt arousal more often than do injections on the non-dominant side. We have supposed that the explanation of these findings lies in the fact that man's language influences and activates many mental processes in both hemispheres even though the words themselves and their symbolic meanings are recorded and played back through a unilateral keyboard and its associated memory recording system. But whatever the explanation, patients with severe aphasia do sometimes create a moderate amount of clinical difficulty in applying the rule that hemispheric lesions cause stupor or coma only when they are either relatively acute, bilateral and diffuse, or when they exert downward displacement on, or compression of, the diencephalon.

CEREBRAL METABOLISM AND CONSCIOUSNESS

Generally speaking, cerebral metabolism increases or decreases in parallel with changes in mental alertness or states of altered consciousness but with some interesting and still puzzling exceptions. Overall metabolism, as reflected in the rate of oxygen consumption by the brain, declines more or less in parallel with the degree of functional depression. The mean rate of oxygen use during mental alertness is about 3·5 c.c/100 gm. of brain per minute. With conditions that rapidly affect the brain, a fall in oxygen consumption of about 10–20 per cent accompanies confusional or obtunded states, whilst patients in coma for any reason generally have a level of cerebral oxygen consumption which is 50–60 per cent of normal. In most instances the decline in oxidative metabolism cannot be attributed to any lack of substrate so must be the result and not the cause of the depressed cerebral state.

With evolving or chronic cerebral abnormalities the rate of the brain's metabolism can decline considerably more than in acute disturbances without being associated with a reduction in the on-off qualities of consciousness, although such patients are usually demented. For example, rates of oxygen consumption in awake patients can be as much as 30–40 per cent below normal in chronic senile dementia and in the Wernicke–Korsakoff syndrome.[14] These figures are based on the Kety–Schmidt method of estimating cerebral metabolism and give, if anything, a falsely high impression of brain metabolism compared to normal since the method measures oxygen consumption only in tissue perfused by blood, and it has no way of estimating the amount of brain that has totally disappeared.

Metabolic analyses clearly mark sleep and coma as different states. The cerebral oxygen consumption remains at or above normal levels during sleep, but declines in all examples of coma thus far studied.

PATHOLOGICAL CONDITIONS IMPAIRING CONSCIOUSNESS

Although a dismayingly long list of diseases which affect the brain can cause stupor or coma (Table 2), they all do so by interfering with the physiological mechanisms that underlie the conscious state. Thus, for an illness to blunt consciousness significantly it must either bilaterally and diffusely interfere with the functions of the cerebral hemispheres, or it must interrupt brainstem arousal mechanisms or it must do both. Most if not all conditions that exert these pathological effects fit into one of three categories: supratentorial mass lesions, subtentorial mass or destructive lesions, and metabolic brain disease.

Supratentorial mass lesions rarely if ever directly destroy or depress enough of the cerebral hemispheres to cause stupor or coma. Rather, they interfere with consciousness by secondary effects, inducing vasomotor changes and an increased tissue bulk which produces an enlarging mass in the supratentorial cavity that gradually radiates out from the initial lesion. This mass with its advancing margin of

tissue dysfunction compresses, displaces and disrupts the bilaterally located deep diencephalic arousal mechanisms that lie close to the level of the tentorial notch in the region of the diencephalic midline. With supratentorial mass lesions stupor or coma implies incipient transtentorial herniation and will be accompanied by neurological signs and symptoms which betray such a course of rostral-caudal deterioration.

Subtentorial Mass or Destructive Lesions cause stupor or coma by compressing or destroying the paramedian reticular formation which stretches in the posterior fossa between the lower third of the pons and the midbrain-diencephalic junction. This same area of paramedian reticulum contains the nuclei and fiber pathways that regulate respiratory, pupillary, oculomotor and somatic motor functions; consequently a mechanical or ischemic brainstem lesion which is big enough to impair the neural structures that regulate consciousness almost always also produces changes in some of these other functions, and these are of very precise localizing value.

The remaining and largest group of diseases causing altered consciousness is made up of *metabolic and disseminated disorders*. Some metabolic diseases cause stupor or coma mainly by depressing the cerebral hemispheres, others mainly by affecting brainstem functions, still others by impairing both. The key to diagnosis is that except in their pre-terminal stages very few of the metabolic encephalopathies depress either all levels of the brain to the same degree or only a small focal region, and the resulting clinical signs of multifocal dysfunction betray the diagnosis.

CLINICAL SIGNS IN COMA

A meticulous attention to clinical signs often gives the key to the diagnosis of the unresponsive patient. Since dysfunction either of the hemispheres, the brainstem, or both together can lead to stupor or coma, what one seeks are physical signs which indicate whether various regions of these respective structures are operating normally or abnormally. The way these signs combine, and evolve, answers the always nagging question as to whether purely psychogenic factors could underlie the unresponsive state; with that disposed of, these signs usually discriminate quickly and accurately between supratentorial, subtentorial, and metabolic causes of coma. Once a disease has been put into one of these major categories it is comparatively straightforward to choose the proper specific tests to give the exact diagnosis.

The parameters that yield the most information about the category of coma are the pattern of breathing, the state of the pupils, the condition of the extra-ocular movements with their associated oculo-vestibular reflexes, and the pattern of the somatic motor responses to stimulation. The advantage of examining these particular functions is that each of them is distinctively influenced by nervous structures located, respectively, at hemispheric, diencephalic, midbrain, and pontine levels; and each of them is therefore altered in a clinically recognizable way when disease at one or more of those levels affects the structures relevant to its particular function. Purely psychological responses by the patient to various intensities of stimulation are not given much weight in this scheme because, once patients have developed a significant impairment of consciousness, fluctuations in their psychological responses are unhelpful in reaching an anatomic or etiologic diagnosis. The level of alertness in stuporous patients sometimes fluctuates a good deal without the underlying disease state changing in any detectable way. More sustained improvement or deterioration tells more about the degree of neurological involvement than its location in the brain and thus is more useful in judging the clinical course than in diagnosing its cause. Clinical descriptions of psychological responses are preferable to grading coma as "light" or "deep". Certainly, as already mentioned, quantitation based on motor reactions to noxious stimuli cannot be more than crude. Nor will the presence or absence of psychological responses to noxious stimuli accurately differentiate between psychogenic and physiologic causes of unresponsiveness. Since reliable physiologically based criteria will make this differentiation, it is rarely necessary or justified to create tissue-damaging pinches or scratches to evaluate an unarousable subject.

The Pattern of Breathing

Breathing serves a behavioral as well as a metabolic function in man and this dual purpose places the regulation of its patterns under the influence of the forebrain as well as of several different levels of the brainstem.[12]

Bilateral disease or depression of the cerebral hemispheres or diencephalon impairs two normal influences on breathing. One is the tonic cerebral stimulus which normally activates rhythmic breathing, keeping it going when chemoreceptor stimuli cease to barrage the lower brainstem centers. The other is the inhibitory or damping influence which normally restrains the reflex respiratory responses of lower centers to chemoreceptor stimulation. Depression or interruption of these two influences leads to the unstable respiratory pattern of Cheyne–Stokes respiration (CSR). The mechanism is as follows: with bilateral cerebral dysfunction, the ventilatory response to a rise in $PaCO_2$ is excessively large and consequently over-ventilation lowers the $PaCO_2$ to a level which no longer stimulates the chemoreceptors. Since the tonic cerebral activating stimuli are also in abeyance, breathing stops until the CO_2 threshold is reached again; it then responds excessively to the next wave of venous blood CO_2 that has passed unrefreshed through the unventilated lungs during apnea. Once initiated the oscillation tends to continue indefinitely in regularly recurring, periodic cycles with a period length equal to approximately twice the lung-to-brain circulation time.

Damage or depression of the paramedian reticulum of the midbrain and rostral pons results in a regular, sustained pattern of hyperpnea called *central neurogenic hyperventilation* (CNH). In pure form this abnormality is relatively rare although well-documented. A commoner respiratory disturbance accompanying posterior diencephalic-midbrain lesions is a mixture of primary and secondary hyperventilation, with vigorous over-breathing accompanying pulmonary pathology, which itself may be partly of neurogenic origin.

Injury to the tegmentum of the lower pons or medulla strikes directly at the centers which control the elemental inspiratory-expiratory rhythm, the result being *apneustic* or *ataxic* breathing patterns or depression to apnea. Such irregular breathing, due to lower brainstem damage, has a chaotic and unpredictable pattern, in contrast to the regularly and predictably periodic waxing and waning of CSR.

The Pupils

Neural centers and pathways at every level of the brainstem, from the diencephalon to the pons, affect the size and reactivity of the pupils, making their diameter, shape and response important clues in diagnosis. Compression or damage to the anterior hypothalamus blocks the sympathetic outflow from that structure and produces a small pupil which retains its reaction to light. Damage to the posterior diencephalic tegmentum blocks the incoming light reflex, leaving a wide (4–6 mm.) pupil that, lacking a tonic (light) stimulus to contract, spontaneously fluctuates (hippus). Damage to the third nerve outflow interrupts the parasympathetic efferent fibers and dilates the pupil, the width depending on how complete the interruption. By contrast, destruction of the third nerve nuclei in the midbrain is usually bilateral because the nuclei essentially adjoin each other; it interferes with both the sympathetic (adjacent descending pathways) and the parasympathetic (Edinger–Westphal nucleus) pupillary innervation so that midposition (3–5 mm.) fixed pupils are the result. Pontine tegmental lesions if unilatreal interrupt one descending sympathetic pathway, if bilateral interrupt both, and pupillary constriction is the result. This is especially intense with pontine hemorrhage when the pupils shrink to pinpoint size and the light reflex may disappear for several hours.

Oculomotor Control

Knowledge of oculomotor function is crucial in appraising unconscious states. The necessary nuclear centers and inter-connecting pathways for full reciprocal oculomotor activity lie in the brainstem between the pons and the midbrain either within the substance of the reticular formation of just dorsal to it, and these ocular pathways respond reflexly to the powerful space-orienting influences of the labyrinthine-vestibular system as well as to the proprioceptive receptors of the neck. When the cerebral hemispheres function normally their effect is to suppress the reflex vestibular-oculomotor influence. But when the hemispheres are depressed or damaged vigorous oculovestibular reflexes emerge, and produce appropriate yoked eye movements as long as the brainstem is intact. Thus a purely hemispheric depression or lesion causing coma is accompanied by strong oculovestibular reflex responses but, since the oculomotor pathways and the reticular formation lie juxtaposed in the brainstem, no midbrain or pontine lesion can interrupt consciousness

COWS

cold opposite / warm same

Dolls

Hesel

without also interfering with reflex or direct oculomotor control.

The oculomotor responses are readily tested clinically. To test for the *oculocephalic responses*, the examiner grasps the patient's head and turns it briskly to one side or the other or flexes or extends it. Each new position should be held briefly while observing the position of the eyes. With an intact reflex response, the eyes turn opposite to the direction of the head movement as if lagging behind (like doll's eyes), then return gradually and steadily to the primary position. A more vigorous and reliable stimulus is caloric irrigation with a small amount of ice water which tests the oculovestibular response. Only 1 c.c. is required to elicit a satisfactory reflex[11] but care must be taken to inject the fluid against the aural tympanum, yet not to damage that structure. An intact and normally functioning cerebrum inhibits this response and centers the eyes so that only quick-phase nystagmus away from the irrigating stimulus is observed. With an intact brainstem, but a depressed cerebrum, the eyes tonically deviate to the side of the ice-water irrigation. Depression of both the cerebrum and the brainstem deadens the system and caloric irrigation then elicits no ocular movement.

Motor Behavior

As with respiration, pupillary, and oculomotor activity, motor behavior alters in fairly distinctive patterns when injury or depression affects, respectively, the cerebrum, the midbrain or the low brainstem: the resulting clinical signs give useful localizing information. Discrete injury to the motor pathways of the cerebrum gives rise to the well-known patterns of mono- or hemiplegia. More diffuse impairment of the hemispheres, particularly of frontal lobe function, gives rise to a plastic-like increased resistance to passive stretch, called *paratonia* or *Gegenhalten*. Tonic palmar or plantar grasp reflexes often accompany strongly developed paratonia.

Noxious stimulation often evokes characteristic motor responses after injury to the cerebrum or brainstem. A standard stimulus of pressing the superior rim of the orbit with the thumb is usually adequate to elicit a response without producing tissue damage. Deeply placed injuries to the hemispheric motor pathways are often accompanied by the emergence of *decorticate* responses; the upper extremity flexes at elbow, wrist and digits and the lower forcefully extends with the foot in plantar flexion. Motor dysfunction emanating from a more caudal level, between the posterior diencephalon and upper pons, gives rise to the *decerebrate response* with extension and pronation of the upper extremity accompanying the extended ipsilateral lower extremity. Tegmental pontine damage results in either generalized flaccidity, or flaccidity in the upper extremities accompanied by a flexor response in the lower.

CLINICAL PATTERNS

The clinical changes that accompany dysfunction at each level of the brain evolve with different patterns according to whether the cause of psychological unresponsiveness stems from supratentorial, subtentorial, metabolic, or psychogenic diseases (Table 1). Some of the commoner causes of stupor and coma that lie within each of these categories are listed in Table 2.

TABLE 1

CLINICAL FINDINGS WITH ALTERED CONSCIOUSNESS

Level of Damage or Depression	Respiration	Pupils	Caloric Responses	Motor Response
None (psychogenic states)	eupnea or hyperventilation	2–3 mm. reactive	quick-phase nystagmus bilaterally	appropriate or absent
Cerebral hemispheres	sighing, eupnea, Cheyne Stokes (CSR)	2 mm. reactive	tonic conjugate deviation	paratonia, paretic
Diencephalon, central	eupnea or CSR	1·5–2 mm. reactive	tonic conjugate deviation	paretic or decorticate
Uncal herniation	eupnea or central hyperventilation (CNH)	unequal, dilated on side of hernia	incipient III nerve weakness	paretic on same or opposite side to pupil; paratonia
Midbrain	CSR or CNH	midposition (4–6 mm.), fixed irregular	sluggish or internuclear ophthalmoplegia	decorticate→decerebrate
Pontine	apneustic, cluster or ataxic	pinpoint, often temporarily fixed	absent	decerebrate or lower extremity flexor response
Medullary (consciousness not lost)	ataxic or apnea	small (2 mm.) reactive	unaffected	flaccid or lower extremity flexor response

Supratentorial Mass Lesions cause coma by causing compression and eventually displacement and bilateral ischemia of the diencephalon. Sooner or later, progressive supratentorial lesions cause herniation of the uncus of the temporal lobe (uncal herniation) or of the central diencephalic structures through the tentorial notch (central herniation) and shortly thereafter the process results in irreversible brainstem damage. Therefore the signs of impending transtentorial herniation, including stupor and coma, usually warn that if the disease is left to itself the patient will soon reach the point of therapeutic no return.

TABLE 2

THE CAUSE OF COMA IN 386 PATIENTS FROM
A LARGE HOSPITAL SERIES [13]

I. Supratentorial Mass Lesions		69
Epidural hematoma	2	
Subdural hematoma	21	
Intracerebral hematoma	33	
Cerebral infarct	5	
Brain tumor	5	
Brain abscess	3	
II. Subtentorial Lesions		52
Brainstem infarct	37	
Brainstem tumor	2	
Brainstem hemorrhage	7	
Cerebellar hemorrhage	4	
Cerebellar abscess	2	
III. Metabolic and Diffuse Cerebral Disorders		261
Anoxia or ischemia	51	
Concussion and postictal states	9	
Infection (Meningitis and encephalitis)	11	
Subarachnoid hemorrhage	10	
Exogenous toxins	99	
Endogenous toxins and deficiencies	81	
IV. Psychiatric Disorders		4

The clinical signs of supratentorial masses often begin with signs and symptoms of focal hemispheric dysfunction: hemiparesis, "cortical" somatic sensory abnormalities, visual field defects, aphasia, or seizures. But this self-revealing unilaterality often disappears or becomes submerged as bilateral cerebral dysfunction and coma develop. The clinical giveaway for supratentorial lesions is that they start in the cerebrum, produce the first clinical signs of their pathological effects from there, and thenceforth their ill-effects progressively move down the brain in a steady rostral-to-caudal wave. This wave is rarely disrupted, and then only by the dynamic changes of an ill-timed lumbar puncture or the sudden rupture of a hemorrhage or abscess into the ventricular system, either of which can precipitate acute cerebellar tonsillar herniation and medullary failure. Other than with these rare catastrophes, clinical signs in patients with supratentorial mass lesions reflect rostral-caudal deterioration which leads to the diagnosis: functions disappear as if their sources were being serially sectioned away from top to bottom and the characteristic changes that signify the loss of one function (i.e. of respiratory, pupillary, oculomotor or somatic motor activity) never precede or lag the loss of the others by more than one functional brain segment.

To give an example: signs of cerebral hemispheric dysfunction are never accompanied by any signs of pontine dysfunction until everything in between has disappeared.

Subtentorial Lesions cause coma by compressing or destroying both sides of the central reticular core of the brainstem. Unavoidably, such damage includes nuclei and pathways lying either within the reticulum or immediately adjacent to it and which influence pupillary and oculomotor control and usually respiratory and somatic motor function as well. Defects in these neighboring functions always identify subtentorial dysfunction and point to its being the primary problem when they can be observed in association with the onset of unconsciousness.

Metabolic Dysfunction of the brain almost always gives itself away clinically because very few metabolic diseases depress all parts of the brain to an equal degree and at an equal rate. Most metabolic encephalopathies spare the pupillary light reflexes (severe anoxia, atropine-like drugs and large doses of glutethimide stand excepted) and many also exert an unequal depressing effect on the other functions described here (i.e. on breathing, pupillary, oculomotor or somatic motor control); in metabolic coma one function is lost whilst another is preserved even though both originate at the same anatomical level. Structural or compressive brain lesions do not exert such a selective effect at several different levels at once and this serves to discriminate these lesions.

Metabolic encephalopathies have many characteristics which, while not pathognomonic, point an arrow in their direction. Non-aphasic confusion or lethargy often introduces the early stages; the metabolic disturbances often induce a compensatory hyper- or hypoventilation unaccompanied by other signs of brainstem dysfunction; unilateral pupillary or oculomotor palsies are lacking; motor weakness occurs, but seldom unilaterally; when asterixis and multifocal myoclonus occur, they are almost diagnostic.

Psychogenic Unresponsiveness is diagnosed by the absence of any sign of physiological dysfunction. Respiration is eupneic or tachypneic; the pupils remain responsive to stimulation unless the charade includes the use of mydriatics; the closed eyelids blink at a physiological rate and close briskly after being passively raised; caloric stimulation evokes quick-phase nystagmus; and motor reflexes and responses are either physiological, absent or bizarre. If available the electroencephalogram is normal but since a relatively normal EEG can also accompany certain comatose states, this by itself does not suffice to separate psychological from organic illnesses affecting consciousness.

PROGNOSIS IN COMA AND THE DIAGNOSIS OF BRAIN DEATH

During recent years respirators, cardiac assistive devices and advances in medical intensive care have given rewarding life to many who otherwise would have succumbed to acute illness or brain injury. At the same time, these remarkable supportive services have enabled the bodies of a certain number of hopelessly brain-damaged persons to survive almost indefinitely, creating heavy emotional and financial burdens on families and hospitals. In these unfortunate circumstances two questions face the physician. Can he say with assurance when the brain has irreversibly died with no chance of recovering even the primitive hindbrain function necessary to support vegetative existence? and, with all humility, can he predict accurately in less severely injured patients which ones will never recover enough consciousness to give life any meaning? As it turns out, the first, which is much the smaller-sized social and economic problem, can usually be readily answered by clinical analysis alone, while present information suggests that the second is often impossible to resolve until so much time has elapsed that the outcome is almost self evident.

Brain Death occurs when irreversible damage to the cerebral hemispheres and brain stem is so severe that the nervous system can no longer maintain internal homeostasis, i.e. autonomous respiratory, circulatory and temperature-regulating functions. Although mechanical methods may preserve the peripheral organs temporarily, circulatory failure invariably develops within a few days or at most a few weeks and the heartbeat then ceases. Proof that the brain has been long dead in such instances come from the invariable finding of extensive autolysis of the organ at the autopsy table.[1a,6a]

Table 3

Clinical Criteria for the Diagnosis of Brain Death Employed at Cornell Medical Center

1. The Nature and Duration of Coma

(a) The cause must be unequivocally structural disease (e.g. trauma, neoplasm, etc.) or of clearly known anoxic origin.

(b) There must be no chance that depressant drugs or hypothermia contribute to the clinical picture.

(c) Signs of absent brain function must persist at least 12 hr. under direct observation.

2. Cerebral Cortical Function must be Absent

(a) Behavioral or reflex responses above the foramen magnum level must be lacking to noxious stimuli applied anywhere on the body.

(b) The electroencephalogram properly recorded[9a] must be isoelectric for 60 min. at an amplitude of 50 μV./cm.

3. Brainstem Function must be Absent

(a) The pupils must be fixed to a strong light stimulus and without evidence of peripheral third nerve injury.

(b) Oculovestibular responses must be absent.

(c) There must be no motor activity whatsoever in structures innervated by cranial nerves.

(d) Spontaneous respiration must be absent. If the patient is on a respirator there must be no breathing movements despite being removed from the respirator for 3 min. (receiving diffusion oxygen) and having a normal arterial PCO_2 at the start.

(e) The circulation may be intact.

(f) Purely spinal reflex responses may be retained.

Several large series of empirical clinical observations, including data from several hundred patients in our own institution[1a,2a,8a] indicate that when all clinical signs of cerebral and brainstem function disappear for more than an hour or so in a patient with a structural or anoxic brain injury, recovery never occurs despite extended reanimation efforts. The criteria for brain death consists of identifying the absence of any signs of function emanating from the brain stem or forebrain in a subject known to have received either a structural or anoxic injury (Table 3). Hypothermia or depressant drug ingestion must be ruled out, because, alone or combined, these conditions can produce the illusion of brain death in recoverable patients.[3a] On the other hand, primitive motor responses or stretch reflexes in the spinal segments do not belie the fact that the brain has died, since the isolated spinal cord can function independently of higher structures. How long signs of function must be absent to fully assure oneself that the brain is truly dead, and not merely depressed, is not conclusively established from available evidence. The Harvard Committee requires 24 hr. under observation[2a] to conclude that the brain is dead. Many patients will not maintain cardiac activity for that long when the brain is gone and many centers, including our own, have established a 12 hr. period of no observed functions as sufficient, since we have observed no patient who met the criteria listed in Table 3 for even a 6 hr. period who later survived. (The main reason for choosing the shorter, but responsibly dependable, period is to gain healthier visceral organs for transplantation.) Extensive laboratory tests add little that is essential when an experienced physician applies the full clinical criteria for brain death. However, for the reassurance of all concerned and possibly for medical-legal purposes it seems wise to insist that a properly applied and recorded electroencephalogram detect no cerebral electrical activity for 60 min.[9a] An alternative is to demonstrate that no contrast material enters the cerebral circulation with a properly performed carotid angiogram.

Irreversible Coma, sometimes called the apallic syndrome, occurs when brain damage is permanently so severe that the individual thereafter never regains the capacity for external homeostasis, i.e. is unable to adjust his thoughts or behavior in any major way to the environment even though vegetative regulation is preserved. The pathology of irreversible coma usually is limited to extensive laminar necrosis of the cerebral cortex, demyelination of the subcortical white matter or focal infarctions of the brainstem reticular formation. Unfortunately, prognosis is an uncertain thing in such severely damaged patients and available clinical studies provide very little direct data to guide one's judgements during the early hours or days after even severe insults to the brain.[7a] However, a few variables can be cited which weight the scales:

(1) Age. The young brain often recovers from injuries which are fatal or permanent in older patients. This holds particularly true in traumatic head injury but even with anoxic or infectious damage almost no children remain permanently in coma whilst few patients

older than 50 years recover sentient behavior after being unconscious for a week or more.

(2) Nature of the lesion. The outcome after anoxic-ischemic lesions is more difficult to predict than after trauma, where several workers have found that the degree and quality of neurological recovery closely relates itself to age and the duration of consciousness.[4a] No accurate predictions can be offered for patients who suffer from non-anoxic metabolic coma, sence even elderly patients can survive and fully recover after, for example, a week or more of profound barbiturate-induced coma.[13]

(3) Extent and course of neurological lesion. The more extensive and severe a traumatic or anoxic injury, the less likely is the brain to recover and the longer the signs of severe injury last the worse becomes the outlook. Signs of severe brainstem injury always worsen the prognosis: although the presence of fixed pupils, absent oculovestibular responses, motor decerebration or flaccidity and apnea can be recovered from when they last for a few brief minutes after the insult, the forecast becomes less encouraging as each succeeding half hour passes. On the other hand as long as one can observe neurological improvement, at first from one day to the next and later from one week to the next no one can predict from presently available guidelines how far recovery will go.

Predicting the outcome for unconscious or acutely neurologically injured patients is difficult and delicate. The lack of well controlled and documented clinical information in the literature may be partly explained because few physicians have carefully examined the problem, but it is also because rough-and-ready early clinical prognostic guesses about neurological outcome have often proved sadly wrong in the past.

FURTHER READING

[1] Brierley, J. B. et al. (1971) "Prolonged Survival with Isoelectric EEG and Normal Respiration after Cardiac Arrest," Lancet, 2, 560–565.
[2] Chase, T. N., Moretti, L. and Prensky, A. L. (1968), "Clinical and Electroencephalographic Manifestations of Vascular Lesions of the Pons," Neurology, 18, 357–368.
[3] Economo, C. von. (Trans. by K. O. Newman), (1931), Encephalitis Lethargica: Its Sequelas and Treatment. Oxford University Press.
[4] Kemper, T. H. and Romanul, F. C. A. (1967), "State Resembling Akinetic Mutism in Basilar Artery Occlusion," Neurology, 17, 74–80.
[5] Lassen, N. A. (1959), "Cerebral Blood Flow and Oxygen Consumption in Man," Physiol. Rev., 39, 183–238.
[6] Magoun, H. W. (1963), The Waking Brain, Springfield: Charles C. Thomas.
[7] Mauthner, L. (1890), "Zur Pathologie und Physiologie des Schlafes nebst Bemerkungen über die 'Nona'," Wien. klin. Wschr., 40, 961, 1001, 1049, 1092, 1144, 1185.
[8] Medical Research Council Brain Injuries Committee (1941), A glossary of psychological terms commonly used in cases of head injury. Medical Research Council War Memorandum Nr. 4. London: HMSO.
[9] Moruzzi, G. (1963), "Active Processes in the Brainstem During Sleep," Harvey Lect., 58, 233–297.
[10] Moruzzi, G. and Magoun, H. W. (1949), "Brainstem Reticular Function and Activation of the EEG," Electroenceph. clin. Neurophysiol., 1, 455–473.
[11] Nelson, J. R. (1969), "The Minimal Ice Water Caloric Test," Neurology, 19, 577–585.
[12] Plum, F. (1970), "Neurological Integration of Behavioral and Metabolic Control of Breathing," Ciba Foundation, Hering Breuer Centenary Symposium, Breathing. (R. Porter, Ed.). London: Churchill.
[13] Plum, F. and Posner, J. B. (1972), Diagnosis of Stupor and Coma, 2nd edition. Philadelphia: F. A. Davis.
[14] Shimojyo, S., Scheinberg, P. and Reinmuth, O. (1967), "Cerebral Blood Flow and Metabolism in the Wernicke–Korsakoff Syndrome," J. Clin. Invest., 46, 849–854.
[1a] Alderete, J. F., Jeri, F. R., Richardson, E. R., Sament, S., Schwab, R. S. and Young, R. R. (1968), "Irreversible Coma: A Clinical Electroencephalic and Neurologic Study," Trans. Amer. neurol. Ass., 93, 16–18.
[2a] Beecher, H. K. et al. (1968), "A Definition of Irreversible Coma," JAMA, 205, 85–88.
[3a] Bird, T. and Plum, F. (1968), "Recovery from Barbiturate Overdose Coma with Prolonged Isolectric Electroencephalogram," Neurol., 18, 456–460.
[4a] Carlson, C. A., VonEssen, C. and Lofgren J. (1968), "Factors Affecting the Clinical Course of Patients with Severe Head Injuries," J. Neurosurg., 29, 242–251.
[5a] Davis, J. N. and Plum, F., Prediction of Neurological Outcome in Anoxic and Metabolic Coma. In press.
[6a] Kraymer, W. (1963), "From Reanimation to Deanimation," Acta neurol. (Scand.), 39, 139–153.
[7a] Miller, H. and Stern, G. (1965), "Long Term Prognosis of Severe Head Injury," Lancet, 1, 225–229.
[8a] Mollaret, P. and Goulen, M. (1959), "Le coma dépassé," Rev. Neurol. 101, 3–15.
[9a] Silverman, D., Masland, R. L., Saunders, M. G. and Schwab, R. S. (1970), "Irreversible Coma Associated with Electrocerebral Silence," Neurology, 20, 525–533.

4. INTELLIGENCE

R. C. OLDFIELD

INTRODUCTION

Less than a century ago the words *intelligence* and *intelligent* were scarcely ever used with concrete reference to any particular person or class of persons. Today both words, and the concepts, hazy or many-faceted, which lie behind them are central in western society. The story of how this change came about is complex, but comprises two somewhat distinct and irreconcilable features. The first arises from post-Darwinian comparisons of man with other animal species, especially in relation to intelligently adaptive behaviour, and this led to attempts to define *intelligence* in such a way as to assist such comparisons and to obtain some measure of it in both human and sub-human species. The second important factor was a consequence of increasing pre-occupation with the techniques of education, particularly in relation to the obviously wide variation in individual capacities to benefit by their application. Thus, very broadly speaking, the word *intelligence* brings two things to mind. One is the capacity for behaviour well-adapted to the demands of the complex and varied environment in which human beings live, and especially in those cases where novelty is required. The other is the ability to perform certain types of mental operation, generally ones relating to the logical structure of the material, whether verbal or not, presented as stimulus. It need hardly be emphasized that the connection, or lack of it, between these two aspects has been a fruitful source of controversy. Indeed, what Lashley wrote in 1929 remains true today:

The whole problem is in confusion. It is uncertain whether we are justified in dealing with intelligence as a single function, as an algebraic sum of all functions, or as the sum of a few selected ones. There is further involved the problem of valuation. So long as we judge intelligence in terms of the effectiveness of integration (success in life or school for example), we are unlikely to discover any simply physiological correlate. On the other hand, attempts to formulate it in terms of the completeness or complexity of integration are baffled by the lack of any effective measures of these attributes.

But today these confusions arouse less concern, and attempts at any overall unitary definition have been largely abandoned. Comparison between men and animals in terms of intelligent behaviour has tended in the past forty years to be specific rather than general and largely confined to developmental aspects, though quite latterly questions of communication and language, rather than problem-solving, have been to the fore.[5]

Of great contemporary consequence are the differences between the idea of intelligence as part of our common stock-in-trade of everyday discourse and judgement on the one hand, and on the other that notion of it which issues in the numerical assessment of a mental attribute arrived at on the basis of performance of a number of standard tasks chosen partly in accordance with tradition, and partly with certain statistical considerations in mind.[8] As an everyday concept, "intelligence" may arise as an element in our judgement of intellectual capacity, as relating to the development of a child or as a criterion of occupational viability. It may, too, crop up in a privative sense as when we recognize its greater or lesser absence in the sub-normal child or the older dement. The idea also has qualitative nuances and the word *intelligent* has different flavours of valuation according to its precise verbal context—it can even suggest a faint but effective disparagement, as it does in French. But the word and the concept are now ineradicable, however dangerous or ludicrous may be the misunderstandings involved in its use.

When, on the other hand, we turn to the apparently greater precision of the intelligence test approach we encounter grave difficulties both as to the ultimate meaning of what is measured and as to the applicability of the figures obtained to any real human situation. In the former connection long and bitter controversy has revolved around the question of whether or not any single unitary attribute is being measured.[9,11] In the latter it is often objected that, particularly in the educational field, the figures may be not only of little practical utility, but dangerously misleading. Others[2] have pointed out that conventional tests are largely concerned with mental operations within closed systems and have little to do with "creative" thinking.

It must not be thought, however, that measures of intelligence are devoid of usefulness. Binet and Simon's pioneer efforts, for example, enabled children to be effectively screened to ascertain which were incapable of normal schooling, and the American Army Alpha Test similarly excluded those recruits whose potential military activity might more assist the enemy than their own comrades. And there are other connections, many neurological, in which, used comparatively or differentially, intelligence measures can be of substantial value.

MEASURES OF INTELLIGENCE

Within the practical and, hopefully, scientific field of neurology we may accept that "Intelligence is what Intelligence Tests measure". Intelligence tests may be be classified in various ways and one distinction is that between "group" and "individual" tests. The former can be administered to a number of people simultaneously, and these are chiefly used in educational connections. "Individual" tests have to be administered to each subject separately and are applied in clinical settings. The former we shall not further consider, though measures of intelligence derived from them may occasionally be encountered in clinical documents. (Such figures should be treated with caution.) Many individual tests derive historically from the pioneer forms developed by A. Binet and T. Simon at the turn of this century. Binet invented the term Intelligence Quotient (IQ) which he defined as the ratio of an individual's *Mental Age* (MA) to his *Chronological Age* (CA), multiplied by 100. The Binet–Simon Test—later revised and presented in two equivalent alternative forms by Terman and Merrill—consists of a number of sub-tests with items of graded difficulty *linked to age*. The precise details of the scoring process whereby the MA is calculated need not detain us, except to note that it is so arranged that a child scoring the *mean score* for those of his age in the whole population on which standardization was carried out shall have an MA equal to his CA. The IQ is thus a measure of an individual's superiority or inferiority compared with his coevals. (Precisely the same kind of measure could be applied to stature.) This conception of the IQ has obvious disadvantages. In the first place, actual performance on the kind of age-graded tests incorporated in the battery does not increase above the age of 17 or so, and thus no provision is made for the application of the IQ to adults.

Secondly, it is found that performance on this kind of task actually falls off progressively after attaining a maximum at around the same age, as shown in Fig. 1. In connection with children, especially the subnormal, the MA is often preferred as a measure. To say that a child of 13 scores the same as an average child of 7 seems to provide a more telling indication of disability than the statement that his IQ is 54. For the literal-minded, however, both versions have their dangers.

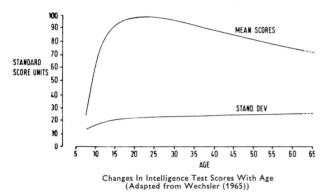

Changes In Intelligence Test Scores With Age
(Adapted from Wechsler (1965))

FIG. 1.

A second distinction to be made is that between *verbal* and *performance* tests. The latter were originally introduced to offset varying standards of educational level and verbal sophistication in different individuals, and to evade difficulties in communities with different mother tongues. In fact not all so-called performance tests involve actual physical activity, and the difference is often rather one between *verbal* and *non-verbal* types. These latter commonly employ *visual* material, very often in geometrical or diagrammatic form. Among tests involving actual visuo-constructive performance (that is, manipulation of objects) we may cite as an outstanding example the Kohs' Block Test, while one primarily involving not actual manipulation but visual thinking is the Raven–Penrose Progressive Matrices.[7] This latter test is of outstanding utility and invokes thinking which may be very largely free of verbal elements.

The emphasis now is no longer on the determination of MA but upon performance scores in a variety of selected tasks. A definition of the IQ in these terms can, as proposed by Wechsler,[10] be given as the ratio of the score attained by a given individual to the *expected* (or average) found *among his coevals* in an appropriate sample of the population at large, multiplied as before by 100. In practice, such a definition of the IQ involves some points of statistical complexity for which the reader must be referred to Chapter 2 of Wechsler's book. We must, however, take account of the fact that the raw scores on different tests and sub-tests may differ in statistical distribution. Varying dispersion requires scores to be expressed as normal deviates* when we wish to make comparisons between scores on different tests and sub-tests. It is customary to relate these deviates to a convenient arbitrary mean, such for instance as in Sub-Tests

* Values expressed using the standard deviation as unit.

in the Wechsler Adult Intelligence Scale (WAIS)[10], where the figure adopted is 10.

We may indeed take WAIS* as a model to illustrate a number of points in the application of intelligence tests in neurology and neuropsychology. WAIS falls into two parts, the *Verbal* comprising six sub-tests (Information, Comprehension, Arithmetic, Similarities, Digit Span, Vocabulary) and *Performance* (Digit Symbol, Picture Completion, Block Design, Picture Arrangement, Object Assembly). For details of the actual character and content of these sub-tests reference should be made to Wechsler[10] and to the Manual supplied with the set of test material. Procedures for calculating from raw scores the Verbal IQ, Performance IQ, and overall WAIS IQ are to be found in the Manual, as are those for the Sub-Test scores, which as we shall see loom large in the applications we are concerned with.

Clinical circumstances and purposes may often render nugatory or impossible the administration of the whole of a test such as WAIS. (Where, however, overall IQ measures are desired, it is important to remember that figures derived from different tests are *not* directly comparable. At best the product-moment correlation between two tests may have been determined and if this is high a fairly close prediction of the score that would be obtained on Test A may be made from the actual value found on Test B.) Confining ourselves for the moment to WAIS, it is important to know which of the Sub-Tests give the best estimates of—i.e. are most highly correlated with—the overall Test IQ. For a population ranging in age from 25–34, for instance, the two lowest (product-moment) correlations are those for Digit Span at 0·56 and Object Assembly at 0·58. The two highest, both at 0·84, are for Information and Vocabulary. By employing a combination of these two Sub-Tests a satisfactory estimate of the total Verbal IQ may be obtained, the correlation being 0·94. On the Performance side, the best pairs are Block Design plus Picture Arrangement, and Digit Symbol plus Block Design, the corresponding correlation in each case being 0·92.†

APPLICATIONS OF INTELLIGENCE TESTS IN NEUROLOGY AND NEUROPSYCHOLOGY

Now that we have gained some idea of the character and structure of an Intelligence Test by reference to one particular model we may consider the uses to which such procedures may be put. It must be stressed at the outset that our present terms of reference relate to the assessment of *Intelligence* and we are not concerned with the use of component parts of such tests in the estimation of

* WAIS was preceded by the Wechsler–Bellevue Test which offers two alternative forms. There is also the Wechsler Intelligence Scale for Children (WISC).

† It may be generally noted that some tests for use in one country may for various reasons require modification in another, even when the respective languages are the same or closely similar. This is very evident in the case of the Information Sub-Test and a provisional British equivalent to the original American version is available. In a more subtle way this will apply to the Vocabulary Sub-Test, and for this and other reasons some workers in Britain prefer the use of the Mill Hill Vocabulary.[6]

particular functional deficits.[4] Neuropsychologists generally may often select one or another Sub-Test for this latter purpose—the Block Design Sub-Test is, for example, very useful in the study of visuo-spatial disorders associated with right posterior cortical lesions. We, on the other hand, have to do with Intelligence and its alterations, and this implies a need to select such test components as may so far as possible be unaffected by any specific defects such as aphasia or apraxia. With this proviso in mind, here are some practical examples of the use of Intelligence Tests in neurological work.

(1) Patients have been subjected to some surgical or other therapeutic procedure, and we wish to know its effect on their general Intelligence. One example, now rather a matter of past history, is given by operations involving removal or disconnection of the frontal lobes, whether for psychiatric purposes or in treatment of neoplasms. Another is hemispherectomy, or large-scale extirpation of hemispheric tissue, for the alleviation of epilepsy. In such cases it is of obvious practical importance to ascertain how far the advantages of the operation may be offset by some degree of resulting general intellectual deficit. The outcome of frontal lobe extirpation and disconnection were the subject of a number of large-scale investigations of this kind[1,3,12] with, it must be confessed, rather conflicting conclusions. Two points are, however, worth making. The first is the surprisingly large amount of frontal tissue which may be removed, at least unilaterally, without any very notable deficit in IQ terms being occasioned. The second is that some at least of the conflict of view arises from the difference between short-term and long-term effects. So far as hemispherectomy and other operations (notably temporal lobe excision) for the relief of epilepsy are concerned actual gains of IQ have been reported. These may be attributed to freeing the brain of morbid tissue whose disordered working might have depressed the intellectual functions. In the case of epilepsy, too, the period between onset and operation may be a factor if continued seizures induce an irreversible mental deterioration measurable in IQ terms.

(2) Another clinical question which not infrequently arises, especially with older patients, is that of the extent to which a general intellectual deterioration, whether resulting from arterio-sclerosis or primary cortical degeneration, may underlie and possibly exaggerate a more specific deficit of recent origin such as a receptive dysphasia. Much attention has been directed to the study of mental deterioration as such in terms of the changing relationships between different Sub-Tests. Thus in WAIS some test components tend to retain their premorbid values to a far greater extent than others and the former are known as "Hold" as opposed to the latter group of "Don't Hold" tests. The "Hold" Sub-Tests are Vocabulary, Information, Object Assembly and Picture Completion, while the latter are Digit Span, Similarities, Digit Symbol and Block Design. Some workers like to use a *Deterioration Coefficient* calculated as

$$(\text{Hold—Don't Hold}) \div \text{Hold}$$

But in a neurological setting where circumscribed lesions and focal defects are commonly involved, use of some of these test components will be likely to be precluded and such numerical data as may be obtainable will best be assessed in a less formal fashion. Such assessment may nevertheless be very useful inasmuch as a considerable amount of cortical degeneration may exist without interfering with some patients' daily lives, its effects only coming to the surface in the face of some fresh specific cerebral insult. (The reader will recall that the *general* effects of ageing are already offset by the construction and standardization of tests such as the WAIS.)

(3) Even where no question of actual dementia arises, it may often be desirable to form a more precise assessment of a patient's pre-morbid intellectual capacity than can be obtained from the accounts of his relatives or from his occupational or socio-economic status. Here careful selection of the Sub-Test to be used is required. The Kohs' Block Design Sub-Test, for instance, affords a reasonable indication of a patient's intellectual status, but would be wholly inappropriate in any case where the right hemisphere may be the site of a lesion. Again, among Sub-Tests the best indicators of intellectual status are Vocabulary and Information. In the presence of an aphasia, administration of the latter may prove difficult or impossible. But even where the speech disorder is quite severe it is surprising how well a Vocabulary Test can be carried out—in the last resort by use of the Multiple Choice version of the Mill Hill Test. In such a case, therefore, a fair and objective notion of pre-morbid intelligence may be gained by combining this test with the Block Design.

(4) Another very important application of intelligence testing relates to research rather than to clinical assessment or prognosis. It frequently happens that in trying to determine the functions of this or that part of the cerebral hemispheres we have to compare performance on appropriate tasks either between two groups of patients with different types of lesion or between one group of patients and a group of normal subjects. It is obviously important to be sure that any differences found are not due to adventitious sampling differences in intelligence as between the two groups. Here again it may be difficult or undesirable to apply a full test battery, and the comparison will have to be made on a selection of sub-tests which are unaffected by the focal psychological deficits shown by the patients.

CONCLUSION

The upshot of this very brief account may be given as follows:

(1) Intelligence, if regarded biologically as some unitary capacity for adaptive behaviour in complex and novel circumstances and possibly correlated with some single aspect of neural function, is a notion which as yet has failed to develop effective links with quantitative empirical treatment. If, in the second place, we try to define it as some single source of intellectual capacity manifesting itself in varied tasks which have an underlying logical structure, we can only say that progress on the

theoretical side has been disappointing. But this has not meant that practical systems of quantitative assessment have not proved viable and useful in a variety of fields. For example cut-off values of IQ as obtained from a given test may be established and validated for screening purposes in occupational guidance and selection. Again, as we have seen, a number of significant issues in neurological practice and science may be handled by the use of measures of intelligence, often in a comparative or differential way.

(2) It cannot be too strongly emphasized that however weak the theoretical basis of intelligence measurement may appear to be, nothing can justify either lack of expertise in the administration of the tests or thoughtless use of the figures resulting from them. Bandying mere IQ figures about regardless of the method by which, and the circumstances in which, they were obtained can be worse than useless—indeed sometimes positively harmful.

(3) Useful as the prevailing concept of measurable intelligence may be in neurology, neither clinician nor scientist can accept that notion as sufficient in the last resort. A *general* notion of intelligence certainly includes reference to its use in *social* situations of varied kinds, but it is abundantly clear that, within wide limits, performance in such situations by no means correlates with measures of IQ. Such misalignment may be seen in a more exaggerated form in some neuropathological conditions. We need only remind ourselves of the peculiar and often bizarre disturbances of judgement and adaptive behaviour which may afflict the victim of a severe frontal lobe lesion to feel convinced that much work remains to be done in the field of "Intelligence"—even though any universally acceptable definition of it should forever elude us.

FURTHER READING

[1] Hebb, D. O. (1952), "Man's Frontal Lobes—a Critical Review," *Arch. Neurol. Psychiat. Chicago*, **68**, 293–313.
[2] Hudson, L. (1966), *Contrary Imaginations*. Methuen, London; also Penguin, Harmondsworth (1968).
[3] Klebanoff, S. G., Singer, J. L. and Wilensky, M. (1945), "Psychological Changes in Organic Brain Lesions and Ablations," *Psychol. Bull.*, **42**, 585–623. (Findings for frontal lobes summarized in (7) Table 48.)
[4] Newcombe, F. (1969), *Missile Wounds of the Brain—A Study of Psychological Deficits*. Oxford Neurological Monographs, Oxford University Press.
[5] Premack, D. (1970), "A Functional Analysis of Language," *J. exp. Anal. Beh.*, **14**, 107–125.
[6] Raven, J. C. (1958), *Extended Guide to using the Mill Hill Vocabulary Scale*, revised edition. London: Lewis (Reprinted 1962).
[7] Raven, J. C. (1960), *Guide to the Standard Progressive Matrices*. London: Lewis.
[8] Vernon, P. E. (1950), *The Structure of Human Abilities*. London: Methuen.
[9] Vernon, P. E. (1966), "Development of Current Ideas about Intelligence Tests," in *Genetic and Environmental Factors in Human Ability*, Vol. 2, Eugenic Society Symposia (J. E. Meade and A. S. Parkes, Eds.). Edinburgh and London: Oliver & Boyd.
[10] Wechsler, D. (1958), *The Measurement and Appraisal of Adult Intelligence*, 4th edition. Baltimore: Williams & Wilkins (Reprinted 1965).
[11] Wiseman, S. (Ed.) (1967), *Intelligence and Ability—Selected Readings*. Penguin Modern Psychology WPS5. Penguin, Harmondsworth (Reprinted 1968).
[12] See also references in Chapter 13 of (10).

5. MEMORY

FREDA NEWCOMBE

INTRODUCTION

Memory plays a vital role in the organization of behaviour and the exploitation of information from the environment. It is dependent on the efficiency of the sensory channels and influenced by such factors as attention, expectation and interest. Remembering is an active process.[5] Hence the importance of coding and rehearsal, the relevance of visual-image strategies, and the highly systematized "place" codes of famous memorists from the Greek orator, Simonides, to the contemporary Russian journalist, Shereshevski.[17]

Some of the conditions that influence learning and recall have been satisfactorily defined—at least in the laboratory. Less is known about the mechanisms of memory and their physiological and anatomical basis. Different facets of these problems have been explored in the study of normal and pathological memory functions. Experimental psychologists propose at least three distinct stages in the processing of sensory information: brief images of material seen or heard that decay within a second or so, short-term memory (e.g. the time required to read and dial an unfamiliar telephone number or hear and repeat a string of digits), and long-term memory (or the storage and retrieval of information over an indefinite period of time).

The concept of short- and long-term memory refers to stages of memorizing that overlap but may be differentiated and tested experimentally. It is not to be confused with the clinical distinction between recent and remote memory, which indicates the span of time covered by past memories and is assessed from the case history. Neurologists and neuropsychologists use both concepts in their examination of amnesic conditions, and also distinguish between amnesia for events preceding trauma (retrograde amnesia—RA), the transient confusional state that may ensue (post-traumatic amnesia—PTA), and the difficulty in learning and remembering new information that may persist (anterograde amnesia).

Termed independent part of music composition

The diagnosis of amnesia rests on careful scrutiny of the evidence. Forgetting a fact or groping for a word are common enough experiences, even before the onset of old age; and they do not necessarily signify an amnesic or an aphasic disorder. Complaints of bad memory or difficulties in concentration are ubiquitous but the diagnosis of amnesia is appropriate only when the disturbance of memory functions is salient and not the inevitable consequence of perceptual disorder, fluctuations of attention, or generalized intellectual deterioration. Testing of delayed memory is crucial; the patient should be asked to recall test material—word-lists, short stories, or patterns—minutes and hours after the initial presentation. Even so, the impairment has to be clearly delineated in terms of the time sequence and the type of material that is forgotten. Clinical and test data have then to be interpreted in the light of the age, occupation, and interests of the patient; and they have to be compared with his performance in other tasks of skill and ability in order to determine whether the impairment of memory is disproportionately great.

In considering the memory deficits associated with neurological disorders, a crucial distinction has to be made between global or generalized impairment of memory functions and specific deficits usually associated with focal, unilateral lesions. Generalized disorders of memory—failure to recall people, places and events—may follow head injury, Korsakoff's psychosis, encephalitis, bilateral hippocampal resection, and severe anoxic damage (provoked by status epilepticus, carbon monoxide poisoning, hanging, or severe loss of blood). Examples of these global amnesic conditions will be described in the next section.

GLOBAL AMNESIAS

Closed head injury causing loss of consciousness almost invariably results in retrograde and post-traumatic amnesia. The RA often shrinks to a short period of time during recovery, whereas the PTA is of more fixed duration although difficult to assess accurately, since patients may have lucid intervals during this period. The end of the PTA is marked by the return of continuous memory and usually exceeds the period of disturbed consciousness noted by the clinician. In the case of a severe injury, the RA may extend for months or even years but gradually shrinks over time, leaving a permanent but often quite short amnesia for events immediately preceding the injury. A few striking images associated with the accident—the galloping horse or bus tyres—may be transiently recalled during the period of confusion and may even be incorporated in confabulatory accusations[39]; but these isolated fragments of memory are not usually recalled when the patient has permanently regained consciousness.

Detailed clinical studies of over a thousand cases of traumatic amnesia[40,41] have shown that a long RA is almost invariably associated with a long period of PTA, and that the length of the PTA is a reliable index of the severity of the injury.[42,46] A clear-cut relationship

between length of PTA and persistent memory disorders has also emerged in another study of the long-term effects of closed head injury;[36] and it has been suggested that disturbances of memory are often the most striking and lasting consequences of such injury.

The even more profound amnesic deficits associated with Korsakoff's psychosis have been extensively studied during the chronic stage of the illness.[47] Memory for events—recent and remote—is grossly deranged. Although the patient may talk coherently, and even achieve average scores in standard intelligence tasks, he can not give an account of his activities during the past year, week, or even hour. This defect can not be detected by routine clinical tests of digit span, for the patient's span—or "primary memory"[52]—is usually intact. He could look up a telephone number and dial it correctly but forget to whom he was intending to speak.

Important items of personal history can not be recalled or are misplaced in time and context. Family members, and even the patient himself, are often reported to be very much younger—as if time tags were lost or else the poverty of memory has the effect of telescoping time. Confabulation may be flagrant during the acute phase of the illness. During the long, chronic coda, the patient may admit to his inability to answer questions that probe memory, or reply in a vague and evasive fashion. His errors show paramnesic condensation: names and events are confused and combined, and also misplaced in time. New information is also vulnerable and he may not be able to recall a name or an episode for more than a few minutes. Nevertheless, he often does not seem to be aware of the extent of his disability and repudiates its cause, but recognizes that he lives in hospital surroundings. Describing a typical patient, Talland[47] wrote: "it appears as if he was sitting there without a thought crossing his mind, without registering any of his surroundings". Indeed, a group of patients, assembled for conversation and discussion "subsided into silence".

A comparable amnesic defect may, in rare cases, follow encephalitis, characterized by a dense and persistent RA with an impairment of recent memory and learning.[37] The patient is usually aware of the gravity of his disability but may be so handicapped by it that some form of institutional care is required. One patient had a dense RA for eleven years and patchy amnesia for about twenty years. Although disoriented in time, he retained skills and knowledge acquired before his illness. Six months after its onset he described his condition in these terms: "I'm in a dream. You don't know how awful it is. I get thousands of impressions and they don't mean anything."

These dream-like sensations have also been reported by another patient following bilateral medial temporal-lobe resection. The operation, carried out in 1953 when the patient was twenty-seven years old and handicapped by intractable epilepsy, resulted in a profound and persistent derangement of memory functions which has subsequently been studied in detail.[25,26,29,44] Like the encephalitic patients, he is aware of his disability: "You see, at this moment everything looks clear to me, but what happened just before? That's what worries me. It's like waking from a dream; I just don't remember."

The patient can recall incidents of his early life but has an RA for one or two years preceding the operation. The anterograde amnesia, or failure to remember ongoing events, is profound. He has difficulty in finding his way about in the vicinity of his home and in recognizing his neighbours. Thirteen years after his operation, he directed his examiners to the street where he used to live before the operation.

This patient rapidly forgets new material presented to him in an experimental situation: pairs of clicks, tones, light flashes, colour shades and nonsense patterns can be discriminated normally if presented without delay but, with an interval of 60 sec. between the paired stimuli, his responses barely exceed the level of chance (Prisko,[35] cited by Milner[28]). He has a normal digit span and can remember three digits for a quarter of an hour, if allowed to rehearse them continuously. But a chance distraction, a knock on the door, a tap on his shoulder, is enough to impair recall. Five years ago, this patient was observed by the writer, working at a delayed matching-to-sample experiment in which he again matched normally if there was no delay between presentation of sample and matching response, but failed to make any correct matches if the delay was greater than 5 sec. Correct responses were rewarded with nickels and at the end of the session he had earned several dollars. Tucking them into his wallet, he was unable to account for them and could not describe how he had spent the afternoon.

The behaviour of this patient, however, contrasts sharply with that of the classical Korsakoff cases in that, apart from the inevitable dependency on a sheltered life with his parents, he appears essentially normal and does not show the apathy and personality change associated with the latter condition. The level of his performance on standard intelligence tests is somewhat higher than it was before the operation and he now obtains above-average scores. The purity of this type of amnesic deficit, therefore, makes it of especial interest for the study of memory mechanisms.

An analogous deficit, in the sense that it is not secondary to disorders of intelligence and personality, can sometimes be observed in association with third ventricle tumours.[56] A patient with a colloidal cyst of the third ventricle, who was recently examined in the Department of Neurological Surgery, showed this selective impairment of memory functions. The deficit was particularly striking in the conventional test of story recall[53]; he attended to the story, trying hard to recall its gist, but succeeded in repeating only a few items. On delayed recall an hour later, without forewarning, he could not recall any items; nor did he benefit from cues, often selecting the wrong item when offered a choice. He was topographically disorientated in the hospital, and was impaired in a spatial task, failing to learn a 10-choice point maze in 25 trials. Thus, there was objective evidence that the impairment of memory was generalized and not restricted to verbal material.

In contrast, no impairment could be detected in spontaneous speech, reading, writing and spelling; and he obtained average scores in a standard intelligence test. After the insertion of a ventriculo-atrial shunt there was a marked improvement in memory functions. Two months post-operatively, he was able to recall the main items of a story and the gist of it when tested without forewarning an hour later. He had no topographical difficulties and his performance in the maze-learning task was normal.

Transient amnesic conditions are of special interest, demonstrating that the memory deficit may in some instances be traced to a failure in the mechanism of retrieval. Old memories have not been destroyed; they cannot be recalled during the amnesic period. An informative case of concussion amnesia has been discussed by Fisher[14]: a forty-one-year-old housewife fell backwards from a low chair, rose to her feet, did not recognize her sister-in-law, and asked what had happened. Initially, she showed a profound memory loss with an RA for many years. Four hours later, there was a slight improvement in her memory for past events; she could then recall the death of her mother and brother and give further details of personal history although her responses were vague and stereotyped. She was orientated after approximately 10 hr. On examination the following day there was no evidence of RA and the neurological examination was normal.

Fisher commented that his patient perceived most sensory data during the amnesic period and concluded that "a traumatic insult to the memory mechanism can occur with complete sparing of the neural basis of alertness". He also drew attention to the transient loss of memories covering a long span of time, suggesting that the loss of recent memories is too often emphasized.

Transient global amnesias of sudden onset and without a known precipitating cause, have sometimes been reported in patients over the age of fifty years.[15,31] The condition is probably attributable to small vascular lesions and is accompanied by mild confusion. In most cases, however, the patient behaves normally, and the amnesia may not be detected; but the history occasionally suggests that a transient RA may extend over a period of years until the episode ends (usually after a few hours), leaving a permanent amnesia only for the attack itself. A patient recently examined in this Department, reported an episode of transient global amnesia which started during a game of bowls and came to an end when the patient found himself at home later that afternoon. He had a hazy memory of vertical strips moving across his line of vision during the amnesic episode, in the course of which he had driven home in the rain. The moving strips were presumably windscreen wipers—an isolated fragment of memory from a period of 2 hr. of which nothing else could be recalled.

MATERIAL-SPECIFIC MEMORY DEFICITS

In sharp contrast to these global memory impairments are the selective failures of recall associated with focal or unilateral brain lesions. These have been well-documented following unilateral temporal-lobe excisions for the relief of focal epilepsy.[24,26] They include the characteristic verbal memory loss (e.g. difficulty in assimilating and recalling stories, notably after delay) following left temporal-lobe excisions and impairment of non-verbal, visual memory (e.g. difficulty in the recognition of faces and nonsense-figures) after right temporal-lobe excisions. A selective impairment in verbal memory and learning tasks has also been found in patients with tumours or vascular lesions of the left hemisphere[3] and in ex-servicemen with focal gunshot-wounds of the left temporo-parietal region.[32] A case in the latter group serves to illustrate this point.

A classics scholar, who incurred a large temporo-parietal missile wound at the age of twenty-three and whose PTA lasted for more than 4 weeks, lost permanently all knowledge of Latin and Greek. But he regained sufficient command of his native language to achieve a second-class honours degree in history within 3 years of wounding. Some 20 years later, having succeeded in publishing two mediaeval inventories in the course of his work as a county archivist, he still had great difficulty in conventional story-recall tasks. The verbal memory deficit was of a restricted nature and could be countered by the intelligent use of *aides-mémoire*.

Verbal memory impairment is not invariably accompanied by the characteristic word-finding difficulties of dysphasia. Dysphasic patients, nevertheless, often show verbal memory deficits, more marked in rote memory tasks than in recall of substance.[58] Notwithstanding these deficits, they may remember without difficulty ongoing events in their lives. They are usually well orientated topographically and may perform efficiently in tasks involving the retention of visual and spatial data.

The selective visual or spatial memory losses seen after focal lesions of the right hemisphere are not so readily detected, not least because patients like other members of this western culture are adept at using verbal cues to increase efficiency and circumvent impairment. Certain categories of stimuli, however, may uncover non-verbal, memory deficits; these include musical sounds, abstract paintings, places and visual stimuli with reduced cues, e.g. fragmented faces or overlapping nonsense figures.[27] The recognition of photographs of faces has proved a difficult task not only for epileptic patients with right temporal-lobe excisions but also patients with tumours or vascular lesions of the right hemisphere;[6] and impairment of face-recognition in real-life situations (prosopagnosia) has been reported in patients with lesions at the junction of the right parietal, temporal and occipital lobes.[16] In addition, there is convincing experimental evidence that associates difficulties in visual perception and visual retention tasks with lesions in the posterior area of the right hemisphere.[49]

These aspects of hemispheric asymmetry have been discussed in relation to right-handed patients. Less is known about hemispheric organization of function in left-handed patients. Empirical evidence suggests that approximately two-thirds of left-handed subjects have speech represented in the left hemisphere but virtually nothing is known of the representation of visuo-spatial skills in this group and the problem is further complicated by the fact that left-handed subjects themselves show a variety of different patterns of handedness.

The possibility of intra-hemispheric specialization of function has also to be considered. Different aspects of memory may be disturbed by lesions in different regions of the hemisphere[21] and there is some evidence of modality-specific memory loss: patients with left temporal or left temporo-parietal lesions may show marked difficulty in repeating and recalling auditorily presented digits, letters and words, although their performance may approach the normal if the same material is presented visually.[22,50]

In the past, there has also been considerable discussion as to the role of the frontal lobes in memory but little hard data to link amnesic deficits with lesions confined to this area. On the other hand, some of the deficits that have been associated with frontal lobe disease—erratic sampling of stimuli, failure to inhibit previous responses, or distractability—may be factors that limit performance in certain types of memory task. Much experimental work is required, however, before this evidence of restricted deficit can be assimilated into a coherent description of the memory network.

ANATOMICAL AND PHYSIOLOGICAL BACKGROUND

As far as these selective, material-specific deficits are concerned, the study of patients with unilateral, temporal lobe resections has illustrated the important role of the medial temporal lobes and also the clear-cut relationship between severity of memory impairment and extent of hippocampal removal.[28] Experimental stimulation of the temporal lobes before surgical excision has also implicated this region of the brain, but has produced contrasting effects: in some cases, sharp memories have been evoked, including words and scenes,[33] in others, a reversible amnesia for events preceding stimulation.[7]

Concerning the global amnesias, the anatomical data have been comprehensively reviewed by Brierley[8]; and evidence has been provided by medial, bilateral temporal lobe resection[43] and also by post-mortem studies of patients with Korsakoff's psychosis[2] showing that the critical site was the medial diencephalon, especially the medial dorsal nuclei. A careful review of the anatomical evidence[1] also noted the association between amnesic deficits and inflammatory necrosis of the medial temporal lobes (as observed in herpes simplex encephalitis), and athero-sclerotic or embolic occlusion of the posterior cerebral arteries. The latter condition, resulting in bilateral infarction of the medial temporal lobes, particularly the hippocampal and para-hippocampal convolutions and fornices, may cause severe global amnesia.

It is therefore not surprising that there was no evidence of cortical damage in the 54 brains from the series of 300 amnesic cases described by Adams, Collins and Victor[1], although Adams[2] has pointed out that it cannot be assumed that the neo-cortex does not play a part in mnemonic integration. On the contrary, he suggests that the neo-cortex may be concerned with specific skills whereas the hippocampal, diencephalic mechanisms are part of a universal circuit for memory and learning.

Different pathways or circuits, however, may provide for different storage systems and different ways of processing sensory input. A review of the evidence to date from comparative work suggests that associative learning, for example, is essentially linked to subcortical systems, and that contingency learning (or the modification of behaviour by reward and punishment) may be cortically stored or represented.[38] By the same token, the patterns of early infant behaviour are probably closely related to a brain-stem reward system whereas the conceptual activity and decision-making that is required of the maturing human being may depend on the integrity of the cortex.

Motor skills and habits may also be mediated by separate systems. The philosopher, Ryle (cited by Posner,[34]) had already made the distinction between remembering *that* and remembering *how*. Talland[48] referred to Kohnstamm's Korsakoff patient who learned new music but did not recall the following morning that he had accompanied a singer in the hospital concert. Another patient who recovered from tuberculous meningitis learned to type during the amnesic period and retained the skill subsequently although he had no recollection of acquiring it (cited by Symonds[45]). Finally, the patient described earlier, who has had a profound and relatively pure amnesic deficit following bitemporal resection, has learned perceptual-motor skills and demonstrated retention of these skills on subsequent testing although unaware of the fact that he has had any previous experience or training in them.[28]

The principal systems of the brain concerned with learning and recall appear to be the temporal lobes and the associated limbic pathways, but the role of the hippocampus is still the subject of speculation. It is seldom suggested that long-term memories are in some sense stored there but rather that these structures are essentially involved in the process of consolidation. Their functions may include inhibiting irrelevant activity and amplifying weak cortical traces. The relationship between the limbic system and arousal or certain emotional states may also serve to strengthen the consolidation of memories; and experimental work has suggested that material learned in conditions of high arousal is better retained after a lapse of time, than similar material acquired in the reverse condition.[20]

There is even less agreement regarding the neurophysiological and biochemical basis of these processes. Neurophysiological models still propose that the stages of perceiving and registering events are based on electrical changes at the synapse. The processes of consolidation and long-term storage, however, may be mediated by macro-molecular changes, associated with protein synthesis. Evidence for the molecular hypothesis has been based largely on learning experiments in animals and presumed transfer of training from donor to recipient.[10]

Neurophysiological and biochemical hypotheses concerning memory functions are not mutually exclusive and are still schematic in nature. Furthermore, assuming that protein synthesis plays an essential role in memory storage, it is not at all clear whether its role is unspecific, or directly concerned with the coding of information.[19] If a functionally-valuable protein can be produced, however, and if it is possible "to add orderliness to brain cells of one individual by incorporation of gene material from another"[18] then some of the problems of impaired memory—perhaps attributable to increased entropy of brain cells with age—will be closer to solution.[18]

amt. of energy unavailable for work during a natural process.

REVIEW

These speculations seem at present remote from the immediate concern of the clinician whose task is to present a factual description of amnesic deficit. It may be legitimate to enquire how much the theoretical and clinical problems have in common and what information the two disciplines may share. There are perhaps three main lines of agreement. These concern the distinction between short- and long-term memory, the consolidation hypothesis, and the emphasis on difficulties of retrieval rather than decay of memory traces.

The two-component (short-term and long-term) view of memory has been strongly supported by both experimental and clinical evidence, despite Melton's[23] eloquent defence of a unitary concept. It envisages a short-term memory store, holding a limited amount of information for a limited period of time and organized in terms of simple sensory dimensions (e.g. sound and time of arrival), and a long-term memory process that acquires coherent structure through meaning and association.[9] These two storage systems may have different physical locations and possibly different retrieval mechanisms; and this formulation accords with clinical evidence of dissociated deficits in short- and long-term memory. A Korsakoff patient, for example, usually has no disturbance of primary memory but a severe impairment in retrieving remote memories or acquiring new information.

The concept of consolidation is also reinforced by both clinical and experimental findings. Since Müller and Pilzecker[30] proposed that memories require time for consolidation and that consolidation could depend on subcortical reverberation, this concept has been evoked to explain the RA associated with head injury[41] or electro-convulsive shock treatment.[12,55] Evidence for the consolidation hypothesis has been the subject of several critical reviews[13] and has received powerful support from physiological experiments on learning, extinction and imprinting.

The problem of retrieving memories is familiar enough in everyday life, including the tip-of-the-tongue phenomenon and the immediate recognition of an item despite inability to recall it spontaneously. Unexpected sensuous cues—notably, a scent or a taste—may evoke long-forgotten but nonetheless vivid fragments of memory. Similarly, patients with a long period of retrograde

(1) perception
(2) coding (engram) = consolidation
(3) retrieval

amnesia may be cued-in, years after an accident, by revisiting people or places previously forgotten.[57] These data suggest that it is not the memory trace which has disappeared but its address which has been temporarily mislaid.

Reversible retrograde amnesia provides further support for this proposition, and has been experimentally observed when temporal lobe cortex was stimulated prior to surgical excision.[7] The two patients concerned were not able to remember recent events of several days preceding stimulation and sometimes had a brief amnesia for subsequent events. The RA was transient and the length of the amnesia was a function of the intensity or duration of stimulation. Finally, even amnesic patients do not forget all the new material presented to them in learning experiments: they make intrusion errors (recalling previously presented material) and they can retrieve material in certain experimental conditions.[51]

There is not always such a close fit between theory and clinical findings. Theoretical models of memory concerned with the establishment of long-term traces do not take into account the extensive RA which may follow acute intracranial disease such as tuberculous meningitis[59] or trauma; and laboratory experiments which emphasize the role of interference (by similar lists of words or nonsense syllables, for example) do not closely simulate the context of memory and learning in daily life.[34] The experimental psychologist studies information processing and perhaps also individual differences in the selection and categorization of this information. The clinician has to describe the nature of impairment and relate it to what is known of the aetiology of the lesion and its anatomical and physiological background.

There is, nevertheless, common ground for research which could include problems of filtering and retrieving information. And what is forgotten? An item—the context in which it occurred, its associations, or its tag? Forgetting itself must be an important aspect of behaviour. Most of the daily bombardment of the senses has to be ignored in order to assimilate interesting and useful information in accordance with some kind of coded hierarchy that the brain has developed with time and experience. "Men are things that think a little but chiefly forget."[4]

The study of ageing may also have a bearing on these problems. Much of the performance decrement with age has been attributed to a decline in short-term retention;[54] and the memory impairment shown by elderly subjects—in experimental conditions at least—has been linked with deficiencies both in coding and retrieving input.[11] This type of research as well as the study of the various forms of amnesia may contribute towards a further understanding of the processes involved in discrimination and creative remembering.

FURTHER READING

[1] Adams, R. D. (1970), "The Anatomy of Memory Mechanisms in the Human Brain," in *The Pathology of Memory*, pp. 91–106. (G. A. Talland and N. C. Waugh, Eds.). New York: Academic Press.

[2] Adams, R. D., Collins, G. H. and Victor, M. (1962), "Troubles de la Mémoire et de l'Apprentissage Chez l'Homme; Leurs Rélations avec dés Lésions des Lobes Temporaux et du Diencéphale," in *Physiologie de l'Hippocampe*, pp. 273–296. Paris: Centre National de la Récherche Scientifique.

[3] Barbizet, J. and Cany, E. (1970), "A Psychometric Study of Various Memory Deficits Associated with Cerebral Lesions," in *The Pathology of Memory*, pp. 49–64 (G. A. Talland and N. C. Waugh, Eds.). New York: Academic Press.

[4] Barbusse, H. (1962), *Under Fire*. London: Dent.

[5] Bartlett, F. C. (1932), *Remembering: A Study in Experimental and Social Psychology*. Cambridge: University Press.

[6] Benton, A. L. and Van Allen, M. W. (1968), "Impairment in Facial Recognition in Patients with Cerebral Disease," *Cortex*, **4**, 344–358.

[7] Bickford, R. G., Milder, D. W., Dodge, H. W., Svien, H. J. and Rome, H. P. (1958), "Changes in Memory Function Produced by Electrical Stimulation of the Temporal Lobe in Man," *Res. Publs Ass. Rev. nerv. ment. Dis.*, **36**, 227–243.

[8] Brierley, J. B. (1966), "The Neuropathology of Amnesia," in *Amnesia*, pp. 150–180 (C. W. M. Whitty and O. L. Zangwill, Eds.). London: Butterworths.

[9] Broadbent, D. E. (1970), "Physiological Aspects of short-term and long-term Memory," *Proc. roy. Soc. Lond.*, **175**, 333–350.

[10] Byrne, W. L. (1970), "Introduction," in *Molecular Approaches to Learning and Memory*, xi–xxiii (W. L. Byrne, Ed.). New York: Academic Press.

[11] Craik, F. I. M. (1968), "Short-term Memory and the Aging Process," in *Human Aging and Behavior*, pp. 131–168 (G. A. Talland, Ed.). New York: Academic Press.

[12] Cronholm, B. (1970), "Post-ECT amnesias," in *The Pathology of Memory*, pp. 81–89 (G. A. Talland and N. C. Waugh, Eds.). New York: Academic Press.

[13] Deutsch, J. A. (1962), "Higher Nervous Function: the Physiological Bases of Memory," *Ann. Rev. Physiol.*, **24**, 259–286.

[14] Fisher, C. M. (1966), "Concussion Amnesia," *Neurology*, **16**, 826–830.

[15] Fisher, C. M. and Adams, R. D. (1964), "Transient Global Amnesia," *Acta Neurol. Scand.*, **40**, 1–83.

[16] Hécaen, H. (1962), "Clinical Symptomatology in Right and Left Hemispheric Lesions," in *Interhemispheric Relations and Cerebral Dominance*, pp. 215–243 (V. B. Mountcastle, Ed.). Baltimore: The Johns Hopkins Press.

[17] Hunter, I. M. L. (1970), *Memory*. London: Penguin (Revised edition).

[18] Hydén, H. (1970), "The Question of a Molecular Basis for the Memory Trace," in *Biology of Memory*, pp. 101–119 (K. H. Pribram and D. E. Broadbent, Eds.). New York: Academic Press.

[19] John, E. R. (1970), "Summary: Symposium on Memory Transfer," in *Molecular Approaches to Learning and Memory*, pp. 335–342 (W. L. Byrne, Ed.). New York: Academic Press.

[20] Kleinsmith, L. J. and Kaplan, S. (1963), "Paired-associate Learning as a Function of Arousal and Interpolated Interval," *J. exp. Psychol.*, **65**, 190–193.

[21] Luria, A. R. (1971), "Memory Disturbances in Focal Brain Lesions," *Neuropsychologia*. In press.

[22] Luria, A. R. and Karasseva, T. A. (1968), "Disturbances of Auditory-speech Memory in Focal Lesions of the Deep Regions of the Left Temporal Lobe," *Neuropsychologia*, **6**, 97–104.

[23] Melton, A. W. (1967), "Implications of short-term Memory for a general Theory of Memory," in *Human Memory and Learning*, pp. 295–316 (N. J. Slamecka, Ed.). New York: Oxford University Press.

[24] Milner, B. (1958), "Psychological Defects Produced by Temporal Lobe Excision," *Res. Publs Ass. Res. nerv. ment. Dis.*, **36**, 244–257.

[25] Milner, B. (1962), "Les troubles de la mémoire accompagnant des lésions hippocampiques bilatérales," *Colloques Internationaux du Centre National de la Récherche Scientifique*, No. 107, 258–272.

[26] Milner, B. (1966), "Amnesia Following Operation on the Temporal Lobes," in *Amnesia*, pp. 109–133 (C. W. M. Whitty and O. L. Zangwill, Eds.). London: Butterworths.

[27] Milner, B. (1968), "Visual Recognition and Recall after Right Temporal-lobe Excision in Man," *Neuropsychologia*, **6**, 191–209.

[28] Milner, B. (1970), "Memory and the Medial Temporal Regions of the Brain," in *Biology of Memory*, pp. 29–50 (K. H. Pribram and D. E. Broadbent, Eds.). New York: Academic Press.

[29] Milner, B., Corkin, S. and Teuber, H.-L. (1968), "Further Analysis of the Hippocampal Amnesic Syndrome," *Neuropsychologia*, **6**, 215–234.

[30] Müller, G. F. and Pilzecker, A. (1900), "Experimentelle Beiträge zur Lehre vom Gedächtnis," *Z. Psychol.*, **1**, 1–288.

[31] Mumenthaler, M. and von Roll, L. (1969), "Amnestische Episoden Analyse von 16 eigenen Beobachtungen," *Schweiz. med. Wschr.*, **99**, 133–139.

[32] Newcombe, F. (1969), *Missile Wounds of the Brain: a Study of Psychological Deficits*. Oxford: The Clarendon Press.

[33] Penfield, W. and Roberts, L. (1959), *Speech and Brain-Mechanisms*. Princeton: Princeton University Press.

[34] Posner, M. I (1970), "Representational Systems for Storing Information in Memory," in *The Pathology of Memory*, pp. 173–194 (G. A. Talland and N. C. Waugh, Eds.). New York: Academic Press.

[35] Prisko, L. (1963), "Short-term Memory in Focal Cerebral Damage." Unpublished Ph.D. Thesis, McGill University. Cited by Milner, B. (1970), "Memory and the Medial Temporal Regions of the Brain," in *Biology of Memory*, pp. 29–50 (K. H. Pribram and D. E. Broadbent, Eds.). New York: Academic Press.

[36] Richardson, F. (1963), "Some Effects of Severe Head Injury," *Develop. Med. Chld. Neurol.*, **5**, 471–482.

[37] Rose, F. C. and Symonds, Sir C. P. (1960), "Persistent Memory Defect Following Encephalitis," *Brain*, **83**, 195–212.

[38] Russell, I. Steele (1966), "Animal Learning and Memory," in *Aspects of Learning and Memory*, pp. 121–171 (D. Richter, Ed.). London: Heinemann.

[39] Russell, W. R. (1959), *Brain: Memory: Learning*. Oxford: The Clarendon Press.

[40] Russell, W. R. (1971), *The Traumatic Amnesias*. Oxford: The Clarendon Press.

[41] Russell, W. R. and Nathan, P. W. (1946), "Traumatic Amnesia," *Brain*, **69**, 280–300.

[42] Russell, W. R. and Smith, A. (1961), "Post-traumatic Amnesia in Closed Head Injury," *Arch. Neurol.*, **5**, 4–17.

[43] Scoville, W. B. (1954), "The Limbic Lobe in Man," *J. Neurosurg.*, **11**, 64–66.

[44] Scoville, W. B. and Milner, B. (1957), "Loss of Recent Memory after Bilateral Hippocampal Lesions," *J. Neurol. Neurosurg. Psychiat.*, **20**, 11–21.

[45] Symonds, C. P. (1966), "Disorders of Memory," *Brain*, **89**, 625–644.

[46] Symonds, C. P. and Russell, W. R. (1943), "Accidental Head Injuries: Prognosis in Service Patients," *Lancet*, **1**, p. 7.

[47] Talland, G. A. (1965), *Deranged Memory*. New York: Academic Press.

[48] Talland, G. A. (1970), "Interaction Between Clinical and Laboratory Research on Memory," in *The Pathology of Memory*, pp. 273–279 (G. A. Talland and N. C. Waugh, Eds.). New York: Academic Press.

[49] Warrington, E. K. and James, M. (1967), "Disorders of Visual Perception in Patients with Localized Cerebral Lesions," *Neuropsychologia*, **5**, 253–266.

[50] Warrington, E. K. and Shallice, T. (1969), "The Selective Impairment of Auditory Verbal Short-term Memory," *Brain*, **92**, 885–896.

[51] Warrington, E. K. and Weiskrantz, L. (1970), "Amnesic Syndrome: Consolidation or Retrieval?" *Nature*, **228**, 628–630.

[52] Waugh, N. C. and Norman, D. A. (1967), "Primary Memory," in *Human Memory and Learning*, pp. 316–330 (N. J. Slamecka, Ed.). New York: Oxford University Press.

[53] Wechsler, D. (1945), "A Standardized Memory Scale for Clinical Use," *J. Psychol.*, **19**, 87–95.

[54] Welford, A. T. (1958), *Ageing and Human Skill*. London: Oxford University Press.

[55] Williams, M. (1966), "Memory Disorders Associated with Electroconvulsive Therapy," in *Amnesia*, pp. 134–149 (C. W. M. Whitty and O. L. Zangwill, Eds.). London: Butterworths.

[56] Williams, M. and Pennybacker, J. B. (1954), "Memory Disturbances in Third Ventricle Tumours," *J. Neurol. Neurosurg. Psychiat.*, **17**, 115–123.

[57] Williams, M. and Zangwill, O. L. (1952), "Memory Defects after Head Injury," *J. Neurol. Neurosurg. Psychiat.*, **15**, 54–58.

[58] Zangwill, O. L. (1946), "Some Qualitative Observations on Verbal Memory in Cases of Cerebral Lesions," *Brit. J. Psychol.*, **37**, 8–19.

[59] Zangwill, O. L. (1969), "Amnesia," *Science Journal*, **5**, 75–79.

6. PERSONALITY

M. E. HUMPHREY

Regardless of his attitude to psychosomatic medicine, the neurologist can hardly pretend that the study of human personality is outside his domain. As Zangwill[18] (1950) pointed out, "Whatever our views on the relation of body and mind, there can be no doubt that personality is intimately bound up with the functions of the central nervous system. Although the nature of the connection is wholly obscure, it is evident to every medical man that personality is profoundly affected by pathological changes in the brain" (p. 203). Where the latter are sufficiently gross the individual may appear to suffer a complete loss of personality, leading a vegetative existence in an institution and becoming almost unrecognizable to those who knew him in his intact state. With lesser degrees of damage the disturbance of personality is usually more subtle, yet this may be the most prominent if not the only sign of a cerebral lesion. Certain kinds of intracranial tumour, notably meningioma, have been found more frequently in psychiatric than in other kinds of patient (Patton and Sheppard,[11] 1956). Even where the neurologist has staked his claim at an early stage of the illness he will often need to enlist the help of his colleagues in the field of mental health.

Although any kind of neurological disorder *may* result in personality change, for the purposes of this chapter there are advantages in focusing on two areas of the brain which appear to be particularly vulnerable in this respect, namely the frontal and temporal lobes. Here a lesion of any kind, whether traumatic, neoplastic or epileptogenic, can have a profound effect on how the patient conducts himself both privately and in his relationships with other people. Reference will also be made to the psychiatric aspects of brain damage, including the personality changes sometimes associated with amnestic and aphasic conditions. Finally we shall discuss the uses and limitations of psychological testing in neurology.

APPROACHES TO THE STUDY OF PERSONALITY

Even if the average layman is not troubled by the meaning of "personality", it may be worth noting that psychologists have given some thought to this question. Allport[1] (1963) devoted a whole chapter of his book to definitions and concluded that personality is "the dynamic organization within the individual of those psychophysical systems that determine his characteristic behaviour and thought" (p. 28). The word is believed to derive from the Latin *persona* (*per sonare* = to sound through), which was the actor's mask worn in Greek drama as an aid to character portrayal. The chameleon-like capacity to be "all things to all men" is fortunately denied to most of us, yet it remains true that differences of opinion about a man's personality are partly due to the different contexts in which he is judged. Social life imposes a façade, and the manner in which we present ourselves to others is influenced by the cues we receive from them. It is therefore important to bear in mind that even the healthiest individual may exhibit marked personality changes according to the social context in which he is performing. In calling him an "individual", however, we are inferring the existence of an underlying hard core which constitutes a recognizable self. It is doubtful, indeed, whether any psychologist could hope to improve upon one of the Oxford English Dictionary definitions (slightly adapted) of personality as "an assemblage of qualities which makes each individual unique".

While it is necessary to take a broad view of what is meant by personality, there are two related concepts which can be defined more precisely. *Temperament* is used by psychologists to refer to the individual's emotional nature as governed primarily by his heredity. Personality and temperament are sometimes treated as interchangeable terms but the distinction is legitimate. *Character* is again liable to misuse but should properly be confined to moral attributes—or as Allport neatly expressed it, character is "personality evaluated". These observations are no idle exercise in semantics since inter-professional communication is greatly aided by exact use of terms. It seems appropriate that at the level of clinical description the neurologist should be concerned with the more global concept of personality rather than with temperament or character, and like any other physician he is more interested in detecting changes (which may of course be relatively superficial) than in penetrating the individual's essential nature.

Although he cannot be expected to share the psychologist's concern with the niceties of classification and with the measurement of personality he ought nevertheless to cultivate a nodding acquaintance with the main schools of thought. These can conveniently be brought under three headings:

(1) Psychodynamic

This is the approach made famous by Freud* and his followers or dissenters, and lays principal stress on the infantile roots of personality development. Among the many criticisms raised is that it relies almost entirely on unverified self-report. Some of the original postulates were undoubtedly extravagant, but a more balanced account is beginning to emerge now that the significance of events in later childhood—which may or may not reinforce earlier events—is becoming acknowledged (Clarke,[4] 1968). For exploring complex developmental problems there is nothing to rival the psychoanalytical method, yet apart from the speculative element reduction to fundamental causes is seldom a practical possibility even in psychiatry, where organic disease can usually be ruled out.

(2) Constitutional

This approach again derives from psychological medicine even if Kretschmer[7] (1925) began from totally different premises. He observed a relationship not only between physique and mental illness but also between type of illness and premorbid temperament, and came to regard both physical and mental characteristics as expressions of a genetic tendency. The more elaborate research of Sheldon and his co-workers[13] (1942) continued this line of investigation, and it is now generally agreed that the *somatotype* (which was Sheldon's term for the composite rating of physique based on the three components of fat, bone and muscle, and linearity or height/weight ratio) can provide clues to individual temperament. However, such clues are far from reliable. Not only have subsequent workers failed to reproduce Sheldon's high correlations, but the somewhat ill-defined relationship between temperament and personality has precluded any widespread use of this method for clinical purposes.

(3) Dimensional

This is where psychologists have come into their own, and the pioneer work of Cattell and Eysenck has set the stage for a vast amount of research relying mainly on paper-and-pencil tests requiring the subject to answer a wide variety of questions about himself.† A mathematical technique known as factor analysis has been used to extract clusters of items from questionnaire data, and bipolar dimensions of personality have been isolated. The Eysenck Personality Inventory consists of two scales only, designed to measure extraversion and emotional stability, whereas the 16 Personality Factor questionnaire is as wide-ranging as its title implies. Whereas Eysenck's restricted dimensions are at least intelligible, Cattell's exuberant fancy has led him into strange neologisms for describing qualities that have not become enshrined in ordinary discourse. The interpretation of statistical

---

* It is intriguing to recall the Freud himself was a neurologist before he became a psychoanalyst.

† For a critical review of this work *see* Vernon (1964).

patterns is always controversial, and we are certainly a long way from consensus on the factors that need to be measured for an all-embracing chart of human personality.

We can now set aside these theoretical issues and face up to the fact that most of our ideas on the neurological basis of personality have evolved from clinical description. There have been many studies of patients with brain lesions both diffused and circumscribed, but few have made extensive use of specialized techniques of personality assessment.

THE FRONTAL LOBES

At one time these were looked upon as "silent" areas of the brain because, in contrast to the dramatic handicaps ensuing from damage to the motor and speech areas, a man could appear to be relatively unaffected by lesions of either frontal lobe. However, the possibility of profound personality changes was indicated by the case of Phineas Gage, who in 1848 suffered the misfortune of having a crowbar driven through the front of his skull. Massive damage to the frontal lobes was confirmed at autopsy 12 years later, and meanwhile he was described as "fitful, irreverent, indulging at times in the grossest profanity (which was not previously his custom), manifesting but little deference for his fellows, impatient of restraint or advice when it conflicts with his desires, at times pertinaciously obstinate, yet capricious and vacillating. . . ." The first world war provided cases of penetrating missile wounds of the frontal lobes, yet the interest of the medical profession was not fully aroused until patients undergoing radical surgery for removal of frontal tumours were studied in the years leading up to the second world war (Brickner,[3] 1936, Rylander,[12] 1939). The results were extraordinarily variable, yet gradually a pattern began to emerge. Whilst intellectual changes were often reported (especially where refined methods of examination had been used), the main emphasis was on personality disturbance. Broadly speaking this might take one of two forms: either the patient would become a caricature of his former self, with exaggeration of his salient characteristics, or else he would veer towards the opposite extreme, as though repressed tendencies had suddenly been released. The significance of previous personality was increasingly recognized as a clue to present reactions—where the individual had habitually held himself on a tight rein, for example, the likelihood of gay abandon was enhanced. (Even today, however, we are still far from being able to predict individual consequences, though response to alcohol might be expected to offer a few pointers.)

As the results from these studies accumulated it became plausible to infer that the frontal lobes had some kind of *regulatory* function, shaping the deployment of intellectual resources and the pursuit of long-term goals. This notion was supported by experimental work on chimpanzees, who were found to have difficulty in retaining objectives and in performing a sequence of actions after bilateral removal of the frontal areas. In the same way a man who all his life had shown a capacity for sustained application to the task in hand, and for planning his life in an orderly way, might after frontal lobe interference become aimless and improvident. Social judgement was also liable to become affected, with a loss of tact and sensitivity. Moreover, self-control would give way to impulsiveness with apparent failure to envisage the consequences of reckless behaviour. The writer can vividly recall, even after a lapse of at least 15 years, the case of a middle-aged man whose frontal tumour had been heralded by a series of grotesque practical jokes, such as turning a hose on his neighbours.

This behaviour pattern has come to be known as the "frontal lobe syndrome". This does not mean that it cannot occur after injury to other parts of the brain, merely that in its most clearly defined form it appears to be associated with frontal lesions. It constitutes a difficult problem in management since often it is the relatives who suffer more than the patient. An example of chronic frontal lobe syndrome is the ex-army officer who was seen by the writer in the course of following up a group of war casualties in 1950–51. He had made a good physical recovery but had been unable to resume his civilian occupation because of his impetuous, childlike behaviour. His social responses were comically inappropriate and his wife complained that he had become sexually overdemanding. The acquisition of self-restraint and the ability to bear frustration, notably absent in the first two years of life, is a painful process which continues throughout the school years and early adulthood. We can now see that it may depend on the activity of the frontal lobes and their subcortical connections.

The degree to which the restraints imposed by society are "internalized" will vary from person to person, and in some cases the lessons have been learned only too well. The over-socialized individual may become a prey to chronic anxiety and compulsive rituals, since he has an exaggerated need to control his sexual and aggressive impulses and to maintain an impeccable front in the presence of others. The clinical and experimental observations already referred to have provided a rationale for the operation of *prefrontal leucotomy*, introduced by the Portuguese neurologist Egas Moniz in 1935. In the early post-war years this was developed on a fairly wide scale where the mental illness had proved severely incapacitating and had responded poorly if at all to treatment. Briefly it consisted in severing the nerve-fibres connecting the frontal cotex with the thalamus. A number of neurosurgeons began to specialize in this procedure, and a colourful account of 300 cases followed up from a social and psychiatric standpoint was published by Partridge[10] (1950). But it soon became clear that the standard operation had undesirable side-effects, and in many cases the price for relief from stress had to be paid in terms of lethargy and reduced social competence. So it became a matter of searching for a technique of minimal intervention that would bring sufficient symptomatic relief without at the same time depriving the patient of all initiative and concern for others. Orbital undercutting and cingulectomy were variants of this nature, and accounted for a proportion of the 10,000 leucotomies that had been performed by the mid-1950s.

During the past decade the operation fell largely into disuse but there are signs of a revival at some centres including St. George's Hospital in London, where Sir Wylie McKissock helped to establish the technique and his successor Mr. Alan Richardson has been developing a cryogenic stereotactic approach to the lower medial quadrants of the frontal lobe and cingulate gyrus (limbic leucotomy). By this method the lesion can be accurately pinpointed and brain damage reduced to an absolute minimum. It is too early to assess the long-term results of this modified operation, but there is every prospect that the patient's basic personality will remain intact if it has not already been impaired by chronic mental illness. Such were the findings of Strom-Olsen and Carlisle[16] (1971) who studied the after-effects of another stereotactic operation (involving bi-frontal tractotomy of the orbital cortex by means of radioactive yttrium 90 seeds) and found significant loss of self-control in only 4 out of 150 patients.

Unfortunately, quite apart from possible erosion of basic personality, there is still a tendency to use surgical intervention as a last resort after all other tactics have failed. This means that in many cases intractable social problems will have built up over the years in such a way as to limit the possibilities of effective rehabilitation. Remarkable success stories can nevertheless be quoted, as in the following case:

A housewife of twenty-seven had developed complicated washing rituals over the past six years. The illness had begun shortly after her marriage which happened to coincide with the birth of an illegitimate child to her sister. She had become fearful of contamination in general and impregnation in particular, but this did not prevent her from producing a child after two years of marriage. At the time of her admission to hospital she had been confined to one room for at least a year and her husband was obliged to bring a bucket for her urine. Evacuation of her bowels was a weekly ceremonial at her mother's home some twelve miles distant, and it took her four hours to have a bath. Window checking and other precautions made bedtime an agony, and the marriage was on the point of breaking up. A wide variety of treatments had made no impact. Three months after the operation of limbic leucotomy she was virtually symptom-free and the couple were hoping to experience for the first time the satisfactions of a normal married life.

Equally striking successes have been reported with the earlier hit-or-miss style of operation, yet the greater control afforded by stereotaxis is surely welcome. In some cases the symptoms persist but with a considerable abatement of the associated tension. The decision to operate cannot even with this latest refinement be undertaken lightly, and the quality of the pre-morbid personality must be evaluated with particular care.

THE TEMPORAL LOBES

The peculiar subjective experiences associated with temporal lobe dysfunction were first noted by Hughlings Jackson, but personality changes did not come into the limelight until about 20 years ago. An earlier landmark was an EEG study of psychopaths, who were found to display a raised incidence of abnormality especially in the temporal regions, with or without epilepsy (Hill and Watterson,[6] 1942). This gave rise to the suspicion that psychopathic conduct, the origin of which has always been mysterious, might have an organic basis. Further impetus came from studies of temporal lobectomy for the relief of epilepsy. Much of the evidence relating personality factors to the temporal lobes is in fact derived from epileptic patients.

The evaluation of research findings is complicated by so-called psychomotor attacks, comprising various forms of quasi-automatic behaviour which may or may not coexist with *grand mal* fits. What does appear to be established, however, is that—particularly as compared with the frontal areas—the temporal lobes are sensitive to epileptic discharge. In confining our review to this type of abnormality we must bear in mind that some of the alleged personality changes may be related to the social repercussions of the epilepsy rather than to the cerebral disturbance as such. It should be noted also that the concept of an "epileptic personality", characterized by aggression, irritability and suspiciousness, has been seriously challenged on the grounds that it is rarely seen outside an institution. Perpetual confinement might bring out latent tendencies of this kind even in the most stable of persons.

A conference on the clinical significance of the temporal lobe was organized by the Royal College of Physicians and Surgeons of Glasgow in 1968, and the proceedings have been fully reported (Herrington,[5] 1969). Despite conflict and confusion in the findings from different studies, the reader is recommended to consult this volume for an overall view of current knowledge and speculation. Aggressive behaviour is a recurrent theme, and the disposition towards violence and unprovoked assault in the established temporal lobe epileptic bears no obvious relationship with the occurrence of *grand mal* fits. Social factors are likely to be relevant, since Ounsted *et al.*[9] (1966) found this type of disorder to be commoner in young men with a poor home background.

A psychotic-like illness resembling schizophrenia has also been described in association with temporal lobe epilepsy (Slater *et al.*,[14] 1963). The whole gamut of hallucinatory and delusional experiences was observed but paranoid thinking tended to predominate. The question of whether the two illnesses are causally related, or whether they are coincidental, has not been finally settled.

PSYCHIATRIC DISABILITY AFTER BRAIN DAMAGE

Lishman[8] (1968) has published a psychiatric analysis of 670 cases of penetrating head injury from World War II (the Oxford series). Psychiatric disability was taken to include all aspects of intellectual, emotional and behavioural disturbance manifested between 1–5 years after injury, and was correlated with depth and extent of brain damage. Its incidence varied between different regions of the brain but was higher following damage to the left hemisphere, especially the temporal lobe. Part of this association may have been due to the effects of dysphasia and general intellectual impairment, which are known to be much commoner with lesions of the dominant hemisphere; however, in almost half of the dysphasic cases psychiatric disability was mild or absent. In relying on documentary evidence Lishman was unable to explore in any detail the mechanisms whereby neurological disorder led to psychiatric symptoms, and he made no attempt to take into account social factors.

In the writer's experience even complete motor aphasia does not necessarily result in personality change. Obviously much will depend on the patient's normal mode of handling frustration and on the reactions of his family and immediate associates. Receptive defects with preservation of speech fluency, while less common, may give rise to more severe problems of personal and social adjustment. A man with a temporo-parietal lesion not only had difficulty in grasping what was said to him but bewildered his listeners by the frequent intrusion of jargon into his speech. By dint of sheer practice the writer learned to communicate with him and found himself acting as interpreter during the neurologist's ward rounds. At one time the patient displayed what might easily have been mistaken for a paranoid reaction, since he accused the nursing staff of having stolen his clothes. Careful explanation of the reasons for their removal had failed to get through to him. Any deficit interfering with normal communication is liable to produce secondary disturbances of this kind, and the same applies to the Korsakov syndrome and other amnestic states.

While there are advantages in studying the effects of specific lesions such as gunshot wounds, much can also be learned from the commoner disorders of civilian practice. Storey[15] (1970) followed up 261 patients 6 months to 6 years after a subarachnoid haemorrhage and assessed personality changes mainly from the statements of other informants. He found evidence of impairment in 41 per cent and improvement in 5 per cent, the latter being attributed to a leucotomy-like effect. Impairment was largely proportional to the amount of brain damage as indicated by neurological signs, and the most frequent change was an increase in anxiety and irritability with loss of vitality.

THE CONTRIBUTION OF PSYCHOLOGICAL TESTS

Since a mere list of psychiatric symptoms is unlikely to tell the whole story of a patient's personality change the help of a psychologist is sometimes invoked. It would be heartening to record that major contributions had been made towards the problem of personality assessment, but in fact most of the psychologist's work with neurological patients has been concerned with cognitive disabilities. Technically the measurement of personality is still somewhat unsatisfactory as compared with intelligence testing, and few of the available instruments meet the criteria of reliability and validity. As already indicated, the EPI measures two aspects of personality which Eysenck

himself would relate to fundamental properties of the central nervous system. A move towards extraversion is common in the brain-injured population, especially where the frontal lobes are involved, whilst neuroticism—defined as the disposition to break down under stress—is likely also to arise. For research purposes it is useful to include measures of this kind even if their value in an individual case is limited. A particular drawback of Eysenck's Neuroticism Scale is that scores are heavily influenced by transitory mood states and current preoccupations.

A more elaborate device used widely with psychiatric patients is the Minnesota Multiphasic Personality Inventory (MMPI), which yields nine clinically defined scales (Depression, Hysteria, Hypochondriasis, etc.) and a measure of deviation towards the interest pattern of the opposite sex. It also incorporates four measures of test-taking attitude and in this respect is superior to most other tests of this nature, which make little or no allowance for the subject who either over-dramatizes his suffering or alternatively "fakes good". However, apart from confusing symptoms with enduring personality traits, it is inordinately lengthy (550 items) for many neurological patients. A variety of other schedules exist and the interested reader is referred to Anastasi[2] (1968).

In an attempt to escape from the bias inseparable from self-assessment procedures some psychologists have favoured the use of *projective* techniques. Briefly, these present the subject with an uncertain stimulus—such as an ambiguous picture—to which he is asked to respond in his own fashion. Not knowing what is expected of him, he is forced to draw on his inner resources and may thus unwittingly betray hidden feelings and attitudes. The best known examples are the Rorschach inkblots and the Thematic Apperception Test (TAT). Unfortunately so much depends upon the intuition of the examiner, and reliability even in skilled hands is so low, that these methods are a long way from commanding universal respect.

Finally we should at least mention the techniques of the psychophysiologist even if these have not yet won their way to routine use. Many hospital departments of psychology have the equipment for galvanic skin response and other methods of monitoring reactions to stress. Extension of clinical observation into the laboratory is well within the psychologist's scope although at present comparatively few patients repay investigation of this kind.

Long experience of psychological testing is apt to breed a certain scepticism as to its value in the realm of personality assessment, though it remains essential where disorders of memory, learning and thinking are concerned. Perhaps, indeed, there is no substitute for careful clinical appraisal, using both direct observation and the testimony of others. Relatives and nursing staff will predominate among the latter but occasionally it may be necessary to interview an employer, landlord or other outsider. Time spent in building up a composite portrait in this way is likely to prove more rewarding than a similar or longer period expended on personality tests of dubious validity.

CONCLUSION

Personality is an important topic for the neurologist and it is regrettable that he receives no training in the psychological aspects. An experienced physician can be relied upon to develop his own skills in this area, but even he might stand to benefit from more frequent contact with clinical psychologists. Above all it is desirable that medical students should at an early stage be taught the elements of the theory of personality before they are directed during their clinical training towards greater awareness of the person behind the illness. In the present state of knowledge it would be unwise to lay down a rigid format for recording personality traits, but students should be encouraged to look for enduring characteristics rather than fleeting tendencies. Even the mature practitioner can fall into alarmingly stereotyped habits of recording, with the result that only one or at most two features receive attention. The men who have forsaken a medical career to write best-selling novels are doubtless exceptional, yet any reasonably alert doctor has a wealth of opportunity for capturing what Medawar in another context has called the "uniqueness of the individual".

I am indebted to Prof. O. L. Zangwill for guidance in the preparation of this chapter, and to my colleague Dr. Desmond Kelly for his observations on stereotactic leucotomy.

FURTHER READING

1 Allport, G. W. (1963), *Pattern and Growth in Personality*. New York: Holt, Rinehart and Winston.
2 Anastasi, A. (1968), *Psychological Testing*, Ch. 17. New York: Macmillan.
3 Brickner, R. M. (1936), *The Intellectual Functions of the Frontal Lobes*. New York: Macmillan.
4 Clarke, A. D. B. (1968), "Learning and Human Development," *Brit. J. Psychiat.*, **114**, 1061–1077.
5 Herrington, R. N. (1969, editor), "Current Problems in Neuropsychiatry: Schizophrenia, Epilepsy, the Temporal Lobe," *Brit. J. Psychiat.*, Special Publication No. 4.
6 Hill, D. and Watterson, D. (1942), "Electroencephalographic Studies of Psychopathic Personalities," *J. Neurol. Psychiat.*, **5**, 47–65.
7 Kretschmer, E. (1925), *Physique and Character*, 2nd English edition, 1936. London: Kegan Paul.
8 Lishman, W. A. (1968), "Brain Damage in Relation to Psychiatric Disability after Head Injury," *Brit. J. Psychiat.*, **114**, 373–410.
9 Ounsted, C., Lindsay, J. M. M. and Norman, R. M. (1966), *Biological Factors in Temporal Lobe Epilepsy*. London: Heinemann.
10 Partridge, M. A. (1950), *Prefrontal Leucotomy*. Oxford, Blackwell.
11 Patton, R. B. and Sheppard, J. A. (1956), "Intracranial Tumours found at Autopsy in Mental Patients," *Amer. J. Psychiat.*, **113**, 319–324.
12 Rylander, G. (1939), *Personality Changes after Operations on the Frontal Lobes*. Copenhagen. English edition, Oxford University Press.
13 Sheldon, W. H. and Stevens, S. S. (1942), *The Varieties of Temperament*. New York: Harper.
14 Slater, E., Beard, A. W. and Glithero, E. (1963), "The Schizophrenia-like Psychoses of Epilepsy," *Brit. J. Psychiat.*, **109**, 95–150.
15 Storey, P. B. (1970), "Brain Damage and Personality Change after Subarachnoid Haemorrhage," *Brit. J. Psychiat.*, **117**, 129–142.
16 Ström-Olsen, R. and Carlisle, S. (1971), "Bi-frontal Stereotactic Tractotomy: A Follow-up Study of its Effects on 210 Patients," *Brit. J. Psychiat.*, **118**, 141–154.
17 Vernon, P. E. (1964), *Personality Assessment—A Critical Survey*. London: Methuen.
18 Zangwill, O. L. (1950), *An Introduction to Modern Psychology*. London: Methuen.

7. INTER-HEMISPHERIC PARTNERSHIP AND INTER-HEMISPHERIC RIVALRY

MACDONALD CRITCHLEY

"If I forget thee . . . let my right hand forget her cunning . . . let my tongue cleave to the roof of my mouth."

Psalm 137

From naked eye anatomy the cerebrum appears as being made up of two comparable hemispheres. Although some morphologists more than a century ago considered that minor structural differences could be discerned between the right and the left halves, their observations were not always accepted as factual, and in any event the alleged differences were by no means obvious. For nearly 200 years, however, clinicians have realized that from a pathophysiological standpoint the two hemispheres are anything but equipotential. Twins they may be, but dynamically speaking, non-identical.

Historical

At one time the problem was a topic of earnest discussion among philosophers: then came many decades of neglect, followed recently for a variety of reasons by a revival of interest.

One of the classic pioneer writers was A. L. Wigan whose monograph *The Duality of the Brain* appeared in 1844. Forty-five years later came another important contribution in H. Maudsley's article upon "The Double Brain". The missing manuscript of Dax, which dated from 1836 though it did not appear in print until 1865, had already drawn attention to the clinical fact that speech impairment was more likely to follow lesions of the left half of the brain than the right, an observation which had quite independently been made by P. Broca in 1865. Shortly afterwards came a series of profound though speculative writings by Hughlings Jackson upon the duality of the brain, with its clinical and physiological implications.

Maudsley believed that the brain was fundamentally a double organ, ministering to one single function, namely that of one body. The two hemispheres, however, did not show activities which were entirely correspondent or equivalent. Consciousness could probably exist at one moment in one hemisphere and at the next moment in the other. Ordinarily the left hemisphere could be regarded as the more richly endowed. Maudsley was interested in the fact that non-identical manual skills could be carried out simultaneously by the two hands, the performer moreover being able to engage in some independent activity. A pianist for instance, would be able to converse while in the throes of musical execution. Such conjoint activity of the two hemispheres must surely imply the operation of some single "compound centre", or governing principle. This, he believed, must be looked for in relation to the hemispheres, not above them, but somewhere below. Maudsley spoke of Nature's parsimony in ordaining that merely one half of the brain was adequate for speech. It seemed to him that Nature had shown more concern about physical propagation than intellectual creativity, in that the destruction of merely one testicle would not impair the generative capacity.

Hughlings Jackson was among the first to bring into his ideas of cerebral bilaterality the factor of manual preference, an important subject which had hitherto been overlooked. While accepting the conception of the duality of the brain, he re-emphasized in 1874 that its two halves were not duplicates as regards their function. As far as words were concerned, the left hemisphere was the "leading half". He was a century ahead of his contemporaries in believing too that the right hemisphere might also play some role in the manipulation of speech. His idea was that the left half of the brain represented the means by which one converses, for damage to it renders one speechless. This hemisphere is the one which is concerned with the voluntary reproduction of words. But the right hemisphere also plays a part in that it is that side of the brain whereby verbal propositions are *received*. It is also concerned with the automatic reproduction of movements of words and the revival of their images. The two halves of the brain should not be looked upon merely as duplicates, but rather as two juxtaposed singles. In many of his early papers, Jackson stressed the importance of handedness, for he was one of the earliest writers to correlate the syndrome of speech-impairment and a left hemiparesis, with an inherent sinistrality which had been present as a pre-morbid constitutional factor. From a phylogenetic point of view the representation of the two sides of the body in each side of the brain is "more equal"—as Jackson put it—the lower we go in the animal

scale. Whether this is literally the case is open to debate, and not so long ago Pribram expressed the opinion that a lack of equipotentiality exists in sub-human mammals, but in a rudimentary form.

Somewhere along the line—and it is not easy to determine just when and by whom—the hypothesis of cerebral dominance took origin. The term is an unsatisfactory one, for it suggests a suzerainty of the cerebral hemispheres over some other unnamed structure of the brain. What is no doubt implied, though not explicitly stated, is a relative preponderance of one half of the cerebrum over the other. It would have been more appropriate to refer to an "inter-hemispheric" dominance, or to a cerebral rivalry.

Anatomical Considerations

Before examining this factor of rivalry, it is convenient to consider the means whereby integration between the activities of the two halves of the brain takes place. Obviously this is mediated by such anatomical structures as the chiasma, the commissures and fornices, and particularly the corpus callosum.

This last-named is a conspicuous landmark of cerebral morphology which did not escape the vigilance of Galen. A fuller description was given by Vesalius (1543) who referred to the Greek term *tyloeides* (peg-like) and *psalidoeides* (arch-like). Nonetheless, this structure was relatively neglected by the early anatomists and physiologists. T. Willis (1664) and M. Malpighi (1665, 1666) probably the first to use the term "tough structure" or corpus callosum. Willis pointed out that this bridge-like structure took origin from the ashen-grey substance of both hemispheres, its function being to convey spirits to a broad field "as under a free and open sky". This connecting structure was concerned with the arousal of memory and phantasy with concomitant appetite and local motion. In other words, it could be looked upon as the seat of imagination.

For more detailed anatomical studies of the corpus callosum, one has to turn to the treatises of F. Vicq d'Azyr (1786) and J. C. Reil (1809).

Callosal Lesions: Callosal Agenesis

Lesions of the corpus callosum were virtually unidentified until Liepmann (1900) and his pupil O. Maas, called attention to the clinical phenomenon of apraxia in all its diversity. In view of the pattern of subtle symptoms which follow a lesion of this commissural structure (left-sided kinetic apraxia: profound loss of recent memory) it seemed extraordinary how little disability often followed destruction of this structure. At the same time paediatricians became aware that an inborn absence of a corpus callosum could be associated with so little disablement as often to evoke surprise when revealed at eventual autopsy. Of course, infants born without a corpus callosum frequently display other congenital abnormalities, some of them neural, other extraneural. Moreover, the "absence" of a corpus callosum is often relative, in that a few commissural strands may perhaps be demonstrated at post-mortem dissection.

It may well be the case that more searching clinical tests would uncover a number of minor deficits in these patients. Jeeves (1965) for example examined 3 patients known to have callosal agenesis and found that performances involving bimanual coordinated manipulation were below average, while one showed a marked impairment in the transfer of learning. However Saul and Sperry three years later found that an adult with callosal agenesis gave normal test-scores when examined by their special techniques, to be mentioned later. The whole topic of congenital absence of the corpus callosum has been admirably discussed in the monograph written by Unterharnscheidt, Jachnik and Gött (1968).

The relative silence of the corpus callosum, clinically speaking, led to various light-hearted expressions of opinion. Thus McCulloch said that the only obvious function of this structure is to transmit epileptic seizures from one side of the body to the other. Lashley's flippancy went even further when he suggested that the corpus callosum existed merely to keep the two hemispheres from sagging.

Aside from such provocative quips, it can scarcely be gainsaid that the corpus callosum assists inter-hemispheric coordination in motor, sensory and visual activities. The body of experimental and clinical data to support this contention is considerable.

Manual Skills: Language

One simple example may be quoted, namely the acquisition of manual skills. One hand in isolation may be trained in the execution of an intricate and highly organized performance. At the same time the corresponding opposite hand is unobtrusively attaining a similar skill to a minor yet not negligible degree. The use of chopsticks at the table is a difficult and wholly unfamiliar procedure for the average Caucasian subject; nonetheless, it is a skill which can be eventually mastered. A Chinese acquires this art at an early age, and for reasons of social usage amounting to a veritable taboo, he manipulates the chopsticks exclusively with the right hand. But should the Chinese subject be requested to use chopsticks with the left hand for the very first time in his life, he can do so. The performance may look awkward, but the Chinese will demonstrate a far greater deftness than an unpractised Caucasian trying to control chopsticks with his master hand (Critchley). In other words, the Chinese not only achieves a right-sided manual skill which is presumably correlated with an engram or memory-trace in the left cerebral hemisphere, but at the same time he must have been unwittingly laying down a similar though fainter mechanism in the opposite half of the brain, that is to say, the right side.

The idea, first promulgated perhaps by K. U. Smith (1951), receives abundant support from the electromyographic researches published by Černáček 1959, 1961, 1966 and by Podivinsky 1963, 1964, 1966, who found that during voluntary contraction of one limb electro-myographic activity could be detected in the symmetrical muscles of the opposite side. This transcallosal irradiation took place more readily from the major to the minor hemisphere, than conversely.

Some years ago the question was posed as to the location and nature of the central mechanism controlling an unpaired or azygos organ of exquisite motor skill and perceptual sensitivity. (Critchley.) Two examples were quoted: the elephant's trunk and the prehensile tail of the spider-monkey. No answer has as yet been adduced as to whether one hemisphere is concerned, or both, and if the latter is the case, the extent to which inter-hemispheric connections come into play. Or indeed, whether some unpaired controlling mechanism exists.

Whether or not manual preference is a property peculiar to men—the evidence being complicated and somewhat contradictory—there can be no dispute but that language is essentially a human prerogative. The necessary rider is that in man, alone among animals, one cerebral hemisphere preponderates in function.

Despite the experiences of over a century, the threefold tie-up between language, inter-hemispheric inequality, and "handedness" remains obscure as regards its *raison d'être*. Not until early in this century did neurologists begin to seek explanations for this clinico-anatomo-physiological linkage. The greater importance of the left hemisphere quâ speech could not be satisfactorily explained merely on the basis of the superior motor skills of the right hand. The division of labour between the two hands in day to day activities does not seem enough to explain the imbalance of the two halves of the brain with regard to speech. Many professional skills are bimanual and yet asymmetrical, as in the case of experienced typists, pianists, violinists, surgeons. Nevertheless, in such executants language continues to be "represented" (to use an unfortunate term) within the dominant or major hemisphere. At one time it was suspected that it was the acquisition of the art of writing, a linguistic modality which is both artificial and asymmetrical which endows the opposite cerebral hemisphere with a special rank in the faculty of language. E. Weber in 1904 was probably the first to state this hypothesis explicitly and unequivocally, believing that the act of writing rather than simple right-handedness was the all-important factor. He quoted a case recorded by Bramwell, of a strongly left-handed man of 36 who, as the result of a lesion of the left hemisphere, sustained a right hemiplegia and a loss of speech. But this patient, although a sinistral, had always utilized his right hand for writing. The idea was that on this account the "speech-centre" [*sic*] had been displaced from the right to the left side of the brain. Weber went on to stress the vulnerability of the delicate mechanism of writing. Penmanship is not only personally idiosyncratic—as borne out by graphologists and forensic handwriting experts—but it may subtly reflect the changing mood of the writer. Such exquisite sensitivity must surely indicate a corresponding complexity of central control, and determine the lateralization of the "speech centre".

Other interesting ideas are stimulated by Weber's

hypothesis. If it were really the case that the act of writing is all-important in determining the sidedness of the central mechanism of language, then it would follow that subjects who had never acquired the ability to write would not be endowed with such a one-sided speech-centre: according to Weber's notion both halves of the brain should be equipotential. One would, therefore, expect to find little or no enduring speech-disorder in children, and also in adult illiterates when victims of unilateral brain-disease.

What is the clinical evidence? True, young children rarely show severe aphasia after a lesion of the brain, whether it be left-sided or right-sided. Or, if some speech-impairment does follow, it rarely persists for long. This observation, which is rarely if ever questioned, brings up the hypothesis of an elasticity of the relatively immature brain. It is also compatible with Weber's idea that unilateral localization of the speech-centre of the brain depends in part upon whether the person in question wrote much or little prior to the onset of disease.

If these ideas are valid then one would furthermore expect one-sided brain lesions (ischaemic, traumatic, neoplastic) to be followed by little or no aphasia in the case of illiterates. Oddly enough there has never been an adequate series of case-reports emanating, as one might expect, from developing countries, which throws any light upon this matter. The experience of aphasiologists alerted to this question assuredly allows them to assert that aphasia can and does occur in illiterates afflicted with brain-damage. Certain matters, however, remain obscure. Is the left or the right hemisphere the more vulnerable one quâ speech-functions in illiterates? Is the pattern of dysphasia in the literate and the illiterate identical? And, in particular, does speech-impairment—should it occur at all—clear up earlier or later in those who have been educationally deprived?

Weber raised another interesting debating point. Mindful of the meagre references to speech-loss in historical times, he wondered whether this was so because of the restriction of the art of writing to a rarified caste made up of the academic élite. Hence he suggested that the syndrome of dysphasia was something of a rarity until the nineteenth century.

However ingenious this idea, it is probably untenable. Even in the remote past there is evidence which pertains not to language, of course, but certainly to manual preference. Among the wall paintings made by Magdelenian and Aurignacian man (50,000–30,000 B.C.) runs a recurring theme, namely a life-size handprint. What these marks signify we do not know. It is intriguing to observe that the majority of these palm-prints are of a left hand. Whether they are direct imprints of the left hand; or whether they are outline drawings of the left executed by the right, we cannot say. As Lewis Carroll remarked "There must be a moral in this somewhere, if only I could find it . . ."

Judging from the shape of the stone implements used in pre-history, dextrals and sinistrals were approximately equal in numbers (Paresin); right-handedness possibly did not preponderate until the bronze age.

Cerebral Dominance

This is the opportunity to stress that it is anything but a simple or straightforward task to determine which cerebral hemisphere is the dominant one; or better which is the senior partner in inter-hemispheric collaboration. Mere enquiry as to whether the subject is right- or left-handed is not enough. Nor does Wada's test—useful though it be within its limits—give us the definitive answer. Footedness and eyedness as well as the preferred direction of automatic lateral gaze are matters of substance, for mere manual preference is not necessarily paramount.

A straightforward decision as to which constitutes the master hand requires a whole battery of tests. These in turn are not equal in validity nor comparable in essence. Some, like the choice of a particular hand for writing, may represent nothing more than a manual skill ordained by instruction rather than natural preference. Other activities, like the use of a fork, spoon, knife, chopsticks, may reflect socio-cultural prejudices rather than instinct. Some actions, like the wielding of a bat by a cricketer or baseball player, are bimanual, and here again the technique adopted by an individual exponent may be decreed rather than chosen. Some other clues indicative of handedness are automatic, unwitting and untaught. For instance there is the way in which one unscrews the cork from a champagne bottle using the bare hands. Here also belongs the manner of clasping the two hands or folding the arms. It could be argued that this type of enquiry represents the most reliable index of manual preference, in that social mores and the acquisition of a manual skill through instruction are irrelevant.

A study of a large enough series of normal subjects will no doubt eventually make it possible to establish an individual's laterality quotient or index of motor dominance; that is to say, a formula representing the extent of inter-hemispheric rivalry. The outcome may well show a varying degree of ambivalence, so that no one person is ever likely to display a complete or absolute unilateral cerebral superiority. What will doubtless emerge is that a subject will prove to be, say, 75 per cent left-brained and 25 per cent right-brained; or perhaps 90 per cent as against 10 per cent.

This will be no simple undertaking, however, for as a preliminary it will entail a statistical assessment of the relative value of each individual component of a constellation of tests which seek to determine handedness, footedness and eyedness. Some tests may well rate as far more significant than others. Anatomical indications of cerebral dominance are constantly being sought as giving as unequivocal evidence of which is, or was, the leading hemisphere, or even the preferred hand. If Geschwind's interesting measurements of the convolutional masses were ever to be confirmed up to the hilt and carefully correlated as regards handedness, it would give us only a hint as to which hemisphere was the one more concerned with the faculty of language. We should continue our quest for some extracerebral clue as to hemispheric leadership, one which we could utilize not only on the cadaver but on the living subject even though he be unconscious. The efforts which have been made so far have proved disappointing. These include such anthropometric and morphological indices as comparative limb-size; contrastive dermatoglyphs; the ectodermo-mesenchymal index on the optic papilla; nailbed formation; venular patterning on the hands; asymmetry in the resting tonus of the limb musculature; and the positioning of the hair-whorl. Černáček has found the skin-temperature to be higher on the dominant hand, while, according to Cigának optokinetic nystagmus, induced in the conscious subject, is slower to the sub-ordinate side.

The question also rises as to the extent to which the laterality quotient correlates with cerebral maturity. In other words, does a child's formula of inter-hemispheric leadership steadily alter as he grows older? And does there gradually come about a state of reduced rivalry? Already there is some evidence to this effect. Most writers place the beginnings of cerebral dominance at approximately the age of 4 years.

Hemispherectomy

Over the last two decades the question of inter-hemispheric collaboration has been both complicated and clarified by the introduction of at least two bold neurosurgical interventions.

The first of these was the practice of hemispherectomy in certain selected cases of gross perinatal one-sided brain-damage. The clinical syndrome of infantile hemiplegia, mental defect, intractable epilepsy and grave behavioural disturbances, came to be regarded as an indication for surgical extirpation of the abnormal half of the brain. It was as though the diseased tissue was something more than a mere passenger, or non-contributor to the mental well-being of the organism: its rôle was more like that of a "squalid nuisance", as Churchill put it. Removal of these cicatricial orts was found to bring about an un-expected control of the epilepsy and improved comport-ment, at the expense of little if any increase in the physical disability. In other words, the patient seemed to get along better with merely half a brain than he did when he was endowed with one healthy hemisphere and one which was little more than a fragment of bad brain.

Such cases, encountered less often nowadays, were probably not subjected before and after operation to the type of experimental psychological and psychiatric investigations which we would currently require.

Split-brain Procedures

The other neurological venture was ushered in 10 years ago with the work of Vogel, Bogen, Fisher, Gaz-zaniga and Sperry.

In an attempt to control certain cases of intractable epilepsy, it was decided to make a complete division of the corpus callosum together with section of the anterior and hippocampal commissures and sometimes the massa intermedia as well. That a satisfactory and sustained improvement in the seizure-incidence followed, is a remarkable event, discussion of which is not germane to this article. Of more immediate interest were the effects upon the patients' motor and perceptual efficiency and their patterns of behaviour.

In the first place, as far as ordinary day-to-day hap-penings were concerned, no obvious detriment occurred, and in the realm of vision, no consistent visual symptoms. Nevertheless, under appropriate testing, using searching neuropsychological procedures, clinical and experimental, bizarre anomalies came to light after the procedure of "commussurotomy" (to employ reluctantly this hybrid terminology). The appropriate techniques entailed an apparatus so constructed that objects could be displayed separately before the right and the left fields of vision. In these circumstances, patients would correctly describe and put a name to objects flashed tachistoscopically to the right visual field. When, however, the same procedure was applied to the left field of vision, the subject would deny having seen more than perhaps a flash of light. If the stimulus was exposed to both right and left fields, there would be no "carry-over" from one field to the other, and the patient would give the impression of being blind in the left half of the field.

However, if all verbal intervention was dispensed with, it was found that the patient was perfectly capable of selecting out of an array of articles before him the one which had just been exposed within his left visual field and which he had actually denied having seen.

With combined visuo-motor tests, an inter-hemispheric breakdown could also be demonstrated, as shown by a dyspraxia. Imitation of complicated digito-manual ges-tures from right to left or left to right was found not to be possible. Likewise, such patients were able to copy simple designs better with the left hand than the right, but when verbal material was concerned the situation was reversed. The same state of affairs applied to olfaction. Although the subjects could be proved to perceive odours from either nostril, they could name them only when the stimulus impinged upon the left side. This also applied to cross modal olfacto-tactual matchings, provided they were projected to the same hemisphere.

With more and more elaborate procedures entailing other perceptual modalities, it appeared as though no "cross-talk" could take place between one half of the brain and the other. The two hemispheres remained disconnected, and the results, though not obvious to casual observation, were found to transcend motor and sensory confines. "Each has its own faults, feelings, awareness, learning and memory, even its own sphere of consciousness and leads its own independent existence." Sperry, whose may studies upon patients with transsected commissures have been so valuable and stimulating, has expressed the opinion that each hemisphere is endowed with "much more than half a mind", and that the left hemisphere remains dominant even after "commissuro-tomy" while the minor right hemisphere tends slowly to decline in function. Sperry spoke of the "prerogative of the right half of the brain", namely an ability to think in a generally "artistic", qualitative and synthetic fashion and to cope with matters of space and form. Bogen suggested that these specific modes of thinking might be termed "appositional", in contrast to the "propositional thought" (Hughlings Jackson) characteristic of the leading hemisphere. By "appositional", Bogen had in mind a capacity on the part of the right brain, for the apposing or comparison of perception, schemata, engrams. "Apposition" has of course a very specific meaning in lexicology and is perhaps not quite appropriate in this context. Indeed Bogen modestly admitted the limitations of this term, its virtue being that it is homologous with "propositional" while at the same time it is sufficiently ambiguous to warrant provisional use.

The Minor Hemisphere

The past 30 years have witnessed a revival of interest in the possible rôle of the non-dominant hemisphere in health and disease. The preponderating importance of the major half of the brain in respect of language has tempted many neurologists and psychologists to enquire whether any specific properties can in comparable fashion be associated with the minor half. Much of the evidence adduced is based upon those symptoms which have followed one-sided disease, and therefore concerns the lateralization of cerebral *dysfunction*. This is no place to discuss or even to list the various clinical phenomena which have been at one time or another correlated with disorder of the minor half of the brain. To do so could constitute an important chapter in itself. One faculty alone contrasts with language as evidence of integrity of the dominant hemisphere, namely music.

The evidence is diverse in type. Part of it derives from the experience of dichotic listening. Thus, by channelling simultaneously different sounds into the two ears of a normal subject, Milner found that numbers and words are perceived better in the right ear, while music and changes in pitch are of greater importance to the left. The inference was that the minor half of the brain is more concerned with musical thinking, appreciation and expression, than the major side, which concerns itself more particularly with language. Many other writers have collected similar arguments. How these are compatible with the partial acoustic decussation in the brain-

stem is not clear. The results of right versus left temporal lobectomies have been compared and contrasted. Here again, several authors have concluded that the minor temporal lobe is the one which is chiefly bound up with musical thought. The relative incidence of amusia after localized lesions of the brain has been touched upon over the years but only sketchily, and in the present state of knowledge it would be rash indeed to attempt to make any conclusions of a dogmatic character.

It is obvious to an aphasiologist that the subject of amusia is still perilously insecure, and that it stands on a par with the descriptive status occupied by speech-pathology in the last century. Music is a highly complex faculty which embraces musical execution, vocal and instrumental; musical perception, identification and aesthetic appreciation; as well as musical imagery, memory and recall. Amusia is a subject which clambers for attention for it might well prove as intriguing and rewarding a subject as aphasia was to Broca and Jackson a hundred years ago.

Commonsense reservations upon any hypothetical duality of brain-function as between music and language are required when faced with any alleged and unlikely antinomy between lyric and melody. It is straining credibility to imagine that music as comprising at one and the same time song and articulate language, should stem from the activities of opposite halves of the brain. Speech and song differ in degree rather than in fundamentals. Herbert Spencer, as long ago as 1857, stressed that song represents the outcome of excited feelings which exaggerate the properties of loudness, timbre, pitch, intervals and rate of variation. The distinctive traits of song are, he said those of emotional speech intensified and systematized. To stretch the argument *ad absurdum*: if we talk with our major hemisphere and sing with our minor, by what cerebral legerdemain do we contrive to cope with those intermediate vocalizations, i.e. chanting and recitative? Where within this mythical dichotomy does poetry properly belong? To seek to separate the lyric from the melody is absurd, as every professional knows. To quote the much seasoned but untutored Edith Piaf . . . "A song isn't a tune on one side and words on the other; they are a unity."

8. COMMUNICATION: RECOGNITION OF ITS MINIMAL IMPAIRMENT

MACDONALD CRITCHLEY

When the topic of communication and especially that of its breakdown comes up for consideration by neurologists, it is a matter of speech and language which is particularly envisaged. The three terms, however, are not synonyms to be used interchangeably. Speech entails the reception as well as exteriorization of ideas and

feelings by way of verbal channels, that is, through the use of words. Language implies something much more fundamental for it includes the encoding and decoding of messages by means of a diversity of media, some of which do not entail the use of words. Thus it would be quite in order to refer to the language of gesture, or of the dance. The term might also include a number of agreed signal-systems, so that it would not be inappropriate to apply it to pictorial art; Braille; and the morse code. Even the homely phrase "language of flowers" is acceptable.

Speech, and to some degree language, being a structure built up on "words" encompasses sounds or graphic marks which "stand for" some abstract idea of concrete object; hence they are being utilized as "symbols". Although the term "symbol" offends certain linguists, it is nevertheless acceptable to most who deal with the psychology and the pathology of language. A symbol, as opposed to a sign or a signal, can be used to refer to something which is out of sight, though not out of mind of course. It can be employed in the context of the past and the future, as well as the present. This malleability of a verbal symbol has been spoken of as its "time-binding" property (Korzybski). The art of juggling with these symbols allows of considerable creativity, that is, employment in novel situations. This property has been called "open-endedness" (Chomsky). In addition speech also utilizes a number of words which are used as "fillers" being low in reference function but important within the somewhat artificial setting of grammar. Here belong the articles, prepositions and conjunctions.

"Communication" is somewhat different for it may by-pass the manipulation of words, and concern itself simply with a traffic in signs and signals which cannot be symbolic for they are products of immediacy. It would be correct to speak of "animal communication"—but not of animal language or animal speech—for the utilization of verbal symbols is a human prerequisite. No sub-hominid species employs any system which can truly be rated as speech even though in some instances, as in the case of bees, and also dolphins, the communicative code is elaborate. Similarly, no community of man, however lowly in the scale of sophistication is devoid of language, often indeed one of great syntactical complexity.

Not surprisingly language and speech, being essentially the prerogative of homo sapiens, are vulnerable to a variety of disease-processes being exquisitely sensitive to mal-functioning. Best known instance is the phenomenon of aphasia, though other aberrations of speech may be identified. Moreover, when ontogenetic development is concerned, the appearance of speech in one or other of its modalities, is at times late in maturation.

This vulnerability of language under the stress of pathology contrasts with the relative insensitivity of animal communication to acquired lesions of the brain. Nothing really comparable with aphasia is met with among animals even after extensive brain-resections (Lashley; Clinton Woolsey; Denny-Brown . . . personal communications). It is true that in the literature there have been a few references to the contrary, *vide* "aphasia" in parrots, (de Allende–Navarro); loss of barking after surgical ablation in dogs, (Katzenstein); and acquired mutism in Capuchin apes (Rothmann). These observations are quite exceptional, however, and not altogether convincing.

Disorders of communication, as they present themselves in medical practice, belong to one or more of the following categories:

(1) Impairment of the mature faculty of language, i.e. aphasia or dysphasia.
(2) Delayed maturation, in a child, of one or more aspects of language.
(3) Anomalous speech as met with in psychotic patients (dements; schizophrenes).
(4) Psychologically determined disorders of speech, including the various hysterial anomalies.
(5) Disorders of phonation or of articulation.
(6) Mixed pictures of complex aetiology.

Of the foregoing (1), (2) and (3) belong firmly within the category of language as opposed to speech. Number (5) is to be regarded entailing disorders of speech rather than language, although in some cases (e.g. dysarthria) concomitant affections of language may be discerned. The aetiology of (4) and (6) sometimes bestrides both speech and language, as for example in cases of verbal dyspraxia.

Aphasia makes up an important chapter in neurological practice. Although it has been familiar to clinicians for well over a century, and a topic of considerable discussion, the subject of aphasiology is one which is obscure and often misunderstood. It offers abundant opportunities for extended study.

An important aspect of the aphasia-problem, although it is very rarely referred to in current teaching, deserves discussion in some detail. This topic concerns the means whereby the very earliest cases of affection of speech may be detected clinically.

THE DETECTION OF MINIMAL DYSPHASIA

The condition about to be discussed entails those subtle impairments in the manipulation of language which constitute the earliest signs of an ingravescent dysphasia. The term "manipulation" is used advisedly, as intending to embrace the act of verbal communication not only in its receptive and expressive aspects, but also the phenomenon of internal reverbalization. This same conception can also apply to the very late stages of recovery after a previous episode of an aphasia. Minimal dysphasia may be so mild as to pass unnoticed during the give and take of ordinary social intercourse. Usually the patient himself is unaware of any detriment in his use of language, unless of course he should happen to be professionally concerned with literature in the widest sense, creative perhaps or merely critical. In this event the victim is only too aware that some falling-off is taking place in his professional competency. As might be expected, specially searching tests are usually required to demonstrate the existence of a minimal dysphasia, and also its extent.

Boller (1968) writing upon this topic stated "the preparation of a test highly sensitive to aphasic expressive defects is a task which has not yet been solved, and which deserves to be more thoroughly investigated. The main difficulty with such a test seems to be the risk that, by increasing the verbal difficulty, it will be made more susceptible to non-specific deficits, which frequently accompany cerebral lesions."

Even earlier, a few aphasiologists had devised tests which subjected the patient to relatively stressful situations in order to bring into the open an underlying speech disorder, receptive or expressive. Head's hand-eye-ear test belongs here, and indeed Head was at one time criticized by some of his colleagues for employing a technique which was not strictly linguistic in nature. Even earlier Pierre Marie had brought out his "three paper test", which is a useful procedure for uncovering a minimal receptive defect of language. We may also recall the technique devised by Thomas and Roux, as well as the "Test of the Absurd Story" used by Weisenburg and McBride, both of which are useful in demonstrating minimal degrees of dysphasia.

The battery of tests for the detection of a minimal dysphasia—or "latent" dysphasia to use the terminology of Pichot—needs to be extended.

Poverty of Speech

An overall reduction in linguistic spontaneity is one common indication of a minimal dysphasia. Although the patient can keep pace with his interlocutor and betray no obvious shrinkage of his vocabulary, he seems reluctant to embark upon the seas of conversation. Inordinately protracted periods of silence are evident when the patient with ingravescent dysphasia is observed in the home, at the conference table, or in the Board Room. He can and will reply to questions adequately enough. If sufficiently inspired, he can pose questions on his own initiative. In general, however, he appears unwilling to break silence with pertinent observations or even with small talk.

This impoverishment of speech is all the more striking when it shows itself in one who had hitherto been looked upon as constitutionally somewhat garrulous, and anything but squeamish of talking in company. Loquacity is a trait which often increases with ageing, and when the reverse occurs, the possibility of a very early disorder of language should be suspected.

More tangible still is a poverty of written speech. Unless the patient happens to depend for his livelihood upon his writings and is therefore compelled to work, he now begins to express himself on paper with greater rarity, and what he writes is far less free than even his spoken speech. With the onset of minimal dysphasia, the reluctance to put pen to paper or to use a typewriter becomes increasingly evident, showing itself in a diminished correspondence on the part of a letter-writer, and in the attenuated output of a diarist.

In contrast, however, one must not overlook the occasional phenomenon of an *over-reaction* which a minimal dysphasiac may display. Instead of an impoverishment of speech, an undue talkativeness, or inordinate resort to letter-writing, may sometimes represent the very earliest signs of a commencing language-disorder. The explanation is simple. During the course of conversation, the verbosity of the one who is actually speaking ordains that for the moment he is master in the use of linguistic tools, and the interlocutor's chances of introducing unexpected or difficult material are considerably lessened. This phenomenon of aggressive loquacity in some early dysphasiacs does not take place at a conscious level.

Poverty of Speech: Its Linguistic Nature

A verbatim record of the early dysphasiac's spontaneous talk or written work may serve as material for linguistic analysis. Various features may be demonstrable:

(a) There may be an exaggerated discrepancy between the vocabulary which may be looked upon as accessible, available, or get-at-able, and the other vocabulary which is actually in common use. In other words, this gap between the potential and the habitual vocabularies which exists in most normal individuals, widens considerably in incipient dysphasiacs.

In normal circumstances the difference between the two vocabularies correlates with the intellectual level and educational status, for in the case of the poorly literate there is but little to choose. Despite this natural difference in normal subjects, minimal dysphasiacs also show a widening gap, the pragmatical vocabulary or the one that is ordinarily utilized becoming more attenuated than the other.

(b) This disparity is also shown by estimating the Type/Token ratio of verbal diversification, or TTR. "Token" refers to the sum-total of words used; while "type" indicates the number of *different* words employed. Ordinarily the lower the ratio the smaller the verbal diversity, and this would be likely to characterize the spontaneous writings of a latent dysphasiac.

(c) A reduced sentence-length may be found especially in the written compositions of a patient with very early dysphasia. In spoken speech this phenomenon may be less evident, because of a complicating stylistic or even syntactical imperfection whereby sentences trail off unfinished, or else become cluttered up with parenthetical clauses, asides, after-thoughts, and qualifications. This type of verbal mannerism is less likely to show itself on paper.

(d) An estimate of the verb-adjective ratio might be revealing. However, to establish beyond all question a minimal deterioration in the manipulation of speech, knowledge is required of the patient's pre-morbid linguistic competency and habits. This may be available in the case of an author who is slowly developing a dysphasia by reason of a slow-growing brain-tumour. When such data are accessible for analysis, it may well become obvious that verbs are reduced in number, while concrete nouns, and more particularly adjectival forms show a relative increase. Such an altered ratio is most striking in the case of the demotic speech of an ill-educated pre-aphasiac. In such, one expects to find a greater incidence of those all-purpose adjectives with almost meaningless fragments of vernacular and which loom so large in the utterances of the barely

Howard Cosell of neurology

literate. Under the stress of growing language-impairment these increase both relatively and absolutely.

(e) An enhanced employment of clichés and trite word-clusters is demonstrable. Practised speakers and experienced writers are less liable to betray in their speech and correspondence any contamination with those oft-recurring phrases which are relatively low in reference-function or "meaning". Those who are less well endowed educationally, tend to slip into this habit of usage in a manner which becomes almost idiosyncratic and personally identifiable. Both types of individuals, when under the influence of a minimal dysphasia, are apt to have an increased recourse to platidudinous phraseology, which might even border on sheer rigmarole.

Except for the last of these linguistic phenomena, the foregoing features are best observed in the written essays of the pre-aphasiac. However, an increased resort to a stale, hackneyed and threadbare style of verbiage is particularly evident in the articulate utterance of a patient with minimal dysphasia, and is far less conspicuous in his written compositions.

Gratuitous Redundancy

This is a phenomenon which I have described elsewhere, and which may be defined as "the interpolation by a patient with mild aphasia, of verbiage which is comparatively low in reference-function, although not wholly beside the point". Such gratuitous redundancy shows itself particularly well in the course of naming tests. In such circumstances, the patient uses too many words, not contenting himself with a simple nomination of the article presented to him. Perhaps it is an over-reaction against an inability to hit upon *le mot juste*, the ideal and most satisfying expression eluding him for the moment. Thus, shown an object, the patient with minimal dysphasia may be hesitant in recalling the exact term, but then having eventually found it, feels it incumbent to proceed to amplify it unnecessarily. Confronted with a wrist-watch, for instance, the patient may after a pause identify it and then go on to say . . . "My husband has a beauty, but then he's got everything!" Or, shown an electric torch battery, the patient, after naming it may add . . . "a new battery; just a one-cell, just a one-cell . . . I don't know what voltage; just one, I think. . . ." Perhaps the origins of gratuitous redundancy lie in the fact that these extrapolated phrases are devoid of any purpose other than a social one, the additional words serving merely to oil the wheel of the small-talk of inter-personal relationships. Gratuitous redundancy is in many ways on a par with the phatic communion of primitive peoples (Malinowski), and the regressive metonymy of leucotomized patients (Petrie).

Defective Exemplification

This expression refers to an inability to recite a series of instances exemplifying some given common property. This faculty is sometimes referred to as a process of "word production". For example, the patient may be directed to enumerate as rapidly as possible as many examples of, say, birds, flowers, fruit, fishes or makes of automobile. Slightly more difficult would be the attempt to name articles which are endowed with a common quality or property e.g. heaviness, sharpness, the colour red, and so on. A test of this sort is in its nature a higher level abstraction and it taxes severely the ability to cull up examples possessing a common denominator. Occasionally the patient succeeds by virtue of carrying out this test at an utterly concrete level. Thus he may enumerate appropriate articles which are lying immediately within his view; or he may resort to a series of clues afforded by a clear visual imagery.

There is a marked similarity between the performance of a dementing patient in the course of this last test and one who is afflicted by the earliest beginnings of true aphasia. In other words, the manoeuvre of a search for defective exemplification in minimal dysphasiacs may also reveal comparable defects in patients with lesions of either cerebral hemisphere (Boller). Two possible explanations arise. Either an impaired word-production is to be regarded as a non-specific index of a cerebral lesion irrespective of its location; or, it could be a true and delicate test of minimal dysphasic deficit, but one which may result from lesions either of the dominant or of the non-dominant hemisphere. This idea brings up the question whether right-brain lesions in right-handed subjects could at times also be associated with subtle disorders of language. *yes*

Recitation or Recapitulation

A searching linguistic test is to request the patient to narrate (or to commit to paper) a resumé of some well-known fable, story, allegory or incident which should be familiar to him. For example, he might be directed to summarize in a few words the story of "Red Riding Hood", or the parable of the "Good Samaritan". The victim of minimal dysphasia will betray considerable difficulty in giving a succinct, crisp, logical and correctly sequenced account of an incident of this kind, which one would ordinarily expect to be both simple and accessible.

Even harder is the task of immediately retailing back to the examiner a story *told to him for the first time*. It is not necessary for the patient to repeat verbatim the words of the examiner as in the case of the Babcock story. Many instances can be taken as a model. It would be appropriate to borrow one or two of Luria's Russian *fabliaux*, as for example, the "Jackdaw and the Dove" story. (A jackdaw dyed his feathers white and joined a community of doves. As soon as his hoarse cries were heard he was rejected. Disconsolately he returned to his former tree-tops, only to be chased away when the other jackdaws saw his colouring).

Sequential linguistic tasks, that is those presented in succession, are particularly difficult for a patient with minimal dysphasia. One technique for demonstrating the ability to cope with serial tasks which we again owe to Luria, is to declaim two short descriptive sentences to the patient who is then required to say them back at once to the examiner. Two examples may be given: (a) "On the edge of a forest a hunter killed a wolf"; followed by: (b) "The appletrees in the garden are in bloom". The victim of minimal aphasia may hopelessly confuse these unrelated statements, even though he may be able to repeat well enough each sentence alone. The patient's difficulty can be increased by separating the test-phrases (a) and (b) first of all by a brief interval, e.g. 30 sec.; and secondly by a similar gap *which has been deliberately occupied by interpolated conversation*. In such circumstances the early dysphasiac may often be said to display a "loss of selectivity" of memory-traces, whereby items of the two sentences fuse, with the introduction of verbal contaminations and perseverations.

The difficulties may be increased by introducing three sentences instead of two. Each of them may be quite brief, e.g. "The sea is cold. The moon is shining brightly. The streets are crowded."

Another device for bringing to the surface an incipient or latent dysphasia while again introducing the factor of selectivity, is by way of an *extended naming test*. Shown a succession of common objects, the patient may identify each one well enough, and furthermore when presented with a collection of articles he may pick out to command one item after another. However, *if he is shown two or three articles simultaneously* (e.g. watch, key, collar-stud) he may experience embarrassment in serial naming. Or, confronted with a collection of articles, and told to pick out—not one—but three objects, he may be hesitant or even at a complete loss. Such errors are particularly likely to occur if the articles displayed are hardly "common" articles, but objects which are a trifle unexpected and out of the ordinary.

Other elaborations of these naming and isolating techniques can be used in order to bring out an underlying incohate dysphasia. Thus, the patient with a number of objects before him may be directed to *manipulate* rather than merely identify them. For example, he may be instructed to "pick up the collar-stud and *put it inside the match-box*". This may prove too much for the patient, although a moment before he may have correctly identified both articles singly as well as in combination.

This technique recalls the so-called "Token Test" devised by De Renzi and Vignolo (1962). Their test is a useful one and has been carefully studied in patients with aphasia, with brain-injured patients who are also aphasic, and in controls. By this means it was possible to uncover mild *receptive* defects in aphasiacs even in those who had been looked upon as instances of pure motor aphasia. In devising this test, the authors took great care to ensure that the procedure was brief in duration; that special apparatus or printed material was not required; that the instructions were so simple as not to tax the dysphasiac's memory; and that the task should entail the maximum linguistic difficulty with the minimum intellectual stress. The materials of their "Token Test" consist of 20 pieces of paper, in 5 colours, 2 shapes, and 2 sizes. The patient is first told to touch one of these papers; and then to touch *two* of them. Gradually the instructions become

more elaborate, e.g. by introducing a choice ("touch the blue circle *or* the red triangle"); or the factor of position ("place the blue circle *on* the red rectangle"); or of succession ("touch the blue circle *after touching* the red rectangle"); or of condition ("touch *all* the circles *except* the green one").

This particular test has many merits. Its principal drawback lies in the use of the term "Token" in this connection—a term which is totally unacceptable—for in linguistic science "token"—as we have already discussed—has a very special connotation, as well as a precise definition, viz. "each particular occurrence of a speech unit, spoken or written". De Renzi and his colleagues would have been on less ambiguous grounds had they spoken of "Items" rather than "Tokens". Perhaps the best solution would be to perpetuate eponymity and to speak of the "De Renzi–Vignolo test".

Another useful elaboration of this type of test-situation, is to tell the patient to pick up (or point to) this article or that, *against a competing background of irrelevant noise*. This factor of noise can be brought in by switching on music; or by introducing some distracting element of sound, but best of all by some acoustic handicap of a linguistic character. This last-named can be furnished by an assistant reading aloud a paragraph from a book during the testing procedure.

Linguistic Recall

This faculty may be impaired in cases of minimal dysphasia but not come to light until specially penetrating procedures are brought to bear. For example, the examiner may recite to the patient a series of ten substantives of a familiar sort.* The examinee is then immediately asked to recount these same ten words. Or—to step up the inherent difficulty—to recap the series after a silent gap of 30 sec.; or after a similar interval filled with interpolated talk. Finally the patient may be confronted with a much longer series of words (either verbally or in print)† within which he is expected to pick out the original ten words which the examiner has recited. Here then are four variants of the same test, of graduated difficulty.

Comprehension and Explanation of Various Trite Linguistic Whimsicalities

This test is similar to, but not identical with, the routine clinical procedure whereby a patient is asked to explain ceratin well-known proverbs. Here the test is directed to an assessment of verbal juggling rather than of thinking. In this particular test for minimal dysphasia, the patient is presented with not a proverb, but a phrase which he is requested to paraphrase or explain. In the English

---

* Inkwell, potato, scissors, bottle, feather, herring, book, electric torch, cigarette, cricket bat.

† Steak, pig, feather, pen, rose, inkwell, scissors, pencil, pipe, cabbage, egg, cigarette, matches, electric bulb, carpet, chair, bottle, football, shirt, cap, newspaper, potato, cricket bat, magazine, bloater, pork, biro, fork, clothes peg, corkscrew, herring, thimble, cigar, wristwatch, boots, razor, key, cabbage, umbrella.

language suitable test-phrases include such *doubles entendres* as "Players please"; or strained obscure metaphors like "it's in the bag", "the horse's mouth"; or truncated aphorisms like "the hair of the dog". In such circumstances the linguistic abilities of the minimal dysphasiac are taxed severely. It is a matter of opinion whether the difficulty lies in an imperfect comprehension, or in defective formulation, or in both.

Analogies and Multiple Choice Quizzes

Here the patient is presented with three words—spoken or printed—and is expected to supply the logical fourth term. The following are examples:

winter, snow: autumn, ...?
mother, daughter: father, ...?
lion, teeth: eagle, ...?
motor-car, engine: boat, ...?
bird, wing: dog, ...?

In these five instances, words like rain, fog, son, claws, sails, oars, paws, legs, would be acceptable.

A similar test entails the search for a second word in a common-place phrase which entails either metonyms or contrasts, e.g.

wet and ?
health and ?
fish and ?
black and ?
big and?

Here any such words as windy, dry, happiness, strength, disease, chips, white and small would be appropriate.

Still easier for the testee is the linguistic task of word-finding when he is assisted by a multiple choice type of presentation, e.g.

water, thirst: food .... (hunger, meal, mouth)
tree, branch: hand .... (feet, fingers, glove)
regiment, soldiers: library .... (readers, books, reading room)
winter, snow: autumn .... (falling leaves, harvest, rain)

The patient is required to underline the words which are appropriate.

A banal test-situation which is a considerable burden to the capacities of a patient with minimal dysphasia can be found in crossword puzzles. In utilizing this procedure as a deliberate aphasiological procedure one should avoid clues which are abstruse and which depend almost entirely upon obscure literary allusions. Verbal play, puns and anagrams are permissible provided they are not too recondite. The following constitute suitable examples:

Clue: "I'm buried in a small hill. Not a sea" (Number of letters 5).
Answer: Timor.
Clue: "English viewpoint?" (Number of letters 5).
Answer: Angle.

Clue: "If ham's off, you'll have to go hungry" (Number of letters 6).
Answer: Famish.
Clue: "Good folk? Few believe in them nowadays" (Number of letters 7).
Answer: Fairies.

This type of linguistic examination is unsuitable for general use, but should be reserved for patients whose pre-morbid educational standing is recognized as being high or appropriate. A minimal dysphasia might come to light in this way, but only in the case of an individual known to have been a keen contestant in crossword puzzles of the standard set by *The Times*, the *Observer*, or the *Daily Telegraph*.

Comprehension of Instructions Involving Sequential or Temporal Components

Here one explores the patient's ability to follow and retain a fairly complicated request. The command may be associated with the factor of time-interval. Thus, again following Luria, one may say to the patient "I shall count: and when I have got up to 12, and not before, raise your hand . . . one . . . two . . . three . . . four . . ." and so on.

Or the patient can be faced with a succession of positive and negative tasks, such as: "When I make a *fist*, lift up your *hand*. When I raise my *forefinger*, you make a *fist*. When I lift up my *hand*, do nothing." This complicated instruction which the patient attempts to obey, may be repeated a number of times, his actual responses being carefully observed and recorded.

Sentence-building

Here the patient is shown a series of cards upon each one of which is printed a single word—noun, verb, adjective, adverb, article, preposition, conjunction. The patient is required to arrange these cards so as to form a grammatical and sensible sentence, preferably as lengthy as possible. Thus a normal control subject would have no difficulty in promptly aligning the cards to form some such sentence as the following "Today the weather is wet, windy and cold, while yesterday it was quite warm and sunny." A performance of this kind would be quite beyond the capacity of a minimal dysphasiac, even though he had been able to read and understand perfectly the printed word on each individual card.

Tests such as the foregoing make up a battery of investigations which, in conjunction, will uncover very mild communicative detriments. Note that every one of these tests is essentially clinical in nature, and depends upon little more than pencil and paper together with the efficient utilization of the examiner's five senses. Elaborate equipment, electrical devices, ancillary aids are dispensed with. But to utilize clinical methods adequately, experience, judgement, patience and intellectual honesty are essential. Every movement on the part of the patient, every gesture, articulate utterance, hesitation, interjection, must be noted, timed, and recorded scrupulously. If the observed data do not entirely conform with the examiner's expectations they must not be glossed over or brushed aside. These "negative cases", these discrepancies, may be all-important occurrences, and not just irritating irrelevancies. The history of Science shows how often advances have been made simply by focusing attention upon unexpected, exceptional or non-conforming phenomena. In exploring the garden of language-behaviour, the neurologist must emulate the industry of the bee. To quote Francis Bacon, changing only the last word: "The men of experiment are like the ant; they only collect and use; the reasoners resemble the spiders, who make cobwebs out of their own substance. But the bee takes a middle course, it gathers its material from the flowers of the garden and of the field, but transforms and digests it by a power of its own. Not unlike this is the true business of aphasiology."

9. PSYCHOSURGERY

M. R. BOND

Mental function is complex and debate continues about the extent to which its different components are relatively discrete and independent. However, certain aspects of mental activity have been defined and may be measured, for example intellectual functions such as memory and concept formation, or aspects of emotion like personality and drive. It is clear that each form of activity may influence the others to a greater or lesser extent, and further may also affect physical activity or response. Thus perceptual deficits or disorders of language may profoundly affect cognition, and emotions influence autonomic and somatic function.

It has long been known that brain injury may be associated with changes in mental activity and behaviour, but the first successful attempt to influence emotion by direct surgical intervention did not take place until 1937 when Moniz introduced leucotomy.

At first it was accepted that in order to influence one aspect of mental function favourably it was inevitable that others would also be changed. This soon became unacceptable and the last twenty years have seen the introduction of a series of different operations each claiming to alter specific aspects of disturbed mental activity with the minimum of effect upon normal functions. During the same period the introduction of drugs capable of relieving symptoms of mental illness led to a great reduction in the demand for psychosurgery. However, the increasing availability of selective operations together with the recognition that some patients and certain symptoms are resistant to drug treatment has led to a limited return of interest in psychosurgery. As the basis of selective operations is founded upon a belief that different mental functions depend on separate anatomical structures or systems, albeit with much overlap, it is important first to review the development of concepts in which attempts have been made to relate the physiological function of the brain and its anatomy to mental activity. (*See also* Sec. VI, Chs 4, 5 and 6).

AN ANATOMICAL BASIS FOR EMOTION

In 1878 Broca used the term "the great limbic lobe" to describe the cingulum, and the frontal and medial temporal structures which surround the hilum of each hemisphere.

The region is common to all mammals and is phylogenetically older than the cortex of man. It was suggested that here lay the source of man's "brute instincts" as opposed to his intelligence. Cannon[1] (1927) proposed that the location of neural patterns responsible for emotion lie in the regions of the thalamus and hypothalamus. He held that there is a reciprocal control system between the cerebral cortex and these centres, which discharge caudally producing the complex physiological changes associated with emotion, at the same time discharging to the hemispheres to activate appropriate psychological processes which give rise to experiences such as anxiety, anger and pleasure. Von Economo commented that the cingulate gyri are part of the cortical representation of the autonomic system.

In 1937 Papez[10] synthesized existing theories of emotion with his own observations upon the anatomical links between frontal, temporal and cingulate cortex, and the hypothalamus. He suggested that the limbic lobe with its central connections provides a cortical centre for a variety of emotional and viscerosomatic activities, whereas intellectual functions occur in the neocortex. According to his theory the basic mechanism for elaboration of emotion lies in the "limbic system" formed by the hypothalamus, anterior thalamic nuclei, gyrus cinguli, hippocampus, and their connections (Fig. 1). Papez observed that in rabies, a disease associated with intense anxiety or apprehension and paroxysms of range or terror, the Negri bodies are found chiefly in large ganglion cells of the hippocampus. This led him to believe that central processes underlying emotion could be built up in the hippocampal formation before being transmitted through the fornix to the mammillary bodies. From the latter they would pass through the mammillo-thalamic tracts of Vicq d'Azyr to the anterior nuclei of the thalamus, then being projected to the cortex of the cingulate gyrus. Further spread to the cortical regions would activate psychological processes specific to them. It was also proposed that nerve impulses originating in the somatic and visceral receptors would pass through the ventral nuclei of the thalamus to the mammillary bodies to enter the limbic system where they too would activate the appropriate psychological activities or feelings. In a later review of this theory McLean[8] commented, "there are indications that the phylogenetically older brain, classically known as the rhinencephalon, is largely concerned with visceral and emotional function, and in contrast to the neopallium this region has many strong

LIMBIC SYSTEM·

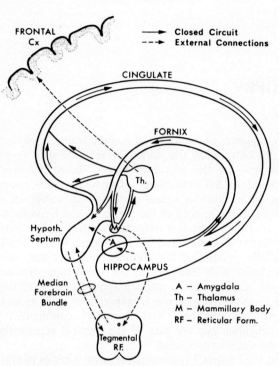

Fig. 1. A schematic representation of the relationship of the cortical and subcortical components of the limbic system.

connections with the hypothalamus for discharging its impressions." More recently doubt has been cast on the role suggested by Papez for the limbic system, as evidence has emerged that it plays a significant part in the function of memory.

The Frontal Lobes

Originally regarded as "silent areas" the frontal lobes are now known to play a major part in intellectual function, aspects of personality, mood and autonomic activity. The neocortex subserves decision making, the goal-seeking activities of concentration and perseverance, and abstract thought. The orbital and medial cortical areas are more primitive cytologically and indeed form part of the "great limbic lobe" of Broca. They are intimately involved in the control of autonomic activity, which is related to the experience of anxiety. In 1894 Spencer[12] obtained autonomic responses from the orbital cortex stimulation of which led to respiratory arrest in the cat, dog, rabbit and monkey. Others have observed similar effects in man, also noting increases in blood pressure, dilatation of the pupils and alterations in visceral tone. These are easily recognized as the substrate of physical changes associated with fear, anger, anxiety and a variety

of psychosomatic disorders including hypertension, peptic ulceration and others. Ablation of orbital cortex, or of the anterior part of the cingulate gyrus in monkeys, renders them more docile, easily tamed and free from fear of man. Isolation of the area from the hypothalamus in man forms the basis of modified leucotomy for the treatment of severe anxiety or depression.

Clinical studies show a marked difference between the results of damage to the supero-lateral and inferior surfaces of the frontal lobes. The former is associated with profound intellectual change whereas the latter primarily affects the degree of emotional tension or depression. These differences in the psychological functions of the two areas are now fully accepted and most psychosurgical operations on the frontal lobes are designed to interrupt the central connecting fibres of the medial orbital cortex whilst sparing those passing to and from the superolateral surface. The anterior part of the cingulate gyrus, the insula, medial and inferior aspect of the temporal lobe resemble the orbital cortex both cytologically and functionally. All four regions are closely interconnected and act as an effector zone for the physiological responses of emotion and are therefore regarded as the area of the brain concerned with the highest representation of visceral function. When Le Gros Clark described thalamo-cortical projection fibres radiating from the dorso-medial nucleus of the thalamus to the frontal neocortex he stressed that this acts as an afferent pathway for excitation of psychological activity represented by different subjective experiences as distinct from the effector system of the medial frontal, temporal and anterior cingulate regions.

The Temporal Lobes

On the basis of early anatomical studies the temporal lobes were considered to be concerned primarily with olfaction and gustation. These activities have been relegated to a minor position as the lobes have wide ranging functions including cortical representation of autonomic activity, short and long term memory, hearing and equilibration. The posterior part of the dominant lobe is concerned with speech and each has rich connections with adjacent cortical areas, and deeper parts of the limbic system.

The lobes are regarded phylogenetically and functionally as two regions. The first consists of medial structures including the amygdala and periamygdala regions, the hippocampus, uncus and the dentate gyrus. The second is formed by the remaining cortex and temporal lobe lying lateral to the hippocampal fissure. This region of neocortex has reciprocal connections with the older medial structures which in turn connect it with the remainder of the limbic system. The medial regions of the hemispheres interconnect through the anterior commissure, and exchange fibres with the primitive orbital cortex, but they have no direct links with the thalamus or with other parts of the neocortex, except that of the temporal lobe.

The precise function of medial structures has not yet

been fully evaluated. There is a profuse afferent inflow to the hippocampus, chiefly from somatic and exteroreceptive sources, and to the amygdala from visceral receptors. Ablation studies in animals and man indicate that the hippocampus is involved in short term memory function, that the amygdala may inhibit or augment hypothalamic functions such as eating, drinking and aggressive activities, and that both are also closely linked to the recticular formation of the brain stem.

The results of bitemporal lobectomy are striking but effects differ between man and the higher primates. Klüver and Bucy[5] (1939) reported that in monkeys the procedure produced bizarre changes in behaviour. These included a compulsion for animals to examine every object orally, a failure to persist in avoiding noxious stimuli, gross alterations in dietary habits, indiscriminate hypersexuality, and loss of fear and aggressiveness. In man however, the predominant change following bilateral lobectomy is a profound defect of short term memory, and even when surgery is confined to bilateral removal of medial structures including the hippocampus and parahippocampal gyrus a permanent memory deficit is produced. Loss of function is primarily concerned with registration of new information exceeding the amount that may be consciously retained. Thus, there is also loss of ability to add new information to the memory store, but long term memory and previously acquired perceptual skills remain unaffected. Unilateral lobectomy produces less obvious changes. Removal of the dominant lobe impairs verbal memory regardless of whether information is heard or read. Following excision of the non-dominant lobe recognition and recall of non-verbal, visual and auditory patterns are affected. (*See* Sec. IV, Ch. 3).

Interest has also centred upon experiments in cats in which hypersexuality and perversion caused by amygdaloidectomy have been abolished by destruction of the ventromedial nuclei of the thalamus. Further studies reveal that the tuber cinereum is also responsible, in part, for sexual function but its destruction produces polyuria and alterations in temperature control in addition to changes in sexual behaviour.

The functions of the temporal neocortex are numerous as evidenced by the rich variety of sensory and emotional experiences encountered in any study of temporal lobe epilepsy. In brief, stimulation of the cortex in conscious man evokes memories, changes in mood, alterations in perception, space and time. It may produce a sense of unreality, excitement, apprehension or fear. Visual, gustatory or olfactory hallucinations occur, and vague sensations referred to the viscera are not infrequent. Williams[15] (1966) commented, "however complex these experiences may be, if they are intermittent, stereotyped and arising as a result of disturbed brain function they constitute a form of local epilepsy in which the origin of the disturbance lies in the temporal lobe but in which the train of events widely transcend its anatomical boundaries". Thus temporal lobectomy, unlike most operations upon the frontal and cingulate cortex, is designed to prevent the repeated complex psychomotor events or

seizures rather than to relieve continuing states such as anxiety or depression.

PRINCIPLES OF PSYCHOSURGERY

The surgeon is concerned with the following three main categories of mental disorder of which only the first two are dealt with in this section.

(1) Certain symptoms associated with neuroses, and psychoses.
(2) The mental symptoms associated with intractable epilepsy originating in the temporal lobe.
(3) Dementia and disorders of personality, mood, drive and cognition, secondary to hydrocephalus or intracranial space-occupying lesions.

Surgery for the first two groups has developed in different centres to a great extent during the past three or four decades. Thus the control of neurotic symptoms, and to a lesser extent those of the psychoses has been achieved chiefly through operations on the frontal lobes, cingulate gyri and thalamic nuclei, whereas the psychological disturbances of temporal lobe epilepsy have stimulated the development of techniques confined to that region of the brain.

Frontal Lobe Operations

In 1937 Moniz[9] published the first clinical report of the operation of leucotomy which he had devised and for which he was later to be awarded a Nobel Prize. He demonstrated significant improvement in a small number of psychotic patients after injecting alcohol into the white matter of their frontal lobes. Subsequently, frontal lobotomy was widely adopted by surgeons and psychiatrists as a method for the treatment of many forms of mental illness, but mostly in patients confined to mental hospitals. Although the earlier patients were usually grossly disturbed mentally it soon became apparent that the operation needed modifications because even in these patients it produced marked deterioration in personality, drive and cognitive function.

Pre-frontal Leucotomy

Freeman and Watts[3] (1942) devised the "standard leucotomy" in which only the central core of frontal white matter was divided, with sparing of the cortex. This was done blind using a brain cannula inserted through bilateral burr holes, making segmental cuts with the widest part of the arc medially. A very large number of patients were treated in this manner and although the gross changes seen after lobotomy were reduced and mortality was only approximately 2 per cent, dissatisfaction remained because intellectual and personality defects were still produced. These became more obvious when the operation began to be used for less seriously disturbed patients who after operation quite often showed diminished drive with loss of ability to plan ahead, egocentricity and loss of social responsibility. Occasionally, drastic physical deterioration occurred with striking metabolic and trophic changes culminating in wasting and death. Approximately a quarter of schizophrenic patients showed improvement; usually a lessening of agitation and aggression. Almost half those with depression gained some relief but indiscriminate selection of patients and lack of carefully controlled studies have rendered accurate assessment of this operation difficult.

Subsequent modifications in surgical techniques, mostly between 1949 and 1958, led to increasing awareness that symptomatic improvement could be achieved with very little or no change in cognitive function or drive. Two of these operations, topectomy and rostral leucotomy were only modifications of a standard leucotomy, and as such showed no advantage over that procedure. However, physiological studies of brain and behaviour led to the development of operations on the anterior part of the cingulum, and infero-medial fibre tracts of the frontal lobes. These connect medial and inferior frontal cortex with the hypothalamus and may be divided from the above, as in bimedial leucotomy, or from the anterior pole of the lobe as in the cortical undercutting operations.

Cingulumectomy

This operation was described by Le Beau[7] in 1952. It was based upon the functional and cytological similarity of the cingulum, orbital cortex, insula and medial temporal regions. All are autonomic effector areas and it was found that the operation produced mood changes with a reduction of the subjective experience of anxiety in addition to its physical manifestations. It proved to be of value in chronic anxiety states and obessional neurosis where tension was extreme. Damage to other aspects of personality and cognition seldom occurred but unfortunately improvement tended to be temporary for many patients; perhaps because only one of four functionally similar areas was destroyed permitting the recurrence of symptoms.

Bimedial Leucotomy

In bimedial leucotomy white matter is divided in a plane extending from the line of the coronal suture above to the sphenoid ridge below. The incision is 2 cm. wide and divides thalamo-frontal fibres from medial, anterior and part of the orbital cortex. However, it does not sever all fibres from the primitive medial and posterior orbital region which is a main autonomic centre.

Depression arising suddenly, without an obvious precipitating cause, in persons with previously well preserved personalities (endogenous depression) appears to be the symptom most amenable to treatment. Depression of the reactive type and symptoms of obsessional states may be relieved but usually only for short periods. Contra-indications include a poor premorbid personality and a past history of aggression or anti-social behaviour, because patients with such features may show an exacerbation of previous personality maladjustments.

Cortical Undercutting

Undercutting operations were introduced by Scoville[11] (1949) and although various forms were developed, only the orbital undercut is now regarded as valuable. This originally entailed division of all white matter lying immediately beneath the cortex in the plane of the orbital roof. The incision extended from the frontal pole to the level of the anterior clinoid processes. As some patients showed a degree of emotional disinhibition and cognitive loss after operation the procedure was modified, restricting undercutting to the medial cortical areas only.

Anxiety and depression were the symptoms most frequently relieved and less success was gained in the treatment of obessional thought disorder and hypochondriasis. Patients who improved most had been ill for less than five years, and had had a good premorbid personality. Schizophrenic patients, and those with a poor premorbid personality adjustment, frequently deteriorated further. The incidence of post-operative epilepsy was 9 per cent and this was regarded as an unwelcome physical complicating factor.

Frontal Tractotomy

With the experience of many restricted orbital undercutting operations Knight concluded that only the posterior 2 cm. of the incision was important for symptom relief. This was in line with the neurophysiological studies on primates carried out by Fulton, who had concluded that the posterior medial orbital cortex should be the main area for surgical isolation in man.

The posterior-medial agranular cortex is separated from the head of the caudate nucleus by a narrow band of white fibres known as the substantia innominata. For anatomical reasons these fibres are inaccessible by direct approach from above, but in 1964 Knight[6] introduced a stereotaxic method for implanting seeds of yytrium 90 into the tract. Although only a small area of destruction results fibres passing to and from inferior and medial frontal, and medial temporal regions are inactivated.

Results of treatment reveal that severe intractable endogenous depression is relieved in as many as 70 per cent of patients. Under half of those with obsessional neurosis respond, whilst relief from symptoms is seldom experienced by patients with reactive depression or hysterical disorders. The operation is valueless in the treatment of chronic pain. Mortality is virtually unknown and alterations in drive and cognitive function have not been reported. Thus it appears that stereotaxic tractotomy has a higher success rate for the disorders described than bimedial leucotomy or restricted orbital undercutting; consequently the social benefits to the patient and his family are correspondingly greater.

Thalamotomy

Destruction of thalamo-frontal fibres at their origin from the dorsomedial nucleus of the thalamus provides an alternative method of altering emotional experience. In 1949 Wycis and Spiegal[13,15] devised a stereotaxic approach to this area but their results showed that the method was no more effective in relieving symptoms than the simpler and less time-consuming procedure of standard leucotomy. Stereotaxic lesions have also been tried in the anterior thalamic nuclei, the posteroventromedial region, the pulvinar and medial and lateral hypothalamic areas. For each site claims have been made that anxiety and depression are reduced, but the number of cases treated is few and the complexity of the procedures has militated against their adoption.

The effect of ablation of the ventromedial nuclei in cats, mentioned previously, has aroused interest in the application of similar operations in man in the treatment of sexual perversion. A very small number of men with a history of repeated homosexual offences against pubertal boys were treated with a reduction of their sexual drive and abolition of homosexuality. Although apparently successful in these cases, the scope of this form of treatment is very limited and its place in psychosurgery has not yet been fully evaluated.

To conclude, the limitations of psychosurgery involving the frontal, cingulate and thalamic regions are becoming clear and at the same time indications for patient selection more precise. It is now possible to change certain mental activities with little or no damage to drive and cognitive function. The chances of success are increased where the illness is well circumscribed, the history short, and where there is evidence of a sound premorbid personality, good social adjustment and a potentially reversible disorder with one symptom predominating. The presence of long-standing neurotic disorders, personality defects, aggression, poor social adjustment or a diagnosis of schizophrenia seriously reduce the chances of success.

Surgery for Mental Disorders Originating in the Temporal Lobe

In the treatment of disorders of temporal lobe origin the surgeon is frequently confronted with the dual problem of seizure control (*See* Sec. IV, Ch. 3) and the relief of psychological disturbances, which are often a major feature of the illness. Thus James[4] wrote "The total disability or incapacity of the patient who is a sufferer from temporal lobe epilepsy is not due only to the occurrence of the seizures. In fact the seizures themselves may become of minor significance as a cause of disability which is predominantly due to the serious changes of personality that develop. Disturbances of aggression, intolerance of frustration, impulsiveness, changes in sexuality, egotism and mood disorder are then of greater significance than the seizures themselves."

The personality changes associated with temporal lobe disorders vary considerably in nature and duration. Formerly it was held that epileptics developed a specific type of personality with slowness of thought and expression, inability to separate relevant from unimportant facts, and difficulty in moving from one thought pattern to another. Mood was thought to be unstable, with swings from despair to elation. Aggression, suspicion of others or the development of frank paranoid delusions were also thought to be a feature of the disease. However, such a combination of symptoms seldom occurs, but lesser degrees of personality disturbances are not infrequent. The main changes are increased irritability and

aggressiveness, often with paranoid states which at times reach psychotic proportions, and neurotic disorders. They tend to follow the onset of epilepsy by some years. Violent outbursts of irritability or overt aggression are more frequent in younger male patients and such acute disturbances often occur in relation to individual seizures, or an overall increase in the seizure rate. With increasing age depressive episodes and delusional states become more common than aggressive outbursts and they too may herald a seizure or occur in the postictal period. Neurotic disorders may vary in type and show little relationship to seizures although they may become more marked with an increase in seizure frequency. The neuroses encountered in temporal lobe disorders are often related to the difficulties in social adjustment encountered by epileptics especially when they have a poor social background with a family history of epilepsy. Thus approximately 30 per cent of patients have relatives with temporal lobe EEG abnormalities of whom 12 per cent have seizures. There is also a higher incidence of psychiatric illness and disordered home life in patients with temporal lobe epilepsy than in the normal population.

It appears that disorders of personality and behaviour are related to abnormal electrical activity in the temporal lobe. The effects upon social adjustment reflect interaction between the individual and his environment, and psychological maladjustment will be greatest when the temporal lobe abnormalities arise in early life, and where there are long-standing disturbances in the patient's immediate environment.

The success of temporal lobectomy for the relief of epileptic seizures depends upon removal of those areas of brain which are the site of the primary epileptic discharge. This is most likely to occur when there is a discrete pathological lesion confined to the anterior third of one temporal lobe and where the EEG abnormality is focal. Surgery was at first limited to the local excision of the epileptogenic foci in the temporal cortex and although seizure relief was gained it later became apparent that unilateral lobectomy, with removal of the lateral cortex and medially placed structures, including the hippocampus and amygdala, was more effective. According to Falconer[2] this is because the most common causes of focal intractable temporal epilepsy are mesial temporal sclerosis or hamartoma formation, both of which occur primarily in the medial part of the lobe. Thus it is currently the practice to remove all temporal lobe structures for a distance of 6 cm. from the anterior pole leaving only the superior temporal gyrus, should the operation be performed on the dominant hemisphere.

The effects of operation can be considered in terms of seizure relief, alterations in psychological function and social readjustment.

The studies of James[4] (1960) and Falconer and Serafetinides[2] (1963) indicate total relief of seizures may be expected in just over 50 per cent of patients, with a significant reduction of seizure frequency in a further 10–30 per cent. In Falconer's series 70 per cent had either mesial temporal sclerosis, or small tumours medially situated.

Of the outward changes in psychological function described earlier, a deficit of verbal learning following lobectomy on the dominant side is the only one likely to produce practical difficulties for patients. Although recovery does eventually occur but it may take three to five years from the time of operation. It is generally stated that unilateral surgery does not interfere with memory function but there are indications that a disturbance of recent memory occurs in 10 per cent of patients after lobectomy.

Slightly more than half the patients with psychiatric disturbances show a significant improvement in their mental state after operation although such changes, with the exception of lessened aggression, are not closely correlated with seizure relief. Exclusion of patients with below normal intelligence increases the proportion of those showing recovery by a further 10–15 per cent. In addition to lessening of irritability and aggressiveness, sexuality tends to improve with increased drive and potency; but impotence does occasionally occur. Although mood stability is increased, acute post-operative depression occurs in 10–20 per cent of patients. This form of illness may affect as many as 50 per cent of patients in the two years following operation but fortunately most of the disorders respond to conventional anti-depressant treatment.

Active psychosocial aftercare is mandatory if patients are to gain full benefit from operation and this should include psychotherapy, outpatient support, early readmission in the event of acute relapses and occupational rehabilitation. These measures are especially important for patients with disturbed family backgrounds, and those with neurotic disorders.

Social adjustments include improved working ability, interpersonal relations and the use of leisure. These, together with increased sexual attainment, are greatest in patients from good social backgrounds where there is little or no history of mental illness in the family and where the patient is of normal intelligence with epilepsy of late onset. If, in addition, epilepsy is secondary to a definite unilateral organic lesion the chances of recovery are improved still further.

Patients who show least improvement tend to have further seizures after operation, a poor family background, a lower level of intelligence and a higher incidence of psychopathy and psychosis. Frequently examination of such patients fails to reveal a focal lesion in the temporal lobe although it is the source of an EEG disturbance.

A major problem arises when the patient presents with bilateral EEG disorders. If there is a marked discrepancy in the degree of abnormality removal of the worst affected lobe may give seizure relief but there is a risk of severe memory impairment. For situations where such differences do exist it has been suggested by Turner[14] that seizure control can be gained by cutting white fibre tracts connecting epileptogenic areas to other parts of the brain. This involves dividing either the isthmus of the lobe by a coronal section through its upper quadrant, 1 cm. from the tip, or by dividing the uncus rostrally from the main body of the hippocampus caudally thereby destroying the central connections of the amygdala. In patients with intractable epilepsy associated with bouts of rage and violence a significant reduction in symptoms has been achieved with relief from seizures in approximately 65 per cent of patients. This technique has not yet been widely practised and a final decision concerning its effectiveness cannot be made until further studies have been performed.

The indiscriminate use of psychosurgery in its early years led to a high and unacceptable morbidity. The resulting disenchantment with this form of treatment coupled with optimism that the development of psychotropic drugs would eliminate the need for surgery, drastically reduced the demands for its use. However, the current realization that the effectiveness of drug therapy is still far from satisfactory, together with increasing improvements in the results obtained by the use of refined surgical techniques has reawakened optimism that psychosurgery has a limited, but well defined role in the relief of symptoms of mental illness.

FURTHER READING

1 Cannon, W. B. (1927), "The James–Lange Theory of Emotion: A Critical Examination and Alternative Theory," *Amer. J. Psychol.*, **39**, 10.
2 Falconer, M. A. and Serafetinides, E. A. (1963), "A Follow-up Study of Surgery in Temporal Lobe Epilepsy," *J. Neurol. Neurosurg. Psychiat.*, **26**, 154.
3 Freeman, W. and Watts, J. W. (1942), *Psychosurgery: Intelligence, Emotion Social Behavior Following Prefrontal Lobotomy for Mental Disorders*. Springfield, Ill.: Charles C. Thomas.
4 James, I. P. (1960), "Temporal Lobectomy for Psychomotor Epilepsy," *J. ment. Sci.*, **106**, 543.
5 Klüver, H. and Bucy, P. C. (1939), "Preliminary Analysis of Function of the Temporal Lobes in Monkeys," *Arch. Neurol. Psychiat.*, **42**, 979.
6 Knight, G. C. (1964), "The Orbital Cortex as an Objective in the Surgical Treatment of Mental Illness. 450 Cases of Open Operation and the Results of Development of the Stereotaxic Approach," *Brit. J. Surg.*, **51**, 114.
7 Le Beau, J. (1952), "The Cingular and Precingular Areas in Psychosurgery (Agitated Behaviour, Obsessive Compulsive States, Epilepsy)," *Acta psychiat. Neurol. Scand*, **27**, 305.
8 McLean, P. D. (1949), "Psychosomatic Disease and the 'Visceral Brain', Recent Developments Bearing on the Papez Theory of Emotion," *Psychosom. Med.*, **11**, 338.
9 Moniz, E. (1937), "Prefrontal Leucotomy in the Treatment of Mental Disorders," *Amer. J. Psychiat.*, **93**, 1379.
10 Papez, J. W. (1937), "A Proposed Mechanism of Emotion," *Arch. Neurol. Psychiat.*, **38**, 725.
11 Scoville, W. B. (1949), "Selective Cortical Undercutting as a Means of Modifying and Studying Frontal Lobe Function in Man," *J. Neurosurg.*, **6**, 65.
12 Spencer, W. G. (1894), "Effect Produced Upon Respiration by Faradic Excitation of the Cerebrum in the Monkey, Dog, Cat and Rabbit," *Philos. Trans.*, **185B**, 609.
13 Spiegal, E. A. and Wycis, H. T. (1949), "Physiological and Psychological Results of Thalamotomy," *Proc. R. Soc. Med.*, **42**, Suppl. p. 84.
14 Turner, E. A. (1969), "A Surgical Approach to the Treatment of Symptoms in Temporal Lobe Epilepsy," *Current Problems in Neuropsychiatry. Schizophrenia, Epilepsy, the Temporal Lobe* (R. N. Herrington, Ed.). Publ. Headley Bros. for the Royal Medico-Psychological Association.
15 William, S. D. "Temporal Lobe Epilepsy," (1966), *Brit. med. J.*, **1**, 1439.
16 Wycis, H. T. and Spiegal, E. A., *Thalamotomy: Neurosurgical Aspects*, ibid., p. 12.

1. CONTROL OF THE CEREBRAL CIRCULATION

A. MURRAY HARPER

The past decade has seen an explosion in studies of the cerebral circulation due to the refinement of techniques of measurement and the introduction of the radioactive inert gas clearance methods. In spite of the proliferation in experiments attempting to unravel the factors controlling the cerebral circulation, there is perhaps more disagreement now than ever before. It is agreed generally that the alteration of various physiological parameters will change cerebral blood flow, but there is considerable controversy about underlying mechanisms. This chapter gives a brief account of the principal factors which affect cerebral blood flow and a summary of the present theories of its control.

Arterial Pressures

The perfusion pressure of the brain is defined as the mean arterial blood pressure minus the cerebral venous blood pressure—the latter being influenced by changes in the intracranial pressure and vice versa. The long held theory that the cerebral blood flow depended passively on the arterial blood pressure has been discarded only relatively recently. It is now recognized that the normal brain has the ability to "autoregulate" in response to changes in arterial blood pressure. Autoregulation can be defined as the maintenance of a relatively constant blood flow in the face of changes in perfusion pressure (Fig. 1). This figure is based on an experimental study in which the arterial blood pressure was altered by graded haemorrhage. Over a wide range of blood pressures the cerebral blood flow alters little, and it is only at

low mean arterial blood pressure (in man probably below 50 mm. Hg.) that the limits of autoregulation are reached and the flow then begins to decrease with pressure.

Observation of the pial blood vessels through a window in the skull shows that when the arterial blood pressure is reduced the pial arteries and arterioles dilate. Similarly, when the blood pressure is increased the pial arteries and arterioles constrict. The change in cerebro-vascular resistance produced by dilation or constriction serves to maintain a relative constancy of flow during changes in pressure. However, these changes in calibre of the cerebral vessels are not instantaneous; various times— from 30 sec. to 2 min.—have been reported for the establishment of autoregulation following an acute change in arterial blood pressure.

Autoregulation is always observed in the normal brain; but in the abnormal brain there are many circumstances where autoregulation is reduced or absent (Fig. 2).

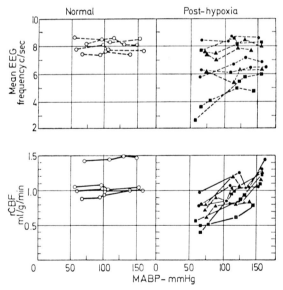

FIG. 2. Responses of regional cortical blood flow to changes in arterial blood pressure before (left) and 1½–2 hr. after an episode of cerebral hypoxia. (From J. Freeman and D. H. Ingvar, 1968, *Exp. Brain Res.* **5**, 61; reproduced by kind permission of the authors and publishers.)

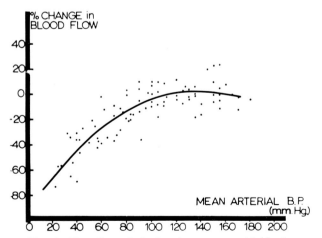

FIG. 1. The effect of altering the mean arterial blood pressure on blood flow through the cerebral cortex. (From A. M. Harper, 1965, *Brit. J. Anaesth.*, **37**, 225 reproduced by kind permission of the publishers.)

Impaired autoregulation may be observed even after the cerebral blood flow has returned to normal after the post-hypoxic hyperaemia (*vide infra*). Similarly, it is fairly well established that autoregulation can be lost following ischaemic brain damage. Following metrazol induced seizures it has been shown that autoregulation is impaired for up to 60 min. Autoregulation may also be reduced where there is pre-existing cerebral vasodilation —due to cerebral hypoxia or hypercapnia for instance— although there are some reports that claim that auto-regulation can be "re-set" to a higher level of blood flow when the stimulus to increased cerebral blood flow is physiological (such as hypercapnia).

Venous Pressure

Just as the cerebral vessels can autoregulate to changes in arterial blood pressure, so can they autoregulate to changes in venous pressure. When coughing, for instance, there are presumably marked changes in cerebral venous pressure; but experimental studies have shown that the cerebral venous pressures can be raised to quite high levels without affecting the cerebral blood flow.

MECHANISM OF AUTOREGULATION

As pointed out before, the mechanism of autoregulation is the dilation of the small cerebral arteries and arterioles when the blood pressure is reduced, and their constriction when the blood pressure is increased. The stimulus to this dilation or constriction is a matter of some controversy. There are three classical theories which can be described under the headings:

> Metabolic
> Myogenic
> Neurogenic

Metabolic

When the blood pressure falls there is a momentary reduction in cerebral blood flow. During this period the tissue pO_2 will fall; there will be a build-up of tissue pCO_2, and a fall in tissue pH. As all of these can result in cerebral vasodilation, it has been suggested that one or all of these factors might act as the control signal in a feedback system controlling the diameter of the cerebral arterioles and therefore helping to maintain a constant flow. Although some experimental work has been produced which shows a lactacidosis of the cerebral extracellular fluid during an arterial pressure drop, studies of the absence of autoregulation following seizures show no association between autoregulation and chemical regulation.

Myogenic

This theory postulates that the cerebral arteries and arterioles have an inherent smooth muscle tone and that an increase in distending pressure will result in contraction, and a decrease in distending pressure a dilation (the Bayliss effect). In other words, it has been suggested that the smooth muscle in the cerebral vessels could be

similar to that of the ureter or intestine, where the frequency of contraction increases the more they are stretched. There is no direct evidence either to support or refute the myogenic theory.

Neurogenic

The influence of the autonomic nervous system on cerebral blood flow will be discussed later in this chapter. It has been claimed recently that autoregulation is impaired following cervical sympathectomy. However, other workers have claimed that autoregulation is preserved when tests are made several weeks after cervical sympathectomy. Also it has been shown that autoregulation was intact in a patient with idiopathic, orthostatic hypotension in which there was gross impairment of the sympathetic nervous system.

Cerebrospinal-fluid Pressure

The cerebral blood flow can also autoregulate to changes in CSF pressure. Figure 3 shows a relative constancy in blood flow during considerable alterations in CSF pressure—induced by infusing fluid into the

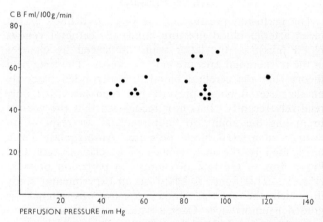

Fig. 3. The effect of changes in cerebral perfusion pressure induced by infusing fluid into the cisterna magna. (In baboons.)

cisterna magna in the experimental animal. However, the autoregulatory response to increase in CSF pressure differs according to the rate of development and the cause of the intracranial hypertension—the magnitude of the CSF pressure rise required to produce a substantial fall in blood flow being very variable. Compensatory mechanisms, such as a rise in systemic blood pressure, also help to preserve the cerebral blood flow, and it has been observed recently that during intracranial hypertension there may even be periods of increased flow associated with the Cushing response.

It is also interesting to note that a recent experimental study showed that there was absence of autoregulation to intracranial hypertension following cervical cord section. However, it would be premature to produce this as evidence for a neurogenic control of autoregulation mentioned previously.

BLOOD GASES

Carbon Dioxide

Changes in the carbon dioxide tension of the arterial blood have long been recognized as having a potent influence on the cerebral circulation. A rise in $PaCO_2$ causes an increase in cerebral blood flow and a fall in $PaCO_2$ a decrease (Fig. 4). Raising the $PaCO_2$ from the

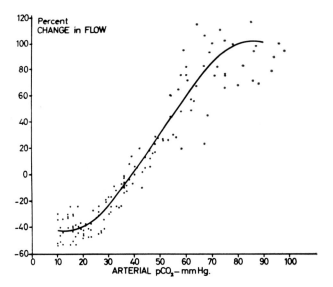

FIG. 4. The effect of gradually changing the $PaCO_2$ by adding CO_2 to the anaesthetic mixture or by hyperventilation. Zero reference point is at $PaCO_2$ of 40 mm. Hg. (From A. M. Harper and H. I. Glass, 1965, *J. Neurol. Neurosurg. Psychiat.* **28**, 449; reproduced by kind permission of the publishers.)

normal value of 40–80 mm. Hg. more than doubles the blood flow. Lowering the $PaCO_2$ to 20 mm. Hg. approximately halves the blood flow, but below 20 mm. Hg. there appears to be little further decrease in flow. This is probably because the flow has been reduced to such an extent that the counter-acting effect of cerebral tissue hypoxia is becoming evident. This will tend to dilate the cerebral vessels and prevent any further decrease in flow. Similarly at $PaCO_2$ values above 80 mm. Hg., further increases in blood flow are relatively small.

A recent observation has been that the increase in flow during hypercapnia is greater if the $PaCO_2$ is raised suddenly and acutely. For instance, the gradient of the $PaCO_2$/flow relationship will be approximately 3 ml. change in flow for every 1 mm. change in $PaCO_2$ if the $PaCO_2$ is raised suddenly from 40 to 60 mm. Hg. However, if the change in $PaCO_2$ is made slowly over several hours, the gradient for the same range will be only 1·5–2.

The cerebral vessels seem able to adapt to chronic changes in $PaCO_2$. If the $PaCO_2$ is held at very high or very low levels for long periods of time, the cerebral blood flow tends towards normal levels.

As with autoregulation, there are circumstances in which the CO_2 response can be reduced or absent. In arterial hypotension the CO_2 response is reduced, and in severe

hypotension can be absent altogether (Fig. 5). Following clinical cerebro-vascular accidents, reactivity to CO_2 may be lost in the area of brain immediately affected and sometimes in the surrounding areas.

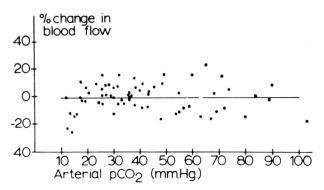

FIG. 5. The effect of changes in $PaCO_2$ during profound hypotension (mean arterial blood pressure 40–50 mm. Hg.). (From A. M. Harper and H. I. Glass, 1965, *J. Neurol. Neurosurg. Psychiat.*, **28**, 449; reproduced by kind permission of the publishers.)

Because CO_2 is such a potent cerebral vasodilator, it is often suggested that it might be a useful therapeutic tool in the treatment of cerebral circulatory insufficiency. In severe hypotension, however, the cerebral arterioles are probably already near to maximal vasodilation and CO_2 then has no further effect on the cerebral circulation (Fig. 5). Similarly, the cerebral vessels surrounding an infarcted area of the brain are already dilated due to tissue hypoxia. Under these circumstances the administration of CO_2 is potentially hazardous as it will dilate the vessels in the normal areas of brain, thereby "stealing" blood from the compromised cerebral tissue. Indeed the opposite therapy may be indicated and some workers have produced evidence to show that hyperventilation, by constricting the normal cerebral vessels, can divert blood to the hypoxic tissue.

Mechanism of CO_2 Response

Three possible mechanisms for the reactivity of the cerebral vessels to CO_2 can be considered.

Firstly, it has been shown that CO_2 can cause relaxation of isolated strips of vascular smooth muscle and could therefore act directly on the smooth muscle of the cerebral vessels.

Secondly, it has been suggested that CO_2 acts by changing the pH of the extracellular fluid of the brain or of the vascular smooth muscle itself. It has been shown by Scandinavian workers, using a micropipette technique, that the instillation of bicarbonate-free CSF around a cerebral arteriole caused a marked dilation. Conversely, the instillation of CSF with a high bicarbonate content caused a marked constriction. The postulate is that CO_2 (being rapidly diffusible) will either build up locally in areas of increased cerebral metabolism, or will diffuse across the capillaries into the extracellular fluid in hypercapnia, thus raising the H^+ ion concentration around the

238 SCIENTIFIC FOUNDATIONS OF NEUROLOGY

cerebral arterioles, and causing vasodilation. This hypothesis does not receive support from experiments in which, during prolonged hyperventilation, it was found that the cerebral blood flow remained low, despite a return to normal of the CSF pH. However, it is an attractive postulate and deserves attention.

Thirdly, it has been suggested that the reactivity of the cerebral vessels to CO_2 is under neurogenic control. It has been claimed that the CO_2 response is lost when lesions are made in certain areas of the mid-brain and restored again when these lesions are subsequently stimulated. This assertion awaits confirmation as direct infusion of blood of high pCO_2 into the internal carotid artery has been shown to increase blood flow in the regions of the brain within its distribution—regions which do not include the mid-brain centres. Similarly, infusion of blood of high CO_2 content into the vertebral artery did not increase blood flow in regions of the brain fed by the internal carotid artery.

Another group of workers have suggested that the CO_2 response is reduced following section of the vagus and carotid sinus nerves, but this claim has not yet been confirmed. There is, however, substantiation for a reduction in the CO_2 response following stimulation of the cervical sympathetic, which has been reported by several groups of workers (Fig. 6). However, this one observation hardly justifies a hypothesis for the neurogenic control of the CO_2 reactivity of the cerebral vessels and the evidence

at the moment is more in favour of a local metabolic control as described above.

Oxygen

The cerebral blood flow reacts in the reverse direction to changes in the arterial oxygen tension, a fall in PaO_2 producing a rise in blood flow. However, there is a threshold for this phenomenon and it is only at PaO_2 below 50 mm. Hg. that marked increases in blood flow are observed. At a PaO_2 of 30 mm. Hg. the cerebral blood flow is more than doubled (Fig. 7).

On the other hand, raising the PaO_2 causes only slight changes in cerebral blood flow. The administration of 100 per cent oxygen (1 atm.) will reduce cerebral blood flow by approximately 10 per cent and the administration of oxygen at 2 atm. by just over 20 per cent. The effects of hyperbaric oxygen on the cerebral circulation will be dealt with in more detail in Chapter VII, 4.

The mechanism of the vasodilator effect of low PaO_2 has not been finally resolved. There is some evidence that O_2 can act directly on isolated perfused vessels, dilation being observed when the perfusate has a low pO_2. It has also been shown recently that the increase in cerebral blood flow at PaO_2 of less than 50 mm. Hg. is accompanied by a decrease in pH on the surface of the cortex. Therefore, it seems likely that hypoxia below a critical level increases the H^+ ion concentration of the extracellular

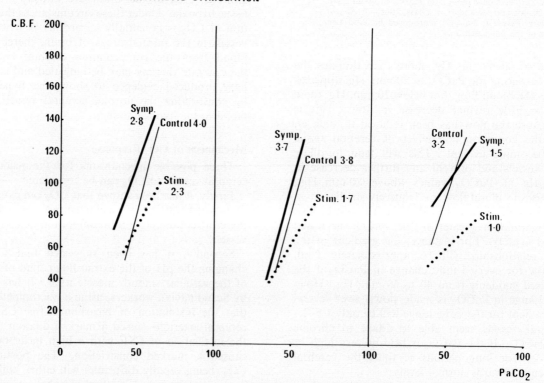

Fig. 6. CO_2 responses before and after unilateral cervical sympathectomy and during electrical stimulation of cervical sympathetic in baboons (ml. CBF change per mm. Hg. change in $PaCO_2$). (From A. M. Harper, V. D. Deshmukh, J. O. Rowan and W. B. Jennett, in *Brain and Blood Flow*; ed., Ross Russell, Pitman: London, 1970, by kind permission of the editor and publishers.)

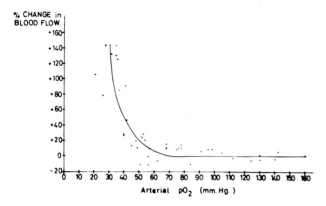

FIG. 7. Effect of arterial hypoxia on cerebral blood flow. (From D. G. McDowall, 1966, in *Oxygen Measurements in Blood and Tissues*; ed., Payne and Hill; Churchill, London.)

fluid of the brain, which results in arteriolar vasodilation—a similar mechanism to that described in the section on CO_2.

Suggestions that neurogenic mechanisms might be involved in hypoxic vasodilation have been put forward but never substantiated.

pH

As seen in Fig. 8 changes in the intravascular pH do not affect cerebral blood flow provided the $PaCO_2$ is unchanged. In metabolic acidosis and alkalosis only slight changes in pH of the extracellular fluid of the brain are observed—and no change in flow has been noted.

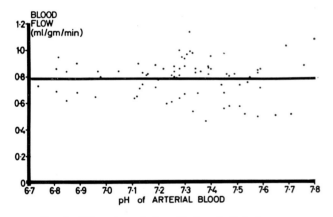

FIG. 8. Effect of metabolic acidosis and alkalosis at constant $PaCO_2$ on blood flow through the cerebral cortex. (From A. M. Harper and R. A. Bell, 1963, *J. Neurol. Neurosurg. Psychiat.* **26**, 341; reproduced by kind permission of the publishers.)

The effect of local instillation of bicarbonate-free CSF around the cerebral arterioles has been discussed in the section on CO_2. There seems little doubt that the alteration of the pH of the extracellular fluid around the cerebral arterioles can influence their diameter—acid solutions causing a dilation and alkaline solutions a constriction.

Cerebral Flow and Function

There is increasing evidence that changes in cerebral "function" can result in changes in cerebral blood flow. It has been shown in the cat that shining a light in the eyes causes an increase in blood flow in the occipital lobe. The administration of analeptic drugs, such as metrazol, causes marked increases in cerebral blood flow which are accompanied by increases in cerebral oxygen uptake. Correlations between EEG frequency and cerebral blood flow have been reported in the experimental animal and in elderly patients with psychiatric symptoms.

That cerebral blood flow was related to function was predicted in the latter part of the nineteenth century by Roy and Sherrington, and from their work grew the idea of the intrinsic chemical control of the cerebral circulation which helped explain the teleological implications of the reactions of the cerebral vasculature to carbon dioxide. It would not be unreasonable to assume that if a part of the brain started to function at a higher rate there would be an increased utilization of oxygen to meet the increased metabolic requirements. An increase in oxygen consumption would result in an increased output of carbon dioxide, which would produce cerebral vasodilation at the local level and thus maintain an adequate supply of blood to the tissue. As has been mentioned previously, the main control signal could be the extracellular pH which would be altered by a change in pCO_2. Similarly, the cerebral vasodilation seen in hypoxia is a mechanism to maintain a supply of blood adequate for the metabolic requirements of the brain tissue. Again this can take place merely at the local level and the main control signal could also be changes in the pH of the extracellular fluid.

The hypothesis of a local intrinsic chemical control of the cerebral circulation has been the mainstay of classical thinking for many years. However, it now appears that there are situations in which CO_2 responsiveness may be present but that autoregulation to blood pressure changes is lost. One must therefore be wary of ascribing local chemical regulation based on metabolic requirements to the same mechanism as autoregulation to blood pressure changes.

NEUROGENIC CONTROL

There is abundant evidence that the cerebral blood vessels have a nerve supply. The main arteries contributing to the circle of Willis have a rich adrenergic supply but this is less pronounced in the smaller cerebral arteries and arterioles. Although early studies of the effect of sympathetic stimulation on the diameter of the pial arteries showed a very modest vasoconstriction, the general consensus of opinion has been that the cerebral circulation is independent of neurogenic control.

However, there is no doubt that nerve fibres are present and it would be logical to assume that they have some function. It is doubtful whether division of the cervical sympathetic chain influences cerebral blood flow but it is interesting to note that the CO_2 response is reduced during stimulation of the sympathetic nerve in the neck. Figure 6 shows the gradient (i.e. the ml. change in blood flow per mm. Hg. change in $PaCO_2$) of the cerebral blood flow following a rise in $PaCO_2$ from approximately 40 to 60 mm. Hg. Following cervical sympathectomy there is little change in gradient. However, during stimulation of the nerve, there is a considerable reduction in the magnitude of the blood flow response (*see also* Fig. 9).

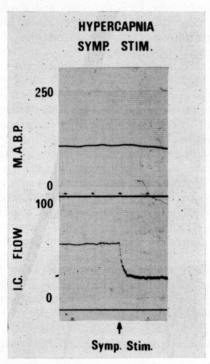

FIG. 9. Effect of sympathetic stimulation on internal carotid artery blood flow as measured with an electromagnetic flowmeter. (From A. M. Harper, V. D. Deshmukh, J. O. Rowan, and W. B. Jennett, in *Brain and Blood Flow;* ed., Ross Russell; Pitman, London, 1970; reproduced by kind permission of the editor and publishers.)

Before ascribing the cerebral blood flow reduction to constriction of the cerebral arterioles, it is important to consider whether this phenomenon could not be due to constriction of the arteries in the neck, such as the internal carotid. As the brain is supplied by three major arteries (two internal carotids and the basilar) it has, under normal circumstances, a considerable reserve of blood supply. Ligation of one internal carotid artery may not affect the blood flow to any part of the brain, but there will be a pressure drop in the arteries going to the territory of the ligated major vessel. This pressure drop will stimulate the usual autoregulatory process and it is the resulting vasodilation in the affected area which maintains a constant flow. Where there is pre-existing vasodilation the CO_2 response will be less marked. Figure 10 shows the reduction in the gradient of the CO_2 response following unilateral and bilateral carotid ligation. It is possible that, under the artificial conditions of sympathetic stimulation in the neck, a similar mechanism is operating.

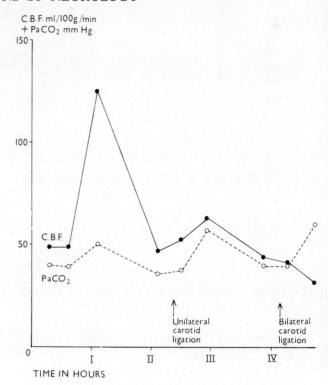

FIG. 10. Effect of unilateral and bilateral carotid artery ligation on the CO_2 response. The CO_2 response is reduced after unilateral and abolished after bilateral ligation, although the normocapnic flow is less severely affected.

In other words, the major arteries supplying the brain, which have a fairly dense adrenergic nerve supply, are constricted—not enough to change the cerebral blood flow under normal circumstances, but enough to reduce the CO_2 response.

It has also been reported recently that division of the vagi and carotid sinus nerves in the neck will reduce the CO_2 response. This work awaits confirmation.

A central neurogenic control of the cerebral circulation has also been suggested. One group of workers have reported abolition of the CO_2 response following cryogenic lesions in certain regions of the mid-brain. Fairly large increases in cerebral blood flow have been reported following electrical stimulation of particular areas of the brain stem. However, it is extremely difficult to distinguish between neurogenic vasodilation and generalised or local increases in cerebral metabolism which could affect cerebral blood flow by local tissue changes in pCO_2 and pO_2. In the past, claims have been made at various times that there are cerebral vasodilator fibres in the Vth, VIIth, IXth and Xth cranial nerves. The changes in cerebral blood flow produced by stimulation of these nerves are inconsistent and unreliable. Two recent studies have claimed that the hypotensive (dilatory) phase of autoregulation can be blocked by anticholinergic drugs, and that the hypertensive (constrictive) phase of autoregulation can be removed by section of the cervical cord at C5.

In summary then the function of the autonomic nerve fibres accompanying the cerebral vessels is still obscure, and the only clear-cut piece of evidence that has emerged from several studies is that stimulation of the cervical sympathetic can reduce the CO_2 response. However, it is not known whether it is the major vessels in the neck or the cerebral arterioles which are most affected. As yet, there is no absolutely convincing evidence to shake the long-held hypothesis that the cerebral circulation is under local metabolic control and is relatively independent of neurogenic influences.

MISCELLANEOUS FACTORS

There are some other factors which can influence cerebral blood flow under rather unphysiological conditions, but which may be of clinical significance.

Blood Haematocrit and Viscosity

Severe anaemia can increase cerebral blood flow but it is difficult to dissociate the effects of the anaemia *per se* from the vasodilatory effect of reduced oxygen content of the blood. Polycythaemia vera, however, can result in a decrease in cerebral blood flow. The latter result can possibly be explained on the grounds of changes in blood viscosity. It has been shown that the deliberate alteration of blood viscosity, by the infusion of packed red cells and high molecular weight dextran, diminishes the CO_2 response of the cerebral vessels. A CO_2 response only half the normal has been observed when the blood viscosity is doubled.

Temperature

The cerebral blood flow has been reported to fall by 6–7 per cent per degree centigrade fall in oesophageal temperature. This reduction in blood flow could be ascribed to fall in $PaCO_2$ and cerebral metabolic rate during hypothermia. However, the blood flow still decreased in experiments in which the $PaCO_2$ was maintained at 40 mm. Hg. during cooling. Neither a direct effect of cold on the cerebral blood vessels nor an increase in blood viscosity during cooling can be ruled out.

Cardiac Output

Changes in cardiac output do not directly influence cerebral blood flow unless the arterial blood pressure falls below the autoregulatory limit or other parameters such as the $PaCO_2$ are altered.

DRUGS

Only a very brief summary can be given of the effect of pharmacological agents on the cerebral circulation.

Anaesthetic Agents (*See also* Chapter IX, 4)

The barbiturates, when given in doses sufficient to produce unconsciousness, lower cerebral blood flow in proportion to the fall in cerebral metabolic rate. On the other hand, some of the volatile anaesthetics, such as trilene, methoxyflurane and halothane, increase cerebral blood flow in spite of a fall in metabolic rate.

The effects of the neuroleptanalgesic drugs, such as phenoperidine, droperidol and fentanyl, are rather more uncertain—partly because the cat (on which much of the early experimental work was done) responds to these drugs in quite a different way from the dog, primate or man. However, it has been reported that droperidol and phenoperidine together do not cause major alterations in blood flow, but that fentanyl, especially when preceded by droperidol, can decrease the cerebral blood flow and the cerebral oxygen uptake by about 50 per cent.

Sympathomimetic Drugs

When administered under "normal" circumstances of $PaCO_2$ and other variables, there is general agreement that neither adrenaline nor noradrenaline has marked effects on cerebral blood flow. If the blood pressure rises, the cerebral blood vessels will constrict in the usual autoregulatory fashion to maintain a constant cerebral blood flow. Direct infusion into the carotid artery of doses of noradrenaline insufficient to change the arterial blood pressure do not affect the cerebral circulation.

However, under certain "abnormal" circumstances, it is becoming apparent that noradrenaline can affect cerebral blood flow in quite striking ways. For example it can significantly reduce cerebral blood flow when administered during hypercapnic cerebral vasodilation (Fig. 11). In addition, it has been shown that noradrenaline can reduce cerebral blood flow during the autoregulatory phase of induced hypotension. In other words, while noradrenaline appears to have little effect on the cerebral circulation under normal circumstances, it appears able to constrict cerebral vessels where there is pre-existing cerebral vasodilation. It is still not clear whether the site of action is the cerebral arterioles or the larger cerebral arteries.

There have been no reports that angiotensin, given either intravenously or through a carotid artery, significantly influences cerebral blood flow.

Blocking Agents

There is considerable confusion about the effects of alpha and beta blocking agents on the cerebral circulation. There have been some reports stating that alpha blocking agents cause modest increases in cerebral blood flow and other reports denying this. Much work remains to be done on this subject, but it is interesting to note that experimentally induced acute cerebral arterial spasm can be reversed by the local application of the alpha blocking agent phenoxybenzamine.

Cerebral Vasodilators

There are many drugs on the market which are claimed to increase cerebral blood flow. Few of them have any

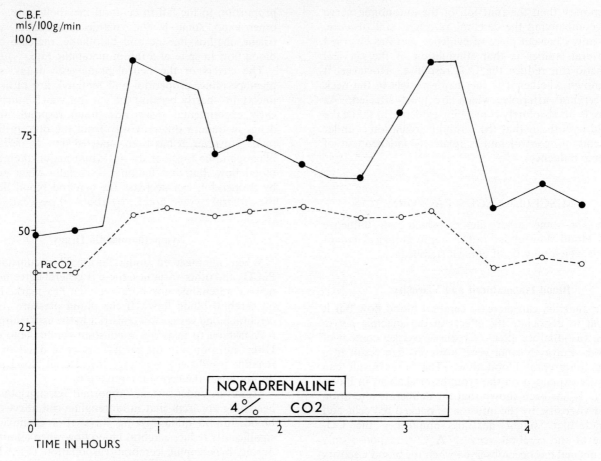

FIG. 11. Effect of intracarotid infusion of noradrenaline during hypercapnic vasodilation. A quite striking decrease in cerebral blood flow can be noted during infusion. The $PaCO_2$ was held at 54 mm. Hg. during the CO_2 administration.

effect when tested on the experimental animal under strictly controlled and "normal" physiological conditions. However, this does not mean that they were not vasodilators in conditions of generalized reduction in cerebral blood flow—for instance, in the elderly, confused patient.

Leaving aside the volatile anaesthetics, the most potent cerebral vasodilators are carbon dioxide and papaverine. The action of the latter drug is exceedingly transient and therefore hardly suitable for clinical use. The general concept of the clinical use of cerebral vasodilators has come under attack in recent years because of observations of the "steal phenomenon". It appears that where there is a local area of cerebral circulatory insufficiency, the small vessels in and surrounding that area are dilated due to hypoxia. If a vasodilator such as CO_2 is now administered, the vessels in the normal parts of the brain will dilate thereby "stealing" blood from the already dilated vessels in the hypoxic area of the brain. Some authorities have even suggested that, under the circumstances of regional insufficiency of the cerebral circulation, the patient should be hyperventilated to constrict the normal cerebral vessels in the hope of forcing more blood through the hypoxic area. This theory may hold in some patients, some of the time. But there have been quite a few reports showing an increase in cerebral blood flow when a vasodilator was administered to patients with focal areas of

cerebral ischaemia. It is possible that the response of patients may be infinitely variable depending on the extent of the lesion, anatomical considerations of the cerebral vasculature and other parameters.

CONCLUSIONS

The cerebral circulation shows a remarkable capacity to remain constant—only hypercapnia, hypoxia and extreme hypotension affect it to any marked extent. The classical concept has been that there is an intrinsic control of the cerebral circulation, geared to meet the metabolic requirements of the brain. Evidence is accumulating that the control signal for this could be the H^+ ion concentration of the cerebral extracellular fluid.

There is now no dispute that the cerebral blood flow can remain constant over a wide range of perfusion pressures. The mechanism of this autoregulation is still uncertain but its absence is certainly a sign of a sick brain.

Until a very few years ago, it was generally accepted that the autonomic nervous system played little, if any, part in the control of the cerebral circulation. In recent years, experiments designed to try to relate some purpose to the autonomic nerve fibres which accompany the cerebral arteries have produced conflicting results. It is still a matter of dispute whether these nerves have any more functional significance than the vermiform appendix; but much further work remains to be done in this field.

Finally, in an era when measurements of regional cerebral blood flow are being increasingly used in clinical practice—in the ward, clinic and operating theatre—it is important to measure the variables which are known to influence cerebral blood flow and to take them into account in interpreting any measurement of the cerebral circulation.

ACKNOWLEDGMENTS

The material for Fig. 3 was obtained in collaboration with Dr. I. A. Johnston, Mr. J. O. Rowan and Professor W. B. Jennett; for Fig. 10 in collaboration with Dr. D. Sengupta and Dr. V. D. Deshmukh, and for Fig. 11 in collaboration with Dr. V. D. Deshmukh.

FURTHER READING

Much of the original work by many authors and detailed references for the points discussed in this chapter can be found in the following:

Bain, W. H. and Harper, A. M. (Eds.) 1966, *Blood Flow Through Organs and Tissues.* Edinburgh: Livingstone.
Brock, M., Fieschi, C., Ingvar, D. H., Lassen, N. A. and Schürmann, K. (Eds.) 1969, *Cerebral Blood Flow.* Springer-Verlag.
Harper, A. M. and Jennett, W. B. (1972), "Control of the Cerebral Circulation," *Excerpta med.* To be published.
Ingvar, D. H. and Lassen, N. A. (Eds.) 1965, "rCBF. Proc. of 2nd Int. Symposium," *Acta Neurol. scand.*, Suppl. 14.
Ingvar, D. H., Lassen, N. A., Siesjö, B. K. and Skinhøj, E. (Eds.) 1968, "CBF and CSF–Proc. of 3rd Int. Symposium," *Scand. J. Lab. clin. Invest.*, Suppl. 102.
McDowall, D. G. (Ed.) 1969, *Cerebral Circulation.* Boston: Little, Brown & Co.
Ross Russell, R. W. (Ed.) 1970, *Brain and Blood Flow*, "Proc. of 4th Int. Symposium," London: Pitman.

2. THE NEUROPATHOLOGY OF BRAIN HYPOXIA

J. B. BRIERLEY

The energy requirements of the brain are provided by the oxidative metabolism of glucose. If the supply of oxygen is reduced below a critical level, as a result of gross depression of circulation or respiration, consciousness is lost after a few seconds (8–10 sec. after circulatory arrest and 17–20 sec. after breathing 100 per cent nitrogen). Evidently the oxygen reserves within brain tissue and its contained blood at any one time are very small. On the other hand the known carbohydrate content of the brain would support metabolic activity for 5–10 min. in the absence of glucose in the bloodstream. Other metabolic intermediates may sustain energy-yielding reactions for up to 90 min.[6] Thus a major reduction in the supply of oxygen can lead to unconsciousness and brain damage far more rapidly than the withdrawal of glucose.

The energy-yielding reactions of the brain may also be depressed or arrested in the presence of normal supplies of oxygen and glucose by substances which poison the oxidative enzymes (largely within the mitochondria) of neurons.

The above considerations provide a basis for a classification of those categories of hypoxia that are known to result in brain damage.

THE TYPES OF BRAIN HYPOXIA

(1) Stagnant.
  (a) Ischaemic local or generalized *arrest* of blood flow.
  (b) Oligaemic local or generalized *reduction* in blood flow.

(2) Hypoxic, reduced oxygen content of the inspired air leading to hypoxaemia.
(3) Histotoxic, poisoning of neuronal oxidative enzymes.
(4) Hypoglycaemia (oxyachrestia), a deficiency of the substrate glucose.

In each type the alterations at the neuronal level are the same and consist of "ischaemic cell change", which is a destructive process leading to the disappearance of the cell, but the differences between each type are in the distribution of neuronal damage or loss in the brain.

Ischaemic Cell Change

In the human brain the study of ischaemic cell change, and particularly its early stages, is made difficult by the presence of histological artefacts. These are due partly to the variable delay between death and autopsy, and partly to the slow penetration of the fixative in which the brain is immersed. Artefacts can also be encountered in the brains of experimental animals particularly when the brain is removed immediately after death and immersed in a fixative. The commonest histological artefacts encountered in human and experimental animal brains are hyperchromatic neurones ("dark cells"), pale, swollen and vacuolated neurones ("water change") and also perineuronal and perivascular spaces. All these artefacts are absent when the brain of a normal animal is fixed by intravascular perfusion *in vivo* and removed at least 2 hr. later. This method of fixation is essential for the early recognition of

9

unequivocal ischaemic cell change and is the reason why evidence from rat, rhesus monkey and baboon brains is combined with that from human brains in the following description of the evolution of ischaemic cell change.

It is important to stress that the time course of ischaemic cell change is influenced only by the size of the cell, being more rapid in small neurones than in large. The severity of the hypoxic insult can influence only the number of nerve cells affected.

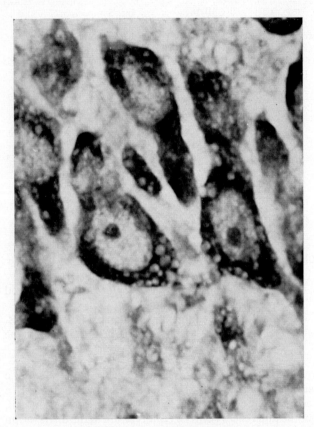

FIG. 1. Typical microvacuolation in pyramidal neurones of rat hippocampus. The small vacuoles are separated by darkly-staining cytoplasm and the nuclei are normal. Paraffin section: cresyl fast violet. ×1,500.

The earliest stage of the ischaemic process has been called "microvaculation" by Brown and Brierley.[11] The cell is not swollen and its nucleus is normal. Apparently empty vacuoles lie within cytoplasm of normal or slightly increased staining intensity (Fig. 1). In electronmicrographs, microvacuoles are seen to be expanded mitochondria with variable disorganization of their cristae (Fig. 2). Some neurones are more or less surrounded by the expanded processes of astrocytes.

In the rat brain microvacuolation has been seen when perfusion-fixation was carried out immediately after exposures to nitrogen (with interruption of blood flow in one common carotid artery) of only 5 min. in one animal and 15 min. in another.[12] Microvacuolation has been identified in the brain of the rhesus monkey 20 min. after a period

of profound hypotension and in both species it can be recognized up to 4 or 5 hr. after a hypoxic insult, when the next stage appears.

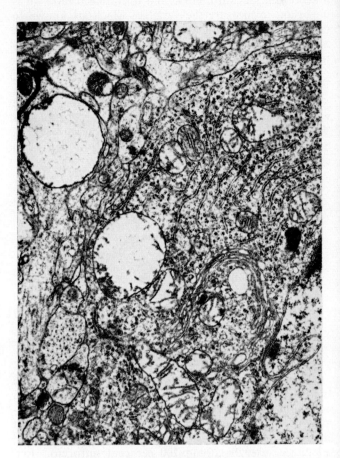

FIG. 2. Electron micrograph showing that microvacuoles are swollen mitochondria. Within their double membranes the cristae are greatly disorganized. ×12,000.

The next stage is that of classical ischaemic cell change. The neurone is variably shrunken and the nucleus is darkly stained and triangular. The cytoplasm shows some eosinophilia and blue or mauve staining with Luxol fast blue and perhaps some residual microvacuoles (Fig. 3). Corresponding electron micrographs show an increased density of the cytoplasm with accumulation of ribosomes. There is some expansion of the vesicles and vacuoles of the Golgi complex and of the cisternae of the endoplasmic reticulum; there is increased density of the nucleus (Fig. 4). In the rat and monkey brain this stage appears after survivals of 0–30 min. and persists for about 24 hr.

The following stage of ischaemic cell change with incrustations differs from the preceding by the presence of small spherical or irregular bodies lying on or close to the cell surface (Fig. 5). The electron microscope has shown that these incrustations represent irregular peripheral portions of the cytoplasm which are of high electron density (Fig. 6). They do not appear to originate from synaptic structures.

The stage of incrustations has been seen in the rat brain after a survival of ½ hr. and after 1½ hr. in the monkey. It persists in large rat neurons up to about 24 hr. and in those of the monkey brain for about 48 hr. Later, the incrustations disappear, the cell body becomes progressively more homogeneous and pale staining and a shrunken nucleus surrounded by ghost-like remnants of cytoplasm may persist for ten days or more.

because the lumina of capillaries are reduced by a combination of expanded perivascular astrocytic processes, swollen endothelial cells and the formation of intravascular blebs. "No re-flow" was only extensive after a circulatory arrest of 7·5 min. or more after which considerable brain damage would be inevitable. However, the latter has not been described nor has it yet been demonstrated that non-filling vessels are surrounded by more dead neurons than those in which post-ischaemic perfusion is normal.

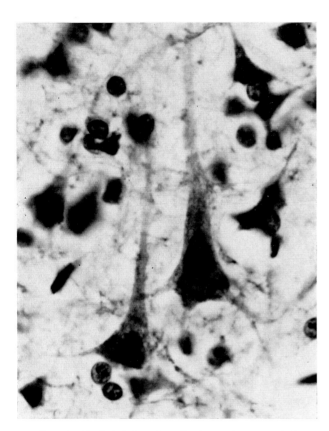

FIG. 3. Typical ischaemic cell change in neocortical pyramidal cells. There is reduced Nissl substance in the cytoplasm and the nucleus is shrunken, triangular and dark-staining. Paraffin section, cresyl fast violet and luxol fast blue. × 850.

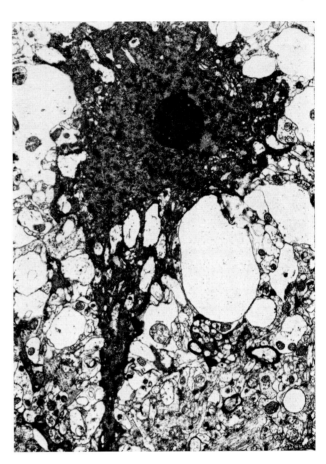

FIG. 4. Electron micrograph showing ischaemic cell change with some residual microvacuoles. The cytoplasm and nucleus are very dense and there are many swollen astrocytic processes around the cell. × 5,700.

The point in the time course of ischaemic cell change at which the process becomes irreversible cannot yet be defined with precision. Most probably mitochondria that are greatly swollen and have lost virtually all traces of cristae cannot be reconstituted. This situation obtains during the late stages of microvacuolation and thus after a survival of 30 min. or even less in small neurons and a little later in large nerve cells.

While ischaemic cell change is the most important primary effect of a hypoxic/ischaemic stress there is a possibility that additional neurons may be imperilled by a delayed secondary ischaemic insult represented by the "no re-flow phenomenon" described by Ames *et al.*[2] This phenomenon implies that after a period of circulatory arrest blood flow is not restored in particular regions of the brain

STAGNANT HYPOXIA

Ischaemic Hypoxia

An arrest of blood flow within a single artery results in the formation of an infarct. This usually occupies some fraction rather than the whole of the arterial territory. At an early stage there is a very variable combination of ischaemic neurons and damaged nerve fibres within a peripheral zone of white matter oedema. Haemorrhage may or may not be present and ultimately the infarct becomes an area of scar tissue often containing cystic spaces.

Overall ischaemia of the brain is most commonly the result of cardiac arrest, which may be associated with either preceding or succeeding periods of reduced brain blood flow, or both. If the cardiac arrest is of abrupt onset and termination brain damage will be generalized in at least the neocortex and cerebellum. A short period of cardiac arrest combined with appreciable periods of reduced brain blood flow before or after the event will lead to a concentration of ischaemic alterations along the arterial boundary zones of the fore- and hindbrain.

brain. Until such information is available neither these findings, nor those of any other experimental study, justify the conclusion that a period of 5–7 min. of arrest of circulation in the human brain can be exceeded with safety.

The macroscopic appearances of the brain after circulatory arrest reflect the extent of neuronal destruction and the duration of survival. After a few hours or days the brain may appear normal externally in the usual slices; swelling is by no means usual and when present is seldom gross. As survival increases, the weight of the brain

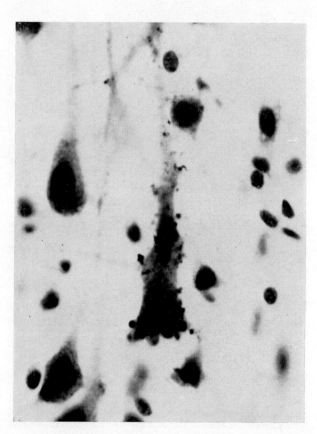

FIG. 5. Typical ischaemic cell change with incrustations lying on the cell surface. Celloidin section, cresyl fast violet. ×1,000.

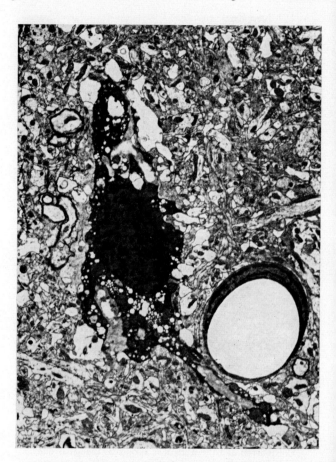

FIG. 6. Electron micrograph showing that incrustations correspond to irregular and very dense areas of cytoplasm on the surface of the cell. ×4,300.

At normal body temperature the upper limit of circulatory arrest compatible with clinical recovery and no demonstrable brain damage is 5–7 min. Recently Hossmann and Sato[19] submitted the cat brain to 1 hr. of ischaemia by clamping the innominate and subclavian arteries and lowering the blood pressure. It was stated that "electron-microscopy revealed the structural preservation of the cortex after the recovery of function". However, the morphological study was restricted to well-fixed portions of the sensorimotor cortex. Later, Olsson and Hossmann[19] found "light microscopical changes were consistently present in the cerebral cortex when ischaemia lasted more than 8 min. . . .". The clinical status of the animals after the longer and shorter periods of circulatory arrest has not been described, nor has the full neuropathology in each

decreases, atrophy of cortical gyri and of cerebellar folia becomes evident and there is expansion of the ventricular system. The hippocampi may seem shrunken and necrosis may be obvious in the caudate and lentiform nuclei.

Microscopic examination of the brain reveals at once that all neurons are not equally damaged. Regions which show total destruction and others that are intact both occur within a spatial pattern that is virtually constant from case to case. This pattern of "selectively vulnerable areas" is the central feature of the neuropathology of all types of hypoxia and is seen to its fullest extent after circulatory arrest.

In the *cerebral cortex* ischaemic alterations diminish in frequency from the occipital lobes forwards and also from the depths of sulci towards the crests of gyri. The third, fifth and sixth laminae are more vulnerable than the second and fourth (Fig. 7).

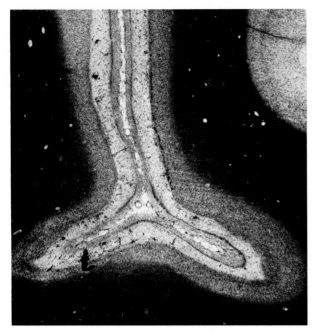

FIG. 7. Typical laminar necrosis of the third cortical layer. Celloidin. Heidenhain. ×18.

In the *hippocampi* the Sommer sector (h. 1) is most vulnerable and is followed by the endfolium (h. 3–5) while h. 2 is the most resistant portion (Fig. 8).

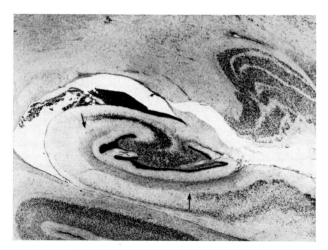

FIG. 8. Neuronal destruction in the Sommer sector (h.1— between arrows) of the hippocampus. Cresyl fast violet. ×7.

The superficial or corticomedial portion of the *amygdaloid nucleus* is more resistant than the basolateral and severe damage in the latter can lead to expansion of the tip of the inferior horn of the ventricle.

Involvement of the *caudate nucleus* and *putamen* is not invariable and ranges from limited alterations along the lateral borders to necrosis with cyst formation. Ischaemic damage within this range is less frequent in the *globus pallidus*.

In the *thalamus*, damage hardly ever attains the level of infarction and the anterior, dorsomedial and ventrolateral nuclei are the most vulnerable. When neocortical damage is severe retrograde neuronal degeneration will be present in the related nuclei if survival is protracted.

Within the hypothalamus, the *mamillary bodies* are virtually the only nuclei to show damage although this is rare in adults and relatively common in infants and children.

The influence of age upon the distribution of ischaemic alterations is clearly seen in the *brain stem*. In the adult, damage is usually restricted to the reticular zones of the substantiae nigrae, the inferior colliculi and the medulla olives. In infants and young children there may be the additional involvement of the third nerve nuclei, the motor and spinal nuclei of the fifth nerve, the vestibular nuclei and the nuclei gracili, cuneati and solitarii in the lower medulla.

In the *cerebellum* the Purkinje cells are most vulnerable and the granule cells the most resistant.

Oligaemic Hypoxia

Within a single artery a critical reduction in blood flow may lead to an infarct with the pathological features already described. The brain damage due to *overall* oligaemia is determined by the rate at which the blood pressure falls, the lowest pressure attained and its duration and also by the rate at which it returns to normal. A moderate fall in brain perfusion pressure does not lead to a reduction in brain blood flow because of vasodilatation and the consequent reduction in cerebrovascular resistance. When vasodilatation is maximal this process of "autoregulation" ceases and blood flow will then fall parallel to the perfusion pressure.

Adams et al.,[1] have shown that when brain oligaemia is due to systemic arterial hypotension the ensuing ischaemic brain damage conforms to one of three patterns.

(i) Ischaemic damage is concentrated along the *boundary zones* between the territories of the major cerebral and cerebellar arteries and is minimal or absent in the hippocampi. In the neocortex damage is most frequent and most severe in the parieto-occipital regions at the junction of the anterior, middle and posterior cerebral arterial territories. It decreases towards the frontal and temporal poles along the anterior/middle and middle/posterior cerebral arterial boundary zones respectively.

This pattern of damage is most often seen after a conscious subject has collapsed because of a sudden reduction in cardiac output due to coronary occlusion, cardiomyopathy or viral myocarditis; but in anaesthetized subjects a hypotensive episode may occur during dental or neurosurgical procedures, particularly in the sitting position.[5] The view of Zulch[31,32] that the boundary zone pattern of damage was a consequence of a major and abrupt fall in systemic blood pressure was confirmed by the experiments of Brierley and Excell[6] and Brierley et al.[8].

Hypotension was produced in rhesus monkeys by the injection of a ganglion-blocking agent, supplemented by 20° head-up tilt of the table and by bleeding. Respiration failed early but mechanical ventilation ensured continued normal arterial oxygenation. Brain perfusion pressure fell below 25 mm. Hg. and values for brain venous oxygen tension of 10 mm. Hg. or less were evidence of the greatly reduced brain blood flow. The duration of profound hypotension required to produce boundary zone lesions (Fig. 9) was estimated from the time course of the somatosensory cortical evoked responses.[23]

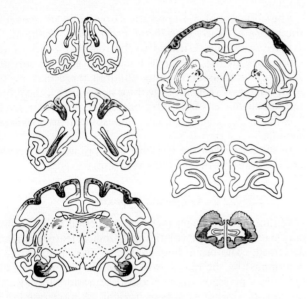

FIG. 9. Distribution of ischaemic damage along arterial boundary zones after profound systemic hypotension (*M. Mulatta*).

(ii) Ischaemic alterations are *generalized* in the cortex of cerebrum and cerebellum, minor or absent in the hippocampi and severe in the thalami and cerebellum.

This pattern of damage has been identified in the brains of patients anaesthetized at the time of either heart block, brief cardiac arrest followed by cardiac massage or the postural hypotension due to head-up tilt. These cases are rare and the final state is usually one of decerebration. It seems that this generalized type of brain damage is caused by hypotension of relatively slow onset but of long duration. Probably early vasodilatation combined with a slowly falling perfusion pressure ensure that a critical level of blood flow is not restricted to the boundary zones but affects all arterial territories more or less equally. This type of brain damage has only been reproduced in the experimental primate if there has also been a rise in intracranial pressure.[8]

(iii) *Generalized* ischaemic alterations in the cortex of cerebrum and cerebellum showing a marked *accentuation along the arterial boundary zones*.

This combination is quite frequent and is seen when a conscious subject collapses as a result of cardiac infarction, brief cardiac arrest followed by massage, or a period of post-operative hypotension without obvious cause. Consciousness is seldom regained. The observed brain damage suggests the implication of sudden hypotension in the genesis of the boundary zone lesions and a more sustained period of hypotension with reduced blood flow in the genesis of the generalized alterations. This pattern of damage has not been produced in the "profound hypotension" model of Brierley *et al.*[8] but is the only pattern of damage found following the primary hypoxic hypoxia represented by atmospheric decompression (*vide infra*).

HYPOXIC HYPOXIA

The belief that brain damage can result from a simple reduction in the oxygen tension of arterial blood for sufficient time is still widely held. A large literature relates nervous dysfunction and proven brain damage to the hypoxaemia resulting from either obstruction of the respiratory passages, pulmonary hypoventilation, the inhalation of inert gases or exposure to high altitude. However, these reports are virtually devoid of such critical physiological data as the degree and duration of the hypoxia, the corresponding blood-gas tensions and the usual parameters of the circulation.

In experimental primates brain damage has not been produced by exposure to a mixture of 94 per cent nitrogen and 6 per cent oxygen for 7 hr.,[4] nor by exposure to pure nitrogen for brief periods (Brierley and Meldrum, unpublished findings). In the latter series, cardiovascular collapse after up to 3 min. set an upper limit to the exposure. Resuscitation was required in order to secure recovery and ultimately the brains were normal.

In baboons and Rhesus monkeys a less severe but more prolonged hypoxic hypoxia may lead to neurological impairment and brain damage. This type of hypoxia is represented by atmospheric decompression to an altitude of 37,500 ft. which has been simulated in a decompression chamber containing the experimental primate. Brain damage was greater in the baboon than in the rhesus monkey but in both species consisted of ischaemic alterations centered upon the arterial boundary zones of fore- and hind brain.[7,28] This neuropathological pattern was in fact indistinguishable from that following profound arterial hypotension with normal arterial oxygenation (Fig. 10). The occurrence of boundary zone lesions as a consequence of a primary hypoxia is not fully explicable, if only because physiological and neuropathological studies have not yet been carried out on any single group of animals. In the seven non-survival animals of Ernsting and Nicholson[14] respiratory rate rose during the first minute of the exposure to 160 mm. Hg. abs. (37,500 ft.) and was maintained for 2·5–12·0 min. after which it slowed progressively. The end-tidal pO_2 fell to 17–20 mm. Hg. at 1·5 min. while arterial pO_2 fell to 11–12·5 mm. Hg. in 1·5 min. and to 7 and 8 mm. Hg. in two animals surviving beyond 15 min. Systemic arterial pressure showed a slight initial fall followed by a transient rise to a level 20–40 mm. Hg. above control levels at about the fifth minute. Then, in three animals blood pressure fell progressively until death; in three it remained above 80 mm. Hg. and in one it remained above 55 mm. and started to fall at the 18th minute. In another series of fifty M. Mulatta submitted to decompression, only one-third to one-half showed brain damage. Clearly, in the

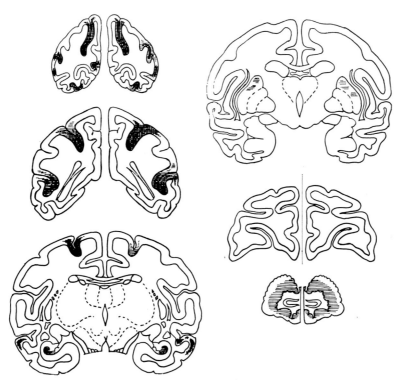

FIG. 10. Distribution of ischaemic damage along arterial boundary zones
after atmospheric decompression (*M. Mulatta*).

above study the four potential survivors whose brains might or might not have been normal do not justify the conclusion that the boundary zone distribution of brain pathology after decompression ". . . could be produced by arterial hypoxaemia in the absence of systemic hypotentions". In the absence of parallel physiological data in animals with proven brain damage, some reduction in brain perfusion pressure during a period of known profound hypoxaemia is the only hypothesis that can account for the boundary-zone distribution of the ischaemic alterations. This implies that hypoxic hypoxia can produce brain damage only through the medium of a secondary depression of the myocardium.

HISTOTOXIC HYPOXIA

Although it has long been recognized that histotoxic hypoxia is brought about by the inhibition of intraneuronal oxidative enzymes, the precise mechanisms of this inhibition and their earliest effects have not yet been defined at a fine structural level. Only the two most familiar examples of the histotoxic group will be considered here, carbon monoxide and cyanide. It is noteworthy that the latter has been studied very extensively because of its effects on white matter but hardly at all where its effects on the neuron are concerned.

(i) *Cyanide.* The clinical and neuropathological effects of sodium and potassium cyanide and of hydrocyanic acid are closely similar. Respiration is depressed or arrested while cardiac action is little affected. Epileptic seizures are common and consciousness is seldom regained, Neuropathological reports are few and none is detailed. Schmorl[30]

described softening in each globus pallidus of a case surviving 36 hr. but there was no histological description. Edelmann[13] presented the macroscopic and microscopic features of the brain of a man dying 23 hr. after exposure to HCN. There was early necrosis in each lentiform nucleus with emphasis on the globus pallidus. Lambert,[21] in a case surviving 16 days after exposure to HCN, described haemorrhages in the white matter and also loss of neurones in the frontal cortex and the cerebellum.

The first experimental studies were those of Meter[25] in dogs and rabbits. Ischaemic necrosis was seen in the cerebral cortex, hippocampi, globi pallidi and substantia nigrae. There was early softening in the white matter, particularly in the corpus callosum. A similar picture was described in the rat by Hicks.[18]

Haymaker *et al.*[17] administered cyanide compounds to dogs by inhalation or intravenous injections and survivals were up to 14 days. Ischaemic damage was seen in frontal and parietal cortex and also in the striatum, globus pallidus and substantia nigra. It was less frequent in thalamus and cerebellum and infrequent in the white matter. All animals surviving more than 14 hr. became comatose and apnoeic and convulsions occurred in seven. Blood pressure was not recorded and the degree and duration of hypoxaemia are not known. As yet there has been no study of the effects of cyanide in experimental primates.

It will be evident from this brief review that the damage observed in human and experimental animal brains cannot be attributed to histological hypoxia alone as the possible contributions of hypoxaemia, oligaemia and convulsions have not yet assessed.

(ii) *Carbon Monoxide*. The ability of carbon monoxide to produce brain damage is due only in part to the inhibition of oxidative enzymes. By virtue of its combination with haemoglobin to form the stable compound carboxyhaemoglobin, it also gives rise to an "anaemic hypoxia", i.e. a reduced oxygen-carrying capacity of the blood.

Meyer[26] reviewed the neuropathology caused by carbon monoxide in man and experimental animals and concluded that "all changes have the appearances and typical localization of anoxia and/or ischaemia". Early necrosis of the globus pallidus is a common feature and is sometimes associated with necrosis in the globus pallidus while ischaemic alterations are common in the cerebral cortex and cerebellum.

HYPOGLYCAEMIA

In the human hypoglycaemia may lead to brain damage when the associated coma is irreversible, i.e. it does not respond to the administration of glucose. When brain damage does occur Meter[26] has stated "the findings in the literature show some variation but there is no doubt that they closely resemble those which occur in other types of anoxia". Hypoglycaemia may be due to overdosage with insulin in the treatment of diabetes, the excessive production of insulin by an islet-cell tumour of the pancreas and the injection of insulin in the treatment of psychoses. It may also occur as an idiopathic condition in infants and as the potentially brain-damaging component of "white liver disease".[22]

The majority of the very numerous experimental studies have been carried out in sub-primates with immersion fixation of the brain, so that histological artefacts account for many of the remarkably diverse neuronal alterations that have been reported. Up to the present time, there have been only three studies of hypoglycaemia in primates. Finley and Brenner produced hypoglycaemic coma in M. Mulatta by the intramuscular injection of insulin. The brains were fixed by immediate immersion in formalin. The large vacuoles seen in the cytoplasm of many neurons after a survival of only a few hours may well have been the artefact of "water cell change" while after survivals of 9 hr. or more, typical ischaemic cell change was described. In this series blood pressure, blood oxygenation and respiration were not monitored.

In order to study the long-term neurological and neuropathological effects of controlled and uncomplicated hypoglycaemia Kahn and Myers[20] injected insulin subcutaneously in lightly anaesthetized young adult rhesus monkeys and monitored blood pressure, the EKG, blood gas tensions, acid-base status and blood glucose. Mechanical ventilation was sometimes used to maintain normal oxygenation of the blood. Blood glucose fell to 20 mg./100 ml. after $1\frac{1}{2}$–3 hr. In eleven animals profound hypoglycaemia lasted from 4–10 hr. and was terminated by the intravenous injection of glucose. Survivals ranged from 10 days to 9 months with permanent neurological impairment and proven brain damage in seven. In these animals, blood glucose averaged 12·1 mg./100 ml. for 6·1 hr. Con-

vulsions occurred in five of the seven, not during profound hypoglycaemia but during the recovery phase.

The neuropathological alterations consisted of nerve cell loss and variable gliomesodermal reaction in the striatum, cerebral cortex and hippocampus in decreasing order of frequency.[27]

Rhesus monkeys were also used by Meldrum et al.[24] in order to see if "ischaemic cell change" was the earliest stage of brain damage after hypoglycaemia uncomplicated by epileptic activity, cerebral hypoxia or brain swelling. Under light pentobarbitone anaesthesia, a chronic preparation allowed the continuous monitoring of biochemical and physiological variables including the EKG, EEG, somatosensory evoked cortical potentials, arterial and venous sinus blood pressures and intracranial pressure. Blood glucose, blood cases and pH were determined in intermittent, simultaneous blood samples. Hypoglycaemia was induced by the intravenous injection of insulin (660–1,880 I.U.) over periods of 2–7 hr. and was terminated after 2–8 hr. by the injection of glucose. After survivals of $\frac{1}{2}$–15 hr. the brains were fixed by per-aortic perfusion with a formalin-acetic acid-methanol mixture (FAM).

Eight of fifteen animals showed unequivocal brain damage after survivals of $\frac{1}{2}$–4 hr.[9] This took the form of a sequence of neuronal alterations that began with typical microvacuolation after a survival of $\frac{1}{2}$ hr. and passed through ischaemic cell change to ischaemic cell change with incrustations after a survival of 4 hr. With one exception, blood pressure was well maintained in these animals, there was no hypoxaemia and no epileptic activity. Intracranial pressure was not significantly raised and there was no postmortem evidence of brain swelling. In one animal ischaemic neuronal alterations were concentrated along the boundary zones between the anterior and middle cerebral arterial territories. In this animal cerebral perfusion pressure had fallen to 28–32 mm. Hg. for 30 min. while the blood glucose did not fall below 34 mg./100 ml. Neither this degree of hypoglycaemia nor the hypotension would have resulted *per se* in brain damage so that the existence of the latter suggests that one factor could potentiate the effects of the other.

In the other seven animals blood glucose was below 20 mg./100 ml. for more than 2 hr. The neocortex was involved in all seven and particularly in the parietal and occipital lobes. The hippocampi, corpora striata and cerebellar Purkinje cells were each involved in one animal.

Thus this study has demonstrated that ischaemic cell change is the neuronal alteration due to uncomplicated hypoglycaemia and its time course was closely similar to that defined in the brain of M. Mulatta after profound systemic hypotension.[10] It also suggests that a nadditional element of hypoxia may potentiate the effects of an initial hypoglycaemia, a combination that exists in perhaps the majority of human cases. It is therefore not surprising that the reported neuropathology or hypoglycaemia in man includes nerve cell damage or loss in the 3rd, 5th and 6th layers of the cerebral cortex, zones h. 1 and h. 3–5 of the hippocampus, the corpora striata (but hardly ever the globus pallidus), and certain thalamic nuclei, while cerebellar damage is usually moderate or even absent.

The report of Anderson *et al.*[3] suggested that in the human infant hypoglycaemia resulted in a very different neuropathological picture. Neuronal alterations including chromatolysis with cytoplasmic vacuolation in some and fragmentation of nuclear chromatin in others were quite generalized and without any suggestion of the pattern of "selective vulnerability" as seen in the adult. In view of the similarity between some of the reported neuronal alterations and autolytic changes, these findings must be treated with reserve until their confirmation by others.

CONCLUSIONS

It will be apparent from the above remarks, that the neuropathology of "brain hypoxia" is passing through a phase of critical reassessment. It is no longer possible to endorse the classical view that all microscopic alterations seen in sections of the brain are of equal significance and must therefore be presented in detail in every case. There is a growing awareness that some degree of histological artefact is inescapable in every human brain. In the particular context of brain hypoxia such artefacts are of critical importance when survival is very short and neuronal alterations still subtle. They are of far less consequence when survival is a matter of weeks, months or years. One important contribution of experimental studies in animals has been to present the earliest stages of the neuronal reaction to hypoxia in material optimally fixed by *in vivo* perfusion. The experimental approach is also valuable because it alone permits the exposure of the brain to hypoxia initially of a single type; and by no means of appropriate physiological monitoring it also permits the recognition of secondary factors. An important example is the demonstration that a primary hypoxic hypoxia can only bring about brain damage through the medium of a secondary reduction in brain perfusion due to a reduced cardiac output.

FURTHER READING

[1] Adams, J. H., Brierley, J. B., Connor, R. C. R. and Treip, C. S. (1966), "The Effects of Systemic Hypotension upon the Human Brain. Clinical and Neuropathological Observations in 11 Cases," *Brain*, **89**, 235–268.

[2] Ames III, A., Wright, R. L., Kowada, M., Thurston, J. M. and Majno, G. (1968), "Cerebral Ischaemia. II, The No-reflow Phenomenon," *Amer. J. Path.*, **52**, 437–453.

[3] Anderson, J. M., Milner, R. D. G. and Strich, S. J. (1967), "Effects of Neonatal Hypoglycaemia on the Nervous System: a Pathological Study," *J. Neurol. Neurosurg. Psychiat.*, **30**, 295–310.

[4] Bogaert, L. Van, Dallemagne, M. J. and Wegira, R. (1938), "Recherche sur le besoin d'oxygène chronique et aigue chez Macacus Rhesus. Absence de lésions expérimentales des centres nerveux après intoxication par l'oxyde de carbone, le nitrite de soude et l'appauvrisement de l'air en oxygène," *Arch. Internat. de méed. exp.*, **13**, 335–378.

[5] Brierley, J. B. (1970), "Systemic Hypotension—Neurological and Neuropathological Aspects," *in Modern Trends in Neurology*—5, Chap. 9, pp. 164–177 (D. Williams, Ed.). London: Butterworths.

[6] Brierley, J. B. and Excell, Barbara J. (1966), "The Effects of Profound Systemic Hypotension upon the Brain of M. Rhesus. Physiological and Pathological Observations," *Brain*, **89**, 269–298.

[7] Brierley, J. B. and Nicholson, A. N. (1969), "Neuropathological Correlates of Neurological Impairment Following Prolonged Decompression," *Aerospace Med.*, **40**, 148–152.

[8] Brierley, J. B., Brown, A. W., Excell, Barbara, J. and Meldrum, B. S. (1969), "Brain Damage in the Rhesus Monkey Resulting from Profound Arterial Hypotension. I: Its Nature, Distribution and General Physiological Correlates," *Brain Research*, **13**, 68–100.

[9] Brierley, J. B., Brown, A. W. and Meldrum, B. S. (1971a), "The Neuropathology of Insulin-induced Hypoglycaemia in a Primate (M. Mulatta); Topography and Cellular Nature," in *Brain Hypoxia* (J. B. Brierley and B. S. Meldrum, Eds.), Chap. 22, 225–229. Clinics in Developmental Medicine, 39/40. Spastics Internat. Med. Publ. Heinemann, London.

[10] Brierley, J. B., Brown, A. W. and Meldrum, B. S. (1971b), "The Nature and Time Course of the Neuronal Alterations Resulting from Oligaemia and Hypoglycaemia in the Brain of Macaca Mulatta," *Brain Research*, **25**, 483–499.

[11] Brown, A. W. and Brierley, J. B. (1968), "The Nature, Distribution and Earliest Stages of Anoxic-ischaemic Nerve Cell Damage in the Rat Brain as Defined by the Optical Microscope," *Brit. J. exp. Path.*, **49**, 87–106.

[12] Brown, A. W. and Brierley, J. B. (1971), "The Nature and Timecourse of Anoxic-ischaemic Cell Change in the Rat Brain. An Optical and Electron Microscopic Study, in *Brain Hypoxia* (J. B. Brierley and B. S. Meldrum, Eds.), Chap. 6, 49–60. Clinics in Developmental Medicine 39/40. Spastics Internat. Med. Publ. Heinemann, London.

[13] Edelmann, F. (1921), "Ein Beitrag zur Vergiftung mit gasförmiger Blausäure insbesonder zu ben dabei auftretenden Gehirnveranderungen," *Dtsch. ztschr. f. Nervenheilk.*, **72**, 259–287.

[14] Ernsting, J. and Nicholson, A. N. (1971), "Respiratory and Cardiovascular Status of Rhesus Monkeys Exposed to an Environmental Pressure of 160 mm. Hg. abs. (11,430 m)," in *Brain Hypoxia* (J. B. Brierley and B. S. Meldrum, Eds.), Chap. 16, 162–169. Clinics in Developmental Medicine 39/40. Spastics Internat. Med. Publ. Heinemann, London.

[15] Finley, K. H. and Brenner, C. (1941), "Histologic Evidence of Damage to the Brain in Monkeys Treated with Metrazol and Insulin," *Arch. Neurol. Psychiat.*, **45**, 403–438.

[16] Geiger, A., Kawakita, Y. and Barkulis, S. S. (1960), "Major Pathways of Glucose Utilization in the Brain in Brain Perfusion Experiments *in vivo* and *in situ*," *J. Neurochem.*, **5**, 323–338.

[17] Haymaker, W., Ginzler, A. M. and Ferguson, R. L. (1952), "Residual Neuropathological Effects of Cyanide Poisoning. A Study of the Central Nervous System of 23 Dogs Exposed to Cyanide Compounds," *Milit. Surg.*, **3**, 231–246.

[18] Hicks, S. P. (1950), "Brain Metabolism *in vivo*. (i) The Distribution of Lesions Caused by Cyanide Poisoning, Insulin-hypoglycaemia, Asphyxia in Nitrogen and Fluoro-acetate Poisoning in Rats," *Arch. Path.*, **49**, 111–137.

[19] Hossmann, K.-A. and Sato, K. (1970), "The Effect of Ischemia on Sensorimotor Cortex of Cat. Electrophysiological, Biochemical and Electronmicroscopical Observations," *Z. Neurol.*, **198**, 33–45.

[20] Kahn, K. J. and Myers, R. E. (1971), "Insulin-induced Hypoglycaemia in the Non-human Primate. 1: Clinical Consequences," in *Brain Hypoxia* (J. B. Brierley and B. S. Meldrum, Eds.), Chap. 19, 185–193. Clinics in Developmental Medicine 39/40. Spastics Internat. Med. Publ. Heinemann, London.

[21] Lambert, S. W. (1919), "Poisoning by Hydrocyanic Acid Gas, with Especial Reference to its Effects upon the Brain," *Neurol. Bull.*, **2**, 93–105.

[22] *Lancet* (1969), "Encephalopathy and Fatty Infiltration of Viscera in Children. Leading Article," ii, 473–475.

[23] Meldrum, B. S. and Brierley, J. B. (1969), "Brain Damage in the Rhesus Monkey Resulting from Profound Arterial Hypotension. II: Changes in the Spontaneous and Evoked Electrical Activity of the Neocortex," *Brain Research*, **13**, 101–118,

[24] Meldrum, B. S., Horton, R. W. and Brierley, J. B. (1971), "Insulin-induced Hypoglycaemia in the Primate: Relationship Between Physiological Changes and Neuropathology," in *Brain Hypoxia* (J. B. Brierley and B. S. Meldrum, Eds.), Chap. 21, 207–224. Clinics in Developmental Medicine 39/40. Spastics Internat. Med. Publ. Heinemann, London.

[25] Meyer, A. (1933), "Experimentelle Vergiftungsstudien. III. Über Gehirnveranderungen bei experimenteller Blausäurevergiftung," *Ztschr. ges. Neurol. Psychiat.*, **143**, 333–348.

[26] Meyer, A. (1963), "Intoxications," in *Greenfield's Neuropathology*, Chap. 4, 235–287 (Blackwood, W., McMenemey, W. H., Meyer, A., Norman, R. M. and Russell, Dorothy S., Eds.). London: Arnold.

[27] Myers, R. E. and Kahn, K. J. (1971), "Insulin-induced Hypoglycemia in the Non-human Primate. II: Long-term Neuropathological Consequences," in *Brain Hypoxia*, Chap. 20, 195–206 (J. B. Brierley and B. S. Meldrum, Eds.). Clinics in Developmental Medicine 39/40. Spastics Internat. Med. Publ. Heinemann, London.

[28] Nicholson, A. N., Freeland, Susan A. and Brierley, J. B. (1970), "A Behavioural and Neuropathological Study of the *Sequelae* of Profound Hypoxia," *Brain Research*, **22**, 327–345.

[29] Olsson, Y. and Hossmann, K.-A. (1971), "The Effect of Intravascular Saline Perfusion on the *Sequelae* of Transient Cerebral Ischemia. Light and Electron Microscope Observations," *Acta Neuropath. (Berl.)*, **17**, 68–79.

[30] Schmorl (1920), "Gehirn bei Blausäurevergiftung," *Münch. med. Wschr.*, **67**, 913.

[31] Zülch, K. J. (1953), "Neue Befunde und Deutungen aus der Gefässpathologie des Hirns und Rückenmarks," *Zbl. allg. Path.*, **90**, 402.

[32] Zülch, K. J. and Behrend, R. C. H. (1961), "The Pathogenesis and Topography of Anoxia, Hypoxia and Ischemia of the Brain in Man," in *Cerebral anoxia and the electroencephalogram*, Chap. 14, 144–163 (H. Gastaut and J. S. Meyer Eds.). Springfield, Ill.: Thomas.

3. CLINICAL EFFECTS OF CEREBROVASCULAR DISEASE

RALPH ROSS RUSSELL

INTRODUCTION

Cerebral infarction now accounts for as many as 85 per cent of cases of stroke, the remainder being due to subarachnoid and intracerebral haemorrhage. It follows that any study of cerebral vascular disease must first consider the mechanism of ischaemia and of vascular occlusion in the brain.

The special features which distinguish the cerebral circulation from that in other regions result from the exceptional vulnerability of cerebral tissue to anoxia and from the unusual anatomical arrangement of the cerebral arteries.

Occlusive change affects vessels as large as the aorta and as small as arterioles. The effect of ischaemia on cerebral tissue depends on the degree and rapidity of the obstruction and on the availability of other routes of blood supply. Occlusion of a penetrating intracerebral artery, for instance, regularly gives rise to a small softening since there are few anastomoses above a capillary level. On the other hand occlusion of the carotid or vertebral artery in the neck is not as a rule followed by cerebral ischaemia since the remaining extracranial arteries and the Circle of Willis immediately accommodate an increased blood flow. The total flow to the brain remains almost unaltered. Occlusion of a main cerebral artery distal to the Circle of Willis is usually followed by infarction, the extent of which is variable and is governed by the availability of collateral blood from surrounding vascular beds, via leptomeningeal anastomoses.

Even in the presence of good collateral vessels, occlusion of an artery reduces the pressure in the distal segment so that normal blood flow in its vascular territory can only be maintained by a compensatory reduction in cerebrovascular resistance (autoregulation). Should vascular reactivity be impaired or should pressure fall further, e.g. as a result of systemic hypotension, the limits of autoregulation may be reached and a focal reduction in blood flow may occur.

Not only the severity but the location of ischaemic lesions in the brain is influenced by collateral blood supply. In middle cerebral artery occlusion collateral flow occurs from the adjacent anterior and posterior cerebral artery territories and the zone of maximum ischaemia is in the Sylvian area (mid-field infarction). By contrast in carotid occlusion where the collateral blood flow utilizes the Circle of Willis the zone of maximal ischaemia, if the circulation is inadequate, lies in the border zone between middle and anterior cerebral artery territories (end-field infarction). Multiple and extracranial occlusion also produces border zone infarction, the pattern of which reflects the sites and degree of occlusion.

The importance of oedema and of secondary changes in the blood vessels themselves has previously been underestimated. Although vascular tissue is less sensitive to anoxia than are neurons the patency of the microcirculation is the determining factor in infarction. Experimental studies have shown that ischaemia impairs the reactivity of cerebral blood vessels to pressure changes and to vasoactive agents, and in clinical practice zones of impaired vascular reactivity may be found even after minor degrees of ischaemia. Unreactive and ischaemic blood vessels tend to become permeable to protein, especially under conditions of raised arterial or venous pressure. The resultant extracellular oedema, together with swelling of glial cells, tends to compress the capillary vascular bed which can lead to further ischaemia. Contributory factors are haemoconcentration and increased viscosity resulting from plasma leakage which may lead to further vascular stasis.

The effects of cerebral oedema are not confined to the microcirculation and larger arteries such as the posterior cerebral may be kinked and occluded by brain swelling. A cerebral infarct is thus not simply the consequence of an inadequate supply of oxygen and metabolites but is the end result of a complex series of events, some vascular and some neural, culminating in blockage of the capillary bed. Many of these events are delayed and amenable to treatment.

DIAGNOSIS

The Clinical Setting and Predisposing Factors

Cerebrovascular disease includes a wide range of pathological processes, and four primary considerations arise when considering the diagnosis of a patient presenting with a stroke:

(1) What is the site and extent of the damaged area?
(2) Is the underlying process vascular or non-vascular?
(3) If vascular, is the brain damage due to ischaemia or to haemorrhage?
(4) What is the underlying arterial lesion?

Only when these questions have been answered can appropriate treatment be applied.

Cerebral Thrombosis

The pathology of most types of occlusive vascular disease in the brain, the heart or the limbs is atherosclerosis, and patients with clinical symptoms in one site are at an increased risk from another. The risk of cerebral infarction for instance is three times as great in patients with coronary disease, even after adjustment for differences in blood pressure. There are, however, some epidemiological differences between cerebral and myocardial infarction which have not yet been explained.

The male predominance in cerebral infarction is much less marked than in cardiac infarction, although at younger age groups women still show a lesser incidence. There are also minor discrepancies in geographical and racial distributions and in the overall incidence in succeeding decades which suggest differences in pathogenesis, but the mortality statistics on which these are based may be unreliable.

Hypertension, diabetes and hyperlipidaemia are common to all the clinical types of atheromatous vascular disease, ischaemic heart disease, stroke and intermittent claudication. However, hyperlipidaemia has been shown to be related to stroke only in the younger age groups. Hypertension is a most important risk factor contributing not only to atherogenesis but to the clinical onset of stroke. Moreover, by contributing to heart disease, it adds further to the risk.

Differences in environmental factors between cerebral and cardiac infarction are also apparent. Obesity and lack of exercise for instance, which are associated with an increased risk of cardiac infarction, appear to be unrelated to cerebral infarction. Cigarette smoking, however, is associated with all the major types of ischaemic disease including cerebral infarction.

Arterial disease other than atheroma is unusual in the carotid system. Giant cell arteritis may involve the external carotid and ophthalmic branches, less commonly the main trunk of the vertebral and internal carotid in the neck, but spares intracranial portions of these arteries. Takayasu's disease, an idiopathic vasculitis, is encountered in large arterial trunks and a similar condition is described affecting intracranial arteries in children.

Rarely the cerebral arteries may become involved in endarteritis secondary to local inflammation, e.g. in tuberculous, or syphilitic meningitis, in mucomycosis, or following tonsillar abscess in childhood. In other forms of systemic vasculitis involvement of the arteries of the brain is unusual, although it may occur in systemic lupus erythematosis and in acute rheumatic fever.

Indirect trauma to the carotid artery in the neck by sudden stretching and tearing of the intima may initiate thrombosis and thromboembolism. Direct trauma by penetrating injury in the tonsillar fossa or during tonsillectomy also occur and is commonest in childhood. In exceptional cases the vessel may be occluded as a result of dissecting aneurysm or fibromuscular hyperplasia.

In some instances thrombosis occurs in cerebral arteries which are relatively free of atheroma, the abnormality being supposedly in the coagulation or haemostatic mechanisms of the blood or in its physical properties rather than in the wall of the artery. In this category are included vascular occlusion secondary to polycythaemia, leukaemia, or sickle cell disease, as a remote complication of carcinoma, of oestrogen-progestin treatment, or of heavy cigarette smoking.

Cases previously diagnosed as Buerger's disease of the brain, are probably instances of widespread thrombosis of cerebral arteries secondary to carotid occlusion.

Cerebral Embolism

Although in clinical practice the heart is still the commonest source of embolism to the brain, dislodgement of fragments of thrombus or atheromatous material may also take origin from ulcerated lesions in large arteries. The age range in cerebral embolism is wide, reflecting that of the underlying disorder. In cardiac embolism both heart disease and disordered conduction are aetiological factors, the former being the more important; thus mitral stenosis with atrial fibrillation is a common cause of embolism, mitral stenosis in sinus rhythm is an uncommon cause and atrial fibrillation alone is a rare cause. Myocardial infarction often results in the formation of intraventricular thrombus, portions of which may be dislodged as emboli in the first few weeks after infarction. Other varieties of heart disease which may be complicated by embolism are endomycardial fibrosis, atrial myxoma and cardiac myopathy. Emboli derived from the cardiac valves in rheumatic valvular disease or from valvular protheses are usually small and give rise to minor episodes of ischaemia. In bacterial endocarditis or in nonbacterial (marantic) endocarditis the vegetations are larger and may occlude a major cerebral artery.

Cerebral Haemorrhage

There is now good evidence that spontaneous intracerebral haemorrhage usually seen in association with chronic hypertension is due to rupture of miliary microaneurysms on the small arteries of the striate system. Patients are usually men in middle age. Intracerebral haemorrhage may also occur in patients with acute hypertension (e.g. malignant hypertension, acute nephritis, drug-induced hypertension, porphyria, toxaemia of pregnancy) and in these cases probably results from fibrinoid necrosis. Other causes of spontaneous intracerebral haemorrhage, excluding haemorrhage into tumour, are developmental defects of the arteries (arteriovenous malformation, berry aneurysm, Marfan syndrome, pseudoxanthoma elasticum, Ehlers–Danlos syndrome) or acquired arterial lesions such as polyarteritis nodosa, or mycotic aneurysm. Multiple haemorrhagic lesions may occur in blood disorders such as leukaemia or thrombocytopenic purpura, or during anticoagulant treatment.

CLINICAL FEATURES

The relatively sudden development of a focal neurological deficit within the territory of one of the cerebral arteries constitutes the stroke syndrome. A rapid increase in signs over a period of minutes, hours or rarely days, is followed, if the patient survives, by a period of stabilization and then of recovery, marking the process as vascular in nature. Strokes with a prolonged onset usually progress in a fluctuating, saltatory or intermittent fashion rather than gradually. In many cases it is possible to decide on clinical grounds into which of the three main pathological groups, thrombosis, embolism or haemorrhage, the patient falls. In other cases, especially where the deficit is mild, or the history inadequate, a clinical distinction may be impossible.

Cerebral Thrombosis

A few general principles are useful in arriving at a clinical diagnosis when taken in conjunction with the patient's age, vascular state and predisposing factors:

(i) The single and most reliable feature is a history of repetitive minor ischaemic episodes in the same vascular territory. These are much less common in cerebral embolism, and are rare in haemorrhage.

(ii) The focal deficit develops in a step-wise or intermittent fashion usually over some hours or longer. Rapid resolution of the symptoms may take place, especially in the early stages. The onset of a stroke during a period of hypotension, reduced cardiac output, cardiac failure, pulmonary embolism, sleep or dehydration is suggestive of infarction.

(iii) The occurrence of a second stroke in the site of a previous hemiplegia is suggestive of infarction rather than haemorrhage.

(iv) Consciousness is usually preserved at the onset of the stroke and headache is not prominent (except in some cases of carotid or vertebral artery occlusion). Frank epileptic seizures are uncommon though focal twitching may be noticed by the patient.

(v) Certain groups of signs are highly characteristic of cerebral thrombosis since they are limited to the vascular territory of a single branch artery. Such groups are the lateral medullary syndrome (occlusion of posterior inferior cerebellar artery or vertebral artery), monoplegia or isolated aphasia without hemiparesis (a cortical branch of middle cerebral artery), pure

motor or sensory hemiparesis (lacunar infarction in the striate system), dysarthria with clumsiness of the upper limb, unilateral internuclear ophthalmoplegia (lacunar infarction in the pons), complete homonymous hemianopia (calcarine branch of the posterior cerebral artery).

(vi) Absence of a carotid or brachial pulse suggests thrombosis, though haemorrhage may occasionally occur beyond a carotid occlusion.

Carotid Thrombosis

Thrombosis of the main trunk of the carotid artery exhibits some clinical features not found in occlusions of the intracerebral vessels. Occlusion of the common carotid or brachiocephalic artery may be detected by the absence of pulsation in the neck and arms and by a delay in superficial temporal pulse. Internal carotid occlusion cannot be detected by palpation with any certainty but increased prominence of temporal or facial branches of the external carotid artery may be seen on the side of the occlusion. A localized systolic bruit over the carotid bifurcation usually signifies internal carotid artery stenosis and the sudden disappearance of such a bruit may indicate occlusion. An identical murmur may, however, be found in cases of complete carotid occlusion presumably due to diversion of blood through the external carotid, which may itself show atheromatous narrowing. Internal carotid stenosis, especially if mild or if almost complete, may exist without any murmur. In some cases failure of the cardiac sounds to be conducted up one carotid may suggest a proximal occlusion. The natural history of strokes due to carotid disease often consists in a number of transient ischaemic attacks, usually in the middle cerebral territory, and probably due to embolism. Transient attacks in middle and anterior cerebral artery territories on the same side are suggestive of carotid disease and if attacks also involve the eye carotid disease is virtually certain. Some cases of carotid thrombosis exhibit an ingravescent stroke-in-evolution extending over some days. This may be due to gradual propagation of the thrombus into the origins of the middle and anterior cerebral arteries.

Ocular Signs in Carotid Disease

The occurrence of repeated attacks of uniocular visual loss is a feature in many cases of carotid atheroma. In the majority the carotid artery is narrowed rather than blocked and the attacks are due to embolism. Although transient ischaemia may affect hemisphere and retina they are rarely involved simultaneously. Permanent loss of vision is not common since even if the origin of the ophthalmic artery is occluded, blood supply to the globe is maintained by collateral flow from external carotid branches. Only when propagated thrombus extends into the branches of the ophthalmic artery does severe ischaemia of the retina occur.

Ocular bruits may occasionally be heard over the contralateral or ipsilateral eye in cases of internal carotid occlusion and are presumed to originate from large collateral arteries or from stenosis in the carotid siphon.

A partial Horner's syndrome (miosis and ptosis, but no change in sweating) is an occasional feature of acute thrombosis of the internal carotid, due to interruption of the blood supply to the sympathetic plexus surrounding the artery. When occlusion begins at the distal end of the internal carotid, an oculomotor nerve palsy may be an early feature.

There is recent interest in chronic ocular ischaemia in multiple extracranial artery occlusion. Patients with bilateral common carotid occlusion may experience transient amaurosis of one or both eyes on exercise or during minor degrees of postural hypotension. In the early stages venous dilatation, peripheral microaneurysms and soft exudates may be seen in the retina and the central retinal artery collapses with slight digital pressure on the globe (low pressure retinopathy). At a later stage a prominent circular arteriovenous anastomosis develops around the disc and vision becomes permanently impaired due to widespread retinal haemorrhage. Finally episcleral venous enlargement, neovascularization of the iris, cataract formation and thrombotic glaucoma may occur. A similar situation exists in caroticocavernous fistula when arterial pressure in the ophthalmic artery is reduced while venous pressure in the ophthalmic veins is raised. The perfusion pressure across retinal capillaries is reduced resulting in an ischaemic retinopathy with widespread haemorrhage and peripheral microaneurysms.

Cerebral Embolism

The sudden appearance of a stroke in a young patient is always suggestive of cardiac embolism, especially if a valvular lesion is present and if the patient is normotensive and free from arterial disease. A clear cut distinction from cerebral thrombosis is often impossible since portions of mural thrombus may become detached as emboli during the process of arterial occlusion. A number of clinical features are useful in diagnosis:

(i) The evolution of the neurological deficit is extremely rapid with none of the fluctuating or step-wise features of thrombosis. The onset is often during normal activity and a history of many transient attacks in the same territory is not commonly obtained. Short-lived headache is sometimes a feature, possibly due to arrest of the embolus at the carotid bifurcation.

(ii) Short-lived focal or generalized seizures may occur as the initial event. Preservation of full consciousness with a severe hemiplegia is suggestive of embolism. Rapid recovery over 24 hr. from an apparently severe stroke is not uncommon and forms an important point of distinction from intracerebral haematoma. The middle cerebral artery territory is much the commonest site for embolism.

(iii) The most commonly overlooked lesion in the heart is a silent or atypical myocardial infarction. An ECG examination should be routine practice. Evidence of previous or pre-existing systemic emboli to mesenteric renal, splenic, or limb arteries strongly favours embolism.

Cerebral Haemorrhage

Although cerebral haemorrhage in general carries a higher mortality and morbidity than infarction, pathological studies show that haemorrhage frequently arrests spontaneously, extravasated blood being then absorbed leaving a small trabeculated cavity. Cerebral haemorrhage should thus be considered in the differential diagnosis of even minor cerebrovascular events.

(1) Elevated blood pressure is found in the majority of patients on admission. The level of pressure often shows some decrease in the following days from an initially high level but signs of chronic hypertension are usually evident in heart and retina. Cerebral haemorrhage does not usually cause death within a few minutes except where haemorrhage occurs in the pons or unless there is a massive extension into the ventricles. The temporal profile of a haemorrhagic stroke is of progressive worsening over a few hours. Initially the neural deficit may be slight and localized to one limb and the patient may be fully alert and ambulant. Steady increase in the degree and extent of paralysis is accompanied by a corresponding decline in the level of consciousness. Vomiting and headache, the latter sometimes localized to the side of the haematoma is usual but not invariable.

(2) In contrast to cerebral thrombosis the occurrence of minor prodromes in the days preceding the stroke is exceptional. A diurnal onset during activity is the rule and is sometimes directly related to episodes of elevated systemic blood pressure, produced for example by straining, emotional stress or sexual intercourse. An onset during sleep is unusual except in patients on hypotensive drugs, when recumbency may produce dangerous hypertension. The occurrence of epileptic seizures or vomiting and the presence of neck stiffness at the early stages of a stroke favours cerebral haemorrhage rather than infarction. Fresh retinal or preretinal haemorrhages suggests subarachnoid or intracerebral bleeding.

(3) Whereas recurrence of haemorrhage is common in subarachnoid bleeding from aneurysm, re-bleeding is rare in intracerebral haemorrhage. Should the bleeding stop spontaneously the degree of recovery may be remarkably complete. Continuing coma or secondary worsening after a few days with or without the development of papilloedema and in the presence of an accessible haematoma is an indication for surgical treatment.

Localizing Signs in Cerebral Haemorrhage

Haemorrhage occurs in certain well-defined sites, namely internal capsule, cerebellum, subcortical white matter and pons. The last is usually rapidly fatal but in other sites early clinical diagnosis has an important bearing on treatment and prognosis. Capsular haemorrhage is usually designated as lateral ganglionic (putaminal) or medial ganglionic (thalamic).

Putaminal haemorrhage produces a flaccid hemiplegia, hemianaesthesia and hemianopia developing over some hours. Conjugate eye movements are usually absent towards the hemiplegic side. Early hemisphere swelling with distortion of the brain stem is indicated by an enlarged fixed pupil on the ipsilateral side, often with abduction of the eye or with failure of full movement on passive head rotation and by bilateral extensor plantar responses. Cheyne–Stokes respiration, bilateral fixed pupils, loss of pharyngeal reflexes, hyperpyrexia, decerebrate posturing on painful stimulation foreshadow a fatal conclusion.

Thalamic haemorrhage is often less extensive than in the putamen and evidence of old small haemorrhages may be found at autopsy. Headache and evidence of leakage of blood into the cerebrospinal fluid is usually present. Ocular signs are highly characteristic of haemorrhage in this area due to extension of the haematoma downwards into the upper mid brain. Voluntary and reflex vertical eye movements may be lost with pupils constricted and unreactive. At rest the eyes are convergent and depressed and may show skew deviation. Involvement of the thalamic nuclei is shown by marked hemianalgesia or mild hemiparesis. Dysphasia may occur if the lesion is on the dominant side. Surgical evacuation of the haematoma is impossible since it is deeply placed in the hemisphere. In non-fatal cases recovery may be considerable although the thalamic syndrome and hemichorea are occasional sequels.

In **cerebellar haemorrhage** the haematoma produces a clinical state evolving over some hours and characterized by headache, vomiting, severe vertigo and falling. Ipsilateral hemiplegia may be detectable but there is often no marked paralysis. There is constantly a forced deviation of the eyes away from the lesion and paralysis of ipsilateral conjugate gaze. Vestibulo-ocular reflexes are lost, there is a progressive depression of consciousness and both plantar responses are extensor. Pupils are usually constricted.

Subcortical white matter. Bleeding in this site is normally in the occipital and parietal lobe and may extend for some distance in an antero-posterior direction, splitting but not destroying white matter. A complete homonymous hemianopia is the most prominent feature, accompanied by hemianaesthesia and mild hemiparesis, and often with confusion, spatial disorientation and dysphasia. Haemorrhage in this situation frequently arrests spontaneously and the superficial situation of the bleeding makes it particularly suitable for surgical evacuation.

TRANSIENT ISCHAEMIC ATTACKS

Transient ischaemic attacks are focal cerebrovascular episodes recovering within minutes or hours and tending to recur in a stereotyped fashion. They may be the prelude to a major stroke in the same vascular territory or may occur without further sequel. Since full clinical recovery occurs it is assumed that no structural damage to the nervous system has taken place although neuropathological examination in some cases of transient ischaemia has shown numbers of small areas of softening unsuspected during life. In general the shorter, milder and more stereotyped the attacks the less likely are they to result in structural damage.

Occlusive Attacks

Not all ischaemic attacks have the same aetiology; in some, occlusion or narrowing of a regional artery occurs during the attack and the symptoms cease when the normal lumen is restored. This category includes attacks resulting from embolism, from temporary compression of extracranial arteries during neck movements and possibly from temporary oedema.

Evidence from angiography, from direct observation of the retina and from pathological studies has shown that emboli do not necessarily produce a stable vascular occlusion but tend to fragment and become dislodged into smaller vessels, in some cases dissolving completely and restoring a normal circulation. The stability of emboli is determined by size and composition, the small recently formed fibrin platelet aggregates being rapidly dispersed while older organized thrombi or fragment of arterial wall or cardiac valve produce a permanent occlusion. The acceptance that many transient ischaemic attacks in the carotid territory are embolic has important practical application. Patients with transient ischaemia in the forebrain or retina should have a carotid arteriogram examined for local mural irregularities indicating atheromatous ulceration on which a mural thrombus may form. Such lesions do not necessarily result in stenosis. They most often occur in the carotid sinus and they may produce no bruit.

External Compression

Although it is known from pathological and radiological studies that in many elderly subjects rotation and extension of the neck may compromise the lumen of the vertebral arteries and occasionally of the carotid artery, it is relatively infrequent for attacks of cerebral ischaemia to be provoked by neck movements. The reason is presumably the adequate size of the remaining neck vessels and the free communication at the Circle of Willis. Cases of bilateral internal carotid artery occlusion lack these reserve channels and in this group rotation or extension of the head may provoke attacks of ischaemia in the vertebrobasilar circulation. Cases with marked inequality of the vertebral arteries may similarly experience ischaemia when the larger vessel is narrowed during neck movements. Occasionally arterial narrowing may take place at a single point and surgical removal of one osteophyte may be curative. More often narrowing takes place at a number of levels and limitation of neck movement by a collar is the only practical solution.

Disturbance of Homoeostasis

In the second variety of transient ischaemia the attacks are due to a regional breakdown in homoeostasis and not to any temporary change in vascular calibre. If a branch vessel is permanently occluded the territory around the occlusion may continue to receive an adequate blood supply through collateral channels although at a decreased perfusion pressure. This area is vulnerable to further fall in blood pressure since the limit of autoregulation will be reached earlier in this area than in surrounding normal brain. Transient ischaemia due to this mechanism is uncommon in clinical practice but may be encountered in patients with generalized extracranial artery disease. Attacks are usually brief, stereotyped and are commoner in the vertebrobasilar than in carotid territory. The onset is seldom as sudden as with embolism. A fall in systemic blood pressure due to defective baroceptor function or to cardiac dysrhythmia may accompany the attack.

Reactivity to the metabolic stimulus of CO_2 may be preserved even in presence of vascular disease, but in clinical practice respiratory disorders with elevated $PaCO_2$ are associated with generalized rather than localized cerebral effects. However vasodilatation in extracerebral tissues in the presence of extracranial vascular disease may lead to redistribution of blood between the vascular beds at the expense of blood flow to the brain (steal syndrome). This mechanism operates in the vertebrobasilar system in some cases of subclavian occlusion when a temporary increase in blood flow to the arm via the vertebral artery may coincide with hind brain ischaemia. Other cases show vertebral reflux but no cerebral symptoms presumably due to compensatory increase in flow up the remaining vertebral artery. Since atheromatous narrowing or occlusion commonly involves more than one artery and since there are a number of possible communications between external carotid branches and branches of the vertebral or thyrocervical arteries a variety of routes of collateral blood have been described, e.g. between vertebral and external carotid in occipital muscles, between two external carotids by superior thyroid branches. In such cases there may be reversal of blood flow in the vertebral or carotid arteries. A distinction should be drawn between such collateral arrangements and the steal syndrome; the latter term should be reserved for cases showing evidence of intermittent ischaemia in distal cerebral vascular beds as a result of diversion of blood.

By a similar mechanism cases with proximal occlusion of the common carotid or innominate arteries may experience ischaemia of the forebrain or retina when external carotid flow is increased. An arteriovenous fistula in the carotid siphon may also present with intermittent ischaemic symptoms due to diversion of blood and in cerebral arteriovenous malformation many of the symptoms may be ischaemic in origin.

INVESTIGATIONS

While in many cases it is possible to distinguish the type of vascular lesion by clinical features alone, ancillary investigations are often necessary.

Lumbar Puncture

This is advisable in the majority of cases. Red cells and xanthochromia are important evidence of intracerebral haemorrhage or subdural haematoma. Encapsulated haemorrhage may show no change in CSF or exceptionally a leucocyte reaction. A rise in cells and protein (up to 100 cells/cm. mm. and up to 500 mg. per cent protein) may occur in severe cases of infarction, although the CSF is usually normal. Vascular occlusion secondary to chronic meningeal inflammation (e.g. syphilis), may be missed if the CSF is not examined. Although embolic infarction is often haemorrhagic in type, the presence of blood in the CSF is exceptional.

Arteriography

There is little place for carotid arteriography in the early stages of a completed occlusive stroke, except as a confirmation of the diagnosis and to exclude other lesions, especially metastases. Even as a confirmatory investigation it is unreliable since in 50 per cent no vascular occlusion is found. The fact that many arteriograms are normal is probably due to fragmentation of emboli. In addition a deterioration in the clinical condition of the patient is frequently seen after arteriography at this stage; this is usually temporary.

In cerebral haemorrhage arteriography may be valuable in excluding ruptured berry aneurysm and in showing the extent and location of a haematoma. It should only be performed, however, on patients in whom surgery is being considered, i.e. patients with hemispheric haematoma whose condition has stabilized after the initial haemorrhage.

In suspected cerebellar haemorrhage, early carotid arteriography is indicated to detect ventricular enlargement, since early surgical intervention has been shown to be effective.

In patients who have experienced one or more minor strokes or transient ischaemic attacks in the same carotid territory, and with clinical evidence of neck vessel disease, absent pulsation or bruit, arteriography is indicated provided the general state of the patient is fit for arterial surgery.

Carotid arteriography is also justified in patients in this category with no carotid bruit, although the abnormalities which are discovered are often multiple and intracranial and not amenable to surgical treatment.

Arteriography is indicated in cerebral embolism only in the very early stages when it is suspected that a large embolus has impacted at the carotid bifurcation.

Ophthalmodynamometry

This relatively crude technique gives an estimation of ophthalmic artery pressure. Blood pressure and intra-ocular pressure must be taken into account when evaluating results and small differences between two sides should be interpreted with caution. Significant reduction, especially in systolic readings, is found on the affected side in most cases of carotid occlusion and of severe stenosis. A normal result does not, however, exclude an obstructive lesion, since an efficient anastomosis between branches of the facial and ophthalmic arteries in the orbit develops rapidly. Prolongation of the arm-retina circulation time may be found on the side of an occluded carotid, but is usually normal in the case of carotid stenosis. Oscillometric tests on the orbit may also show decrease in the amplitude of pulsation on the side of carotid occlusion.

Ultrasound

Echoencephalography is a useful diagnostic screening test in obtunded or severely ill patients suspected of harbouring an intracerebral or extracerebral haematoma, when displacement of midline structures may be detected. It has the great asset of being non-traumatic and repeated measurement may aid the evaluation of treatment. Dilatation of the lateral ventricles as a result of cerebellar haemorrhage may also be detected in some cases.

Significant displacement (more than 3 mm.) within a few hours of onset is strong evidence for intracranial haematoma. Displacement developing after 24 hr. may be due to cerebral oedema consequent on infarction.

Radioactive Brain Scan

Conventional brain scanning (see Ch. IX: 5) shows an increased uptake of isotope in many cases of cerebral infarction. The percentage of positive scans is greatest (about 75 per cent of cases) in the second and third week after onset and decreases thereafter until by 12 weeks the great majority have returned to normal. In the first week only about 25 per cent of cases show increased uptake and a positive scan at this time should suggest the possibility of a cerebral tumour presenting as a stroke.

The infarction must be moderately large to be detectable and must be situated in the hemisphere within the distribution of the three main cerebral arteries. Brain stem or cerebellar infarctions are not detectable. Cases with transient ischaemia and those with small strokes recovering rapidly also give negative results. A positive result early in such a case should suggest a cerebral tumour. Positive brain scans may also occur in intracerebral or subdural haematoma and arteriovenous malformation.

EEG

A single electroencephalogram is of little value in the diagnosis of cerebrovascular disease, but repeated records are more informative. There is a poor correlation between clinical deficit and EEG abnormality but in general the EEG reflects the site and extent of cerebral damage rather than its pathological basis.

Lower brain stem ischaemia and small lesions in all areas are usually associated with normal records. Involvement of the upper brain stem reticular formation either directly or as a result of brain swelling or haematoma, produces bilateral synchronous slow activity, with maximal amplitude in frontal areas. Focal abnormalities are often obscured.

In cerebral infarction without loss of consciousness, focal slow activity (delta or theta range) is usually found within a few hours of the stroke. Foci resolve slowly over about 4 weeks, depending on the extent of injury. Diminution of alpha rhythm may persist. Cortical infarction results in more prominent slow activity than subcortical, and thalamic lesions may produce diffuse unilateral slow activity.

Rapid resolution of a marked slow wave focus is evidence for a vascular lesion rather than a neoplasm. In general the more normal the record the better the prognosis but in the later stages the persistence of marked clinical deficit with a normal EEG is an unfavourable sign. While slow activity persists the possibility of clinical improvement remains.

PREVENTATIVE TREATMENT

Anticoagulant Treatment

Controlled trials of anticoagulant treatment using prothrombin antagonists have been carried out in four main groups of occlusive vascular disease: completed stroke, transient ischaemic attacks, progressing stroke and cerebral embolism.

There are many differences between the various studies in regard to the number of patients, criteria of diagnosis, length and type of follow-up, and quality of control.

Completed Stroke

The majority of investigators studying the effect of anticoagulants on recurrence of infarction in patients suffering a cerebral infarct have shown no benefit in the treated group (Hill, Marshall and Shaw, 1962; Baker, Schwartz and Rose, 1966). In these two studies the treated group had more infarcts in the follow-up period and the incidence of cerebral haemorrhage was also greater. In other trials (McDowell and McDevitt, 1965) the treated group appeared to show fewer infarcts, though the risk of haemorrhage was again evident. Conclusions from published reports are that following a completed stroke anticoagulants are contraindicated in the presence of hypertension; if there is any doubt about the diagnosis of cerebral infarction; or if there is impaired renal or hepatic function or peptic ulceration. In other patients, anticoagulant treatment if precisely controlled may offer a small beneficial effect in preventing further infarction but this scarcely outweighs the risks of treatment.

Transient Ischaemic Attacks

Many independent studies have shown anticoagulants to be effective in reducing substantially the number of transient ischaemic attacks. The number of patients subsequently developing cerebral infarction is also reduced, although the incidence of death is much the same in the two groups due to the increased number of fatal cerebral haemorrhages in the treated group.

The length of time for which treatment is necessary has not been determined, but the benefit is not merely in the short term, being apparent for at least 3 years after initiation of treatment.

Progressive Stroke

This group comprises patients showing increasing neurological deficit while under observation. The group is a heterogeneous one, and the diagnosis of ischaemic vascular disease is often in doubt. Evaluation of the published reports is difficult and numbers are small. Most workers conclude that twice as many patients in the control group show continued deterioration as in the treated group, and anticoagulants (heparin followed by warfarin) improve the immediate prognosis in such patients. Duration of treatment is usually a few weeks.

Cerebral Embolism

Cerebral embolism arising from a cardiac source should be treated by anticoagulation, since this has been shown to produce a substantial reduction in the risks of subsequent emboli. (Carter, 1957; McDevitt, 1961.) In cardiac emboli recurrence is particularly likely in the first few days and anticoagulants should be administered as soon as possible after diagnosis in spite of the risks of haemorrhage into a recent ischaemic infarct.

In patients with mitral stenosis and atrial fibrillation, anticoagulants are to be continued indefinitely unless both valvular lesion and dysrhythmia are corrected. In embolism following myocardial infarction, anticoagulants should be continued for about 6 weeks and slowly discontinued. Anticoagulants are contraindicated in bacterial endocarditis because of the risks of intracerebral haemorrhage.

Fibrinolytic Treatment

In vivo fibrinolysis is mediated by plasmin, the proteolytic enzyme derived from an inactive precursor plasminogen by the action of specific activators. Activators can be extracted from almost all tissues; usually plasma contains very low levels but increased amounts occur after exercise, various drugs (e.g. adrenalin) and in disease states. The activator extractable from urine (urokinase) has been prepared in a pure form.

Plasmin has little substrate specificity but the potentially harmful effects of widespread release of proteolytic enzymes are controlled by the existence of plasminogen in both soluble and gel phase, the latter being found in fibrin thrombi. Widespread activation of soluble plasminogen is prevented by inhibitors, except in the vicinity of thrombi where gel phase plasminogen (which is more susceptible to activation) is converted to plasmin. Activators for clinical use should thus have an affinity for gel phase plasminogen. Thrombolytic agents employed clinically to date have various actions:

Long-term increase in plasma thrombolytic activity has been produced by phenformin-oestradial combination with the object of preventing or limiting fibrin formation. No conclusive beneficial results in patients with thromboembolic disease are yet available. Drugs mediating short-term release of endogenous plasminogen activator are too toxic for clinical use.

Intravenous injection of a purified fraction of Malayan pitviper venom (Arvin) an enzyme resembling thrombin, produces virtual defibrination but with relatively few haemorrhagic complications. It is thought that endogenous fibrinolytic activity is increased although this has been difficult to demonstrate *in vitro*. Promising clinical results have been reported in venous thromboembolism but not so far in cerebral vascular disease.

Streptokinase is a potent activator of plasminogen but has proved unsuitable for overall clinical use because of antigenicity and haemorrhagic complications. The latter are particularly serious in the brain. Urokinase is non-antigenic, more predictable in action and causes only minor upset of coagulation mechanism. It has been shown to promote lysis of fresh pulmonary emboli and its action on cerebral arterial occlusions is at present under investigation. It has the advantage of acting at multiple sites wherever fibrin formation is occurring and may be especially suitable for patients with widespread arterial disease. Its disadvantages are its high cost and the need for intravenous administration.

Treatment of Hypertension

Reduction of blood pressure in patients with overt cerebral vascular disease has been discouraged in the past on the supposition that the blood flow to the damaged area of brain would be further compromised by reducing perfusion pressure. This consideration is valid shortly after infarction or transient ischaemia, or cerebral haemorrhage, when it has been shown a localized area of brain has lost autoregulation and when pressure levels are unstable. After this phase has passed the cerebral arteries of hypertensive patients regain reactivity (albeit reduced). Reduction of blood pressure in hypertensive patients following a completed stroke has been shown to lessen the incidence of further strokes (Carter, 1970). Although episodes of systemic hypotension may occur in hypertensive patients under treatment, they rarely lead to cerebral infarction.

There is evidence that segmental arteriolar (microaneurysmal) change the pathological lesion underlying both spontaneous haemorrhage and lacunar infarction, is strongly associated with chronic hypertension. Recent lesions may be found in the brain after many years of raised blood pressure. The benefit of hypotensive therapy is probably due to prevention of further lesions of this type, with healing or thrombosis of existing microaneurysms.

General Measures

There are a number of factors known to be associated with arterial disease or thrombosis, which should be treated although it has not so far been proved that a beneficial effect ensues in a patient already affected by a stroke. The most important of these are diabetes, some types of hyperlipidaemia, anaemia, polycythaemia, heavy cigarette smoking and oral contraceptive medication. Other more general measures of even less certain efficacy are reduction in hours of work, regular modest exercise, and the treatment of superadded affective disorder.

FURTHER READING

Achar, V. S., Coe, R. P. K. and Marshall, J. (1966), "Echoencephalography in the Differential Diagnosis of Cerebral Haemorrhage and Infarction," *Lancet*, **1**, 161–164.

Aring, C. D. and Merritt, H. H. (1935), "Differential Diagnosis Between Cerebral Haemorrhage and Cerebral Thrombosis," *Arch. intern. Med.*, **56**, 435–456.

Baker, R. N., Schwartz, W. S. and Rose, A. S. (1966), "Transient Ischaemic Attacks, Report of a Study of Anticoagulant Treatment," *Neurology* (*Minneapolis*), **16**, 841–847.

Bull, J. W. D., Marshall, J. and Shaw, D. A. (1960), "Cerebral Angiography in the Diagnosis of the Acute Stroke," *Lancet*, **1**, 562–565.

Carter, A. B. (1957), "The Immediate Treatment of Cerebral Embolism," *Quart. J. Med.*, **26**, 335–348.

Carter, A. B. (1970), "Hypotensive Therapy in Stroke Survivors," *Lancet*, **1**, 485–489.

Cole, F. M. and Yates, P. O. (1967), "The Occurrence and Significance of Intracerebral Microaneurysms," *J. Path. Bact.*, **93**, 393–411.

Daley, R., Mattingly, T. W., Holt, C. L., Bland, E. F. and White, P. D (1951), "Systemic Arterial Embolism in Rheumatic Heart Disease," *Amer. Heart J.*, **42**, 566–581.

Denny-Brown, D. (1960), "Recurrent Cerebrovascular Episodes," *Arch. Neurol. (Chicago)*, **2**, 194–210.

Dimant, S., Moxon, C. T. and Lewtas, N. Z. (1956), "Cerebral Angiography in a Neurosurgical Service," *British med. J.*, **2**, 10–16.

Fisher, C. M. (1954), "Occlusion of the Carotid Arteries," American Medical Association, *Arch. Neurol. Psychiat.*, **72**, 187–204.

Fisher, C. M. (1961), "Clinical Syndromes in Cerebral Arterial Occlusion," in *Pathogenesis and Treatment of Cerebrovascular Disease*, pp. 151–177 (W. S. Fields, Ed.). Springfield: Thomas.

Gunning, A. J., Pickering, G. W., Robb-Smith, A. H. T. and Russell, R. W. R. (1964), "Mural Thrombosis of the Internal Carotid Artery and Subsequent Embolism," *Quart. J. Med.*, **33**, 155–195.

Hill, A. B., Marshall, J. and Shaw, D. A. (1962), "Cerebrovascular Disease: Trial of Long Term Anticoagulant Therapy," *Brit. med. J.*, **2**, 1003–1006.

Fletcher, A. P. (1970), "Current Status of Thrombolytic Agents," pp. 148–157 in *Cerebrovascular Survey Report* (Revised) (R. G. Siekert, Ed.). Minnesota: Whiting, Rochester.

Kiloh, L. G. and Osselton, J. W. (1966), *Clinical Encephalography*, 2nd edition. London: Butterworths.

McDevitt, E. (1961), in *Cerebral Vascular Disease* (C. H. Millikan, Ed.). New York: Grune-Stratton.

McDowell, F. and McDevitt, E. (1965), "Treatment of Completed Stroke with Long Term Anticoagulants," in *Transactions of the 4th Princeton Conference*, pp. 185–199 (R. G. Siekert and J. P. Whisnant, Eds.). New York: Grune-Stratton.

McKissock, W., Richardson, A. and Walsh, L. S. (1960), "Spontaneous Cerebellar Haemorrhage," *Brain*, **83**, 1–9.

McKissock, W., Richardson, A. and Walsh, L. S. (1961), "Primary Intracerebral Haemorrhage, a Controlled Trial of Surgical and Conservative Treatment in 180 Unselected Cases," *Lancet*, **2**, 221–226.

Marshall, J. and Popham, M. G. (1970), "Radioactive Brain Scanning in the Management of Cerebrovascular Disease," *J. Neurol., Neurosurg. Psychiat.*, **33**, 201–4.

Meyer, J. S. and Denny-Brown, D. (1957), "The Cerebral Collateral Circulation," *Neurology (Minneapolis)*, **7**, 447–458.

Millikan, C. (1970), "Anticoagulant Treatment in Cerebrovascular Disease," in *Cerebrovascular Survey Report* (Revised) (R. G. Siekert, Ed.). Minnesota, U.S.A.: Whiting, Rochester.

Mitchell, J. R. A. and Schwartz, C. J. (1965), *Arterial Disease*. Oxford: Blackwell.

Morax, P. V., Aron-Rosa, D. and Gautier, J. C. (1970), *Bulletin des Societes d'ophtalmologie de France, Rapport annuel.*

Rhoton, A. L., Klinterfuss, G. H., Lilly, D. R. and Ter Pogossian, M. M. (1966), "Brain Scanning in Ischaemic Cerebrovascular Disease," *Archives Neurol.*, **14**, 506–511.

Romanul, F. C. A. and Abramowicz, A. (1964), "Changes in Brain and Pial Vessels in Arterial Border Zones," *Arch. Neurol. Psychiat. (Chicago)*, **11**, 40–65.

Russell, R. W. R. (1963), "Observations on Intracerebral Aneurysms," *Brain*, **86**, 425–442.

Russell, R. W. R. (1970), "The Origin and Effects of Cerebral Emboli," in *Modern Trends in Neurology* 5 (D. Williams, Ed.). London: Butterworths.

Sheehan, S., Bauer, R. B. and Meyer, J. S. (1960), "Vertebral Artery Compression in Cervical Spondylosis," *Neurology (Minneapolis)*, **10**, 968–986.

Toole, J. F. (1964), "Reversed Vertebral Artery Flow, Subclavian Steal Syndrome," *Lancet*, **1**, 872–873.

4. HYPERBARIC OXYGEN

IAIN McA. LEDINGHAM

The fact that cellular hypoxia is the final common pathway of many pathological processes accounts for the continued pursuit of methods to prevent its appearance or diminish its severity. One technique which has been subjected to scrutiny during the past decade is hyperbaric oxygenation, i.e. the administration of oxygen at pressures greater than atmospheric but not usually exceeding 3 atmospheres absolute (ATA).

Soon after its introduction into clinical medicine, however, the limitations of hyperbaric oxygenation became obvious and it is perhaps appropriate to place these in perspective at the outset of this brief review. Oxygen toxicity[4,12] was and is likely to remain the greatest obstacle to the clinical exploration of pressures greater than 3 ATA and even at lesser pressures a definite restriction to the duration of safe exposure to hyperbaric oxygen has emerged.[7,37] Oxygen toxicity must not be regarded, however, as a wholly disadvantageous phenomenon since its controlled application forms the basis of the use of hyperbaric oxygen as an antibiotic.[41] Less well known but to the clinician scarcely less disconcerting than oxygen toxicity was the vasoconstrictive influence of hyperbaric oxygen particularly with its use in regional ischaemia.[30] In a few clinical circumstances this vasoconstrictive influence is an advantageous feature e.g. in reducing raised intracranial pressure.[26]

Undoubtedly one of the limitations of hyperbaric oxygen which has prevented the more widespread clinical investigation of the method has been the cost, physical bulk and inconvenience of the facilities required to deliver oxygen under hyperbaric conditions. These take the form either of a one-man pressure vessel in which only the patient is exposed to increased pressure or a large walk-in pressure vessel which contains both patient and attendant staff.[22]

Oxygen Transport and the Vascular Effects of Hyperbaric Oxygen

At a pressure of 3 ATA arterial oxygen content is increased above normal by about one third (6–7 ml. of O_2/100 ml. blood), the greater part of which is in the form of dissolved oxygen in the plasma (resulting in an increase in arterial oxygen tension to 2,000 mm. Hg.). In spite of this substantial increase in arterial oxygen tension mechanisms exist which maintain tissue oxygen tension at near normal values. Of these mechanisms, regional vasoconstriction is the most important although cardiac output is also significantly reduced. In the intact organism the mechanism of vasoconstriction is complex. In the brain, for example, the vessels appear able to constrict in response both to a primary increase in arterial oxygen tension[15] and to a secondary fall in arterial carbon dioxide tension resulting from hyperventilation.[19] Furthermore, under certain conditions the cerebral vessels may actually dilate in the presence of hyperbaric oxygen. These conditions are encountered when the arterial carbon dioxide tension is held constant and the increase in arterial oxygen tension is of such a magnitude as to completely saturate cerebral venous blood with oxygen (Fig. 1). An increase in cerebral tissue carbon

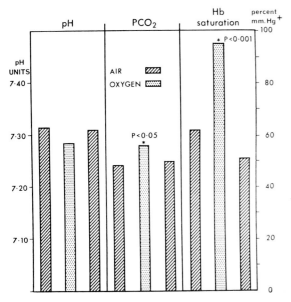

FIG. 1. Changes in sagittal sinus pH, carbon dioxide tension and haemoglobin oxygen saturation with oxygen breathing at 3 ATA in dogs. Because of complete saturation of the venous haemoglobin with oxygen at 3 ATA, the carbon dioxide tension increased significantly, with a corresponding decrease in pH.

dioxide tension consequent on diminished carbon dioxide transport is assumed to be the factor responsible for the resultant vasodilatation. Within the brain considerable fluctuations in regional blood flow have been shown to occur[20] and the coincidence of these regional flow changes and fluctuations in local tissue oxygen tension may be related to the onset of convulsions which are one of the features of oxygen toxicity.

Although reduced blood flow tends to negate the effect of raised arterial oxygen tension, in most instances a small net gain of oxygen to the tissues occurs. One possible

exception may be the retina. Dogs exposed to oxygen at 3 ATA for single exposure of up to 4 hr. develop retinal microinfarcts.[25] The likelihood that ischaemia rather than a direct toxic action of oxygen is responsible for these lesions is indicated by the fact that the simultaneous administration of carbon dioxide protects the retina from this adverse effect of hyperbaric oxygen.

The extent to which the vascular effects of hyperbaric oxygen may be modified by ischaemia and hypotension is not clear but vasoconstriction in the brain and heart can be overcome by increased carbon dioxide tension and in the periphery by certain pharmacological preparations.

Oxygen Toxicity

All living tissue deteriorates when exposed to excessive pressure of oxygen. The rate at which this deterioration occurs is dependent on many factors, the two principal of which are the absolute pressure of oxygen and the duration of exposure.

At pressures in excess of 2·5 ATA (1,900 mm. Hg.) oxygen toxicity in intact animals predominantly affects the central nervous system and commonly presents in two forms—*grand mal* convulsions (the onset of which may occur within a few minutes of oxygen breathing) and persistent paralysis. In man hyperoxic convulsions do not lead to long term neurological *sequelae*.[10] Persistent paralysis occurs after repeated brief exposure to hyperbaric oxygen and in the rat necrotic lesions of the globus pallidus, substantia nigra and anteromedial horn cells of the spinal cord have been described.[2] The distribution and histological appearances of these lesions are unlike those of ischaemia or hypoxia.

Certain anaesthetic agents (e.g. pentobarbitone) can effectively eliminate hyperoxic convulsions but paradoxically increase the susceptibility to persistent paralysis. A reduction in cerebral metabolic rate seems a likely explanation for the anticonvulsant effect of the barbiturates but this hypothesis has been weakened by the observation that some other agents which are equally effective in reducing metabolic rate, do not prevent convulsions.[12] Persistent paralysis has not been recorded in man.

Ever since oxygen was incriminated as the primary causative factor in retrolental fibroplasia of new born infants the eye has been a source of interest to those concerned with oxygen toxicity. Additional pathological changes which have been described[27] include visual cell death, retinal detachment and microinfarct (cytoid-body formation). In man bilateral contraction of the peripheral visual fields occurs after a minimum of 3 hr. of oxygen breathing at 3 ATA and recovers quickly on resumption of air breathing. Individual susceptibility to optic oxygen toxicity has been described in man particularly when a history of ophthalmic disease exists.

At pressures below 2·5 ATA the brain and central nervous system are less obviously affected. This zone of hyperbaric pressure, however, may hold greater dangers for the clinician than the higher pressure range where signs of oxygen toxicity are more dramatic. Exposure to lower pressures of oxygen leads to changes predominantly in the lungs.[7,18,38] The process is insidious, ill-defined and, after a particular time interval, irreversible. The outcome may vary from death in a few hours or days if oxygen administration is continuous, to non-fatal pulmonary changes (mainly affecting the vessels) if oxygen administration is intermittent. Man exhibits a similar response to hyperoxia to that of most other mammals in that respiratory distress begins to occur within about 5 hr. of the onset of oxygen breathing at 2 ATA.[7,8] A fall in arterial oxygen tension occurs only late in pulmonary oxygen toxicity probably after the underlying changes have become irreversible. Information about the later stages of pulmonary oxygen toxicity in man is almost entirely lacking but in a recent prospective study[3] on patients with irreversible brain damage who were being ventilated with either air or 100 per cent oxygen at normal pressure, impairment of lung function was significantly worse in the oxygen group after 40 hr., the most sensitive indicator being an increase in the alveolar-arterial oxygen tension gradient.

Pulmonary oxygen toxicity may be modified by anesthesia,[5] intermittent positive pressure ventilation,[39] the presence of an inert gas,[33] hypoxaemia[40] and periodic respiration of air at normal pressure.[1]

At a cellular level little is known about the basic biochemical changes which occur during exposure to higher oxygen tension although the function of many enzyme and coenzyme systems is disrupted. Haugaard[12] in his review of the mechanisms of oxygen toxicity, indicates that only some of the metabolic-inhibiting effects of oxygen are likely to be important *in vivo*. Amongst these are the oxidation of SH-containing coenzymes, inactivation of iron- and SH-containing enzymes and flavoproteins, damage to cell membranes by lipid peroxidation and oxidation of such substances as glutathione and ascorbic acid. It is uncertain whether oxygen exerts its damaging effects by simple mass action or via the formation of free radicals.

PHYSIOPATHOLOGICAL STUDIES

In clinical practice hyperbaric oxygen has been put to a wide variety of uses, some more logical than others. The following physiopathological account does not purport to be comprehensive and is orientated towards topics of neurological interest with which the author has some familiarity.

Prevention of Cerebral Hypoxia

The ability, albeit limited, of the brain to store oxygen may be demonstrated in human volunteers subjected to temporary ocular circulatory occlusion. Visual blackout occurs in 12 sec. with oxygen at normal pressure and in 50 sec. with oxygen at 3 ATA.[29] In a study on dogs,[34] simultaneous occlusion of the carotid and vertebral arteries led to flattening of the cortical electroencephalogram within 1 min. during air breathing at normal pressure while no change was observed after similar vascular occlusion for up to 30 min. with oxygen at 2 ATA.

Hyperbaric oxygen obviously provided additional time for the development of adequate collateral circulation.

In patients undergoing internal carotid artery ligation, when cerebral blood flow is reduced by more than 25 per cent the likelihood of neurological damage is high. An increased arterial oxygen content might compensate, to some extent, for this reduction in flow and might maintain cerebral oxygenation above a critical level. In 17 patients, anaesthetized with trichlorethylene, undergoing carotid surgery in a pressure chamber at 2 ATA, cerebral blood flow did not fall significantly with oxygen (Table 1).

TABLE 1

HYPERBARIC CAROTID SURGERY SERIES
21 PAIRS OF OBSERVATION (MEAN ± S.E.)

	Air	OHP
Cerebral blood flow (ml./100 g./min.)	49·5 (±3·9)	47·4 (±4·7)
ΔA–V O$_2$ content (ml./100 ml.)	5·41 (±0·37)	4·72 (±0·37)
O$_2$ consumption (ml./100 g./min.)	2·54 (±0·18)	2·07 (±0·16)

The arterio-venous oxygen content difference fell and there was a small but statistically significant reduction in oxygen consumption which could not be attributed to changes in arterial carbon dioxide tension, mean arterial pressure and oesophageal temperature. The mean jugular venous oxygen tension rose from 36–56 mm. Hg. suggesting an improvement in cerebral oxygenation (Fig. 2). On the other hand, in spite of the absence of long term neurological *sequelae* in any of the patients, there was no objective evidence that hyperbaric oxygen *per se* was the factor which protected against the occurrence of post-operative neurological problems. One patient whose EEG flattened after 10 sec. of carotid clamping on air exhibited similar EEG changes after 15 sec. on oxygen. In a separate clinical study, Jacobson[14] and his colleagues observed a decrease in the amplitude of the left frontoparietal EEG after 1 min and 21 sec. during air ventilation and after 2 min. and 15 sec. with oxygen at 2 ATA.

The choice of anaesthetic agent in these procedures would appear to be important. Cerebral vasoconstriction consequent on halothane anaesthesia was thought to account for the fact that oxygen at 2 ATA conferred no protection on a series of dogs subjected to middle cerebral artery occlusion.[16] Trichlorethylene has less obvious effects on the cerebral circulation while chloroform produced a marked elevation of jugular venous oxygen tension in a clinical study on 2 patients breathing oxygen at 2 ATA.[24]

Several groups of workers investigating the practical feasibility of hyperbaric oxygen storage during cardiac surgery have not been impressed by the extra time made available to the surgeon during a period of total circulatory standstill. In addition, the combination of hyperbaric oxygen and hypothermia has not extended, to any remarkable degree, the period of safe circulatory arrest beyond that resulting from hypothermia alone. Although the disappointing nature of these results is conceded, it is nevertheless important not to underestimate the value of even 2 or 3 min. of added time during a period of circulatory arrest. It is partly on this basis that Bernhard et al.[6]

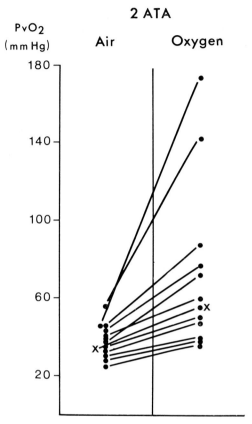

FIG. 2. Jugular venous oxygen tension (PVO$_2$) in 12 patients exposed to *air* and *oxygen* at 2 ATA prior to carotid endarterectomy. All PVO$_2$ values increased with oxygen.

have operated on patients with aortic and pulmonary stenosis with arterial oxygen tensions, at 3 and 4 ATA of 1,300–2,200 mm. Hg. A considerable weight of evidence also exists to suggest that following a period of circulatory standstill, cardiac resuscitation and defibrillation are more successfully achieved in an environment of oxygen at increased pressure.

Treatment of Cerebral Hypoxia

Extracranial or cerebral arterial occlusion leading to neurological deficit would be considered a suitable indication for hyperbaric oxygen therapy only if it were of recent onset, since permanent brain damage of brain tissue must inevitably result within a very short period of time. Heymen et al.[13] described the response of 22 patients treated with oxygen at 2–3 ATA for periods up to 5 hr. although the majority of exposures did not exceed 1 hr. Dramatic improvement in neurological function occurred in 4 patients, the improvement persisting in 2; in the other 2 the neurological deficit recurred a few hours after removal from the hyperbaric chamber and repeated brief

exposures to pressurized oxygen were associated with only temporary clinical improvement. In 6 other patients there was some evidence of clinical recovery immediately after onset of hyperbaric oxygenation but the neurological deficit returned during decompression. The remaining 12 patients did not improve in any way. The authors concluded that in some patients neuronal structures remained viable for some hours after loss of function in acute cerebral ischaemia. In such circumstances an increase in oxygen delivery might reverse cellular ischaemia and prevent death of tissue. During this study hyperbaric oxygen treatment was of short duration; longer exposure might have been successful in achieving more beneficial results although the ever present danger of oxygen toxicity has to be considered.

Elsewhere in this volume the effects of hyperbaric oxygen on cerebral oedema and raised intracranial pressure are discussed. In general, experimental observations indicate that hyperbaric oxygen exerts a beneficial influence in reducing raised intracranial pressure and increasing survival in animals subjected to cerebral trauma of various sorts. In patients, improvement in neurological signs is commonly observed but these effects are usually short lived and withdrawal of oxygen may be associated with worsening of the neurological deficit. Very few studies have been performed to determine the influence of hyperbaric oxygen on cerebral oedema following cardiac arrest. In a recent experimental study, all control animals subjected to a period of cerebral ischaemia died within 14 hr. All animals given oxygen at 3 ATA for 2–3 hr. after the ischaemic insult survived.

Air Embolism and Associated Conditions

The use of compressed air or oxygen in the treatment of air embolism and decompression sickness is logical since the size of a gas bubble in a vessel or in the tissues will diminish as the surrounding gaseous pressure increases.

Air embolism, a particularly tragic consequence of certain forms of thoracic surgery and of certain investigative procedures involving the injection of air, has been shown to respond well to hyperbaric oxygen in experimental animals. Lundgren and Thomson[23] demonstrated a close relationship between the level of increased pressure and the fluctuation of neurological signs in a patient suffering from cerebral air embolism treated with compressed air. In the treatment of decompression sickness, pressurized oxygen instead of air was recommended by Goodman[11] in 1964 to reduce the total barometric pressure required for such therapy. The risks to staff within the pressure vessel were thereby reduced and the efficiency of the treatment was little altered.

Generalized Hypoxaemia

Hypoxic hypoxaemia may arise from several causes and is usually relieved with oxygen at normal pressure either alone or with the addition of positive pressure ventilation. In only a few instances would oxygen at greater pressures be required and although there is no doubt that a low arterial oxygen can be corrected in this way, most patients requiring these high concentrations of oxygen have very severe underlying pulmonary pathological changes.

The danger of oxygen toxicity arises when high concentrations of oxygen even at normal atmospheric pressure are administered for prolonged periods of time. A compressed-air pressure vessel can be used to lower the concentration of oxygen. It is not known in clinical practice whether this procedure would diminish the danger of oxygen toxicity but the hypothesis is supported by some experimental evidence.[31]

Carbon Monoxide Poisoning

Carbon monoxide has an affinity for haemoglobin approximately 250 times greater than that of oxygen and also affects the dissociation of the remaining oxyhaemoglobin. Tissue death occurs as an indirect result of hypoxia rather than of any direct toxic action of the gas. Apart from its lethal effects, carbon monoxide poisoning is associated with prolonged, if not permanent, damage to several tissues of the body including the brain,[9] the peripheral nerves and the heart.[17] The muscle and skin changes which have been described may be attributed, in many instances, to a combination of hypoxia and local pressure ischaemia.

Two factors are of particular importance in the treatment of carbon monoxide poisoning—the partial pressure of oxygen in pulmonary capillaries and alveolar ventilation. Carbon monoxide metabolism is negligible in man and therefore the lungs offer the only pathway for excretion of the gas. Oxygen at 2–2·5 ATA is the optimal pressure for treatment in that the maximum rate of excretion of carbon monoxide is combined with freedom from acute cerebral oxygen toxicity. Tissue hypoxia is relieved almost as soon as this pressure of oxygen is breathed since oxygen requirements are largely met by oxygen dissolved in plasma without utilization of oxyhaemoglobin. Experimental evidence of the efficiency of oxygen at 2–2·5 ATA in clearing the blood stream of carbon monoxide and relieving tissue hypoxia is abundant.[28] In the absence of hyperbaric oxygen, a mixture of 5–7 per cent dioxide in oxygen offers the best alternative method of resuscitation.

Clinical experience with hyperbaric oxygen has not been so clear cut. There appear to be two facets to the problem and these can best be presented with reference to a recent study[36] performed in a defined population within the United Kingdom. The overall mortality from coal gas poisoning in this region was 40 per cent. As is common, the great majority (96 per cent) died before reaching hospital and the only method of improving this figure would be to provide hyperbaric oxygen facilities as a mobile service. No evaluation of this procedure has been described although experience indicates that several mobile units would be required in a densely populated area for such a service to be of practical value. Only a very small number of those admitted to hospital (2 per cent) subsequently died and this confirms the findings of other centres in the United Kingdom.[21] Hyperbaric oxygen, under these circumstances, has little or no part to play in

improving survival but may contribute to lowering the morbidity in this condition. Prolonged delirium complicated 20 per cent of patients recovering from carbon monoxide poisoning in the previously mentioned study and only 50 per cent of the patients received any form of oxygen therapy. Clearly carbon monoxide poisoning receives less energetic treatment in some centres than the condition justifies and hyperbaric oxygen has been reported to be capable of eliminating much of the long term neurological *sequelae*.[35]

One of the reasons advanced for the protracted delay in recovery of consciousness in patients with severe carbon monoxide poisoning has been the development of cerebral oedema. As indicated previously, hyperbaric oxygen can reduce raised intracranial pressure resulting from cerebral oedema but clinical evidence of the value of hyperbaric oxygen at this stage of carbon monoxide poisoning is lacking. Sluijter,[32] in an experimental study, was unable to demonstrate any beneficial influence of hyperbaric oxygen in delayed recovery of consciousness following severe poisoning although the protective influence of hypothermia was readily demonstrable.

Shock

Information gained from laboratory experiments suggests only a limited role for hyperbaric oxygen in the treatment of shock. In certain specific circumstances e.g. hypovolaemia, severe anaemia and carboxyhaemoglobin-aemia, oxygen at increased pressure provides a rapid improvement in oxygen transport while primary disorders such as fluid loss and haemoglobin deficit are being corrected. The ability of oxygen at 2 ATA to restore cerebral cortical oxygen consumption to normal during severe haemorrhagic hypotension in dogs is demonstrated in Table 2. In shock secondary to impaired myocardial

TABLE 2

THE EFFECT OF OXYGEN AT 2 ATA ON CEREBRAL CORTICAL BLOOD FLOW AND OXYGEN CONSUMPTION (MEAN ± S.E. OF THE MEAN) IN HYPOTENSIVE DOGS, INDICATING RESTORATION OF NORMAL OXYGEN CONSUMPTION.

Experiment	Blood Flow (ml./gm./min.)	Oxygen Consumption (ml./gm./min.)
Control (air)	0·83 ± 0·24	0·052 ± 0·007
Hypotension (air)	0·50 ± 0·11[a]	0·038 ± 0·003[b]
Hypotension (O$_2$ at 2 ATA)	0·48 ± 0·12[a]	0·059 ± 0·009

[a]$P < 0.005$
[b]$P < 0.01$

function, experimental and clinical data support the value of hyperbaric oxygen in selected patients. Evidence favouring the use of hyperbaric oxygen is perhaps most tenuous in septic or endotoxin shock but in this respect is little different from most other forms of therapy.

Other clinical applications of hyperbaric oxygen have been described in previous reviews[21,30,41] and the reader is directed to these for a detailed discussion of the method in infection, chronic vascular disorders, resuscitation of the newborn and radiotherapy.

If a concluding comment may be ventured, it is that a much deeper understanding of oxygen toxicity must emerge before any further progress can be made in the application of hyperbaric oxygen in clinical medicine. At the present time too little is known for safety.

FURTHER READING

1 Ackerman, N. B. and Brinkley, F. B. (1966), "Development of Cyclic Intermittent Hyperbaric Oxygenation as a Method for Prolonging Survival during Chronic Hyperbaric Exposure," *Surgery*, **60**, 20–27.

2 Balentine, J. D. (1968), "Pathogenesis of Central Nervous System Lesions Induced by Exposure to Hyperbaric Oxygen," *Amer. J. Path.*, **53**, 1097–1109.

3 Barber, R. E., Lee, J. and Hamilton, W. K. (1970), "Oxygen Toxicity in Man: Study in Patients with Irreversible Brain Damage," *New Engl. J. Med.*, **283**, 1478–1484.

4 Bean, J. W. (1965), "Factors Influencing Clinical Oxygen Toxicity," *Ann. N.Y. Acad. Sci.*, **117**, 745–755.

5 Bean, J. W. and Zee, D. (1966), "Influence of Anesthesia and CO_2 on CNS and Pulmonary Effects of O_2 at High Pressure," *J. appl. Physiol.*, **21**, 521–526.

6 Bernhard, W. F., Navarro, R. U., Yagi, H., Carr, J. G., Jr. and Barandiaran, L. (1966), "Cardiovascular Surgery in Infants Performed under Hyperbaric Conditions," *Vascular Dis.*, **3**, 33–41.

7 Clark, J. M. and Lambertsen, C. J. (1971), "Pulmonary Oxygen Toxicity," *J. appl. Physiol.*, **30**, 739–752.

8 Dewar, K. M. S., Smith, G., Spence, A. A. and Ledingham, I. McA. (1971), "The Effect of Hyperoxia on Airways Resistance in Humans," *J. appl. Physiol.*, in press.

9 Garland, H. and Pearce, J. (1967), "Neurological Complications of Carbon Monoxide Poisoning," *Quart. J. Med.*, **36**, 445–455.

10 Gillen, H. W. (1966), "Oxygen Convulsions in Man," in *Proceedings of the Third International Conference on Hyperbaric Medicine*, pp. 217–222 (I. W. Brown and B. G. Cox, Eds.). Washington: National Academy of Sciences.

11 Goodman, M. W. (1964), "Decompression Sickness Treated with Compression to 2–6 Atmospheres Absolute. Report of Fourteen Cases, Discussions and Suggestions for a Minimal Pressure-oxygen Breathing Therapeutic Profile," *Aerospace Med.*, **35**, 1204–1212.

12 Haugaard, N. (1968), "Cellular Mechanisms of Oxygen Toxicity," *Physiol. Rev.*, **48**, 311–373.

13 Heyman, A., Saltzman, H. A. and Whalen, R. E. (1966), "The Use of Hyperbaric Oxygenation in the Treatment of Cerebral Ischemia and Infarction," *Circulation*, Suppl. 2, **33**, 2027.

14 Jacobson, I., Bloor, K., McDowall, D. G. and Norman, J. N. (1963), "Internal Carotid Endarterectomy at 2 Atmospheres of Pressure," *Lancet*, **2**, 546–548.

15 Jacobson, I., Harper, A. M. and McDowall, D. G. (1963), "The Effect of Oxygen under Pressure on Cerebral Blood Flow and Cerebral Venous Oxygen Tension," *Lancet*, **2**, 549.

16 Jacobson, I. and Lawson, D. D. (1963), "The Effect of Hyperbaric Oxygen on Experimental Cerebral Infarction in the Dog. With Preliminary Correlations of Cerebral Blood Flow at 2 Atmospheres of Oxygen," *J. Neurosurg.*, **20** (10), 849–859.

17 Jaffe, N. (1965), "Cardiac Injury and Carbon Monoxide Poisoning," *S. Afr. med. J.*, **39**, 611–615.

18 Kistler, G. S., Caldwell, P. R. B. and Weibel, E. R. (1967), "Development of Fine Structural Damage to Alveolar and Capillary Lining Cells in Oxygen-poisoned Rat Lungs," *J. Cell Biol.*, **33**, 605–628.

19 Lambertsen, C. J., Kough, R. J., Cooper, D. Y., Emmel, G. L., Loeschcke, H. H. and Schmidt, C. F. (1953), "Oxygen Toxicity. Effects in Man of Oxygen Inhalation at 1 and 3·5 Atmospheres upon Blood Gas Transport, Cerebral Circulation and Cerebral Metabolism," *J. appl. Physiol.*, **5**, 471–486.

20 Leatherman, N. E. and Bean, J. W. (1967), "Continuous Recording of Changes in Brain Blood Flow by a Probe," *J. appl. Physiol.*, **25**, 585–588.

21 Ledingham, I. McA. (1967), "Current Status of Hyperbaric Oxygen Therapy," in *Modern Trends in Pharmacology and Therapeutics*, pp. 96–111 (W. F. M. Fulton, Ed.). London: Butterworths.

22 Ledingham, I. McA. (1968), "Hyperbaric Oxygen Equipment," *Brit. J. Hosp. Med.*, Equipment Suppl., p. 35.

23 Lundgren, C. E. G. and Thomson, R. A. (1968), "Air Embolism and Babinski Reflex," *Brit. med. J.*, **1**, 559.

24 McDowall, D. G., Jennett, W. B., Bloor, K. and Ledingham, I. McA. (1966), "The Effect of Hyperbaric Oxygen on the Oxygen Tension of the Brain During Chloroform Anaesthesia," *Surg. Gynec. Obstet.*, **122**, 545–549.

25 Margolis, J., Brown, I. W., Fuson, R. L. and Moor, G. F. (1966), "A New Ocular Manifestation of Oxygen Toxicity," in *Proceedings of Third International Conference on Hyperbaric Medicine*, p. 133 (I. W. Brown and B. G. Cox, Eds.). Washington: National Academy of Sciences.

26 Miller, J. D., Ledingham, I. McA. and Jennett, W. B. (1970), "Effects of Hyperbaric Oxygen on Intracranial Pressure and Cerebral Blood Flow in Experimental Cerebral Oedema," *J. Neurol. Neurosurg. Psychiat.*, **33**, 745–755.

27 Nichols, C. W. and Lambertsen, C. J. (1969), "Effects of High Oxygen Pressures on the Eye," *New Engl. J. Med.*, **281**, 25–30.

28 Norman, J. N. and Ledingham, I. McA. (1967), "Carbon Monoxide Poisoning: Investigations and Treatment," in *Carbon Monoxide Poisoning*, p. 101 (Bour and Ledingham, Eds.). Amsterdam: Elsevier.

29 Saltzman, H. A., Anderson, B., Hart, L., Duffy, E. and Sieker, H. O. (1965), "The Retinal Vascular and Functional Response to Hyperbaric Oxygenation in Normal Subjects and in Patients with Retinal Vascular Disease," in *Hyperbaric Oxygenation*, p. 202 (I. McA. Ledingham, Ed.). Edinburgh: E. & S. Livingstone.

30 Schraibman, I. G. and Ledingham, I. McA. (1969), "Hyperbaric Oxygen and Regional Vasodilatation in Pedal Ischemia," *Surg. Gynec. Obstet.*, **129**, 761–767.

31 Shanklin, D. R. (1967), "The Influence of Total Pressure on the Pulmonary Toxicity of Oxygen," *Amer. J. Path.*, **50**, 46a.

32 Sluijter, M. E. (1967), "The Treatment of Carbon Monoxide Poisoning by Administration of Oxygen at High Atmospheric Pressure," in *Carbon Monoxide Poisoning*, p. 123 (Bour and Ledingham, Eds.). Amsterdam: Elsevier.

33 Smith, G., Clarke, G. M., Sandison, A. T. and Ledingham, I. McA. (1971), "Acute Pulmonary Oxygen Toxicity: Effects of Nitrogen and Pathological Findings," *Amer. J. Physiol.*, in press.

34 Smith, G., Lawson, D. D., Renfrew, S., Ledingham, I. McA. and Sharp, G. R. (1961), "Preservation of Cerebral Cortical Activity by Breathing Oxygen at 2 Atmospheres of Pressure During Cerebral Ischemia," *Surg., Gynec., Obstet.*, **133**, 13–16.

35 Smith, G., Ledingham, I. McA., Sharp, G. R., Norman, J. N. and Bates, E. H. (1962), "Treatment of Coal Gas Poisoning with Oxygen at 2 Atmospheres Pressure," *Lancet*, **1**, 816–819.

36 Smith, J. S. and Brandon, S. (1970), "Acute Carbon Monoxide Poisoning—3 years Experience in a Defined Population," *Postgrad. med. J.*, **46**, 65–70.

37 Spencer, F. C., Bosomworth, P. and Ritcher, W. (1966), "Fatal Pulmonary Injury from Prolonged Inhalation of Oxygen in High Concentrations," in *Proceedings of the Third International Conference on Hyperbaric Medicine*, p. 189 (I. W. Brown and B. G. Cox, Eds.). Washington: National Academy of Sciences.

[38] Trapp, W. G., Patrick, T. R. and Oforsagd, P. A. (1971), "Effect of High Pressure Oxygen on Alveolar Lining Phospholipids," *Amer. J. Physiol.*, **221**, 318–323.

[39] Trapp, W. G., Yoshida, S. and Grant, A. (1967), "Prolonged Hyperbaric Oxygenation under Positive Pressure Anesthesia," *Canad. med. Ass. J.*, **96**, 365.

[40] Winter, P. M., Gupta, R. K., Michalski, A. H. and Lanphier, E. H. (1967), "Modification of Hyperbaric Oxygen Toxicity by Experimental Venous Admixture," *J. appl. Physiol.*, **23**, 954–963.

[41] Zobell, C. E. and Hittle, L. L. (1967), "Some Effects of Hyperbaric Oxygenation on Bacteria at Increased Hydrostatic Pressures," *Canad. J. Microbiol.*, **13**, 1311–1319.

5. SURGERY FOR OCCLUSIVE VASCULAR DISEASE

GAVIN D. SMELLIE

In practical terms, the surgery of occlusive vascular disease affecting the brain is the surgery of atherosclerotic extracranial arteries.

Its aims are to increase cerebral blood flow by re-boring (endarterectomy) or bypassing a tight arterial stenosis or block, to prevent eventual thrombosis in a stenosed artery and to get rid of a source of micro-emboli by removing an ulcerated atheromatous plaque, whether it is reducing cerebral arterial blood flow or not. The common sites of atheroma formation in the main arteries supplying the brain are shown in Fig. 1.

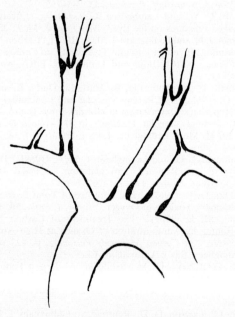

FIG. 1. Common sites of atherosclerotic plaques affecting the extracranial arteries.

Operations on the extracranial arteries have been reported in increasing numbers since the mid-1950's, thanks to the pioneering operations to relieve stenosis of the common carotid bifurcation, performed by Eastcott, Pickering and Rob in Great Britain and De Bakey, Crawford, Morris and Cooley in the United States of America.

It is salutary to remember that the treatment by surgical methods of cerebral occlusive vascular disease is still controversial. We have no sure statistical grounds for recommending surgery. Properly controlled studies of patients treated conservatively and by operation, matched for mode of onset, severity of deficit and pattern of lesions are not yet available. When such studies are reported, they will likely reflect the work of experts which the inexpert cannot hope to emulate.

Yet no surgeon, however expert, should enter light-heartedly into operating on the arteries supplying a patient's brain: the consequences to the patient of surgical misadventure are much too serious.

LAMINAR AND TURBULENT FLOW

The behaviour of fluid flowing along a system of tubing can be extremely complex. This contributor makes no pretence of being an initiate, and records his debt to Weale's book on surgical haemodynamics.[15] Much of the theoretical work in this field has concerned flow 'in rigid tubes' of Newtonian fluids, i.e. homogeneous fluids whose viscosity is constant at all velocities. The study of flowing blood is complicated by its not being a Newtonian fluid, and by the fact that it flows in a pulsatile fashion along elastic vessels which do not maintain a uniform diameter.

Blood, like any fluid, flows from an area of high to an area of low pressure and it was generally thought that flow stopped at once should this pressure difference be removed. However, it has been shown by Manteuffel-Szoege[12] in chick embryos and also in dogs, that despite the arrest of the heart, blood continues to travel along the arteries and veins for several minutes. If the venous return to the arrested heart of a dog is obstructed, pressure in the veins can become positive and arterial pressure negative while blood continues to pile up in the veins. The only possible explanation for these phenomena is that the blood is propelled by its own kinetic energy.

Normally, the flow between two vessels at different pressures can be shown to increase when the pressure difference is increased. There are, however, physical and biological reasons why this increase in flow is limited: continual raising of blood pressure will not produce a parallel rise in flow. Cerebral blood flow is directly dependent on blood pressure only below a systolic pressure of 60–70 mm. Hg. Above this level, autoregulatory mechanisms maintain an optimal constant steady flow, but in the first few days after a stroke, autoregulation of cerebral blood flow is defective.[1]

Blood flow along a vessel is also influenced by the calibre and length of the vessel and the viscosity of the blood. Ideally, blood flows smoothly along the blood vessel in a series of sleeves or laminae moving at different speeds. The lamina next to the vessel wall moves most slowly and the central core moves most quickly. When this orderly progression (laminar flow) is disturbed, flow is said to become turbulent, and this is the normal type of flow in the chambers of the heart. In the blood vessels, turbulence can be caused by stenoses or dilatations, or sometimes by very rapid flow (flow murmurs).

Turbulence is not usually seen in healthy arteries. Once it occurs, an increase in pressure would be needed to maintain flow at its pre-turbulence level. The most usual cause of turbulence is the presence of atheroma, plaques of which increase in size by a process of thrombosis and mural incorporation of the thrombus.[16]

BRUITS

A bruit usually denotes an abnormality of flow in an artery due to turbulence or jet formation. Before coming to this conclusion regarding a particular artery other causes of bruit, such as a propagated cardiac murmur, have to be excluded.

If a bruit is due to a stenosis in an artery, this means that the lumen is about 50 per cent stenosed; lesser degrees of stenosis cause turbulence which can be shown to produce vibrations, but these are not heard with the stethoscope at this stage in the formation of the stenosis. The vibrations have to penetrate the arterial wall to be heard and the stiffness of the wall of the artery influences the loudness of the bruit.

A very loud murmur indicates a critical stenosis: further stenosis causes the bruit to become quieter, until it disappears often just before the artery finally blocks. Thus a soft murmur over a big vessel can mean either a stenosis which is affecting flow very little if at all, or else a stenosis on the point of occlusion. In the carotid, due to flow being strongly prograde in diastole, a critical stenosis may produce a machinery murmur. Kartchner et al.[11] have examined patients with symptoms of cerebrovascular insufficiency by displaying audiofrequency recordings, taken from the neck, on an oscilloscope and photographing the result. Recordings were made from above, below and directly over the carotid bifurcation on each side. Arteriograms were also employed and it was found that stenoses seen on arteriography but not clinically detectable, were sometimes detectable on the audiovisual record. On follow-up by the audiovisual recording method combined with arteriography, several patients developed significant stenoses and audible bruits after several years.

The authors were able to show the development of the bruit as seen on the oscilloscope. Their method of recording from three points along the course of the carotid could pick out bruits from more proximal stenoses. Such stenoses had a muffling effect on a carotid stenosis, making the bruit quieter than might be expected. At the same time, the proximal stenosis propagated its own bruit on occasion into the neck.

In conclusion it is clear that a bruit detected on a single occasion, and in particular its quality, is unreliable evidence of the degree of stenosis.

POST-STENOTIC DILATATION

At the carotid bifurcation, when there is a sharp stenosis, a small post-stenotic dilatation of the internal carotid is sometimes seen (Fig. 2). At this point, the arterial wall

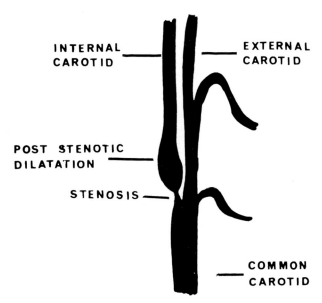

FIG. 2. Tracing of an arteriogram showing critical stenosis and post-stenotic dilatation.

is thinned somewhat, and histological studies of post-stenotic dilatations have shown damage to elastic tissue in the media and increased fragility of the wall. For a post-stenotic dilatation to occur, the stenosis must be short and critical with a reduction in diameter of the vessel to between 1/3 and 1/4 of the original. The flow should be turbulent, pulsatile and of an adequate volume and velocity.

The cause of post-stenotic dilatation is not clear and many theories have been put forward to explain it. The wall of the artery beyond the stenosis may be weakened by being struck by jets of blood coming, at high speed, through the stenosis. A post-stenotic dilatation can be reproduced in an elastic rubber tube by forcing a pulsatile flow of fluid through a suitable stenosis for a sufficient time. The dilatation is reversible at first but later is permanent even if the system is de-pressurized.

The production of turbulence by the stenosis causes the vessel walls to vibrate and it is thought that the impact of pressure waves striking the walls unevenly produces points of high stress and leads to structural fatigue. If a vibrating reed is inserted in a thin latex tube without its touching the walls and the tube filled with water under pressure of 130 mm. Hg., the impacts of increased pressure waves cause a local dilatation opposite the vibrating end of the reed, due to structural fatigue.

One of the most interesting theories is that of structural fatigue of the vessel wall caused by cavitation, a phenomenon that may be partly responsible for the bruit. Water, because of its comparatively high surface tension, is a very effective medium for cavitation, which occurs when a fluid is quickly compressed and decompressed. During the decompression phase, gases dissolved in the fluid come out of solution as bubbles. Once the pressure amplitude returns to a high enough level and the initial radius of the bubbles is less than a critical value, the bubbles collapse. This sudden collapse is known as cavitation and can result in the release of comparatively large amounts of energy almost instantaneously.

VENTURI TUBE

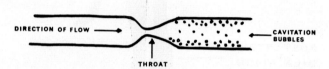

DIRECTION OF FLOW →

← CAVITATION BUBBLES

THROAT

FIG. 3. Cavitation bubbles collect downstream near the wall of the tube.

Cavitation is known to occur in Venturi tubes (Fig. 3). When fluid flows through such a tube, as the inlet velocity increases, pressure at the throat of the tube decreases (Bernouille's theorem). In certain flow conditions, the pressure at the throat may be lower than the vapour pressure, in which case a foaming mixture of water and bubbles can be seen on the downstream side of the throat. The bubbles tend to congregate near the wall of the tube.

The similarity between the Venturi tube and a sharp critical stenosis (Fig. 2) is obvious and it is possible that cavitation on the downstream side of the stenosis causes fatigue failure of the arterial wall followed by post stenotic dilatation. The wall of the carotid is not likely to be subjected to stress for long as critical stenoses are probably progressive and the special haemodynamic requirements for the formation of a post-stenotic dilatation are unlikely to be sustained for more than a few months.

ARTERIAL STENOSIS

Arterial stenoses, as we have seen, may be a source of emboli, can damage the arterial wall (post-stenotic dilatation) and can cause a reduction in flow before finally causing occlusion and thrombosis of the artery.

It is surprising how much the lumen of an artery must be reduced before flow is interfered with. While there is controversy regarding what constitutes a significant stenosis, there is fairly general agreement that the lumen must be constricted by 50 per cent (some workers think the value is much higher) before there is interference with flow.

The haemodynamic resistance depends on the length of the stenosis, the minimum cross-sectional area, the shape of the channel and the shape of the inlet and outflow segments. Brice et al.[3] studied patients undergoing carotid ligation in the treatment of aneurysms on the circle of

Willis; having clamped off the external carotid artery and applied a progressive clamp with micrometer regulation to the common carotid artery, they measured flow with an electromagnetic flowmeter. They found that the carotid artery (average cross section 35·8 sq. mm.) had to be constricted to between 2 and 4 sq. mm. with a stenosis 3 mm. long, before there was any change in blood flow or pressure gradient. This represents a reduction of the lumen of the average internal carotid of between 80 and 90 per cent. They also noted that a round constriction had less effect than a slit-like one of equal cross-sectional area.

Although the gradient across a stenosis is often measured at endarterectomy and its absence confirmed at the end of the operation, the essence of the circulation is blood flow.[5] This cannot be assured by measurement of pulse and pressure but only by direct measurement of flow. They confirm that flow in a system is not affected by a localized lumen constriction until the constriction is very pronounced and they state, furthermore, that the nature of a gradient in pressure across a constriction has no predictable relation to flow taking place.

SURGICAL ASPECTS OF CEREBRAL BLOOD FLOW

In a normal man, according to Roberts et al.[13], the internal carotid arteries supply about 90 per cent of the blood flow to the brain. The rest travels in the vertebral arteries. These figures hold good when the head is in the neutral position, facing to the front. These authors removed the brain from 20 cadavers varying in age from newborn to 78 years. Fluid was pumped into the aortic arch which had been isolated along with the innominate, left common carotid and left subclavian arteries intact. The vertebral and internal carotid arteries were cannulated where they entered the skull, and flow in these vessels was measured in various positions of the head. Moving the head through a normal range of movement resulted, in every cadaver studied, in a position being arrived at during which no flow was recorded in one of the four arteries. Flow was more readily obstructed in the older patients by change in position. No one position of the head occluded a certain vessel in all individuals. All cadavers showed alteration in flow with changes in position.

It was concluded that in man, maximal flow is found in the internal carotid vessels when the head is in the neutral position as regards rotation of the cervical spine and as regards flexion and extension of the neck. It can be seen from these findings how, if one or more of the main arteries to the brain is occluded or severely stenosed, turning or tilting the head may impair flow through the remaining arteries and lead to fainting and other neurological symptoms and signs.

Roberts et al.[13] have shown that if the head was turned, say, to the right side, blood flow through the left common carotid was always reduced, sometimes by as much as 25 per cent. Complete occlusion of one common carotid resulted in an increase in flow of from 13 to 38 per cent in the opposite common carotid. In the vertebral arteries, turning the head away from the side being measured cut down the flow by between 9 and 23 per cent.

The above findings were the result of measuring blood flow using electromagnetic flowmeters in patients who had no symptoms of cerebrovascular disease and who were undergoing neck dissection for other reasons. When one or more of the arteries supplying the brain are gradually affected by disease, the situation may be very different. Indeed many cases have been recorded of patients suffering an occlusion of both internal carotid arteries with little or no impairment of cerebral function. However, only 13 such cases were found in one investigation of 1,500 patients with atherosclerotic cerebrovascular disease. In 17 cases recently reviewed, collateral circulation of varying patterns and degrees was shown in all patients, but only 4 patients were able to return to work.

The incidence of extracranial arterial disease among unselected patients with atherosclerotic cerebrovascular disease is unknown, because investigation is justified only in those with certain syndromes; post-mortem studies are also subject to some bias. It has been shown that 74·5 per cent of 3,788 patients who had 4-vessel angiography for symptomatic cerebrovascular disease had surgically accessible lesions, but in one-third of these there was also an inaccessible lesion.[8] The most careful clinical examination, including palpation and auscultation of the neck, may fail to reveal evidence of even gross arterial lesions and there is really no substitute for angiography in making the diagnosis. However, most series fail to show any angiographic abnormality in up to a third of patients; it seems likely that their symptoms are due to transitory embolization or to structural disease in vessels too small to be visualized radiologically.

Measurement of the total cerebral blood flow using the Kety–Schmidt technique, in patients with incapacitating cerebrovascular insufficiency, has shown that those with severe lesions of the great vessels at the aortic arch or multiple lesions of both carotid and vertebral arteries may have impairment of total cerebral blood flow, correctable by the appropriate endarterectomy. Patients measured between attacks of cerebral ischaemia and without neurological deficit at the time of measurement mostly have normal total cerebral blood flow. Studies of total cerebral blood flow may not accurately reflect regional cerebral blood flow, which can be normal despite the presence of an area of local cerebral ischaemia; nor is the finding of an adequate flow under resting conditions any guarantee that there are adequate reserves to deal with stress conditions—such as variations in blood pressure or $PaCO_2$.

How a patient fares when one or more of the arteries supplying his brain become stenosed or occluded depends on what sort of collateral circulation his brain can get through the circle of Willis and through intra- and extra-cranial collaterals. The patient's circle of Willis is his birthright: he may be unlucky and be born with a poor one. In about 50 per cent of adults, the circle is "abnormal" in that the anterior or posterior communicating arteries are hypoplastic. There is a greater incidence of abnormality than this in patients with cerebral infarcts at post-

mortem. If a patient is fortunate in having a good collateral circulation to his brain, a stenosed extracranial artery may block without causing symptoms. Paradoxically, if the patient is having symptoms, they may clear up when the artery blocks if they have been due to microemboli breaking loose from a diseased part of the affected artery.

It can be shown that, given a good collateral circulation with cross-flow between both sides of the brain, an operation which will increase flow in one extracranial artery may improve total cerebral blood flow. The patient's symptoms may then be dramatically relieved despite stenoses of his remaining extracranial arteries. There are many convincing recorded cases of just such a result, and they are sufficiently dramatic to overthrow the old notion that brain cells are either fully functional or dead. Clearly, there are a few patients whose poor general cerebral function is due to ischaemia and not to infarction. These patients may be expected to improve greatly, if not return to normal, once adequate cerebral blood flow is restored by surgery.

Many patients have been noted to have symptoms suggestive of vertebro-basilar ischaemia, yet associated with carotid stenosis and relieved by carotid endarterectomy. Also, the patient's symptoms may arise from the carotid territory opposite to the side of the carotid stenosis yet again be relieved by carotid endarterectomy. Such clinical observations support the aim of trying to improve critically low regional cerebral blood flow by increasing total cerebral blood flow.

SMALL STROKES

Small strokes, or transient ischaemic attacks, by the usual definition, do not last longer than an hour. They may have many causes including blockage of a cerebral vessel with restoration of adequate flow by the collateral circulation. Cerebral arterial spasm may play a part as may transient lowering of local cerebral blood flow due to arterial stenosis. Hypertension, hypotension, polycythaemia and interference with vertebral artery flow by osteophytes on the cervical spine have also been blamed. Most likely of all, small strokes may be due to emboli coming from a plaque of atheroma (Fig. 4).

Large arteries of the size of the carotid are nourished by the vasa vasorum and by diffusion from the blood in the lumen. The nutritional watershed lies in the substance of the media. The capillaries from the vasa vasorum cannot venture nearer to the lumen on account of the high tissue tension, but once the intima thickens, due to atheroma, capillaries from the vasa vasorum can invade it. Small blood vessels can also arise from the luminal surface and invade the plaque. Nevertheless, the nutritional balance is fine and easily upset by sudden growth of the plaque due to mural thrombus formation.[16] The plaque may then become necrotic in its depths and may ulcerate.

Emboli from such a plaque may be composed largely of platelets—the white bodies seen moving along the retinal vessels during attacks of transient monocular blindness.

Should the plaque ulcerate the emboli may contain atheromatous debris, and later a more mixed type of thrombus.

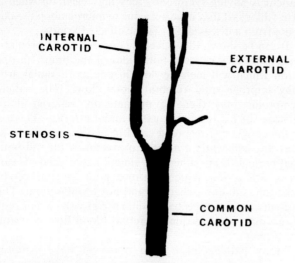

FIG. 4. Tracing of an arteriogram showing an ulcerated atheromatous plaque in the interval carotid. The plaque does not interfere with flow but is a source of micro-emboli.

If small strokes are thought to be brought about by carotid stenosis, carotid endarterectomy should be urgently considered as in 75 per cent of cases only one or two small strokes occur before the patient suffers a major stroke. The average time between a small stroke affecting the carotid territory and a major stroke, has been found to be 14 months. The equivalent figure for the vertebral territory is 23 months.

CAROTID ENDARTERECTOMY

This is the commonest operation used in the treatment of cerebrovascular insufficiency. The objectives in the operation, technically, are to remove the atheromatous plaque without leaving loose intima distally, to leave a smooth arterial wall and to achieve a blood-tight closure. The artery must be carefully closed, for if it is narrowed (Fig. 5) the reconstruction may thrombose. If the arteriotomy is closed with a patch, this must not be too large (Fig. 6) or the carotid bifurcation will be too commodious, and turbulent flow with eddy formation may occur and clot be deposited, with the risk of later embolization. If vein is used for patch material it may stretch a little, but on the other hand it "takes" as a free graft and can resist infection. Dacron or Teflon used as a patch is readily available, does not stretch, but remains as a foreign body. Should it become infected, the prognosis for the reconstruction and for the patient could be serious with a grave risk of haemorrhage. The state of the repair may be assessed by operative angiography before closing the wound, but this has its technical difficulties. The ultimate functioning of the operated artery can be reliably assessed only by post-operative angiography; this should be done by remote arterial puncture, either by the femoral brachial or through the common carotid low in the neck. By no means all surgical series include post-operative angiograms and it is as well to realize that complete relief of transient ischaemic attacks may follow an operation which has resulted in complete thrombotic occlusion of the internal carotid artery. This operation entails clamping of common, internal and external carotid arteries during the actual removal of the plaque and the arterial reconstruction. Whilst many patients can tolerate this, cerebral ischaemia may occur in a matter of minutes, particularly if the opposite internal carotid is also occluded.

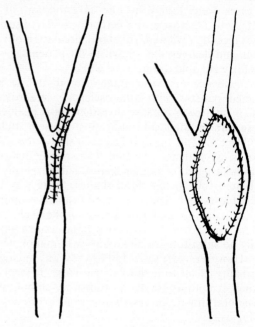

FIG. 5. Bad arteriotomy closure with narrowing and liability to thrombosis of the reconstruction.

FIG. 6. Patch angioplasty closure with too-large patch leaving aneurysmal dilatation prone to turbulent flow and clot formation.

Unfortunately no readily available reliable test has been devised to predict whether or not the clamping will be tolerated, and most surgeons use a by-pass to ensure adequate cerebral perfusion during operation without requiring the surgeon to work against the clock. A No. 10 French gauge polythene catheter (internal diameter 2·5 mm.) is adequate, and is placed across the bifurcation from common to internal carotid artery, in the lumina of which it is snared (Fig. 7). Measurements of cerebral blood flow using radio-active tracers have shown perfusion to be normal with such a shunt in position (Jennett et al.[10]). In a series of 300 consecutive carotid endarterectomies Thompson and his associates, using a shunt routinely, have had an instance of death or severe post-operative deficit in only 0·67 per cent. They have also operated on 40 patients who had occlusion of the opposite carotid without a single death or severe neurological deficit.

There are surgeons who prefer to avoid a shunt, considering that it impedes the operator and that during its insertion intimal damage may occur. They may operate under local anaesthesia in order to monitor CNS function continuously and to have immediate warning of cerebral ischaemia, or they may attempt to improve cerebral oxygenation by one of several techniques. One is to reduce oxygen usage by operating under hypothermia. When the body is cooled to 30°C, oxygen consumption is decreased by 55 per cent. But the heart is liable to arrhythmias and difficult to defibrillate when cold should the need arise. Bleeding and clotting times are prolonged: the platelet count falls. Blood viscosity rises and there is a tendency to metabolic acidosis.

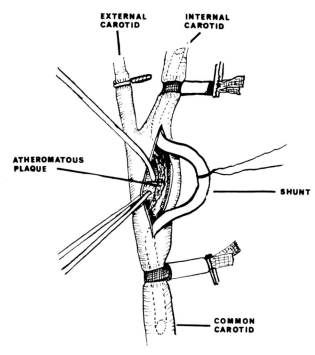

FIG. 7. Carotid endarterectomy. Blood flow to the brain is maintained through a polythene shunt while a dissector separates the plaque from the wall which is held in dissecting forceps.

Another is to produce cerebral vasodilatation by hypercarbia and use of high oxygen content in the inhaled gases. However, there is increasing clinical and experimental evidence to suggest that this may be unsuccessful in improving the oxygenation of areas of brain that are threatened by ischaemia. This is because vasodilatation may already be maximal in such compromised parts of the brain, due to local metabolic factors, and the result of inducing hypercarbia is then to dilate the vessels in the remaining (normal) part of the brain; as a consequence there may be an internal steal of blood away from the affected area, which might eventually be less well off than previously. Whether or not a by-pass is used, it is important to avoid hypoxia or hypotension during operation because this will certainly increase the risk of ischaemic brain damage.

ACUTE STROKES AND TOTAL CAROTID OCCLUSION

There is a difference of opinion on the role of surgery in the acute stroke. Some surgeons are still enthusiastic about attempting to perform endarterectomy on the blocked carotid responsible for the stroke. They argue, supported by statistics, that the sooner a blocked artery is tackled surgically, the better the chance of removing propagated clot before it becomes organized and, therefore, the better the chance of restoring flow. Many such successful restorations have been reported.

Against such a view is the undoubted fact that an occasional patient with an acute stroke is made very much worse by restoring flow to the affected cerebral hemisphere. Such patients die of brain swelling, some with a haemorrhagic infarct. The more profound the stroke before surgery, the greater the mortality following surgery.

Anoxic damage to the walls of small blood vessels in an infarct is an important factor in causing bleeding into the infarct. Anaemic cerebral infarcts can be created in the monkey brain and their progress studied. Softening is maximal at a week and healing of the infarct takes eight weeks. By giving the animals anticoagulants and raising their blood pressure, haemorrhage can be induced in recent infarcts.

The dangers of restoring arterial blood flow to a cerebral infarct must be set against the possible benefits. Most surgeons have become discouraged from operating on patients with profound strokes as the mortality is anything from 20 to 60 per cent. The same applies to strokes that are rapidly deteriorating. While rapidly improving strokes do not merit emergency investigation, they should be investigated with a view to operation as soon as they become stable. Eastcott[7] considers the totally occluded internal carotid artery to be a complete contraindication to operation.

The internal carotid artery may become blocked by a major embolus, usually arising in the heart. As there is no time for a collateral circulation to develop, a profound stroke often results. The good results that attend embolectomy in the limbs using Fogarty balloon catheters have not been duplicated in dealing with carotid emboli. The reasons for this are that while tissues in a limb will survive for six hours without a blood supply, brain tissue so deprived will survive for only a few minutes. Also, the carotid artery pursues a tortuous course inside the skull— a course that balloon catheters find difficult to follow.

Gillespie[9] advises an aggressive policy, carrying out angiography and operation within a few hours of the stroke, as there have been dramatic if rare successes following embolectomy. Very often, unfortunately, the emboli cannot be removed. The risk of haemorrhagic infarction, already mentioned, has to be remembered.

Where there is no embolic source and the occlusion of the internal carotid is thought to be thrombotic, many surgeons are prepared to operate. Thompson states that a totally occluded internal carotid artery can be opened up successfully in 20 per cent of cases as long as a month after the stroke. He has found arteriograms useful in predicting a successful outcome, by showing filling of the ophthalmic artery, the siphon or distal internal carotid on the occluded side via collaterals from the external carotid of the same side, the vertebral, or from the other side of the brain via the circle of Willis. He has also found that on occasion the internal carotid was patent distal to the occlusion at the bifurcation. Usually, a blocked artery propagates clot up to the first collateral, and in order to explain his curious findings, Thompson[14] wonders if an abnormally placed ascending pharyngeal branch arising from the internal carotid might be responsible for sustaining retrograde flow and keeping the carotid patent.

The key to successful reconstruction of the blocked internal carotid artery has proved to be a good back-flow. If the back-flow was poor or the carotid represented by a fibrous cord, the attempted reconstruction has failed.

ARTERIAL BY-PASS

When an artery is stenosed or blocked, a by-pass of the obstruction is easier to perform and less liable to thrombosis in the long term than an endarterectomy in many cases.

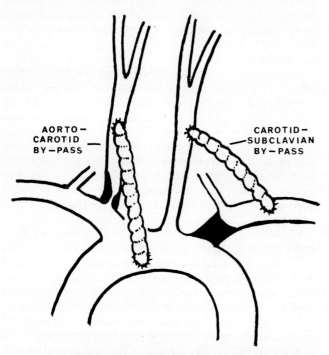

AORTO-
CAROTID
BY-PASS

CAROTID-
SUBCLAVIAN
BY-PASS

FIG. 8. Dacron by-pass grafts inserted to relieve stenosis of the right common carotid artery causing cerebral ischaemia and thrombosis of the left subclavian artery causing "subclavian steal" (see text).

Figure 8 shows a patient with severe stenosis of the right common carotid, overcome by a tube of knitted dacron joined end-to-side between the aortic arch proximally and the patent common carotid distal to the obstruction. Such an operation demands a thoracotomy. This is a major undertaking in a patient with advanced atherosclerosis, and can lead, even in the best hands, to a mortality of over 5 per cent.

Figure 8 also illustrates blockage of the left subclavian. This can cause reversed flow in the left vertebral artery, particularly on vigorous use of the left arm (subclavian "steal"). A knitted 8 mm. dacron tube is shown joining the normal left common carotid and the left subclavian artery distal to the block. This allows the carotid to perfuse the left upper limb as well as the brain and to restore

normal flow to the vertebral artery. It might be supposed that such a by-pass would divide the normal carotid arterial blood flow between brain and limb in such a way that use of the arm would dangerously diminish the supply to the brain. These fears have proved groundless in practice. Both with the carotid and in other situations in the body, the artery being asked to supply two territories instead of its normal one, has responded with a marked increase in flow.

An experimental model was set up by Barner et al.[2] using 10 dogs in which they constructed a by-pass graft between the carotid and subclavian arteries distal to the vertebral artery. Ligation of the subclavian with the by-pass clamped resulted in reversal of vertebral flow in 9 of the animals, the greatest change being from +36 to −100 ml./min. Opening the by-pass caused cephalad flow to be restored in the vertebral artery in 8 animals and a marked reduction in the reversed flow in the rest. Distal carotid flow was not appreciably disturbed.

After stimulating the brachial plexus to simulate exercise of the ipsilateral limb, distal carotid flow fell by 15 per cent on average and subclavian flow increased from 100 to 400 per cent. The authors calculated that with strong use of the arm in a man with such a by-pass constructed, there might be a reduction in cerebral blood flow but noted that review of 12 such cases in the literature had not confirmed these theoretical fears.

Indeed de Bakey and Crawford have employed extrathoracic by-pass grafts when possible, with increasing frequency of recent years to avoid an endarterectomy, simplify the procedure and reduce the mortality associated with thoracotomy and endarterectomy of the great vessels.

CONCLUSION

There are many differing opinions on the usefulness of surgery in the treatment of cerebrovascular ischaemia. The literature abounds with varying reports ranging from great success to little change. Yet it is probably true to say that patients suffering from transient ischaemic attacks are usually relieved of their symptoms by operation and that the long-term patency of the internal carotid following endarterectomy is good. The ultimate place of surgery in the treatment of cerebrovascular insufficiency is as yet undecided. We must keep an open mind on the subject and await the results of controlled trials.

FURTHER READING

[1] Agnoli, A., Fieschi, C., Bozzao, L, Battistini, N. and Precipe, M. (1968), "Autoregulation of Cerebral Blood Flow. Studies During Drug-induced Hypertension in Normal Subjects and in Patients with Cerebral Vascular Diseases," *Circulation*, 38, 800–811.

[2] Barner, H. B., Rittenhouse, E. A. and Willman, V. L. (1968), "Carotid-subclavian By-pass for 'Subclavian Steal Syndrome'," *J. Thorac. Cardiovasc. Surg.*, 55, 773–782.

[3] Brice, J. G., Dowsett, D. J. and Lowe, R. D. (1964), "The Effect of Constriction on the Carotid Blood Flow and Pressure Gradient," *Lancet*, 1, 84–85.

[4] Brock, M., Fieschi, C., Ingvar, D. H., Lassen, N. A. and Schurman, K. (Eds.) (1969), "Cerebral Blood Flow. Clinical and Experimental Results," An International Symposium held in Mainz, April 10–12, 1969. Berlin: Springer.

[5] Cannon, J. A., Lobpries, E. L., Herrold, G. and Frandenberg, B. S. (1960), "Experience with a New Electro-magnetic Flowmeter for Use in Blood-flow Determinations in Surgery," *Ann. Surg.*, **152**, 635–647.

[6] Clauss, R. H. and Ray, J. F. (1968), "Pharmacologic Assistance to the Failing Circulation," *Surg. Gynec. Obstet.*, **126**, 611–631.

[7] Eastcott, H. H. G. (1969), *Arterial Surgery.* London: Pitman.

[8] Fields, W. S., North, R. R. and Hass, W. K. *et al.* (1968), "Joint Study of Extracranial Arterial Occlusion," *JAMA*, **203**, 955–968.

[9] Gillespie, J. A. (1969), "The Surgical Treatment of Internal Carotid Artery Lesions," in *Extracranial Cerebrovascular Disease and its Management* (J. A. Gillespie, Ed.). London: Butterworths.

[10] Jennett, W. B., Harper, A. M. and Gillespie, F. C. (1966), "Measurement of Regional Cerebral Blood Flow During Carotid Ligation," *Lancet*, **2**, 1162–1163.

[11] Kartchner, M. M. and McRae, L. P. (1969), "Auscultation for Carotid Bruits in Cerebrovascular Insufficiency," *JAMA*, **210**, 94–97.

[12] Manteuffel-Szoege, L. (1970), "Paradoxes of Haemodynamics," XIXth International Congress of European Society of Cardiovascular Surgery, July 2–4, 1970, Warsaw.

[13] Roberts, B., Hardesty, W. H., Holling, H. E., Reivich, M. and Toole, J. F. (1964), "Studies on Extracranial Cerebral Blood Flow," *Surgery*, **56**, 826–833.

[14] Thompson, J. E. (1968), *Surgery for Cerebrovascular Insufficiency* (*Stroke*). Illinois: Thomas.

[15] Weale, F. E. (1966), *An Introduction to Surgical Haemodynamics.* London: Lloyd-Luke.

[16] Woolf, N. (1970), "Aspects of the Pathogenesis of Atherosclerosis," in *Modern Trends in Vascular Surgery* (J. A. Gillespie, Ed.). London: Butterworths.

[17] Zulch, K. L. and Behrend, R. C. H. (1961), "The Pathogenesis and Topography of Anoxia, Hypoxia and Ischaemia of the Brain in Man," in *Cerebral Anoxia and the Electroencephalogram*, Chap. 14 (J. S. Meyer and H. Gastaut, Eds.). Illinois: Thomas.

6. SPINAL CORD CIRCULATION

R. WÜLLENWEBER

The vascularization of the spinal cord has been the subject of numerous investigations down the centuries, even Vesalius having shown an interest in it. During the last few decades morphological questions about the spinal circulation have been intensively studied.[8,11,19] Some disparity of opinion persists about the arterial circulation in the watershed zones and regions of distribution; Clemens[2] has produced evidence of the unusual arrangement of the venous drainage system. Certain functional and pathological characteristics of the spinal blood supply can be deduced from these morphological studies.

Assertions about the functional behaviour of morphologically different vessels in the spinal cord must be examined with great care. This applies also to the direction of blood flow at different spinal levels. From C1–D3/4 the main direction of flow appears to be downwards and between D9/10 and D3/4 in a cranial direction. A functional watershed between these two areas has been assumed, and this should lie at the level of D4. There may also be another watershed in the region of D12/L1. There are several opinions also about the role played by the lateral vessels in connection with the direction of stream. The theory which best agrees with the physiological and pathophysiological observations states that the blood flow between C1–3, coming from the vertebral artery, flows downwards and at the level of C3–6 meets an upwardly directed flow from the ascending ramus, whilst the descending ramus sends flow downwards to the region of C6–D3/4. It could be accepted as experimentally proved that in the descending branch of the radicular artery there is a caudally directed flow. Flow direction in the anterior spinal artery has not yet been established but is apparently subjected to marked local fluctuations. Conditions in the dorsal complex of vessels

are not yet definitely known but the idea of a mosaic of varying flows is generally accepted. According to the anatomical evidence a cross-section of the spinal cord has blood circulating in opposing directions, streaming centrifugally out of the sulcus arteries and centripetally into the marginal branches. Probably there is an overlap of neighbouring regions of supply rather than a genuine collateral circulation.

The anatomical structure of the spinal venous systems are so complex that up to now the direction of the blood flow has scarcely been studied. From the centre of the spinal cord there should be a steady horizontal flow outwards towards the periphery alongside the centripetal drainage into the sulcus branches. The blood coming from the upper cervical segments must flow down either into the root veins or up into cranial sinuses. The radicular vena magna takes up the main blood flow from the caudal segments, which implies the assumption of flow in a cranial direction (towards the radicular vena magna). Theories about functional supply regions and border regions in man have been deduced from several hydrodynamic models that postulate that under physiological conditions an adequate blood supply is assured for each spinal segment, whilst under pathological circulatory conditions some border regions are presumed to be particularly vulnerable.

METHODS OF EXAMINATION OF THE SPINAL BLOOD FLOW

The methods used for estimating cerebral blood flow, in particular isotope techniques, cannot be applied to the spinal blood flow because of the complexity of supply. Angiographic methods have hitherto been difficult because of the small size of the vessels and the superimposition of bony structures. Measurements of the circulation time with a fluorescence method applied to the lumbar cord in dog and rabbit under serial angiographic control have been limited to the thoracic level. The use of thermo-electric methods were also limited to animal experiments until the development of plaque electrodes permitted examination in man. Polarographic examinations allow an estimation of the oxygen tension in spinal cord tissue.

Results of Animal Experiments

Spinal Circulation Time

Measurement of the circulation time with fluorescent marker and serial angiographic control reveals considerable physiological deviations. The dog shows a circulation time of 1·9–3·4 sec, the rabbit between 1·1 and 3·5 sec. In the dog the spinal circulation time is about twice as long as that in the brain.

Quantitative Measurements of Spinal Blood Flow

Using a method of particle distribution it has been shown that the whole spinal cord in cat has an average blood flow of 19·28 ml/100 g/min.[5,6] There are variations according to the level, the cervical cord showing a value of 19·2, the thoracic 16·79 and the lumbosacral 20·05 ml/100 g/min.[15]

Regulation of the Spinal Blood Flow

There are discrepant opinions about the dependency of the spinal blood flow on the systemic circulation. Under physiological conditions in rabbit the spinal blood flow shows some independence from arterial pressure changes.[3,1] However, polarographic examinations in the dog showed a close relationship between the spinal blood flow and the general circulation which agreed with studies undertaken utilizing heat clearance techniques.[12] These latter results imply a pressure-passive relationship for the spinal blood flow. However, more recent work indicates that within the range 60–160 mms Hg pressure the spinal circulation does not depend upon the mean arterial pressure providing $PaCO_2$ and PaO_2 are normal.[4,5,6,10,14] At $PaCO_2$ above 55 Torr on the other hand there was no evidence at all for autoregulation, whilst older observations[1,3,12] indicated only a limited sensitivity of the spinal haemodynamics to alterations in $PaCO_2$. According to recent work $PaCO_2$ has a significant effect on all spinal segments. There are considerable quantitative differences between different segments, with bigger alterations of the circulation with the same variation in $PaCO_2$ in the cervical and lumbosacral cord than in the thoracic cord. But overall there is no longer any doubt that $PaCO_2$ is as important for the regulation of the spinal blood flow as it is for cerebral blood flow. There is no definite relation between PaO_2 changes between 60 and 140 mm Hg and spinal cord blood flow as long as $PaCO_2$ and mean arterial blood pressure remain within the normal range. In circumstances of hypercapnia on the other hand there is within this range a significant negative correlation between PaO_2 and blood flow.

Influence of Vaso-active Substances

Extensive investigations using thermoprobes on dwarf pigs, and testing numerous pharmaceutical substances, have shown no differences in the influences of these substances on the spinal as compared to the cerebral blood flow.

Investigation of Spinal Blood Flow in Man

Methods

Examination of the spinal circulation in man became possible only after development of techniques that could be used without exposing either the cord or the patient as a whole to any danger. Adapting a method developed by Hensel for skin blood flow measurements we have used thermoprobes consisting of two gold electrodes in a plaque of synthetic material. The principle of heat clearance, on which this method is based, depends on the continuous measurement of the effect of the transfer of heat into the blood stream. A plaque of synthetic material can be loosely applied to the spinal cord surface and held there with a cotton pledglet. One advantage of this method is that the part to be measured can be seen, although it is suitable only for short-term observations since the position of the measuring probes must be continually monitored in order to avoid artefacts which could develop from small haematomas underneath the probes. The value obtained can be considered only as a measure of the relative blood flow and so far it has not been possible to devise a method for making a truly quantitative estimation. The observations have all been made in the course of neurosurgical operations under controlled ventilation with gas and oxygen and neurolept-analgesia. The patients were often on the operating table in the sitting position, in order to avoid any compression of the thorax or the abdomen. This group of patients included some with spinal tumours and others with intractable pain undergoing cordotomy or root section; there was therefore the opportunity to study circulatory regulation under both physiological and pathological conditions.

Measurements Under Physiological Conditions

In these patients without spinal cord compression the influence of $PaCO_2$ was first explored by removing the CO_2 absorber from the closed system and rebreathing, or alternatively by subjecting the patients to a brief period of apnoea by briefly switching off the ventilator. The final value of the CO_2 concentration of the expired air was 5·5–6·5 per cent. A rapid increase of blood flow lasting a minute could be observed (Fig. 1); after replacement of the CO_2 absorber, there was an equally quick decrease; until after approximately two minutes the original level was regained. A delayed increase of blood flow was found in cases in which there had been previous hyperventilation to an expired CO_2 level of 3·5–4·0 per cent. In accordance with the findings in animal experiments spinal blood flow in man reacted consistently to alterations of $PaCO_2$.

The injection of vasoconstrictor (Arterenol) was followed by an immediate increase in spinal blood flow, running parallel to the increase in systemic blood pressure (Fig. 2).

However, the spinal blood flow soon returned to the original level whilst the increase of the systemic blood pressure was maintained for some time. By contrast when a vasodilator (Halothane) was used a short term decrease of spinal blood flow was observed parallel to the decrease of systemic blood pressure; later there was a prolonged increase in spinal circulation although throughout the period of halothane administration the systemic blood pressure remained slightly lower than normal (Fig. 3). These results lead to the conclusion that autoregulation exists in the spinal circulation as well as in the

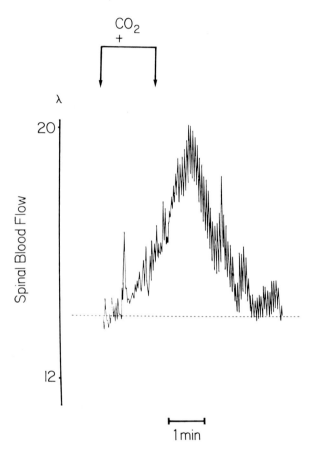

FIG. 1. Effect of hypercapnia (by removing CO_2 absorber) on spinal blood flow in anaesthetized male aged 65, undergoing high thoracic cordotomy.

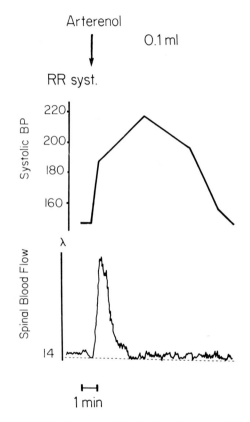

FIG. 2. Effect of vasoconstrictor (arterenol) on spinal blood flow and systolic arterial blood pressure in anaesthetized man.

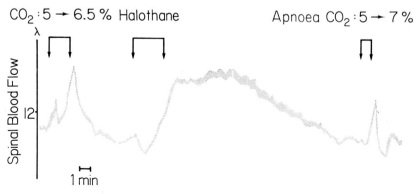

FIG. 3. Effect of hypercapnia and of halothane on spinal blood flow: female aged 40 undergoing cervical cordotomy.

cerebral circulation. After injection or inhalation it takes up to one minute for the full flow change to occur. It seems likely that the mechanisms are similar to those in the cerebral circulation since there are no fundamental differences in the experimental findings.

Measurements Under Pathophysiological Conditions

In the case of the spinal cord compression due to extramedullary tumours (neurinoma, meningioma) it appeared that when there was hypercapnia an increase in blood flow was observed, although the blood flow curve showed some irregularity and the blood flow increase was not as consistent as under normal conditions. For

apnoea. According to these results it seems that auto-regulation—the ability to maintain constant blood flow independent of blood pressure—is abolished in the tumour region. Cord sections show an ischaemia produced by tumour pressure and the tissue hypoxia causes maximal vasodilatation. The already dilated vessels cannot respond to raised CO_2 tension by any further dilatation and therefore, as in the cerebral steal syndrome, results in diversion of blood to those spinal cord regions with a reactive vascular system and autoregulation still intact. Contrary to this spinal steal effect, an inverse steal effect can be shown in cases of intramedullary tumours when the CO_2 tension is reduced with resulting vasoconstriction

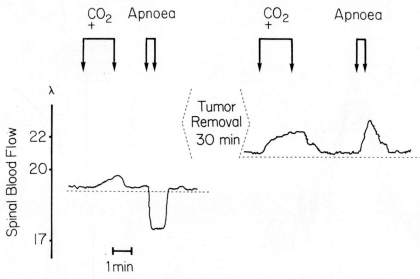

FIG. 4. Effect of hypercapnia before and after removal of an intramedullary tumour (recording from close to tumour).

technical reasons the thermal probes could only be applied about a centimetre away from the tumour, on the spinal cord surface, so that there was no evidence about the direct influence of the tumour compression. Moreover most of the compression by the tumour had been eliminated by the opening of the dura so that the conditions did not exactly correspond with the pathological situation with the dura closed.

In the case of intramedullary tumours (glioma, ependymoma) the thermal probe could be placed directly on the spinal cord surface near the caudal part of the tumour. During the removal of the tumour the blood flow could be continually recorded although there were occasionally movement artefacts. In contrast with the results under physiological conditions the intramedullary tumours showed very little or no blood flow increase during hypercapnia produced by the removal of the CO_2 absorber; when a brief period of apnoea was allowed a massive decrease of spinal blood flow in the tumour region was observed (Fig. 4). The opposite conditions were found after the tumour had been removed and the spinal blood flow on the whole increased markedly. If the CO_2 tension was raised by removal of the CO_2 absorber and rebreathing then a distinct blood flow increase was found as with

of the other vessels in the unaffected segments (Fig. 5). This vasoconstriction is followed by an increase in blood flow in the ischaemic segments, where autoregulation is abolished. The same observation was also made after injection of an efficient vasoconstrictor (Aminophyllin). No alteration in flow was found with this drug in the normally functioning spinal cord but in the ischaemically compromised cord near a tumour it caused an increase in spinal blood flow (Fig. 6). The marked decrease of spinal blood flow during apnoea cannot be explained by a steal effect alone since the CO_2 concentration obtained was about the same as that produced by rebreathing. In the observations during neurosurgical operations haemodynamic factors related to respiration may have an additional influence, since many of the patients were breathing spontaneously. During apnoea intrathoracic pressure was increased and this would have repercussions on the epidural spinal venous plexus, resulting in a pressure increase; this might be expected to decrease the arteriovenous pressure drop in the spinal cord. The role played by the CSF pressure in spinal cord blood flow under various conditions is still not clear since measurements in man have been undertaken only with the dura open. Certainly there is a close relationship

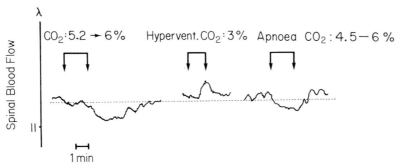

FIG. 5. Spinal steal effect associated with hypercapnia, and increase in flow with hypocapnia in male aged 5 with cervical spongioblastoma.

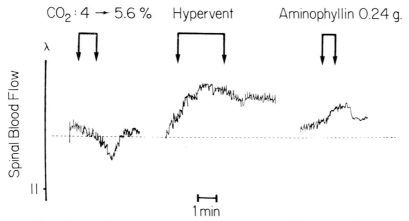

FIG. 6. Increase in flow associated with hypocapnia, and with vasoconstrictor, in male aged 44 with cauda equina ependymoma.

between pressure increase transmitted via the jugular veins to the spinal venous plexus and CSF pressure, as is known from the Queckenstedt test. Because of this it seems likely that the reverse effect also operates and that a primary increase in CSF pressure might affect the veins. Any alteration in arteriovenous pressure difference would be expected to have a more damaging influence on the spinal circulation in segments threatened by ischaemia associated with loss of autoregulation.

The question of the nervous regulation of spinal blood flow in man has not been verified as fully as in the cerebral circulation. Animal experiments which showed a segmental increase of blood flow after peripheral stimulation could not be verified in man. Account has to be taken of the difficulty of segmental localization during surgical procedures. Spontaneous waves independent of respiration, but with a frequency of about two per minute, were repeatedly observed, which raises the possibility of a spontaneous fluctuation in vasomotor tone in the spinal vascular system. Summarizing, it can be stated that the phenomenon of autoregulation, as it is understood in the cerebral circulation, exists also in the spinal circulation. Both steal effect and inverse steal effects seem probable under pathological conditions.

CLINICAL AND THERAPEUTIC IMPLICATIONS

The pathogenesis of spinal blood flow disturbances is complex and single causal factors can seldom be identified. Jellinger[8] has proposed the following classification:

1. **Functional blood flow disturbances,** in which he includes all those which are not based on organic alterations of the spinal cord vessels and which include circulatory disturbances the origin of which lies outside the spinal cord.

2. **Structural blood flow disturbances** due to anatomical abnormalities in the spinal vessels. Disorders of the systemic circulation and cardiac function may in some cases lead to critical reduction of the blood supply of the spinal cord. This can also occur by an increase of local vascular resistance due to vasoconstriction as well as compression of spinal vessels by external pressures. Other factors which may operate differently at different levels of the spinal cord include intrinsic as well as extrinsic abnormality. They include not only lesions of the spinal vessels but also the connections between the inflow and outflow regions and spinal vascular system. Occasionally there is direct involvement of the spinal vessels by local atherosclerosis, apart from the effect of generalized atherosclerosis and hypertension on the spinal vascular system. Inflammatory vascular conditions accompany specific infections, such as meningitis and myelitis, and may have substantial effects on the spinal circulation whilst conditions such as angiitis obliterans or arteritis nodosa are decided rarities. Mechanical damage to the vascular system may play a role in various spinal conditions such as spinal compression and trauma. There are also secondary effects of disease in large vessels, such as aortic aneurysm and consequences of surgical treatment of

this condition. Vascular malformations of the cord include both arterial and venous lesions. Thrombosis of the spinal vessels are relatively unusual as is embolism. Spinal complications after angiography or spinal anaesthesia may be due to a toxic effect on the vascular system but it is difficult to distinguish this from mechanical iatrogenic damage.

Because of the different vascularization of the spinal cord at different levels not all regions are uniformly affected in the case of reduction of blood supply. Certain regions are particularly sensitive to such circulatory disturbances, including the junctional areas which count as functional endartery regions such as the thoracocervical junction. Deficiency of arterial supply usually causes necrosis in a circumscribed region and the neurological deficit reflects the distribution of the artery concerned.

Damage may result from disturbances in venous outflow systems with resulting haemorrhagic infarction which, in the case of partial blockage, may be limited to perivascular foci, but with more extensive lesions may produce a transverse spinal lesion.

There is no doubt that vascular factors play an important part in the development of the clinical picture in cases of trauma or spinal cord compression. In particular neurological deficits which are not limited to the site of actual injury may well be explained by disturbances of spinal blood flow. It is very difficult to assess the part played by haemodynamic and metabolic factors in a complex situation such as arises after trauma. Even the morphological substrata of this kind of injury seldom offers an adequate explanation for the clinical picture. The same applies to injuries of the cervical cord after whiplash trauma, where the mechanical lesions may affect not only the spinal cord and its own vascular system but also the vertebral arteries. The same holds for prolapsed intervertebral disc in the cervical region.

The conservative treatment of spinal blood supply disorders should first of all take into account the phenomenon of steal effects. Thus the administration of vasodilators may not be as helpful as might be expected and indeed may be contraindicated. It is obviously important to avoid any treatment which might cause a drop in systemic blood pressure. It is important to avoid increased intrathoracic and intra-abdominal pressure which may lead to congestion of the spinal epidural venous plexus and in turn to a drop in the arteriovenous pressure difference. It is important to maintain adequate oxygen saturation and adequate ventilation. For instance we have had the experience of an 18 year old patient with a transverse lesion at D8 who suffered a massive pulmonary embolism. He improved slowly after this but there was a long period of serious deterioration in the neurological state, which was attributed to insufficient spinal blood supply secondary to respirator insufficiency. In all conditions when there may be disturbances of spinal blood flow, it is important to emphasize the necessity for maintenance of the general circulation and adequate oxygen carriage.

FURTHER READING

[1] Capon, A. (1961), *Acta neurol. belg.*, **61**, 227.
[2] Clemens, H. J. (1961), *Die Venensysteme der menschlichen Wirbelsäule*. Berlin: de Gruyter.
[3] Field, E. J., Grayson, J. and Rogers, A. F. (1951), *J. Physiol.*, **114**, 56.
[4] Flohr, H. (1968), *Pflügers Arch.* **302**, 268.
[5] Flohr, H., Brock, M. and Pöll, W. (1970), *Pflügers Arch.*, **316**, H. 3/4.
[6] Flohr, H., Pöll, W. and Brock, M. (1971), in *Brain and Blood Flow*, p. 406 (R. W. Ross Russell, Ed.). London: Pitman.
[7] Golenhofen, K., Hensel, H. and Hildebrandt, G. (1963), *Durchblutungsmebungen mit Wärmeleitelementen in Forschung und Klinik*." Stuttgart: Thieme.
[8] Jellinger, K. (1966), *Zur Orthologie und Pathologie der Rückenmarksdurchblutung*. Wien. New York: Springer.
[9] Kessel, Guttman, Maurer (1971), *Neuro-Traumatologie*, Bd. II. München–Berlin–Wien: Urban & Schwarzenberg.
[10] Kindt, G. W., Tucker, T. B. and Huddlestone, J. (1971), in *Brain and Blood Flow*, p. 401. London: Pitman.
[11] Lazorthes, G. and Zadeh, O. (1962), *Rev. Neurol.*, **106**, 535.
[12] Otomo, F., Wolbarsht, M. C., Van Buskirk, C. and Davidson, M. (1960), *J. Nerv. Ment. Dis.* **131**, 418.
[13] Palleske, H. and Hermann, H. D. (1968), *Acta neurochir.*, **19**, 73.
[14] Palleske, H. (1968), *Acta neurochir.*, **19**, 217.
[15] Smith, H. C., Pender, I. W. and Alexander, S. C. (1969), *Amer. J. Physiol.*, **216**, 1158.
[16] Taylor, A. R. (1951), *J. Bone Jt Surg.*, **33B**, 543.
[17] Tönnis, D. (1963), "Rückenmarkstrauma und Mangeldurchblutung," *Beitr. Neurochir.*, H.5. Leipzig: J. A. Barth.
[18] Wüllenweber, R. (1969), *D.Z. Nervenheilk.*, **195**, 33.
[19] Zülch, K. J. (1954), *D.Z. Nervenheilk.*, **172**, 81.

SECTION VIII

1. CEREBROSPINAL FLUID

RALPH H. JOHNSON

INTRODUCTION

The medical student of the last century was taught the value of blood letting, purging and blistering in the treatment of hydrocephalus. His textbook* also advised the use of mercury of digitalis and, after reporting some apparently successfully treated patients, the author added about these cases:

"Where the theory of a disease is obscure, facts are of considerable value".

The physician of that time no longer followed Galen's teaching that the cerebrospinal fluid (CSF) was formed by the brain, stored in the ventricles, and then excreted through the nose. However the physiological background of "water-on-the-brain" was, contrary to the above aphorism, still a mystery.

Over the intervening century and a half since that time, knowledge of the circulation and nature of the CSF has lagged behind information on other systems. Thus, at a 1957 Symposium, the chairman asked:

"Do we really know where, how and why the cerebrospinal fluid is produced and absorbed, and is it a secretion, excretion or transudate?" (Mitchell, in *Ciba Foundation Symposium*, 1958.)

Since those words were written research has added much to our knowledge of CSF, although studies of metabolites have indicated that none of the questions has a simple answer. The *Ciba Foundation Symposium* (1958) provides a useful review up to 1957 and this has been advanced by Davson's valuable monograph (1967).

This review indicates some of the more recent literature related to cerebrospinal fluid. Other chapters describe the pathophysiology of hydrocephalus and therefore go into detail about the formation, circulation, and absorption of CSF. This section summarizes some of that information and discusses its composition.

PRODUCTION AND CIRCULATION

In the adult about 130–140 ml. of the cavity enclosing the brain and spinal cord is occupied by cerebrospinal fluid. It has a very low specific gravity (1·005) and is secreted continuously into the ventricles, chiefly from the ventricular choroid plexuses. The process of secretion is probably an active one as the newly formed secretion differs slightly but significantly from a plasma ultrafiltrate (Table 1). Further evidence is that production of CSF is reduced by the carbonic anhydrase inhibitor, acetazoleamide (Diamox).[15] Filtration is probably a

* *Edinburgh Practice of Physic, Surgery and Midwifery* (1803), Vol. II, p. 304. London, for booksellers in London, Edinburgh and Glasgow.

factor, however, as large molecules fail to enter the CSF due to the interposition of the blood-brain barrier. This appears to depend on the vascular endothelium as large molecules are readily able to pass through the pia and the endothelium is common to the blood-brain and blood CSF interfaces. After formation from the choroid plexuses the fluid then passes out of the ventricles, by way of the foramina of Luschka and Magendie, into the subarachnoid space. It is then absorbed into the venous system via the arachnoid villi. The mean rate for CSF formation is about 0·35 ml./min. and the rate of flow from the ventricles can be studied. Observations have been made of the rate of disappearance from the ventricles of ^{131}I albumin by means of serial scanning with a scintillation counter.[3]

TABLE 1

NORMALLY ACCEPTED VALUES OBTAINED AT LUMBAR PUNCTURE

Pressure (at lumbar puncture)	50–200 mm. H$_2$O
Volume	120–140 ml.
Specific gravity	1·003–1·008
Cells adults	0–5 mononuclears
infants	0–20 mononuclears
Total proteins (mostly albumin)	10–45 mg./100 ml.
Globulin	0–6 mg./100 ml.
Colloidal gold (Lange)	000110000
Urea nitrogen	5–10 mg./100 ml.
Creatinine	0·4–2·2 mg./100 ml.
Non-protein nitrogen	12–30 mg./100 ml.
Uric acid	0·3–1·5 mg./100 ml.
Glucose	50–85 mg./100 ml.
Sodium	144 mEq/l.
Chloride	120–130 mEq/l.
Calcium	4–7 mg./100 ml.
Phosphate	1·2–2·0 mg./100 ml.
Magnesium	1–3 mg./100 ml.
Potassium	2·06–3·86 mEq/l.
Cholesterol	0·06–0·5 mg./100 ml.

The experimental procedure of ventricular perfusion[33] has provided a precise and physiological method for studying CSF secretion and absorption. These studies have allowed definition of several mechanisms regulating the composition of CSF. The concentration of electrolytes is very similar to blood but active mechanisms are probably involved as there is relative independence of the concentrations in CSF of changes in the plasma. There is also an extremely rapid exchange of small molecular weight substances between the CSF and the extracellular fluid of the brain and spinal cord. This exchange has an important influence on the constitution of the fluid and there has been a considerable interest over the last decade in the brain metabolites, which probably enter the CSF by diffusion.

The concentrations of solutes such as sucrose in the CSF are always less than in the brain. This is because passage into brain and CSF is restricted by the respective blood-brain and blood-CSF barriers and by the continual drainage back into the blood by the arachnoid villi which give no restraint to the passage of the solutes. The cerebrospinal fluid normally acts as a "sink" preventing the extracellular fluid of the brain from achieving a true equilibrium with the blood plasma. It appears that the escape of ions and metabolites from the brain occurs by diffusion and it is unlikely that the process adds much in terms of volume to the cerebrospinal fluid.[17]

FUNCTION

The CSF not only acts as a buffer to external pressure waves but may act as a means for removing metabolites from cerebral tissue. Its many other activities are probably dependent upon its hydrogen ion concentration which affects ventilation, cerebral blood flow, and also probably brain metabolism. The changes depend upon alterations in the brain's extracellular fluid pH, with which the CSF pH is in equilibrium. In view of its low glucose content it is highly unlikely that it is nutrient.

ABSORPTION

As CSF is secreted continuously a mechanism for outflow into the vascular system is required. The route is via the arachnoid villi which are essentially evaginations of the subarachnoid space into the dural venous sinuses. It also appears that a subsidiary pathway is via the large spinal veins around the emerging nerve routes. These are highly permeable and allow relatively free flow of cerebrospinal fluid, as well as of protein and also small particles, into the blood. The physical factor favouring the passage of CSF from the subarachnoid space into the vascular system is the higher hydrostatic pressure in the CSF pathways.

It has been suggested that the return of water to the blood stream could depend upon a difference of colloid osmotic pressure due to the protein difference between the two fluids. However, as Davson[14] has pointed out, this is unlikely because it would lead to an accumulation of protein in the CSF and would require the membranes to be impermeable to protein. Electron microscopical studies have raised the possibility that this difficulty could be overcome if protein was absorbed from the CSF by phagocytes in the arachnoid villi walls. These possibilities can now be discarded as a result of elegant experiments by Davson, Hollingsworth and Segal.[16]

Further evidence for the effect of hydrostatic pressure is that several investigations have indicated that the rate of absorption is linearly related to intraventricular pressure (Fig. 1).[31] The rate of absorption is not affected by acetozoleamide (Diamox), and it is therefore probably not an active process.[11] The figure indicates that fluid will accumulate if some of the characteristics of either the absorptive process, the rate of formation, or the outflow pressure, change. This problem is further considered in Chapter IX: 3.

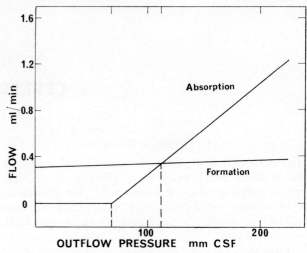

FIG. 1. Superimposed regression lines for CSF formation and absorption as a function of outflow pressure. The intercept at 112 mm. indicates the pressure at which formation and absorption are equal. The pressure at which absorption is zero is also indicated. (From Cutler *et al.* (1968), by kind permission.)

COMPOSITION

The composition of the CSF is close to that of an ultrafiltrate of plasma but differs in certain important respects (Table 2). The fluid is normally clear and colourless; it can be discoloured by blood due to haemorrhage into the central nervous system or local trauma at the time of puncture. Xanthochromia (a yellow tint) may be present in the supernatant fluid after haemorrhage and disappears after 3–4 weeks in the absence of further haemorrhage. It may also occur in meningitis, brain abscess and stasis below a block (Froin's syndrome). The CSF can also be discoloured in jaundice and if a dye, such as acriflavin, is present.

TABLE 2
THE COMPOSITION OF CSF (AVERAGE VALUES)
COMPARED WITH PLASMA (ADAPTED FROM JENNETT[26])

Constituent	Ratio CSF: plasma	CSF	Plasma	Units
pCO₂	1·28	50·2	39·5	
Chloride	1·21	125	103	
Sodium	1·03	144	140	mEq/1.
Bicarbonate	1·01	25·1	24·8	
Magnesium	0·8	2·4	3	
Urea	0·8	12·0	15	mg/100 ml.
Glucose	0·64	64·0	100	
Potassium	0·52	2·1	4	mEq/1.
Calcium	0·33	1·7	5	
Protein	0·0033	20·0	6,000	mg./100 ml.
Cholesterol	0·0002	0·14	175	

Routine clinical observations have followed changes in cell count, pH, sugar, electrolytes and total protein (Table 2). Some details follow about observations upon these constituents. Research in the last decade has added, in particular, to our knowledge of the gammaglobulin fraction and details are given. Much information has also accumulated about other substances including lipids, cerebral amines, tissue enzymes and vitamins. This review concludes with a discussion of these topics. Some of the concentration values of these substances, together with changes which may occur in them, are given in Table 3.

fluid may be normal. The rise in cell count may be observed only two to three days after the development of symptoms.

A variety of cells other than white blood cells may be found in the CSF in association with different conditions, and if appropriate preparations are made the pathologist may be able to make observations of considerable diagnostic value (see Chapter IX: 8).

TABLE 3

SOME OF THE BIOCHEMICAL CONSTITUENTS OF THE CSF WITH NORMAL VALUES, TOGETHER WITH CHANGES IN DISEASE STATES

Constituent	Normal Values	Units	Abnormal Shift	Disorder	References
pH	7.307 ± 0.01 (SEM)		↓ 7.239 ± 0.044	Haemorrhagic CSF	Froman and Smith (1967)
Bicarbonate	22.9 ± 1.0 (SEM)	mEq/l.	↓ 16.71 ± 2.1	Haemorrhagic CSF	Froman and Smith (1967)
Lactate	0.93 ± 3.7 (SEM)	mEq/l.	↑ 8.21 ± 2.7	Haemorrhagic CSF	Froman and Crampton Smith (1967)
Glutamine	8.71 ± 2.5 (SD)	mg./100 ml.	↑22.83 ± 5.52 ↓41.50 ± 5.18	Chronic hypercapnia Hepatic coma	Jaikin and Agrest (1969)
Sugar	68.7 ± 10.6 (SD)	mg./100 ml.		Bacterial meningitis including TB (glucose oxidase method)	Bradley *et al.* (1968)
Chloride	126 ± 1.6 (SD)	mEq/l.	↓ lowest: 99	Tuberculous meningitis	Breyer and Kanig (1970).
Immunoglobulin (IgG)	9.0 ± 5.2 (SD)	% total protein	↑ 18.9 ± 10.7	Multiple sclerosis Myeloma	Riddoch and Thompson (1970)
5-hydroxindol-3-ylacetic acid (5H1AA)	15.7 ± 1.8 (SEM)	μg./ml.	↑ 27.7 ± 5.2 38.0 ± 5.0	Air in CSF space Oral tryptophan	Eccleston *et al.* (1970)
	10.38 ± 1.8 (SEM)	μg./ml.	↑ 233.30 ± 1.05 15.80 ± 2.07 60.10 ± 3.3 50.40 ± 7.80	Recent CVA Old CVA Quadriplegia (recent) Paraplegia (recent)	Misra *et al.* (1967).
Creatine phosphokinase (CPK)	$0-1.5$	i.u./l.	↑ 8	Cerebral tumours	Nathan (1967)
Lactate dehydrogenase (LDH)	8.4 ± 3.7 (SD)	i.u./l.	↑ 85	Metastatic tumours	Davies-Jones (1970)
Glutamic oxalacetic transaminase (GOT)	4.4 ± 1.4 (SD)	i.u./l.	↑ 16.8	Metastatic tumours	Davies-Jones (1970)
Folate	23.6 ± 2.0 (SEM)	μg./ml.	↓ 16.0 ± 2.1	Anticonvulsant therapy	Wells and Casey (1967)

Cells

The normal lymphocyte count is 0–5 white cells/mm.[3] and may be raised in infections and in many other disorders including demyelinating diseases. In multiple sclerosis a slight rise in the CSF cell count may occur in one in four of cases, although only 2 per cent of the total have more than 20 cells/mm.[3,32] These authors did not, however, relate the changes to the clinical condition.

Methods of examination usually require the sample to be concentrated. The introduction of a simple sedimentation method[42] has overcome the problem of distortion which occurred with earlier techniques. The nature of a cellular deposit can therefore be studied more satisfactorily.

It should be noted that an aseptic meningitis (of presumably viral origin) may rarely present with symptoms of headache, vomiting, and meningism, and yet the spinal

Hydrogen Ion Concentration

The subject of CSF pH and its control have recently been reviewed by Cameron,[5] and its role in ventilation was the subject of symposia in 1964[4] and another reported in 1968.[24]

The hydrogen ion concentration is normally maintained within very narrow limits at a pH of about 7.31 and is primarily determined by the level of PCO_2. There is a direct relationship between PCO_2 in the CSF and hydrogen ion concentration in clinical situations, such as chronic hypercapnia.[29] The range is much smaller than that of blood and the pH may change in the opposite direction to that of blood in certain situations.

Pulmonary ventilation is chiefly regulated by the chemical state of the arterial blood, particularly its CO_2 tension ($PaCO_2$) as appreciated by chemoreceptors in the medulla of the brain. Neuronal reflexes also play their part via this respiratory centre system. Changes in O_2 tension cause adjustments of ventilation via the chemoreceptors of the aortic and carotid bodies and not via a direct action on the medulla.

The part the CSF pH plays in the central regulation of ventilation is uncertain but two groups of experiments suggest that it is involved. If an experimental metabolic acidosis is produced by feeding the subject with ammonium chloride, the blood pH falls and the CSF pH rises. An increase, albeit small, in ventilation occurs probably as a result of the CSF alkalosis.

The second series of experiments depends upon perfusion of the ventricular system of the brain with solutions of differing pH and pCO_2 concentrations[19] which produced changes in ventilation independent of blood changes. In general the pH and pCO_2 of CSF changes in the same direction as those of blood in acute respiratory acidosis and alkalosis whereas in metabolic pH changes the tendency is for CSF to go in the opposite direction.

It thus appears that changes in CSF pH have some part in the control of respiration through their exact importance may be small compared with those due to the effect of blood pCO_2. It has been suggested, however, that the effect of blood changes may depend secondarily upon changes in the CSF as there is free exchange between blood and CSF CO_2.

Changes in metabolites from the brain may also modify the initial effect of an alteration in ventilation. Thus chronic hypercapnia results in an increased production of ammonia by cerebral tissue. Nevertheless blood and CSF ammonia levels are not increased but the CSF glutamine is raised.[25] It therefore appears that glutamine may be considered an ammonia carrier. It could be an important method for removing ammonia from the brain and also influence CSF pH and hence respiration.

The pH of the CSF, and hence of the extracellular fluid of the brain, may also play a part in the vascular resistance changes in the brain.[5] Cerebral anoxia and acidosis probably interfere with normal autoregulation of the vessels.[24]

Blood enters the CSF as a result of severe head injury, spontaneous subarachnoid haemorrhage, rupture of a vessel or aneurysm, or during neurosurgery.

Hyperventilation is frequently observed after serious head injuries and a variety of brain lesions, and has been attributed to damage or irritation of specific regions in the central brain stem.[37] If the former explanation were correct then as the $PaCO_2$ falls the arterial pH should rise and the pH of the CSF should also rise above normal. Froman and Smith,[21, 22] however, have investigated a series of patients with a variety of intracranial lesions and measured the changes in pH of CSF. The CSF's were consistently more acid than normal (pH 7·2) and the bicarbonate concentration was reduced. Since it is recognized that a change in pH of CSF influences ventilation they postulated that the hyperventilation did not result from brain damage but resulted from the low CSF pH, due perhaps to metabolism or breakdown of blood in the CSF. Froman and Smith then produced evidence that the fall in pH may be associated with a rise in lactate concentration.

This probably results from the glycolytic action of the enzyme systems of the shed blood cells, glucose being metabolized to lactic acid via the anaerobic Embden-Meyerhof pathway. These observations fitted with diminution of CSF sugar concentration associated with subarachnoid haemorrhage, which had previously been unexplained. It therefore appeared that the metabolic effects of blood in CSF results in a primary CSF acidosis with a pattern of acid-base values previously noted to follow hypoxia and after being at a high altitude.

That the cause for hyperventilation in subarachnoid haemorrhage is an acidosis due to an increased lactate content in the CSF has since been questioned. Lane, Rout and Williamson[30] found that a given CSF lactate was probably associated with *less* hyperventilation in those with haemorrhage than those without and on this, and other evidence, they concluded that in most cases of hyperventilation in acute cerebrovascular disease a neurogenic drive is responsible. The explanation for hyperventilation when head injury occurs has therefore gone full circle in the last decade.

Sugar

The laboratory investigation of meningitis has depended upon CSF cell counts and sugar concentration as well as on culture of the fluid. The effectiveness of therapy could be assessed by following the changes in CSF. The determination of sugar was originally thought to be unreliable in tuberculous meningitis treated with intrathecal streptomycin. It has been shown, however, that the streptomycin interferes with some methods. This is not, however, the case with the Glucose-Oxidase method.[1] The CSF glucose is about the same as that of the blood in ventricular CSF but 10–20 mg./100 ml. less than that of blood in cisternal and lumbar fluids. It is increased in diabetic hyperglycaemia and sometimes in viral encephalitis and syphilis. It is reduced in hypoglycaemia, bacterial or fungal infections and rarely in tumours of syphilis if a gross pleocytosis is present. It should be noted that it may be normal in viral infections and also in tuberculous meningitis.

In some situations, as in CSF rhinorrhoea, it can be important to distinguish CSF from serous fluids. The estimation of sugar, and also electrophoresis for protein in the fluid, can then be a useful guide.

Electrolytes

Electrolyte concentrations are kept constant within narrow ranges with the exception of phosphate, in which the range is much greater. It has long been recognized that the chloride concentration may be diminished in the majority of cases of tuberculous meningitis. It may, however, be normal in early stages of the disease. This change may also be found occasionally in other inflammatory disorders, particularly of the meninges. Inflammation may also be associated with an increased concentration of inorganic phosphate and a decreased content of magnesium.[2] Breyer and Kanig[2] studied a series of 1,000 cases of neurological disease and in spite of the extent of their work no other important clinical correlates were observed and the chloride concentration remains the most useful electrolyte estimation for differential diagnosis for tuberculous meningitis, although diagnosis ultimately depends upon identification of the organism by microscopy or culture.

Protein

A raised total protein level is found in a wide variety of pathological conditions. The highest levels are found when there is a spinal block. Other causes include spinal tumours, particularly neurofibromas even without a block, cerebral tumours, recent infarction or trauma.

The concentration of protein in the CSF is lowest in the ventricles and highest in the lumbar theca. During pneumoencephalography it is usual to find a significant fall in the protein content of successive specimens, which is more marked when the initial lumbar CSF protein is raised.[18] This is probably due to the dilution of lumbar CSF by ventricular or cisternal fluid which is displaced downwards.

The value of protein estimation in the CSF has altered in perspective, and it must be remembered that laboratories have varying standards of accuracy. New techniques such as those of immunoelectrophoresis and microelectrophoresis have already shown themselves of value in particular in the diagnosis of multiple sclerosis, neurosyphilis, and collagenoses. Even when the total protein is normal, the gamma globulin portion may be abnormally high, as indicated by immunoelectrophoresis.

The upper limit of the *gamma globulin* content for "normal" spinal fluid lies between 13 and 16 per cent of the total protein, the exact level being dependent upon the method of assay. Elevation is often considerable in multiple sclerosis (MS) and this change has become generally accepted at present as the best laboratory indication of MS.[32] It has superseded the colloidal gold reaction (the "Lange" curve), because a paretic Lange curve (with a negative Wasserman reaction) is found in only one in ten patients with MS. The gamma globulin may also be raised with neurosyphilis, gliomas, cerebral infarction and infections as well as disorders, such as collagen diseases and carcinoma, which cause high serum globins even though there may be no clinical evidence of neurological involvement. Because of the large number of disorders in which the gamma globulin may be raised several investigations have studied the level above which MS is most likely. Prineas, Teasdale, Latner and Miller[38] found that 44 per cent of all patients with MS had a gamma globulin above 29 per cent of total protein (Fig. 2). There were high levels in neurosyphilis, diseases associated with high serum globulin levels and certain encephalitides, but otherwise fewer than 5 per cent of patients with other neurological diseases exceeded this percentage. No correlation was found between the gamma globulin level and the duration or clinical activity of the disease, or the presence or absence of a paretic Lange curve. Other authors have, however, found a relation with the Lange curve (e.g. Riddoch and Thompson[39]) which is probably because gamma

globulin causes precipitation of colloidal gold. Those cases with a negative Lange but with a raised gamma globulin may occur because of inhibition of colloidal gold precipitation by other substances such as albumin. There was, however, a correlation with the extent of clinical neurological involvement and with the spinal-fluid white-cell count. Prineas *et al.* pointed out that a recent lumbar puncture or myelogram invalidated the test.

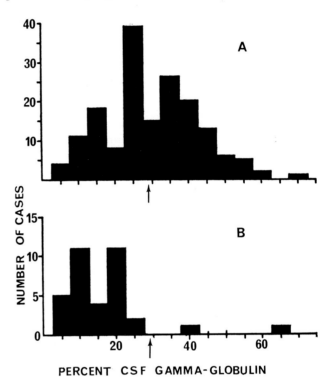

Fig. 2. The percentage of spinal-fluid gamma-globulin in (A) multiple sclerosis, (B) cervical spondylosis. The arrow indicates the upper limit in "miscellaneous" neurological diseases (mean + 2 S.D.); 44 per cent of patients with multiple sclerosis have a level above this. (From Prineas *et al.* (1966), by kind permission.)

Electrophoresis has indicated that the gamma globulin fraction of serum consists of four major classes of immunoglobulins, IgA, IgG, IgM and IgD. Their occurrence in neurological disorders has been studied by Riddoch and Thompson.[39] They did not find IgD although it had been reported by other workers examining CSF; IgA and IgM were raised in fluids with a high total protein and they appear to have no diagnostic value. IgG, which is the major part of the gamma globulin fraction in most cases, was found in all specimens they examined; 62 per cent of their cases with multiple sclerosis had raised levels above those they accepted as normal.

If high percentages of IgG could also be found in the serum of patients with multiple sclerosis the diagnosis of this disorder would be facilitated. Unfortunately several series have indicated that the CSF changes are not consistently reflected in the blood.[27] This supports the suggestion that the abnormal globulin is formed locally in the nerve tissue or from the white cells in the CSF and not by diffusion from the plasma. Kolar *et al.* failed to find any distinct pattern of immunoglobulin change in MS which would allow the diagnosis to be confirmed with certainty.[27, 28]

Raised immunoglobulins may also be found in the CSF in myeloma, when the changes also occur in the blood. They may also occasionally be related to plasma cell deposits within the brain, but this is very unusual.

The raised gamma globulin may also be of diagnostic value in subacute sclerosing panencephalitis, in which immunoglobulin-G (IgG) is probably produced locally within the nervous system. The level may exceed 50 per cent of the total protein in this disorder. Other inflammatory disorders with high IgG levels are post exanthematons and postvaccinial "allergic" encephalomyelitis.

Para-albumins

Abnormalities of serum albumin may be found in some genetic situations, and in many pathological disorders such as those which cause hypoalbuminaemia, e.g. cirrhosis, nephrotic syndrome, or collagen diseases. These changes are reflected in the CSF and therefore abnormal albumins, "para-albumins", may appear in the CSF. They may also appear without any changes being found in the serum albumins. In this situation their appearance in the CSF indicates a pathological process in the central nervous system. The change is not, however, very specific and occurs with any disorder causing oedema of the brain parenchyma.[27]

Lipids

Certain constituents of the CSF are in higher concentration than in the serum and indicate that, although it is in most respects an ultrafiltrate of plasma, some part of it must result from active transport or from synthesis by nervous tissue. The latter may be the explanation for the higher level of myoinositol, which is one of the constituents of certain cerebral lipids.[23] The levels of all lipids are raised above normal in some patients with acute exacerbations of multiple sclerosis and possibly also in children. They are low in acute bacterial meningitis and in some patients with dementia.

In general the determination of CSF lipids is of no diagnostic importance (Cumings[8]). The possible exception is in Refsum's disease in which there is considerable elevation of one fatty acid (phytanic acid) level in association with a markedly raised protein. The level is not necessarily related to a rise in cerebral phytanates (Skrbic and Cumings[41]).

Cerebral Amines

The amines found in the brain each have a peculiar distribution and it has been proposed that they may serve as transmitter agents or modulators of cerebral activity. Their study offers a possibility of providing a pharmacological basis for further understanding the functions of these areas and also therapy in disorders such as Parkinsonism. The metabolites from these substances enter the blood or CSF and should provide an index of turnover

of the amines, although complex variables are involved.[34]

Studies have been made of dopamine, noradrenaline and 5-hydroxytryptamine (5HT). Dopamine and noradrenaline are found in the extrapyramidal system and in autonomic centres in the midbrain. 5HT is also found in midbrain nuclei and their connections and it may be involved in the neuronal control of sleep, temperature and other central autonomic processes. Evidence for the limited region in which 5HT is metabolized in the brain has come from studies of the effect of oral administration of the amino-acid tryptophan. This is a precursor of 5HT, and observations of lumbar CSF have indicated that there is a considerable lag in the rise in the level of its metabolite, 5-hydroxyindol-3-ylacetic acid (5H1AA). The delay is probably due to the time taken for it to diffuse down from the brain to the lumbar space,[19] suggesting that it is produced in the brain rather than the spinal cord. Further evidence for the lower levels of 5H1AA in the spinal cord region is given by Misra, Singh and Bharagara,[33] who studied quadriplegics and paraplegics.

Interest has also concentrated upon homovanillic acid (HVA) from dopamine as well as 5-hydroxyindol-3-ylacetic acid (5H1AA) from 5-HT. Thus patients with endogenous depression appear to have a selective alteration of 5-hydroxyindoles in the brain. Patients with Parkinsonism show impaired metabolism of 5-hydroxyindoles and also dopamine. So far attempts to correlate the improvement of Parkinsonism as a result of L-DOPA therapy with changes in dopamine activity of the CSF have been very limited. The change in the homovanillic acid (HVA) and hence of dopamine, its precursor, has been studied by Curzon, Godwin-Austin, Tomlinson and Kantamaneni.[10] Although they found a positive correlation between L-DOPA dosage and HVA concentration, they found no clear relationship with degree of benefit. These authors did, however, consider that there was evidence that increased brain synthesis of dopamine (and hence of HVA levels in the CSF) was necessary for a therapeutic response to L-DOPA.

A considerable rise in the metabolites also occurs after tissue infarction due to cerebro-vascular accidents (Misra et al.[33]).

Several workers have investigated the physiological role of catecholamines and 5H-T in animals, particularly in temperature regulation, by injecting them and observing the response, and also by cross perfusion experiments. Feldberg and Meyers[20] injected 5HT into the lateral ventricles of a cat. This produced a prolonged rise in body temperature, whereas similar injections of noradrenaline had the opposite effect. There appear, however, to be species differences.[7] Another experimental situation has been the cross perfusion of CSF from the third ventricle of one monkey into the third ventricle of another. When the donor was heated the temperature of the recipient fell, and vice versa. Although one explanation for these findings is that the amines are transmitter substances released at central thermoregulatory synapses it is also possible that they are effective by alteration of blood flow. The blood flow changes could be independent of any primary involvement of the amines in the regulation of body temperature.

Tissue Enzymes

Tissue enzymes are released into body fluids as a result of disease processes and their determination may be useful in assessing a patient's progress. Measurements of serum levels have been particularly useful in this way in muscle disorders such as myocardial infarction, muscular dystrophy and polymyositis. The increases in enzyme activities in extra-cellular fluid result from the damage of cells. As far as the central nervous system is concerned the brain is normally impermeable to the enzymes and therefore any changes that occur are usually only detectable in the CSF. Although several enzymes, such as creatine phosphokinase, lactate dehydrogenase and glutamic oxaloacetic transaminase have been found to be raised in the spinal fluid in association with pathology of the nervous system, the initial hopes that their determination might be of value in diagnosis has only been justified to a very limited extent.

Creatine phosphokinase may be measured in the CSF by several techniques.[35] There is no correlation with the level found in serum or with CSF protein or cell counts. The normal value is exceeded in tumours (60 per cent of Nathan's series) and in some patients with cerebrovascular disease. The usefulness of the investigation awaits further studies. It was originally suggested that it might be helpful in determining the status of hydrocephalus but this is now doubtful. In Nathan's series of 100 cases an absence of elevation in multiple sclerosis, dementia and in most cases of idiopathic epilepsy was noted and he suggested that the investigation might prove useful in differential diagnosis.

Further observations have failed to support this suggestion and it has been concluded that "an increased spinal fluid creatine phosphokinase level was not diagnostic for any particular disease".[40] The diagnostic value of CPK estimation therefore appears to be limited to one use: a raised level suggests the presence of neurological disease.

Lactate dehydrogenase (LDH) and glutamic oxalacetic transaminase (GOT) determinations have also produced conflicting results but studies by Davies-Jones[12,13] have indicated that elevation of both enzymes was associated with metastatic carcinoma of the CNS whereas patients with primary tumours had normal levels. Davies-Jones pointed out that most of the primary tumours he studied were benign and that highly malignant primary tumours might also show similar enzyme changes. It would appear that their determination could eventually prove of more value than that of creatine phosphokinase in that raised LDH and GOT levels were only found in the patients with malignant tumours. The value of the test may be greater because the changes are independent of any consistent rise in CSF protein.

LDH also rises after cerebrovascular accidents and frequently reaches a maximum 24–72 hr. after the event. There is no definite relation to other changes in the CSF such as cell count, xanthochromia or protein concentrations. The behaviour of the other enzymes in the CSF is irregular but a rise in GOT and of transaminases is seen in about 50 per cent of patients with large infarcts.

Although many investigations have been carried out into changes in CSF enzyme activities the results have been very variable apart from those already discussed. It can be concluded that the estimation of CSF enzymes is of limited practical value compared with their estimation in serum.

Vitamin B$_{12}$ and Folate

Patients with epilepsy receiving anticonvulsant therapy may develop megaloblastic anaemia. They may also show a steady deterioration of mental performance. The anaemia will respond well to folic acid but in some an increase in fits will occur unless B$_{12}$ is then given as the level of this vitamin may fall when treatment is instituted with folic acid. The development of symptoms appears to be related to the CSF level of folate. There is a positive correlation between serum and CSF folate levels, the latter being more concentrated, and normally three times that of blood and if it falls below the blood level, then retardation and dementia may become severe. The reason for the higher concentration in CSF than in blood is not known.

Apart from the high proportion of subnormal folate levels in drug-treated epileptic patients, the mean levels in most other disorders does not differ from controls.[43] An association between folate deficiency and tuberculosis has, however, been noted. The deficiency may be present in epileptics without anaemia being present and may occur with several anticonvulsants, particularly with phenytoin.

CONCLUSION

Just over a decade ago Professor Mitchell asked fundamental questions about the CSF and pointed to the "need to recognize the chinks no less than the chasms in our understanding" (*Ciba Foundation Symposium*, 1958). Our knowledge of the CSF has extended considerably but although some of its pathophysiology is better understood, "chasms" still exist in our biochemical knowledge. Davson's monograph is the most useful summary of research up to 1967 and yet much of our knowledge of cerebral amines, tissue enzymes, and even the immunoglobulins, has developed since that time. Sir George Pickering once wrote that he regarded scientific research as an intellectual adventure. In this little known area the researcher is just beginning his journey.

FURTHER READING

[1] Bradley, W. G., Ayyar, D. R., Freed, A. H. de C., Woolf, I. L., Cassells-Smith, A. J. and Wilkinson, R. H. (1968), "Streptomycin and CSF Sugar," *Brit. med. J.*, **4**, 454.

[2] Breyer, U. and Kanig, K. (1970), "Cerebrospinal Fluid Electrolyte Disturbances in Neurological Disorders," *Neurology*, **20**, 247–253.

[3] Brocklehurst, G. (1968), "Use of Radio-iodinated Serum Albumin in the Study of Cerebrospinal Fluid Flow," *J. Neurol. Neurosurg. Psychiat.*, **31**, 162–168.

[4] Brooks, C. McC., Kao, F. F. and Lloyd, B. B. (1966), *Cerebrospinal Fluid and the Regulation of Ventilation.* (Report of a Symposium, New York, 1964.) Oxford: Blackwell.

[5] Cameron, I. R. (1969), "Acid-base Changes in Cerebrospinal Fluid," *Brit. J. Anaesth.*, **41**, 213–221.

[6] Ciba Foundation Symposium (1958), *The Cerebrospinal Fluid, Production, Circulation and Absorption*. (G. E. W. Wolstenholme and C. M. O'Connor, Eds.). London: J. & A. Churchill.

[7] Cooper, K. E. (1966), "Temperature Regulation and the Hypothalamus," *Brit. med. Bull.*, **22**, 238–282.

[8] Cumings, J. N. (1971), "The Lipidoses," in *Handbook of Clinical Neurology* (P. J. Vinken and G. W. Bruyn, Eds.). Amsterdam: North Holland Publishing Co. In press.

[9] Cunningham, D. J. C. and Lloyd, B. B. (1963), *The Regulation of Human Respiration*. Oxford: Blackwells Scientific Publications.

[10] Curzon, G., Godwin-Austin, R. B., Tomlinson, E. B. and Kantamaneni, B. D. (1970), "The Cerebrospinal Fluid Homovanillic Acid Concentration in Patients with Parkinsonism Treated with L-DOPA," *J. Neurol. Neurosurg. Psychiat.*, **33**, 1–6.

[11] Cutler, R. W. P., Page, L., Galicich, J. and Watters, G. V. (1968), "Formation and Absorption of Cerebrospinal Fluid in Man," *Brain*, **91**, 707–720.

[12] Davies-Jones, G. A. B. (1969), "Lactate Dehydrogenase and Glutamic Oxalacetic Transaminase of the Cerebrospinal Fluid in Tumours of the Central Nervous System," *J. Neurol. Neurosurg. Psychiat.*, **32**, 324–327.

[13] Davies-Jones, G. A. B. (1970), "Lactic Dehydrogenase and Glutamic Oxalacetic Transaminase of the Cerebrospinal Fluid in Neurological Disease," *J. Neurol. Sci.*, **11**, 583–591.

[14] Davson, H. (1956), *Physiology of the Ocular and Cerebrospinal Fluids*. London: J. & A. Churchill.

[15] Davson, H. (1967), *Physiology of the Cerebrospinal Fluid*. London: J. & A. Churchill.

[16] Davson, H., Hollingsworth, G. and Segal, M. B. (1970), "The Mechanism of Drainage of the Cerebrospinal Fluid," *Brain*, **93**, 665–678.

[17] Davson, H. and Segal, M. B. (1969), "Effect of Cerebrospinal Fluid on Volume of Distribution of Extracellular Markers," *Brain*, **92**, 131–136.

[18] Dykes, J. R. W. and Stevens, D. L. (1970), "Alterations in Lumbar Cerebrospinal Fluid Protein During Air Encephalography," *Brit. med. J.*, **1**, 79–81.

[19] Eccleston, D., Ashcroft, G. W., Crawford, T. B. B., Stanton, J. B., Wood, D. and McTurk, P. H. (1970), "Effect of Tryptophan Administration in 5H1AA in Cerebrospinal Fluid in Man," *J. Neurol. Neurosurg. Psychiat.*, **33**, 269–272.

[20] Feldberg, W. and Myers, R. D. (1964), "Effects on Temperature of Amines Injected into the Cerebral Ventricles. A New Concept of Temperature Regulation," *J. Physiol. (Lond.)*, **173**, 226–237.

[21] Froman, C. and Smith, A. C. (1966), "Hyperventilation Associated with Low pH of Cerebrospinal Fluid after Intracranial Haemorrhage," *Lancet*, **i**, 780–782.

[22] Froman, C. and Smith, A. C. (1967), "Metabolic Acidosis of the Cerebrospinal Fluid Associated with Subarachnoid Haemorrhage," *Lancet*, **i**, 965–967.

[23] Garcia-Buñuel, L. and Garcia-Buñuel, V. M. (1965), "Cerebrospinal Fluid Levels of Free Myoinositol in Some Neurological Disorders," *Neurology*, **15**, 348–350.

[24] Ingvar, D. H., Lassen, N. A., Sicujö, B. K. and Skinhøj, E. (Eds.) (1968), "CBF and CSF International Symposium on Cerebral Blood Flow and Cerebrospinal Fluid," *Scand. J. Clin. Lab. Invest.*, **22** (Suppl. 102).

[25] Jaikin, A. and Agrest, A. (1969), "Cerebrospinal Fluid Glutamine Concentration in Patients with Chronic Hypercapnia," *Clin. Sci.*, **36**, 11–14.

[26] Jennett, W. B. (1967), "The Central Nervous System," in *Scientific Foundations of Surgery* (Wells, C. and Kyle, J., Eds.). London: Heinemann.

[27] Kolar, O. J., Ross, A. T. and Herman, J. T. (1969), "Para-albumins in Cerebrospinal Fluid," *Neurology*, **19**, 826–833.

[28] Kolar, O. J., Ross, A. T. and Herman, J. T. (1970), "Serum and Cerebrospinal Fluid Immunoglobulins in Multiple Sclerosis," *Neurology*, **20**, 1052–1061.

[29] Lane, D. J., Howell, J. B. L. and Stretton, T. B. (1970), "The Effect of Dichlorphenamide on Blood and Cerebrospinal Fluid Acid-base State in Chronic Ventilatory Failure," *Clin. Sci.*, **39**, 391–406.

[30] Lane, D. J., Rout, M. W. and Williamson, D. H. (1971), "Mechanism of Hyperventilation in Acute Cerebrovascular Accidents," *Brit. med. J.*, **3**, 9–12.

[31] Lorenzo, A. V., Page, L. K. and Watters, G. V. (1970), "Relationship Between Cerebrospinal Fluid Formation, Absorption and Pressure in Human Hydrocephalus," *Brain*, **93**, 679–692.

[32] McAlpine, D., Lumsden, C. E. and Acheson, E. D. (1965), *Multiple Sclerosis, A Re-appraisal*. London and Edinburgh: E. & S. Livingstone.

[33] Misra, S. S., Singh, K. S. P. and Bharagara, K. P. (1967), "Estimation of 5-hydroxytryptamine (5HT) Level in Cerebrospinal Fluid of Patients with Intracranial or Spinal Lesions," *J. Neurol. Neurosurg. Psychiat.*, **30**, 163–165.

[34] Moir, A. T. B., Ashcroft, G. W., Crawford, T. B. B., Eccleston, D. and Guldberg, H. C. (1970), "Cerebral Metabolites in Cerebrospinal Fluid as a Biochemical Approach to the Brain," *Brain*, **93**, 357–368.

[35] Nathan, M. J. (1967), "Creatine Phosphokinase in the Cerebrospinal Fluid," *J. Neurol. Neurosurg. Psychiat.*, **30**, 52–55.

[36] Pappanheimer, J. R., Heisey, S. R., Jordan, E. F. and Downer, J. de C. (1962), "Perfusion of the Cerebral Ventricular System in Unanaesthetized Goats," *Amer. J. Physiol.*, **203**, 763–774.

[37] Plum, F. and Swanson, A. G. (1959), "Central Neurogenic Hyperventilation in Man," *Arch. Neurol. Psychiat.*, **81**, 535–549.

[38] Prineas, J., Teasdale, G., Latner, A. L. and Miller, H. (1966), "Spinal-fluid Gamma-globulin and Multiple Sclerosis," *Brit. med. J.*, **2**, 922–924.

[39] Riddoch, D. and Thompson, R. A. (1970), "Immunoglobulin Levels in the Cerebrospinal Fluid," *Brit. med. J.*, **1**, 396–399.

[40] Sherwin, A. L., Norris, J. W. and Bulcke, J. A. (1969), "Spinal Fluid Creatine Kinase in Neurologic Disease," *Neurology*, **19**, 993–999.

[41] Skrbic, T. R. and Cumings, J. N. (1969), "Phytanic Acid in Tissue Lipids in Rrefsum's Disease," *Clin. Chin. Acta*, **23**, 17–21.

[42] Sörnäs, R. (1967), "A New Method for the Cytological Examination of the Cerebrospinal Fluid," *J. Neurol. Neurosurg. Psychiat.*, **30**, 568–577.

[43] Wells, D. G. and Casey, H. J. (1967), "*Lactobacillus* Casei CSF Folate Activity," *Brit. med. J.*, **3**, 834–836.

2. THE CEREBRAL EDEMAS

W. EUGENE STERN

The study of cerebral edema has been plagued by multiple complexities:

(1) Lack of agreement as to definitions and the modifications of definitions necessary to accommodate new laboratory observations.

(2) Lack of tissue homogeneity throughout the brain, causing area-dependent differences in cellular and tissue responses.

(3) The non-homogenous distribution of solutes when introduced into the cerebrospinal fluid (CSF).

(4) Species differences in laboratory animal models whereby the sizes of tissue fluid compartments vary in relation to brain size.

(5) Ontogenetic differences in the behavior of brain tissue.

(6) Artifacts and pathological factors introduced in tissue preparation or preservation.

(7) Difficulties inherent in using the human brain as an experimental model and the pitfalls of correlating results from animal models with those encountered in the clinical condition.

Cerebral edema is an abnormal state which, although not peculiar to man's diseased brain, probably has some unique features when encountered in man.[49]

COMMON DENOMINATOR

Evidence cannot support a unitarian concept of cerebral edema but does suggest that the common denominator of all the cerebral edemas is an increase in water in the extravascular portion of brain tissue (excluding the CSF spaces). Accompanying the increase in brain tissue water (irrespective of what other patterns of chemical changes occur) is an increase in tissue bulk. The tumefaction, if of sufficient magnitude, has its own important influences on intracranial mass dynamics. Although edema produces increases in tissue bulk, it is not to be confused with other processes which alter bulk and which may be coexistent, e.g. vascular tree engorgement, increased cerebral blood flow, increased volume of cerebrospinal fluid as in the case of CSF pathway obstruction. Some authors have made distinctions between "swelling" and "edema" which seem to contribute little to our understanding, especially in view of the derivation from the Greek, in which "oedema" means swelling.

EXPERIMENTAL MODELS

In the experimental models developed to study the problem, edema-inducing techniques produce effects which may differ, depending on the agent utilized. Structural (anatomical), biochemical, and physical aspects of the phenomena have come under analysis.

Edema in the Absence of Membrane Structural Damage

Edema in the absence of breakdown in the blood–brain barrier (minimal or absent disturbance of capillary and cell membrane selectivity) is encountered in its simplest form when *water intoxication* occurs (administration of a water load in excess of 10 per cent body weight, plus exogenous antidiuretic hormone). Swelling of astrocytic processes is produced in the gray matter; in the white matter, the astrocytes also swell (even to the point of rupture), as do the extracellular spaces.[31,50] The other glial elements, the capillary endothelium, and the neurones do *not* participate in the anatomical change, although neuronal dysfunction and, hence, neural deficit do, indeed, occur. This form of edema is generalized in the cerebral hemispheres, although detailed analyses of areal differences have not been made. The structural change produced by water intoxication has been compared by Wasterlain and Torack[50] with those changes produced by other edema-inducing techniques. Their data, presented in table form, illustrate the unique characteristic of this form of edema. The demonstrated integrity of the basement membranes and capillary endothelial cells, together with evidence of dilution of brain tissue sodium and potassium, a fall in brain tissue fluid osmolality, and the absence of vital dye staining, have led to the conclusion that, in this type of edema, the water has passed from the vascular tree into the tissue under the influence of osmotic gradients.[46]

Another edema encountered experimentally in the absence of demonstrable ultrastructural damage to membranes and intercellular functions is that produced by *organic tin compound intoxication*.[25,44,50] The edema fluid in this condition is found within myelin clefts (splits in the myelin lamellae) leading to large, clear vacuoles without obvious communication with the extracellular space of white matter. Although some evidence supports an accompanying gray matter astrocytic swelling, the dominant finding is in the white matter. Unlike the edema fluid of water intoxication, that of organic tin intoxication reveals an *increase* in sodium and chloride. There is no albumin penetration or vital dye staining, and the fluid is probably an ultrafiltrate of plasma. Space and compartment labelling data also provide supporting evidence that the spaces of fluid in tin intoxication are not in direct communication with the extracellular space. It would appear that temporary alterations in permeability or transport mechanisms account for the edema, i.e. the tin inhibits oxygen consumption and, hence, oxidative phosphorylation in the mitochondria. How this influences myelin sheath or membrane selectivity, permeability, or transport is not clear, although findings in various experimental models have been reported.[2,10,35,44]

Edema in Association with Structural Damage

In the presence of intact tissue membranes, water may be expected to respond to the creation of osmotic gradients, and in the example of the cerebral edemas of water intoxication and triethyl tin poisoning, the edema fluid itself can be removed from the tissue by such osmotic activity.[27] By contrast, many forms of edema are associated with not only a paralysis of physiological activity of cell membranes but also rupture thereof (anatomical injury and necrosis).

The edema of *inflammation*, such as is produced by the implantation of pellets of bacterial endotoxins, does not appear to mimic that of tin or water intoxication. The gray matter (astroglia or oligodendroglia?) cell processes swell, and the extracellular space in the white matter increases, even in the absence of tissue destruction. Vital dye staining also appears, indicating a protein-rich edema fluid.[19]

Clasen *et al.*[10] have pointed out that, with the exception of water intoxication and tin poisoning (with its very limited clinical implications), edema fluid is not an ultrafiltrate of plasma but, rather, contains a lower concentration of sodium and chloride than does serum. It should be noted, however, that such edema fluid may be sodium and chloride poor relative to serum, but rich relative to normal brain tissue.

Techniques producing focal lesions have been utilized in attempts to create a model analogous to perifocal edema accompanying clinical disease, e.g. neoplasm, abscess, and trauma. In most studies these techniques have resulted in well-documented increases in blood-brain barrier permeability in close proximity to the focal lesion with decreasing concentration of the signs of edema as one moves away from the site of insult. Almost always, concomitant tissue destruction occurs at the epicenter of the process.

An important concept to recognize, as has been emphasized by Bakay,[2] is that, although a break may occur in the physical integrity of tissues at the site of insult, the edema process will extend along tissue pathways to remote parts of the brain where tissue integrity persists. Such demonstrations by isotope-tagged substances, proteinaceous tracers such as ferritin, and vital dyes reveal gradients of edema which may involve (as in the case of inflammation-inducing implants) the entire brain in small animals. Thus, several of the techniques which produce focal brain insult result in sequential changes with areal gradation, in contrast to those accompanying the more diffusely distributed disturbances produced by water and tin intoxication.

A frequently studied form of focal insult is that produced by *focal freezing* over a cerebral hemisphere utilizing a column of frozen isopentane or frozen CO_2. Such an insult produces a hemorrhagic lesion with tissue damage and death. In the *cortex*, the major change, apart from tissue destruction and hemorrhage, is the swelling of one glial component (probably the astroglia). No cortical extracellular space enlargement occurs. In the *white matter*, however, there is both astroglial swelling and extensive enlargement of extracellular spaces. Tracer substances are found in high concentration near the lesion, especially in relation to capillaries, and are seen to diminish as the distance away increases. The edema fluid (which appears to be iso-osmolar with plasma in such lesions) is presumably derived from plasma, is protein-rich, and is distributed in a gradient of decreasing intensity as one moves away from the lesion. The routes taken in distribution of the edema fluid in the gray matter appear to be both intracellular and extracellular, although no increase in extracellular space is seen in gray matter. The presence of particulate tracers, e.g. proteinaceous ferritin, in swollen glial cells confirms the intracellular process. In the white matter, the extracellular route is dominant.[26,45] The major alteration in the natural barriers appears to be at the site of injury rather than throughout the edematous region. This observation is of some importance relative to the possible effectiveness of osmotic agents in removing water from regions where intact membranes permit osmotic gradients to be created.

If the edema fluid is iso-osmolar with plasma, then, clearly, a steeper gradient will be needed between plasma and brain tissue fluid to effect the same bulk water movement than if the fluid is hypo-osmolar, as in the case of water and, possibly, tin intoxication.

Other techniques of producing focal edema include: exposure of the cortex; insults with nitrogen gas jets; introduction of pellets of metals, inorganic chemical compounds, experimental tumors, or psyllium seeds into the brain; exposure to ultrasonic or laser energy; ionizing radiation; prolonged compression by balloons; intravascular oil injections; direct laceration of the cortex and subcortical tissues; and exposure to radiofrequency energy.[4,41,44]

The Composite Picture of "Traumatic" Edema

The picture emerges that the *cortex* response is primarily that of intracellular swelling of the astroglia. Although some debate has taken place as to the ultrastructural criteria of astrocytes compared with other glial elements, the weight of opinion favors the astrocytic location of cortical edema. The *white matter* responds also with astrocytic swelling but occurring with an increase in extracellular space, consonant with the long-known observations made upon human brain material. The edema fluid usually is characterized by an increase in sodium and chloride content as compared with that of normal brain, and, therefore, the brain tissue examined usually shows an increased sodium/potassium ratio if not a fall in potassium content due to the dilution of tissue potassium by plasma. When the process produces tissue death and fracture of capillary membranes, such as occurs with most of the techniques described, the edema fluid is characterized by increased amounts of proteinaceous substances and other constituents, either occurring spontaneously or injected artificially into the vascular stream. A reversible proteinaceous edema has been described which is an exception to the concept that tissue destruction is at the heart of large molecule escape from the vascular compartment (*see below*).

TEMPORAL CONSIDERATIONS

The tempo of the evolution of the edema following a single, time-certain insult will vary. The peaks of the processes have been documented. Rovit and Hagan[41] found maximal edema 24–48 hr. after lesion-production by radiofrequency energy. Water intoxication edema is obvious 2 hr. after the administration of a water load. (CSF pressure rises within 30 min. of intravenous water administration.) Freezing-induced edema has been identified 4 hr. after injury, reaching a peak 24–48 hr. thereafter.[20] Laser energy-induced edema also appears to be maximal at 48 hr. following exposure. As might be expected, exposure to a toxic material such as triethyltin requires a matter of days before neurologic deficit appears with which cerebral edema may be associated.

Shaw et al.[42] studied autopsied case material from man following ischemic infarction (with arterial occlusion and minimal hemorrhage). By documenting transtentorial herniations and midline shifts from their own material and by correlating the data with previously reported cases fulfilling similar criteria, they constructed a temporal concept of swelling: The process was well developed in 24 hr., reached a maximum on the third or fourth day, and usually was gone in 2 weeks.[3]

Whatever shifts of water occur to produce it, the influence of edema upon brain bulk can approach critical values for survival; at such times, the confining nature of the intracranial cavity may limit the process by physical barriers. That such physical limitation occurs is revealed by the experience of cranial expansion witnessed following massive cranial decompression operations.[7]

There are two forms of cerebral insult worthy of special mention: the edema accompanying cerebral neoplasia and that associated with anoxic insults.

SPECIAL CEREBRAL EDEMAS

Edema with Neoplasia

Few experimental models of brain neoplasms have been studied with reference to the accompanying edema process. Inoculated mouse and rabbit gliomas and sarcomas produce the familiar response of the gray matter, i.e. a swelling of glial cell processes. When these rupture, as they do occasionally, in the superficial white matter, there is an increase in extracellular space. In the deep white matter, the edema fluid is found extracellularly.[1,16] Tracer studies would indicate that the edema fluid is protein-rich and that the barriers to protein molecules and other particulate matter are penetrated. Bakay[2] likens the process to that accompanying trauma, but study of the process which accompanies spontaneously occurring tumors is required, since the inoculation of the animal is, in itself, traumatic.[22] The vast experience gained with clinical material before the advent of ultrastructural studies is still worthy of recognition.[20]

In 1966 two studies were reported on the pathology of human cerebral edema.[1,30] Both included ultrastructural analyses, one limited only to the edema associated with gliomas while the other contained a predominant number of neoplasms; no distinctions were reported between the edema accompanying neoplasm, abscess, or hematoma. The process is identified as predominately an extracellular one, but in both cortex and white matter the cytoplasmic processes of the astroglia also are swollen, notably about vascular structures. Occasional breaks in cellular-limiting membranes give some increase in extracellular space in the cortex. The main changes are seen in the deeper layers of cortex and in white matter where the extracellular spaces are enlarged, as are the periaxonal spaces. Glial cell membranes in the white matter also can be broken, but the extracellular spaces are enlarged in the white matter in the absence of such fractures. As might be anticipated, cellular debris is found floating in the extracellular space when cell membranes are broken. The chemical analysis of this form of edema demonstrates the familiar pattern of a rise in sodium and chloride content in both gray and white matter, especially the latter, and a fall in gray matter potassium, that is, the potassium in the potassium-rich cells is diluted by the potassium-poor fluid derived from the vascular compartment. The altered selectivity of the vascular endothelium (and possibly the basement membranes) in neoplasms may be recognized in vivo by observing the appearance of intravascularly injected fluorescein, which labels serum protein, and from gradients of concentrations of radioactive isotopes similarly injected.

In the example of neoplastic tissue per se, we are dealing with structures which are and have been abnormal throughout their neoplastic existence. This is in contrast to normal tissue which is subsequently altered by other pathological processes. Thus, the neoplasm is associated with a variable degree of abnormal fluid exchange through "loose" junctions at the capillary endothelial level and, perhaps, widened intercellular clefts between the investing perivascular glial end-feet.

Reulen et al.[39] analyzed human surgical material sampled in grossly appearing edematous regions adjacent to a variety of surgically exposed central masses (neoplasms, hematomas, and foci of trauma) as well as from areas remote from the discussed sites. Both gray and white matter water content rose, the latter to two to three times that of the former. Although histologic studies were not made, high-energy phosphates and glycolytic metabolites were analyzed. Creatinine phosphate and adenosinetriphosphate (ATP) were decreased, whereas adenosinediphosphate (ADP), adenosinemonophosphate (AMP), and inorganic phosphate were increased in the areas of increased water uptake which, on gross examination, were considered to be edematous. Their data also suggested an increased anaerobic glycolysis of the edematous tissue. This work leaves in doubt whether the ATP reduction seen in association with tin intoxication is a specific white matter enzyme inhibition caused by tin as Torack[48] proposed or whether it might also be a basis for edema in other diseased states.

That neoplasms which are accompanied by edema but which also act as mass-compressing lesions do not necessarily produce the edema by a process generated within the tumor is recognized when we note the edema which occurs after prolonged balloon compression or extradural fragments of kelp (laminaria). (*See* Zülch in reference 20).

Edema with Infarction (Not Anoxia)

Cerebral infarction with death of tissue is associated with mass effects upon brain tissue,[42] and the pattern of edema findings is similar to that which accompanies the edema of trauma, e.g. cold-induced injury. Whether or not anoxic insults to the brain produce edema has also been of interest to clinicians. Plum et al.[37] found little evidence of edema in rats subjected to carotid ligation and exposed to decreased oxygen tension in the inspired air unless necrosis was present. Bakay[2] considered that anoxia caused cerebral edema only when accompanied by severe hypercarbia, such as under the circumstances of an arterial pH < 6.75 and an O_2 saturation < 25 per cent.[3] Regrettably, these studies did not determine whether there was an increase in water content of the tissue and although increased cerebrospinal fluid pressure was documented, the effects of hypercarbia upon that function are recognized as being independent of the occurrence of edema. We would rely on the more recent data of Norris and Pappius[33] who, while observing profound neurological sequelae in their experiments with cats, found that no edema accompanied hypoxia, with or without hypercarbia, in the absence of histological damage.

A Reversible, Non-traumatic Proteinaceous Edema

In our consideration of the edemas which accompany trauma, the edema fluid is seen to contain large particles which are derived from plasma and which probably have gained their extra-vascular location from disruption of capillary cell membranes, that is, tissue destruction. Whether severe venous stasis in the brain can produce edema without vessel disruption (hydrostatic edema), is still a moot point, and most evidence suggests otherwise; nevertheless, one very important piece of work requires emphasis. Barlow's group[12] has shown clearly that a functional derangement may occur in the brain with extravasation of water *and albumin* (iodinated human serum albumin) related to the duration of the functional abnormality. Prolonged pentylenetetrazol-induced seizures caused an increase in albumin in all brain tissue sampled: cortex, white matter, and especially the thalamus, with significant water increases noted in the latter. The reversibility of these abnormalities with administration of dexamethasone will be discussed below, but these findings are important in that structural damage is presumed not to be an immutable condition for the accumulation of proteinaceous edema fluid in cerebral tissue. That there may well be other edema-producing stimuli which act in a similar fashion must be entertained.[1] This consideration is relevant to that edema which accompanies neoplasms (*vide supra*) and to the extravasation of protein-rich fluid by tumors exposed to cisternal CSF pathways, e.g. the 8th nerve neurilemomas.

THE INTRA- AND EXTRACELLULAR PROCESS OF EDEMA ACCUMULATION

In the presence of both intracellular and extracellular edema fluid accumulation, the question may be asked: Is this accumulation sequential or more or less simultaneous, and if the former is true, in what order does the process take place? In the gray matter, the question is redundant, for there is little change in the spaces between cells other than the limited pools of fluid which may accumulate if swollen cells fracture. In the white matter, the site of the most severe changes in almost all the edemas, the evidence from time sequence studies supports the concept that the fluid appears extracellularly first and intraglially second. The astrocyte is the dominant partner in association with some oligodendrocytic participation.[1,17,18]

The possibility that the intracellular swelling seen in the astroglia may be of more than one fundamental type (such as a difference in reaction between cortical and white matter astrocytes)[48] has been raised by indirect evidence suggesting that, at times, the glial processes of cortical astrocytes behave as an "extracellular" space with a higher sodium and chloride content than in other cells.[15,44] This question is as yet unresolved, as is the question of how the edema fluid reaches the astroglia, whether through the capillary cells or through their junctions. Outside the capillary, the prevailing concept is that the intercellular clefts, not the glial cytoplasm, serve as the main pathway for rapid fluid, electrolyte, and larger molecular access to deeper tissue. The reader is referred to the excellent review of Kuffler and Nicholls.[23]

When the edema-producing process destroys the fine anatomical relationships, the mechanisms involved in edema fluid accumulation become more obvious and defy the sophisticated analysis implied in the above comments which apply to a structurally "intact" system and to the edema accumulation which occurs at sites remote from injury.

The role of *pinocytosis* is not fully elucidated but is probably not great in the rapid accumulation of edema fluid, although it may be important in the transport of particulate matter and in the resolution of the process, e.g. in the uptake of large molecules.

Only Part of the Elephant

Until the full spectrum of biochemical derangements has been comprehended for the various etiological entities which are associated with cerebral edema, it is difficult to ascribe a cause and effect relationship to a single physio-chemical system. Systems studied in isolation may be truly part of the whole picture, but a single pigment doesn't make a painting. This applies to the interesting observation on the highly effective way in which *serotonin* produces edema when injected intracerebrally. If the etiological mechanism (such as trauma) releases free serotonin in the brain and if its mode of action is to disrupt the cement of the vascular-endothelial cellular barrier, as has been suggested, then we have another stroke on the canvas but still not the whole concept.[34] Each experimental protocol may have its variable; thus the edema of the periventricular cerebral tissue in *hydrocephalus* has been found to be pressure-dependent,[32] whereas the edema associated with iso-osmolal surface perfusion of primate cortex is a linear function of potassium ion concentration.[5]

THE BASIS OF THERAPY

And so not only do we have a variety of techniques to produce edema, some of which are akin to clinical entities and which vary quantitatively and qualitatively in the edema associated with them, but so do we recognize a broadening complex of pathogenetic mechanisms, one or more of which in varying combinations may be at work, some primary and some secondary to more fundamental preceding mechanisms.

To the extent that we can appreciate these different mechanisms, so then may we be able to offer rational therapy.

An analysis of the therapeutic armamentarium available to combat the cerebral edemas reveals that certain modes of treatment approach a *reversal* of one or more of the primary derangements of function; others are directed toward *altering normal tissue*, and still others influence the remote or secondary effects of the altered mass dynamics. A rigorous criterion of effective therapy would be the complete reversal of the structural and biochemical abnormalities of the edematous tissue. Such a search is made in the laboratory since, in man, the opportunity is rare for the analysis of pre- and post-therapeutic tissue taken from the same individual.

Steroid Therapy

Since their introduction into clinical medicine by Galicich and French,[14] glucosteroids have gained acceptance as valuable therapeutic agents. However, not all experimental work has supported the efficacy of steroid therapy in the control of cerebral edema, most likely because of the great variability in techniques used for evaluation. Thus, in the work of Clasen and associates,[8] the insult was massive and the animals were sacrificed 12 hr. after injury. These data are pertinent because Pappius and McCann,[36] also studying cold-induced edema, found that the objective laboratory findings of beneficial effects of steroids were not measurable until the *second* 24 hr. after injury. In the study by Benson et al.,[4] laser energy was used in rats and produced a coagulation necrosis with remote changes, suggesting that the edema-producing lesion was leaking fluid from tissue disruption and that the fluid accumulation was conceivably *irreversible* in its pathogenesis.

Steroid therapy (dexamethasone) in experimental triethyltin-induced edema in rabbits protects against clinical deterioration, restricts the edema to focal areas, and reduces the biochemical changes to a significant degree.[47] The study by Long et al.[28] on dogs and rabbits which were rendered edematous by psyllium seed and balloon techniques demonstrated clearly a quantitative improvement in light microscopic and ultrastructural changes as well as in the clinical state in glucosteroid-administered animals. These same workers reported similar beneficial effects of steroid therapy on the ultrastructural criteria of edema in patients with intracranial neoplasms and other mass lesions.[29,30] Of necessity, comparable patients rather than the same patients served as their control group. The maximal effects were seen on astrocytic cytoplasm and extracellular fluid accumulation in the white matter.

Reconstitution of the deranged transport systems for sodium and water is the suggested mode of action of the steroid. In cerebral edema associated with experimental cerebral neoplasia, the interesting observations of Kotsilimbas et al.[21] that steroid therapy may produce some of its effects by inhibiting tumor growth should not be overlooked in assessing the mode of steroid action. The work by Rovit and Hagan[41] on focal radio-frequency injury-induced edema in cats demonstrated the salutory effects of prophylactic combined with post-injury therapy and emphasized important aspects of steroid use: some reparable tissue must be available for the steroid to influence; necrotic tissue cannot be salvaged. The steroid appears to correct a functional derangement, perhaps stabilizing cell membranes and influencing local enzyme systems with a resulting decrease in transcellular water and electrolyte shifts. The earlier that therapy can be instituted, preferably in advance of the edema-initiating mechanism, the better the possibility of favorable results. Although pre-insult therapy is impossible in cases of human head injuries, treatment before the peak of the process is practical in more slowly-evolving processes.

It appears that no two edemas will be influenced by steroids to the same degree. Factors which tend to render an edema "susceptible" to beneficial influence include: (1) the earliest possible institution of therapy in the pathogenesis of the edema-producing process; (2) a slow rather than catastrophic tempo of the disease mechanism; (3) a process which produces a mass of destroyed tissue which is below a critical volume, and which will not cause death to the patient before the benefits of therapy can be realized (24 hr.); and (4) a process which, even in the presence of some irreversible tissue destruction, is surrounded by functionally reparable and potentially viable structures. Eisenberg et al.[12] demonstrated that dexamethasone reduces the increased brain vascular permeability to protein and water uptake which is induced by prolonged seizures. One or more of the above factors may explain the lack of success of steroid therapy in ameliorating experimental cerebral infarction[38] but would not necessarily vitiate the results of a careful clinical trial.

The beneficial effects of steroids may be seen clinically before they can be recognized by the microscope or test tube. This may be because our measuring tools are imprecise or, more likely, because we may not be measuring, or know how to measure, other variables. The possible effects of steroids on tumour growth have been noted; steroids also influence neural activity, influencing excitability and central recovery processes.[51] They may also have a direct action opposing that of serotonin at the capillary level.[34]

Although a comprehensive critique of steroid therapy is not appropriate in this chapter, a word is in order in view of the compelling evidence in favor of the value of steroid administration in the prevention and treatment of many edemas. There is the need for an awareness of the probable increased incidence of gastrointestinal bleeding attendant upon its use, especially following intracranial surgical procedures.[6]

Osmotic Agent Therapy

From the time of the well-known work of Weed and McKibben in 1919, osmotically active agents (including magnesium sulphate, sodium chloride, sucrose, glucose, urea, isosorbide, mannitol, glycerol, sodium succinate, sodium lactate) have been employed to combat cerebral edema. The principle governing their use has been the creation of an osmotic gradient in favor of raising the osmotic pressure of the intravascular compartment above that of the edematous tissue with which it exchanges fluid so that water will pass from the tissue into the bloodstream. If tissue injury exists to permit the easy passage of an intravascular molecule into the edematous zone, then no gradient can be established; it follows that to be effective, a selective barrier (even though relative only) must exist for edema fluid to be drawn into the vascular system. Osmotic agents do not alter the fluid or the chemical content of severely disrupted and hemorrhagic tissue except by their own presence.[9]

Overall brain bulk reduction does occur with osmotic agent therapy, primarily through the mechanism of drawing water from normal brain or from altered brain which retains tight vascular endothelial junctions. Thus, osmotic agents, if they create a gradient of about 35 milliosmoles, can produce a net decrease in brain bulk even when large areas of unresponsive necrosis exist. The increase in cerebral blood volume attendant upon the use of such agents as urea is insufficient to cancel the effects of the removal of water which is redistributed into the vascular tree.[46] Whatever substance is used to create the beneficial osmotic gradient (depending upon the barrier selectivity—vascular endothelium and junctions, the basement membranes, and cell membranes), as it enters the brain tissue, its concentration in that tissue rises as the vascular compartment's concentration falls. Such dynamic shifts can cause a reversal of the desired bulk changes. For acute alterations in brain water in the therapy of cerebral edema, urea is the agent of choice; for more prolonged use, mannitol or glycerol may possess advantages derived from less permeability. The disadvantages of hyperosmolar states as produced by the repetitive administration of osmotic agents deserves special note.

The *reverse* of a desired osmotic gradient can aggravate cerebral edema and can be contributed to by the administration of improper solutions in parenteral fluid maintenance. Five per cent dextrose in water, a commonly used solution, when administered intravenously, can produce brain hydration, that is, the rapid distribution of glucose in body tissues is followed by a relatively faster fall in the blood than in the brain and a consequent passage of water into brain tissue.[13]

Hypothermia Therapy

Temperature reduction of the brain by a variety of techniques (hypothermia) has been applied in the therapy of the cerebral edemas. The rationale has been based on the known reduction in the metabolic requirements of the brain at hypothermic temperatures with a resulting protective effect upon damaged but potentially recoverable cells or metabolic systems (the recovery of or protection of ATP) and on the demonstrated reduction in intracranial pressure due, in part at least, to a reduced cerebral blood flow. In a study by Rosomoff, hypothermia to 25°C applied to dogs subjected to standard cold-induced lesions reduced the size of the hemorrhagic and (presumably) edematous lesion as well as the mortality thereof.[40] Although in Rosomoff's work the criteria for the definition of cerebral edema were not fulfilled, the further work of Laskowski et al.[24] supported the general thesis that hypothermia retards or reduces the astrocytic and extracellular changes seen in the edema accompanying cold injury.

A reduction in metabolic activity as a result of hypothermia also may explain the potentiating effect which hypothermia appears to have on the influence of urea in reducing intracranial pressure. Such an observation highlights the many other biochemical systems which may also be retarded, thereby reducing the accumulation of edema fluids. Neither the experimental nor the clinical evidence is sufficiently crisp to assign a place for the application of hypothermia in the management or prevention of the edemas, particularly if applied after the edema-producing process has been initiated. Although clinical application for this purpose has received little recent attention and, in fact, has been largely discarded (primarily because of the complex technology involved and the complications attendant thereto), nevertheless well-controlled studies are needed before intelligent final judgments can be rendered.[3]

Other Therapeutic Endeavors

For a discussion of certain of the nonoperative methods of controlling increased intracranial pressure as a *sequel* to the edema-initiating process or the edema itself, the review of Shenkin and Bouzarth[43] is of value. With the exception of steroids, most nonsurgical methods directed against cerebral edema have the effect of redistributing fluids between two or more of the following intracranial compartments (at times with a net loss of fluid): the intracranial vascular compartment, the cerebrospinal fluid compartment, and the brain water compartment. The importance of the bulk changes which may accompany shifts of edema fluid into the latter compartment can be realized from the estimate by Pappius[35] that in focal cold injury in cats, a 45 per cent increase in volume of the affected tissue (mainly white matter) occurs. Furthermore, if any significant portion of the glial elements participates in swelling, the estimate that they (the glia) constitute about 50 per cent of brain volume has special meaning with respect to altering brain bulk.[11]

Although neurones do not appear to share in the swelling as seen structurally, they may have their function altered; axonal compression may be severe, and, although conjectural at present, they may have their metabolism changed because of the accompanying glial changes.

The mass intracranial shifts producing brain stem distortion, hemorrhage, and death are the final catastrophic results of massive uncontrolled edema. A small change in one may be sufficient to tide the patient over a critical phase of edema. It is primarily the influence of the edema fluid upon the intracranial mass relationships, as well as upon neural function directly, that gives the edema its lethal reputation. Even so, if the patient can be shepherded through the peak of the process, the altered intracranial mass relationships may linger for days or weeks (as revealed by persistent shifts of tissue), yet the patient may be clinically recovered.

FURTHER READING

[1] Aleu, F. P., Samuels, S. and Ransohoff, J. (1966), "The Pathology of Cerebral Edema Associated with Gliomas in Man," Report Based on Ten Biopsies, *Amer. J. Path.*, **48**, 1043.

[2] Bakay, L. (1968), "Changes in Barrier Effect in Pathological States," *Prog. in Brain Res.*, **29**, 315.

[3] Bakay, L. and Lee, J. C. (1965), *Cerebral Edema*. Springfield, Illinois: C. C. Thomas.

[4] Benson, V. M., McLaurin, R. L. and Foulkes, E. C. (1970), "Traumatic Cerebral Edema; an Experimental Model with Evaluation of Dexamethasone," *Arch. Neurol.*, **23**, 179.

[5] Bourke, R. S., Nelson, K. M., Naumann, R. A. and Yound, O. M. (1970), "Studies of the Production and Subsequent Reduction of Swelling in Primate Cerebral Cortex under Iso-osmotic Conditions *in vivo*," *Exp. Brain Res.*, **10**, 427.

[6] Cantu, R. C., Amir-Ahmadi, H. and Prieto, A. (1968), "Evaluation of the Increased Risk of Gastrointestinal Bleeding Following Intracranial Surgery in Patients Receiving High Steroid Dosages in the Immediate Postoperative Period," *Int'l. Surg. Sect.* 1, **50**, 325.

[7] Clark, K., Nash, T. M. and Hutchison, G. C. (1968), "The Failure of Circumferential Craniotomy in Acute Traumatic Cerebral Swelling," *J. Neurosurg.*, **29**, 367.

[8] Clasen, R. A., Cooke, P. M., Pandolfi, S., Carnecki, G. and Bryar, G. (1965), "Hypertonic Urea in Experimental Cerebral Edema," *Arch. Neurol.*, **12**, 424.

[9] Clasen, R. A., Cooke, P. M., Pandolfi, S., Carnecki, G. and Bryar, G. (1965), "Steroid-antihistaminic Therapy in Experimental Cerebral Edema,' *Arch. Neurol.*, **13**, 584.

[10] Clasen, R. A., Pandolfi, S., Russell, J., Stuart, D. and Hass, G. M. (1968), "Hypothermia and Hypotension in Experimental Cerebral Edema," *Arch. Neurol.*, **19**, 472.

[11] Dennis, M. J. and Gerschenfeld, H. M. (1969), "Some Physiological Properties of Identified Mammalian Neuroglial Cells," *J. Physiol.*, **203**, 211.

[12] Eisenberg, H. M., Barlow, C. F. and Lorenzo, A. V. (1970), "Effect of Dexamethasone on Altered Brain Vascular Permeability," *Arch. Neurol.*, **23**, 18.

[13] Fishman, R. A. (1953), "Effects of Isotonic Intravenous Solutions on Normal and Increased Intracranial Pressure," *Arch. Neurol. Psychiat.*, **70**, 350.

[14] Galicich, J. H. and French, L. A. (1961), "Use of Dexamethasone in the Treatment of Cerebral Edema Resulting from Brain Tumors and Brain Surgery," *Amer. Practit.*, **12**, 169.

[15] Hartmann, J. F. (1966), "High Sodium Content of Cortical Astrocytes," *Arch. Neurol.*, **15**, 633.

[16] Herzog, I., Levy, W. A. and Scheinberg, L. C. (1965), "Biochemical and Morphologic Studies of Cerebral Edema Associated with Intracerebral Tumors in Rabbits," *J. Neuropath.*, **24**, 244.

[17] Hirano, A., Zimmerman, H. M. and Levine, S. (1965), "Fine Structure of Cerebral Fluid Accumulation: VI. Intracellular Accumulation of Fluid and Cryptococcal Polysaccharide in Oligodendroglia," *Arch. Neurol.*, **12**, 189.

[18] Hirano, A., Zimmerman, H. M. and Levine, S. (1965), "Fine Structure of Cerebral Fluid Accumulation: VII. Reactions of Astrocytes to Cryptococcal Polysaccharide Implantation," *J. Neuropath.* **24**, 386.

[19] Katzman, R., Gonatas, N. and Levine, S. (1964), "Electrolytes and Fluids in Experimental Focal Leukoencephalopathy," *Arch. Neurol.*, **10**, 58.

[20] Klatzo, I. and Seitelberger, F. (1967), *Brain Edema* (Proceedings of the Symposium, Sept. 11–13, 1965, Vienna). New York: Springer-Verlag.

[21] Kotsilimbas, D. G., Meyer, B. A., Berson, M., Taylor, J. M. and Scheinberg, L. C. (1967), "Corticosteroid Effect on Intracerebral Melanomata and Associated Cerebral Edema," *Neurology*, **17**, 223.

[22] Krigman, M. R. and Manuelidis, E. E. (1965), "Morphological and Permeability Changes in the Cerebral Parenchyma Adjacent to Heterologous Intracerebral Tumors," *J. Neuropath.*, **24**, 49.

[23] Kuffler, S. W. and Nicholls, J. G. (1966), "The Physiology of Neuroglial Cells," *Ergebn. Physiol.*, **57**, 1.

[24] Laskowski, E. J., Klatzo, I. and Baldwin, M. (1960), "Experimental Study of the Effects of Hypothermia on Local Brain Injury," *Neurology*, **10**, 499.

[25] Lee, J. C. and Bakay, L. (1965), "Ultrastructural Changes in the Edematous Central Nervous System: I. Triethyltin Edema," *Arch. Neurol.*, **13**, 48.

[26] Lee, J. C. and Bakay, L. (1966), "Ultrastructural Changes in the Edematous Central Nervous System: II. Cold-Induced Edema," *Arch. Neurol.*, **14**, 36.

[27] Levy, W. A., Taylor, J. M., Herzog, I. and Scheinberg, L. C. (1965), "The Effect of Hypertonic Urea on Cerebral Edema in the Rabbit Induced by Triethyltin Sulfate," *Arch. Neurol.*, **13**, 58.

[28] Long, D. M., Hartmann, J. F. and French, L. A. (1966), "The Response of Experimental Cerebral Edema to Glucosteroid Administration," *J. Neurosurg.*, **24**, 843.

[29] Long, D. M., Hartmann, J. F. and French, L. A., (1966), "The Response of Human Cerebral Edema to Glucosteroid Administration; an Electron Microscopic Study," *Neurology*, **16**, 521.

[30] Long, D. M., Hartmann, J. F. and French, L. A. (1966), "The Ultrastructure of Human Cerebral Edema," *J. Neuropath.*, **25**, 373.

[31] Luse, S. A. and Harris, B. (1960), "Electron Microscopy of the Brain in Experimental Edema," *J. Neurosurg.*, **17**, 439.

[32] Lux, W. E., Hochwald, G. M., Sahar, A. and Ransohoff, J. (1970), "Periventricular Water Content Effect of Pressure in Experimental Chronic Hydrocephalus," *Arch. Neurol.*, **23**, 475.

[33] Norris, J. W. and Pappius, H. M. (1970), "Cerebral Water and Electrolytes," *Arch. Neurol.*, **23**, 248.

[34] Osterholm, J. L., Bell, J., Meyer, R. and Pyenson, J. (1969), "Experimental Effects of Free Serotonin on the Brain and its Relation to Brain Injury," *J. Neurosurg.*, **31**, 408.

[35] Pappius, H. M. (to be published), "Chemistry and Fine Structure of Various Types of Cerebral Edema," *Riv. Patol. nerv. ment.*

[36] Pappius, H. M. and McCann, W. P. (1969), "Effects of Steroids on Cerebral Edema in Cats," *Arch. Neurol.*, **20**, 207.

[37] Plum, F., Posner, J. B. and Alvord, E. C., Jr. (1963), "Edema and Necrosis in Experimental Cerebral Infarction," *Arch. Neurol.*, **9**, 563.

[38] Plum, F., Posner, J. B. and Alvord, E. C., Jr. (1963), "Effect of Steroids on Experimental Cerebral Infarction," *Arch. Neurol.*, **9**, 571.

[39] Reulen, H. J., Medzihradsky, F., Enzenbach, R., Marguth, F. and Brendel, W. (1969), "Electrolytes, Fluids, and Energy Metabolism in Human Cerebral Edema," *Arch. Neurol.*, **21**, 517.

[40] Rosomoff, H. L. (1959), "Experimental Brain Injury During Hypothermia," *J. Neurosurg.*, **16**, 177.

[41] Rovit, R. L. and Hagan, R. (1968), "Steroids and Cerebral Edema: The Effects of Glucocorticoids on Abnormal Capillary Permeability Following Cerebral Injury in Cats," *J. Neuropath.*, **27**, 277.

[42] Shaw, C. M., Alvord, E. C., Jr. and Berry, R. G. (1959), "Swelling of the Brain Following Ischemic Infarction with Arterial Occlusion," *Arch. Neurol.*, **1**, 161.

[43] Shenkin, H. A. and Bouzarth, W. F. (1970), "Clinical Methods of Reducing Intracranial Pressure; Role of the Cerebral Circulation," *New Engl. J. Med.*, **282**, 1465.

[44] Stern, W. E. (1965), "The Contribution of the Laboratory to an Understanding of the Cerebral Edemas," *Neurology*, **15**, 902.

[45] Stern, W. E., Abbott, M. L. and Cheseboro, B. W. (1966), "A Study of the Role of Osmotic Gradients in Experimental Cerebral Edemas," *J. Neurosurg.*, **XXIV**, 57.

[46] Stern, W. E., Coxon, R. V. (1964), "Osmolality of Brain Tissue and its Relation to Brain Bulk," *Amer. J. Physiol.*, **206**, 1.

[47] Taylor, J. M., Levy, W. A., Herzog, I. and Scheinberg, L. C. (1965), "Prevention of Experimental Cerebral Edema by Corticosteroids," *Neurology*, **15**, 667.

[48] Torack, R. M. (1965), "The Relationship Between Adenosinetriphosphatase Activity and Triethyltin Toxicity in the Production of Cerebral Edema of the Rat," *Amer. J. Path.*, **46**, 245.

[49] Tower, D. B. (1968), "Delineation of Fluid Compartmentation in Cerebral Tissues," *Prog. Brain Res.*, **29**, 465.

[50] Wasterlain, C. G. and Torack, R. M. (1968), "Cerebral Edema in Water Intoxication," *Arch. Neurol.*, **19**, 79.

[51] Woodbury, D. M. and Vernadakis, A. (1966), "Effects of Steroids on the Cerebral Nervous System," *Meth. Hormone Res.*, **5**, 1. (Academic Press: New York).

3. HIGH PRESSURE HYDROCEPHALUS

A. N. GUTHKELCH

To survey the large, complicated and sometimes contradictory body of evidence which constitutes our knowledge of high-pressure hydrocephalus, we must have some definite base, even if this is in places none too secure.

CSF CIRCULATION

We can start with the following three fundamental propositions:

(1) The bulk of the cerebrospinal fluid (CSF) is *secreted* within the choroid plexuses, though some arises from the interstitial fluid of the brain. The rate of secretion per gram of choroid plexus per minute is roughly constant (and species-specific) in normal subjects, possibly rising very slightly in a linear fashion with increasing intracranial pressure (ICP); but in hydrocephalus it may perhaps fall—also slightly—as the ICP rises beyond normal limits (Fig. 1). The rate of CSF formation is probably a little lower in hydrocephalic (0·30 ml./min.) than in normal children (0·35 ml./min.), while in normal adults the rate is a little higher still being 0·40 ml./min. (Lorenzo, Page and Watters, 1970).

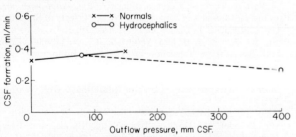

FIG. 1. Relationship between CSF formation and pressure in normal and hydrocephalic subjects. (From Lorenzo, Pagel & Walters (1970), who state that the difference of both lines from horizontal is not statistically significant.)

(2) The CSF *circulates* through the ventricular system, which it leaves by way of the foramina of Luschka and Magendie, and thence through the basal cisterns and the rest of the subarachnoid space to the arachnoid villi. Obstruction at any point of its flow leads primarily to proximal dilatation of the pathway; but since this implies distension of the brain also, and only the subarachnoid space and its contained blood vessels intervene between the enlarging brain and the unyielding skull, it follows that this space is soon obliterated and a further secondary block is established distal to the original obstruction and outside the ventricular system.

(3) Absorption mostly occurs through the minute valve-systems which make up the arachnoid villi, more particularly in the region of the sagittal sinus. The opening pressure of the valves is related to the pressure within the cerebral venous sinuses, being about 68 mm. CSF in man. There is evidence to suggest that in experimental animals there is also an increasing *gradient* between ventricular and sinus pressures, which in turn would help to promote more rapid absorption (Sahar, Hochwald and Ransohoff, 1970). Unlike the situation on the production side, the rate of absorption rises rapidly and in linear fashion from zero at 68 mm. CSF pressure to about 1·5 ml./min. at 250 mm. in normal subjects. Two variations from the normal pattern of absorption have been described in hydrocephalics. In Type I the opening pressure is higher than normal but the slope of the absorption curve is unchanged; in Type II the opening pressure is normal but the slope of the curve is decreased or even negative (Lorenzo, Page and Watters, 1970). However, mixed forms of these two defects can occur.

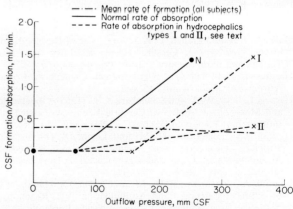

FIG. 2. Relationship between CSF formation/absorption and pressure in normal and hydrocephalic subjects.

There are almost certainly other absorptive pathways, notably through the ependyma and perhaps also along the perineural sheaths of the spinal nerves; the relative importance of these probably varies with the intracranial pressure and with the degree of patency of the CSF pathways as a whole. However, the literature abounds with examples of the difficulty of distinguishing between, for example, exchange of labelled ions or molecules across a membrane and actual net transport of ions or other substances from one side of this to the other. Even now one must be cautious in assessing the importance of these subsidiary routes of absorption.

In the short term, the mean intracranial pressure (ICP) must be that determined by the point of balance between CSF production and absorption; it follows from the slopes of the lines in Fig. 2 that large variations in the rate of production will be followed by less change in ICP than variations of equal magnitude in the rate of absorption.

OTHER FACTORS

1. Periodic Fluctuations in ICP

Of these there are three, those due to the arterial pulse, those due to respiration and the slow waves of increased pressure ('X' waves) of which the cause is still unknown. The mean amplitude of ICP fluctuations due to respiration and the 'X' waves remains roughly constant whatever the perfusion pressure, whereas that resulting from the arterial pulse rises sharply when ICP is greater than 150 mm. CSF.

It has been suggested that these large oscillations of pressure provide the main mechanical force which causes ventricular dilatation in high-pressure hydrocephalus. They have recently been studied by Shulman and his colleagues (unpublished) in relation to what these workers have termed the capacitance (C) of the brain, defined as follows:

$$C = \frac{V_{in} - V_{out}}{P' - P}$$

where V_{in} is the volume of fluid (CSF) introduced into the system and V_{out} that absorbed during the same period, P and P' the initial and final ICP respectively. When the rate of introduction is rapid V_{out} can be neglected and the equation reduces to

$$C = \frac{V_{in}}{P' - P}$$

If ICP is plotted against total volume of CSF, then the resulting curve (Fig. 3) implies that the greater the initial pressure in the system, the greater the increment of ICP resulting from small increments in volume—as for instance with each arterial pulsation—and the less the cerebral capacitance.

2. Ventricular Size and Distensibility

It has been mentioned elsewhere (Chapter VIII: 4) that once ventricles have become dilated, the amount of pressure required to maintain this state of dilatation, and presumably also the increase of pressure required to cause

yet further distension, may be less than was required to cause the *initial* dilatation. This would follow from what has been called the "hydraulic press" effect, by which the total force applied to the surfaces (internal and/or external) of the cerebral hemispheres is given by $F = P \times A$ where F is the force, P the pressure and A the area of the surfaces. For constant P, an increase in A implies an increase in F also.

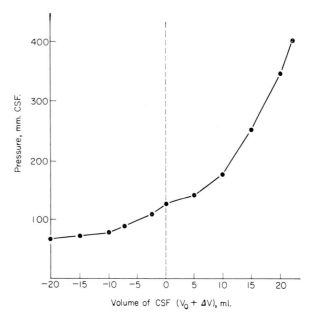

FIG. 3. Pressure/volume curve in a hydrocephalic infant. (Data kindly supplied by Dr. K. Shulman.)

3. Ventricular Dilatation and Cerebral Blood Flow (CBF)

As also mentioned elsewhere (Chapter VIII: 4), the onset of hydrocephalus is correlated with a decrease in CBF, presumably due to greater resistance in the cerebral capillary bed, and clinical improvement after a shunting procedure is in proportion to increased CBF thereafter.

WHY DO THE VENTRICLES DILATE?

It has already been pointed out that CSF production tends to occur at a rate which varies little with ICP. If there is obstruction to its free flow, then plainly something must give way. When the obstruction is outside the ventricular system the dilatation occurs first in the lateral ventricles, then in the third ventricle, then in the aqueduct of Sylvius. This might be because the arterial pressure waves are progressively dissipated the further one goes from the choroid plexuses which produce them. But a more likely explanation seems to be that the more compact nuclei of the brain stem offer a greater resistance to dilatation of CSF pathways than the white matter surrounding the ventricles. When the CSF circulation is blocked in experimental animals, tears rapidly appear in the ventricular ependyma beneath which the white matter becomes pale and swollen due to an accumulation of intercellular fluid—presumably CSF (Clark and Milhorat, 1970). In this state it can be shown to be penetrated by, for example, labelled proteins, to a depth of several millimetres, probably with disruption of its fibres. This weakened tissue is presumed to be specially vulnerable to compression. Local differences in resistance of the periventricular white matter may account for some of the irregularity of contour which is frequently seen in cases of hydrocephalus, though many other factors, including infarction, doubtless play a part. How close in the normal subject must be the balance between production and absorption of CSF is evident when one realizes that as small an excess as 5 ml./day, or little more than 1 per cent of total production, must necessarily lead to a very gross hydrocephalus within a month.

Of the return to normal pattern of the ventricular system following successful surgical control of hydrocephalus very little seems to be known, except that undoubtedly the ventricles begin to contract and the cortical thickness to increase within a few days, as can be shown by ventriculography. Presumably the protein and liquid which has been lost from the previously compressed tissues is replaced as the ICP returns to normal. But clinical experience suggests that in many cases there has been irreversible neuronal damage, since the intelligence of children whose hydrocephalus has been surgically controlled or has apparently gone into remission is, particularly in respect of visuospatial relationships, lower than normal. Such children have special difficulty in making a meaningful appraisal of a complicated visual pattern and may show impaired intermanual matching of tactile stimuli, possibly due to previous stretching of the *corpus callosum* and consequent partial interhemispheric disconnection (Miller and Sethi, unpublished). It has not been shown that there are any other special features of dementia due to hydrocephalus without other progressive organic brain disease. Some authors have claimed to identify a typical hydrocephalic behaviour pattern but this, if it exists, probably results from the fact that in any case of generalized brain damage, verbal ability tends to be relatively less severely affected than performance.

DIAGNOSIS OF HIGH-PRESSURE HYDROCEPHALUS

In infants the picture of enlarged head, bulging fontanelle, dilated scalp veins and down-turned ("setting sun") eyeballs is familiar enough, though care must be taken to exclude subdural haematoma. Recently, because almost all cases of infantile hydrocephalus of whatever origin tend to be treated by some sort of a shunting procedure, there has been a temptation to neglect a detailed examination of the cause of the obstruction. This must be resisted. Not only will occasional intraventricular and posterior fossa tumours be missed, but there is also evidence of a difference in prognosis and in liability to future shunt revisions in cases of hydrocephalus of differing origin.

No single diagnostic method is uniformly satisfactory in all cases. If air ventriculography is practised, one has to beware of too complete a replacement lest the ventricles subsequently collapse and subdural haematomas

result; yet the use of small volumes of air ("bubble ventriculography") requires considerable care and experience and incomplete examination may result in a tumour being missed. Positive-contrast methods are valuable. If 2–3 ml. of Iodophendylate (Myodil, Pantopaque) is injected into a lateral ventricle and positioned in the frontal horn an estimate of the thickness of the cortex can be made, following which the medium can be directed through the foramen of Munro and thence into the rest of the ventricular system under direct vision. This method has been practised by the author for more than 20 years with few reactions although it has recently been criticized on the grounds that the substance causes quite severe changes in the linings of the CSF pathways of dogs, particularly after the previous induction of hydrocephalus. More practically, this method has the disadvantage that it yields incomplete information about the lateral ventricles and their contents and none about the subarachnoid space. The use of the water-soluble medium methyl-glucamine iothalamate (Conray) obviates the first disadvantage, in that it diffuses rapidly throughout the ventricular system; but when this is very large the medium becomes unduly diluted with resulting poor visualization. However, there have recently been reports that a larger quantity than the 5–6 ml. of 60 per cent aqueous solution which is usually recommended can be injected without reactions, one author mentioning the use of as much as 40 ml. This method also has the great advantages over the use of air or iodophendylate that the whole ventricular system is visualized at once, the patient's head does not have to be moved, and only a few films need to be exposed.

The gross changes in the angiogram in a case of hydrocephalus are well known but Raimondi (1969) has demonstrated the possibility of making an accurate distinction between non-communicating and communicating hydrocephalus by careful study of the circle of Willis and its branches in infants. Other writers are now beginning to apply somewhat similar concepts to an analysis of the angiographic changes resulting from differing types of hydrocephalus occurring in adults. The use of the radioisotopes in the diagnosis of high pressure hydrocephalus is described elsewhere (Chapter IX: 5).

By intraventricular injection of the dye phenosulphonephthalein, once fairly widely used in clinical practice to distinguish between communicating and non-communicating hydrocephalus, Milhorat and Clark (1970) have shown that there is intraventricular absorption of CSF in hydrocephalus and confirmed the secondary block in the arachnoid cisterns at tentorial level in cases of severe obstruction of the aqueduct or fourth ventricle.

Of non-surgical diagnostic techniques, echoencephalography can, in some hands, give information on ventricular size but is not at present sufficiently reliable to replace the standard neuroradiological manoeuvres.

LESIONS CAUSING INCREASED CSF PRODUCTION AND THEIR EFFECTS

Whatever the situation in experimental animals choroid plexus papilloma is the only pathological condition which causes high pressure hydrocephalus by oversecretion of CSF in man, and even here the evidence is equivocal. Most cases of this tumour occur in infants, and its existence should be suspected when hydrocephalus, particularly with asymmetrical dilatation of the ventricles, is accompanied by a xanthochromic CSF, resulting from repeated spontaneous haemorrhage. Adequate ventriculography is essential if they are not to be missed, for the clinical signs are often no more than those of increased intracranial pressure, accompanied in half the cases by papilloedema (which is unusual in most forms of infantile hydrocephalus).

Is the ventricular dilatation which is a regular feature of these cases really the result of CSF over-production? Although instances are on record in which, following the institution of ventricular or lumbar drainage, the amount of CSF collected was, for a few hours or days, considerably greater than the normal rate of CSF formation, it is also true that when any case of high-pressure hydrocephalus is relieved in this way, the ventricular system rapidly shrinks, and the brain substance with its vascular bed re-expands. This would result in an apparent excess of CSF production for the period in question. In some cases of choroid plexus papilloma, the hydrocephalus is unilateral, occurring only on the side of the tumour despite any absence of blockage of the foramen of Munro; this suggests that perhaps increased pulsation, rather than increased production, is the causative factor. In others the hydrocephalus persists after removal of the tumour and it has been pointed out that the repeated haemorrhages associated with these tumours may give rise either to ependymitis or to obstruction of the basal cisterns, which in turn could lead to hydrocephalus.

It is interesting to note that in one of the frequently quoted cases (Fairburn, 1960) a ventricular pressure of 300 mm. was observed in a child from whom a 13 gm. choroid plexus papilloma was later removed. If one takes the weight of the normal human choroid plexus as a little over 2 gm. and assumes that (1) the papilloma secreted CSF at a normal rate in proportion to its weight and (2) the rate of absorption was normal, a balance between production and absorption would in fact have been struck at an outflow pressure of about 300 mm. CSF (cf. Fig. 2). On the other hand, the actual daily rate of drainage of CSF in Fairburn's case (the outflow pressure being kept at 50 mm.) ranged between 400 and 960 ml./day, whereas on the basis of overproduction of CSF as the sole cause of the elevated pressure one would have expected figures of 6 times normal (approx. 3 l./day). The discrepancy is more easily explained by assuming an increased outflow resistance; Johnson (1958) showed that simple decompression of the posterior fossa, thus opening the CSF pathways, could reduce the hourly drainage from the lateral ventricle of a case of choroid plexus papilloma of the fourth ventricle to negligible limits, although the tumour was not removed.

We must conclude that the possibility that hydrocephalus associated with choroid plexus papilloma results from overproduction of CSF is not excluded, but that probably some other factor, such as a change in rate of absorption due to outflow obstruction, also operates in most cases.

PATHWAY OBSTRUCTIONS AND THEIR EFFECTS

Rather than retracing familiar ground by a classification of the various causes of "obstructive hydrocephalus," this section looks at the total situation associated with these.

It has been conventional to classify the causes of obstruction of the CSF pathways into intraventricular (non-communicating) and extraventricular (communicating), and this terminology has some value in encouraging an analysis of the primary cause. But the more one looks at the realities of the clinical situation the more one is impressed by the frequency with which multiple obstructions are found in any given case. This possibility has already been touched upon in the previous section, and it has been recognized for years that hydrocephalus associated with the Arnold–Chiari malformation may arise from any one or more of the following:

(1) Aqueduct stenosis.
(2) Exit foramen obstruction.
(3) Basal cistern block at the level of the foramen magnum (both (2) and (3) are due to the downward displacement of the cerebellum).
(4) Basal cistern block at tentorial level, because of the disproportion in size between the subtentorial compartment of the skull and its contents in cases of rachischisis (Verbiest, 1953).

If in any case of high-pressure hydrocephalus the obstruction is intraventricular and at the level of the upper end of the aqueduct, the effect is one of generalized distension of the cerebral hemispheres and of the walls of the third ventricle. In this situation both the lateral and the third ventricles tend to enlarge into the subarachnoid space at tentorial level due to distension in the former case of the choroidal fissure, in the latter of the suprapineal recess. These compete with one another, so to speak, for extra space, with the result that eventually a diverticulum of one, but only one, of them may be formed. This diverticulum causes a secondary extraventricular obstruction of the subarachnoid pathway. Similarly, when the obstruction is of the foramina of Luschka and Magendie the third and fourth ventricles distend to the point at which the aqueduct is taken up into them and again there is secondary occlusion, this time by expansion of the midbrain, at tentorial level. To either of these may be added an element of obstruction of the outflow pathways due to the distension of the cerebral hemispheres which has already been described.

One other sort of pathway obstruction should be mentioned. From time to time one sees cases in which pouch-like diverticula occur within the subarachnoid space itself, probably as a result of localized thickening and obstruction due to the effects of previous haemorrhage or infection. These, when untreated, have a tendency to progressive enlargement which is probably due to temporary alterations in the pressure relationships between the inside and the outside of the pouch, partly perhaps the regular variations associated with the arterial pulse, but probably also—as in Williams' (1970) hypothesis of the production of syringomyelia—because the wave of high pressure produced by coughing, etc., is preferentially propagated through the wide mouth of the pouch, giving rise to a momentary pressure gradient between the hollow interior and the mesh-like subarachnoid space around it. (Dott's view that the pressure wave is propagated along the arteries which lie within the pouch is difficult to sustain in the light of the fact that the mouth of the pouch is usually large in comparison with the diameter of any of the arteries which may traverse it.) As a result these apparently harmless, open-mouthed pouches can in fact grow to a considerable size. When they simply occupy the cisterna magna, they can be explored and dissected out. But a small number force their way through the tentorium from the posterior fossa, distorting the midbrain and giving rise to severe and even fatal symptoms; their effects can be relieved by the usual shunting procedures but dissection of this type of pouch is dangerous and best avoided (writer's data, also Gardner, W. J., personal communication).

OUTFLOW OBSTRUCTIONS

The discovery of the valves by which CSF passes from the subarachnoid space to the sinuses has not resulted in any special modification of surgical practice, and at present it is uncertain whether these are true micropores, open to the passage of protein molecules, as argued by some, or whether they are filters closed by a fine and intact membrane, as suggested by others. The two different curves of rate of absorption for a given pressure which are found in hydrocephalus have already been described (p. 296, Fig. 2). One has normal opening pressure with low absorptive rate and the other high opening pressure with normal rate of increase of absorption as the ICP increases further. This suggests two different sorts of obstruction, the one analogous to a narrow outflow tube and the other to a sticky valve; but we cannot yet relate this information to specific causes, nor use it in counteracting them. Possibly the further development of isotope studies will be of assistance here. In the meantime, we can only treat this most distal of blocks by the conventional method of a proximal shunt of some sort.

PRINCIPLES AND OBJECTIVES OF TREATMENT

Bearing in mind the slopes of the curves for rates of production and absorption of CSF at different ICP's (Fig. 2) one can see that high-pressure hydrocephalus should be more easily controlled by increasing the latter than by reducing the former. So it proves to be in practice. Although such drugs as acetolazamide (Diamox) reduce the rate of CSF formation and hence the ICP up to a point, they are not effective over a long period. Similarly, despite the distinguished advocacy of Scarff in a number of communications presenting the results of choroid plexectomy in cases followed over many years, few surgeons have found his methods applicable to the treatment of

acute hydrocephalus, particularly as it arises in early infancy; choroid plexectomy can never be complete in man—the plexus within the third ventricle, for example, cannot safely be destroyed—and the growing body of evidence in favour of considerable CSF production by the ependyma and even in the subarachnoid space diminishes the logical basis for plexectomy—always provided, of course, that a satisfactory alternative is found.

When the cause of a case of intraventricular obstruction can be removed, then obviously this is the method of choice. It was in the management of irremovable but acquired obstructive lesions that Torkildsen's ventriculocisternostomy first found favour—and is still practised today. In congenital cases, however, the problem is rather different because there has always been an obstruction, either within the aqueduct of Sylvius or by obliteration of the exit-foramina of the fourth ventricle. The brain has been distended for so long that the basal cisterns and subarachnoid pathways over the hemispheres have never developed—or have become secondarily obliterated—with the result that simple relief of the intraventricular block does no more than convert a non-communicating to a communicating hydrocephalus. Unfortunately, the few proposed ways of directly facilitating CSF absorption— e.g. by the use of valved drains or mechanical pumps inserted directly from the subarachnoid space into the sagittal sinus—have proved ineffective. We are left with the problem of creating an artificial absorptive mechanism inserted into that part of the CSF pathway proximal to the obstruction which is most conveniently available (normally the right lateral ventricle) which is then drained into one or other of the body cavities. But before we consider in detail the various mechanical devices by which this may be achieved and the destination of the CSF when removed, it is helpful to ask what exactly the surgeon is trying to achieve when he attempts to control hydrocephalus as such.

We have already noted that even in severe and rapidly progressive cases of hydrocephalus, the net imbalance between production and absorption must be relatively small in volume—though the work of Milhorat and his colleagues (1970) also suggests that hydrocephalic changes such as ventricular dilatation and permeation of the subependymal white matter by CSF commence within a matter of hours. Equally, as Torkildsen first showed, a return to near normal size of a previously dilated ventricular system occurs within days in the human subject; the immediate collapse of the fontanelle and diminution in the circumference of the head of a hydrocephalic infant after the successful insertion of, e.g. a ventriculo-atrial shunt is evidence of the same process and the shrinkage of the ventricles themselves can be demonstrated either radiographically or by echo-encephalography.

The multiplicity of changes which are known to follow the induction of experimental hydrocephalus must presumably also occur in the clinical situation in man with resultant damage to brain structure and function, yet the evidence of a negative correlation between cortical thickness and intelligence (for example) remains unclear except for extreme cases. Moreover, on following the growth curves of the heads of hydrocephalic children treated by ventricular drainage with, e.g. the Holter valve, one finds that only those valves which open at a low pressure (50 mm.) are successful in actually restoring the growth curve to normal as distinct from preventing further divergence therefrom. On the other hand clinical experience suggests that it is often those infants in whom drainage is, as it were, too efficient, so that the ventricles return to normal or even below normal size, who also show the greatest degree of shunt-dependency and who most often need revision-operations. This may be partly because the small area of the ventricular walls diminishes the amount of CSF which can be reabsorbed through them, partly because the narrowness of the ventricle may cause obstruction of any drainage catheter lying within it. This leads us into a dilemma. Is the primary objective of treatment of high pressure hydrocephalus the restoration of a constant, normal level of ICP even at the expense of abnormal rates of CSF production and absorption, or the correction of an imbalance between these two, leaving the pressure to adjust itself? This question is discussed later.

DIVERSIONARY (SHUNTING) PROCEDURES

Much work has been done and much written on the use of diversionary procedures but it is proposed here to limit discussion to the principles involved and how they are applied rather than to discuss details of techniques and complications.

The early attempts at diversion of CSF into some body cavity whence it could be either excreted or reabsorbed were technically unsuccessful in most cases because of a tendency to clotting of blood within their lumina or around their ends. With the development of plastic tubing and the use of silicone-coating it became possible to establish more reliable long-term drainage systems. At first these were non-valvular, the most popular being a direct connection between either the ventricle or the spinal theca at one end, and the pleura, the peritoneum or the ureter at the other. Of these the last-named was mechanically the most effective but this operation necessitated the sacrifice of a healthy kidney while the constant voiding of CSF from the bladder led to a persistent salt-deficiency which could be fatal. Direct intrapleural or intraperitoneal drainage avoided electrolyte-loss but had the serious disadvantage that in some subjects frequent revision operations were required, since they proved relatively intolerant of the tubing and formed adhesions around its lower end. Both methods, however, were less than ideal in principle in that the only limit to the amount of CSF drainage, and therefore to reduction of ICP, was the absorptive or excretory capacity of the drainage-system itself.

The next stage was the development of a number of valvular devices all of which had in common the idea of restricting drainage to times at which the ICP exceeded a given height. There are in effect two groups of these. In one a small compressible chamber is interposed between two one-way valves, in the other a single valve is situated at the outflow end of the device.

In each case the CSF is diverted from the ventricle through a catheter, which may be angled in order to fit securely against the skull, and which has multiple inlet holes or protective flanges to prevent blockage by the choroid plexus; to this may be attached a small reservoir capable of being punctured repeatedly in order to sample the ventricular fluid or instil antibiotics. The outflow catheter leads either into the right atrium of the heart via the internal jugular or common facial veins, or into the pleural or peritoneal cavity. When the peritoneal cavity is used various devices such as loosely wrapping the end of the catheter in plastic sheeting, placing it above the liver or in the lesser peritoneal sac have been used in order to diminish the danger of obstruction by adhesions. None is ideal.

Until recently all these shunt systems had in common the principle of a valve which operated at a constant pressure, following which CSF drainage continued at the limiting rate of the system until the ICP fell below the opening pressure of the valve. But this is not, either theoretically or practically, the only way in which to approach the problem. It has already been mentioned that the actual imbalance between production and absorption of CSF may be quite small and yet cumulatively give rise to gross hydrocephalus within a few weeks or months, and that over-enthusiastic drainage may lead to an undesirable state of shunt-dependency. This latter could be counteracted by draining only so much CSF as was necessary to correct clinical evidence of increased ICP at intervals determined by the appearance of increased fontanelle-tension in infants or of such symptoms as headache, vomiting and irritability in older patients. The New York University (NYU) valve is designed to work on this principle. It comprises a single one-way valve which is inserted under the scalp and is attached on one side to a ventricular catheter and on the other to a pleural or peritoneal catheter in the usual way. It is opened by digital pressure, which is maintained for as long as seems to be required to correct the increased ICP, at first at regular intervals of a few hours, but later as infrequently as the subject can tolerate without symptoms. A safety by-pass opening at a high pressure can if necessary be built in to mitigate the possibility of a sudden dangerous rise in ICP. The intention is therefore to control the hydrocephalus by a *constant volume* rather than a *constant pressure* system. This device remains under trial but has shown itself effective in a small series of cases. It cannot of course be used to divert the CSF into the blood-stream, since thrombosis would tend to occur around the intravascular end of the tube between periods of flushing, and would involve the same liability to obstruction as constant pressure devices used in the same way. However, it avoids the serious morbidity attached to the various ventriculo-atrial shunts and resulting from such complications as bacteraemia, nephrosis and superior caval obstruction.

There is a long way to go both in our understanding of the mechanics of high-pressure hydrocephalus and in its treatment, but recent years have seen a very healthy expansion of our knowledge and increasing attention to the fundamental principles of the pathophysiology of the

CSF pathways, over and above what might be called the gadgetry of therapeutics.

FURTHER READING

Clark, R. G. and Milhorat, T. H. (1970), "Experimental Hydrocephalus," Part 3, *J. Neurosurg.*, **32**, 400–413.

Fairburn, B. (1960), "Choroid Plexus Papilloma," *J. Neurosurg.*, **17**, 166–171.

Johnson, R. T. (1958), "Clinicopathological Aspects of the CSF Circulation," in *The Cerebrospinal Fluid*, Ciba Foundation Symposium. London: J. & A. Churchill.

Lorenzo, A. V., Page, L. K. and Watters, G. V. (1970), "Relation-ship between CSF Formation, Absorption and Pressure in Human Hydrocephalus," *Brain*, **93**, 679–692.

Milhorat, T. H. and Clark, R. G. (1970), "Some Observations on the Circulation of Phenolsulfonphthalein in CSF," *J. Neurosurg.*, **32**, 522–528.

Milhorat, T. H., Clark, R. G. and Hammock, M. K. (1970), "Experimental Hydrocephalus," Part 2, *J. Neurosurg.*, **32**, 390–399.

Raimondi, A. J. (1970), "Angiographic Diagnosis of Hydrocephalus in the Newborn," *J. Neurosurg.*, **31**, 550–560.

Sahar, A., Hochwald, G. M. and Ransohoff, J. (1970), "CSF and Cranial Sinus Pressures," *Arch. Neurol.* (*Chicago*), **23**, 413–418.

Verbiest, H. (1953), "The Arnold–Chiari Malformation," *J. Neurol. Neurosurg. Psychiat.*, **16**, 227–233.

Williams, B. (1970), "Current Concepts of Syringomyelia," *Brit. J. Hosp. Med.*, **4**, 331–342.

4. NORMAL PRESSURE HYDROCEPHALUS*

ROBERT G. OJEMANN

INTRODUCTION

The clinical syndrome of normal pressure hydrocephalus has now become well established. Also termed occult hydrocephalus, low pressure hydrocephalus, normotensive hydrocephalus, and hydrocephalic dementia, the syndrome consists of a fairly well defined group of neurological symptoms and signs associated with lumbar cerebrospinal fluid (CSF) pressures of less than 180 mm. and no clinical evidence of increased intracranial pressure; normal plain skull films; and marked ventricular enlargement on pneumoencephalogram (PEG) with little or no air entering the cerebral subarachnoid spaces. Recently, the presence of an abnormal isotopic cisternogram with persistent ventricular activity has been included in the description of the syndrome. Improvement in symptoms usually follows establishment of a CSF shunt.

ETIOLOGY AND PATHOLOGY

Normal pressure hydrocephalus develops insidiously, often in association with some specific pathological process but in some patients in the absence of a recognizable etiological factor. Documented pathological processes underlying the syndrome include subarachnoid hemorrhage,[2,3,8,9,11,12,14,18,19] trauma,[2,8,10–12,14,15,18,19] intracranial tumor,[1,11,14,18,19] meningitis,[12,19] aqueduct stenosis[14,18,19] and ectasia of the basilar artery.[5,8]

In cases of hydrocephalus developing after spontaneous subarachnoid hemorrhage, trauma, infection and tumor operation, the block in the CSF flow is usually due to scar in the basal cisterns, but on occasion may be in the supratentorial subarachnoid space. It is known that scarring in the subarachnoid space results from the effects of blood or inflammation, and it appears that a similar pathological process is present in the idiopathic cases. The possibility certainly exists that the block seen in these patients relates to a forgotten episode of head trauma or to an unrecognized hemorrhage.

NEUROLOGICAL SYMPTOMS AND SIGNS

The clinical syndrome of normal pressure hydrocephalus has been well summarized.[1,18,19] Cardinal symptoms are mental change and disturbance of gait. Although mental changes usually appear first, the order of symptom appearance is not invariable. On more than one occasion, gait disturbance was the prominent symptom. Headache was not a feature in our patients or in those reported in the literature. Occasional falling spells with brief impairment of consciousness were noted, but frank seizures did not occur.

Mental changes never appeared dramatically but developed unobtrusively over a period of weeks or months, depending on the underlying cause. An initial mild forgetfulness for time and events was soon combined with a slowing-up of mental processes and physical activity. Spontaneity of action decreased, less conversation was initiated by the patient, and apathy was apparent; reduction of activity rather than hyperactivity was the rule. Conspicuous uninhibited or aberrant behavior was seen in only one patient, and politeness, good humor and social graciousness were usually retained. Although insight was absent or limited, delusions, hallucinations, paranoia, delirium, spasms of laughing and crying, and nonsensical or irrational speech were each present in only occasional cases. Frank dysphasia was absent in the early stage of the illness, and comprehension of language was always preserved; calculation was frequently slow and inaccurate. In the most advanced cases, mutism, advanced hypokinesia, abulia and intermittent interruption of behavior were prominent. When memory impairment became severe, abnormalities in speech, writing, drawing and copying often developed.

---

* Portions of this have previously appeared in the *Journal of Neurosurgery* and in *Clinical Neurosurgery* and are reproduced here with the permission of the Editors.

The disturbance of gait was often difficult to characterize. In the mildest derangement, the patients walked slowly on a wide base with slightly zigzag steps in a manner described by relatives as "sloppy" and "careless". The ill-defined term gait ataxia was often applied. There were usually no clear cerebellar signs. Tandem walking was difficult. The deficit increased until walking, standing, arising and even turning over in bed finally became impossible without assistance.

Dysarthria did not occur. In the early stages, patients spoke briskly and responded promptly, but in the advanced stages speech was slow and quiet, sometimes reduced to a whisper. An unexplained nystagmus was seen several times but papilledema was never a feature. Movements of individual limbs were slow, with an absence of tremor or rigidity, although in one case tremor, bradykinesia and anteropulsion mimicked parkinsonism. Lower limbs were always more affected than upper. Tendon reflexes tended to be increased, especially in the legs and plantar responses were often extensor. Sucking and grasping reflexes appeared in the late stages.

Urinary incontinence, not a feature in the early stage, appeared in some degree with the progression of the illness.

On two occasions a porencephalic cyst was associated with reversible focal signs. One of these patients had suffered a cerebral trauma and the other had had an intracerebral hematoma from a vascular malformation.

Although some of the more prolonged cases appear to reach a plateau, the course of the illness is slowly downward, with fluctuation from day to day or week to week.

RADIOLOGICAL FINDINGS

Skull Films

Skull films are usually normal, with no evidence of changes characteristic of chronic increased intracranial pressure.

Pneumoencephalography

PEG demonstrates marked enlargement of the ventricular system, similar to that seen with elevated CSF pressure. The increase in size is most prominent in the frontal horns, where ventricular span is usually greater than 50 mm. on the brow-up anteroposterior (A-P) films. Enlargement of the 3rd and 4th ventricles is frequently found, but there are no changes characteristic of the syndrome (Fig. 1).

In the typical case, no air enters the cerebral subarachnoid space above the basal cisterns, even when specific efforts are made to effect entry of air into the convexity subarachnoid space. In our series there were some types of cases in which there was filling of a varying portion of the cerebral subarachnoid space, most frequently in the inferior frontal region or in the region of the Sylvian cisterns. This finding should be distinguished from that seen with the typical case of atrophy in which enlarged, dilated subarachnoid spaces are seen over the cerebral convexity.

Marked deterioration in neurological symptoms and signs occurs in some patients after PEG. When this happens, it helps to confirm the diagnosis of normal pressure hydrocephalus, but an absence of worsening in the patient's condition does not exclude the syndrome. A few patients have shown temporary elevation of CSF pressure after the PEG.

Angiography

An accurate estimation of ventricular size can be made from the A-P venous phase of the angiogram by noting

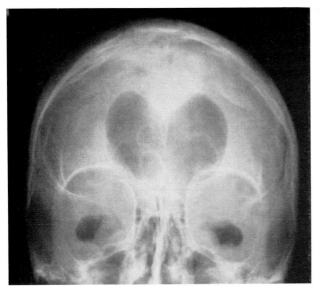
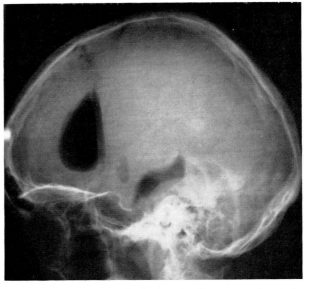

FIG. 1. PEG (A–P and lateral) three days after cisternogram. Note that no air has entered the cerebral subarachnoid space even though the patient has been turned to fill temporal horns and air was injected into the basal cisterns with the head extended.

the position of the subependymal veins. Angiography, however, is not the primary diagnostic procedure in most of the patients with this syndrome since detailed evaluation of the subarachnoid space reveals much more diagnostic information.

CEREBROSPINAL FLUID STUDIES

Lumbar Puncture

Numerous reports have now documented the fact that hydrocephalus may exist when careful measurement of CSF pressures from the lumbar subarachnoid space with the patient in the lateral recumbent position has shown pressures of less than 180 mm. of water. This finding has been confirmed in a few cases by recordings of the pressure over a period of several hours.

In some patients with normal pressure hydrocephalus, particularly those who have suffered a subarachnoid hemorrhage, elevation of CSF pressure may occur early

in the course of the illness but the symptoms of hydrocephalus may not appear until the pressure has returned to normal (*see Mechanism*).

Cerebrospinal Fluid Absorption

Measurement of CSF absorption has been proposed as a method of recognizing occult hydrocephalus. Saline infused at a rate of approximately twice the normal rate of CSF formation in patients with normal absorption capacity produces a predictable rise in the CSF pressure, while in abnormal situations the CSF pressure rises abruptly. In adults with occult hydrocephalus due to specific etiological factors the capacity to absorb added fluid was reduced, but in 13 of 14 patients with Alzheimer's disease the infusion test was normal.[13]

Isotope Cisternography

The isotope test is done by injecting 100 μc. of high specific activity radioiodinated serum albumin (RISA) into the lumbar subarachnoid space or cisterna magna.

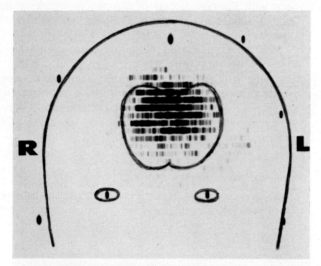 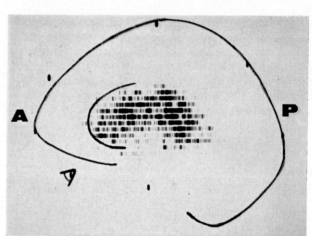

Fig. 2A. RISA cisternogram (A–P and lateral) 24 hr. after injection of 100 microcuries of RISA into the lumbar subarachnoid space. Essentially all of the isotope has entered the lateral ventricles.

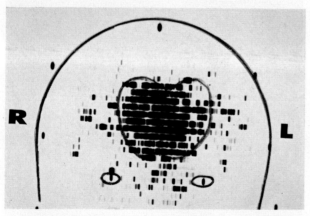 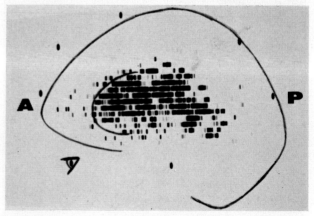

Fig. 2B. RISA cisternogram (A–P and lateral) at 48 hr., with minimal flow into basal cisterns. Apparent increase in density of concentration in ventricles is due to increase in sensitivity of recorder, which has also increased background counts in adjacent area.

(Reproduced with the permission of the Congress of Neurological Surgeons, from *Clinical Neurosurgery*, Volume 18, Williams and Wilkins Co., Baltimore, 1971.)

Abnormal studies are usually characterized by one of the following features: persistent ventricular filling with delayed clearance and reduction or absence of flow in the cerebral subarachnoid space; transient ventricular filling with delayed or normal convexity flow; no ventricular filling but delayed flow over the cerebral surface; and abnormal concentration in cystic areas of pathology.

Several reports[2,4,11,14,16,18,19] have confirmed the fact that, in the typical case of normal pressure hydrocephalus, when the PEG shows enlarged ventricles with no air in the convexity subarachnoid space the isotope scan will be abnormal, with essentially all of the activity in the ventricles and very little reaching the surface of the cerebral hemisphere, even 48 hr. after injection (Fig. 2a and b). A normal scan usually excludes a problem in CSF flow. Difficulty arises, however, from the fact that there are a number of variations between the absolutes of a definitely normal and a definitely abnormal scan.

A review of 18 adult patients with communicating hydrocephalus, most of whom had normal lumbar puncture pressures, showed that when isotopic clearance from the ventricles occurred in 24–48 hr. they seldom responded to surgical therapy.[16] Preliminary evidence suggested that prolonged retention of the isotope in the ventricle was a favorable prognostic sign.[14] The use of this test in differentiating normal pressure hydrocephalus from atrophic disease is discussed below.

RESPONSE TO SURGICAL TREATMENT

Following insertion of a satisfactory shunt, the most rapid improvement is usually noted in mental symptoms. Incontinence also clears but gait is usually slow to improve and some residual deficit may persist. The rate of recovery varies greatly. Improvement may be noted within a few hours of surgery but may not begin for several days or weeks.[18,19]

DIFFERENTIAL DIAGNOSIS

Patients with normal pressure hydrocephalus of unknown etiology have been separated from the large group of adults presenting with dementia. Experience has indicated that patients with Alzheimer's disease or other primary dementing illnesses do not benefit appreciably from a ventriculovenous shunt.[11,14,18,19,20]

In Alzheimer's disease, the principal symptom is loss of memory, to which are later added defects in calculation, speech and thinking. Gait disturbance is rarely an early manifestation. Late in the course of the illness mental slowness develops and then incontinence appears. Deficits usually develop over several years, while in the majority of patients with normal pressure hydrocephalus the evolution is a period of months. Pneumoencephalography clearly differentiates the two entities in most cases, with patients with Alzheimer's disease showing dilated ventricles and large pools of air in the widened sulci in the cerebral subarachnoid spaces, while those with normal pressure hydrocephalus show a lack of air in the subarachnoid space.

In Alzheimer's disease, the RISA CSF flow study reveals either a normal appearance[2] or transient ventricular filling with a delayed but normal cerebral convexity flow pattern.[4] Some patients, as noted below in Groups 1B and 1C, present a clinical picture with some features of both normal pressure hydrocephalus and cerebral atrophy. Indeed, both processes may be present, and the response to therapy is determined by the relative severity of each process.

Another important area of differential diagnosis is the intracranial tumor whose sole manifestation is the symptoms and signs of hydrocephalus (see Group 2C). The PEG is crucial for full evaluation of these cases. The tumor is usually in the midline causing partial obstruction of the ventricular system.

TABLE 1*

SUMMARY OF 50 CASES OF NORMAL PRESSURE HYDROCEPHALUS

Group	No. of Cases	Etiology	Age (years)	Sex	Clinical Syndrome	Cerebral Subarachnoid Space (PEG)	Response to Treatment†	Follow-up (years)
1A	5	Unknown	61–77	5F	Typical	Complete obstruction	Good to excellent	1–11
B	6	Unknown	62–77	3F 3M	Typical	Partial obstruction	Fair to good	1–4
C	7	Unknown	63–77	3F 4M	Atypical	Partial obstruction	None to fair	1–4
2A	12	Subarachnoid hemorrhage	26–67	7F 5M	Variable	Complete obstruction	Fair to excellent	1–4
B	11	Trauma	18–78	2F 9M	Variable	Variable	Fair to excellent	1–9
C	5	Intracranial tumour and surgery	47–62	1F 4M	Typical	Variable	Good to excellent	1–7
D	3	Meningitis	49–65	2F 1M	Typical	Complete obstruction	Good to excellent	1–2
E	1	Aqueduct stenosis	54	1F	Typical	Partial obstruction	Excellent	3

* *See* reference 19 for complete explanation.
† Excellent—returned to previous activity; normal or nearly normal examination.
Good—returned to previous activity with minor residual symptoms.
Fair—definite improvement in symptoms but unable to resume previous level of activity.
None—no appreciable change.

CLASSIFICATION OF CASES

For purposes of analysis, we have divided our cases into two large groups (Table 1). Group 1 consists of those patients with complete or partial CSF obstruction in whom no definite etiology could be established to account for the enlarged ventricular system and neurological symptoms. Group 1 is subdivided into three categories, dependent on characteristics of the clinical syndrome, radiographic features and response to surgical treatment. Group 2 includes those patients with a complete or partial CSF obstruction in whom there is a specific etiological factor to explain the development of the hydrocephalus. At times, the clinical syndrome is superimposed on some degree of residual deficit from the underlying disease process. On rare occasions focal neurological deficits are noted in association with porencephalic cysts. Group 2 is subdivided into etiological factors.

Group 1A

Included in this category are patients who have the typical clinical syndrome, radiographic evidence of enlarged ventricles with no filling of air in the convexity subarachnoid space, and a good response to a shunt operation. Several reports[1,8,10–12,14] have confirmed the presence of this syndrome in a small percentage of adults presenting with dementia of undetermined etiology.

Group 1B

Characteristic of these patients are symptoms and signs closely resembling those typical of normal pressure hydrocephalus although PEG shows not only large ventricles but also some air entering the surface CSF pathways above the tentorium, albeit large areas of the convexity remain unfilled. Response to treatment is variable, but in the majority of patients there is a good recovery with ability to function at a near normal level.

Group 1C

These patients were distinguished by histories and findings more typical of Alzheimer's or a related dementing illness, but their PEGs demonstrated partial lack of filling of the cerebral subarachnoid space, rather than the large dilated areas characteristic of atrophy. In these cases there was usually little or no response following shunt placement.

In both Groups 1B and 1C, there are some cases in which it is probable that both hydrocephalus and atrophy co-exist. Response to treatment depends on the relationship between these two processes. In some cases improvement from the shunt procedure may last for several months or longer, only to be followed by deterioration clearly related to degenerative disease.

Group 2A: Subarachnoid Hemorrhage

The historical facts relating the development of normal pressure hydrocephalus to subarachnoid hemorrhage have been well summarized.[3] It is not uncommon to observe mild to moderate ventricular dilatation soon after subarachnoid hemorrhage. Often there is a temporary increase in CSF pressure, but in some cases symptoms of hydrocephalus develop when the pressure has returned to or has been persistently normal. Symptoms may seem to begin almost immediately after the hemorrhage but more commonly onset is delayed for three weeks or longer.[18,19]

Improvement of hydrocephalic symptoms is usually evident within a few days of placement of the ventriculo-venous shunt. Neurological deficits related to the effect of the hemorrhage have not usually been altered with treatment of the hydrocephalus, but there are exceptions to this general rule.[19]

Group 2B: Trauma

Hydrocephalus is a rare complication following head trauma and has been recognized for many years. Only recently, however, with the recognition that symptoms due to hydrocephalus may be present with normal CSF pressure has the higher frequency of this complication been realized. The largest series reported to date includes 20 cases of hydrocephalus of all types following severe head injury.[15]

Presumably, the cause of CSF obstruction, which may be in either the basal cisterns or cerebral subarachnoid space, is scarring following subarachnoid hemorrhage. Symptom onset may be delayed for a considerable period of time after the initial injury, an interval of several months occurring in some reported cases.[19] Persistent signs of brain dysfunction following a severe injury may indicate that hydrocephalus is present, and in some cases there may be a positive response to surgical treatment.

Group 2C: Intracranial Tumors and Surgery

Partial obstruction of the ventricular system from a mass lesion may be associated with normal CSF pressure and symptoms related only to the ventricular enlargement.[1,19] Symptoms may also be related to obstruction of the basal cisterns following intracranial surgery, most commonly posterior fossa operations.

Group 2D: Meningitis

A few adult cases of meningitis with either persistent or delayed onset hydrocephalus have been reported.[19]

Group 2E: Other

Other causes of normal pressure hydrocephalus include aqueduct stenosis and ectasia of the basilar artery.

MECHANISM

Considerable discussion has taken place regarding the causal factors in the normal pressure hydrocephalus syndrome. In our series, all of the patients with idiopathic hydrocephalus and most of those with a specific etiological factor showed a block to passage of air or isotope in the subarachnoid space, usually at the level of the basal cisterns, but in some cases higher in the cerebral subarachnoid pathway, from a mass lesion or aqueduct obstruction. Autopsies done on two patients with idiopathic normal pressure hydrocephalus demonstrated a block due to scar tissue in the subarachnoid space,[19] which has also been the finding after subarachnoid hemorrhage.

The dual question of what constitutes normal CSF pressure, and whether the entity of normal pressure hydrocephalus does in fact really exist, has been raised. This problem has been considered in detail and it has been found that careful measurements in patients with normal pressure hydrocephalus have repeatedly shown pressures below 140 mm.[6] Another factor supporting the reality of the syndrome is that there are no clinical signs or symptoms of increased intracranial pressure, and no radiographic evidence of changes normally associated with a long-standing increase in CSF pressure.

Several explanations have been offered to clarify the relationship of enlarged ventricles to normal CSF pressure. The mechanisms will be discussed below, but it is certainly possible that more than one factor may be important, particularly since improvement in symptoms following shunt insertion is, as previously noted, quite variable.

Intermittent High CSF Pressure

The possibility of intermittent, or initially high, CSF pressure should be considered. Certainly this may be the case in some patients with subarachnoid hemorrhage, but often the symptoms of hydrocephalus persist or even develop after the pressure has returned to a normal range. In view of the clinical and laboratory findings presented by these patients, it seems unlikely that persistent high pressure plays a role in most cases of normal pressure hydrocephalus.

Activation of Early-Life Arrested Ventricular Enlargement

This problem has been discussed in detail.[17] In some cases of arrested hydrocephalus the patient may never show any symptoms. In others, head trauma may aggravate the underlying situation and cause the appearance of signs of increased intracranial pressure. There are, however, patients in whom the course is one of gradual onset of symptoms.

Although this process may be present in a few cases, the lack of any change on plain radiographic films coupled with the rapid shrinking of the ventricles and improvement in symptoms following a shunt operation makes it unlikely that arrested ventricular enlargement is a frequent cause of the normal pressure hydrocephalus syndrome.

Force-Pressure Relationships

In his original article on normal pressure hydrocephalus, Hakim,[9] and then Hakim and Adams[10] proposed the "hydraulic press effect" to explain the clinical symptoms resulting from large ventricles under normal pressure. In brief, their hypothesis assumes that early in the course of the illness there is some mechanism which produces an increase in pressure, which, in turn, causes ventricular enlargement. When all factors come into balance, even with the relief of the cause (whatever it may be) of the initial increased pressure (however mild that increase may be), the ventricles remain enlarged and neurological symptoms persist. This is explained by the fact that the total force applied to the cerebral hemispheres is the pressure per unit area multiplied by the total area $(F = P \times A)$. With the ventricles enlarged, the total area is markedly increased and therefore a lower or "normal" pressure is all that is necessary to maintain an increased force against the cerebral tissue.

Pulsatile Force and Loss of Lipid and Protein

It has been postulated[6] that expansion of the ventricular system might relate to the rapid loss of protein and lipid from the white matter, which, in turn, might be activated by "intermittent peaks of pressure exceeding those of the normal ventricular system". This ventricular expansion could result from the purely physical mechanism of "slow relaxation after sudden expansion" from the pulsatile force.

Alterations in Cerebral Blood Flow

Xenon-133 clearance after intracarotid injection has been used to study cerebral blood flow in normal pressure hydrocephalus and atrophy.[7] It was found that blood flow was reduced by approximately 20 per cent in patients with cerebral atrophy and by 40 per cent in those with normal pressure hydrocephalus. Blood flow has also been measured before and after a shunt operation.[8] In these cases, postoperative increase in blood flow correlated well with clinical improvement, and a close correlation was noted between the percentage decrease in ventricular size and the percentage increase in mean flow. Whether this reduction in cerebral blood flow is due to secondary changes in metabolism from ventricular expansion or is a primary cause of the syndrome has not been established.

Change in Direction of CSF Flow

Isotopic CSF flow studies shed some light on the problem of ventricular enlargement with normal pressure. Normally the isotope ascends to the basal cisterns into midline or temporal subarachnoid space and Sylvian fissure, then over the cerebral hemisphere, to be absorbed in the parasagittal area. In RISA flow studies in patients with normal pressure hydrocephalus who have a block in the subarachnoid space, the flow is into the ventricular system, with the result that the normal current flow out of the ventricles is reversed and the spinal fluid seeks alternate routes of absorption. The excess fluid absorbed through the ventricular wall into the adjacent tissues may well change the properties of that tissue and allow for expansion under normal pressure. As previously noted, there may be alterations in protein and lipids in the tissue immediately adjacent to the walls of hydrocephalic ventricles. Under these circumstances it is possible that no increase in pressure would be necessary. Once the process reaches equilibrium, the "hydraulic press" mechanism of $F = P \times A$ may be important in the maintenance of the process.

Comment

It seems unlikely that a single explanation will account for all aspects of the syndrome of normal pressure hydrocephalus. Several mechanisms working singly or in combination account for the development and maintenance of enlarged ventricles with normal pressure and the associated neurological symptoms and signs.

FURTHER READING

[1] Adams, R. D., Fisher, C. M., Hakim, S., Ojemann, R. G. and Sweet, W. H. (1965), "Symptomatic Occult Hydrocephalus with 'Normal' Cerebrospinal-fluid Pressure: A Treatable Syndrome," *New Engl. J. Med.*, **273**, 117–126.

[2] Bannister, R., Gilford, E. and Kocen, R. (1967), "Isotope Encephalography in the Diagnosis of Dementia Due to Communicating Hydrocephalus," *Lancet*, **2**, 1014–1017.

[3] Barnett, H. J. M. (1969), "Some Clinical Features of Intracranial Aneurysms," in *Clinical Neurosurgery*, Vol. 16, pp. 43–72 (R. G. Ojemann, Ed.). Baltimore: The Williams & Wilkins Co.

[4] Benson, D. F., LeMay, M., Patten, D. H. and Rubens, A. B. (1970), "Diagnosis of Normal-pressure Hydrocephalus," *New Engl. J. Med.*, **283**, 609–615.

[5] Ekbom, K., Greitz, T. and Kugelberg, E. (1969), "Hydrocephalus Due to Ectasia of the Basilar Artery," *J. Neurol. Sci.*, **8**, 465–477.

[6] Geschwind, N. (1968), "The Mechanism of Normal Pressure Hydrocephalus," *J. Neurol. Sci.*, **7**, 481–493.

[7] Greitz, T. (1969), "Cerebral Blood Flow in Occult Hydrocephalus Studied with Angiography and the Xenon 133 Clearance Method," *Acta radiol.*, **8**, 376–384.

[8] Greitz, T., Crepe, A., Kalmér, M. and López, J. (1969), "Pre- and Postoperative Evaluation of Cerebral Blood Flow in Low-pressure Hydrocephalus," *J. Neurosurg.*, **31**, 644–651.

[9] Hakim, S. (1964), *Algunas observaciones sobre in presion del L.C.R. sindrome hidrocefalico en el adulto con "presion normal" del L.C.R.* Tesis de grado. Colombia: Universidad Javeriana, Bogotá.

[10] Hakim, S. and Adams, R. D. (1965), "The Special Clinical Problem of Symptomatic Hydrocephalus with Normal Cerebrospinal Fluid Pressure: Observations on Cerebrospinal Fluid Hydrodynamics," *J. Neurol. Sci.*, **2**, 307–327.

[11] Heinz, E. R., Davis, D. O. and Karp, H. R. (1970), "Abnormal Isotope Cisternography in Symptomatic Occult Hydrocephalus," *Radiology*, **95**, 109–120.

[12] Hill, M. E., Lougheed, W. M. and Barnett, H. J. M. (1967), "A Treatable Form of Dementia Due to Normal-pressure, Communicating Hydrocephalus," *Canad. med. Ass. J.*, **97**, 1309–1320.

[13] Hussey, F., Schanzer, B. and Katzman, R. (1970), "A Simple Constant-infusion Manometric Test for Measurement of CSF Absorption. II. Clinical Studies," *Neurology* (*Minneap.*), **20**, 665–680.

[14] LeMay, M. and New, P. F. J. (1970), "Radiological Diagnosis of Occult Normal-pressure Hydrocephalus," *Radiology*, **96**, 347–358.

[15] Lewin, W. (1969), "Preliminary Observations on External Hydrocephalus after Severe Head Injury," *Brit. J. Surg.*, **55**, 747–751.

[16] McCullough, D. C., Harbert, J. C., Di Chiro, G. and Ommaya, A. K. (1970), "Prognostic Criteria for Cerebrospinal Fluid Shunting from Isotope Cisternography in Communicating Hydrocephalus," *Neurology* (*Minneap.*), **20**, 594–598.

[17] McHugh, P. R. (1964), "Occult Hydrocephalus," *Quart. J. Med.*, **33**, 297–312.

[18] Ojemann, R. G., Fisher, C. M., Adams, R. D., Sweet, W. H. and New, P. F. J. (1969), "Further Experience with the Syndrome of 'Normal' Pressure Hydrocephalus," *J. Neurosurg.*, **31**, 279–294.

[19] Ojemann, R. G. (1971), "Normal Pressure Hydrocephalus," in *Clinical Neurosurgery*, Vol. 18 (G. T. Tindall, Ed.). Baltimore: The Williams & Wilkins Co. In press.

[20] Taveras, J. M. (1968), "Low-pressure Hydrocephalus," in *Neuro-ophthalmology*, pp. 293–309. (J. L. Smith, Ed.). St. Louis: C. V. Mosby Co.

5. PHYSIOPATHOLOGY AND MANAGEMENT OF INCREASED INTRACRANIAL PRESSURE

DOUGLAS MILLER and HUME ADAMS

INTRODUCTION

A wide range of pathological lesions eventually cause a rise in intracranial pressure (ICP), and indeed often become symptomatic or life-threatening only when they do so. Consequently, clinicians are frequently concerned with recognizing when ICP is, in fact, raised and with instituting measures to counteract this potentially dangerous situation. Although certain diffuse pathological processes in the brain may cause raised ICP without any marked brain shift, most lesions are localized and produce internal herniations and brain shifts, with the development at some stage of pressure gradients. To some extent these shifts compensate for expanding lesions and it is not uncommon, now that ICP can be continuously monitored, to observed brain shifts at a time when ICP is not actually raised; of course, ICP may have been previously high and may later become high again. It is, therefore, important not to equate shift with increased ICP, and indeed it may be difficult at times to know with certainty whether the patient's clinical state is mainly the result of shift or of persistently raised ICP. Nevertheless, the clinician most often has to treat a patient with both shift and raised pressure and must consider the treatment of both.

In this chapter both are considered as part of a dynamic process. After reviewing the evolution of ideas about these topics, the conventional neuropathology common to all expanding intracranial lesions is summarized. Factors which modify ICP, and the effect of increased ICP on intracranial and extracranial physiological function, are then dealt with. The clinical features and principles of management constitute the final section.

THE EVOLUTION OF IDEAS ON INCREASED INTRACRANIAL PRESSURE

Historically, the dominating influence on thinking about intracranial pressure was the Monro–Kellie doctrine. This originally stated (in 1824) that the intracranial contents consist of brain and blood within a rigid un-yielding container, the skull; because both were incom-pressible, the implication was that cerebral blood volume would remain constant at all times. This concept had to be modified to take account of the cerebrospinal fluid (CSF) volume, and by the end of the 19th century it was generally accepted that as an intracranial mass lesion increased in size a compensatory reduction of CSF and blood volume could, for a time, prevent or modify any increase in ICP. Only when this compensatory capacity was becoming exhausted would ICP increase. This con-cept was translated into clinical terms by Kocher who, at the turn of the century, defined four stages of cerebral compression. The first, or compensated stage, was characterized by little or no change in the clinical status of the patient despite the expansion of a mass lesion, because of a compensatory reduction in the volume of the other intracranial constituents. In the second stage there was some headache and drowsiness as compensatory mechan-isms were becoming exhausted. In the third stage, when ICP was thought to be increasing to high levels, there was pronounced depression of the conscious level, an increase of systemic arterial pressure (SAP), bradycardia and irregular respiration. The fourth (pre-terminal) stage was characterized by deep unconsciousness, bilateral fixed dilated pupils and a progressive reduction of SAP.

At this time Cushing, working for Kocher, investigated changes in the systemic circulation during cerebral compression. He increased ICP in anaesthetized dogs up to and beyond the level of SAP and observed that, as ICP approached SAP, there was a sharp increase in SAP which he ascribed to an attempt by the brain to maintain its blood flow, the triggering mechanism of this pressor response being medullary ischaemia.

The assertions of Kocher and Cushing were challenged during the 1920's and 30's by two clinical observations; firstly, that some patients with severe brain damage and the clinical features of cerebral compression were found on lumbar puncture to have a normal CSF pressure; secondly, elevations of SAP were observed in patients with cerebral compression when the lumbar CSF pressure was far below SAP. It was many years before these appar-ent conflicts were resolved(see page 315).

In 1938, Jefferson's classical review of the clinical features of the tentorial pressure cone led in turn to a better understanding of the other types of shift that occur in response to expanding intracranial mass lesions. By 1959 it had been established in human studies by Johnson and Yates and in experimental animals by Thompson and Malina that, in addition to tentorial herniations with supratentorial mass lesions, the entire brain stem could be forced in a downward axial direction and it was suggested that the Cushing response was triggered not by any absolute level of ICP, but by mechanically produced medullary ischaemia, consequent on stretching of the perforating branches of the relatively fixed basilar artery. There was, at this stage, therefore, a tendency to ascribe nearly all of the symptoms of cerebral compression to the effects of brain shift and little or none to the level of ICP.

In the early 1960's several publications reversed, to some extent, the emphasis on brain shift. Lundberg and his colleagues pioneered the use of continuous long-term intra-ventricular pressure recording in patients suffering from a wide variety of intracranial lesions, including tumours and trauma (see Lundberg, Chapter IX: 3). They found extremely high levels of ventricular fluid pressure (VFP) in many patients and demonstrated pressure waves which could attain a level of 100 mm Hg. (1,360 mm. H$_2$O) not only in patients with persistently increased ICP but also in patients in whom ICP was relatively low most of the time.

In 1964 and 1965 Langfitt and his colleagues published two sets of papers which clarified and resolved many of the previous discordant observations on increased ICP. The first group of papers dealt with transmission of ICP within the supratentorial space and across the tentorium to the posterior fossa. If ICP was increased in experi-mental animals by infusing saline into the lumbar sub-arachnoid space, the increased pressure was transmitted freely throughout the craniospinal axis; thus the same pressure was measured from the cisterna magna, the lateral ventricles and the supratentorial extradural and subarach-noid spaces. When ICP was slowly increased by inflating a balloon in the supratentorial subdural space of Rhesus monkeys, the ICP in the subarachnoid space of the poster-ior fossa was initially the same as that in the supratentorial subarachnoid space; this period was followed by pro-gressive impaction of brain in the tentorial hiatus, during which there was a progressive failure of communication of pressure from the supratentorial compartment to the posterior fossa; when impaction was complete any further increase of supratentorial subarachnoid pressure was not transmitted to the posterior fossa; indeed pressure in the posterior fossa and lumbar subarachnoid space could return to normal, despite rising supratentorial pressure. Expansion of a subdural balloon in the supratentorial compartment thus produced a *pressure gradient* between the subarachnoid spaces of the supratentorial compart-ment and the posterior fossa. If infratentorial pressure was increased at this stage by infusing CSF into the lumbar subarachnoid space, transmission of pressure across the tentorium could be restored, but only for a short period. Failure of transmission of ICP across the blocked tentorial hiatus was indicated not only by the development of a pressure gradient, but also by loss of recorded pulsation in the pressure recordings from the posterior fossa and lumbar subarachnoid space.

Within the supratentorial compartment, subarachnoid pressure was the same as pressure recorded from the ventricle and the overlying extradural space, but when increased ICP was generated by an extradural mass lesion, the pressure within this lesion greatly exceeded the pressure transmitted to the underlying subarachnoid space because of the elasticity of the dura; pressure recorded from the contralateral extradural space was the same as subarachnoid and intraventricular pressure.

The second series of papers from Langfitt's group dealt with cerebrovascular responses to an expanding supratentorial mass lesion and represented an attempt to re-define Kocher's 4 stages of cerebral compression under controlled conditions, with direct measurements of arterial and intracranial pressure and cerebral blood flow in experimental animals. Stage 1, the period of spatial compensation, was characterized by a minimal increase in ICP despite slow inflation of an extradural balloon. In stage 2, at the end of the period of spatial compensation, ICP began to rise significantly until even small injections into the balloon produced large increases of ICP; even after inflation of the balloon had been stopped, prolonged increases of SAP and ICP occurred. These pressure waves could also be triggered off by hypercapnia and hypoxia once this critical stage had been reached. In stage 3, progressive decompensation occurred following repeated pressure waves. At this time ICP was approaching SAP and there was slowing of the EEG; eventually ICP reached the level of SAP and EEG activity disappeared. While the balloon remained inflated changes in arterial PCO$_2$ had no effect on ICP, while induced changes in SAP caused almost the same change in ICP. This was termed "cerebral vasomotor paralysis" by Langfitt to emphasize the lack of response of cerebral vessels to what were normally vaso-active stimuli. Even at this stage, however, rapid deflation of the balloon could result in return of ICP to normal and some return of EEG activity. In stage 4, which was a gradual transition from stage 3, decompensation had become irreversible, SAP fell rapidly and death was inevitable. Deflation of the balloon during the final stage resulted in a transient fall of ICP followed by a rapid return of ICP to the level of SAP, and an induced increase of arterial pressure by vasopressor agents caused a parallel increase in ICP, even after the balloon had been removed from the skull.

These important and fundamental studies by Langfitt's group have provided a much needed explanation and synthesis of clinical observations from the time of Kocher to the work of Lundberg and ushered in the current clinical and experimental investigations of raised ICP and cerebral blood flow and metabolism.

THE PATHOLOGY OF INTRACRANIAL EXPANDING LESIONS

Any intracranial expanding lesion, whether it be a tumour, an abscess, a haematoma or a large swollen infarct will produce distortion and shift of the brain. These lead in turn to secondary, often vascular, sequelae in other vital structures. Deformity may develop remarkably quickly in association with a rapidly expanding lesion, but it tends to be maximal when the lesion is expanding very slowly. As shift and distortion contribute to the spatial compensation referred to above, they can occur in the absence of any significant increase of ICP. In contrast, when the lesion is expanding rapidly, secondary vascular sequelae may occur in the presence of minimal distortion. The pattern of deformity inevitably depends not only on the rate of enlargement but also on the site of the expanding lesion.

Supratentorial Expanding Lesions

The commonest variety will be dealt with first, viz. a space-occupying lesion within a cerebral hemisphere. As the lesion expands, so also does the hemisphere: the surface of the brain is pressed against the unyielding dura, gyri are flattened, sulci are narrowed and, as CSF is displaced from the subarachnoid space, the surface of the brain becomes dry. The lateral ventricle on the side of the lesion and the third ventricle become reduced in size and there is lateral shift of the mid-line structures, viz. the pericallosal arteries, the interventricular septum and the third ventricle, away from the lesion (Fig. 1). At autopsy the dura

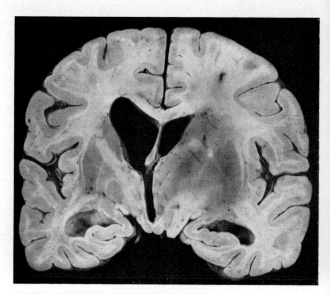

FIG. 1. *Lateral shift* of mid-line structures caused by a diffuse astrocytoma in the right cerebral hemisphere. The interventricular septum and the third ventricle are displaced to the left and the right lateral ventricle is of reduced size.

may be so tense that it is difficult to incise it without damaging the underlying cortex, and there may be deformities on the surface of the brain where it has been in contact with bony prominences on the base of the skull, e.g. the jugum sphenoidale and the lesser wing of the sphenoid bone. If the expanding lesion has been present for a long time, cerebral cortex may actually push through the dura to form numerous small nodules on its outer surface.

The next stage is the development of internal herniae, viz. displacement of brain tissue from one intracranial compartment to another.

A **supracallosal hernia** (subfalcine or cingulate hernia) is usually the first to appear, particularly with frontal and parietal lesions: the ipsilateral cingulate gyrus herniates under the free edge of the falx producing downward displacement of the roof of the ipsilateral ventricle and selective displacement of the pericallosal arteries away from the mid-line (Fig. 2). Although a supracallosal

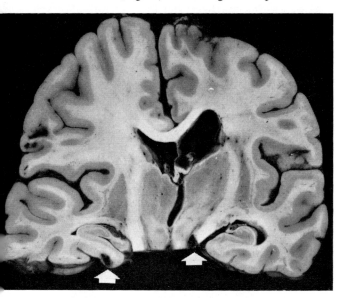

FIG. 2. *Internal herniae* produced by a left subdural haematoma. In addition to the lateral displacement shown in Fig. 1, the cingulate gyrus has herniated under the falx to produce a *supracallosal hernia*. This has produced downward displacement of the roof of the left lateral ventricle and selectively severe shift of the peri-callosal arteries. There is also haemorrhage in the left hippocampal gyrus (arrow) in the groove produced by a *tentorial hernia* and a haemorrhagic infarct in the *contra-lateral cerebral peduncle* (arrow) where it has been compressed against the tentorium.

hernia may not materially affect the clinical state of the patient, it is of importance to the neuroradiologist. A small wedge of haemorrhagic pressure necrosis can occur in the cortex of the cingulate gyrus where it is in contact with the falx and, occasionally, when the circulation through the pericallosal arteries is severely impaired, widespread infarction may occur in the territories which they supply.

A **tentorial hernia** (uncal or lateral transtentorial hernia) viz. herniation of the uncus and the medial part of the ipsilateral hippocampal gyrus through the tentorial incisura (Fig. 3) is of much greater clinical significance because of its consequential effects on other structures. It characteristically occurs when the expanding lesion is in the temporal lobe or in the lateral part of the middle cranial fossa, but it may occur in association with any supratentorial expanding lesion. As the medial part of the temporal lobe pushes towards the mid-line and over the free edge of the falx, the mid-brain is narrowed in its transverse axis, the aqueduct is compressed, and the contralateral cerebral peduncle is pushed against the opposite free edge of the tentorium. The ipsilateral

oculomotor nerve becomes compressed between the petroclinoid ligament or the free edge of the tentorium and the posterior cerebral artery to produce pupillary dilatation, loss of light reflex, oculomotor dysfunction and ptosis. Dilatation of the pupil is the earliest consistent sign of a tentorial hernia and may occur before there is any impairment of consciousness. As the hernia enlarges it produces a distinct groove on the upper surface of the adjacent cerebellar hemisphere; a pressure gradient develops between the supratentorial and infratentorial subarachnoid spaces; a wedge of necrosis, often accompanied by haemorrhage, appears along the line of the groove in the uncus and the hippocampal gyrus (Fig. 2); and focal infarction may occur in the contralateral cerebral peduncle where it is pressed against the edge of the tentorium (Fig. 2). The clinical syndrome of this type of tentorial herniation has been differentiated from that of caudal displacement of the diencephalon and upper brain stem by Plum and Posner, but both types of hernia are usually found in the end-stage seen by the neuropathologist.

Caudal displacement of the diencephalon and the rostral mid-brain (central transtentorial herniation) is often preceded by herniation of the hippocampal gyrus and occurs particularly in response to expanding lesions in the frontal, parietal and occipital regions. Its particular clinical importance is that interference with diencephalic function leads to impairment of intellect and then of the conscious level. Minor degrees of caudal displacement are less apparent even in a properly fixed brain than the lateral shifts already described, but when the condition is advanced the mamillary bodies are displaced backwards and downwards, the pituitary stalk is compressed and the posterior part of the floor of the third ventricle comes to lie below the level of the tentorial incisura. Focal in-farction may occur in the mamillary bodies, and in the

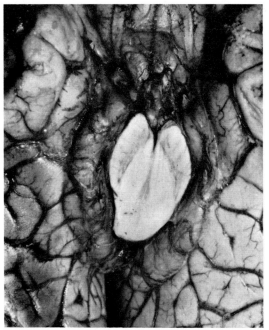

FIG. 3. There is a large *tentorial hernia* on the left of the illustra-tion and a smaller one on the right. The mid-brain is narrowed.

anterior lobe of the pituitary gland due to impairment of blood flow through the long hypothalamo-hypophysial portal vessels. A clinical sign associated with downward displacement of the posterior part of one or both hippocampal gyri is impairment of upward gaze due to downward pressure on the tectal plate. Displacement of the oculomotor nerves is now more severe and focal haemorrhage (Fig. 4) is frequently seen in the nerve where it is

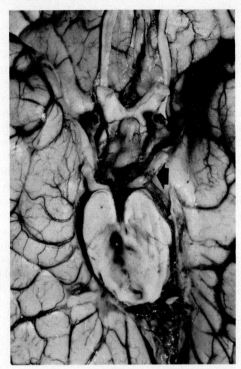

FIG. 4. In addition to a small *tentorial hernia* on the right of the illustration, there is *haemorrhage into the ipsilateral oculomotor* nerve where it crosses the posterior cerebral artery (arrow). The contralateral oculomotor nerve is sharply looped over the posterior cerebral artery but there is no haemorrhage into it. There is also *focal haemorrhage* into the tegmentum of the lower mid-brain.

looped round the posterior cerebral artery. Infarction often occurs in the posterior cerebral arterial territory as a result of distortion and compression of its main trunk: the infarction is usually haemorrhagic and restricted to the cortex on the medial and inferior aspects of the occipital lobe (Fig. 5) but it can be more widespread, implicating the entire circumference of the occipital lobe, the hippocampal and fusiform gyri and the posterior part of the thalamus. The anterior choroidal artery may be similarly affected. When tentorial herniation and caudal displacement are severe, focal flattening and/or haemorrhage into the oculomotor nerve and infarction in the posterior cerebral arterial territories may be bilateral even when the tentorial hernia is unilateral. Tentorial herniation may, however, sometimes be bilateral, particularly when the space occupying lesion is near the mid-line.

Haemorrhage and infarction in the mid-brain and pons is another event associated with lateral and caudal displacement of the brain stem. Emphasis is usually placed on haemorrhage as this is obvious to the naked eye, but

microscopical examination often shows that ischaemic infarction is more widespread than frank haemorrhage. Both types of lesion occur mainly adjacent to the mid-line in the tegmentum of the mid-brain and in the tegmental and basal parts of the upper pons (Fig. 4). Considerable controversy exists as to their pathogenesis: it is unlikely that they are related solely to venous obstruction or to the increase in blood pressure frequently associated with raised ICP (the pressor response referred to below) in view of the frequent occurrence of ischaemic infarction as well as haemorrhage, but these factors may well contribute to the final picture. Emphasis therefore has to be placed on caudal displacement of the relatively mobile brain stem and the relative immobility of the vertebrobasilar arterial system. As a consequence of this, the perforating vessels are subjected to shearing strains which in turn lead to spasm, infarction and/or haemorrhage.

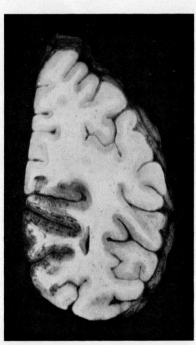

FIG. 5. There is *haemorrhagic infarction* of the cortex on the medial aspect of the lower half of the right occipital lobe. The primary lesion was an acute subdural haematoma on the right.

A **tonsillar hernia** (foraminal impaction, cerebellar cone) viz. downward displacement of the cerebellar tonsils through the foramen magnum may also occur in association with a supratentorial space-occupying lesion: impaction may be sufficiently severe to produce haemorrhagic infarction of the tips of the tonsils which can actually separate from the cerebellum and be found postmortem in the spinal subarachnoid space. The occurrence of a tonsillar hernia in the absence of a tentorial hernia in a patient with a supratentorial expanding lesion may at first seem surprising, but it is readily explicable if one recalls that there is great individual variation in the size of the tentorial incisura, and that the tentorium itself is able to bulge downwards. A small incisura precludes the occurrence of a large tentorial hernia, but not compression of the mid-brain by the hippocampal gyri or caudal displacement of the brain stem. It is in such cases that the leaves of the tentorium tend to be displaced downwards resulting in a reduction in the vertical axis of each cerebellar hemisphere, the upper surface of which becomes distinctly concave upwards, a reduction in the volume of the posterior fossa and, ultimately, a tonsillar hernia.

An essentially similar sequence of events to that already described occurs in association with supratentorial extracerebral collections such as an extradural or subdural haematoma. One difference observed is that convolutional flattening associated with a subdural haematoma is often restricted to the contralateral hemisphere. When brain swelling is diffuse and bilateral, the ventricles become small and symmetrical and there is no lateral shift of the mid-line structures. Tentorial herniae may occur but they are usually relatively small and often bilateral, their size depending to some extent on the rate of brain swelling and the size of the tentorial incisura. Caudal displacement of the diencephalon and the brain stem may be as severe as with a unilateral expanding lesion.

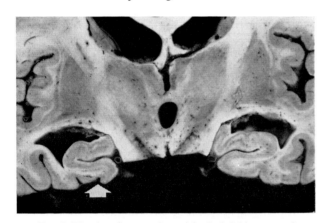

FIG. 6. The shrunken scar (arrow) in the left hippocampal gyrus immediately lateral to the medial part of its crest is indicative of a *previous tentorial hernia*. A left subdural haematoma had been evacuated one month previously.

If, as a result of treatment, distortion and herniation of the brain regress, evidence of the previous episode often remains; this can often be seen with the naked eye, but sometimes only on microscopy. The most characteristic lesion is a small shrunken wedge-shaped scar along the hippocampal gyrus (Fig. 6). A similar lesion is less frequently seen in the cingulate gyrus as a result of a previous supracallosal hernia. If the episode has been severe, there may be evidence of previous medial occipital infarction or focal brain stem haemorrhage and/or infarction.

Infratentorial Lesions

Hydrocephalus is the commonest abnormality associated with mass lesions in the posterior fossa, whether they be in the fourth ventricle, in the cerebellum or extracerebellar. This in turn leads to enlargement of the cerebral hemispheres, convolutional flattening, ballooning of the third ventricle and compression of hypothalamic structures

against the sphenoid bone. When the lesion is not in the mid-line, the aqueduct and fourth ventricle are compressed and displaced to the other side. Tonsillar herniation tends to be more severe than with a supratentorial expanding lesion. It may also produce compression of the medulla whose anteroposterior axis can become greatly reduced: in severe cases a distinct groove occurs where the ventral aspect of the lower medulla is compressed against the anterior margin of the foramen magnum. Microscopical examination in such cases often demonstrates focal infarction in the medulla. Occasionally, the posterior inferior cerebellar arteries may be compressed to such an extent that infarction occurs in the inferior part of one or both cerebellar hemispheres. Herniation of the cerebellum may also occur in an upward direction— the so-called *reversed tentorial hernia:* if the lesion is expanding very slowly, upward herniation of the superior vermis of the cerebellum can produce considerable distortion of the hippocampal gyri. Occasionally compression of the superior cerebellar arteries may lead to infarction in the superior part of one or both cerebellar hemispheres.

Other Effects

A long-sustained moderate increase of ICP is conventionally associated with erosion of bone, particularly of the posterior clinoid processes. There may also be erosion of the lesser wings of the sphenoid bone and of the orbital plates (Fig. 7). Enlargement of the pituitary

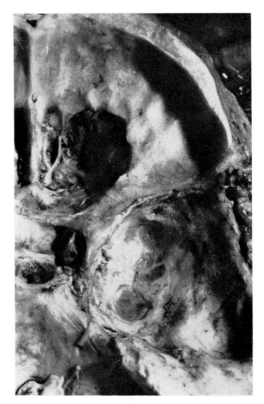

FIG. 7. *Erosion of bone* in the right anterior and middle cranial fossae caused by a slowly growing glioma in the right cerebral hemisphere.

fossa is attributed to downward pressure on the diaphragma sellae. Certainly, a deeply cupped diaphragma sellae is often seen post mortem in patients with slowly expanding space occupying lesions. In younger patients, separation of sutures may be a conspicuous abnormality but the so-called "beaten silver" appearance is now thought to be of considerably less diagnostic importance than it was in the past.

External herniae occur when there is a defect in the skull: these may simply amount to the protrusion of small "nubbins" of cortex through burr-holes, but, if an external decompression has been undertaken, a large part of a cerebral hemisphere may herniate through the gap in the calvaria. This procedure is intended to reduce midline shift, internal herniae and caudal displacement of the diencephalon, but as the herniated brain tissue itself tends to swell and become necrotic, the reduction of shift is often less than one might anticipate.

DYNAMICS OF INCREASED INTRACRANIAL PRESSURE

Traditionally, in measuring ICP from the lumbar subarachnoid space during lumbar puncture, the pressure has been expressed in mm. H_2O or more correctly, mm. CSF. This has been largely a matter of convenience as it is a simple matter to measure the height of the column of CSF displaced into a vertical graduated column attached to the spinal needle. This may be converted into mm Hg. by dividing by 13·6, the specific gravity of mercury. This unit permits a direct comparison of ICP with SAP and should become standard for expressing measurements of ICP, whether obtained from the lumbar subarachnoid space or the supratentorial compartment.

Normal ICP shows small variations with the arterial pulse and with respiration, but little change with induced changes of SAP. As ICP increases, the magnitude of the "arterial" pulse wave in the ICP trace increases also. The method of obtaining a mean pressure from the pulsatile record also becomes important. As yet there is no fixed convention, but since mean SAP is obtained from

$$\frac{\text{systolic pressure} + 2 \times \text{diastolic pressure}}{3}$$

it would seem logical for mean ICP to be derived in the same way.

In assessing the effects of any agent upon ICP, the fundamental relationship to consider is the *volume/pressure curve*, viz., the relationship between ICP and the volume of any addition to the intracranial contents. The exponential form of this curve (Fig. 8) was implicit in the descriptions of cerebral compression given by Kocher, and confirmed in experimental animals by Langfitt and his co-workers. Initially, the addition of small volumes to the intracranial contents produces little change in pressure; but once this begins to rise then smaller and smaller increments of volume produce larger and larger increases in pressure. The exact volume required to produce a given pressure is dependent upon several factors, including the volume of the cranial cavity, the ability of the skull to expand (e.g. in young children), the elasticity of the dura,

the time taken for the increase in volume, the relative proportions of CSF, blood and brain present in any individual and the ability of the brain to herniate out of any compartment, which is in turn partly related to the configuration of the tentorial hiatus and the foramen magnum.

RELATIONSHIP BETWEEN INTRACRANIAL PRESSURE and VOLUME of SPACE OCCUPYING LESION

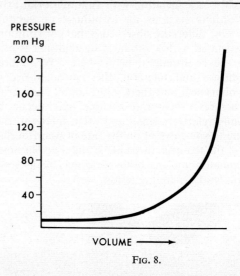

Fig. 8.

Any increase in cerebral blood flow (CBF) due to cerebral vasodilatation will, by augmenting the volume of intracranial blood, cause a rise in ICP; normally, this is rapidly compensated and the pressure change is small. But when compensatory mechanisms have already been partly utilized, such as when there is an intracranial space occupying lesion, the same amount of cerebral vasodilatation may produce a much larger increase in ICP. The increase in cerebral blood volume is most likely to occur in the thin-walled cerebral veins (*see* McDowall, Chapter IX: 4). This important application of the volume/pressure curve was clearly shown by the studies of McDowall and Jennett and their colleagues who demonstrated that volatile anaesthetic agents, which are known to increase CBF, produced only a small increase of ICP in patients with normal CSF pathways, but caused enormous increases in ICP in the closed head in patients with intracranial space occupying lesions. This principle also explains why hyperventilation, which causes cerebral vaso-constriction, may produce a marked reduction of ICP when this is high and a much smaller effect when ICP is at a normal level. Hypercapnia, hypoxia and volatile anaesthetic agents all increase ICP; hypocapnia, hyperbaric oxygen, hypothermia and neurolept-analgesic agents all reduce ICP, but the magnitude of these changes is dependent not only on the vaso-active properties of the agent, but also on the cerebrovascular reactivity and the intracranial volume/pressure status of the patient at that particular time.

Of the pressure waves described by Lundberg (*see* Chapter IX: 3), the most important type clinically is the plateau A wave in which ICP may reach 100 mm Hg. or more. There seem to be several triggering mechanisms for such waves, but the one common feature is that it indicates a "tight brain" on the steeply ascending portion of the volume/pressure curve. As the brain becomes "tight" it becomes increasingly important that the method used for measuring ICP be isovolumetric, as any displacement of CSF will significantly alter ICP.

TRANSMISSION OF INTRACRANIAL PRESSURE

Although the craniospinal axis has for long been regarded essentially as a hydrostatic system throughout which all pressures are equally distributed, important modifications are required in the light of more recent observations. Thus, there is considerable variation in the stress/strain relationships of the various constituents of the craniospinal axis; skull and dura are highly elastic, i.e. a deforming force produces a pronounced tendency for the material to return to its former configuration, while brain tissue is more plastic, i.e. it tends to yield and conform to a distorting force. Cerebral blood vessels fall somewhere between. Even within the CSF pathways, pressure gradients may develop if obstruction occurs at certain isthmuses, namely, the tentorial notch and the foramen magnum.

This has important implications for the measurement of increased ICP. With supratentorial expanding lesions, pressure measurements must be from the supratentorial compartment if they are to be valid. It is only since the widespread adoption of continuous recording of pressure from the lateral ventricles or from the supratentorial subdural or extradural spaces that the frequency with which high levels of ICP are encountered in various types of brain lesion has been fully appreciated. This contrasts with the frequent finding of normal CSF pressure in the lumbar subarachnoid space in patients with supratentorial mass lesions. It is now clear that this is due to a tentorial block causing a pressure gradient between the supra- and infra-tentorial compartments.

Fitch and McDowall have added another dimension to tentorial block by demonstrating that, with intermittent expansion of an extradural balloon in the supratentorial space in experimental animals, the addition of halothane which is a cerebral vasodilator, causes an increase in the pressure gradient between the supra- and infra-tentorial compartments and often unilateral pupillary dilatation, suggesting that the addition of halothane, even when the balloon was not being expanded, had exacerbated tentorial herniation.

Low ICP in the posterior fossa due to complete tentorial block may not, however, be uniform. Langfitt's group have recently shown that in experimental animals with high supratentorial pressure due to expansion of a subdural balloon but with normal pressure in the cerebello-pontine cistern as a result of tentorial block, pressure within the fourth ventricle was the same as supratentorial pressure. Tentorial block, therefore, may not protect the brain stem itself from the direct effects of increased supratentorial ICP.

Pressure recorded from the lateral ventricle in a patient with a brain tumour is assumed to be the pressure existing throughout the entire supratentorial compartment. Even this may not be a valid assumption, as it is possible that pressure gradients can build up within the brain itself owing to the capacity of brain tissue to yield to a distorting force. Pressure gradients within brain substance in the supratentorial compartment have been demonstrated in experimental animals, but only in relation to very rapidly expanding intra-cerebral lesions. In most clinical situations, because lesions expand more slowly, the gradient of pressures around an intracerebral mass should be small relative to the absolute level of ICP but, nevertheless, it is conceivable that there is a range of different cerebral tissue pressures surrounding an expanding lesion. At the present time satisfactory direct evidence for or against the existence of significant pressure gradients within cerebral tissue must be regarded as still lacking.

EFFECT OF INTRACRANIAL PRESSURE ON CEREBRAL BLOOD FLOW

Not only do changes in cerebral blood flow (CBF) affect ICP, but there is also a reciprocal relationship. The question now to be considered is what effect increased ICP has on CBF. Since the clinical study of Kety, Shenkin and Schmidt in 1948, it has been generally accepted that levels of ICP over 30 mm Hg. are associated with a reduction of CBF. Several groups of workers have, however, shown that moderate increases of ICP (up to 30 mm Hg.) cause no change in CBF.

The effect of ICP on CBF must be considered in relation to the level of SAP, however, and Zwetnow and his colleagues have defined cerebral perfusion pressure (CPP) during increased ICP as the difference between SAP and ICP. In their experiments the infusion of mock CSF into the cisterna magna of dogs resulted in a diffuse increase in ICP with no brain shift; in this situation CBF remained constant until CPP fell below 40 mm Hg. Beyond this point there was a sharp fall of CBF. The same relationship has been found in the baboon by Rowan and his co-workers using the same method of increasing ICP. Thus, it has been argued that the important factor in determining CBF is not the exact level of ICP, but its relationship to SAP. Both groups of workers concluded that this maintenance of CBF during the increase in ICP produced by CSF infusion was a type of autoregulation analogous to the well-established autoregulation of CBF to changes of arterial pressure (see Harper, Chapter VII: 2). Miller and his co-workers supported these conclusions by showing that the maintenance of CBF in the face of rising ICP was present only as long as autoregulation of CBF to altered arterial pressure was maintained; when autoregulation was impaired, e.g. by preceding hypotension or hypoxia, a subsequent increase of ICP caused an immediate reduction of CBF. The relationship between CPP and CBF was now represented by a straight line, the gradient of which corresponded to the degree of loss of autoregulation; thus the steeper the gradient, the less effective is autoregulation. CBF could then be maintained by elevating SAP, which in turn increased CPP.

Strictly speaking, CPP is the difference between the mean pressure in the arteries entering the subarachnoid space and the mean pressure inside the cerebral veins as they leave the subarachnoid space to enter the dural venous sinuses. When CPP is defined as the difference between arterial and intracranial pressure, it is assumed that the subarachnoid venous pressure is close to ICP. Shulman has shown this to be so for moderate increases of ICP produced by CSF infusion, but great caution should be exercised before assuming that this situation holds also for expanding intracranial lesions, cerebral oedema or other conditions which occur clinically.

When a diffuse rise of ICP is produced by CSF infusion, the head of pressure along the length of any cerebral vessel (CPP) is the same as the transmural pressure at the arterial end of the cerebrovascular system. Since ICP is the extravascular pressure, it can be postulated that the stimulus for autoregulation of CBF to the decreased pressure head produced by increased ICP is, in fact, the transmural pressure at the arterial end of the capillary bed. Support for this hypothesis comes from work by Ekstrom-Jodal and colleagues, who showed that when CPP was diminished by increasing cerebral venous pressure, but without changing transmural pressure (by performing the experiment with the calvarium removed so that ICP remained at zero) there was a diminution of CBF although autoregulation to altered arterial pressure was still intact.

This mechanism, however, does not take into account the possible effects of an expanding intracranial lesion in causing venous compression. Langfitt has argued that the cerebrovascular resistance may be regarded as a series of resistances starting in the larger cerebral arteries and proceeding through the capillary bed to include resistances at the venous end, both in the thin-walled veins and in the dural sinuses themselves. Compression of the venous end of the system, sufficient to cause an increase in resistance here, can be balanced by a decrease in resistance at the arterial end in order to preserve CBF at a constant level. This is clearly a problem which requires further investigation.

The potential effect of increased ICP on CBF is sometimes dramatically demonstrated during attempted angiography in patients *in extremis* from cerebral compression, when contrast medium fails to enter the subarachnoid portions of the carotid or vertebral arteries. Such a situation is almost invariably pre-terminal. At autopsy, there may be no obstructive lesion within the lumen of the distal part of the carotid artery and the condition has been referred to as "false block of the carotid". Failure of the contrast medium to enter the cranial cavity is usually accepted as meaning that ICP is the same as or only very slightly less than SAP, so that there is no pressure head available to carry the contrast medium through the cerebral vasculature. This has been confirmed in several cases by direct measurements of ICP and SAP taken at the time of angiography, but this is not always the case. We have observed a patient in whom no visualization of the internal carotid beyond the siphon could be obtained at angiography; SAP and ICP were almost equal at this stage; on repeat angiography, following reduction of ICP by aspiration of fluid from the ventricles, the same

failure of contrast medium to enter the brain was observed. Brierley has recorded this phenomenon in primates after a period of severe cerebral ischaemia; contrast medium failed to enter the cranial cavity, despite the restoration of normal ICP and SAP, and in the absence of any demonstrable block in the carotid arteries or their main branches. In certain circumstances, therefore, other factors have to be invoked in order to explain the failure of contrast medium to perfuse the head. These may be very slow flow with pooling of contrast in the carotid siphon, distortion of the carotid artery due to cerebral shift, or factors operating at capillary level which prevent forward flow of the column of blood from the carotid arteries.

It would seem inevitable that in any situation a very low CPP should produce widespread ischaemic damage in the brain. Adams and Brierley and their colleagues have shown that this is certainly so in man, and also in experimental animals, when ICP is not raised and the low CPP is due to arterial hypotension. However, there is as yet no positive evidence that diffuse ischaemic brain damage occurs when ICP is high and CPP is low, except in the highly artificial context of the so-called "respirator" brain which neuropathologists are encountering with increasing frequency. These are the brains removed from patients who, it would appear, must have reached the stage of total decompensation prior to being maintained on artificial ventilation for varying periods of time; in this situation the brain is virtually totally dead and "autolysis" has proceeded during the period of artificial ventilation. Raised ICP and a low CPP could conceivably contribute to the high incidence of ischaemic brain damage observed in patients dying as a result of a head injury (*see* Adams and Graham, Chapter X: 7) or of a ruptured intracranial aneurysm, and to some of the ischaemic damage conventionally associated with brain shift and increased ICP, but this remains to be substantiated.

Another inconsistency between CPP and CBF is sometimes seen in patients with benign intracranial hypertension in whom continuous monitoring of VFP has been carried out. At times, ICP may so closely approach SAP that CPP is less than 10 mm Hg., yet the patient remains conscious, implying that CBF has not been seriously reduced. One can only speculate as to the underlying haemodynamics of this situation; one possible cause of the sharp rise in ICP is the occurrence of cerebrovascular dilatation in an already tight brain, the tendency for CBF to increase being counteracted by a falling CPP. Lack of depression of conscious level in such cases may be related more to absence of brain shift than to the actual level of CBF attained at the height of the pressure wave.

In considering the inter-relationships of SAP, ICP, CPP and CBF the final question one must ask is whether it is possible for ICP to increase above SAP in clinical conditions. If zero CPP means no CBF then it is hard to see how ICP can go on rising above SAP; haematomas should stop expanding and oedema should stop forming if there were no supply of blood. On the other hand at autopsy, when SAP is zero, ICP in some cases appears still to be increased as the dura can still be very tight.

VFP has now been continuously monitored in over 200

patients in the Institute of Neurological Sciences, Glasgow; seldom, if ever, has ICP been observed definitely to rise above SAP; most apparent recordings of this are due to baseline drift of the transducer or faulty calibration. Any excess of ICP over SAP that has been observed has been small and of short duration.

THE VASOPRESSOR RESPONSE AND CEREBRAL BLOOD FLOW

The vasopressor response to increased ICP originally described by Cushing was thought by him to be an attempt by the ischaemic medulla to increase its blood supply. There has been much dispute about the stimulus for its production and its efficacy in increasing blood flow in the medulla and in the rest of the brain. There is no doubt that it indicates clinically that cerebral compression has reached an advanced and most serious stage.

The Cushing response consists of an increase in SAP in response to an increase in ICP, accompanied by bradycardia. The increase in SAP is often preceded by a transient fall in SAP. One of the confusing aspects of the response, as elicited in experimental animals, has been that the threshold levels of ICP required to produce the pressor response vary greatly with different methods of increasing ICP, with different animals and even with repeated trials in the same animal. This variation persists even when differing levels of SAP are taken into account. The vasopressor response can be elicited by a diffuse increase of ICP (CSF infusion into the lateral ventricles, the cisterna magna, the lumbar subarachnoid space or the supratentorial subarachnoid space), by expansion of supratentorial and infratentorial balloons, by downward pressure on the cut end of the mid-brain, by direct local pressure on the floor of the 4th ventricle and parts of the spinal cord, by ischaemia produced by bilateral vertebral artery ligation, and by hypoxia. The final common pathway appears to be ischaemia and/or hypoxia in the lower half of the floor of the 4th ventricle; the pressor response is mediated by the sympathetic outflow and can, therefore, be blocked by cervical cord section or sympathectomy and may be augmented by experimental decerebration. The bradycardia component originates in the same area of the 4th ventricle, but is mediated by the vagus nerve, and so may be blocked by vagotomy. The transient fall in SAP at the beginning of the Cushing response is thought to arise from receptors in the ventral medulla.

The effectiveness of the Cushing response in increasing CBF or in restoring CBF to normal depends upon the degree to which SAP can rise beyond ICP, i.e. whether CPP is increased and on other factors which are more difficult to define precisely, but probably relate to flow conditions at the capillary level. It is generally agreed that by the stage at which Cushing responses appear, normal autoregulation of CBF has been abolished. Thus, the greater the CPP that is attained during the Cushing responses, the higher ought to be the CBF. In practice, however, CBF is often not increased during a Cushing response despite the attainment of a high CPP and, in such an instance, it is likely that local factors either at capillary level or causing compression of the venous outflow may be responsible for the failure to restore normal CBF.

CEREBROVASCULAR DYSFUNCTION AND INCREASED ICP

Normal cerebral pial arteries dilate when SAP falls, and constrict when it rises in an attempt to preserve a constant flow. They also dilate and constrict when arterial PCO_2 is raised or lowered respectively. Such changes in vascular diameter have been confirmed by CBF measurements. These normal responses become disturbed by cerebral tumours, ischaemia (focal and generalized), by hypoxia (anoxic and stagnant) and cerebral trauma. It is not surprising, therefore, that during the sequence of events leading to severe cerebral compression, normal vascular responses are lost. The progressive impairment of normal responses is important, however, because of its implications in the treatment of raised ICP. As ICP rises and CPP falls, CBF is at first maintained by progressive arterial dilatation, possibly followed by increasing SAP; during this period hypercapnia causes pronounced increases in CBF and ICP. When this capacity has been exhausted, however, further increases in ICP result in cerebral ischaemia; at this stage the administration of CO_2 does not cause any further increase in either ICP or in CBF. Because cerebral resistance vessels are already maximally dilated to try to maintain flow despite a reduced perfusion pressure, it may be proposed that it is impossible for them to dilate any further; but the vessels also cannot constrict because it can be shown that hyperbaric oxygen or hyperventilation, both cerebral vasoconstrictors under normal circumstances, cause no reduction in ICP or in the already reduced flow at this stage. The normal vasomotor responses to CO_2 and oxygen have, therefore, been lost, supporting Langfitt's term "cerebral vasomotor paralysis". If there is now a sharp increase in SAP due to a vasopressor response the ICP may increase in parallel and there is no net increase in CPP, or in CBF.

In the situation described, vasomotor paralysis is a generalized phenomenon in the brain. Studies of regional CBF in multiple areas in patients with brain tumours have shown, however, that there may be loss of reactivity to CO_2 in isolated areas adjacent to the tumour. In these circumstances the phenomenon of *cerebral steal* may occur. When CO_2 is administered, blood flow increases in normal regions, whereas in the unresponsive region flow is unchanged or may actually be decreased. When hyperventilation is instituted the opposite may occur, namely a decrease of flow in normal brain and a small increase in flow in the abnormal area. This was at first ascribed to a simple redistribution of flow within the cerebrovascular bed, but Brock has recently proposed that the changes in flow in abnormal regions of brain actually represent impaired autoregulation and passive responses in these areas to changes in CPP or local tissue perfusion pressure. Thus, when CO_2 is administered, ICP rises and CPP falls. Flow is maintained in normal brain by active autoregulation, whereas reduced blood flow in the abnormal area of brain is a passive response to the decrease in CPP. With hyperventilation, most of the cerebral blood vessels constrict and ICP and CBF fall. In the small area which is unresponsive to the change in CO_2, the flow now increases passively because of the increase in CPP which has resulted from the fall in ICP. This is an interesting hypothesis, but since it hinges upon the validity of the definition of CPP as the difference between arterial and intracranial pressure in a situation in which both mass lesions and changes in arterial CO_2 are responsible for changes in ICP, it remains to be substantiated. Meyer has put forward the simpler proposal that blood is squeezed out of the abnormal area of brain during hypercapnia by the increase in volume of normal brain.

PRESSURE/FLOW DISSOCIATION IN THE CEREBRAL CIRCULATION

When ICP is increased in patients due to cerebral mass lesions, head injury or subarachnoid haemorrhage, CBF does not show the fairly close relationship to CPP which is found when increased ICP is produced in experimental animals by CSF infusion. Even in animal models this relationship is much less consistent when ICP is raised by expanding focal masses or experimental oedema. This inconsistency remains even when allowance is made for any impairment of autoregulation. Other factors must be affecting CBF independently of ICP, as measured; alternatively, local brain tissue pressures, which are different from measured ICP, have to be invoked to explain the findings.

Ames and his colleagues have shown that after a period of total cerebral ischaemia in experimental animals, parts of the brain fail to reperfuse and have called this the "no re-flow phenomenon". They have ascribed it to obstruction of capillaries due to sludging of their contents and swelling of their walls. A similar phenomenon has been observed by Hekmatpanah through a cranial window after a sharp elevation of ICP by inflation of a subdural balloon. Following a pressure wave in a patient, if temporary arrest of the cerebral circulation has occurred, areas of the brain may possibly fail to re-perfuse despite the return of SAP and ICP to favourable levels.

The effect of cerebral oedema on CBF has been studied experimentally using cryogenic lesions. CBF is reduced or absent at the centre of the lesion regardless of the levels of SAP and ICP. This corresponds with the microscopic observation of congested dilated blood vessels with complete stasis of corpuscular elements within them. This is the necrotic zone and flow changes in this area are due to local capillary obstruction. On the periphery of the lesion CBF is reduced; this may be related in part to raised ICP since in one study carried out with the calvarium open and presumably normal ICP, pronounced hyperaemia was observed in this peripheral zone. Reduction of CBF in the peripheral zone may, therefore, be due to a combination of impaired autoregulation and reduced CPP, due to the increase in ICP. Flow approaches normal levels with progressive distance from the cryogenic lesion, suggesting that autoregulation has remained intact here.

Reduced blood flow in areas of cerebral oedema raises an important point of definition. True oedema, or fluid in the extracellular space, is a feature of *white matter* oedema. In grey matter, where the greater part of CBF exists and is measured by isotope washout techniques, the excess fluid is intracellular in astroglial processes. Since these abut on capillaries and may intrude upon their lumina, it is a controversial point whether flow is being reduced by increased ICP, increased tissue pressure or by mechanical capillary obstruction. If the reduction in CBF in areas of cerebral oedema is due primarily to an increase in ICP or local tissue pressure, autoregulation at the arterial end of the system must be impaired.

EFFECTS OF INCREASED ICP ON OTHER SYSTEMS

We have already described how alterations of arterial PCO_2 and PO_2 may, by affecting CBF and cerebral blood volume, influence ICP. Increased ICP can in turn be associated in a causal way with alterations in blood gases and the respiratory pattern, although it remains uncertain whether this is due primarily to pressure or to brain shift. However caused, these blood gas disturbances may then start a vicious circle of increasing ICP and worsening brain shift.

Many patients with cerebral compression are found to have low arterial PO_2. This may often be ascribed to pulmonary atelectasis and the resulting arterio-venous shunting and ventilation/perfusion inequalities. There is some evidence from animal experiments, however, to suggest that lesions of the brain stem may directly affect arterial PO_2. Two mechanisms have been proposed. Increased ICP and brain shift may cause ventilation/perfusion inequality in the lungs directly with a fall in arterial PO_2. This has been ascribed to pulmonary vasoconstriction; since the fall in PO_2 can be prevented by alpha-adrenergic blocking agents, it is thought to be due to a sympathetic discharge and may therefore represent the respiratory corollary of the Cushing response. The second mechanism proposed is that increased ICP or brain stem shift affect central respiratory chemoreceptors located in the ventro-lateral part of the medulla, depressing respiration, and producing a resultant fall in arterial PO_2 and an increase in arterial PCO_2. In occasional patients with increased ICP, mostly after a head injury, sudden severe, often fatal, pulmonary oedema may develop. Its cause has not, so far, been satisfactorily explained.

Increased respiratory activity, "hyperpnoea", is common in patients with increased ICP and precedes the well-recognized respiratory slowing and apnoea seen in terminal brain compression. This hyperpnoea is probably most often due to a hypoxic drive in response to a low arterial PO_2, attempting to return it to normal levels. True central neurogenic hyperventilation, with a slightly increased arterial PO_2, is a rare phenomenon. Pronounced hypocapnia causes marked CSF lactacidosis, independent of blood lactate levels, which tends in time to reverse the respiratory CSF alkalosis. It is not yet clear whether this plays a part in prolonging or worsening spontaneous hyperventilation.

The most striking effect of increased ICP on the cardiovascular system is the vasopressor response described by

Cushing. This is mediated by the sympathetic and para-sympathetic outflows from the brain stem and acts on the peripheral resistance vessels and the conducting tissues of the heart. Evidence is now accumulating to suggest that increased ICP and/or brain shift may directly affect the myocardium also.

Abnormalities of the ECG pattern have long been recognized in patients with acute brain damage. Similar ECG abnormalities have been produced experimentally by hypothalamic stimulation and prevented by cervical cord section. In a survey of 231 patients dying in this Institute from acute brain damage (e.g. intracranial haemorrhage, tumour or infection or following head injuries) Connor found multiple areas of focal myocardial necrosis in 8 per cent and proposed that this might be the reason for the ECG changes. Similar myocardial lesions have been produced experimentally in mice by injecting blood into the parietal subarachnoid space; the incidence of these lesions was reduced by adrenalectomy and pre-treatment with atropine and reserpine. The cause of the myocardial damage under these circumstances, which are all likely to be associated with increased ICP, has been ascribed to vagal or sympathetic overactivity, excessive release of catecholamines in the myocardium, or a combination of these factors. Subendocardial haemorrhage in the outflow tract of the left ventricle is another post-mortem feature associated with acute brain damage.

Erosion, ulceration and even perforation of the oesophagus, stomach, duodenum and jejunum is observed not infrequently in patients suffering from head injuries or intracranial haemorrhage. Although the underlying mechanism is not yet clear, similar lesions have been produced by stimulation of the hypothalamus in cats. Another frequent finding in patients dying as a result of severe brain damage is acute congestion, often with ulceration of the mucosa of the trigone of the bladder.

It is tempting, therefore, to postulate that in the late stages of cerebral compression, when increased ICP and brain shift are severe, sympathetic and vagal discharges occur, which may affect not only the blood pressure and heart rate, but also the pulmonary arterioles, the myocardium and the mucosa of the upper digestive tract and bladder.

CLINICAL DIAGNOSIS OF INCREASED ICP

Many of the symptoms and signs conventionally associated with raised ICP may be caused by other factors. Severe headache, bursting in quality, may be related to shift or distortion of cerebral blood vessels and distension of the pain-sensitive dura mater. Vomiting, occurring often in the morning and often unassociated with nausea, may be related more to shift or distortion of the medulla than to the level of ICP. Vomiting of this type is seen in association with tumours involving the 4th ventricle and may occur before ICP is increased.

Papilloedema is probably the only feature of the "Cushing triad" which is truly causally related to increased ICP; transient bilateral visual obscurations, often related to change of posture, are also indicative of increased ICP and are of considerable clinical importance since they are a warning that permanent visual loss due to the papilloedema may occur if increased ICP is not soon relieved.

Bradycardia and increased SAP are unreliable signs; recent studies on patients with increased ICP have shown that these signs are frequently absent even when the ICP is in excess of 75 mm Hg. (1,000 mm. H_2O). Bradycardia and arterial hypertension are more likely to be caused by brain stem distortion or ischaemia than by any absolute level of ICP. What makes the clinical diagnosis of raised ICP difficult is that brain distortion often co-exists; there may be little more than increasing headache with some restlessness and a decreasing level of consciousness to indicate that ICP is rising and even these signs may not be due directly to the pressure changes; impairment of the conscious level may be a result of caudal displacement of the diencephalon and mid-brain. One of the revelations of continuous monitoring of ICP has been that in some patients ICP may exceed 75 mm Hg. for periods of several minutes with no symptoms whatsoever.

Other signs commonly seen in patients with increased ICP, namely pupillary dilatation, decerebrate rigidity and respiratory irregularity are due either to tentorial and tonsillar herniation or to direct involvement of the brain stem by the lesion, with or without ICP being high at that particular time.

The presence of increased ICP can only be suspected on clinical grounds; it must be confirmed by direct measurement. Lumbar puncture will give information on the true ICP only if there is free communication of pressure within the craniospinal axis. In patients with supratentorial mass lesions, particularly if there are any signs suggestive of tentorial herniation, it is likely that such free communication of pressure has been lost and lumbar puncture is not only misleading but dangerous because, due to the subsequent leakage of CSF into the spinal epidural space, any pressure gradient may be increased. Furthermore, the changing pattern of ICP over a period of time can be followed only by continuous measurement; one cannot say that a patient does not have increased ICP until this has been monitored continuously for 12–24 hr., from the supratentorial compartment, using an isovolumetric technique, which requires a pressure transducer and chart recorder.

MANAGEMENT OF INCREASED ICP: GENERAL PRINCIPLES

The basic principle is to treat the patient, not merely the level of ICP; reduction of raised ICP is useful only insofar as it improves the neurological status of the patient. It may, however, be difficult at times to define "neurological improvement". When presented with a patient in whom raised ICP is suspected, many questions have to be answered and certain decisions taken before embarking upon a specific form of treatment. In this section these matters are dealt with in the order of their priority for the patient.

Before attempting to elucidate the often complicated pattern of cause and effect in the pathogenesis of increased

ICP, the primary consideration is to ensure that the principal substrates essential for continued cerebral metabolism are available, so that during the time taken for a more accurate assessment of the patient further clinical deterioration due to extracranial causes may be prevented. The main factors are oxygen, glucose, haemoglobin and SAP. The airway must be clear, there should be an adequate partial pressure of oxygen in the inspired air, and pulmonary function should be sufficient to permit oxygen transfer to arterial blood and satisfactory clearance of carbon dioxide. Pulmonary function has to be considered particularly in patients with an acute head injury who may have pulmonary atelectasis, arteriovenous shunting or oedema related to brain damage, as well as concomitant chest injuries. At this stage it should be mentioned that caution may need to be exercised before attempting to correct any inadequacy of the oxygen supply by having the patient breathe 100 per cent oxygen. There is some experimental evidence to suggest that during cerebral compression the normal chemical control of respiration is impaired, so that increased oxygen may result in apnoea, due to removal of hypoxic drive. Finally, the level of mean SAP should be kept well above 60 mm Hg., which is about the lower limit for autoregulation in normal patients. Low arterial pressure in the patient with a head injury is often indicative of other injuries, such as a pelvic fracture or a ruptured spleen.

The second stage in the management of the patient in whom increased ICP is suspected is to determine whether or not pressure *is* increased and, if so, its cause, and to what extent that increase is responsible for any deterioration in the patient's condition. The cause of the increased ICP will, in part, determine the choice of method used for reducing ICP.

Increased ICP is due to an increase in the volume of one or more of the normal intracranial constituents, or the addition of extraneous volume (tumour, abscess, haematoma). The constituents most commonly increased are CSF (hydrocephalus), cerebral blood volume (vasodilatation due to hypercarbia and/or hypoxia), or brain water (cerebral oedema). The level of ICP caused by any particular lesion will be related only partly to the volume of the lesion; other factors such as speed of development, CSF blockage and concomitant vasodilatation and cerebral oedema may all be important. Most important is the net effect of all factors, viz. the "tightness" (or its reciprocal, the compliance) of the brain. This raises the important point of how to determine the "tightness" of the brain, i.e. at which point on the volume/pressure curve the patient is at that particular time. This can be established only by the careful and controlled withdrawal and/or addition of CSF during continuous pressure monitoring.

If it is decided to try to reduce ICP as a definitive manoeuvre, it must be quite clear why this is being done. There are four main purposes in reducing intracranial pressure. Firstly, it may be reduced as a diagnostic measure to try to determine whether increased ICP is, in fact, playing a significant role in producing the patient's neurological dysfunction; secondly, as a temporary

measure in the operating theatre during craniotomy, to improve operating conditions; thirdly, in patients with a rapidly expanding intracranial lesions, to "buy time" prior to definitive surgical treatment of the lesion; finally, in patients with persistently raised ICP, in whom no surgical lesion is present, or in whom surgery has already been carried out, it may be helpful to control ICP over a period of days or even weeks. At all stages it must be quite clear why ICP is being reduced as this represents only one step in an overall management plan, the purpose of which is the optimum delivery of oxygen and energy yielding substrates to the brain.

SPECIFIC THERAPY

The basis of all methods of reducing ICP is to increase the volume available for functioning brain, either by increasing the volume of the effective cranial cavity, or by reducing the volume of one of its constituents, viz. CSF, cerebral blood volume and brain water, or by removal of an extraneous mass lesion or non-essential part of the brain.

Cerebral Decompression

The removal of part of the skull was the first approach to the treatment of increased ICP resulting from brain tumours. The procedure is seldom if ever carried out for that purpose today. As a temporary measure, e.g. after head injury surgery or the technically difficult removal of a benign brain tumour, when a period of brain swelling may be expected, the provision of an external decompression may be useful.

Clearly, if a mass lesion such as an extradural haematoma or meningioma is removable, then that is the obvious treatment. Associated brain swelling may call for other measures. A larger internal decompression, temporary external decompression or other pressure reducing agents may also be required.

Dramatic clinical improvement may follow aspiration of blood, pus or cyst fluid. In general, the best clinical results of fluid aspiration result from removal of fairly large volumes of fluid, greater than that required simply to reduce ICP to normal. This suggests that the beneficial effects are due to alleviating brain shift rather than reducing high ICP. Improvement is only temporary, however. Repeated aspiration or delayed definitive removal of the lesion may be required.

When a brain tumour is infiltrating widely and is occupying a silent area of the brain, then an adequate internal decompression may be obtained, combined with removal of all or part of the tumour, by deliberately resecting part of the brain. Areas which may be resected without adding materially to the patient's neurological deficit are one frontal lobe or the anterior 5 cms. of either temporal lobe; resection of one occipital lobe will cause only a contralateral hemianopia and is certainly justified when this deficit is already present.

In cases of severe brain swelling, the beneficial effects of decompression are considerably diminished by continued swelling of the remaining brain; it is therefore, essential to correct exacerbating factors, such as hypoxia or hypercarbia, particularly when combined with arterial hypertension. In all of the decompressive methods of reducing ICP, the ameliorating effect on the patient's neurological status is due at least as much to the correction of mid-line cerebral shift and the reduction of brain herniation and downward axial displacement of the brain stem as to relief of increased ICP. This important factor has to be taken into account when considering the use of any of the non-surgical methods of reducing ICP, when there is relatively less effect on brain shift than ICP.

Reduction of CSF Volume

A temporary reduction of ICP may be obtained by the removal of CSF through lumbar puncture only when there is full communication between the supra- and infra-tentorial compartments. This is present in communicating hydrocephalus which may occur after some head injuries, subarachnoid haemorrhage or meningitis. If such communication is not present, removal of CSF from the lumbar subarachnoid space is not only ineffective in reducing supratentorial ICP, but it is also dangerous.

When a suitable burr hole is present, removal of CSF by needling the lateral ventricle is often used. The effectiveness of this method depends to some extent on the size of the ventricles because, if they are small, they are difficult to locate and it may be impossible to obtain a sufficient volume of CSF. It depends also on the tightness of the brain, which will determine how great a volume of fluid has to be removed to obtain a satisfactory reduction in pressure. If the ventricle contralateral to a supratentorial mass lesion is tapped, the removal of CSF may actually accentuate mid-line shift, although it reduces ICP.

The main application of ventricular puncture is probably during craniotomy, as an aid to opening the dura and to facilitate the exposure of structures at the base of the brain, e.g. aneurysms of the circle of Willis or pituitary tumours. Continuous catheter drainage of CSF from the lumbar subarachnoid space or lateral ventricle throughout the operative procedure is, however, more effective. Outside the operating theatre, external ventricular drainage may be used to permit reduction of ICP over longer periods of time; a catheter in the lateral ventricle is connected to a drainage reservoir set at a pre-determined height above the head. This technique is practicable only in patients with enlarged ventricles and has to be of limited duration because of the danger of infection in this open system. Limited external drainage may be combined with continuous monitoring of ICP. This method is again limited by the size of the ventricle because, if CSF is withdrawn from small ventricles, the ICP recording may be lost at a crucial stage as the ventricular wall collapses round the end of the catheter; furthermore, attempting to re-establish the recording by uncontrolled injection of fluid into the ventricular catheter under these conditions may be a hazardous procedure because, on the steep part of the volume/pressure curve, the addition of even a small volume of fluid may cause an enormous increase in ICP.

As a long-term solution to relieve increased ICP when the ventricles are enlarged, CSF may be shunted from the lateral ventricle to the right atrium or the peritoneal cavity. Such shunting procedures may be done before, during or after surgical measures aimed directly at the cause of increased ICP.

Reduction of Brain Water

Hypertonic Solutions

These solutions increase cerebral intravascular osmotic pressure and withdraw brain water into the bloodstream. To be effective the agent must reach the brain and is therefore dependent on an adequate CBF, and it must remain largely intravascular which requires that the blood-brain barrier system for this agent is intact. In fact, the blood-brain barrier systems are not complete even under normal conditions for any of the agents currently in use and depend to some extent on the relative vascularity of different parts of the brain. When breakdown of the blood-brain barrier has occurred in the area of a cerebral lesion, osmotic withdrawal of water from this area will be less effective than in areas where the barrier systems are intact; there is corroborative evidence from experimental studies of focal cerebral oedema to show that hypertonic solutions tend to reduce brain water more in normal brain than in the lesion itself. After the rapid intravenous administration of a hypertonic solution in a patient with increased ICP, pressure begins to fall within five minutes. The duration of this effect depends upon several factors, viz. the rate of disappearance of this agent from the bloodstream, the rate at which it diffuses into the brain, thus reducing the osmotic gradient between blood and brain, and the volume/pressure status of the patient. Furthermore, ICP may be primarily increased by a lesion which is able to continue expanding despite this form of treatment.

When hypertonic solutions are administered, SAP may rise because of the concomitant increase of total blood volume. In severe brain compression, when autoregulation is impaired throughout the cerebral vascular bed, this rise in SAP may lead to an increase in cerebral blood volume. If there has been little osmotic withdrawal of extravascular fluid, there will then be a further increase in ICP, the extent of which is related to the volume/pressure status of the patient and the degree of vasomotor paralysis. The net effect of hypertonic solutions in certain situations can then be to raise, not lower, ICP. This effect is not infrequently seen in patients *in extremis* from cerebral compression.

A much discussed phenomenon of hypertonic solution therapy is "rebound" in which, as the effect of the hypertonic solutions passes off, ICP rises to a higher level than it was before treatment was started. Several factors contribute to this late rise in ICP; the eventual passage of the agent into cerebral tissues, the reduction of its intravascular concentration which can lead to reversal of the osmotic gradient, and the continued increase in volume of an expanding brain lesion or brain swelling. As the brain re-expands when the effect of the hypertonic solution wears off, it does so into a space which has been reduced by increased oedema in any abnormal regions in the brain and possibly also by cerebrovascular dilatation and by an increased CSF volume due to its increased production or decreased absorption; the net result may be a pronounced increase in ICP beyond the level before treatment was begun.

Mannitol has now replaced urea as the hypertonic solution of choice; the advantages claimed are that it is relatively inert metabolically, that it remains extracellular for a longer period of time and that there is less rebound in ICP after its administration. Oral glycerol has been employed to reduce ICP; it is less effective than the intravenous agents in terms of degree of reduction of ICP, but it may be used over long periods of time without causing the disturbances in water and electrolyte balance which may accompany prolonged administration of intravenous hypertonic solutions. Glycerol may also be administered intravenously.

The question of the most effective dose and the frequency of administration of hypertonic solutions has not yet been settled. With the use of continuous ICP monitoring, the precise effect on ICP and its duration can be easily measured and the agent titrated against the ICP. From such studies it appears that mannitol is often better administered in smaller doses and more frequently than the 4–6 hourly intervals customarily employed. This method is preferable to awaiting the reappearance of drowsiness, pupillary dilatation or decerebrate rigidity which simply show that brain swelling has again progressed to the point of causing cerebral herniation. Whatever the dose, however, it must be administered rapidly in order to maximize the osmotic gradient.

Recent work in patients with head injuries and strokes suggests that hypertonic mannitol and glycerol solutions may sometimes increase CBF, independently of changes in SAP and ICP.

Glucocorticoids

Powerful glucocorticoids have now found wide application in the treatment of brain swelling, particularly in peritumoural oedema, swelling related to brain infarcts and cryogenic brain lesions and, to a lesser extent, in cerebral trauma. When a satisfactory result has been obtained from steroid therapy, ICP is reduced, pressure waves aborted and cerebral angiography may show that brain shifts are reduced. The exact mechanism of action of steroids in brain oedema has not yet been elucidated and is certainly complicated, involving tissue interchange at the capillary level in both the normal and abnormal tissue; CSF formation is probably affected as well. Furthermore, clinical improvement has been recorded when no reduction of ICP was produced. This subject is dealt with more fully in Chapter VIII: 3. The dangers of high dosage systemic steroid therapy have to be balanced against the beneficial effects. If steroids have had no effect on ICP or neurological status within 24 hr. of administration, they should be stopped forthwith.

Systemic Diuretics

Although hypertonic mannitol and urea solution act also as diuretics, their actions on the brain are not dependent on this systemic effect, and other diuretic agents, such as frusemide, have little effect on ICP. Dehydration of the patient is less emphasized now than formerly, as the dangers of gross electrolyte imbalance outweigh the chance of preventing cerebral oedema, as this may still occur in the presence of systemic dehydration. On the other hand, it is important to avoid over-hydration as this may exacerbate cerebral oedema, although studies of the relationship between moderate systemic over-hydration and brain oedema are scanty.

Reduction of Cerebral Blood Flow

The last component of the intracranial contents which may be reduced therapeutically is the intravascular blood pool. Although the actual volume reduction produced by cerebral vasoconstriction may be a small one, a significant fall in ICP may be obtained if the volume/pressure curve is at its steep portion.

Hyperventilation

Hyperventilation was popular for many years as a means of reducing brain bulk during craniotomy and was proposed by Lundberg and his colleagues in 1959 as a method for reducing ICP over periods of days or weeks in ward patients. Controversy still exists as to its indications, limitations and possible complications. Certainly, hyperventilation produces a significant decrease in ICP (averaging 30 per cent) in most cases of intracranial hypertension; at extreme levels of ICP, when brain damage is severe and the responsiveness of cerebral blood vessels to CO_2 has been lost, hyperventilation will not reduce ICP. Hyperventilation also tends to increase arterial PO_2; in particular, hypoxia due to inadequate ventilation will be corrected and this may contribute considerably to the benefits of hyperventilation therapy in the management of cerebral trauma and increased ICP. Most controversy relates to the possibility of reducing cerebral oxygenation as a result of the fall of CBF and Bohr shift of the oxyhaemoglobin dissociation curve caused by the respiratory alkalosis. A pronounced reduction of arterial PCO_2, to less than 25 mm Hg. causes a reduction of cerebral venous PO_2 to around 20 mm Hg., drowsiness in conscious human subjects and the appearance of slow waves on the EEG; there is also an increase in brain tissue and CSF lactate without an increase in pyruvate, so that the lactate: pyruvate ratio is increased. The same changes have been observed in cerebral hypoxia of both stagnant and hypoxic types and provide evidence for the theory that the changes produced by hypocapnia are indicative of cerebral hypoxia. In support of this is the observation that the EEG and biochemical changes may be reversed by the administration of hyperbaric oxygen, despite continuing hypocapnia. The hypocapnic reduction of CBF is, however, a self-limiting phenomenon, because cerebral hypoxia itself causes vasodilatation which counteracts the hypocapnic vasoconstriction; thus, when the hypoxic vasodilator stimulus is removed by hyperbaric oxygenation, a greater reduction of CBF is seen at the same level of arterial hypocapnia. The real question is whether the hypoxia produced by this degree of reduction of CBF is harmful to the patient or is a physiological feed-back mechanism to correct the vaso-constricting effect. Although normal brain may not be adversely affected, damage may be intensified in abnormal regions.

The production by hypocapnia of reversed intracerebral steal near brain tumours and focal infarcts during regional CBF studies has led to the suggestion that hyperventilation may be beneficial in focal cerebral ischaemia and head injury. Initial optimism arising from experimental observations that hyperventilation reduced the size of cerebral infarcts has not been sustained by further animal studies, and clinical trials have not established the benefits of passive hyperventilation in patients with focal ischaemic brain damage, although there is evidence in favour of passive hyperventilation for some patients with head injury.

To hyperventilate the unconscious patient who already has an endotracheal tube or tracheostomy, the tidal volume and/or rate of respiration may simply be increased. For many patients, however, the institution of prolonged hyperventilation means that tracheostomy is required. Once arterial PCO_2 has been reduced to an optimum level of between 25 and 30 mm Hg. it is comparatively easy to maintain it at this reduced level. If hyperventilation is going to reduce ICP the effect will be apparent within 5 min., so that the decision can quickly be made as to whether hyperventilation should continue or not. If it is to be continued for long periods, an arterial PCO_2 level close to 30 mm Hg. is optimal.

Hyperbaric Oxygen

The wider implications of the administration of oxygen at high pressure to patients with brain damage are considered at length in Chapter VII: 5 and it is considered here only as a means of reducing ICP. Elevation of arterial PO_2 to levels in excess of 1,000 mm Hg. by hyperbaric oxygen at 2 atmospheres absolute will rapidly reduce increased ICP by approximately 30 per cent despite a constant level of arterial pressure and PCO_2. The reduction in ICP is due to cerebral vasoconstriction, the mechanism thus being similar to that of hypocapnia. Oxygen is a weak vasoconstrictor, however, and any increase in arterial PCO_2 will immediately negate the effect of the increased oxygen. Reduction of ICP by oxygen depends on retention of cerebrovascular responsiveness; thus, neither hypocapnia nor hyperoxia will reduce ICP when vasomotor paralysis has supervened.

It can be predicted from experimental data that the best effects of both hyperoxia and hypocapnia in reducing ICP should be seen when the area of brain damage is localized and comparatively small relative to the normal brain where cerebrovascular function is intact; patients with lesser degrees of brain damage should respond best to hyperbaric oxygen and this impression is borne out in the few clinical reports available.

Administration of hyperbaric oxygen is more complicated than hyperventilation. The patient may be placed in a small one-man compression chamber filled with oxygen; in this situation, however, the patient is inaccessible during treatment, so that the technique is not suitable for the confused or unconscious patient who requires airway care. The importance of this is that any resultant increase in arterial PCO_2 will over-ride the effect of the oxygen.

The preferable method of treatment is to place the patient in a large "walk-in" type of pressure chamber which is filled with air. Routine monitoring and nursing care are thus uninterrupted and only the patient breathes 100 per cent oxygen.

Hypothermia

Reduction of body temperature will lower ICP by several mechanisms. Reduction of whole body metabolism reduces arterial PCO_2 with a consequent fall in CBF. Reduction of cerebral metabolism reduces the cerebral demand for blood, which also reduces CBF. There may be a direct effect on cerebral vessel walls causing vasoconstriction and an increase in blood viscosity, both of which increase cerebrovascular resistance. The common factor in the reduction of ICP is a reduction of CBF and cerebral blood volume. In addition, hypothermia reduces CSF production. Whether reduction in cerebral metabolism actually protects neural tissue from reduced oxygen delivery due to increased ICP and reduced CBF is doubtful. Experimental results have been more optimistic than clinical experience, in that hypothermia applied before or during the creation of a brain lesion seems to be effective in reducing the ill-effects of that lesion. (This applies also to hypocapnia and hyperoxia). Studies in which the agent is applied only after a fixed time interval from the production of the lesion, i.e. a closer approach to the clinical situation, are notably less successful in limiting or reducing the size of such experimental brain lesions.

Although hypothermia was widely used for many years during neurosurgical anaesthesia and in the management of patients with severe head injuries and other forms of brain damage, its value is still much disputed and its use has been discontinued in many centres. In practice, temperatures of around 30°C are used in the closely controlled conditions of the operating theatre whereas in the ward management of patients with increased ICP, the optimum temperature is higher (32–35°C). Shivering to restore body temperature poses problems; there may be a considerable metabolic acidosis, and the administration of agents such as promazine to reduce shivering may reduce SAP and interfere with the clinical appraisal of the neurological status of the patient.

CONCLUSIONS

In summary, management of the patient with increased ICP must in the first instance be directed towards the maintenance of an adequate supply of blood, glucose and oxygen to the brain. The cause of the increase in ICP must be sought, not only the pathological lesion, but also the mechanism by which ICP has become raised. The method of treatment should be appropriate to the cause and should be monitored carefully throughout the period of treatment, bearing in mind that reduction of a brain shift is at least as, if not more, important to the patient's well-being than a reduction of ICP. The physician should always be ready to change the treatment for a more effective one; greater emphasis must be placed on the importance of carefully monitoring the effects of therapeutic agents which may in themselves have dangers in their administration. Finally, the treatment of increased ICP is only one facet in the management of a patient with a brain lesion and must never be regarded as a definitive treatment.

FURTHER READING

Adams, J. H., Brierley, J. B., Connor, R. C. R. and Treip, C. S. (1966), "The Effects of Systemic Hypotension upon the Human Brain," *Brain*, **89**, 235–268.

Ames, A.III, Wright, R. L., Kowada, M., Thurston, J. M. and Majno, G. (1968), "Cerebral Ischaemia II. The No-reflow Phenomenon," *Amer. J. Path.*, **52**, 437–454.

Berman, I. R. and Ducker, T. B. (1969), "Pulmonary, Somatic and Splanchnic Circulatory Responses to Increased Intracranial Pressure," *Ann. Surg.*, **169**, 210–216.

Brierley, J. B., Brown, A. W., Excell, B. J. and Meldrum, B. S. (1969), "Brain Damage in the Rhesus Monkey Resulting from Profound Arterial Hypotension. 1. Its Nature, Distribution and General Physiological Correlates," *Brain Res.*, **13**, 68–100.

Brierley, J. B., Meldrum, B. S. and Brown, A. W. (1971), "Posthypoxic Brain Swelling: Physiological and Anatomical Aspects," in *Brain Hypoxia*, pp. 136–144 (Brierley and Meldrum, Eds.). London: Heinemann.

Brock, M. (1971), "Cerebral Blood Flow and Intracranial Pressure Changes Associated with Brain Hypoxia," in *Brain Hypoxia*, pp. 14–19 (Brierley and Meldrum, Eds.). London: Heinemann.

Cantu, R. C., Ames, A.III, Doxon, J. and DiGiacinto, G. (1969), "Reversibility of Experimental Cerebrovascular Obstruction Induced by Complete Ischaemia," *J. Neurosurg.*, **31**, 429–431.

Connor, R. C. R. (1968), "Heart Damage Associated with Intracranial Lesions," *Brit. med. J.*, **3**, 29–31.

Cushing, H. (1902), "Some Experimental and Clinical Observations Concerning States of Increased Intracranial Tension," *Amer. J. med. Sci.*, n.s. **124**, 375–400.

Ekstrom-Jodal B. (1970), "On the Relation Between Blood Pressure and Blood Flow in the Canine Brain with Particular Regard to the Mechanism Responsible for Blood Flow Autoregulation," *Acta physiol. scand.* Suppl., 350.

Fitch, W. and McDowall, D. G. (1971), "Effect of Halothane on Intracranial Pressure Gradients in the Presence of Intracranial Space-occupying Lesions," *Brit. J. Anaesth.*, **43**, 904–912.

French, L. A. and Galicich, J. H. (1964), "The Use of Steroids for Control of Cerebral Oedema," *Clin. Neurosurg.*, **10**, 212–223.

Hawkins, W. E. and Clower, B. R. (1971), "Myocardial Damage After Head Trauma and Simulated Intracranial Haemorrhage in Mice: The Role of the Autonomic Nervous System," *Cardiovascular Research*, **5**, 524–529.

Heiskanan, O. (1964), "Cerebral Circulatory Arrest Caused by Acute Increase of Intracranial Pressure," *Acta neurol. scand.*, **40**, Suppl. 7.

Hekmatpanah, J. (1970), "Cerebral Circulation and Perfusion in Experimental Increased Intracranial Pressure," *J. Neurosurg.*, **32**, 21–29.

Hoff, J. T. and Reis, D. J. (1970), "Localization of Regions Mediating the Cushing Response in the Central Nervous System of the Cat," *Arch. Neurol.*, **22**, 228–240.

Javid, M. (1961), "Urea in Intracranial Surgery," *J. Neurosurg.*, **18**, 51–57.

Jefferson, G. (1938), "The Tentorial Pressure Cone," *Arch. Neurol. Psychiat.*, **40**, 857–876.

Jennett, W. B., Barker, J., Fitch, W. and McDowall, D. G. (1969), "Effect of Anaesthesia on Intracranial Pressure in Patients with Space-occupying Lesions," *Lancet*, **i**, 61–64.

Johnson, R. T. and Yates, P. O. (1956), "Clinico-pathological

Aspects of Pressure Changes at the Tentorium," *Acta radiol.*, **46**, 241–249.

Kety, S. S., Shenkin, H. A. and Schmidt, C. F. (1948), "The Effects of Increased Intracranial Pressure on Cerebral Circulatory Functions in Man," *J. clin. Invest.*, **27**, 493–499.

Langfitt, T. W. (1969), "Increased Intracranial Pressure," *Clinical Neurosurg.*, **16**, 436–471.

Langfitt, T. W. and Kassell, N. F. (1966), "Non-filling of Cerebral Vessels During Angiography: Correlation with Intracranial Pressure," *Acta neurochir.*, **14**, 96–104.

Langfitt, T. W., Kassell, N. F. and Weinstein, J. D. (1965), "Cerebral Blood Flow with Intracranial Hypertension," *Neurology (Minneap.)*, **15**, 761–773.

Langfitt, T. W., Weinstein, J. D. and Kassell, N. F. (1965), "Cerebral Vasomotor Paralysis Produced by Intracranial Hypertension," *Neurology (Minneap.)* **15**, 622–641.

Langfitt, T. W., Weinstein, J. D., Kassell, N. F. and Simeone, F. A. (1964), "Transmission of Increased Intracranial Pressure. I Within the Craniospinal Axis," *J. Neurosurg.*, **21**, 989–997.

Langfitt, T. W., Weinstein, J. D., Kassell, N. F. and Gagliardi, L. J. (1964), "Transmission of Increased Intracranial Pressure. II. Within the Supratentorial Space," *J. Neurosurg.* **21**, 998–1005.

Lundberg, N. (1960), "Continuous Recording and Control of Ventricular Fluid Pressure in Neurosurgical Practice," *Acta Psychiat. Scand.*, **36**, Suppl. 149.

Lundberg, N., Kjällquist, A. and Bien, C. (1959), "Reduction of Increased Intracranial Pressure by Hyperventilation," *Acta Psychiat. Neurol. Scand.*, **34**, Suppl. 139.

McDowall, D. G. (1969), "Cerebral Circulation," *Int. Anaesth. Clin.*, Vol. 7.

Meyer, J. S. and Welch, K. M. A. (1972), "Relationship of Cerebral Blood Flow and Metabolism to Neurological Symptoms," *Progress in Brain Research*, **35**, 285–348.

Miller, J. D. and Ledingham, I.McA. (1971), "Reduction of Increased Intracranial Pressure," *Arch. Neurol.*, **24**, 210–216.

Miller, J. D., Ledingham, I.McA. and Jennett, W. B. (1970), "Effects of Hyperbaric Oxygen on Intracranial Pressure and Cerebral Blood Flow in Experimental Cerebral Oedema," *J. Neurol. Neurosurg. Psychiat.*, **33**, 745–755.

Miller, J. D., Stanek, A. E. and Langfitt, T. W. (1972), "Concepts of Cerebral Perfusion Pressure and Vascular Compression During Intracranial Hypertension," *Progress in Brain Research*, **35**, 411–432.

Moody, R. A., Ruamsuke, S. and Mullan, S. (1969), "Experimental Effects of Acutely Increased Intracranial Pressure on Respiration and Blood Gases," *J. Neurosurg.*, **30**, 482–492.

Plum, F. and Posner, J. B. (1966), *The Diagnosis of Stupor and Coma.* Davis: Philadelphia.

Richardson, A., Hide, T. A. H. and Eversden, I. D. (1970), "Long-term Continuous Intracranial Pressure Monitoring by Means of a Modified Subdural Pressure Transducer," *Lancet*, **ii**, 687–690.

Rosomoff, H. L., Clasen, R. A., Hartstock, R. and Bebin, J. (1965), "Brain Reaction to Experimental Injury after Hypothermia," *Arch. Neurol.*, **13**, 337–345.

Rowan, J. O., Harper, A. M., Miller, J. D., Tedeschi, G. M. and Jennett, W. B. (1970), "Relationship Between Volume Flow and Velocity in the Cerebral Circulation," *J. Neurol. Neurosurg. Psychiat.*, **33**, 733–738.

Shulman, K. (1965), "Small Artery and Vein Pressures in the Subarachnoid Space of the Dog," *J. surg. Res.*, **5**, 56–61.

Thompson, R. K. and Molina, S. (1959), "Dynamic Axial Brain-stem Distortion as a Mechanism Explaining the Cardio-respiratory Changes in Increased Intracranial Pressure," *J. Neurosurg.*, **16**, 664–675.

Weinstein, J. D., Langfitt, T. W., Bruno, L., Zaren, H. A. and Jackson, J. L. F. (1968), "Experimental Study of Patterns of Brain Distortion and Ischaemia Produced by an Intracranial Mass," *J. Neurosurg.*, **28**, 513–521.

Wise, B. L. and Chater, N. (1961), "Effect of Mannitol on Cerebrospinal Fluid Pressure," *Arch. Neurol.*, **4**, 96–98.

Zwetnow, N. N. (1970), "Effects of Increased Cerebro-spinal Fluid Pressure on the Blood Flow and on the Energy Metabolism of the Brain," *Acta Physiol. Scand.*, Suppl. 339.

1. ELECTRICAL ACTIVITY OF THE BRAIN

DAVID HELLERSTEIN and REGINALD G. BICKFORD

Electrical activity of the brain is both diverse in its manifestations and complex in its relation to normal function and cerebral pathology. In spite of intense study during the last 40 years since Berger's discovery, we remain today largely ignorant of the basic mechanisms generating these rhythms. Nevertheless, a large and diagnostically useful field of knowledge relating pathology to disturbances of cerebral rhythm has developed in clinical encephalography and this short account will emphasize these practical features. At the same time it will offer some concepts relating these rhythms to more basic membrane and synaptic theory.

BASIC MECHANISMS[4,5,9,10,16]

Nerve cells generate three fundamentally different kinds of electrical activity: resting membrane potentials; action potentials, and synaptic potentials. Of the three, synaptic potentials are of particular interest to the clinician since they summate to produce the electrical activity observed in the electroencephalogram. In this section we will examine the nature of the electrogenic cellular events giving rise to these potentials and consider the physical laws governing their relationship to the cortical macropotential, or brain wave, familiar to clinicians.

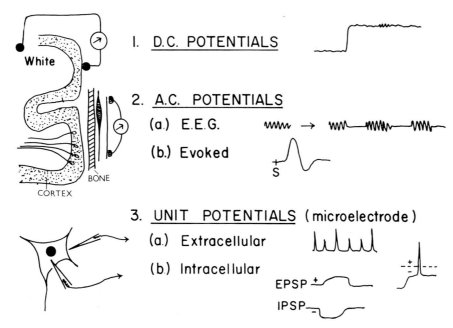

FIG. 1. Varieties of electrical activity which can be recorded from the brain. Note that the scalp recording system is separated from the brain by skull, muscle and skin. Muscle and skin are active biologic generators which often distort recordings made from the scalp.

The electrical activity of a complex organ such as the brain has many aspects, which are summarized in Figure 1. There are three main categories of *output* which are distinguished by the physical nature of the electrical events (DC potentials, AC potentials, unit potentials) and by the nature of the recording instrumentation and physiological strategy needed to record them effectively. Let us begin with the basic mechanisms underlying these varied manifestations.

The Resting Membrane Potential[4,16]

The cell membrane is a thin, highly resistive medium separating two conductors, the intracellular and extracellular media, and therefore behaves like a capacitor (Fig. 2A). In addition, there is an electrogenic pump located within the membrane that moves positively charged sodium ions from the internal to the external medium (Fig. 2B). This transfer leaves the interior of the cell with a net negative charge and the extracellular medium with a net positive charge (Fig. 2C). These equal charges attract each other and move through the conductive media to lie opposite each other across the resistive membrane surface (Fig. 2D); thus the cell membrane "capacitor" is charged, which creates a potential making the inside of the cell 60 or 70 millivolts negative with respect to the extracellular medium.

During an action potential these relations are temporarily disrupted: (1) for about a millisecond the cell membrane becomes very permeable to Na^+; (2) since Na^+ is in low concentration within and high concentration outside the cell Na^+ flows in, discharging the membrane capacitance and even charging it slightly positive; as the membrane permeability to Na^+ ends, a positive charge is

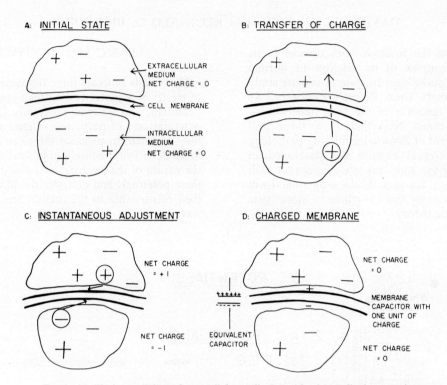

FIG. 2. (A) The intracellular and extracellular media are conductive media that contain many ions but no net charge. They are separated by a highly resistive cell membrane. (B) The electrogenic sodium pump moves positive sodium ions across the cell membrane, creating equal and opposite charges in the intra- and extracellular media. (C) These charges attract each other and since the media are conducting the charges move to face each other across the cell membrane. (D) The result is a charged membrane separating the two uncharged conducting media. This is electrically equivalent to a charged capacitor, hence a potential difference, or voltage, can be measured across the cell membrane.

The Action Potential[9,10,16]

The inside of the cell membrane is kept sodium-poor by a combination (1) of the sodium pump that removes Na^+ from the cell, and (2) the cell membrane that is impermeable to Na^+ and keeps it out. Potassium, however, is relatively more free to flow across the membrane because the resting cell membrane is slightly permeable to potassium. The negative potential within the cell, maintained by the sodium pump, attracts the positive K^+ ion into the cell, where it is concentrated. This continues until the K^+ concentration is so high that the tendency for K^+ to enter because of the negative potential is balanced by the tendency for it to leave because of the high K^+ concentration. Hence potassium is said to be *in equilibrium* with the resting membrane potential.*

* We have, for simplicity, omitted reference to the chloride ion here and below. The actual equilibrium involves both K^+ and Cl^- ions, and places the resting membrane potential between the equilibrium potentials for these ions.

left within the cell. (3) The membrane now becomes extremely permeable to K^+. Prior to the beginning of the action potential the high internal K^+ concentration was in equilibrium with the negative potential; however, as the cell becomes positive this equilibrium is disturbed, with both the positive potential and the concentration tending to drive K^+ out. (4) As the membrane permeability to K^+ increases, K^+ therefore moves out of the cell, carrying its positive charge with it and leaving a negative charge on the inner membrane of the cell once more. This process continues until the negative potential thus created just balances the tendency for K^+ to leave; i.e., until K^+ is in equilibrium and the resting membrane potential is restored. (5) As the resting potential returns, the permeability of the membrane to K^+ also returns to its low resting state, and the action potential is complete. Since relatively few K^+ and Na^+ ions are involved, the concentration of these ions inside and outside of the cell are essentially unchanged from their initial values. The entire sequence of events lasts one or two milliseconds.

The Synaptic Potential[5]

During synaptic potentials a different sequence of events with a longer time course occurs: (1) under the influence of a humoral synaptic transmitter the subsynaptic membrane becomes permeable to certain ions. In an excitatory post-synaptic potential (EPSP) the permeability to Na^+ predominates. (2) Hence, as in an action potential, Na^+ rushes in, discharging the membrane although not actually making it positive since other ions also contribute. (3) The membrane permeability then drops to resting levels, and there is *no* opening of the gates to K^+ as in the action potential. (4) Hence the K^+ cannot re-establish its equilibrium rapidly but must slowly penetrate the membrane, limited by the very low permeability that the resting membrane shows to K^+, a process that typically takes from 5 to 10 msec., depending upon the particular cell type.

Inhibitory potentials are smaller, with the synaptic transmitter acting to increase the permeability of the subsynaptic membrane to Cl^-, K^+ and other ions although *not to Na^+*. This clamps the membrane at a potential which is an average of the equilibrium potentials for the participating ion types, which may even be below the resting membrane potential, hyperpolarizing the cell. Such IPSP's may be as brief as EPSP's or last up to hundreds of milliseconds.

Generation of Extracellular Potentials[6,14]

For a potential that is generated across a cell membrane to contribute to the extracellular macropotential recorded as the EEG, 3 criteria must be met:

(1) Each individual nerve cell must produce a potential that is detectable at some distance from the cell proper.
(2) The contribution of different nerve cells within the generating population must reinforce rather than cancel one another.
(3) The time course of the cellular membrane events must be consistent with the macropotentials to which they give rise.

Let us first consider the possible contribution of the resting membrane potential to cerebral macropotentials. Since the brain waves of current practical use to the clinician vary with time and the resting potential is stationary, the resting potential fails according to criterion (3) above, and cannot be the underlying generator. In addition, it can be shown that the resting membrane potential cannot be detected outside of the cell; hence this potential also fails criterion (1), and is therefore not the generator of the stationary or D.C. potentials of the brain which some investigators have suggested are correlated with behavioral states.

It would appear that the action potential is a good candidate for macropotential generation, and for years it was believed that brain waves were formed from the envelopes of numerous action potentials. Many subsequent experiments have cast serious doubt on this hypothesis. In 1933 Bartley and Bishop implanted the vagus nerve into rabbit brain tissue and found that stimulation of the nerve produced no potentials comparable to brain waves that could be detected with macroelectrodes[1]. More recent studies have shown that there is often little correlation between single unit action potentials and macropotentials, and that under certain conditions brain waves are present when no action potentials at all can be detected. It is now generally accepted that only under special circumstances are action potentials significant components of cerebral macropotentials, and such circumstances usually include direct or indirect massive synchronous stimulation of the large fiber tracts of the brain[14]. All three of the criteria required above are met only poorly by the action potential hypothesis; thus, (1) they are not detected at large distances from the generator. (2) Potentials generated in neighboring cells often do not summate and may cancel each other, and (3) the time course of the action potential, commonly lasting 1 or 2 msec., makes it difficult to account for brain waves with periods in the tens or hundreds of milliseconds range.

Synaptic potentials, with a time course of tens to hundreds of milliseconds, do satisfy criterion (3), and as we shall show below they also satisfy criteria (1) and (2), making them a likely source of EEG macropotentials. Understanding these events requires a detailed study of the flow of current that takes place during a synaptic potential.

Sources and Sinks

The extracellular medium, considered by itself, consists of a three dimensional continuum studded with numerous "holes" where the cells lie. If an EPSP occurs at some locus on a cell, then positive charge (Na^+) enters *into* the cell at that point from the extracellular medium (Fig. 3A). As far as this medium is concerned, it loses charge into a region bounding one of the holes. Hence this region is called a *current sink*. A fundamental rule of current flow in neural tissue is that if the extracellular medium is losing current into a "hole" at some point, then at some other point or points on the boundary of that "hole" an equal current is coming back into the extracellular medium (Fig. 3B). Such regions are called *current sources*.

The reason for this equality of source and sink strength is that the intracellular medium is a conductor, and the membrane is a capacitor. As positive charge flows into a cell during an EPSP, for example, a charge builds up within the cell. These positive charges repel each other, and since the intracellular medium is a conductor the charges move away from each other until they line the inner surface of the cell membrane, whose high resistance stop their progress. But the membrane is a capacitor, and if a charge enters one side or plate of a capacitor an equal charge must leave the other side or plate. Since the other "plate" of the membrane capacitance faces the extracellular medium, a charge coming to lie on the inner face of the membrane forces an equal charge into the extracellular medium. Since all charges that enter the cell through the EPSP "sink" come to lie on the inner surface of the membrane, an equal amount of charge is returned to the extracellular medium. Hence the total source strength for

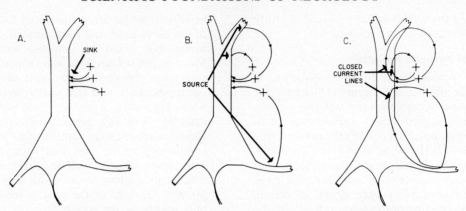

FIG. 3. (A) Positive charge leaves the extracellular medium as it enters a cell during an EPSP, creating a current sink at that locus in the extracellular medium. (B) For each such sink a source of equal strength must appear along the cell boundary. (C) Hence current flows along continuous lines: from source to sink extracellularly, and from sink to source intracellularly.

this cell is equal to the total sink strength. The extracellular medium, too, is a conductor, and like the intracellular medium it will not support a buildup of charge. Thus current flows in continuous lines, from sink to source in the intracellular medium, and closing the loop by flowing from source to sink in the extracellular medium (Fig. 3C). These lines can be extremely short or very long, but whenever current flows across a cell membrane it creates a source and a sink of equal strength somewhere along the cell's boundary with the extracellular medium, and current flows continuously along lines connecting the two.

Dipole[16]

The concept of a *dipole* is important to the understanding of synaptic potentials as macropotential generators. A dipole is defined as a source and sink of equal strength (or equivalently an equal positive and negative charge) separated by a short distance and is represented graphically as an arrow pointing from sink to source (from − to +). It has magnitude, the product of the source strength and the distance separating the poles; and direction, the direction in which the arrow points.

Consider a hypothetical cell with a single large dendrite, and suppose that a synapse on the cell body is activated, generating an EPSP there (Fig. 4). Positive charges (Na⁺) enter into the cell, depolarizing the cell body which therefore becomes a sink. Since current lines are closed this current must flow through the cell and flow out somewhere else across the cell membrane, creating a source of equal strength and closing the current loop. To the external medium it appears that there is a sink at the soma, the locus of the EPSP, and a source of equal strength distributed along the dendrite. This distributed source may be approximated by a single source located at some intermediate point along the dendrite. We therefore have a *dipole* configuration: a source and sink of equal strength separated by a short distance. Such dipoles are important because the potentials created by them can project a considerable distance from the generating cell (criterion 1), and potentials from a population of such cells oriented in the same direction will add to produce a macropotential (criterion 2).

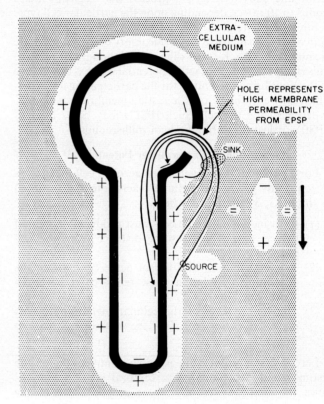

FIG. 4. During an EPSP at the soma of a cell with a single dendrite, current flows into the soma creating a sink there, and out of the cell along the dendrite creating a distributed source. This may be approximately by a single source (represented by the large +) and an equal sink (the large −). A source and sink, separated by a small distance, define a dipole, represented by the arrow.

Realistic Cell Shapes

Consider a stellate cell with many dendrites oriented radially and symmetrically about the soma. An EPSP at the soma will produce a sink there (Fig. 5), with sources distributed along the dendrites. Thus each dendrite will have associated with it a small dipole represented in the figure by arrows. By the symmetry of the cell geometry each dipole will be paired with another dipole on the other

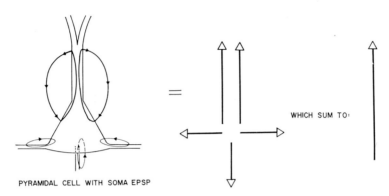

STELLATE CELL WITH SOMA EPSP

WHICH SUM TO ZERO

PYRAMIDAL CELL WITH SOMA EPSP

WHICH SUM TO:

FIG. 5. An EPSP at the soma of a stellate cell produces a symmetrical distribution of sources and sinks about the center of that cell. This gives rise to radially oriented dipoles, which cancel each other out and produce no net dipole field.

An EPSP at the soma of a pyramidal cell produces an asymmetrical field by virtue of the large current flow through the apical dendrite. The resulting dipoles do not cancel in the axial direction, giving rise to a net dipole generator parallel to the apical dendrite.

side of the cell pointing in the opposite direction. Such dipole pairs tend to cancel, and the potential of such a pair will not be detected at any significant distance away. Hence such a stellate cell will not produce a potential that can be measured far from the cell, and a collection of such cells, each activated by an EPSP on its *soma*, will not sum to produce a macropotential, failing criteria (1) and (2). (This is not to say that such cells never produce macropotentials: a PSP to a single stellate cell *dendrite* will set up an asymmetrical current flow distribution, and such fields can project over significant distances.)

As a more complex example consider an EPSP to the soma of a pyramidal cell, which contains a short basal dendritic skirt attaching directly to the soma, and a long thick apical dendrite ending in an arborization similar to the basal skirt. We again produce a sink at the level of the soma, but because the apical dendrite is bigger than the basal dendrites and its large diameter offers a lower resistance to current flow, an asymmetry is produced and there will be relatively more sources distributed along the apical than along the basal dendrites. Although we again have a collection of dipoles pointing outward, as in the stellate cell, because of the asymmetry of source distribution the dipole from the apical dendrite will be much larger than the other dipoles, and there will not be complete cancellation. *Hence there will be a net dipole pointing outward along the apical dendrite.*

The key to production of a net dipole field is *asymmetry*. Where fields are symmetrical so that every dipole pointing in one direction is matched by a dipole pointing in the opposite direction, there will be cancellation. Only with asymmetry will net dipoles be generated, which can then be detected at large distances. Symmetrical fields of sources and sinks, which cannot sum, are referred to as "closed fields", whereas asymmetrical fields, which always have a net dipole component and the capacity to sum, are called "open fields"[13].

Generators of the Electroencephalogram

Since pyramidal cells are by far the most abundant cells in cerebral cortex, and since they lie in sheets giving rise to layers of parallel dipoles of large area, they are peculiarly suited for generating gross brain potentials and are considered to be responsible for most of the potentials recorded from the scalp by electroencephalography[6]. The contribution of basal ganglia and thalamus is relatively small, for three reasons: the subcortical structures are further from the electrode, hence the potential they project to the electrode will be reduced; cells in these structures are individually more symmetrical than in cortex, hence individual cell fields will tend to be a "closed field" pattern, failing criterion (1); and even open fields of randomly oriented adjacent neurons will tend to cancel each other, failing criterion (2).

The Shadowing Theorem[7,8,11,17]

How do the potential fields produced by a population of cells containing dipole generators combine to produce a gross cortical macropotential? The answer to this question calls upon a very important concept for electrophysiologists, generally known as the solid angle theorem for a dipole layer, which we shall call *the shadowing theorem*[11,17]. This theorem applies to potentials generated by a dipole layer.

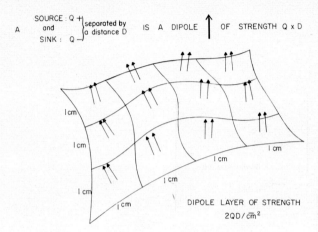

FIG. 6. A sheet containing an array of dipoles oriented perpendicular to the surface of the sheet is called a *dipole layer*. The strength of the dipole layer is equal to the total strength of the individual dipoles in one unit area of the surface.

A dipole layer is any surface in which dipoles are distributed with their axes oriented perpendicular to the surface. The *dipole strength* of such a layer is really a density, and is defined as the summed magnitude of all the dipoles in a unit area of the surface (Fig. 6). The shadowing theorem requires:

(1) that the generator be a dipole layer
(2) that the generator be a dipole layer *of constant strength*, i.e., a dipole layer whose density of dipoles is constant over its entire surface.

It applies to any dipole surface of any strength, size, shape, and distance from the recording electrode, and in this generality lies its power.

The theorem itself is perhaps easier to understand than the definitions and constraints noted above. Consider a dipole layer of any shape or size, situated at some distance from a recording electrode. The shadowing theorem states that this surface may be replaced with another, simpler surface of equal strength, and that the simpler surface will produce the same potential at the recording electrode. Suppose that the recording electrode is a bright source of light (Fig. 7). This light will illuminate the potential generator, however twisted and contorted its surface. Let us insert a new surface between the light and the original generator so that the new surface casts a shadow on the generator. If we trim the new surface around its edges so that it exactly shadows the old generator and no more

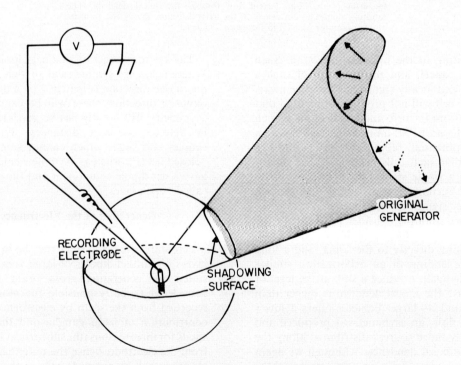

FIG. 7. The Shadowing Theorem. A dipole field of constant strength, the "original generator", produces a certain potential at the recording electrode. If: (1) a source of light is placed at the recording electrode, (2) a new surface is found which casts a shadow that exactly covers the original generator, and (3) a dipole field of strength equal to that of the original generator is created on the shadowing surface, then the potential produced at the recording electrode by the shadowing surface will equal the potential produced by original generator.

than the old generator, and if we fill the new surface with a dipole layer of strength equal to the original generator, then *the potential produced by the new surface at the recording electrode will exactly equal the potential produced there by the original generator*. Although it may appear that we have accomplished little, merely replacing one surface with another, we have in fact made the problem much simpler. We may choose as we wish the shape although not the outline of the new surface, and the potential produced by the simpler equivalent surface is usually easy to compute. The most useful application of this theorem, however, has been less as a numerical predictor of brain potentials and far more as a conceptual tool for their qualitative analysis and understanding.

As an application of this principle, consider the visual evoked potential. In response to a flash of light impulses from all over the retina are relayed to the visual cortex at the occipital pole of the brain. It is believed that afferent impulses synapse upon the apical dendrites of pyramidal cells, producing a large negative component to the evoked potential on the cortical surface. Let us analyze this potential, applying the principles that we have discussed to predict the spatial distribution of potential that might be measured by an array of EEG electrodes on the surface of the scalp.

The EPSP arriving at the level of the apical dendrite allows Na^+ to enter the cell there, producing a current *sink*. The equal sources for such a sink must come from the rest of the cell, the soma and basal dendrites which lie below, and such equal sources and sinks separated by a short distance create a dipole oriented away from the cortical surface. Because of this orientation with sinks (which are equivalent to negative charges) nearest the surface, the potential there will be negative. Since pyramidal cells lie in layers within cortex a dipole layer is created, and with uniform illumination of the retina we might suppose that the dipole strength will be reasonably constant over the visual cortex. Hence the shadowing theorem is applicable.

What about projection of the potential to the scalp? Although between cortex and surface are layers of CSF, connective tissue, blood, bone, muscle, and skin, their principle effect is to reduce the amplitude of potentials passing through them, and to a first approximation we may continue to apply the shadowing theorem *qualitatively* to potential distributions on the scalp surface. Nevertheless, the task seems hopelessly complicated by the numerous convolutions of cerebral cortex in the visual region. The shadowing theorem simplifies this problem.

Consider a single sulcus whose walls contain a synchronously activated layer of pyramidal cell dipoles (Fig. 8). To a recording electrode a distance away, the near wall of the sulcus will largely shadow the far wall, but the orientation of the dipoles of the two walls will be opposite. Hence the contribution to the potential of neurons within the sulcus will essentially cancel, permitting us to ignore the cortical convolutions and to replace a convoluted cortex with a smooth one. Thus primary visual cortex may be *represented* as a small smooth cap on the occipital pole (Fig. 9).

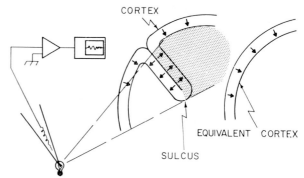

FIG. 8. If a source of light is placed at the site where an electrode is recording the EEG, the near wall of a sulcus will shadow the far wall. If the strength of the dipole layer is constant throughout the sulcus, then the magnitude of the potential produced by the near and far walls will be equal. However, since the dipoles are oriented in opposite directions, the potentials they produce are of opposite sign, and will cancel. Their contribution to the EEG can therefore be ignored, and the cortex replaced by an equivalent cortex without convolutions.

Prediction of the potential distribution is now easy. Let us "shadow" this cap with a small spherical surface placed a fixed distance from our recording electrode. As we move the electrode about the scalp, the area of this surface will change depending upon the distance and angle of the cortical cap. Since the "shadow" area produces a potential equal to the true potential of the cap, the larger this area the greater the magnitude of the evoked potential. Fig. 9

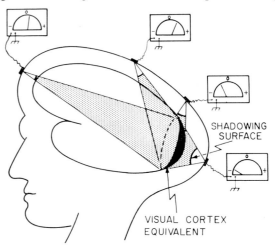

FIG. 9. During the visual evoked response a small cap on the occipital pole is activated as dipole layer generator. Shadowing surfaces at different portions of the scalp predict the magnitude of the potential at these loci. Since the shadowing surfaces chosen are all the same distance from their corresponding electrode, comparison of the size of the different shadowing surfaces predicts the relative size of the potential measured. The sign of a potential is determined by whether the shadowing surface darkens the inner or outer surface of the dipole layer.

demonstrates this graphically. Near the occipital pole the area of the shadowing surface is largest, as is therefore the visual evoked potential. Moving further away, the potential quickly falls to zero and then becomes *positive* as the concave side of the cap and therefore the positive or source direction of the dipole layer comes into view. This positive potential increases and finally becomes small again as the distance between cap and recording electrode make the shadowing surface small. This potential distribution is an accurate description of the field actually observed during the visual evoked potential[2]. Thus by using the shadowing theorem it has been possible to simplify the convoluted shape of a cortical generator, and to predict the potential distribution of an important cortical response.

A Closer Look at Projection to the Scalp—Spatial Resolution

As potentials generated in cerebral cortex project to the surface of the scalp, spatial resolution is lost; thus it is not uncommon to find epileptic patients who appear free of interictal spiking on scalp EEG examination, whose EEG at operation displays a distinct, localized epileptogenic spike focus. This is due in part to the effects of shunting and insulating layers between cortex and scalp, as mentioned above, but it is also due to distance; once again the shadowing theorem helps supply the explanation.

The shadowing surface for the epileptogenic region is far smaller on the sphere surrounding the scalp electrode than at the cortical surface, hence the potential at the scalp will be reduced. More important, however, is the observation that at the scalp the shadowing surface for the epileptic focus is very small in comparison to the shadowing surface for the cortex as a whole. Thus at the scalp the spike focus potentials will tend to be lost in the potentials generated by the rest of the cortex. On the cortical surface the spike generator area represents a large percentage of the total shadowing area for the entire cortex, and an epileptic spike is unlikely to be swamped in extraneous potentials projected from healthy cortex. This discussion applies equally well to any small area of cortex, epileptic or not, and we may conclude that for a potential to be observed by an electrode placed on the scalp it must arise from a relatively large synchronous area of cerebral cortex; in other words, the spatial resolution of the scalp electroencephalogram is poor.

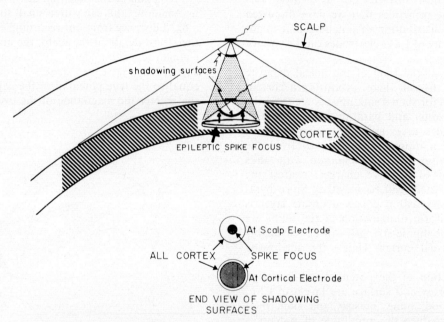

Fig. 10. A comparison of potentials measured at the scalp and on the cortex. An epileptic focus is represented here as a disk embedded in cerebral cortex, and recording electrodes are placed on the cortical surface and on the scalp. Two shadowing surfaces are drawn on a single sphere surrounding each electrode: the first shadows the entire cerebral cortex and the second, contained within the first, shadows the epileptic focus. An end view of these spherical surfaces is shown below the cortex, one sphere for each electrode. The central disk shows the shadowing surface for the epileptic focus; the outer circle shows the shadowing surface for the entire cortex.

Consider, for example, an epileptic focus lying within cerebral cortex, and let us record from it with two electrodes, one located on the cortex immediately overlying the focus, and the second lying on the scalp surface a cm or two away (Fig. 10). Let us draw two shadowing surfaces on a small spherical surface surrounding each electrode: one surface shadowing the epileptogenic focus, and the other surface shadowing the entire neighboring cortical surface.

ELECTROENCEPHALOGRAPHY—BASIC PRINCIPLES[12]

Recording techniques

Since the EEG is one of the lowest voltage of the biologic rhythms commonly encountered, its registration carries a requirement of good instrumentation and excellence in recording technique. Because of the high gain employed (10^6 voltage amplification) the instrumentation is prone to pick up a large variety of artifacts of extracranial origin which can appear indistinguishable from genuine brain activity. Artifacts are usually divided into instrumental and biologic categories. The EEG electrode with its metal-electrolyte interface together with the electrolyte-skin interface are sources of electrical fluctuation which can simulate all known forms of normal and abnormal EEG activity. The most important and difficult artifacts encountered are those generated by biologic structures in the vicinity of the brain. These include:

(1) *Eye blinking and eye rolling*. These generate slow waves due to the battery like properties of the eye globe (this has a corneal-retinal potential of about 1 millivolt).
(2) *Muscle*. This produces a large variety of wave forms ranging from spikes to rhythms which are often difficult to distinguish from brain activity.
(3) *Tongue*. This is charged (glossokinetic potential), and its movements during speaking or reading may cause spurious activity to appear in the EEG.
(4) *EKG*. This artifact, generated by the heart, whose amplitude depends on the geometry of the neck region may be mistaken for a spike discharge. It causes particular difficulty in the isopotential record.
(5) *Skin*. This gives rise to slow shifts in potential.

There is an extensive literature concerned with the recognition of these and other artifacts[12].

Sampling Techniques

A major problem in EEG is its limited ability to sample brain function in both space and time, to an extent and depth which a clinician might require. Thus, the brain is a large organ much of whose EEG generating cortex is on the inferior and medial surface not readily accessible to scalp electrodes. Some of these anatomic sampling problems can be overcome by the use of special electrodes (such as nasopharyngeal or implanted depth leads). Only the latter techniques bring the whole volume of the brain under surveillance; however, their use can be justified in only rather special cases. A further difficulty is that adequate coverage of accessible cortex cannot be achieved with the 8 channels of the EEG amplification commonly available. This problem requires a variety of recording strategies (so-called montages) which systematically sample the brain in an orderly sequence.

There is also a problem in the time sampling of EEG activity since the usual tests last only about 45 minutes. In diseases such as epilepsy in which abnormal discharges occur intermittently, the test may fail to sample a critical time period and negative results will be obtained. It is important to bear this in mind when the significance of a negative finding is discussed in the EEG report. In response to these problems electroencephalographers have used a variety of "activation" techniques in order to increase the probability of recording abnormal discharge. The common ones used are:

(1) Hyperventilation (usually for 3 minutes) which by reducing CO_2 levels causes cerebral constriction and activation of spike-wave and spike discharges and occasionally induces seizures.
(2) Visual stimulation by means of a strobe light at frequencies ranging from 1 to 25 flashes per second.
(3) Periods of drowsiness or sleep.

In some cases a more dynamic and flexible approach to a patient's problem may be required, so that there is an attempt to produce environmental conditions under which the patients seizure usually occurs. This might require the use of TV or music stimulation in pattern sensitive or musicogenic epilepsy suspects.

THE NORMAL EEG

Spontaneous Potentials

As indicated in Figure 1 the EEG is one aspect of electrical activity by the brain. The waves commonly encountered in the EEG are classified by frequency as follows:

(1) 0·5 to 3 Hz—Delta
(2)   4–7 Hz—Theta
(3)   8–13 Hz—Alpha (Adult)
(4)   18–35 Hz—Beta

An alpha rhythm is present in each hemisphere and the amplitude is maximal in the parieto-occipital regions. As already indicated these rhythms are thought to arise from fluctuating membrane (synaptic) potentials in the soma-dendritic tree. Their precise origin is not understood and no useful function has yet been assigned to them. Nevertheless they are highly responsive to a variety of influences listed below which gives them considerable research interest and diagnostic importance.

Factors influencing the EEG:

(a) *Changes with level of consciousness* (*drowsiness, sleep coma, anesthesia, etc.*, Figure 11). The eye opening effect leading to blocking of the alpha rhythm (See Figure 12) is often designated as an alerting response. This effect is usually attributed to the desynchronization of the idling alpha rhythm by visual input, but the fact that the effect can sometimes be obtained in darkness indicates that more complex factors are operative.
(b) *Changes with maturation*. The alpha rhythm undergoes maturation changes with age which are summarized in Figure 13. The mechanism underlying such a progressive shift in frequency is not presently understood.
(c) *Changes with chemical environment*. These are numerous, but common ones include: hypocania, hypoglycemia and anoxia.
(d) *Changes with drugs*. These include anesthetics, convulsants, etc.
(e) *Changes in pathologic conditions*. The most dramatic change in the EEG occurs in pathology and is thought to result from alterations in neuronal synchronization. Some of the mechanisms are shown in Figure 14.

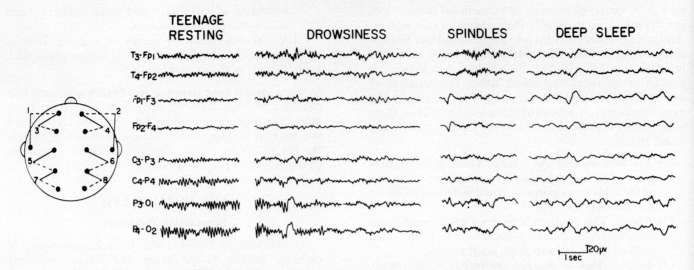

FIG. 11. Changes in EEG with drowsiness and sleep in normal subject. Note disappearance of alpha rhythm in drowsiness, the appearance of spindles and K complexes in deeper sleep. The rapid eye movement stage is not shown.

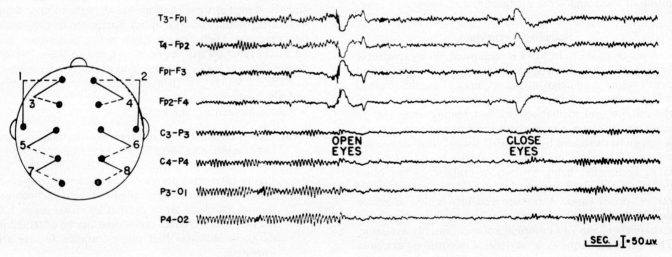

FIG. 12. Alpha rhythm in normal subject showing blocking with eyes open and reappearance with closing the eyes. There is eye blink artifact in the upper 4 channels during opening and closing.

Evoked Potentials

The evoked potential is a complex cortical response containing components triggered by the arrival of an input at the cortex and its later elaboration. In animals the components can be separated by special techniques such as laminar recording, but the responses obtained from the scalp in the human are often difficult to relate to the animal observations. While the responses in man are usually small they can be enhanced by computer summation techniques. Even so there remains a difficult problem

of response contamination from contiguous generators such as the eyes (ERG, and oculogram) skin, and muscle.

In spite of these difficulties evoked responses have considerable promise for the future in both clinical and research applications. Thus the vertex evoked potential in man, a midline response thought to arise from the non-specific system, has found useful application in the detection of the perceptual deafness in infants. In research, the contingent negative variation[15] has aroused interest because of its relation to learning and habituation situations (Fig. 15).

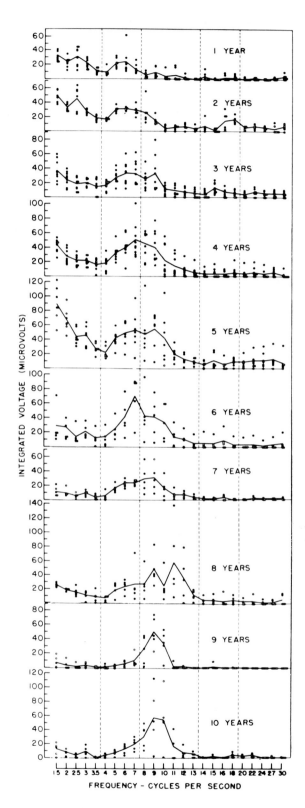

FIG. 13. Frequency changes in the occipital alpha rhythm with age from 1 year to 10 years in normal subjects (10 subjects per year). The dark line represents the mean for each age. Notice the gradual shift towards the right with the establishment of an approximate adult pattern at 10 years.

Clinical EEG

The changes in the EEG which occur in disease are due either to reduction in output of neuronal generators or to the effect of anomalous synchronization of neuronal elements which produces a variety of wave patterns. When neuronal output is reduced so that the EEG is no longer detectable the isoelectric EEG results. This is of diagnostic importance in the establishment of brain death. Diagnosis involves problems of separating amplifier and biologic noise (particularly EKG artifact) from genuine brain activity.

The anomalies of synchronization which give rise to the large variety of patterns encountered in clinical EEG can be conveniently classified as follows:

(1) *Arrhythmic Wave Forms* (Delta Waves). The characteristic EEG pattern is of a slow 0·5 to 3 Hz wave which has the qualities of a random process without repetition or specific pattern. Arrhythmic discharge is commonly produced by localized mass lesions such as tumors (Fig. 16).

(2) *Specific Wave Forms* (spikes, sharp waves, triphasic waves, etc.). These seem to be generated by a local neuronal programming mechanism which exists in normal cortex, but is not normally activated (strychnine is an example of a local activator which, when applied to normal cortex, produces spikes). In disease such wave forms are commonly produced by scar processes (Fig. 17).

(3) *Diffuse Specific Patterns*. The classical example is the spike and wave discharge of petit mal (Fig. 18) which appears to be a disorder of the diffuse thalamic system although its precise origin is not understood.

(4) *Diffuse Nonspecific Patterns*. These are a commonly occurring series of rhythms which bear a close relation to sleep and coma mechanisms. There is some evidence to indicate that they arise from brain stem synchronizing systems. The changes which include both fast and slow diffuse system discharge are commonly seen with drugs (anesthetics, tranquilizers, anticonvulsants, etc.), but also in clinical conditions associated with impaired consciousness.

A descriptive classification of wave forms commonly encountered in clinical EEG is shown diagramatically in Fig. 19 (Mayo System).

Computer Processing of the EEG[3]

Many parameters of the EEG have been quantitated by computer techniques. These methods cannot be reviewed here but one of the most effective, spectral analysis, provides a compact summary of frequency components in normal and abnormal conditions (Fig. 20).

FURTHER READING

[1] Bartley, S. H. and Bishop, G. H. (1933), "Factors Determining the Form of the Electrical Response from the Optic Cortex of the Rabbit," *Amer. J. Physiol.*, **103**, 173–184.

[2] Bourne, J. R., Childers, D. G. and Perry, N. W., Jr. (1971), "Topological Characteristics of the Visual Evoked Response in Man," *Electroenceph. clin. Neurophysiol.*, **30**, 423–436.

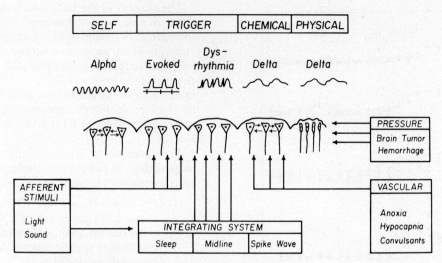

FIG. 14. Diagram of suggested mechanisms of EEG synchronization operative in normal and pathologic states.

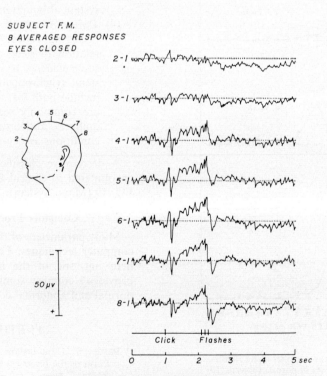

FIG. 15. Example of the contingent negative variation recorded in man. The CNV is the negative wave that occurs between the sound and light stimuli and builds progressively in amplitude as a result of this stimulus association.

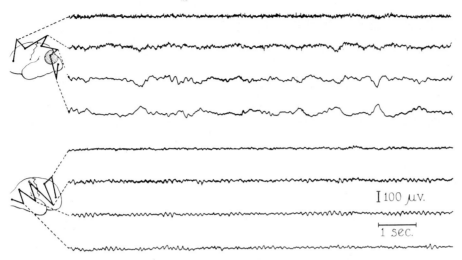

FIG. 16. Example of a delta focus with arrhythmic slow waves in a patient with a left parietal tumor.

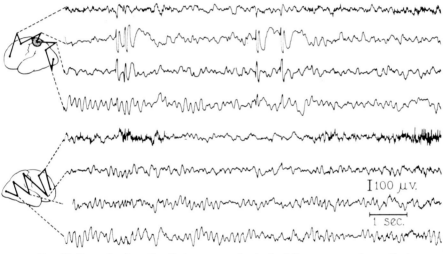

FIG. 17. Example of a spike discharge occurring in the left sensory area in a patient with a scar lesion.

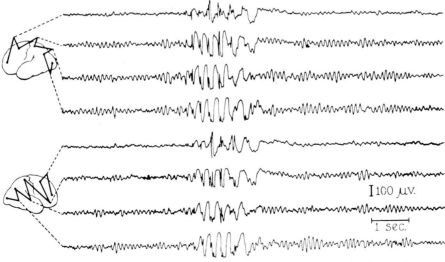

FIG. 18. Example of a spike-wave discharge occurring in a patient suffering from petit mal attacks.

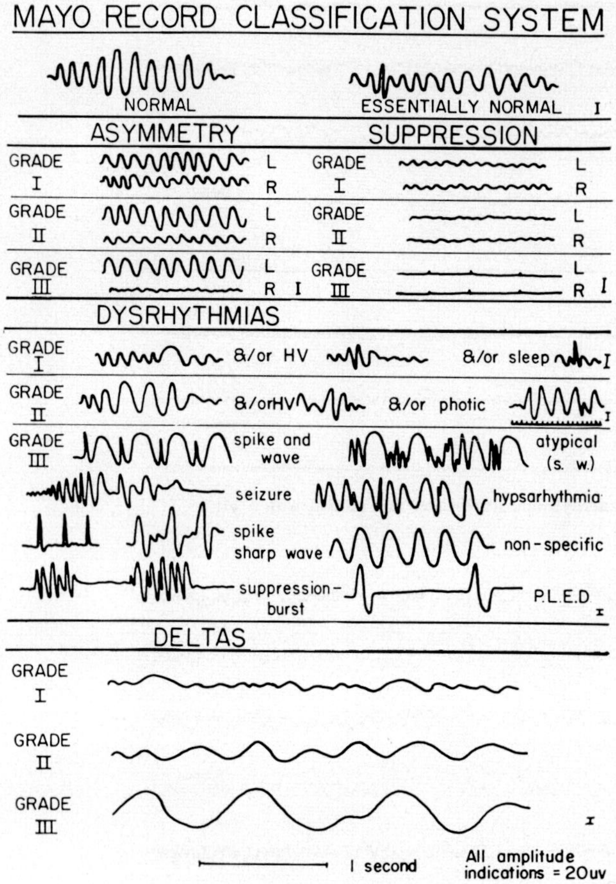

MAYO RECORD CLASSIFICATION SYSTEM

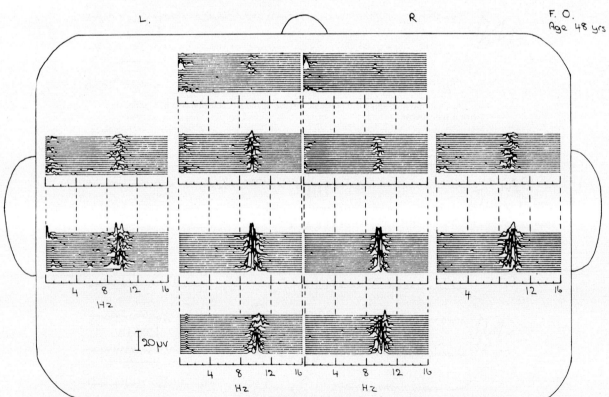

NORMAL

ESSENTIALLY NORMAL   I

ASYMMETRY   SUPPRESSION

GRADE I		L	GRADE I		L
GRADE II		L	GRADE II		L
GRADE III		L R I	GRADE III		L R I

DYSRHYTHMIAS

GRADE I		δ/or HV		δ/or sleep I
GRADE II		δ/orHV		δ/or photic I
GRADE III		spike and wave		atypical (s. w.)
		seizure		hypsarhythmia
		spike sharp wave		non-specific
		suppression-burst		P.L.E.D I

DELTAS

GRADE I

GRADE II

GRADE III   I

⊢———————⊣ I second   All amplitude indications = 20uv

FIG. 19. Mayo classification system for normal and abnormal EEG records. It shows the main categories of normal, asymmetry, suppression, dysrhythmia and delta and the gradings within these categories.

L.   R   F. O. Age 48 yrs

4   8   12   16
Hz

I 20µv

4   8   12   16
Hz

4   8   12   16
Hz

4   12   16

FIG. 20. A method of representing the EEG as displayed frequency spectra. Time rises vertically four seconds per spectral line. The EEG is on a normal subject age 48 years. Note the clear definition of the alpha peaks and the absence of appreciable slow wave activity. (Bickford *et al.*, San Diego Biomed. Sympos., 1972.)

[3] Brazier, M. A. B. (1961), "Computer Techniques in EEG Analysis," *Electroenceph. clin. Neurophysiol.*, Supplement No. 20.

[4] Cole, K. S. (1968), *Membranes, Ions and Impulses.* Berkeley: University of California Press.

[5] Eccles, J. C. (1964), *The Physiology of Synapses.* Berlin: Springer-Verlag.

[6] Fessard, A. (1959), "Brain Potentials and Rhythms—Introduction," in *Handbook of Physiology*, Section 1, Vol. 1, pp. 255–259 (J. Field, H. W. Magoun, and V. E. Hall, Eds.).

[7] Fourment, A., Jami, L., Calvet, J. and Scherrer, J. (1965), "Comparaison de L'EEG recueilli sur le scalp avec l'activité élémentaire des dipoles corticaux radiaires," *Electroenceph. clin. Neurophysiol.*, 19, 217–229.

[8] Gloor, P., Vera, C. L. and Sperti, L. (1963), "Electrophysiological Studies of Hippocampal Neurons. I," *Electroenceph. clin. Neurophysiol.*, 15, 353–378.

[9] Hodgkin, A. L. (1964), *The Conduction of the Nervous Impulse.* Liverpool: Liverpool University Press.

[10] Hodgkin, A. L. and Huxley, A. F. (1952), "A Quantitative Description of Membrane Current and its Application to Conduction and Excitation in Nerve," *J. Physiol. London*, 117, 500–544.

[11] Jami, L., Fourment, A., Calvet, J. and Thieffry, M. (1968), "Étude sur modèle des méthodes de détection EEG," *Electroenceph. clin. Neurophysiol.*, 24, 130–145.

[12] Kooi, K. A. (1971), *Fundamentals of Electroencephalography.* New York: Harper and Row.

[13] Lorente De Nó., R. (1947), "Action Potential of the Motoneurons of the Hypoglossus Nucleus," *J. cell. comp. Physiol.*, 29, 207–287.

[14] Purpura, D. P. (1959), "Nature of Electrocortical Potentials and Synaptic Organizations in Cerebral and Cerebellar Cortex," *Int. Rev. Neurobiol.*, 1, 47–163.

[15] Walter, W. G. (1964), "The Contingent Negative Variation: an Electrocortical Sign of Significant Association in the Human Brain," *Science*, 146, 434.

[16] Woodbury, J. W. (1965), "Chapter 1: The Cell Membrane: Ionic and Potential Gradients and Active Transport; Chapter 2: Action Potential: Properties of Excitable Membranes," in *Physiology and Biophysics*, 19th edition, pp, 1–72 (T. C. Ruch and H. D. Patton, Eds.).

[17] Woodbury, J. W. (1965), "Potentials in a Volume Conductor," in *Physiology and Biophysics*, 19th edition, pp. 85–91 (T. C. Ruch and H. D. Patton, Eds.).

2. ELECTROMYOGRAPHY

J. A. SIMPSON

ELECTROMYOGRAPHY

This science is the assessment of neuromuscular function by studying the action currents or variations in electrical potential associated with muscular activity. It does not indicate the strength of muscular contraction, though there is a correlation between electrical activity and the tension produced by contraction. Simultaneous recording of tension and electrical activity is desirable for quantitative studies but unnecessary for diagnostic electromyography. The latter depends on an analysis of:

(a) The recruitment of muscle and its control by the nervous system during graded voluntary effort.

(b) The amplitude and time course of electrical potentials associated with activity of motor units.

(c) The occurrence of spontaneous electrical discharges from muscle.

From these data it is possible to recognize abnormalities of innervation or of structure of motor units in muscle and to define these abnormalities operationally. The abnormality may be correlated with other clinical data to suggest the nature of pathology in the nervous system or muscle. Electromyography alone cannot provide a nosological diagnosis.

CONTROL OF MOVEMENT

Movements, whether voluntary or involuntary, result from the contraction or controlled relaxation of groups of muscles and rarely, if ever, of a single muscle only. This is effected by contraction of muscles acting as prime movers and reciprocal relaxation of their antagonists. The reciprocity between, for instance, flexor and extensor muscles of a limb appears to be determined by the activity of spinal cord interneurones. The action of the prime movers is provided with a firm base by contraction of synergists which stabilize the joints, and by appropriate adjustments of posture. The postural adjustments are largely under the control of the extrapyramidal motor system and the visual, vestibular and spinal reflexes. Voluntary movements require the participation of the contralateral pre-central gyrus of the cerebral cortex acting through the corticospinal tract. The timing and degree of contraction and relaxation of the muscles of the synergy are regulated by feedback loops utilizing spinal reflex arcs from length and tension receptors in muscle and tendons, and coordinated by the cerebellum, especially when a movement involves more than one segment of a limb.

The actions of the upper motor neurones from the motor area of the cortex, the extrapyramidal motor system and the cerebellum are brought directly or indirectly to the cells of the anterior horn of spinal grey matter or motor cranial nuclei from which the lower motor neurone runs to a group of muscle fibres ("motor unit"). Thus the lower motor neurone is the "final common path" for all efferent impulses directed at the muscle and the groups of anterior horn cells may be considered to "represent a muscle" in the same sense as the cells of the motor cortex "represent a movement".

Further detail on the central control of movement is not required in this chapter. Since the lower motor neurone is a final common path, the elemental components of the electromyogram do not depend on the origin of a motor drive to the motoneurones. The motor unit and its action potential are defined below.

Electromyography in Kinesiology

A consequence of this fact is that it is not possible to state by examining an EMG trace whether the activity resulted from voluntary or involuntary innervation. There is therefore no advantage in studying the detailed structure of motor units in the electromyography of the dyskinesias. The disorder of function consists in the inappropriate timing and quantification of motoneurone discharge, its distribution in synergic muscles and others which are normally unrelated, its relationship to target seeking and the economy with which this is achieved. For these purposes needle electrodes are unnecessary except as a means of localized recording from deeply situated muscles. In most instances surface electrodes are adequate, the degree of amplification is moderate, and a recording device with a limited temporal discrimination is suitable. A polygraph with multichannel pen or similar galvanometer is appropriate as this will permit simultaneous recording of the activity of many muscles.

Abnormalities of the timing of muscular contraction may be measured with sufficient precision for most purposes. The amplitude of the recorded activity is, however, a poor indication of the degree of muscular contraction. Quantitative methods, described below, may be used but it should be noted that amplitude also depends on the size of the electrode and the proximity of active muscle fibres. The selective pick-up of needle electrodes makes it particularly difficult to compare one channel with another. Failure to recognize these points invalidates many of the orthopaedic and kinematic studies using EMG recording.

DYSKINESIAS

There is nothing to distinguish the EMG trace from a contracting muscle in the dyskinesias except that the activity is involuntary but compounded of normal motor unit activity. The following basic types of involuntary movement occur in different varieties recognized by distribution and associated abnormalities on neurological examination.

Myoclonus

There is a salvo of grouped motor unit potentials within a single muscle or a group of muscles. It lasts for about 100 msec. and the twitch or jerk may be sufficient to displace the limb.

Tremors

These are rhythmical movement disorders characterized by regular repetition of the contraction of certain muscles or groups of muscles.

Physiological Tremor

This is of low amplitude and is seen when the normal subject maintains a posture. The frequency is influenced by age. It is 5–6 Hz. at 2–9 years, increases progressively to 10 Hz. at 20 years, then slows again after 40 years of age. Proprioceptive feedback and supraspinal tonic impulses play a dominant role in maintaining the amplitude and regularity of this type of tremor. It is modified by limb position, the load carried, fatigue and closure of the eyes. Nervous tension, thyrotoxicosis, alcoholism, many toxic states, and a familial tendency may exaggerate it and it is diminished or absent in myxoedema and afferent neuropathy (including tabes dorsalis).

Tremor of Parkinsonism

There are two types. A tremor at rest (4–7 Hz.) has bursts of motor unit action potentials with intervening silent periods during which similar bursts may be recorded from antagonists. It disappears during sleep and is diminished or absent during voluntary movement. The other type, action tremor, is faster and probably represents an exaggerated physiological tremor. This form modulates the myotatic reflex when the muscle is passively stretched, constituting the 'cog-wheel tremor' which is typical of Parkinsonism. The anatomical and physiological basis for these tremors is still being argued.

Clonus

This is a rhythmical movement (5–6 Hz.) brought on by abruptly stretching an extensor muscle. It is maintained by contraction alternating between that muscle and its antagonist. It is due to a cycle of muscle contraction followed by relaxation which occurs because the muscle spindles are unloaded during the contraction phase, the whole cycle being exaggerated in the presence of an upper motor neurone lesion.

Cerebellar Dyskinesia

The dysmetria, dyssynergia, dysdiadokokinesia and intention tremor of cerebellar disease which cause ataxia of movement are due to improper timing and distribution of motor impulses to the muscles of a synergy and are found in both postural and kinetic voluntary activity. There is no EMG discharge at rest and the content of each burst of activity is of normal type. The abnormality of contraction is recognized by its inappropriateness of length and timing.

Athetosis

The involuntary movement of the limbs in this type of dyskinesia is slow, maintained, and non-rhythmical. Agonist and antagonist muscles frequently contract simultaneously, but the tonic activity of each is otherwise indistinguishable from voluntary innervation by EMG criteria.

Spasmodic Torticollis and Torsion Dystonia

These are similar disorders of the neck, trunk and proximal limb musculature.

Chorea

In the non-rhythmical abrupt involuntary movements of chorea the reciprocal innervation is retained.

In short, polygraphic studies are useful for documenting involuntary movements for research purposes but electromyography alone has little to offer in the diagnosis of the dyskinesias.

GRADATION OF MUSCULAR CONTRACTION

The Motor Unit

Sherrington coined the term "motor unit" to include the whole axon of the motoneurone from its hillock in the perikaryon down to its terminals in the muscle and the group of muscle fibres to which the latter are distributed. The term is commonly used to embrace the whole motoneurone or, more loosely, to describe the group of muscle fibres supplied by one motoneurone. The latter usage is implied by the EMG terminology in which "motor unit potential" applies to the compound action potential of the group of muscle fibres and not to the nerve action potential. There is a one-to-one relationship between the muscle and nerve potentials as there is normally an "all or none" relationship between the two if neuromuscular transmission is normal and so the (muscular) motor unit action potential is a reliable "marker" of motoneurone activity.

Gradation of Muscular Contraction

In the resting muscle no motor unit activity can be detected, even by small (needle) electrodes inserted into the muscle belly. "Tonic" activity depends on reflex innervation of the muscle from stretch, vestibular impulses, etc. When motoneurones are depolarized by excitation from supraspinal or extraspinal afferent fibre activity, motoneurones are recruited in order of threshold. Each fires at a slow rate (6–10/sec.) and irregularly, but with increasing depolarizing pressure the rate increases to a characteristic rate for that unit (15–30/sec.) and the rhythm is more regular. At the same time, motoneurones are recruited from a previously subliminal fringe as the depolarizing pressure rises above their firing threshold. The strength of contraction of the muscle is therefore increased by two mechanisms: (i) increased firing rate of motor units; (ii) recruitment of new units. The latter mechanism is the main one. Firing rates do not continue to rise as maximum mechanical effect is produced when the twitch responses of the muscle fibres are fused into a tetanus. This relatively slow rate has the additional advantage that fatigue of motoneurones is unlikely to occur. Rotation of units is therefore unnecessary and probably only occurs in certain limited circumstances.

With the needle electrodes commonly used, muscle fibres belonging to a number of motor units are within the pick up range of the electrode so that with maximum contraction the number of motor unit action potentials recorded is too great for individual motor unit potentials to be identified. The summed activity recorded is termed an "interference pattern". (The author prefers "full recruitment pattern", Fig. 1.) If muscle contraction is reduced the pattern simplifies as motor units cease firing; individual unit potentials can then be identified ("reduced pattern"). With minimal contraction only one or two motor unit potentials may be recorded ("discrete" or "single unit" activity). To observe the firing pattern of single motor units during moderate or strong contraction it is necessary to use very fine needle or wire electrodes with limited pick up area carefully placed close to a fibre of the required motor unit. In practice it is rarely possible to achieve such discrimination for more than a few motor units and this can only be achieved by sacrificing information regarding the innervation ratio.

Muscle Fibre Types

Muscle fibres differ in their speed of contraction and relaxation and this is to some extent related to their chemical constitution. Thus fast-twitch (white) and slow-twitch fibres (red) have been recognized in some animals. The distinction is less clear in mammalia and particularly in the human where, if they exist, the different fibre types are mixed in each muscle. By modern histochemical techniques a number of different fibre types may be identified and there is evidence that each motoneurone innervates only one type of muscle fibre. The fibre type is apparently determined by the motoneurone, as shown by cross-innervation experiments. For present purposes it is unnecessary to go into details about this aspect of muscle physiology but some mention of it is required as the possibility exists that the different fibre types (and hence their motoneurones) are differentiated functionally, e.g. for phasic and tonic activity. This consideration is important as it throws doubt on the Sherringtonian concept of the "final common path" which postulates that all motoneurones are similar and used for phasic or tonic, voluntary or reflex functions according to the dictates of the central nervous system.

Phasic and Tonic Motoneurones

Experimental studies on the cat and rat strongly suggest that motoneurones may be specialized for one or other type of activity. Japanese electromyographers claim to be able to differentiate tonic from phasic (kinetic) motor units in the human according to the firing rate at which discharge becomes regular. Critics, including the writer, consider that these parameters depend on feed-back control from muscle spindles, tendon organs, and the Renshaw loop, and hence consistent with the Sherringtonian view. This is an important point requiring elucidation.

Firing Rate and Recruitment in Disease

Recording from a concentric needle electrode of suitable size (0·07 sq. mm.) most normal muscles at maximum voluntary innervation will produce a fully recruited "interference" pattern as defined above. If the pattern is "incomplete" or shows single unit activity, it is necessary to ensure that full effort is being exerted if the contraction is voluntary, or that the stimulus is maximal if it is evoked reflexly or by electrical stimulation. With this proviso, a reduction in the pattern indicates poverty of motor units available for recruitment—i.e. there is a disorder of lower motor neurones. This may be due to disease of the motoneurone cells (e.g. poliomyelitis, amyotrophic lateral

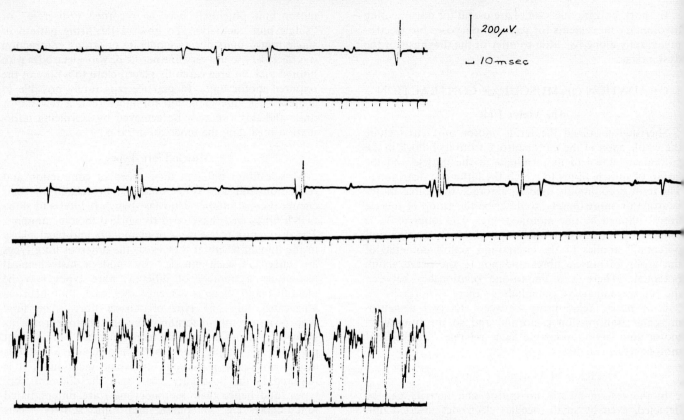

Fig. 1. EMG of normal muscle: (i) slight voluntary contraction recruits four motor units firing at 4–9/sec.; (ii) two motor units synchronize temporarily (note possibility of confusion with polyphasic units is not observed for adequate time); (iii) maximum voluntary contraction with fully recruited ("interference") pattern. Calibration: 200 μV. and 10 msec.

sclerosis) or of the peripheral axons (radiculoneuropathy, peripheral neuritis). The surviving motor units generally fire at faster rates than normal (30–60/sec. for limb muscles). This is not of diagnostic significance as it is due to diminished inhibitory feedback and so the increased firing frequency may also be present in myogenic disease. Failure of recruitment is confined to neurogenic disease, provided that myopathy is not so severe that large areas of muscle are replaced by fat or fibrous tissue.

Further discrimination between neurogenic and myogenic lesions depends on: (i) analysis of the innervation ratio, (ii) presence of spontaneous electrical activity. This requires an understanding of the anatomy of the motor unit, the motor unit action potential, and the pathological responses of nerve and muscle to disease.

Innervation Ratio and Distribution
of Muscle Fibres

The number of mucle fibres innervated by one motoneurone, the innervation ratio (I.R.) differs from one muscle to another. For various practical reasons this ratio is difficult to determine with accuracy. Most of the limb muscles have large units (I.R. 1000:1), whereas motor units of the face (I.R. 700:1), and sphincter muscles (I.R. 50:1) have fewer fibres. The extraocular muscles have particularly small numbers of muscle fibres for each motor unit (I.R. 6–30:1). These differences determine the units of increment of tension in the muscle. The

number of muscle fibres also influences the dimensions o the motor unit action potential.

There is good histological and EMG evidence that th muscle fibres of a single motor unit are scattered in group through a cross section of about 30 sq. mm. in a muscl belly. The unit is not coterminous with the primar fascicles of muscle. The dispersion is such that no singl needle electrode can record the activity of all of its fibres (Multilead electrodes are available for mapping th anatomical distribution of motor units.)

There may be a reduction in the innervation ratio i disease. This is particularly so in myopathic disorder owing to the loss of functioning muscle fibres more o less at random within motor units. It has been suggeste that a "terminal neuronitis" may have the same resul but this concept lacks adequate confirmation. In dis orders of peripheral nerves, especially traumatic lesions regenerating neurones may have a reduced innervatio ratio in the so-called "nascent units".

In non-traumatic disease there is almost invariably recovery or compensatory process *pari passu* with th destructive one. In myopathies this is seen as hypertroph of muscle fibres but development of new fibres is excep tional and incomplete, the innervation ratio and the anato mical distribution remain reduced. The restorativ process is not sufficient to make a significant contributio to the electrogenesis of the motor unit action potential. I lesions of the lower motor neurone, on the other hand there is active regeneration of surviving neurones which develop new branches at the endplates, the terminal branching, and more rarely proximally. These fibres make contact at random with denervated muscle fibres which may have belonged originally to another moto-neurone. In this way the surviving regenerating neurones acquire a high innervation ratio and have an enlarged anatomical distribution.

THE ELECTRICAL SIGNS OF MUSCULAR ACTIVITY

The action currents or potential variations associated with muscular activity are recorded by volume conduction. The usual rules of recording in this situation are applicable, notably that the potential field drops by (approximately) the square of the distance from its potential maximum and propagated action potentials cause triphasic deflections at one or both electrodes, depending on whether the reference ("inactive") electrode is remote or within the potential field.

Electrodes

The amplitude, the duration and the rate of change of potential depend on the characteristics of the electrodes and in particular their size. For recording the activity of motor units it is usual to employ concentric needle electrodes. The "active" or exploring electrode is the bared tip of an insulated wire firmly secured within a cannula which is a hypodermic or similar hollow needle which acts as the "indifferent" electrode. As the latter averages the potential field over its whole length, the most significant contribution to the potential difference between electrodes is that of the central core but the "indifferent" electrode is only relatively so. As the needle has a bevelled tip the active electrode "sees" an electrical field in the direction faced by the bevel. Alternatively, a sewing needle insulated except at the tip may be used (so-called "monopolar" electrode) referred against a remote electrode which may be another needle or a surface metal plate. The potential difference between the two electrodes is amplified by a push-pull amplifier with a bandwidth of 0·5 Hz–10,000 Hz. and displayed on an oscilloscope. This avoids the inertia of galvanometers but problems of time-constant and other distortions must be considered. Recording on magnetic tape is convenient but introduces further distortions. Those intending to do serious work must become familiar with the properties of different electrodes and recording systems and the use of earth leads. A loudspeaker is usually used for auditory monitoring as the human ear is very sensitive to variations in frequency.

Single Fibre Potential

The action potential of a single muscle fibre recorded in volume is a triphasic (positive–negative–positive) deflection of which the negative phase has the greatest amplitude ("spike") and so is most readily detected at a distance. As just described, the measurements vary

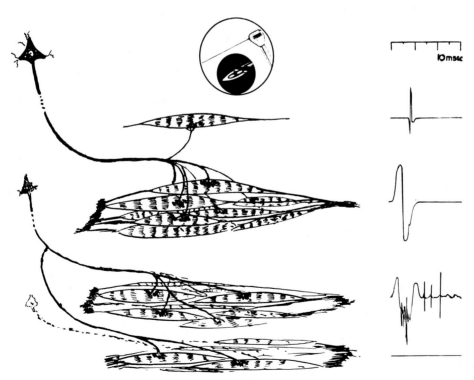

FIG. 2. Interpretation of muscle action potentials recorded by concentric needle electrode (inset). On left, diagram of intact motor unit (above) and degenerated unit in which some muscle fibres are re-innervated by collateral branching from a surviving axon which therefore has a greater complement of muscle fibres. On right: (a) action potential of single muscle fibre; (b) normal motor unit; and (c) motor unit with collateral branching. The latter shows a polyphasic motor unit potential with "parasites".

according to the electrodes used and the distance from the generator. With the usual concentric needle electrode the peak–peak amplitude is 100–1000 μV. and the duration rarely exceeds 5 msec (Fig. 2a).

Motor Unit Potential

This is the action potential expressing the activity of that part of (the muscle fibres of) a single motor unit which is within the recording range of the electrode. (Figs. 1, 2b). It is recognized by its consistent relation to contraction of the muscle. As those fibres nearest the exploring electrode contribute most voltage, the "picture" varies if the intra-muscular needle is rotated, inserted or withdrawn, but if left in one position the potential is relatively constant. (Muscle movement introduces slight changes.) If all muscle fibres were synchronously fired by the motoneurone, the motor unit potential would be of high voltage but with the same time characteristics as the potential of each single fibre since these would sum. However, there is a temporal dispersion which is mainly due to the scatter of endplates in the innervation zone. For this reason the amplitude is less than would be anticipated (100–1,000 μV.), the duration longer (12 ± 3 msec. but different in various muscles) and each phase may be inflected (Fig. 3a). The potential is described as "polyphasic" if there are more than three crossings of the baseline. With the usual electrodes, the incidence of polyphasic potentials is only about 4 per cent in limb muscles but much higher in the facial and extra-ocular muscles. The latter have a lower innervation ratio so that there is less summing of single fibre potentials.

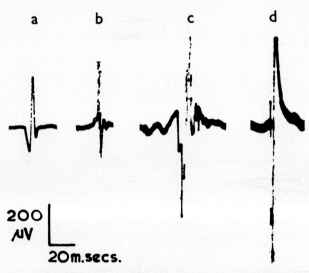

Fig. 3. The motor unit action potential: (a) normal; (b) myopathy; (c) polyneuritis; (d) amyotrophic lateral sclerosis.

200 μV 20m.secs.

In diseases which reduce the innervation ratio the incidence of polyphasic motor unit potentials with normal or slightly reduced amplitude and/or overall duration is significantly increased. This is characteristic of myogenic disease but, as pointed out above, motor units formed by newly regenerated motoneurones may have similar characteristics (e.g. in the Kugelberg-Welander syndrome).

When the innervation ratio is increased owing to collateral branching, the motor unit potential becomes enlarged and tends to be polyphasic (Figs. 2c, 3c). This is particularly so when the endplate zone is widened as in peripheral neuropathy. The overall duration may then be 15–20 msec. or longer. The amplitude may be increased but not necessarily so. Large units increased in amplitude more than duration (and hence more synchronous and less polyphasic) are characteristic of the increased innervation ratio associated with disease of the anterior horn cells (poliomyelitis, amyotrophic lateral sclerosis) (Fig. 3d). The causation of these "giant unit potentials" is uncertain. It is possible that they are actually due to synchronized firing of more than one motoneurone. It may not be possible to discriminate between polioclastic disease and peripheral neuropathy without additional techniques such as measurement of conduction velocity.

Synchronization of Motor Unit Potentials

In the normal subject, adjacent motor units fire asynchronously throughout a graded contraction of muscle (leading to an "interference pattern"). Some units normally fire synchronously especially at the onset of contraction and many do so when effort is maximal causing a 40–50 Hz. Piper rhythm. When fatigue occurs the synchronization causes a coarse visible tremor. Synchronization with lesser degrees of effort is very characteristic of spinal cord disease with involvement of motoneurones. Grouped firing leading to tremor also occurs in disorders of the basal ganglia. This is to be distinguished from iterative firing.

Iterative Discharge

In hypocalcaemia, and other states associated with lowered accommodation of neurones (p. 52), the motor unit action potentials may occur in pairs ("doublets") or as triple discharges ("triplets"). The time interval between each discharge of a doublet or triplet remains consistent (2·5–20 msec.) and the group repeats at intervals corresponding to the normal intervals between single discharges for the appropriate degree of innervation. With further decrease of accommodation trains of motor unit potentials ("multiplets") occur in response to voluntary, reflex, or evoked stimulation and when accommodation breaks down altogether there is spontaneous iterative firing of many units. This causes the muscular spasm of tetany. Iterative responses should not be considered diagnostic of latent tetany unless the time constant of accommodation of the peripheral nerves is lowered. Similar changes of accommodation of axons or muscle fibres occur in diseases of these structures and lead to spontaneous discharges of various types.

SPONTANEOUS ACTIVITY
Myokymia

Continuous spontaneous muscular contractions of a vermicular type, myokymia, are found in three conditions:

Facial Myokymia

This is occasionally associated with brain stem lesions (pontine glioma; multiple sclerosis) but more commonly as a benign disorder of orbicularis oculi associated with exhaustion. Presumably of central origin, the motor units of the facial muscles discharge continuously.

Generalized Myokymia

Widespread continuous undulating movements of face, tongue, limbs and trunk occur in the absence of muscular cramp, wasting or weakness. The movements are shown by EMG to be small tetanic series rather than twitches.

Schultze's Myokymia

Similar spontaneous movements are associated with painful spasms provoked by active or passive movements. There are prolonged bursts of repetitive motor unit potentials. There is no detectable weakness but muscle biopsy may show denervation atrophy.

Stiff-man Syndrome

Progressive, fluctuating muscle rigidity with episodes of painful cramp and associated tachycardia and sweating constitute the "stiff-man syndrome". Pharmacological studies suggest that in one type the persisting α-neurone activity shown by EMG is due to abnormal gamma-motor system activity. Another type which is not relieved by diazepam is described as skeletal and autonomic over-activity from an excess of spontaneously liberated transmitter substance at efferent nerve terminals ("quantal squander"). The motor unit potentials are grouped into triplets or multiplets as in tetany. The hyperexcitability of distal branches of motoneurones has been attributed to a "neuromyositis". It is reduced by hydantoinates and blocked by curare. This type closely resembles tetany. A similar rigidity occurs after severe prolonged hypothermia.

Tetany

The occurrence in latent tetany of iterative firing on voluntary innervation has already been described. When the accommodation of peripheral nerve is almost completely abolished, spontaneous discharge of iterative trains of action potentials occurs from axons as well as nerve cells. The effect of hypocalcaemia is potentiated by anoxia. Where the anoxia is local (as under a compressive cuff) the spontaneous firing of nerve originates in ischaemic segments of nerve.

Tetanus

The spasms of tetanus are of a different nature. They are not truly spontaneous, being evoked reflexly. The reflex excitability of motoneurones is increased by the exotoxin blocking the action of inhibitory interneurones, especially the Renshaw system.

Isolation of Motoneurones

A spontaneous rigidity due to continuous muscular activity occurs in rare disorders of the spinal cord in which the motoneurones are de-afferented and isolated from all projection systems including inhibitory interneurones.

Fasciculation

Spontaneous discharge may occur randomly at infrequent intervals from motoneurones which are metabolically abnormal but still capable of conducting nerve impulses. The site of origin is unknown. It is most common in slowly degenerating conditions of the lower motor neurone cells such as amyotrophic lateral sclerosis, progressive muscular atrophy, or syringomyelia but may occur with more peripheral disorders (radiculitis, cervical rib neuropathy and rarely peripheral neuropathy). In these conditions it is associated with other signs of denervation.

Benign fasciculation is not related to denervation and has a good prognosis. It may be a form of generalized myokymia (p. 346).

In fasciculation, the spontaneous nerve impulse activates a normal or large motor unit so the motor unit potential has a normal morphology or it may be large and polyphasic (Fig. 4). Iterative firing is rare, the discharge occurring singly at random. The muscle fibres of the motor unit contract with sufficient power to cause a visible twitch of a bundle of muscle fibres, but not to displace a limb segment.

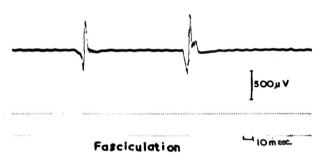

FIG. 4. Fasciculation potentials. Firing is random. The two potentials recorded originate in different groups of muscle fibres. Calibration: 500 μV. and 10 msec.

To study the morphology of fasciculation potentials the oscilloscope may be triggered by the fasciculation potential which is then displayed on the "scope" after being introduced to the Y-plate via a delay line.

Fibrillation

This term should be restricted to spontaneous contractions of single muscle fibres (as distinct from the whole unit involved in fasciculation). This type of involuntary activity is characteristic of denervated muscle fibres but is also found in myogenic lesions. It is common in myositis and other acquired myopathies but is not rare in hereditary muscular dystrophy.

The fibrillation potential, being the action potential of a single muscle fibre (or in some instances a few muscle fibres) is triphasic with a total duration which does not usually exceed 5 msec. The duration and amplitude (100–1000 μV.) depend on the type of intramuscular electrode used to record it. Fibrillation potentials occur repetitively and are not influenced by nerve impulses (Figs. 5, 8).

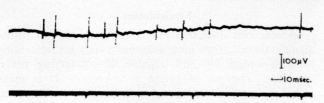

Fibrillation

FIG. 5. Fibrillation potentials. These are spontaneous, firing in short trains, and have the configuration of potentials from single muscle fibres. Calibration: 100 μV. and 10 msec.

End-plate "Noise"

A needle electrode inserted into the end-plate zone of a normal muscle records low voltage negative monophasic potentials occurring in irregular sequence. They are usually less than 100 μV. and of brief duration (0·5–2 msec.) but may be accompanied by larger (up to 300 μV.) biphasic (usually negative-positive) potentials which occur irregularly. These potentials are considered to be spontaneous miniature end-plate potentials recorded extracellularly.

Insertion Activity

Movement or insertion of a needle electrode in a muscle commonly provokes irregular high frequency potentials, mainly positive-going (Fig. 6). These are probably injury

suggests that they originate at and propagate away from the tip of the recording needle (Fig. 8).

Myotonic Response

This is defined as a high frequency repetitive discharge of either biphasic (positive–negative) spikes or positive waves induced by different means. It may occur as an after-discharge following voluntary contraction, on movement of the needle, or on percussion of the muscle (Fig. 9). The amplitude and frequency of the potentials wax and wane and this is associated with a characteristic musical sound which increases then decreases in pitch. The elements of the discharge may differ widely but include positive sharp waves and single fibre potentials as well as potentials of motor unit type. True myotonic response is confined to myotonia congenita and myotonia dystrophica.

A similar response but without the waxing and waning of frequency is found in polymyositis, paramyotonia and the related condition of hyperkalaemic periodic paralysis (adynamia episodica hereditaria of Gamstorp). In glycogen storage diseases of muscle there may be "pseudo-myotonic" bursts of single fibre potentials or bizarre high frequency polyphasic potentials.

Bizarre High Frequency Potentials

The usual circumstances of these are listed above. They may also be found in neurogenic atrophy. The action

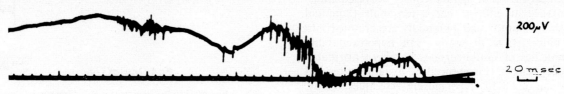

FIG. 6. Insertion activity, provoked by movement of the needle electrode. Calibration: 200 μV. and 20 msec.

potentials. In normal muscle the burst of activity is brief and does not outlast the needle movement. In pathological muscle—either denervated or undergoing necrosis from myogenic disease—the insertion activity is commonly prolonged. When it continues on arresting the needle movement it is difficult to know whether to classify the spontaneous potentials as insertion activity, fibrillation potentials, or positive sharp waves.

Positive Sharp Waves

These are slow waves with rapid onset which occur repetitively, usually associated with needle insertion or movement injury. When recorded at a monopolar needle exploring electrode the initial potential change is in a positive direction, followed by a slower exponential change in the negative direction which may continue into a prolonged negative phase of smaller amplitude (Fig. 7). The total duration usually exceeds 10 msec. and may be 100 msec. or more. Positive sharp waves (sometimes called "saw-tooth potentials") are recorded in chronically denervated muscle, particularly in amyotrophic lateral sclerosis, but are also common in muscle necrosis due to myositis and other acquired myopathies. They are probably injury potentials. The positive initial deflection

potentials are usually polyphasic, repeating 10–150/sec. with very uniform frequency, shape and amplitude. They generally start and stop abruptly. Their source is uncertain. They have been attributed to altered excitability of the muscle cell membrane, to muscle spindles and to fine nerve terminals. Wherever they originate they are almost certainly a form of injury potential.

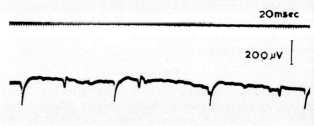

Positive Injury Potential

FIG. 7. Positive sharp waves ("saw-tooth potentials") from a patient with amyotrophic lateral sclerosis. Calibration: 200 μV. and 20 msec.

Electromyographic Localization of Muscular Weakness

The previous sections have described the features to be observed in carrying out an electromyographic

MYOGENIC   POTENTIALS

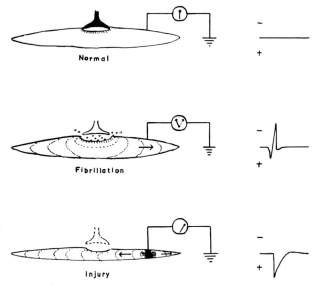

FIG. 8. A concentric electrode with large shaft as "indifferent" electrode may be treated as a "monopolar" recording electrode with respect to a closely adjacent muscle fibre. In the absence of voluntary activity no potential variation is recorded from a normal muscle fibre at a distance from the endplate. Fibrillation or other potentials propagating past the stigmatic electrode cause a positive–negative–positive variation. Potentials originating at and propagating away from the stigmatic electrode cause a positive "saw-tooth" potential.

examination. No single feature is diagnostic of one disease. Correlation of them permits an operational description of neuromuscular function in physiological terms. This must then be integrated with clinical (and possibly histological) data to make a nosological diagnosis. The following are the main categories (*see also* Table 1).

Dystonias and Dyskinesias

There are defects of timing and coordination of muscles with involuntary movements. The motor unit potentials are fully recruited and normal in morphology. There is no excess of insertion activity and no spontaneous myogenic activity.

Denervation

The coordination of the muscle synergy is normal. Recruitment is reduced. Surviving motor units fire at increased rate for the tension produced. The morphology of the motor unit potentials may be normal, small and polyphasic (in regenerating units), prolonged and polyphasic (where there is collateral re-innervation) (Fig. 10), or polyphasic and of high amplitude (usually with central causes of denervation) (Fig. 11). Insertion activity may be increased. Fasciculation, fibrillation and positive potentials may be recorded. The probability of each feature differs with central and peripheral causes (Table 1) but it may be impossible to determine the level of the lesion causing neurogenic atrophy of muscle if the disorder is polioclastic or axonal. If there is primary demyelination the signs of denervation are associated with diminished conduction velocity of the motor nerve fibres.

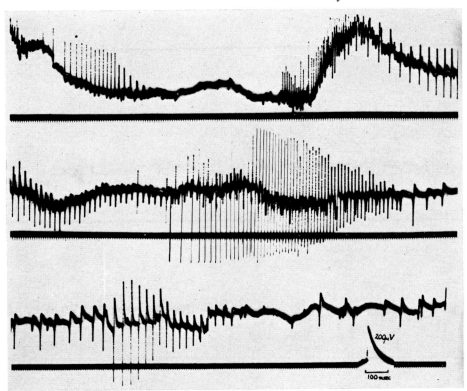

FIG. 9. Myotonic discharge provoked by moving the needle electrode in the muscle.
Calibration: 200 μV. and 100 msec.

TABLE 1

SUMMARY OF EMG FINDINGS

	Maximum Recruitment Pattern	Motor Unit Action Potentials				Spontaneous Activity				
		Polyphasic* %	Mean Amplitude* %	Mean Duration* %	Mean Territory (dia.)* %	Insertion Activity	Positive 'Injury' Potentials	High Frequency Bursts	Fibrillation Potentials	Fasciculation Potentials
Normal	I	0–10	100	100	100	+	−	−	Local	Occ.
Ant. horn cell disease	I → R → D	10–20	110–1,000	100–200 parasites [b]	100–250	++	+++	Occ.	++	++
Peripheral neuropathy	I → R → D	10–30	70–150	85–250	50–300	++	++	Occ.	+++	+
Myositis	I → R	15–30	40–85	75–100	70–95	+++	++	++	++	−
Myopathy [a]	I → R → D	15–50	40–85	75–100	70–95	±	+	+	+	− [d]
Dystrophia myotonica	I → R	15–50	40–85	75–100	70–95	+++	++	+++ [c]	+	−
Congenital myotonia	I	0–10	100	99–100	100	+++	++	+++ [c]	Local	−

[a] Muscular dystrophy, congenital myopathy, acquired myopathies other than myositis.
[b] One or more single fibre action potentials regularly occurring, 5–10 msec. after main potential.
[c] Waxing and waning in frequency and amplitude.
[d] Fasciculation occasionally in thyrotoxic myopathy.
* Absolute measurements depend on anatomical site, age, and electrode characteristics.

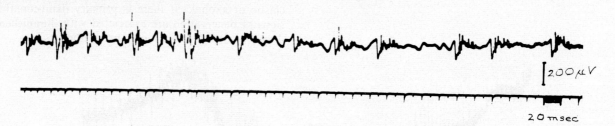

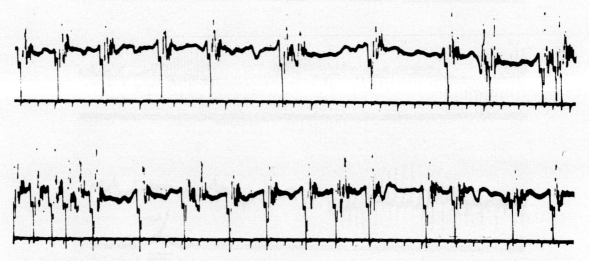

FIG. 10. Polyneuritis. EMG pattern reduced to "single-unit activity", the surviving unit potential being polyphasic and of increased amplitude and duration. Maximum effort in upper and lower traces. Note firing rate faster than normal. Calibration: 200 μV. and 20 msec.

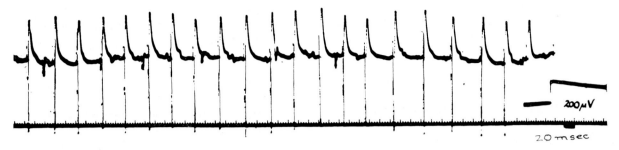

FIG. 11. Amyotrophic lateral sclerosis. Maximum voluntary contraction. Single-unit activity consisting of "giant units". Calibration: 200 μV. and 20 msec.

Myopathic Lesions

The coordination of the muscle synergy is normal. Recruitment is full but motor units may fire at faster rates than normal. The proportion of motor unit potentials which are polyphasic but with normal or reduced duration and/or amplitude is significantly increased (Fig. 12).

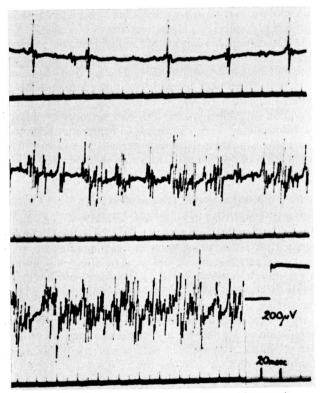

FIG. 12. Hereditary muscular dystrophy. Motor unit potentials are of small amplitude and duration; many are polyphasic; maximum effort recruits a full "interference" pattern. Calibration: 200 μV. and 20 msec.

Insertion activity is normal or reduced in congenital myopathies and hereditary muscular dystrophies with the exception of those associated with myotonia. Increased insertion activity sometimes amounting to "pseudomyotonic" discharge is characteristic of acquired myopathy. This includes polymyositis with or without other evidence of connective tissue disease, carcinomatous myopathy, and endocrine myopathies. There is no electrodiagnostic distinction between the myopathies of the various "collagen" disorders, or between one endocrine disease and another. (Examples are thyrotoxic myopathy and steroid myopathy.) In addition to increased insertion activity, the acquired myopathies show marked spontaneous activity of fibrillation and positive saw-tooth varieties. Fasciculation is rare but occurs in thyrotoxic myopathy. Spontaneous activity is less common in hereditary muscular dystrophy except for a slow fibrillation discharge which is rather characteristic.

QUANTITATIVE ELECTROMYOGRAPHY

For purposes of diagnosis the electromyographer depends on recognition of the phenomena described above. In denervation atrophy the reduction of recruitment is a good indication of the extent of denervation, bearing in mind the statistical requirements of a sampling technique. In myopathic disease this parameter is not available and it may be difficult to be sure of the abnormality of the EMG in early disease. To provide the clinician with a measure of the severity of muscular disease a number of quantitative techniques have been described.

Mean Potential Duration

Measurement of an adequate sample of motor unit potentials provides clear distinction between myogenic and neurogenic atrophy. The method is less satisfactory to distinguish between early myopathy and normal muscle. Only low threshold units are amenable to measurement.

Motor Unit Territory

By multielectrode recording the territory inhabited by muscle fibres of a motor unit may be measured. It is decreased in myopathy and increased in neurogenic atrophy if re-innervation is present (Table 1).

Mean Potential

The average potential of the interference pattern from surface electrodes follows the tension produced by the muscle with sufficient fidelity to use this method in kinesiology studies but it does not have diagnostic value.

Voltage-tension Curves

Electronic integration of the EMG from surface electrodes produces a voltage which is proportional to the tension. The regression line of voltage against load is increased with primary muscle disease. The method is useful for research studies but not sufficiently sensitive to detect early myopathy or the carrier state in Duchenne muscular dystrophy.

Frequency Analysis

A Fourier analysis of the EMG in myopathic diseases shows a higher proportion of high frequency components than normal. The method is relatively insensitive.

Spike Counts

Assessment of the amount of polyphasic activity in an interference pattern by counting spikes visually or electronically has been tried with limited success.

Counts of Change in Direction of Potential in an Interference Pattern

This procedure, using a special analyser and computer, has more theoretical justification and is claimed to have clinical value.

EVOKED MUSCULAR ACTIVITY

The electromyographic methods described above require the collaboration of the patient in production of controlled contraction or complete relaxation of muscles. This is impossible with young children and nervous subjects. Electrical stimulation of muscle has the disadvantage that the muscular response is virtually synchronous so there is little advantage in using needle electrodes except to limit the pick up area.

Graded Stimulation

Little use has been made of measurements of the parameters of the evoked response of muscle to graded stimulation of the motor nerve. It is sometimes possible to estimate the number of motor units in a muscle.

Paired or Repetitive Stimulation

The response of muscle to a pair or a train of stimuli is valuable provided that the stimulus is supramaximal. Variations in the amplitude and duration of the response occur in disorders of neuromuscular transmission and in some disorders of muscle.

Refractory Period

After a single shock is applied directly to a muscle fibre it is refractory to further stimuli for a short interval of time. For a very brief time there is an absolute refractory period in which the muscle cannot be excited by any stimulus, no matter what its strength. This is followed by the relative refractory period when a sufficient stimulus may be effective.

Refractoriness depends on the recovery time after depolarization and the total refractory period is approximately of the same duration as the action potential. In normal human muscle it is 2·2–4·6 msec. In muscular dystrophy (and sometimes in dystrophy carriers) it is reduced to about 30 per cent of the normal value.

The refractory period is due to properties of the membrane of the muscle. Nerve membrane shows similar phenomena but only at rates of stimulation much faster

than used in human studies. The following discussion refers to whole muscle not single fibres, so gross electrodes (normally on the surface) are necessary to record the phenomena. A train of stimuli recurring within the refractory period of nerve or muscle will cause a first maximal response followed by submaximal but nondecrementiny responses to the succeeding shocks. (When a group of fibres is stimulated some may respond to alternate stimuli.) This is *Wedensky inhibition*. It is not a true inhibitory phenomenon and is not related to transmission failure at the neuromuscular junction. It is probably of little importance in physiological activity.

Progressive Changes of Muscle Polarization

In chronic hypoxia and hypokalaemic states, alternating responses, progressive decrement, or sudden reduction to a new level of evoked action potential may be seen in a supramaximally stimulated muscle at stimulation rates of 20–50/sec. This has not been fully studied but it is probably due to defective repolarization of the muscle fibres as the first response after a brief rest is subnormal. It is not prevented by anticholinesterases.

During a paralytic episode of familial periodic paralysis there is gradual reduction in the amplitude of the muscle potential evoked by single shocks as the blood potassium level falls. This was formerly considered to be due to hyperpolarization of the muscle fibres by intracellular migration of potassium, but this has not been confirmed by intracellular measurements of membrane potential. There are hypokalaemic and hyperkalaemic forms. The explanation of the failure of the action potential and twitch mechanisms is uncertain.

Failure of Neuromuscular Transmission

Reduced muscular response to a second neural stimulus more than 5 msec. after a test shock is not due to the refractory period or other polarization phenomena. Full-sized muscular response is obtained by direct stimulation of the muscle postsynaptically. The decrement is due to failure of transmission at the neuromuscular junction. The associated progressive muscular weakness is *myasthenia*. The amount of acetylcholine released by serial stimulation of a motor nerve decreases progressively if the rate of stimulation exceeds the rate of mobilization of transmitter substance from stores in the nerve terminals. Normally, however, the amount liberated by each shock is much in excess of that required to produce endplate potentials exceeding the threshold for triggering propagated action potentials in the muscle fibres. Tetanization must be prolonged (for a period depending on stimulus frequency) before there is insufficient to stimulate the muscle fibres. There is, therefore, a normal "safety factor". Any lesion which lowers the safety factor causes an early decrement of the muscle response to repetitive stimulation. Progressive failure of acetylcholine production is temporarily arrested or reversed by facilitated ejection of transmitter due to an effect of fast stimulation on the nerve terminals. This is only seen when the safety factor is so reduced that decrement of evoked response is seen in the first 10 seconds or so.

Symptomatic Myasthenia

Safety factor is reduced by any disorder causing dying back of the lower motor neurones (motor neurone disease (ALS), poliomyelitis, syringomyelia, peripheral neuropathy), but the myasthenic response is rare until the neurone has almost ceased to function. Facilitated release is not seen. A decremental response is also a temporary feature in an early stage of some acquired muscular diseases—polymyositis, dermatomyositis, systemic lupus erythematosus, and carcinomatous myasthenia (Fig. 13).

Myasthenia Gravis

Decrementing response of the compound muscle action potential to paired or repetitive supramaximal stimuli separated by 10 msec. or more cannot be due to membrane properties of nerve or muscle, but may result from lowering of the safety factor for neuromuscular transmission. Nerve action potential remains normal and the response to direct muscular stimulation is normal. This may be present in myasthenia gravis (and the first response is sometimes also subnormal).

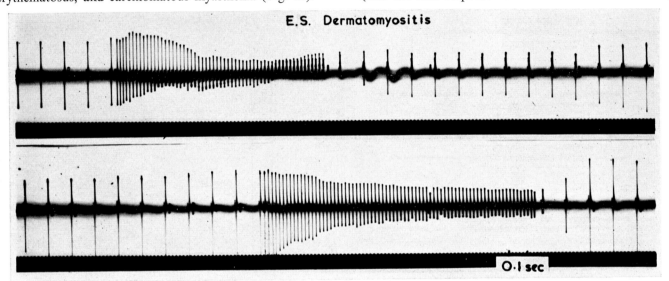

FIG. 13. Symptomatic myasthenia in polymyositis. Supramaximal nerve stimulation. Surface recording of evoked muscle potentials.

It is uncertain whether there are pre- or post-junctional causes (or both) for the loss of safety factor in this group, but facilitated release is common and may be a dominant feature. This may point to the integrity of the nerve terminals. In this group of disorders the response to a single stimulus is often subnormal; repetitive stimulation at slow rates (3–10/sec.) causes a decrementing "myasthenic" response, but at fast rates (20–50/sec.) there is progressive facilitation (300 per cent or more) which is sustained. This is particularly striking in carcinomatous myasthenia (Eaton-Lambert syndrome) associated with small-cell carcinoma of the bronchus and other tumours, but it is not exclusive to that state (Fig. 14).

With a train of stimuli ("tetanus") the defect varies with the interval between stimuli. Even at rates as low as 3/sec. there may be an immediate and progressive decline in voltage for the first few responses. The voltage of the evoked response may then continue with little further change; it may continue to decrement, or it may temporarily increase in size. Sometimes the decremental response at slow stimulation is replaced by incremental response at fast stimulation. Commonly no abnormality is seen unless the muscle has first been fatigued or rendered ischaemic (Fig. 15). There may or may not be post-tetanic potentiation. Commonly this is followed by "post-activation exhaustion" for 10–30 min.

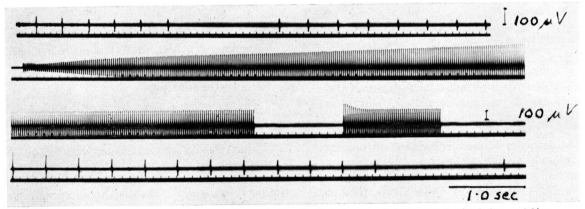

FIG. 14. Carcinomatous myasthenia. Recording as in Fig. 13. Note decrementing response to stimulation at 2·3/sec. and incrementing response to stimulation at 50/sec. Calibration: 100 μV. and 1·0 sec.

The findings on examination depend on the degree of reduction of safety factor for transmission and the recent activation history of the muscle. The safety factor is strikingly restored by anticholinesterase drugs. Various pharmacological analogues have been proposed for the loss of safety factor in myasthenia gravis. It can be entirely accounted for by the morphological changes at the endplates which appear to be damaged by an immunological process.

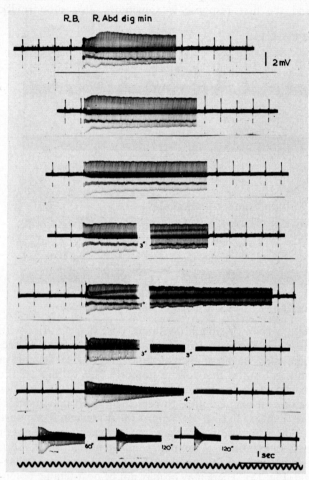

FIG. 15. Myasthenia gravis. Recording is continuous apart from brief breaks of durations indicated on trace. Supramaximal stimulation of right ulnar nerve at 4 and 50/sec. showing delayed myasthenic response and post-tetanic facilitation.

Galvanic Stimulation of Muscle

When a long pulse of unidirectional current (about 100 msec.) is passed longitudinally through a muscle it stimulates muscle fibres at lower threshold than nerve fibres owing to the longer chronaxie of the muscle. This type of stimulation may provoke fibrillation of denervated muscle before the appearance of spontaneous fibrillation. The latent period decreases as muscle degeneration proceeds and the amplitude of fibrillation potentials increases at the same time.

The same phenomenon occurs with slowly rising or "triangular" pulses of current which may therefore be used to detect early denervation by selective stimulation

of denervated muscle. The response is due to the lowered power of accommodation of denervated muscle. A similar change is found in myotonic muscle and accounts for the repetitive firing noted above.

Measurement of Accommodation

When a depolarizing stimulus is applied gradually to a nerve or muscle fibre the threshold for stimulation is higher than the threshold for abrupt (rectangular) pulses of short duration. This is due to accommodation—a metabolic process tending to restore polarization and depending on oxygen and calcium ions.

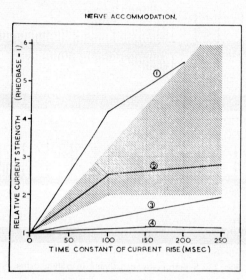

FIG. 16. The time course of accommodation is measured by charting the progressive rise in threshold which occurs when slowly rising currents are used. The shaded area represents the normal range and (2) is a mean value. (1) Increased accommodation in hypercalcaemia; (3) decreased accommodation in spontaneous hypothermia; (4) hypocalcaemic tetany.

Breakdown of accommodation in peripheral nerve fibres is responsible for the spontaneous iterative firing of nerve fibres which causes clinical tetany or, in lesser degree, the "doublet", "triplet" or "multiplet" responses to stimulation described on page 346. The time constant of accommodation is measured from a plot of firing thresholds to slowly rising electric currents of different rates of rise. (The time constant (λ) is the reciprocal of the slope of the line connecting these points.) Accommodation is lowered by hypocalcaemia, hypomagnesaemia, hypoxia, hyperkalaemia and hypothermia. It is raised by hypercalcaemia (Fig. 16).

Intensity–Duration Curve

The minimum current which will stimulate, regardless of its duration, is the *rheobase* of the tissue. If the duration of stimulation is progressively reduced the threshold stimulus increases. (The time factor depends on the type of stimulator.) *Chronaxie* is the time required for a stimulus of twice the rheobase. It is therefore a measure of the time constant of the intensity–duration curve (Fig. 17). As nerve degenerates its chronaxie lengthens and the rheobase rises until eventually the nerve fibres are not excitable. If the stimulus is applied to a "motor point" (where a motor nerve enters a muscle) the muscle fibres continue to respond by direct stimulation after the nerve can no longer be stimulated, but its rheobase is much higher and its chronaxie very much longer than the nerve's. The technique is complicated by certain practical difficulties but has some advantages of simplicity which render it useful as a screening test. It is particularly valuable in the differential diagnosis between myositis and denervation which may be difficult by electromyography. It is also useful for following the progress of reinnervation.

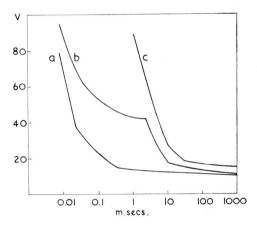

FIG. 17. Intensity–duration curve: (a) normal muscle; (b) partial denervation; (c) total denervation.

Galvanic–Tetanus Ratio

Similar information may be obtained by plotting the ratio of thresholds to a prolonged rectangular stimulus ("galvanic") and a short rectangular pulse or rapidly alternating current ("tetanic"). This is, in effect, plotting two points on the intensity–duration curve so its value is restricted to the extreme situations—normal or complete denervation.

Nerve Conduction Velocity

The conduction velocity of a nerve fibre is proportional to its diameter. It is calculated by measuring the time required for an action potential (evoked by electrical stimulation) to traverse a known length of nerve. A muscular response may be used as an index but, to eliminate the uncertainty introduced by slowing in the terminal branches and delay at the neuromuscular junction, it is necessary to measure the latency from two points on the nerve and, by subtraction, obtain the time-difference between the two cathodal points. For afferent fibres or antidromic conduction it is necessary to record the (compound) nerve action potential, using superimposed oscilloscope traces or an averaging computer to extract the low-voltage nerve action potential from "noise".

Conduction velocity is decreased by any lesion causing demyelination or marked constriction of nerve fibres. (With compressive lesions, as in entrapment syndromes, the reduced velocity may be quite local (Fig. 18).) Axonal or nerve cell lesions do not cause slowing until dying back occurs, with Wallerian-type degeneration of axon and myelin. Thus, a finding of significantly reduced conduction velocity invariably means damage to the peripheral nerve, but neuronal-axonal damage is possible without slowing.

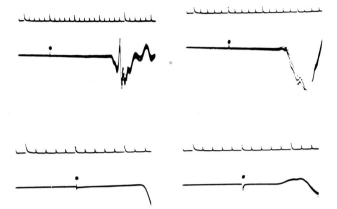

FIG. 18. Motor nerve conduction velocity. Right carpal tunnel syndrome. Supramaximal stimulation of right (a, b) and left (c, d) median nerves at elbow (a, c) and wrist (b, d). Time of stimulation is marked by a spot. After a delay due to conduction of the nerve impulse, the action potential of abductor pollicis brevis is recorded by surface electrodes. Time marks are 1 and 5 msec. (scale varies). The latency at the right wrist is twice that at the left, but the additional latency due to stimulating at the elbow is substantially the same on each side.

SUMMARY

It will be seen that no single electrodiagnostic test provides an answer to a diagnostic problem, but a combination of electromyography, nerve conduction, nerve excitability, and neuromuscular transmission studies will usually permit a statement about the physiological state of nerves and muscle which are accessible to stimulation and detection. The further interpretation of the pathophysiological information can only be made along with other clinical or histological data. Like the microscope, electrophysiology extends the range of the human senses. It does not replace them, but enables earlier recognition of abnormal function.

FURTHER READING

Buchthal, F. and Rosenfalck, A. (1966), "Evoked Action Potentials and Conduction Velocity in Human Sensory Nerves," *Brain Research*, **3**, 1–122.

Buchthal, F. and Rosenfalck, P. (1966), "Spontaneous Electrical Activity of Human Muscle," *Electroencephalography and Clinical Neurophysiology*, **20**, 321–336.

Coërs, C. and Woolf, A. L. (1959), *The Innervation of Muscle*. Oxford: Blackwell.

Guld, C., Rosenfalck, A. and Willison, R. G. (1970), "Technical Factors in Recording Electrical Activity of Muscle and Nerve in Man," *Electroencephalography and Clinical Neurophysiology*, **28**, 399–413.

Kaeser, H. E. (1970), "Nerve Conduction Velocity Measurements," in *Handbook of Clinical Neurology*, i, 116–196 (P. J. Vinken and G. W. Bruyn, Eds.). Amsterdam: North-Holland Publishing Co.

Lenman, J. A. R. and Ritchie, A. E. (1970), *Clinical Electromyography*. London: Pitman.

Licht, S. (Ed.) (1961), *Electrodiagnosis and Electromyography*. Connecticut: Licht.

Magladery, J. W., McDougal, D. B. and Stoll, J. (1957), "Electro-physiological Studies of Nerve and Reflex Activity in Normal Man, I, II, III and IV," *Bulletin of Johns Hopkins Hospital*, **88**, 265–519.

Simpson, J. A. (1962), "The Clinical Physiology of the Lower Motor Neuron," *Developmental Medicine and Child Neurology*, **4**, 55–64.

Simpson, J. A. (1966), "Disorders of Neuromuscular Transmission," *Proceedings of the Royal Society of Medicine*, **59**, 993–998.

Walton, J. N. (Ed.) (1969), *Disorders of Voluntary Muscle*, 2nd edition. London: Churchill.

3. MONITORING OF THE INTRACRANIAL PRESSURE

NILS LUNDBERG

METHODS

Since lumbar puncture was introduced as a clinical procedure by Quincke in 1891, the CSF pressure has been used as a measure of the intracranial pressure (ICP). The CSF pressure is well defined as the pressure just necessary to prevent escape of fluid into a needle introduced into the subarachnoid space or ventricular system.[2] Of course, its value depends on to what extent it is representative of the pressure in other compartments of the cranial cavity. We know that there may be considerable differences in pressure between separate parts of the cranio-spinal cavity, as when there is a tentorial pressure cone or, as shown by Langfitt,[9,10] when an intracranial balloon is rapidly expanded. Apart from such limitations, pressure variations seem to be transmitted between the brain and the CSF—and vice versa—almost as freely as in a homogeneous fluid or semifluid compartment, and the use of the CSF pressure as a standard measure of the ICP is justified.

However, there are several reasons for rejecting the conventional method of assessing the ICP by a once-only measurement of the lumbar CSF pressure. One is the possible existence of a cranio-spinal block, which means false values and the risk of acute herniation. The dynamic nature of the intracranial pressure in cases of intracranial hypertension and the risk of leakage at the side of the needle *in situ*[18] may also cause misleading measurements.

Recently, attempts have been made to monitor the ICP by means of miniature stress-sensitive transducers implanted in the subdural or epidural space (for references *see* 26). Such measurements are influenced by different parameters, such as elasticity of surrounding tissues, local tissue reaction, shape and size of the probe, etc. Only by referring such "pressures"—or, properly speaking, stress-strain relationships[12]—to the CSF pressure, can they be used for quantitative assessment of the ICP.

To be meaningful, therefore, monitoring of the ICP should be based on continuous recordings, either of the ventricular fluid pressure (VFP) in a closed hydrostatic system with insignificant elasticity, or by stress-sensitive transducers placed intracranially.

An electronic technique for recording the VFP in neurosurgical patients was introduced by Guillaume and Janny in 1951.[4] An elaborate method for continuous recording of the VFP has been used in clinical work in this department since 1956.[14] In order to minimize the risk of intracranial infection, to benefit from technical developments and to make the equipment easier to handle, the original method has since undergone modifications,[22] but its main features are unchanged (Fig. 1). A technique for monitoring the ICP by an epidural transducer[20] has recently been introduced in this department and the epidural "pressure" related to the VFP by simultaneous recordings.

Recording of the Ventricular Fluid Pressure

The ventricle, preferably the right frontal horn, is punctured with a flexible thin-walled polyvinyl catheter with an outer diameter of 1·5 mm.* The ventricular end of the catheter is closed and rounded off and provided with two side-holes within 10 mm. of the tip. At the time of puncture it is mounted on a specially designed stopcock ("head-cock") with two nozzles, one for the ventricular catheter and one for the plastic tubing leading to the transducer. The other opening of the head-cock is closed by a perforated cap fitted with a rubber washer through which a stylet may be inserted into the ventricular catheter. On puncture the ventricular catheter is fitted with the stylet, which should not obstruct the lumen, and connected to the recording apparatus. By these means the puncture can be made under pressure control which makes it easy to know when and at which depth the tip penetrates into the ventricle without letting out fluid. The ventricular catheter is tightly fixed in the burr-hole by a rubber plug. Thus, traumatization of the brain tissue due to movements of the catheter is minimized and also a guarantee against leakage is obtained. After closure of the wound the head-cock is fixed to the skin by sutures (Fig. 1).

The ventricular catheter is connected to a diaphragm transducer and the pressure is recorded by a specially designed ink-writing recorder. The transducer may be fixed on the patient's head (Figs. 1A and B) or on a separate stand where it is movable upwards and downwards for adjustment of the reference level to the position of the patient's head (Fig. 1C). This adjustment is facilitated by a water level; the recorder writes linearly

---

* Cat. No. 18–032, Eschman, England.

A

B

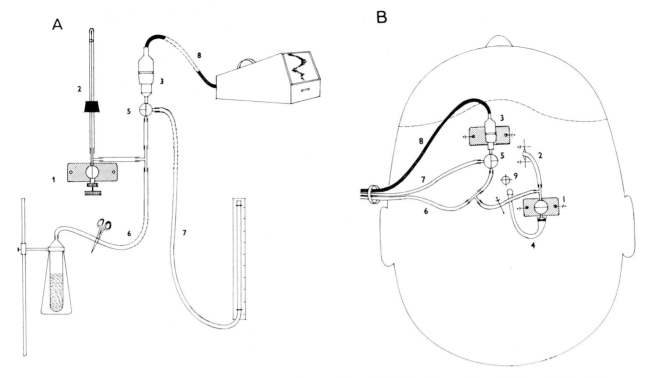

Fig. 1, A and B. Schematic drawing of the set-up for recording of VFP when the transducer is fixed on the head. In A the ventricular catheter is fitted with stylet and rubber plug, i.e. ready for ventricular puncture under pressure control. (Sundbärg *et al.*)

1—Head-cock
2—Ventricular catheter
3—Transducer
4—Rubber catheter for sampling and ventriculography
5—Three-way stopcock

6—PVC tube for drainage of CSF
7—PVC tube for calibration
8—Cable to recording apparatus
9—Bregma

and with square coordinates within a range of −10 to +100 mm. Hg. on a 10 cm. wide paper moving with a speed of 12 cm./hr. Calibration of the apparatus can be done electrically or by means of an open bore fluid manometer connected to the transducer. CSF can be drained, occasionally or continuously, into a closed, thin-walled rubber bag which is kept inside a bottle, and is vertically movable on a stand (Fig. 1). For quantitative measurements of the ventricular fluid pressure, the equipment may be supplemented by an electronic analyser (*see* p. 364).

Measures Against Infection

The risk of infection (*see below*) has prompted modifications of the technique. One aim has been to protect the fluid system from contamination from without, another to get as much as possible of the fluid-containing parts autoclavable or disposable. At present all tubings and connections are autoclaved and kept as disposable sets ready for immediate use. The pressure chamber of the transducers are sterilized by being kept filled with antiseptic solution (25 per cent glutaraldehyde).

Connecting the ventricular catheter with the transducer, filling the system with fluid and all other preparations for ventricular puncture are done under strict aseptic conditions in the operating theatre. All measures that require opening of the fluid system while recording is going on, e.g. calibration, sampling of CSF, insufflation

of air for pneumography, are also done with strict adherance to aseptic technique.

Samples of CSF for cell-counts and cultures are taken every second or third day. The CSF is withdrawn from the stopcock at the outer end of the ventricular catheter. After one week of continuous recording, all tubings and the transducer are exchanged and samples of fluid from various parts of the system are cultured. On removal of the ventricular catheter the tip of the catheter and the rubber plug are also cultured.

Antibiotics are not given unless cell-counts, cultures or clinical symptoms indicate infection of the CSF spaces.

Epidural Recording

The transducer* has the shape of a coin 2 mm. thick and 12 mm. in diameter. It is inserted into the epidural space through a burr-hole and placed 3–4 cm. from the border of the hole with the pressure sensitive membrane facing the dura.[20] For routine use the same equipment used for recording of the VFP is connected. When the two pressures are recorded simultaneously the two transducers are connected to a two-channel potentiometer recorder.

Preliminary results of simultaneous recording of VFP and epidural pressure[26] showed that rapid deviations in the

* Manufactured by the Central Institute for Industrial Research, Oslo, Norway.

C

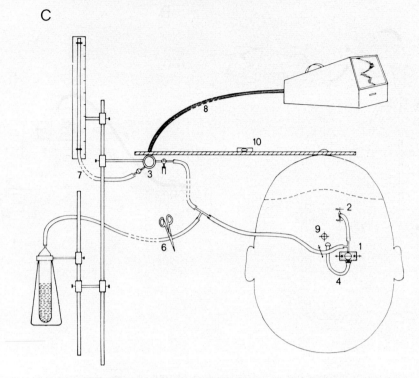

Fig. 1, C. Schematic drawing of the set-up for recording of VFP when the transducer is movable on a stand (Sundbärg *et al.*).

1—Head-cock
2—Ventricular catheter
3—Transducer with one two-way and one three-way
    stop cock
4—Rubber catheter for sampling and ventriculography
6—PVC tube for drainage of CSF
7—PVC tube for calibration
8—Cable to recording apparatus
9—Bregma
10—Water-level

VFP tracing were reflected by similar deviations in the epidural pressure tracing. Under standard conditions there was a linear correlation between the two pressures, the epidural pressure being constantly higher than the VFP. The difference ranged between 10 and 40 mm. Hg.; it increased in proportion to the pressure level, the slopes of the regression lines varying slightly in different patients. Deviations from the linear correlation between the two pressures were observed under certain conditions, e.g. after lowering a high intracranial pressure by removal of fluid.

The results of simultaneous recordings of the VFP and the epidural pressure indicate that the latter may give adequate information about variations in the ICP and with certain limitations permit approximate quantitative assessments of the actual VFP level. One disadvantage of the miniature transducers has been that they have not been designed for calibration in relation to atmospheric pressure during the recordings. Recently a device has been presented which seems to solve this problem.[23] Technical development will certainly give us implantable transducers which are reliable enough to justify widespread use in clinical neurosurgery, especially in cases in

which there is no need for drainage of fluid or instillation of gas for pneumography and no demand for strictly quantitative measurements.

PATIENT STUDIES

The present material includes 848 patients admitted to the neurosurgical department during the years 1956–1970. The main indication for recording of the VFP was diagnosed or suspected intracranial hypertension. Only patients in whom monitoring of the ICP was presumed to be of appreciable diagnostic and/or therapeutic advantage were selected, in particular patients in whom obstruction of the fluid pathways could be presumed. The diagnoses of the patients are given in Table 1.

Complications of Recording of the VFP

Hemorrhage and Local Reaction of Brain Tissue

The ventricular puncture or the indwelling ventricular catheter did not cause clinically significant intracranial hemorrhage in any case. After the puncture a slight asymptomatic admixture of red blood cells was sometimes found in the fluid samples and in one case

TABLE 1

	1956–1960	1960–1970
Verified intracranial tumour	98	331
Non classified intracranial tumour	2	8
Non verified or suspected intracranial tumour	6	72
Carcinomatosis (or sarcomatosis) of meninges	4	7
Brain abscess	3	9
Intracranial hemorrhage	5	53
Ischemic vascular lesion	3	15
Hydrocephalus	13	65
Head injury	2	62
Papilledema, "pseudo-tumour cerebri"	5	22
Encephalitis, meningitis		10
Miscellaneous	2	51
	143	705

ventriculography showed a filling defect in the punctured ventricle, interpreted as an intraventricular clot.

Histologic investigation of the tract in the brain caused by the ventricular catheter showed that the diameter of the necrosis was small (0·5–2 mm.) in diameter, that the secondary cell reaction was slight and that the recording time had little influence on the extent of necrosis and degree of secondary reaction.[14] X-ray examination of the skull in 35 patients, > year after recording of the VFP by the present technique, showed no signs of calcification in the catheter tracts. After conventional ventricular puncture for ventriculography such calcification has been found in 13·3 per cent and are considered to signify hemorrhage and traumatization of brain tissue around the tract.[3]

Intracranial Infection

The first 130 patients in the present series were studied with regard to cell-counts, cultures and post mortem signs of intracranial infection.[14] All findings indicating intracranial infection could be explained by the original disease or by measures other than the VFP recording.

In a subsequent series (705 cases, 1960–1970) pathologic cell-counts, positive cultures and clinical symptoms of infection in the CSF occurred with varying frequency during different periods. This is illustrated by Fig. 2.[22]

Sequelae

Sequelae in the form of epileptic seizures or other functional disorders of the brain ascribable to the VFP recording have not been observed in our series.

Comments

With the present method, traumatization of the brain tissue by the ventricular catheter is slight and probably significantly less than with the conventional technique of single ventricular puncture for ventriculography or drainage of fluid. On the other hand the indwelling ventricular cannula involves a certain risk of bacterial

contamination of the CSF spaces which cannot be neglected. This risk has been a perpetual challenge since the method was adopted in clinical work. During the first ten years it was not a problem of significance, but as demonstrated by Fig. 2 the number of positive cultures and clinical infections increased considerably during the period 1966–1968, prompting us to face the question whether continuous recording of the ventricular fluid pressure could be used as a routine aid in clinical work.

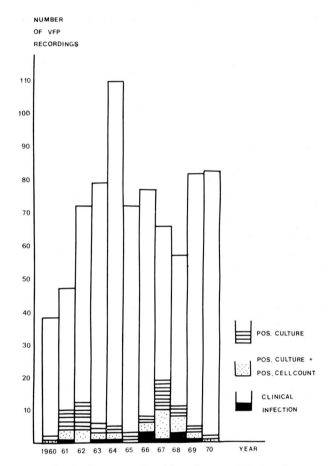

FIG. 2. Frequency of positive culture, pathologic cell-counts, and clinical infections during the period 1960–70. The cultured samples of CSF and the samples for cell-counting were withdrawn from the ventricles during the recording and when the ventricular catheter was removed at end of recording. *See text.* (Sundbärg *et al.*)

Search for possible causes revealed, among other things, that the antiseptic fluid Septin+, a quartinary ammonium base used earlier for sterilization of ventricular catheter, tubings and pressure chamber of the transducer was not reliable and that many infections appeared after pneumography, in particular after ventriculography, performed in the X-ray department. Furthermore, the cultures showed that bacteria which are usually regarded as non-pathogenic such as *sarcina*, *chromobacter* and *Staphylococcus albus* may colonize in the extracranial part of the fluid system and even propagate intracranially and give rise to meningitis.

The favourable trend during the last two years (Fig. 2) has convinced us that the risk of infection can be satisfactorily controlled and that the present technique is sufficiently safe to permit routine use in cases in which control of the intracranial pressure is important and particularly in cases in which ventriculography, drainage of CSF or intraventricular administration of drugs may be indicated as well. If monitoring of the ICP is the only purpose and there is no demand for strictly quantitative measurements it would be justified to use epi- or subdural recording instead. If these techniques are otherwise equally useful, epidural recording is preferable because it certainly involves less risk of intracranial infection and damage to the cerebral cortex.

STANDARDS

When measuring the spinal fluid pressure by the usual open fluid manometer the point of puncture is usually used as zero and the pressure is given in millimetres of fluid. There is no reason to preserve these conventions when the fluid pressure is measured in the ventricles by means of an electronic technique.

In order to simplify calibration, a reference level that roughly corresponds to the uppermost part of the CSF spaces at the time of measurement was originally chosen. The calibration is then easily done by placing the transducer approximately 1·5 cm. below the uppermost point of the head by means of a water level. With this reference level and calculated on the basis of accepted values for the normal spinal CSF pressure[19] the range of a normal VFP in the supine strictly horizontal position ("standard position") would be 1–10 mm. Hg.[14] A pressure level above 15 mm. Hg. should definitely be regarded as pathological provided that the patient is awake, relaxed and has normal respiration. If the transducer is fixed to the head, instead of being moved when the position of the head changes, then these figures are, of course, not valid for any position of the head. However, by fixing the

transducer near the sagittal midline in front of the coronal suture, the divergences would be negligible, provided that the patient is in the supine position. If there is a need for strictly quantitative assessments, e.g. to distinguish between a normal and a pathologically elevated pressure, the measurements should be done with the patient in the standard position.

The ICP should always be given in millimetres of mercury, for the purpose of easily relating it to the arterial and venous blood pressures. In particular, the difference between the mean arterial pressure and the VFP ("cerebral perfusion pressure") is of clinical interest[21] (Figs. 4 and 21).

CLINICAL APPLICATION

The following routine is usually employed in those patients with intracranial expanding lesions who have been selected for monitoring of the ICP.

The recording is started one or two days before the planned operation. Urgency sometimes makes immediate drainage of fluid necessary; otherwise the pressure is recorded for at least two hours to obtain information of the intracranial dynamics. In some patients it may be necessary to keep the pressure on a low level, usually between 10–20 mm. Hg., for some days before operation in order to relieve the brain stem or optic nerves from stress.

Pneumography is done under pressure control.[1,14] In most cases the procedure is started by lumbar insufflation of gas. If filling of the intracranial fluid spaces is insufficient, gas is insufflated and fluid withdrawn through the ventricular catheter. The risk of deterioration after pneumography due to acute elevations of the ICP is well known and has been an argument for immediate operation after pneumography. This routine may be discarded if the VFP is recorded and fluid can be drained at any moment (Fig. 3). Unless operation is urgent for other reasons it will usually be delayed for one or two days after pneumography.

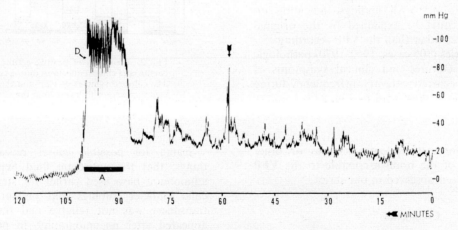

FIG. 3. Case 130 A.M., 57-year-old man. *Verified metastasis in the left frontal lobe.* Intracranial hypertension with marked plateau waves preoperatively (see Fig. 12). Recording of the VFP 4–6 hr. after *ventriculography* (Lundberg, *Acta Psychiat. & Neurol Scand.*, 1960). Arrow—patient coughs; A—attack of unconsciousness, marked periodic breathing of the Cheyne–Stokes' type, clonic convulsions succeeded by tonic flexion of the arms; D—drainage of fluid; a few minutes later, the tonic–clonic phenomena had ceased and consciousness had returned to former state.

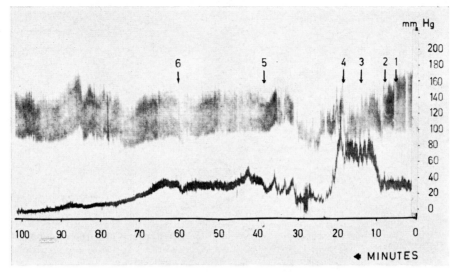

FIG. 4. Case 581 A.N., 50-year-old man. *Verified metastasis in left cerebellar hemisphere.* Spontaneous plateau waves before operation. Simultaneous recording of the VFP (lower tracing) and the arterial blood pressure in femoral artery (upper tracing) before and after induction of general anesthesia. The anterior axillary line was used as common reference level. Note the reduction of the "perfusion pressure" after administration of neuroleptic drugs. 1–3—Intravenous administration of atropine, fentanyl and benzperidol; 4—intubation; 5—connection to respirator; 6—intravenous infusion of urea.

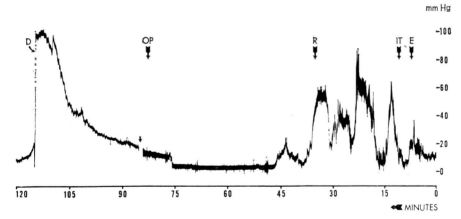

FIG. 5. Case 129 K.B., 60-year-old man. *Verified glioma in basal ganglia and third ventricle.* Spontaneous plateau waves of increasing duration before operation. Recording of the VFP during operation (Torkildsen shunt, general anesthesia with controlled respiration). Note the rise in VFP after the patient had been turned to the prone position with head bent forward. (Lundberg, *Acta Psychiat. & Neurol. Scand.*, 1960.) E—administration of evipan + succinylcholine; IT—intubation; R—respirator connected; OP—operation started; D—drainage of fluid.

Recording of the VFP during operations under general anesthesia has proved very valuable. Among other things it has taught us and our anesthesiologists that induction of, and subsequent disturbances during, general anesthesia may provoke dangerous acute elevations of the ICP in patients with intracranial hypertension (Figs. 4, 5 and 21). Drainage of fluid or administration of hypertonic solutions should be started before the induction in those patients. Recording of the VFP also helps to detect malfunction of the respirator, inappropriate positioning of the patient and other things that might jeopardize optimal operative conditions. Furthermore, during the operation the indwelling ventricular catheter facilitates adequate drainage of fluid without additional traumatization of the brain (Fig. 5).

After the operation it is our policy to record the VFP, without drainage, for the early detection of a hematoma, the failure of a shunt or any other cause of postoperative intracranial hypertension (Fig. 6). Apart from urgent situations fluid should not be drained unless the surgeon has decided either to reopen the wound or to resort to non-surgical treatment. Usually the ventricular catheter is removed 3–5 days after the operation.

In patients with severe traumatic brain injury or

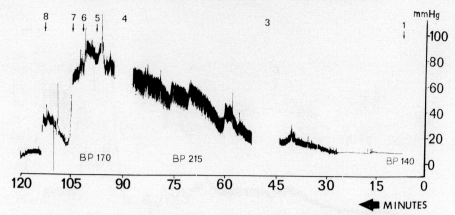

FIG. 6. Case 644 A.P., 55-year-old woman. *Verified metastasis in left cerebellar hemisphere. Postoperative hematoma.* Slightly increased ICP preoperatively, no plateau waves. Recording of VFP immediately after the operation (removal of tumour in the sitting position).

1—End of operation
3—Transfer to the ward
4—Transfer back to the operating theatre

5—Intubation
6—Respirator connected
7—Reoperation begins
8—Dura re-opened

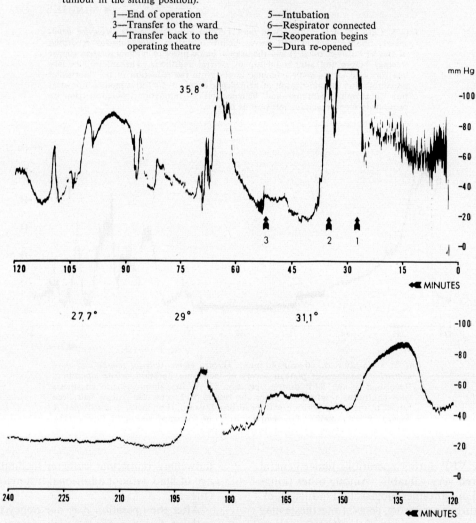

FIG. 7. Case 172 B.K., 30-year-old woman. *Severe traumatic brain injury; local contusion of the left temporal lobe.* Operation under hypothermia: Removal of contused left temporal lobe. Recording of the VFP 4–8 hr. after accident, before and during induction of hypothermia. The first part of the tracing (uppermost right) shows a very high pressure-level (60–80 mm. Hg.). Figures above the curve indicate rectal temperature in centigrades. The lower tracing is an immediate continuation of the upper one. (Lundberg, Troupp & Lorin, *J. Neurosurg.*, 1965.) Arrow 1—Sudden rise to a pressure far above the range of the apparatus (>115 mm. Hg.) accompanied by respiratory arrest; artificial respiration started immediately and a respirator was connected soon thereafter. Arrow 2—Infusion of urea. Arrow 3—Cooling begins.

subarachnoid hemorrhage, information obtained from the VFP tracings may serve as a guide to treatment. Measures to reduce intracranial hypertension such as drainage of fluid, controlled hyperventilation, hypertonic solutions, hypothermia, and corticosteroids become more rational if the indications are based on, and the results are controlled by, monitoring of the ICP[5,8,14,16] (Figs. 7 and 9).

In cases of hydrocephalus recording of the VFP may be used for checking the effect of a shunt operation. However, it should not be used routinely in hydrocephalic infants before or after ventriculo-atrial shunting because of the risk of bacterial colonization in the shunt.

INTERPRETATION OF THE VFP TRACINGS

Two main kinds of information may be gained from the VFP records, i.e. about the pressure level and about the variations of the pressure.

Pressure Level

In many cases a rough estimation of the pressure level is all that is needed. For this purpose the following categories may be used:

normal level ($1 < 10$ mm. Hg.),

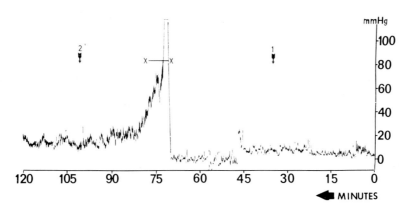

FIG. 8. Case 614 V.Å., 52-year-old man. *Saccular aneurysm of the basilar artery, subarachnoid hemorrhage, basal arachnoiditis and hydrocephalus.* Recording of the VFP six weeks after first bleeding (preliminaries for a planned shunt operation). First part of tracing shows a pressure-level within normal range. The rapid rise in pressure to >115 mm. Hg. was caused by a *rupture of the aneurysm and rebleeding* as proved by typical symptoms and subsequent lumbar puncture. 1—Awake, slightly confused; X–X—headache, stuporous; 2—drowsy, agitated, severely confused.

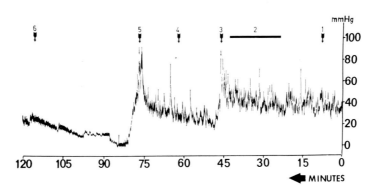

FIG. 9. Case 614 (see Fig. 8). Recording of the VFP two days after the tracing in Fig. 8. The pressure level was now considerably elevated and the patient was still somewhat drowsy and confused. The tracing shows two incidents of rapidly increasing VFP (arrows 3 and 5) accompanied by temporary deterioration. At the second incident, alarming symptoms including respiratory standstill and stupor occurred. Bother elevations were cut short by drainage of fluid. Similar occurrences necessitated continuous drainage of fluid while waiting for the shunt operation.

1—Awake, slightly drowsy
2—Increasingly restless and confused
3—Release of fluid
4—Stuporous
5—Respiratory arrest (two minutes), release of fluid
6—Awake, very drowsy, respiration adequate

slightly increased (11–20 mm. Hg.),
moderately increased (21–40 mm. Hg.),
severely increased (>40 mm. Hg.).

However, a quantitative representation of the tracing may be useful. Such a representation may be obtained in different ways. One is to calculate the mean pressure during a period of, say, one hour by reading single values at predetermined intervals. Such mean values have been used for evaluating the relation between the VFP level and symptoms and signs of intracranial hypertension.[14]

Alternatively we have used a specially constructed electronic analyzer, connected to the recording apparatus, which reads the pressures at predetermined intervals (0·1–10 sec.) and groups them into 13 classes.[7] At any time the counts of the different classes can be read and a frequency diagram drawn. This method gives a more varied picture including gross variations, basic level, etc., and makes it easy to survey the changes in pressure during long periods without uncoiling the paper roll. It has been used for studying the effect of corticosteroids[8] and different hypertonic solutions on the ICP and has also proved valuable in daily clinical work.

Variations of the VFP

(1) Pulse and respiration. Variations caused by the arterial pulse and the normal respiration are present in all tracings unless they are ironed out by damping. They increase in amplitude when the pressure level rises (Fig. 6). Until now we have not attached any special importance to these variations of the VFP. As a rule they are damped by an adjustable clamp on the tube between the ventricular catheter and the transducer.

Apart from these rhythmic variations the tracings show a variety of irregular and short-lasting deflections both at a normal and, more markedly, at a pathologically increased pressure level. These variations are related to straining, coughing, movements of the head, etc. If the patient is ventilated by a respirator they may completely disappear.

(2) Other rhythmic variations. Analysis of the tracings from patients with severe disturbance of cerebral functions revealed two kinds of pathologic rhythmic variations.[14] One showed a frequency of $\frac{1}{2}$–2 waves/min. related to periodic breathing of the Cheyne–Stokes' type (Figs. 10 and 11). The frequency of the other varied between 4–8/min., and they were found to coincide with similar waves in tracings of the arterial blood pressure, so-called Traube–Hering–Mayer waves (Fig. 12).

The clinical importance of these rhythmic variations is limited. Cheyne–Stokes' breathing is known to occur normally during sleep, at least for short periods and short sequences of Traube–Hering–Mayer waves can also be seen under normal conditions. If persisting for long periods rhythmic variations of the VFP may be a sign of dysfunction of the brain stem. The appearance of rhythmic variations with a frequency of about 1/min., i.e. signifying periodic breathing, may also signal circulatory or respiratory disorders of other origin.

(3) Plateau waves. In patients with intracranial hypertension variations of the ICP sometimes give the VFP tracing a typical plateau-shaped appearance. This third type of pressure variation differs entirely in character and significance from the others. Being closely related to acute cerebral symptoms in patients with intracranial hypertension, this phenomenon deserves to be discussed in detail.

Definition and Occurrence of Plateau Waves

Plateau waves are characterized by a sudden elevation in pressure, continuation of the pressure on a high level for some time, and finally a rapid fall to or below the original level (Figs. 13 and 14). If fully developed they show a considerable height and duration, usually ranging between 60–160 mm. Hg. and lasting for 5–20 min.

Plateau waves may occur with varying intervals—from many hours to a few minutes. Sometimes they appear in sequences with regular intervals giving the curve a rhythmic appearance (Fig. 17). They have been observed

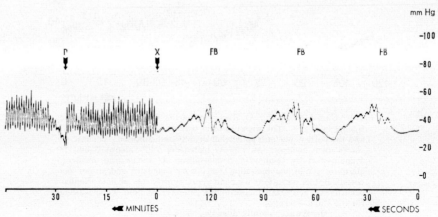

Fig. 10. Case 130 (see Fig. 3). Recording of the VFP performed during final stage when the patient was comatose and had continuous Cheyne-Stokes' breathing (Lundberg, *Acta Psychiat. & Neurol. Scand.*, 1960). FB—Forced breathing; X—change of paperspeed from 6 in./min. to ordinary speed (12 in./hr.); P—painful stimulation.

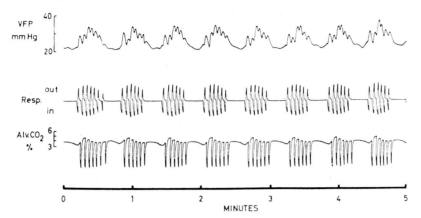

FIG. 11. Case 130 (see Fig. 3). Patient drowsy with marked Cheyne–Stokes' breathing. Polygraphic registration of VFP and respiration by a themistor in face mask and alveolar CO_2 by an infrared analyzer. (Kjällquist, Lundberg & Pontén, *Acta Neurol. Scand.*, 1964.)

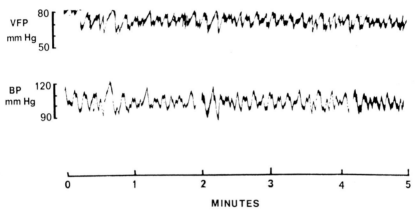

FIG. 12. Case 134 S.B., 34-year-old man. *Verified malignant glioma in right parietal region.* Frequent, large plateau waves preoperatively. Simultaneous recording of VFP and arterial blood pressure in the femoral artery (BP). The tracings represent the horizontal part of a plateau wave. *Note—* Waves with a frequency of about six per minute synchronously appearing in both tracings (Traube–Hering–Mayer waves). (Kjällquist, Lundberg and Pontén, *Acta Neurol. Scand.*, 1964.)

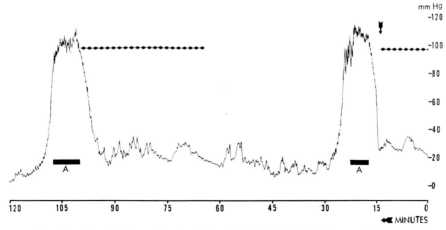

FIG. 13. Case 130 (see Fig. 3). Intermittent headache for three months before admission. Recording of the VFP after admission showed huge spontaneous plateau waves occurring with intervals varying between 20 min. and 2 hr. Between the waves the patient was torpid and somewhat disorientated but fully conscious. The plateau waves were accompanied by attacks which were at first misinterpreted as epileptic seizures (Lundberg, *Acta Psychiat. & Neurol. Scand.*, 1960). A—Attacks of restlessness followed by unconsciousness, and clonic movements followed by flexor rigidity of the arms.

exclusively in cases with a moderate or severe increase of the mean VFP (> 20 mm. Hg.). Almost all cases with plateau waves have papilledema. As a rule plateau waves do not occur in patients with extremely high pressure levels (> 50 mm. Hg.). However, in such cases the final failure of cerebral circulation may be preceded by a rapid rise of the VFP to a still higher level (Fig. 16).

Plateau waves have been recorded in patients with intracranial hypertension of various origin, e.g. supra- and infratentorial tumors, carcinomatosis of the meninges, intracranial hematoma, subarachnoid hemorrhage and traumatic brain injury. They are most often seen in cases of intracranial tumor and meningeal carcinomatosis, less often in traumatic cases and not at all in cases of infantile hydrocephalus. In a mixed series of 48 non-traumatic cases, admitted for suspected space-occupying intracranial lesions, plateau waves were recorded in 21.[14] In 52 cases of severe traumatic head injury plateau waves were recorded in 12 cases.[28]

Clinical Significance of the Plateau Waves

It is an old observation that symptoms and signs of increased intracranial pressure have a tendency to appear acutely, and often in the form of transitory attacks. Such attacks have been given a number of different names such as cerebellar seizures, tonic fits, *crises toniques*, mesen-cephalic (diencephalic, decerebrate) seizures, acute in-carceration, brain stem seizures, acute herniation or coning, etc. Various mechanisms have been suggested for explaining the episodic appearance of the symptoms, such as epileptic discharge or intermittent obstruction of the fluid pathways.

After we began to use continuous recording of the VFP in clinical work, it soon became clear that acute transitory symptoms, as well as acute deterioration in patients with intracranial hypertension, were almost always accom-panied by acute elevations of the intracranial pressure of the plateau wave type. The signs and symptoms most

commonly observed during typical plateau waves were headache, nausea, vomiting, facial flush, air hunger, forced or irregular or periodic breathing, changes in pulse frequency, rise in blood pressure, involuntary micturition, restlessness, confusion, motor agitation, changes in the level of consciousness and various motor phenomena such as clonic movements and tonic rigidity of the limbs.

The plateau waves pertain to a certain stage in the course of a progressive intracranial hypertension. To begin with they may be of moderate height and duration and not accompanied by any symptoms. During the later stages they may augment in size, and especially in duration, and they eventually become accompanied by signs and symptoms of increasing severity and duration (Figs. 14, 15 and 16). There is, however, no consistent relationship between the height of the plateau wave and the severity of the accompanying symptoms. During certain conditions moderate elevations in pressure may be accompanied by alarming symptoms, even respiratory stand-still. Factors of importance seem to be the degree of deformation of the brain stem, infratentorial location of the lesion, systemic circulatory insufficiency, and circulatory or metabolic disturbances of the brain.[15] On the other hand huge waves with a height of more than 100 mm. Hg. may occasionally occur without or with only slight symptoms.

Increasing duration and height of the plateau waves, and decreasing intervals between them are always ominous signs predicting a state of continuously high pressure and lasting signs of brain stem dysfunction preceding the final catastrophe (Figs. 15, 16 and 17). Usually the symptoms disappear promptly after the fall in pressure, whether this occurs spontaneously or is produced by drainage of fluid. However, one single plateau wave accompanied by severe symptoms may be followed by a lasting deterioration even if the pressure returns to the base line.

Thus, transitory elevations of the ICP of the plateau wave type, whether suspected on the basis of clinical symptoms or diagnosed by monitoring of the intracranial

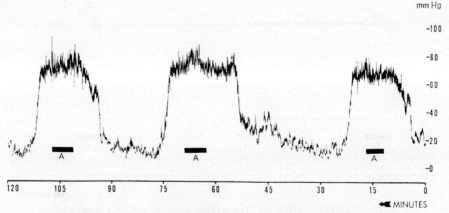

Fig. 14. Case 136 W.P., 60-year-old man. *Verified glioblastoma in central part of right cerebral hemisphere.* Spontaneous plateau waves recorded on fifth day after admission. Between the waves the patient was somewhat torpid and drowsy. During the waves, the following symptoms were noted: restlessness, headache, stupor, flushing of the face, involuntary micturition, Parkinson-like tremor and tonic flexion of the arms, increased rigidity of the neck and the limbs. (Lundberg, *Acta Psychiat. & Neurol. Scand.*, 1960.) A—Attacks of involuntary motor activity.

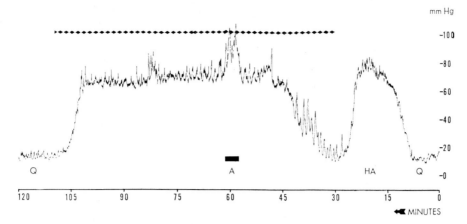

FIG. 15. Case 136 (see Fig. 14). Plateau wave of long duration recorded four days after the graph in Fig. 14. The patient was stuporous during the whole wave as indicated by the dotted line. (Lundberg, *Acta Psychiat. & Neurol. Scand.*, 1960.) Q—Awake, confused; HA—headache; A—attack of generalized clonic movements.

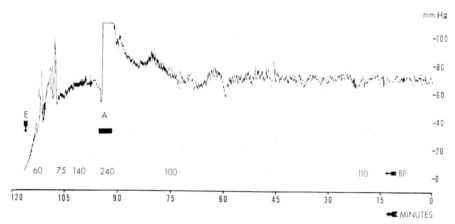

FIG. 16. Case 136 (see Fig. 14). Recording of the VFP 10 days after the graph in Fig. 14 during the final stage 2 hr. before death. The patient was in deep coma and had a shallow, regular respiration. The VFP had been on a high, even level at about 70 mm. Hg. for 4 hr. For no apparent reason it suddenly rose to a level much higher than could be recorded—one may guess to above 200 mm. Hg. At the same time, the blood pressure rose to 240 mm. Hg. After a few minutes both the intracranial and the arterial pressures dropped critically and soon reached about the same level, indicating general vasoparalysis and cessation of cerebral blood flow. Artificial respiration was not given and after a short while the heart stopped beating. (Lundberg, *Acta Psychiat. & Neurol. Scand.*, 1960.) BP—systolic arterial blood pressure; A—respiratory standstill, opistotonus; E—cardiac standstill.

pressure, should always be regarded as a warning signal. They indicate impending deterioration, spontaneous or precipitated by pneumography, induction of anesthesia or operation, or the like.

PATHOGENESIS OF THE PLATEAU WAVES

Continuous recording of the VFP in a number of patients with plateau waves has made it possible to study this phenomenon in detail and to form a hypothesis of its pathogenesis. Some elucidating observations are illustrated by Figs. 18 to 21.

Figure 19 demonstrates that a moderate increase of the ICP (in this case induced by injection of gas for ventriculography) can produce a secondary elevation in pressure in a patient with spontaneous plateau waves. After having reached a high level, this secondary elevation stopped, thus giving the curve an appearance similar to that of a spontaneous plateau wave. After removal of the same amount of gas + fluid the pressure fell to a level considerably above the initial level, indicating a net addition to the intracranial content. Injection of the same amount of gas with the same rate into the ventricles of a patient with a normal or slightly increased ICP provoked no, or only an insignificant secondary elevation. The phenomenon shown in Fig. 18 could also be produced by pressure on a subtemporal decompression from without.[1] Langfitt and his group have been able to produce a similar secondary rise of the ICP and fluctuations similar to plateau waves in animals by inflating an intracranial balloon.[11,12]

As already mentioned (p. 366) plateau waves have not been observed in hydrocephalic infants in spite of the VFP being considerably increased. Furthermore, in patients with frequently occurring plateau waves, subtemporal

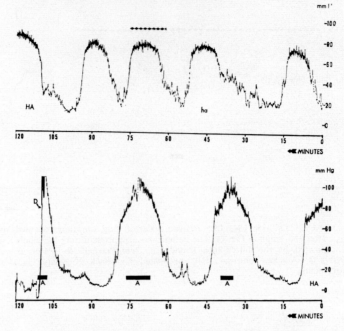

FIG. 17. Case 134 (see Fig. 12). Preoperative recording of a continuous sequence of plateau waves. *Note*—the increasing height of the waves and the simultaneously increasing severity of the symptoms. During the last wave, the pressure rose higher than the apparatus could write (>115 mm. Hg.). The patient became unresponsive and his condition was more alarming than during previous waves. After drainage of fluid, he soon recovered. (Lundberg, *Acta Psychiat. & Neurol. Scand.*, 1960.) ha—slight headache; HA—severe headache; A—attack of drowsiness, rise of blood pressure, varying pulse-frequency, air-hunger and hyperpnea, involuntary micturition, thirst, nausea, stiffness of the neck and weakness of the left arm; D—drainage of fluid.

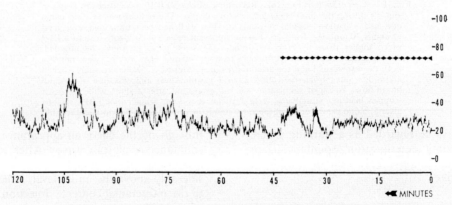

FIG. 18. Case 134 (see Fig. 12). Recording of the VFP four days after *subtemporal decompression*. Should be compared with the preoperative graph in Fig. 17. The patient was completely relieved of the former attacks and did not complain of headache. (Lundberg, *Acta Psychiat. & Neurol. Scand.*, 1960.)

decompression has resulted in a reduction or even disappearance of the plateau waves (Figs. 17 and 18).

Taken together these clinical and experimental observations suggest that the rigid skull and a reduction of the spare space in the cranial cavity or other facilities for compensation of intracranial pressure/volume variations is a prerequisite for plateau waves to occur. They also indicate that the elevation in pressure in the beginning

of a plateau wave is caused by dilatation of cerebral resistance vessels and that this vasomotor reaction may be elicited by an initially relatively moderate increase of the ICP—spontaneous or induced.

This suggestion is supported by the study illustrated in Fig. 20,[24] the main result of which was the consistent finding of an increased cerebral blood volume during plateau waves. An equally consistent finding was that

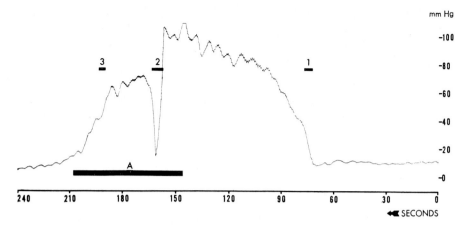

FIG. 19. Case 143 E.S., 62-year-old man. *Verified carcinomatosis of the meninges. Operated cancer of the stomach.* Recording of the VFP during pneumography. Frequent spontaneous plateau waves before the examination. The tracing shows secondary rise of the VFP induced by a primary rise to about 40 mm. Hg. produced by insufflation of gas. *Note:* that withdrawal of about the same amount of fluid + gas leaves the VFP on a level considerably above the initial one, indicating a net addition to the intracranial content. (Lundberg, *Acta Psychiat. & Neurol. Scand.,* 1960.) 1—Injection of 10 ml. oxygen in five seconds; 2—withdrawal of about 12 ml. fluid + oxygen; 3—withdrawal of 5 ml. fluid; A—stupor.

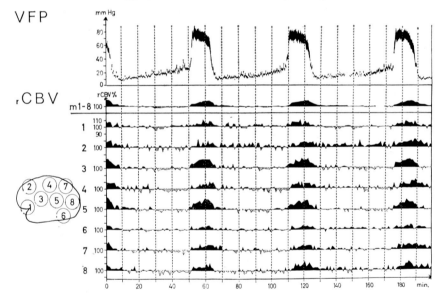

FIG. 20. Case 611 A.E., 28-year-old woman. *Non-verified central glioma in left hemisphere.* Fairly regularly occurring spontaneous plateau waves with a frequency of about one per hour. Simultaneous recording of VFP and *regional cerebral blood volume* (rCBV). The CBV was measured in eight regions of the left hemisphere. The uppermost CBV tracing represents the mean of the eight regions. *Note:* that the VFP decreases *during* the plateau waves whereas the CBV at the same time increases and that the CBV remains unchanged while the VFP slowly rises *between* the waves. (Risberg, Lundberg and Ingvar, *J. Neurosurg.,* 1969.)

during the plateau waves the VFP decreased at the same time as the cerebral blood volume was increasing, while *between* the plateau waves the cerebral blood volume remained constant in spite of a slow increase of the VFP. This discrepancy between the VFP and the cerebral blood volume indicates that apart from the intracranial blood volume at least one more volume variable is involved. There are strong reasons for believing that this variable is the intracranial CSF volume.[2,25,12]

Figure 20 evokes speculation about the role of the CSF flow in the production of plateau waves. The tracing

indicates that CSF is squeezed out from the intracranial fluid spaces during the plateau waves until the pressure falls to a critical level when intracranial hemodynamics are restored, and that the fluid spaces are refilled between the waves until the pressure rises to a level where vasodilatation occurs. Judging from the form of available VFP tracings this mechanism may be a contributory factor in most but not in all cases and may also explain why pressure waves sometimes occur in regular sequences (Fig. 17).

Figure 21 shows simultaneous recording of the VFP and the systemic arterial blood pressure before and during induction of general anesthesia in a patient with spontaneous plateau waves. It demonstrates that plateau waves may occur without any increase of the systemic arterial blood pressure. This phenomenon has been observed in other cases of spontaneous plateau waves[6] and also in patients in whom VFP elevations of the plateau wave type were precipitated by induction of general anesthesia (Fig. 3). However, there are also cases in which the elevation in VFP is accompanied by a marked increase of the blood pressure (Fig. 16).

Our investigation includes studies of the cerebral vessels by angiography and the cerebral blood flow by the isotope clearance technique of Ingvar and Lassen.[17] Angiography showed wider arteries when the pressure was high during a plateau wave than when it was low between two waves. The parasagittal veins on the convexity of the cerebral hemispheres were equally well filled in both instances. Measurements of the cerebral blood flow showed that the flow was lower during the plateau waves. This paradoxical discrepancy between dilatation of the cerebral arteries and increase of the cerebral blood volume on one side, and decrease of the cerebral blood flow on the other, suggests some kind of obstruction of the draining veins.[12]

intracranial pressure. It is probable that a purely mechanical effect obstructs the draining veins causing slowing of the CBF and further congestion of the brain.

As mentioned, this process may occur without any rise of the systemic arterial blood pressure. However, the rise in arterial blood pressure which sometimes accompanies the plateau waves may certainly contribute to the rise in ICP. In his animal experiments Langfitt found involvement of a "pressure response" in the process leading to secondary elevation of the ICP induced by expanding an intracranial balloon.[11]

The dilatation of cerebral resistance vessels forms a link of primary significance in this hypothetical chain of events. It is tempting to assume that the plateau wave phenomenon is related to the autoregulation of the cerebral blood flow, by which a reduction of the perfusion pressure is compensated for by dilatation of cerebral resistance vessels. In any case, if there is a "tight" situation inside the skull, i.e. if we are on the steep part of the pressure/volume curve,[12] small elevations of the ICP may elicit a secondary rise in pressure of the plateau wave type—temporary or lasting. Such small initial elevations might be produced by various causes, e.g. ventriculography, intubation, volatile anesthetics, increase in $PaCO_2$,

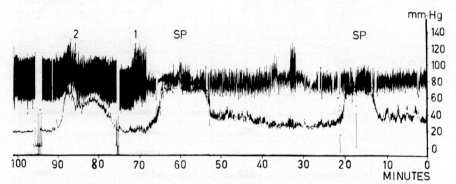

FIG. 21. Case 579 M.N., 26-year-old woman. *Verified glioblastoma in left frontal lobe.* Irregularly occurring spontaneous plateau waves before operation. Simultaneous recording of VFP (lower tracing) and arterial blood-pressure in femoral artery (upper tracing, damped during first two-thirds of recording) before and during induction of general anesthesia. A horizontal level through the right atrium was used as common reference level. *Note:* that the blood pressure does not rise during the plateau waves, resulting in a marked reduction in "perfusion pressure". Nevertheless, the patient got only slight headache and a feeling of unreality during the waves. (Lundberg *et al.,, Progress in Brain Research,* 1968.) SP—spontaneous plateau wave; 1—intravenous administration of fentanyl + benzperidol; 2—intubation.

On the basis of these observations the following hypothesis has been formulated:

Under normal conditions variations of the cerebral vascular resistance and consequent variations of the intracranial blood volume are readily compensated for, probably mainly by the ability of the CSF to pass into and out of the cranial cavity. If the facilities for "spatial buffering"[12] are insufficient because of a space-occupying lesion, such variations may instead initiate a chain of events characterized by the reciprocal relationship between elevation in ICP and dilatation of cerebral resistance vessels. Such vasodilatation means that a greater part of the systemic blood pressure is transmitted to thin-walled vessels of the cerebral vascular bed. The result is swelling of the brain from congestion and a general increase of the

epileptic discharge, painful stimuli, emotional stress, vomiting, coughing or straining; and last, but not least, by the slight additional expansion of an intracranial hematoma, and by refilling of the CSF spaces after a previous wave (Figs. 17, 20).

Acute elevation of the ICP may influence cerebral function in two ways, either by causing local compression and distortion of the brain stem or by reducing the "cerebral perfusion pressure" to subliminal values. From Figs. 4 and 21 it is clear that the "perfusion pressure" may be greatly reduced during plateau waves but also that a considerable reduction may cause only mild symptoms. In cases of carcinomatosis of the meninges, plateau waves accompanied by severe cerebral symptoms have been observed without any signs of a tentorial or tonsillar pressure cone, as seen by encephalography, angiography or post mortem examination.[14] It is probable that a local stress on the brain stem as well as a general reduction in "perfusion pressure" causing cerebral ischemia may be responsible for symptoms during plateau waves.[21]

It still remains to be explained why the elevation in pressure usually stops at levels between 60 and 100 mm. Hg., why the pressure remains at this level and why it falls critically after some time. These questions are related to the nature of the reaction by which an elevation of the ICP produces vasodilatation. Whether this reaction is of a "neurogenic" or a "metabolic" or a "myogenic" origin is still under discussion.

One may assume that the transport mechanisms of the intracranial CSF as well as respiratory brain stem reflexes also participate in giving the plateau waves their typical shape. The relation between respiration and plateau waves is of particular interest because it has clinical implications. In many cases the critical fall in pressure at the end of a plateau wave is preceded by spontaneous hyperpnea, and artificial hyperventilation may reduce the size and frequency of plateau waves and even abolish them completely.[13,14] On the other hand even controlled respiration with a consistently low $PaCO_2$ is no guarantee against the occurrence of plateau waves[13,14] (Fig. 5). Furthermore, simultaneous recording of the VFP and the PCO_2 of the expiratory air showed that there may be a lag of several minutes between the reduction in PCO_2 and the fall of the VFP.[6] These observations suggest that the vasodilatation, which is assumed to occur during plateau waves, makes the vessels resistant to hypocapnia, but not to such a degree that the beneficial effect of controlled respiration is disqualified.

FURTHER READING

[1] Cronqvist, S., Lundberg, N. and Pontén, U. (1963), "Cerebral Pneumography with Continuous Control of Ventricular Fluid Pressure," *Acta Radiol.*, 1, 558–564.

[2] Davson, H. (1967), "Physiology of the Cerebrospinal Fluid," London: J. & A. Churchill.

[3] Falck, B. (1951), "Calcifications in the Track of the Needle Following Ventricular Puncture," *Acta radiol.*, 35, 304–308.

[4] Guillaume, J. and Janny, P. (1951), "Manométrie Intracranienne Continue. Intérêt de la Méthode et Premiers Résultats," *Rev. Neurol.*, 84, 131–142.

[5] Johnston, I. H., Johnston, J. A. and Jennett, B. (1970), "Intracranial-Pressure Changes Following Head Injury," *Lancet*, i, 433–436.

[6] Kjällquist, Å., Lundberg, N. and Pontén, U. (1964), "Respiratory and Cardiovascular Changes During Rapid Spontaneous Variations of Ventricular Fluid Pressure in Patients with Intracranial Hypertension," *Acta Neurol. Scand.*, 40, 291–317.

[7] Kullberg, G. and Sundbärg, G. (1970), "A Method for the Automatic Statistical Analysis of Intracranial Pressure Recordings," Proceedings of Scand. Neurosurg. Soc. 22nd Ann. Meeting, Stockholm, 1970, *Acta Neurol. Scand.*, 46, 631.

[8] Kullberg, G. and West, K. A. (1965), "Influence of Corticosteroids on the Ventricular Fluid Pressure," *Acta Neurol. Scand.*, 41, Suppl. 13/II, 445–452.

[9] Langfitt, T. W., Weinstein, J. D., Kassell, N. F. and Simeone, F. A. (1964), "Transmission of Increased Intracranial Pressure. I. Within the Craniospinal Axis," *J. Neurosurg.*, 21, 989–997.

[10] Langfitt, T. W., Weinstein, J. D., Kassell, N. F. and Gagliardi, L. J. (1964), "Transmission of Increased Intracranial Pressure. II. Within the Supratentorial Space," *J. Neurosurg.*, 21, 998–1005.

[11] Langfitt, T. W., Weinstein, J. D. and Kassell, N. F. (1965), "Cerebral Vasomotor Paralysis Produced by Intracranial Hypertension," *Neurology (Minneap.)*, 15, 622–641.

[12] Langfitt, T. W. (1969), "Increased Intracranial Pressure," *Clin. Neurosurg.*, 16, 436–471.

[13] Lundberg, N., Kájllquist, Å. and Bien, Ch. (1959), "Reduction of Increased Intracranial Pressure by Hyperventilation," *Acta Psych. et Neurol. Scand.*, Suppl. 139.

[14] Lundberg, N. (1960), "Continuous Recording and Control of Ventricular Fluid Pressure in Neurosurgical Practice," *Acta Psych. et Neurol. Scand.*, Suppl. 149.

[15] Lundberg, N. and Pontén, U. (1963), "Some Observations on Postoperative Ventricular Fluid Pressure," *Acta Neurol. Scand.*, 39, 264–265.

[16] Lundberg, N., Troupp, H. and Lorin, H. (1965), "Continuous Recording of the Ventricular-Fluid Pressure in Patients with Severe Acute Traumatic Brain Injury: A Preliminary Report," *J. Neurosurg.*, 22, 581–590.

[17] Lundberg, N., Cronqvist, S. and Kjällquist, Å. (1968), "Clinical Investigations on Interrelations Between Intracranial Pressure and Intracranial Hemodynamics," *Progress in Brain Research*, vol. 30, 70–75, Cerebral Circulation. Amsterdam: Elsevier Publ. Co.

[18] Lundberg, N. and West, K. A. (1965), "Leakage as a Source of Error in Measurement of the Cerebrospinal Fluid Pressure by Lumbar Puncture," *Acta Neurol. Scand.*, 41, Suppl. 13/I, 115–121.

[19] Merritt, H. H. and Fremont-Smith, F. (1937), *The Cerebrospinal Fluid*. Philadelphia: W. B. Saunders Co.

[20] Nornes, H. and Serck-Hanssen, F. (1970), "Miniature Transducer for Intracranial Pressure Monitoring in Man," *Acta Neurol. Scand.*, 46, 203–214.

[21] Pontén, U., Kjällquist, Å., Lundberg, N. and Nilsson, L. (1968), "Monitoring of the Cerebral 'Perfusion Pressure' in Patients with Intracranial Hypertension. A Preliminary Report." Proceedings of Scand. Neurosurg. Soc. 20th Ann. Meeting, Uppsala, 1967. *Acta Neurol. Scand.*, 44, 251.

[22] Pontén, U., Månsson, B., Månsson, M. and Sundbärg, G. (To be published.)

[23] Richardson, A., Hide, T. A. H. and Eversden, I. D. (1970), "Long-Term Continuous Intracranial-Pressure Monitoring by Means of a Modified Subdural Pressure Transducer," *Lancet*, ii, 687–690.

[24] Risberg, J., Lundberg, N. and Ingvar, D. H. (1969), "Regional Cerebral Blood Volume During Acute Transient Rises of the Intracranial Pressure (Plateau Waves)," *J. Neurosurg.*, 31, 303–310.

[25] Ryder, H. W., Espey, F. F., Kimbell, F. D., Penka, E. J., Rosenauer, A., Podolsky, B. and Evans, J. P. (1953), "The Mechanism of the Change in Cerebrospinal Fluid Pressure Following an Induced Change in the Volume of the Fluid Space," *J. Lab. clin. Med.*, 41, 428–435.

[26] Sundbärg, G. and Nornes, H. (1970), "Simultaneous Recording of the Ventricular Fluid Pressure and the Epidural Pressure." Proceedings of Scand. Neurosurg. Soc. 22nd Ann. Meeting, Stockholm, 1970. *Acta Neurol. Scand.*, 46, 634–635.

[27] Troupp, H. (1967), "Intraventricular Pressure in Patients with Severe Brain Injuries," *J. of Trauma*, 7, 875–883.

[28] Troupp, H. (1969), Personal Communication.

4. ANAESTHESIA FOR NEUROSURGERY

D. GORDON McDOWALL

This chapter consists of a discussion of some of the special features of neurosurgical anaesthesia. It is not intended to be a comprehensive account, because a great part of anaesthetic practice in neurosurgery involves well-established principles that apply to the whole field of anaesthesia, and also because several comprehensive texts are available on the subject.[19,22,29]

PHARMACOLOGY AS APPLIED TO NEUROSURGICAL ANAESTHESIA

Anaesthetic drugs used in neurosurgery can be divided into three main groups: induction agents, muscle relaxants, and maintenance anaesthetics. However, many other drugs are used in the preparation and care of the patient before, during and following operation.

Induction Agents

Almost invariably the induction of anaesthesia is by the intravenous route and barbiturates are the commonest drugs used, mainly thiopentone or methohexitone.

Methohexitone is metabolized more quickly than is thiopentone, but if only a small induction dose is used there is probably no difference in the duration of action, since this is established by cerebral wash-out of the drug and not by metabolic degradation.[46] The rate of breakdown does not become important unless repeated doses are given, or unless the drug is administered as a continuous infusion. Methohexitone may produce less hypotension on induction and is therefore often used when difficulty is anticipated in maintaining a satisfactory blood pressure.

Barbiturates are respiratory depressants and therefore assisted or controlled ventilation should be used when they are administered to patients with space-occupying lesions or raised intracranial pressure. In neurosurgical practice induction with barbiturates is commonly followed by the administration of a muscle relaxant and the institution of controlled ventilation. Following induction and during the onset of muscle paralysis adequate ventilation must be maintained; indeed, hyperventilation during this phase is preferable, since a period of apnoea is bound to occur during intubation.

Barbiturates themselves reduce cerebral blood flow and cerebral metabolism in parallel, provided respiratory depression is avoided.[40] During light thiopentone anaesthesia both flow and metabolic rate are reduced by about a third, while in deep thiopentone anaesthesia the reduction is to a half. As a result, cerebrospinal fluid pressure falls after the injection of barbiturates.[18]

An alternative induction technique employs large doses of **fentanyl** (*see below* for pharmacology) in the range 0·4:0·8 mg., but if this is done the powerful respiratory depressant action of the drug must be countered by early control of ventilation. It is also important to administer a muscle relaxant soon after the intravenous dose of fentanyl, otherwise muscle rigidity may occur which makes controlled ventilation by mask difficult or impossible.

Ketamine is a drug which has recently been introduced as an induction and maintenance agent. It has the unusual attribute of stimulating the circulation so that blood-pressure and heart rate rise.[4] Rather substantial increases in intracranial pressure have been reported, implying increased cerebral blood flow.[9] It was originally thought that an adequate cough reflex was maintained during anaesthesia with ketamine, but recent evidence indicates that this may not invariably be so.[48] Respiratory obstruction can also occur, and these two factors indicate that patient monitoring during ketamine anaesthesia should be as complete as during other forms of general anaesthesia. A further drawback is the occurrence of unpleasant dreams during recovery from ketamine in a proportion of adult patients.

Muscle Relaxants

Suxamethonium continues to be the only relaxant with a truly rapid onset of action, and so it is used almost invariably for the acute case or in those situations where only a brief period of paralysis is required, e.g. in order to insert an endotracheal tube. The muscle fasciculations which result from its depolarizing action elevate both intra-abdominal and central venous pressure and therefore also raise cerebrospinal fluid pressure. Suxamethonium, even in the absence of fasciculation, causes a small and brief elevation of intracranial pressure.[15] The muscle fasciculations, which have a rather marked effect on intracranial pressure, can be reduced by the prior administration of a small dose of a non-depolarizing relaxant, e.g. gallamine, but the action of suxamethonium after such a non-depolarizing relaxant is less predictable.

Among the non-depolarizing relaxants several new drugs have been introduced, and of these pancuronium appears to have the virtue of avoiding the hypotension seen not infrequently with tubocurarine. The non-depolarizing relaxants appear to be without direct effect on intracranial pressure.[45]

The importance of full muscular relaxation in neurosurgery cannot be over-estimated, for it is not sufficient merely to avoid the patient "fighting the ventilator". If relaxation becomes less than complete, then returning muscle tone reduces the chest wall compliance and increases the abdominal wall resistance to the descent of the diaphragm. In this way central venous pressure, cerebral venous pressure and cerebrospinal fluid pressures all increase. The surest way to titrate relaxant requirements correctly is to make routine use of a simple nerve stimulator. This is particularly true of pancuronium, where the dosage requirements appear to vary rather widely from patient to patient.

Maintenance of Anaesthesia

Inhalational Drugs

Nitrous Oxide is one of the most insoluble of the anaesthetics in blood, and so excretion of the drug is more rapid than with other anaesthetics.

Nitrous oxide appears to be a mild cerebral vasodilator; thus, on changing from halothane/air to halothane/nitrous oxide anaesthesia, cerebral blood flow increases.[26,33] Since it has been demonstrated[1] that cerebral oxygen uptake is depressed by 23 per cent by N_2O, cerebral blood flow is in excess of metabolic requirements.

Theye and Michenfelder[49] also found an increase in cerebral blood flow in dogs when nitrous oxide was administered, but contrary to the results of Alexander et al.[1] they observed an increase in cerebral metabolism with 70 per cent N_2O, as compared with the air breathing values.

The effect of N_2O on CSF pressure is disputed; some report an increase[20,26] while others find no change.[11] The effect certainly cannot be great, for the mean CSF pressure in a group of patients anaesthetized with nitrous oxide/oxygen and ventilated to normocapnia was within the normal range for conscious man.[32] Of more significance is the effect of nitrous oxide on intracranial pressure after air has been introduced into the subarachnoid space during air encephalography. Under such circumstances nitrous oxide moves into the intracranial air collection in exchange for nitrogen, and since the solubility of nitrous oxide in blood is 30 times that of nitrogen, the net gas exchange is greatly in favour of expansion of the intracranial gas bubble. The CSF pressure therefore rises, on some occasions markedly.[43] For this reason some have recommended the use of nitrous oxide in place of air as the injected gas for gas encephalography.

Halothane is of intermediate blood-solubility, so that recovery is moderately quick, except after prolonged administration when considerable quantities are absorbed into fat. It is a hypotensive drug, particularly when combined with tubocurarine or ganglion-blocking drugs. The hypotension seems to arise principally from myocardial depression rather than from peripheral vasodilatation.[10] There is no period of post-operative analgesia after halothane anaesthesia; indeed, it has been suggested that the drug is antianalgesic.

Halothane is a cerebral vasodilator producing increases in cerebral blood flow in proportion to the inhaled concentration; 0·5 per cent increasing flow by 11 per cent; 1·2 per cent by 15 per cent; and 2·0 per cent by 24 per cent.[30,51] Greater inspired concentrations depress blood-pressure so markedly that cerebral blood flow falls (Fig. 1).

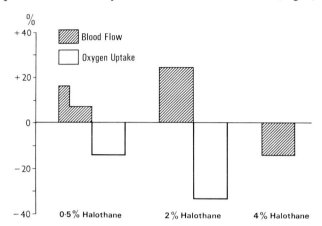

FIG. 1. The effects of halothane on cerebral cortical blood-flow and cerebral cortical oxygen uptake in the dog. Halothane is a cerebral vasodilator and flow is increased more by 2% than by 0·5% inspired concentration. Furthermore, the vasodilation with 0·5% is not fully maintained with time, flow being higher in the first 20 min. of administration than later; 4% halothane reduces cerebral blood flow because of the associated hypotension. The depression of cerebral cortical oxygen uptake is greater with 2% than with 0·5% halothane. (Reproduced from *Brit. J. Anaesth.*, by courtesy of the publishers.)

Cerebral metabolic rate is depressed so that oxygen uptake of the cortex is reduced by 14 per cent with 0·5 per cent inspired halothane, and by 33 per cent with 2·0 per cent halothane[30] (Fig. 1). Theye and Michenfelder[50] found a reduction in $CMRO_2$ of 17 per cent in light halothane anaesthesia, but no further reduction with deep halothane.

On account of the increased cerebral blood flow, and therefore the increased cerebral blood volume, there is an increase in cerebrospinal fluid pressure with halothane which is proportional to the inspired concentration.[32,35,45] The increase in cerebrospinal fluid pressure is much greater in patients with intracranial space-occupying lesions (Fig. 2).[23]

Halothane is also a powerful dilator of skin vessels, a fact of some value in deliberate hypothermia.

Trichloroethylene is a very blood-soluble agent, so that recovery from anaesthesia is slow. It is, however, a potent analgesic, though this action is of less importance in neurosurgery than in other types of surgery. It produces less hypotension and less respiratory depression than halothane, and so it is sometimes a useful adjuvant to nitrous oxide/oxygen anaesthesia during either spontaneous or controlled ventilation. Trichloroethylene, especially in high concentrations, may lead to tachypnoea, but this does not necessarily lead to CO_2 retention;[47] indeed, hypocapnia often results from trichloroethylene tachypnoea in the intubated patient (Barker, J., personal communication).

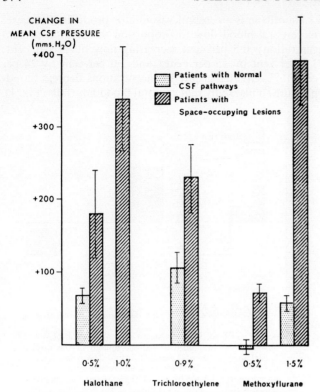

FIG. 2. Increases in CSF pressure (means ±S.E.) produced by the volatile anaesthetics: halothane, trichloroethylene and methoxyflurane, in patients with and without intracranial space-occupying lesions. The values measured were obtained after 10 minutes' administration during controlled normocapnic ventilation. On account of the short duration of administration, blood anaesthetic concentration was still below inspired, especially with methoxyflurane. Furthermore, at 10 min. CSF pressure was still rising, so the values shown do not represent the peak values which would be attained with longer periods of administration. (Reproduced from *International Anesthesiology Clinics*, by courtesy of the publishers.)

Trichloroethylene is also a cerebral vasodilator and a depressant of cerebral oxygen uptake. CSF pressure increases with its use to the same degree as with halothane (Fig. 2).

Cyclopropane has unusual effects on cerebral blood flow and cerebral oxygen uptake,[2] but its explosive nature virtually excludes it from neurosurgical use.

Methoxyflurane is very blood-soluble, so that excretion is slow at the end of anaesthesia. During wash-out it provides a degree of post-operative analgesia. The drug produces hypotension and respiratory depression of similar degree to halothane. The occasional occurrence of renal toxicity has been reported.[39] Cerebrospinal fluid pressure increases (Fig. 2) and so methoxyflurane is probably another cerebral vasodilating anaesthetic.

Ether and Chloroform are both cerebral vasodilators. They are, however, hardly ever used in neurosurgical practice; the former on account of its explosive properties, and the latter because it produces hepatic and renal toxicity.

Intravenous Supplements

Certain of the agents used for induction are also employed for maintenance, for example, the intravenous infusion of a barbiturate—usually methohexitone. The clinical advantages claimed are a reduction in the cerebral metabolic requirements and a reduction in intracranial pressure.

Neuroleptic and analgesic drugs are increasingly being employed in place of volatile anaesthetic agents; commonly used are the neuroleptic droperidol 5–20 mg. and the analgesics fentanyl 0·1–0·2 mg.; phenoperidine 1–2 mg. or pentazocine 30–60 mg. Droperidol is a butyrophenone which acts as a tranquillizer, a sedative, an antiemetic and an alpha adrenergic blocker. It is administered either as a premedicant, when its lack of respiratory depression is of value, or intravenously prior to induction of anaesthesia. Its antiemetic action is of particular importance in neurosurgical anaesthesia. Its hypotensive effect is usually mild, but can be severe especially in the hypovolaemic patient and in the sitting position. The analgesic drugs fentanyl, phenoperidine and pentazocine differ mainly in their duration of action, with fentanyl being the shortest acting—at about 15–20 min.—and phenoperidine the longest at 30–60 min. after intravenous administration.

Anaesthesia consisting of nitrous oxide, analgesic supplement and relaxant is a very light form of anaesthesia and, if the dosage has been correctly judged, it is a technique of anaesthesia from which recovery of full consciousness is quick and complete. Since these drugs are respiratory depressants it is important to ensure that ventilation is adequate and to use nalorphine almost routinely at the end of surgery after administration of fentanyl or phenoperidine, and certainly more often than following general surgical procedures. Otherwise a patient with a raised intracranial pressure may exhibit brain shift due to sudden CO_2 retention on return to the ward. An antagonist to pentazocine is methyl phenidate.

THE IMPORTANCE OF INTRACRANIAL PRESSURE CHANGES PRODUCED BY ANAESTHESIA

The level of intracranial pressure can be altered by many factors during anaesthesia; the most important of these are:

(1) hypercapnia from respiratory obstruction or ventilatory inadequacy;
(2) elevated intrathoracic pressures from faulty anaesthetic circuitry or from inadequate muscular relaxation;
(3) pressure on the veins in the neck, usually as a result of poor positioning of the patient on the operating table.

Hypoxic hypoxia, of course, also produces high intracranial pressure but is, hopefully, an uncommon feature of modern anaesthesia. Ischaemic hypoxia due, for example, to sudden hypotension on induction, is accompanied by a normal or low intracranial pressure but is followed by high pressure during the period of reactive hyperemia. This is probably a factor in some of the "tight brains" discovered by the neurosurgeon on decompressing the skull. Good anaesthetic technique in neurosurgery consists, therefore, of the avoidance of these major determinants of elevated intracranial pressure.

Intubation is the stage at which it is most difficult to avoid sudden large increases in intracranial pressure, even with impeccable anaesthetic technique.[3] Even so, a smooth induction with thiopentone, followed by gentle progression to controlled hyperventilation after a relaxant other than suxamethonium, and rapid intubation with minimal neck distortion, will all minimize intracranial pressure swings.

The anaesthetic drugs themselves, however, also have effects on intracranial pressure; in particular the increased cerebral blood flow which accompanies administration of the volatile agents leads to elevated intracranial pressure by the following sequence of events:

Volatile anaesthetic administration

↓

Cerebral arteriolar dilatation

↓

Increased blood flow

↓

Elevation of pressure in the major cerebral veins and intracranial sinuses because of the fixed outflow orifices

↓

"Backfiring" of this pressure into the small thin-walled cerebral veins

↓

Dilatation of these small veins, with consequent increase in intracranial blood volume

↓

Elevation of intracranial pressure

The point to note from this sequence is that it is not principally the dilatation of the cerebral arterioles which causes the expansion of the intracranial blood volume because, in the brain, as elsewhere, the volume of the arterioles is small. It is the dilatation of the high-capacity veins, resulting mechanically from the elevated venous sinus pressures, which accounts for the major part of the volume change. Under experimental conditions cisterna magna and sagittal sinus pressures during halothane administration change in parallel, as would be predicted from the schema shown above (Fig. 3).

Of course, volatile anaesthetic drugs can increase intracranial pressure through the mechanism of respiratory depression; but even under conditions of controlled ventilation and normocapnia halothane, trichloroethylene and methoxyflurane have been shown to elevate CSF pressure in patients without intracranial pathology.[32]

In patients with intracranial space-occupying lesions, the intracranial pressure, as measured in one lateral ventricle, increases much more markedly than in patients without such pathology[23] (Fig. 2). The increased sensitivity of ICP to volatile anaesthetics is, presumably, the

result of cerebral compression produced by the space-occupying lesion. As an intracranial tumour expands, additional space is found within the skull by translocation of CSF and cerebral venous blood out of the intracranial space. During this compensated phase intracranial pressure changes only slightly. Eventually a stage of cerebral compression is reached, when only a small further

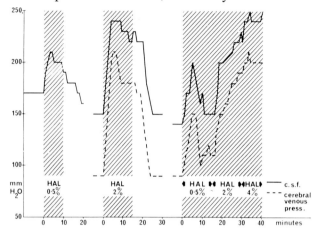

FIG. 3. Changes in intracranial CSF pressure and cerebral venous (superior sagittal sinus) pressure in one dog with different halothane concentrations. Note the parallel changes in sinus venous pressure and CSF pressure. (Reproduced from *Anaesthesia*, by courtesy of the publishers.)

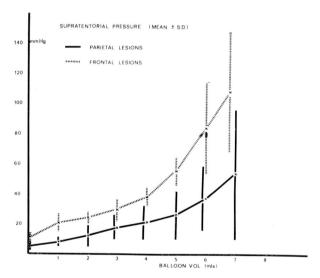

FIG. 4. Relationship between intracranial pressure and balloon volume during progressive expansion of an extra-dural balloon at 2 ml./hr. in 5 dogs with parietally-placed balloons and 5 with frontally-placed balloons. A phase of compensated pressure increase is followed by a phase of decompensation. (Reproduced from *Brit. J. Anaesth.*, by courtesy of the publishers.)

expansion of the tumour produces a very great increase in pressure. This is illustrated in Fig. 4, where the intracranial pressure response to the gradual expansion of an intracranial balloon in the dog is shown. At a certain stage in this process intracranial compression reaches a critical state, when a small further increase in balloon volume produces a large increase in pressure.

When the intracranial contents are critically compressed, similar large increases in intracranial pressure can be produced by the administration of cerebral vasodilators, e.g. halothane. This situation is illustrated diagrammatically in Fig. 5, and experimentally in Fig. 6; the latter figure shows that halothane produces greater increases in intracranial pressure at high balloon volumes, i.e. when intracranial compensation is nearly exhausted. Further support for this concept comes from the work of Richardson *et al.*[41] who observed that in patients with intracranial tumours those who exhibited "plateau waves" had the greatest pressure rises when halothane was administered; it being generally accepted that plateau waves are evidence that intracranial compensation is nearly exhausted.

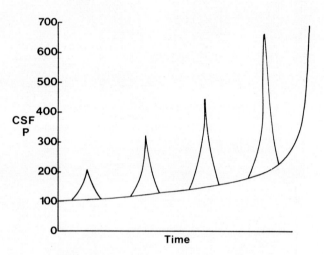

Fig. 5. A schematic diagram showing relationship between intracranial pressure and time (or volume of an expanding space-occupying lesion). The increases in intracranial pressure which might be expected to be produced by halothane administration at different stages are shown superimposed.

It is, of course, important to consider whether these elevations of intracranial pressure have any clinical significance. It is very improbable that the absolute value of intracranial pressure reached has any clinical importance, for its relevance would result from resistance offered to cerebral perfusion. Since, in the case of volatile anaesthetics, the intracranial pressure rises as a result of increased flow, it is difficult to conceive of the increased intracranial pressure leading to a generalized decrease in flow (regional flow changes are discussed below). However, a mechanism by which these intracranial pressure changes might be important would be through the production or accentuation of intracranial pressure gradients; for example, if halothane were to raise the intracranial pressure more in the intracranial compartment containing the tumour (due to greater compression of the brain in this compartment) than it raised intracranial pressure in adjacent compartments, gradients of pressure would be established which would tend to produce brain shift, herniation and impaction.

A study designed to explore this possibility has been reported by Fitch and McDowall,[8] who inflated intracranial balloons in dogs at the rate of 1 ml./30 min. and observed the effects of halothane at each 1 ml. increment in balloon volume. They measured intracranial pressure in the supratentorial space (i.e. in the compartment with

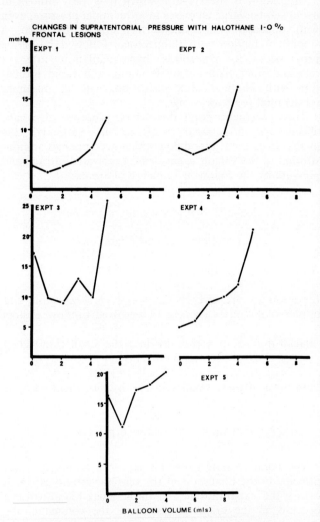

Fig. 6. The increases in intracranial pressure produced by 10 min. of 1% inspired halothane in dogs with extracranial balloons of increasing volumes. It will be seen that, as the balloon volume increased, the effect of halothane on intracranial pressure was magnified. (Reproduced from *Brit. J. Anaesth.*, by courtesy of the publishers.)

the tumour) and in the posterior fossa. As the tumour expanded gradients of pressure developed across the tentorium, but the most important finding in the present context was that halothane, at certain critical stages, would greatly and quickly accentuate the transtentorial pressure gradients (Fig. 7). As further evidence that halothane increased brain compression at the tentorium, it was observed that the first dilatation of one pupil occurred during periods of halothane administration in 8 of the 10 animals. The authors conclude that at certain critical stages in the expansion of intracranial space-occupying

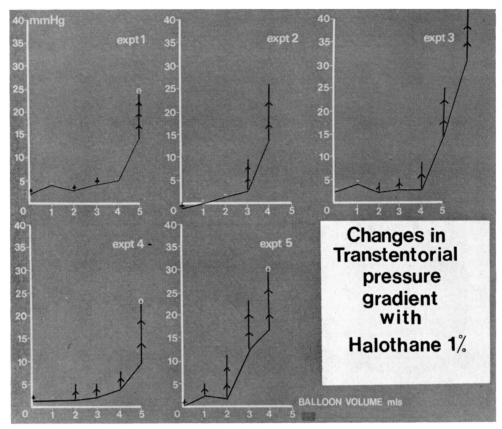

FIG. 7. The effect of 10 min. of 1% halothane administration on the transtentorial pressure gradient in 5 dogs with extradural balloons. The continuous line indicates the relationship between transtentorial pressure gradient and balloon volume in the absence of halothane, and the vertical arrows show the increases in that gradient produced by halothane. The open circles indicate the points of first dilatation of one pupil.

lesions, the administration of 1 per cent halothane can—even during controlled normocapnic ventilation—lead to brain shift and impaction.

The other mechanism by which the change of intracranial pressure produced by volatile anaesthetics could be detrimental would be through the mechanism of intracerebral "steal"; thus the cerebral vasodilatation produced in normal areas of brain by volatile anaesthetics might not occur in areas of trauma or compression because of tissue oedema and acidosis. In this event, the effect of the volatile agent would be to "steal" blood from the "bad" areas of brain in order to over-perfuse the normal areas. Furthermore, the increased flow to the normal areas would elevate intracranial pressure, and this generalized increase in intracranial pressure would further compress the capillaries and venules of the area of damaged or diseased brain where tissue pressure would already be high. Therefore, although the intracranial hypertension produced by volatile anaesthetics is unlikely to impair total cerebral flow, it may lead to regional flow depression in abnormal areas of brain.

All the considerations discussed above apply only to the closed skull, for when the skull has been decompressed any anaesthetically-induced increase in cerebral blood volume merely displaces CSF out through the wound. The time course of the changes is also important,

for it has been observed in experimental animals that the effect of the volatile agent on intracranial pressure reaches a peak and then declines towards base line values.[32] Definition of the time-scale of such adaptive changes in man still awaits elucidation.

Since adaptation occurs in this way, and since the effect of a volatile anaesthetic agent on intracranial pressure is proportional to the inspired concentration, it may be possible to avoid major changes in intracranial pressure gradients, if the anaesthetic agent is introduced slowly and progressively starting with low concentrations. The effect of prior hyperventilation and/or dehydrating agents is likely to be beneficial.

Daily experience in many neurosurgical centres indicates that volatile anaesthetic drugs can be used safely in patients with space-occupying lesions, presumably because the drugs are employed carefully and with moderate hyperventilation. Major difficulties are most likely to be experienced in situations in which relatively inexperienced anaesthetists administer volatile agents without due caution and in the presence of spontaneous ventilation. Neuroradiological investigations under general anaesthesia often provide such conditions. Similar factors may apply when a case of multiple injuries, with undiagnosed head injury, is given an anaesthetic for some orthopaedic procedure, especially since spontaneous ventilation with halothane is a commonly-used technique in such cases.

Replacement of volatile anaesthetics by intravenous supplementation with neuroleptanalgesic drugs avoids all these problems, since these intravenous supplements, in the presence of controlled ventilation, cause either no change in intracranial pressure or a fall.[7]

ANAESTHETIC TECHNIQUES IN NEUROSURGERY

For Neuroradiological Studies

Pneumo-encephalography

This procedure is often associated with severe headache and with nausea and vomiting, especially when the position of the head is changed. On account of these unpleasant effects some centres perform the investigation under general anaesthesia, though in the author's opinion adequate analgesia can be produced in the conscious patient with fentanyl or pentazocine after premedication with droperidol or perphenazine to reduce vomiting.

A satisfactory technique is premedication with droperidol 5 or 10 mg. and atropine (incidentally, 0·3 mg. atropine is adequate in premedication and reduces the discomfort produced by larger doses). An opiate may also be given in premedication if the patient's condition allows. On arrival in the neuroradiology room the adequacy of sedation is assessed and, if necessary, a further 5 mg. of droperidol is given intravenously. However, since hypotension on adopting the sitting position is the commonest difficulty, the total dosage of droperidol—which is an alpha-blocking agent—should be restricted. If hypotension does occur, wrapping the legs in Esmarch's bandages and intravenous methylamphetamine or other vasopressor may be effective. In the author's experience, however, the most useful manoeuvre is to infuse 200–500 ml. dextran rapidly.

As soon as the patient is in the sitting position and the blood-pressure has been checked, the first dose of analgesic is given, e.g. fentanyl 0·1–0·2 mg. depending on age and weight. While the lumbar puncture proceeds the effect of the analgesic on respiration is assessed and further increments of 0·05 or 0·1 mg. fentanyl given. On account of the respiratory depression it is wise to give oxygen throughout, via nasal cannulae or catheter.

Occasionally, pneumo-encephalography has to be performed in disorientated, unco-operative patients, and here intravenous diazepam often provides adequate tranquillization. If not, then intravenous (2 mg./kg.) or intramuscular ketamine (5–10 mg./kg.) is very useful.

Pneumo-encephalography in babies and young children is usually performed under general anaesthesia consisting of nitrous oxide/oxygen/halothane with spontaneous ventilation. Since some of the head positions required involve extreme neck movement, the endotracheal tube has to be very well-secured. An excellent alternative method is provided by the use of ketamine, provided care is taken to immobilize the head because of the spontaneous muscle activity which occurs, and which otherwise produces jerking of the head and neck.

If nitrous oxide is employed during pneumo-encephalography, the expansion of intracranial air collections by the nitrous oxygen/nitrogen exchange already discussed should be borne in mind.

Carotid and Vertebral Angiography

The practice varies widely between centres, in that some use local anaesthesia—particularly for unilateral carotid angiography—while others employ general anaesthesia. If general anaesthesia is used then the technique chosen should avoid sudden increases in intracranial pressure, particularly where a space-occupying lesion is suspected. Another important factor is that the technique used must not produce hypotension, for this will make puncture of the artery unnecessarily difficult, while in cases of subarachnoid haemorrhage the blood pressure must not be allowed to rise since further bleeding may be induced. Finally, since most of these radio-diagnostic procedures are followed by a major operation, it is necessary to remember that the use of halothane may, in a few cases, produce halothane sensitization which may lead to hepatic damage should halothane be used again during the subsequent operative procedure.[38]

The following technique meets these points: Induction is with either thiopentone or droperidol/fentanyl, followed by non-depolarizing muscle relaxant. Hyperventilation is employed prior to intubation and moderate hyperventilation with nitrous oxide and oxygen thereafter. Supplementation is with small doses of fentanyl. This technique avoids both the hypotension and the intracranial pressure changes associated with halothane. However, halothane is used in patients with subarachnoid haemorrhage if the blood pressure shows any tendency to increase above normal values.

Moderate hyperventilation, in addition to avoiding the intracranial hypertension of spontaneous ventilation with halothane, is of assistance in producing high quality radiographs for the following reasons:

(1) The slowing of cerebral circulation transit time with hypocapnia lengthens and separates the arterial, capillary and venous phases, giving the radiologist more time to follow the transit of the radio opaque dye.
(2) The reduction in capillary flow reduces the "background" opacity from dye in the capillaries.
(3) The phenomenon of reverse cerebral "steal" may on occasion lead to the routing of more dye through the tumour circulation.

That these are not mere armchair predictions is shown by the work of Samuel and colleagues[44] who found that the radiographs obtained during hypocapnia were of greater diagnostic value than those taken during moderate hypercapnia.

If an opiate analgesic is employed for supplementation then any respiratory depression at the end of the investigation must be reversed with nalorphine.

For Surgery on the Major Vessels in the Neck

The problem here is that the cerebral circulation may be compromised during surgery on the neck vessels. It is well-known that, although a proportion of patients will tolerate occlusion of one carotid artery for the time necessary for carotid endarterectomy, not all will do so. In order to forecast which patients will withstand a period of arterial occlusion equal to that required in disobliteration a trial occlusion is produced and cerebral oxygenation monitored either by EEG analysis or in the conscious patient by testing for neurological deficit. The EEG is, unfortunately, not always a reliable guide during this procedure, and, because of this, some surgeons prefer to operate under local anaesthesia.

The anaesthetist has tried in various ways to provide additional protection to the brain during surgery on the carotid vessels by:

(i) increasing cerebral perfusion with carbon dioxide;[17]
(ii) by increasing cerebral perfusion through elevation of blood pressure;[27]
(iii) by producing deep anaesthesia, usually with halothane;
(iv) by inducing general hypothermia.

The concept of employing deliberate hypercapnia can be criticized on the grounds that it may merely lower cerebrovascular resistance on the side of the patent carotid and so "steal" blood flow which would otherwise have crossed to supply the compromised hemisphere. Deliberately increasing blood-pressure would seem a more hopeful procedure, in that normal areas of brain will auto-regulate to hold flow constant while affected areas, in which local perfusion pressure has fallen below auto-regulatory limits, should benefit. Deep anaesthesia, by lowering cerebral oxygen requirements, is theoretically attractive but suffers the disadvantage that cerebral perfusion pressure may be severely impaired. Hypothermia, though routinely used in a few centres, is generally considered to complicate the operation unnecessarily.

In assessing these methods of cerebral protection measurements are often made of jugular venous oxygenation. This may be useful insofar as it is known that jugular venous PO_2 values below 20 mm. Hg. should probably not be accepted. However, a normal value for jugular venous oxygen is no guarantee that areas of severe hypoxia do not exist within the wide drainage territory of the jugular bulb.[36]

An approach with good experimental backing is to induce anaesthesia with methohexitone and maintain it with nitrous oxide/oxygen, plus a methohexitone drip to depress cerebral oxygen requirements. Control of ventilation and lowering of arterial PCO_2 to the range 25–30 mm. Hg. may help to divert blood from normal brain to ischaemic areas by the inverse "steal" mechanism. Finally, elevation of blood-pressure with a vasopressor infusion may be helpful.

Those who work in centres with large walk-in hyperbaric oxygen chambers may decide to operate on such cases under hyperbaric oxygenation,[24] which has the twin advantages of increasing cerebral oxygenation and constricting cerebral vessels in normal brain[21] but not in ischaemic brain.[14] (*See also* Chapter VII : 4.)

For Intracranial Operations[29]

The main points have mostly been discussed already but can be summarized.

(1) Minimal doses of the induction agent in order that recovery of consciousness may be rapid.
(2) Avoidance or caution in the use of volatile agents until the skull has been opened.
(3) The use of intravenous supplements, e.g. pentazocine, fentanyl or methohexitone.
(4) Moderate hyperventilation with nitrous oxide/oxygen in order to reduce brain bulk and intracranial pressure and to decrease the dosage of supplemental agents required; the reverse "steal" mechanism may be of value with some pathological lesions. The level of arterial PCO_2 should not be below 25 mm. Hg., otherwise tissue acidosis from lactate formation may result.[12] The optimum level is probably between an arterial PCO_2 of 25 and 30 mm. Hg.

There is a good deal of confusion about the effect of hyperventilation on "brain bulk", largely based on Rosomoff's finding that total brain water and brain solids are not reduced by hyperventilation.[42] However, in the same paper Rosomoff showed that brain blood volume is reduced by hyperventilation, and of course brain blood volume constitutes an important part of "brain bulk"—at least as the term is used clinically. This reduction of brain blood volume by hyperventilation provides a useful reduction in brain bulk. The increase in CSF volume which balances the fall in blood volume during hyperventilation does not constitute a problem during intracranial surgery.

(5) The use, when indicated, of osmotic dehydrating agents perhaps combined with diuretics.
(6) Control of blood-pressure with either intravenous agents, e.g. hexamethonium or trimetaphan or with halothane once the skull is open.
(7) Careful reversal of relaxants and narcotics before the patient leaves the anaesthetist's direct observation.

A particular problem arises in the case of surgery in the posterior fossa and concerns the use of spontaneous or controlled ventilation. If the latter is employed one loses the warning sign of respiratory irregularities should the surgeon encroach too closely on vital medullary centres. Some hold that if such encroachment occurs an adequate warning is given by ECG changes,[37] while others believe that respiratory irregularities may occur in the absence of ECG abnormalities and so provide an earlier warning. Some of these respiratory abnormalities are of a subtle nature and require continuous display of tidal volume and frequency for their detection.[28]

If spontaneous ventilation is used then the selection of anaesthetic technique poses considerable problems, in that the use of either halothane or opiate supplementation will lead to increased intracranial pressure in patients who commonly have considerable posterior fossa compression.

Furthermore, it is more difficult to maintain a satisfactory blood-pressure in the sitting patient under anaesthesia with spontaneous ventilation than during controlled ventilation. The reason for this seeming paradox is that the former technique demands a deeper level of anaesthesia, and this more than reverses the benefit of maintaining the thoracic pump action on venous return.

SPECIAL TECHNIQUES IN NEUROSURGICAL ANAESTHESIA

Deliberate Hypotension

Deliberate hypotension is widely used in neurosurgical anaesthesia, usually for surgery of intracranial aneurysms. Only relatively brief periods of hypotension are required, and these can be produced with halothane plus trimetaphan, phenactropinium or hexamethonium. Guanethedine may be added, if necessary, to prevent the pressure "escaping" through tachycardia.[16] The effect of hypotension on cerebral blood flow has been exhaustively studied in man and animals.[5,13,25] Unfortunately, almost all this information applies to the healthy cerebral circulation, which can certainly withstand extreme hypotension. In neurosurgical work the anaesthetist often has the advantage that he can assess the cerebral vasculature by studying the available angiograms before deliberately lowering the blood-pressure. Even so, cerebral spasm may appear subsequent to angiography, and so be present at the time of surgery. The safety of hypotensive anaesthesia in the presence of such spasm is uncertain, though the clinical experience of those centres which commonly employ the technique is encouraging.

Increasingly, intra-arterial blood-pressure monitoring and central venous pressure measurement are employed when deliberate hypotension is invoked.

Hypothermia

The use of hypothermia to protect the brain during periods of surgical interference with the cerebral circulation is declining in the U.K. (see Table 1) though on the North American continent its use is apparently increasing, and at the expense of deliberately induced hypotension.[22] A few British centres, however, use the technique commonly; expressed as a percentage of major intracranial operations, the Midland Neurosurgical Centre and Wessex use hypothermia in 15 per cent of cases, Glasgow in 20 per cent and Liverpool in 30 per cent.[31] The most commonly used technique of anaesthesia for hypothermia consists of controlled ventilation with nitrous oxide/oxygen, supplemented with either halothane or intravenous analgesics. Cooling is usually produced with circulating-water blankets, though at least one centre commonly using hypothermia employs total patient immersion in a bath.

The reasons for the decline in popularity of hypothermia appear to be that an increasing number of neurosurgeons doubt its necessity in the majority of these cases. The occurrence of complications ascribable to hypothermia does not appear to be a major reason for rejection

of the method, since the experience of most anaesthetists is that serious arrhythmias are extremely rare. The fact remains that ventricular fibrillation does occasionally occur and, if it does, resuscitation is complicated by the difficulty of defibrillating the cold heart.

TABLE 1

USE OF HYPOTHERMIA AS PERCENTAGE OF MAJOR NITRACRANIAL OPERATIONS

Aberdeen	3%
Belfast	5%
Birmingham	10%
Bristol	10%
Cambridge	0%
Dublin	0%
Dundee	0%
Edinburgh	0%
Glasgow	20%
Hull	1%
Leeds	2%
Liverpool	30%
London	
Atkinson Morley's	0%
Brook General	0%
Central Middlesex	1%
Guy's-Maudsley-King's	0%
Sick Children	0%
London	3%
Maida Vale	0%
Middlesex	3%
National	<1%
St. Bartholomew's	<1%
S.E. Metropolitan	0%
Manchester	2%
Midland Neuro-s	15%
Newcastle	2%
Oxford	0%
Plymouth	1%
Sheffield	3%
Swansea	0%
Wessex	15%

Reproduced from *Brit. J. Anaesth.*, (1971) **43**, 1084, by kind permission of the publishers.

MONITORING DURING NEUROSURGICAL ANAESTHESIA

Blood-pressure

There appears to be a considerable increase in direct intra-arterial monitoring of blood-pressure during neurosurgery. This increase is obviously mainly concerned with operations where a sudden major haemorrhage is anticipated, or where deliberate hypotension is to be used to aid surgical treatment of aneurysms and vascular tumours.

Central Venous Pressure Measurement

This is another monitoring technique the use of which is increasing. In addition to its value in the estimation of blood loss, air can be aspirated through the catheter should air embolism occur.

Monitoring for Air Embolism

Two advances in this field have been the increasing use of the oesophageal stethoscope and the introduction of an ultrasonic detector which, when strapped to the precordium, will give an audible alarm should air appear within the field of the ultrasonic beam.[34] The trouble with the latter is that it may be too efficient a detector of intravascular air, since it will readily signal the introduction of only a few mls. of air. Furthermore, because the ultrasonic alarm operates in an "all or none" fashion, it cannot indicate the gas volume which has triggered the signal. Nonetheless, the instrument may have a place in routine neurosurgical monitoring, especially in the sitting position, because its alarm can be used to indicate:

(a) that further precautions against air embolism should be taken in the surgical field, and

(b) that careful reappraisal of other signs is required, including trial aspiration through the central venous catheter.

The ultrasonic detector has the advantage over all other methods of detecting air embolism, that it is a continuous monitor.

End Tidal CO_2 Monitoring

Great emphasis is placed on the importance of control of arterial P_aCO_2 in discussions of neurosurgical anaesthesia, yet very few neurosurgical anaesthetists routinely monitor end tidal CO_2. Experimental evidence discussed in Chapters VII: 1 and VIII: 5 leads to the clinical rule that, to produce the minimum intracranial blood volume compatible with adequate cerebral perfusion and oxygenation, the arterial PCO_2 should be close to 25 mm. Hg. To produce this arterial P_aCO_2 regularly and routinely during anaesthesia by means of intuitive inspiration or clinical acumen is unlikely, so that end tidal CO_2 monitoring should be routine in neurosurgical anaesthesia. That this is a practical proposition can be demonstrated from the experience of neurosurgical centres abroad, particularly in West Germany. Furthermore, the continuous display of end tidal CO_2 can provide another warning of air embolism.

The reasons for the slow introduction of routine end tidal CO_2 monitoring are mundane; the apparatus is expensive and water vapour in the expired air tends in time to reach the detector unless care is taken. The errors introduced by the presence of anaesthetic gases in the detector can readily be allowed for. The apparatus currently most commonly available for end tidal CO_2 monitoring was designed for highly accurate research work and so is expensive. Accuracy of this degree is unnecessary, and there is a clinical need for a rugged monitor which will monitor end tidal CO_2 to an accuracy of about 3–4 mm. Hg., or 0·5 per cent CO_2.

Monitoring of Neuromuscular Transmission

Reference has already been made to the great importance of full muscular relaxation in maintaining a low intracranial pressure and a lax brain. To check that this has been achieved requires the use of a nerve stimulator, an instrument which combines all the virtues of low cost, high reliability and portability. This simple instrument is

also of value, of course, in ensuring that full reversal of the relaxant has been produced at the end of the procedure.

Other Monitoring

Adequate monitoring during major neurosurgical procedures will obviously also include ventilatory gas volumes, ECG, temperature and, on occasions, blood gas measurement.

FURTHER READING

[1] Alexander, S. C., Cohen, P. J., Wollman, H., Smith, T. D., Reivich, M. and Van der Molen, R. A. (1965), "Cerebral Carbohydrate Metabolism During Hypocarbia in Man," *Anesthesiology*, **26**, 624.

[2] Alexander, S. C., James, F. M., Colton, E. T., Gleaton, H. R. and Wollman, H. (1968), "Effects of Cyclopropane on Cerebral Blood Flow and Carbohydrate Metabolism in Man," *Anesthesiology*, **29**, 170.

[3] Cooper, R., Hulme, A. and Chawla, J. G. (1970), "Changes in Cortical Blood Flow, I.C.P., and other Variables During Induction of General Anaesthesia," *Proc. 4th Internat. Symp. Regulation C.B.F.* p. 327 (R. W. Ross Russell, Ed.). London: Pitman.

[4] Dundee, J. W., Bovill, J., Knox, J. W. D., Clarke, R. S. J., Black, G. W., Love, S. H. S., Moore, J., Elliott, J., Pandit, S. K. and Coppel, D. L. (1970), "Ketamine as an Induction Agent in Anaesthetics," *Lancet*, **1**, 1370.

[5] Eckenhoff, J. E., Enderby, G. E. H., Larson, A., Davies, R. and Judevine, D. E. (1963), "Human Cerebral Circulation During Deliberate Hypotension and Head Up Tilt," *J. appl. Physiol.*, **18**, 1130.

[6] Fitch, W., Barker, J., Jennett, W. B. and McDowall, D. G. (1969), "The Influence of Neuroleptanalgesic Drugs on Cerebrospinal Fluid Pressure," *Brit. J. Anaesth.*, **41**, 800.

[7] Fitch, W. and McDowall, D. G. (1969), "Hazards of Anesthesia in Patients with Intracranial Space-occupying Lesions," *Internat. Anesth. Clinics*, **7**, No. 3, 639.

[8] Fitch, W. and McDowall, D. G. (1971), "Effect of Halothane on Intracranial Pressure Gradients in the Presence of Intracranial Space-occupying Lesions," *Brit. J. Anaesth.*, **43**, 904.

[9] Gardner, A. E., Olson, B. E. and Lichtiger, M. (1971), "Cerebrospinal Fluid Pressure During Dissociative Anesthesia with Ketamine," *Anesthesiology*, **35**, 226.

[10] Gersh, B. J., Prys-Roberts, C., Reuben, S. R. and Baker, A. B. (1970), "The Relationship Between Depressed Myocardial Contractility and the Stroke Output of the Canine Heart During Halothane Anaesthesia," *Brit. J. Anaesth.*, **42**, 560.

[11] Gordon, E. and Greitz, T. (1970), "The Effect of Nitrous Oxide on the Cerebrospinal Fluid Pressure During Encephalography," *Brit. J. Anaesth.*, **42**, 2.

[12] Granholm, L. and Siesjo, B. K. (1969), "The Effects of Hypercapnia and Hypocapnia upon the Cerebrospinal Fluid Lactate and Pyruvate Concentrations and upon the Lactate, Pyruvate, ATD, ADP, Phosphocreatine and Creatine Concentrations of Cat Brain Tissue," *Acta physiol. scand.*, **75**, 257.

[13] Harper, A. M. (1966), "Autoregulation of Cerebral Blood Flow; Influence of the Arterial Blood Pressure on the Blood Flow Through the Cerebral Cortex," *J. Neurol. Neurosurg. Psychiat.*, **29**, 398.

[14] Harper, A. M., Ledingham, I.McA. and McDowall, D. G. (1965), "The Influence of Hyperbaric Oxygen on Blood Flow and Oxygen Uptake of the Cerebral Cortex in Hypovolaemic Shock," in *Hyperbaric Oxygenation* p. 342. (I.McA. Ledingham, Ed.) Edinburgh: Livingstone.

[15] Halldin, M. and Wahlin, A. (1959), "Effect of Succinylcholine on the Intraspinal Fluid Pressure," *Acta anaesth. scand.*, **3**, 155.

[16] Holloway, K. B., Holmes, F. and Hider, C. F. (1961), "Guanethidine in Hypotensive Anaesthesia," *Brit. J. Anaesth.*, **33**, 648.

[17] Homi, J., Humphries, A. W., Young, J. R., Beven, E. G. and Smart, J. F. (1966), "Hypercarbic Anaesthesia in Cerebrovascular Surgery," *Surgery*, **59**, 57.

[18] Horsley, J. S. (1937), "The Intracranial Pressure During Barbital Narcosis," *Lancet*, **1**, 141.

[19] Hunter, A. R. (1964), *Neurosurgical Anaesthesia*. Oxford: Blackwell.

[20] Jackson, A. S. and Ball, C. G. (1971), "Intracranial Pressure in the Dog at Constant Anesthetic Depth," *Proc. Annual Meeting Amer. Soc. Anesth., Scientific Programme, Atlanta Meeting*, p. 159.

[21] Jacobson, I., Harper, A. M. and McDowall, D. G. (1963), "The Effects of Oxygen Under Pressure on Cerebral Blood Flow and Cerebral Venous Oxygenation," *Lancet*, **2**, 549.

[22] Jenkins, L. C. (1969), *General Anesthesia and the Central Nervous System*. Baltimore: Williams and Wilkins.

[23] Jennett, W. B., Barker, J., Fitch, W. and McDowall, D. G. (1969), "Effect of Anaesthesia on Intracranial Pressure in Patients with Space-occupying Lesions," *Lancet*, **1**, 61.

[24] Jennett, W. B., Ledingham, I.McA., Harper, A. M., McDowall, D. G. and Miller, J. D. (1970), "The Effects of Hyperbaric Oxygen on Cerebral Blood Flow During Carotid Artery Surgery," *Proc. 4th Internat. Congr. Hyperbaric Medicine* (J. Wada and T. Iwa, Eds.). Tokyo: Igaku Shoir.

[25] Kaasik, A. E., Nilsson, L. and Siesjo, B. K. (1970), "The Effect of Arterial Hypotension upon the Lactate, Pyruvate and Bicarbonate Concentrations of Brain Tissue and Cisternal Cerebrospinal Fluid upon the Tissue Concentrations of Phosphocreatine and Adenine Nucleotides in Anaesthetised Rats," *Acta physiol. scand.*, **78**, 448.

[26] Laitinen, L. V., Johansson, G. G. and Tarkkanen, L. (1967), "The Effect of Nitrous Oxide on Pulsatile Cerebral Impedance and Cerebral Blood Flow," *Brit. J. Anaesth.*, **39**, 781.

[27] Lyons, C., Clark, L. C., McDowell, H. and McArthur, K. (1964), "Cerebral Venous Oxygen Content During Carotid Thrombintimectomy," *Ann. Surg.*, **160**, 561.

[28] McCleery, W. N. C. (1971), *Respiratory and E.C.G. Changes During Posterior Brain Operations*. In preparation.

[29] McComish, P. B. and Bodley, P. O. (1971), *Anaesthesia for Neurological Surgery*. London: Lloyd-Luke.

[30] McDowall, D. G. (1967), "The Effects of Clinical Concentrations of Halothane on the Blood Flow and Oxygen Uptake of the Cerebral Cortex," *Brit. J. Anaesth.*, **39**, 186.

[31] McDowall, D. G. (1971), "The Current Usage of Hypothermia in British Neurosurgery," *Brit. J. Anaesth.*, **43**, 1084.

[32] McDowall, D. G., Barker, J. and Jennett, W. B. (1966), "Cerebrospinal Fluid Pressure Measurement During Anaesthesia," *Anaesthesia*, **21**, 189.

[33] McDowall, D. G. and Harper, A. M. (1965), "Blood Flow and Oxygen Uptake of the Cerebral Cortex of the Dog During Anaesthesia with Different Volatile Agents," *Acta neurol. scand.*, Suppl. 14, 146.

[34] Maroon, J. C., Edmonds-Seal, J. and Campbell, R. L. (1969), "An Ultrasonic Method for Detecting Air Embolism," *J. Neurosurg.*, **31**, 196.

[35] Marx, G. F., Andrews, C. and Orkin, L. R. (1962), "Cerebrospinal Fluid Pressure During Halothane Anaesthesia," *Canad. Anaesth. Soc. J.*, **9**, 239.

[36] Meyer, J. S., Gotch, F., Tazaki, Y., Hanaguchi, K., Ishikawa, S., Nouailhat, F. and Symon, L. (1962), "Regional Cerebral Blood Flow and Metabolism in vivo," *Arch. neurol.*, **7**, 560.

[37] Michenfelder, J. D., Gronert, G. A. and Rehder, K. (1969), "Anesthesia for Neurosurgical Procedures," in *A Decade of Clinical Progress, Clinical Anesthesia, Series* 3, p. 384 (L. W. Fabian, Ed.). Oxford: Blackwell.

[38] Mushin, W. W., Rosen, M. and Jones, E. V. (1971), "Post Halothane Jaundice in Relation to Previous Administrations of Halothane," *Brit. med. J.*, **2**, 18.

[39] National Academy of Sciences; Committee on Anesthesia (1971), "Statement Regarding the Role of Methoxyflurane in the Production of Renal Dysfunction." *Anesthesiology*, **34**, 505.

[40] Pierce, E. C., Lambertsen, C. J., Deutsch, S., Chase, P. E., Linde, H. W., Dripps, R. D. and Price, H. L. (1962), "Cerebral Circulation and Metabolism During Thiopental Anaesthesia and Hyperventilation in Man," *J. clin. Invest.*, **41**, 1664.

[41] Richardson, A., Hide, T. A. H. and Eversden, I. D. (1970), "Long-term Continuous Intracranial-pressure Monitoring by Means of a Modified Subdural Pressure Transducer," *Lancet*, **2**, 687.

[42] Rosomoff, H. L. (1963), "Distribution of Intracranial Contents with Controlled Hyperventilation: Implications for Neuroanesthesia," *Anesthesiology*, **24**, 640.

[43] Saidman, L. J. and Eger, E. I. (1965), "Changes in Cerebrospinal Fluid Pressure During Pneumoencephalography Under Nitrous Oxide Anesthesia," *Anesthesiology*, **26**, 67.

[44] Samuel, J. R., Grange, R. A. and Hawkins, T. D. (1968), "Anaesthetic Technique for Carotid Angiography," *Anaesthesia*, **23**, 543.

[45] Sondergard, W. (1961), "Intracranial Pressure During General Anaesthesia," *Dan. med. Bull.*, **8**, 18.

[46] Swerdlow, M. (1962). "G 29, 505. A Comparison with Thiopentone and Methohexitone," *Brit. J. Anaesth.*, **34**, 558.

[47] Talcott, D. A., Larson, C. P. and Beuchel, D. R. (1965), "Respiratory Effects of Trichloroethylene in Man," *Anesthesiology*, **26**, 262.

[48] Taylor, P. A. and Towey, R. M. (1971), "Depression of Laryngeal Reflexes During Ketamine Anaesthesia," *Brit. med. J.*, **2**, 688.

[49] Theye, R. A. and Michenfelder, J. D. (1968a), "The Effect of Nitrous Oxide on Canine Cerebral Metabolism," *Anesthesiology*, **29**, 1119.

[50] Theye, R. A. and Michenfelder, J. D. (1968b), "Effect of Halothane on Canine Cerebral Metabolism," *Anesthesiology*, **29**, 1113.

[51] Wollman, H., Alexander, S. C., Cohen, P. J., Chase, P. E., Melman, E. and Behar, M. G. (1964), "Cerebral Circulation of Man During Halothane Anesthesia," *Anesthesiology*, **25**, 180.

5. RADIOISOTOPES IN DIAGNOSIS

J. O. ROWAN

INTRODUCTION

Isotopes of an element have atomic nuclei which each contain the same number of protons but different numbers of neutrons, i.e. they have the same atomic number but different mass numbers. Since an atom, being electrically neutral, has equal numbers of protons and electrons, and since the chemical behaviour of an atom depends on the number and arrangement of its orbital electrons, isotopes of the same element have the same chemical properties. The ratios of neutrons to protons in the atomic nuclei of stable isotopes lie within a limited range. If the neutron–proton ratio is outwith this range, the isotope will be unstable and will disintegrate spontaneously with emission of radiation, i.e. it will be a radioisotope.

The energy of the emitted radiation is measured in electron volts. An electron volt is the energy gained by an electron when it is accelerated through a potential of 1 V. The practical units are:

Mega electron volt (MeV.) = 10^6 electron volts (eV)
Kilo electron volt (KeV.) = 10^3 electron volts (eV.)
(1 eV. = $1\cdot6 . 10^{-19}$ joules)

During radioactive decay a definite fraction of the total number of parent atoms disintegrate in unit time producing a new daughter product; the disintegration rate (or the radioactivity) is therefore decreasing in an exponential fashion. The expression commonly used to describe the radioactive decay rate is the half life, $T\frac{1}{2}$, which is the time taken for the radioactivity to decrease to half its initial value.

The unit of radioactivity is the curie (Ci.). This is the activity when the disintegration rate is $3\cdot7 \times 10^{10}$ disintegrations per second. The curie is subdivided into the following units:

Millicurie (mCi.) = 10^{-3} curies = $3\cdot7.10^7$ disintegrations per second.

Microcurie(μCi.)= 10^{-6} curies = $3\cdot7.10^4$ disintegrations per second.

The levels of radioactivity administered to patients undergoing diagnostic tests can vary from about 1 μCi. to 10 mCi.

Radiation

The two most common types of radiation met with in clinical diagnostic practice are Beta radiation and Gamma Radiation.

Beta Radiation

Beta radiation consists of very light negatively charged particles (electrons), or positively charged particles (positrons), travelling at high speed. These Beta particles result from spontaneous conversions of neutrons into protons and protons into neutrons within radioactive nuclei. The negatively charged electrons result from nuclei rich in neutrons, and the positively charged positrons from nuclei rich in protons. The Beta energy spectrum from any radioisotope has a continuous distribution from very small values up to a characteristic maximum energy ranging from about $0\cdot025$–$3\cdot1$ MeV.

Beta particles are very easily absorbed, e.g. Krypton 85 Beta radiation, with a maximum energy of 670 KeV., has a maximum range of only $2\cdot6$ mm. in water and $0\cdot2$ mm. in lead.

Gamma Radiation

Gamma radiation is electromagnetic radiation similar to X-rays but having higher frequency and thus shorter wave length. It is in fact not possible to distinguish between the higher frequency X-rays and the lower frequency gamma rays but it is common practice to denote only those rays originating from atomic nuclei as gamma rays. It should be noted that gamma radiation may result from radioactive changes which also produce Beta particles. It is propagated in definite energy bundles or quanta called photons travelling at the speed of light. The amount of energy in each photon is characteristic of the frequency and is given by the equation:

$E = h\mu$ where h is Plancke's constant and equals $6\cdot6.10^{-27}$ erg. seconds and μ is the frequency of the radiation.

Gamma rays are highly penetrating and the effective range depends on energy. For mono-energetic gamma radiation the intensity decreases exponentially with distance travelled in the absorption medium.

i.e. $I = I_0 e^{-\mu x}$ where μ is the linear absorption coefficient, x is the distance in centimetres, I_0 is the intensity of the incident radiation, I is the resultant intensity.

In practice, the quantity known as the half value thickness is used to describe the attenuation power of a particular medium to gamma radiation from a known radioisotope. The half value thickness is the thickness of the absorber required to reduce the intensity of the incident radiation to half its initial value.

For Tc 99 m. the tissue half value thickness equals 46 mm.

The lead half value thickness equals $0\cdot3$ mm.

The sodium iodide half value thickness equals $2\cdot3$ mm.

Gamma rays passing through matter can be absorbed in several ways (Fig. 1):

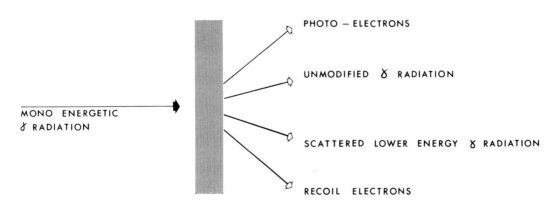

PHOTO – ELECTRONS

UNMODIFIED γ RADIATION

MONO ENERGETIC γ RADIATION

SCATTERED LOWER ENERGY γ RADIATION

RECOIL ELECTRONS

FIG. 1. Absorption of gamma radiation.

(1) A proportion of the photons will strike orbital electrons and eject them from their orbits. These photons will then disappear and the resultant available energy gives kinetic energy to the photo electrons. This is the photo-electric effect and is true gamma ray absorption. The orbital electrons in the ionized atom are immediately re-arranged and a characteristic X-radiation (fluorescent radiation) is emitted. This absorption effect occurs mainly with relatively low energy gamma rays and high atomic weight absorbing materials.

(2) A photon striking a free or loosely bound electron, indirectly, causes the electron to recoil and this leaves the photon with less energy and hence longer wave length. The change in wave length depends on the change in direction of the photon. This process is known as Compton scatter and is more significant in materials of low atomic weight. If a photon strikes an electron which is firmly bound to the nucleus, and the electron recoils, then the nucleus will recoil with it, and in this case the photon energy loss is negligible.

(3) With high energy gamma rays, the formation of positron electron pairs in the absorbing medium becomes important. However, this process requires a minimum of 1·02 MeV. and is rarely met with in clinical diagnostic practice, since the energy of the radiation from the commonly used radioisotopes is much less than this.

Therefore, with radiation from diagnostic radioisotopes, a gamma ray photon will only cease to exist as a result of an interaction leading to the photo-electric effect. In Compton scatter the photon only loses part of its energy.

The result of true absorption of a gamma ray is the ejection of an electron with a considerable amount of kinetic energy. The ionization caused by the secondary electrons produced either in the gas or ejected from the walls of the detector provides a means of detecting gamma rays in gas filled radiation detectors.

It is worthwhile noting that when positrons have travelled about 2 or 3 mm. from their parent atoms they are reduced to thermal velocities. Each positron then combines with an electron. The pair are then annihilated and two photons of gamma radiation each with an energy of 0·51 MeV. are produced. These photons proceed in opposite directions, 180° apart. It is this interaction which allows coincidence counting to be used in positron scanners, where a relatively high degree of resolution can be obtained in the region between two gamma ray detectors without the use of lead collimators.

Detection of Radiation

Most detectors commonly met with in clinical practice make use of two main effects arising from the interaction of beta and gamma radiation with matter. These are ionization of gases and scintillation effects.

Gaseous Ionization Detectors

When radiation passes through a gas, some of the neutral atoms of the gas are stripped of orbital electrons. This process is called ionization and the resultant positively and negatively charged particles are called ions. If these ions are not subject to an electric field they will eventually re-combine to form neutral atoms. However, if an electric field is set up between two electrodes placed in the gas the negative ions will be attracted to the positively charged electrode and the positive ions to the negatively charged electrode, thus forming an electric current. This current can be used as a means of detecting the passage of radiation through the gas.

With relatively low voltages, say 200, the current resulting from the ionization due to a single beta or gamma ray is very small, but the current from a number of such events can be measured to monitor the incident radiation. This current can be as low as 10^{-12} A. The detector using this principle is called an ionization chamber.

If the voltage between the electrodes is raised, the ions gain sufficient energy to ionize other gaseous atoms by collision, and these in turn produce further ions (i.e. a multiplication process results). An output pulse for each beta or gamma ray can then be detected at the electrodes. If the field strength between the electrodes is kept within defined limits, the size of these output pulses will be proportional to the energy of the incident radiation. A detector employing this principle is known as a proportional counter.

When the voltage between the electrodes is raised to the point where the multiplication process reaches saturation, the amplitude of the output pulses is independent of the energy of the incident radiation. Such a detector is called a Gieger–Müller counter. Inert gases, such as Argon, are commonly used in these detectors. Another gas is normally added to quench the electrical discharge so that it is not prolonged after the detection of a single ray. Gases used for this purpose are ethyl alcohol or a halogen such as bromine. With organic vapour counters, the operating voltage is of the order of 1,000 V. while for halogen counters it can be about half this value.

When the count rate detected by a Geiger–Müller counter from a constant source of radioactivity is plotted against operating voltage, a characteristic plateau shaped curve is obtained. In the plateau region the count rate is independent of applied voltage and therefore the requirement for voltage stability is less stringent than for other types of radiation detectors.

Since practically all incident beta particles are absorbed within the sensitive volume of a Geiger–Müller counter it makes a very good detector for beta radiation.

Scintillation Detectors

When radiation is absorbed by sodium iodide, light scintillations are produced in the crystal. These light scintillations are detected by a device known as a photo-multiplier. The photo-multiplier face is placed in contact with a single crystal of sodium iodide activated with thalium. Silicon grease or paraffin oil is used to provide good light transmission. The light is made to fall on a photo cathode inside the photo-multiplier glass envelope and electrons are emitted. These electrons under the influence of electric fields are made to fall on other electrodes called dynodes, causing emission of secondary electrons. This process is repeated a number of times so that for 1 electron emitted at the photo cathode about 10^6 electrons are available at the output.

The amplitudes of output pulses from a scintillation counter are proportional to the energy of the radiation absorbed in the crystal. Thus the scintillation detector can be used as a spectrometer, because an energy spectrum will result in a corresponding pulse height distribution. The relationship between energy and pulse height is subject to statistical variation, so that a particular energy is represented by a relatively broad peak of pulse height distribution.

The efficiency of counting will depend on the size of the crystal and will vary with energy. The higher the energy of the incident radiation, the greater the probability that it will pass through the crystal without being detected.

For gamma ray detection a single crystal of sodium iodide activated with thalium is normally used. The high atomic number of iodine assures good absorption of gamma rays and the crystal is transparent to the fluorescent light emitted. Sodium iodide must be protected from the atmosphere as it is hygroscopic. It is therefore encased in a thin aluminium alloy with a layer of diffuse reflector to improve the collection of light.

Radiation Measurement

Any radiation measuring instrument consists of a detector, a pulse processing system, and a data display system (Fig. 2).

The most commonly used detectors are Geiger–Müller counters and sodium iodide scintillation counters, although solid state *p-n* junction detectors are being used more and more.

in an output pulse. The detector efficiency is defined as the ratio of the number of rays counted to the number of rays striking the detector. For gamma rays with Geiger–Müller counters this is of the order of 2 per cent and with scintillation counters it can vary from 30 to 90 per cent.

Scintillation detectors are normally collimated, i.e. they are shielded (usually with lead) such that there is a high sensitivity to gamma ray photons arising from a defined field of view, whilst most rays originating from outside the field of view are absorbed in the lead. Correct design of these collimators is essential if it is hoped to detect gamma radiation from only part of the body or if comparative measurements are to be made between various tissue regions. A unity gain pre-amplifier is often mounted in the scintillation detector housing. This is used to "match" the output impedance of the detector to the impedence of the signal cable connecting the detector to the main amplifier, thus preventing distortion of the output.

A high voltage unit is required to supply a voltage to bring the detector to the correct operating conditions; for Geiger counters this voltage can be between 400 and 1,000 V. while for scintillation detectors it is normally of the order of 1,000 V. Since with scintillation counters the gain of the photo-multiplier is highly dependent on the supply voltage the high voltage unit must be well stabilized.

In scintillation detector channels the pulses are normally processed in three steps:

(1) Amplification.
(2) Pulse height analysis.
(3) Counting.

(With Geiger counter channels, pulse height analysis is

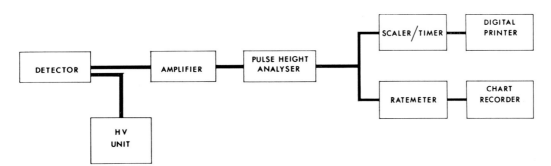

FIG. 2. Radiation-measuring system.

It should be remembered that only a fraction of the rays emitted by the source are detected. This fraction depends on:

(1) Geometry—many of the emitted rays do not enter the sensitive volume of the detector.

(2) Attenuation—due to absorption in the medium between the source and the detector.

(3) Scatter—due to rays being reflected away from or towards the detector.

(4) Detector efficiency—not every ray entering the sensitive volume of the detector will necessarily result

not required since in this case the detector output pulses are all the same size and after amplification these pulses are fed directly to the counting system.)

The pulses from the scintillation detector are amplified linearly. This must be done with accuracy and minimum pulse distortion. The pulses are then passed to a pulse height analyser which provides a variable lower amplitude, threshold setting and a variable window width control providing an upper level at a set voltage above the threshold level such that only input pulses having amplitudes falling within these two levels will initiate an output pulse. Since the amplitude of the pulses coming from the amplifier are proportional to the energy of the radiation striking the crystal, these two levels can be calibrated in energy. The pulse height analyser ensures discrimination against background radiation, rays whose energies have been degraded due to Compton scatter, photo-mutiplier noise, and radiation from any other radioisotope which may be present.

The pulses from the pulse height analyser are then counted using a scaler or rate meter. A scaler is normally used with an accurate electronic timer to display the total number of pulses received in a given time interval or the time taken to record a given number of pulses. The average count rate can then be calculated by dividing the number of counts recorded by the time interval. The number of counts and the time interval are normally displayed on electronic indicator tubes and in many modern systems they can also be written out on a fast digital printer. However, in cases where the radioactivity is changing very rapidly it is sometimes convenient to measure the changing count rate directly. In this case a rate meter is used and provides an output DC voltage which is proportional to the pulse rate. This voltage is normally displayed on a front panel meter calibrated in pulses per second and an output is provided so that the voltage can be displayed on a strip chart recorder to obtain a recording of pulse rate as a function of time.

Errors in Counting

There are three categories of errors which can arise in the attempt to measure radiation. These are:

(1) Instrumentation errors.
(2) Statistical errors.
(3) Dynamic errors.

Instrumentation Errors. These can result from malfunctioning equipment or from faults in measurement procedure. Radiation measuring equipment has to be checked at frequent intervals so that any deviation from the optimum working conditions can be detected at an early stage and corrected. This checking procedure should be carried out on a routine basis and should involve checks on the ageing of detectors, high voltage instability, pulse resolution and faulty cables and connectors. The measuring procedure should be planned such that any changes in the measuring conditions which occur (e.g. change in background count rate) can be detected and corrected. Any calculations involved in the measurement should also be thoroughly checked.

Statistical Errors. All nuclear events are random in character and as a consequence if successive counts are taken over a short period of time, using the same detector exposed to a constant source of radiation, there will be variations in the results obtained. Thus there is a high probability that a single observation of a small number of counts will give an inaccurate estimate of count rate. The statistical accuracy can be improved by increasing the number of counts in each observation. The standard deviation of an observation of N counts is $\sqrt{N}$. This

means that if the average number of counts observed in a unit of time is N, then 95 per cent of the results will lie within the range $N \pm 2\sqrt{N}$. If $N = 100$, then 5 per cent of the observations will result in counts below 80 or above 120, since the standard deviation will be 10 (or 10 per cent). If the time during which observations are made, or the source strength, were increased such that $N = 10,000$, the resultant standard deviation would be only 100 (or 1 per cent), giving a more accurate estimate of count rate.

Associated with each radiation measurement is a background count rate which arises from external sources such as stored radioactive material, naturally occurring radioisotopes, and, to a lesser extent, ionization due to cosmic rays. This background count rate also varies statistically and contributes to the overall inaccuracy of the final result. If N_0 is the number of counts observed in time t, and N_b is the background count rate in the same time, the true count $N_c = N_0 - N_b$ and the standard deviation is $\sqrt{N_0 + N_b}$. In general, if the ratio of the source count rate to the background count rate is greater than 10–1, the effect of the background is negligible. This ratio can be improved by increasing the source strength but with patient investigations the administration of large doses of radioactivity has to be avoided and efforts must therefore be made to keep the background count rate as low as possible.

When radiation is being measured there is inevitably a dead time involved in each measurement. After detecting a beta or gamma ray the apparatus is insensitive to further radiation for a period which for Geiger counters is of the order of 200–300 μsec. The detection process is much faster with scintillation counting and the dead time is normally determined by the scaler or ratemeter and is of the order of 1 μsec. If R_0 is the observed count rate in counts per second and the dead time is t seconds, then in each second there will be a time $R_0 t$ when the detector will be insensitive to counts. The true count rate will then be given by

$$R_c = \frac{R_0}{1 - R_0 t}$$

If $t = 300$ μsec., and $R_0 = 1,000$ c./sec. then,

$$R_c = \frac{10^3}{1 - 10^3 . 3.10^{-4}}$$
$$= \frac{10^3}{1 - 0\cdot3}$$
$$= 1\cdot43.10^3 \text{ c./sec.}$$

i.e. the true count rate is greater by 43 per cent than the observed count rate. With an observed count rate of 100 counts per second this difference will be only 3 per cent. A scintillation counter channel with 1 μsec. dead time would have a loss of only 1 per cent with a count rate of 10,000 c./sec.

Dynamic Errors. If the radioactivity is changing rapidly, e.g. when isotopes with short physical or biological half lives are being used, short counting times must be selected, otherwise the results will be grossly inaccurate. This means that if a rate meter is being used a low time constant must be selected (i.e. the counts must be averaged over a shorter period). Large statistical fluctuations in measured count rate will of course result. This leads to conflicting requirements since for good statistics one requires many counts and for dynamic accuracy the time intervals should be short. A compromise must be effected using sensitive detectors, and where possible increased doses of short lived isotopes, to improve counting statistics without increasing radiation hazard to the patient, and also by using high speed counting systems so that rapid changes in activity can be followed.

Cerebral Investigations

A great deal of confusion arises from the various terms used in the investigation of intracranial disease employing radioisotopes. Differentiation has to be made not only between the various procedures but also between the different types of detecting apparatus involved. Methods used in the investigation of the cerebral circulation will be considered later. Table 1 lists the terms used to describe other radioisotope procedures commonly employed.

TABLE 1

Investigation	Route of Isotope Administration	Detecting Apparatus	Result
Brain scinti-scanning	Intravenous	Rectilinear Scanner	Scintiscan
Brain scinti-photography	Intravenous	Scinticamera	Scintiphoto
Isotope cisternography	Lumbar theca	Rectilinear Scanner or Scinti-camera	Isotope Cisternogram
Isotope ventri-culography	Lateral ventricle	Rectilinear Scanner or Scinti-camera	Isotope Ventriculo-gram

Brain Scintiscanning

Localization of Brain Lesions

A number of radiosotopes in different chemical forms have been used with varying degrees of success in localizing brain lesions. It has been found that many plasma carried substances will concentrate more in lesions than in normal brain tissue. It is presumed that this results from a selective focal breakdown of the blood brain barrier, the only blood/tissue transport mechanism normally operating in the brain being a carrier mediated one. A brain scintiscan can therefore, be thought of as a blood–brain barrier map. Why some lesions should concentrate isotopes much more actively than others is not clear, but it does appear to be related to the vascularity or the acuteness of the lesion. In addition, certain isotopes may

still remain in certain types of lesion after the level of the tracer in the blood stream has become very low. This is thought to be due to intracellular transfer and binding.

The lack of discomfort and risk to the patient has made this investigation very useful in neurological practice. The introduction of short-lived isotopes has led to even further acceptance of brain scanning as a diagnostic tool. If the investigation is negative, the patient may be spared further tests, but if the investigation is positive it will usually be supplemented by neuroradiological contrast studies. However, as confidence increases a number of neuro-surgeons are prepared to operate on the basis of scintiscans alone if they are consistent with the clinical signs. It should be remembered, however, that angiography and brain scintiscanning provide different types of information. The angiogram indicates the distribution and velocity of an opaque medium in the blood while the scintiscan indicates the distribution of the blood–brain barrier.

Instrumentation

In the first scanning systems, the radiation detector was moved manually over the patient's head and where a high count rate was obtained ("hot spot"), a tumour was suspected. Initially, Geiger–Müller detectors were used, but these were replaced by scintillation counters because of the much higher gamma ray counting efficiency of the latter. The problem is to detect the relatively low level of activity within the brain with sufficient statistical accuracy so that changes in activity due to a lesion can be displayed. The introduction of narrow angle collimators greatly improved spatial resolution and therefore the usefulness of the scanning result. The restricted field of view which results from collimation, however, reduces the count rates and provides poorer statistics and a great deal of effort has subsequently gone into overcoming this by improving the counting efficiency of scanning systems and by increasing the activity of the dose injected, using suitable short lived radioisotopes. To be really useful, a brain scan should be made up of at least 10^4 counts.

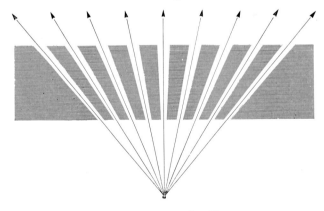

FIG. 3. Focused multi-hole collimator.

Multi-hole collimators were designed to increase sensitivity for a particular degree of collimation (Fig. 3). These collimators are very useful with low energy gamma ray emitters such as technetium 99 m. (140 KeV.) and mercury 197 (77 KeV.) but becomes less effective for high energy emitters, such as gold 198 (410 KeV.). They are optimally effective at a specified distance with spatial resolution falling off at other distances. The position of the patient is, therefore, important and any movement of the patient during the scan can be critical. Depth is also an important consideration when interpreting results and anatomical variations set practical limits on collimator efficiency. Increased depth also means increased attenuation and difference in adjacent areas on a scan could be due to differences in depth. However, one advantage in brain scintiscanning over other organ scanning investigations, such as liver and thyroid scanning, is that the aim is to detect areas of *increased* uptake which are in general more easily detected than areas of decreased uptake.

At the present time the most common type of scanning machine consists of a collimated 3 or 5 in. thalium activated sodium iodide crystal scintillation detector which is made to move automatically in successive parallel paths over the patient's head. The detector output pulses are amplified and pass to a pulse height analyser and hence to a rate meter. The final display can be in the form of a photoscan on X-ray film or as a series of black or coloured dots on white paper. To produce the photoscan, the pulses from the pulse height analyser can be made to switch on the electron beam in a cathode ray tube, while the voltage output of the ratemeter, which is proportional to count rate, controls the tube EHT level and thus the intensity of the light spots, which are time integrated using X-ray film. As a result the phososcan is made up of black dots on X-ray film which increase in number and density as the count rate increases. To produce a coloured dot scan, pulses from the pulse height analyser are made to operate a solenoid tapper, while the ratemeter output voltage causes a carriage, carrying a ribbon divided linearly into a number of colours, to move to and fro such that, as the count rate changes, the ribbon colour beneath the tapper changes. Thus, the colour of the dots as well as their number, changes with the detected count rate. With the simple monochromatic print-out the pulse height analyser output controls the number of dots produced. Other types of print-out such as coloured digits indicating the variation in count rate are occasionally employed. Also in some systems, a fixed count rate is fed to the tapper of a colour printer and reliance is placed on dot colour change alone. Often in these systems, a logarithmic colour ribbon is used providing colour change enhancement at high count rates.

The positron scanner employs two scintillation detector probes situated on opposite sides of the patient's head. As explained in the introduction, positrons are rapidly annihilated resulting in pairs of 510 KeV. gamma ray photons travelling in opposite directions. The positron scanner electronic system is arranged such that a count is registered only when a gamma ray is detected simultaneously by both detectors. Thus the field of view is limited to the region between the detectors obviating the need for large amounts of lead in collimation, although, of course, some shielding is required to minimize the background radiation, due mainly to scatter from the rest of the body. The positron scanner offers high sensitivity and good spatial resolution. The sensitive region between the detectors is symmetrical and the response is unaffected by lateral movements of the source since as it moves away from one detector it becomes closer to another. However, only a few expensive radioisotopes are positron emitters; many have short half-lives and have to be produced using a cyclotron, and toxicity can also be a problem.

The main requirements for a brain scintiscanner are good spatial resolution and high sensitivity, to provide good counting statistics. Each view has to be carried out as quickly as possible to reduce the effect of gross patient movement.

Choice of Radioisotope

Gamma rays with energies less than 50 KeV. are largely absorbed in the skull and consequently are of little use in brain scintiscanning. Gamma rays with energies above 500 KeV. can provide collimation and detection problems due to their high penetrating power. Rays with energy between 75 and 200 KeV. are normally considered ideal for brain scintiscanning and associated techniques. This is one of the most important factors in choosing a suitable isotope for the investigation.

In recent years a great deal of work has been expended, in attempting to find radioisotopes with the ideal characteristics for brain scanning. In order to obtain high count rates as great a dose of activity as possible has to be injected. The boundary conditions here are set by the maximum radiation dose that the patient can be safely exposed to. The radiation hazard to the patient can be reduced if radioisotopes with short physical half-lives or short biological half-lives are used. This means that if the isotope decays rapidly, or is removed rapidly from the body, relatively high activity doses can be given without increasing the radiation hazard to the patient. It is also very helpful if the tracer emits few or no beta particles since, due to absorption within the body, these rays contribute to the hazard to the patient without contributing to the external detected count rate. These characteristics, are properties of the radioisotope technetium 99 m., which has a physical half life of 6 hr. and insignificant beta radiation. The technetium is obtained from a generator (sometimes known as a "cow"), containing molybdenum 99 absorbed on to an alumina column. This generator is produced in a sterile form and is normally replaced once per week. The technetium while in equilibrium with the molybdenum decays with the molybdenum half-life of 67 hr. The technetium is eluted prior to use, by passing sterile physiological saline through the generator, and the radioisotope is collected as sodium pertechnetate ($NaTcO_4$). Up to 10 mCi. of technetium 99 m. can be injected into a 70 kg. patient with no more radiation hazard than 500 μCi. of iodine 131, mercury 197 or mercury 203, the previous most used scanning agents. The gamma ray energy of 140 KeV. leads to good gamma ray detection external to the skull and yet satisfactory collimation can be achieved without excessive amounts of lead.

A number of investigators have reservations concerning the localizing properties of technetium. However, the physical properties of technetium are so ideal for brain scintiscanning that it is still accepted as generally the most useful isotope. This is especially true for initial screening investigations. However, it may well be that where a technetium scan result is equivocal it should be followed by an investigation using another radioisotope such as mercury 197 or iodine 131. De Chiro has suggested that since both experimental and human pathological results have indicated that human serum albumen is a biologically favourable tumour localizing agent, it might be useful to combine the favourable physical characteristics of technetium 99 m. with the useful biological characteristics of human serum albumen in brain scintiscanning. Technetium labelled human serum albumen should be useful in localizing cerebral vascular lesions and by using different times between injection and investigation for neoplastic and vascular lesions optimum contrasts between lesion and normal brain might be obtained.

Indium 113 m., the daughter product of tin 113, has also been used recently for brain scanning. It has a half-life of 99·5 min. and emits gamma rays with 320 KeV. energy. Indium is also eluted from a generator but in this case hydrochloric acid is used. A new generator needs to be replaced only after 3 months since the half life of tin 113 is 118 days. With indium more lead is required for collimation and strict control is necessary over injection times.

The Procedure

Many centres prepare patients for technetium scanning by giving 250 mg. of potassium perchlorate orally, or 50 mg. potassium iodide intravenously, in order to block the thyroid. Furthermore, it has been found that potassium perchlorate also blocks the choroid plexus which has been shown to selectively concentrate technetium with a tendency to produce false positive scans. Oral potassium perchlorate is normally given up to half an hour before the radioisotope injection, but intravenous potassium iodide is given immediately before. 5–10 mCi. of technetium 99 m., in the form of sterile sodium pertechnetate, is then given intravenously and 30 min. to 2 hr. later the patient is scanned with at least one anterior and one lateral view, although often a posterior view is also required.

cavity. The convexity halo is made up of isotope in the scalp, bone, meninges and in blood in large surface vessels and sinuses. In attempting to detect the abnormal it is extremely important to note the normal distribution pattern within the head.

There are various ways of calibrating the scanner, although most of these involve taking a count over a "hot spot" and a count over a "cold spot" to define the required density or colour range. In this laboratory it is standard practice to take the "hot spot" count over the eyes and the "cold spot" count over the centre point of one cerebral hemisphere. The temporal and occipital muscle also take up technetium and the posterior fossa region is largely obscured using the standard calibration procedure. When a posterior fossa lesion is suspected, the scanner can be set up with the "hot spot" over one parotid gland.

In scintiscanning, parasagittal tumours and other hemisphere lesions are normally well defined. Meningiomas, malignant gliomas and metastatic tumours normally have a high scanning detection rate, since in these cases isotope tumour to brain ratio is normally high (up to 100:1). Low grade gliomas show very little more uptake of isotope than normal brain tissue and they are therefore difficult to detect. Recently infarcted brain also shows areas of increased uptake. However, on retesting about four weeks later the high uptake area is no longer apparent, allowing a differentiation to be made between infarct and tumour which will show the same or greater uptake. Subdural haematomas also take up isotope readily. In most cases it is not possible to distinguish between cerebral infarction and tumour after only one scan investigation. Although, in this respect, claims have been made for selenium 75 which rapidly clears from the blood stream, while remaining concentrated in tumour tissue.

SCINTIPHOTOGRAPHY

Considerable time is required to complete a scintiscan, even if only two views are taken. This has serious limitations for dynamic studies and also limits the use of extremely short lived isotopes, as in these situations a

TABLE 2

GAMMA RAY EMITTING ISOTOPES COMMONLY USED IN BRAIN SCINTISCANNING AND SCINTIPHOTOGRAPHY

Radioisotope	Chemical Agent	Half Life	Energy of Main Emission	Activity Injected	Typical Injection Scan/Time
Technetium 99 m.	Pertechnetate	6 hr.	140 KeV.	5–10 mCi.	30 min. to 2 hr.
Indium 113 m.	Chelate	99·5 min.	320 KeV.	5 mCi.	30 min. to 1 hr.
Mercury 197	Chloromerodrin	64 hr.	77 KeV.	0·5 mCi.	4 hr.
Mercury 203	Chloromerodrin	47 days	279 KeV.	0·5 mCi.	4 to 24 hr.
Iodine 131	Human serum albumen	8 days	360 KeV.	0·4 mCi.	4 to 24 hr.

Scintiscan Interpretation

The scintiscan of the head shows a halo of high activity around the edge of the convexity, in the high vascular area in the region of the eyes, and in the region of the parotid glands with very little radioactivity within the cranial

stable condition does not exist during the scanning time (15–20 min. per view) and many ill patients find it impossible even to lie moderately still for these periods of time. Increased activity doses have been used to provide increased count rates so that the scanning speed can be increased. However, the time saved in this way has not been considerable. Specially designed scanners have been produced to improve the situation still further. One such improvement has a detector probe employing ten parallel 2 in. scintillation crystals optically coupled through light pipes to 10 photomultipliers tubes. This ten crystal detector is moved over the patients' head at a uniform speed and since all the detectors are moved together, the scanning speed is effectively increased. The detected isotope distribution is then displayed on an oscilloscope.

However, the instrument used most frequently in the attempt to overcome these basic scanning problems, is the scinticamera (gamma camera). There are a number of different types but all of them consist of a stationary detector which responds continuously to radiation from the whole area of interest within the defined field of view producing a complete image. Scinticamera exposure times are of the order of 2 or 3 min. for each view of the brain using technetium 99 m., this is about 5–10 times faster than brain scanning.

There are a number of different designs of scinticamera but the type in use in most centres is based on the original design by H. O. Anger. A present day Anger scinticamera employs a large single crystal of thalium activated sodium iodide, 11 in. diameter and $\frac{1}{2}$ in. thick. A number of multihole collimators are usually supplied to cope with the energies of the radiation emitted by different radioisotopes. Pin hole collimators can also be supplied to provide high resolution images of small organs, such as the thyroid, by image enlargement at the crystal. Gamma radiation incident on the crystal results in flashes of light which are viewed by a hexagonal array of 19 photomultipliers. The pulse height distribution obtained from these photomultipliers corresponds to a particular light flash location in the crystal, and therefore also to the location in the field of view from which the gamma ray originated. An energy signal, and two position co-ordinate signals are computed electronically from this distribution. A pulse height analyser selects pulses corresponding to the energy of the gamma rays emitted from the radioisotope within the patient, discriminating between background and scattered radiation. The selected energy pulses are used to produce a "bright up" pulse on a cathode ray tube, while the co-ordinate pulses are fed to the X and Y deflection plates. In this way, the radioactivity distribution within the field of view is displayed as a series of light flashes on a cathode ray tube screen. By using Polaroid film, 35 mm. film, or X-ray film, these light flashes can be integrated with respect to time. A storage oscilloscope can be employed to permit immediate viewing of the activity distribution. This can be useful for checking the correct positioning of the patient thus saving time and film. By amplifying the selected X and Y co-ordinate pulses, and by using suitable analogue to digital converters to define the amplitudes of these pulses in digital form, the scinticamera can be interfaced to a digital computer which can be used to store the result, provide field uniformity corrections, and carry out statistical analysis on the result. The data can be analysed in various ways at leisure, and in this

way the overall usefulness of the scinticamera can be extended.

The Anger scinticamera design has been modified to produce displays of the distribution of positron emitting isotopes within a patient. These modifications have taken several forms. In each case the image detector which is placed on one side of the patient's head, is the same as that used in the scinticamera employed for detecting gamma activity distribution, except for the fact that no collimator is used. A detector known as the focal detector is placed on the other side of the patient's head. In the simplest form of positron camera, the focal detector is a single scintillation counter. The annihilation photons are detected by both the image and focal detectors and by use of coincidence circuitry, a two dimensional display of the distribution of the positron emitting isotope within the patient can be obtained without the use of collimators. This simple type of positron camera is very insensitive, as many of the annihilation photons miss the focal detector and are not recorded. In order to increase sensitivity, other types of focal detector have been designed. One type employs a detector assembly similar to the image detector while another type consists of a bank of 19 scintillation counters situated about 20 in. from the patient. This latter type is the one most often found in practice. When annihilation radiation is detected by the centre scintillation counter of the focal detector, the coincidence scintillations in the image detector are shown on the display oscilloscope without change of position. However, when annihilation photons are detected, by other counters, a correction signal is sent from the focal detector to the image detector position computing circuit, so that the position of the light flash on the oscilloscope is changed. Since this correction is exact for only one plane, there is a "plane of best focus" between the image and focal detectors. This plane can be set electronically. Since no collimators are used, positron cameras have high sensitivity. However, it should be noted that these cameras can be easily overloaded causing deterioration in their characteristics. The resolution is good for planes deep within the subject, although there is a limited depth of focus above and below the plane of best focus beyond which the resolution becomes unacceptable. Under electronic control each plane in the subject can be displayed in sharp focus. Here a shallow depth of focus is required and is obtained by placing the focal detector close to the subject. This is analogous to taking a series of tomograms. However, it has to be remembered that the remarks made earlier regarding positron radiopharmaceuticals in relation to positron scanners are also applicable in relation to positron cameras. Three other types of scinticamera are in current use and these will be described briefly.

(1) The Autofluorscope

This instrument employs a rectangular mosaic of 293 thalium activated sodium iodide crystals, each of which is 3/8 in. in diameter and 2 in. thick. They are packed in an array measuring 6 × 9 in. with 1 cm. separation between centres. The light scintillations in the crystals are passed to an array of photomultipliers by means of light pipes in such a way that it is possible to identify in which crystal the interaction has occurred. Because of their thickness, the crystals are good radiation absorbers providing a good response to high energy gamma radiation. The resolution is good but, of course, is limited by crystal diameter. After processing, the information is displayed on a cathode ray tube.

(2) Image Tube Scinticamera

There are a number of different designs but basically in this type of scinticamera, a multi-hole collimator allows gamma rays to fall normally on to a fluorescent screen. This fluorescent screen is similar to that used in an ordinary X-ray image intensifier tube. The fluorescent coating on one side of the glass screen glows as a result of gamma radiation falling on it. This light causes electrons to be liberated from the photo electric surface on the other side of the screen resulting in an electron image of the gamma activity distribution. As a result of electron acceleration and reduction in size, the image produced at a collector screen is an intensified version of that produced at the fluorescent screen. This intensified image is then optically coupled to a photo cathode of an optical image intensifier resulting in an overall brightness gain of about 50,000.

(3) Spark Chambers

These systems make use of the fact that a gas discharge can produce a considerable amount of light. An electric field is set up in a chamber as in a Geiger–Müller counter. The filling gas is an Argon–Neon mixture with alcohol or iodine vapours as a quenching agent. Gamma radiation entering the chamber interacts with the silver on a coated glass window producing electrons which cause a spark discharge. The spark is extremely bright and can be recorded using Polaroid film. However, gamma ray detection efficiency is low resulting in poor sensitivity. Also no energy discrimination is possible. With low gamma ray energies and using good collimation, good spatial resolution is theoretically possible.

Isotope Cisternography

Investigation of the movement of CSF along normal and abnormal pathways using radioisotope tracers can yield useful information in cases of hydrocephalus and rhinorrhoea. It has been found that when sodium pertechnetate, the normal scintiscan agent, is injected into the CSF by lumbar theca puncture, it is not transported with the CSF but is absorbed within a short distance of the injection site and fails to be distributed throughout the subarachnoid spaces. This is presumably because of its small molecular size. For investigations employing this tracer route iodine 131 labelled human serum albumen, or technetium 99 m. labelled human serum albumen, are usually used. Because of large molecular size these tracers are carried along with the CSF and are absorbed mainly in the cortical subarachnoid spaces. For this investigation technetium 99 m. labelled human serum albumen combines the favourable physical characteristics

of technetium 99 m with the favourable biological characteristics of albumen. 2 mCi. of technetium 99 m. labelled human serum albumen are usually injected providing less radiation hazard to the patient, than 100 μCi. of iodine 131 labelled human serum albumen. The resulting high count rates and the 140 KeV. energy of the technetium 99 m. gamma rays allow use to be made of a scinticamera. When the investigation is to be carried out for a period greater than 30 hr., either iodine 131 labelled human serum albumen or a combination of iodine 131 human serum albumen and technetium 99 m. human serum albumen has to be used in order to overcome the problems of low count rates due to the short physical half life of technetium 99 m. Injections of large amounts of protein have to be avoided to reduce the possibility of meningitis. Even with injections of 500 μg. protein, a reaction may occur, the symptoms of which can usually be reduced by use of an antihistamine.

If a scintiscanner is used for the investigation it can prove advantageous to have an X-ray image superimposed on the photoscan to allow for comparison of anatomical detail. Use of a scinticamera will reduce the time required for each view, but it also provides a more flexible arrangement when various projections are required. This can be of real value in cases of rhinorrhoea where, if it is hoped to gain any useful information, it is necessary to place the patient in a position where CSF leakage will occur. With these patients the investigation may be augmented by placing cotton swabs in the nostrils and then later measuring the swab activity using a well scintillation counter.

Investigations into communicating hydrocephalus involve determining whether or not the tracer appears in the cortical subarachnoid spaces 24 or 30 hr. after injection. In cases of blockage, the tracer tends to enter the ventricular system. Isotope cisternography can prove to be a very useful complementary test to air encephalography.

Isotope Ventriculography

Whereas sodium pertechnetate has been found to be of no value in isotope cisternography, it has proved useful in isotope ventriculography. Studies have shown that when sodium pertechnetate is introduced directly into the lateral ventricles and the ventricular system is totally obstructed, the activity within the head decays with the 6 hr. physical half life of technetium indicating little or no absorption. This fact has been made use of in monitoring the efficiency of surgical CSF shunts in children and adults as well as in the diagnosis of hydrocephalus.

INVESTIGATION OF THE CEREBRAL CIRCULATION

Both radioisotopes which tend to diffuse physically between blood and tissue (diffusible isotopes) and radioisotopes which remain in the blood stream during the time of the investigation (non-diffusible isotopes) have been used to investigate the cerebral circulation.

Diffusible Tracers

Choice of Radioisotope

The tracer employed should be metabolically inert and should diffuse rapidly between blood and tissue. The radioisotopes commonly used are:

    (a) Krypton 85:
half life 10·6 years
main emissions—670 KeV. beta radiation
                   510 KeV. gamma radiation
    (b) Xenon 133:
half life 5·27 days
main emission—81 KeV. gamma radiation

The maximum range of Krypton 85 beta rays in tissue is only 2·6 mm. Therefore, the use of beta counting techniques is limited to measuring flow in the exposed brain cortex. Only 0·4 per cent of the total Krypton 85 disintegrations gives rise to emission of 510 KeV. gamma radiation, resulting in low count rates and the need for considerable amounts of lead in collimation to define the field of view at this energy. As a consequence, Xenon 133 has been more widely used in recent years. Perhaps with the advent of improved solid state radiation detectors with dimensions of the order of 2 or 3 mm. in diameter, beta radiation may become the means by which cerebral blood flow will be measured in very small defined regions of the brain using needle probes.

Method

Methods using diffusible tracers are based on the Fick principle which states that the quantity, Q, of a substance, taken up by an organ at a specific time, t, is the product of the blood flow, F, and the arterio venous difference for that substance at that time, $C_{at} - C_{vt}$.

i.e. $Qt = F(C_{at} - C_{vt})$

$$F = \frac{Qt}{C_{at} - C_{vt}}$$

The flow in a period, T, is found by integration.

i.e.
$$F = \frac{\int_{o}^{T} Qt \, dt}{\int_{o}^{T} (C_{at} - C_{vt}) \, dt}$$

If C_{Bt} is the concentration of the substance in brain tissue at time, t, and W_B is the weight of the brain tissue, then,

$$Q_t = C_{Bt} W_B$$

If equilibrium is reached within the time, T, the concentration of the substance in the brain tissue will be equal to the final venous concentration C_{VT} multiplied by a constant, λ, the partition co-efficient (which expresses the ratio of the solubility of the substance in brain tissue and blood.)

$$F = \frac{C_{VT} W_B \lambda}{\int_{0}^{T} (C_{at} - C_{Vt}) \, dt}$$

(The brain concentration will be exactly equal to the final venous concentration only where the solubility of the tracer in brain tissue and in blood are equal, i.e. when $\lambda = 1$)

$$\frac{F}{W_B} = \frac{C_{VT} \lambda}{\int_{0}^{T} (C_{at} - C_{Vt}) \, dt}$$

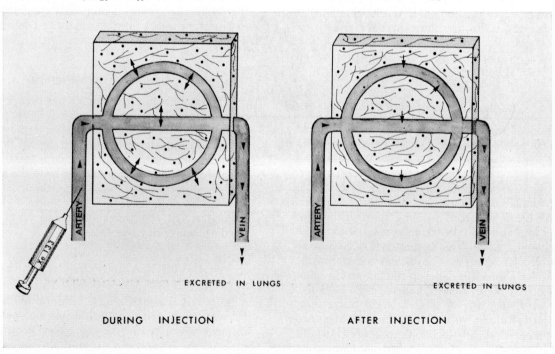

EXCRETED IN LUNGS   EXCRETED IN LUNGS

DURING INJECTION   AFTER INJECTION

FIG. 4. Xenon clearance technique.

It is usual to express the cerebral blood flow measurement in flow per 100 gm. weight of tissue per minute.

The first successful technique based on this principle did not use a radioisotope tracer but used stable nitrous oxide. This was the well-known Kety–Schmidt method, where the patient inhaled nitrous oxide over a 10 min. period. However, this technique involved sampling of arterial and venous blood to obtain serial measurements of nitrous oxide content. The use of a radioactive tracer overcomes the problems of estimating the amount of nitrous oxide in the blood since standard radioactive counting techniques can be employed.

However, by employing intracarotid artery injections of Xenon 133 and externally mounted radiation detectors to monitor the clearance of the tracer from brain tissue, the need for blood sampling is obviated. Furthermore, by using this technique, cerebral blood flow in defined regions of the brain can be measured instead of in the brain as a whole.

When Xenon 133 dissolved in saline is injected into the internal carotid artery the tracer is carried to the cerebral tissue (Fig. 4), equilibration between blood and tissue takes place rapidly. Furthermore, since the inert gas is highly soluble in air, about 95 per cent of the tracer reaching the lungs is excreted so that there is no significant recirculation. On completion of the injection the fresh arterial blood containing no radioisotope clears the tracer from the tissue, and the rate of this clearance depends on ths blood flow.

Detection and Data Processing Systems

A number of collimated scintillation detectors are mounted around the head. The size of the detectors and the degree of collimation are chosen to define the regions of the brain to be studied. The output pulses from each detector are fed to pulse height analysers and the selected pulses can then be processed as follows:

(1) The pulses can be fed to a multitrack magnetic tape recorder with a "downstream monitoring" head, such that any chosen channel can be monitored by a ratemeter and scaler to allow immediate data analysis, (if desired all channels could be monitored in this way). A paper chart recording of the ratemeter output will give the shape of the clearance curve, while the scaler will display the total number of counts recorded (i.e. the area under the clearance curve).

This is the simplest way of storing the data so that various types of analysis can be carried out on all channels at some later stage. However, the tape recording system can impose definite dead time limitations on the acceptable count rate, and if these limits are exceeded, serious loss of counts will result.

(2) The pulses can be fed through a multiplexing system to a multi-channel analyser operating in "multi-scaler mode" and the data can be stored in the instrument's ferrite core memory in the form of time histograms with selectable time intervals. This is an improvement although, depending on the multiplexing system, the method may also be dead time limited.

However, in general these systems have to write out the stored data so that analysis can be carried out.

(3) The pulses can be fed on-line to a laboratory digital computer where again the data can be collected in the form of time histograms. However, in this situation, in addition to the data being stored in a ferrite core memory, use can also be made of magnetic tape files. Analysis can be carried out using the computer and the results for every regional channel can be obtained in a very short time.

Sources of Error

Eagerness to measure cerebral blood flow in smaller and smaller regions of the brain can be accompanied by the temptation to use systems which are unable to provide the necessary spatial resolution.

The regions of the brain defined by some systems have been assessed using point sources. The response of a scintillation detector to a point source of radiation depends on:

(a) The inverse square of the distance of the source to the detector.
(b) The area of the crystal exposed to radiation.
(c) The attenuation produced by the intervening tissue.

In the situation where cerebral blood flow is being measured, the source is not a point and using this kind of assessment is misleading, because due to the inverse square law effect it tends to suggest that the effective volume from which gamma radiation is being detected is confined to a localized region close to the scintillation detector (Fig. 5). However, if thin infinite uniform sources perpendicular to the axis of the detector are considered, then the detector response to such a source is independent of the source-to-detector distance. This is the result of the fact that the detector response to any point source within the extended source is inversely proportional to the square of the source to the detector distance, whereas the area of the extended source "viewed" is directly proportional to the square of the source to detector distance and the two squared distance factors cancel. However, in the practical situation, the detector response will fall off with distance from the detector due to absorption within the intervening tissue, but this reduction in response is not as severe as that predicted by point source assessment. If a multi detector system has been designed using a point source assessment, there will be considerable overlap in the adjacent detector fields of view and the idea of well defined regions of measurement using such a system is questionable.

This situation is aggravated even more due to Compton scatter within the tissue of the 81 KeV. gamma rays of Xenon 133. If large pulse height analyser window widths are employed, a significant percentage of the detected rays in fact originate outwith the collimated detector field of view. This again limits the regionality of the measurement. Using Xenon 133 as the tracer the optimum setting of the lower threshold on the analyser is of the order of 75 KeV. eliminating all first order scatter

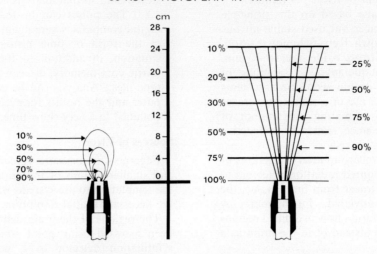

FIG. 5. Point source response compared with plane source response for a collimated scintillation detector. (After F. C. Gillespie, "Some factors influencing the interpretation of regional blood-flow measurement using inert gas clearance techniques". *Blood Flow Through Organs and Tissues*, 1968. Published by permission of E. and S. Livingstone Ltd.)

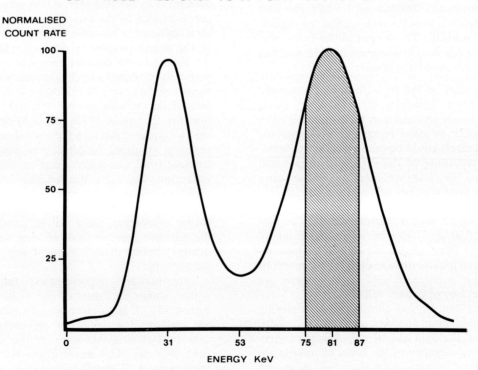

FIG. 6. Xenon 133 energy spectrum in air, showing the 81 KeV gamma ray peak and the 31 KeV X-ray peak. The shaded area indicates the "window width" necessary to eliminate all first-order scatter greater than 60°.

greater than 60° (Fig. 6). Naturally, this reduces the counting sensitivity, and as the detector size is reduced more and more in the attempt to measure the cerebral blood flow from smaller regions of the brain, the effect on counting sensitivity is considerable. Moreover if the comparison of cerebral blood flow measurements from different small regions of the brain are to be meaningful, then not only must all the electronic channels be set up accurately in the same way, each detector gamma ray energy response must be the same, otherwise each detector will be "looking at" regions of different size.

The accuracy of cerebral blood flow measurement using the clearance technique also depends on the uniformity of partial pressure of Xenon within the tissue. This becomes a problem where the region under consideration is small and consists of inhomogeneous tissue. At microscopic levels, in a situation where flow is high, the Xenon partial pressure will decrease more rapidly than where flow is low and as a result partial pressure gradients can be set up around different tissue boundaries. The inert gas will then diffuse from areas of high mean partial pressure to areas of low mean partial pressure altering the mean rate of clearance from both regions. The lower the mean flow in the whole region the more significant this effect will be, and this further imposes a lower limit on the size of the region from which meaningful cerebral blood flow measurements can be made. If measurements are being made from a region of fast flow, and from an adjacent region of slow flow, diffusion of Xenon will take place between regions and this will modify the clearance curves obtained.

At the present stage of detector development, and using Xenon 133 as the radioactive tracer, it must be questionable if there are any advantages to be gained in attempting to measure cerebral blood flow from more than about eight different regions of the brain. With the introduction of cyclotron-produced isotopes with energies in the region of 200 KeV. (such as Xenon 127) it should become more feasible to use gamma cameras interfaced to laboratory computers for the measurement of regional cerebral blood flow. However, there will still be a limit to the size of region of the brain from which cerebral blood flow can be measured accurately. The versatility of a gamma camera-computer system make it very attractive.

Cerebral Blood Flow Calculations

Since after injection has ceased, the arterial blood contains no tracer, the Fick equation for the clearance technique can be written as:

$$dQ = -FC_V \, dt$$

where dQ = the change of quantity of tracer in the tissue in time, dt
F = the blood flow
C_V = the venous concentration of the tracer
As before, $Q = C_B W_B$ where C_B is the concentration of tracer in tissue, and W_B is the weight of brain tissue.

Therefore, $dC_B = -\dfrac{F.C_v}{W_B} dt$

$$C_V = \frac{C_B}{\lambda}$$

where λ is the partition coefficient.

$$\frac{dC_B}{C_B} = -\frac{F}{W_B \lambda} \, dt$$

The solution of this differential equation is

$$C_B = C_{BO} \, e^{-\frac{F}{W_B \lambda} \cdot t}$$

where C_{BO} is the concentration at time O.

This is an equation of an exponential decay and will result in a straight line when points are plotted on semi-log paper. Two exponential components can be extracted from the clearance curve after intra carotid injection. These are understood to represent the distribution of flows in grey matter and in white matter of the brain. The exponential stripping process can be carried out manually by plotting the clearance curve on semi-log paper and fitting a straight line to the latter part of the curve. This defines the slow component and by subtraction from the initial part of the curve the fast component can be found. This, of course, can be done more accurately and more quickly using a computer.

The slopes of the two components can be expressed as half times, $(T\frac{1}{2})$, (the time taken for any point on the line to decrease to another of half its value). From these $T\frac{1}{2}$ values, flow values can be calculated for grey matter and white matter from the following equations.

$$\text{Flow (grey matter)} = \frac{\lambda_g \times \log_e 2 \times 100 \times 60}{T\frac{1}{2} \text{ (fast component)}}$$

$$= \frac{3370}{T\frac{1}{2} \text{ (fast component)}}$$

$$\text{Flow (white matter)} = \frac{\lambda_\omega \times \log_e 2 \times 100 \times 60}{T\frac{1}{2} \text{ (slow component)}}$$

$$= \frac{6237}{T\frac{1}{2} \text{ (slow component)}}$$

where $T\frac{1}{2}$ = the half time in seconds
λ_g = the partition co-efficient for grey matter
λ_w = the partition co-efficient for white matter.

The mean cerebral blood flow through the whole region of the brain under study can be calculated from the peak count rate obtained and the area under the clearance curve using the formula

Mean flow (ml./100 g./min.)

$$\frac{(H_{max} - H_{10}) \times \lambda_B \times 100 \times 60}{A_{10}}$$

where H_{max} = the peak count rate of the clearance curve
H_{10} = the count rate 10 min. after injection
A_{10} = the area under the clearance curve,
i.e. the total number of counts recorded in 10 min.
λ_B = the partition co-efficient for whole brain.

This relation was basically formulated by Zierler, but it can also be proved using the more general occupancy principle enunciated by Orr and Gillespie.

The use of a 10 min. measurement period is a practical approximation. In cases of very slow flows, tracer clearance may have to be monitored for a longer period.

Inhalation Technique

Perhaps the most clinically attractive technique of measuring cerebral blood flow is the Xenon 133 inhalation technique introduced by Mallet and Veal in 1963 and also developed by Obrist. In this method Xenon 133 is inhaled by the patient for 1–5 min. and the brain tissue clearance curve is monitored by externally mounted detectors. This technique is completely atraumatic since no arterial punctures or blood samples are necessary. However, there are two major disadvantages. During inhalation, all the body tissues take up Xenon and as a consequence there is appreciable re-circulation which distorts the clearance curve. A correction is applied by measuring the Xenon activity in the expired air, which reflects the arterial concentration. The clearance curves are also distorted due to isotope in the extra cranial tissues. It would appear that the real practical use of this technique will be to determine only fast component flows, using computer analysis to carry out the exponential stripping procedure and apply the necessary corrections.

Application

Knowledge of cerebral blood flow can help neurosurgeons to decide whether or not it is safe to operate, for example, in the situation where spasm is present during subarachnoid haemorrhage. Cerebral blood flow measurements in the operating theatre may indicate which surgical procedure is best, such as when estimating the risk of cerebral ischaemia during carotid ligation. Post-operative measurements of cerebral blood flow may increase the knowledge concerning a patient's recovery. Furthermore, knowledge of the state of the cerebral circulation in cases of raised intracranial pressure can be invaluable.

Non-Diffusible Tracers

Since the measurement of cerebral blood flow using the Xenon clearance technique necessitates intra carotid injection and a fair amount of data processing, there have been a number of attempts to find a less traumatic and simpler alternative. A method proposed by Oldendorf, utilized the measurement of the circulation time of a non-diffusible isotope. The method was taken up by other workers and has been applied to patients with various intracranial disorders.

The method basically consists of injecting a bolus of a non-diffusible isotope intravenously (0·5 mCi. iodine 131 labelled hippuran and 1 mCi. Technetium 99 m. have been used) and monitoring the passage of radioactivity through the brain by means of an externally mounted collimated scintillation detector. After amplification and pulse height analysis, the detector output pulses are fed to a ratemeter, the output of which is filtered and electronically differentiated to give a recording of rate of

change of count rate (activity) with respect to time (Fig. 7). The peaks of this bi-polar curve indicate the maximum rate of entry of activity and the maximum rate of exit of activity into and from the detector field of view. The time interval between those peaks is the mode circulation time.

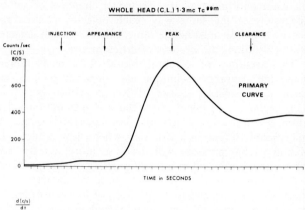

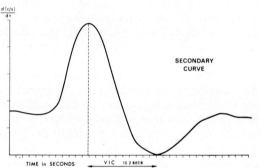

FIG. 7. (a) Recording of activity/time curve after a Bolus injection of a non-diffusible radioisotope. (b) Recording of rate of change of activity/time curve.

The relative simplicity of this method makes it attractive to clinicians but the information one can acquire about the circulation in this way is limited. The method provides an index of velocity and not a measure of cerebral blood flow and theory shows that under conditions of changing radius, the flow through tubes will change more markedly than velocity. On the other hand any changes in blood viscosity will also tend to effect the velocity. Furthermore, in a series of 200 patients studied in the Institute of Neurological Sciences, in Glasgow, many patients with gross intracranial pathology showed no abnormal circulation velocity, although the average mode circulation time for groups of patients with ischaemia, haematoma and subarachnoid haemorrhage was increased. However, this is of limited value since when faced with an individual patient the clinician is very likely to be confronted with a mode circulation time result which will be within the expected range for normal patients. This is due to the rather wide range of mode circulation times found in normal subjects. The assumption that changes in flow will be reflected in changes in velocity is valid in such restricted circumstances that it seems unwise to base clinical decisions on such measurements.

FURTHER READING

1 Glasstone, S., *Source Book in Atomic Energy*. D. Van Nostrand Company Inc.
2 Stanton, L., *Basic Medical Radiation Physics*. Butterworths.
3 McAfee, J. G., Fueger, C. F., Stern, H. S., Wagner, H. N. and Migita, I. (1964), "Tc[99 m]. Pertechnetate for Brain Scanning." *Journal of Nuclear Medicine*, 5, 811–827.
4 Oldendorf, W. H., *Detection of Brain Tumours using Radioisotopes*. Private Communication.
5 De Chiro, G., Ashburn, W. L. and Grove, A. S., "Which Radioisotope for Brain Scanning?" *Neurology*, Vol. 18, March, 1968.
6 Stern, H. S., Goodwin, D. A., Schaffel, V. and Wagner, H. N., "In[113 m]. for Blood-Pool and Brain Scanning," *Nucleonics*, Vol. 25, No. 2, pp. 62–65, 68, February, 1967.
7 Anger, H. O. (1958), "Scintillation Camera," *Rev. Sci. Inst.*, **29**, 27.
8 Anger, H. O. (1963), "Gamma Ray and Positron Scintillation Camera," *Nucleonics*, **21**.
9 Bender, M. A. and Blau, M. (1963), "The Autofluorscope," *Nucleonics*, **21**.
10 *Proceedings of the Workshop on Computer Processing of Dynamic Images from an Anger Scintillation Camera, St. Louis, Missouri, January, 1971*.
11 Ter-Pogossian, M. M., Niklas, W. F., Bull, J. and Eichling, J. O. (1966), "An Image Tube Scintillation Camera for use with Radioactive Isotopes Emitting Low Energy Photons," *Radiology* **86**, 463.
12 Horwitzh, N. H., Lofstrom, J. E. and Forsaith, A. L., (1966), "A Comparison of Clinical Results Obtained with a Spark Imaging Camera and a Conventional Scanner," *Radiology*, **86**, 830.
13 Bannister, R., Gilford, E. and Kocen, R., "Isotope Encephalography in the Diagnosis of Dementia due to Communicating Hydrocephalus," *Lancet*, November, 1967.
14 Di Chiro, G., Ashburn, W. L. and Briner, W. H., "Technetium Tc[99 m]. Serum Albumen for Cisternography," *Arch. Neurol.*, Vol. 19, August, 1968.
15 Lassen, N. A. and Ingvar, D. H. (1961), "The Blood Flow of the Cerebral Cortex Determined by Radioactive Krypton," *Experientia* (*Basel*), **17**, 42–43.
16 Harper, A. M., Glass, H. I., Steven, J. L. and Granat, A. H. (1964), "The Measurement of Local Blood Flow in the Cerebral Cortex from the Clearance of Xenon 133," *J. Neurol. Neurosurg. Psychiat.*, **27**, 255.
17 Gillespie, F. C. (1968), "Some Factors Influencing the Interpretation of Regional Blood Flow Measurements using Inert Gas Clearance Techniques," in *Blood Flow Through Organs and Tissues* (Brain and Harper, Eds.). Edinburgh: Livingstone.
18 Zierler, K. L., "Equations for Measuring Blood Flow by External Monitoring of Radioisotopes," *Circulation Research*, Vol. XVI, April, 1965.
19 Orr, J. S. and Gillespie, F. C., "Occupancy Principle for Radioactive Tracers in Steady State Biological Systems," *Science*, Vol. 162, 138–139, October, 1968.
20 Mallet, B. L. and Veall, N. (1963), "Investigation of Cerebral Blood Flow in Hypertension using Radioactive Xenon Inhalation and Extracranial Recording," *Lancet*, i, p. 1081.
21 Rowan, J. O., Harper, A. M., Miller, J. D., Tedeschi, G. M. and Jennett, W. B. (1970), "Relationship Between Volume Flow and Velocity in the Cerebral Circulation," *J. Neurol. Neurosurg. Psychiat.* Vol. 33, 733.
22 Rowan, J. O., Cross, J. N., Tedeschi, G. M. and Jennett, W. B. (1970), "Limitations of Circulation Time in the Diagnosis of Intracranial Disease," *J. Neurol. Neurosurg. Psychiat.*, Vol. 33, 739.

6. THERAPEUTIC RADIATION

ROBERT TYM

INTRODUCTION

Ionizing radiations are beams of photons or atomic particles that have sufficient energy to penetrate the body and by splitting electrons from tissue molecules create highly reactive ions in the tissues. Their "radiation" effect is produced by these ions acting as chemical poisons to the cells. Radiation therapy relies firstly on the control of the physical characteristics of the radiation, secondly on the control of the biological effects of the chemical poisoning and lastly on the delineation of the tissue to be destroyed in order to protect the rest of the patient. The aim of this chapter is to foster in the mind of the clinician an intuitive—a mind's eye—grasp of these three factors as they apply to the treatment of brain tumours, avoiding the infinite wealth of complex detail that is the special delight of the physicist, the chemist and the radiobiologist.

IONIZING RADIATION

There are two forms of radiation that have to be considered, namely photons and atomic particles.

Photons

The non-physicist can best think of photons as weightless particles, travelling at the speed of light but differing from each other in the amount of energy they possess and hence in their physical behaviour. The universal energy unit for photons is the **Electron Volt** ($= 1.6 \times 10^{-12}$ ergs) but in the energies used in radiation therapy they are usually expressed in units of a thousand, million or billion-fold as KeV., MeV., or Bev. (10^9). A simple classification of photons is best based on their energy for there is no difference between a "gamma ray" photon of 1.33 MeV. from cobalt[60] and an "X-ray" photon of 1.33 MeV. produced by an X-ray machine (Fig. 1).

There is a difference in *beams* of photons from radioactive sources such as cobalt[60] which are all of one or two distinct energies, and beams of photons from an X-ray machine which have mixtures of energies. An X-ray beam designated as 150 *kV*. (not KeV.) means that the most energetic photons are of 250,000 eV.

Some of the energy of photons is transferred to the

constituents of any matter with which they collide (interact). By energy transfer at the moment of interaction a photon of a little above 2 eV. can produce an excited atom or molecule by displacing one of its electrons from one orbit to an orbit of higher energy nearer the nucleus—the photon then proceeds on its way, deflected in another direction, with 2 eV. of energy less than before the interaction. It is the photons of about 2 eV. ("light waves") that are the power source of the photochemistry of the retina and the photosynthesis of the leaf.

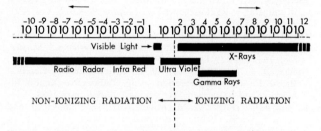

FIG. 1. Photon energy in electron volts (log scale)

Energy transfers of about 4 eV. are capable of destroying organic molecules by breaking strong organic bonds. A transfer of about 35 eV. is sufficient to eject an electron right out of a molecule and produce a pair of **Ions**. Statistically it requires photons of about 100 eV. to be sure of producing ionizations in tissue so that the term **Ionizing Radiation** is reserved for beams of photons (or atomic particles, *see* below) that are capable of producing

produce them any more deeply. The sinister effects of X-ray photons of more than 10^5 eV. is due to their ability to produce ionizations on the surface and still have enough energy to continue producing them throughout the depths of the body.

Atomic Particles

The kinetic energy imparted to atomic particles by "radioactive" atomic nuclear disintegrations or by atomic particle accelerators is also measured in electron volts and the energy transfers at their interactions with tissue molecules produce the same type of ionizations and subsequent chemical changes that follow photon interactions. The *probability* of particles interacting with tissue atoms depends upon their kinetic energy (speed) and their charge (any atom that is to be accelerated artificially has to be stripped of at least one of its electrons so that it becomes responsive to a magnetic field). Slowly travelling, heavily charged particles more readily interact, and transfer more of their energy per micron of their track through tissue, than fast, lightly charged or uncharged particles (*see* Table 1).

Any atomic configuration is called a **Nuclide** and is specified by giving the number of its protons (Z) and neutrons (N) which make up the nucleus (usually the mass (A) is used where $Z + N = A$). Using the convention $_Z$(chemical symbol)^A. $_6C^{14}$ denotes a nuclide of 6 protons and 8 neutrons. Since there are 6 positively charged protons there must be 6 negatively charged electrons in order to give a neutral atom and this number of electrons gives the nuclide the chemical characteristics

TABLE 1

COMMONLY USED ATOMIC PARTICLES FOR IONIZING RADIATION

Electrons	Small, negatively charged particles orbiting the atomic nucleus. Referred to as *beta rays* when given off spontaneously by a disintegrating (radioactive) nuclide and *delta rays* when ejected from atoms by photon or particle interaction—but best called electrons and designated by their energy in electron volts.	Mass = 0·0005 Charge = −1
Protons	Charged particles that form part of the atomic nucleus. The hydrogen nucleus consists of a sole proton so that protons can be considered hydrogen atoms with the single orbiting electron stripped off.	Mass = 1·0 Charge = +1
Neutrons	Uncharged particles which add to the mass but not to the charge of the nucleus. Hydrogen has no neutrons. They cannot be accelerated artificially because they have no charge and their source is always atomic nuclear disintegrations.	Mass = 1·0 Charge = 0
Alpha Particles	The nuclei of helium atoms consisting of two protons and two neutrons. They are sometimes referred to as *alpha rays* when given off by radioactive atoms or produced by particle or photon interaction but better thought of as helium atoms with the two electrons stripped off.	Mass = 4·0 Charge = +2

Any atom can have some or all of its electrons stripped off and be accelerated into part of a beam; the *charge* of the particle depends upon how many electrons it has lost and the *mass* depends upon the sum of protons and neutrons in the nucleus.

interactions that eject electrons and produce ions. The secondary chemical changes that follow the sudden appearance of these highly reactive ions within the cell are the basis of radiation chemistry, radiobiology and ultimately radiation therapy.

The higher energy ultra-violet light photons (*see* Fig. 1) can produce ionizations but they do so only on the surface of the body—after energy transfers sufficient to produce surface ionizations there is not enough energy left to

of carbon. A difference in the number of neutrons alters the mass and makes it another **Isotope** of carbon. If a nuclide is unstable and has a likelihood of disintegrating by emitting photons and particles it is **Radioactive**. The post-disintegration nuclide retains its chemical characteristics and hence its name (e.g. carbon) as long as it only emits neutrons and photons; but if protons are lost electrons must go too, to keep it neutral, and it becomes a nuclide of another **Element**, the different chemical characteristics of the new element depending upon its different shell of electrons.

The **Chart of the Nuclides** shows all the isotopes of all the elements and their percentage abundance; for the radioactive ones it shows the rate at which they disintegrate (expressed as a half life), the photons and atomic particles they emit and their energy, and the nuclide that is left.

THE EFFECTS OF IONIZING RADIATION ON CELLS

Qualitative

Chemical changes in the cell begin at the moment of exposure to radiation. Much of the initial damage is short-lived as electrons in many of the excited atoms and molecules re-distribute themselves back into their normal orbits, many ruptured organic bonds reform and many ion pairs re-combine—the energy gain appearing as heat. But where ions do not re-combine their single unpaired electron makes them **Highly Reactive Free Radicals** which go on to disrupt other molecules, large and small, within the cell.

Free radicals are more numerous and persist longer in tissue where oxygen is freely available. Severe degrees of hypoxia protect tissues (paradoxically called the **Oxygen Effect**) because fewer reactive free radicals are formed and those that are have an increased tendency to re-combine. Chemicals containing sulphydryl groups also have a **Radiation Protection** effect similar to that of hypoxia but act by "mopping up" the free radicals at an early stage.

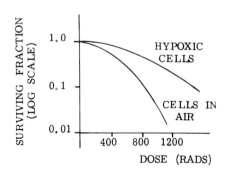

FIG. 2. X-Ray dose response curve for human cells in tissue culture.

The subsequent radiation damage is essentially a slow chemical poisoning affecting DNA and RNA, with consequent far-reaching effects both for the damaged cell and its progeny. A radiated cell may die soon after the exposure, indicating a high sensitivity to chemical poisoning, or die much later; on the other hand, it may lie quiescent, nursing a chemical wound.

It is not surprising that chemicals have been found that mimic some or all of these biological end effects of radiation and can be given as drugs—they were termed "radiomimetic drugs" and are now part of cancer chemotherapy, being used as alternative or adjuvant methods of cancer treatment.

Quantitative

Most photons or particles of the *primary beam* that enter the body interact with tissue atoms and after yielding some of their energy proceed on as part of the *secondary beam*—the rest of the secondary beam consisting of accelerated atomic fragments and new photons from the interactions. The *difference in energy* between the *entry beam* (the primary beam) and the *exit beam* (any non-interacted primary beam and any unspent secondary beam) represents *energy that has been absorbed*. The **Dose** to the body is a measure of this absorbed energy that has gone into the fragmentation of tissue atoms, chemical changes in tissue molecules and (to a very insignificant extent) heat production. The unit of dose is the **Rad** = the absorption of 100 ergs/gm. (of tissue). A tumour dose of 5,000 rads implies that each gram of tumour has absorbed $5,000 \times 100$ ergs. The total or *integral dose* given to the body during a tumour radiation includes those rads given to the tumour and those rads given unavoidably to normal tissue on the way in and out —it is given in **Gram-rads**. If the whole body receives an evenly distributed dose it is given in **Rads, Total Body Dose**. An accidental exposure of 500 rads, Total Body Dose, would give a 50 per cent chance of death to an adult human.

The difference between the **Rad** and the **Roentgen** is that the former measures absorption of energy by an unspecified absorber (usually tissue), but the roentgen, by specifying the absorbing material and measuring the electrical charge from ions formed by the radiation, becomes more a measure of the number of photons or particles in a beam of any given energy. *The ROENTGEN is the radiation sufficient to produce one electrostatic unit of electricity in 1 c.c. of air at NTP*. The measurement by an ammeter of the electric current produced by ions in a closed box of air interposed in the beam is therefore a measure of the total energy to which the body is being exposed and hence a form of dosimetry.

However, the amount of energy absorbed is *not* necessarily an accurate measure of biological damage. The protective action of hypoxia has been mentioned and other factors influencing the biological effectiveness of radiation include:

(a) The sensitivity of the cell at the time of radiation.
(b) The rate of radiation.
(c) The distribution of the energy deposition within the cell.

(a) **The sensitivity** of cells to the *lethal* effects of radiation varies but is broadly determined by a "law" enunciated sixty years ago by Bergonie and Tribondeau stating that it is "*. . . directly proportional to the reproductive activity of the cell and inversely proportional to the degree of differentiation of the cell . . .*".

The devastating effects of radiation on the cells of an early foetus are to be expected since all cells are rapidly dividing. The lethal effect of a moderate dose of radiation on the whole adult animal is determined by the most sensitive cells in the body, usually the most rapidly dividing ones, namely the gut epithelial cells and the haemopietic cells. (Gonadal cells are equally sensitive but whilst they are vital to the propagation of life their survival does not influence the survival of the individual.) Animals exposed to a moderate but lethal total body dose die of intestinal haemorrhage or leucopenia or both within a few days.

Following a much larger dose, however, the animal dies much more quickly, within minutes or hours, from an overwhelming chemical toxicity occurring in every cell of the body. Death in these circumstances is characterized by an acute central nervous system failure with epilepsy and apnoea. The lethal poisoning of the animal's nervous system kills the animal by poisoning but without first killing the neurons and it pre-empts the slower but no less lethal effects of leucopenia and intestinal haemorrhage. The neurons themselves are highly resistant to the *lethal* effects of radiation, in keeping with the above "law" because they never divide—but their *function* is highly sensitive to chemical change. Two well-documented phenomena illustrate this functional sensitivity of neurons—the sensitivity of spontaneous epilepsy in certain strains of mice to minute doses of radiation, and the sensitivity of animal behaviour, that is, conditioned reflexes, to very low doses of brain radiation. There is little clinical evidence of this neuron-sensitivity in therapeutic brain radiation, however. *Radiation sickness* is proportional to the total dose of radiation given in any part of the body at one time and is attributed to radiation-induced chemical toxins that circulate and affect the brain secondarily.

Most tumour cells do not divide as rapidly as gut epithelial, haemopietic or even skin cells and their apparent lack of differentiation does not always make up for this in terms of radiation sensitivity: consequently, tumour cells are rarely the most sensitive in the body and not necessarily more sensitive than adjacent normal cells in the tissue radiated. The *therapeutic ratio* attempts to relate the dose that surrounding normal tissue will tolerate to the dose required to kill neoplastic tissue.

Sensitivity applied to tumours can be given many connotations and a rapid "melting away" of tumours in response to radiation, if followed by an equally rapid re-appearance, is a less desirable form of sensitivity than a slow disappearance with a good chance of no recurrence.

(b) **The rate of radiation.** A dose of 3,000 rads given in 30 min. will produce roughly the same biological end effect as a dose of 6,000 rads that is evenly divided and given at 10 weekly intervals (*see* Fig. 11). This is because if given enough time all cells can recover from radiation damage to some extent provided the dose has not been too high and the damage not too severe to kill them outright. There are several reasons why it is thought more prudent clinically to give divided doses when radiating tumours.

(1) Many tumour cells that are dormant or hypoxic at the time of one exposure may become more sensitive

later if death of surrounding tumour allows their share of oxygen to increase and stimulates them into more active growth.

(2) Different phases of the mitotic cycle give slightly differing sensitivities to the cells, and cells in a resistant phase at one exposure may be in a sensitive phase at the next exposure.

(3) There is a smaller total dose to the body at each sitting, decreasing the likelihood of radiation sickness.

(4) Normal tissue surrounding the tumour will have a greater chance of recovery from the effects of a number of low doses of unavoidable radiation than it would from one large one. (*See* the initial, fairly flat part of the response curve—Fig. 2.)

(5) If normal cells die after one dose then extra time will allow replacements of capillary endothelial cells, astrocytes or microglia to migrate to the scene before the next dose.

(6) Experiments on animals suggest that divided doses induce fewer mutations in normal cells—inferring fewer post-radiation meningeal sarcomas in therapeutic radiation of the brain.

(7) It is always hoped, but it has yet to be proved, that normal cells recover relatively more from multiple small doses than do neoplastic cells.

(c) **The distribution of the energy deposition in the cell** varies with the energy and whether it is photon or particle radiation. When photons or atomic particles travel through tissue the energy they transfer per unit length of track—*The Linear Energy Transfer* (LET, in units of *electron-volt per micron*)—increases with particle charge and decreases with particle or photon energy. When a helium (alpha) particle with a charge of +2 slows down it loses nearly all its energy in the last few microns before it stops; the effect on the cell in which it does stop is like that of a miniature red-hot poker. The consequent disruption is enough to kill, if not to over-kill, the cell, overwhelming even the protective effect of hypoxia, and yet leaving an adjacent cell unscathed. The same dose per gram of tissue delivered by photons has a different spatial and temporal distribution and this smoothing-out in time and space of the ionizations may cause little individual cell disruption and no cell death. The biological effect of the photons will be less. The **Relative Biological Effectiveness** (RBE, a ratio) relates the biological effectiveness per gram of tissue of the same dose of various types of radiation to the biological effectiveness of "standard" 250 kV. photons from an X-ray generator, which is taken as unity. The RBE varies from 0·8 for very high energy photons that have evenly scattered ionizations, to 5·0 for very heavy fully ionized particles such as carbon or the violent reactions of neutrons. The RBE falls off again with still larger atoms and greater charge as energy is dissipated in over-killing any one cell. Biological effectiveness is not a precise term; it depends upon exactly which biological end-effect is used for its measurement. Nonetheless, it is because of Relative Biological Effectiveness that the measurement of any inadvertent radiation dose in rads alone is insufficient as a means of monitoring its harmful biological effects to man. The Roentgen Equivalent, Man (**Rem**, a number) is a better measure of harmfulness. Rem = rad dose of the particular radiation × RBE of the particular radiation.

A "safe" dose of radiation for occupational exposure (if anything capable of breaking chromosomes can be called safe) is said to be 5 rem per year total body dose—about one routine chest X-ray (0·02 rem) every week-day of adult life. For the general population one tenth of this is barely tolerable and even so is a probable contributor to the increasing incidence of leukaemia.

The translation of these principles of radiobiology into the practice of radiotherapy depends upon the solution of several problems, not the least of which are those imposed by the absolute physical and geometrical characteristics that must be considered next.

RADIATION THERAPY

This can either be applied *internally* from implanted or injected radioactive molecules or applied *externally* from X-ray generators, radioactive sources or particle accelerators.

Internal Radiation

(a) Internal Implanted Sources (to be considered here as fixed "point" sources for the sake of simplicity but obviously they can be of any shape).

(i) The number of photons or particles emerging in all directions per unit of time depends upon the rate of disintegration of the radioactive source, the **Activity**, (the **Specific Activity** is the activity per gram). The unit is the **Curie** = $3·7 \times 10^{10}$ *disintegrations per second* (usually used as a milli- or micro-curie). The dose to tissue depends upon the amount of radioactive material used, its activity, its half-life, the time that it is in contact and the energy of its radiation. A gold[198] implant is usually left in place since its half-life is 65 hr. and after 390 hr. (six half-lives) the dose rate is a negligible (1·6 per cent) of what it was at the time of implanting. Radium, on the other hand, has a half-life of over one thousand years and must be removed when the dose has been given.

(ii) The energy of the emitted photons of particles (and hence the effective penetration) is a characteristic of the isotope used: with electron emitters however, it is not one single energy but a *range* of energies that is the characteristic of the isotope, with an average energy (denoted $\bar{E}$) and a maximum energy (denoted E max).

(iii) With increasing distance from the point source the *flux* (the number of photons or particles crossing a unit area in a unit time) decreases not only according to the inverse square law but also according to the rate of absorption of the photons or particles by the tissue (the absorption coefficient of the tissue).

These three factors determine the distribution of the dose.

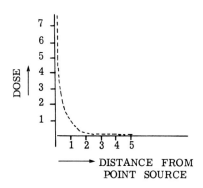

FIG. 3. Curve of the inverse square law.—The dose distribution curve for a point source of photons.

The *Dose Distribution Curve for Photons* (Fig. 3) is, in effect, the curve of the inverse square law (because the loss of dose from tissue absorption of the emitted photons is matched by scattering of dose from secondary radiation).

The *Dose Distribution Curve for Electrons* (Fig. 6, for strontium[90]) is a composite curve combining:

(i) The "bell-shaped" distribution curve of electron energies (which varies from isotope to isotope and is not necessarily a symmetrical curve—Fig. 4).

(ii) The curve of the distribution of energy transfer with distance (linear energy transfer) for each single electron (Fig. 5). (The small, shaded asymptotic tail is due to secondary photons emitted as the result of collisions and is known as **Bremstralung Radiation**.)

(iii) The curve of the inverse square law, as for photons (Fig. 3). These 3 curves combined give the curve of Fig. 6; the scale used in Fig. 6 relates to the distance travelled by the electrons of strontium[90].

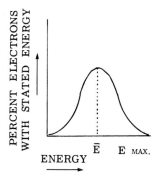
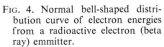
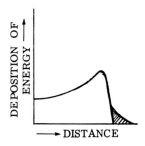

FIG. 4. Normal bell-shaped distribution curve of electron energies from a radioactive electron (beta ray) emmitter.

FIG. 5. The linear energy transfer of a single electron.

With internal radiation from implants the aim is to deliver as large a dose as possible to the tumour, including the tumour capsule, and as small a dose as possible to the immediately adjacent normal tissue. But if the capsule is to be radiated then there must be some radiation beyond. With a point source of photons, when the distance from the source is doubled the dose is reduced to one quarter, i.e. the dose has a very rapid fall-off (*see* Fig. 3, the curve of the inverse square law). When the distance is doubled from a point source of electrons the dose is reduced—but to more than one quarter (*see* Fig. 6). On purely geometrical grounds, therefore, a point source of photons is always better than a point source of electrons for radiating a tumour and its capsule from within and sparing as much as possible the adjacent normal tissue.

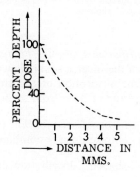

FIG. 6. Dose distribution curve for a point source of electrons. SR^{90}

Because of its symmetry and the ease of access to it the pituitary gland and its tumours has been the site of implantation of many internal radiation sources. A spherical pituitary tumour 2 cm. in diameter (volume = 4 c.c.) is probably the upper limit for treatment by a single point source of photons. Radiation emanating from the centre which gives a dose of 4,000 rads to the capsule will give a fall-off dose down to 1,000 rads 1 cm. away, and this is a barely tolerable dose to the optic nerves, chiasm and hypothalamus. Were the tumour to be 4 cm. in diameter (volume = 32 c.c.) and the dose to the capsule was again 4,000 rads from a single point source, the fall-off to 1,000 rads would be over 2 cm., being absorbed by a dome-shaped 100 c.c. volume of overlying brain and cranial nerves.

The normal pituitary gland is small (1 c.c.) and being spheroidal in shape can be almost resolved into two spheres and radiated with two point sources. A very high, destructive dose can be given in comparative safety (Fig. 7) and a fall-off of dose from 15,000 rads at the capsule to 5,000 rads 4 mm. away just preserves the third nerves.

The bony floor of the sella and the mucosa of the roof of the sphenoid sinus are in danger of necrosis from intra-sellar photon radiation but by compromising on fall-off by using an electron emitter (yttrium^{90}) the penetration of the bone is reduced and very little radiation reaches the mucosa. Nevertheless, radiation necrosis of bone does occur from this form of intra-sellar therapy and has been followed by CSF rhinorrhoea and secondary, often fatal, meningitis. This complication is less frequent following the use of an yttrium^{90} implant screwed into the sellar floor

(Fig. 8)—as long as the sellar floor is thick enough for the screw of the source to be held rigidly in one place the bone is protected to some extent. Even this ingenuity does not guarantee effective destruction of all the normal gland in every case—anatomical variation, amongst other things, being always one step ahead of any technique.

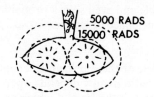

FIG. 7. Isodose curves for two point sources of photons implanted into the pituitary gland.

FIG. 8. Yttrium^{90} screw implant into the sella.

For the eradication of the normal pituitary gland or of small intrasellar tumours all other methods have now been superseded by the per-nasal trans-sphenoidal micro-neurosurgical approach. For larger pituitary tumours with moderate suprasellar extensions removal at open cranio-tomy followed by an application of a paste containing yttrium^{90} powder to the lining of the sella is most effective. The surgery of large or small pituitary tumours is always best followed by external radiation—no surgical method can remove every tumour cell.

(b) Internal Diffusible Sources (not often used in CNS radiation therapy although they have sometimes been injected into the CSF).

To the physical factors already mentioned that govern the dose distribution from static implanted sources, must be added two biological factors of *selective tissue uptake* and *biological half-life* that affect the dose distribution from soluble radioactive compounds that can be given orally, injected intravenously or instilled into body cavities.

External Radiation

(a) Photons. There is a difference in the dose distribution between high and low energy photons, illustrated in an idealized Fig. 9 by superimposing a dose distribution curve upon a coronal section of a head.

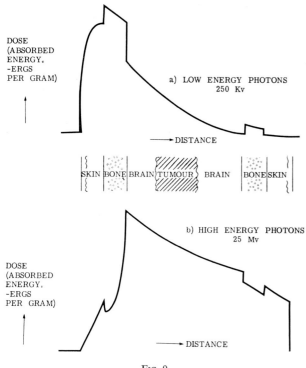

DOSE (ABSORBED ENERGY. -ERGS PER GRAM)

a) LOW ENERGY PHOTONS 250 Kv

→ DISTANCE

SKIN │BONE│BRAIN│TUMOUR│ BRAIN │BONE│SKIN

b) HIGH ENERGY PHOTONS 25 Mv

DOSE (ABSORBED ENERGY. -ERGS PER GRAM)

→ DISTANCE

FIG. 9.

(1) *Low Energy Photons* (250 kV., Fig. 9a). The photons arrive at the skin and some immediately interact with tissue atoms, releasing a shower of relatively low energy secondary electrons and secondary photons which deposit their energy within a very short distance. It is the skin and subcutaneous tissue at the entry site, therefore, that absorbs the most energy and receives the highest dose. On hitting the more dense bone the amount of energy deposited per unit of distance is increased and the absorbed energy per gram (which is how dose is measured) is also increased in this instance. With continued passage through the head the successive photon interactions steadily decrease the energy of the beam and when the tumour is reached its dose is much lower than that at the skin and bone on the way in. The dose to the skin on the far side is minimal. (The *dose* to bone varies greatly with varying radiation energies and may be higher or lower than the dose to the tissue on either side of it, sometimes resulting in bone necrosis without other tissue necrosis.)

(2) *High Energy Photons* (25 mV., Fig. 9b). At the moment of impact with the skin a shower of secondary electrons and photons is again produced. Their greater energy sends them further, and predominantly in a forward direction (the sideways scattering of radiation is less with increasing energy). They travel almost to the surface of the tumour before most of their energy is given up. The dose at the skin on the way in is less than the dose at the skin on the way out.

Perhaps the most important ratio is the dose at the skin (whether exit or entry) to the dose at the tumour. In these somewhat idealized diagrams (Figs. 9a and b) it is 2:1 for the low energy beam and 1:2 for the high. With deep tumours, therefore, high energy radiation increases the possible dose from one beam if the skin is to be protected from radiation damage. By virtue of the reduced sideways scattering with high energy photon beams, other beams can be brought in from other directions to increase the tumour dose without endangering skin or too much normal brain from the overlapping of radiation fields.

The geometrical complexities of matching the dose from several overlapping beams to the three dimensions of a tumour are considerable. A computer is commonly used by the physicist to produce a treatment schedule that confines the radiation to any shape required by the physician. Unfortunately there is no comparable accuracy on the part of the physician in delineating the size and shape of most tumours in the brain and so a good deal of the physicist's expertise goes unrewarded clinically.

The obliging symmetry of the pituitary gland and most of its tumours had attracted as much inventiveness for its external as for its internal radiation. With conventional methods of external radiation, using approximately 1 MeV. photons from a cobalt[60] source, the minimum treatment field is a 5 cm. cube (125 c.c.), so that the adjacent hypothalamus and diencephalon always get the same dose as the pituitary itself. This should be borne in mind in the radiation treatment of secreting pituitary tumours—benefit might be secondary to radiation depression of releasing factor production from the hypothalamus rather than to depression of hormone production from the radiated tumour itself.

(b) Atomic Particles. (1) *Charged Atomic Particles* can be accelerated to great speeds (800 MeV. of kinetic energy and more) by using massive machinery (which, incidentally, takes up quite a few acres of ground) and a very narrow beam can be produced which has much less sideways scatter than a photon beam of similar energy. Using stereotactic techniques this beam can be accurately directed to the pituitary gland or to any small target in the head. Electrons are not used for this sort of beam because they are too light—regardless of their speed they are, like ping-pong balls, too easily deflected in all directions: there is less sideways scattering with the much heavier protons and helium particles, which behave more like cannon balls in comparison.

The energy of a mono-energetic proton or helium (alpha) particle beam just before it enters the head can be so adjusted by aluminium or water absorbers that it reaches just as far as some desired target in the head and no further. There is a peak of energy transfer at the end of the beam—the target—as the particles slow and stop (the peak of energy at the end of a particle beam was first described by Bragg, an English physicist, and is known as the Bragg peak). The dose distribution curve for the beam is similar to that of a single electron shown in Fig. 5. Using the large accelerators in Harvard and Berkeley, California, to produce particle beams, large doses of external radiation can be concentrated in the pituitary, sparing the hypothalamus, providing there is not a tumour larger than 4 c.c. which is a critical volume for this, as well as for internal radiation, though for different reasons. Doses of from 7,000 to 12,000 rads have been used, but the lower end of this range seems to be excellent for acromegaly, giving adequate suppression of growth hormone production in about half the cases without at the same time producing pan-hypopituitarism.

Ideal as these knife-like beams of particles at first seem to be there are still many physical and geometrical constraints and very often an adequate dose of radiation cannot be given to the gland or to a whole tumour; as with other forms of radiation the ideal is rarely if ever realized.

(2) *A beam of fast* (14 MeV.) *neutrons* can penetrate deeply into tissue and the nuclear interactions of these neutrons with oxygen and other tissue atoms produce high LET secondary radiation that is capable of killing hypoxic tumour cells. But because neutrons are heavy the fall-off dose with depth due to scattering and absorption cancels out a lot of the benefits and in the end leaves a neutron beam no more clinically effective than a much cheaper beam of about 1 MeV. photons from a cobalt[60] source, which penetrates tissue so much further.

(3) The rationale of *Boron Capture Therapy* was based upon the physical property of a high probability of inter-action (capture) that boron atoms and slow neutrons have for each other. The interaction causes the boron atom to disintegrate into a stable atom of lithium and an 8 MeV. helium (alpha) particle. If the interaction takes place intracellularly the helium nucleus will travel about the length of the cell and produce enough ionizations to kill it.

A wan hope that the brain cancer cells could be enticed to take up certain compounds selectively—an enticement to which, throughout the history of cancer research, the cancer cell anywhere in the body has shown a marked resistance—prompted the somewhat premature building of a huge slow neutron-producing atomic reactor with an operating room arranged below it. The arrangement still awaits the discovery of a boron compound—or any compound—that has the property of going into malignant cells and no others. However, any compound that was selectively taken up by cancer cells, boron containing or not, would so revolutionize cancer therapy that the atomic reactor would be forgotten in the rush to use the compound more rationally. The failure of the boron capture project is a sad comment on those who put action before clear thinking and its failure is monumental not only because of its cost and size.

TUMOUR BIOLOGY AND RADIOTHERAPY

The elegant quantitative radiobiological studies on cultures of single, separate cells in suspension or growing separately on plates (Fig. 2) have unfortunately not been followed by any commensurate success with solid tumours or tumour explants. Yet sensible extrapolation of the cell culture data must be relevant to solid tumours despite the difficulty of comparable experimental design. Compared with the logarithmic growth of cell cultures little is known about the cell kinetics of solid tumour growth—the hypothetical mathematical models are relatively simple and to some extent supported by experiment but there appear to be many obscure variables in practice.

A solid tumour of 1 mm³ is barely visible to the naked eye but has grown from one original malignant cell, through twenty-two generations, to two million cells. At this stage its size is beginning to impede the diffusion of oxygen into it and metabolites out of it, and continued growth at the previous rate depends upon a properly constructed vasculature—something that cannot be guaranteed in any experimental situation or even in all natural ones. Its rate of increase in size therefore ceases to be exponential and instead is governed by the caprice of the blood supply, or by growth of the cells that can be supplied by surface diffusion. (It is the independence of any intrinsic vasculature which makes ascites "tumours" a favourite *in vivo* experimental model.)

Intrinsic cerebral tumours, the gliomas, parasitize the normal blood supply or grow their own vessels or do both. Tumours whose cells freely infiltrate through the surrounding normal brain cause little disruption of neurons and fibre tracts and have access to the normal blood supply (curve I in Fig. 10). Tumours whose cells remain mostly aggregated (curve II in Fig. 10) and displace normal tissue must develop their own vessels and the larger they become the more likely they are to outgrow their blood supply, and as this fails tumour hypoxia and central necrosis develop. Tumours of each type, diffuse or aggregated, may be the same size—in that they are composed of the same number of malignant cells—and their cellular growth kinetics may be similar, but their clinical and histological presentations may be very different.

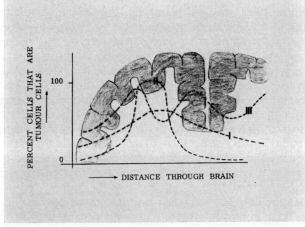

FIG. 10.

The bizarre cell morphology seen at the centre of tumours that remain aggregated—the deformed mitotic figures, the giant cells, the pleomorphism and anaplasia—may be a reflection of severe growth constraints on both tumour cells and normal cells due to overcrowding and starvation, rather than an indication of an inherent morphological characteristic of the cells of one "type" of tumour. An "anaplastic" cell from the centre of a glial tumour has been seen to regain all its characteristic finery of dendrites and intra-cellular structure when rehabilitated in an optimum culture environment outside the body. Indeed such a cell often becomes indistinguishable from a normal astrocyte in tissue culture. When a biopsy is taken from where blood supply is abundant, at the periphery of an aggregated glial tumour or in the midst of an infiltrating, diffuse glioma, there are *no* morphological criteria for distinguishing any one single malignant astrocyte from any one normal astrocyte. In these sites local overcrowding and hence morphological degeneration of cells is postponed by the motility of successive generations of tumour cells that travel through surrounding normal brain at random. Eventually, however, cells of a diffuse glioma infiltrating in one direction will meet cells infiltrating back again, and randomly placed regions of local overcrowding will develop, giving the appearance of a multi-centric tumour (curve III in Fig. 10). But that term should not necessarily imply that there is more than one tumour, or that the one tumour present started from more than one cell—even if its different "centres" end up being in different hemispheres of the brain.

A large glioma seen on cutting the brain in the post-mortem room is the end result of from 5 to 10 years continuous growth; such observations as: ". . . highly malignant looking . . ."; ". . . appears to be more malignant (in one or another region) . . ."; or ". . . appears to have 'changed its spots' . . ."; are based upon conjecture and are of doubtful meaning in the absence of cellular growth kinetic data. Anaplasia, pleomorphism and necrosis may signify nothing more than local overcrowding. Certainly there is much soundly based correlation between histology and clinical prognosis—but there is also a lot of neuropathologically embroidered nosolgy based on an attempt to classify beyond any natural distinctions. All intrinsic tumours are *sui generis* but their similarities are greater than their differences.

Little information is available on the *in vivo* cellular growth kinetics in human malignant glial tumours—but they can be investigated without detriment to the patient. Small amounts of tritiated thymidine can be injected intravenously and will label all the cells in the body that are at that moment synthesizing DNA prior to cell division. After tumour biopsy at operation those tumour cells that were about to divide at the time of the thymidine injection can be recognized by autoradiography. By juggling the delay between the injection or injections of tritiated thymidine and the biopsy, and by giving a few hours before the biopsy a small intravenous dose of a colchicine derivative, which holds all cells entering mitosis in the easily recognizable metaphase for several hours after injection, proportions of labelled and unlabelled mitotic cells can be ascertained. From the cell counts, and by the simplest of deductions, the time the tumour cells spend in DNA synthesis (S-phase), and the time spent between S-phase and mitosis (G$_2$-phase)—8 hr. and 5 hr. respectively—are not very different from any other cells in the animal kingdom. Applying the data to the

most acceptable mathematical model of growth—the so-called stem cell model which has a fraction of the cells actively dividing and a fraction of the cells that are not (at least not dividing for some considerable time, but resting in the co-called G$_0$-phase) the doubling time of the actively dividing tumour cells appears to range from 5 to 20 days with a mean of 12 days. The fraction of G$_0$-phase—presently non-dividing—cells appears to be from one third to one half. This non-dividing fraction, together with a randomly distributed death rate amongst all tumour cells, gives a doubling time of the *tumour* (the time it takes the tumour to double its size) of about 3 months, considerably longer than the doubling time of the actively dividing *tumour cells* themselves which is up to 3 weeks.

A tumour that starts from one cell and doubles its size every 3 months takes 5 years to reach 1 mm.[3] and another 5 years to reach 100 cm.[3]—even longer if necrosis continually reduces the number of viable cells. It is common for epilepsy to ante-date the more obvious clinical presentation of a tumour by 5 years or more, and if a tumour of 1 cmm. can be accepted as epileptogenic then this clinical observation is consistent with tumour growth rates of this order.

Tumours growing in "silent" regions of the cerebral hemisphere remain undetected until they reach a critical volume of about 100 c.c., at which stage they give rise to significantly raised intracranical pressure and distortion of the brain stem.

Continued growth at the rate of doubling in size every 3 months would imply reaching a size of 200 c.c. in the next 3 months and 400 c.c. in the 3 months after that. But a functioning organ such as a vascular tree cannot expand so rapidly and remain efficient, because vascular failure with consequent tumour necrosis will eventually slow the rate of increase in size. However, *any* increase in size of the tumour will be associated with rapid clinical deterioration of the patient, once it has passed the critical size for seriously disturbing the intracranial hydrodynamics and the critical size for distorting the brain stem. Despite the dramatic appearance of the rapidly deteriorating patient and the large, expanding and partly necrotic tumour, there is *no* justification for invoking a change in the growth rate. The tumour cells can be assumed to be dividing at the same rate as they were at the time of inception of the tumour, perhaps 10 years before, and the tumour itself, if there is any change, is doubling its size at a slower rate than before because of the necrosis within it.

Unfortunately it is at this late stage of tumour development that surgery and radiotherapy are so often expected to influence the clinical course. It is hardly surprising that at this stage the elegant radiation dose-response curve for cells in tissue culture (Fig. 2) appears to have so little relevance. The factors which contribute to the survival of the patient himself, and to the survival of the cells of the tumour during a course of radiation, and which therefore contribute to the variability and unpredictability of the clinical response to either surgery or radiation must be considered alongside this classical dose response curve of single cells. These factors can be listed.

(a) After 10 years or so of growth tumour cells will have infiltrated widely throughout the brain, from lobe to lobe, hemisphere to hemisphere, down the brain stem, and even along the walls of the ventricles and over the whole neuraxis via the CSF. Recurrence can be anywhere—but a recurrence in the brain stem, for example, would produce devastating clinical effects out of all proportion to its size. Accurate delineation of the tumour being impossible the radiation dose must on occasion be given to the whole neuraxis, as is becoming routine for juvenile medulloblastomas and ependymomas in which CSF seeding is as common as any other form of spread. Where dissemination has been permitted into the peritoneum or blood stream because of a CSF shunting procedure, or into the lymphatics of the scalp where a tumour is infiltrating through a decompression, there is no such ready answer. The death from radiation of 99·9 per cent of tumour cells in a tumour whose total volume was 100 c.c. would still leave ten million healthy tumour cells scattered at random through the brain from which continued growth may continue at the previous rate. Had prior surgery been able to reduce the tumour bulk to 1 c.c. the same radiation dose would still leave one hundred thousand surviving cells, needing about 6 years to regrow to 100 c.c. (or 2×10^{12} cells).

(b) Many hypoxic cells will be protected from the effects of radiation and yet later regain a blood supply sufficient to enable them to resume an active part in continued growth. Attempts to reduce the number of cells protected by hypoxia by radiating the patient in hyperbaric oxygen are not necessarily successful since many cells are too distant from functioning capillaries to benefit from any increase in the partial pressure of oxygen.

(c) At any one time a large latent fraction of tumour cells (those in G_0-phase) is not actively dividing and may be considerably less susceptible than the other fraction to the lethal effects of radiation. If these cells, possibly 40 per cent of the total, survived the radiation they need only re-enter the division cycle and divided two or three times to return the tumour to its previous volume.

(d) Despite the apparent "malignancy" of malignant glioma cells they divide considerably less often than the cells of many other tissues in the body. On that score they are less susceptible to radiation damage than the skin and hair follicles of the scalp, and probably than the capillary endothelium of normal cerebral blood vessels. Even when the scalp is protected from a high dose, by using high energy beams through multiple portals of entry, there is often a temporary, sometimes a permanent depilation within a few weeks of treatment. Varying amounts of adjacent normal or sparsely infiltrated brain cannot be so protected, and will receive the full tumour dose. The non-tumorous capillaries and arterioles eventually show endothelial proliferation leading to an obliteration of the lumen.

The mechanism of *radiation necrosis of brain* appears to be delayed ischaemia from vascular failure. However, clinically it often comes on very rapidly and apparently over a large region of brain at the same time, although the delay after treatment may be from a few months to 5 years. Histological changes in the neurones and glial elements—the fattening of the cell bodies and the blunting of the dendritic processes—may be a non-specific change due to radiation and ischaemia. But the appearance is not unlike the changes seen in experimental allergic encephalomyelitis and the sudden regional onset after so many years makes an iso-immune concept attractive for at least part of the effect. There is an earlier, often clinically transient, demyelination that is supposedly due to oligodendroglial damage and which sometimes and unaccountably responds to high doses of steroids.

At autopsy many years after radiation therapy there is often very little to find that can account for the progressive neurological deterioration evident in so many cases in the terminal months or years. Relatively few viable tumour cells are seen with no dramatic regions of necrosis or gliosis; the assumption must be that neurones have degenerated and died one by one leaving no trace but insufficient normal tissue to support life. Neuronal cell counts to support this would be difficult.

The *Time-Radiation Dose* response curve for radiation necrosis of normal human brain (Fig. 11) has been published by Lindgren and radiation necrosis is therefore usually avoided to-day. But either due to mistakes in dosimetry or to unpredictable and capricious responses of some brains and spinal cords all forms continue to be seen occasionally.

To these radiobiological factors must be added the mechanical factors derived from brain swelling, alterations in cerebral blood flow or CSF circulation and distortion of the brain stem that can follow radiation damage, haemorrhagic necrosis or cyst formation. It soon becomes a matter of little surprise that the overall clinical response of the patient with an intracranial tumour to any therapy may often seem capricious.

The criteria by which success or failure of treatment of intracranial tumours are judged are imprecise, to say the very least. Survival is certainly a poor guide, but once an attempt is made to judge the quality of surviving life the matter becomes intuitive, obviating a scientific answer. Clinical trials designed to answer the question of whether or not patients with gliomas benefit from radiation treatment are doomed to failure because the experimental errors introduced by the large number of uncontrollable and unassessable variables are far greater than any differences from the small but definite advantages that radiation confers on certain patients in certain circumstances. That there is not always a clearly defined scientific basis for radiotherapy is no reason for dismissing it. Radiation, like surgery, can remove malignant tissue and it can be similarly justified on a basis of informed empiricism. Radiotherapeutic practice depends upon this

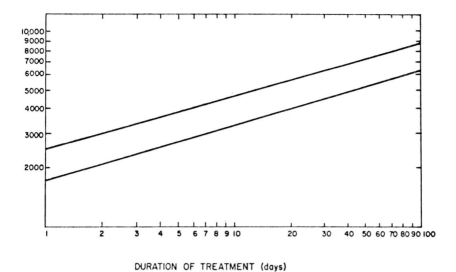

DURATION OF TREATMENT (days)

FIG. 11. Time-dose curves—Radionecrosis in human brains

empiricism, with its careful control of each individual radiation field and dose in order to minimize ill effects, and competent clinical observation of each individual to gauge results. It is this empiricism and nothing else which suggests that external radiation (often in surprisingly low doses) will relieve the paraplegia caused by an extra-dural spinal metastasis from Hodgkin's disease or other lymphomata often as fast and effectively as surgery will, but this is not so for compression from a prostatic metastasis: patients will have as good a chance of normal life span with an optic nerve glioma or a fibrillary astrocytoma provided they have proper surgery regardless of whether they have radiotherapy, but practically the opposite is true for children with cerebellar medulloblastomas or neuroblastomas: even the most deft surgery is unlikely to compete with radiation in the management of Rathke pouch cysts. But what appears true today in one centre of radiotherapy or neurosurgery will not necessarily appear to be true always.

FURTHER READING

Bacq, Z. M. and Alexander, P. (1961), *Fundamentals of Radiobiology*. London: Pergamon Press.

Bouchard, J. J. (1966), *Radiation Therapy of Tumours and Diseases of the Nervous System*. Philadelphia: Lea & Febiger.

Brain Research, VII, 1 (January 1968). "Special Issue on Pathogenesis of X-irradiation Effects in the Monkey Cerebral Cortex."

Code of Practice for the Protection of Persons against Ionizing Radiations Arising from Medical and Dental Use (1964). London: H.M.S.O.

Johns, H. E. and Cunningham, J. R. (1969), *The Physics of Radiology*, 3rd edition. Springfield, Illinois: Thomas.

Lebedenskiy, A. V. and Nakhil'nitskaya, Z. N. (1963), *Effects of Ionizing Radiation on the Nervous System*. Amsterdam/London/New York: Elsevier Publishing Company.

7. PRINCIPLES OF STEREOTAXIC SURGERY AND LESION MAKING

JOHN W. TURNER

INTRODUCTION

Stereotaxic surgery is a method of "closed" surgery whereby it is possible to act upon a deeply placed and otherwise virtually inaccessible region of the central nervous system. Stereotaxic surgery has evolved for three main reasons:

(1) Both theoretical considerations and empirical observations suggest that some patients can be helped by surgical action aimed at modifying the function of deeply placed structures in the central nervous system. Although most stereotaxic surgery is ablative at present, it seems possible that methods of enhancement or facilitation by pharmacological, biochemical or electrical means may evolve.

(2) There are difficulties and dangers, particularly of damage to neighbouring structures, in the direct approach to many deeply placed parts in the central nervous system by open surgical techniques.

(3) The internal anatomy of the brain shows reasonable consistency (although this point will be qualified later) and it is possible to identify most structures radiologically, either directly or by intermediate radiological reference points.

As virtually any point in the central nervous system can now be reached safely by the stereotaxic technique, its possible applications are enormous. However, the current practical applications of stereotaxic surgery are not dealt with in this chapter; suffice it to say that the following are the chief areas of use of the technique:

(1) Disorders of movement and tone.
(2) Intractable pain.
(3) Mental and behaviour disorders.
(4) Epilepsy.
(5) Biopsy.
(6) Implantation.

The stereotaxic technique involves several steps which are detailed in each section. Briefly, the steps are as follows:

The stereotaxic instrument, which is rigidly fixed to the skull, carries an adjustable holder for the probe or electrode which is eventually guided to the target region. A stereotaxic atlas is used to define the coordinates of the target point in relation to the brain and to radiologically identifiable reference points. By this means it is possible to relate the coordinates of the target to the instrument. An electrode of small diameter may then be inserted through a burr hole and directed towards the target; by stimulation or recording this can provide functional confirmation of the site of the tip of the probe prior to the production of a permanent lesion at the target site.

Stereotaxic procedures are usually performed under local anaesthesia so that with the patient's full co-operation it is possible to achieve the most satisfactory result and to avoid unwanted side-effects while the permanent lesion is being made.

STEREOTAXIC INSTRUMENT

Many different stereotaxic instruments have been devised but they can be rationalized and classified according to the type of co-ordinate system they use. This may be one of the three systems namely, rectangular, cylindrical or spherical.

Rectangular Co-ordinate System

This was the method adopted by Horsley and Clark in their original method of 1908. Three mutually perpendicular reference planes can be established within the brain, namely, sagittal (ZX), horizontal (XY) and frontal or coronal (YZ); these intersect at the origin O (Fig. 1). It is possible to identify any point within the brain by giving its directed distances along the three axes from the point of origin. In other words, the co-ordinates of the target point P can be uniquely identified as $P(x, y, z)$; in the figure $P(3, 6, 1)$ indicates that P is 3 mm. anterior, 6 lateral and 1 above the zero point.

In the Horsley and Clark system for animals the co-ordinates of the target with respect to the origin O in the brain are identical with the co-ordinates of the target with respect to the origin O of the instrument. That is, the origins coincide at the intersection of the mid-sagittal,

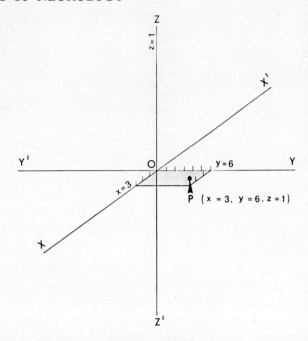

O = Zero point of instrument.

P = Target point.

FIG. 1. Rectangular co-ordinate system.

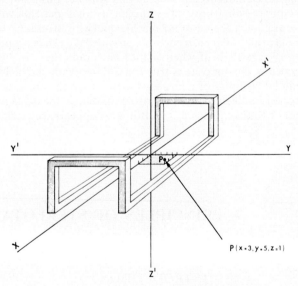

FIG. 2. Rectangular co-ordinate system.

frontal and horizontal planes. Therefore, the target point $P(x, y, z)$ can now readily be reached by direct transfer of the target point co-ordinates to the stereotaxic frame as in Fig. 2. In practice, the electrode carrier is moved to a position corresponding with the co-ordinates in two axes, while the electrode itself is advanced along the vertical axis as in Fig. 3.

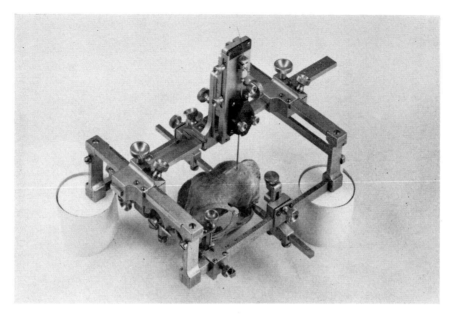

FIG. 3. Stereotaxic instrument with cat skull.

In 1947, Spiegel and Wycis were the first to describe the stereotaxic method in the human. In their original method the frame was fixed to the skull by a plaster cast and the basic rectangular co-ordinate system was used. In a later model the stereotaxic frame was attached rigidly to the skull and an angled electrode carrier was employed. In the human in particular it is not always desirable, convenient or safe to advance the electrode along the vertical path which may pass through venous channels or important cortical or sub-cortical areas. It is necessary to select an entry path at an angle to the rectangular co-ordinates but this can be inconvenient and will complicate the procedure with further calculations. Various devices have been evolved to overcome this problem. The most elegant method is to arrange for the target point, whose rectangular co-ordinates have already been defined, to become the centre of a sphere (Fig. 4). As the radius of a sphere always passes through its centre, any point on the surface of the sphere can be chosen as the site of entry of the centrally directed electrode. In practice, a semi-circular arc is used rather than the full sphere. In this limited sense, spherical co-ordinates are being used, since the point of entry of the electrode could be defined in these terms.

In the stereotaxic method of Leksell (Fig. 5), the head is fixed rigidly to the frame on which the rectangular co-ordinates of the target point are identified. The semi-circular arc is then moved until the centre of the sphere which it represents, coincides with the rectangular co-ordinates set up on the frame. The method allows access for the electrode via any point of the head within the limits of the physical location of the parts of the frame and the anatomy of the patient.

In the method used by Todd and Wells (Fig. 6) and by Rand and Wells, the head is attached rigidly to a base ring, and is moved along the X and Y axis and can also

be rotated around a Z axis, along which the semicircular arc is moved until its centre corresponds with the target point.

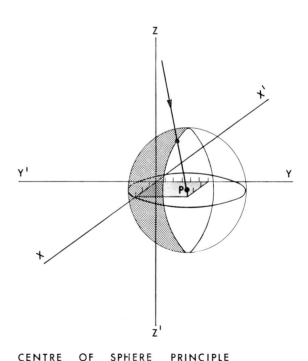

CENTRE OF SPHERE PRINCIPLE

FIG. 4. Rectangular co-ordinate system. Centre of sphere principle.

In the method used by Van Buren, the frame has a three point fixation over a small area of the skull. Attached to the frame are racks which allow three dimensional movements, with respect to the fixed points on the head.

Fig. 5. Stereotaxic instrument of Leksell.

Fig. 6. Stereotaxic instrument of Todd-Wells.

Adjustment is made so that the centre of a sphere, of which a large arcuate electrode carrier represents a part, coincides with the target.

In the method of Riechert, the system is similarly based on the rectangular co-ordinate system with appropriate corrections for a relations factor (based on the relationship with measurements made in a model and the patient) and for X-ray distortion. The co-ordinates are then transferred to a phantom or mechanical analogue on which the derived target point is charted. Although the system has a semicircular arc, it is not adjusted to bring its central point to coincide with the target as in the previously mentioned methods. Spherical co-ordinates are used to relate the target point and the electrode tip. With the help of the phantom, however, calculation is avoided as the angular readings on the semicircular arc and electrode holder of the phantom can be transferred directly to the apparatus on the patient.

Cylindrical Co-ordinate System

In the cylindrical co-ordinate system the target point P can be identified with respect to O by an angle and two distances. The origin O is considered to be the pole, hence the term "polar" applicable to both cylindrical and spherical co-ordinate systems, the principle of which is illustrated in Fig. 7. First, consider the co-ordinates of point P' in two dimensions only, with respect to O the origin. The polar co-ordinates of P' can be identified by

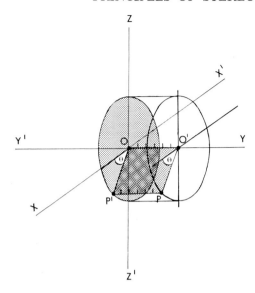

P (y, r, θ)

P'–P = y = 6

P'–O = r

P'OX = θ

FIG. 7. Cylindrical co-ordinate system.

one distance r (the radius of the cylinder) and one angle θ, that is $P'(r, \theta)$. Now a three dimensional system using cylindrical co-ordinates can be considered to be similar to the above with the addition of a third co-ordinate y which is the distance along the Y axis (i.e. the long axis of the cylinder). The cylindrical co-ordinates of the target point are therefore $P(y, r, \theta)$. In practice, P lies in a parasagittal plane at a distance y from the fixed midsagittal plane.

The method of Gillingham (Fig. 8), modified from Guiot, illustrates a type of apparatus in which cylindrical co-ordinates could be considered as the underlying principle. The sagittal bar is fixed at three points in the precise midline of the brain as defined radiologically. The electrode passes in a parasagittal plane at an absolute distance y from the midsagittal plane. The co-ordinates of the target point now require definition in two dimensions only.

Spherical Co-ordinate System

The spherical co-ordinate system is one of the polar co-ordinate systems in which the target point P can be identified with respect to O the origin or pole, by two angles and one distance (Fig. 9). The system can be compared with the cylindrical co-ordinate system and as a further step away from the rectangular co-ordinate system, replacing one linear measurement by one angular measurement.

P can be considered as lying on the surface of a sphere whose radius is ρ. This is a different distance from r in the cylindrical co-ordinate system since it is the radius of the sphere and not the cylinder, as can be seen by reference to Figs. 7 and 9. The angle θ is retained as the angle $P'OX$ on the midsagittal plane, as in the cylindrical co-ordinate system. The angle POY is ϕ. In practice it is measured as if it were projected on to the YZ plane.

The instrument described by McCaul (Fig. 10) and the Planisphere of Ward employ the principles of spherical polar co-ordinates. The instrument is attached by the socket of a ball-and-socket joint to the skull at a burrhole site. The rotatable ball carries a directing rod and later the electrode. With the directing rod in place, but not inserted into the brain, the angle the directing rod makes with a line drawn between the target point and the central point of rotation of the ball and socket joint, can be ascertained from X-ray examination in the AP and lateral views. Thus the angular measurements, θ, and

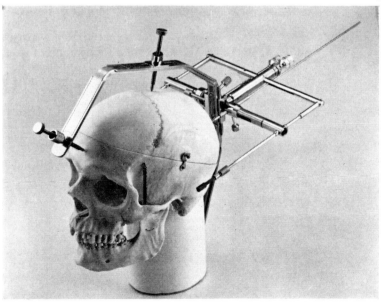

FIG. 8. Stereotaxic instrument of Gillingham.

the equivalent of ϕ are obtained. The distance ρ can also be derived but not measured directly as foreshortening of this length always occurs since the line is never in a plane perpendicular to the X-ray beam.

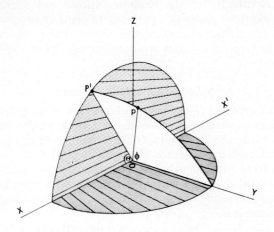

$P (P, \theta, \phi)$

$PO = \rho$

$P'OX = \theta$

$POY = \phi$

Fig. 9. Spherical co-ordinate system.

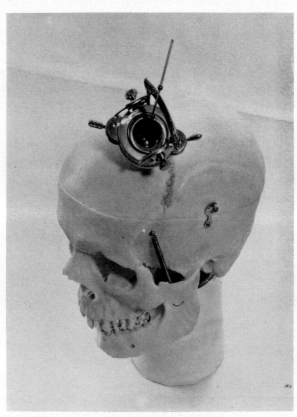

Fig. 10. Stereotaxic instrument of McCaul.

With regard to the practical implications in stereotaxic surgery, an instrument should be accurate, simple, universally applicable, and allow for the comfort of the patient and adequate observation of the patient. The mechanical accuracy of the commercially available stereotaxic instruments is usually quite acceptable (of the order of less than 1 mm.). Rigid fixation of the instrument to the patient's skull is more comfortable than other methods of attachment and also necessary for accuracy. The patient is more comfortable when the instrument is light and allows some head movement and when it is not fixed to an operating table, and it is valuable to be able to use the instrument when the patient is in different positions and to be able to adjust the patient's position if necessary. The cost and compatibility of associated radiological and lesion-making equipment must also be considered. For example, the cost of installing appropriate radiological equipment, particularly structural building alterations for tele-radiology, may be considerable. Whichever instrument and co-ordinate system is used, an almost obsessional attention to the details of the procedure is required and of course careful counter-checking of co-ordinates, calculations and the transfer of measurements is advisable. Familiarity with one instrument with its co-ordinate system leads to confidence in its use and is normally to be recommended, but it may not be universally applicable to all aspects of stereotaxis.

ANATOMICAL ATLAS FOR STEREOTAXIS

As the stereotaxic method evolved, and any target in the central nervous system could be assailed on a theoretical or empirical basis, it was natural and necessary that atlases of the brain should become available. They defined the shape, size and relationship of target structures to each other and to a rectangular system of the brain. In experimental animal work the construction and use of a stereotaxic atlas was relatively straightforward, because cranio-cerebral topography is reasonably constant and external bony landmarks can be used as reference points to form the basis of a rectangular coordinate system of the brain. There are two major considerations which complicate the construction and use of the human atlas and therefore the stereotaxic method.

Reference Points

Human cranio-cerebral topography is inconstant. Although external bony landmarks show roughly consistent relationships with internal structures, they are not reliable enough for precise localization of internal structures and to form the basis of a coordinate system of the brain. It is therefore necessary to employ internal reference points which can be identified radiologically; those intermediate radiological reference points include the anterior commissure, posterior commissure, foramen of Munro and pineal body. The anterior and posterior commissures are probably most commonly used. These reference points can readily be seen on the midsagittal section of the brain (Fig. 11) and can be outlined

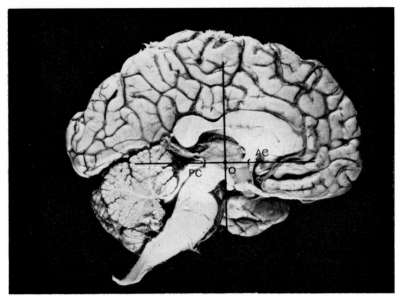

FIG. 11. Mid-sagittal section of brain. Note anterior AC and posterior PC commissures.

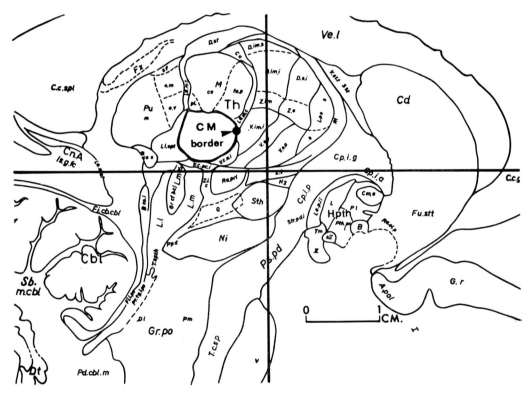

FIG. 12. Anterior border of nucleus centro-medianum indicated on parasagittal section at laterality of 10 mm. on Plate 46 from Atlas of Schaltenbrand and Bailey. The intercommissural and mid-commissural lines are shown.

radiologically in the anterior and posterior walls of the midline third ventricle (Fig. 16); a rectangular co-ordinate system of the brain can then be built around them. The horizontal and midsagittal planes pass through both anterior and posterior commissures with the frontal plane perpendicular to them both. The point of intersection of the three planes at the midcommissural point (MCP) is the zero and from this reference point it is possible to give the rectangular co-ordinates of any target or structure. The Atlas of Schaltenbrand and Bailey shows a series of brains which have been sectioned at intervals in each of the three planes. Each section is identified by its plane of section and the metric distance from the zero point. The use of co-ordinates can be illustrated in the following example. In the management of a patient with intractable pain it may be decided to destroy the nucleus centro-medianum (centre mediane CM), whose boundaries must therefore be defined. The rectangular coordinates of the most anterior part of the boundary of the nucleus, marked on the section S1, 10 (Fig. 12), can be given as posterior 4·5, lateral 10, horizontal +5. Thus the co-ordinates of one boundary of the target structure relative to zero point and to intermediate radiological reference points have been established. It is then necessary to find the co-ordinates of the intermediate radiological reference points relative to the stereotaxic instrument and thereby relate the target region to the stereotaxic instrument.

Variability

A further problem arises due to the variation from one brain to another. Variability is found in the size and shape of the subcortical targets and in the distances between them. Of particular importance is the variability in the distance and direction between a structure and reference points of the brain. The relationships generally assume a gaussian distribution. In Fig. 13 the frequency

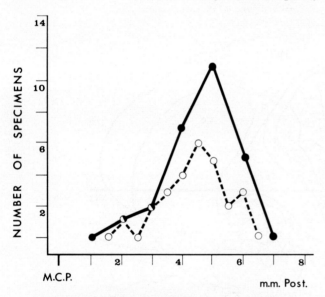

FIG. 13. Frequency distribution curve of relation of anterior boundary of nucleus centro-medianum to the mid-commissural point. (From Andrew and Watkins, 1969.)

distribution of the distance of the anterior boundary of the nucleus centro-medianum (CM) from the midcommissural plane is shown. Frequency distribution curves related to other reference points may be similar or show a widespread or bimodal character. Considering the nucleus centro-medianum further, the mean distance from the midcommissural plane to the anterior boundary of CM is 4·4 mm., with a standard deviation of 1 mm. (data obtained from Andrew and Watkins, 1969, in 26 observations). Therefore, in a given patient it can be assumed with 95 per cent certainty that the anterior boundary of CM will lie between 2·4 and 6·4 mm. posterior to the midcommissural plane. Conversely, there is a one in twenty chance of this particular point lying outside the wide limits of 4 mm.—a not inconsiderable chance of an appreciable error in this complex region of the brain. A coronal variability profile of nuclear centro-medianum

at its peak incidence was constructed from data of its most medial, lateral, superior and inferior limits. The mean of each boundary is shown in Fig. 14 together with

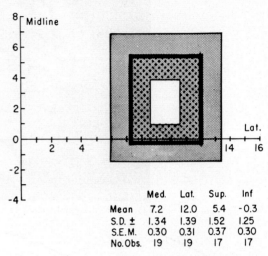

NUCLEUS CENTRO-MEDIANUM - 18P.

	Med.	Lat.	Sup.	Inf
Mean	7.2	12.0	5.4	-0.3
S.D. ±	1.34	1.39	1.52	1.25
S.E.M.	0.30	0.31	0.37	0.30
No.Obs.	19	19	17	17

FIG. 14. Coronal variability profile of nucleus centro-medianum. The horizontal axis lies in the foramen of Munro/posterior commissure plane. The plane of the coronal section lies 18 mm. posterior to the foramen of Munro. (From Andrew and Watkins, 1969.)

1 standard deviation on either side, into which range 66 per cent of the population falls. Conversely in 33 per cent of the population it will lie beyond the shaded areas. The practical consequence must follow that if atlas co-ordinates are used as the sole basis for siting a stereotaxic lesion, the lesion will be so misplaced in a proportion of cases as to be ineffective in treating the patient's problem and may also result in undesirable side effects due to involvement of neighbouring structures.

Van Buren made a variability study by superimposing outline diagrams of the human basal ganglia of 26 hemispheres with reference to various internal landmarks and structures including CM at a laterality of 10 mm. (Fig. 15). Again considering CM, the anterior border appears on the average to lie 18 mm. behind the anterior commissure and 3 mm. above the intercommissural line. Although in this case the anterior commissure has been used as the reference point the coordinates with reference to the mid-commissural point can be computed and can be given as P(posterior 6, lateral 10, horizontal plus 3).

It can be seen that while on the average the co-ordinates of this particular point (that is the anterior border of CM), exhibit moderately good uniformity in the three atlases quoted, the variability studies show that there is a potentially large error in translating the coordinates of a target from a stereotaxic atlas to the brain of an individual patient.

The practical implications therefore are that while it is obviously essential to derive the precise brain co-ordinates of a target structure from a stereotaxic atlas, it is necessary to realize that there is significant individual variation from one brain to another, that it is impossible to be dogmatic about the actual numerical co-ordinates which will give the best therapeutic results, and that other means of confirming the localization of the probe are required.

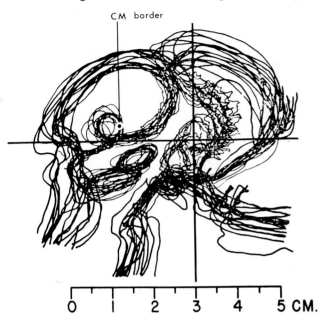

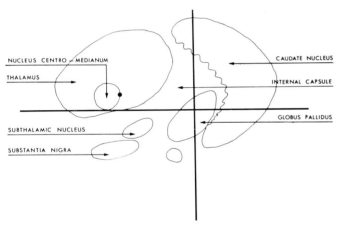

FIG. 15. Parasagittal section at laterality of 10 mm., showing (upper) variability of superimposed outline drawings and (lower) approximate mean borders of the named structures. The anterior border of nucleus centromedianum is indicated. The axes lie along the intercommissural plane, and a frontal plane through the anterior commissure which is the reference point. (After Van Buren and MacCubbin, 1962.)

RADIOLOGICAL CONTROL

It is clear that if internal landmarks are to be used, a method for their display in two planes must be available and for this radiological means are employed.

Direct Radiological Visualization

The target structure can occasionally be displayed directly by plain radiographs, for example the bony limits of the pituitary fossa, or a partially calcified tumour.

It may be possible to establish the co-ordinates of a target directly by ventriculography, and vascular lesions can similarly be defined by angiography.

Intermediate Radiological Reference Points

In most instances the target structure is not visible directly and intermediate radiological reference points are used (Fig. 16). When the target point lies some distance from the zero point other intermediate radiological reference points are used and are selected on the basis of:

(1) The closeness and constancy of relationship of the intermediate radiological reference point to the target.
(2) The ease and clarity of display radiologically.
(3) Convenience in the particular stereotaxic method. For example, in cerebellar stereotaxic surgery for disturbances of tone, it is clearly more appropriate to relate the target point to reference points in the fourth rather than third ventricle.

Magnification and Distortion

Since the rays of an X-ray beam diverge and the object of interest in stereotaxic surgery cannot be placed immediately against the radiographic film, magnification and distortion of the object will occur. The amount of magnification will be proportional to the ratio of object-to-film distance to focus-to-object distance. The magnification of linear measurements complicates the translation of radiological measurements and co-ordinates into absolute measurements based either on direct radiological visualization or intermediate radiological reference points. In the latter case, differences in rotation of the axes of the brain and axes of the stereotaxic instrument may add a further complication and source of error (Fig. 17). Distortion of both linear and angular measurements occurs when the plane in which they lie is not perpendicular to the X-ray beam; for example, foreshortening of the linear measurement will occur as in the spherical co-ordinate system.

It is possible to combat the problems in a number of different ways. By fixing the distances between the X-ray focus, the object and the film it is possible to make the magnification factor constant and to make due allowance in the calculation and translation of co-ordinates.

When the X-ray focus-to-object distance is increased considerably, as in tele-radiology, the magnification factor becomes quite small. For example, at a focus-to-film distance of 4 metres, the magnification factor can be below 3 per cent. By using the central beam of X-rays magnification and distortion problems are considerably reduced. By using a moving slit diaphragm it is possible to measure absolute distances on the film in the direction of movement.

By using polar co-ordinates, it is possible to reduce the number of linear measurements and to make use of angular measurements (*see above* θ and ϕ). However,

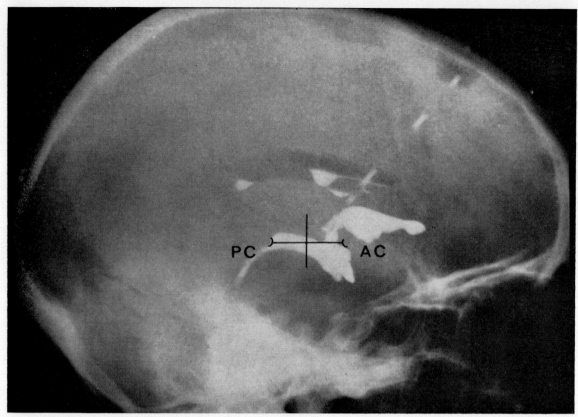

FIG. 16. Myodil ventriculogram. The anterior AC and posterior PC commissures together with the intercommissural and mid-commissural lines are shown.

even with angular measurements distortion may occur and one linear measurement remains in both polar co-ordinate systems (i.e. the direct distance ρ or r along the line between the target and zero point of the instrument).

By setting up a mechanical, photographic or other analogue combining the stereotaxic instrument, the radiological system and the patient's brain, together with its reference points and the desired target point, it is possible to obtain a correction for X-ray magnification and distortion, and also for errors due to rotation of the axes of the stereotaxic instrument with respect to those of the patient's brain (Schaltenbrand, 1959; Dawson, 1969).

Contrast Media

In order to demonstrate the internal radiological reference points a contrast medium is required to outline the ventricular system. Formerly a lumbar air encephalogram was performed to outline the reference points and often gave very adequate pictures but on occasions the commissures, for example, were difficult to visualize. In addition, such a procedure could be disturbing for the patient and other methods are now available.

Ventriculography is most satisfactory and is performed via a burrhole or twist drill-hole. The lateral ventricle is penetrated by a cannula or catheter and the contrast medium is instilled. Air or positive contrast media may be used. Air, being lighter than cerebro-spinal fluid, remains at the uppermost part of the system and may give inadequate contrast, particularly in a narrow

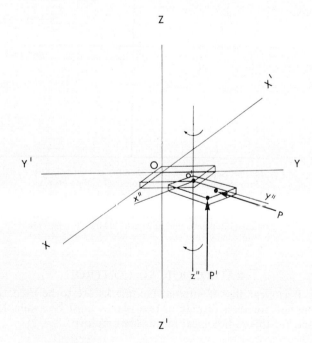

O' = Intermediate Reference Point
P = True Target Point
P' = False Target Point (Rotational Error)

FIG. 17. Rotational error around Z axis.

third ventricle. With positive pressure air-ventriculography it is possible to show both commissures more clearly but for a limited time. An advantage of the use of air is that fewer side reactions are encountered compared with the positive contrast media.

Myodil (iophendylate, pantopaque) provides dense contrast outline of the intermediate radiological reference points (Fig. 16) and does not become absorbed being in oily solution. Being rather heavy it sinks to the lowest point in the ventricular system and in order to outline the commissures it is necessary to position the patient appropriately. Patients may complain of pain in the leg due to lumbar nerve root irritation, but side-effects due to myodil are seldom encountered and it is used as the contrast medium of choice by many people.

Conray ventriculography will often give good contrast of the ventricular system including the third ventricle, but it is absorbed within minutes. This water-soluble medium is considerably less dense than myodil, but it still tends to sink to the most dependent part.

FUNCTIONAL LOCALIZATION

While anatomical studies of variability enable the degree of accuracy of the electrode striking a target to be predicted, the requirements for an individual patient are that the chances of missing the target should be reduced to a minimum. Having employed the atlas and the radiological method to the limit of their combined accuracy and usefulness, it is still necessary to use local search techniques in order to discover the precise position of the electrode tip in relation to the target in that individual patient. Various methods of achieving this objective are available but each uses the same sequence: a stimulus is applied, the response observed, the result interpreted and then appropriate action is taken. A target may thereby be identifiable directly. If, however, there are no direct means of identification, indirect means by defining the surrounding structures may be used.

Eventually, by these methods, it will be possible to compile a comprehensive dictionary of functional localization in the central nervous system which will be complementary to the human anatomical atlas as an aid to the stereotaxic surgeon.

1. Mechanical

The minor local damage resulting from the introduction of a probe into a target site may result in observable changes in the patient. The most dramatic demonstration of this effect is during the treatment of Parkinsonian tremor. It frequently happens that when the electrode reaches the target site in such a patient the tremor ceases. This effect is usually a good indication that the electrode is situated correctly. After a little time, however, the tremor will usually return unless a permanent and larger lesion is made. It is worth noting that simple passage of a fine probe through the brain does not seem to be associated with clinical evidence of permanent damage to the tissues through which it passes.

2. Thermal

At the periphery of an expanding thermal lesion, such as a radio-frequency or cryogenic lesion, there is a zone of reversibly blocked neural activity. The reversibility of this zone can be of great usefulness in avoiding permanent side effects due to the lesion extending into a structure beyond the target region. If depression of function of the structure can be recognized by immediate behavioural or other counterparts these can be watched for during the lesion-making process; if such signs are observed, the heating or cooling can be discontinued. For example, if a lesion is being made in the ventro-lateral nucleus of the thalamus, the patient can be forewarned that if paraesthesiae occur he should immediately inform the surgeon. The observation of paraesthesiae by the patient will suggest that the periphery of the lesion is beginning to involve the sensory relay nucleus lying posterior to the target region. By discontinuing the heating or cooling, the side effect usually disappears. Similarly, the appearance of a mild contra-lateral hemiparesis will suggest that the lesion is encroaching on the cortico-spinal pathways in the internal capsule. Drowsiness may suggest encroachment medially.

Naturally, the use of these indications of correct or incorrect electrode placement demands that the patient should be conscious and able to co-operate. If general anaesthesia is necessary, other methods of confirmation of localization are necessary. Similarly, where immediate clinical effects are not produced by the lesion at the target site and surrounding areas are relatively "silent", these simple methods of confirmation are inadequate.

3. Depth Stimulation

The application of an extra-cellular electrical stimulus during passage of an electrode towards the target site may result in clinical, electrical, or other responses, which may indicate the position of the electrode in relation to the target.

Equipment

Stimulator. The stimulator may provide a constant voltage or constant current output. While the latter will provide the required constant stimulus, a disadvantage is that a high and damaging voltage may occur when a high series resistance is present and, that if capacitative elements are present, discharge current will occur after the stimulator has been turned off. A disadvantage of the constant voltage stimulator is that because of variable series resistance (for example, as the electrode is being advanced) the applied electrical stimulus to the cell membranes will vary.

Waveform. As the most effective stimulus causing discharge of the surface membrane of nerve cells is one having a fast rise time, short duration rectangular pulses are the most common waveform to be used. Both duration and strength of current are important. With pulses of very short duration the threshold of excitation may not be reached, even if the current strength is high. Similarly, at low current strengths, threshold may not be reached even with long duration pulses. Monophasic, in contrast to bi-phasic pulses, will result in polarization at the electrode tip, which under conditions of high current strengths may result in the production of an electrolytic lesion.

Electrodes. Electrodes are of metal and should pre-rerably be non-polarizable. Monopolar stimulation may result in distant effects due to current spread. Bi-polar stimulation may be preferable but if the interelectrode distance is small, observable clinical effects may not occur in spite of stimulation in an area where they would be expected. When stimulating in "silent" areas, there is a danger of obtaining false positive results due to current spread to neighbouring areas or of producing local damage if the applied current is high.

Safety. For reasons of safety it is important to provide an isolation transformer between the stimulator and the patient in order to ensure that there is no possible means by which the patient can receive a high voltage, particularly mains, shock.

Application

In practice, for example, a constant voltage stimulator providing bi-phasic or monophasic square waves of 1 msec. duration fed to a concentric bi-polar metal electrode via a stimulus isolation unit, has proved of use. Threshold voltages for the production of clinically observable effects being reached at 0·5 V or less. Electrical stimulation may be of assistance in many situations. In percutaneous cordotomy, monopolar electrical stimulation can help to provide information about the localization of the electrode tip. Stimulation at 100 c./sec. with 1 msec. pulses resulting at very low threshold in the experience of

clonic movements may suggest stimulation of the anterior horn cells.

Apart from many situations where clinical or behavioural effects can be observed, stimulation in "silent" areas may result in electrically or biochemically observable events. Low frequency (8/sec.) short duration bi-polar stimulation in the nucleus centro-medianum may result in recognizable "recruiting responses" being observed on the cortical electrical record.

Figure 18 shows the results of stimulation at a threshold of 1 V or less at the tip of a bi-polar concentric electrode as it was progressively passed forwards along a track to the thalamus and the globus pallidus in the treatment of a patient with Parkinsonism. The electrode traverses the lateral ventricle (VeL), then the thalamus including the pulvinar (Pu), the sensory relay nucleus of the thalamus (Vci), intermediate nucleus (Vime), ventral oral nucleus (Vop, Voa) and reticular envelope of the thalamus (Rt), followed by the posterior limb of the internal capsule (Cpip) and the globus pallidus (Pm, Pl.). "Pins and needles" on the right side of the face were reported by the patient at sites 1 and 2. At site 3 an involuntary withdrawal response of the right arm was noted. At site 4, she reported an unpleasant sensation in the right side of the body. At site 5 no subjective or objective response was noted. During stimulation at many sites along the electrode track in this dominant hemisphere, no disturbance of speech or language function occurred.

4. Depth Recording

Extracellular recording of electrical activity of neural tissue during the passage of an electrode towards the target site is the most precise method of localization in certain

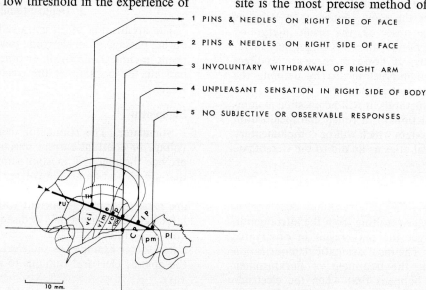

1 PINS & NEEDLES ON RIGHT SIDE OF FACE

2 PINS & NEEDLES ON RIGHT SIDE OF FACE

3 INVOLUNTARY WITHDRAWAL OF RIGHT ARM

4 UNPLEASANT SENSATION IN RIGHT SIDE OF BODY

5 NO SUBJECTIVE OR OBSERVABLE RESPONSES

10 mm.

FIG. 18. Depth stimulation. Electrode track with sites and results of stimulation, superimposed on Plate 47 of Atlas of Schaltenbrand and Bailey.

pain in the contra-lateral lower limb, is a good indication that the tip is correctly located in the spinothalamic tract. Clonic movements in the ipsilateral limbs synchronous with low frequency stimulation may suggest that the tip is located in the cortico-spinal motor pathway; while local

parts of the central nervous system. One method depends on the observation of an evoked electrical response at the recording point after application of a distant stimulus, preferably physiological, although other stimuli may be used. It depends, of course, on the ability to produce evoked responses in the target or neighbouring structures. A further method depends on the recognition of a pattern of electrical activity which is characteristic of a specific structure and this will provide evidence of the location of the electrode tip.

Equipment

Electrode. Several points must be borne in mind when choosing the electrode. (1) A fine micro-electrode with high impedance will generate more internal noise than a larger tip, but it will "see" a small region of neural activity of only a few cells and at times single cell recording is possible. (2) A large tip with low impedance will generate less noise but will "see" many units rather indistinctly and there will be more "tissue noise". (3) The size of the functional structure from which recording is to be performed, for example, recording evoked sensory responses in the sensory relay nucleus from tactile stimulation of the thumb, may extend over only a few tens of microns and it will be necessary to use an electrode tip of an appropriate order of magnitude to obtain clear results. In other words, the finer the electrode tip, the greater the precision. (4) With fine microelectrodes, distortion and attenuation of the signal will occur as the result of capacitive shunting (Fig. 19) if a high tissue

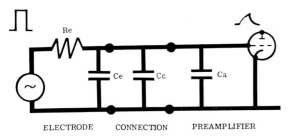

ELECTRODE   CONNECTION   PREAMPLIFIER

FIG. 19. Capacitative shunting.

electrode resistance (Re) is combined with appreciable capacitance in the electrode (Ce), its connections (Cc) to the pre-amplifier, and the first stage of the pre-amplifier (Ca). These effects will depend on the time constant ($T = RC$) of the recording system in relation to the signal level and its time course. For example, the instantaneous response will be reduced by two-thirds if the time constant is equal to the time course of the signal. The effects will be frequency dependent and the higher frequencies will be more affected than the lower frequencies. (5) A further disturbance results from the effective series capacitance brought about by the unavoidable tissue electrolyte/electrode junction. If current is drawn from the signal source, polarization will tend to occur at the electrode tip with loss of slowly changing DC signals. If, in fact, these signals are not of interest, the disturbance can be ignored and capacitative coupling amplification can be used to advantage.

It is possible to overcome these effects of distortion and attenuation by feeding the signal from the electrode into a system with a very high input impedance such as a cathode follower circuit which effectively prevents flow of current from the signal source, thereby effectively eliminating the shunting capacitance (Ce + Cc + Ca). It is always necessary to use short connections (to reduce Cc) between the electrode and cathode follower.

Tungsten is often selected as the metal of choice as it is rigid, can be sharpened to a fine point, is relatively inert and can be coated with platinum. Electrode tips ranging from a few microns to a hundred or more microns in diameter are commonly used.

Amplifier. Either a single ended amplifier or a differential amplifier may be used. However, it is preferable to use a balanced differential amplifier in order to reduce the interference of unwanted biological signals, such as the ECG or extraneous noise, generated for example by mains power cables, fluorescent lamps, switches, motors or electromechanical devices and diathermy. A locally produced signal will present the two electrodes with different out-of-phase potentials while distant or interference signals will be seen by both electrodes in-phase and of equal value. These latter signals are amplified but balanced out so that no output will result from them. The out-of-phase local signal is amplified but not balanced out and is therefore passed on to the next stage. Mains hum may inadvertently be introduced into the recording system in other ways and particularly by ground loops which may occur when more than one earth point is used.

A direct coupled amplifier is necessary where slowly changing or steady potentials are to be recorded. Otherwise, where the information concerns only spatial and temporal relations between events rather than the precise waveform, the simpler capacity coupled amplifier is adequate. By reducing the band pass of the amplifier, noise can be reduced.

Display. The signal having been successfully isolated undistorted, and then amplified, can be displayed. It is commonly found that audio-monitoring is very satisfactory in picking up "spike" signals. The amplified signal is played through a loudspeaker and can be heard by the ear which detects the signal amidst the "noise", often more successfully than the eye can detect the signal on a cathode ray oscilloscope. Because the biological signal can often be predictably repeated and "noise" is random, it is possible by repeating the biological signal a large number of times and the application of the averaging technique to retrieve the original low level biological signal from the random "averaged-out" noise. Permanent records can be obtained by photographing the signal on the cathode ray oscilloscope screen, or by the use of an ultraviolet oscillograph. Tape recording allows data processing to be undertaken at a later stage or on-line analysis and reference to the dictionary or functional atlas.

Application. Depth electrical recording may be of assistance in many situations where it is possible to arrange that evoked potentials can be elicited from the target region or related neighbouring structures, or where these structures have a characteristic pattern of electrical activity. In the treatment of disorders of movement and tone, it may be decided to undertake stereotaxic surgery. For example,

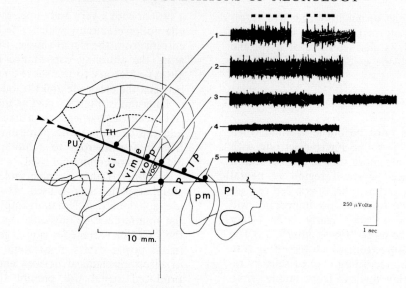

FIG. 20. Depth recording. Electrode track with sites of recording and
oscillographic traces, superimposed on Plate 47 of Atlas of Schaltenbrand
and Bailey.

a parkinsonian patient with unilateral tremor, not adequately helped by drugs, including L-dopa or a patient
with intention tremor due to multiple sclerosis, may
benefit from a lesion in the ventro-lateral nucleus (ventro-
oral nuclei of the lateral nuclear region of Hassler).

The figure (Fig. 20) shows an oscillographic display of
the depth electrical recording (patient IS) using a tungsten
micro-electrode penetrating progressively more anteriorly
towards a pallidal reference point. The track of the
electrode as well as the records at various points along
the track are shown superimposed on the parasagittal
outline drawing of Schaltenbrand and Bailey Atlas at a
laterality of 15 mm. In particular, the internal capsule
(Cpip)), the thalamus (Th) and the globus pallidus (Pm,
Pl) are shown. The record (1) at 19 mm. behind the pallidal point shows the evoked responses from the sensory
relay nucleus of the thalamus (Vci) resulting from tactile
stimulation of a small area of the right upper lip. The
times of tactile stimulation are shown by the bars above the
record. Other tactile evoked potentials were obtained
along the electrode track between 19·5 mm. and 17 mm.
behind the pallidal point. Further anteriorly (2) the
thalamic record from the ventro-oral area, the target, is
shown. The transition (3) from the cellular regions of the
thalamus (Vop, Voa) and its reticular envelope (Rt) to
the fibre region of the posterior limb of the internal
capsule (Cpip) is shown, in the trace which has been
recorded during advancement of the electrode. There is
reduction in the background and cell activity as shown by
the narrowing of the trace and lack of "spikes". The
"silence" of the internal capsule is seen in tracing 4. The
transition (5) from the fibre region of the internal capsule
to the cellular region of the globus pallidus (Pm, Pl) is
heralded by recurrence of spike activity. The results of
depth stimulation in this patient were less precise than
depth recording as may be seen by comparing the results
of the above records of depth stimulation and recording
(Figs. 18 and 20).

From the complete results of such recording, it is possible with great precision to define the boundaries of the
various structures traversed. The size and the position of
the proposed lesion anterior to the sensory relay nucleus
and posterior to the internal capsule can be calculated and
correctly sited with respect to these structures as defined
in this particular patient. A good therapeutic result
should follow and side effects avoided.

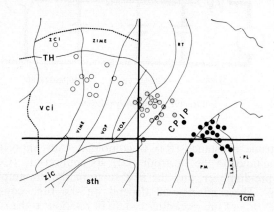

○ ANTERIOR LIMIT OF SENSORY EVOKED POTENTIALS

◉ POSTERIOR ⎫
            ⎬ LIMIT OF "SILENCE" OF INTERNAL CAPSULE
● ANTERIOR ⎭

FIG. 21. Depth recording. Scatter diagram of results of
depth electrical recording in 21 patients at laterality of
15 mm. superimposed on Plate 47 of Atlas of Schaltenbrand and Bailey.

In the preceding case it can be seen that the boundaries
between the structures as defined by depth recording
correspond fairly well with the boundaries as shown on
the Atlas of Schaltenbrand and Bailey. However, in a
series of 21 patients where recording was performed, at
the same laterality of 15 mm., a scatter diagram (Fig. 21)
has been constructed of the points of the most anterior

limit of sensory evoked responses, and the posterior and anterior limits of "silence" of the internal capsule. The points have been plotted with reference to the mid-commissural plane and corrected for radiological magnification. They are superimposed on the appropriate plate of the Atlas of Schaltenbrand and Bailey. It can be seen that considerable variability occurs from one brain to another which is in agreement with the previous section on the anatomical atlas for stereotaxis.

5. Impedance Method

Since the electrical impedance of the white matter is greater than that of grey matter, it is possible by passing an alternating current and deriving the change in impedance recorded during advancement of an electrode, to define the boundary between white and grey matter.

The impedance will be related to the frequency of the current, and to the capacitance of the tissues as well as resistance. It is also possible to derive the change in phase angle which occurs as the electrode passes between grey and white matter since it will depend on the changing capacitance of the tissues. A low strength alternating current at say 1 Kcps is passed from the small tip of the advancing electrode and the recorded impedance will reflect the nature of the tissue in the vicinity of the tip.

The method has been employed to provide confirmation of the track of an electrode in cerebral stereotaxis. It is also used in percutaneous cordotomy, particularly in indicating the point at which the electrode passes from the cerebrospinal fluid in the subarachnoid space into neural tissue.

LESION MAKING

The final objective of stereotaxic surgery is usually to destroy a defined structure or volume of neural tissue. The aim is to create a lesion which can be accurately tailored to the target site in size and shape. The target will previously have been defined by a stereotaxic atlas in the "average" brain and displayed by electrophysiological or other techniques in the particular patient under observation. Unfortunately, the tissues to be destroyed are not homogenous. Grey and white matter of the central nervous system have different susceptibilities to destructive agents, so that lesions tend to "track". Neighbouring blood vessels, ventricles and leptomeninges may also affect the size and shape of the lesion, for example, by creating "heat sinks". In addition to these inherent difficulties in the tissues of creating a lesion of predictable size and shape, an ideal lesion-maker has not yet been devised. An ideal lesion-maker would be safe, reliable, simple, capable of producing a reversible lesion and a definitive lesion of predictable dimensions. It would be universally applicable throughout the stereotaxic field where a destructive lesion was required. Very many methods of creating a lesion have been employed, including mechanical, chemical, physical (heat or cold), electrolytic, ultrasonic and radioactive.

In many methods of lesion-making, it is possible to standardize all but one variable. During the process of acute lesion-making, it is invaluable to be able to observe the clinical effect that it has on the patient's symptomatology and to watch for clinical side effects. Chronic implantation of electrodes may also be employed with more long term testing and gradual enlargement of the permanent lesion.

Mechanical Lesion

A mechanically produced lesion can be created by means of a knife of spring steel which is protruded from the tip of a probe. Alternatively, an extrudable wire loop can be used. The lesion is created by rotating the probe through 360°, the extent to which the cutting edge protrudes and therefore the volume of the lesion can be varied. Observations on experimental lesion have been rather disappointing, showing that the lesions tend to be unpredictable in size, shape and extent (Carpenter, 1952). This is apparently due to interruption of small blood vessels resulting in haemorrhage or ischaemia in the distribution of the vessels.

Chemical Lesion

While chemically produced lesions were frequently used in the early days of human stereotaxic surgery, they are now less commonly employed. The toxic material tends to track back along the needle and to diffuse along tissue interfaces, with resultant irregularity and unpredictability in the size and shape of the lesion.

Physical Lesion

At relatively small deviations from the normal body temperature of 37°C, neural function can be temporarily blocked. The limits of reversibility are probably in the region of 0°C and 45°C. A permanent lesion can be created by increasing the temperature differential to lethal levels. A temperature gradient is set up between a region of lethal temperature and normal body temperature. At some point along this gradient is a zone of reversibly inactivated tissue. As the temperature differential is increased the reversible zone progressively moves outwards away from the region of damaging temperature and in front of the permanent lesion. Temperature-dependent lesions are most commonly created using a radio-frequency lesion-maker or a cryogenic lesion-maker. As the temperature difference between blocking and lethal temperatures at low temperatures is greater than the difference at high temperatures, the cryogenic lesion may well have a higher margin of safety. The zone of reversibility which surrounds these lesions is a great advantage of both methods. For example, the unwanted side effects which may develop as a lesion advances into regions outwith the target site, can be reversed by discontinuing the heating or cooling system. Other advantages of the radio-frequency and cryogenic lesions are that they are relatively consistent and predictable in their dimensions with good demarcation of their boundaries, probably due to the poor thermal conductivity and steep temperature gradients in neural tissue.

I. Heat

1. Radio-frequency Thermal Lesion

Mode of Action. When radio-frequency current is passed through neural tissue, energy is dissipated in the form of heat which can be employed to create a lesion. The amount of heat generated will depend on current density. If the temperature reaches lethal levels, coagulation necrosis occurs.

Equipment. The equipment consists essentially of a source of high frequency alternating current, connections, and a unipolar electrode insulated except for its tip. The "spark" gap electro-cautery has been used for many years in neurosurgery (Cushing, 1928), to obtain haemostasis by heat coagulation and can be used successfully to produce a satisfactory lesion in stereotaxic surgery. However, the output from such a machine tends to be rather erratic. A more controllable output can be obtained by means of a valve operated radio-frequency power generator (Aronow, 1960), producing continuous sinusoidal alternating current. Frequencies between 0·5 Mc. and 2 Mc. have largely been used. At higher frequencies a real problem of capacitative shunting with loss of power eventually reaching the electrode tip may occur, particularly if the probe is long, or of small diameter or thinly insulated. It is, of course, essential that the insulation should be intact. The uninsulated tip of the electrode may measure between 2 and 8 mm. in length, depending on the size of the lesion required. While it is possible to measure the radio frequency voltage and current of the generator, these measurements do not always reflect accurately the actual power output into the neural tissues at the tip of the electrode. Therefore, whenever possible it is of more value to measure the tip temperature as an indicator of the power being dissipated as heat in the tissues. The temperature at the tip of the electrode can be monitored by a thermocouple or thermistor which reflects the temperature in the surrounding brain tissue.

By means of a feed back mechanism to the generator, it is possible to maintain the temperature of the tip of the electrode at a preselected level. Because the heating is generated in the tissues and not in the electrode tip, the recorded temperature may, however, be lower than the tissue temperature. A time lag also occurs. The temperature gradient in the tissue is usually very steep as the energy absorption varies with the fourth power of the radial distance from the source of energy (Aronow, 1960), and is responsible for the relatively clean boundary of the lesion.

Determinants of Lesion Size and Shape. The *size* of the lesion will be related to several factors.

(1) **Temperature.** Lesion size was plotted against rising temperature and an almost linear relationship was observed, with a constant electrode tip length of 5 mm. and diameter of 0·042 in. and over periods of 2 min. (Fig. 22).

(2) **The Dimensions of the Electrode Tip.** Lesion size was found to rise with increasing size of electrode tip when maintaining temperature and time constant (Fig. 23).

(3) **Time.** Although the size of the lesion is also dependent on the duration of current flow, it is a non-linear relationship. It was found (Pecson *et al.*, 1969) that the lesion rapidly increased in size reaching 50 per cent of its ultimate size within 2·5–5 sec. from the time that the tip reached the predetermined temperature of 65°C. The rate

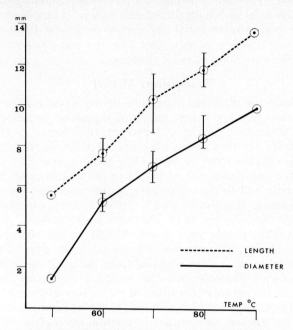

Fig. 22. Radio-frequency lesion. Average lesion size plotted against temperature. Time and tip size constant. (From Alberts *et al.*, 1966.)

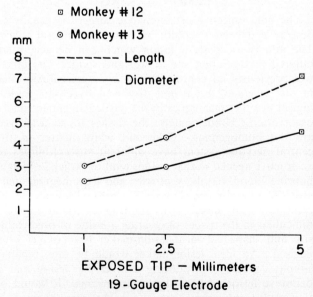

Fig. 23. Radio-frequency lesion. Lesion size plotted against tip dimensions. Time and temperature constant. (From Alberts *et al.*, 1966.)

of increase then steadily diminished until the maximum dimension was reached within 30 sec. (Fig. 24). With larger tip dimensions, equilibrium takes longer but appears to be complete within about one minute.

The *shape* of the lesion is dependent to some extent on the shape of the electrode. Side-protruding electrodes and partially insulated electrodes have been designed for special purposes. In addition, chronic electrode placement in contrast to the more commonly practised acute lesion may also be used. An advantage of this method is that the size of the lesion can be gradually increased over a long period of time. When high temperatures are produced around the electrode tip, boiling and gas formation may occur resulting in an abrupt change in the readings of RF voltage and current.

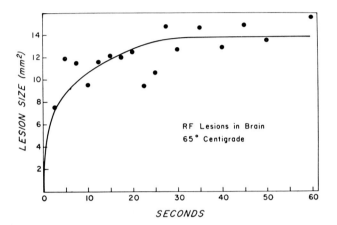

Fig. 24. Radio-frequency lesion. Average lesion size plotted against time. Temperature and tip size constant. (From Pecson *et al.*, 1969.)

Pathology of Lesion. Unipolar lesions are discrete in size, show a clear-cut edge and an absence of gross reaction, whereas bi-polar lesions show inconsistent patterns of destruction (Smith, 1966). The histological appearance of the unipolar RF lesion varies with the time of survival. Lesions a few days old show a central cavity produced by the electrode itself, surrounded by a wall of coagulation necrosis, beyond which is an irregular zone of softening and a further zone of demyelination. The longer standing lesions may resemble old cystic infarcts containing a gelatinous tissue in a central cyst surrounded by scar tissue. When lesions involve both grey and white matter they are seen to be more extensive in the more susceptible white matter. The presence of an adjacent "heat-sink" such as a ventricle containing cerebrospinal fluid will influence the size and shape of the lesion. Vascular complications may occur, particularly in patients with vascular disease such as hypertension and diabetes.

The practical implications of using RF lesions are as follows:

(1) Temperature controlled lesions are much preferable to power "controlled" lesions.
(2) The duration of current flow should be sufficient to allow maximum lesion size to be achieved, the size of the lesion being controlled by temperature. The size of the electrode should be chosen appropriate to the size of the lesion required.
(3) Unipolar lesions are preferable to bi-polar lesions.
(4) Checking and maintenance of the equipment,

particularly the electrodes and connections is important in the achievement of consistent results and safety of the patient.

The radio frequency lesion has applications throughout the stereotaxic field and is probably the most widely used method of producing small localized lesions of reasonably predictable size and shape in the brain or spinal cord under acute or chronic conditions.

2. Induction Heating Lesion

Mode of Action. A metal conductor placed in an alternating magnetic field will become heated, primarily due to the eddy currents set up within it. If such a conductor is placed in the brain, a heat-dependent lesion can be created. As in the other temperature-dependent methods, a zone of reversibly inactivated tissue will advance ahead of the permanently damaged tissue.

Equipment. The method employs an induction coil through which an alternating current of moderately high frequency is passed. An inert stainless steel rod of high magnetic permeability is inserted stereotaxically into the predetermined target point. The induction coil is then placed around the head and orientated so that the long axis of the rod lies at 90° to the plane of the coil, and radio frequency current then passed through the coil.

Determinants of Lesion Size. The degree of heating of the rod, and therefore the size of the lesion, depends on the efficiency of the coupling system, which will depend on the characteristics of the generator system, the physical properties and size of the metal conductor and its orientation and position within the magnetic field. In human stereotaxy where the rod is small and the distance from the coil is large, coupling is poor and it is necessary to use a powerful generator system.

Pathology of Lesion. Experimental and human lesions have been shown to be uniform, circular in shape and with no associated distant tissue injury (Carpenter, 1952; Walker, 1966).

With regard to the practical applications of the method, it is said to be simple and safe and is controllable within the limits of clinical observations. The temperature dependent zone of reversibility is a safety factor. An advantage of the method lies in the absence of the necessity of performing a further surgical procedure should the lesion require enlargement. However, its practical use at the present time is limited.

3. Thermocautery Lesion

The method employs the simple device of placing a heating element of resistance wire at the tip of an electrode and passing an electrical current through the element. The size of the lesion will be determined by the temperature developed at the tip of the electrode, the size of the probe and the duration of heating. Experimental lesions produced by this method in the cat were reported to be inconsistent in size and shape (Carpenter, 1952), but temperature monitoring of the electrode tip can yield more consistent lesions in the experimental animal.

II. Cryogenic Lesion

Mode of Action. It is well known that cooling can be employed to block function in neural tissue temporarily. A permanent lesion develops when the temperature is further reduced and congelation of the tissue occurs. Reversible lesions probably occur down to about 0°C. Lethal temperatures appear to be somewhere above -12°C in tissue (Fraser, 1967). Freezing of the tissue to a solid state is lethal. The mechanism by which tissue death occurs may be due to rupture of cell membranes, denaturation of protein molecules, crystallization, dehydration, thermal shock or vascular stasis and ischaemia.

Cooling is usually achieved by means of a liquefied gas which absorbs heat from the adjacent tissue when it changes its state from liquid to gas, the latent heat required for vaporization of the gas is extracted from the tissues. Alternatively, a compressed gas is used which absorbs heat when it is allowed to expand (Joule–Kelvin effect). This effect is shown by a change in the temperature of a gas when it is allowed to expand freely. The change in temperature is proportional to the change in pressures and most gases at ordinary temperatures become cooled. Observations on the temperature changes in the tissues involved in the progressing lesion, show an initial fall in temperature followed by a plateau. A third phase of continued cooling then occurs. The second phase is presumably due to heat absorption by the process of the latent heat of crystallization occurring in the lesion. It is at this stage that irreversible changes occur.

Equipment. A vacuum-insulated cannula carries the liquefied gas, for example liquid nitrogen, to the uninsulated tip where heat exchange occurs with cooling of the tissues by vaporization or expansion of the gas. Liquid nitrogen at a temperature of -196°C is capable of producing extremely low temperatures down to -160°C in the brain tissue. A thermocouple at the tip of the cannula records temperature. By means of a feedback mechanism from the thermocouple, the temperature of the tip can be maintained at a preselected level or altered as required, by changing the flow of liquid or compressed gas. At the conclusion, removal of the probe is deferred until thawing has been completed.

Determinants of Lesion Size. The size of the lesion will be related to (i) the temperature differential between the probe tip and the brain, (ii) the size of the probe tip, and (iii) duration of application. The selected temperature at the uninsulated tip of the probe is important in determining the size of the lesion. A steep temperature gradient exists between the probe tip and the surrounding brain. For example, the temperature at 2 mm. distance from the tip of -196°C was -56°C, at 4 mm. distance the temperature was -24°C and at 8 mm. the temperature was -12°C. Beyond the frozen lesion is a zone of reversibly inactivated tissue. As the temperature differential is increased by the flow of liquid nitrogen through the probe, the size of the permanent lesion increases. There is an almost linear relationship between the diameter of the lesion and the temperature (Fig. 25). The size of the probe tip will also markedly affect the size of the lesion. It is possible to select the size of probe according to the size of lesion required. The size of the lesion is time dependent, particularly when using very low temperatures in order to produce a large lesion. Repeated freeze-thaw cycles increase the size of the lesion and are of particular use when large lesions are required. Up to 6 or 7 repetitive cycles of freezing and thawing may be required before the maximal lesion is produced.

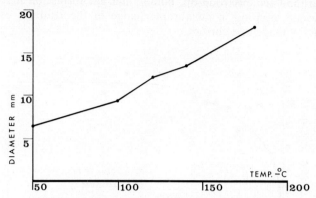

Fig. 25. Cryogenic lesion. Diameter of lesion plotted against temperature. Time and tip size constant. (From data in Gill *et al.*, 1968.)

Pathology of the Lesion. The histological features of the cryo-lesion are similar to those of an ischaemic infarct. The lesions are essentially haemostatic, sharply circumscribed and delineated from surrounding normal tissue. There is a thin reactive zone bordering the zone of destruction. There is no gross haemorrhage in the necrotic tissue or the surrounding nerve tissue. Major arteries do not suffer necrosis of their muscular wall and this enhances the margin of safety of the method. However, with the recycling repeated freeze-thaw method, lesions tend to be more haemorrhagic.

With regard to the practical implications of the method, the duration of the freezing process should be sufficient to allow maximum lesion size to be achieved; the size of the lesion being controlled by temperature. The size of the probe should be chosen appropriate to the size of the lesion required. Small diameter probes, even where available, are particularly delicate and require considerable care in handling. The cryogenic lesion has wide applications in stereotaxic surgery of the brain under acute conditions.

Electrolytic Lesion

Mode of Action. When a potential difference is applied between electrodes in the body tissues, a migration of ions occurs; anions, in particular chloride, migrating towards the anode. Chlorine, hypochlorite and oxygen are evolved at the anode whilst hydrogen in particular is evolved at the cathode. Both chemical and mechanical effects are responsible for the lesion. Bleaching and coagulation of protein occurs around the anodal lesion, probably due to the hypochlorite and chlorine. The mechanical effect, which is due to the release of gas, is particularly marked at the cathode. The cathodal lesion is larger and more irregular than the anodal lesion, and possibly responsible for distant effects. The anode is therefore almost always used as the lesion-making electrode.

Equipment. Electrolytic lesions have been used since, and even before, the advent of stereotaxis itself (Horsley, 1908). Electrolytic lesions continue to be used but mainly in experimental work. The equipment which is simple and cheap provides a constant current source, delivering only a low current level as the passage of high current strengths tends to produce irregular lesions. The electrode which is insulated, apart from its tip, may be made of platinum coated tungsten wire. The platinum provides an inert pole while the tungsten provides rigidity and strength and can be sharpened to a fine point if necessary. The indifferent electrode has a wide area of electrical contact with the patient and is placed at a sufficient distance to prevent directional effects.

Determinants of Lesion Size. The size of the lesion will be determined by the strength of current, size of electrode, and duration of current flow. Using an electrode tip of 0·010 in. diameter and 2 mm. length, it was found (Mullan, 1965) with anodal lesions that maximum size was achieved within approximately 1 min. for current strengths of 0·75 mA. and less. Currents above 2 mA. showed marked irregularity even at the anode. The importance of a smoothly and uniformly ground tip to the electrode has been emphasized (Carpenter, 1952).

Pathology of the Lesion. The anodal lesion is characterized by a central cavity surrounded by a zone of coagulation outside which is a zone of softening. In the zone of coagulation the nerve cells show tigrolysis, the nucleus becoming small and darkly staining. Thrombosed vessels are seen which later undergo dissolution although the elastic lamina is relatively resistant. In the oedematous zone, small cavities are noted and often a line of cleavage. Sections made of lesions produced three weeks before death are marked by phagocytes in the inner zone of softening (Horsley, 1908). Capillaries in the periphery where nerve cells may appear damaged are dilated but not thrombosed. In this zone which is beyond the macroscopic lesion, neural cells may appear damaged.

Applications. With regard to the practical applications of the electrolytic lesion, it has its greatest usefulness in making small discrete lesions of only a few millimetres diameter, for example, in the experimental animal and in human spinal cord surgery. However, even in the spinal cord other methods of lesion making are more commonly employed. Nevertheless, it is a simple, inexpensive method which is reasonably well controllable at low current levels and may have applications in regions where it would be advantageous to pass the smallest possible probe and where a small lesion is required.

Ultrasonic Lesion

Mode of Action. Compared with the widespread use of diagnostic ultrasound, the use of ultrasound for lesion making is much less common. Ultrasound becomes destructive at high intensities. At the ultrasonic frequencies used for lesion making (e.g. 1 Mc./s.), sound waves behave in ways comparable with light waves and travel in straight lines. Reflection and refraction occur and focusing is possible. Tissue fluids are a good conductor of ultrasound but attenuation occurs in air. It is absorbed strongly by bone and reflected at tissue interfaces. At the higher frequencies better focusing can be achieved but absorption in the tissues increases rapidly and poor penetration occurs. The energy of ultrasound is dissipated as heat and this is the principal mechanism underlying the production of the focused ultrasonic lesion. However, the high frequency mechanical vibration of ultrasound may lead to shearing forces and to breakdown and cavitation in the tissues (Wells, 1970). Increased permeability and damage to cell membranes occur and the larger molecules and enzymatic activity may be affected. Particle streaming may also be responsible for part of the damage.

Equipment. Ultrasound is produced by applying a high frequency alternating current across a piezo-electric crystal, causing it to vibrate at the applied frequency which is usually made to coincide with the resonant frequency of the crystal. The emitted ultrasound is focused and beamed into the brain to the target point. Because of the loss of power which occurs at air/fluid interfaces, air must be excluded between the ultrasonic source and the target site. It is necessary to remove part of the skull because of the marked absorption of ultrasound by bone and the resultant heat production.

Determinants of Lesion Size. Lesion size will depend on the intensity and time of dissipation of ultrasound energy at the target site. The intensity will depend on the power output of the ultrasonic generator, the distance and nature of intervening structures between the generator and the target site and the focusing arrangements. With focused ultrasound it has been possible to produce controllable lesions, often of elliptical shape, the long axis of the ellipse lying in the long axis of the beam of ultrasound. Lesions of 0·5–7 mm. in extent have been made in experimental animals.

Pathology of Lesion. The lesion is usually sharply demarcated and laminated:

(1) There is a central core of intensely staining necrotic tissue in which the architecture has largely been preserved.

(2) An intermediate zone consists of pale staining tissue with marked disruption of cells and fibres, often resulting in a punched-out appearance.

(3) There is a very narrow peripheral zone in which minor cellular damage has occurred. Gliosis later occurs in this zone. The blood vessels in the lesion are often less affected than the neural and neuro-glial cells, but thrombosis and distant ischaemic effects may occur.

Practical Implications. While ultrasonic lesions have been used in human stereotaxis, general acceptance of the method has been lacking. An advantage of the method is that no electrode penetrates the brain. However, this carries the disadvantage that depth recording and stimulation are not possible, and except within the limits of clinical observation during lesion making functional localization is not possible.

Radionecrotic Lesion

The use of the radionecrotic lesion is dealt with in detail under therapeutic radiation, suffice to say that in stereotaxic surgery such methods can produce very satisfactory lesions in terms of size, shape and reproducibility. However, delay in the development of the lesion and irreversibility of side effects should they occur, can be important disadvantages.

FUTURE PROSPECTS

In the future it would seem that there are several areas for progress in the field of stereotaxic surgery:

(1) Stereotaxic instrumentation may show rationalization so that there may be a reduction in the number of instruments which are similar in all but relatively minor details. Nevertheless, continued search for simplicity and universality must occur; further exploration of polar co-ordinate systems may prove worthwhile.

(2) It will be necessary to select new and better target sites for modifying different aspects of brain function in order to extend the usefulness of the stereotaxic technique in the management of human illness.

(3) Improved methods of confirming that the target has been located will evolve. Depth electrical recording and stimulation will help considerably, but other methods, particularly biochemical, will be necessary. The compilation of a truly functional stereotaxic atlas or "dictionary" will be of immense value.

(4) While methods of lesion making have improved considerably, perfection has not yet been achieved and refinements will probably occur.

(5) The use of the stereotaxic technique to supplement or to enhance biological function may well develop in contrast to the present purely destructive lesions.

FURTHER READING

Andrew, J. and Watkins, E. S. (1969), *A Stereotaxic Atlas of the Human Thalamus and Adjacent Structures*. Baltimore: The Williams and Wilkins Co.

Alberts, W. W., Wright, E. W. and Feinstein, B., *et al.* (1966), "Experimental Radio-frequency Brain Lesion Size as a Function of Physical Parameters," *J. Neurosurg.*, **25**, 421–423.

Aronow, S. (1960), "The use of Radio-frequency Power in Making Lesions in the Brain," *J. Neurosurg.*, **17**, 431–438.

Carpenter, M. B. and Whittier, J. R. (1952), "Study of Methods for Producing Experimental Lesions of the Central Nervous System with Special Reference to Stereotaxic Technique," *J. comp. Neurol.*, **97**, 73–131.

Dawson, B. H., Dervin, E. and Heywood, O. B. (1969), "The Development of a Mechanical Analog for Directing and Tracking the Electrode During Stereotaxic Operations. Technical note," *J. Neurosurg.*, **31**, 361–366.

Fox, J. L. (1970), "Experimental Relationship of Radio-frequency Electrical Current and Lesion Size for Application to Percutaneous Cordotomy," *J. Neurosurg.*, **33**, 415–421.

Fraser, J. and Gill, W. (1967), "Observations on Ultra-frozen Tissue," *Brit. J. Surg.*, **54**, 770–776.

Gaze, R. M., Gillingham, F. J. and Kalyanaraman, S., *et al.* (1964), "Microelectrode Recordings from the Human Thalamus," *Brain*, **87**, 691–706.

Gill, W., Fraser, J. and Carter, D. C. (1968), "Repeated Freeze-thaw Cycles in Cryosurgery," *Nature*, **219**, 410–413.

Gillingham, F. J. and Donaldson, I. M. L. (Eds.) (1969), *Third Symposium on Parkinson's Disease*. Edinburgh: Livingstone.

Horsley, V. and Clark, R. H. (1908), "The Structure and Functions of the Cerebellum Examined by a New Method," *Brain*, **31**, 45–124.

Mullan, S., Mailis, M. and Karasick, J., *et al.* (1965), "A Reappraisal of the Unipolar Anodal Electrolytic Lesion," *J. Neurosurg.*, **22**, 531–538.

Nashold, B. S. and Huber, W. V. (Eds.) (1966), "Second Symposium on Parkinson's Disease," Supplement to *J. Neurosurg*.

Pecson, R. D., Roth, D. A. and Mark, V. H. (1969), "Experimental Temperature Control of Radio-frequency Brain Lesion Size," *J. Neurosurg.*, **30**, 703–707.

Schaltenbrand, G. and Bailey, P. (Eds.) (1959), *Introduction to Stereotaxis with an Atlas of the Human Brain*, vols. I–III. Stuttgart: Georg Thieme Verlag.

Smith, M. C. (1966), "Pathological Findings Subsequent to Stereotactic Lesions," *J. Neurosurg. Suppl.*, **24**, 443–445.

Spiegel, E. A., Wycis, H. T., Marks, M. and Lee, A. J. (1947), "Stereotaxic Apparatus for Operations on the Human Brain," *Science*, **106**, 349–350.

Spiegel, E. A. and Wycis, H. T. (1952), *Stereoencephalotomy (Thalamotomy and Related Procedures), Part I. Methods and Stereotaxis Atlas of the Human Brain*. London: Heinemann.

Spiegel, E. A. and Wycis, H. T. (1962), *Stereoencephalotomy (Thalamotomy and Related Procedures) Part II. Clinical and Physiological Applications*. New York: Grune and Stratton.

Spiegel, E. A. and Wycis, H. T. (Eds.), *Advances in Stereoencephalotomy*. Basel: Karger.
Vol. 1: *Stereotaxic Surgery* (1963). Reprint from *Confin. Neurol.*, Vol. 22, No. 3–5.
Vol. 2, Part I: *Methodology and Extrapyramidal System* (1965). Reprint from *Confin. Neurol.*, Vol. 26, No. 3–5. Part II: *Pain, Convulsive Disorders, Behavioral and Other Effects of Stereoencephalotomy* (1966). Reprint from *Confin. Neurol.*, Vol. 27, No. 1–3.
Vol. 3: *Dyskinesias, Sensory, Emotional and Mental Aspects. Methods and Various Stimulation Effects* (1967). Reprint from *Confin. Neurol.*, Vol. 29, No. 2–5.
Vol. 4: *Recent Clinical and Theoretical Applications of Stereoencephalotomy* (1968). Reprint from *Confin. Neurol.*, Vol. 31, No. 1–2.
Vol. 5: *Extrapyramidal, Sensory, Convulsive and Behavioral Disorders. Recent Techniques* (1970). Reprint from *Confin. Neurol.*, Vol. 32, No. 2–5.

Stellar, S. and Cooper, I. S. (1968), "Mortality and Morbidity in Cryothalamectomy for Parkinsonism. A Statistical Study of 2,868 Consecutive Operations," *J. Neurosurg.*, **28**, 459–467.

Taren, J., Guiot, G., Deroe, P. and Trigo, J. A. (1968), "Hazards of Stereotaxic Thalamectomy. Added Safety Factor in Corroborating X-ray Target Localization with Neurophysiological Method," *J. Neurosurg.*, **29**, 173–182.

Van Buren, J. M. and MacCubin, D. A. (1962), "An Outline Atlas of the Human Basal Ganglia with Estimation of Anatomical Variants," *J. Neurosurg.*, **19**, 811–839.

Walker, A. E. and Burton, C. V. (1966), "Radio-frequency Tele-thermocoagulation," *J. Amer. med. Ass.*, **197**, 700–704.

Waltz, J. M. and Cooper, I. S. (1967), "Temperature Gradients, the Blood Brain Barrier and the Brain Tumour," *Bull. Millard Fillmore Hospital*, **14**, 96–102.

Warwick, R. and Pond, J. (1968), "Trackless Lesions in Nervous Tissues Produced by High Intensity Focused Ultrasound (High-frequency Mechanical Waves)," *J. Anat.*, **102**, 387–405.

Watkins, E. S. (1965), "Heat Gains During Electrocoagulation Lesions," *J. Neurosurg.*, **23**, 319–327.

8. BRAIN BIOPSY

HUME ADAMS

Brain biopsy has been available as a diagnostic method for many years but it is not as widely used as it might be. Brain tissue can be subjected to a considerable number of highly specialized research techniques but the aim of this chapter is to define at a more routine diagnostic level the value and limitations of brain biopsy by outlining the types of condition for which it may be used and the principal techniques which will ensure the maximum yield of information.

VALUE OF BIOPSY

It is well to remember that in recent years the development of neuroradiological and neurophysiological techniques, together with other methods such as scintiscanning, the gamma camera and isotope ventriculography, has led to the more accurate identification of focal lesions within the brain and the positive recognition during life of such diverse conditions as normal pressure hydrocephalus and neocortical death. The clinician is increasingly expected to make a precise pathological diagnosis in patients who, in previous years, might have simply been accepted as cases of "stroke", "dementia" or "cerebral atrophy"; and as medical and surgical treatment becomes possible for more conditions there is a natural demand for the recognition (or exclusion) of treatable conditions rather than the acceptance of diagnostic labels on the balance of clinical probabilities. There are many modern laboratory techniques such as the examination of peripheral nerve or rectal biopsies, CSF cytology and the application of sophisticated biochemical and neurochemical techniques to CSF, blood and urine which can provide a wealth of information relevant to diseases of the brain without recourse to an actual brain biopsy, but there remain many conditions where the final diagnosis can be made or confirmed only on the basis of examination of brain tissue itself. If it transpires that a patient suffering from some progressive condition has a subacute inflammatory disorder of the brain, the relatives can at least be assured that the disease is an acquired one. On the other hand if the presence of a hereditarily determined disease is established, genetic counselling can be offered on the basis of a firm knowledge of its nature. Information derived from brain biopsies has also contributed to the more accurate classification of many progressive cerebral disorders, to a better understanding of their nature and, in some diseases, to a more accurate assessment of the prognosis.

Brain biopsy is most commonly used by neurosurgeons as the final diagnostic procedure in a patient with a focal intracranial lesion. The lesion suspected is most often a tumour, but the biopsy may disclose an inflammatory lesion or a recent swollen infarct. The need for brain biopsy in such circumstances is readily accepted. Its second common use—often referred to as primary cortical biopsy—is in the patient with a subacute or chronic progressive cerebral disorder of diffuse character such as occurs in presenile dementia, subacute sclerosing panencephalitis, the leucodystrophies or neuronal storage diseases. Some clinicians believe that there is rarely justification for primary brain biopsy because it is unlikely to lead to the institution of specific treatment and as it entails a formal, albeit minor, neurosurgical procedure; brain biopsy, however, is probably no more traumatic than ventriculography and there is no evidence to suggest that it is more hazardous than percutaneous renal or liver biopsy. As a result of a questionnaire sent to a group of experienced neurologists—all Directors of Clinical Establishments either in Europe or the U.S.A.—Biemond[3] suggests that "primary cerebral biopsy is an admissible diagnostic procedure when—

(1) one is convinced of the presence of a chronic progressive cerebral disorder of diffuse character accompanied by dementia;

(2) all other possible diagnostic methods have already been tried and have failed to provide sufficient diagnostic certainty;

(3) the general condition of the patient permits it;

(4) several specialists are in agreement regarding the indication;

(5) permission has been obtained from the parents or the relatives respectively, after the limited aim of the procedure has been fully explained in an understandable manner;

(6) modern diagnostic possibilities are exploited to the fullest in the examination of the material obtained".

The last of these is by no means the least important and is inevitably conditioned by the facilities which are immediately available, but every effort must be made to exploit to the full properly taken brain biopsies, and unless laboratory facilities and staff experienced in their interpretation are available, biopsy is neither advisable nor justified.

BIOPSY TECHNIQUE

In the majority of cases this simply entails a burr-hole and aspiration of tissue from a *focal lesion* in the brain through a cannula: an attempt should always be made to obtain tissue from the lesion and not merely cyst fluid or necrotic material. The experienced neurosurgeon usually knows when he has obtained only oedematous tissue and time will be saved if he proceeds with a second aspiration biopsy without waiting for a negative tumour report from the laboratory.

SCIENTIFIC FOUNDATIONS OF NEUROLOGY

Once the decision to take a *primary cortical biopsy has* been reached, there should be joint consultation between the clinical and laboratory staff to decide the best site for the biopsy (it may be advisable to select primary and secondary sites at this stage lest it transpires later that it is not technically feasible to obtain an adequate biopsy from the former), and the techniques by which it should be examined. Most biopsies are taken from the frontal or the parieto-occipital regions and should consist of a 1·0–1·5 cm. cube of tissue composed of meninges, cortex and white matter excised by sharp disection before using diathermy. If only a few small pieces of cortex and/or white matter are obtained the chances of establishing a firm diagnosis are greatly reduced. The tissue is then transferred at once to the laboratory staff who ideally should be in attendance in the theatre suite so that the specimen can be subdivided and placed in the appropriate containers with the minimum of delay.

EXAMINATION OF BIOPSY MATERIAL

Tissue Smears

This method was established originally for examining small aspiration biopsies in suspected cases of intracranial tumour and is the most widely used technique in the diagnosis of acute neurosurgical illnesses. It is the counterpart of the more conventional frozen section technique of the general pathologist. Some laboratories still prefer to cut frozen sections of aspiration biopsies of the brain, but this is technically more difficult than the preparation of smears and only a small fraction of the biopsy can be examined in any one section. The smear technique on the other hand is quick and simple, and several portions of even a small biopsy can be sampled. Its principal disadvantage is that it is basically a cytological diagnosis because tissue architecture is distorted and sometimes completely destroyed by the technique. In our experience this disadvantage is more than compensated for by the detailed cytological features that can be seen in smears compared with frozen sections, and by the ease with which numerous parts of the specimen can be screened. Thus a diagnosis of metastatic carcinoma may often be confidently based on a small group of tumour cells in a smear otherwise composed of normal or reactive cells. Such a group would be less likely to appear in a single frozen section. Although the smear technique was introduced for the rapid diagnosis of cerebral tumours, many other cell types can be readily identified, e.g. gemistocytic astrocytes in reactive gliosis, lipid phagocytes in cerebral infarction, and polymorphonuclear leucocytes, lymphocytes or plasma cells in inflammatory lesions. Indeed the light perivascular cuffing by lymphocytes and plasma cells which occurs in encephalitis is often more obvious in smears than in paraffin sections.

Smears may be stained by a variety of techniques, e.g. 1 per cent toluidine blue, polychrome methylene blue, Mann's eosin methylene blue or by the Papanicalaou technique; none has any particular advantage and the usual policy adopted in any one laboratory is to adhere to one technique and to become as competent as possible

in interpreting the results. Clinicians should realize, however, that the level of accuracy of a smear diagnosis does not attain that of formal histological sections, even in experienced hands: it is therefore the policy in most laboratories to confirm the preliminary smear diagnosis in paraffin sections and some tissue should, wherever possible, be set aside for this purpose.

Frozen Sections

These may be used either as an aid to the immediate diagnosis of an intracranial lesion or as part of the more formal study of primary biopsies from patients with chronic neurological illnesses. There is little to commend the use of frozen sections in the examination of small soft brain biopsies: the production of good sections is technically rather difficult and unless sections are cut at numerous levels, thus wasting tissue that might be used for other purposes, only a very limited portion of the biopsy can be examined under the microscope. The technique, however, is invaluable when the biopsy is too tough for the preparation of smears. Another advantage, when fairly large pieces of a tumour are available, is that tissue architecture is preserved.

 The principal role that frozen sections play in the examination of a brain biopsy is in the diagnosis of neuronal storage disorders or diffuse demyelinating diseases as most of the abnormal lipid substances to be identified dissolve out during the preparation of paraffin sections. They are also useful in the diagnosis of organic dementia. These applications are dealt with in greater detail below in the relevant sections.

Paraffin Sections

This is the sheet anchor of histological diagnosis and paraffin sections should be prepared from every brain biopsy. Disadvantages are that the sections are not normally available for about 48–72 hr. after the operation and that many substances dissolve out of the tissue in the course of processing. A particular advantage is the ease with which serial sections can be cut from a small biopsy.

Celloidin Sections

Because of the time required for their production, celloidin sections are rarely prepared from brain biopsies as a rapid diagnosis is usually required. In our experience they are, however, less prone to technical artefact than paraffin sections and remain the method of choice for the production of thick sections from large pieces of brain where there is a need to assess the general topography of grey and white matter. This type of investigation is particularly appropriate for the examination of excised temporal lobes in patients with temporal lobe epilepsy.[6]

Microbiological Examination

If there is even the slightest suspicion of an inflammatory process when a biopsy is taken, or if there are any features suggestive of inflammation in a preliminary smear, brain tissue should be taken at that time for bacteriological and virological examination; this may lead to a considerable saving in time in establishing a precise diagnosis. Tissue removed at biopsy is particularly suitable for the isolation of virus in acute encephalitis as virus may often be isolated from the brain when it is not present in the CSF.[1] The rapid and accurate identification of viruses has assumed increasing importance since it has been suggested that certain agents such as iodo-deoxyuridine (a DNA inhibitor) may be of value in the treatment of acute encephalitis due to DNA viruses such as herpes simplex virus.[16] Tissue to be used for virus isolation should be placed in a special transport medium.[10] Tissue removed at brain biopsy can also be utilized in the search for transmissible agents in chronic neurological illnesses such as Creutzfeldt–Jakob disease.

Chemical Analysis

This more highly specialized type of investigation tends to be undertaken in particular centres. The tissue can be analysed quantitatively for its lipid content or examined by thin layer chromatography. Blackwood and Cumings[4] have used very successfully a combined chemical and histological approach to brain biopsies. This is particularly relevant to the neuronal storage diseases and the leucodystrophies where biochemical criteria have now been so firmly established that they are often of greater diagnostic significance than those made by the histologist.

Electron Microscopy

As recently as 1970 Peters[19] has observed that "the nervous system is still *terra incognita* as far as electron microscopy is concerned". Much of our current knowledge of the ultrastructure of brain has inevitably been based on studies in animals but ultrastructural diagnostic criteria have now been established for several diseases of the nervous system as a result of the examination of brain biopsies, e.g. the several types of intracytoplasmic body that occur in the neuronal storage disorders (*vide infra*). At a diagnostic level the electron microscope can also be used in the identification of virus particles[11] and in the classification of cerebral tumours. The examination of properly fixed samples from a brain biopsy has great potential as there is still a need for the proper correlation of ultrastructural features and those of classical neuropathological histology in diverse processes such as cerebral infarction, hypoxia, oedema, inflammation and dementia. To attain perfect fixation there must be close co-operation between the surgeon and the laboratory staff.

Tissue Culture

Tissue culture provides an opportunity of studying living cells under defined conditions. Its general use and potential have been reviewed by Lumsden[14] but in the context of the current chapter this type of investigation has been used particularly in the examination of intracranial tumours. These tumours grow readily in culture and the various types of tumour retain *in vitro* their essential biological characteristics.[15] Therefore although still really a supplementary and research method it could be of diagnostic value as it can on occasions be more certain than histology in the final diagnosis when a biopsy is extremely small. Tissue culture has also been used to clarify the histogenesis of cerebral tumours and may be a means of assessing their response to various types of treatment and of elucidating the possible contribution of oncogenic viruses in the causation of human gliomas.

DIAGNOSTIC APPLICATIONS OF BRAIN BIOPSY

Intracranial Tumours

The smear technique is the method of choice for the examination of needle biopsies of suspected cerebral tumours. When the pathologist is experienced with this technique the diagnostic accuracy is high, but as already indicated the interpretation of smears is more difficult than that of paraffin sections. There is, therefore, nothing to be gained by the pathologist examining the smear "blind" as a diagnostic exercise: if he knows the age and sex of the patient, the site of the biopsy and any other relevant clinical features or operative findings, he will be in a better position to assess the probabilities and the diagnostic accuracy will be correspondingly higher.

It should also be more widely recognized that smear diagnoses come into two groups—those where a genuine immediate diagnosis is required and those where the need is really for a "same-day" diagnosis. Diagnostic accuracy will inevitably be higher when the pathologist is not under pressure to provide an immediate diagnosis within a few minutes. The neurosurgeon should therefore make it clear to the pathologist if he is waiting in theatre, perhaps in the middle of a craniotomy, and requires to know the nature of the lesion before deciding what to do next. More often biopsy is carried out through a burr-hole in a patient suspected of having a malignant tumour so situated that removal is not a practical proposition: in these circumstances the surgeon hopes to avoid a major operation if he can confirm the nature of the tumour beyond doubt, and he can usually wait an hour or so for the result. If it is negative, however, or the pathologist suspects a benign tumour, then he will probably wish to obtain more tissue either by repeating the biopsy or by undertaking craniotomy to confirm the diagnosis. Occasionally patients deteriorate after biopsy, especially those with malignant tumours, and the surgeon should know the nature of the tumour within a few hours in order to be able to decide whether or not to intervene in the event of such deterioration.

When the smear is being examined the pathologist must first ask himself "is it or is it not a tumour?". This question can usually be answered in the affirmative within seconds, unless the biopsy is composed entirely of necrotic

...ureless material. If the appearances are not immediately suggestive of a tumour, at least three smears should be screened systematically at low and intermediate magnifications for any evidence of tumour: this is the reason why it often takes longer to issue a negative report than a positive one. The experienced pathologist soon finds it easy to recognize normal brain tissue without having recourse to high magnification because, at this stage, it is the overall picture of the smears rather than the appearance of individual cells that is important. When stained with toluidine blue, grey and white matter tend to have a distinctive homogeneous blue colour that is not seen in tumours and in such smears the temptation to look at small groups of cells at high magnification should be resisted.

A particular problem in the examination of smears is to distinguish between tumour and intense reactive changes, particularly in the thicker parts of a smear. The nuances of this distinction cannot be illustrated in the present text but it should be recalled that reactive gliosis is particularly severe adjacent to a recent cerebral infarct and in acute necrotizing encephalitis; also that groups of lipid phagocytes are only rarely seen in smears from a tumour, that gemistocytic astrocytes have a characteristic appearance that makes them fairly readily distinguishable from tumour cells, that vascular proliferation is not restricted to tumours, and that light perivascular cuffing may occur in and adjacent to gliomas and metastatic carcinoma as well as in encephalitis. The close admixture of tumour astrocytes and normal cells in a well differentiated diffuse astrocytoma, or the presence of occasional tumour cells in the reactive gliosis around a glioma, are particularly difficult problems, while necrotic structureless material may occur in an infarct as well as within an anaplastic tumour.

When it is apparent that there is a tumour in the smear the next question is "what type of tumour is it and could it be a meningioma?". The latter point is simply a reminder that meningiomas may vary greatly in appearance in smears and that every effort must be made not to overlook this diagnostic possibility. Information as to the site of the biopsy may make it much easier to reach a diagnosis: thus the sheets of fairly uniform round or oval cells that are characteristic of *oligodendroglioma* can be closely mimicked by a *pituitary adenoma*. Another relatively simple diagnosis is *metastatic carcinoma*, because of the conspicuous epithelial appearances of the cells and the prominent nucleoli in their nuclei: metastatic carcinoma is frequently of such a characteristic appearance that even the presence of a few clumps of cells in an otherwise normal smear—clumps of cells that are readily identifiable at low magnification—may allow of a positive diagnosis. Other features suggestive of metastatic carcinoma are the juxtaposition of tumour cells and normal brain tissue and the tendency the tumour cells show to become detached from each other and from blood vessels in the smear. This is in marked contrast to the *astrocytomas* where the tumour cells tend to adhere to each other and particularly to blood vessels with the result that a rather papillary pattern results. Because of the clarity of cytological detail in smears, variations in the size and shape of cells, binucleate and multinucleate cells, and mitotic figures can be readily identified with the result that some idea of the grade of malignancy of the tumour can be gained. The number of fibrils present varies greatly and, as many may be formed by smear artefact, not much significance should be attached to their presence. *Ependymomas* often have a prominent papillary architecture and the cells are distinctly pseudo-epithelial in appearance. Tumours of the *choroid plexus* are highly papillary and, were it not for their bulk, could hardly be distinguished from normal choroid plexus, the possible presence of small portions of which in smears should always be borne in mind. *Medulloblastoma* composed of sheets of small cells with scanty cytoplasm and with varying numbers of mitotic figures is also usually fairly easy to recognize once the pathologist is sufficiently experienced to distinguish between cerebellar granule cells and medulloblastoma cells: a useful feature is that Purkinje cells are usually scattered among normal granule cells.

Meningiomas can be very easy to diagnose in smears if numerous cell whorls and groups of typical arachnoidal cells are present: unfortunately they can also be very difficult to diagnose even when the pathologist has a great deal of experience in examining smears. A source of error leading to the mistaken diagnosis of meningioma is the occasional presence of groups of arachnoidal cells, presumably a contaminant in the biopsy from the surface of the brain, in some other types of tumour. Glomeruloid proliferation of small vessels in an anaplastic astrocytoma may also mimic the cell whorls of a meningioma. If meningioma is even suspected, however, the policy should always be to raise this possibility with the surgeon at once, lest even this slight suspicion is an indication for a further biopsy or a more extensive exploration. As the more fibroblastic meningiomas are difficult to smear, a frozen section is often more appropriate. The same may be said of some *Schwannomas*, but the presence in smears of interweaving bands of greatly elongated Antoni type A cells and groups of loosely packed polygonal cells of varying shape and size of Antoni type B tissue often makes the diagnosis straightforward. Distinguishing the various types of cerebello-pontine angle tumours in smears is sometimes particularly difficult as meningioma, Schwannoma, haemangioblastoma and fibrillary astrocytoma have several similar features: if the biopsy from a cerebello-pontine angle tumour is fairly large, frozen sections are particularly helpful as tissue architecture is preserved. Finally, many of the less common intracranial tumours have highly characteristic appearances in smears, e.g. craniopharyngioma, microglioma and chordoma.

In our experience the commonest problem encountered in smear diagnosis is to differentiate between an anaplastic astrocytoma and a poorly differentiated carcinoma: this has to be accepted as a limitation of smear diagnosis but such a distinction is rarely of immediate significance to the neurosurgeon, and it is sometimes difficult to resolve even in paraffin sections of a small biopsy.

Another technique which may help in the diagnosis of intracranial tumours is examination of the CSF for tumour cells: these are usually present in the CSF in cases of diffuse meningeal carcinomatosis or gliomatosis,[13] but they may also occur in association with a more focal lesion. As CSF protein is characteristically raised in cases of diffuse meningeal tumour and the sugar decreased,[13] the CSF should be examined routinely for tumour cells in cases of subacute meningitis of undetermined aetiology. It is probably appropriate to mention here that CSF rarely contains only "polymorphs" or "lymphocytes" because large mononuclear cells of reactive type, plasma cells and eosinophil polymorphs are frequently seen when stained preparations of the centrifuged deposit from fluids with an increased cell count are screened routinely by a pathologist.

Encephalitis

We have found the smear technique of considerable value in the immediate diagnosis of acute necrotizing encephalitis due to herpes simplex virus. The soft necrotic tissue obtained from such brains is not suitable for frozen section but is eminently so for smears. Indeed, perivascular cuffing and infiltration of the perivascular brain tissue by atypical mononuclear cells, and reactive astrocytes, hypertrophied microglial cells, and lipid phagocytes are often more apparent in smears than in the subsequent paraffin sections. As essentially similar abnormalities may be found adjacent to a brain abscess, acute necrotizing encephalitis cannot be diagnosed with certainty simply on the basis of smears. Where, however, it is the policy to treat such cases with iododeoxyuridine this can be started forthwith on the basis of the smear pending further confirmation of the diagnosis.[16] Immunofluorescent studies for virus antigen and electron microscopic examination for viral particles[11] may also be carried out on suitably preserved smears but the simple stained smear will always be the first available for examination. Samples of the biopsy should also be taken for virus isolation in a suitable transport medium,[10] as the isolation of virus from CSF is generally less successful than its isolation from brain tissue.[1] Serological studies are also of value, but results are never available immediately as paired sera taken about 10 days apart have to be compared: hence the importance of obtaining and storing the first specimen as early in the course of the disease as possible. In suspected cases of acute necrotizing encephalitis the biopsy should be taken as near as possible to the medial temporal lobe structures in the more severely affected hemisphere.[2] As further anti-viral agents become available it seems likely that brain biopsy will assume increasingly greater significance in suspected cases of acute viral encephalitis.

Primary cortical biopsy is often undertaken in suspected cases of subacute sclerosing panencephalitis, although the diagnosis can now be established with a reasonable degree of certainty on the basis of the clinical and EEG findings and the titres of complement fixing antibody to measles virus in the serum and CSF. Smears taken from a biopsy in such a case will again show perivascular cuffing by inflammatory cells, but in most cases the typical features are more readily seen in sections of a block of tissue incorporating cortex and white matter. The advice of the virologist is essential before biopsies are taken from such cases in view of the recent development of techniques which have allowed of the isolation of complete measles virus from biopsies taken from cases of subacute sclerosing panencephalitis.[12]

Leucodystrophy and Neuronal Storage Disorders

It is in this field that combined histological, histochemical, neurochemical and ultrastructural examinations have been particularly fruitful, not only as a means of reaching a definite diagnosis but also in accurately defining subdivisions in the major groups of these diseases. By conventional histology using frozen and paraffin sections and a relatively limited number of techniques the diagnosis of the major sub-types can be established with a fair degree of certainty, e.g. sudanophilic and metachromatic leucodystrophy, Krabbe's disease and amaurotic family idiocy. Blackwood and Cumings[4] have clearly demonstrated how combined histological and neurochemical studies can increase the number of cases in which a positive diagnosis can be obtained: thus in sudanophilic types of diffuse demyelinating disease there is characteristically a diminution of phospholipids and the presence of esterified cholesterol, while in metachromatic leucodystrophy, hexosamine and sulphatide are increased in association with the loss of phospholipids. Thin layer chromatography can demonstrate the sulphatide abnormality particularly clearly.

In the amaurotic family idiocies and in Niemann–Pick's disease the nature of the lipid storage material in neurones is remarkably similar in histological preparation, but they can be satisfactorily separated chemically, particularly by identifying various abnormalities in gangliosides in thin layer chromatography. In Tay–Sach's disease there is a large absolute and relative increase in G_{M2}—sometimes referred to as the "Tay–Sach's ganglioside"—while in late infantile amaurotic family idiocy the increase is in G_{M1}.[4,17,22] Several other variants of gangliosidosis, due basically to the deficiency or absence of lysosomal hydrolase enzymes, have now been identified. The ganglioside pattern is also abnormal in Niemann–Pick's disease and in Gaucher's disease.

Electron microscopy is becoming increasingly important in the study of neuronal storage disorders as various characteristic intracytoplasmic bodies have now been identified,[7] e.g. membranous cytoplasmic bodies (MCB's) in Tay–Sach's disease, membranovesicular bodies (MVB's) in juvenile lipidosis and curvilinear bodies in the specific type of neurovisceral storage disease identified by Duffy et al.[8] The identification of such structures helps in the classification of these storage disorders.

Presenile and Senile Dementia

This is another group of diseases in which brain biopsy has been fairly widely used. As they are chronic and progressive illnesses with protean clinical features and often come to have many symptoms in common, it is difficult to reconstruct the course of the illness and to assess the chronology and the symptomatology in any one type of dementia if the diagnosis is not established until the brain has been examined post mortem. Early accurate diagnosis might help to solve some of these problems as the patient could then be followed up and the progress of the disease charted, compared with others, and its natural history defined. This is the premise on which the series of Sim and his colleagues[20,21] is based. It would be wrong to suggest that all the defined types of organic dementia can be identified as the result of a brain biopsy, but at least in Alzheimer's presenile and senile dementia a reasonably confident diagnosis can be made if there are in the biopsy numerous senile plaques and examples of neurofibrillary change. Thus 34 of the 59 cases described by Sim fell into this group. Furthermore, useful information has been obtained about the nature and the origin of plaques and the alterations in neurofibrils in Alzheimer's disease by histochemical, enzyme histochemical and ultrastructural investigations. No specific changes were seen in 17 of the 59 cases described by Sim and his group but in other smaller groups the histological findings were those of arteriopathic cerebral atrophy, chronic meningo-encephalitis and subacute spongiform encephalopathy. This group also suggested that it might be possible to diagnose Pick's disease by brain biopsy but this is open to question in view of the fact that the more specific changes of Pick's disease are related to the medial temporal lobe gyri. The examination of a brain biopsy can also contribute to a positive diagnosis of Creutzfeldt–Jacob disease and on the basis of the ultrastructural examination of two such biopsies Gonatas et al.[9] came to the conclusion that the status spongiosus which is such a characteristic feature of Creutzfeldt–Jacob disease is brought about by dilatation of both astrocytic and neuronal processes. Biopsies from cases of this type can also be used as a source of material in the search for other transmissible degenerative diseases of the brain.

Other Conditions

Many diseases of the nervous system are diagnosed, often fortuitously, as a result of the examination of brain biopsies taken from patients with suspected intracranial tumours or expanding inflammatory processes. There are numerous other fields, however, where information obtained from a formal brain biopsy could be of considerable value. Thus, in the context of cardiac arrest, when a patient appears to be making some degree of recovery of brain stem and spinal cord function, it would often be helpful if the extent and severity of neocortical damage could be defined for, if this is profound, it is unlikely that there will be any useful recovery of consciousness or intellect. The examination of a fairly generous brain biopsy, preferably from the occipital lobe, could shed a considerable amount of light on the circumstances existing in any individual case.[5] This type of investigation could also be relevant to the diffuse neocortical damage associated with status epilepticus or profound hypoglycaemia, but not to the majority of cases with ischaemic brain damage or head injuries as, in both of these conditions, cortical damage is focal rather than diffuse. In recent years there has been a considerable amount of interest in progressive multifocal leucoencephalopathy culminating in the cultivation of a papova like virus from a single case post mortem:[18] if this disease were positively diagnosed more often during life by biopsy, more intensive investigations could be undertaken in an effort to determine its aetiology.

CONCLUSION

The types of technique to which brain biopsies could be subjected are very numerous and many that have been reported reflect various research interests, e.g. enzyme histochemistry, phase contrast microscopy, the identification and quantification of catecholamines in the brain and the analysis of fractions obtained by ultracentrifugalization. It is likely that some of these will become routine in the future, particularly in the sphere of stereotaxic surgery for movement disorders, but it is hoped that this chapter will help to clarify the current principal uses of brain biopsy.

FURTHER READING

1. Adams, J. H. (1969), "Acute Necrotizing Encephalitis," *Brit. J. Psychiat.*, Special Publ. No. 4, *Current Problems in Neuropsychiatry*, pp. 35–39.
2. Adams, J. H. and Jennett, W. B. (1967), "Acute Necrotizing Encephalitis: A Problem in Diagnosis," *J. Neurol. Neurosurg. Psychiat.*, **30**, 248–260.
3. Biemond, A. (1965), "Indications, Legal and Moral Aspects of Cerebral Biopsies," *Proc. Vth Inter. Congr. Neuropath.* (F. Luthy and A. Bischoff, Eds.), pp. 372–275. Amsterdam: Excerpta Medica.
4. Blackwood, W. and Cumings, J. N. (1965), "The Combined Histological and Chemical Aspects of Cerebral Biopsies," *Proc. Vth Inter. Congr. Neuropath.*, pp. 364–369. Amsterdam: Excerpta Medica.
5. Brierley, J. B., Adams, J. H., Graham, D. I. and Simpson, J. A. (1971), "Neocortical Death after Cardiac Arrest," *Lancet*, ii, 560–565.
6. Corsellis, J. A. N. (1969), "Some Observations on the Pathology of the Temporal Lobe," *Brit. J. Psychiat.*, Special Publ. No. 4, *Current Problems in Neuropsychiatry*, pp. 31–34.
7. Crome, L. C. and Stern, J. (1967), in *Pathology of Mental Retardation*, p. 239. London: Churchill.
8. Duffy, P. E., Kornfield, M. and Suzuki, K. (1968), "Neurovisceral Storage Disease with Curvilinear Bodies," *J. Neuropath.*, **27**, 351–370.
9. Gonatas, N. K., Terry, R. D. and Weiss, M. (1965), "Electron Microscopic Study in Two Cases of Jakob–Creutzfeldt Disease," *J. Neuropath.*, **24**, 575–598.
10. Grist, N. R., Ross, C. A. C., Bell, E. J. and Stott, E. J. (1966), in *Diagnostic Methods in Clinical Virology*. Oxford: Blackwell.
11. Harland, W. A., Adams, J. H. and McSeveney, D. (1967), "Herpes-simplex Particles in Acute Necrotizing Encephalitis," *Lancet*, ii, 581–582.
12. Horta–Barbosa, L., Fuccillo, D. A., London, W. T., Jabbour, J. T., Zeman, W. and Sever, J. L. (1969), "Isolation of Measles Virus from Brain Cell Cultures of Two Patients with Subacute Sclerosing Panencephalitis," *Proc. Soc. exp. Biol. (N.Y.)*, **132**, 272–277.

13 Hughes, I. E., Adams, J. H. and Ilbert, R. C. (1963), "Invasion of the Leptomeninges by Tumour," *J. Neurol. Neurosurg. Psychiat.*, **26**, 83–89.

14 Lumsden, C. E. (1968), "Nervous Tissue in Culture," in *The Structure and Function of Nervous Tissue*, Vol. 1 (G. H. Bourne, Ed.). London and New York: Academic Press.

15 Lumsden, C. E. (1971), in *Pathology of Tumours of the Nervous System* (D. S. Russell and L. J. Rubinstein, Eds.), Chap. 14. London: Arnold.

16 Marshall, W. J. S. (1967), "Herpes-simplex Encephalitis Treated with Idoxuridine and External Decompression," *Lancet*, ii, 579–580.

17 O'Brien, J. S. (1969), "Five Gangliosidosis," *Lancet*, ii, 804.

18 Padgett, B. L., Walker, D. L., Zurhein, G. M., Eckroade, R. J. and Dessel, B. H. (1971), "Cultivation of Papova-like Virus from Human Brain with Progressive Multifocal Leucoencephalopathy," *Lancet*, i, 1257–1260.

19 Peters, A., Palay, S. L. and Webster, H. de F. (1970), in *The Fine Structure of the Nervous System*, p. xv. New York: Harper and Row.

20 Sim, M., Turner, E. and Smith, W. T. (1966), "Cerebral Biopsy in the Investigation of Presenile Dementia: Clinical Aspects," *Brit. J. Psychiat.*, **112**, 119–125.

21 Smith, W. T., Turner, E. and Sim, M. (1966), "Cerebral Biopsy in the Investigation of Presenile Dementia: Pathological Aspects," *Brit. J. Psychiat.*, **112**, 127–133.

22 Suzuki, K., Suzuki, K. and Kamoshita, S. (1969), "Chemical Pathology of G_{M1}—Gangliosidosis," *J. Neuropath.*, **28**, 25–73.

9. NEUROCHEMISTRY

J. N. CUMINGS

INTRODUCTION

The origins of the basic scientific study of the brain can be traced from the middle of the nineteenth century through such chemists as Thudichum, Warburg, Page, Krebs and Peters, but the application of basic knowledge to neurological disorders in man has mainly taken place in the last 30 or so years. While in the past year or two a number of treatises have been published regarding basic neurochemistry, often in animals, only a few have been devoted to pathological changes found in the nervous system or in biological fluids in human disease. It is possible to mention in some detail only a few pathological conditions in the space available, hence certain diseases or groups of disorders have been chosen to illustrate some of the biochemical principles involved and of the methods of approach to the problems of interest to the neurologist. Thus the questions of transmission of nerve impulses, of γ-amino-butyric acid, acetylcholine and electrolytes in epilepsy, of amines in parkinsonian-like conditions, and the biochemistry of muscle diseases have all been omitted.

Hepatolenticular Degeneration (Wilson's Disease)

Although patients with this condition were described just prior to the commencement of this century, the real clinical features and pathology were enunciated by Wilson in 1911 who, however, was unaware of its biochemical basis. While isolated analyses for various metals were made from 1913 onwards it was not until 1948 that a clear demonstration of an abnormality of copper metabolism was propounded. At that time it was suggested that this condition was due to an inborn error of metabolism resulting in a deposition of copper in the tissues, especially in the brain and liver and that this abnormality caused the clinical and pathological features. While this enabled methods of treatment, namely BAL and penicillamine, to be suggested and to prove efficacious in prolongation of life, it did nothing to indicate the metabolic chain of events leading to this biochemical abnormality.

Although many have studied a variety of aspects concerning copper metabolism, it is still far from clear how the abnormality arises or what enzyme defect, for one there must be, is actually present. A brief survey of the present state of knowledge may assist in understanding this problem, but fuller details can be found elsewhere.[4,14]

There is normally a close balance between absorption and excretion of copper taken in the daily diet, whereas in hepatolenticular degeneration the patient is always in positive balance. Normally the absorbed copper, loosely bound to albumin is transferred to an apocaeruloplasmin in the liver to be firmly bound to an α_2 globulin known as caeruloplasmin. The enzyme responsible for this transfer is not known, but assuming its presence and action, at least 95 per cent of the transported copper is bound in this way and levels of caeruloplasmin and of copper remain fairly constant in the blood serum of the normal subject at 20–40 mg./100 ml. and 90–120 μg./100 ml. respectively.

The bound copper is neither deposited in tissues, except in trace quantities, nor excreted, except in small amounts (up to 30 μg. a day) in the urine. The subject with hepatolenticular degeneration, however, does not bind copper in this manner so that the serum levels of both caeruloplasmin and copper are low, less than 15 mg./100 ml. and 40–60 μg./100 ml. respectively, while the circulating copper being loosely bound is both taken up by tissues and excreted in the urine in excess.

It has not been possible to demonstrate abnormality in the structure of caeruloplasmin in patients or of apocaeruloplasmin using immunological techniques and, in fact, a few patients may even show normal levels of this enzyme at some stage of the disease. Yet Sahgal, Needleman and Boshes (1969), after studying the peptide subunits from caeruloplasmin, found a greater concentration of basic peptides from patient caeruloplasmin as compared to the normal pattern. It is also suggested that copper-binding is less effective in hepatolenticular degeneration. It had been anticipated that this condition was due to a defect in an enzyme, and that this enzyme was caeruloplasmin, but there is as yet little evidence to substantiate this, and a number of factors against it. There is no evidence to support the view that the liver is incapable of synthesizing caeruloplasmin or apocaeruloplasmin but it may be that copper cannot be transferred in the liver to the globulin concerned, or that this transfer takes place more slowly. Considerable progress has resulted from *in vitro* studies relating to the functions and kinetics of caeruloplasmin, but the findings have little or no place in human pathology.

Despite all the unsolved problems relating to exact mechanisms the results of therapy in proven cases have been remarkably good. A practical problem sometimes arising relates to the definitive diagnosis in sibs of young patients and to some older subjects not clinically typical. Probably the increased amount of copper in the liver or the relatively gross increase in urinary copper after a dose of penicillamine are the best biochemical guides in diagnosis,[5] although isotopic studies such as those of Walshe may also be valuable.

Refsum's Disease

For many years after Refsum in 1945 had described a condition inherited by a rare recessive gene, no biochemical or other studies yielded any clues as to its nature, and the only abnormality found was a raised CSF protein. Klenk and his colleagues in 1963 reported that some tissues as liver and kidney as well as blood contained a considerable amount of phytanic acid (3,7,11,15-tetramethylhexadecanoic acid), which branched-chain fatty acid was rarely found in the normal subject. Since then others have demonstrated a similar excess in the urine, nerve, muscle and CSF with almost no increase in the brain.[5] The findings of excess phytanic acid appears to be of diagnostic significance.

The accumulation of a compound, such as phytanic acid, does not necessarily mean that the clinical features are the result of its presence in the tissues, but it usually stimulates the neurochemist to investigate the significance of the variation from normal. It was immediately suggested that there was an inborn error in the degradation pathway for branched-chain fatty acids and Eldjarn and colleagues suggested various metabolic routes that could be affected. Finally Steinberg, Herndon, Uhlendorf, Mize, Avigan and Milne (1967) suggested that the enzyme

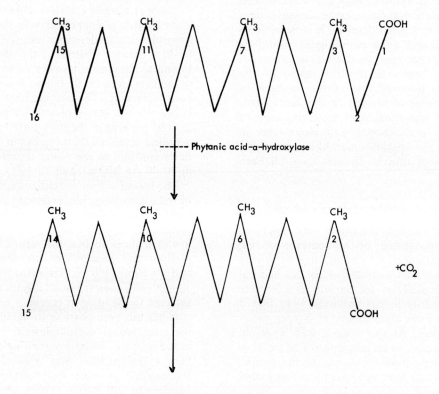

Fig. 1. Diagrammatic representation of first stage in degradation of phytanic acid.

phytanic acid-α-hydroxylase is completely or partially absent. The site of action is shown in Fig. 1 somewhat as a diagrammatic representation of the earlier stages of the metabolic pathway.

It should be mentioned that various enzymes can be measured from cultured cells or from the actual fluid of the amniotic cavity in pregnant women at around the 12th week of pregnancy and that this examination may assist in the prenatal diagnoses of a number of diseases. Uhlendorf and Herndon (1969) have demonstrated phytanic acid-α-hydroxylase in normal amniotic fluid.

Skrbic and Cumings (1969) have also shown that there are raised levels of cholesterol in the liver, heart and kidney in patients dying of this condition and have suggested that this may be a factor in the fatal progression of the disease.

Conditions Related to Vitamin Abnormalities

Thiamine Deficiency

There are a number of disorders of the beri-beri type in which raised pyruvate levels have been found and where the prompt administration of thiamine results in clinical improvement. Although relatively rare, Wernicke's encephalopathy, seen usually in chronic alcoholism, can most commonly be regarded as due to thiamine deficiency.

Many experiments in animals, as well as in human volunteers have been carried out to determine the nature of the clinical features resulting from an absence of thiamine in the diet, and most of the changes obtained have paralleled those found in human disease and can be relieved by appropriate therapy.[12]

Subacute Combined Degeneration of the Spinal Cord

Although this condition is causally related to a deficiency of vitamin B_{12} and there is some evidence that B_{12} is concerned with the reduction of disulphide compounds to the —SH form, little is known of the basic biochemistry of this disorder. Blood pyruvate levels may be raised in untreated cases with a return to normal following therapy resulting in clinical improvement.

Polyneuritis

Apart from the neuritic or polyneuritic lesions associated with vitamin B_1 and B_{12} deficiencies there are now known to be other types of polyneuritis associated with metabolic disorders such as some bacterial infections, with various chemical compounds and some, such as the Guillain–Barré syndrome, which are of unknown nature.

The blood pyruvate metabolism test of Williams, Mason, Power and Wilder (1943) and the therapeutic use of large doses of B_1 has enabled some distinction to be made between the various groups, but the greater proportion of the patients studied cannot be placed in well defined and separate categories. An absence of the coenzyme thiamine pyrophosphate, which is one of the enzymes responsible for pyruvate oxidation, can indirectly be shown to be responsible by means of the pyruvate metabolism test as well as by the levels of blood transketolase. The latter enzyme which is present in red blood cells

and which needs thiamine pyrophosphate for its action is reduced in some of these conditions and methods for its estimation have been described.

Experimental as well as occasional examples of accidental production of polyneuritis in man by organophosphorus compounds and by acrylamide have occurred. Human cases of disease from the neurotoxic activity of tri-o-cresyl phosphate (TOCP) have been known since 1930 and it has been demonstrated that lesions occur mainly in sensory nerve terminals and that nerve fibres are damaged. It has been shown that conversion of the relatively stable TOCP to a cyclic metabolite takes place in the body by hydroxylation of a methyl group and that this cyclic compound is an esterase inhibitor which produces the neurotoxic lesions. Thus in animals there is a fall in red blood cell acetylcholinesterase as well as a similar reduction in muscle tissue.

Other compounds besides TOCP which can cause similar lesions are parathion, mipofax as well as diisopropyl fluorophosphonate (DFP).

Apart from the neuropathies associated with diabetes and acute porphyria about which relatively little is known from a biochemical aspect, the other interesting condition is cyanide neuropathy, both from tobacco smoke and from a diet of cassava in Nigeria, South America and Congo. There appears to be little doubt from the work of Wilson (1965) and others that the neuropathy, which mainly affects the optic nerve, results from an inability to detoxicate cyanide to thiocyanate. This is normally carried out by an enzyme (rhodanese) and it may be that this enzyme is reduced in some subjects, who are rendered sensitive to substances containing cyanide such as cassava. It should be added that there is a possibility that vitamin B_{12} may play a role in these body reactions.

Lipid Disorders

A very large number of lipid disorders have now been described clinically but it is only in the last decade or two that many of the basic biochemical abnormalities have been determined. The lipid diseases are now generally considered to belong to the group of disorders described by Garrod as inborn errors of metabolism and in an increasing number of them the enzyme responsible is now known. Genetic studies have been made in many of these conditions.[8]

Chemical study of the brain, and to some extent of other parts of the nervous system, has shown the large amount of lipid present and Table 1 illustrates this fact.

The lipids are built up, and broken down, by specific enzymes at each metabolic step, although from many studies, such as those of Payling Wright and his colleagues, it has been shown that many lipid structures, such as myelin, once formed may not change significantly during later life. Thus the prenatal and early natal periods of growth are extremely important as Dobbing (1968) has attempted to show, more particularly in animals.

Each of the lipids, as sphingomyelin, cerebroside, sulphatide and ganglioside, are built up from fatty acids and one such metabolic pathway, that for sphingomyelin,

TABLE 1

LIPID COMPOSITION OF THE BRAIN

Substance	White Matter	Cortex
Total lipid	50–70	20–45
Total phospholipid	22–28	20–28
Sphingomyelin	6–10	3–7
Lecithin	4–6	4–8
Phosphatidylethanolamine	2–3	1·5–2·5
Phosphatidylserine	3–5	3–4·5
Phosphoinositide	0·7–1·5	0·7–1·2
Total cholesterol	12–16	5–8
Esterified cholesterol	0–0·8	0–0·5
Cerebroside	12–14	5–7
Sulphatide	1–3	0·5–1·0
Proteolipid protein P	6–8	3–4
Water (%)	64–73	81–86

In g./100 g. dry tissue.

is illustrated in Fig. 2. It is obvious that an absence of an enzyme responsible for one of the various steps in the pathway could result in an abnormality. In the example shown in Fig. 2 when sphingomyelinase is absent or reduced sphingomyelin is increased with deposition in certain cells and organs, and clinically Niemann–Pick's disease results. Similar variations from the normal can be shown for many other diseases.

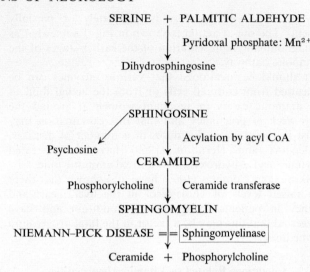

FIG. 2. Sphingomyelin pathway.

It is thus possible to present in a diagrammatic manner the abnormalities that are found in a number of lipid diseases and these can be seen from Fig. 3. These lipid diseases, with the characteristic lipid present in many of the tissues occur not only in man but also in animals, for

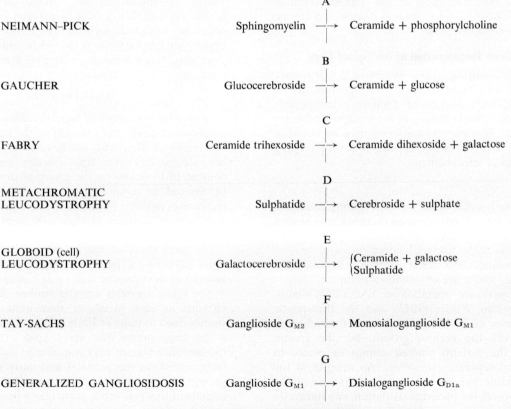

A–G are the sites of the enzymatic deficiencies.

FIG. 3. Essential metabolic pathways in lipid diseases (schematic).

the author has seen metachromatic leucodystrophy in pumas and generalized G_{M1} gangliosidosis in a cat. (*See* Fig. 4).

A classification of some human lipid diseases is given in Tables 2 and 3, the former table listing those which can be regarded as sphingolipidoses and the latter includes the

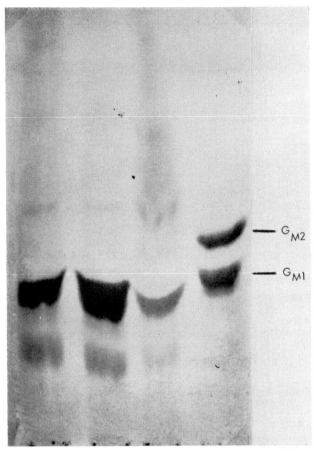

FIG. 4. Thin-layer chromatogram of lipid extract of cerebral white matter, cortex and liver from a cat (from left to right), stained to show the ganglioside abnormality of an increase in G_{M1}. On the right are authentic G_{M1} and G_{M2} markers.

TABLE 2

(1) THE SPHINGOLIPIDOSES

Disease	Lipid Deposited	Deficient Enzyme
Niemann–Pick	Sphingomyelin	Sphingomyelinase
Gaucher	Glucocerebroside	β-glucosidase
Fabry	Ceramide trihexoside	Ceramide trihexosidase
Metachromatic leucodystrophy	Sulphatide	Sulphatidase
Globoid (cell) leucodystrophy	Galactocerebroside	Galactosidase or Cerebroside sulphotransferase
Tay-Sachs	G_{M2} ganglioside	Hexosaminidase A
Generalized gangliosidoses	G_{M1} ganglioside	β-galactosidase
Generalized gangliosidoses	G_{D1a} ganglioside	?

various forms of mucopolysaccharidoses and a few miscellaneous interesting disorders. It will be seen at once that some conditions, such as that known as "amaurotic family idiocy", have been omitted. Reference will be made to this later.

Most of these conditions were originally investigated on cerebral tissues obtained at autopsy and the specific lipid determined biochemically.[3] Later biopsy material was obtained from the brain, rectum and appendix and definitive diagnosis made during life.[1]

Examples of the results found in five specific cases of cerebral lipid disease are shown in Table 4 where the changes from the normal composition of the brain are clearly seen.

TABLE 3

LIPID DISORDERS

(2) OTHER LIPID CONDITIONS

THE MUCOPOLYSACCHARIDOSES

	Substance deposited
Type 1 Gargoylism (Hurler)	Chondroitin sulphate B and heparin-heparitin sulphate
Type 2 Gargoylism (Hunter)	
Type 3 Sanfilippo	Heparitin sulphate
Type 4 Morquio	Kerato-sulphate
Type 5 Scheie	

MISCELLANEOUS

Disease	Substance increased	Enzyme involved
Refsum	Phytanic acid	Phytanic acid-α-hydroxylase
Wolman	Triglyceride and esterified cholesterol	Acid esterase
Hand–Schüller–Christian	Cholesterol	
Farber	Glycolipid	
Alexander		
Canavan		

TABLE 4

CEREBRAL LIPIDS IN SOME OF THE LIPIDOSES

Substance	Metachromatic Leucodystrophy	Globoid (Cell) Leucodystrophy	Tay-Sachs	Generalized Gangliosidosis	Primary Demyelination
	White matter (M 7)	White matter (F 10/12)	Cortex (M 1½)	Cortex (F 11/12)	White matter (F 45)
Total phospholipid	9·4	14·5	15·1	19·7	21·2
Total cholesterol	3·3	0·6	6·1	4·9	12·0
Esterified cholesterol	0·3	0·05	0·2	0·3	2·4
Cerebroside	0·4	2·3	—	2·6	⎰ 12·1
Sulphatide	9·2	0·4	—	—	⎱
N-acetyl neuraminic acid	0·07	0·13	0·6 (85)*	0·4 (75)†	0·36
Water (%)	82·0	80·2	82·2	84·2	79·0

Results in g./100 g. dry tissue.
* Figure in brackets is per cent of G_{M2}.
† Figure in brackets is per cent of G_{M1}.

TABLE 5

ENZYME ABNORMALITIES IN SOME LIPID DISEASES

Disease	Reported Enzyme Deficit	Site of Enzyme	Relative Amount of Enzyme
Gaucher	Glucocerebrosidase	Skin fibroblasts	3%
		Leucocytes	
Neimann–Pick	Sphingomyelinase	Spleen	1%
		Leucocytes	8%
Tay-Sachs	Hexosaminidase A	Liver	5%
		Muscle	0
		Blood ?	0
		Brain	0
Generalized Gangliosidosis	β-D-galactosidase	Brain	30%
Metachromatic Leucodystrophy	Aryl sulphatase	Leucocytes	10%
		Brain	1%
Globoid (cell) Leucodystrophy	Cerebroside sulphotransferase	Brain	30%
Fabry	Ceramide trihexosidase	Small intestine	0·5%

Recently Brady and his colleagues have shown that examination of tissue or cell culture as well as red and white cell examinations, frequently with the use of iso- topes, has enabled the specific enzymic disturbance to be detected during life[2] and even prenatally when using amniotic fluid, as for example in Tay-Sachs disease.[7] Table 5 lists the sites where it is possible to determine lack of activity of the enzymes of the various diseases.

Studies have also been made by a number of workers relating to the composition of myelin and of microsomes in brain tissue, both normal and in a variety of diseases such as metachromatic leucodystrophy, globoid (cell) leucodystrophy, Tay-Sachs disease and in demyelinating conditions, as multiple sclerosis. These can be said to support the view that there is a genetic abnormality present in many of these conditions, probably from birth resulting in abnormal myelin or microsomes. There are somewhat similar and suggestive features in studies of white matter in cases of multiple sclerosis.

The fatty acid composition of whole cerebral white matter and cortex, as well as of cerebrosides and sul- phatides have been determined in most of the diseases just mentioned as well as in phenylketonuria, together with the various ganglioside fractions especially in diseases affecting ganglioside metabolism. However, although of great scientific interest these studies do not great assist the neurologist.

Discussion of a number of disorders has been deliber- ately omitted, partly as they do not primarily affect the brain and partly because they are very rare and little is known of their basic biochemistry. In addition there are a group of conditions commonly belonging to a group called "amaurotic family idiocy", a label in itself erroneous clinically, and with no accurate biochemical background. In fact there is very good evidence that one large section of this group, known as Batten's disease, is a ceroid lipofuscinosis of unknown aetiology. Until more is discovered biochemically about these conditions it is desirable for the neurochemist to beware of adding to the present confusion.

An attempt has been made to show how knowledge of a basic biochemical defect will bring light to the character- istic clinical and pathological features of a few neurological diseases, and it is anticipated that within the next decade many more will be found to have a biochemical basis for their aetiology.

FURTHER READING

1 Blackwood, W. and Cumings, J. N. (1966), "The Combined Histological and Chemical Aspects of Cerebral Biopsies," in *Proceedings of the Vth International Congress of Neuropathology in Zurich*, 1965, pp. 364–371, International Congress Series No. 100 (F. Lüthy and A. Bischoff, Eds.). Amsterdam: Excerpta Medica Foundation.

2 Brady, R. O. (1970), "Prenatal Diagnosis of Lipid Storage Disease," *Clin. Chem*, **16**, 811–815.

3 Cumings, J. N. (1960), "Abnormalities of Lipid Chemistry in Cerebral Lipidoses and Demyelinating Conditions," in *Modern Scientific Aspects of Neurology*, pp. 330–354 (J. N. Cumings, Ed.). London: Edward Arnold Ltd.

4 Cumings, J. N. (1968), "Biochemistry of the Basal Ganglia," in *Handbook of Clinical Neurology*, Vol. 6, pp. 116–132 (P. J. Vinken and G. W. Bruyn, Eds). Amsterdam: North-Holland Publishing Co.

5 Cumings, J. N. (1971), *Inborn Errors of Metabolism in Neurology.* Hughlings Jackson Lecture, Royal Society of Medicine, **64**, 313–322.

6 Dobbing, John (1968), "Vulnerable periods in developing brain," in *Applied Neurochemistry*, pp. 287–316 (A. N. Davison and John Dobbing, Eds.). Oxford and Edinburgh: Blackwell Scientific Publications.

7 Okada, S. and O'Brien, J. S. (1969), "Tay-Sachs Disease: Generalized Absence of a Beta-*d*-N-acetylhexosaminidase Component," *Science*, **165**, 698–700.

8 Pratt, R. T. C. (1967), *The Genetics of Neurological Disorders.* London: Oxford University Press.

9 Sahgal, V., Needleman, S. B. and Bosches, B. (1969), "Studies of Peptide Maps of Ceruloplasmin in Wilson's Disease," *Trans. Amer. neurol. Ass.*, **94**, 335–336.

10 Skrbic, T. R. and Cumings, J. N. (1969), "Phytanic Acid in Tissue Lipids in Refsum's Disease," *Clin. chim. Acta*, **23**, 17–21.

11 Steinberg, D., Herndon, J. H., Uhlendorf, B. W., Mize, C. E., Avigan, J. and Milne, G. W. A. (1967), "Refsum's Disease: Nature of the Enzyme Defect," *Science*, **156**, 1740–1742.

12 Thompson, R. H. S. and Cumings, J. N. (1968), "Diseases of the Nervous System," in *Biochemical Disorders in Human Disease*, 3rd edition, pp. 451–487 (R. H. S. Thompson and I. D. P. Wootton, Eds.). London: J. and A. Churchill.

13 Uhlendorf, B. W. and Herndon, J., Jr. *See* Nadler, H. L. (1969), "Prenatal Detection of Genetic Defects," *J. Pediat.*, **74**, 132–143.

14 Walshe, J. M. (1967), "The Physiology of Copper in Man and its Relation to Wilson's Disease," *Brain*, **90**, 149–176.

15 Williams, R. D., Mason, H. L., Power, M. H. and Wilder, R. M. (1943), "Induced Thiamine (Vitamin B$_1$) Deficiency in Man; Relation of Depletion of Thiamine to Development of Biochemical Defect and of Polyneuropathy," *Arch. intern. Med.*, **71**, 38–53.

16 Wilson, J. (1965), "Leber's Hereditary Optic Atrophy: A Possible Defect of Cyanide Metabolism," *Clin. Sci.*, **29**, 505–515.

Biochemical Aspects of Neurological Disorders, First Series (1959) (J. N. Cumings and M. Kremer, Eds.). Oxford: Blackwell Scientific Publications.

Biochemical Aspects of Neurological Disorders, Second Series (1965) (J. N. Cumings and M. Kremer, Eds.). Oxford: Blackwell Scientific Publications.

Biochemical Aspects of Neurological Disorders, Third Series (1968) (J. N. Cumings and M. Kremer, Eds.). Oxford: Blackwell Scientific Publications.

Applied Neurochemistry (1968) (A. N. Davison and John Dobbing, Eds.). Oxford and Edinburgh: Blackwell Scientific Publications.

Handbook of Neurochemistry Vol. 1 (1969) "Chemical Architecture of the Nervous System," (Abel Lajtha, Ed.). New York: Plenum Press.

Handbook of Neurochemistry, Vol. 2 (1969) "Structural Neurochemistry," (Abel Lajtha, Ed.). New York: Plenum Press.

Myelination (1970) (A. N. Davison and Alan Peters, Eds.). American Lecture Series No. 782. Springfield, Illinois: Charles C. Thomas.

SECTION X

1. LATE EFFECTS OF HEAD INJURIES

BRYAN JENNETT

Many months after a head injury a patient may complain of persisting symptoms affecting either physical or mental function or both. Entirely new complications may also develop, either in patients with residual complaints or in those who have already made a complete recovery. These late complications, which may follow either mild or severe injuries, are relatively unusual; they include epilepsy, intracranial infection, and carotico-cavernous fistula. In each of these, as with persisting physical and mental sequelae after severe injuries, the relationship to the injury is fairly obvious; but the basis for the subjective physical and mental symptoms frequently encountered after mild injuries, the so-called post-concussional or post-traumatic syndrome, remains a matter of controversy. The various sequelae can indeed be arranged according to how strongly they are related to the severity of injury (Table 1).

sources to verify that there are no striking discrepancies in respect of three features in particular.

1. The Population Studied

Probably the only consecutive series of head injuries followed up for long periods are those from the Armed Services; yet these constitute a special group of young and healthy males in the unusual social setting which military service and subsequent pension (or veteran) status entails. Other reported series are mostly comprised of residual complainers, with a further bias introduced by the context in which they have come under observation— whether seen by physician, surgeon or psychiatrist and whether referred for treatment, for routine follow-up or for medico-legal purposes. It is also becoming clear that the head injured population in civilian life is not a random

TABLE 1

SEQUELAE OF HEAD INJURY

	Strongly Related to Severity of Injury	*Less Strongly Related*	*Unrelated*
Mental	Apathy Euphoria Loss of social restraint Intellectual deficits Marked memory defects	"Poor concentration" "Poor memory" "Slowness"	Fatigue Irritability Insomnia Nervousness Anxiety Depression
Physical	Dysphasia Hemianopia Motor disorders — spasticity / ataxia / tremor Perceptual disorders	Anosmia Vertigo Epilepsy	Headache Sensitivity to noise Dizziness (sans vertigo) Pain at site of injury

(Derived from data of Lishman[8] and Russell and Smith.[17])

DISCREPANT REPORTS

The whole field of persisting symptoms after head injury is full of paradoxes, with remarkable recoveries after severe injuries and prolonged complaints after trivial ones. Some of the disparities between the experience of different authors are, however, more apparent than real, in that they derive from the use of widely differing criteria in the description either of the original injury or of the effects attributed to it, or of both. Whilst there seems little prospect of reaching agreement about these criteria it is wise when comparing data from different

sample of the population at risk, and that the social and psychological factors which contributed to the original injury may likewise influence the sequelae of that injury, or at least the patient's reaction to them.

2. The Severity of the Injury

What should be taken to constitute "a head injury" has never been defined. Hospital doctors will tend to think of patients either with loss of consciousness or with skull fracture; but there are many with only scalp lacerations

441

whom it cannot be denied have suffered a head injury. However, in most contexts head injury implies damage to the brain, or the risk of this developing as a result of complications. Damage to the scalp and skull indicates the possibility of underlying brain damage but not its certainty; unconsciousness indicates beyond doubt that there has been brain damage. But it is undeniable that such damage can occur without a fracture or any blemish on the scalp, and, especially when it is of a focal nature, without loss of consciousness or amnesia.

When an injury produces unconsciousness its duration is often taken to indicate the severity of the diffuse brain damage. But what shall be held to mark the return of consciousness? Is it when the patient first speaks, or when he recognizes his relatives, or when continuous ongoing memory returns? Dysphasia may delay the return of speech, whilst many patients suffer a prolonged period of confusion after beginning to speak; whether or not relatives are recognized is often a matter of opinion. The return of continuous memory, which marks the end of post-traumatic amnesia (PTA), is more readily assessed, and commonly occurs some time after the patient has begun to talk and even to behave fairly normally; it seems that the capacity of the brain to store day-to-day memories is one of the last functions to return after the kind of diffuse injury associated with blunt (acceleration-deceleration) injury. The return of continuous memory usually coincides with reorientation, an accurate awareness of time and place. But what makes the PTA so valuable as a means of assessing severity is that it can be ascertained some time after injury, without reference to original case records or to the evidence of other informants. The patient himself is asked when he woke up, whether it was by the roadside, in the ambulance or in the hospital ward. And if the latter, whether on the day of injury or later than that. When the PTA lasts several days it may be difficult to decide its exact duration, but this is not crucial because once PTA has lasted this long the severity of the injury is no longer in doubt. A classification of severity which depends only on the determination of PTA within broad limits was originally proposed by Ritchie Russell in 1934 and has subsequently been used in many reports both of missile and non-missile injuries in the British literature:

            <1 hour   —mild
            1–24 hours—moderate
            1–7 days —severe
            >7 days   —very severe

The practice of quoting a mean or average PTA (or duration of coma) for a series of patients is to be deplored, unless the range and standard deviation are also quoted, because most such series include a few cases with exceptionally prolonged unconsciousness which make the average misleading.

The criterion of unconsciousness and PTA as evidence of brain damage is reliable only for the diffuse brain damage due to acceleration-deceleration injury, the pathology of which has been discussed in another chapter (p. 478). Focal brain damage from penetrating injuries, whether due to missile or non-missile injury, may cause

focal neurological dysfunction, such as dysphasia or hemiparesis, without loss of consciousness or amnesia, or with a disproportionately brief period of altered consciousness.

3. Assessment of Sequelae

Whether or not a patient is judged to have sequelae depends very largely on whether he complains of them or whether the doctor specifically searches for evidence of persisting dysfunction. Some reports regard return to work as evidence of full recovery; others require a faultless run through a careful neurological examination and psychometric test battery. Obviously some men back at work may be suffering significant sequelae, whilst measurable mental or physical defects may cause little or no disability. When changes in social behaviour are the sole evidence of sequelae it is particularly important to consider these in the context of the pre-traumatic state, because an injury may well be blamed for what proves to be a long-standing behavioural disorder.

In the following review of specific sequelae it has seemed best, for the sake of clarity, to deal separately with persisting residua of severe injuries, with the post-concussional syndrome, and with newly developing late complications; of course a patient may suffer more than one of these types of late effect.

PERSISTING PHYSICAL RESIDUA

After blunt (acceleration-deceleration) injuries, which comprise the majority of civilian cases, primary brain damage is often widespread and there may be secondary diffuse or local brain damage in addition (see Chapter X : 6). Nonetheless it is useful in clinical practice to consider persisting symptoms as reflections of damage predominantly in the cerebral hemisphere, in the brain stem and cerebellum, or in the cranial nerves, recognizing that this does not imply that damage has been confined to any one of these regions.

Cerebral Hemisphere

Damage here may result from contusions of the cortex, from haematomas on the surface or within the brain, or from the effects of vascular occlusion. Cortical contusions, the commonest hemisphere lesion, are most frequent in the subfrontal and temporal regions, well away from the motor or sensory cortex, the optic pathways or speech areas; therefore it is only a relatively small number of injuries that result in persisting hemisphere dysfunction.

Dysphasia

This is a particularly disabling disorder, both in the early and late stages of recovery. Patients with dysphasia spend longer in hospital than those with comparable injuries but without language dysfunction, and their rehabilitation is made difficult by the communication problem which arises between the patient and the staff. This can readily lead to misunderstandings and frustrations, especially if those who deal with the patient are not familiar with neurological symptomatology and mistakenly believe the patient to be obtuse, or even deliberately disobedient, when in truth he simply does not understand the instructions he has been given. The same difficulty may persist even after the patient returns to work, looking physically fit and otherwise well, particularly if his duties include giving or taking orders or entering items on paper. Not infrequently dysphasia is misinterpreted by the patient or those around him as evidence of intellectual loss or memory disorder; such deficits may indeed accompany disordered language function but the different handicaps should be distinguished as far as possible. Failure to recognize mild dysphasia is a frequent explanation of unexpectedly slow progress in rehabilitation or of unusual difficulties in resettlement. In the experience of Walker and Erculei[24] dysphasia following missile injuries rarely persisted without other evidence of hemisphere damage (i.e. sensori-motor hemiparesis). However, the disability attributable to sensori-motor dysfunction was often trivial compared with that resulting from dysphasia. The same probably goes for blunt injuries, although focal features of this kind are very much less common.

Even in the absence of obvious dysphasia, disabilities are likely to be greater following damage to the dominant hemisphere. Not only does this result from the relatively greater handicap of losing the skills of the dominant hand but certain subtle disorders in the sphere of mental functioning are more seriously affected. The long-term effects of a hemisphere lesion may depend also on the degree of dominance which the individual patient has developed; many sinistrals are in reality only weakly right brain dominant and may therefore make a better recovery after unilateral hemisphere damage, whichever side of the brain has been damaged. Similarly age is crucial, in that dominance seems not to be irrevocably determined before mid-childhood, whilst the allocation of function between areas within a hemisphere is also a process which matures gradually during post-natal development. The astonishing recoveries which children quite frequently make after injuries which in adults would having devastating permanent effects is commonly attributed to this greater degree of flexibility and resilience in cortical and subcortical functioning which is characteristic of the young brain.

Sensori-motor Deficits

Motor hemiplegia commonly shows the same pattern of recovery as that due to cerebral infarction, in that the function of the lower limbs return earlier and more completely than of the upper limb, and the proximal movements both sooner and better than the distal. But hemisphere damage is seldom as extensive as is common with infarction in the middle cerebral artery territory; this, together with the younger age of most patients, makes for a more satisfactory recovery than is usual after a major stroke. Indeed hemisphere deficits recover on the whole much better than cranial nerve lesions or motor disorders attributed to brain stem or cerebellar damage. However, the time scale of this recovery can be very extended and Miller and Stern[12]

showed that significant degrees of further recovery, as in the improvement of dysphasia, can occur more than two years after injury.

Homonymous hemianopia is an occasional persisting defect but need not constitute a major disability if the patient consciously compensates for it. Sometimes a limb which has powerful individual movements is relatively useless because of cortical sensory loss or damage of the parietal association areas, resulting in apraxia and agnosia.

Cranial Nerve Lesions

Damaged cranial nerves recover only slowly and many patients completely recovered in all other respects may have persisting cranial nerve dysfunction. The disability which this occasions is seldom great, yet these lesions account for a sizeable proportion of permanent neurological signs after head injury. Sometimes the nerves are damaged in their extracranial course (in the orbit or face) and care must be taken not to regard such a cranial nerve lesion as *a posteriori* evidence of brain injury.

Anosmia (*see also* Chapters V : 4, 6)

This is the commonest cranial nerve lesion, but in only a minority does it result from major injuries involving the floor of the anterior fossa. More often the injury has been mild or moderate (more than half have PTA < 1 hr.); in such cases the blow has often been occipital, leading presumably to contre-coup damage of the olfactory fibres at the cribriform plate. Recovery of olfaction sometimes occurs after these mild injuries, usually within 3 months. A great deal of the flavour of food is lost with the sense of smell, but trigeminal taste survives (salt and vinegar). Anosmia deprives a person of much pleasure, and of the protection of being able to smell burning or escaping gas.

Lesions of the Visual Pathways

Optic nerve lesions can result from very mild injuries, particularly in children. Fracture into the orbit or optic canal is unusual and the frequent occurrence of an inferior altitudinal hemianopia suggests a vascular mechanism. Total lesions are associated with loss of the light reflex and within 3 weeks the disc is pale if the lesion is permanent; when recovery occurs some sight usually returns within a few days. Chiasmal lesions give characteristic field defects, and may be associated with CSF rhinorrhoea (via the sphenoidal sinus) or with pituitary insufficiency.

Eye Movements

Squints and diplopia can result from mechanical distortion of the visual axes by fracture of the walls of the orbit, especially the floor. Nystagmus commonly results from injury to the vestibule or the brain stem; lesions in the latter site occasionally cause complex abnormalities of conjugate movements so bizarre as to make hysteria suspect.

Much more common, however, is an isolated third or sixth nerve palsy due to tentorial herniation or petrous fractures respectively; but either may result from damage in the superior orbital fissure. Third nerve lesions are commonly associated with pupillary dilatation and fixation, and with ptosis; upward gaze is usually most affected, and is the last movement to recover. Sixth nerve lesions show a marked tendency for late recovery and surgical attempts to correct squints by operations on the muscles should always be postponed for at least a year after injury.

Facial Palsy

Damage is sustained in the intra-osseous course due to petrous fracture, usually associated with the bleeding from the ear; but in 40 per cent no fracture is identified. Although usually obvious soon after injury the palsy is occasionally delayed by a few days; such delayed paralysis almost always recovers, and can often be prevented by the early administration of steroids.[1]

Eighth Nerve

Disturbances of hearing and vestibular function can be demonstrated in a high proportion of blunt head injuries, including many who have been only mildly injured, as judged by the duration of PTA. Such dysfunction is frequently revealed only by formal neuro-otological examination including provocative tests and electrical recording Chapter V : 3. Before these tests were devised the common complaints of vertigo and hyperacuisis were commonly regarded as hysterical or neurotic, and certainly subjective vestibular symptoms commonly resolve in time. Conductive deafness is most commonly due to middle ear bleeding and recovers as blood is absorbed, but sometimes the ossicles are knocked out of position, and the resulting conductive deafness can then be improved only by surgical restoration of the chain of ossicles. End organ damage does occur on occasions and pure tone audiometry may help to distinguish this from conductive deafness, or from lesions in the central connections. Neurogenic deafness tends to persist, but as it is usually unilateral the disability is not too great.

MENTAL DISORDERS AFTER HEAD INJURY

"That a man with a hurt brain should have a disturbed mind is to be expected"—   C. P. Symonds, 1942.[18]

It cannot be disputed that every severe injury, defined as one followed by >24 hr. PTA, has been associated with a profound disturbance of normal mental activity in the early post-traumatic period. Accepting the current view that even brief unconsciousness is always associated with some degree of permanent structural change in the brain, it must be assumed that the physical substrate of mental function is always impaired to some extent after severe head injury; and indeed there are those who hold that some persisting alteration in mental function can always be detected if the search is assiduous enough. Unfortunately the methods which are available for assessing mental function are very insensitive, even when applied to those features, such as intellectual performance or memory, which are to some extent measurable. Personality change, which is perhaps the most consistent post-traumatic feature, is peculiarly difficult to quantify, but it would be misleading to reject, as valid evidence of sequelae, all those abnormal features which cannot be measured. And it is important also to avoid the logical fallacy of regarding absence of evidence as evidence of absence of mental impairment.

Mental sequelae are best regarded as falling into one or more of five categories (Table 2). In general the organic syndromes, both non-specific and specific, show a close correlation with brain damage whilst in the case of the non-organic syndromes pre-traumatic psychosocial maladjustment may be found. But it is important to emphasize that neither the presence of organic brain damage, nor the discovery of psychiatric abnormalities, proves that the symptoms complained of are due wholly to either mechanism. However, it is possible to indicate which individual mental symptoms are commonly correlated with severity of brain damage, or with the physical sequelae which are associated with such damage (Table 1).

Mental disorder (or disturbed mental function) seems

TABLE 2

MENTAL SEQUELAE OF HEAD INJURY

1. General organic dementia (non-specific)	disorders of—personality / intellect / memory
2. Local organic syndromes (specific)	frontal—severe behavioural problems right hemisphere—visuo-spatial deficit left hemisphere—defective verbal skills without dysphasia
3. Post-concussional syndrome (Post-traumatic)	subjective mental and somatic features
4. Accident neurosis	prolongation and exaggeration of post-traumatic syndrome
5. Psychosis	depression schizophrenia

the best term to embrace all the sequelae set out in Table 2. It is arguable whether dysphasia and gross perceptual defects should be regarded as mental disorders; no one can doubt that these affect certain aspects of mental function, but then so does hemiplegia or hemianopia, as far as the performance of many tests are concerned. The following terms are sometimes used to include the whole range of post-traumatic mental symptomatology: "psychological, psychiatric, emotional, affective, functional behavioural, intellectual or subjective symptoms". Many of these terms refer to only one aspect of mental function whilst some of them ("functional" and "psychological") suggest that the symptoms are not related to brain damage, whilst "psychiatric" is apt to imply only neurosis or psychosis. For these reasons they seem less appropriate than "mental disorder", as an inclusive term.

General (Non-specific) Organic Dementia

The features of this syndrome resemble those encountered in a wide range of diffuse structural brain disorders, such as ageing, arteriosclerosis and pre-senile dementia; Indeed the comment is often made by near relatives that the injury seems to have aged the patient by several year. Three types of disorder can be recognized.

1. Personality Change

This is both the most consistent feature and the most difficult to measure or describe. Even though the patient may have made a satisfactory recovery and good social adjustment his spouse may avow that he is not the man she married. These more subtle changes can usually be recognized as lesser degrees of those features which occur in a florid form in more severely damaged patients, and can be categorized as disturbances of drive, of affect and of social restraint or judgement.

Drive is usually reduced, and the apathy which results may be described as laziness, sloth or simply slowness. Circumstances may enable a man to carry out his work satisfactorily, with the support of a structured environment and perhaps an overseer or foreman; yet once home at night, and left to his own devices, he may fail to follow previous leisure pursuits, preferring to dream away the evening in an armchair. This lack of drive can be an obstacle to successful rehabilitation, and is difficult to deal with other than by a near relative acting as a daily goad.

Affect most often changes in the direction of euphoria which, combined with lack of drive, may result in the patient's under-estimating his disabilities, and claiming to be better than he really is; this may well lead to a miscarriage of justice when the time comes to award damages. Emotional lability, with the unexplicable bouts of crying, or less often laughter, sometimes occur; patients with insight may explain that these represent the outward signs of emotion and are not mirrored by a corresponding inner feeling, and in that event they are more distressing to the onlooker than to the patient. But some do complain of bitterly experienced frustration, usually related to their physical or mental handicap and the slowness of recovery, and this in turn may lead to secondary depression.

Social restraint and judgement are qualities rarely appreciated until they being to fail. A lack of consideration for the feelings of others, tactlessness if you will, is the commonest feature. But there may be general disinhibition, talkativeness and a degree of childishness (to contrast with the appearance of ageing mentioned earlier—but is not senility described as second childhood?).

2. Intellectual Deficits

The existence of numerous tests of intelligence is apt to result in undue emphasis on this aspect of the mental sequelae. These tests tend to be overweighted with verbal tasks and are therefore liable to make patients with left hemisphere lesions appear more intellectually disabled than they really are. In a brilliant study of patients 20 years after missile injuries which had been restricted to the right or left hemispheres Newcombe was able to show that there was little or no impairment of general intelligence, even when specific tests for right or left hemisphere function showed a definite abnormality, providing patients with clinically obvious dysphasia were excluded. General IQ tests sample a variety of abilities which tend to be closely correlated in normal subjects, but which may be differentially affected by focal lesions; yet the concept of focal representation of intellectual skills has survived the 100 years since its proposal by Hughlings Jackson and others. It must also be remembered that intelligence tests tend to sample a lifetime of experience in developing conceptual activities, rather than the present physiological adequacy of the brain. To the extent that they measure the ability to solve problems they may test a very unusual activity, as far as many patients are concerned; it is easy to forget what creatures of habit many men are, and how relatively seldom innovation or problem-solving is called for. A further difficulty arises from the effect on intellectual activity of other mental changes, such as lack of drive, anxiety, distractability and general slowness—quite apart from specific mental syndromes and physical disabilities. Newcombe's[14] very localized lesions rarely occur with blunt head injury, but it is interesting that she found that bilateral lesions caused more severe and long-lasting effects. She also commented that patients who complained most of "poor concentration" often had superior scores, and this emphasises the value of objective tests whenever possible. She found no tendency for deterioration over 20 years, either in non-specific or specific psychological performance, although few of her patients had yet reached the sixties when premature ageing might be expected in the previously damaged brain; Walker and Erculei[24] likewise found little evidence of deterioration with ageing.

3. Memory

To complain of a bad memory is respectable, and as a symptom it may in fact refer to general intellectual impairment, or to dysphasia ("can't remember words"). Apart from these false amnesias true impairment of memory is a very consistent feature after head injury; in view of the universality of immediate post-traumatic amnesia it is hardly surprising that some such disorder should persist in many patients. This may be reflected in a learning defect, which may have a specific flavour if it is predominantly for verbal or visuo-spatial material. Patients normally have good insight into their memory defect and if otherwise fairly intelligent may compensate by keeping a book or diary, or using other cues. Sometimes the memory loss is so profound as to resemble a Korsakoff syndrome, and in such cases there is probably a specific lesion affecting the limbic system and its frontal connections bilaterally.

The extent to which these three components of organic dementia may be independently affected is a matter of some controversy. There are those who claim that memory is not a specific mental modality, and that it is impaired *pari passu* with intellectual deterioration. As for the relationship between personality change and intellectual impairment most modern reports seem to imply considerable independence, and make no reference to the clearly expressed views of Reynell[15] who claimed that personality change was so consistently associated with intellectual loss that he was suspicious of the validity of personality change if it was not accompanied by intellectual loss; on the contrary he frequently found intellectual deficits without personality change. At the same symposium, however, Kremer[15] commented on the striking disagreements between different observers as to the presence or absence of personality change, and this may account for the variety of opinions about this relationship.

Local (Specific) Organic Syndromes

The site and extent of the brain damage is relatively certain only when there has been penetration by small missile fragments, or other sharp objects. What is known about the association of certain sequelae with damage in certain anatomical areas rests either on such injuries (Newcombe)[14] or on the study of patients undergoing cortical excisions for epilepsy (Milner);[23] but the sequelae which follow blunt (acceleration-deceleration) injuries are so similar, that it seems reasonable to assume a similar correlation. These injuries commonly cause widespread cortical contusions, most frequent in the temporal poles and the under-surface of the frontal lobes but haematomas may cause focal damage elsewhere Chapter X : 6.

Frontal Lobe Syndromes

Two distinct syndromes are encountered, according to whether the brunt of the damage has been suffered by the convexity of the frontal lobe or the orbital cortex. Intellectual deficits characterize the convexity lesions and there is a lack of drive and a tendency to tackle problems with a fixed strategy, there being a comparative inability to innovate or to change direction as different tasks demand this. Milner[23] has interpreted this as an inability to suppress a preferred mode of response. Orbital lesions cause serious personality and behavioural abnormalities, usually without any intellectual deficit. Social disinhibition, as described under general organic dementia, assumes a more extreme form with euphoria, hyperactivity and aggression; this may involve sexual activities and lead to criminality. Whilst very marked deviations of behaviour are almost confined to frontal lesions quite definite behavioural changes are found in some patients believed to have no frontal damage.

Right Hemisphere Lesions

Specific visuo-spatial difficulties may be revealed by highly specialized tests, but in Newcombe's[14] series few of the patients complained of handicaps attributable to this particular deficit. Some had difficulty in recognizing faces, or in visualizing familiar scenes or pictures.

Left Hemisphere Lesions

Even when those with clinically detectable dysphasia are excluded, deficits in verbal skills can often be detected. These include registration, learning and retention of verbal material. In Lishman's[8] series, which included many with dysphasia, there was a marked correlation between left hemisphere lesions and what he termed "psychiatric disability", and this was largely due to damage to the left temporal lobe; he also found a marked association between generalized intellectual impairment and damage to the left hemisphere which Newcombe with her severe lesions did not find.

Post-concussional (Post-traumatic) Syndrome

This comprises a constellation of subjective complaints which are remarkably consistent from one patient to another, and which can be grouped into those relating to mental function and those associated with somatic sensations (Table 1, column 3). Mental symptoms include irritability and short temper, poor concentration and loss of confidence, nervousness and fatigue. Headache is frequent, usually described as a tight band round the head or a feeling of pressure; sometimes localized pain at the site of impact is associated with tenderness. Vertigo is common and is often precipitated by sudden postural changes of the head; dizziness, which cannot be recognized as including a false sensation of movement (vertigo), is also a frequent complaint, and it may likewise be precipitated by postural factors, such as sudden rising.

The need to offer alternative titles for this syndrome bespeaks an altering attitude to it which arises from changing views both about concussion and about the basis of the symptoms which may follow it. For many years the term concussion was limited to the short-lived stunning effect of a mild head injury and it carried the implication, postulated by Trotter[20] in 1924, that the pathological basis was a functional neuronal disturbance without any structural brain damage. In labelling certain symptoms after injury as "post-concussional" the inference was that these also had no basis in organic pathology. Improved neuropathological techniques have, however, revealed that the mildest brain injury, if sufficient to cause even brief amnesia, produces permanent brain damage of some degree. Moreover Symonds[19] has argued cogently that the patient who remains unconscious for hours or days may well have suffered an injury which differs in quantity rather than quality from the milder injury—that there need not necessarily be contusions or lacerations of the brain, or a secondary complication such as oedema or haematoma, to account for prolonged unconsciousness, as traditional concepts would require. Given a concept of concussion which embraces injuries of widely varying severity the term post-concussional might be taken to mean no more than post-traumatic; and as concussion seems likely to mean very different things to different people for some time to come—whether they adopt Trotter's or Symonds' view—it could be frankly misleading to continue using this term.

Coincident with the discovery that even mild concussion has a structural basis, investigation of patients following mild injuries has revealed physiological abnormalities which might account for some of the somatic symptoms commonly complained of. A high incidence of abnormalities in caloric response and of latent nystagmus has been found when vestibular function is tested using electro-nystagmography in patients complaining of vertigo 3–12 months after minor injuries but who showed no neurological signs on routine examination. Many of these patients also had asymmetrical high-frequency hearing loss, which caused difficulty in auditory discrimination, that is to say in understanding rather than in hearing speech. The pathological basis for these abnormalities would appear in many cases to be local damage in the middle ear—labyrinthine concussion, loose otoliths, disarticulation of the ossicles; but lesions in the eighth nerve or its brain stem connections may also play a part. Certainly there seems good reason to explain vertigo and hyperacuisis on an organic basis.

The circulation time through the head has been shown by isotope techniques to be prolonged even several weeks after head injury which suggests that functional abnormalities of the circulation may account for headache and for postural dizziness. An alternative explanation for some symptoms is musculo-skeletal damage to the cervical spine. It cannot be doubted that an impact to the freely moving head must always place some strain on the neck; Jacobson[23] has shown that headache, psychological symptoms and vertigo may occur quite frequently in patients who have had neck injuries without any head injury.

The natural history of the post-traumatic syndrome is towards resolution, but the time taken varies considerably and it is this which appears to depend on the patient's personality and on how confidently he is managed by his medical advisers. The duration of disability after milder injuries was greatly reduced early in World II by abandoning the traditional custom of keeping all head injuries in darkened rooms, with visitors and reading forbidden. This, and the undoubted fact that the syndrome is much more commonly encountered after apparently mild injuries, requires an explanation. The protection which severe injury appears to confer may well stem from two consequences of such an injury. One is that the patient remains oblivious of all the unpleasantness of the early

stages, the cerebral irritation and confusion which have so worried his relatives, and the period of meningism from subarachnoid haemorrhage. For him the illness begins the day he comes out of his PTA, free of headache and surrounded by people who are relieved that he has regained his senses, and who indeed expect little of him for weeks or months and for whom every step forward in recovery seems little short of a miracle. Much less care and consideration is extended to the victim of a mild injury, which may be equally or even more upsetting for the patient, who wakes up in strange surroundings with a bad headache, bewildered by what has happened to him; yet within a few days he is expected to pull himself together and even return to work, with the facile reassurance that nothing serious has happened to him.

Accident Neurosis

The demonstration that concussion and some of its sequelae may have an organic basis might be thought to have settled the vexed issue of whether or not the post-traumatic syndrome is organically based, or the result of a psychological reaction to injury. Thirty years ago Charles Symonds[18] and Aubrey Lewis argued, in a symposium at the Royal Society of Medicine in London, that to try to separate physiogenic from psychogenic mechanisms, or organic from functional symptoms, was unnatural, unprofitable and misleading. At the same Society in 1966, however, Henry Miller[13] devoted an address to doing just that. In his view the post-concussional syndrome is a special instance of "accident neurosis", a condition which he described in 1961.[10,11] His view is based on a wide experience of medico-legal practice, but there are reasons to doubt whether such a view can be applied to head injuries in general. Indeed many of his observations are compatible with the view that the post-traumatic syndrome is in fact suffered by most patients with mild or moderate injury, whilst the amount of distress it causes, or the length of time for which it persists, may well depend on factors such as the personality of the patient and on whether or not litigation is expected. This view allows that exaggeration or prolongation of some of the features of the post-traumatic syndrome may well depend on the development of a secondary neurosis. It is to this situation that many of Miller's observations are relevant—that most sufferers have had an injury in potentially litigious circumstances, are in the lower socio-economic classes, have preceding emotional instability and are below average intelligence. Having deprived these patients of the comfort of an organic explanation for their symptoms Miller will not even allow some of them the relatively respectable label of neurosis, but castigates them with the harsh judgement of malingering. In this situation the role of the lawyer must not be overlooked, concerned as he is to press the patient to recall and embellish all his complaints in order to help his cause. The diagnosis of accident neurosis will be on the firmest ground when applied to patients who have sustained a blow on the head without subsequent amnesia (post-concussional syndrome *sine* concussion). But when there has been

Blunt Head — 5% c̄ most early — recurrence 25%.
have seized
Late →
after 8 wks
75% c̄ 50% of pts develop
it in 1st yr but up to 4 [?]

448   SCIENTIFIC FOUNDATIONS OF NEUROLOGY

undoubted brain damage it would seem wise to try to discover where the balance lies between organic and psychogenic factors, the interplay of which is by no means confined to injury to the head, rather than to conclude too readily that the doctor's inability to find an obvious explanation for the symptoms indicates that they originate in the patient's imagination.

EPILEPSY

This complication tends to occur in the first week after injury, or to be postponed until more than 3 months after injury. This enables a distinction to be made between early (first week) and late epilepsy; the latter tends to persist and is an important cause of continuing disability after a head injury, occurring as it quite often does in patients who have otherwise made a good recovery. Although epilepsy is much less common after non-missile than after missile injury (c. 10 per cent compared with c. 35 per cent), blunt injuries are so common that they have become an important cause of symptomatic epilepsy. There is much less variation in the incidence of epilepsy after missile wounds than after non-missile injury, and as the latter are of most concern in civilian practice (in most countries!) the following account refers only to this type of injury: a note on missile injuries is included at the end.

Early Epilepsy
(First week after injury)

In many reports epilepsy occurring soon after injury is considered separately. Most often such fits are discarded from the main analysis, in the belief that they reflect a transitional state of the recently injured brain and have no significance for the future. However, some authors have claimed that early epilepsy does increase the risk of epilepsy in the future, but others reject altogether the case for considering fits at this stage after injury in a special category.

Definition and Identity

Those who do recognize early epilepsy define it variously, but none defends his definition of how early is early (Table 3). In a closely observed series of 1,000 consecutive blunt head injuries Lewin and Jennett[4] recorded 46 patients having the first fit of their lives within the first week after injury, whilst only 1 patient developed a fit

during the next 11 weeks. They therefore proposed that the first week was an appropriate definition for early epilepsy. In a further study of over 400 patients who suffered epilepsy within 8 weeks of injury Jennett[5] showed that epilepsy begins in the first week very much more frequently than in any of the subsequent 7 weeks. Epilepsy in the first week after injury has other characteristics which distinguish it from epilepsy occurring later

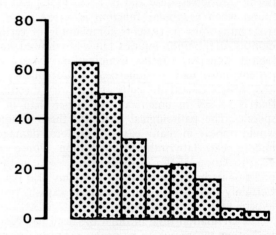

FIG. 1. The incidence of late epilepsy after depressed fracture with various combinations of predisposing factors.

TABLE 3

CHARACTER OF EARLY AND LATE EPILEPSY
(non-missile injuries)

Time After Injury to First Fit	Focal Motor Attacks		Recurrence of Epilepsy	
Week 1	175/441	42·6%	36/147	24·8%
Weeks 2–8	7/41	17·1%	29/41	70·7%
>3 months	7/218	3·2%	195/254	76·8%

P < 0·01
P < 0·001
P < 0·001
P not sig.

(Table 4). Focal motor fits are very much more common in the first week, whilst temporal lobe seizures seem not to occur. Epilepsy in the first week is much less likely to persist than epilepsy first appearing during the next 7 weeks, which is almost as likely to persist as epilepsy which is delayed for 3 months or more after injury. Thus fits occurring during the first few weeks (after the first) should be regarded as "late" epilepsy developing sooner than usual, rather than as delayed "early" epilepsy. This study confirmed the view of Earl Walker: "It is generally considered that patients having attacks within the first weeks of a head injury usually have focal fits and the prognosis is better than in those developing seizures later." But it seems that these conclusions are justified only for epilepsy occurring during the first week, and that the term "early epilepsy" should be confined to fits in this period. When a patient who has had a fit in the first week also has one or more fits during the next few weeks he must be regarded as having suffered both early and late epilepsy. His risk of suffering persisting epilepsy is high by reason of his having already developed late epilepsy, even though at the end of the first week a more favourable outlook would have been given (i.e. before he had had a late fit).

Incidence and Cause of Early Epilepsy

The relative consistency among estimates of the frequency of early epilepsy, even when based on varying periods after injury, is explained by the fact that 90 per cent of the first month's cases occur during the first week (Table 1). For an unselected series of non-missile injuries admitted to hospital Jennett's estimate of 5 per cent developing early epilepsy agrees well with the experience of others, when allowance is made for their wider definition of early epilepsy. Early epilepsy is commoner after more severe injuries, whether judged by duration of PTA, or the presence of skull fracture, of neurological signs, or of subarachnoid haemorrhage, or the development of intracranial haematoma (Table 3). Early epilepsy is commoner under the age of 5 than after that age and in this age group frequently occurs after relatively trivial injuries; at this age it seems less likely to be followed by late epilepsy.

Significance of Early Epilepsy

In most cases a fit in the first week is of no immediate consequence, representing no more than additional evidence of damage in the cerebral hemisphere, which is probably already obvious from other features. Complications such as intracranial haematoma or infection may be associated with epilepsy, but this is never the sole sign of such a development; that a patient has had a fit would not in itself be sufficient reason for altering management, for example by undertaking neuroradiological investigation or opening the skull. If status epilepticus develops, however, life may be threatened unless active measures are undertaken forthwith and the seizures brought under control.

What is more significant about early epilepsy, even if limited to a single fit in the first week, is that it increases the risk of late epilepsy very considerably (Table 4). This tendency to late epilepsy after early epilepsy is independent of the duration of PTA, of whether or not there has been a depressed fracture and of the age of the patient. But the increased risk associated with early epilepsy is most striking in patients who have suffered

	Cases Followed	Late Epilepsy	%Epilepsy
No early epilepsy	868	29	3·3
After early epilepsy	147	36	24·8
$p = \, < 0.001$			

neither depressed fracture nor an intracranial haematoma, because such patients very rarely develop late epilepsy unless they have an early fit, in contrast to those with these other complications which in themselves predispose to late epilepsy.

Late Epilepsy
(more than 1 week after injury)

About 5 per cent of patients admitted to hospital with a non-missile injury develop epilepsy during the next 4 years. Rather more than half the cases have their first fit within a year of injury, but a quarter do not develop this complication until more than 4 years after injury. Most patients followed for more than 2 years after their first late fit prove to have had repeated seizures, half of them continuing to suffer more than one attack a month. In about half the patients some fits have a recognizably focal pattern and in about half of these temporal lobe seizures are recorded (i.e. in a quarter of all patients with late epilepsy).

The likelihood of developing late epilepsy depends on the nature of the injury and on the early complications. Early epilepsy and intracranial haematoma each increase the risk of late epilepsy, and do so independently of each other and of the duration of PTA. Depressed fracture also increases the risk, but this effect is marked only in injuries associated with prolonged PTA; this suggests that a combination of local and diffuse brain damage is necessary before an injury becomes highly epileptogenic. Penetration of the dura and early epilepsy also each add to the risk of late epilepsy after depressed fracture, which ranges from <5 to >60 per cent according to different combinations of these three factors[6,23] (Fig. 1). Age and site of fracture appear of little significance in determining this risk. Nor does the way in which the fracture has been treated seem to affect the incidence of late epilepsy; thus epilepsy was no more frequent when bone fragments were replaced than when they were removed, nor was the incidence higher in a series in which no elevation of depressed fragments was carried out at all, although such a group of patients is biased with less severely depressed fractures.[7] There can be little doubt that epilepsy after depressed fracture is a reflection of local and diffuse brain damage inflicted at the time of injury, and is not due to continuing pressure of bone fragments on the brain.

These studies do not provide much hope that the incidence of epilepsy will be reduced by any change in management, and this has also been the experience with missile injuries (*vide infra*). However, it is now possible to reassure many patients previously considered at risk that their chances of developing epilepsy are quite low—for example, 20 per cent of those with a depressed fracture have less than 5 per cent risk of late epilepsy. Moreover those in a high risk category can be identified; anticonvulsants can then be prescribed and account taken of the possibility of epilepsy developing when giving advice about the future.

Epilepsy after Missile Injury

Missile injuries do not form quite such a homogeneous group as might at first appear and it must not be assumed that series of "battle injuries" or "combat casualties" consist only of missile injuries. Even among those that are due to missiles a distinction should be made between those which penetrate the skull and those which do not, even though there is good evidence that even tangential missile wounds may cause underlying cortical contusion. Only if these factors are kept in mind can apparent discrepancies between recent reports be understood (Table 5).[2,3,16,21,22]

the risk only by one and a half times; it is therefore of much less significance after this type of injury.

Factors which increase the epilepsy rate after missile injury are the site of the fracture (epilepsy most likely after parietal and least likely after frontal and occipital polar injury); deep penetration of the brain (>3 cm.); dural penetration; the duration of PTA; and the occurrence of acute intracranial haematoma. Within any one series infection does appear to increase the risk of epilepsy somewhat, but the greatly reduced infection rate following injuries in World War II, compared with World War I, has made no obvious difference to the overall incidence of epilepsy.

Over half the patients have developed epilepsy within a year of wounding, even excluding early fits. There is some difference of opinion as to whether long delays in onset are more common after missile than non-missile injuries. More than half the patients suffer from fits with a focal component, but the majority of patients have major seizures although the onset may be focal. In patients followed for several years after their first fit it is common to find that epilepsy ceases or becomes very infrequent; this occurs in about half the patients but this tendency to remission shows no constant relationship to the severity of injury, persisting signs or the time of onset of epilepsy; if frequent fits once develop, however, remission is unlikely. A consequence of this high rate of cessation, together with the delayed development of epilepsy, is that the *prevalence* of epilepsy in any group of head injuries may at some stages be only about half the incidence; 40 per cent of the population at risk may suffer epilepsy at some stage after injury, but at any one time only 20 per cent are suffering from repeated seizures.

TABLE 5

EPILEPSY AFTER MISSILE INJURY

All combat injuries	28%	of 739	Walker and Jablon	World War II
	23·8%	of 407	Caveness	Korea
All missile injuries	34%	of 317	Ascroft	World War I
	35·1%	of 211	Caveness	Korea
	33·9%	of 295	Walker	World War II
	32%	of 221	Evans	Korea
Missile injury penetrating dura	43·0%	of 820	Russell and Whitty	World War II
	41·0%		Ascroft	
	42·0%		Caveness	
Missile injury with dura intact	22·0%		Ascroft	
	23·8%		Caveness	

Whilst late epilepsy is a much more common complication after missile than after non-missile injury, early epilepsy occurs equally frequently after the two types of injury. As a consequence only 5 per cent of patient with late epilepsy after missile injuries have had early epilepsy, compared with 14 per cent for non-missile injuries or 23 per cent for non-missile depressed fractures. Whereas early epilepsy after a non-missile injury quadruples the likelihood of late epilepsy, after a missile injury it increases

FURTHER READING

[1] Briggs, M. and Potter, J. M. (1971), "Prevention of Delayed Traumatic Facial Palsy," *Brit. med. J.*, **3**, 458.

[2] Caveness, W. F., Walker, A. E. and Ascroft, P. B. (1962), "Incidence of Posttraumatic Epilepsy in Korean Veterans as Compared with those from World War I and World War II," *J. Neurosurg.*, **19**, 122.

[3] Caveness, W. F. (1963), "Onset and Cessation of Fits Following Craniocerebral Trauma," *J. Neurosurg.*, **20**, 570.

[4] Jennett, W. B. and Lewin, W. (1960), "Traumatic Epilepsy after Closed Head Injuries," *J. Neurol. Neurosurg. Psychiat.*, **23**, 295.

[5] Jennett, W. B. (1969), "Early Traumatic Epilepsy. Definition and Identity," *Lancet*, **i**, 1023.

[6] Jennett, W. B. (1962), "Epilepsy after blunt head injury," London: Heinemann.

[7] Jennett, B. and Miller, J. D. (1972), "Infection after Depressed Fracture of Skull," *J. Neurosurg.*, 36, 333.

[8] Lishman, W. A. (1968), "Brain Damage in Relation to Psychiatric Disability after Head Injury," *Brit. J. Psychiat.*, 114, 373.

[9] London, P. S. (1967), "Some Observations on the Course of Events after Severe Injury of the Head," *Ann. roy. Coll. Surg. Engl.*, **41**, 460.

[10] Miller, H. (1961), "Accident Neurosis," *Brit. med. J.*, **2**, 919.

[11] Miller, H. (1961), "Accident Neurosis," *Brit. med. J.*, **2**, 992.

[12] Miller, H. and Stern, G. (1965), "The Long-term Prognosis of Severe Head Injury," *Lancet*, **i**, 225.

[13] Miller, H. (1966), "Mental After-effects of Head Injury," *Proc. roy. Soc. Med.*, **59**, 257.

[14] Newcombe, F. (1969), *Missile Wounds of the Brain*. Oxford University Press.

[15] Paterson, A., Reynell, W. R. and Kremer, M. (1944), "Discussion on Disorders of Personality after Head Injury," *Proc. roy. Soc. Med.*, **37**, 556.

[16] Russell, W. R. and Whitty, C. W. M. (1952), "Studies in Traumatic Epilepsy. 1. Factors Influencing the Incidence of Epilepsy after Brain Wounds," *J. Neurol. Neurosurg. Psychiat.*, **15**, 93.

[17] Russell, W. R. and Smith, A. (1961), "Post-traumatic Amnesia in Closed Head Injury," *Arch. Neurol.*, **5**, 4.

[18] Symonds, C. P. (1942), "Discussion on Differential Diagnosis and Treatment of Post-contusional States," *Proc. roy. Soc. Med.*, **35**, 25.

[19] Symonds, C. (1962), "Concussion and its Sequelae," *Lancet*, **i**, 1.

[20] Trotter, W. (1924), "On Certain Minor Injuries of the Brain," *Lancet*, **i**, 935.

[21] Walker, A. E. (1957), "Prognosis in Post-traumatic Epilepsy. A Ten-year Follow-up of Craniocerebral Injuries of World War II," *J. Amer. med. Ass.*, **164**, 1637.

[22] Walker, A. E. and Jablon, S. (1961), *A Follow-up Study of Head Wounds in World War II*, V.A. Monograph. U.S. Government Printing Office, Washington, D.C.

[23] Walker, A. E., Caveness, W. F. and Critchley, M. (Eds.) (1969), *Late Effects of Head Injury*. Springfield, Illinois: Charles C. Thomas.

[24] Walker, A. E. and Erculei, F. (1969), *Head Injured Men*. Springfield, Illinois: Charles C. Thomas.

2. BACTERIAL INFECTIONS OF THE CENTRAL NERVOUS SYSTEM

R. J. FALLON

INTRODUCTION

Infection of the central nervous system by bacteria, fungi or parasites almost invariably constitutes a medical emergency. Rapid and accurate clinical and laboratory diagnosis is necessary not only to save life but also to prevent disability. This chapter will deal mainly with bacterial infection of the central nervous system which is the commonest type of non-viral infection and which may, as with meningococcal disease especially in North and West Africa, reach epidemic proportions. It must, however, be remembered that parasites may affect the nervous system either directly as in cysticercosis, or indirectly as in cerebral malaria. The need for rapid and accurate diagnosis has become more urgent not only as the range of therapeutic agents available for the treatment of infections has become more extensive, but also because pathogenic micro-organisms have developed resistance to many of these agents. The development of resistance of *Neisseria meningitidis* to sulphonamides in many areas of the world is a good example of this disturbing trend. It is impossible to gauge the weight of infection of the central nervous system in different parts of the world because ascertainment and recording of infection are far from complete. However, in 1969 there were 1,481 cases of bacteriologically proven meningitis reported to the Public Health Laboratory Service from the United Kingdom and this total is certainly an underestimate of the true incidence of infections in Britain because many will have been rendered bacteriologically negative by antibiotic therapy prior to admission to hospital.

Infections affecting the central nervous system may conveniently, if somewhat artificially, be considered as follows: (1) Those principally affecting the brain; (2) Infections of the meninges; (3) Extradural infections; and (4) Those which affect the nervous system by the action of exotoxins.

The nervous system may be infected in one of three ways: (a) by penetrating injury; (b) by extension from adjacent structures; and (c) by blood stream spread.

In the first instance almost any organism may be introduced; in the second, which is the commonest source from which a cerebral abscess originates, the organisms involved are more clearly defined, i.e. those that infect the nasal sinuses (such as *Haemophilus influenzae* or *Streptococcus pneumoniae*), or the middle ear. *Staphylococcus aureus* which gives rise to osteomyelitis of the spine or skull may be another causal agent of this type of infection. In the third instance some organisms are well recognized as often infecting by this route (e.g. *N. meningitidis*).

Parasites which affect the brain directly travel either by routes (b) or (c).

It follows therefore that many structures may be implicated in infections affecting the nervous system (a factor which may be of considerable importance in determining treatment, e.g. recurrent meningitis due to a skull-fracture involving the nasal sinuses does not only require antibiotic therapy but also neurosurgical repair of the lesion) and this must be borne in mind when reading this chapter.

In this chapter the features of the different kinds of infection are set out briefly and then the laboratory diagnosis will be considered so that the clinician may be aware of what lies behind the report he receives from the laboratory. Finally the features of the most important infecting organisms will be considered together with the therapeutic agents currently recommended for dealing with these infections.

INFECTIONS AFFECTING THE CENTRAL NERVOUS SYSTEM

Infections of the brain

Broadly speaking these may be either acute or chronic and may be due to bacteria, fungi or parasites.

Diffuse infection of the cerebral substance, i.e. encephalitis, is usually due to viruses but may be found in non-localizing cerebral infections due to bacteria. Meningo-encephalitis is associated with some bacteria and parasites and will be discussed under the heading of infection of the meninges. The commonest infection of the brain is an abscess. Cerebral abscess may be acute or chronic. Abscesses due to pyogenic bacteria are usually acute but may persist for some time if treated by antibiotics, the abscess then being rendered sterile, or the infection at least being suppressed. Even if not treated, abscesses may persist undetected for months if vital areas of the brain are not involved. In some instances, e.g. a brain-abscess due to *Strep. pneumoniae* arising in the course of bronchiectasis, the causal agent may be inferred but usually the cause is more obscure and can be ascertained only by culture of pus obtained at operation. The diverse species of bacteria that may be isolated from brain abscesses are illustrated by the figures for 100 of the brain abscesses from which bacteria were isolated, treated at the Western

Regional Neurosurgical Centre at Killearn Hospital, Glasgow during the years 1958–70. The pus in many other abscesses was sterile on culture probably due to prior antibiotic therapy.

It is significant that many of these organisms are found in the respiratory tract as pathogens affecting the middle ear and that over 50 per cent of the abscesses originated from this site or from sinuses.

Chronic infections of the brain may be due to organisms which give rise to chronic infections elsewhere. Hence *Mycobacterium tuberculosis* may give rise to a tuberculoma which may persist for years or may manifest itself as a space-occupying lesion. *Treponema pallidum* may give rise to general paralysis of the insane. There are many other manifestations of syphilitic infection of the brain but these are now rare and will not be discussed further in this brief survey.

Parasites may invade the brain-substance and give rise to focal lesions. This is well seen in cysticercosis where the *Cysticercus cellulosae*, an intermediate stage of the porcine tapeworm *Taenia solium*, may migrate to the brain and produce hydrocephalus, epilepsy, pareses of cranial nerves or mental disturbance. Rarely *Entamoeba histolytica* may invade the brain and give rise to abscess-formation.

There is evidence to suggest that larvae of the ascarids *Toxacara cati* and *T. canis*, adult forms of which normally inhabit the intestines of cats and dogs, may invade the brain giving rise to epilepsy. The protozoon parasite, *Toxoplasma gondii*, for which the cat is an intermediate host, can infect the brain. This occurs as a congenital

TABLE 1

BACTERIOLOGICAL FINDINGS IN 100 BRAIN ABSCESSES

One Organism Isolated*		More than One Organism Isolated	
Gram positive species		*Two organisms isolated*	
Streptococci:		Proteus and non-haemolytic strep.	5
Haemolytic	5	Proteus and other Gram +ve cocci	5
Aerobic non-haemolytic	18	Proteus and Gram —ve bacilli	3
Anaerobic non-haemolytic	6	Coliform and diphtheroid	1
Pneumococcus	3	Coliform and micrococci	1
	— 32	*Staph. aureus* and micrococci	1
		Staph. albus and diphtheroid	1
			— 17
Staphylococci:			
Aureus	14		
Albus	3	*Three organisms isolated*	
"Micrococci"	2	Proteus, *Strep. faecalis* and Staph. sp.	1
Actinomycetes	— 19	*Neisseria catarrhalis*, diphtheroids	
Diphtheroids	5	and micrococcus	1 2
Candida albicans	1		—
	1		19
Gram negative species			
Proteus	11	*Sources of infection*	
Escherichia coli	9	Ears	48
Haemophilus	2	Sinuses	8
Klebsiella	1	Blood	13
	—	Fractured skull	4
	81	Others	3
		Unknown	24

* *Note*: 17 showed more than one organism on the Gram film of pus.

infection giving rise to the tetrad of chorio-retinitis, hydrocephalus or microcephaly, psychomotor retardation and cerebral calcification. Acquired infection in children may give rise to encephalitis. Several varieties of flukes including schistosomes may affect the brain. Trypanosomes commonly invade the central nervous system giving rise to sleeping sickness.

Parasites may also affect the brain indirectly as in cerebral malaria. Here the affected erythrocytes adhere to the walls of the cerebral capillaries blocking them so as to give rise to areas of cerebral anoxia and necrosis with resultant coma and death.

Clinical Diagnosis. From what has been said diagnosis of infection of the brain may be looked upon as relatively simple in acute infections, particularly if these comprise a diffuse encephalitis. The diagnosis of a less acute infection may be difficult, as the onset is often insidious and the patient may complain only of vague ill-health extending over many weeks. A history of head-injury or local sepsis should be regarded as important as is any history suggestive of embolic phenomena or of disease, such as infective endocarditis, where infected emboli *may* occur. Focal signs may aid in the localization of a lesion but the causal agent will often be unknown. A developing abscess will produce evidence of a space-occupying lesion with headache, nausea and focal neurological signs. Rupture of an abscess into the subdural space will give rise to the manifestations of acute meningitis. Parasites may often reveal their presence only by causing epilepsy. Cerebral malaria is a medical emergency being a disease of acute onset. The patient will give a history of recently having been in a malarious area and of having received inadequate antimalarial therapy. The clinical picture is that of a patient with fever and a rapidly decreasing level of consciousness. The patient may be jaundiced. Diagnosis is of extreme urgency as once the patient has become unconscious the prognosis is grave.

Infection of the Meninges

Meningitis is commonly an acute condition and, like brain-abscess, may be caused by a wide variety of infective agents and may be due to injury or to a spread of infection from neighbouring structures, and hence may precede or coincide with infection of the brain in these circumstances. It may be a sequel to neurosurgery. However, unlike what applies to brain-abscess, there are some infective agents which are very common compared with the others and furthermore meningitis is often associated with bacteraemia, although it is not always certain that the presence of bacteria in the blood-stream precedes their presence in the meninges. The pattern of meningeal infection varies with age and geographical location. Table 2 gives an indication of the present situation in Great Britain and Eire.

In neonates and young infants the commonest infecting micro-organisms are the aerobic Gram-negative bacilli normally found in the gut with *Escherichia coli* predominating. Others such as Proteus sp., Klebsiella sp. and *Pseudomonas aeruginosa* may also cause neo-natal meningitis. Meningitis in the new-born is often preceded

by prenatal or immediately postnatal pneumonia or other septic process. Maternal infection is another important predisposing cause. Many cases of meningitis in this age-group present a congenital neurological abnormality such as meningo-myelocoele, hydrocephalus or spina bifida. "Coliform" meningitis is uncommon in later life. In the young child meningitis is most commonly due, in Great Britain, to *N. meningitidis*, with *H. influenzae* being found less frequently. The converse is true in North America. These organisms are most uncommon in meningitis occurring in later childhood and in adult life in Great Britain, but in conditions where susceptible subjects are in close contact with carriers, such as in

TABLE 2

NUMBER OF CASES OF BACTERIAL MENINGITIS REPORTED TO THE PUBLIC HEALTH LABORATORY SERVICE FROM LABORATORIES IN THE UNITED KINGDOM AND REPUBLIC OF IRELAND 1967–69. THE ORGANISMS ARE LISTED IN ORDER OF FREQUENCY.

Bacterial Species	No. of Cases	Bacterial Species	No. of Cases
Meningococcus	1274	Proteus	98
Haemophilus	1015	Pseudomonas	66
Pneumococcus	907	Listeria	62
Escherichia coli	199	Other coliforms	48
Staphylococcus	152	Klebsiella	32
Mycobacterium tuberculosis	140	Other species	30
Streptococcus	118		

Table reproduced by kind permission of the Editor, from *Brit. Med. J.*, **3**, 114 (1970).

armed forces camps and in North and West Africa where epidemics occur in the dry season, meningococcal infection will affect all age-groups. Pneumococcal meningitis is a severe infection with a more grave prognosis than meningococcal or *H. influenzae* meningitis and may occur in all age-groups. It commonly arises after local sepsis, or with extension from the nasal cavity through fine skull-fractures or through a congenital dermal sinus and may recur if the track is not closed. Other bacterial agents are much less common as can be seen from Table 2 and will be discussed in brief in section B.2.

Meningitis may be caused by the fungus *Cryptococcus neoformans*. This is very uncommon in Great Britain but must always be borne in mind in a patient with the picture of a meningitis of insidious onset and chronic course.

Until recently parasites were not recognized as a course of meningitis, but in recent years meningo-encephalitis due to the free-living saprophytic amoebae of the *Naegleria* genus has been described from several parts of the world including Great Britain. It has been shown experimentally that amoebae of the *Hartmanella* genus can give rise to meningo-encephalitis in experimental animals, but their pathogenic role in man is less clear at present.

Clinical diagnosis. The diagnosis of acute pyogenic meningitis in children and adults is usually straightforward in the conscious patient. The complaint of headache, perhaps with vomiting, fever and, in children, convulsions together with the finding of signs of meningeal irration—rigidity of the neck, a positive Kernig's sign and, in later cases, head-retraction, all point to the diagnosis. In neonates and infants the manifestations of meningitis are far less obvious, and the child may present in the early stages with lethargy, irritability, anorexia, vomiting and unexplained fever. Convulsions may occur. A bulging fontanelle may be present in infants, but neck-stiffness and a bulging fontanelle are rare in the new-born.

In leptospiral meningitis the signs and symptoms may be far less severe. Conjunctival injection and perhaps jaundice are important findings as is the history of occupational exposure to infection in sewer-workers, miners, farmers and dog-owners.

Tuberculous and cryptococcal meningitis are usually of slow onset, although tuberculous meningitis may occasionally be relatively acute. Normally a history of headache and anorexia, and perhaps occasional vomiting over one to three weeks is obtained in cases of tuberculous meningitis, whereas in cryptococcal meningitis the course is usually one of months. Again, in both conditions the signs of meningitis are to be found.

The manifestations of meningitis may occur in other conditions such as encephalitis or subarachnoid haemorrhage, and in meningism accompanying acute infections, as well as in intracranial abscess. Occasionally other infections, such as spinal osteomyelitis, may simulate meningitis. The definitive diagnosis depends upon examination of cerebro-spinal fluid and other laboratory investigations which will be discussed in section B.1.

Extra-dural Infections

These may affect the nervous system directly by pressure. They may also simulate conditions such as meningitis. By spreading to the nervous system, as in middle ear sepsis, they may give rise to meningitis. Spinal osteomyelitis may produce an extradural abscess compressing the cord, with consequent neurological signs and symptoms. Examination of the spinal fluid may be confusing here, because there may be an increase in cells. Extra-dural hydatid cysts may also occasionally cause compression of the spinal cord.

Intoxication

Bacterial toxins may have a profound effect upon the nervous system and it would be inappropriate to conclude any discussion of the various infections of the nervous system without mentioning this important aspect of neurological disease. The principal conditions are tetanus, botulism and diphtheria. Tetanus is caused by the powerful exotoxin produced by *Clostridium tetani*. Any injury, even one so trivial as virtually to escape detection, may give rise to tetanus as a result of the wound being infected with *Cl. tetani*. Although deep wounds favour multiplication of this anaerobic bacterium, even superficial abrasions may be infected and give rise to tetanus. The exotoxin diffuses from the site of injury and affects the nervous system resulting either in local tetanus—which is often followed by generalized tetanus—or in generalized tetanus alone. The neurological lesion in tetanus comprises a disturbance of the regulation of the reflex arc which results in simultaneous contraction of prime movers and their antagonists. The response to a stimulus is also heightened so that spasms of the limbs and trunk occur and may become extremely violent and exhausting.

Botulism is the most severe form of food-poisoning and is due to the ingestion of food contaminated by the exotoxin produced by *Clostridium botulinum*. This toxin, which is the most powerful bacterial toxin known, results from the multiplication of *Cl. botulinum* in food under anaerobic conditions, e.g. inadequately heat-treated canned food, or vacuum-packed raw smoked fish. The toxin, which can be destroyed by boiling, affect neuromuscular transmission with resulting weakness spreading to all muscles. The disease is almost unknown in this country. Recently, cases have been recognized as being due to the eating of fish-products contaminated with *Cl. botulinum* type E.

Diphtheria is an uncommon disease in Great Britain at the present time. As with tetanus and botulism, the disease is due to a powerful exotoxin—in this case that produced by *Corynebacterium diphtheriae*. This toxin affects the peripheral nerves giving rise to segmental demyelination. The area principally affected is that which is adjacent to the dorsal root ganglia. The common clinical manifestations are palatal paralysis early in the disease with paralysis of accommodation appearing during the third or fourth week. Generalized polyneuritis develops later, with widespread motor paralysis and sensory loss.

LABORATORY DIAGNOSIS

Routine Procedures

Laboratory diagnosis is directed towards establishing whether the patient's condition is due to infection; the recognition of the infective agent; and, in the case of bacterial infection, the most appropriate antibiotic for the eradication of the infection. Where pus is available from a brain-abscess or an open wound, this is dealt with in the same manner as pus from any other site, i.e. Gram film and culture incubated under aerobic (preferably with added carbon dioxide), and anaerobic conditions with antibiotic sensitivity tests.

In almost all other cases, examination of the cerebro-spinal fluid is essential. The principal exceptions to this would be the obvious cases of tetanus, where the patient should be disturbed as little as possible, diphtheria and botulism. Because many cases of bacterial meningitis are accompanied by septicaemia, blood-cultures should always be performed. Where parasite infestation is suspected, faeces should be examined for ova, and the blood for parasites. Serology is of value in the diagnosis of leptospiral meningitis, meningo-encephalitis due to *Mycoplasma pneumoniae*, neurosyphilis, and of some parasitic infestations—especially toxoplasmosis and filariasis. This technique has also been found to be helpful in the diagnosis of some atypical cases of meningococcal meningitis.

Examination of the blood may reveal the circulating toxin in cases of botulism. A full haematological examination is essential. The differential white count will demonstrate whether the patient has a pyogenic process or not (and this may be helpful in cases of brain-abscess and osteomyelitis where the diagnosis may be difficult). A blood-film will help to reveal the diagnosis in cases of cerebral malaria, trypanosomiasis or filariasis, and is essential in any patient who has recently visited an area where these diseases are endemic. The rare occurrence of malaria following a blood-transfusion should not be forgotten.

Examination of the Cerebro-spinal Fluid. Primary examination of the fluid is macroscopic then microscopic. At lumbar puncture the operator should note the nature of the fluid obtained—whether clear, turbid or purulent, if blood-stained whether this is uniform, as in subarachnoid haemorrhage, and, in some cases, traumatic haemorrhage from intrathecal veins; or whether the fluid becomes less blood-stained as more is withdrawn as may occur in traumatic haemorrhage. In the latter case an attempt should be made to collect a separate specimen of the less heavily blood-stained fluid for laboratory examination. Cerebro-spinal fluid is normally crystal clear, and any deviation from this, apart from traumatic haemorrhage, is pathological. Apart from turbidity the fluid is inspected for the presence of a fine protein clot ("spiderweb clot") which may develop on standing. Such a clot sometimes develops in fluid from cases of *M. tuberculosis* or occasionally other organisms. Where the protein-level of the fluid is high the fluid may clot spontaneously.

The first microscopical examination aims at establishing the number of cells in the fluid, and is performed on the uncentrifuged specimen. Where blood is present, a differential cell-count may be of value in order to estimate (by comparison with the circulating blood) whether there is an actual increase in white cells in the fluid, or not.

Any large cells should be observed for motility and, if there is any doubt, a wet preparation of the fluid should be made and examined, preferably under phase contrast, for the characteristic motile amoebae associated with amoebic meningo-encephalitis. Normal fluid contains no more than 3–5 white cells per cubic millimetre. Whilst the cell-count is being performed, an aliquot of the fluid should be centrifuged to deposit cells and any micro-organisms which may be present. The supernatant fluid is separated for biochemical analysis, the deposit being used to make films for microscopical examination. A film should be made to establish the type of cells present in the fluid and the proportion of the total cell-count which they form, and another for examination for bacteria. Where the history is suggestive of amoebic meningo-encephalitis or cryptococcal infection, wet films should be made from the deposit and examined under phase contrast in the former case, and in an Indian ink preparation in the second when capsulated yeast bodies will be seen. If the history, or the clinical and biochemical findings are suggestive of tuberculous meningitis, a special film is made. Here four or five drops of cerebro-spinal fluid are placed on a slide, each drop being allowed to dry (without spreading) before another drop is layered on the same site.

The film for establishing the cell-type may be stained either with methylene blue or with Leishman's stain, that for general bacteriology with Gram's stain and that for examination for *M. tuberculosis* by the Ziehl–Neelsen method. Some workers have reported favourably on the use of the fluorescent antibody technique for the rapid diagnosis of the commoner forms of meningitis (i.e. meningococcal, *H. influenzae* and pneumococcal).

In untreated meningitis due to pyogenic bacteria the cellular exudate will consist almost entirely of polymorphonuclear leucocytes whereas in infections due to leptospira, *M. tuberculosis*, *T. pallidum*, *C. neoformans* or viruses, lymphocytes will predominate. Occasionally in early infection due to viruses or *M. tuberculosis* or in *Leptospira ictero haemorragiae* meningitis as opposed to that due to *L. canicola* there may be a predominance of polymorpho-nuclear leucocytes in the exudate. Typical findings in different infective conditions are shown in Table 3.

A Gram-stained film should be examined for the presence of bacteria. If lymphocytes only are present, it is unusual to see any bacteria in the fluid, but if polymorpho-nuclear leucocytes predominate, a careful search of the film should be made before recording the result as negative. If the patient has received antibiotics the fluid may well contain polymorpho-nuclear leucocytes but no organisms. If bacteria are present, a tentative diagnosis may be reached on examination of the film. A film containing Gram-negative kidney-shaped cocci in pairs is virtually diagnostic of meningococcal meningitis, whereas Gram-positive cocci in pairs are suggestive of pneumococcal infection. Gram-negative rods are found in haemophilus infection as well as those due to coliform bacteria. The organisms associated with meningitis will be discussed in more detail below.

The presence of bacteria in a film is always of importance but, especially in the absence of pus cells, care must be taken to exclude the possibility that either the container in which the spinal fluid was collected or the stain solution are contaminated with bacteria. For this reason, wherever possible new containers should be used for the collection of spinal fluid.

If tuberculous meningitis is suspected either from the clinical history or from the finding of a lymphocytic exudate with a decrease in glucose (*vide infra*), the thick film stained either by Ziehl Neelsen or auramine method must be examined in detail perhaps for an hour or more by different observers for the presence of acid-alcohol-fast bacilli. This examination must be exhaustive, because of the great importance of finding the tubercle bacillus in view of the slow rate of growth of the organisms in culture. The finding of an acid-fast bacillus is virtually diagnostic of tuberculous meningitis, as meningitis due to other mycobacteria is rare.

The supernatant fluid is observed for xanthochromia which, in the presence of blood, would support the diagnosis of subarachnoid haemorrhage, and is then analysed for the glucose and protein content. The chloride

Condition	Appearance	Cells	Protein mg./100 ml.	Sugar mg./100 ml.	Film	Culture
Normal	Sparkling clear	0–5/mm.³ lymphocytes	20–40	45–70	—	—
Localized brain abscess	Clear or slight haze	6–100 lymphocytes predominating	10–120	Normal	—	—ve
Pyogenic meningitis	Cloudy or turbid	Over 500 (usually over 1,000) polymorphs	80–500	0–40 (usually 10–30)	Bacteria present in 50–60% (if untreated case)	+ve in 90% (less if case partially treated)
Tuberculous meningitis	Clear or slight haze (may be with fine clot)	100–500 lymphocytes (may be polymorphs early in disease)	100–500	0–40 (usually 30–40)	Very scanty AAFB in Ziehl–Neelsen	+ve (L–J medium)
Leptospiral	Clear or slight haze	50–500 lymphocytes (? polymorphs in Weil's disease)	50–100	Normal	—	—ve

The ranges given represent the usual case. Atypical cases may fall well outside the figures given.

content may also be determined but this is much less informative than the glucose and protein levels. Typical levels are shown in Table 3. A glucose-content of less than 45 mg./100 ml. is suspicious, and below 40 mg./100 ml. is pathological being commonly due to bacterial or fungal meningitis but may be found in hypoglycaemia or diffuse malignant invasion of the meninges. It is common to find only a slight reduction below 40 mg./100 ml. in early tuberculous meningitis but in pyogenic meningitis the level is usually less than 30 mg./100 ml. It is important to note that in about 15 per cent of culturally proven cases of bacterial meningitis, even in the presence of large numbers of polymorphs in the fluid, the glucose-level may be above 45 mg./100 ml. The protein-content is almost always raised above 40 mg./100 ml. but this is also the case in non-bacterial meningitis.

The deposit is then inoculated on to suitable culture media under both aerobic (plus 5–10 per cent carbon dioxide) as well as anaerobic conditions. If tuberculous meningitis is suspected, two Lowenstein–Jensen slopes should also be inoculated. If cryptococcal meningitis seems possible, Sabouraud's medium should be inoculated and cultures incubated both at 37°C and at room temperature.

Most organisms other than *M. tuberculosis* will grow after overnight incubation at 37°C, but cultures should be incubated for a further 24 hr. and anaerobic broth cultures should be Gram filmed after 48 hr. and subcultured at that time.

As mentioned previously, blood cultures should be taken, and if leptospiral meningitis is suspected, special media (e.g. Korthof's) should be used for blood-culture.

As indicated in Table 2 a wide range of bacteria may give rise to meningitis. However, most cases are due to a fairly limited range or organisms. A brief survey of the principal features of the more usual organisms is given below.

Characteristics of Organisms Commonly giving rise to Infections of the Central Nervous System

(a) **Neisseria Meningitidis.** The meningococcus is the commonest cause of bacterial meningitis in Britain. It is carried in the nasopharynx and gives rise to disease only in a proportion of carriers. Clinical disease is commonest in children but epidemics may occur in young adults in conditions of overcrowding such as armed forces' camps. Epidemics also regularly occur in the dry season in Nigeria and North Africa. Meningococcal infection may present as meningitis or as a septicaemia with a haemorrhagic rash in which the meningitis may play a notable or, as in the fulminating septicaemia associated with the Waterhouse–Friderichsen syndrome, a much less prominent part. In fact, in some of the cases of the latter syndrome, death may occur with little or no meningeal involvement, and even in those who survive, the first lumbar puncture may reveal a virtually normal fluid.

Neisseria meningitidis is a Gram-negative diplococcus which grows in 24–48 hr. on enriched media such as chocolate blood agar or Mueller–Hinton medium in an atmosphere of 5–10 per cent of carbon dioxide in air. It is recognized by its morphology, biochemistry, a positive oxidase reaction and agglutination with antisera. Four classical groups of meningococci have been internationally accepted for many years—A, B, C and D. Of these, Group A is the serotype associated with widespread epidemics, whereas Groups B and C are more common in inter-epidemic periods. Group D strains are rarely isolated. In recent years, types X, Y and Z have been described in Europe and have been recognized in the U.S.A. Serotype Y, in particular, has been associated with widespread carriage in U.S. military camps. Types X and Y have been isolated also from cases. Apart from one instance in America, disease due to type Z strains has not been reported. However, recently several cases have been observed both in Glasgow and Dundee. Two further serotypes designated 135 and 29E have been seen fairly frequently in U.S. Army camps, and strains related to type 135 have been identified in Scotland.

Meningococci are sensitive to a wide range of antibiotics including benzyl-penicillin. However, one of the disturbing developments in recent years has been the emergence of sulphonamide-resistant strains. These were first identified in the U.S.A. and belonged to Groups B and C, but more recently not only have similar observations been made in Europe and Great Britain, but epidemics due to sulphonamide-resistant Group A strains have also occurred in both Africa and Greece. As antibiotics (with the possible exception of rifampicin) are much less efficient at eradicating *N. meningitidis* from the naso-pharynx than sulphonamides, the emergence of sulphona-mide-resistant strains is especially disturbing because a prime weapon for halting an epidemic by treatment of cases and *carriers* had been lost. The specific antigen is poly-saccharide in nature and type-specific polysaccharide vaccines have been produced which give rise to type-specific protection. Future developments in this field will obviously be of considerable interest and possible importance to those working in areas where epidemics occur.

From what has been said, it is more important than ever to combine penicillin with sulphonamides in the treatment of meningococcal infection, and the treatment of infection by sulphonamide alone can no longer be recommended. In fulminating disease, steroids have an important supportive part to play, even though the plasma cortisol levels may be raised.

(b) Haemophilus Influenzae. Meningitis due to this organism is confined to the young child and is rare in later childhood and in the adult. This organism does not give rise to epidemics although, like the meningococcus, the causal strain may be carried in the nasopharynx. Capsulated strains of *H. influenzae* fall into six types (a to f) first described by Pittman. With rare exceptions only type b is associated with meningitis. As in meningococcal meningitis the causal organism may commonly be isolated from blood taken at the onset of disease.

H. influenzae is a tiny Gram-negative cocco-bacillus but in the spinal fluid larger bacillary and filamentous forms are commonly seen. Capsular material is liberated into the spinal fluid so that if antiserum to Pittman type b *H. influenzae* is layered on top of a small amount of the fluid in a capillary tube or Pasteur pipette a precipitate will form at the interface. This is a useful rapid diagnostic test to help differentiate this type of meningitis from that due to other Gram-negative rods.

H. influenzae grows on enriched media such as chocolate-agar, and the addition of 5–10 per cent carbon dioxide to the atmosphere may facilitate growth. The organism may be recognized by its morphology, and agglutination by Group b antiserum as well as its dependence on certain growth factors. It is sensitive to most antibiotics although only moderately so to benzyl-penicillin. Despite its sensitivity *in vitro* to ampicillin, which is a bactericidal drug, the response may be disappointing and the drug of choice remains the bacteriostatic drug chloramphenicol. Cephaloridine in particular has given unsatisfactory results in the treatment of this condition.

(c) Streptococcus pneumoniae. This organism gives rise to meningitis in all age-groups. Pneumococci are normally found in the upper respiratory tract and may presumably invade the nervous system directly from this site. This is certainly true in cases of recurrent meningitis where the organism is usually a pneumococcus which gains access to the subdural space from the nasal sinuses through a fine skull-fracture. Many cases of pneumococcal meningitis give a history of head-injury and pneumococcal meningitis is the commonest form of meningitis secondary to head-injury. As with other forms of meningitis blood-culture taken before treatment has been started may yield pneumococci. Pneumococcal meningitis is associated with a thick purulent exudate which, in fatal cases, covers the brain and, in a case presenting in life, may be too thick to flow unaided through the lumbar puncture needle giving the impression of a "dry tap".

The pneumococcus is a capsulated Gram-positive diplococcus, grows well on ordinary horse blood-agar and indeed grows poorly on chocolate blood-agar. Strains grow better in an atmosphere of 5–10 per cent carbon dioxide and some strains may grow poorly in the absence of carbon dioxide. The typical colonies, smooth and shining with the "draughtsman" appearance, are easy to recognize but occasionally highly capsulated strains may give rise to large mucoid colonies which could be mistaken for colonies of coliform bacteria. Pneumococci are highly sensitive to benzyl-penicillin and also sul-phonamide *in vitro* as well as to cephaloridine. Despite this the response of cases of pneumococcal meningitis to penicillin therapy is disappointing, the disease carrying a 20–30 per cent mortality even in the face of penicillin in large doses. Recently cephaloridine therapy has been tried with encouraging results and this is currently the drug of choice.

(d) Escherichia coli. This organism and other Gram-negative bacilli normally found in the large bowel such as *Klebsiella aerogenes*, Proteus sp., and *Pseudomonas aeruginosa* (pyocyanea) are usually found in neonatal meningitis. Neonatal meningitis is frequently associated with intra-uterine infection, difficult delivery and prematurity. It may result from umbilical sepsis and may also result from heavy contamination of the infant's environment such as incubators infected with *Ps. aeruginosa*, for example.

These organisms grow well on ordinary laboratory media such as blood-agar and in addition a medium such as McConkey's neutral-red bile-salt-lactose agar will aid in their identification. If Gram-negative rods are seen on the Gram stained film of spinal fluid from a new-born infant they can be assumed, for the purposes of immediate treatment, to be "coliform" bacteria, as infection with *H. influenzae* in this age-group is rare. A direct antibiotic sensitivity test should be set up so that rational therapy can be commenced as soon as possible because the antibiotic sensitivity-patterns of coliform bacteria vary widely and therapy must be guided by laboratory results. The most resistant organism is *Ps. aeruginosa*. This is usually sensitive only to gentamicin, colistin (polymyxin E) and carbenicillin in therapeutic dosage and it is wise to include one of these drugs in the initial "blind" treatment of neonatal meningitis. Penicillins and amino-glycosides are not only bactericidal in activity but are frequently synergistic, so that a combination of ampicillin and gentamicin would be rational until full bacteriological results are available.

(e) **Mycobacterium tuberculosis.** Unlike other forms of bacterial meningitis, tuberculous meningitis is usually of slow and insidious onset. For this reason a history of a slowly progressive illness with lethargy, anorexia and then vomiting developing over 1–2 weeks with signs of meningitis, points strongly to this diagnosis. All age-groups, except young infants, may be affected, although children and young adults are more susceptible than older persons because miliary tuberculosis, of which meningitis is a complication, is commoner in these age-groups. Although BCG vaccination commonly protects against tuberculosis and especially the miliary form, rarely cases may be seen with a valid history of vaccination. The tubercle bacillus because of its waxy envelope can be stained only by special techniques such as the Ziehl–Neelsen stain. Similarly it differs from other bacteria in its slow rate of growth—commonly 3–4 weeks, but up to 8 weeks on occasion before colonies can be seen with the naked eye on media such as Lowenstein–Jensen medium. Because it is imperative that a rapid diagnosis should be made and therapy begun, the examination of the stained film is of paramount importance in diagnosis.

Despite the emergence of drug-resistant strains of *M. tuberculosis* those isolated from cases of meningitis are usually sensitive to the three primary drugs streptomycin, iso-nicotinic acid hydrazide and para-amino salicylic acid, and these should be used in full dosage until the results of antibiotic sensitivity tests are available in 6–11 weeks time. Streptomycin may be given intrathecally at first as well as intramuscularly, and steroid therapy helps to prevent the formation and organization of exudates which otherwise might result in the development of hydrocephalus.

(f) **Staphylococci.** These may give rise to meningitis particularly in the latter part of the neonatal period as a result of colonization after birth in which case the causative organism will be *Staphylococcus aureus*, or following the insertion of a ventricular drain for the relief of hydrocephalus when the Spitz–Holter valve may be colonized by *Staphylococcus albus*. Whereas *Staph. aureus* is usually sensitive to cloxacillin, lincomycin, fusidic acid, cephaloridine and possibly to many other drugs, the sensitivity pattern of *Staph. albus* is unpredictable and

infections with this normally saprophytic species may be very difficult to treat and may only be terminated by removing the valve.

These Gram-positive cocci grow well on ordinary laboratory media and are differentiated by their ability to clot plasma. *Staph. aureus* produces the enzyme coagulase which will clot plasma, whereas *Staph. albus* is always coagulase negative.

If the Gram film of the spinal fluid, particularly from a neo-nate shows Gram-positive cocci tending to occur in clumps as well as singly, cloxacillin therapy should be commenced pending the results of sensitivity tests.

(g) **Listeria monocytogenes.** Listeria meningitis occurs in the young as a neo-natal infection, acquired from the mother either before or during birth, and also occasionally in middle-aged adults. In the last named cases the origin of the infection is unknown although this organism is an animal pathogen. *L. monocytogenes* is a short Gram-positive rod and may be mistaken for a "diphtheroid". However, the distinctive diagnostic feature is that this organism shows a characteristic "tumbling" motility when cultures are left at room temperature. This motility ceases at 37°C. The organism is sensitive to most of the common antibiotics and successful treatment has been reported with chloramphenicol as well as ampicillin. Other organisms that are encountered in central nervous system infections include streptococci of various types (especially in babies in the later neonatal period), Salmonella, Mima sp., Brucella sp., and the anaerobic organisms Bacteroides sp. and *Cl. welchii*. Other species may be found from time to time. Syphilitic meningitis is now a rarity but should be considered in obscure cases. Diagnosis is by serological methods.

Cryptococcal meningitis is caused by the fungus *Cryptococcus neoformans* recognized as capsulated budding yeasts in an Indian ink-stained film of spinal fluid. The yeasts may not be found unless the fluid is centrifuged for longer than is usual for cells and bacteria. The cell-response in this disease tends to be lymphocytic and the sugar-content of the fluid is below 40 mg./100 ml. Treatment is with 5-fluorocytosine or amphotericin B.

Amoebic meningitis due to *Naegleria* is diagnosed, as previously noted, by recognition of amoebae in the spinal fluid. Treatment is with amphotericin B and (in case *Hartmanella sp.* are present) sulphadiazine.

Should a treated case of bacterial meningitis not respond adequately to treatment the possibility of a subdural collection of pus should be investigated and treated by aspiration.

In cases of intoxication the diagnosis is essentially clinical, and treatment with antitoxin is an urgent necessity. Penicillin will help to eradicate *C. diphtheriae* and *Cl. tetani* but antibiotics have no curative effect and play no part in the management of botulism.

In all cases close co-operation between the clinician and laboratory is essential. Not only will this enable prompt and specific treatment to be undertaken in cases due to the commoner infective agents but will expedite diagnosis in more obscure conditions. In this way damage to the nervous system may be kept to a minimum.

FURTHER READING

Apley, J., Clarke, S. K., Roome, A. P. G., Sandry, S. A., Saygi, G., Silk, B. and Warhurst, D. C. (1970), "Primary Amoebic Meningo-encephalitis in Britain," *Brit. med. J.*, **i**, 596.

Brain, Lord (1962), *Diseases of the Nervous System*. Oxford University Press.

Christie, A. B. (1969), *Infectious Diseases*: *Epidemiology and Clinical Practice*. Livingstone.

Dalton, H. P. and Allison, M. J. (1968), "Modification of Laboratory Results by Partial Treatment of Bacterial Meningitis," *Amer. J. clin. Path.*, **49**, 410.

Feldman, H. A. (1968), "Toxoplasmosis," *New Engl. J. Med.*, **279**, 1370, 1431.

Love, W. C., McKenzie, P., Lawson, J. H., Pinkerton, I. W., Jamieson, W. M., Stevenson, J., Roberts, W. and Christie, A. B. (1970), "Treatment of Pneumococcal Meningitis with Cephaloridine," *Postgrad. med. J.*, **46**, Supplement 155.

Watkins, J. S., Campbell, M. J., Gardner-Medwin, D., Ingham, H. R. and Murray, I. G. (1969), "Two Cases of Cryptococcal Meningitis, One Treated with 5-Fluorocytosine," *Brit. med. J.*, **3**, 29.

Woodruff, A. W., Bisseru, B. and Bowe, J. C. (1966), "Infection with Animal Helminths as a factor in causing Poliomyelitis and Epilepsy," *Brit. med. J.*, **i**, 1576.

3. SLOW VIRUS INFECTIONS OF THE NERVOUS SYSTEM

WILLI K. MÜLLER

INTRODUCTION

The late Dr. Sigurdsson[12,17] of the Keldur-Institute in Reykjavik during a series of lectures at London University introduced for the first time the term "slow infection" together with an entirely new concept of virus activity. This was a novel conception, because—in those times—nearly everybody's mind was occupied by the entero-virus infections as the prototype of diseases caused by viruses. Processes differing from this prototype, like infections through the herpes group persisting for lifetime or some rabies infections notorious for the long delay between infection and onset of clinical signs, were considered as a curiosity rather than as an indication that things may take a quite different course if an organism is confronted with pathogenic viral agents. Even nowadays, when the existence of slow infections is widely accepted, such prejudices seem to persist, when people speak about "slow viruses" instead of slow virus-infections, implying in this way that some peculiar group of viruses may exist, which may produce unexpected effects. But Sigurdsson was apparently thinking of a particular process, rather than of a particular group of agents, interesting as this concept might be in itself. Traces of such a second process, differing from an otherwise common type of viral infection, can be found everywhere, or perhaps—if we were better informed—traces of a second, a third and a fourth process. We have, for example, in connection with the generally quite harmless dengue which is an arbovirus infection of man, epidemics of a very dangerous haemorrhagic encephalitis produced by just the same viruses as the harmless equivalent. The haemorrhagic encephalitides for their part, by way of the haemorrhagic encephalitis of Hurst, are in some way connected with the demyelinating diseases of man. The recent observation that the Epstein-Barr virus, known to be involved in a neoplastic disease of man, is the causal agent in most of the cases of infective mononucleosis, another relatively harmless disease of man, represents such an indication. With the subacute sclerosing panencephalitis as a second process in connection with the common measles infection in childhood, we are, last but not least, just approaching the centre of the contemporary interest in slow virus-infections. Scrapie, Visna and Maedi, the classical slow infections of sheep, cannot be used as an argument for the existence of a particular group of "slow viruses", because we do not yet know the harmless and more common equivalent of those diseases. It is not surprising, therefore, that the attempt to establish a particular group of viruses as CHINA (Chronic Infectious Neuropathic Agents)[6] never became widely accepted.

Sigurdsson established three criteria for slow infections:

(1) A very long initial period of latency, lasting from several months to several years.

(2) A protracted course after the appearance of clinical signs, usually ending in serious disablement or death.

(3) Limitation of the infection to a single host species, with anatomical lesions in only a single organ or tissue system.

He added: "These last statements have to be modified as knowledge increases." We are now in this process of modification, not only in relation to "lesions in only a single organ or tissue system", but also with regard to the "limitation to a single host species". But opinions as to which diseases are actually covered by these criteria and which are not, differ considerably. It is not clear whether all the PTI (Persisting Tolerated Infections) of Hotchin[6] are quite the same thing as slow virus-infections or whether they represent a process to some extent apart from the classical slow virus-infections. Therefore it is not clear precisely which diseases of proven viral aetiology should be treated in an article about slow virus-infections, e.g. rabies, the rubella complications of man, and many others. On the other hand, there are several diseases considered to represent slow viral infections, but still no proof exists for this opinion—among them some of the most important neurological diseases of man, such as multiple sclerosis, amyotrophic lateral sclerosis and postinfective Parkinsonism. It would be even worthwhile to approach some muscle-diseases with slow virus-infection in mind.

We still know too little about slow virus-infections to be able to formulate a clear systematic classification. Therefore the only thing possible would be to restrict ourselves to a simple enumeration and description of all those diseases which undoubtedly belong to this group, depicting each of them with its own interesting peculiarities. In the present circumstances, it seems preferable to restrict one's remarks to a nucleus of the most interesting diseases, such as subacute sclerosing panencephalitis, multifocal leucoencephalitis and the Jakob–Creutzfeld disease on the one hand, and Scrapie, Kuru and the transmissible mink encephalopathy on the other; to give a brief description of the clinical features of these disorders; to compare the clinical data with experimental findings; and then to enter fully into the field of scientific controversy and speculation about the matter. For a more complete access into the matter the reader is referred to the existing literature,[6,12,16,40] some of which contain a large bibliography. Furthermore, there are two unofficial papers[16,17] from the NIH, Bethesda, Md., listing the literature on Scrapie and Kuru up to the beginning of 1969. In addition to these standard works, our bibliography is restricted to articles and books which are either not contained in those works or which cannot be readily identified. This present article may appear somewhat unbalanced in favour of the scrapie complex, but there is a strong feeling that this is "the pot where the rabbit lies in the pepper", as a German proverb says.

SLOW VIRUS-DISEASES CONNECTED WITH PAPOVA-LIKE VIRIONS

Subacute Sclerosing Panencephalitis (SSPE)

Following Greenfield, the denomination "Subacute sclerosing panencephalitis" is nowadays used to include several groups of neurological diseases which have been reported by various authors in different countries, such as the "subacute sclerosing leucoencephalitis" of van Bogaert and the "subacute inclusion body encephalitis" of Dawson.

Most of those cases comprised young people or children of school-age, even though a number of cases have also been observed in adults. Apparently these patients contracted a disease of fairly uniform picture, though different authors have emphasized some variability. Three phases, or rather levels of a continuously progressive evolution rather than well-demarcated stages, are discernible. The process starts with some alteration of intelligence and personality, detected first by the scholastic achievements, which slowly deteriorate, amounting to the loss of recently acquired knowledge and the incapacity for assimilation of new knowledge. With the onset of myoclonic movements or hyperkinesis, patients reach the second phase, which is marked by convulsions, visual disorders and disorientation,

going on to a state of functional decortication. Finally the patient lies rigid and unconscious in a flexion contraction. The eyeballs are in continuous movement. The body is agitated by myoclonic jerks. In a condition of marasmus and central hyperthermia the patient perishes after a period ranging from a few months to 2 years (maximally 9 years) after the onset of the first clinical signs.

In the earlier phases, the EEG is slow and dysrhythmic. Later, with the appearance of myoclonic jerks, typical high amplitude, low frequency waves are regularly found. The CSF cells are normal or slightly increased in number. Later a paretic type of gold curve is found. A marked increase in and qualitative changes of IgG's in serum and CSF are particularly characteristic of this disease.

Histologically the disease is described as a panencephalitis with gliosis and a somewhat discrete breakdown of myelin-sheaths. Within the neurons and oligodendroglial cells acidophil inclusions are found.

Many authors, impressed by these typical inclusion bodies, originally thought that there might be some connection with herpes simplex encephalitis, but a few years ago Conolly and his co-workers found high antibody titres against measles virus in patients with SSPE.[40] These findings were confirmed by many other investigators. Such antibody titres are extremely high in both serum and CSF, increasing during the course of the disease. By immuno-fluorescent methods, the connection between the cerebral lesions and an antigen reacting with anti-measles sera could be demonstrated. There was no staining with antibodies against distemper-virus, and only little staining with antibodies against rinderpest-virus, two agents belonging to the same group as measles-virus. Therefore, a connection between SSPE and a persistent measles infection is the present concept of SSPE. Katz et al.[22] were able to transmit the process to ferrets by direct intracerebral injection of biopsy material even when this material had been kept in tissue-culture for some time. Two weeks after injection the animals developed an encephalitis with just the same EEG-changes as in SSPE of man. Barbanti-Brodano et al.,[3] members of the same group of investigators, found by electron microscopy two types of virus-particles in tissue-cultures of such biopsy material—a myxovirus-like particle budding from the surface of the infected cell, and a spherical Papova-like virion without envelope, in the cytoplasm of the cells.

Progressive Multifocal Leucoencephalitis (PML)

The disease entity known as "Progressive multifocal leucoencephalitis" (PML) has only recently been described. Aström et al. found it to have been first described by M. Hodgkin. Later, similar cases were reported, namely in connection with malignant tumours. By reason of the multifocal nature of the lesions, the clinical picture is somewhat variable, depending on their localization within the cortex, cerebellum or brain-stem. Histologically, perivascular demyelinization, hypertrophy of astrocytes and oligodendrocytes leading at times to the formation of giant cells, are conspicuous. Within the astrocytes, acidophil inclusions can be detected. Spongiform changes are also to be found.

By electron microscopy Zu Rhein et al.[42] found Papova-like virions in glial cells of patients with this disease.

Jakob–Creutzfeld Disease

In the same year 1920 both Jakob and Creutzfeld described independently cases of the same clinical and pathological entity, also known as "spastic pseudosclerosis" or "subacute spongiform encephalopathy". The cases of Jakob belonged to one family. The disease generally starts rather late, between 50 and 60 years of age, though Seitelberger reported some cases in children. At the onset patients complain of neurotic-like symptoms and of diffuse pains in the muscles. The speech later becomes dysarthric. Signs of spasticity appear together with extrapyramidal manifestations. Mental disturbances are common. In some cases a cerebellar syndrome seems to be predominant, while in other cases part of the symptomatology resembled that of amyotrophic lateral sclerosis. Death supervenes after a period ranging from several months to about 4 years.

The brains show macrogliosis, loss of neurons and a status spongiosus. The gyrus precentralis seems to be the site of predilection, but other cortical regions are also damaged, excepting only the parietal and occipital areas. The striatum and thalamus are often involved. Degeneration of the pyramidal tract is found.

Recently the disease has been successfully transmitted to the chimpanzee by Gibbs et al.[15,16] Vernon et al.[41] found by electron microscopy in the brains of such patients, two types of particles: larger particles resembling myxoviruses, and smaller particles of Papova-like morphology. In addition, they described nucleoprotein-like filamentous structures in cytoplasmic fragments, or in the extracellular spaces.

SLOW VIRUS-DISEASES CONNECTED WITH AGENTS WITH UNUSUAL PROPERTIES

Scrapie of Sheep

Scrapie, the classical virus disease of sheep, although better studied than any other of the slow virus-diseases, remains the most contradictory and enigmatical. It is, or was, a naturally occurring disease in sheep-flocks in Great Britain, France, Germany, Iceland and several other European and non-European countries. In Britain the first evidence of this disease can be detected in some reports dating from the early eighteenth century (Palmer,[12,17] McGowan[12,17]). The first clear veterinary description, apparently as a well-known entity, was given in Germany by Leopoldt in 1759,[25] and in France by Paulet[33] late in the eighteenth century. The latter author quoted a book of travels by Eggert Olafson in the seventeenth century, where a disease of sheep in Iceland with all the characteristics of scrapie was mentioned. Thus, the disease seems to be of some antiquity. The history of investigation, nevertheless, has differed in each country. In Germany the clinical and epidemiological interest in this disease started in the late eighteenth century, due to

an epidemic-like occurrence, and had its peak during the nineteenth century with many transmission experiments. It would have culminated in the first successful transmission by Cassirer,[12,17] if he had not neglected his result, because the incubation period seemed to be too unusual to him. In France, at the same time, interest was constant, but rather less intensive than in Germany, culminating in the first description of the characteristic brain lesions by Besnoit and Morel[12,17] and in the first clear transmission from sheep to sheep by Cuille and Chelle.[12,17] In Great Britain the disease received but little attention until the twenties of this century, when large-scale experimental work was started. This still goes on, and has provided us with most of our present knowledge about scrapie.

In addition, some less important variations exist of rather local character. The disease seems to occur in two main clinical forms, according to the presence or absence of scratching. Generally, the process starts with changes in behaviour: stubborn reactions, spontaneous or provoked, are described; jerky movements of the ears; stretching of the head—sometimes in an opisthotonos-like fashion; shivering and fasciculation of muscles, especially of the neck; and a strange gait resembling that of a donkey, and known as the "cuddy trott". Stockman[12,17] emphasized early periods of intense thirst. Later a slight tremor of the head can be observed. The animals show a tendency to lag behind the moving flock. In the scratching form of the disease a constant and frenzied nibbling predominates. The animal typically starts to bite at the skin of the root of the tail, then the hind legs and later the trunk. Sheep rub these parts of the body against posts or walls, until the skin and fleece become severely damaged. Only rarely does nibbling begin on the forelimbs. Later a weakness of the hind-limbs appears. If such an animal becomes frightened, it falls and tries to move away by rudder movements of the fore-legs. Complete paresis, however, is rather rare. The gait is staggering, apparently more on account of ataxia than by actual paresis. A threshold test has been used by German farmers and veterinarians, in which an animal is unable to pass quickly over some threshold or beam, without stumbling; this seems to reveal dysmetria. There is some difference of opinion whether true convulsions ever occur; the existence or non-existence of convulsions seems to be a matter of focal variations. Severe emaciation is considered to be one of the most constant symptoms. Starting at a relatively early phase of the disease, this wasting is not connected with loss of appetite or any disorders of digestion. After several weeks or months the animal dies, apparently from oedema of the lung and a complete inanition. The annual loss in flocks with natural scrapie seems to be about 10 per cent in Britain and as much as 30 per cent in Iceland. English authors generally deny any sex-incidence, while most German authors are convinced that many more rams than ewes contract this disease; the ratio noted is about 3 : 1.

One of the most prominent histological features is the more or less intensive vacuolization of neurons in the brain and spinal cord. A definite status spongiosus of the ground substance is often found. By Cajal's staining methods, a typical enlargement of astrocytes is revealed, which is nowadays considered to be the true histological proof for the existence of scrapie in a specimen. Beck et al.[12,17] from a large series of naturally affected sheep brains, emphasized severe destruction in the nuclei paraventricularis and supraopticus of the hypothalamus. A slight enlargement of the adrenal cortex, namely the zona reticularis, seems to be a very common finding, even in experimental scrapie. Weihermüller[17] found consistent changes in the thyroid glands as confirmed by Brownlee.[12,17] Bosanquet et al.[12,17] observed specific lesions in voluntary muscles and on that account considered scrapie to be a primary muscle-disease. This observation, although based on a large series, was never confirmed; it is one of the contradictory observations in this disease.

The susceptibility to scrapie seems to differ widely in different sheep-strains. Furthermore, there is no doubt that the offspring of affected animals in the naturally occurring disease are more often affected than the offspring of healthy animals. Parry et al.,[12,17] who never observed any lateral spread in their flock, assumed therefore that scrapie is a hereditary disease *strictu sensu*, due to a recessive autosomal gene. Sigurdsson,[12,17] on the other hand, found after eradication of the whole sheep-population in the area where the disease is endemic in Iceland, that a few years later scrapie reappeared in the new flocks which were imported from a region where scrapie had never existed, with eventually the same annual loss as before. He therefore concluded that scrapie must depend on some local factor such as possibly a vector. This connection with some local factors had been one of the strong impressions of the earlier English authors. The concept of scrapie as a venereal disease has often been advanced by German and French veterinarians, also by some of the earlier British authors (Stockman,[12,17] McFadyean.[17])

Scrapie can easily be transmitted to goats, mice, rats and hamsters. Depending on the species, on the level of adaptation to the species, on the amount of agent contained in the inoculum, and on the route of infection, the incubation period varies between a few months and several years, with the shortest incubation periods in mice and the longest in sheep and goats. The agent grows in tissue-cultures[8] of infected mouse-brains. It has a strong affinity to tissue-debris and to cell-membranes. Furthermore, it is resistant to boiling, to formalin-treatment and to several other chemicals which destroy most other known viruses. By UV measurements its size was found to be exceptionally small, but the authors hesitated to give a rigid interpretation, apparently because of some refraction problems.[24] Reports of a successful dialysis of the agent seem to be now definitely refuted.[28] It was never possible to demonstrate any antibody-formation during the scrapie-process. There seems also to be no interference or reaction to interferon, but the agent may interfere with infections by a virus of the tick-borne encephalitis-complex.[1] There seems to be no viraemia. On the other hand, the agent can be detected in almost every tissue of the infected organism. The site of entry into the organism is probably of particular importance for the disease-process, because, after peripheral application only, activity can be found very soon in spleen and lymph nodes; furthermore, the agent seems to spread along adjacent peripheral nerves to the spinal cord, ascending thence to the brain. The symptom of scratching or non-scratching depends upon the particular material used for inoculation, suggesting the existence of different strains of the agent.

Kuru in Man

Localized to a small tribe of stone-age people in the distant highlands of New Guinea, there exists a progressive and fatal disease of the nervous system which the natives call Kuru, and which was fully described for the first time by Gajdusek et al.[12,15] The process starts with difficulties in maintaining balance. After a steadily increasing disability, ataxia of the trunk becomes the prominent feature. Flickering movements around the lips, fasciculation and a fine tremor are reported as typical signs. In the advanced stages, jerky movements resembling myoclonus, athetosis or chorea; slurred speech and rigidity, appear. The disease ends in a state of dementia, total incoordination and flexion contraction. Patients die in marasmus after a period of 2–24 months.

The brains of those patients reveal a widespread neuronal degeneration, astrocytic hypertrophy and a status spongiosus. In the cerebellum a loss of granule-cells and a moderate to severe loss of Purkinje cells with torpedo-like swellings of the axon are found. PAS-positive plaques can often be observed. Neutral fat-stains show a breakdown of myelin. The similarity between Kuru and scrapie was first noted by Hadlow.[12,15,17]

Because only the tribe of the Fore people and closely related linguistic groups intermarrying with them are affected, the importance of genetic factors becomes obvious. Recently Schaltenbrand et al.[15] described a case very similar to Kuru, occurring in a schoolboy born and brought up in northern Germany, without any contact with New Guinea. The existence of this disease in the Fore tribe is not long standing, and the incidence has decreased recently; an environmental factor of still unknown character has therefore been assumed. Sex-factors seem also to be relevant. The recent spread of the disease is probably due to the ingestion of infected material through the practice of cannibalism.

Kuru can be transmitted to the chimpanzee[12,15] and to the Spider monkey,[15] perhaps—after immuno-suppression—to mice as well (Field[12,15]). By electron microscopy no agent can be detected. The unusual physical properties of scrapie-factor applied also to those of the Kuru-agent.

Transmissible Encephalopathy of Mink (TME)

A particular encephalopathy of mink was first observed in some Wisconsin mink-farms (Hartsough et al.[16]). Hadlow reported the same disease in farms in Idaho.[16]

The disease starts with subtle changes in feeding habits and in cleanliness. A peculiar excitability occurs. The tails are carried high and occasionally convulsions take place. The animals are liable to run in circles, and they show involuntary movements of the feet. Later on they lapse into somnolence. The gait becomes stiff and the hind legs show jerky stepping actions. Finally the animals are no longer able to move. A fine tremor appears. They die in a state of emaciation 3–6 weeks after the onset of the disease.

Widespread lesions can be found in the brains of affected minks. A status spongiosus of the grey matter, astrocytosis and some acidophil cell inclusions are predominant, with the main localization in the dorsal and medial nuclei of the cerebellar peduncles.

The spread from one farm to the other is apparently due to infected food, with an incubation period of about 7 months.

Like the scrapie-agent, the agent of TME shows unusual properties. Zlotnik et al.[17] and Barlow et al.[4] were successful in transmitting it to goats, mice and hamsters. Eckroade et al.[10] were able to transmit the disease to the squirrel monkey and to rhesus monkeys after adaptation. Recently the same authors transmitted scrapie to the mink, thus closing the circle, which makes the identity of both processes highly probable.

THEORIES, HYPOTHESES AND SPECULATIONS

Myxoviruses and Papova-like Virions

In SSPE, after the recent discovery of the causal role of measles-virus, we are confronted by the problem why a few individuals with high antibody-levels in serum and CSF should contract a particular virus disease, while most of the population are protected against reinfection with the same measles-virus for lifetime, by these specific antibodies. One interpretation would be that precisely this high antibody-level might be the cause of the disease, thus explaining SSPE as an auto-immune disease, the antibodies being directed more against the infected cell than against the viral agent. But, the agent being demonstrated as persisting in the infected cells budding from the surface of the cells, the antibodies represent true anti-measles antibodies, with distinct reactions against rinderpest or distemper, and by immuno-fluorescence, sites of virus accretion are stained. Another theory is that of an auxiliary virus-system[23] which assumes a mute and latent presence of a virus of the Papova-group within some cells of the brain. A fresh infection with measles only, by the well-known properties of this viral group to induce a fusion of different cells to a single structure containing several nuclei, would enable those viruses of the Papova-group to infect a new cell. This is an alternative theory, but it does not explain why the measles infection should persist in the presence of high antibody levels, even increasing during the disease-process. Furthermore, the attempt to prove the specific character of the Papova-like virions by immuno-fluorescent methods was unsuccessful. Schumacher and Albrecht[38] were apparently

thinking more of a system of complete and incomplete virus-particles, when they tried to interpret their very similar results. Later, Barbanti-Brodano et al.[3] spoke of a different complexity in different cultures of biopsy-material. Perhaps a finding by Horta-Barbosa et al.[20] could be the key to a better understanding. They found that the neutralizing antibodies of a patient with SSPE were more susceptible to the measles wild virus than to the agent isolated from this patient, but the cytopathogenic effect and the plaque formation of this virus resembled more the vaccine-strain of measles-virus than the wild virus. Sabin[34] as early as 1952, noted unusual findings when two serologically closely related arbovirus strains are present in the same natural disease-focus. Perhaps in some arboviruses we can find a satisfactory model to explain persistent infections in the presence of antibodies. Arboviruses have group- or common-, and type- or strain-antigens. In the face of difficulties with the usual serological methods of deducing the different strains of a subgroup as in the case of dengue or in the so-called TBE-complex, we may suppose that a strong group or common antigen is in such cases combined with a weak type or strain antigen. In a subsequent infection by two of those strains one might expect that the second infection would provoke the group antibodies, but the weak type antigen might be tolerated. It is known that there are arbovirus antigens which can be separated from infectivity, and others which cannot. A logical assumption would be to explain the antigens which are not separable from infectivity, as the type-antigens, and the others as the group antigens. In every virus population we have a certain amount of incomplete particles. If the incompleteness of an individual virus-particle is not genetically determined, we would expect that all complete particles formed are caught subsequently by the high group antibodies present in the serum and elsewhere, while the incomplete particles are tolerated. Should they be infective, they infect new cells, and the newly infected cell produces complete and incomplete particles as before. This would be a persistent tolerated infection in the presence of high antibody levels. Whether high antibody levels are present or not, would depend on the absolute strength of the group-antigen and on the ratio of complete to incomplete particles formed in a given population. This ratio might be genetically determined, and as such, a constant property of a virus subgroup. It is not clear if this model can be translated to the measles-virus system or to other viral systems, where serologically closely related strains exist, or generally to the relations of wild and vaccine strains. The reason why the disease then takes another atypical course is also not explained.

The Spread of Scrapie and Related Diseases

(i) Vector Transmission

A spread of scrapie in animal-houses under experimental conditions is a very rare event. The most common possibility seems to be ingestion of infected organ-material, e.g. connected with fighting of males in mice. Spread by contact only, even in naturally occurring scrapie, is an extremely rare event. Nevertheless events such as these are reported, which cannot be explained by fighting or other ingestion of material. How difficult it is to infect animals merely by contact, however close this contact may be, was recently demonstrated by Field *et al.*[13] In their experience these authors were apparently inclined to think of a vector-transmission in the few cases where such spread occurred. Spontaneous outbreaks of scrapie, not connected with breeding, are well documented throughout the centuries of the history of scrapie. The endemic scrapie in an Icelandic valley seems to be a continuous series of spontaneous outbreaks, rather than one connected with mating and breeding. In valley-farms with a high incidence of scrapie-cases the flocks are in the immediate neighbourhood of farms where scrapie never appears. If scrapie is really vector-transmitted, as Sigurdsson suggested, transmission by flying insects is unlikely, because flying insects—namely *Simuliidae*, the only species suitable for a vector-function existing in this valley—have a rather wide range of activity. A less mobile arthropod, with low action-radius, would be more probable. Local occurrence seems to be one of the most outstanding features of spontaneous scrapie outbreaks. It is quite impossible to quote all the German reports on outbreaks of scrapie after pasturing a flock in a particular meadow, and the disappearance of scrapie after removing the flock to another meadow. The first generation of modern English writers, such as Gaiger,[17] discussed this point in detail. An experiment of Greig and Gordon,[17] pasturing a scrapie-affected flock and a non-affected flock subsequently in the same meadow, was partially successful. That nematodes, the most common parasites of sheep, do not play any vector-role, was demonstrated by Fitzsimmons and Pattison.[17] Ticks and mites would fulfil those topographical conditions. In the early nineteenth century v. Richthofen[31] came to the conclusion that the spontaneous outbreaks of scrapie could be explained only by the influence of some arthropod. He suggested that scrapie was due to the interaction of a mite and received much scorn because of this idea, for he was never able to demonstrate his scrapie-mite. James Hogg, an English shepherd in the early nineteenth century, said that the disease of sheep he described—apparently scrapie—occurred only in places where ticks were found.[37] His report, like those of Bishop[5] and of Stockman,[12,17] are in this regard of little value, because they all regarded louping-ill and scrapie as identical. Brownlee[7] found *Demodex* mites in the genital organs of sheep with scrapie, but unfortunately he was arguing in terms of a direct causal connection rather than of a vector transmission, and one could hardly see how *Demodex*, with its feeding-habits, could play a vector-role for scrapie. Were bloodsucking mites or ticks the vector, then mice too would be expected to be involved. As far as we know, no large-scale examination of field-mice has been made. On the contrary mice have always been considered as a susceptible, but naturally unaffected animal, a concept which is dubious, since naturally occurring scrapie-like changes in mice within a German laboratory colony have been demonstrated by Henn *et al.*[19] In a yet unpublished study, mice of the scrapie-farms of Iceland were found to show not infrequently extensive vacuolization of neurons in the brain and spinal cord. Both species—*Mus musculus* and *Apodemus sylvaticus*—were involved. Therefore we can conclude that the hypothesis of vector transmission of natural scrapie by ticks or mites, with mice as the host reservoir, as in arboviruses of the TBE-complex but without the usual alimentary infection, would explain the facts. However, not enough data are known about this matter. This question may also be of importance for the Kuru problem. A small rodent, carrying the infected vector and imported by European ships to New Guinea, could have reached the Fore region long before any European came there, or the vector after adaptation to indigenous rodents or the agent after adaptation to indigenous vector and rodents. The fondness of the stone-age people for small rodents as a favoured article of diet (Alpers[16]), suggests many opportunities for infection in the case of humans.

(ii) Heredity *v.* Congenital–Connatal Transmission

Any concept of genetic properties in a disease which can be transmitted indefinitely to other animals by injection of infected material, raises important theoretical problems. On the other hand, if there are no demonstrable chromosome aberrations, the question arises whether a disease which may be transmitted to the offspring by both the parents, the latter being in a latent or carrier state of the disease, could be distinguished from a hereditary disease merely by statistical methods. One argument for a connatal transmission is shown by the high constancy of the age of onset in naturally diseased sheep-flocks. In most of the animals the process starts in the second year of life. An onset before the end of the first year of life is unanimously denied by all observers. An onset after the second year of life is unusual. This corresponds with the incubation period in experimental scrapie after peripheral application of the agent.

One mechanism of connatal contamination might be found in the vector hypothesis alone. It is known that ticks and mites select the inguinal region of domestic animals, where the skin is comparatively thin and therefore easy to penetrate. In that same area lymph- and blood-vessels are easily available. This is of essential importance for the larvae and nymphae of ticks and for all stages of the smaller mites. Therefore, during the mating act the parasites of the ram could attach themselves to the ewe, and during birth the lamb could be attacked by the hungry larvae, which are only waiting for a young animal, because the skin of the mother cannot be penetrated by them. However, one can scarcely believe this to be the only manner of connatal contamination, because—however small the larvae of some mites are and difficult to detect with the naked-eye—it is improbable that so many careful observers would have consistently overlooked such parasites.

Congenital transmission of the agent to the embryo or the fertilized egg by the infected uterine mucosa is a possible route of infection, for Eklund, Kennedy and

Hadlow[12,17] found high scrapie-activity in the uterus of experimentally infected animals. Concerning congenital transmission by the father, one experiment was done with semen of an infected ram (Palmer[17]) but with negative results. However, one must take into consideration that the semen was obtained by ampoule stimulation. There is not much likelihood that the testis is an organ of scrapie propagation. Eklund, Kennedy and Hadlow[11,17] could find no scrapie activity in the testes of experimentally infected males, unlike most of the other tissues. Again, the incidence of natural scrapie in castrated animals is apparently the same as in others. Therefore, if one assumes scrapie-activity in semen, this would be brought about more by the co-products of the accessory glands—prostate or vesicles—than by the main organ. Whether an artificially produced semen corresponds in all respects, including those co-products, with that produced by the natural way, is not known.

Further questions in connection with connatal transmission are discussed in the next chapter.

(iii) Scrapie as a Venereal Disease

Reports that a ewe or a ram, after mating with an infected partner, contracted scrapie some time later, are fairly numerous in the German, French and early English literature, but this event apparently was not the rule. Other reports are even more interesting: Ewes, with formerly normal offspring, after mating with a certain ram, produced normal offspring in the next season, but all later offspring contracted scrapie, even if the ewe was subsequently mated only with healthy rams (Stockman,[12,17] McFadyean,[17] Frank,[14] Kanert,[21] Seer[39]). Attempts were made to find an anatomical substratum for this venereal and connatal transmission. Stockman[12,17] found "very distinct purplish patches" in the urethra of affected rams, extending forwards for some distance from the neck of the bladder. Bertrand et al.,[12,17] reading this report, recalled similar findings by Girard,[17] who described 100 years before, some blackish plaques in the bladder of an affected ram. There were only two rams at their disposal both of which were negative. But in the uteri of affected ewes they found haemorrhagic plaques; the difference in regard to a large group of control animals was highly significant. Brownlee,[12,17] in an attempt to confirm their results, was finally unable to do so in his material, but he found polymorph cells in the uteri of his ewes, which he connected with the French reports. The localization of Stockman's lesions would correspond exactly with the site where the urethra is compressed by the prostate.

The Unusual Properties of the Scrapie Agent

To be resistant to boiling and even autoclaving for a short time; to endure formalin treatment and even boiling in formalin, to react otherwise than any known viruses, even the smallest ones, against UV-irradiation; these are indeed unusual properties for an agent. Doubts whether scrapie is due to an infection with a virus in the common use of this term, seem to be justifiable, because nucleoproteins, necessary for the self-perpetuation of a virus,

would not be able to tolerate all those things. Thus it happens yet again that with the scrapie problem we come into conflict with the present valid models. As before, we have to determine whether facts are known which would allow us a means, however complicated it may be, of avoiding such a conflict. Each of these unusual properties, in itself, has occasionally been described in connection with some known animal or plant viruses. Instead of assuming a complete mechanism of self-perpetuation for some membrane polysaccharides, Field[17] proposed the concept of some small nucleoprotein covered and protected by a polypeptide or polysaccharide. Quite recently, however, he seems to have departed somewhat from this concept and to assume a more complicated linker system, composed of a commensal propagating non-pathogenic subvirus, a normal cell-membrane and no self-replicating linkage material. He has suggested that many susceptible animals contain this non-pathogenic subvirus and that only the addition of the linker, contained in certain diseased tissues, would initiate the scrapie process. One of the questions arising would be whether this small element of nucleoprotein, or this subvirus, were an agent sui generis, or an incomplete part of a known virus. Which known virus would we have to look for, should we want to ascertain the most likelihood agent for such a function? Knowing the difficulties of differentiating true scrapie from louping-ill we would find it advisable to start with testing this virus for its qualification. In sheep it causes a meningo-encephalitis. Both diseases were distinguished 40 years ago on clinical and histological grounds, but since the detection of the SSPE aetiology we know more about the reliability of clinical and histological arguments for and against relations between two neurological diseases. Mindful of a vector hypothesis for scrapie transmission, the vector for louping-ill and for scrapie might prove to be the same. This would explain the ecological circumstances in Scotland. However, in France and Germany louping-ill has never been observed, but there we have the closely related tick-borne encephalitis. The different strains of this virus are known for their tendency to produce persistent infections of tissue-culture systems (Mayer,[27] Libikova et al.[26]). They can be shown to remain for a long time at the site of inoculation. A subacute or chronic skin disease of man, erythema chronicum migrans, is connected with antibodies against this virus (Samovich); is transmitted by ticks and shows a segmental spread along the peripheral nerves (Bammer et al.[2]). A virus isolated from the affected area of skin is closely related with tick-borne encephalitis-virus, but differs in some biological properties (unpublished observation). Epidemic vertigo seems to be another and abortive form of disease in man (Müller and Hopf[29]). A vertigo-like disease, known in France as "tourni", in Germany as "Drehkrankheit", was often confused with scrapie in sheep. This disease is aetiologically very heterogenous, partly coenurosis, partly listeriosis. A third form, less typical in its symptomatology than coenurosis, less acute and less often fatal than listeriosis, with an epidemiological peak in spring, might be the correlate with epidemic vertigo in man. This "turning disease" is often reported as being in ecological connection with scrapie both in France and in Germany. Rudolphi[32] reported protocols of a sheep flock with observations over a period of 20 years, which showed that every peak of this "turning disease" was followed by an upsurge of scrapie 2–3 years later. These connections are easy to explain, if one assumes a transmission by the same vector. There is, however, the recent report of Albrecht[1] on interference between scrapie and a virus closely related to louping-ill and tick-borne encephalitis. This is the first account of any experimental interaction of scrapie with a known agent. We know that defective particles of an arbovirus may interfere with the complete particle[40] and that even a heat-inactivated arbovirus is still able to induce inter-feron.[18] The viruses of louping-ill and tick-borne en-cephalitis induce antibodies very well and scrapie does not, but would an incomplete particle of those viruses, well covered by a non-foreign material, be recognized as foreign and stimulate antibody production? For our first hypothesis, slow virus-infection as a consequence of the interaction between two closely related virus strains, the viruses of the TBE-complex would be an excellent model. A final story may illustrate the fascination of such speculations upon these matters. Grieg[17] in 1935 pro-duced, together with Gordon, a vaccine against louping-ill, using brain, spinal cord and spleen of infected sheep. Eighteen-thousand sheep were vaccinated. An average of 10 per cent of the vaccinated animals later contracted scrapie, among them sheep of farms where natural scrapie had never been observed before, and sheep of strains but little susceptible to natural scrapie. Greig concluded that scrapie agent was contained in the vaccine, but in terms of our hypothesis one could say that perhaps those animals which had a former contact with the wild virus, contracted scrapie by the interaction of the wild virus antibodies with the vaccine strain of the virus.

The Spread of Scrapie in the Organism

Considering the reports on the spread of scrapie in the organism in natural scrapie and in the experimental disease by peripheral application, we are confronted by a number of fresh problems. We find an early activity in the spleen and lymph nodes on the one hand, a very slow spread along peripheral nerves (Field,[12,17]) and ascending the spinal cord (Eklund et al.[12,17]) on the other hand. In this connection it may be recalled that the first descrip-tion of histological scrapie lesions by Besnoit and Morel[12,17] considered a discrete breakdown of myelin sheaths in the peripheral nerve, more in distal zones rather than close to the spinal roots, as typical as the vacuolization of neurons. Cassirer[12,17] in the same year, confirmed the vacuolization, but he could not detect any changes in the peripheral nerves. Besnoit[17] a year later blamed his particular technique. In France their results were accepted and confirmed, but apparently not else-where. Why should there be this slow involvement of the central nervous system, if spleen and lymph nodes are affected so early? Involvement of the spleen and lymph nodes is a feature which nowadays generally suggests an immune process. Scrapie apparently does not induce

any antibody formation. How does this agent reach the spleen and lymph nodes, if activity in blood and serum can only occasionally be detected, but not regularly so in terms of a viraemia? Are the spleen and lymph nodes in fact the site of primary propagation?[11] The segmental spread along adjacent peripheral nerves, as found in experimental scrapie; the ascending character of the disease, starting generally at the root of the tail in natural scrapie of sheep, suggests that the hind quarter of the animal might be the point of entry in most naturally affected cases. We stated that with vector transmission, the inguinal region could well be the principal site of entrance. With venereal and connatal transmission we argued that the accessory glands of the genital tract and the uterine mucosa might be involved in a scrapie activity, and that if there should actually occur animals in a carrier state without manifest disease-symptoms, this activity must be confined to these genital and perigenital organs. Are they perhaps the organs of primary scrapie growth in natural scrapie? Yet another interesting complex of organ manifestation of scrapie has often been described though rarely appreciated, namely the involve-ment of the endocrine system within the scrapie process. This was an idea held by Oppermann.[17] He initiated the thesis of Weihermüller[17] and was disappointed when this author could not find more lesions than he did. However, there were changes in the thyroid, the adrenal cortex, the pituitary, and the hypothalamus. Minor clinical signs were also present. A transitory period of thirst early in the disease, and later the extreme emaciation, which starts long before the pareses become severe, and which may be explained either as a malabsorption phenomenon or as a syndrome comparable with the Simmonds cachexia of man. Parry[12,17] in his work on the hereditary aspects of scrapie, associated his scrapie-gene with the gene responsible for such features as vigour, appearance, and other characteristics important for breeding, because it was always the best, i.e. strongest animals which were affected with scrapie. German veterinarians almost without exception described this as characteristic of scrapie. In terms of modern medicine these are functions of the endocrine system, including body-strength and sexual activity. Somatotropic and gondatropic effects might be the first clinical signs of scrapie and at times indeed the only signs of the disease. The observations of Beck et al.[12,17] are of particular importance. They found the posterior lobe of the pituitary gland—the storing and release centre—to be devoid of neuro-secretory material. Surprisingly, such material was present in the stalk, and this fact was interpreted as a favourable indication for recovery, even though the animals were in a moribund condition when slaughtered. Possibly some product of the hypothalamus is the material which covers and protects the nucleoprotein of the scrapie particle. The products of the hypothalamus are—it must be borne in mind—furnished as organized droplets which are bound to a small protein molecule, namely neurophysin. They are released from this neurophysin in the posterior lobe of the pituitary. Should an incomplete virus-particle, or a sub-virus, have functional similarities to neurophysin, then such a particle would bind hypothalamic products. Nothing is known for certain on this matter, but should any virus have such properties, it might be expected in the first place to be within an arbovirus, because arboviruses flourish within the nerve-cells of arthropods, and because in anthropods the nervous system and the endocrine system are still undifferentiated. Furthermore, arthropods produce and excrete defensive substances similar to, if not identical with, mammalian hormones (Schildknecht[43]).

The hypothalamic products bound to neurophysin apparently cannot be used by the consumer-cells. This is apparently the function of the hypothalamus itself including the upper stalk. Should such a conjugation occur outside the hypothalamus, there would probably be a lack of the product for the consumer cells as well as a surplus in the blood-stream. This surplus would promptly be removed from the blood, with continuous activity of the blood-cells. The spleen might be the organ, where such a surplus is deposited and destroyed; hence the early intense activity in the spleen. The hypothalamus, on the other hand, would be receiving continuous feed-back signals from the consumer cells. Because the neurosecretory cells apparently produce only one single type of product, an increasing number of cells would be activated in order to produce this single substance, which might be of no essential importance for the organism. However, as a secondary result of such dysfunction, there would be a lack of other hormones and steering substances. This might stimulate the adrenal cortex in its characteristic substitution role, causing hypertrophy. A total breakdown of the whole system follows and the animal perishes in a state of emaciation. Thus, such an event would be due to the bulk of the particles leaving by way of the blood-stream. A secondary effect would be initiated by the particles leaving by way of the smaller nerve-fibres, eventually reaching the lumbo-sacral plexus, later the spinal cord, and eventually the brain. The mechanism would be, in principle, the same, namely deprivation of the last reserves of some hypothalamic substance necessary for the metabolism of neurons. The enlargement of the astrocytes would not then be seen as a benign neoplasia, but rather as an active hypertrophy, due to continuous request-signals proceeding from the affected neuron.

CONCLUSION

It is fascinating to note that throughout the history of studies with scrapie, observers in different countries throughout almost two hundred years, quite independently, have made precisely the same observations, have come to exactly the same conclusions, and have committed at all times just the same errors.

Upon the basis of old, new and quite recent work on slow virus-diseases, a framework of hypotheses has been constructed. Slow virus-infections are regarded as the product of a subsequent infection with two virus strains, which are serologically closely related and which start an infective process in the presence of variably high antibody levels, by strains of the measles virus in SSPE, perhaps by strains of viruses of the tick-borne encephalitis (TBE) complex, a subgroup of viruses in arbovirus group B,

in scrapie and possibly other related diseases. Scrapie was considered to be a natural disease of sheep occurring in two epidemiological forms: the spontaneous type due to vector transmission, and the connatal-venereal type. This latter, connected with a latent and persisting carrier-state, might be autonomous in some flocks where a specially adapted strain of the agent by a continuous chain of venereal and connatal infections in the complete absence of the vector, might simulate a hereditary transmission. Severe epidemic outbreak of the disease may occur by reason of intensive breeding, as in Germany in the early nineteenth century, or through an unusual ingestion of infected material as in the case of TME and perhaps also Kuru. The vectors are presumably ticks or mites, mice being the natural host-reservoir. On account of the feeding habits of the vector, inguinal and perigenital regions of the animal would be the common site of entrance into the organism. As the next step, one of the accessory genital glands or the uterine mucosa becomes infected. These would constitute the organ of primary propagation of the agent. From a functional similarity to neurophysin, the scrapie-subparticle might be capable of binding a hypothalamic product, proceeding to the organ of primary propagation as a steering substance or a prehormone. Covered by this substance, the scrapie-particle would no longer be recognized as a foreign substance, but the organism would register a constant surplus of this material in the blood-stream, owing to feed-back signals from all the consumer cells which are unable to use this substance in the bound form. The surplus in the blood-stream would be removed continuously by way of blood-cells, deposited and destroyed in the spleen. Subsidiary mechanisms would be activated by the organism causing eventually a secondary deficit of other central hormones and which ultimately brings about the death of the organism from inanition. The spread of scrapie from the organ in which it propagates, along the peripheral nerves to the lumbo-sacral plexus, the spinal cord and the brain, would deprive glia and neurons of their last reserves of this same substance. The early involvement of this most sensitive system, would make a neurological symptomatology the most prominent feature of the disease.

This is a logical framework of hypothesis, but still insufficiently supported experimentally. It may be accepted as a demonstration how the facts of scrapie can be variously considered. It must be admitted that even now, too little is known about slow virus-infections.

FURTHER READING

[1] Albrecht, P. (1970), "Immune Status of the Organism during Experimental Scrapie Infection." *Proc. VIth Intern. Congr. Neuropath*, pp. 833–834. Paris: Masson.

[2] Bammer, H. G. and Schenk, K. (1965), "Meningo-Myelo-Radiculitis nach Zeckenbiss mit Erythema chronicum migrans," *Dt. Ztschr. Nervenheilk*, **187**, 25.

[3] Barbanti-Brodano, G., Oyanagi, S., Katz, M and Koprowski, H. (1970), "Presence of Two Different Viral Agents in Brain Cells of Patients with Subacute Sclerosing Panencephalitis," *Proc. Soc. exp. Biol. Med.*, **134**, 230.

[4] Barlow, R. M. and Rennie, J. C. (1970), "Transmission Experiments with a Scrapie-like Encephalopathy of Mink," *J. comp. Path.*, **80**, 75.

[5] Bishop, C. F. (1911), "Notes on a Trypanosome found in a Sheep Tick and its Probable Connection with the Disease known as Louping-ill," *Vet. J.*, **64**, 709.

[6] Brody, J. A., Henle, W. and Koprowski, H. (1967), "Chronic Infectious Neuropathic Agents (CHINA) and other Slow Virus Infections," *Current top. microbiol. immunol.*, p. 40. Berlin–Heidelberg–New York: Springer.

[7] Brownlee, A. (1935), "A Species of Demodex found in Sheep in Britain," *J. comp. Path.*, **48**, 68.

[8] Clarke, M. C. and Haig, D. A. (1970), "Multiplication of Scrapie Agent in Cell Cultures," *Res. vet. Sci.*, **11**, 500.

[9] Clarke, M. C. and Haig, D. A. (1967), "Presence of the Transmissible Agent of Scrapie in the Serum of Affected Mice and Rats," *Vet. rec.*, **80**, 504.

[10] Eckroade, R. J., Zu Rhein, G. M., Marsh, R. F. and Hanson, R. P. (1970) "Transmissible Mink Encephalopathy: Experimental Transmission to the Squirrel Monkey," *Science*, **169**, 1088.

[11] Eklund, C. M. and Hadlow, W. J. (1969), "Pathogenesis of Slow Viral Diseases," *JAVMA*, **155**, 2094.

[12] Field, E. J. (1969), "Slow Virus Infections of the Nervous System," *Int. rev. exp. pathol.*, **8**, 130.

[13] Field, E. J. and Joyce, G. (1970), "Evidence Against Transmission of Scrapie by Animal House Fomites," *Nature*, **226**, 971.

[14] Frank, E. K. (1819), *Gesammelte Erfahrungen über die Traberkrankheit der Schafe. Schriften u. Verh. d. ökon. Ges. i. Königr. Sachsen.* Dresden: Walther.

[15] Gajdusek, D. C. and Alpers, M. P. (1969), *Bibliography of Kuru.* NIH, Bethesda, Md., inoff. print.

[16] Gajdusek, D. C., Gibbs, C. J. and Alpers, M. P. (1965), "Slow, Latent and Temperate Virus Infections," *NINDB Monogr.*, No. 2. PHS 1378. Washington, D.C.: U.S. Gov. Print Off.

[17] Gibbs, C. J., Gajdusek, D. C. and Harvey, J. (1969), Bibliography on Scrapie. *NIH, Bethesda, Md.*, inoff. print.

[18] Goorha, R. M. and Gifford, G. E. (1970), "Interferon Induction by Heat-inactivated Semliki-forest-virus," *Proc. Soc. exp. Biol. Med.*, **134**, 1142.

[19] Henn, R., Müller, W. and Schaltenbrand, G. (1970), "Über eine scrapieähnliche Epizootie der weißen Mäuse und ihre Provokation durch Liquor einer Patientin," *Dt. Ztschr. Nervenheilk*, **197**, 215.

[20] Horta-Barbosa, L., Fuccillo, D. A., Hamilton, R., Traub, R., Ley, A. and Sever, J. L. (1970), "Some Characteristics of SSPE Measles Virus," *Proc. Soc. exp. Biol. Med.*, **134**, 17.

[21] Kanert, (1827), "Beobachtungen, die Ansteckung der sog. Traberkrankheit oder Kreuzdrehe bei den Schafen betreffend," *Möglin'sche Ann. d. Landw.*, **20**, 195.

[22] Katz, M., Rorke, L. B., Masland, W. S., Barbanti-Brodano, G. and Koprowski, H. (1970), "Subacute Sclerosing Panencephalitis: Isolation of a Virus Encephalitogenic for Ferrets," *J. infect. Dis.*, **121**, 188.

[23] Koprowski, H., Barbanti-Brodano, G. and Katz, M. (1970), "Interaction Between Papova-like Virus and Paramyxovirus in Human Brain Cells: A Hypothesis," *Nature*, **225**, 1045.

[24] Latarjet, R., Muel, B., Haig, D. A., Clarke, M. C. and Alper, T. (1970), "Inactivation of the Scrapie Agent by Near Monochromatic Ultraviolet Light," *Nature*, **227**, 1341.

[25] Leopoldt, J. G. (1759), *Nützliche und auf Erfahrung gegründete Einleitung zu der Landwirthschaft.* Berlin, Glogau: Günther.

[26] Libíková, H. and Motajova, M. (1967), "Persistent Infection of a Human Cell Strain with Tick-borne Encephalitis Virus," *Acta virol.*, **11**, 380.

[27] Mayer, V. (1962), "Interaction of Mammalian Cells with Tick-borne Encephalitis Virus. II. Persisting Infection of Cells," *Acta virol.*, **6**, 317.

[28] Mould, D. L. and Dawson, A. McL. (1970), "The Unsuccessful Dialysis of Scrapie Agent from Goat Brain and Spleen," *Res. vet. Sci.*, **11**, 304.

[29] Müller, W. and Hopf, H. Ch. (1967), "Autochthone epidemische Vertigo aus Franken mit Antikörpern gegen das Virus der durch Zecken übertragenen Frühsommer-Meningoencephalitis (FSME-Virus)," *Dt. Ztschr. Nervenheilk*, **190**, 16.

[30] Peters, G. (1970), *Klinische Neuropathologie*, 2. Aufl. Stuttgart: Thieme.

[31] v. Richthofen, A. K. S. (1827), *Die Traberkrankheit der Schafe verglichen mit der sogenannten Schafräucekrankheit.* Breslau: Korn.

[32] Rudolphi, K. A. (1823), "Einige Bemerkungen über die Schafkrankheit, welche das Traben oder Schruckigsein genannt wird," *Möglin'sche Annal. d. Landw.*, **12**, 54.

[33] Rumpelt, G. L. (1776), *Beyträge zu einer Geschichte der Viehsuechen nebst deren Behandlung und Chur. N.d. franz. d. Herrn Paulet.* Dresden: Walther.

[34] Sabin, A. B. (1952), "Research on Dengue during World War II," *Amer. J. trop. Med. Hyg.*, **1**, 30.

[35] Samovich, N. V. (1964), "Circinate erythema in tick-borne encephalitis." (In Russian.) *Sov. Med.*, **3**, 130.

[36] Schilling, M. H. (1821), *James Hogg's, des Ettrik-Schäfers, praktischer Unterricht über die Krankheiten der Schafe, deren Ursachen und zweckmäßige Verhütungsmittel.* Leipzig: Baumgärtner.

[37] Schumacher, H. P. and Albrecht, P. (1970), "Optimal Conditions for Isolation of a Neurotropic Measles Virus from Brain Tissue," *Proc. Soc. exp. Biol. Med.*, **134**, 396.

[38] Seer, H. (1834), *Die Heerdenkrankheiten der Schafe.* Glogau: Fleming.

[39] Sever, J. L. and Zeman, W. (1968), "Conference on Measles Virus and Subacute Sclerosing Panencephalitis," *Neurology*, **18**, 2.

[40] Sreevalsan, T. (1970), "Homologous Viral Interference: Induction by RNA from Defective Particles of Vesicular Stomatitis Virus," *Science*, **169**, 991.

[41] Vernon, M. L., Horta-Barbosa, L., Fuccillo, D. A., Sever, J. L., Baringer, J. R. and Birnbaum, G. (1964), "Virus-like Particles and Nucleoprotein-like Filaments in Brain Tissue from Two Patients with Creutzfeld-Jakob-disease," *Lancet*, **1**, 1970.

[42] Zu Rhein, G. M. and Chou, S. M. (1965), "Particles Resembling Papova Viruses in Human Cerebral Demyelinating Disease." *Science*, **148**, 1477–1479.

[43] Schildknecht, H., Birringer, H. and Maschwitz, U. (1967), "Testosterone as Protective Agent of the Water Beetle Ilybius," *Ang. Chemie.* (Intern. edition), **6**, 558.

4. SPINAL DYSRAPHISM

L. P. LASSMAN

The congenital spinal disorders of the central nervous system result from developmental errors during and following closure of the neural tube in the early weeks of gestation. These anomalies may be grouped together under the heading *spinal dysraphism*; this includes all forms of congenital abnormality occurring in the midline of the back, from uncomplicated abnormalities of the skin associated with spina bifida occulta to pre-vertebral mediastinal or mesenteric cysts, and the lesions may affect the skin of the back, the spinal column, the spinal nerve roots and the gut. Spina bifida is the commonest manifestation and can conveniently be divided into two varieties, spina bifida aperta, the undisguised lesion which is apparent on the day of birth, and spina bifida occulta, the hidden malformation which is far commoner and often not of clinical significance. There are some cases of spina bifida occulta in which the developmental error is not only in the skeleton but also in the surrounding tissues and because of this the spinal cord and cauda equina may be involved. The congenital spinal anomalies are:

(1) Meningocoele and myelomeningocoele—*spina bifida aperta.*

(2) Lesions which may be found in association with *spina bifida occulta*

    (i) Cauda equina adhesions.
    (ii) Dermal sinus.
    (iii) Dermoid cyst.
    (iv) Diastematomyelia.
    (v) Ectopic dorsal nerve roots.
    (vi) Localized angioma of the spinal cord.
    (vii) Neurenteric cyst.
    (viii) Subcutaneous lumbosacral lipoma.

These abnormalities are capable of producing a neurological deficit of varying degrees of severity and surgical treatment at the correct time may either prevent damage to the spinal cord and its nerve roots, or give rise to improvement and even cure in many of the cases.

SPINA BIFIDA APERTA

The lesions in spina bifida aperta may vary considerably from a small parchment-like membrane on the back of a baby without neurological deficit to a large myelomeningocoele occupying several segments and causing complete loss of nervous function in the lower limbs and sphincters. The myelomeningocoele which occurs in the cervical or thoracic regions is usually small, has a narrow neck and seldom contains important nervous tissue.

From the surgical point of view the commonest and most important lesion is the myelomeningocoele in the napkin area. In many of these cases the nerve roots of the cauda equina are adherent to the inner surface of the sac of the myelomeningocoele, causing a loss of distal nervous function of varying degree. It has been advocated that all children suffering from myelomeningocoele should be operated on within the first 24 hr. of life. Recently there has been a change in opinion and most neurosurgeons now agree that this is the optimum time for operation, but that surgery should not be advised in every case. There are cases which are inoperable because of an enormous wide lesion involving many spinal segments and others which should not be considered for surgery for a variety of reasons, particularly those with severe kyphosis or with complete paralysis of the lower limbs and non-functioning hip flexors. In the rare case in which a child in this group survives and appears to develop satisfactorily, apart from the paraplegia, the myelomeningocoele may be excised later to facilitate the nursing, orthopaedic and other methods of treatment used in the rehabilitation of the child.

Before these babies were operated on within the first 24 hr. of life, over 90 per cent died within 6 months of meningitis, progressive hydrocephalus or the complications of paraplegia.

One of the most important complications of myelomeningocoele is hydrocephalus resulting from abnormalities of the circulation of cerebrospinal fluid due to developmental malformation of the hind brain. This anomaly is found in almost every case of myelomeningocoele and is known as the Arnold-Chiari malformation. There is inferior displacement of the cerebellar tonsils through the foramen magnum into the cervical vertebral canal associated with elongation, distortion and inferior displacement of the medulla oblongata and fourth ventricle. There are also dense adhesions which give rise to partial or total obliteration of the cisterna magna and surface subarachnoid pathways of the upper cervical spinal cord.

The development of methods to control hydrocephalus has completely altered the prognosis and, now that meningitis can be easily controlled by antibiotics and early operation, more attention is being devoted to the limb paralysis and limb deformity. It is unlikely that any cases of lower limb paralysis will improve after operation, but in some cases failure to repair the defect at a sufficiently early time will result in increased lower limb paralysis due to drying of the exposed neural tissue. Provided that the myelomeningocoele is closed within the first 24 hr. of life, a large percentage of the babies will survive and if the cases are chosen carefully prior to operation, the children who survive should be able to enjoy a life of reasonable quality. It is surprising how many of these children can be made to walk with or without splintage and there is no doubt that those children who are not paralysed above the knees will walk fairly satisfactorily. In the myelomeningocoeles that have been operated on, paralysis of the bladder and cystitis is very common and therefore investigation from this point of view is essential in the neonatal period, for only careful and continued treatment will avoid the complications of hydronephrosis and chronic bladder infection. Often complete social independence in boys can be achieved by conservative management and the use of the "Downs" male pubic pressure urinal with transverse rubber bag, but in girls ileal or colonic conduit or ureterostomy operations may be necessary. Sometimes a type of automatic bladder will develop, but in any case incontinence is now manageable and will not prevent employment. Research into the electrical control of the bladder continues and eventually this is likely to prove successful and the management of urinary incontinence will become much easier. On rare occasions some of the lesions found in spina bifida occulta do complicate a myelomeningocoele, the commonest being a bone septum associated with diastematomyelia, and some of these lesions can be easily dealt with at the time of the primary operation.

SPINA BIFIDA OCCULTA

The occult form of spinal dysraphism, which is due to incomplete fusion of the embryo in the median-dorsal region, is a bony defect of the spine in which there is no visible exposure of meninges or spinal cord.

In association with it, a syndrome has been described of progressive muscular imbalance and neurological deficit resulting in foot deformity, paresis and in some cases trophic ulceration and incontinence. The lesions are due to extrinsic abnormalities of developmental origin affecting the spinal cord and spinal nerve roots and the syndrome occurs not only in spina bifida occulta, but also in the myelomeningocoele which in many respects is a similar lesion. The main difference is that in spina bifida occulta the neurological deficit, in the majority of cases, comes on after birth and may be steadily progressive. These extrinsic abnormalities that affect the spinal cord are the fibrosed remains of embryonic tissues which are frustrated and fail to develop completely in a normal fashion. The lesions produce their effects gradually by increasingly interfering with nerve conduction, cell function and blood supply or drainage, so that at first only minor effects occur. Later on as the interference increases, the effects become more widespread and severe and only for a time may the tissue damage be repairable, allowing function to recover if the noxious factor is removed. There is a stage beyond this where the nervous tissues are incapable of recovery and, because of this, surgical treatment is undertaken with the intention of preventing further clinical deterioration. Cessation of neurological deterioration assists the treatment of foot and limb deformity in that relapse is unlikely and orthopaedic surgery is successful in the first instance and will not need to be repeated.

The Clinical Syndrome

The patients present for one or more of the following reasons and spina bifida occulta is always present:

(1) External manifestations on the back in the form of lesions of the skin and blood vessels.
(2) An orthopaedic syndrome—e.g. progressive unilateral pes cavo-varus, or paralytic valgus.
(3) An increasing neurological deficit in one or both lower limbs, with or without trophic ulceration.
(4) A neurogenic bladder.

At their worst, the effects of the extrinsic spinal cord anomalies are the same as those seen in cases of spina bifida aperta—paraplegia with incontinence, loss of lower limb and buttock sensation, deformed and paralytic feet and trophic ulcers, although few children or adults progress to this severe degree. In fact, the clinical manifestations of spina bifida occulta are those that occur in spina bifida aperta, with the differences that in the latter condition the process is much more rapid, more severe, and for the most part occurs before birth. Occulta and aperta are basically the same anatomical defect in lesser or greater degree. Other cases present with disorders of the bladder and rectum, which may be there at birth or may not appear until later. The commonest mode of presentation is with the orthopaedic syndrome, starting with an established, but slight cavo-varus deformity of one foot. The affected leg is slightly shorter than the other. The parents complain that the child walks in an odd manner and twists the forepart of his shoe. There may already be changes in the tendon reflexes and possibly trophic ulceration. In time this cavo-varus foot may develop a paralytic valgus deformity and the other limb may also become involved.

The onset of abnormality of one foot may be at any age; some children are born with the early evidence. The commonest age of onset seems to be between four and six years. If the first symptom appears in adult life, it is usually incontinence and there is no abnormality of the lower limbs.

Examination of the Nervous System may show no abnormality of reflexes to begin with, although foot deformity is already established. The lower limb reflexes change as time passes, the ankle jerks and knee jerks may be absent and the plantar responses become extensor. There may be mild spasticity of the affected limb. Sensory changes occur, but in very young children they are difficult to detect and are unreliable unless there is trophic ulceration. It is important to examine the perianal area and the saddle area on the buttocks; changes of sensibility in this region are more easily detected than elsewhere.

Lesions of the Skin and Blood-Vessels. Dysraphic lesions of the skin and blood-vessels on the back are frequently, but not by any means always, present in these cases and give a clear indication of the existence of an underlying bone abnormality. These lesions are:

(a) Abnormal hair on the back, in some cases resembling a horse's tail.

(b) A superficial skin naevus.

(c) A dimple or dimples over the sacrum or near the mid-line higher up, amounting in some cases to a sinus. These dimples are occasionally surrounded by an area of darkly pigmented skin.

(d) A lipoma in the subcutaneous tissues, which is commonly dome-shaped.

All these external cutaneous manifestations may be present together, in combination with each other, or singly. The dermal sinus is important in infants since there may be a deep connection communicating with the subarachnoid space and however minute this channel, organisms can penetrate down it and cause recurrent attacks of meningitis. Lumbosacral lipomas are sometimes mistaken for teratomas and, since they are nearly always attached to the spinal cord or conus medullaris by a fatty fibrous band, are better explored right down to their attachment and removed as a preventive operation. The deep fibrous extension has been the cause of the orthopaedic syndrome in a number of children and can produce bladder symptoms in adults. Very occasionally a bone septum in diastematomyelia is found in association with a lumbosacral lipoma.

Investigations

(1) **Plain X-rays.** In every case spina bifida will be shown on radiological examination. If the lesion found is only a split in the spinous process of the first piece of the sacrum, this is unlikely to be associated with a surgically treatable spinal cord lesion and can be ignored.

(2) **Myelography.** Myodil, Pantopaque or air may be used in this investigation, but it has been found that Myodil gives very satisfactory information and it is usually introduced by the cisternal route with the patient under general anaesthesia. This route of administration is preferred to the lumbar route because in most of the cases the conus medullaris can be expected to lie at a very low level in the vertebral canal and the spinal cord could be damaged by insertion of the lumbar puncture needle. In addition, in cases where the Myodil is introduced by the lumbar route, some of it may leak outside the arachnoid mater and obscure detail in subsequent screening. If this happens the patient will have to be submitted to another examination later on. Myodil escaping outside the arachnoid after cisternal puncture is unlikely to interfere with the radiological examination. An important technique has been developed for demonstrating the level of the conus medullaris and when in the absence of any demonstrable lesion the conus lies lower than the third lumbar vertebra, it has been found that there will be a lesion in the region of the conus and cauda equina.

The Lesions

Diastematomyelia. In the last few years a considerable amount of attention has been paid to diastematomyelia—a bifid state of the spinal cord of developmental origin. This is only one of several congenital anomalies of the spinal cord and its coverings which produce similar clinical findings. It should be emphasized that where diastematomyelia is suspected and not found by radiological methods, other congenital anomalies affecting the spinal cord must be sought.

In diastematomyelia there may or may not be a septum passing dorso-ventrally between the two halves of the spinal cord. This septum may be fibrous, cartilaginous or osseous. The bifid cord is not by itself the cause of symptoms; they are produced by the septum or other associated lesion.

The lesions affecting the spinal cord are extrinsic and for general purposes can be classified in three groups according to their supposed mode of action.

Lesions Causing Traction. These are the commonest and the spinal cord becomes tethered to the subcutaneous tissues, to the vertebral column or to the dura mater. The tethering agent may be an ectopic posterior nerve root, arachnoid adhesions, fatty fibrous adhesions, an abnormally developed filum terminale presenting as a fibrous band attached in an abnormal position, or a fibrous band passing through to the subcutaneous tissues. A septum associated with diastematomyelia may also produce a traction lesion.

Lesions Causing Pressure. These may be: transverse bands of ligamentous origin, usually extradural; inverted laminae, intrathecal lipoma, fatty fibrous tissue associated with defective neural arches, either intrathecal or extradural or both; intrathecal dermoid cysts, or neurofibromata. Septa associated with diastematomyelia may also cause pressure.

Lesions Causing Traction and Pressure. These may be any of the above in combination. They may act together at the same time or either the pressure or traction effect may be exerted separately at different times. It is often impossible to decide which is the cause of the damage.

Selection of Cases for Operation

In selecting cases, three criteria have been laid down, without which a surgically treatable abnormality is unlikely to be found. There must be: abnormality of gait and deformity of the foot, unilateral or bilateral, which is either progressive or associated with neurological deficit, or a neurogenic incontinence; radiological evidence of laminal defects of a greater degree than only of S1; and myelographic evidence of abnormality or a low-placed conus medullaris.

There are two exceptional types of case outside these criteria—those with a discharging sinus or fistula on the back, all of which run the risk of recurrent meningitis, and those cases with a lumbosacral lipomatous swelling, the majority of which have a direct connection from the subcutaneous tissues to the spinal cord. The second group of cases should be operated on as a preventive measure provided that the operation includes an exploration of the spinal cord at the same time as the removal of the lipoma. The lipoma must not be removed superficially without this deep exploration.

Treatment

Treatment consists of laminectomy, exposure and opening of the dura mater, and exploration of the spinal cord. Lesions preventing or likely to prevent movement of the spinal cord or causing pressure are removed. The old notion of a tight filum terminale has a basis of truth, and exploration in the lumbosacral region should include examination of this structure. The dura mater must be opened in every case; many extradural lesions are found and the majority of them continue within the theca; these must be removed and the spinal cord be seen to have no tethering agent.

The operation is undertaken with the chief object of preventing deterioration and there is no mortality. After operation 40 per cent are improved, 15 per cent possibly improved and the remainder are unchanged. Not more than 1 per cent are made worse.

It is believed that laminectomy is justified in all the cases which fulfil the three criteria for operation but it is impossible to determine which of these cases will not benefit. In a series of over 200 cases the symptom least likely to be improved was incontinence that was known to have been present from birth.

For success in the operative treatment of cases of occult spinal dysraphism, the diagnosis must be made before irreversible changes have occurred in the spinal cord or cauda equina and neurological surgeons will not see these cases early enough unless the diagnosis is made by the neurologist, paediatrician or orthopaedic surgeon. With wide experience, preventive operation is sometimes indicated in some patients who simply have external cutaneous manifestations on the back, but the incidental finding of diastematomyelia with a bony septum may not by itself be an indication for operation, although very careful and frequent follow-up of these cases is necessary. Deformity of a foot or feet of neurological origin may cease to progress after operation, but where a neurological lesion is not acting a foot deformity in a young child may progress during growth because the bones of the feet are already deformed. This does not happen in older children. In some cases the deformity before operation is so marked that local treatment is necessary later, but in other cases with a small degree of deformity improvement has taken place after operation and further local treatment then becomes unnecessary.

FURTHER READING

(1) Spina Bifida Aperta

Guthkelch, A. N. (1965), "Thoughts on the Surgical Management of Spina Bifida Cystica," *Acta neurochir. (Wien)*, **13**, 407.

Hemmer, R. (1969), *Dringliche chirurgische Eingriffe an Gehun, Rückenmark und Schädel im frühen Säuglingsalter*, p. 50. Stuttgart: Ferdinand Enke Verlag.

Laurence, K. M. (1964), "The Natural History of Spina Bifida Cystica," *Arch. Dis. Childh.*, **39**, 41.

Mawdsley, T. and Rickham, P. P. (1969), "Further Follow-up Study of Early Operation for Open Myelomeningocele," *Develop. Med. Child Neurol.*, Supplement No. 20, 8.

Sharrard, W. J. W., Zachary, R. B., Lorber, J. and Bruce, A. M. (1963), "A Controlled Trial of Immediate and Delayed Closure of Spina Bifida Cystica," *Arch. Dis. Childh.*, **38**, 18.

Schulman, K. and Ames, M. D. (1968), "Intensive Treatment of 50 Children Born with Myelomeningocele," *N.Y.J. Med.*, **68**, 2656.

(2) Spina Bifida Occulta

Bentley, J. F. R. and Smith, J. R. (1960), "Developmental Posterior Enteric Remnants and Spinal Malformations," *Arch. Dis. Childh.*, **35**, 76.

Gryspeerdt, G. L. (1963), "Myelographic Assessment of Occult Forms of Spinal Dysraphism," *Acta Radiol.*, **1**, 702.

James, C. C. M. and Lassman, L. P. (1960), "Spinal Dysraphism. An Orthopaedic Syndrome in Children Accompanying Occult Forms," *Arch. Dis. Childh.*, **35**, 315.

James, C. C. M. and Lassman, L. P. (1962), "Spinal Dysraphism. The Diagnosis and Treatment of Progressive Lesions in Spina Bifida Occulta," *J. Bone Jt Surg.*, **44B**, 828.

James, C. C. M. and Lassman, L. P. (1964), "Diastematomyelia. A Critical Survey of 24 Cases Submitted to Laminectomy," *Arch. Dis. Childh.*, **39**, 125.

James, C. C. M. and Lassman, L. P. (1967), "Results of Treatment of Progressive Lesions in Spina Bifida Occulta Five to Ten Years after Laminectomy," *Lancet*, **2**, 1277.

Lassman, L. P. and James, C. C. M. (1963), "Lumbosacral Lipomata and Lesions of the Conus Medullaris and Cauda Equina," *Excerpta med. (Amst.)*, p. 139. Int. Cong. Series, No. 60.

Lassman, L. P. and James, C. C. M. (1964), "Spina Bifida Cystica and Occulta; Some Aspects of Spinal Dysraphism," *Paraplegia*, **2**, 96.

Lassman, L. P. and James, C. C. M. (1967), "Lumbosacral Lipomas. Critical Survey of 26 cases submitted to Laminectomy," *J. Neurol. Neurosurg. Psychiat.*, **30**, 174.

Lichtenstein, B. W. (1940), " 'Spinal Dysraphism.' Spina Bifida and Myelodysplasia." *Arch. Neurol. Psychiat. (Chicago)*, **44**, 792.

Schlegel, M. F. (1964), "Spina Bifida Occulta und Klauenhohlfuss, *Ergeb. Chir. u Orthopädie*, **46**, 268.

Till, K. (1965), "Spinal Dysraphism," *Turkish Journal of Pediatrics*, **7**, 3.

Till, K. (1969), "Spinal Dysraphism. A Study of Congenital Malformations of the Lower Back," *J. Bone Jt Surg.*, **51B**, 415.

5. CRANIO–VERTEBRAL ANOMALIES

ARNOLD APPLEBY

The developmental anomalies found in the region of the foramen magnum and upper cervical spine may be skeletal, confined to the neural tissues, or a combination of both. The extent of the neurological signs and the amount of disability are often unrelated to the extent or even the presence of bony abnormalities. It is not uncommon to discover congenital abnormalities in the cervical spine of symptomless patients who have been X-rayed because of trauma. Conversely, patients presenting with a neurological disorder suggestive of a lesion of the foramen magnum show no bony abnormality in approximately 50 per cent of cases. Rarely, a patient with quite gross bony anomalies and neurological symptoms and signs will be found to have an entirely different cause for the neurological abnormality (*see* Fig. 1). Furthermore, neural anomalies in the cranio-vertebral junction quite often do not produce symptoms until the second,

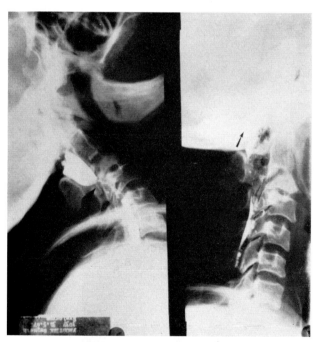

FIG. 1. Myelogram films, prone on the left and supine on the right, of a patient with occipito-vertebral fusion and fusion of C2 and C3. The supine myelogram shows that there is no tonsillar ectopia (arrow), but there is a block due to spondylosis in the prone film.

third and even fourth decades. When, however, the symtoms develop they tend to be progressive and may even prove fatal.

Depending upon the type and the severity of the anomaly concerned, the symptoms have been at various times attributed to:

(1) Constriction of the neural tissues in the region of the foramen magnum due to a tight foramen, basilar invagination or due to intermittent pressure from congenital atlanto-axial subluxation.

(2) Interference with the egress of cerebro-spinal fluid from the foramen of Magendie due to failure of perforation of the rhombic roof resulting in the transmission of the cerebro-spinal fluid pulse wave into the central canal of the spinal cord causing hydromyelia. Gardner (1965) postulated that most, if not all cases of syringomyelia are the result of long standing hydromyelia. The syrinx, unconnected with the obliterated adult central canal is he thinks developed from a breach of the ependyma and lateral dissection of the wall of the canal by the pulsating fluid, the cavity so formed being later isolated by gliosis and developing the histological features of "syringomyelia".

(3) Interference with the blood-supply to the neural tissue in the region of the cranio-vertebral junction.

(4) The development of arachnoiditis and arachnoidal adhesions in the posterior fossa. In the experimental animal, sealing off of the outlets of the fourth ventricle following the introduction of chemical irritants is followed by acute hydrocephalus and syringomyelia. In man distension of the central canal by cerebro-spinal fluid has been shown when the foramen of Magendie has been obstructed by arachnoiditis following meningitis.

(5) Increased intraventricular pressure causing hydrocephalus.

It is likely that the exact causative mechanism varies from patient to patient and depends upon the exact anatomical situation which applies, together with a variable patient-response to the anatomical situation. Such factors as whether there is interference with the blood-supply to the cord, and whether arachnoid adhesions form, probably exert a secondary effect on the course of the disease.

The neurological symptoms may be mistaken for multiple sclerosis, cerebellar tumour, tumour in the upper cervical region, or hydrocephalus. The commonest presentation is that of syringomyelia with some atypical features. A dissociated anaesthesia is often present but in addition to the sensory abnormality, weakness, wasting and reflex change are often present. Thus, because of the common finding of cyst-formation in the upper thoracic region the patient presents with wasting of the hand and development of claw hands. Posterior column sensory abnormality, pain in the back of the neck, cough, headache and drop attacks also may occur.

The variability of the presence of plain radiological signs, the variability of the clinical picture and the fact that these patients can be helped by posterior fossa decompression combine to encourage the neurologist to seek contrast radiological studies to try and arrive at a definitive anatomical diagnosis.

The methods of radiological investigation available are: (1) Routine plain films of skull and cervical spine; (2) Tomography in the coronal and sagittal planes of the cranio-vertebral junction; (3) Positive contrast myelography using myodil (pantopaque) in the supine as well as the prone position; (4) Air encephalography with particular reference to the foramen magnum region; (5) Vertebral angiography; and (6) Ventriculography.

The commonest method of radiological contrast examination is by myelography. Since the true diagnosis can be unsuspected clinically it behoves the neuroradiologist to be aware of the clinical difficulties involved and to be alert to the possibility of congenital anomalies when performing any investigation involving examination of the foramen magnum or upper cervical region.

RADIOLOGICAL FINDINGS

The bony anomalies of the upper cervical and cranio-vertebral regions have been well documented[12] and these may include:

(1) Occipitalization of the atlas. The synostosis may affect the anterior arch, the posterior arch, either lateral mass or a combination of two or more of these sites.

(2) Fusion of the cervical vertebrae. This may occur at any level but is commonest at C2/3.

(3) Anomalies of development of the odontoid. These vary from complete absence to various abnormalities of ossification including a failure of the odontoid to fuse with the body of C2. Such anomalies allow abnormal mobility at C1/2 sometimes amounting to atlanto-axial subluxation, which can readily be demonstrated by taking films in flexion and extension.

(4) Basilar invagination. This abnormality may be present as a primary defect in a proportion of cases and even when this is not apparent on measurement, the angle between the line of the cervical vertebra and the occipital bone may be abnormally acute. Even in the presence of marked bony anomalies the basal angle is usually normal and therefore the presence or absence of platybasia is of little value in the diagnosis of craniovertebral anomalies. (*See* Fig. 2.)

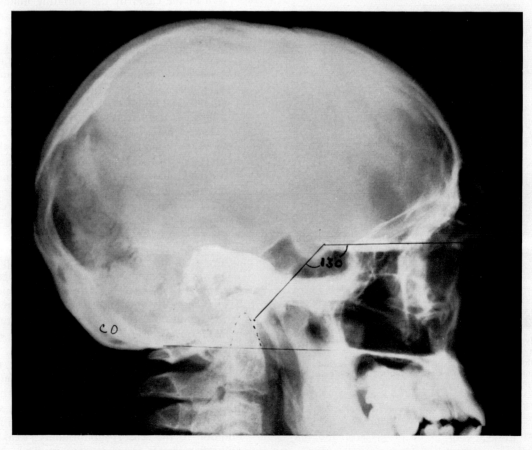

FIG. 2. Patient with basilar invagination and an abnormally shaped clivus but a normal basal angle.

(5) Hydrocephalus. Changes due to arrested or compensated hydrocephalus are apparent in approximately a quarter of cases.

(6) Increased sagittal diameter of the cervical spinal canal. The sagittal diameter of the cervical canal is increased in approximately 50 per cent of cases and tends to occur particularly in those patients whose symptoms began early (Wells, Spillane and Bly[3]).

Radiological Contrast Studies

Supine Myelography may show evidence of descent of some part of the hind-brain, the commonest single abnormality being a variable degree of cerebellar tonsillar ectopia. This produces a filling defect in the lateral view which in the PA view is shown to be bi-lobed in outline. (*See* Fig. 4.)

Occasionally myodil will enter the fourth ventricle which may be shown to be lying at an abnormally low level.

Disintegration of the myodil column and failure to fill the cisterna magna during supine myelography is suggestive of the presence of arachnoiditis. In such cases it is usually difficult and often impossible to decide whether the arachnoiditis is caused by or even accompanied by tonsillar ectopia. (*See* Fig. 7.)

Air Myelography or Encephalography. The use of air as a contrast medium for this purpose is uncommon but Gardner (1965) and Conway (1967) have described the paradoxical findings that during lumbar air encephalography in the erect position the shadow of the spinal cord is narrow.

This may be due to a change in shape of the syrinx, due to the effect of gravity, or to a more complex chain of events put forward by Conway. His explanation is that during the exchange of air and fluid in the erect position, fluid is withdrawn from the surface of the hemispheres and the ventricles expand. Because of the partial obstruction of the outlet of the fourth ventricle, air cannot readily enter, so the expansion of the ventricular system aspirates fluid from the syrinx.

Vertebral Angiography. This examination is rarely carried out, but when performed it usually shows a low caudal loop of the posterior inferior cerebellar artery. This loop is presumably carried down around the ectopic cerebellar tonsils.

RESULTS AND MANAGEMENT

In his original account Chiari (1891) divided hind brain anomalies into four types: (1) Variable displacement of the cerebellar tonsils into the upper cervical canal, unaccompanied by caudal dislocation of the medulla; (2) Variable displacement of the inferior vermis of the cerebellum into the upper cervical canal accompanied by caudal displacement of the lower pons and medulla together with an elongated fourth ventricle; (3) Downward displacement of the medulla with herniation of the cerebellum into a high cervical meningocoele; and (4) Hypoplasia of the cerebellum.

Arnold and his colleagues found that the Chiari type-2 anomaly was invariably associated with spina bifida, and

subsequently it was suggested that this anomaly should be called the Arnold–Chiari malformation. The other three types of Chiari anomalies may not however be associated with skeletal anomalies.

Fifty-nine patients presenting with some form of foramen magnum syndrome have been examined at Newcastle General Hospital during the past seven years. Of these forty-five showed some form of Chiari anomaly, nine had changes suggesting severe arachnoiditis in the region of the foramen magnum, two showed dilatation of the cervical cord without evidence of cerebellar ectopia and three were considered to be completely normal radiologically.

SURGICAL FINDINGS AND RESULTS OF OPERATION

In all, fifty-two cases have been submitted to posterior fossa decompression and high cervical laminectomy. The region of the foramen magnum has been explored and the ectopic tonsils decompressed. No effort was made to uncover the syrinx completely but in most cases its upper pole was visualized.

Except in the eight cases of arachnoiditis the tonsils were lying below the level of the foramen magnum, the amount of tonsillar descent varying from 5 mm. to 3 cm. (*See* Figs. 3 and 4.)

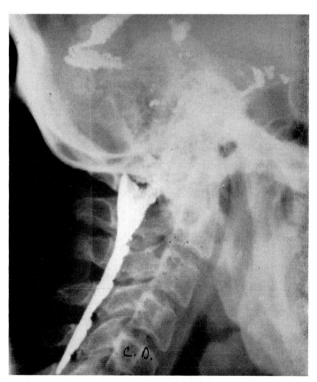

Fig. 3. Supine myelogram of the same patient as Fig. 2, showing cerebellar tonsillar ectopia.

In those cases with arachnoiditis there was difficulty in opening the dura and more particularly in separating the tonsils from each other and from the medulla. The adhesions were extremely vascular and appeared to obliterate the foramen of Magendie. Of the eight cases of

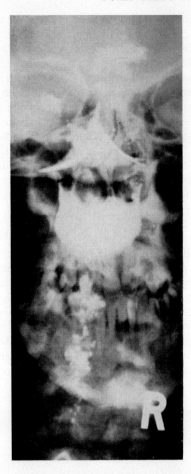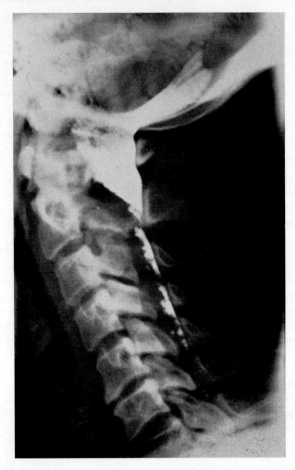

FIG. 4. Postero-anterior and lateral supine myelogram showing tonsillar ectopia, larger on the left side.

arachnoiditis five were thought to have normally placed tonsils and three showed herniation through the foramen magnum.

In the absence of arachnoiditis the foramen of Magendie was found to be occluded by a fine membrane in eight cases. When this was divided a free pulsatile flow of clear cerebro-spinal fluid took place. In all the other patients the foramen appeared to be obliterated by compression from the ectopic cerebellar tonsils and there was a similar flow of cerebro-spinal fluid when they were separated.

In thirty-one patients the opening of the central canal was seen in the floor of the fourth ventricle (see Fig. 6). When seen, this was occluded by a small piece of muscle as suggested by Gardner (1965). In our series of forty-five operations there were no operative or post-operative deaths. A woman of fifty-five at the time of the operation died eighteen months later from acute myeloid leukemia after steady improvement in her neurological state. A male of thirty-six rapidly improved after operation with regard to walking and the use of his right hand; after eighteen months he failed to return to the clinic, and died from severe chronic bronchitis five years after operation. Two patients with chronic arachnoiditis developed post-

operative hydrocephalus requiring drainage operation. Those cases with arachnoiditis appeared to show less improvement and in fact, sometimes deteriorated. Overall the results are that thirty-eight patients showed immediate improvement in neurological deficit on examination, five improved gradually as judged by follow-up of one to two years. Nine patients gained no benefit from operation and three of these suffered serious worsening with no significant recovery. Thermal appreciation joint position sense and ataxia have been particularly improved.

Four cases sufficiently incapacitated to justify surgical treatment have now no neurological deficit. The follow-up on our patients has been between six months and eight and a half years and may not be adequate in a disease of such chronicity. If we extrapolate from Gardner's experience it seems probable that 50 per cent of a group of syringo-myelic patients presenting with a wide spectrum of disability and with radiological evidence of tonsillar herniation will gain significant long-term improvement following posterior fossa decompression. The numerically much smaller problem of arachnoiditis should be considered separately and may well be best treated with ventricular drainage rather than posterior fossa decompression or possibly a combination of both procedures.

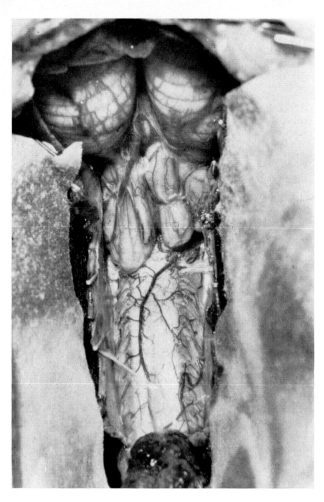

FIG. 5. Same patient as Fig. 4. Occipital bone removed showing elongated low-lying tonsils, the left being the larger.

FIG. 6. Same patient as Figs. 4 and 5. Tonsils separated and a probe in the opening of the central canal of the cord.

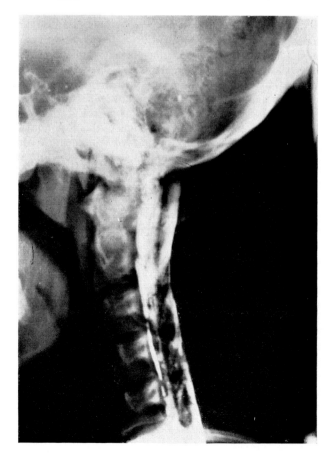

FIG. 7. Supine myelogram showing obstruction to myodil in a patient with arachnoiditis.

FURTHER READING

1 Appleby, A., Foster, J. B., Hankinson, J. and Hudgson, P. (1968), *Brain*, **91**, 131.
2 Appleby, A., Bradley, W. G., Foster, J. B., Hankinson, J. and Hudgson, P. (1969), *J. Neurol. Sci.*, **8**, 451.
3 Chiari, H. (1891), *Dt. med. Wchnschr.*, **27**, 1172.
4 Chiari, H. (1895), *Denkschr. Adad. Wissensch. Wiern. Mathaturw.*, Kl.63, 71.
5 Conway, L. W. (1967), *J. Neurosurg.*, **27**, 501.
6 Gardner, W. J. (1965), *J. Neurol. Neurosurg. Psychiat.*, **28**, 247.

7 Gardner, W. J., Abdullah, A. F. and McCormack, L. J. (1957), *J. Neurosurg.*, **14**, 591.
8 Gardner, W. J. and Angel, J. (1959), *Clin. Neurosurg.*, **6**, 131.
9 Gardner, W. J. and Goodall, R. J. (1950), *J. Neurosurg.*, **7**, 199.
10 Gardner, W. J., Karnosh, L. J. and Angel, J. (1957), *Trans. Amer. neurol. Ass.*, p. 144.
11 McLaurin, R. L., Bailey, O. T., Schurr, P. H. and Ingraham, F. D. (1954), "Myelomalacia and Multiple Cavitations of Spinal Cord Secondary to Adhesive Arachnoiditis. An Experimental Study," *Arch. Pathol.*, **57**, 138.
12 Spillane, J. D., Pallis, C. and Jones, A. M. (1957), *Brain*, **80**, 11.
13 Wells, C. E., Spillane, J. D. and Bligh, A. S. (1959), *Brain*, **82**, 23.

6. THE PATHOLOGY OF BLUNT HEAD INJURIES

HUME ADAMS AND D. I. GRAHAM

In the United Kingdom, trauma is responsible for more deaths in all age groups under 45 than any other single cause, while head injury has been shown to be the single most important factor in deaths due to trauma.[1] In England and Wales alone, with a population of 48·9 million, just over 100,000 patients are *admitted to hospital* every year as a result of a head injury,[31] and the total annual number of *deaths* attributable to head injury, with or without a fracture of the skull, is over 9,000.[30] These facts, coupled with the observation that about 500 people are discharged from hospital every year so severely disabled as a result of a head injury that they will never work again[22] makes it very clear that head injury is responsible for a tragic loss of human resources.

It is unlikely that severe and irreversible brain damage directly attributable to a head injury will ever yield to treatment but it is a fundamental principle that, in many patients, only part of the brain damage is due directly to impact. Indeed the activist philosophy in the management of head-injured patients is based on the knowledge that delayed brain damage frequently occurs as a result of events initiated by the impact, and that some of this is potentially preventable. Brain damage of delayed type is most often due to an intracranial expanding lesion, distortion and herniation of the brain, and raised intracranial pressure. It may be contributed to or even precipitated by systemic factors which either reduce the supply of oxygen to the brain, e.g. blood loss, hypotension or hypoxaemia, or increase the intracranial pressure, e.g. hypoxia, hypercapnia or volatile anaesthetic agents. Thus the pathogenesis of brain damage due to head injury is complex and the clinical spectrum of fatal cases wide. Some patients, because of severe impact injury, remain unresponsive until death which may occur within hours of the injury or be delayed for up to a year or more. Others, who might appropriately be referred to as "talk and die" injuries, are conscious and rational a short time after the injury only to deteriorate and die later as a result of delayed brain damage.

Despite the many detailed investigations that have already been undertaken into the pathology of blunt head injuries, many questions remain unanswered. One reason for this is that the events initiated by a head injury form part of a dynamic and sequential process with the result that the pathologist often finds it curiously difficult to reconstruct the events leading to a fatal outcome. He is also largely limited to the study of fatal head injuries, as only occasionally does he have the opportunity of examining the brain of a head-injured patient who has died of an unrelated cause. A further factor is that certain processes, e.g. Wallerian degeneration in nerve fibres ruptured at the time of impact, take several weeks to become apparent: if the patient dies sooner than this, it may be impossible to detect what may be the principal pathological lesion in the brain. More recently the advent of intensive therapy units has produced a new phenomenon, viz. progressive autolysis of the brain, which occurs when a patient has been maintained on artificial ventilation for several days. These, therefore, are some of the limitations with which the pathologist has to contend when attempting to contribute to the clinico-pathological correlations in a patient who has died as a result of a head injury. The situation is even more difficult if the brain has been sectioned unfixed in an attempt to provide a rapid report, e.g. for forensic purposes. Even an experienced neuropathologist, after dissecting a properly fixed brain, may have difficulty in establishing the precise cause of death: indeed the brain on occasions may appear normal on macroscopic examination. Because of our interest in the pathology of blunt head injuries, we have routinely undertaken a comprehensive histological study of large celloidin sections of brain, frozen sections, and serial blocks of brain stem from such cases. In our experience 30μ celloidin sections are both less prone to technical artefact than paraffin sections, and are more reliable in the identification of the distribution of histological abnormalities such as ischaemic brain damage, loss of nerve cells, and gliosis.

The account which follows is based both on the consensus of current concepts on the pathology of blunt head injuries and on our personal experience with some 400 fatal head injuries. It will also incorporate some preliminary results of an investigation we are undertaking in the Institute of Neurological Sciences on a consecutive series of fatal blunt head injuries over a period of 5 years. This, however, is a biased experience as it is based on patients secondarily referred to a regional neurosurgical unit. It seems likely that the neuropathological findings in head-injured patients dying in a general hospital might not be the same, while those who die shortly after a head injury and are therefore taken to a city mortuary might be different again. For these reasons we think it may be unwise to lay too much emphasis on the proportional incidence of lesions in different series, including our own. Before dealing with the pathology of individual lesions, we shall review briefly current concepts on the mechanism of head injury. These are particularly relevant to the understanding of brain injury directly attributable to impact.

THE MECHANISMS OF BRAIN INJURY DUE TO TRAUMA

Prior to the 1940s, the majority of investigations into the mechanisms whereby an injury to the head produces damage to the brain and upper spinal cord were concerned principally with the phenomenon of concussion. The end of this era was marked by the classical experiments of Denny-Brown and Russell[5] who drew particular attention to the distinction between acceleration concussion and compression concussion. Concussion could be readily produced by subjecting an animal's head to a sufficiently high rate of change of velocity, while concussion produced by a crushing injury required a much greater force to produce the same effect. Since that time, greater attention has been focused on studying the pattern and distribution of identifiable structural changes in the brain with particular reference to *coup* and *contre-coup* lesions. These terms are now firmly established in the literature and are probably still germane in precise experimental work. Unfortunately they tend to be accepted in too literal a sense by pathologists, and probably also by clinicians, in the context of human head injuries. Whereas *coup* lesions are contusions that occur directly below the site of injury, *contre-coup* lesions are located on the side of the brain diametrically opposite to the point of impact.

The forces acting on the brain when the head is injured produce complex movements and deformations that cannot readily be expressed in the terms of simple physical laws. Thus none of the generally held theories explains satisfactorily all aspects of the pathogenesis of brain damage. The damage may be the result of a blunt (non-missile) injury, with which we are dealing almost exclusively in this chapter, or of a penetrating injury. Blunt blows are most common in civilian practice and strike the head broadly, the usual result being a closed injury. The unfixed head may either be struck by a blunt object—an *acceleration* injury or, more commonly in man at least, the head suddenly strikes a blunt object when a *deceleration* injury results. Sharp blows, in contrast, usually produce open brain injuries as a result of penetrating wounds of the skull and dura.

A considerable amount of recent experimental work has been concerned with translational (linear) and rotational (angular) movements of the skull after a blunt blow which, if it is sufficient to produce brain damage, usually causes the head to accelerate. If the impact is directed at the centre of the head, as for example during a frontal or occipital blow, the head moves forward in a straight line and a translational acceleration type of injury results. If the blow is directed eccentrically, the result is a combined translational and rotational acceleration type of injury. The distinction between these two types of acceleration is important in view of the different physical processes they initiate in the brain. Pure translational acceleration creates intracranial pressure gradients, while pure rotational acceleration produces rotation of the skull relative to the brain. Whereas the majority of experimental studies have examined the neuropathological effects of either of these mechanisms in isolation, there is little doubt that many factors participate in the genesis of brain damage in man including distortion of the skull, translation of the head in a straight line, and rotation of the head with twisting of the head on the neck.

Two principal hypotheses have been advanced to account for brain damage incurred at the moment of impact, viz. the skull distortion/head rotation hypothesis and the head translation/cavitation hypothesis. Although rotation of the cerebral mass as a whole had been suspected for many years, its relationship to *contre-coup* lesions was not investigated until Holbourn[13] studied the mechanisms of head injury. He believed that the distribution of shear-strains within the skull-brain system resulting from various types of blow could be predicted, and he explained *contre-coup* lesions on physical principles which he elaborated by experiments on gelatin models. He postulated that brain damage was due to rotational acceleration forces which were more important than transmitted waves of compression and rarefaction. The prime requisite for *contre-coup* damage, therefore, was rotational movement of the head in the coronal, sagittal or horizontal plane or in a combination of these, the movement being transmitted to the brain which glided in its dural compartment. The gliding motion was relatively free except where the brain was confined by bony structures, particularly in the anterior and middle cranial fossae where shear-strains developed which caused laceration of the brain and tearing of blood vessels. Damage was least in those parts of the brain that were free to glide, or under conditions where rotation was minimal. Holbourn's theory accounted more satisfactorily than any previous one for the distribution of the *contre-coup* lesions observed in fatal cases of head injury in man. This theory was supported by the direct observations of brain movement made by Pudenz and Shelden[29] in monkeys fitted with lucite calvaria. They found that when the head was free to move, blows on the head caused swirling rotational movements of the brain within the cranial cavity. The patterns of convolutional motion were determined by the direction in which the head was displaced by the blow. When the head was immobile, the amplitude of brain movement was either considerably reduced or absent. Gurdjian and his colleagues[11] have recently confirmed that, at the moment of impact, the skull and brain move both as a unit and relative to each other. Thus, according to the skull distortion/head rotation hypothesis, important factors in the causation of brain damage are:

(i) deformation of the skull with or without a fracture; and

(ii) sudden rotation of the head which is responsible for the *contre-coup* injuries, for some intracranial haemorrhages, and probably also for concussion.

With regard to the head translation/cavitation hypothesis, it has been widely held that compressive waves generated at the time of a head injury are insufficient to damage the brain, although Gurdjian and Lissner[12] had demonstrated a relationship between traumatic brain damage and intracranial pressure gradients. The reverse concept that negative pressure, particularly at the antipole, i.e. the site diametrically opposite the point of impact, is responsible for cavitation and tissue destruction has been investigated by Unterharnscheidt and his group.[32,37] They showed that when the skull is arrested, the brain, because of its inertia, tends to continue its movement in the same direction. Increased pressure is thus produced on the surface of the brain at the site of impact. Since the brain tends to move away from the internal aspect of the skull at the antipole, a reduced pressure will develop on the surface of the brain there. It can be calculated that the pressures at the site of impact and at the antipole are identical except for their sign. The pressure is proportional to the prevailing acceleration, the distance between the impact pole and the antipole, and the specific gravity of the brain; thus, from a purely theoretical point of view, brain damage due to cavitation is a possibility during transient intracranial pressure changes.

These concepts help to clarify the mechanism of injury in many cases, although there are instances in which other factors seem to be important. The latter include tensile stresses that stretch and deform the brain stem and upper cervical cord at the cranio-spinal junction. The vulnerability of this area has been studied by Friede[7] and by von Gierke[8] who found that concussion indistinguishable from that produced by a blow on the head could be produced by stretching the cervical cord over the odontoid process. They suggested that the pathological basis of experimental concussion was damage to large nerve fibres close to the ventral surface of the upper cervical cord at the level of the first cervical vertebra. Changes in the cell structure in the nuclei of the brain stem were thought to be secondary to the primary fibre lesion. The vulnerability of this region in higher primates to both flexion and extension has also been stressed.[25]

The two main hypotheses for brain injury have been recently re-examined by Ommaya and his group[26] on the basis of the predicted and actual location of *coup* and *contre-coup* lesions and of subdural haematomas in primates after frontal and occipital injuries. They found that, from a purely theoretical point of view, there was a basis for the translation/cavitation hypothesis of brain injury but that discrepancies existed between the theoretically predicted areas of cavitation and the actual distribution of gross lesions found at autopsy both in man and in experimental models. Although this did not mean that cavitation had been disproved as a probable cause of lesions under certain conditions, it did appear that cavitation was not a significant cause of *coup* and *contre-coup* contusions. They postulated that head rotation and skull distortion were both significant in the genesis of brain injury, but recognized that the specific way in which these mechanisms produced brain lesions was not known, and concluded that skull distortion and head rotation helped to explain *coup* and *contre-coup* injuries better than either rotation alone or the translation/cavitation theory. The complexity of the genesis of these lesions was clearly demonstrated by Unterharnscheidt and Higgins[37] who have concluded from the different distribution patterns of primary traumatic lesions that a cylindrically arranged symmetrical pattern occurs after translation/acceleration injury whereas a regularly disposed pattern located close to the midline is found after rotation/acceleration injury, and that both types of acceleration injury contribute to the neuropathological effects of a blunt head injury in man.

Walker[38] has classified head injuries in man on the basis of their pathogenesis into three main categories. The *first* is direct injury from a blow to the head produced either by a moving object striking a stationary head or a moving head striking a stationary structure. Since the majority of blows strike the frontal and occipital parts of the head, the brain tends to rotate about a coronal axis with the result that the inferior parts of the frontal lobes and the tips of the temporal lobes become contused on the sphenoidal ridge. At the same time there is a tendency for veins along the longitudinal sinus to be torn. Lateral blows rotate the brain about a sagittal axis, contusing the brain stem as it strikes the sharp edge of the tentorium, or the parasagittal region as it strikes against the edge of the falx. These rotational blows cause severe shear-strains in the white matter of the hemispheres, as a result of which fibres in the ascending and descending systems may be ruptured. The *second* category is that of transmitted stresses, when patients fall on their feet from a height, the force being transmitted through the legs and spinal column to the base of the brain along the neuraxis to the parasagittal region. The *third* are indirect stresses, when there is sudden movement of the body on the unsupported head, a motion which is frequently described as "whiplash". This results in marked stretching of the upper part of the neck with hyperflexion or hyperextension at the cranio-spinal junction.

THE PATHOLOGY OF HEAD INJURIES

It is often rather difficult to reconcile the divergent views of clinicians and pathologists as to where the line of demarcation should be drawn between what have been referred to in the past as primary and secondary brain damage resulting from a head injury. In the first of the two ensuing sections we shall deal with lesions that appear to us to be directly attributable to impact. Some of these have an *immediate* clinical effect and may be referred to as true impact or primary brain damage. Others, such as intracranial haemorrhage, have a *delayed* effect although the process has been initiated at the time of impact. The second section will be devoted to changes in the brain that are a sequel to the head injury, i.e. changes that are *not* restricted to head-injured patients but may occur in association with a variety of disease processes that affect the nervous system.

Lesions that are generally accepted will be mentioned only briefly while more controversial issues will be dealt with in greater detail.

Lesions Directly Attributable to Impact

Lacerations of the Scalp

These can be of importance as a source of blood loss and an indication of the site of the injury. If there is an underlying fracture, they may be a potential route for subsequent intracranial infection.

Fracture of the Skull

A fracture was present in 78 per cent of our series of fatal blunt head injuries. Thus, although it can usually be taken to mean that the blow has been moderately severe, a fracture is by no means an invariable finding in fatal head injuries. Indeed a patient may die as a direct result of a head injury without there being any evidence of damage to the scalp or a fracture of the skull. On the other hand a patient with a fracture may appear to have only minimal, if any, clinical evidence of brain damage.

A compound depressed fracture, however, is always of importance because it is a potential source for intracranial infection; it is also associated with an increased incidence of post-traumatic epilepsy (see Jennett, Chapter X : 1). Fractures of the base of the skull are also liable to be complicated by intracranial infection, organisms spreading from the air sinuses or the middle ear—hence the clinical importance of CSF rhinorrhea and otorrhea, or an intracranial aerocele, which are indicative of the presence of a route whereby intracranial infection may become established.

Contusions and Lacerations

The pia is supposedly intact over contusions but torn in lacerations: in practice, however, the terms tend to be used synonymously. In the early stages both are haemorrhagic. When healed, they are represented by golden-brown shrunken scars. Contusions characteristically affect the crests of gyri (in contrast to focal ischaemic damage which has a predilection for the cortex within the depths of sulci) but they may extend into the sulci and the digitate white matter. Severe contusions in the frontal and temporal lobes are often associated with acute subdural and intracerebral haemorrhage, when the terms "burst frontal lobe" or "burst temporal lobe" would appear to be particularly appropriate (Fig. 1).

Contusions are the hall-mark of brain damage due to impact and their appearances are so characteristic that it is often possible to state with certainty post-mortem that a patient has experienced a head injury some time, even many years, in the past. They are usually asymmetrical, but although they are frequently more extensive on the side opposite to the one that has suffered the impact, they are only very rarely precisely *contre-coup*, i.e. at the diametrically opposite pole to the site of impact. Contusions related to fractures may occur in any part of the brain but, in any blunt head injury, they tend to affect particularly the frontal poles, the orbital gyri, the cortex above and below the

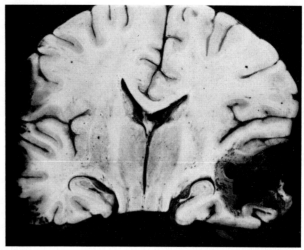

FIG. 1. "Burst" temporal lobe. Contusions on the right temporal lobe are in continuity with an intracerebral haematoma and an acute subdural haematoma. Note the shift of the midline structures to the left, the supracallosal hernia, and the contusions typically restricted to the crests of gyri in the left hemisphere.

Sylvian fissures where the brain is in close contact with the lesser wings of the sphenoid bones, the temporal poles and the inferior aspects of the temporal lobes, and, less frequently, the inferior aspects of the cerebellar hemispheres. Small contusions, often only identifiable microscopically, occur very commonly in the uncinate processes where they are traumatized against the anterior free edges of the tentorium cerebelli. Such contusions have to be distinguished from haemorrhagic necrosis due to tentorial herniation but necrosis of this type always extends posteriorly into at least the anterior part of the parahippocampal gyrus.

Typical contusions are rare in young infants: the characteristic features of a blunt head injury in this age group are grossly visible tears in the white matter, and microscopic tears in the outermost layers of the cortex.[21]

Tearing of Nerve Fibres

Patients who sustain a severe head injury, who are unconscious from the moment of impact until death, and who survive for more than 2 or 3 months, often show extensive degeneration in the white matter of the brain. This has been ascribed by Strich[33,34] to the tearing of nerve fibres by mechanical forces acting at the time of injury. Wallerian degeneration then occurs in the affected myelinated nerve fibres. As this is a slow process in the central nervous system, breakdown products of myelin do not become visible until about 6–8 weeks after the injury: they then continue to form over a period of months and remain identifiable for as long as two years or more. Patients with this type of diffuse degeneration in the white matter may survive for a year or more if intensive nursing care is maintained.

At post-mortem, apart from a few small healed contusions at the conventional sites, the brain may appear remarkably normal on macroscopic examination. In sections, there are almost invariably small, slightly shrunken and often discoloured lesions in the corpus callosum (Fig. 2), and in and adjacent to one or both superior cerebellar peduncles

(Fig. 3). The callosal lesions occur to one side of the midline and may extend over an antero-posterior distance of several centimetres. If the patient has survived several months, there is generalized enlargement of the ventricular system secondary to a reduction in the amount of white matter (Fig. 4). The white matter may also be of increased consistency and the brain stem smaller than normal. Macroscopic abnormalities may, however, be so difficult to identify that the pathologist unaware of this syndrome may find it hard to reconcile the appearances of the brain with a persistent post-traumatic vegetative state.[17]

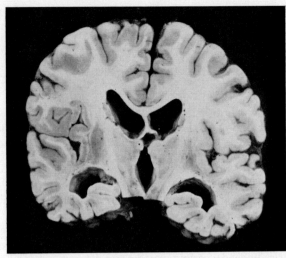

FIG. 4. Diffuse degeneration of the white matter in a male, aged 20, who survived in a vegetative state for 21 months. Note the generalized enlargement of the ventricular system, and the absence of severe contusions.

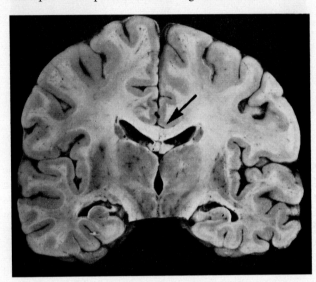

FIG. 2. "Tear" in corpus callosum in a male, aged 29, who survived in a vegetative state for 12 weeks. Note the lesion affecting the full thickness of the corpus callosum immediately to the right of the midline, and the absence of contusions.

The principal histological abnormality is the presence in the white matter of the breakdown products of myelin which can only be satisfactorily demonstrated in frozen sections stained by the Marchi method or with the Sudan dyes. The distribution of degeneration of nerve fibres has been described in detail by Strich.[33] It is usually asymmetrical, and severely degenerated areas may be quite sharply demarcated from apparently normal regions. In the

cerebral hemispheres there tends to be selective involvement of subcortical white matter, the internal capsule (Fig. 5) and the corpus callosum. In the brain stem, the superior cerebellar preduncles, the medial longitudinal bundles, the cortico-spinal tracts and the medial lemnisci are mainly affected (Figs. 6 and 7). There may also be degeneration of nerve fibres in cerebellar folia.

Patients with this type of brain damage have a characteristic clinical course. They are always deeply unconscious

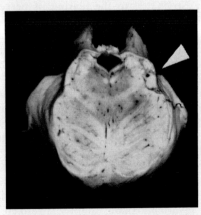

FIG. 3. "Tear" in superior cerebellar peduncle in a male, aged 47, who survived in a vegetative state for 2 months. Note the well-defined lesion in the left peduncle (arrow).

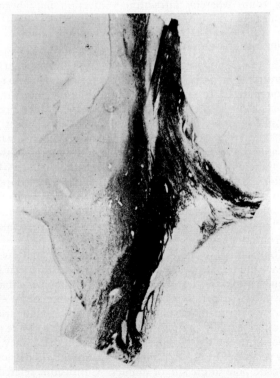

FIG. 5. Diffuse degeneration of white matter in the internal capsule in same case as Fig. 4. Note the abundant Marchi-positive (black) material indicative of degeneration of myelin. Marchi × 3.

immediately after the impact and they remain unresponsive in a post-traumatic persistent vegetative state[17] until death. They often do not have a fracture of the skull and there may be no evidence of raised intracranial pressure based either on direct monitoring of ventricular fluid pressure or on histological examination of the brain.

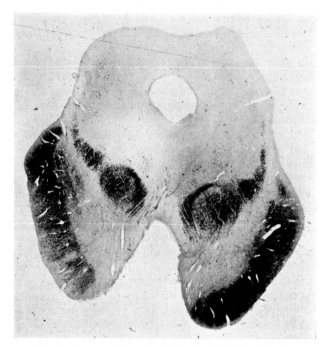

FIG. 6. Degeneration of particular tracts in the midbrain in the same case as Fig. 4. Marchi × 3.

FIG. 7. Degeneration of particular tracts in the pons in the same case as Fig. 4. Marchi × 3.

There is therefore no doubt that diffuse degeneration of the white matter, particularly of long fibre tracts, may occur as a consequence of a severe head injury. But is this degeneration due to the rupture of axons at the time of injury as postulated by Strich? She argues that haematomas and infarcts in the brains of the cases she has examined are far

too infrequent to account for the amount of degeneration present in the white matter, and our experience, albeit on a much smaller series of cases, accords with her view. Her argument is further supported by Holbourn's biophysical studies[13] which have shown that shear-strains occur in the brain as a result of a head injury, and by the frequent occurrence of lesions in the corpus callosum and in the superior cerebellar peduncles which may be attributed to a direct tearing effect. As there seems to be little doubt that every patient with this type of pathology suffers immediate and severe brain damage at the time of impact, it is unlikely that the degeneration in the white matter is secondary to some other, e.g. vascular, complication. Thus it appears highly probable, on the basis of the information available, that degeneration in the white matter in cases of this type is due to the tearing of nerve fibres at the time of injury.

Unfortunately this type of damage can only be identified with certainty if the patient survives for at least 6–8 weeks, and if frozen sections are examined specifically for the breakdown products of myelin. The staining of myelin in paraffin or celloidin sections may appear to be normal for many months while, with routine cell stains, abnormalities may be limited to the presence of hypertrophied astrocytes and microglia, and occasional lipid phagocytes in the affected white matter. Thus, if frozen sections are not examined, the principal pathological abnormality may not be recognized, and severe neurological deficits ascribed to other abnormalities such as the small lesions that almost invariably occur in and adjacent to the superior cerebellar peduncles in cases of this type. If the patient survives for less than 6 weeks, the principal clues suggestive of this type of brain injury are probably retraction balls and microglial stars, but these will be discussed in the next section as they can probably be interpreted as a link between cases with diffuse white matter degeneration and so-called primary brain stem damage.

Primary Brain Stem Injury

This is also a rather controversial problem. Clinicians frequently encounter head-injured patients with signs of brain stem dysfunction which, if present soon after the injury, is usually construed as evidence of primary damage to the brain stem at the moment of impact. It is, however, not always easy to distinguish damage of this type from that attributable to a particularly rapidly expanding intracranial lesion with shift and distortion of the brain, and increased intracranial pressure. The neuropathologist encounters similar problems, as the great majority of head-injured patients who die in a neurosurgical unit have secondary brain stem damage due to raised intracranial pressure. This may mask pre-existing primary brain stem damage or, in patients with very rapidly expanding intracranial lesions, be difficult to distinguish from primary impact damage. The problem is not made any easier by Jellinger and Seitelberger's[15] suggestion that, in head-injured patients, secondary brain stem damage in cases of long survival may have a slightly different pattern from that seen in patients who survive for only a short time. It is, however, difficult to be quite certain that the glial dystrophy they ascribe to long-standing secondary brain stem damage is not due at least in part to degeneration of white matter of the type described in the previous section as it is not clear if they used staining techniques that specifically demonstrate breakdown products of myelin.

The majority of patients with severe primary brain stem damage probably die within a few hours of their injury[35], but there are some patients in our series who have survived long enough to be referred to a regional neurosurgical unit in whom it is reasonable to assume that any abnormalities identified in the brain stem should be ascribed directly to the impact. Firstly they should be unconscious from the moment of impact and have clinical evidence of brain stem dysfunction when first examined. We are reluctant to accept the view[4] that patients with primary brain stem damage, which is severe enough to contribute materially to a fatal outcome, may have a lucid interval. Secondly there should be no evidence of raised intracranial pressure, either from continuous recording of the ventricular fluid pressure[18] or from histological examination of the brain. The preliminary results of a study we are at present undertaking on the brains of patients whose ventricular fluid pressure has been monitored are tending to confirm our view that, provided strict criteria are used, it is possible to state with considerable certainty if the intracranial pressure has been raised, even if the episode of raised intracranial pressure has occurred some time before death. The most significant lesions in this context are focal pressure necrosis in the cingulate

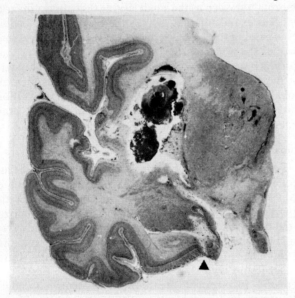

Fig. 8. Left temporal lobe. Note the focal (pale) infarct related to a tentorial pressure groove (arrow). 30μ celloidin section. Cresyl violet × 1·5.

and/or parahippocampal gyri (Fig. 8 and Fig. 2, Chapter VIII : 5) as a result of supracallosal or tentorial herniation respectively, focal ischaemic damage in the medial occipital cortex due to impairment of the blood flow through the ipsilateral posterior cerebral artery, and pressure necrosis in the cerebellum at the site of tonsillar herniation. The final criterion for inclusion in this group of cases is that the histological changes in the brain stem should not consist only of selective neuronal necrosis in the distribution associated with acute cardio-respiratory arrest.

In the context of the pathology of primary brain stem damage, small haemorrhages, axonal retraction balls and microglial stars appear to be the three principal types of lesion. Whereas some of the **haemorrhages** may be large enough to be seen on macroscopic examination, others are so small that they can only be identified with the microscope. They have a fairly characteristic distribution[4,35], viz. in the subependymal tissues around the third and fourth ventricles and in the peri-aqueductal grey matter, in the lateral structures of the brain stem, in the superior cerebellar peduncles and colliculi, and in the basis pedunculi. Tomlinson[35] believes that such haemorrhages are not necessarily responsible for death but are merely indicative of widespread and severe brain damage which is incompatible with survival.

Retraction Balls are masses of axoplasm which form at the severed ends of an axon. They are sufficiently prominent to be easily identifiable in sections stained with many of the routine cell stains but they may be more conspicuous in silver impregnation techniques used for the demonstration of axons. They are impossible to see in sections stained by Nissl's method or with the standard techniques for myelin. Care must be exercised in the interpretation of retraction balls as they occur in circumstances other than rupture of axons due to trauma. They are, for example, found in vast numbers in the brain stem around established infarcts and haematomas from whatever cause. Retraction balls not related to such vascular lesions occur in the brain stem of head-injured patients in several forms:

(i) scattered throughout the white matter in small numbers;

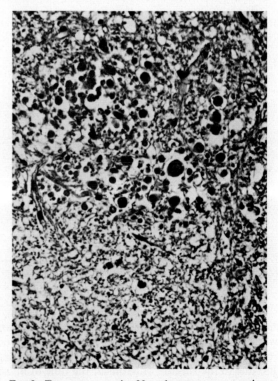

Fig. 9. Tegmentum pontis. Note the numerous retraction balls of varying size and shape. Haematoxylin and eosin × 300.

(ii) as closely packed clusters within the white matter, usually in the tegmental parts of the midbrain or pons, or in the basis pontis (Fig. 9): in this type of lesion, they tend to occur in either vertically or horizontally disposed fibres thus suggesting that there is a correlation between the direction in which the fibres are running and the shear-strains responsible for their genesis;

(iii) small groups immediately adjacent to blood vessels;

(iv) within and around coarsely vacuolated and rare-fied lesions that are most often seen in and immediately adjacent to a superior cerebellar peduncle (Figs. 10 and 11).

Fig. 11. Superior cerebellar peduncle. Note the retraction balls on axons immediately adjacent to a lesion similar to that seen in Fig. 10. Glees and Marsland (silver impregnation) × 300.

Fig. 10. Superior cerebellar peduncle. Note the coarsely vacuolated rarefied lesion. Haematoxylin and eosin × 125.

Microglial Stars are small clusters of hypertrophied microglial cells that are thought to be a cellular reaction at the site of minute tissue tears.[27] They can be identified with routine cell stains but they are more easily seen in sections stained specifically for microglia (Fig. 12). Microglial stars within white matter are highly characteristic of head injury and probably do not occur in large numbers in any other condition.

In our current study on the pathology of blunt head injuries, we have so far examined serial blocks (celloidin, paraffin and frozen sections) of 78 brain stems. The sections have been assessed particularly for haemorrhage, infarction, retraction balls, microglial stars and the breakdown products of myelin. Only 9 of these cases come into the category of potential primary brain stem damage as defined above, viz. they were unresponsive from the moment of impact, did not experience an episode of acute cardio-respiratory arrest, and had no evidence of raised intracranial pressure. In none of these cases were small haemorrhages

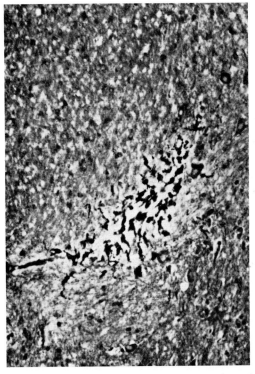

Fig. 12. A microglial star in the pons. Nauomenko and Feigin (silver impregnation) × 200.

of the type described by Tomlinson[35] present: this does not challenge his observations, however, but tends to support his contention that cases with the type of primary brain stem damage that he has described usually die within a few hours of their injury. Four of the 9 cases survived for more than 6 weeks: in each there were focal lesions in one superior cerebellar peduncle and in the corpus callosum, and degeneration of the white matter of the type described in the previous section. In the 2 of the 4 cases who had survived for 6½ and 8 weeks respectively there were numerous microglial stars in addition to early Marchi-positive material. In contrast microglial stars were much less conspicuous in the remaining 2 cases who had survived for longer than 3 months, while the breakdown products of myelin were much more obvious.

In 3 of the 5 cases who had survived for less than 6 weeks, there were no abnormalities in the brain stem. In the remaining 2, there were, in addition to lesions in the corpus callosum, coarsely vacuolated and rarefied lesions containing numerous retraction balls in the superior cerebellar peduncles (bilateral in one) and, in one, there were closely packed masses of retraction balls in the tegmentum pontis. Coarsely vacuolated lesions in the superior cerebellar peduncles were also seen in some of the cases with evidence of raised intracranial pressure: in such cases we are provisionally interpreting these as evidence of impact brain stem damage, the primary damage having preceded the secondary changes due to raised intracranial pressure.

We have examined too few cases at this preliminary stage to allow of any valid conclusions but there is at least some evidence to suggest that the principal evidence of primary injury to the brain stem are groups of retraction balls, lesions in one or both cerebellar peduncles and microglial stars. There is also a high incidence of focal lesions in the corpus callosum (vide infra). If these observations are confirmed in a larger series of cases, it seems likely that patients with clinical and histological evidence of primary brain stem damage and who die within a few weeks of a head injury fall into the same category as patients with diffuse degeneration in the white matter, the main difference being that they do not survive sufficiently long for the breakdown products of myelin to appear. Before it can be established that the tearing of nerve fibres at the time of injury is an important cause of the clinical syndrome of primary brain stem injury, careful studies will have to be made for retraction balls in the white matter of the cerebral hemispheres in patients with the clinical features of primary brain stem damage who survive for only a few days after a head injury. Strich[33] has already identified retraction balls in the corpus callosum, at the junction of the cerebral cortex and digitate white matter, and in the internal capsule in some of the cases she has examined, while Nevin,[24] and Peerless and Rewcastle[28] have shown that the effects of shear injuries on the white matter are of fairly common occurrence after a head injury.

In view of the association between concussion in various experimental animals and damage to nerve fibres in the upper cervical spinal cord as a result of shear-strains at the cranio-cervical junction,[7,8] it might be thought that similar damage would be observed in man. In a study of longitudinal sections of the lower medulla and upper three cervical segments in a consecutive series of 32 blunt fatal head injuries and 16 controls, we found a few retraction balls in only one case of head injury and no microglial stars.

Lesions in the Corpus Callosum

Lindenberg and his group[20] found gross lesions in the corpus callosum in 16 per cent of a large series of head injuries and considered that they were caused by sudden stretching and shearing forces at the moment of impact. In our series, however, gross callosal lesions were present in every case with either diffuse degeneration of the white matter or evidence of primary injury to the brain stem. Furthermore, in our consecutive series of cases, the incidence of lesions in the corpus callosum was 80 per cent. Lindenberg, however, was considering only gross lesions while, in our series, they ranged from microscopic groups of retraction balls and microglial stars, through small infarcts and haemorrhages, to massive tears. Another reason for the apparently discordant results is that many of Lindenberg's cases died within hours of injury whereas all the cases we studied survived long enough to be referred to a neurosurgical unit. In addition, at least a proportion of the lesions in our cases can be attributed to neurosurgical procedures but these are not always easy to distinguish histologically from spontaneously occurring lesions. We tend to agree with Lindenberg and his group that many lesions in the corpus callosum are due to tearing at the time of injury, particularly in cases who remain unresponsive until death, but we are also of the opinion that many are due to supracallosal herniation and to focal ischaemic damage in the territories supplied by the anterior cerebral arteries (vide infra).

Intracranial Haemorrhage

In the great majority of head-injured patients who develop intracranial haemorrhage, the main effects are delayed until the haematoma has attained a size sufficient to cause distortion and herniation of the brain, and raised intracranial pressure. Indeed, the conventional neuropathological features of an expanding lesion are often the predominant findings in the brain (see Miller and Adams, Chapter VIII : 5). Nevertheless the onset of the haemorrhage has to be attributed to the impact.

Haematomas due to a head injury may develop in three principal sites: they may be extradural, subdural or intracerebral. Some degree of subarachnoid haemorrhage is almost inevitable in any severe head injury: it not only accounts to a considerable extent for headache and a stiff neck, but it may also be a contributory factor in the causation of the spasm which is becoming increasingly recognized in carotid angiograms in a proportion of patients with acute head injuries.[23] A discrete subarachnoid haematoma within a Sylvian fissure is a not uncommon finding while massive haemorrhage due to rupture of the basilar artery at the time of impact is occasionally responsible for a rapidly fatal outcome. Intraventricular haemorrhage, when it occurs, is usually a terminal feature due to the extension of an intracerebral haematoma into the ventricular system.

It is not uncommon, particularly with extradural or chronic subdural haematomas, for there to be an interval after the injury during which the patient may be rational and mentally alert only to become comatose later. On the other hand, acute subdural or intracerebral haematomas tend to develop while the patient is still unconscious as a result of brain damage sustained at the moment of impact.

Extradural haemorrhage is usually due to tearing of a meningeal artery; as the haematoma develops it gradually strips the dura from the skull to form a large ovoid mass that progressively indents the adjacent brain. Although about 85 per cent of patients who develop an extradural haematoma have a fracture of the skull[14] which is directly responsible for the tear in the meningeal artery, the original head injury is often apparently trivial. Indeed in many patients who die as a result of an extradural haematoma, there is very little evidence of direct damage to the brain. In children with an extradural haematoma, the incidence of fracture is less than in adults. As the middle meningeal artery is the vessel most frequently torn, the commonest site for an extradural haematoma is in the temporal region. They may also occur in the frontal and parietal regions, or within the posterior fossa. They may also be multiple (usually bilateral) but we have seen two cases where there were two separate unilateral extradural haematomas.

Subdural haemorrhage is attributed to the rupture of small veins which bridge the subdural space and is often bilateral. In contrast to the localized nature of an extradural haematoma, haemorrhage into the subdural space tends to spread diffusely over the hemispheres. Thin *acute* subdural haematomas are an almost invariable finding in severe head injuries, and they are rarely of particular importance except insofar as their volume may be sufficient to take up some of the intracranial space normally available during the period of spatial compensation when there is an expanding intracranial lesion. Occasionally they are large enough to act as expanding lesions but, in contrast to the majority of patients with an extradural haematoma, they are usually associated with contusions of the underlying brain, which may be extensive enough to constitute a "burst lobe" (Fig. 1).

Subacute subdural haematomas, which present between a few days and about two weeks after the injury, also tend to be associated with contusions of the brain: the usual clinical feature in such cases is a failure of the conscious level to improve because of continuing cerebral compression.

Chronic subdural haematoma presents weeks or months after what may have seemed at the time to have been a trivial head injury. Coagulation defects such as haemophilia or long term anticoagulant therapy may occasionally be incriminated in their pathogenesis. The precise aetiology of chronic subdural haematoma is not clear. The clot, which ultimately becomes encapsulated in a membrane, slowly increases in size, probably as a result of repeated small haemorrhages, until it becomes large enough to produce distortion and herniation of the brain. As chronic subdural haematoma is particularly common in older age groups in whom there is already some cerebral atrophy, and as the haematoma expands very slowly, the period of spatial compensation (*see* Chapter VIII : 5), may be so long that there can be considerable distortion of the cerebral hemispheres before there is any significant increase in intracranial pressure (Fig. 13). In untreated cases, however, death is usually due to brain damage secondary to increased intracranial pressure.

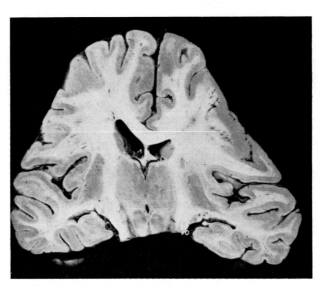

Fig. 13. Bilateral chronic subdural haematoma. Note the severe distortion of the cerebral hemispheres. The haematoma on the right side was the larger: hence the supracallosal hernia to the left and the small right ventricle.

Intracerebral haematoma occurs in some 15 per cent of fatal head injuries.[6] They can be single or multiple and may act as rapidly expanding lesions. Occasionally their development appears to be delayed for several days but it is not clear to what extent this is due to a slowly expanding haematoma or to an actual delay in the onset of haemorrhage. Most intracerebral haematomas are related to contusions of the brain and occur principally, therefore, in the subfrontal or temporal regions or, less commonly, in the cerebellum. They may also occur deep within the hemispheres where they are presumably due to shearing strains affecting small vessels at the time of impact. As indicated in the section dealing with the mechanisms of head injury, there is some relationship between the site of the haematoma and the nature of the injury. If a solitary haematoma is found in the brain of a patient who has suffered a head injury, the possibility of its being due to hypertension or to a ruptured intracranial aneurysm and hence precipitating the injury has to be borne in mind.

Post-traumatic Brain Swelling

This also tends to be a delayed effect and one that is difficult to explain satisfactorily. Some swelling, this term being used in preference to oedema, is frequently found in the white matter adjacent to contusions and around haematomas when it may contribute to the size of an expanding lesion. It may also occur, however, in the form of diffuse swelling of one or both cerebral hemispheres when conventional contusions are mild or even absent. Swelling of one cerebral hemisphere is seen most often in association with an acute subdural haematoma. Swelling of both hemispheres seems to have a particular predilection for children; the original head injury often appears clinically to have been quite trivial yet, 24–48 hours later, the conscious level rapidly deteriorates. At post-mortem, the brain is diffusely swollen and the ventricles small and symmetrical. The results of histological examination in cases with diffuse brain swelling has been unrewarding, abnormalities being restricted to pallor of myelin staining. In some of the cases there has been a history of early post-traumatic epilepsy and this may be causally related to the swelling. Other possible explanations are cerebral vascular dilatation due to vasomotor paralysis[19] or increased vascular permeability resulting from the effect of shear-strains on small vessels at the time of injury.

Other Lesions Attributable to Impact

Other structures such as cranial nerves (particularly the olfactory, the optic and the acoustic nerves) and the cavernous part of the carotid artery may be torn at the time of head injury. So also may the pituitary stalk and, although this is rare, it is of considerable clinical importance because the long hypothalamo-hypophysial portal vessels are torn with the result that there is massive infarction of the anterior lobe. This may not only be a contributory factor to death in the acute phase but later on may be responsible for hypopituitarism. We have seen one case who died some weeks after a head injury and who, it had been noted, tended to respond well when steroids were administered for the control of raised intracranial pressure. At post-mortem there was evidence of previous rupture of the pituitary stalk and massive infarction in the anterior lobe of the pituitary. Atrophy of the posterior lobe occurs if the neural part of the stalk is torn. Rupture of the pituitary stalk is usually associated with a fracture running across the sphenoid bone and a radiologically identifiable fluid level in the sphenoidal sinus as a result of haemorrhage into it. This subject has been fully reviewed by Treip.[36]

Lesions not Directly Attributable to Impact
Sequelae of Intracranial Expanding Lesions

We have already emphasized that intracranial haematomas figure prominently in acute head injuries and that, in a large proportion of such cases, death is attributable ultimately to distortion and herniation of the brain, and raised intracranial pressure. Post-traumatic brain swelling and extensive ischaemic brain damage may initiate a similar sequence of events. The conventional neuropathological features of an intracranial expanding lesion will not be dealt with here as they have been fully described by one of us in Chapter VIII : 5, but the predominant features are supracallosal, tentorial and tonsillar herniae, lateral shift of the midline structures, infarction in the territory supplied by the posterior cerebral artery ipsilateral to the expanding lesion, focal haemorrhage into the oculomotor nerves, and haemorrhage and/or infarction in the brain stem. If the expanding lesion is evacuated, but too late to prevent haemorrhage and/or infarction in the brain stem or in the thalamus, patients may occasionally survive for a considerable time after the head injury. This is another cause of a post-traumatic persistent vegetative state[17] but is, in our experience, a less common cause than diffuse degeneration of the white matter of the type described above.

Ischaemic Brain Damage

Ischaemic brain damage up to and including frank infarction is not uncommon in patients dying as a result of a blunt head injury. The infarcts may be large or small, single or multiple. Some are simply related to contusions particularly in the frontal and temporal lobes when they can be ascribed directly to impact; they are not necessarily restricted to subcortical white matter but may involve the deep white matter, the corpus callosum and the basal nuclei. Others, as already described, are secondary to distortion and herniation of the brain, and raised intracranial pressure; these have a fairly characteristic distribution in the brain stem and in the territories supplied by the posterior cerebral arteries. There is, however, a third category of ischaemic brain damage where, unrelated to contusions, either established infarcts or widespread foci of neuronal necrosis may occur throughout the brain.

We have recently undertaken a neuropathological analysis of 63 consecutive fatal blunt head injuries in an attempt to determine the incidence and distribution of this type of damage.[9,10] The age range was from 1 year 6 months to 85 years, there were 50 males and 13 females, and the length of survival after injury ranged from 6 hours to 7 months. Even when ischaemic damage of the type conventionally associated with raised intracranial pressure, infarction related to contusions, and necrosis due to fat embolism, cardiac arrest or post-traumatic status epilepticus were excluded, we found clearly defined focal ischaemic brain damage in an unexpectedly high proportion of the brains examined.

There was focal ischaemic damage in the *cerebral cortex* in 25 of the 63 cases (40 per cent). In 11 cases (10 bilateral) it was centred on the boundary zones between major

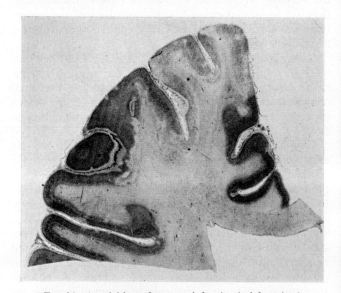

Fig. 14. Arterial boundary zone infarction in left parietal lobe. Note the pale infarct adjacent to the superior border of the lobe in the boundary zone between the anterior and middle cerebral arterial territories. 30μ celloidin section. Cresyl violet × 2. (Reproduced, with permission, from *Brain Hypoxia*, Brierley, J. B., and Meldrum, B. S., Eds. Clinics in Developmental Medicine, Nos. 39/40, William Heinemann Medical Books Ltd., London.)

arterial territories, particularly between the anterior and middle cerebral arterial territories (Figs. 14 and 15), and on the lateral aspect of the occipital lobe in the common boundary zone of the anterior, middle and posterior

brain. The effect of this reduced blood flow will be intensified if the oxygen content of the blood is reduced, e.g. as a result of multiple injuries, chest injuries, respiratory insufficiency due to airway obstruction, pulmonary

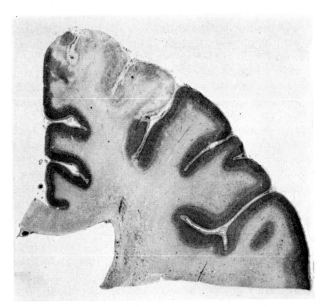

FIG. 15. Arterial boundary zone infarction in right parietal lobe. Same case as Fig. 14. Note boundary zone lesion in similar situation to that in the left hemisphere. 30μ celloidin section. Cresyl violet × 2. (Reproduced, with permission, from *Brain Hypoxia*, Brierley, J. B., and Meldrum, B. S., Eds. Clinics in Developmental Medicine, Nos. 39/40, William Heinemann Medical Books Ltd., London.)

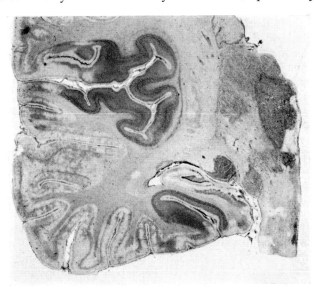

FIG. 16. Multiple foci of necrosis in left temporal lobe. Note the multiple pale lesions in the cortex. There are also infarcts in the thalamus and in the midbrain, and necrosis in the Sommer sector of the hippocampus. 30μ celloidin section. Cresyl violet × 1·6. (Reproduced, with permission, from *Brain Hypoxia*, Brierley, J. B., and Meldrum, B. S., Eds. Clinics in Developmental Medicine, Nos. 39/40, William Heinemann Medical Books Ltd., London.)

cerebral arterial territories. In 9, ischaemic damage involved particular arterial territories—the middle cerebral territory in 5 (2 bilateral), the anterior cerebral territory in 2 (1 bilateral), and both the middle and anterior cerebral territories in 2 (both bilateral): in 2 of these 9 cases ischaemic damage was accentuated within arterial boundary zones. In 5 cases, there were multiple foci of necrosis throughout the neocortex (Fig. 16) and in 2 of these necrosis was accentuated either in arterial boundary zones or within the territory supplied by a particular artery. The *hippocampus* was affected in 49 cases (29 bilateral) and in the great majority of cases this consisted of small foci of neuronal loss. In 17 of these cases the hippocampal lesions were associated with infarcts in the medial occipital cortex. The *cerebellum* was involved in 26 cases, in one of which the ischaemic damage was restricted to arterial boundary zones (Fig. 17). The *basal nuclei* were affected in 51 cases while there was infarction in the *brain stem* in 42 cases.

Possible reasons why such a high incidence of ischaemic brain damage has not been previously reported are that even quite large areas of recent necrosis in the brain may not be identifiable macroscopically and that, in our experience, early ischaemic damage is much more easily seen in thick celloidin sections than in paraffin sections. The pathogenesis of these lesions is complex but clearly depends basically on an inadequate blood flow to the affected parts of the

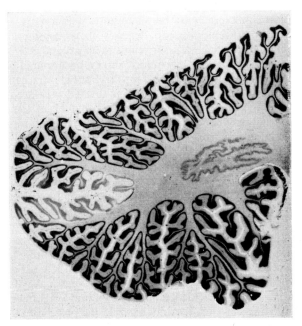

FIG. 17. Arterial boundary zone infarction in left cerebellar hemisphere. Note the recent pale infarct at the dorsal angle in the boundary zone between the superior and the posterior inferior cerebellar arterial territories. 30μ celloidin section. Cresyl violet × 2. (Reproduced, with permission, from *Brain Hypoxia*, Brierley, J. B., and Meldrum, B. S., Eds. Clinics in Developmental Medicine, Nos. 39/40, William Heinemann Medical Books Ltd., London.)

oedema or the development of hypoxaemia as a result of ventilation/perfusion imbalance in the lungs.[2] The ischaemic damage cannot be attributed simply to agonal hypotension as histological reactive changes were so well established in numerous cases that they must have started early in the post-traumatic period. In this respect it is of considerable interest that in 2 cases, where the head injury was apparently trivial, the patients suddenly collapsed some 10 and 20 min. respectively after the injury: in neither case was there an intracranial expanding lesion and in both there was unusually extensive ischaemic brain damage. Cases of this type have also been reported by Strich.[33]

Any attempt to define the nature of the haemodynamic disturbance responsible for this high incidence of ischaemic brain damage must inevitably be rather speculative but occlusive arterial disease in the extracranial and intracranial cerebral vessels did not appear to be a contributory factor in our cases. The most obvious explanation for arterial territory lesions might seem to be distortion of vessels due to brain shift and herniation, i.e. a mechanism similar to that widely accepted for infarction in a posterior cerebral arterial territory in association with an ipsilateral tentorial hernia: however in 4 of the 9 cases with arterial territory infarcts there was no evidence of shift and, in any event, it is difficult to postulate a mechanical basis for bilateral middle cerebral arterial or combined anterior and middle cerebral arterial infarction. On the other hand the frequency of boundary zone lesions in the neocortex and the accentuation of ischaemic damage in these regions in cases with arterial territory infarction and multiple foci of necrosis suggests that a critical reduction in cerebral perfusion pressure must be an important factor.[16] The cerebral perfusion pressure depends to a considerable extent on intracranial pressure and systemic blood pressure but, in the context of a recent head injury, perfusion failure is more likely to be attributable to variations in intracranial pressure than to a reduced systemic arterial pressure. It may be of some importance therefore that 52 of the 63 cases had definite neuropathological evidence of raised intracranial pressure, and that in 26 cases the systolic B.P. had fallen to less than 80 mm. Hg. at some point after the head injury. Furthermore, in this series of cases, vascular narrowing (spasm) and a prolonged circulation time as demonstrated by angiography were not uncommon.[23]

In head-injured patients whose ventricular fluid pressure has been monitored, there is often little correlation between the actual level of intracranial pressure and the clinical evidence suggestive of raised intracranial pressure.[18] It is also becoming clear that, in such patients, there is often little correlation between the level of the ventricular fluid pressure and the incidence and distribution of ischaemic brain damage. This does not exclude the possibility that ischaemic brain damage in the majority of cases is due to a failure of cerebral perfusion, as this may have occurred as a consequence of an episode of systemic hypotension shortly after the injury, prior to admission to hospital. It is of some interest, however, that in patients who have no clinical or pathological evidence of raised intracranial pressure, the incidence of ischaemic brain damage is

relatively low whereas that of diffuse white matter degeneration of the type described above is relatively high.

Infection

Meningitis is a well-recognized complication of a head injury and is due to the spread of micro-organisms through an open fracture of the calvaria or a fracture of the base of the skull. If there is also a tear in the dura, the latter may be associated with a CSF rhinorrhoea or otorrhoea, or an aerocele. In such cases, meningitis is not restricted to the early post-traumatic period but may be delayed for many months: a small traumatic fistula of this type may also be a cause of recurrent episodes of meningitis.

Acute purulent meningitis may be difficult to recognize if it develops within a few days of a severe head injury as the usual clinical features of meningitis are often lacking. In such circumstances the patient simply fails to improve or deteriorates for no apparent cause. If, therefore, there is even the slightest suspicion of post-traumatic meningitis, bacteriological examination of the CSF should be undertaken without delay.

Subdural or intracerebral abscesses are rarer complications of a head injury than meningitis. Infective material may be carried directly into the cranial cavity as a result of a penetrating injury, or may spread secondarily from infection of the scalp, bone or air sinuses.

Progressive Post-traumatic Dementia

Some patients who make a reasonably good or even apparently complete recovery from a head injury, subsequently develop a progressive neurological illness with the features of an organic dementia. Thus examples of Alzheimer's disease, Pick's disease or Jakob-Creutzfeldt disease have been reported after a head injury. Many of these probably cannot be substantiated, but occasionally the temporal relationship between a head injury and the appearance of a progressive organic dementia is such that it is difficult to believe that they are purely coincidental.

It is, however, now generally accepted that there is an organic basis for the "punch-drunk" syndrome which appears to be due partly to the direct effect of multiple minor injuries and partly to certain degenerative changes in the brain. An investigation at present being undertaken by Corsellis[3] has revealed a recurring pattern of damage in the brains of ex-boxers, viz. fenestration of the interventricular septum, the formation of a sizeable cavum between the two leaves of the septum, atrophy and gliosis of folia in the region of the cerebellar tonsils, degeneration of the substantia nigra similar to that found in post-encephalitic or idiopathic Parkinson's disease, and a curiously intense formation of Alzheimer's neurofibrillary tangles in certain parts of the brain.

Current interest in normal pressure hydrocephalus may have an important bearing on head injuries as a proportion of patients who have suffered a moderately severe head injury are found later, either on contrast neuroradiology or at autopsy, to have communicating hydrocephalus which is usually attributed to obliteration of the subarachnoid space by previous subarachnoid haemorrhage. Any correlation between normal pressure hydrocephalus and a previous head injury has not yet been established but it clearly will have to be investigated more fully in the future: we know of at least one patient who, after making a reasonably good recovery from a head injury, developed a slowly progressive organic dementia which was greatly improved by the insertion of a ventriculo-atrial shunt.

CONCLUSION

In this chapter we have attempted a brief resumé of the major neuropathological findings in patients dying as a result of blunt head injuries and have elaborated those aspects which appear to us to be of particular interest. One of our principal concerns has been to separate the features that are due to impact from those that are later developments. We have done this in an attempt to stimulate a more activist approach to the problem of blunt head injuries in the belief that at least a proportion of the delayed effects are preventable or, even if established, reversible. Much work remains to be done but already, by correlating clinical, physiological and neuropathological features in a series of cases, we have been able to gain some insight into the sequence of events that may be initiated by the impact. If some of the suggestions we have made are rather speculative, it is in the hope that further studies will be undertaken to obtain a better understanding of a problem that has both serious social and economic implications.

Acknowledgements. We would like to thank Professor G. Forbes, Regius Professor of Forensic Medicine, University of Glasgow, and his staff for allowing us to examine the brains from cases on whom they had undertaken post-mortem examinations.

FURTHER READING

[1] Capener, N. (1970), "The Ecology of Trauma," *J. clin. Path.*, **23**; *Suppl.* (Roy. Coll. Path.), **4**, 1–7.

[2] Cole, W. G. (1972), "Respiratory Sequels to Non-thoracic Injury," *Lancet*, **i**, 555–556.

[3] Corsellis, J. A. N. (1972), Personal communication.

[4] Crompton, M. R. (1971), "Brainstem Lesions Due to Closed Head Injury," *Lancet*, **i**, 669–673.

[5] Denny-Brown, D. and Russell, W. R. (1941), "Experimental Cerebral Concussion," *Brain*, **64**, 93–164.

[6] Freytag, E. (1963), "Autopsy Findings in Head Injuries from Blunt Forces," *Arch. Path.*, **75**, 402–413.

[7] Friede, R. L. and Arbor, A. (1961), "Experimental Concussion Acceleration. Pathology and Mechanics," *Arch. Neurol.*, **4**, 449–462.

[8] Gierke, H. E. von (1966), "On the Dynamics of Some Head Injury Mechanisms," in *Head Injury*, Chap. 30. (W. F. Caveness and A. E. Walker, Eds.). Philadelphia and Toronto: Lippincott.

[9] Graham, D. I. and Adams, J. H. (1971), "Ischaemic Brain Damage in Fatal Head Injuries," In *Brain Hypoxia*, pp. 34–40 (J. B. Brierley and B. S. Meldrum, Eds.). Spastics International Medical Publications. London: Heinemann.

[10] Graham, D. I. and Adams, J. H. (1971), "Ischaemic Brain Damage in Fatal Head Injuries," *Lancet*, **i**, 265–266.

[11] Gurdjian, E. S., Hodgson, V. R., Thomas, L. M. and Patrick, L. M. (1968), "Significance of Relative Movements of Scalp, Skull and Intracranial Contents During Impact Injury of the Head," *J. Neurosurg.*, **29**, 70–73.

[12] Gurdjian, E. S. and Lissner, H. R. (1944), "Mechanism of Head Injury as Studied by the Cathode Ray Oscilloscope," *J. Neurosurg.*, **1**, 393–399.

[13] Holbourn, A. H. S. (1945), "The Mechanics of Brain Injuries," *Brit. med. Bull.*, **3**, 147–149.

[14] Jamieson, K. G. and Yelland, J. D. N. (1968), "Extradural Hematoma. Report of 167 Cases," *J. Neurosurg.*, **29**, 13–23.

[15] Jellinger, K. and Seitelberger, F. (1970), "Protracted Post-Traumatic Encephalopathy. Pathology, Pathogenesis and Clinical Implications," *J. Neurol. Sci.*, **10**, 51–94.

[16] Jennett, B., Graham, D. I., Adams, H. and Johnston, I. H. (1972), "Ischaemic Brain Damage After Fatal Blunt Head Injury," in *Proceedings of Conference on Cerebro-vascular Disease*. Princeton. In the press.

[17] Jennett, B. and Plum, F. (1972), "Persistent Vegetative State After Brain Damage," *Lancet*, **i**, 734–737.

[18] Johnston, I. H., Johnston, J. A. and Jennett, B. (1970), "Intra-cranial-pressure Changes following Head Injury," *Lancet*, **ii**, 433–436.

[19] Langfitt, T. W., Tannanbaum, H. M. and Kassell, N. F. (1966), "The Etiology of Acute Brain Swelling Following Experimental Head Injury," *J. Neurosurg.*, **24**, 47–56.

[20] Lindenberg, R., Fisher, R. S., Durlacher, S. H., Lovitt, W. V. and Freytag, E. (1955), "Lesions of the Corpus Callosum Following Blunt Mechanical Trauma to the Head," *Amer. J. Path.*, **31**, 297–317.

[21] Lindenberg, R. and Freytag, E. (1969), "Morphology of Brain Lesions From Blunt Trauma in Early Infancy," *Arch. Path.*, **87**, 298–305.

[22] London, P. S. (1967), "Some Observations on the Course of Events After Severe Injury to the Head," *Ann. roy. Coll. Surg. Engl.*, **41**, 460–478.

[23] McPherson, P. and Graham, D. I. (1972), Personal observations.

[24] Nevin, N. C. (1967), "Neuropathological Changes in the White Matter Following Head Injury," *J. Neuropath.*, **26**, 77–84.

[25] Ommaya, A. K. (1966), "Trauma to the Nervous System," *Ann. roy. Coll. Surg. Engl.*, **39**, 317–347.

[26] Ommaya, A. K., Grubb, R. L. and Naumann, R. A. (1971), "Coup and Contre-coup Injury: Observations on the Mechanics of Visible Brain Injuries in the Rhesus Monkey," *J. Neurosurg.*, **35**, 503–516.

[27] Oppenheimer, D. R. (1968), "Microscopic Lesions in the Brain Following Head Injury," *J. Neurol. Neurosurg. Psychiat.*, **31**, 299–306.

[28] Peerless, S. J. and Rewcastle, N. B. (1967), "Shear Injuries of the Brain," *Canad. med. Ass. J.*, **96**, 577–582.

[29] Pudenz, R. H. and Shelden, C. H. (1946), "The Lucite Calvarium—A Method for Direct Observation of the Brain. II Cranial Trauma and Brain Movement," *J. Neurosurg.*, **3**, 487–505.

[30] Registrar General's Statistical Review of England and Wales (1969). London: H.M.S.O.

[31] Report on Hospital In-patient Enquiry (1968), Part I Tables. London: H.M.S.O.

[32] Sellier, K. and Unterharnscheidt, F. (1965), "The Mechanics of the Impact of Violence on the Skull," *Proc. 3rd Inter. Congr. Neurol. Surg.*, pp. 87–92 (A. Bischoff and F. Luthy, Eds.). Amsterdam: Excerpta Medica.

[33] Strich, S. J. (1969), "The Pathology of Brain Damage Due to Blunt Head Injuries," in *The Late Effects of Head Injury*, pp. 501–524 (A. E. Walker, W. F. Caveness and McD. Critchley, Eds.). Illinois: Thomas.

[34] Strich, S. J. (1970), "Lesions in the Cerebral Hemispheres After Blunt Head Injury," *J. clin. Path.*, **23**; *Suppl.* (Roy Coll. Path.), **4**, 166–171.

[35] Tomlinson, B. E. (1970), "Brain-stem Lesions After Head Injury," *J. clin. Path.*, **23**; *Suppl.* (Roy. Coll. Path.), **4**, 154–165.

[36] Treip, C. S. (1970), "Hypothalamic and Pituitary Injury," *J. clin. Path.*, **23**; *Suppl.* (Roy. Coll. Path.), **4**, 178–186.

[37] Unterharnscheidt, F. and Higgins, L. S. (1969), "Neuropathologic Effects of Translational and Rotational Acceleration of the Head in Animal Experiments," in *The Late Effects of Head Injury*, pp. 158–167 (A. E. Walker, W. F. Caveness and McD. Critchley, Eds.). Illinois: Thomas.

[38] Walker, A. E. (1970), "The Pathogenesis and Pathology of Head Injuries," *Proc. 6th Inter. Congr. Neuropath.*, pp. 155–175. Paris: Masson et Cie.

INDEX

INDEX

CAFÉ RACERS

SPEED, STYLE
AND TON-UP CULTURE

Michael Lichter & Paul d'Orleans

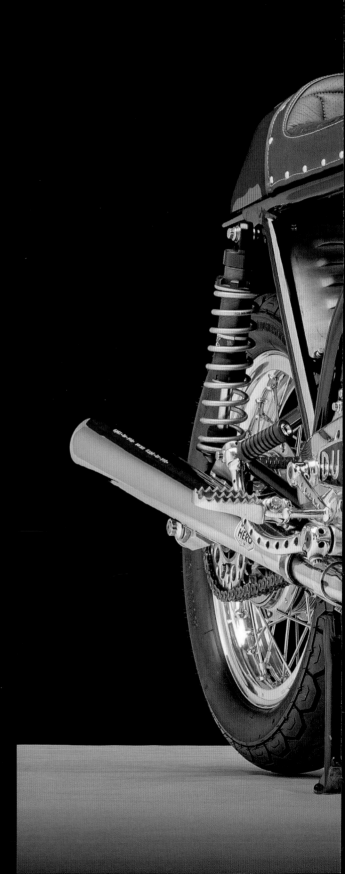

CONTENTS

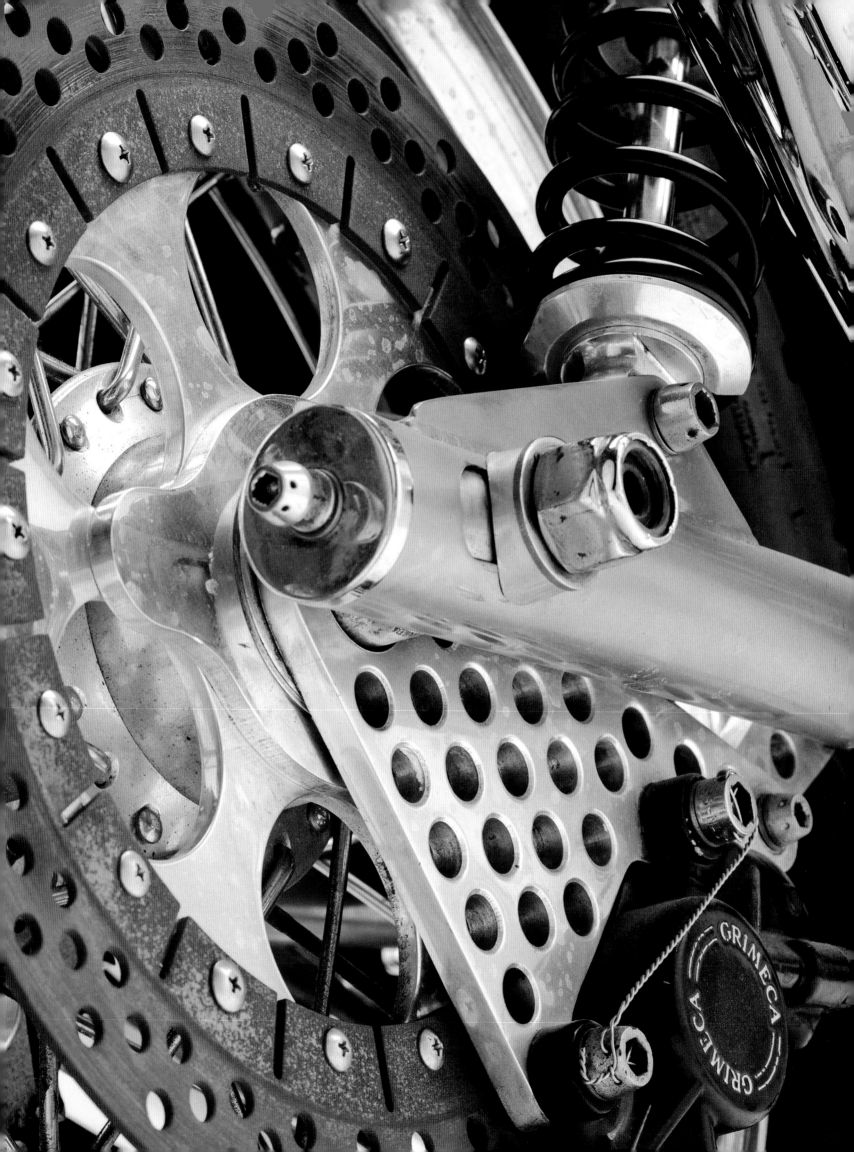

A CAFÉ RACER IN OHIO

Mark Mederski
Director, National Motorcycle Museum USA

IN MY HOMETOWN OF WOOSTER, OHIO, I spent time on a used, street-legal Briggs and Stratton minibike and eventually progressed to a slightly beat-up 1962 Honda 305 Dream, purchased from my slot-car buddy Bob. I needed some magazines to help me find my motorcycling self.

In the 1960s, via *Cycle World,* I could learn about choppers and see ads for banana seats, peanut tanks, long fork tubes, and high bars to give my lightweight Japanese bike or British bike the chopper look. The back pages carried months-old European Grand Prix (GP) racing coverage. These bikes had full fairings, with riders' feet back and butts tucked up against little streamlined decks. Those photos of the racers leaned way over showed riders taking motorcycle performance to an extreme.

I decided I was in with the GP thing; it was about real motorcycle performance, not style. My pal Bob came across an older motorcycle guy, Nelson, who became our mentor. Nelson was into Honda Super Hawks, on which he mounted low bars and moved the adjustable footpegs back at least one notch. That's when I put two and two together: rearsets plus fairings plus bump seats equals GP racing. Nelson was doing the road racer thing for the street, and he was hip to Honda's special parts catalog to race-kit a Super Hawk: long chrome megaphones, velocity stacks, number plates, a special seat, clip-ons, an aluminum rear fender, and alloy rims. He suggested we watch the racing at Nelson Ledges Raceway in Northeast Ohio. We were barely in the gate when castor fumes drifted our way and howling megaphones called to us. This was 1966. We saw Manx Nortons and Matchless G50s along with stripped and race-kitted Hondas and 250cc Yamaha production racers.

The die was cast. Following Nelson's approach, my 1962 Honda Dream soon had low bars and short megaphones and was cut down to resemble a CB92 Super Sports. I bought a Super Hawk in spring of 1969. I swapped the stock risers for flat bars while mounting an early CB450 tank, which was dechromed and molded to look long and sleek like Rickman racers, plus a pretty cool seat I designed and built with two light bulbs behind translucent red plexiglas. I utilized my industrial design studies at Ohio University, doing what Brits like Paul Dunstall and the Rickman brothers had done.

After ditching the stock rear fender and moving the footpegs all the way back, I felt like Mike Hailwood, hunched low, slid back on the seat, pressing my knees into the long fuel tank. With a set of CYB Honda racing megaphones, the noise from the Honda's 180-degree crankshaft sounded just great when wound out on the twisties south of Athens, Ohio. I stuffed some compact glass packs up the megaphones' large reverse cone openings, and that fine megaphone howl was legal, if I stayed off the throttle.

I bought a Honda CB750 in 1970, right after Dick Mann won Daytona on his kitted CR750. I ordered up a full fairing from Grizzly in California, cut a hole for a headlight, and put on some clip-ons. Bob built me some rearsets, since Dunstall rearsets had a bad reputation. I built a seat based on a Rickman item, which was spray-bombed candy apple red to match the factory Honda tank paint. Back out on the roads, I was running much faster than with the old Super Hawk.

Fifteen or twenty years after that 1970 café racer blip in America, these bikes could be purchased over the counter and were called sport bikes. Today ratty and worn-out CB350 and CB750 Hondas are stripped of their sheet metal and mufflers, and with the fitting of a few universal parts fitted such as clubman bars, voilá! They're café racers. There's a lot more moto-culture today than in 1970, with magazines and TV shows dedicated to café racers, and even if some of the bikes are ill-conceived, and their creators have never heard of Mike Hailwood or smelled castor fumes, I really enjoy watching it all happen again.

INTRODUCTION

THE CAFÉ RACER HEYDAY WAS ONLY A MOMENT, a blip on the radar, a mere dozen years in a tradition that began in the earliest days of motorcycling and continues today. That's the tradition of a motorcycle built for speed and a rider bent on achieving it. The original term *café racer* was derogatory South London slang for a young motorcyclist who tore up the highways on hot bike and hung out in roadside cafés, rather than risking himself on the racetrack. The term was soon civilized and became a badge of honor among road riders enamored of speed in 1950s–1960s England.

WHAT IS A CAFÉ RACER?

The label also stuck to the motorcycles themselves, which were already part of a 40-year tradition. Bike factories had explicitly catered to the speed jones of road riders since the 1910s, offering race-tuned—or at least race-associated—bikes for use on public roads. The iconic café racer motorcycles of the 1960s—the BSA Gold Star, the Norton-based specials—did not appear fully formed, but rather evolved over decades. The Gold Star was almost 20 years into its development as a clubman racer when it flowered into the iconic DBD34 in 1956. The distinctive look of the post-1950 Norton Manx inspires café racer builders to this day, but the sports/racing OHC Norton was introduced in 1927 (the CS1). What was new in the 1950s was the universal adoption of swingarms and telescopic forks. These updated the look of racing bikes, even if their engines and gearboxes hadn't changed much since the 1930s. The Triumph twins so popular with 1950s café racers were merely an updated 1930s design, and the same type of rider hammered them down pre–World War II roads.

The classic café racer moment of the late 1950s established a highly visible style. Riders continue to modify their machines in a similar fashion, with low handlebars, rear-set footrests, and an abbreviated seat, because this combination keeps a rider tucked out of the wind. Equally important, it sings the song of speed. Factories today build café racers that echo the classic 1950s shape, because it works. Some of their bikes are retro and some are techno, but they all have roots in a century-old tradition.

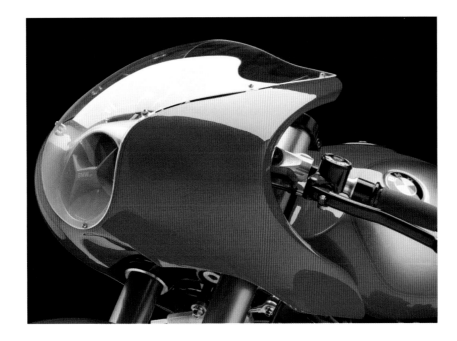

CHAPTER
1

"The first motorcycle race began when the second motorcycle was built."
—*Anonymous*

RACERS ON THE ROAD

THE AXIOM ABOVE IS NOT LITERALLY TRUE. The second motorcycle was built very soon after the first, but an ocean away. Historians disagree on which motorcycle was actually first, but they do know that the earliest recorded motorcycles were built by clever engineers with the same basic ideas and methods, thousands of miles apart and unknown to each other.

The axiom is figuratively true, though. Had Sylvester Roper and Henri-Guillaume Perreaux met with their respective steam-powered creations, you can be damn sure they would have raced! How do I know? Contemporary accounts of both men record their extensive testing of their suprisingly similar beasts on the dusty, horseshit roads of 1867, the year both men invented the motorcycle. Perreaux rode outside his Paris studio near the Tuileries Palace, while Roper made regular trips from his home in Roxbury, Massachusetts, to the Boston Yacht Club and back, a distance of seven miles. Both men developed their ideas, building three- and four-wheel versions of their steam contraptions. But I'd give the competitive edge to Roper, who in 1895 built an improved version of his "steam velocipede," which was a properly developed steam motorcycle.

Roper was motorcycling's first hot rod - and its first martyr. Roper is the patron saint of our two-wheeled passion, and he died for the same sin that stains twenty-first-century bikers: the lust for speed. On June 1, 1896, at the tender age of 73, he was asked to demonstrate his "self propeller," as he called it, on the Charles River Speedway, a banked wooden bicycle racing track in Cambridge. By this date, a few crude petrol-engined moto-bicycles had appeared on bicycle racing tracks. They were immediately engaged as cycle pacers, providing a draft for fast bicyclists during competition. Professional bicycle racing was extremely popular in the late 1800s, and crowds thronged to see the action, especially when the newfangled, unstable, and unreliable motocycle created a fast-moving catastrophe. The petrol engine's bark echoed across the wooden track. Engineers struggled to keep the loud, smoking machines running, trying not to crash the horribly wobbly and high-centered contraptions beneath them, while racing trains of bicycles followed behind. Panting racers on ridiculously high-geared bicycles pressed their front wheels against a rolling bar to keep pace, inhaling smoke and unburned gasoline by the lungful, and all the while trying their damnedest to beat the fellows beside them. It was absolutely worth the price of admission for spectators; meanwhile, racers and race promoters were getting rich.

Roper's steam cycle had a reputation around Boston as the fastest thing moving, period. It was able to "climb any hill and outrun any horse," as Roper stated. He was invited to pace a few cyclists at the Speedway. This, of course, became a race, which Roper won handily; the bicyclists simply couldn't keep up with the steamer's estimated 40 miles per hour. Roper was elated, high on his proof of concept after 30 years' effort making motorcycles. Track officials invited him to show what the hissing beast could to with the leash off, and the 73-year-old inventor was excited to oblige. After a few scorching laps, Roper wobbled and slowed toward his pit "crew"—his son Charles—into whose arms he collapsed, dead. Roper likely had a heart attack from an extremely elevated heart rate in an effort to become the world's fastest human on anything but a train, which by 1896 could travel at 70 miles per hour. Thus, Roper became the first motorcycle fatality—not from a wreck, but from the thrill of riding. Put a sprocket-edged halo on the man; he was the first to get it about motorcycles.

As the infant motorcycle industry wobbled toward stability, Roper's exercise as a bicycle pacer was repeated on tracks around the world, on ever-bigger track machines, with engines from De Dion–Bouton, Marchand, Peugeot, or Anzani. While Roper and Perreaux invented the motorcycle simultaneously, it was the French who planted the seed for the world's motorcycle industry. The big bicycle pacers soon raced against one another more frequently on the banked

A. G. Chapple of the New York Motorcycle Club hard at speed in 1908 during a road trial on his Indian "torpedo tank" single-cylinder sports machine. *Paul d'Orléans collection.*

bicycle tracks of the 1890s, which gave event promoters like John S. "Jack" Prince a few ideas, and the age of board track racing began. These were the first specialized racing machines, totally unsuitable for roadwork.

As far as we know, the first official motorcycle-only road race was held on a one-mile course at Sheen House in Richmond, England, on November 29, 1897. Charles Jarrot won in two minutes eight seconds on his Fournier motorcycle. This means unofficial road racing had been going on prior to the Sheen House race. We know that in France, motorcycles participated in official multivehicle racing (including cars and trikes) as early as 1894, in the Paris-Rouen race. That means the first illegal contests were even earlier.

It's no leap to guess that motorcyclists raced from the first instant, even on unreliable, fire-prone, and dangerous vehicles, and that their pilots were instantly addicted to the sheer joy of speed. Speed is the essential allure of motorcycles.

RACE ON SUNDAY, SELL ON MONDAY

Roper was not selling replicas of his unique steam velocipede—he never even patented his designs—but others were deeply interested in making a profit from moto-bicycles. Charles H. Metz, president of Waltham Enterprises, entered the first known motorcycle speed contest, at the Charles River Speedway, in July 1900. He recorded a time of seven minutes for a five-mile run, beating his competition

The Norton BRS and, later, the Model 16H Sport were about the hottest machines on English roads of the early 1920s. This gent shows the proper attire for fast roadwork: World War I flying goggles, tight-fitting leather gloves and jacket (there's a collared shirt and tie underneath), jodhpurs, knee socks, and a pair of brogues. 1923. *Paul d'Orléans collection*

handily, and sales of his Orient motorcycles thrived after he advertised the win. Demonstrating the worth of machines via races and speed contests became the pattern for motorcycle advertising for the next 100 years.

The first racing motorcycles appeared in catalogs as early as 1903, and the first racers appeared on the road a few years later, as long-distance races became popular with spectators and provided aspiring motorcycle builders with a venue to showcase their products. The rough, unpaved, and cobbled roads of Europe and the United States witnessed reliability trials over hundreds of miles. These were races, of course, but since few machines completed the courses, reliability was tested more than speed. England missed out on the fun, since racing on public roads was illegal there. That led to the creation in 1907 of the Brooklands speedbowl and the Isle of Man Tourist Trophy (TT) motorcycle races. Both tracks were outside the reach of Parliament's stupidity; Brooklands was on private property, and the Isle of Man had its own laws, thank you very much.

THE UR-CAFÉ RACER: NORTON'S BRS

It wasn't long before Brooklands Specials and TT Replicas began appearing in the catalogs of bike makers, supposedly sold for racing only. But in 1916 Norton offered a Brooklands *Road* Special (BRS), which may have been the world's first production café racer. The BRS was a stripped but road-legal racing machine. (Not that any government required roadworthiness testing in those days!) The name says it all: it was a track-racing motorcycle with the speed required to circulate the most famous racing track in the world, but

it was intended for a rider's use on the road. The name acknowledges that a certain type of rider wants a fast and impressive machine for everyday use, one that might never see the hallowed surface of the fastest track on the planet, but that endows its rider with the perfume of the place, the aura of competition and victory, heroic deeds and legends. The name packs a wallop, although it passes without comment as the most natural thing in the world. Of *course* motorcyclists want a road special of their racing machine.

Factories have offered *pur sang* racing bikes for sale since 1903, when Mars advertised its Renntypus. Such racers were unsuitable for road use, being built for speedbowls, with no brakes or clutch, and a hunched-monkey riding position. The BRS was only uncompromising in being stripped of deep fenders and lights, with a fairly high gear ratio for its direct belt drive, and low but not cramping handlebars. It featured the styling that would compromise every café racer for following century and beyond.

Soon other factories, in Europe at least, offered race replicas for the sporting rider or clubman who raced at club events on weekends and likely rode the same machine to work daily. These clubman models, named after specific racetracks in the late 1910s through the late 1950s, became a new genre of motorcycle. The BSA and Velocette and Matchless Clubman models are today recognized as factory café racers. Many postwar machines were identical to prewar models, but with telescoping forks and plunger rear suspension added. If we trace back to the direct predecessors of these machines, we find the Norton BRS, a genius of an idea, catering to tearaways, motorcycle hooligans, hot rods, speed demons, and Promenade Percys.

THE AMERICAN SCENE

While British factories, having experienced a smidgen of racing success at the Isle of Man TT, the Ulster GP, or at Brooklands, quickly labeled their stripped-down models as TT Replicas or Brooklands Specials, and the European factories named machines after their own important races, American factories never offered racing models for hot road use. Specialized tracks in the United States meant flat dirt ovals or banked board tracks of wood, and in the 1910s and 1920s, American track-racing motorcycles were completely unsuitable for road use. The rare moments when Harley or Indian offered road-going racers, (board track machines with gears and brakes), the bikes were invariably destined for Europe, to satisfy a small but important demand for road racers. Americans didn't have the luxury of a ready-made racer on the road, so they had to build their own.

Speed-bent riders have always dropped their handlebars and ditched heavy tinware, but in California, a new breed of hot roadster evolved to modernize older bikes, especially

Hot bikes were a global phenomenon from the beginning of the sport. These Brazilian tearaways are sitting astride two of the fastest road bikes from Europe. The left machine is a circa-1928 Moto Guzzi C4V, the Corsa four-valve, overhead-camshaft sports racer capable of 90 miles per hour. The rider on the right has a TT Replica Rudge, also with a four-valve engine but with pushrod-operated valves. Both bikes have excellent brakes and handling, far exceeding the quality of the roads in Brazil! *Paul d'Orléans collection*

Harley's ubiquitous J model V-twin. The J was tough and could be tweaked for an excellent turn of speed, but its chassis grew outdated by the mid-1920s, as lower, shorter motorcycles supplanted the old long-and-high style of the teens. The California cut-down, or simply the cut-down, became a popular hot roadster. In it the J frame top tubes were lowered and the rear section shortened, requiring pockets in gas tanks to clear the cylinder tops, with smaller diameter wheels suitable for the shorter wheelbase. Their engines were tuned via Ricardo cylinders with extra metal in the combustion chamber roof, giving a higher compression ratio and better breathing for the inlet-over-exhaust Harley engine. Occasionally a second camshaft was added for more positive valve actuation, and in all cases, the machines looked and performed better.

Cut-downs still had to cope with unpaved American roads, so they retained fairly wide cow-horn handlebars for maximum control. By the 1930s, the cut-down look evolved with changes in Harley, Indian, and Excelsior chassis design to a lower seat height with teardrop-shaped saddle tanks. Meanwhile, American Motorcyclist Association (AMA) Class C racing using production-based racing motorcycles took hold. Road riders imitated the stripped look of Daytona sand and dirt-oval racers of the 1930s by removing their heavy front fenders and chopping or bobbing the rear fender. The bob-job was the evolution of the cut-down, the American racer on the road for the next 25 years, until paved road racing courses were built in the States, and American race bikes (the Harley KRTT and XRTT) finally resembled their European cousins. The bob-job (which in later years became simply the bobber) was a direct cousin of the clubman machine (and hence the café racer), but it had evolved to suit its native environment.

THE CLUBMAN RACERS

As the 1930s progressed, European road racing became highly specialized. The big factories like BMW, DKW, Gilera, Velocette, and Moto Guzzi battled each other with multicylinder, overhead camshaft, supercharged exotica. Giant-killer Norton remained true to its durable single-cylinder racers

This 1925 BMW R37 was the factory's first OHV motorcycle and was immediately pressed into service as a racer. This snappily dressed young rider has already established two café-racer standards, having dropped his handlebars and ditched his exhaust for straight-through exhaust pipes. *Motor-Sport-Museum, Hockenreimring*

(using sophisticated double overhead camshaft engines), but the factories offered the average rider nothing to compare with such race machinery. Being sensible, they offered instead road-legal machines with less complexity but a good turn of speed, their aforementioned clubman models. While occasionally raced, these were primarily tailored for the speed merchant. Since speed is expensive, and tuning an engine is laborious handwork, these sports racers were always range-motorcycles. They were the most expensive and desirable items in a catalog, although most riders could only dream of speed's luxury in the economic doldrums of the 1930s.

Even staid factories like BSA offered hot roadsters smeared with racer juice: the original M24 Gold Star (1938)

was named for Wal Handley's 100-plus-miles-per-hour laps of the Brooklands track and is essentially a Brooklands Replica with lights. Norton sold pure racers, but its Manx Grand Prix (1936 onward) could be ordered with full lighting, to get you to the track on time, even if the track was the road outside your door. Velocette would and did sell its KTT (code for TT Replica) as fully road legal, which is why I'm able to ride my 1934 KTT mkIV on California's roads with no lights or silencer. ("They came that way, officer, and are grandfathered into legality.") European marques joined the fray, with *super sport* the typical cue for the clubman. BMW sold the R51SS, a private example of which was raced by Tim Reid in the Isle of Man TT in 1939. Makes like Terrot, Peugeot, and FN sold super sport models, for racing or the sheer joy of a fast machine on the road. Rudge's Ulster (named after the first 90-miles-per-hour race average in the Ulster GP) and Triumph's Tiger 100 both found their way onto America's dirt tracks and roads as global media expanded American riders' consciousness of foreign opportunities.

AFTER THE WAR

War is generally thought to benefit industry and the advance of technology. But World War II didn't do much for motorcycling except to unleash a flood of ex-military, low-performance machines onto the market, which didn't help the sales of new motorcycles in the immediate postwar period. A few manufacturers had been toiling quietly in their off-hours, preparing designs for a postwar return to civilian production, at least in England. Philip Vincent and Phil Irving penned the revolutionary HRD-Vincent Series B Rapide during wartime. It was a giant step in the right direction for the speed-conscious rider, but few riders could afford such extravagance. Like the men who rode their motorcycles, many manufacturers never returned after World War II, and the entire genre of bikes built around bought-in engines from JAP or Rudge or AMC simply disappeared.

Early 1920s: Members of the Oakland Motorcycle Club relaxing with their Harley J Model cut-downs. The top frames have been lowered, requiring the deep pockets in the fuel tanks to clear the valve gear. The middle machine has been converted into a 500cc single-cylinder by blanking off the rear jug. This machine has the most radically modified chassis. None have front brakes! *Rich Ostrander collection*

Nonetheless, riders who wanted a fast machine sorted themselves out in the late 1940s. They carried on riding prewar hotrods or tuned up ex-military bikes while waiting for the industry to wake up to a new reality on the road. In the United States, where populated areas tended to be devoid of twisty roads, the focus remained on dirt tracks and drag racing. The British government needed cash, and it held vital raw materials like aluminum for ransom, forcing motorcycle factories to export or die. That meant they had to sell to America. What America wanted was bigger, faster motorcycles, which the British were happy to supply, increasing the engine capacity of their popular vertical twins from Triumph, Norton, BSA, Royal Enfield, and AJS/Matchless from 500cc to 650cc by 1950. A few of these were converted to café racers in the United States, but enthusiasts of European-style road racing were rare, as few U.S. racetracks were yet paved. The HRD-Vincent marque was unsuitable for dirt-tracking, but it was perfect for U.S. street racing and speed records. The image of Rollie Free at the Bonneville Salt Flats, lying prone atop a Black Shadow at 150 miles per hour in 1948, clad only in his bathing suit, became the most famous motorcycle photograph in the world.

Basil B. Decker, in Washington State, aboard his "Sam Oppie Special." Oppie was a race tuner for the Seattle Harley dealer, and he built 20 to 30 cut-downs with two-cam JDH engines. *Rich Ostrander collection*

THE AMERICAN SPEED CRAVING

The most famous American street racer in the 1940s was Marty Dickerson, although few knew his name. Dickerson was hired in 1948, at the tender age of 19, by the Los Angeles HRD-Vincent dealer Mickey Martin, expressly to ride a new Rapide around the small towns of the Southwest, challenging local riders to unofficial street drags in cars or motorcycles. Dickerson never lost, and quite a few HRD-Vincents were

sold after his exploits, which had the larger effect of cementing the reputation of the Vincent as the fastest thing on wheels, confirmed by Free's and Dickerson's record-breaking exploits on the Bonneville Salt Flats. Dickerson's rivals rode Harleys and Indians (the only U.S. factories left standing after the Depression), but American speed style veered ever farther away from European road racing and toward bob-job imitations of dirt track racers.

On the other side of the Atlantic, European factories built tiny utilitarian motorcycles to weave around the rubble of their bombed-out cities until 1950. Racing was conducted with prewar machines. Germany and Italy were banned from international competition. French and Belgian factories, big race contenders prewar, were hardly visible postwar. So

B.S.A. 500 c.c. O.H.V. Gold Star
Model M 24

Engine. Single cylinder single port O.H.V., 82 mm bore x 94 mm. stroke, 496 c.c.; individually built and bench tested; aluminium cylinder and head; valve seat inserts; cylinder liner; B.S.A. dry sump lubrication with 5-pint oil tank under saddle; oil indicator on engine; enclosed O.H.V. gear; roller bearings on both drive side and gear side of mainshaft, new design silent timing gear; improved tappet construction facilitating adjustment; Amal T.T. carburetter with Burgess air cleaner.

Transmission. Engine shaft cush drive; front chain ½ in. x .305 in., with oil bath; rear chain ⅝ in. x ¼ in. with lower run guard; five plate clutch embodying fabric inserts, on double row ball bearing centre; B.S.A. four-speed close-ratio gearbox; enclosed foot gear change; gear ratios 4.8, 5.2, 8.15, 11.8.

Frame. Triangulated cradle type; 531 tubing; front fork shock absorber with finger adjustment; steering

The now famous B.S.A. Gold Star — the fastest standard sports machine you can buy. It is fitted with **quickly detachable rear wheel.**

damper; 3½-gallon tank; knee grips; Dunlop Fort tyres, 3.00—20 front, 3.50—19 rear; 7 in. dia. x 1⅛ in. wide brakes; spring-up rear stand; lifting handle on rear guard; **quickly detachable rear wheel;** front stand; adjustable footrests.

Equipment. B.S.A. flexibly mounted handlebar with special controls; racing twist grip throttle; ratchet lever for front brake; adjustable Terry saddle; metal toolbox with complete tool kit; inflator; gear-driven Lucas 6-volt Magdyno lighting set with compensated voltage control; tank instrument panel; anti-vibration battery; electric horn; valances to front and rear mudguard; provision for pillion footrests. Prop Stand. Mudguard Pad.

Finish. Black and chromium; chromium tank with matt silver panels; chromium wheel rims with matt silver centres. Wheelbase 54 in.; clearance 4⅝ in.; saddle height 28½ in.

16

First in a long line of iconic Gold Stars, the BSA M24 of 1938 was a Brooklands replica of Wal Handley's very special racing BSA, which lapped that track at over 100 miles per hour—earning an actual gold star for its rider, a small star pin with enameled "100," meant to be attached to one's British Motorcycle Racing Club badge. *Paul d'Orléans collection*

racing in friendly European states was dominated by British machines. Almost all of these were single-cylinder racers from Velocette and Norton, who began supplying pukka racers immediately postwar and of course dominated GP racing in the inaugural World Championships by 1949. Street riders could buy a Norton International or Manx for hot-rodding, but Velocette failed to offer a clubman version of its OHC racers. Other factories did, though, and by the late 1940s, BSA and Matchless once again offered tuned roadsters for the speed addict. The year 1950 was a turning point for all the British and European factories. These countries finally shook off the detritus of war and began to prosper, which meant that riders could afford motorcycles again.

The majority of riders immediately after the war still used motorcycles or sidecars for purely utilitarian reasons, but

with increased prosperity and cheaper cars by 1950, the role of motorcycles shifted permanently (in modern industrial nations) to vehicles of pleasure. Performance has always been the number one selling point for bikes, even when buyers only use them to commute. But the heady optimism of increasing prosperity in the 1950s, plus a growing population of young men whose energies weren't spent on war or supporting a family (yet), meant that motorcycles advertised power and more power, which could finally be used on the improving roads of the United States.

THE LEATHER JACKET AND ROCK-AND-ROLL

The trend across Europe was also toward bigger, faster machines, built for the American market. This trend also meant the locals could enjoy ever-faster machines on their home roads. A new generation of young riders, freed of economic and military concerns, focused instead on simply having fun with their motorcycles.

A wave of pop-culture influences combined in England in the early 1950s to create an entirely new look for young bikers: the swagger of rock-and-roll, faster motorcycles, and the biker aesthetic revolving around the leather jacket. While the zippered leather jacket had been around since the 1930s, it was popularized in films like *The Wild One*. The film was banned in England, but nothing is more alluring than a banned film, and the image of Marlon Brando in his Schott Perfecto jacket became a sexy new icon. In England, Lewis Leathers had been serving motorcyclists and aviators since the turn of the century, and suddenly its designs, such as the Lightning and Plainsman, were absolutely necessary

motorcycle wear. There had been no music associated with motorcycles before the war, but the driving beat of rock-and-roll perfectly suited the rhythmic thunder of a four-stroke vertical twin motor. In no time at all, a flourishing Rocker culture combined all these elements into a distinctive style of moto-clothing that endures to this day.

THE CAFF RACERS

Leather-clad youth on hot new Triumphs and Nortons and Vincents, with dropped handlebars and rearset footrests, were suddenly and spontaneously swarming at transport cafés along Britain's highways. They were looking for

A 1941 Harley JD. *Paul d'Orléans collection*

This 1925 BMW R37 was the factory's first OHV motorcycle, and was immediately pressed into service as a racer. This snappily dressed young rider has already established two café racer standards, having dropped his handlebars, and ditched his exhaust for straight-through exhaust pipes.
Hockenheim Museum

caff racers. In South London slang, that was no compliment—instead of racing on the track, they merely raced from café to café. This, of course, was absolutely true, no matter how many street racers graduated to real track work.

The name stuck, and it lost its sting—just as the term *Impressionism* was initially spat at a late-1800s style of painting but is used admiringly today, and the insult *1%er* became a patch worn proudly by chopper fans in the 1960s. Riders in flashy leather gear (or equally likely, cheaper imitations) were also known as Rockers, after their preferred music and style icons.

THE CLUBMAN'S TT

Thus the rapidly beating heart of fast road riding moved to England in the 1950s. It was the English motorcycle manufacturers who were truly on target in the period, as clubman racing exploded in popularity. While the Isle of Man had been considered the toughest and most important road race in the world since the dawn of the 20th century, Grand Prix racing had by the 1930s become specialized with multiple cylinders, double overhead camshafts, and superchargers, none of which was available to the privateer, and certainly not the road rider. The FIM decided in its wisdom that supercharging was to blame for a rise in unattainable (to the consumer) engine technology. This kind of technology was largely irrelevant and opposed to the core aim of (or justification for) road racing: to improve the breed and advance the science of the motorcycle's engine, chassis, suspension, and so on.

Limitations on GP machines failed to staunch the rapid growth of exotica in postwar racing. Factories are more interested in winning than following noble intentions. But the initiation of a new Clubman's TT at the Isle of Man in 1947, specifically for road-going, privately owned machines, encouraged factories to offer hot roadsters to support the race series. Suddenly, the fastest road machines from all factories were pitted against each other on the most famous track in the world, and it seemed every factory responded quickly with special clubman models or race-tuning kits to (hopefully) transform ordinary machines into racers. As expected, the Norton International and HRD-Vincent and Triumph twins were present, but plenty of less-well-known factories built clubman machines, such as Douglas with its 90+ models, and in the first years of the new TT, Rudge and Excelsior prewar sports racers. AJS/Matchless, BSA, and Velocette were common, and even Royal Enfield and Panthers were given a try.

The following essay captures the essence of the café racer scene.

like-minded riding pals or simply taking a break from scrubbing off the edges of their tires in those prefreeway days. These young congregants were much discussed in both the motorcycling and popular press of the day, in contrast to their prewar forbears, who were discussed in the motorcycling press only, and even then, only occasionally. A dawning (or invented) awareness of youth culture was a hot topic in the trash press of the day, and high-speed motorcycle riding by attractive youth wearing distinctive garb was easy fodder for print media (and when it arrived, on TV too). With the glare of the media spotlight came both fame and derision, as well as a new label. No longer were young tearaways called Promenade Percys or even clubmen. Their stylistic aping of Grand Prix racing machinery, mixed with the reality of young amateurs sitting at transport cafés while their hot machines sat outside, earned them the name of

LONDON'S OTHER CAFÉ RACER CLUB

DAVID LANCASTER

London's Mean Fuckers MC (Motorcycle Club) grew out of a late-1980s melting pot of punk rock's DIY attitude, respect for a good leather outfit, skate culture, and a love of bikes. The classic bike scene was divided into two conservative elements, and each believed it alone held the flame. *Classic Bike* magazine readers shunned home-brewed specials in favor of winter-long, washer-correct restorations, while the "heritage" Rocker movement was stuck in the past. "I was berated by a 59 Club classic section member for wearing a pudding basin on a 1970s Guzzi," recalls Ben Part, an early Mean Fucker, ace photographer, and cofounder of *Sideburn* magazine. Prosper Keating, who would later edit *Fast Classics* magazine, recalls being told, "You shouldn't wear that riding that," but was asked to consider joining the 59 Club as long he "accepted some advice on the wardrobe. They weren't fucking kidding!" Neither camp appealed.

The bikes of choice for the Mean Fuckers in the late 1980s were far from lavish. London's new RUBs (Rich Urban Bikers) sunk their cash into garish OW01 Yamahas, GSXR-1100s, and the like, whose amazing performance and paint schemes were too much in every way for swift urban riding to Mean Fucker tastes. Night racing through London required a punchy, light Triumph or Norton twin, not a 100-horsepower behemoth. Thus, Bonnies, Commandos, Guzzis, and Ducati twins were the rides of choice, and most were café-racered, tweaked, home-painted, or built-up specials. They married rugged performance with a timeless cool.

The Mean Fuckers MC started in the late 1980s on a very small scale, with founders Johnny Campling (with a BSA) and Robert Carr (a Moto Guzzi man) devoted to a certain kind of revivalism, which owed as much to The Clash as to pre-unit Tritons. "The name was the last man standing, that is the last thing we could remember, from a drunken evening with me, Johnny and a guy called Chris Evans," remembers Robert Carr. The club's distinctive signage was set simple and early: at first a hand-stamped aluminum badge, and then a skull sporting a pudding basin. Johnny and his brother Rich Campling were mostly behind the skull, with Carr making the stamped alloy badges "cut by hand, and stamped with a punch set I'd bought at a secondhand shop somewhere."

In its early days (1989 to 1994), the collective would ride mad-fast around central London on Wednesday nights, from South London and North London pubs to the Bar Italia in Soho. (Nobody died.) At those early meetings you'd likely find Matt Davis (now publisher of *DiCE*), artist Conrad Leach, Ben Part (Sideburn), Prosper Keating (*Fast Classics*), along with stylish riders and skilled bike builders like Jake Turner, Nick Walker, Kojo, Cres, Dixie, and others.

The cast coming in and out of this orbit included David Vanian of the Damned, Johnny Stuart (author of the fantastic book *Rockers!*), Paul Simonon of the Clash, and rare, but oh-so-glamorous visits by Chrissie Hynde. The link with the punk ethos that had informed the Mean Fuckers' look and attitude was strong, as Hynde had worked at Malcolm McLaren and Vivienne Westwood's King's Road seminal punk shop Sex before kicking off her musical career with Mick Jones of The Clash and then starting The Pretenders.

Ask members for a description of the Mean Fuckers, and they'll reach for the same word: a club for "misfits." Or, as longtime member Cres puts it: "People I can trust to ride with. Possibly also people with too many motorcycles, and too many sunglasses." Some 25 years later the Mean Fuckers MC remains a group which "seems to have got a life of its own," according to member Nick Walker—still ragged, still elegant.

1962 BSA DBD34 GOLD STAR CLUBMAN

Owner: Herb Harris

- 499cc OHV single-cylinder
- 40 hp
- Single-leading-shoe 190mm front brake
- 1½-in GP carb
- 115 mph top speed
- Built 1956–1963
- Price new £277

THE IMMORTAL GOLD STAR MOTORCYCLE was introduced as BSA's Brooklands Replica (with full road equipment) in 1938, after Wal Handley lapped the Brooklands speedbowl at over 100 miles per hour on an Empire Star model. The actual gold star was an enameled pin, worn with pride on a racer's lapel after a race lap over 100 miles per hour. Wearers of the gold star formed an elite club. Only 141 riders earned the badge between 1922 and 1939, when Brooklands closed for World War II. While Brooklands didn't revive after the war, the "Goldie" lived on, doing an amazing variety of tasks, including tourer, scrambler, trials bike, and full-blooded racer in the Isle of Man Clubman's TT, which it dominated between 1947 and 1956. Every Gold

Star had an all-aluminum cylinder barrel and head. Every motor was hand-assembled and dynamometer-tested, and the dyno results came with every machine.

The ultimate Gold Star model was the DBD34 500cc, introduced in 1956. This was a very fast and uncompromising machine. It had a notoriously tall first gear due to an all-needle-roller, close-ratio gearbox; first gear was good for over 60 miles per hour. The DBD34 was available in three forms: the Catalina scrambler, named after California's Catalina Island GP off-road race; the Touring, with normal handlebars and footrests; and the Clubman, intended for road racing, with clip-ons, rearsets, and a massive 1.5-inch GP racing carburetor.

The Herb Harris 1962 BSA shown at Ton Up! is an immaculate example of the DBD34 Gold Star Clubman. It embodies the magnetic allure of this chrome-and-aluminum street racer. The Gold Star was the real deal, the original café racer, as far more were sold for street use than for track racing. It took a committed rider to use one daily, as kick-starting the 499cc single-cylinder engine took a bit of skill, especially with a full-race GP carb, which had to be tickled for the correct amount of fuel needed to start the beast. After a few healthy kicks, the distinctive muffler (a capped megaphone) barks in response, with a unique mechanical twitter on the overrun. It's a siren song that lured cash from the pockets of speed-crazed riders by the thousands.

1962 NORTON 30M MANX

Owner: Mark Mederski

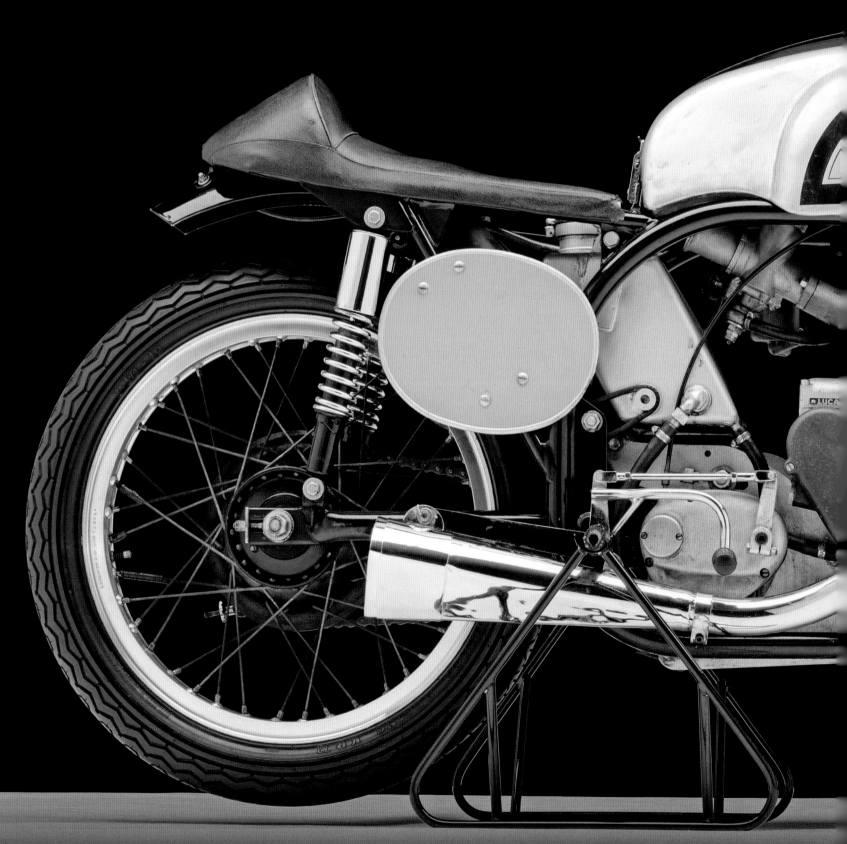

- 498cc shaft-and-bevel OHC
- 54 hp at 7,200 rpm
- 4-leading-shoe front brake
- Magnesium hubs, crankcase, and cambox
- Aluminum tanks and fenders
- 135 mph top speed
- 305 lbs

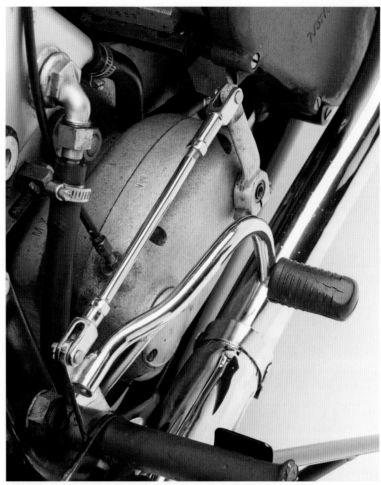

THE MANX WAS NORTON'S PRODUCTION RACER, available to any ambitious rider with cash. Closely based on the factory's Grand Prix machines, the Manx was a top-tier road racer, winning thousands of races from the 1950s through the 1970s and launching the race careers of champions. The Manx's double-loop tube frame was introduced in 1950. Three-time Isle of Man TT winner Harold Daniel nicknamed it the "Featherbed" after declaring his first race test to be like "riding on a feather bed" compared to any other motorcycle.

This 1962 Model 30M, in completely original condition, is the last in a long line of Norton overhead-camshaft single-cylinder racers. They were introduced in 1927 and were legendary race winners around the world for four decades. The name Manx (meaning "from the Isle of Man") was first used on Norton's 1936 Manx Grand Prix model. After World War II, the name was shortened to Manx, in 350cc and 500cc capacities. With its light, strong, full-cradle lugless tube frames and Roadholder telescopic forks, the post-1950 Manx was at the forefront of chassis technology for three decades.

Racing motorcycles require lightweight and strictly functional components, so the Manx has abbreviated front and rear fenders, a very short seat with a bump to give a secure riding position, a wide tank that straddles the parallel frame rails (with a cutaway at the back for the rider's knees), a central oil tank, a swept-back exhaust pipe (necessary when used with a fairing), short handlebars clamped to the frame tubes to keep the rider low and out of the wind, and rear-set foot controls

for a forward-leaning riding position. With spare adornment—Norton's traditional black-and-red pinstripes plus its amazing vampiric logo—the Manx was not only completely modern, but also beautiful in its curt simplicity.

The Manx engine was simple and robust, and by the 1960s, whole Manxes were purchased solely to remove their engines to power Formula Junior Monoposto racing cars. Thus, a glut of perfectly good Norton rolling chassis were available cheaply. These were filled with other engines—Triumphs, Vincents, and BSAs—and became Tritons, NorVins, and NorBSAs. They retained the Manx's good looks—while spawning a completely new genre of motorcycles, café racers.

NORVIN COMET

Builder: Garry Laurence

Owner: Mars Webster

- 1950 Vincent Comet engine
- 499cc OHV single-cylinder
- 30 hp at 5,800 rpm
- Circa 1954 Norton Featherbed frame and forks
- Manx alloy tanks and seat
- Triumph gearbox and conical wheels

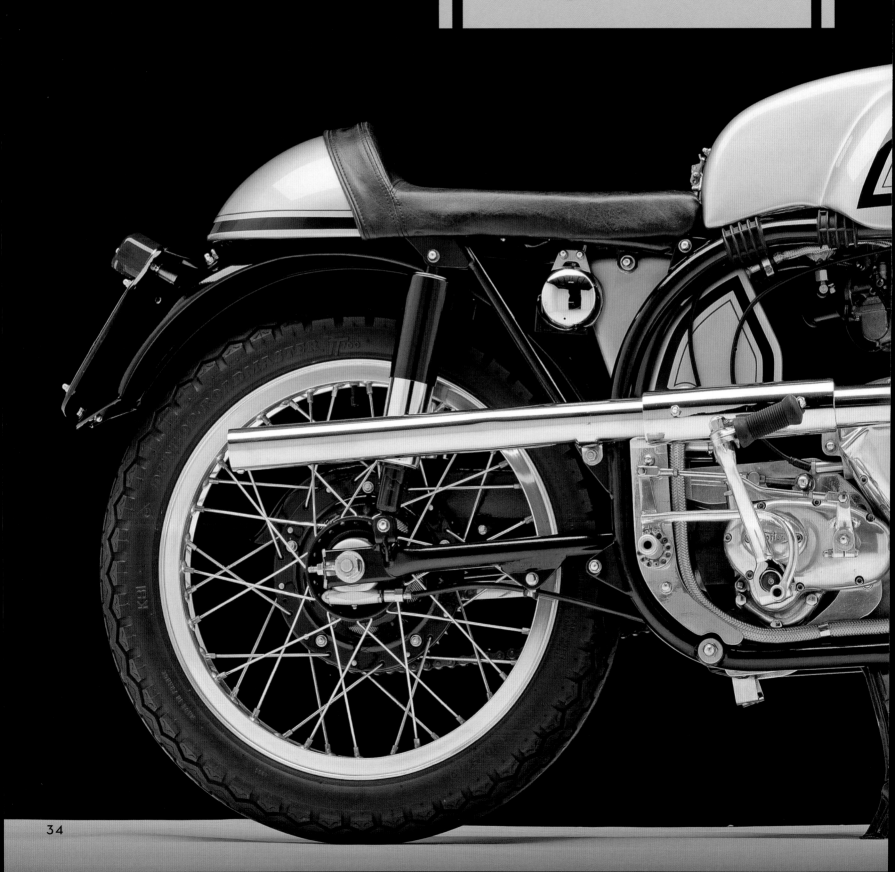

KENTON BOOKS
SUITE NO. 77
315 CHISWICK HIGH ROAD
LONDON
LONDON W4 4HH
UNITED KINGDOM

To: SAM ADAMSON
LIBERTY SPECIALTY MARKETS
20 FENCHURCH STREET
LONDON
EC3M 3AW
UNITED KINGDOM

Please ship this item via **Standard Shipping** no later than two business days from Mon Dec 15, 2014. Note that UPS Ground does not ship to P.O. Boxes, APO/FPO, or U.S. Protectorates.

Alibris Packing Slip

Ordered by: Sam Adamson

Ship to: Sam Adamson
Liberty Specialty Markets
20 Fenchurch Street
LONDON
EC3M 3AW
UNITED KINGDOM

Visit Kenton Books at http://kentonbo.alibrisstore.co.uk again!

PN #	Item ID	Alibris ID	Media Type	Title / Author	Order Date
55547797-1	97643516	B053312620	BOOK	Cafe Racers Paul D'Orleans Michael Lichter	Dec, 15 2014

New pp. 224.

Alibris Return Information

Alibris guarantees the condition of every item as it is described on our Web site. If you are not satisfied that your item is as described, please visit the following page for **important return instructions:**

http://www.alibris.co.uk/returns

All return requests must be submitted via the Alibris Web site. Any item returned without accompanying paperwork and/or more than 60 days after its shipment date will be discarded and you will not be eligible to receive a refund.

Problems? Questions? Suggestions? Send e-mail to Alibris Customer Service at info@alibris.com

THE STANDARD VINCENT CHASSIS, while groundbreaking and radical for 1946, was immediately outdated when Norton introduced the Featherbed frame in 1951. While the single-cylinder Vincent Comet and Meteor models were better handlers with their original Vincent chassis, being much lighter than the big-twin Rapide and Black Shadow models, an easy solution for even better Vincent handling was to shoehorn a Vincent engine into a Norton Featherbed frame. This was a tight fit for the twin, but the Comet's single-cylinder engine and separate gearbox was an easier union.

As Norton Featherbed frames were considered fair game for chassis poaching, the NorVin became a much-admired beast, especially when a Black Shadow engine was used, and for a time NorVin twins were the kings of café racers. Less common are single-cylinder Vincent engines in Norton frames; as the Comet engine has a separate gearbox, it was a far easier proposition to make a set of engine plates for the single. A Comet NorVin, being lighter, makes a much better-balanced whole within the Norton frame, which was designed for the Manx single. And the Comet can be turned fairly easily to racing Grey Flash spec, making a very tasty—and rare—café racer.

1970 VELOCETTE THRUXTON

Owner: Mark Mederski

- 499cc single-cylinder OHV
- 40 hp at 6,200 rpm
- Twin-leading-shoe front brake
- Clip-ons, rearsets, humped seat, and 1 3/8-in GP racing carb as standard
- 115 mph top speed
- Built 1965–1971
- About 1,000 produced

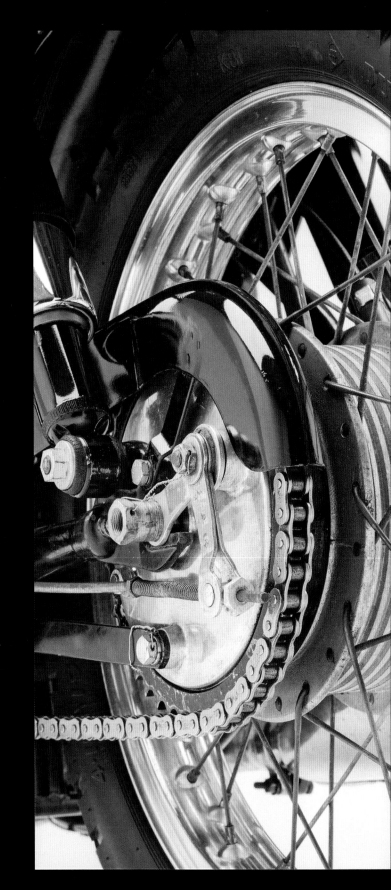

VELOCE WAS A SMALL, FAMILY-OWNED MOTORCYCLE BUILDER near Birmingham, England. It had a reputation for high-quality machines, starting with small two-strokes from 1905. In 1925, Veloce leapt to the forefront of engine technology, producing a light, fast, and durable overhead-camshaft 350cc, the K, which soon proved itself by winning and placing in the Isle of Man Junior TT many times before World War II, plus two 350cc World Championships after the war, in 1949 and 1950. The factory gave up making racing motorcycles in 1952, to focus on what they hoped would be a mass-produced commuter machine, the LE (Little Engine), a 200cc side-valve, water-cooled flat twin, which flopped.

A quick reassessment of priorities meant the introduction of the Venom 500cc single-cylinder sports model in 1955. The Venom was remarkably durable and fast, which Veloce proved by riding one at 100 miles per hour for 24 hours at the Montlhéry speedbowl in 1961, an achievement still never equaled by a 500cc machine.

Thruxton was a racetrack in England, converted from a World War II airfield, where popular 12-hour and 24-hour endurance races were held in the 1960s. Velocette's clubman version of the Venom, with a full catalog of racing parts as standard, won this and other endurance races many times. In 1965 Velocette offered a race replica to the public, the Thruxton, with a very special cylinder head created by Veloce using feedback from dealers and racers in the United States and Australia. The Thruxton proved very fast, exceptionally smooth, and reliable, with beautiful handling, and it won the Isle of Man Production TT in 1967. While nominally built for racing, the Thruxton came with full road equipment, making one hell of a café racer. Mark Mederski's Thruxton is in completely original condition.

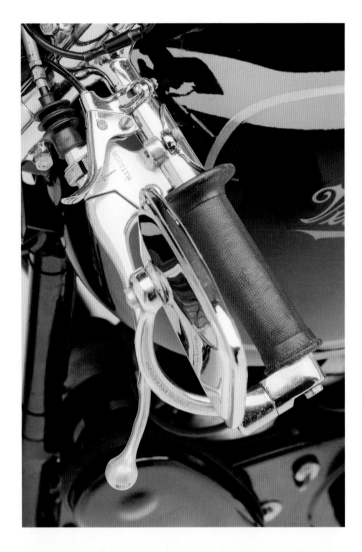

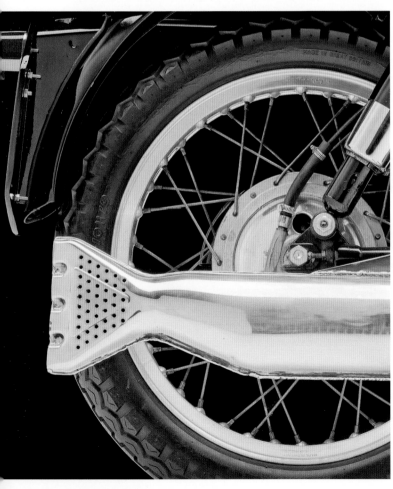

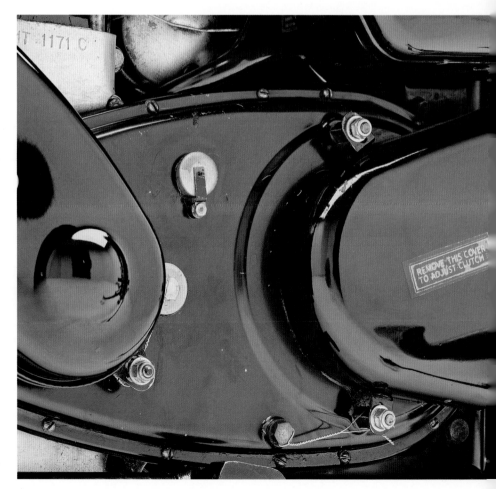

1965 Dunstall Dominator Norton Atlas

- 1965 Norton Atlas 750cc 2-cylinder OHV
- Tuned to 60 hp
- Dunstall bodywork, controls, exhausts, and speed tuning parts
- 130 mph top speed

Owner: Gordon McCall

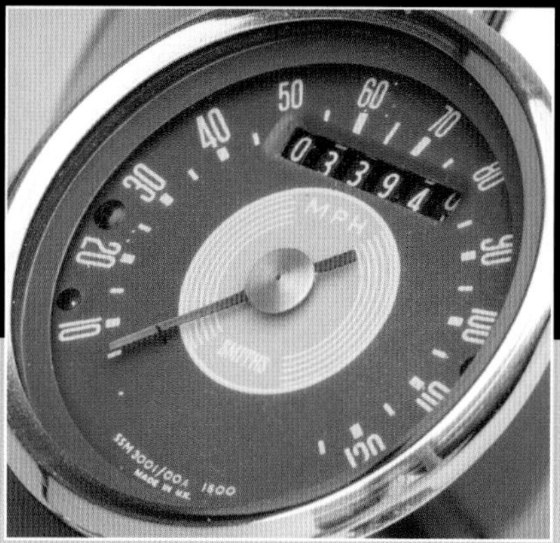

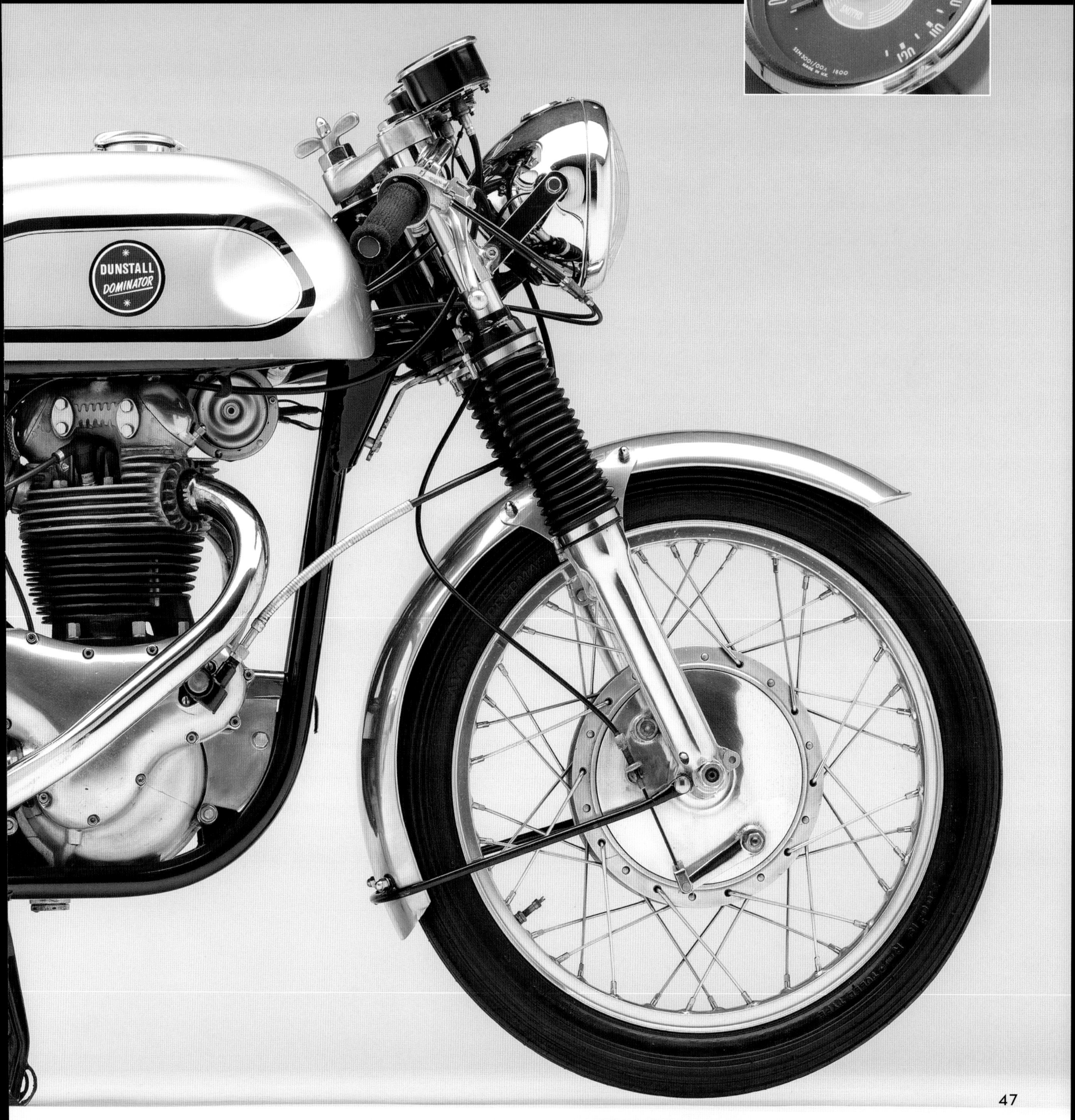

PAUL DUNSTALL WAS A YOUNG RACER of some ability in England in the 1950s. Dunstall tuned his own racing Norton. Recognizing a business opportunity in the difficulty of finding racing parts and bodywork, he began manufacturing his own parts in 1961 and offering them in a mail-order catalog, selling BSA Gold Star–pattern mufflers and Norton Manx look-a-like fiberglass or alloy fuel and oil tanks. Some of these parts were used on racetracks, but Dunstall was really supplying the exploding café racer scene in early 1960s England. Suddenly, it was possible to clad your Triumph, BSA, or Norton with racerlike bodywork, even if it was perfectly ordinary underneath all the race gear.

By 1966, Dunstall was recognized in England as a full-fledged motorcycle manufacturer. He offered Dunstall Dominators like this Atlas in complete and road-ready form. Dunstalls were highly tuned and very fast. In 1967 a Dunstall Norton 750cc Atlas was the fastest road-legal motorcycle you could buy in England, topping 130 miles per hour.

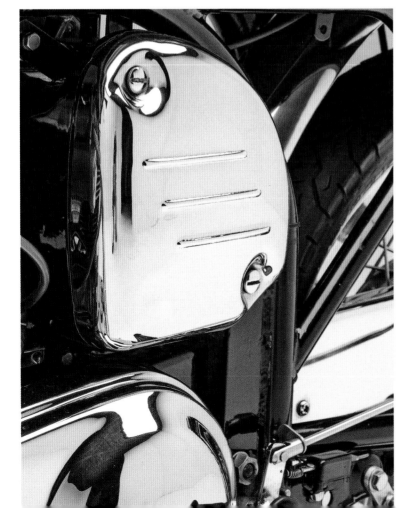

ED NORTON

Builder: Boyle Custom Moto

- 1971 Norton Commando
- 745cc Vertical-twin OHV
- 65 hp at 6,800 rpm
- Aluminum bodywork by Evan Wilcox; stock frame, forks, and wheels

NORTON'S COMMANDO WON BIKE OF THE YEAR five years running in England after its introduction in 1967. With a rubber-mounted engine, it cured the worst attribute of a parallel twin engine: vibration. Suddenly, a highly tuned 750cc British engine was smooth as silk on the road, and it handled almost as well as the legendary Featherbed that preceded it—at least until its Isolastic rubber engine mounts wore out, at which point all bets were off. Still, it was finally possible to ride a big British twin at high speed without losing fillings or shaking parts off the bike, and it hadn't taken a major investment from Norton in a new-generation engine. Rubber-mounting the 1948 motor design extended its life a further eight years . . . and what glorious years they were, with Commandos winning Production races right and left and Battle of the Twins races long after Norton had shut its doors in 1975.

Surprisingly, given the British industry's reputation in the 1970s as "sideburns and flares" men, Norton didn't offer a proper café racer version of the Commando until the 1974 John Player Norton Replica, based on the JPN-sponsored race team's livery and bodywork. As with most "café racer" models offered by the big factories, it was a sheep in wolf's clothing, being completely standard beneath the beautiful bodywork. Norton sold 120 genuine Production Racers—the infamous "Yellow Submarines," of which most did see track time, but many were pure posers on the road. Which, of course, only increased their cool factor.

As with Norton's earlier twins, plenty of owners got busy adding clip-ons and racing tanks to their roadster Nortons. Boyle Custom Moto has taken a modern spin on an old trend, and their Ed Norton bike has an especially cleaned up and lightened Commando chassis with spectacular alloy bodywork. Surprisingly (and distinctively), they've retained the late 1960s pre-disc-era Norton drum brakes; the result is a bike that could have been built in the '60s . . . but is better than any that were.

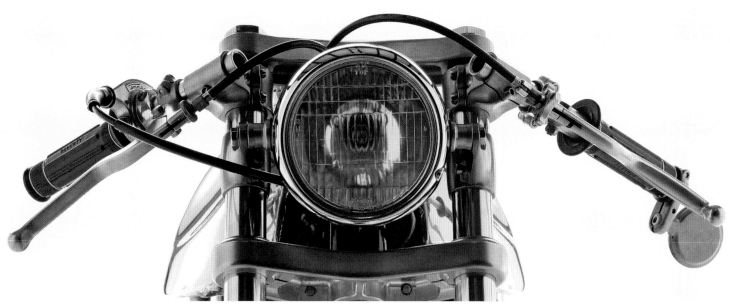

GODET-EGLI VINCENT

Builder: Patrick Godet

Owner: Mars Webster

- Vincent Black Shadow engine
- 998cc OHV V-twin
- 60 hp at 5,500 rpm
- 2002 Patrick Godet Egli frame and bodywork
- Ceriani road race forks
- Fontana front brake
- 378 lbs

THE LEGENDARY VINCENT V-TWIN MOTORCYCLE was the "World's Fastest Production Motorcycle" from 1946 until the 1972 introduction of the Kawasaki Z1. That's a long time to be fastest, and even by the 1950s the "frameless" 1946 chassis of the Vincent was outdated. Speed-crazed bike builders needed good handling to manage the power, so they installed Vincent engines in Norton and other frames, but the best frame of all was built by Swiss Vincent enthusiast Fritz Egli from 1966 onward.

Egli built a new spine frame with a large-diameter tube that holds the oil, a rear subframe with mounts for twin shocks, and a beefier swingarm. The first Egli Vincent won a European hill climb, and suddenly Vincents were winning races again, 11 years after the factory closed. Egli built around 100 of his Swiss creations as café racers, road racers, and touring bikes, all of which were beautifully crafted.

Frenchman Patrick Godet restored an Egli with a Vincent Black Shadow engine and took it to the master for his approval. Egli was so impressed with the machine, he granted Godet a license to build new Egli-framed bikes as Godet-Egli-Vincents. From his workshop in Malaunay, France, Godet now builds Egli-Vincents to order using mostly new components, including new Vincent engines built to just about any capacity and horsepower rating. Godet-Egli-Vincents are no longer restorations, but completely new machines, and are just about the sexiest café racers ever.

RICKMAN METISSE TRIUMPH

Owner: Yoshi Kosaka, Garage Company

- 1967 Triumph Bonneville
- 650cc parallel-twin OHV
- 46 hp at 6,700 rpm
- Top speed 120 mph
- 1974 Rickman Frame, tanks, and forks

THE TRIUMPH BONNEVILLE WAS THE WORLD'S FASTEST PRODUCTION BIKE when introduced in 1959, but its handling was only adequate, and never truly up to GP race standards. By the mid-1960s a new frame improved matters. The Rickman brothers of England began building motocross frames in 1960 of nickel-plated chromoly tubing. These frames were vastly superior to any factory chassis; they immediately began winning world-class motocross races and vexing the big factories. After plenty of televised trouncings of factory teams, Don and Derek Rickman were big stars. They began selling motocross chassis kits, replicas of their race machines. In 1962, they began

to sell road race frame kits, too, with a slightly more stretched-out chassis, reminiscent of Norton's Featherbed, although the Rickman was lighter and looked great in polished nickel. The Rickmans were also known for their beautiful bodywork. When they introduced street bike kits for Triumph engines in 1966, which was basically their road racer chassis with lights, they were ready-made café racers.

The most popular engine to power a Rickman chassis was the unit-construction Triumph twin. But the brothers weren't biased; they also offered engine plates for Velocette and BSA single-cylinder engines and worked in collaboration with Mitchell's of Birmingham to house a batch of spare Royal Enfield Interceptor 750cc engines intended for the late Floyd Clymer's Indian venture. When Mitchell's got stuck with 170 engines, it called the Rickman brothers to work out a deal; the result was the Rickman Interceptor, a gorgeous brute of a café racer. The Rickman brothers continued to make kits for evil-handling Hondas, Kawasakis, and Suzukis throughout the 1970s and 1980s. They still produce frame kits for the vintage café racer and road racing market today.

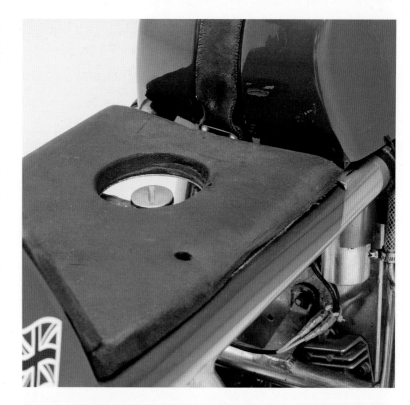

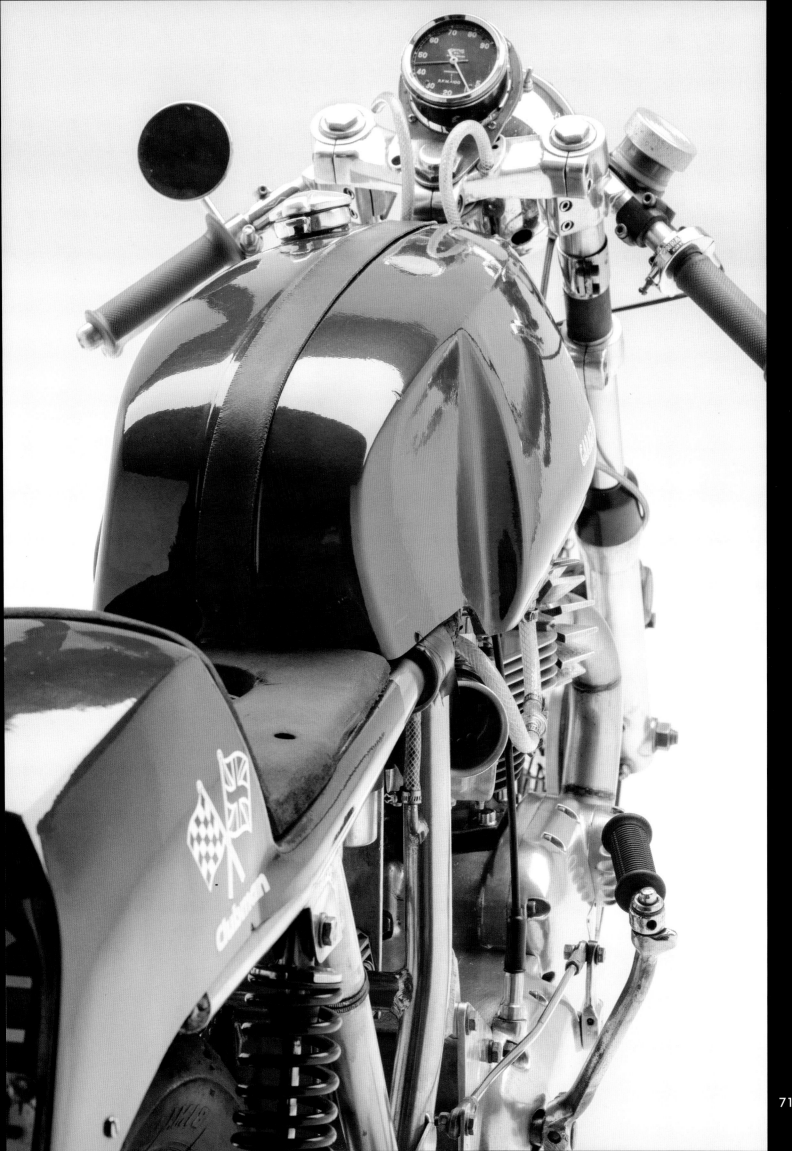

CHAPTER
2

Motorcyclists have modified, upgraded, and improved their
machines since the 1900s, but the trend for customization
really took off in the early 1960s.

SURPRISINGLY, IT WAS THE OLD STALWART GUN MANUFACTURER, Birmingham Small Arms, who snatched up the gauntlet of the clubman's race series. BSA did this with an update of its prewar M24 Gold Star model. It evolved, just as the FIM hoped, into a better, faster, and safer machine, and it ultimately dominated the race series. By 1954, the competition in the 500cc and 350cc categories simply could not equal the Goldie's magic combination of speed, reliability, and handling. The Triumph Tiger 100, while fast, tended to shake itself to bits. The Velocette, Royal Enfield, and AJS/Matchless rivals were simply not fast enough. And Norton's International, with the best chassis of all in the Featherbed post-1950, was never properly developed to the level of its all-conquering Manx brothers.

Increasing success in the Clubman's TT boosted the image of the BSA Gold Star, especially when the epic final variant emerged in 1956. This was the DBD34, a near-perfect

THE RISE OF
THE SPECIALS

café racer, and in practical terms the fastest motorcycle on the road in the late 1950s. The big HRD-Vincent twins were faster, with the slogan *the fastest production motorcycle in the world*, but their production had stopped in 1955. The fastest 650cc Triumph in 1956 was the Tiger 110, nominally good for 110 miles per hour, but riding one at that speed was an exercise in hand-numbing vibration with the risk of turning the engine into a grenade. There was no offering from America or Europe that matched the British bikes for top speed. The BMW R68/69 600cc flat twins were certainly fast enough with 35 horsepower and 100 miles per hour, but their all-black paint and cobby looks didn't shout "teenage sex" in the way of English chrome and metallic paint jobs.

The best thing about the Gold Star was that is looks bested its performance. It was a perfect example of the saying *if it looks right, it is right*. The DBD34 Goldie remains today

If you were lucky, and rich, and inclined towards Italian machines, there was none better in 1973 than the Ducati 750 Super Sport, the fastest production motorcycle in world, proven with a famous win at the Imola 200 ("Italian Daytona") in 1972. While the quality of its paint job and electrics were maligned in the press, none of this dented its reputation as a masterpiece.

a visually perfect motorcycle; the finned mass of its engine is balanced against the swelling curves of its chromed tank, and its swept-back exhaust pipe suggests speed even at a standstill. The patented reverse-cone exhaust has a distinctive bird-like twitter when the throttle is rolled off. The drawback of tall race gearing makes traffic stops a drag. (First gear is good for 70 miles per hour.) But once on the road, a hard throttle twist is rewarded with the miracle of single-cylinder power pulses, giving the rider visceral feedback that every combustion cycle is working hard. Acceleration is felt as a gentle pounding in the backside, without the harsh buzz of two or more cylinders.

Motorcyclists have modified, upgraded, and improved their machines since the 1900s, but the trend for customization really took off in the early 1960s, with the availability of secondhand Norton Featherbed frames. Norton had the wisdom to produce a roadster version of its Grand Prix chassis almost unaltered, although it never offered a roadster version of its fantastic Manx racer. By the early 1960s, spare Featherbeds were easy to source from defunct roadsters

or tired racers, especially when it grew common to rob the Manx's engine for 500cc Formula Junior car racing. The world's best-handling motorcycle frame had a large enough hole in the middle to accommodate virtually any motor. Every motor found a home there at least once, from Hillman Imp and NSU four-cylinder car engines to Harley, Vincent, Triumph, BSA, Royal Enfield, and Velocette motors. At the time, these were called "specials." The term *custom* (or *kustom*) emerged in America in the mid-1960s, with the popularization of the Southern California (SoCal) hot rod and chopper scene.

From all these experiments in mating various engines to the Norton chassis, the Triton emerged as the most sensible and popular mix. Triumph engines were ubiquitous, cheap, and well-supplied with go-faster parts and tuning instructions. The Triton combined the abbreviated good looks of the Norton Manx and the relative reliability of a Triumph, setting the visual tone for café racers from the 1950s on. The popularity of the Triton created the first customizing supplies industry by the early 1960s, as small businessmen like Dave Degens and Paul Dunstall supplied everything a rider needed to convert a sad old Norton twin into a gleaming Manx look-alike.

The first NorVin was built by multiple World Champion John Surtees, who updated the handling of his racing Vincent Black Lightning (Vincent had dropped the *HRD* in 1949) by

OPPOSITE: While Ducati had been building perfect café racers for years, albeit in single-cylinder form, in 1972 they built a big one: the 750 Sport. It was a perfect road-sports machine, fast and utterly beautiful, with impeccable handling and a dead-smooth engine.

While Ducati big-twins were known for exceptionally stable handling, a few chassis builders, such as Fritz Egli (better known to Ton Up! fans for his Vincents), felt there was yet room for improvement. Egli offered a spine-frame chassis kit for the 900SS desmo engine, which didn't improve the looks of the original but did offer quicker steering and bespoke options: an Italian-Swiss café racer.

installing the motor into a genuine 1955 Manx chassis. While never common, the NorVin is considered by some to be the ultimate Norton-based special, combining the fastest engine in the world with the best-handling chassis. The Ton Up! exhibit was graced with a NorVin Comet, the 500cc single-cylinder Vincent engine with a separate Albion gearbox, instead of the in-unit cluster of the big twin. The separate gearbox makes installation in a foreign frame much easier than with the twin, which is shoehorned into the Norton chassis, unless (horrors!) the gearbox casting is cut away first.

By the 1960s, a few of the big English factories offered explicit café racers, such as the Royal Enfield Continental GT and the Matchless G12 CSR (Coffee Shop Racer), which tended toward the lurid in their decoration, with checkered "speed" tape, small flyscreens, or heavy chrome badges. These machines theoretically catered to the type of rider

who might build a Triton. But in truth, their performance could be easily bettered by an earnest special-builder, particularly one who could afford speed tuning parts or even whole chassis from the emerging crop of specialist café racer suppliers.

THE PROFESSIONALS

While other combinations of one factory's chassis with another's engine were fair game in the 1960s (TriBSAs, NorFields, Healy 4s with Ariel 4-cylinder motors, and so on), what riders were really after was a faster, better-handling machine than was offered in the showroom. By 1966, a new business model emerged from the workshops of Derek and Don Rickman, champion motocross and road racers. The Rickman brothers built their own racing frames, which regularly trounced the factory teams, especially in off-road work. They satisfied the clamor for replicas of their lovely nickel-plated frames in 1960 by selling chassis kits, which were stronger, lighter, and had more beautiful bodywork than any other dirt bike of the day. By 1962, a slightly longer Rickman frame was developed for road racing. It was every

In 1974, Norton capitalized on its Formula 750 racing success by cladding a standard 850 Commando in the livery of cigarette manufacturer John Player & Sons, its race sponsor. The "JPN" was actually slower than its unfaired Roadster brother, which was silly, but it certainly looked like a racer. It didn't take much to boost the power of a Commando, but few JPNs were used thus; most were treated as trophies.

While formerly staid Moto Guzzi entered the café scene in 1971 with its V7 Sport, it was the Le Mans Mark 1 of 1976 that hit a home run. Good for over 130 miles per hour, the Le Mans was an instant classic with a rare trifecta: speed, good handling, and reliability. While fussier factory café racers can be found with low mileage, a Le Mans has typically been enjoyed for tens of thousands of miles!

King of the 1970s factory café racers, MV Agusta finally offered a hot roadster version of its Grand Prix–dominating four-cylinder, DOHC racers. The MV 750 Sport appeared in 1971, expensive and exotic—the only two-cam, four-cylinder bike in the world—with gorgeous styling. Motorcyclists wanted this bike so badly, and for so long, we forgave its overweight package.

bit as beautiful and strong as the motocross frame and like the Featherbed, it could house any kind of engine. As usual, not every racing frame saw track time. It took no more effort to install wiring and a headlamp to a Rickman frame and bodywork than to a Norton, and with those—voilà, the last word in café racers was yours. The Rickman brothers took the hint, and by 1966 offered a complete and fully road-legal motorcycle from their racing chassis. The Rickman Triumph became an instant classic and remained in production for nine years as a complete bike.

The Rickman brothers weren't the only small businessmen who noticed the expanding popularity of the café racer. Paul Dunstall, also a successful former racer, began offering speed parts for Norton roadsters in a mail-order catalog in 1961. As the clamor grew for his tuning parts, replica Manx tanks, and Gold Star mufflers, he began to sell street-legal Dunstall Dominators as complete motorcycles in 1966, becoming an officially recognized manufacturer, just like the Rickmans. While the Triumph engine used by the Rickmans and Triton builders was fast, the Norton twin-cylinder engine used by

Dunstall could actually be tuned for more horsepower than the Triumph Bonneville. By 1967 the Dunstall Dominator, a no-nonsense, balls-out café racer, was the fastest street-legal and showroom-stock motorcycle available in the world, good for over 130 miles per hour.

NEWS OF THE WORLD

A stack of books has been written celebrating café racer culture in 1950s England and Rocker hangouts like London's Ace Café. But this hotspot was hardly the only one, nor were its native motorcycles the only bikes in the genre. Factories everywhere woke up to a huge trend in two-wheeled fun by the late 1950s. The Italians have a speed-crazed motoring culture, and they encouraged racing with road-legal motorcycles in long distance postwar events, such as the Moto Giro and the Milano-Taranto races. While Italy's initial postwar period was dominated by under-250cc machines, by the mid-1950s sporting motorcycles of all capacities were available, such as the Moto Guzzi Falcone Sport of 1953, an evolution of the prewar racing Guzzi flat single-cylinder Condor. Factories like Morini, Ducati, Mondial, Benelli, Motobi, and so on all sold sporting small-capacity machines

that fit the description of a café racer in every aspect: low handlebars, rearset footrests, abbreviated seats, alloy rims, good brakes, and great performance.

As Italian manufacturers ramped up their involvement in GP racing in the 1950s, their roadsters got better, too. Ducati's experience in racing, for example, improved its road machines to a high pitch; its Mach 1/Diana of 1962 was the fastest production 250cc motorcycle in the world, capable of over 100 miles per hour, which most contemporary bikes of twice the capacity struggled to reach. Like a half-size Gold Star—and almost as fast—the Mach 1 had looks to match its performance. It was an absolute gem, with beautiful engine castings balanced against shapely fuel tanks and ancillaries. Better still, it was reliable, oiltight, and handled like a razor knife.

Japanese machines began filtering into showrooms worldwide in the late 1950s. The world was astonished by their sheer quality, and the amazing level of technology incorporated into affordable road machines. Honda, for example, first entered international GP racing in 1959, to little fanfare and some derision. Two years later, Honda completely dominated the 125cc and 250cc World Championships. By 1966, Honda had won the World Championship in every category: 50, 125, 250, 350, and 500cc. Understandably, Honda's road machines reflected some of this prowess. The Honda CB92 Benly Super Sports of 1959 was a 125cc miracle, with an OHC twin-cylinder engine with an electric starter, capable of 75 miles per hour. It looked fantastic

standing still and didn't leak a drop of oil. If it didn't scare the pants off every other manufacturer in the world, it should have. Like the word *clubman* in England, the tag *super sports* as applied to European and Japanese bikes could be accurately substituted with *café racer*. All these terms indicated a road machine with track pretensions.

Suzuki and Yamaha both built very fast, small, two-stroke, twin-cylinder machines in the 1960s. These vied for "fastest

250" with the Ducati Mach 1. The Suzuki X-6 of 1965 was also capable of 100 miles per hour. It cultivated a taste for wheelie-popping two-stroke hot rods, which would develop more fully in the 1970s, when the Japanese invasion changed café racers forever.

A SECOND GOLDEN AGE: THE 1970s

By the late 1960s, café racers had become a global phenomenon. Just about every manufacturer in the world catered to the trend, while increasing numbers of small manufacturers offered tuning parts or even whole chassis of their own design. Riders who wanted the café racer look for popular bikes, like the Honda CB450 twin or CB750 four, had a little work to do. This could be as simple as replacing the handlebars with Ace bars or as complex as ditching everything but the motor and purchasing a Rickman chassis while tuning the engine to race standards.

It had been over 15 years since the real heyday of the English Rocker scene, which was current at the birth of rock-and-roll in the 1950s, but was totally retrograde by the mid-1960s—sartorially, musically, and machine-wise.

The rise of scooter-riding Modernists, usually called Mods, who wore the latest fashions and danced to new music like R & B and ska, made the leather-loving Rockers look hopelessly out of date. Their style was no longer hip, and it was no wonder Rockers and Mods fought by the Brighton seaside. Theirs was a clash of the past with the future, as Rocker culture became the property of nostalgists clinging to a remembered (or invented) youth, and the attention of younger riders moved elsewhere.

While Rocker style and music were anachronistic during the rise of Swinging London in the mid-1960s, the Rockers' motorcycle legacy—the clubman racers on the road, the home-built specials, the taste for the intoxicating cocktail of youth and fast motorcycles —only grew in popularity. The focus of the café racer scene began to shift in the late 1960s, as new machines from Italy and Japan were the fastest and most sophisticated. England was no longer the center of the fast-bike universe. No successful Grand Prix motorcycle emerged from a British factory after the AJS Porcupine, which won the World Championship in 1949. No British-made motorcycle won a World Championship after Eric Oliver's Norton Manx sidecar outfit won the sidecar GP way back in 1953. British dominance of GP racing was long over. Grand Prix racing was now dominated by battles between Japanese and Italian machines (and German ones with sidecars). British bikes were still successful in production-based events, like the Daytona 200 in the States. They managed to limp through another decade of racing with occasional wins before vanishing completely.

THE RISE OF THE GLOBAL CAFÉ RACER

In the late 1960s, if one wanted the fastest bike available, a sober assessment of motorcycle market would naturally lead to a conclusion that Italian or Japanese bikes were ripe for "hotting up." The parts catalogs of Honda, Suzuki, and Yamaha all contained a special section of tuning components. These were presumably for racing, but there was no restriction on road use. The Honda 305cc Super Hawk, for example, had a complete racing kit available, which included a five-speed gear cluster, special tachometer, an aluminum rear fender, special racing seat, rearsets, clip-ons, and so on, which could be ordered by individual part numbers. As late as 1987, I was able to order at least half of the items originally listed from 1965 directly from Honda—a remarkable situation!

Engine capacities of sporting street motorcycles grew from a typical "big bike" of 600 to 650cc in Britain and Europe to 750cc and beyond by the early 1970s. Harley had of course offered 883cc and 1000cc Sportsters since 1957, but few were modified into café racers until the trend truly landed in America in the 1970s. This was probably because American motorcycles completely disappeared from international race competition after the 1920s, and Harley battled it out at home with obsolete sidevalve racers until 1968. American hot rodders using the native product generally built dirt track and dragster style street racers, until the Daytona races moved off the beach in 1962, and racers like Cal Rayborn took their XRTT racers across the Atlantic in the 1970s.

The Japanese didn't build café racers for years after the Honda CB92 Benly in 1962. Yet they built fast motorcycles, even if their chassis were barely adequate when ridden hard. To fix this, one could purchase racing forks from Ceriani in Italy or go whole hog with a specialist chassis builder like the Rickman brothers or Colin Seeley, who offered vastly improved frames to fit Japanese engines by 1970. The Rickman Honda CB750 and Rickman Kawasaki Z1 were sold as complete machines in 1974. But that only lasted a year, after which Rickmans were only chassis kits.

The English weren't the only specialist frame builders producing kits and whole machines. Swiss motorcycle racer and chassis builder Fritz Egli developed a radical frame for the big Vincent V-twin in 1968, when it was still the fastest motorcycle engine available, albeit housed in hopelessly outdated cycle parts. Proof of Egli's concept arrived with wins in a European Hill Climb Championship (not to be confused with American-style hill climbing up steep dirt hills), using a 15-year-old engine. The Egli Vincent road bike remains on everyone's list of the all-time coolest café racers.

It has remained in production as a chassis kit by Egli, or later, as a whole motorcycle from Patrick Godet, who was granted a license to build authorized Egli-Vincents at his Malaunay workshop in northern France. While Godet's story is rooted back in Egli's 1968 racer, the Godet-Egli-Vincent is built with a brand-new continuation engine, often of enlarged capacity (well over 1,000cc) and approaching 100 horsepower. It's a modern superbike in vintage clothing!

In the 1970s, it was the Italians who stepped up to provide factory-built café racers. After decades of lightweight, gemlike sports/racers, Benelli, in the thick of battling MV Agusta's four-cylinder GP racers, was the first Italian factory to offer a large-capacity (650cc) sports machine in 1969. It was sold as the Tornado, an oiltight version of a British vertical twin, with a pushrod engine—how retrograde for the Italians! Benelli had other plans, though, and blew away the competition with its six-cylinder OHC 750cc Sei in 1972, the first six-cylinder production motorcycle. Even though it was blatantly copied from the Honda CB500 four-cylinder—a Honda and a half—it was still a technological leap forward.

THE RISE OF THE ESPRESSO RACER

The Benelli Tornado of 1968 coincided with the introduction of the Laverda 750 vertical twin, which was also a blatant copy of a Honda design, this time the CB305 Super Hawk, supersized. The Laverda was introduced in the United States as the American Eagle, which was not quite as absurd as it sounds today; after all, Harley-Davidson owned Aermacchi at the time and was winning GP races in the 350cc category with Italian two-strokes. Not only that, the U.S. motorcycle market was the magnet for global motorcycle production. American riders were waking up to the allure of European GP racing bikes and their street look-alikes, the café racers.

What followed was a second Golden Age of factory café racers. In the 1970s, every factory wanted a piece of the hot rod pie and offered machines to whet the appetite of young street racers. Laverda hotted up its 750 OHC twin with the 750S and SF café racers, and in 1971 it offered a full-tilt production racer. It was the 750SFC, with a distinctive half-fairing and competition orange bodywork, and it decimated the opposition in endurance events like the Barcelona 24 Hours and the Bol d'Or. Laverdas were built like trucks—a bit heavy, but utterly reliable.

The trend for all manufacturers was toward bigger, faster motorcycles, and the Italians truly displaced the English as the kings of the café racer hill by 1971. Ducati introduced its radical L-twin 750GT models to coincide with a new attack on GP racing with a 500cc version of the L-twin, which had some success. It had a lot more success as a 750 production racer, with desmodromic cylinder heads and a hand-built, super hot engine. Paul Smart took one of these amazing factory racers to victory in the 1972 Imola 200 race (the "Italian Daytona"). It was produced as a replica—the 750SS of 1973—and was the fastest production motorcycle in the world, good for 135 miles per hour.

Moto Guzzi hired Leno Tonti to create a new chassis for its reliable transverse V-twin. The V-7 Sport was born in 1971, with a metalflake paint job and shark-gill mufflers. The Sport was a far cry from the bulky police bikes of their previous incarnation, and they handled beautifully. By 1976, the same chassis was used with a hotter engine and new bodywork to create the 850 Le Mans, a masterpiece of innovative styling with its small bikini fairing and low, long looks. That it had 130 miles-per-hour potential from its pushrod engine shows just how serious Guzzi was to enter the café racer game.

By 1972, Laverda had added a cylinder to its 750 twins to create the 3C, a 900cc triple with DOHC engine of robust

construction, with a drawback of extra weight. The 3C was fast and furious, but it was the English importer Slater Brothers who encouraged the factory to produce a total hot rod, the Jota of 1976, which was the new fastest production bike in the world, good for over 140 miles per hour. Café racers were becoming much faster and much heavier than their lithe British predecessors. But the Italians translated decades of racing experience into their chassis design, and the Guzzis, Laverdas, Ducatis, and Benellis all handled impeccably on the road—well enough to make a good rider into a better rider. I speak from experience, having owned quite a few round-case Ducati twins and even a Laverda triple; their stability and sure-footed roadwork gave me the confidence to push my abilities as a rider and improve my game terrifically.

A RIDER'S CHOICE

By 1974, a rider with sporting intentions had a smorgasbord of excellent machines to choose from, all with similar performance and super-sports styling. Ducati offered the 750 Sport, a fantastic café racer. Or if you wanted to be the king

of the hill, you might get lucky and score a 750 Super Sport. While the Ducati's paint and electrical connectors were criticized as shoddy by the press of the day, there was no denying that Fabio Taglioni had penned an absolute masterpiece with his L-twin engine and frame design. Anyone with an eye for beauty could see that the 750SS, with its duck-egg green frame, was a bike for the ages. *Cycle* magazine in 1974 called it "a bike that stands at the farthest reaches of the sporting world—the definitive factory-built café racer," while *Motociclismo* rhapsodized, "to say that the Super Sport 750 was one of the most beautiful sport bikes ever to be made is no exaggeration; it may be considered among the most significant motorcycles of all times."

With perfect café racers like the Guzzi Le Mans and Ducati 750s available, what was the tinkering-minded enthusiast to do? While too few 750SS Ducatis were seen on the roads (most did indeed live on the track), the 750GT and Sport were stripped down and hot-rodded. I owned an example for many years: a 750GT with the full treatment, including a half-fairing from a Laverda 750SFC. While the styling of the Ducati 750 Sport and SS were perfection, riding one on the street was certainly not. The rangy wheelbase, combined with a very long gas tank, forced a rider to stretch far to reach the clip-ons—fine at 80 miles per hour but agony in the city. The GT model has a slightly different frame with a shorter gas tank. Reducing the reach to the handlebars by 2 inches doesn't sound like much, but it makes a huge difference to one's back, making the ride totally acceptable for everyday use with clip-ons. Here's a real rider's secret: the GT makes a more usable café racer than the Sport!

NOT JUST ESPRESSO

The Italians weren't the only ones making strides. BMW finally shed its all-black demeanor and entered the café racer fray in 1973 with the R90S. It had a smoke-fade paint job and small handlebar fairing. Both items were unique and highly innovative for a production machine and were completely unexpected from Munich. The R90S was an instant classic, and while it was hardly the uncompromised track-derived special of the Ducati 750SS or Laverda Jota, for a BMW it was radical and sporting. It fulfilled all the requirements of a BMW—competence, smoothness, quality, and reliability—with enough of a contemporary edge to be hip in any context. While the R90S was celebrated in the press and sold very well, it would be the last Munich-built café racer for many years.

A similar story played out in the United States in 1977. Willie G. Davidson, chief of styling at Harley-Davidson, took note of the global explosion in popularity of café racers. He decided it was time Harley built one of its own. His prototypes of the XL Sportster-based café racer—the XLCR—were built in 1975, and the machine was released in 1977. Davidson's machine had a purposeful brutality and menacing all-black finish (even the exhaust), with a half-fairing more abbreviated than BMW's but larger than the bikini of the Moto Guzzi 850 LeMans. Somehow, that fairing combined well with the XR750s dirt track tail section and a squared off tank, when it all surrounded the Sportster's black iron V-twin engine. It all coalesced into a masterpiece of beautiful toughness. On this point, the press and the public agreed. Where they differed with Harley's then-owner AMF was in the actual performance of the animal. Rather than ramping up the handling and horsepower of its first true café racer, in the XLCR Harley had created a sheep in wolf's clothing. It was vibratory and 20 miles per hour down on performance compared to its competition. What enthusiasts really wanted was the racing XR engine in the XLCR's cycle parts, but no way was the Harley brass going to offer a potentially troublesome race motor for a production machine. Whether the market for a Harley café racer didn't really exist, or word of its foibles stymied sales, the XLCR sold only 3,000 units in 1977 and 1978 and was quietly shelved.

BMW wasn't the only German company interested in performance; race tuner Friedl Münch built tasty Horex café racers until the mid-1960s, using up the last of that defunct company's stock of 400cc OHC vertical twin motors. When they were gone, he turned to NSU 996cc OHC four-cylinder engines from the Prinz car. His first prototype in 1966 had a chassis based on the Norton Featherbed. It weighed a reasonable 480 pounds, with a 55-horsepower engine. A top speed of 115 miles per hour wasn't earth-shattering, but by 1968, NSU produced a hotter engine of 1,177cc, now with over 88 horsepower, which Münch installed in a new chassis. Even with extensive use of magnesium and

© PART B Photography

hand-beaten aluminum, the Münch TTS weighed a staggering 650 pounds, and the name Mammut (Mammoth) stuck. While Münch was a German café racer builder, most of his Mammuts were touring models, although a few were ordered with proper street-racer gear. Production wrapped up—barring a few outrageous one-offs—in 1974.

The Japanese manufacturers didn't sell an out-of-the-box café racer in the 1970s, but that didn't stop owners from doing it themselves. The flourishing trade in replica Manx parts simply shifted to the new interest—replica Honda GP bodywork or Kawasaki racing gear, along with a burgeoning industry in making Japanese four-cylinder machines handle properly under hard use. The Rickman brothers offered frame kits for Honda CB750 and Kawasaki Z-1 engines, which were the first road machines to use disc brakes on both wheels, after collaborating with Lockheed. Colin Seeley built a few chassis to house Suzuki two-stroke engines, while brothers Steve and Lester Harris began building their Magnum chassis for big Japanese engines in 1974. They became famous later in the 1970s for winning the World Superbike Championship. These specialist builders, when they produced road-legal machines, built seriously performance-oriented roadsters, good enough to win races and championships alike.

The English weren't completely out of the scene in the 1970s, as Norton produced two café racer variants of their esteemed Commando, which rightly won 'Machine of the Year' five years running after its introduction in 1968. The Commando was smooth and fast and handled beautifully, even though its engine was a stretched-out design dating back to 1948. On paper it was wrong, but on the road it was so right. Norton had success in production racing in the early 1970s and built its Yellow Submarine 750 Production Racer, which was of course street legal. The Commando was the only real sporting motorcycle left in England by 1972, and the Production Racer was the fastest and best-handling

© PART B Photography

vertical twin ever. It was produced for two years, and in 1974 came the John Player Special (JPS), which was the other kind of factory café racer: a tarted-up roadster with no speed mods, as a styling replica of Norton's last piston-engined racers. The JPS was actually slower than the standard Roadster model, due to the fairing's large frontal area and greater weight.

The disparity between these two Nortons highlights a problem with factory café racers. Plenty are offered with a racy appearance, but to match those looks with actual performance upgrades is expensive business, best left for special production racing models…unless you're an Italian company.

The global craze for fast motorcycles, whether factory-built or home-built, peaked in the 1970s with instantly classic offerings from a dozen manufacturers, large and small. Café racers grew ever closer to real racers, as production racing grew in popularity with riders and thus in importance to manufacturers. It was a second golden age of café racers. This decade produced many of the most iconic motorcycles of the twentieth century. But the rapidly improving chassis and increasingly powerful engines of the 1970s had consequences across the industry, because the best-performing bikes of the decade were café racers, and were definitely not built in Japan. The Japanese certainly noticed.

LOSSA ENGINEERING
CB77

Builder: Lossa Engineering, Jay LaRossa

- 1967 Honda CB77
- 305cc SOHC parallel-twin
- 28.5 hp at 9,000 rpm
- Frame mods, bodywork, and exhaust by Lossa Engineering

THE HONDA CB77 SUPER HAWK was a technical tour de force for Honda, introducing the world to their manufacturing prowess. Nobody else was building a sophisticated twin-cylinder overhead-camshaft bike with an electric starter in 1961. It didn't leak oil, was beautifully manufactured, and had the speed and handling of a much larger bike. The 305cc CB77 was a wake-up call to motorcycle manufacturers around the world, although few companies were able to respond to the juggernaut Honda had already become. In the year the Super Hawk was introduced, Honda won the 125cc and 250cc GP World Championships, after only two years of competing on the global stage.

Honda offered a full race kit of accessories to transform your CB77 into a red-blooded road racer (or hot roadster), but most owners simply made their own café racers, adding Ace bars and big-bore kits from aftermarket suppliers like Webco. Super Hawks were the first Japanese bikes to be altered by artisans in large numbers, partly because so many were sold. So it's appropriate the earliest Japanese café racer in the Ton Up! show is a CB77.

Jay LaRossa grew up in the motorcycle industry. Both his parents' families had dealerships in Los Angeles. As an adult, after years in a day job, he turned to building hot rods and trucks. Then a bout with stage four Hodgkin's lymphoma inspired him to rearrange his priorities, quit working for others, and turn to his first love, building motorcycles. Lossa Engineering in Long Beach, California, is a busy place, and LaRossa is known especially for his tasty and beautifully constructed café racers. This CB77 is stripped down with raw aluminum bodywork, built to resemble 1960s Honda factory GP bikes, which makes a clean and classic street racer.

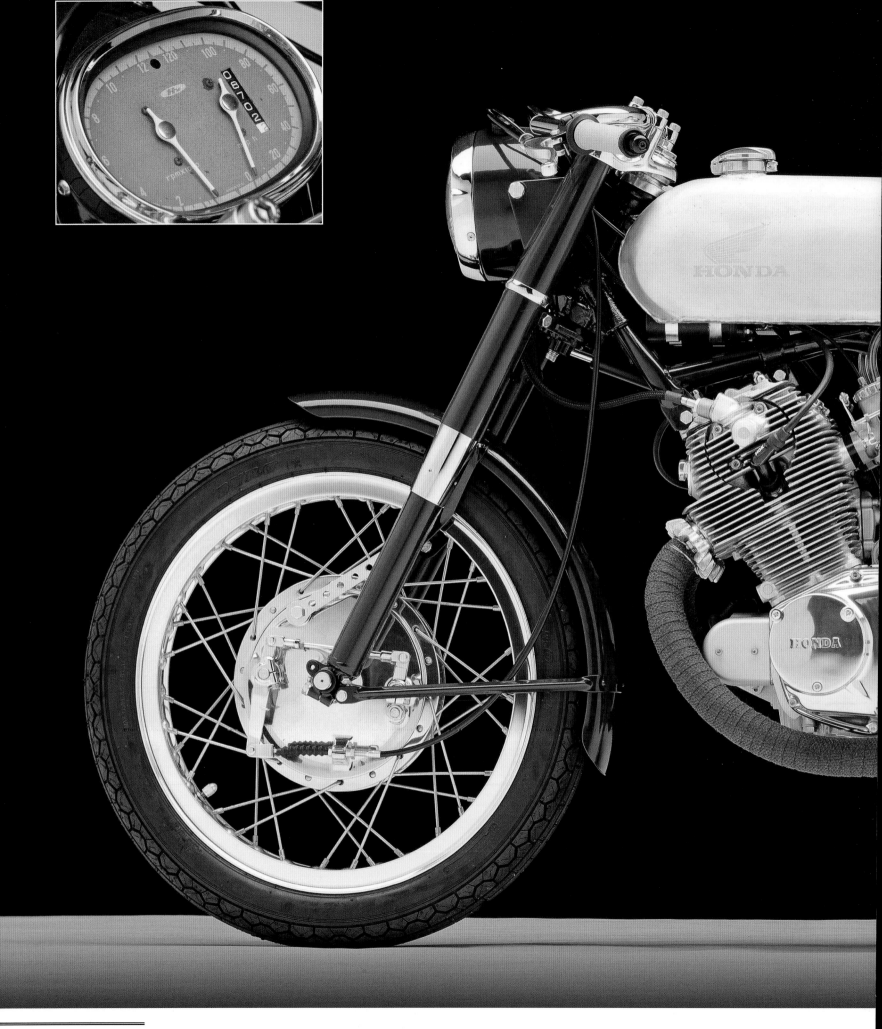

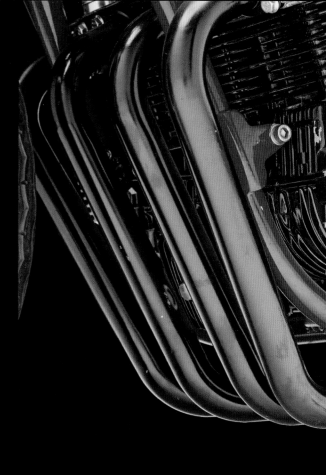

- 1969 Honda CB750 KO
- 836cc 4-cylinder OHC
- 85 hp @ 8,000 rpm
- Arces race forks
- CB750 dual (K) front and rear (F) brakes
- Kawasaki swingarm
- H-D custom oil tank
- Fuel tank handmade by a deceased master panel beater in Ireland
- Carpy-built seat and exhaust

THE HONDA CB750 WASN'T THE FIRST MASS-PRODUCED FOUR-CYLINDER BIKE, but it was the most produced from 1969 onwards, with over 400,000 built between 1969 and 2003. The engine was fast and bullet-proof, and the frame was a decent full-loop design, but the stock forks and shocks were crap, giving mediocre handling. Still, it was so far ahead of its competition technically, and sold at such a reasonable price, that it changed motorcycling forever. Amazingly, at least in retrospect, Soichiro Honda was unsure of the 750's reception, having seen the MV Agusta four-cylinder receive rave reviews but sell poorly. The first engine crankcases were built using "permanent mold casting," which produces a slightly textured finish to the cases, which are often colloquially but incorrectly referred to as "sandcast" crankcases.

Steve Carpenter's CB750 is a first-year "KO" model, produced after the sales success of the model was clear and Honda had begun using die-casting molds. Carpy's CB perfectly captures the British café racer look with a five-gallon "Manx" tank and racing seat, and he's uprated the Honda's handling with top-flight Arces Italian racing forks (from which Ceriani forks are derived) and a robust aluminum I-section Kawasaki swingarm to sort out potential high-speed weaves. The aluminum oil tank is from an old Harley chopper, but it looks perfect between the frame rails. The extensive use of aluminum continues with the speedo bracket and brake master cylinder, all polished and contrasting nicely with the red frame and blackened cylinder barrels.

Now that this Honda handles properly, the pumped 85-horsepower motor can be put to good use! The overall effect is perfection—a well-muscled, all-alloy café racer, looking like it handles and stops as well as it goes.

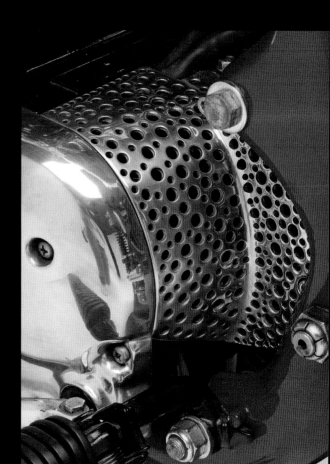

The '69

Builder: Kott Motorcycles

- 1969 Honda CB350T
- Twin-cylinder OHC
- 325cc
- 36 hp at 10,200 rpm
- Suzuki tank
- Kott seat and fairing

HONDA CB SERIES BIKES OF THE LATE 1960S and early 1970s have become hugely popular in twenty-first century café racer culture, being cheap and reliable bases for modification, with good parts availability. The CB350 was introduced in 1968 and built until 1972. With more than 250,000 sold in its four-year run, it was Honda's best-selling motorcycle. It is still common in garages around the world, being essentially bulletproof and given to a very long life. Its simple single-overhead-camshaft engine is robust and powerful enough to keep riders happy, and while the suspension can use an upgrade —like every Japanese bike of the period—the handling is actually well matched to the

performance. With British-inspired styling, the CB350 is one of the nicest-looking bikes of the era as well.

Dustin Kott's version of a CB custom, the ink-blue '69, has had all of Honda's styling scrubbed off, leaving a clean rolling chassis to play with. After detabbing the frame, Kott modified a Suzuki GS750 tank by slimming down a pair of knee indents and built a superslim saddle with perhaps the smallest bump-stop ever seen. The blackened wheel rims showcase the polished wheel hubs and upswept exhaust pipes, and the groovy micro-fairing is the finishing touch, giving the '69 a supercompact street racer vibe.

FULL SPORT DUCATI

Builder: Fuller Hot Rods

- 1974 Ducati 750 GT
- 748cc OHC L-twin
- 60 hp at 7,000 rpm
- 125 mph top speed
- Frame modifications by Fuller Hot Rods

THE ROUND CASE DUCATI TWIN WAS INTRODUCED IN 1971 and was immediately hailed as a masterpiece of design—but not for the quality of its finish. The finish was notoriously dodgy, with inexplicably cheap electrical connectors, considering Ducati's origins as an electrical supply manufacturer in 1926. Regardless, Fabio Taglioni's original 90-degree L-twin engine, with its shaft-and-bevel overhead camshaft drive, was as beautiful as it was effective. The L-twin layout has perfect balance, as good as a flat twin but without the width. The

downside of a horizontal front cylinder is the long wheelbase required to accommodate all that engine.

Taglioni didn't attempt to shorten up his GT, as he'd done with his 500cc GP racing versions of the first L-twins. Instead he expressed his 750 GT as a horse stretched in full gallop, with a rangy wheelbase and extravagant rake to the forks. As a consequence, bevel-drive Ducatis are masters of the high-speed sweeper, feeling utterly stable at any speed. The downside, of course, is that wide handlebars are required for throwing one around tight bends. (Ask how I know!) This, of course, was the opposite of the café racer styling in which the Ducati looked so good. Thus, aggressive mountain-pass riding is hard work and unnatural to the beast. But when the road opens up a little, riding as fast and hard as you like feels completely secure.

When the 750 Sport was released in 1972, it was a beautiful café racer. The next year, the 750 Super Sport appeared, the fastest production bike in the world on the day. But Sports and Super Sports are rare, so touring 750 GTs are often converted to café racers, just as Bryan Fuller has done. Lighter, cleaner, and more minimal than the Ducati originals, Fuller has built a two-wheeled Italian hot rod.

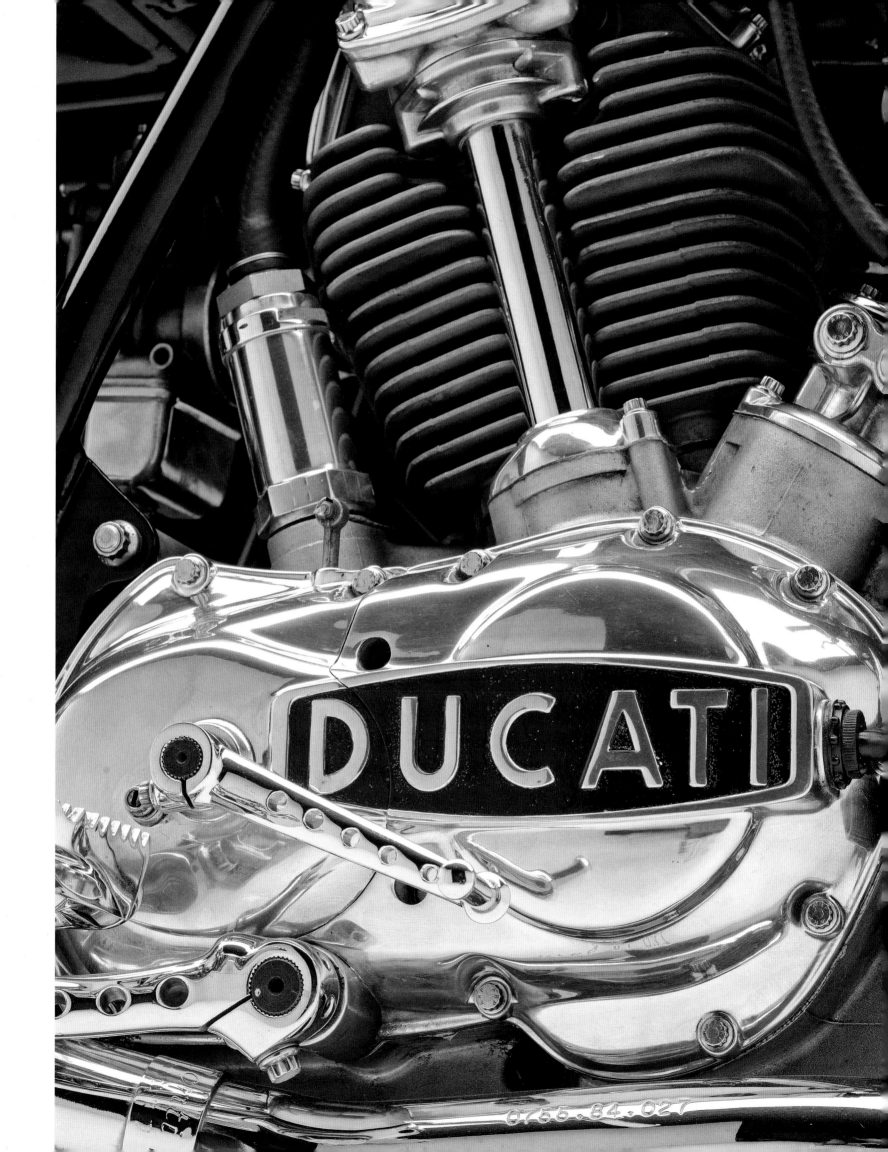

NessCafe

Builder: Arlen Ness

- 1987 Harley-Davidson XR1000
- 998cc OHV V-twin
- 70 hp at 5,600 rpm
- Arlen Ness raked frame, stretched swingarm, exhaust, and bodywork
- Performance Machine brakes

**ARLEN NESS STARTED BUILDING CUSTOMIZED CHOP-
PERS BACK IN 1965.** He built a small chopper parts business
in San Leandro, California, into an empire of name-brand
parts and motorcycles. He's become an institution of the
custom motorcycle world, but his interests never strayed into
café racer turf until he built the NessCafe.

Harley's XR1000 was a street version of its dirt track king,
the XR750, with tightened-up Sportster looks around its
all-aluminum motor. The engine produces terrific and smooth

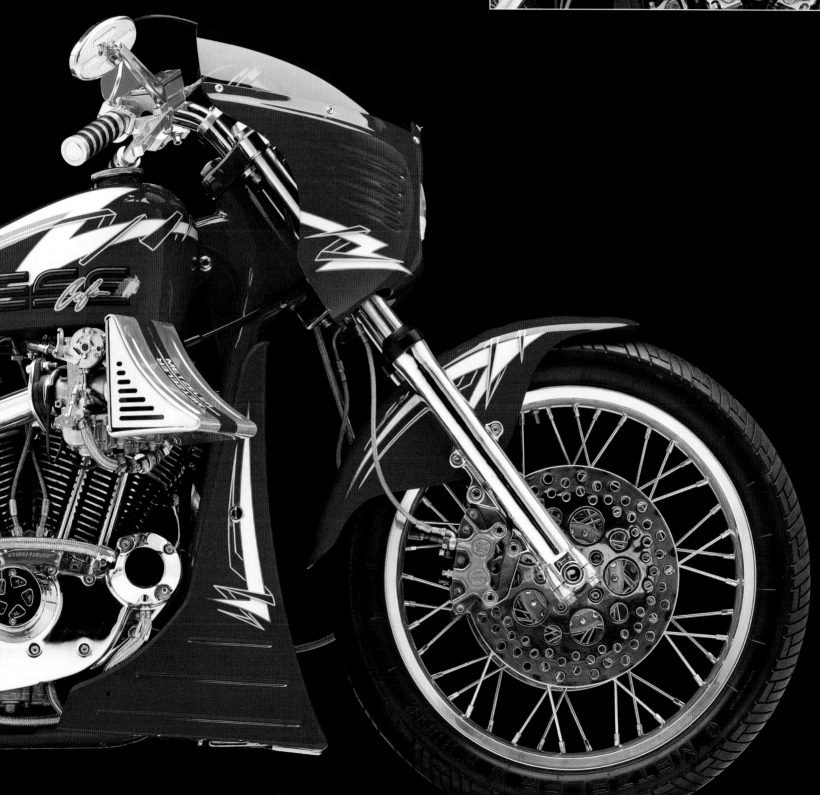

power, but not everyone wants traditional Sportster looks. In building the NessCafe, Ness did a bit of work on the engine, porting the cylinder heads for more power and adding straight exhausts, but it was the chassis that defined the machine. The frame is lowered and lengthened, with stretched swingarm. The small fairing and overall length pushes the look toward drag bike turf, but with uprated suspension and brakes, Ness says it handles as good as it looks. Rumor has it the only café racer he ever built was his favorite rider for many years.

1977 HARLEY-DAVIDSON XLCR

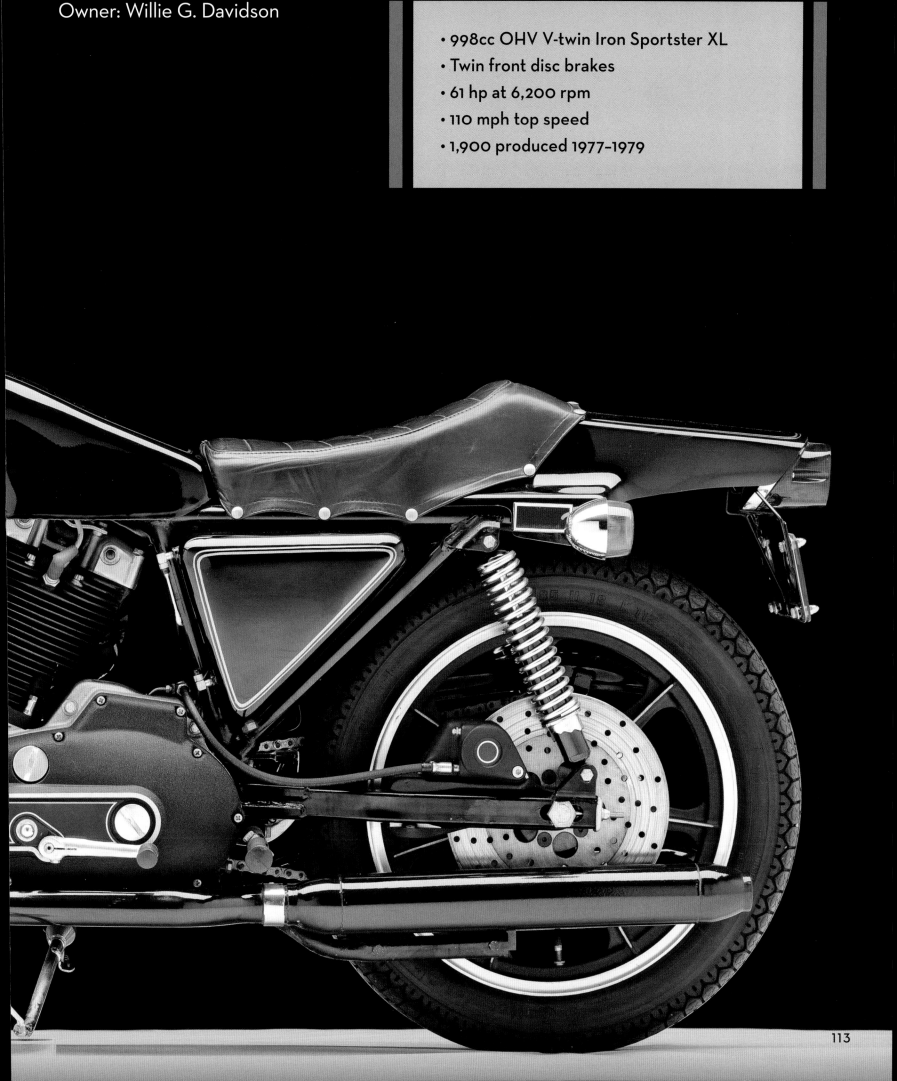

Owner: Willie G. Davidson

- 998cc OHV V-twin Iron Sportster XL
- Twin front disc brakes
- 61 hp at 6,200 rpm
- 110 mph top speed
- 1,900 produced 1977–1979

THE XLCR WAS A RADICAL DEPARTURE FOR HARLEY-DAVIDSON. It was their first-ever—and last-ever—true café racer. Head of Styling Willie G. Davidson began assembling the first prototypes in 1974 for consideration of Harley-Davidson's Board. The Ton Up! exhibit included the prototype's actual blueprint, dated 1975, which Davidson used to convince the company to produce a café racer from its XL Sportster—the XLCR. The board approved, and by 1977 Harley-Davidson began production.

When Davidson drew the lines of the XLCR in 1974, café racers were the hottest new production machines, with BMW's R90S, Ducati's 750S and SS, Desmo singles, Norton's John Player Special Commandos, and Laverda's SF and SFC all capturing the attention of riders craving speed and good looks.

Initial road tests were mixed. Davidson's styling, with its menacing, all-black, macho lines, incorporating a short fairing, unmistakable squared-up tank, the rear seat from an XR750 flat-track racer, and unusual siamesed exhaust pipes earning universal praise. Less praiseworthy were the economies required of a production Harley-Davidson Sportster-based café racer; namely, the standard iron XL engine, with plenty of grunt but too much vibration, and underdeveloped disc brakes that didn't. With attention to the motor and brakes, the XLCR could give performance equal to the promise of its looks, but such attention equaled a much higher purchase price, so the XLCR was considered a sheep in wolf's clothing.

Still, the XLCR was the fastest street Harley available in 1977, and is visually one of the most charismatic Milwaukee motorcycles ever. The XLCR has become hugely collectible, as only 1,900 were produced in its two-year lifespan. It was considered a sales failure at mighty Harley-Davidson, but a smaller European company would have considered it a huge success! The continued popularity of the café racer movement, and the consensus of the XLCR as a classic, has vindicated Davidson's vision.

Flash

Builder: Chabott Engineering

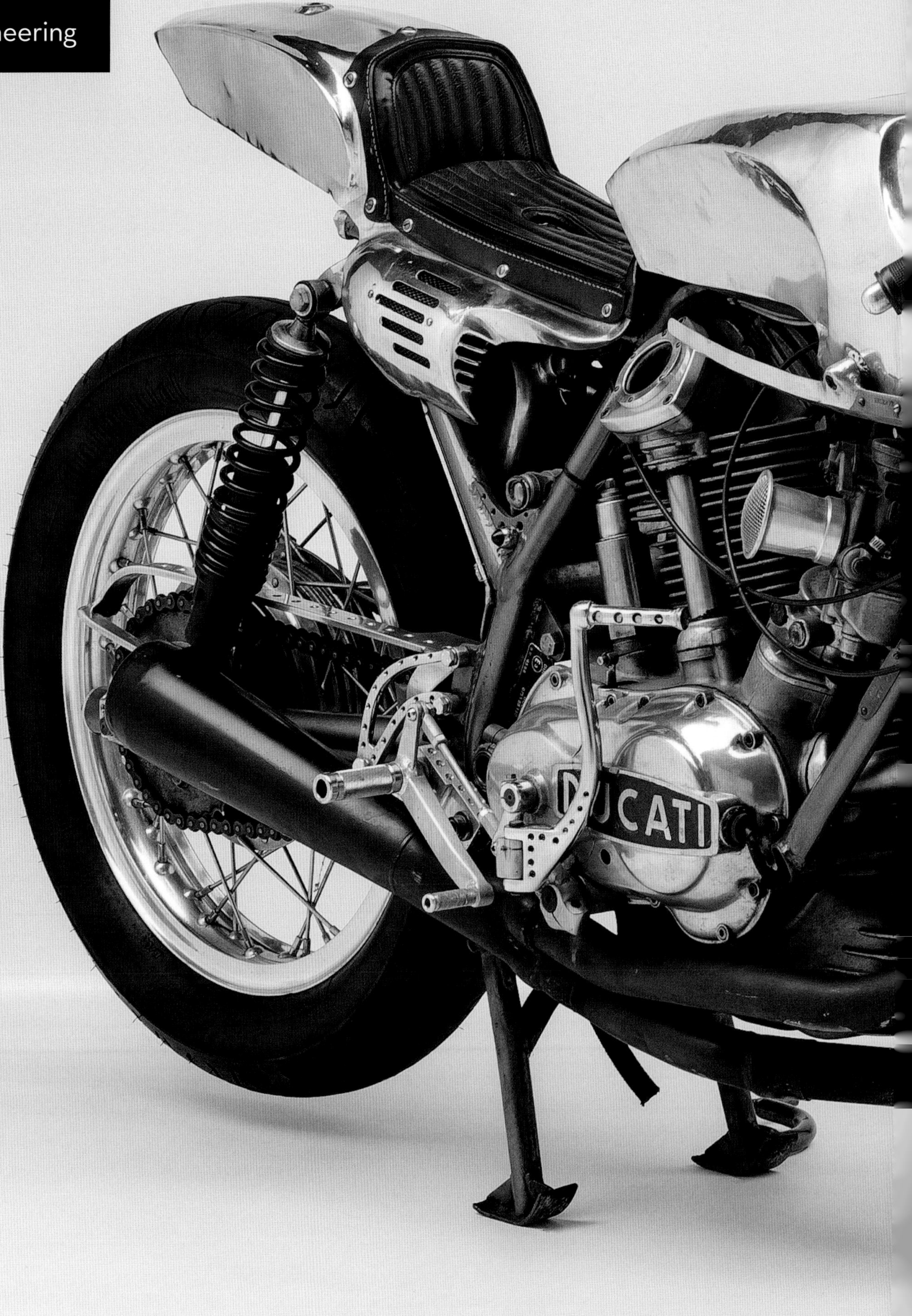

- 1974 Ducati 750cc Sport
- 750cc OHC 90-degree V-twin
- 80 hp at 7,200 rpm
- 125 mph top speed
- Ceriani Road Race forks
- Menani magnesium 4-leading-shoe front brake
- Ducati rear wheel
- Bodywork and exhaust by Shinya Kimura

SHINYA KIMURA BUILT HIS REPUTATION IN JAPAN CUSTOMIZING HARLEYS with his company Zero, but moved to Los Angeles and started coachbuilding a variety of makes several years ago, using the engine and chassis of a motorcycle as the base for his own highly customized vision. The Flash started out as round-case 1974 Ducati 750GT, a safe bet on any list of perfect motorcycles, so why on Earth would anyone make a custom bike from one? Kimura has discovered something different about the graceful and beautifully balanced lines of that engine and frame, a new expression of Taglioni's legendary powerplant.

The Flash contrasts the 90-degree V-twin's perfect primary balance and smoothness with a curiously asymmetric fairing, which emphasizes the left/ride side differences of the primary case and bevel drives. While beautiful, the Ducati is not in fact the same on every side, and it has curious organic shapes formed into its crankcases. Somehow, Kimura has drawn out both the shapeliness of the engine, its lovely bumps and curves, and the implication of speed while standing still in its profile. The velocity-squeezed fuel tank has speed scallops for knee cutaways, matching those on the high and slim tail unit. Yet the delicacy of all that tapered bodywork is offset by the massive drum brakes from a TZ Yamaha held in place by Ceriani Road Race forks. The Flash combines the muscular requirements of a fast motorcycle with bodywork that might have been carved by the wind.

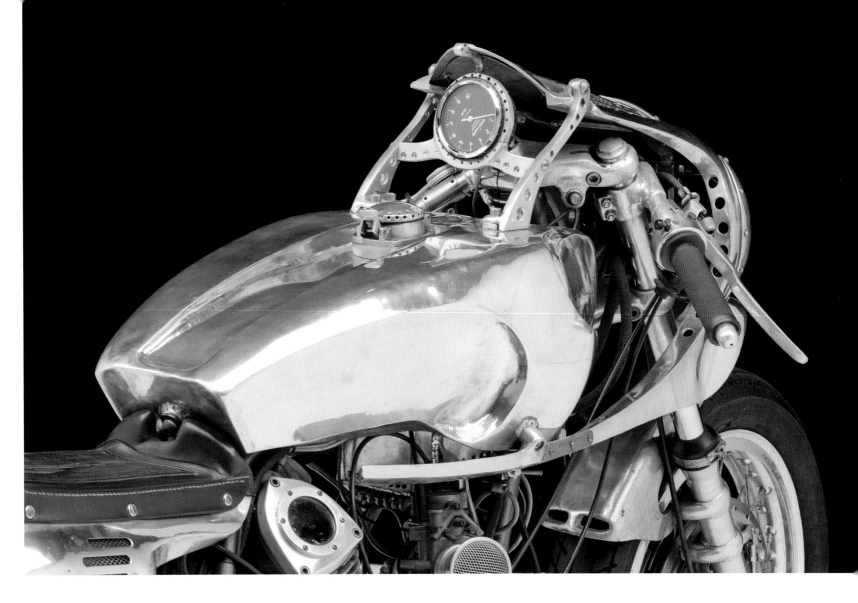

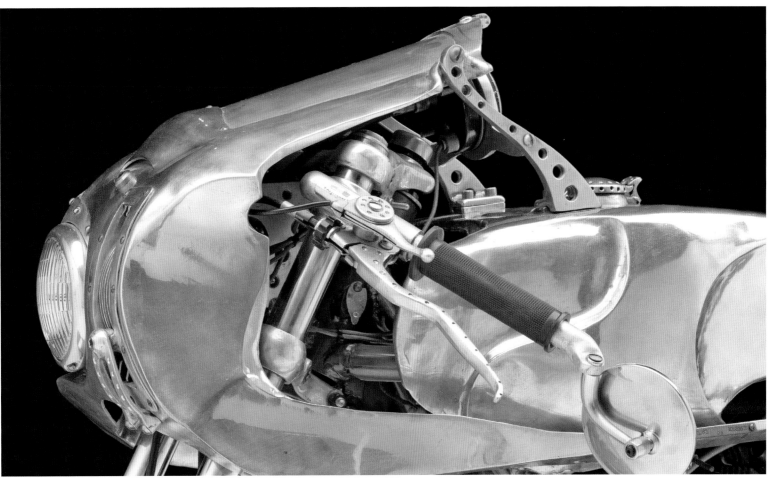

Trackmaster Café

Builder: Danny Erikson

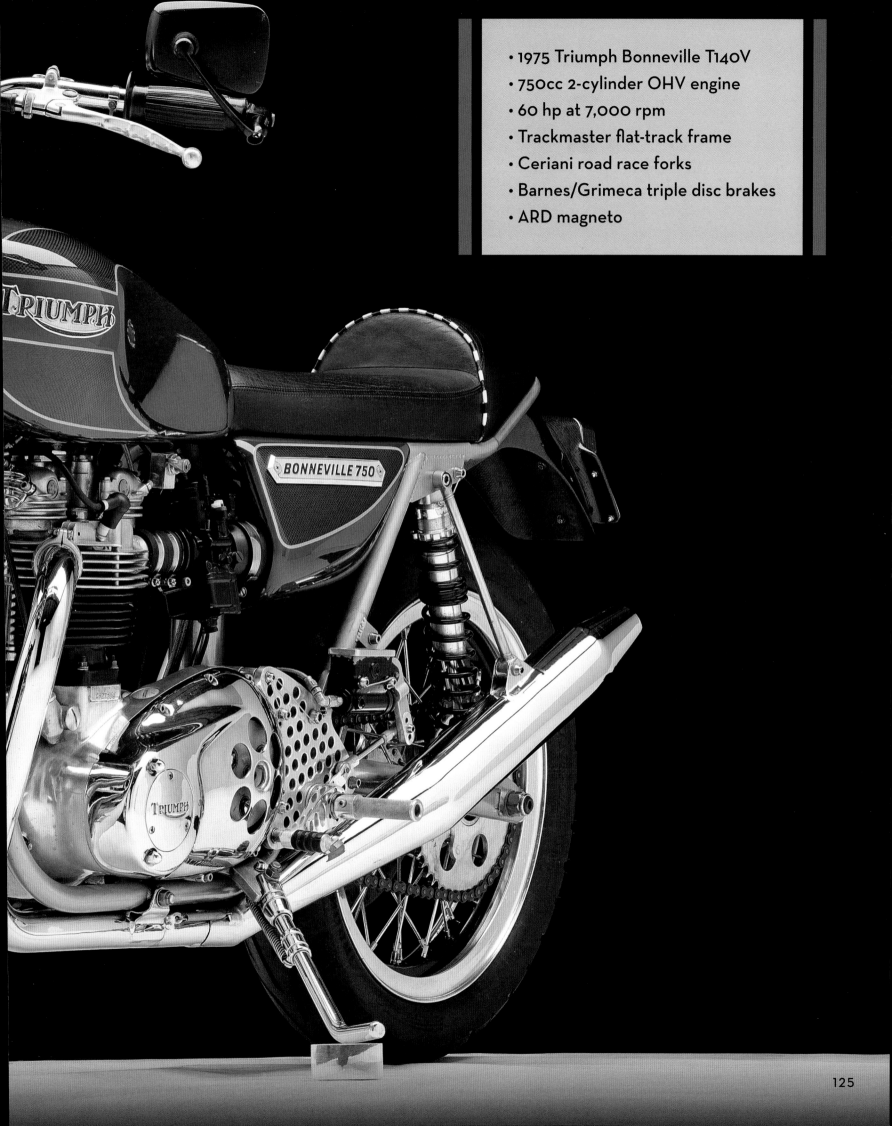

- 1975 Triumph Bonneville T140V
- 750cc 2-cylinder OHV engine
- 60 hp at 7,000 rpm
- Trackmaster flat-track frame
- Ceriani road race forks
- Barnes/Grimeca triple disc brakes
- ARD magneto

THE TRACKMASTER FRAME IS LEGENDARY in American flat track racing history, being the ideal chassis for a Triumph engine to belt around a dirt oval in the 1970s, lighter and stronger than the Triumph original, with that distinctive nickel-plate frame. Trackmaster Triumphs won dirt races across the United States in the 1970s On the West Coast, plenty of them were converted to street trackers , close cousins of café racers created from the same impulse—racers on the road—but with a slightly different aesthetic; American dirt track racing rather than European GP racing.

When *Bike Craft* (and former *Cycle World*) editor David Edwards saw this Trackmaster for sale, he'd already featured the bike in *Cycle World* and had to own it, knowing that its quality, by aircraft technician Danny Erikson, was flawless. The machine is a hybrid—a café tracker—and as such breaks the rules. But café racers were never about rules. They just ended up looking the way they look because that's what fast racing machines look like! Had any rockers from London ever seen a national-level flat track race, they would certainly have considered broadsliding at 100 miles per hour worthy of worship!

XR CAFÉ

Designer: Ray Drea

- 1984 Harley Davidson XR1000
- 998cc OHV V-twin
- 70 hp at 5,600 rpm
- Mike Lange's extensively modified components, motor build, HD frame, and new swingarm; Lock Baker's aluminum bodywork and exhaust

WHAT CAN YOU SAY ABOUT A SELF-TAUGHT PINSTRIPER, graphic artist, and bike customizer who took over Willie G. Davidson's job? You'd start with "obviously damned talented." Drea's greatest passion is creating art, in this case rolling sculpture that delivers smiles on faces around the world, a testament to Harley-Davidson's ability to "free more souls," as Drea puts it! The XR Café was a rare opportunity for him to design a bike without the handcuffs of high-volume production.

Drea built the XR-based café racer for Ton Up! as an homage to his former boss's HD XLCR café racer of 1977, knowing both bikes would be exhibited together. Keeping the tough-guy silhouette of the XLCR, Drea respected the handsome original while moving the aesthetic forward. The heart of his design was the visual adrenaline of the XR1000 motor; while the XR1000 wasn't a pure racer, it was based on the post-1972 all-alloy XR750 flat-track motor, and it had excellent performance even in a slightly detuned package. The motor is capable of serious stuff, as Lucifer's Hammer, an XR1000-based racer with 100 rear-wheel horsepower, showed by winning Daytona in 1983, a product-launch stunt that certainly worked. The XR Café was built around the engine, using materials and components often found in racing, like handmade aluminum bodywork, fatter rubber gripping carbon-fiber wheels, inverted forks, and triple Brembo brakes.

The result, Drea's XR Café, is an enormously appealing motorcycle, and a very rare factory redo of an older machine. It validates the rightness of Davidson's original concept, looking timeless and production-ready. In this age of retro-mad branding, one can only hope Harley might see fit to build a few more café racers.

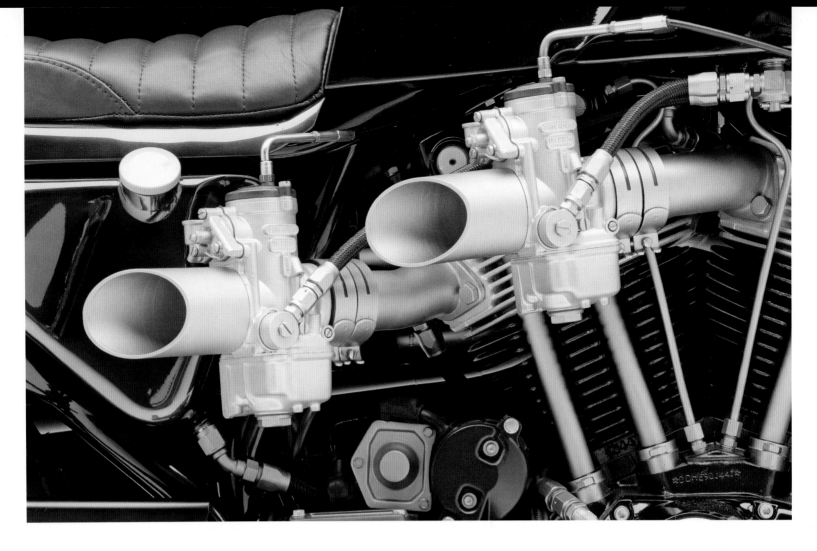

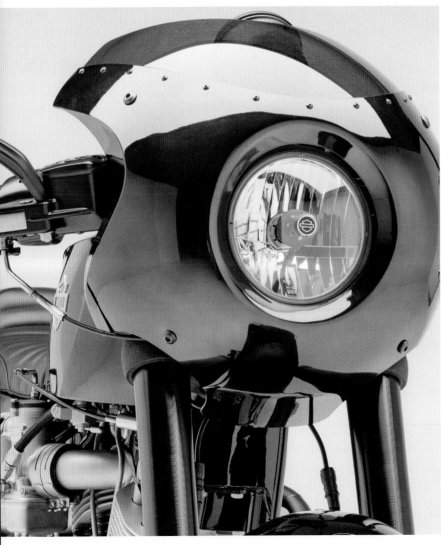

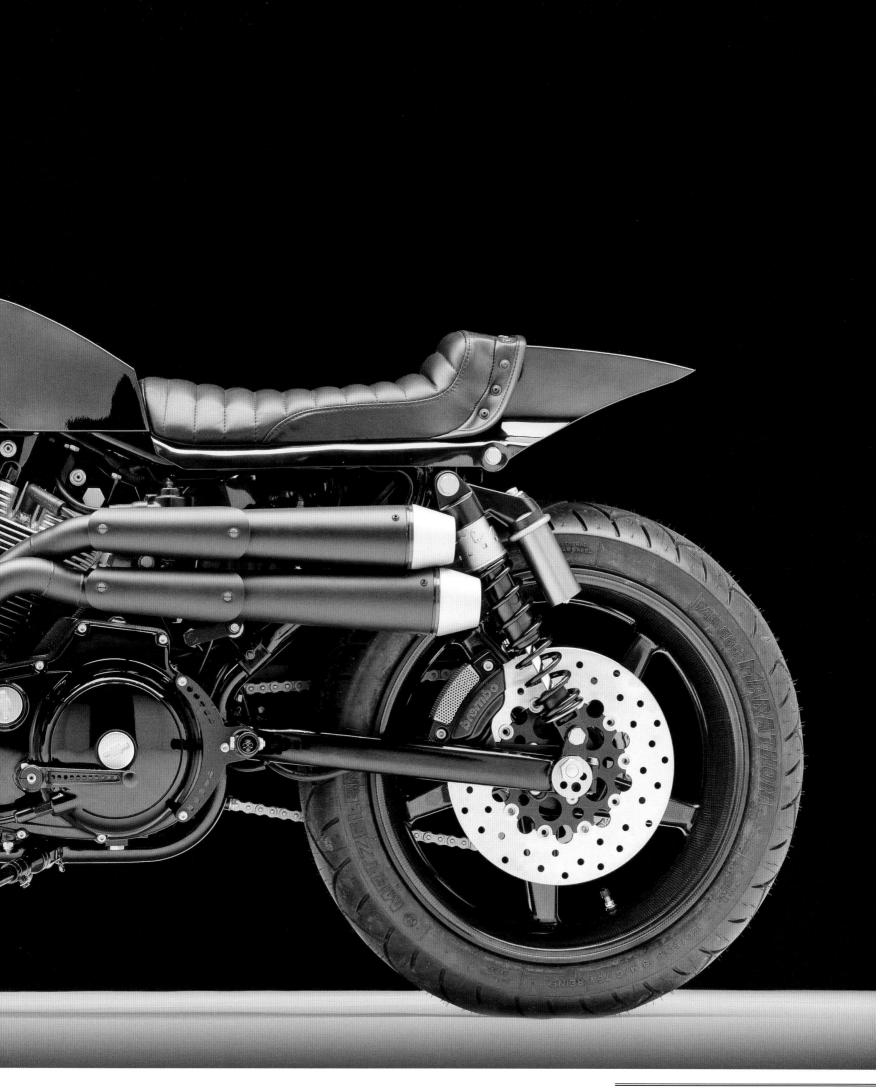

Sporty TT

Builders: Brad Richards, Ry Seidler

- 1999 Harley-Davidson Sportster 883H
- Bored to 1,200cc
- 2-cylinder OHV
- 58 hp at 5,200 rpm

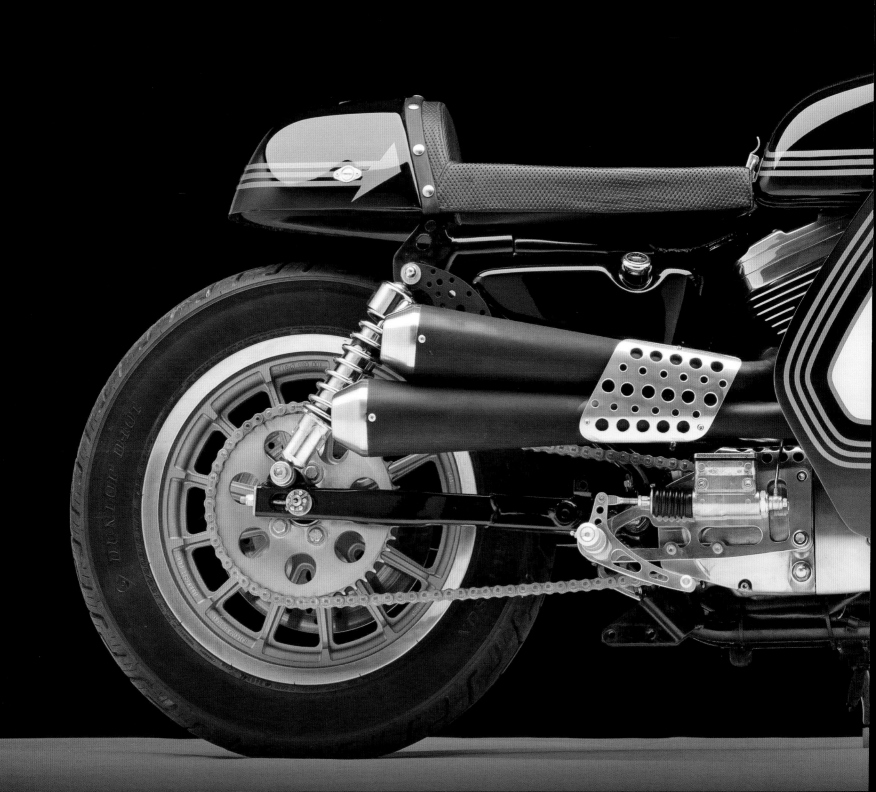

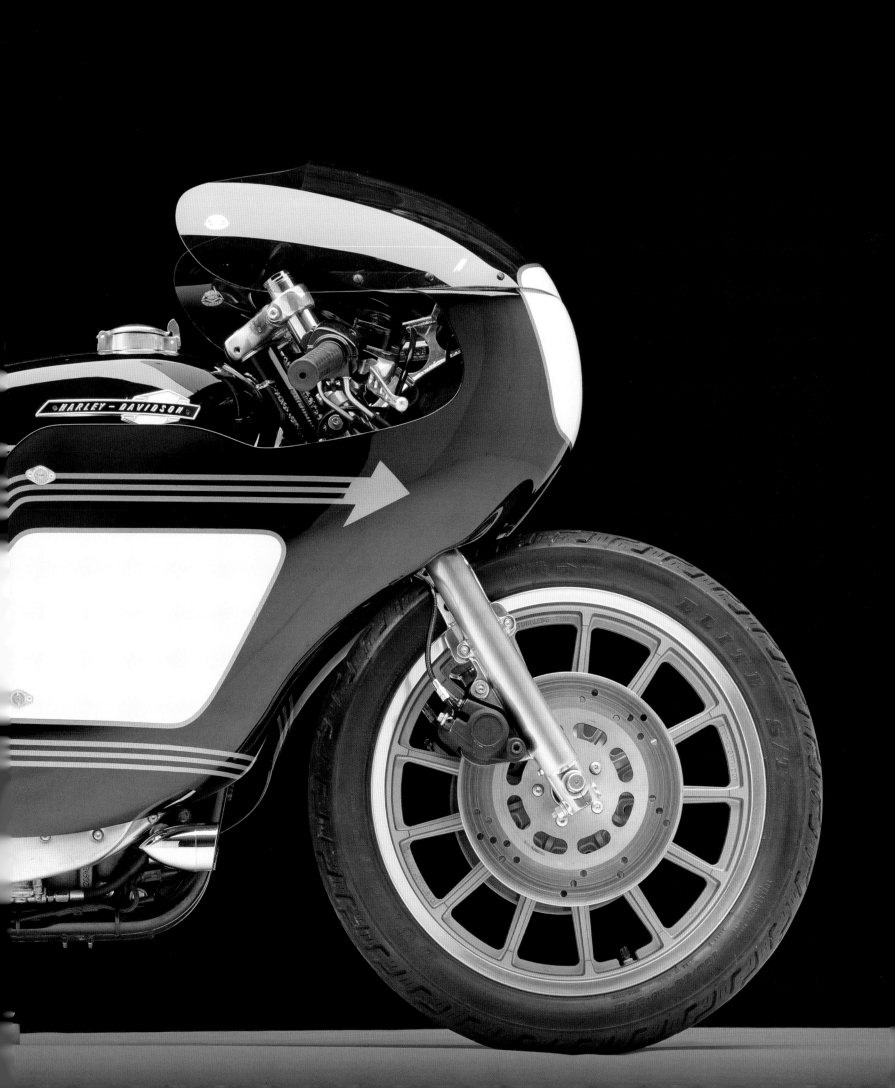

WHILE BRAD RICHARDS DESIGNS TRUCKS FOR FORD, he dreams up cool motorcycles to build in his spare time. When he heard the theme for the 2013 Motorcycles As Art exhibit would be Ton Up! he immediately promised to deliver a machine for display in six months. Richards began with a vision of the immortal Harley XRTT racer, which has served as an inspiration for many street and race replicas, since Harley-Davidson never made a roadster version. Working with talented friends like Ry Seidler, his late-night workshop journey began in earnest.

The Sporty TT takes styling cues from the XRTT, with high sidepipes (made in-house) and a full fairing. The vintage Suzuki gas tank looks surprisingly natural with a modified Ducati seat, and with clip-ons (using stock Harley-Davidson levers) and rear-sets, the whole package is solid. The curious may ask, "Where's the headlamp?" The keen-eyed will spot two tucked into and around the fairing—one in an air scoop, one hidden behind the front wheel. The graphically fantastic paint job ties the whole machine together, and it all adds up to give this mostly stock, Sportster-based custom a full-on road racer look, with a truly professional quality.

CHAPTER
=== 3 ===

The obsession with top-speed plastic sportbikes alienated a huge
segment of the motorcycle buying public.

TARNISHING
THE
GOLDEN AGE

AS THE 1970S FINISHED, the Italians were kings of the café racer hill, but it wasn't long before the second golden age lost its shine. By the late 1970s the British motorcycle industry was dead, although a few specialist chassis builders like Rickman and Harris still built kits for Japanese engines. Japanese bikes were faster and heavier and still handled like camels, even though they did well on the racetrack. Mike Hailwood provided a perfect example when he piloted his Ducati 900SS NCR special to a legendary victory over Suzuki at the Isle of Man Production TT in 1978. In shades of the old 750SS magic, Ducati quickly released a Mike Hailwood Replica 900SS the following year. But Ducati neglected to hide a hand-built racing engine inside the gorgeous body-work; it had fallen to the dark side of the factory café racer scene. (Of course, the 900SS was no slouch in 1980, even though it had never been the fastest production street bike.)

After the heady 1970s, the café racer scene began to fade. Some manufacturers took the idea of a racer on the road too literally, while other companies seemed to lose their way. Laverda had been the late-1970s speed king with the Jota, but in the 1980s it was struggling. Laverda fitted its powerful triple into increasingly touristy models like the 1200RGS, hoping to capture sales. It didn't work, and Laverda hit rocky financial ground. Ducati dropped its shaft-and-bevel OHC engines in favor of the belt-drive Pantah motor, which was very compact and efficient, but hardly the visual masterpiece of Taglioni's original round-case 750cc motor. Worse, Ducati started out at 500cc, which seemed a total capitulation in the speed wars. Moto Guzzi went on a pasta diet, growing heavier and less sporting in the 1980s. And the Japanese didn't find their niche with super-sporting road bikes until the middle of the decade.

East Side Moto Babe Ana Llorente and her Motobécane café racer at the Bonneville Salt Flats for a record run. *Paul d'Orléans*

and a pleasure to ride. Even though it was a mere 350cc two-stroke, its unified qualities gave rise to real affection from its riders, and it became an instant classic. Its formula—a perfectly balanced, light, and quick machine—was exactly what was appealing about café racers. But these qualities were overlooked for many years by the big Japanese factories, who had decided motorcycles belonged to specific categories: sport bikes, tourers, or cruisers. Meanwhile, the universal or standard motorcycle disappeared.

THE RISE OF THE SPORTBIKE

Kawasaki introduced the first of its Ninja series, the GPZ900, in 1986. This started a trend for plastic-wrapped "café racers" called sportbikes. Why weren't these café racers? Because they had no soul. The sales success of the Ninja led the motorcycle industry on a 10-year journey through the wilderness, producing increasingly fast sportbikes with increasingly loud graphics on their totally plastic surfaces, until the Ducati Monster was introduced in 1993 and slapped the motorcycle industry back to reality. Real motorcyclists prefer metal over plastic, thank you, and like the look of machinery, too. The sad reality of the 1986-to-1993 period was that the Monster seemed like such a shock. It should have seemed absolutely normal—a bike without crap covering every surface, a bike that looked like a machine, not an appliance.

The first over-the-counter Japanese café racer for many years was also the last two-stroke sold in America, the Yamaha RZ350 Kenny Roberts Replica of 1986. It was nothing of the sort, of course, the real deal being a technically brilliant, fire-breathing, four-cylinder, two-stroke beast, capable of nearly 200 miles per hour and winning the World 500cc GP Championship in the hands of a masterful and extremely brave rider. The Replica was an excellent road machine with fantastic handling, and although it couldn't compete for top speed with its 900cc rivals, it was extremely well-balanced

The obsession with top-speed plastic sportbikes alienated a huge segment of the motorcycle buying public. Sales of motorcycles began to suffer a long decline. Meanwhile, a generation of faux café racers called squids emerged. Squids are motorcyclists, of course, and therefore we must love them as family, but their devotion to plastic motorcycles had little to do with the machinery, as none was visible. Sportbikes are hyperefficient, blindingly fast, and totally reliable, yet seemed to have been robbed of their spirit; these motorcycles had become mere appliances. As appliances, they were inexpensive, disposable, and increasingly unrepairable for the average home mechanic. For all their incredible performance, nobody seemed to care all that much about the machines per se.

OPPOSITE: Le Mans driver and TV personality Alain de Cadanet aboard the infamous Rollie Free "bathing suit" Vincent, back at the Bonneville Salt Flats. *Paul d'Orléans*

REJECTION OF THE PLASTIC MOTORCYCLE: PUNK AND ROCKERS

A rejection of the plastic motorcycle coincided in the mid-1980s with an underground resurgence of the café racer style. Echoing the 1950s Rocker scene in England, music was the glue binding a new generation of motorcycle enthusiasts—but it wasn't the music of the 1950s. The explosion of Punk and its DIY ethos alerted all manner of artists, writers, photographers, revivalists, and just-plain-motorcyclists to the appeal of black leather and an old motorcycle. Being young, these new riders were attracted to the stylish speed at the core of the café racer scene. It was a short step from a black leather jacket with motorcycle patches and logo pins to a black leather jacket with safety pins and a punk band logo. The mid-1980s economy was crap, with high unemployment among young people, and the punk aesthetic, as demonstrated by its magazines, clothing, and music, was decidedly homemade. It became cool to build things with your hands, and old motorcycles were cheap at the time—especially when they hadn't run in years. An underground café racer scene emerged in London, Paris, Madison, and San Francisco as young enthusiasts of racy vintage bikes formed clubs. The Triton Club of Paris, the Mean Fuckers of London, the Roadholders, the British Death Fleet, and the Vintage Rockers of the San Francisco area were less interested in nostalgia than in enjoying the café racer style, using some of the same machines as café racers had in the 1960s and 1970s.

While the Mean Fuckers in London bumped against a few of the original 1960s Rockers, the rest of the clubs evolved without the disapproval of the inventors of the café racer style. That style was able to evolve, as Manx gas tanks were fitted to Moto Guzzi V-twins, Sportster engines were stuffed into empty Norton frames, and all manner of Japanese machines given the treatment. If you were young and broke,

just like young Rockers in the 1950s, you needed innovation to transform an ordinary machine into something special. You also needed a cheaply acquired donor bike. Luckily, the Classic scene was just emerging, and an old Triumph or Norton or Ducati or BMW was still very inexpensive. That would change by the 1990s, especially for Vincent twins, but even today an average-condition 1960s motorcycle is still affordable, if no longer cheap.

Tridents into clip-on racers. The style became an established genre of motorcycling, not simply a revival or anachronism. The label *café racer* became further divorced from its 1950s English origins and grew into something timeless.

While the motorcycle industry as a whole developed increasingly sophisticated machines at the turn of the twenty-first century, the interest in vintage and custom motorcycles exploded into a huge industry. This explosion touched the café racer scene, too, as builders became better known through popular magazines and even TV shows. By 2006 the rise of Internet motorcycle blogs, like my own The Vintagent (http://thevintagent.com), and websites like Bike EXIF (http://www.BikeExif.com) spread the appeal of café racers as a part of a broader custom motorcycle scene. The interest in customs spread viruslike into global popularity, with builders on every continent and in every large country sending photos of their latest work across the Internet.

CAFÉ RACERS: THE NEW GENRE

Café racer style expanded in the 1990s to include all sorts of machinery—Japanese, Italian, German, and British—anything to which clip-ons or Ace bars could be added and a humped seat bolted on. As British bikes grew more collectible and therefore more expensive, Japanese machines became especially attractive for modification, being cheap and widely available. Thus, CB twins and four-cylinder Hondas, RD Yamahas, and Suzuki two-strokes were the next wave of donor machines for young riders. Meanwhile, older enthusiasts (presumably with jobs) tweaked big Ducati twins, Norton Commandos, and Triumph

THE TRUE APPEAL OF A CAFÉ RACER

As sporting motorcycles became incredibly fast from the 1990s onwards, it grew increasingly clear that speed was not the sole attraction of the café racer. Sportbikes continued

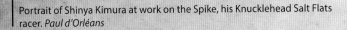

Portrait of Shinya Kimura at work on the Spike, his Knucklehead Salt Flats racer. *Paul d'Orléans*

Vincent Prat of the Southsiders MC with his son, Olivier, and their Bonneville racer Triton, together on the salt. *Paul d'Orléans*

to evolve technically and push boundaries of total performance, while café racers became something else. Until the 1980s, café racers were synonymous with performance, but then motorcycles-as-machines ceased to be beautiful. "Naked" bikes from the Ducati Monster onward celebrate the mechanical nature of a motorcycle, as opposed to styling exercises with plastic and carbon fiber coverings, but does anyone think the contemporary Ducati motor is a visual masterpiece? The same question applies to any contemporary motorcycle engine. When was the last time you thought a new engine was simply gorgeous in itself and would make an exquisite centerpiece to build a motorcycle around? Yet we have no trouble imagining building a bike around an older Triumph engine, or a Vincent twin, or even a Shovelhead. I suggest that this isn't because these engines are old, but because they look like machines, and their function is expressed as character.

The appeal of a café racer (and its predecessors, the clubman racer and the Brooklands/TT Replica) has always been a mix of the swift and the beautiful. Owners of a Ducati 750S or Norton 650SS or BSA Gold Star knew from start that they

were buying a classic, a pinnacle of good design, something to cherish and maintain and take pride in. With the rise of appliancelike sportbikes, café racers have parted ways with pure speed lust and moved toward appreciation of gorgeous machines built for speed. The word *style* is sometimes thrown as an insult, meaning "without substance." But in the case of café racers, style is a mix of aesthetics and function. It has little to do with technology and everything to do what moves us; a beautiful, fast motorcycle.

THE ROADHOLDERS OF SAN FRANCISCO

In 1984, clutching the art degree I'd spent four years earning, I stacked my brushes and books of anarchist theory into borrowed milk crates and made my pilgrimage to San Francisco. I wanted a motorcycle, as I'd previously buzzed around Stockton, California, on a Honda Express. This got me out of high school a whole year early, ferrying me to community college for night classes. I was 21, riding six years already, but normal progress from moped to new Japanese four-cylinder bike was perverted by a friend, his motorcycle, and his magazines.

Velocette enthusiast Dick Casey and his Thruxton café racer. *Paul d'Orléans*

That friend was Jim Gilman, a journeyman printer. Together we manhandled a lithographic press into my mother's basement and set about printing radical posters and books, fomenting revolution while Mom baked cookies. Since 1982 I had been a writer for *Maximum Rocknroll*, the biggest and baddest punk zine of them all. (Remarkably, it's still published.) I mention punk because everyone I knew who liked British bikes passed through the mosh-pit gauntlet. It was our music and our time; the attitude and the style left deep, studded-leather impressions on our little clay souls.

The revolution Jim ignited was not the one he intended. Being a character, he rode a 1957 BMW R50 in what we now call original paint, but was then just an eccentric and worn old bike. He found it under a staircase and bought it for $500. Everything was $500 back then. Our rule for buying bikes was $1 per cc, and we stuck to it for years. Jim had a guilty treasure in his apartment, his secret obsession. His stack of *Classic Bike* magazines, complete from issue number one, didn't fit with his ideal of a propertyless revolution, so he handed them to me. Those magazines were first worn out by my eyes, then my fingers; they became my bible and my pornography. I studied them so hard, their ink stained my corneas, and old motorcycles were all I could see. They changed my life forever, and luckily, I wasn't alone!

I needed a Norton, and I found a 1966 Atlas in Santa Cruz. So I hitched a ride and rode home on Skyline Boulevard, hitting the ton on an open stretch. It was my first ton, and my eyeballs shook so violently from the Altas' vibration I could not see properly. Within a few weeks, I'd added Ace bars, found a jet helmet and goggles, and was transformed into a café racer. Few in San Francisco knew what this meant. I was just a kid on an old bike, but 1984 was the year I grew a motorcycle under my heart.

Munro Motors had become a hangout and used bike emporium. It had previously been a Triumph dealership, but Triumph wasn't a company anymore. There was still a brand new TSX and a Jubilee Bonneville sitting on the floor, dead stock from a dead factory. We had no idea John Bloor had purchased the Triumph name and would revive it. We did know British bikes were really cool, and cheap, and superfun to ride, even though they needed more tending to than a thoroughbred racehorse. But we were young, and these obsolete machines were our thoroughbreds, worthy of the many hours we spent in dark garages tending their needs. We had yet to grow into full-fledged centaurs, the half-man, half-moto creatures we would become.

The seed for the Roadholders MC started the day I met Adam Fisher in the Munro Motors forecourt. He got my Rocker getup, but I was a snob, since he rode a Moto Guzzi V50. Still, he invited me to DNA, the club where he spun discs. We became great friends. He soon found a red 1962 Atlas in beautiful original condition, complete with a pudding basin helmet and black leather jacket. We attracted attention—the only proper Rockers in San Francisco, on period-correct café racer Nortons. We met Josiah Leet while parked in Berkeley having coffee. ("Hey! There's a gang of Mods down the street! Let's kick their asses!") How could you not love a guy like that? He had the getup, too, and Ace bars on his BMW. He introduced us to Bill Charman, who had a 1966 Bonneville and rocked a perfect American-style biker getup: white tee, cuffed jeans, engineer boots, horsehide cop jacket. He's still my best friend. My girlfriend Denise Leitzel, who rode a 1969 Velocette Venom, was smarter than all of us and suggested we form a gang.

We needed a garage. You can't have a gang without a garage; it's the stable for your horses, the church for your congregation, and the oil-stain pentagram for your rituals of initiation, celebration, and drink. So Adam and I found a house together, and it became our clubhouse. Now our gang needed a name. We had a friendly rivalry with the British Death Fleet, named after a newspaper headline about the Falklands War. Adam came up with Roadholders, and hand-painted a silkscreen stencil that night, which meant everyone had a painted biker jacket within the week. The Roadholders MC was born.

Among our members was Rob Tuluie. He was busy studying for his master's degree in physics at University of California Berkeley while developing a ratty but wicked-fast Commando for vintage racing, which double-dutied as his daily rider. Rob raced under a nom-de-plume and kept it all secret from his parents . . . until he graduated, won the championship, built the absurdly powerful TulAris racer

Yoshi Kosaka, proprietor of L.A.'s Garage Company, with his very special supercharged Honda CB750 café racer. *Paul d'Orléans*

using a snowmobile engine, designed the Victory motorcycle chassis, and now heads the Mercedes F1 chassis group. He still has his Roadholders jacket.

None of the Roadholders are in such a hurry as we used to be, but I'm still happy to ride with clip-ons, and grind away the sharp corners of motorcycles around bends. I'm built for speed, and prefer bikes that are, too. In my 20s, my Roadholder days, my relationship to motorcycles matured and made me the rider I am. I'm still a café racer, still a half-motorcycle centaur.

As displayed at Ton Up!, Yoshi Kosaka's Rickman Triumph Bonneville, in original condition. *Paul d'Orléans*

The Mako

Builder: Brawny Built

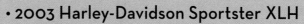

- 2003 Harley-Davidson Sportster XLH
- 1420cc OHV V-twin built and tuned by Mach Motors
- 110 hp at 6,500 rpm
- Brawny Built bodywork and chassis modifications

IT'S A RARE THING THAT A CAFÉ RACER IS INVITED to what appears to be a chopper show, but the Born-Free Show reflects the big changes happening in the world of custom bikes as the definition expands beyond choppers and diggers to include all types of home-modified machines. Builders are crossing boundaries, making any type of bike that appeals to them or suits their donor machine, and the massive exposure of builders and bikes on the Internet has encouraged moto-artisans to expand their horizons.

Brandon Holstein of Brawny Built was an "invited builder" at Born Free 5, and he brought the sister machine of the Mako, which was a hit. The Mako is further developed with a speed-tuned XLH Sportster engine, ported, flowed, overbored, and generally pumped to produce 110 to 120 horsepower. Such performance is astounding from an engine originally rated at 47.5 horsepower and clearly requires chassis upgrades to cope with the speed potential. One of the lessons of 1960s café racers was to find a compromise between the desire for power and the ability to actually use it on the road; a well-balanced machine, however fast, is infinitely preferable to ride than a brute.

Harley-Davidson built over 57,000 Sportsters in 2003, and they are among the most customized motorcycles in the world, but really good Harley café racers are rare. Brawny has added excellent brakes and suspension to help tame its ultra-hot Sportster café racer, which will clearly leave long black streaks down any road and in any gear! The inspiration for the Mako, says Holstein, was "to build a bike that I could blast through the desert at 120 miles per hour. When I plan a bike, it revolves around the type of riding, and for this project, it was high speed." That's music to a café racer's ears.

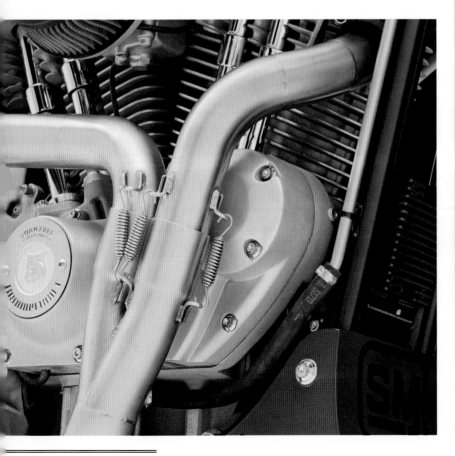

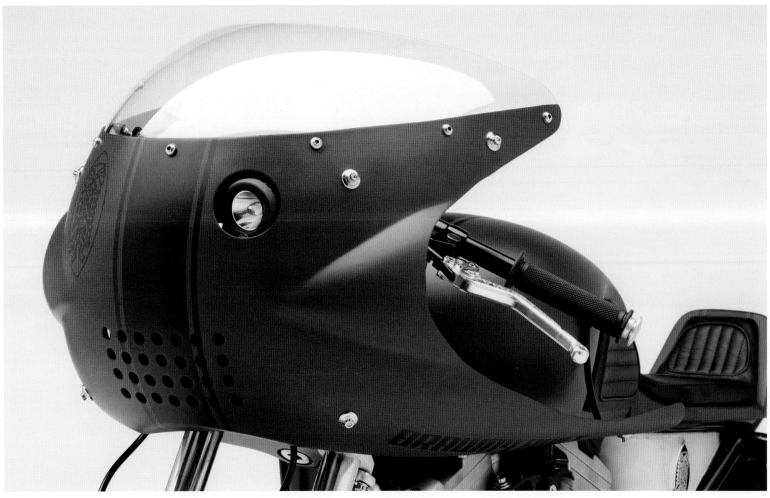

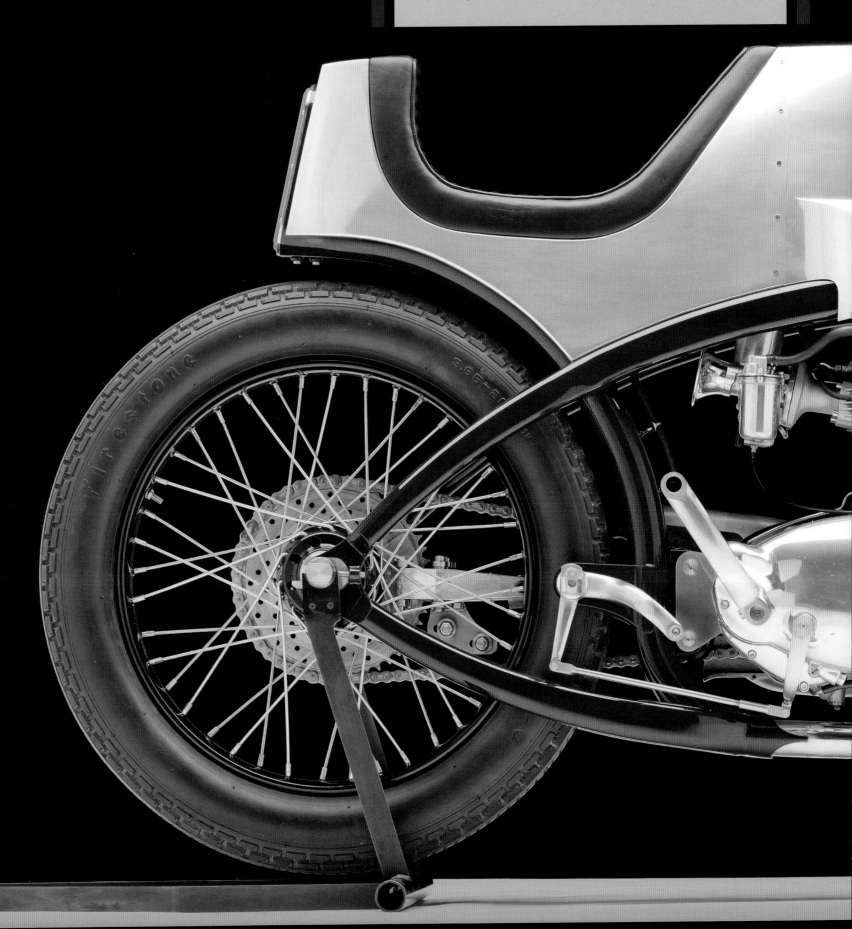

BEEZERKER

Builder: Speed Shop Design

- 1965 BSA A65 650cc 2-cylinder OHV
- 38 hp
- 105 mph top speed
- Frame, bodywork, forks, brakes, and controls all fabricated by Speed Shop Design from aluminum, steel, and stainless

THE 'BEEZERKER' IS AMONG THE MOST ORIGINAL MOTORCYCLES EVER BUILT. It stretches the very definition of the café racer genre. Builder Chris Fletchner uses the visual cues of the Café Racer—dropped 'bars, rearsets, a humped seat, even a tank with bulges echoing the Norton Manx and the Ducati 750SS Imola—but guides these familiar forms on a walk into terra incognita. Fletchner's overall shapes seem inspired by 1930s sci-fi films; this might be Flash Gordon's BSA, but it isn't a film prop—the beast works!

Fletchner's welds, bends, fit, and clearances on the chassis reveal his background as a silversmith; every detail is precisely crafted, with peerless lines and symmetry. The technical brilliance of his design includes the hand-fabricated frame, forks, bodywork, and controls, which are blade-slim and almost Art Deco. The box-section sheetmetal girder forks and the hard-edged tank-seat combo look like they're cut from solid aluminum. The handlebars, controls, and even handgrips are stainless steel. The clutch is engaged by twisting the left grip—unusual, but it works well. The squared-up chassis makes the BSA "power egg" motor look sexily curved and balances all that futuristic extremity. Even the exhaust is cleverly integrated into both the frame and seat unit. To look underneath the motor at the tapered tubing joint where the stainless exhaust pipes join the Amaranth Red–painted frame, is to marvel at Fletchner's exhaustive attention to detail. Specials were always an important part of café racer culture, and the Beezerker is a bit more special than most.

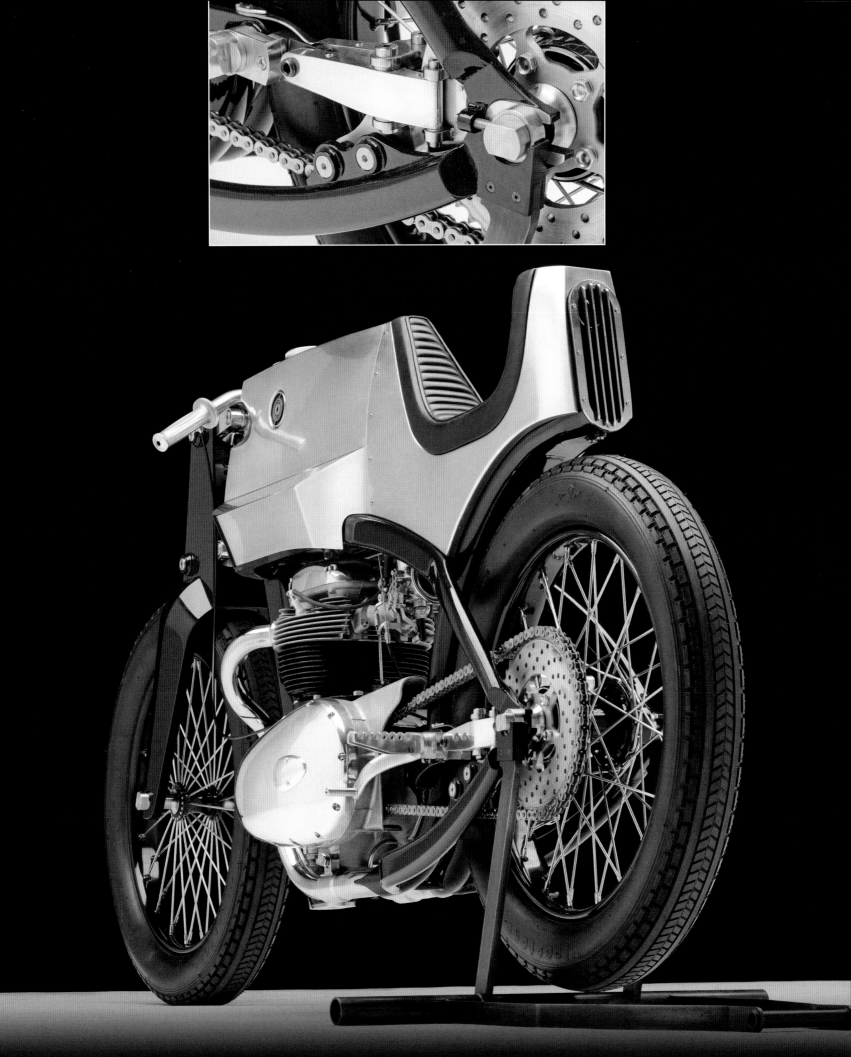

BRASS CAFÉ

Builder: Dime City Cycles

- 1968 Honda CB450
- 505cc twin-cylinder DOHC
- 45 hp at 8,500 rpm
- Bodywork and controls by Dime City Cycles

THE HONDA CB450 WAS A SHOT HEARD ROUND THE WORLD when introduced in 1965. It was the first big street bike from Honda, whose remarkable ambition the world was only beginning to discover. Starting in 1959, Honda went from a complete unknown in GP racing to World Champion within two years in the 125cc and 250cc classes. While manufacturers in Britain and the United States felt secure in their dominance of the large-capacity (over 500cc) global market, Honda's technically superior double-overhead-camshaft middleweight was a clear signal that the times were a-changin'. The CB450 was more reliable and almost as fast as its 650cc rivals from England, and it sold in the hundreds of thousands.

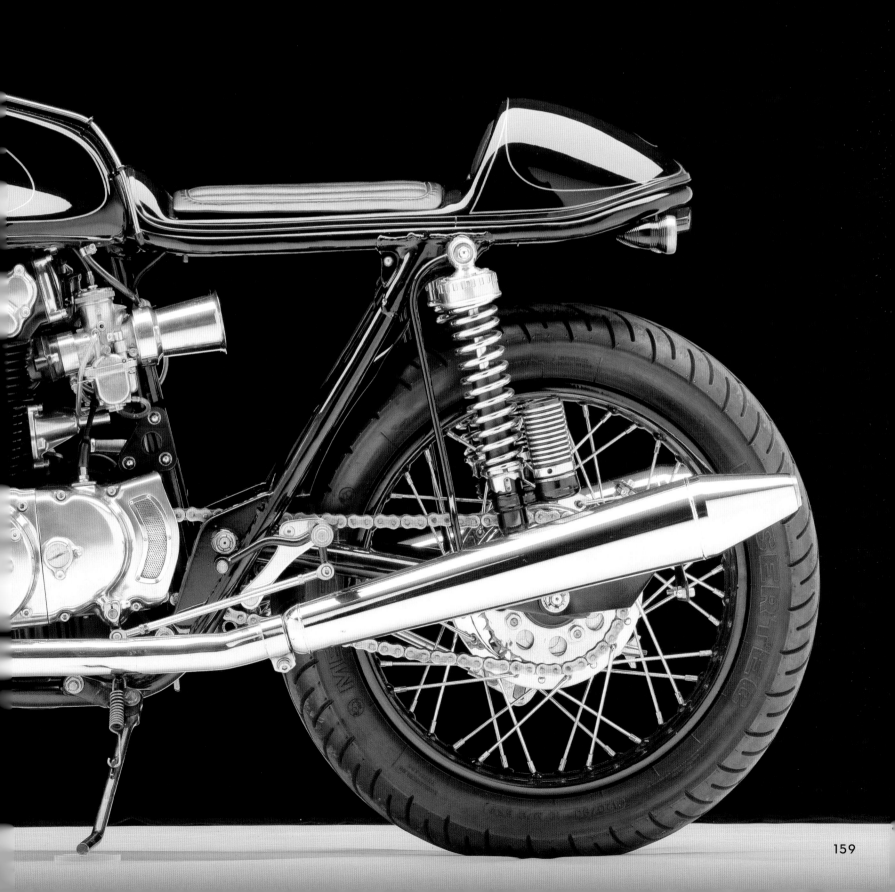

Today, CB Hondas are popular bases for customization for the same reason they were popular in the 1960s and 1970s: they're inexpensive, they're reliable, and they perform well. While prices for good examples are rising, these early Hondas are still relatively common, and with so many built, there's no need to flinch when chopping up a frame to build a custom.

Dime City Cycles has transformed a Black Bomber, the name of the very first CB450s with chrome-panel tanks, into the Brass Bomber by adding slick brass accents to every part of its stunning and sleek café racer. The tank is a stock CB item, with the sides and top cut out and reshaped, while the seat is a custom Dime City Wasp seat atop a reshaped rear frame loop in Dime City's signature style. The engine was overbored and the cams replaced with racing lumps, with the inlet passages reshaped and smoothed. Not many CB450s would pull wheelies—unless they'd broken a clutch cable!—but the Brass Café was built to be a proper Ton Plus machine.

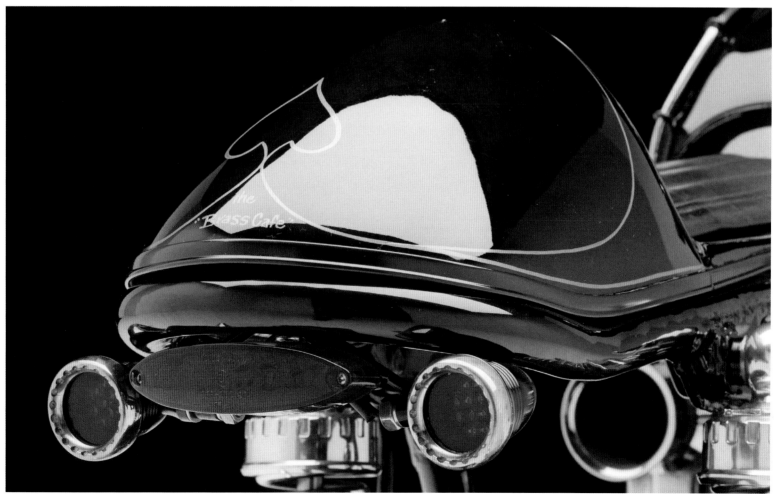

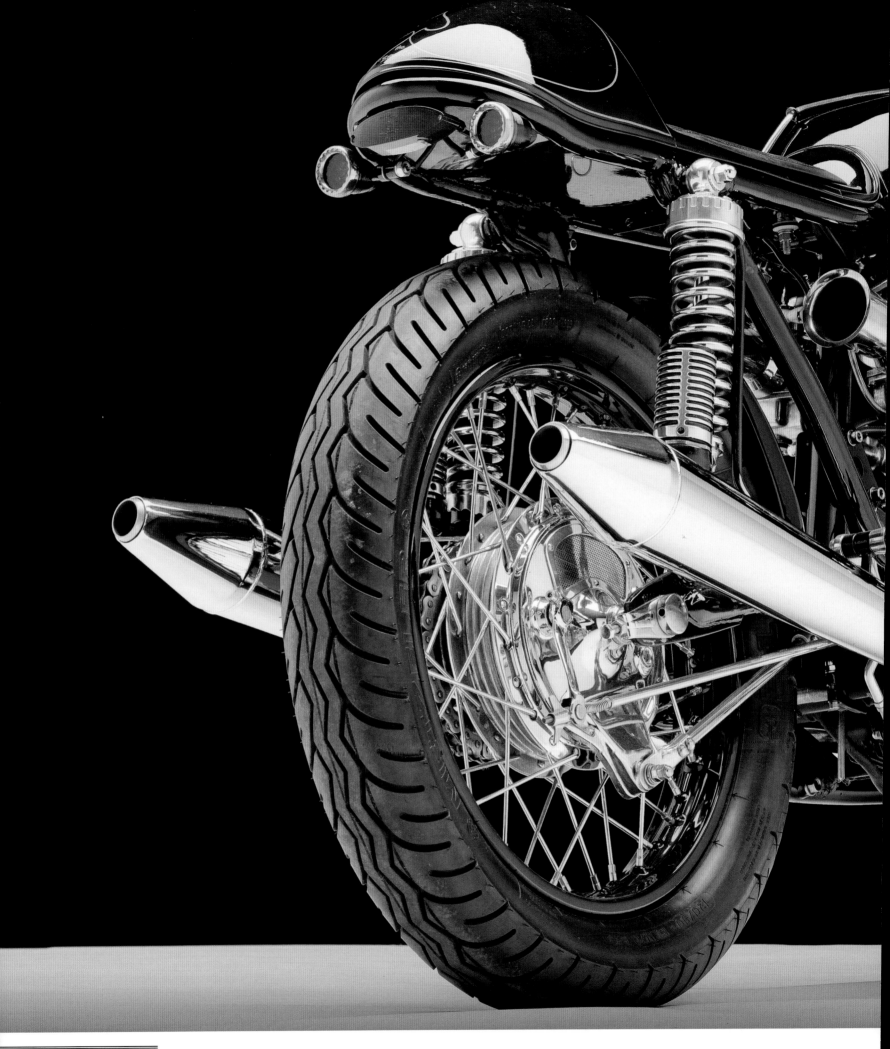

Yamaha Streak

Builder: Steve "Brewdude" Garn

- 1974 Yamaha RD350
- 349cc 2-cylinder 2-stroke
- Tuned to produce 60 hp
- Brew custom frame
- Yamaha R5 forks and modified tank

STEVE GARN IS BEST KNOWN AS A BICYCLE FRAME BUILDER, having supplied international-class road and BMX racers with superlight frames since the 1990s. He's also developed and raced quite a few motorcycles over the years, winning a second-place in the 2012 American Motorcycle Dealer (AMD) World Championship with a hot rod Honda CB 350.

The Brewdude Streak is the first motorcycle frame in the USA to use Reynolds 853 tubing, an ultralight and superstrong alloy; this frame weighs 17.2 pounds! Built to resemble the Featherbed double-loop frame of the Norton Manx, Brewdude has shrunk the Norton design to wrap tightly around a Yamaha RD two-stroke engine. Two-stroke engines are already significantly lighter than comparable four-stroke engines, without camshafts, valves, camchains, and a heavy cylinder head casting. So using a two-stroke engine to save weight is a great starting point for an ultralight motorcycle. This RD's reed-valve two-stroke engine has been tuned to 60 horsepower, resulting in an impressive power-to-weight ratio.

With a total weight of 243 pounds, the Streak weighs a full 130 pounds less than a stock RD350, which is widely considered a light motorcycle! The advantages to handling and acceleration are clear. While the Streak was built for track racing, it is fully road legal, with lights and full electrics, and is indeed a racer on the road.

Doc's Chops Yamaha

Builder: Doc's Chops

- 1982 Yamaha Virago XV920
- 1000cc OHC V-twin
- 65 hp at 8,000 rpm
- Top speed 110 mph
- Frame, seat, and exhaust by Doc's Chops
- Benelli Mojave tank

THE MAJORITY OF 1960S CAFÉ RACERS were built from used, crashed, or discarded bikes—mostly because they were cheap and easy to tune, while their riders were young and broke. While such machines were no longer at the forefront of racing technology, slightly obsolete bikes were still fast enough to satisfy riders' speed cravings and pretty enough to supply the required pose factor.

Today, with 40 years of reliable Japanese bikes available to modify, a few clever builders are rooting through the small ads and salvage yards for uncool bikes to purchase cheaply and customize. The Yamaha Virago is one such machine, deservedly almost forgotten, never legendary, but given a second life by those who are able to look past the cringeworthy 1980s styling or who are too young to have such judgments embedded in their memory.

What Greg Hageman of Doc's Chops saw in the Virago was a large-capacity OHC V-twin motor, robust enough to withstand tuning while keeping reliability. Discarding the original frame and bland 1980s bodywork, Hageman has modified the main frame and added a monoshock swingarm. With a sexy little Benelli tank balanced between the two cylinders, and those chunky enduro tires, the resulting bike is something never imagined in the Ace Café days. But it is certainly a hot and appealing roadster, worthy of inclusion in the café racer canon.

BH 347

Builder: George Kassapakis, See See

Motor Coffee Company

- 1985 Yamaha RZ350
- 347cc parallel-twin water-cooled two-stroke
- 50 hp at 9,500 rpm
- Top speed 125 mph
- Forks and swingarm Suzuki GSXR
- Aftermarket expansion chambers, seat by New Church Customs

THE YAMAHA RZ350 WAS THE LAST TWO-STROKE FAC-TORY CAFÉ RACER (called a "sportbike" by the industry) sold new in the United States (in 1986), due to increasingly stringent pollution regulations. The RZ was a water-cooled version of the venerable RD line of lightweight, reliable, and good-handling two-strokes, plenty of which had Ace handlebars and rear-sets added. The engine was easy to tune, and not many bikes could equal the low weight and good handling of these pocket rockets. Without the weight of camshafts and a valvetrain, two-strokes are much lighter than their four-stroke cousins. And with power pulses twice as often, it's no wonder they dominated GP racing in the 1980s and 1990s, long after they disappeared from U.S. roads!

The RZ was the first mass-production motorcycle with a perimeter frame—tubes wrapped around the engine rather than a central spine or twin top rails. The idea appeared on Gilera's 1938 4-cylinder supercharged Rondine racers, and private frame builders like Seeley and Spondon offered similar designs since the 1970s. The Silk motorcycle of 1975 was the first production bike with a two-stroke water-cooled twin-cylinder engine and perimeter Spondon frame, but the Yamaha RZ is cheap, fun, and has excellent manners. See See has improved handling further with Suzuki GSXR forks and swingarm, and has added sexy upswept expansion chambers for knee-dragging fun. Long live the ring-a-ding!

The American Café

Builder: Skeeter Todd

- 1979 Harley-Davidson XL/XR
- 1,260cc OHV V-twin
- XR1000 heads
- 1979 HD frame and modified forks,
- 1966 HD tank
- Skeeterbuilt oil tank and rear subframe, Brembo brakes

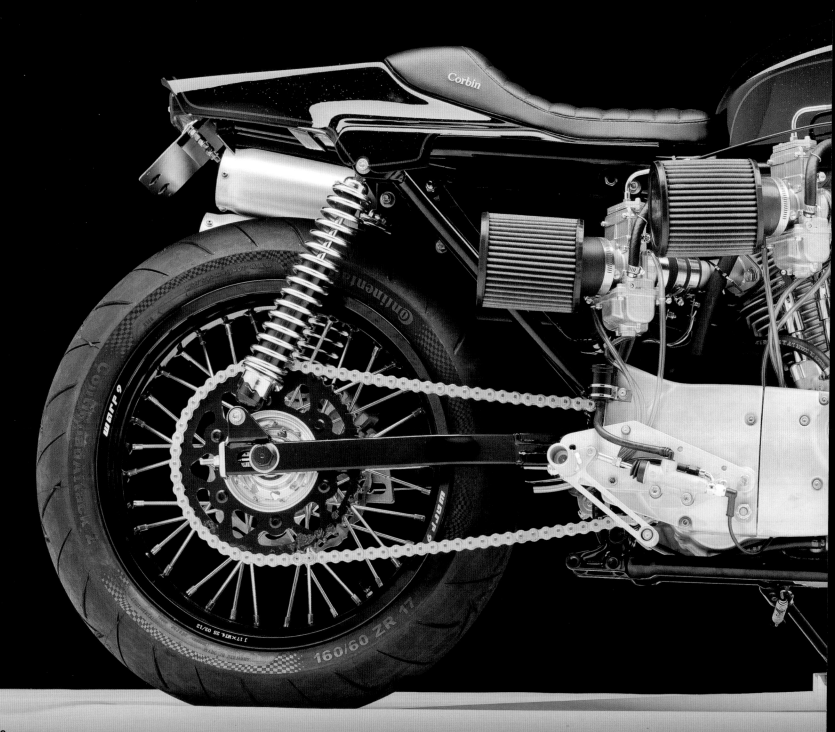

IT TRULY IS A PITY THAT THE SOLE AMERICAN CAFÉ SINCE THE 1950S WAS DAVIDSON'S XLCR, for it's now clear the Harley-Davidson Sportster makes a fine basis for a street racer, especially with 1970s road race style bodywork. Fans of American iron have long built café racers from their roadsters, and Skeeter Todd jumped into the fray for the Ton Up! exhibit with a heavily modified machine, which owes as much to his skill as a machinist as it does to any particular Harley-Davidson engine.

The Harley XR1000 was aimed squarely at the street tracker market, but the engine is fast and smooth and deserves the café racer treatment. Todd built a nearly all-Harley machine, much like Johnny Cash's Cadillac, one piece at a time. The turtle tank is from a 1966 Sportster. The frame is modified from a

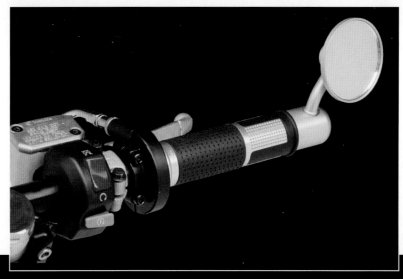

1979 ironhead. The engine is a mix of XL bottom end and XR top end—which is easy to say, but a close look at the actual engine will reveal how different those engines really are. "I wore two footprints in the concrete beside my milling machine, to make this work," says Skeeter. With different pushrod placement and cam positions between the XL and XR models, it took hundreds of hours to make it all work. When asked why he didn't just buy an XR engine, Skeeter says practically, "They're expensive!"

In keeping with the XR style, the American Café uses high pipes and twin carbs, which suggest power and handling. This machine might be assembled from Harley hodgepodge, but Skeeter's skilled work results in a truly all-American café racer.

DEUS EX MACHINA R100S

Builder: Deus Ex Machina

- 1978 BMW R100S
- 980cc flat-twin OHV
- 70 hp at 5,500 rpm
- Deus-built rear subframe, tank, controls; Ohlins forks

WHILE THE 1973 R90S WAS BMW's SOLE ENTRY INTO CAFÉ RACER TERRITORY (until the Concept 90), plenty of BMW's flat twins have been modified as hot roadsters or outright racers since they began production in 1923. Larger-capacity BMWs were especially popular bases for conversion in the 1980s, following the successful exploits of Reg Pridmore in Battle of the Twins racing. Deus has a different take on a contemporary "air head" café bike, with modern forks and a superclean, minimal aesthetic just begging to be thrown around a canyon.

"The inspiration behind this bike is something that didn't look like a BMW," explains Woolie Woolaway, who built the machine. "I tried to change the look of it and to style it around something that was a bit older than the bike was. It's got a big tank and you're all stretched out, so you really feel like you're tucked in behind it." Woolaway deconstructed the frame, removing all the brackets and the old subframe, and built a new chrome-moly subframe, relocating the battery under the seat. The components—rearsets, fenders, controls, tank, seat, brackets, and so on—are all handmade. The front forks are shortened Ohlins. "It's a fun bike . . . a bit faster than I actually expected. It's definitely a one-off."

The BMW is certainly unique, a collage of off-road and road-race influences, and it pushes the traditional boundaries of the café racer style. The folks at Deus don't intend their machines to fit neatly into any particular style, which suits their customers just fine, as they've opened workshops on three continents!

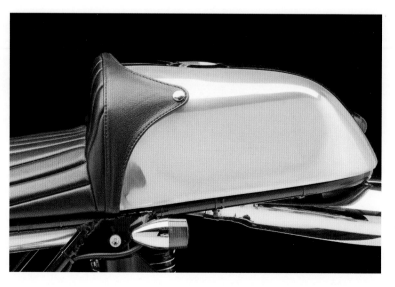

DZ Sportster

Builder: David Zemla

- 2003 883 Harley-Davidson Sportster
- 883cc OHV V-twin
- 50 hp at 4,400 rpm
- RSD wheels/fork brace; Burly Brand seat, fairing, and shocks

SINCE THE XLCR WAS BUILT FOR ONLY TWO YEARS (1977 and 1978), anyone wanting a café racer Harley has to build one for him- or herself. Still, the Sportster has been a popular subject for café modifications since the 1970s, and an entire industry of suppliers is ready to help owners wanting a racier look to transform their ordinary roadsters into something much cooler than stock.

David Zemla and Burly Brand sell bolt-on components, which can transform an ordinary Evo Sportster into a café racer in a single weekend. A case in point is Zemla's personal DZ Sportster, which is modified with off-the-shelf components from several manufacturers, including his own Burly Brand parts: 15-inch Stilleto shocks, Burly café tail section, and the small fairing. Ton Up! contributors Roland Sands Design (the fork brace and Morris wheels) and Boyle Custom Moto (air cleaner) are represented, as are Speed Merchant triple clamps, G-Bones Powell Peralta chain tensioner, and Chainsikle rearsets.

The DZ Sportster is built to be ridden hard. "You can drop it into a corner and just rip out," says Zemla. It's an old tradition: take off the heavy street components, replace them with much lighter and cooler parts, and you've dramatically improved the performance of your street machine. Aftermarket parts suppliers in the 1960s, like Dunstall, sold Triumph and Norton accessories. Today's moto-entrepreneurs focus on Harley-Davidson, although the new Triumphs get their share of attention, too.

CHAMPIONS MOTO BRIGHTON

Builder: Champions Moto

- 2004 Triumph Bonneville
- 865cc twin-cylinder DOHC 4-valve
- 75 hp at 7,400 rpm
- Grimeca brakes; custom frame, bodywork, and exhaust

THE ORIGINAL TRIUMPH BONNEVILLE WAS A GLOBAL FAVORITE for nearly 20 years, combining beautiful looks with excellent power and speed, even if the first versions felt squeamish in hard corners. A change of engine to unit construction in 1963 improved some of the handling issues, and by the time the engine grew to 750cc with a five-speed gearbox and disc brakes, the Bonnie had become reliable and fairly modern. But the end was near. Triumph production at the original Meriden plant ceased in 1983, and it took 17 years for a revamped Bonneville to emerge from the Hinckley factory of John Bloor.

The new Bonnie had big shoes to fill, sharing a name with a motorcycle legend, but enough magic from the original remains to make the new machine an amazingly popular standard motorcycle. It has since become a popular base for modification and

customizing, just like the 1950s to 1970s models, and Triumph nodded to the Bonneville's café racer history by introducing its Thruxton version in 2004.

Champions Moto trumped the factory's own effort with its Brighton, which has been heavily reworked to captured a period café racer look, with plenty of modern touches and a quality of finish rarely found on machines built back in the day. Using traditional Triumph Amaranth Red as found on the original Speed Twin of 1938, the Brighton has 1960s touches like drum brakes (double-sided, Italian, and gold), but the chrome-moly chassis and engine tuning mods (ported heads, hot cams, lightened flywheel) improve significantly on the modern factory's performance. With a professional level of fit and finish, the Brighton looks for all the world like a showroom floor special, but not even Triumph offers a bike this cool.

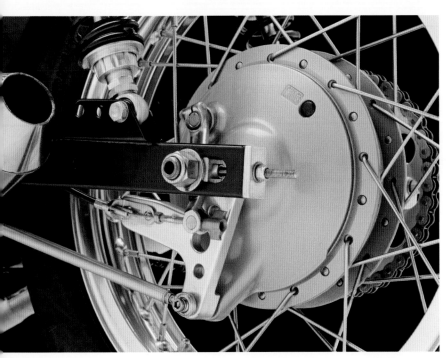

BMW Concept 90

Builder: Roland Sands Design

- 2013 Prototype
- BMW 900cc flat-twin DOHC 4-valve motor
- 115 hp at 8,500 rpm
- Ohlins forks and shocks
- Brembo brakes
- RSD bodywork, wheels, and details

STARTING WITH THE R37 OF 1925, BMW has built many serious sports machines, winning races and world championships ever since. But it didn't succumb to fashion until its first café racer in 1973, the legendary R90S. With its smoked paint job in orange or gray over a silver base and its bikini fairing, the R90S was a clear answer to the café racer craze. It was flamboyant enough to appeal to sideburn-and-flares youth but correct enough to never have passed through an embarrassing stage. These machines have always been in demand, always been classic, and always been cool.

For the 40th anniversary of the R90S, BMW handed custom motorcycle wunderkind Roland Sands its new 900cc prototype, the Concept Ninety, and let him go to work. Roland Sands Design redesigned and built beautiful new bodywork of hand-formed aluminum and carbon fiber, used computer-aided design (CAD) machines to build new "contrast cut" wheels, cylinder covers, and other parts from aluminum, and painted it all up in the familiar Daytona Orange of the original R90s. BMW was wise to collaborate with an outsider, as Sands' version of the Concept Ninety has details that add a serious cool factor. BMW is proud of the stunning collaboration, and Sands has been seen recently in Italy and France doing smoky burnouts and street racing on the Concept 90—as any real café racer should.

Patton Café Racer

Builders: Santiago Choppers, Alain Bernard

- 1996 Moto Guzzi 1100 Sport
- 1064cc 4-valve OHV V-twin
- 90 hp at 7,800 rpm
- Carbon fiber tank, seat, and subframe

MOTORCYCLE FACTORIES FINALLY GOT HIP TO THE ALLURE OF THE CAFÉ RACER in the 1970s, and it was the Italians who really embraced the concept. Ducati, Laverda, and Moto Guzzi produced the fastest and best-handling roadburners in the 1970s and 1980s. It was truly a second golden age of the café racer. The Ducati 750 Super Sport was the fastest motorcycle in the world in 1974, and the Laverda Jota was fastest in 1976. Moto Guzzi produced a classic in its first 850 LeMans, with its long and low chassis, small bikini fairing up front, and fluorescent orange flash paint job.

By the 1990s, Italian bikes were no longer fastest. Moto Guzzis, especially, had been eating too much pasta, gaining weight, and becoming sports tourers rather than trim fighters. Alain Bernard of Santiago Choppers was commissioned by Patton Watches to put this Moto Guzzi 1100 Sport on a carbon fiber diet. With a hacksaw and very light components, he managed to trim 80 pounds, which goes a long way to help performance. The stripped-out look is reminiscent of the Moto Guzzi heyday of Battle of the Twins racing and the victories of John Wittner. The bruising Patton Café Racer reminds Guzzi lovers everywhere that it's still possible to have a light and nimble road dancer, Italian style.

BUCHEPHALUS

Builder: Loaded Gun Customs

- 1967 T120R Bonneville
- Short rod crank
- 803cc
- 65 hp at 7,200 rpm
- Top speed 130 mph (estimated)
- Aluminum chassis and chromoly swingarm by Loaded Gun Customs
- Alloy tank by Junior Burrell, forks and wheels by Buell

AS CAFÉ RACER STYLE EVOLVES, a few builders are going where no café racer has gone before, experimenting with radical chassis designs and extreme styling, even while using traditional motors like this 1967 Triumph Bonneville. Loaded Gun's Kevin Dunworth built the frame for his Bucephalus (named after Alexander the Great's infamous horse) from parallel plates of 7005 aluminum. Dunworth admits this is probably overkill; a lower-spec aluminum would have been lighter and strong enough, as hi-spec aluminum plates are stronger than steel. With chromoly struts between the plates, the frame is built like a bridge while being a superlight chassis, which has all the tensile, compressive, and torsional strength of a much heavier tube frame.

Dunworth hand-fabricated the monoshock swingarm as well. The tank is a handmade replica of a Triumph item, built to fit around the experimental frame. The tank isn't slick, but looks very hand-beaten, in contrast to the rather severe chassis. The seat is held in place by carbon fiber rods, which look delicate as chopsticks but are far more robust than steel tubes. With modern forks and wheels, this Triumph could only be a twenty-first century machine. But with its 1960s engine, the overall effect is that of a retro-future racer.

VICTORY
NessCafé

Builder: Zach Ness

- 2013 Victory Judge
- 1,731cc OHC V-twin
- 85 hp at 5,300 rpm
- 665 lbs

ZACH NESS HAS PRODUCED A BRUISING CAFE RACER from a big-bore contemporary street cruiser. The Victory Judge is all about thunderous power and attitude, with a dollop of muscle car styling and a few cues cribbed from rival Harley-Davidson. The massive 1,730cc engine helps offset the equally massive 665-pound dry weight of the standard Judge. This is not a bike for the faint of heart.

Ness set about lightening the Victory with his own rear subframe, eliminating unnecessary side panels and the rear fender, and adding 10-spoke aluminum wheels with contrast cut details. His NessCafé flirts with automotive styling cues (those wheels), but with his cool bodywork tweaks, a set of high-level exhaust pipes, lowered handlebars, and bump-stop seat, the NessCafé's proportions are visually balanced to make the Victory's 600-pound bulk look perfectly street-able and devastatingly powerful. One cheeky detail not lost in a sea of café racers is the large-diameter speedo atop the fork triple clamps, reminiscent of the Vincent Black Shadow's five-inch speedometer, a bold statement about what matters on this machine: speed, and not much more.

KAFÉ STORM

Builder: Klock Werks

- 2013 Triumph Thunderbird Storm
- 1699cc 2-cylinder DOHC water-cooled
- 97 hp
- Top speed 115mph (electronically limited)
- Frame alterations and bodywork by Klock Werks

TRANSFORMING A "BRUISER CRUISER" LIKE TRIUMPH'S NEW-GENERATION THUNDERBIRD into a café racer takes a lot of imagination and a very dry wit. Ray Klock of Klock Werks chose to treat the Thunderbird as just another Triumph awaiting customization, ignoring the factory "brief" for the machine—a torque monster more suited to boulevard cruising and smoky burnouts than carving canyons.

In building a new rear subframe for the Storm, Klock has moved the Triumph out of traditional H-D turf and back to traditional British lines, even though the 1700cc bike was never intended to link with past Triumph glories at the Ace Café. By hiding the electrics and removing the side panels and other styling clutter, the machine looks significantly lighter, even though this Uzi weighs a ton.

Klock took his inspiration for the Kafé Storm from the headlamp of a 1937 Graham "Shark Nose" automobile; taking cues from the horizontal finning of the Triumph engine and the chrome grillwork of the car, his team blended the rare Graham headlamp (restored by Iverson Automotive) into a home-built fiberglass half-fairing, which resulted in the distinctive shape of the Storm's nose. Another Deco-era influence was the bump-stop seat, which Klock reckoned could be shaped to resemble a 1930s Union Pacific "streamliner" locomotive! The Kafé Storm is something of a locomotive too, being stretched out, heavy, powerful, and built for the long haul.

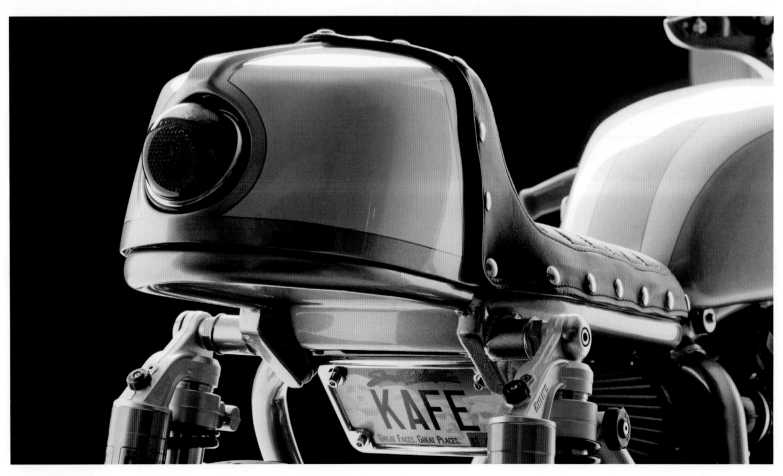

INDEX

First published in 2014 by Motorbooks, an imprint of Quayside Publishing Group Inc.,
400 First Avenue North, Suite 400, Minneapolis, MN 55401 USA

Motorbooks titles are also available at discounts in bulk quantity for industrial or sales-promotional use.
For details write to Special Sales Manager at
Quayside Publishing Group, 400 First Avenue North, Suite 400, Minneapolis, MN 55401 USA.

To find out more about our books, visit us online at www.motorbooks.com.

ISBN-13: 978-0-7603-4582-5

Editor: Darwin Holmstrom
Design Manager: Brad Springer
Book Designer: John Barnett, 4 Eyes Design
Layout: Rebecca Pagel

On the front cover: Flash
On the spine: Kafé Storm
On the back cover: Deus Ex Machina R100RS, Norvin Comet, Ed Norton
On the frontis: XR Café
On the title page: Full Sport Ducati

Printed in China

10 9 8 7 6 5 4 3 2 1